Course	Law of Business Organizations
Course Number	**LAW 4043**
	Patricia Quinn Robertson
	Arkansas State University

http://create.mheducation.com

ISBN-10: 1121647812   ISBN-13: 9781121647817

Contents

Credits

Property, Estates and Bankruptcy 319

Business Ethics 431

Online Supplements 545

Preface Preface

This is the 15th UCC Edition (and the twenty-first overall edition) of a business law text that first appeared in 1935. Throughout its over 75 years of existence, this book has been a leader and an innovator in the fields of business law and the legal environment of business. One reason for the book's success is its clear and comprehensive treatment of the standard topics that form the traditional business law curriculum. Another reason is its responsiveness to changes in these traditional subjects and to new views about that curriculum. In 1976, this textbook was the first to inject regulatory materials into a business law textbook, defining the "legal environment" approach to business law. Over the years, this textbook has also pioneered by introducing materials on business ethics, corporate social responsibility, global legal issues, and e-commerce law. The 15th Edition continues to emphasize change by integrating these four areas into its pedagogy.

Continuing Strengths

The 15th UCC Edition continues the basic features that have made its predecessors successful. They include:

- *Comprehensive Coverage.* We believe that the text continues to excel both in the number of topics it addresses and the depth of coverage within each topic. This is true both of the basic business law subjects that form the core of the book and also of the regulatory and other subjects that are said to constitute the "legal environment" curriculum.
- *Style and Presentation.* This text is written in a style that is direct, lucid, and organized, yet also relatively relaxed and conversational. For this reason, we often have been able to cover certain topics by assigning them as reading without lecturing on them. As always, key points and terms are emphasized; examples, charts, figures, and concept summaries are used liberally; and elements of a claim and lists of defenses are stated in numbered paragraphs.
- *Case Selection.* We try very hard to find cases that clearly illustrate important points made in the text, that should interest students, and that are fun to teach. Except when older decisions are landmarks or continue to best illustrate particular concepts, we also try to select recent cases. Our collective in-class teaching experience with recent editions has helped us determine which of those cases best meet these criteria.
- *AACSB Curricular Standards.* The AACSB's curriculum standards say that both undergraduate and MBA curricula should include ethical and global issues; should address the influence of political, social, legal and regulatory, environmental, and technological issues on business; and should also address the impact of demographic diversity on organizations. In addition to its obvious emphasis on legal and regulatory issues, the book contains considerable material on business ethics, the legal environment for international business, and environmental law, as well as Ethics in Action boxes. By putting legal changes in their social, political, and economic

context, several text chapters enhance students' understanding of how political and social changes influence business and the law. For example, Chapter 4 discusses the ethical issues of recent years, and Chapters 43 and 45 address the mortgage lending crisis, the current credit crunch, and options backdating. Chapter 51's discussion of employment discrimination law certainly speaks to the subject of workplace diversity. Finally, the 15th UCC Edition examines many specific legal issues involving e-commerce and the Internet.

Features

The 15th Edition continues 10 features introduced by previous editions:

Opening Vignettes precede the chapter discussion in order to give students a context for the law they are about to study. Many opening vignettes raise issues that come from the corporate social responsibility crisis that students have read about the last few years. Others place students in the position of executives and entrepreneurs making management decisions and creating new business.

Ethics in Action boxes are interspersed where ethical issues arise, asking students to consider the ethics of actions and laws. The ethics boxes often ask students to apply their learning from Chapter 4, the chapter on ethical and rational decision making. The boxes also feature the most important corporate social responsibility legislation of the last 20 years, the Sarbanes–Oxley Act of 2002.

Cyberlaw in Action boxes discuss e-commerce and Internet law at the relevant points of the text.

The Global Business Environment boxes address the legal and business risks that arise in international business transactions, including being subject to the laws of other countries. By the integration of the global business environment boxes in each chapter, students are taught that global issues are an integral part of business decision making.

Log On boxes direct students to Internet sites where they can find additional legal and business materials that will aid their understanding of the law.

Online Research Boxes close each chapter by challenging students to use their Internet research skills to expand their understanding of the chapter.

Concept Reviews appear throughout the chapters. These Concept Reviews visually represent important concepts presented in the text to help summarize key ideas at a glance and simplify students' conceptualization of complicated issues.

Cases include the judicial opinions accompanying court decisions. These help to provide concrete examples of the rules stated in the text, and to provide a real-life application of the legal rule.

Problem Cases are included at the end of each chapter to provide review questions for students.

Key Terms are bolded throughout the text and defined in the Glossary at the end of the text for better comprehension of important terminology.

Important Changes in This Edition

In this edition, there are many new cases, the text has been thoroughly updated, and a good number of problem cases have been replaced with new ones. The cases continue to include both hypothetical cases as well as real-life cases so that we can target particular issues that deserve emphasis. The 15th UCC Edition continues the development of components that were added to the text's previous edition. Examples of these components are as follows:

- Active **Learning Objectives** open each chapter, and are tied to AACSB standards. LOs inform you of specific outcomes you should have after finishing the chapter. Icons reference each LO's reference within the chapter.

Chapter 1

- Two new text cases on statutory interpretation—both of which are 2011 decisions of the U.S. Supreme Court. One, *Federal Communications Commission v. AT&T*, deals with whether the statutory phrase "personal privacy" applies to corporations. The other, *Kasten v. Saint-Gobain Performance Plastics Corp*, involves an interpretation of a Fair Labor Standards Act provision in light of its purpose and historical context.

Chapter 2

- A discussion of the new federal rules governing discovery of electronically stored information.
- The Dodd-Frank Wall Street Reform and Consumer Protection Act of 2010 is covered throughout the corporations chapters. This important legislation gives shareholders a greater role in corporate governance and expands the liability of corporate officers and those involved in securities transactions. The Dodd-Frank Act receives treatment in Chapters 43, 45, and 46.
- Expanded treatment of class-action issues, including discussion of the U.S. Supreme Court's influential 2011 decision in *Wal-Mart Stores, Inc. v. Dukes*.
- New text case dealing with class arbitration issues (U.S. Supreme Court's influential 2011 decision in *AT&T Mobility v. Concepcion*).

Chapter 3

- *Citizens United v. Federal Election Commission*, the U.S. Supreme Court's landmark 2010 decision, included as new text case in First Amendment section.
- New text case dealing with whether federal law on employment of illegal immigrants preempts Arizona law dealing with same subject (U.S. Supreme Court's 2011 decision in *Chamber of Commerce v. Whiting*).

Chapter 5

- Chapter title changed to "Criminal Law and Procedure."
- *Skilling v. United States*, U.S. Supreme Court's 2010 decision, included as new text case in section dealing with constitutional challenges to criminal statutes on vagueness grounds.

- *Berghuis v. Thompkins*, U.S. Supreme Court's 2010 decision establishing that person held for custodial interrogation must affirmatively speak up in order to invoke right to remain silent, included as new text case in section dealing with Fifth Amendment and *Miranda* warnings.

Chapter 6

- New text case dealing with intentional infliction of emotional distress (*Durham v. McDonald's Restaurants of Oklahoma, Inc.*, Oklahoma Supreme Court, 2011).
- New Global Business Environment box dealing with whether the right of publicity is violated when the relevant activities occurred outside the United States.

Chapter 7

- New introductory problem dealing with duty, breach of duty, *respondeat superior*, and comparative negligence issues (problem based on *Cabral v. Ralphs Grocery Co.*, California Supreme Court, 2011).
- New text case dealing with business owner's potential negligence liability when customer is attacked by third party in parking lot outside business premises (*Kroger v. Plonski*, Indiana Supreme Court, 2010).

Chapter 8

- As new text cases, recent Supreme Court decisions on patent law. Chapter 8 also includes new material on the Trademark Dilution Revision Act of 2006.
- The contracts chapters integrate e-commerce issues at various points. Examples include treatments of the proposed Uniform Computer Information Transactions Act in Chapter 9, shrink-wrap and clickwrap contracts in Chapter 10, and digital or electronic signatures in Chapter 16.
- New— and extensive—discussion of various patent reform issues and changes in U.S. patent law (including, but not limited to, switching the U.S. from a "first-to-invent" approach to a "first-to-file" approach).
- *Bilski v. Kappos*, the U.S. Supreme Court's high-profile 2010 decision dealing with business method patents, included as new text case.

Chapter 9

- *Aceves v. U.S. Bank*, a topical case involving mortgage foreclosure and loan modification.

Chapter 10

- Added the case of *Hines v. Overstock.com* (a topical case involving website terms and conditions).

Chapter 20

- A new section on the preemption and regulatory compliance defenses in product liability cases, and features the Supreme Court's recent *Riegel* decision in that section.
- New text case dealing with alleged design defects and the negligence and strict liability theories (*Branham v. Ford Motor Co.*, South Carolina Supreme Court, 2010).

- New discussion of two key U.S. Supreme Court decisions dealing with possible federal preemption of state product liability claims (*Wyeth v. Levine*, 2009, and *Pliva, Inc. v. Mensing*, 2011).

Chapter 27

- New feature discussing the Patient Protection and Affordable Care Act, which was enacted by Congress and signed into law by President Obama in 2010.

Chapter 30 (Bankruptcy)

- A case from the Madoff bankruptcy, *In Re Bernard Madoff Investment Securities LLC*.

Chapters 35 and 36

- Expanded coverage of the *Restatement (Third) of Agency*, making it the primary source of law for those chapters. Changes include the new *Restatement*'s change in terminology, such as nonemployee agent (instead of independent contractor) and unidentified principal (instead of partial disclosed principal), as well as different definitions for express and implied authority.
- *Ederer v. Gursky*, a decision of New York's highest court, exploring whether partners in limited liability partnership have limited liability to their partners, has been added to Chapter 38.
- The Supreme Court's decision in *Goodyear Dunlop Tires Operations, S.A. v. Brown*, explaining the limits of the *International Shoe* case regarding state jurisdiction over foreign and alien corporations, is a new text case in Chapter 41.

Chapter 41

- A new Ethics in Action box that considers the State of Indiana's grant to Amazon.com of an exemption from the Indiana sales tax in exchange for Amazon's building warehouses in Indiana.
- The Dodd-Frank Act's provisions requiring periodic shareholder approval of executive compensation and expanding liability of officers is covered in Chapter 43.
- The recent Delaware Supreme Court case, *Versata Enterprises, Inc. v. Selectica*, regarding the legality of poison pills, is cited in Chapter 43's coverage of directors' duties when adopting tender offer defenses.

Chapter 44

- As a text case the Delaware Supreme Court's decision in *City of Westland Police & Fire Retirement System v. Axelis Technologies, Inc.*, which delineated the limits of the shareholder inspection right.

Chapter 45

- Securities Regulation, clarifies the distinction between the preliminary and final prospectuses, on the one hand, and the free-writing prospection, on the other.
- The Dodd–Frank Act requirement that the SEC issue rules expanding shareholder proxy solicitation rights is covered in Chapter 45, as is the Act's dictate that the SEC give cash awards to whistleblowers who report securities violations.

- The Securities Regulation chapter also updates information on the cost of complying with Sarbanes–Oxley Act section 404.
- One of the first cases addressing the liability of banks as a result of the current credit crisis, *SRM Global Fund L.P. v. Countrywide Financial Corp.*, is a new text case in Chapter 45.
- The insider trading materials, including a concept review, have been clarified in Chapter 45.
- Chapter 45 new material on the safe harbor for issuers releasing forward-looking information.
- A problem case in Chapter 45 addresses whether Dallas Mavericks owner Mark Cuban may be liable for insider trading.

Chapter 46

- A discussion of the recent Supreme Court case, *Janus Capital Group, Inc. v. First Derivative Traders*, limiting the persons who can have liability under Securities Exchange Act Rule 10b-5.
- The Frank–Dodd Act's imposition of greater liability on brokers and dealers who tout securities is covered in the professional liability chapter.
- New language in Chapter 45's coverage of negligent misrepresentation clarifies the application of the *Ultramares* case.

Chapter 47

- Chapter title changed to "Administrative Law."
- New introductory problem dealing with the saga of the FDA's attempts to regulate tobacco problems (including the Supreme Court's decision that Congress had not given the FDA such authority and the later action by Congress to grant the FDA such authority).

Chapter 48

- Contains new text material discussing recent amendments to the Consumer Product Safety Act.

Chapter 49

- As a new text case, the recent *Leegin* decision, in which the Supreme Court held that vertical minimum price-fixing would be treated under the rule of reason rather than as a per se violation of the Sherman Act.
- Recent Supreme Court cases, such as *EXXON Shipping Co. v. Baker* (Chapter 52), have been integrated in this edition.
- *American Needle, Inc. v. National Football League*—the U.S. Supreme Court's 2010 decision dealing with the concerted action requirement under Sherman Act § 1 and with rule of reason analysis—included as new text case.

Acknowledgments

We would like to recognize Professor Jamie D. Prenkert of Indiana University, who authored the revisions of Chapter 51 (Employment Law).

We would also like to thank the many reviewers who have contributed their ideas and time to the development of this text. Our sincere appreciation to the following:

Sandra Jackson, *Lincoln Land Community College*
Judith Wright, *Indiana University, Kelley School of Business–Indianapolis*
Joseph Zavaglia, *Brookdale Community College*
Kurt Saunders, *California State University–Northridge*
Melanie Stallings Williams, *California State University–Northridge*
George A. Nation III, *Lehigh University*
Christine R. Bork, Esq., *Gloucester County College*
Gideon Mark, *University of Maryland Smith School of Business*
Richard J. Guertin, *Orange County Community College*
Remy C. Orffeo, *Erie Community College*
Floyd Woodard, Jr., J.D., *Indiana University & Purdue University–Indianapolis*

Michael Zugelder, *Old Dominion University*

We also acknowledge the assistance of Professors Sarah Jane Hughes and Dennis Long of the Indiana University Law School, and research assistants Elise Boruvka and Scott Corba.

Jane P. Mallor
A. James Barnes
Thomas Bowers
Arlen W. Langvardt

Agency Law

Part Eight

Agency Law

CHAPTER 35

THE AGENCY RELATIONSHIP

Upon graduating from college, Rita Morales was hired as a software consultant by IPQ Company, a large computer manufacturing and services company. Rita negotiated a high salary and even a nice signing bonus, yet after a few years of work she found that her spending often outstripped her earnings and savings. As her credit card bills piled up, Rita started her own consulting firm. Initially, Rita provided software consulting for her clients only on nights and weekends after she had finished her IPQ work for the day. As her business grew, she began seeing clients during normal weekday working hours and calling them from her office at IPQ. To find new clients, Rita downloaded IPQ's client information from IPQ's database. She contacted over 200 IPQ clients and asked them to switch from IPQ to Rita's business. Over two dozen IPQ clients switched to Rita.

- Do you see any potential problems with Rita's actions?
- What legally and practically can IPQ do to prevent Rita from taking its clients?
- What would an ethical employee in Rita's position do if her income did not meet her expenses?

LO LEARNING OBJECTIVES

After studying this chapter, you should be able to:

1 Know when an agency relationship is created.

2 Understand the distinction between employees and nonemployee agents.

3 Recognize when an agent risks breaching a fiduciary duty.

4 Learn the way agency relationships are terminated.

OFTEN, BUSINESSES ARE LEGALLY bound by the actions of their employees or other representatives. For example, corporations frequently are liable on contracts their employees make or for torts their employees commit. We take such liability for granted, but why should we? A corporation is an artificial legal person distinct from the officers, employees, and other representatives who contract on its behalf and who may commit torts while on the job. Similarly, a sole proprietor is distinct from the people she may employ. How can these and other business actors be bound on contracts they did not make or for torts they did not commit? The reason is the law of **agency.**

Agency is a two-party relationship in which one party (the **agent**) is authorized to act on behalf of, and under the control of, the other party (the **principal**). Examples include a Toyota dealership hiring a salesman to sell cars, Google employing a software engineer to write computer code, and you engaging a real estate agent to sell your home. Agency law's most important social function has been to stimulate commercial activity. It does so by enabling businesses to increase the number of transactions they can complete within a given time. Without agency, for instance, a sole proprietor's ability to engage in trade would be limited by the need to make each of her purchase or sale contracts in person. As artificial persons, moreover, corporations can act only through their agents.

Agency law divides into two rough categories. The first involves legal relations between the principal and the agent. These include the rules governing formation of an agency, the duties the principal and the agent owe each other, and the ways an agency can be terminated. These topics are the main concern of this chapter. Chapter 36 discusses the principal's and the agent's relations with third parties. In that chapter, our main concerns are the principal's and the agent's liability on contracts the agent makes and for torts the agent commits.

Much of the law of agency, which is largely state law in the United States, has been codified or adopted by the state legislatures or their courts in the form of the *Restatement (Third) of Agency* (2006), a project of the American Law Institute (ALI). The *Restatement (Third)* was adopted by the ALI in 2006, replacing the *Restatement (Second)*, which had been the chief source of agency law since its adoption in 1958.

 L01 Know when an agency relationship is created.

Creation of an Agency

Formation Agency is the fiduciary relationship that arises when one person (a principal) manifests assent to another person (an agent) that the agent will act on the principal's behalf and be subject to the principal's control. The agent must also manifest assent to the relationship or otherwise consent to act for the principal and under the principal's control. Agency is a fiduciary relationship because the principal entrusts the agent with power to make contracts for the principal and to possess and use the principal's property. As a fiduciary, the agent must use the entrusted power and property in the best interest of the principal.

As the term *manifested* suggests, the test for an agency's existence is *objective*. If the parties' written or spoken words or other conduct indicate an agreement that one person is to act on behalf of and under the control of another, the relationship exists. The *MDM* case, which follows shortly, applies the *Restatement (Third)* definition of agency. That case shows that an agent is a fiduciary of the principal and not vice versa.

If the facts establish an agency, neither party need know about the agency's existence or subjectively desire that it exist. In fact, an agency may be present even when the parties expressly say that they do not intend to create it, or intend to create some other legal relationship instead.

Often, parties create an agency by a written contract. But an agency contract may be oral unless state law provides otherwise. Some states, for example, require written evidence of contracts to pay an agent a commission for the sale of real estate. More important, the agency relation need not be contractual at all. Thus, consideration required to form a contract is not necessary to form an agency.

Capacity A person has the capacity to be a principal if that person has capacity to do the acts for which the agent has been retained. For example, a person competent to make a contract to purchase a building has the capacity to appoint an agent for that purpose.

Usually, any person may be an agent, including a person who cannot make his own contracts. An agent must merely understand that he is acting for someone else and under his control.

Corporations have the capacity to appoint agents. In a partnership, each partner normally acts as the agent of the partnership in transacting partnership business, and a partnership can appoint nonpartner agents as well. In addition, corporations, partnerships, and other business organizations themselves can act as agents for other business organizations as well as individuals.

Nondelegable Obligations Certain duties or acts must be performed personally and cannot be delegated to an agent. Examples include making statements under oath, voting in public elections, and signing a will. The same is true for service contracts in which the principal's personal performance is crucial, such as, certain contracts by lawyers, doctors, athletes, and entertainers. For example, the guitarist for Lady Gaga may not delegate to another guitarist his duty to perform at a Lady Gaga concert in Soldier Field.

MDM Group Associates, Inc. v. CX Reinsurance Company Ltd.
165 P.3d 882 (Colo. Ct. App. 2007)

MDM Group is an insurance broker. Joseph McNasby, its president, developed an insurance program for insuring ski resorts against the risk that the number of "paid skier days" during a ski season would fall below a specified minimum. CX Reinsurance Co. and others agreed to underwrite insurance policies covering the risk for a year, starting with the 1997–1998 ski season, and issued policies to a number of ski resorts in exchange for premium payments. For the first two years, the policies generated premiums of about $550,000 and $476,000, from which MDM received a commission of 12.5 percent. No claims were submitted under the policies during the first and second seasons.

Before the 1999–2000 ski season, several underwriters declined to renew their involvement. However, CX issued policies for that year, which, because more ski resorts purchased the coverage, generated total premiums of approximately $3 million. MDM received commissions totaling approximately $378,000. Unfortunately, the 1999–2000 ski season was not a good one for the insured resorts. There was little snowfall in the United States until well after the Christmas and New Year's ski holidays, and vacation travel was reduced because of concerns related to the millennium change. All the insured resorts, including Vail and Mammoth, submitted claims. CX negotiated, mediated, and litigated the claims, ultimately paying in excess of $23 million to settle them. As was its right, CX declined to renew the insurance policies after their one-year term expired in May 2000.

MDM initiated this action against CX asserting several grounds for liability, including a breach of fiduciary duty claim. MDM contended that CX, as the principal in an agency relationship with MDM, owed it a fiduciary duty and breached its duty by handling the ski resorts' claims improperly and in bad faith, thereby causing the resorts not to renew their policies and causing MDM to lose renewal commissions. The jury found for MDM and awarded it $6,750,783 in damages. CX appealed to a Colorado appeals court.

Casebolt, Judge

CX contends that MDM's breach of fiduciary duty claim must fail because a principal cannot owe a fiduciary duty to an agent as a matter of law.

A fiduciary duty arises among parties through a relationship of trust, confidence, and reliance. Certain types of relationships give rise to general fiduciary duties as a matter of law, such as attorney-client, principal-agent, and trustee-beneficiary. However, fiduciary duties are owed by only one of the parties in these relationships.

A fiduciary duty arises when one party has a high degree of control over the property or subject matter of another, or when the benefiting party places a high level of trust and confidence in the fiduciary to look out for the beneficiary's best interest.

In the principal-agent context, it is the *agent* who owes a fiduciary duty to the principal as a matter of law. "An agent has a fiduciary duty to act loyally for the principal's benefit in all matters connected with the agency relationship." *Restatement (Third) of Agency,* § 8.01 (2006).

A principal does owe *some* duties to an agent. *See Restatement (Third) of Agency,* §§ 8.13–8.15. However, the "obligations that a principal owes an agent, specified in §§ 8.13–8.15, *are not fiduciary.*" *Restatement (Third) of Agency,* § 1.01 comment e (emphasis supplied).

The jury was wrongly instructed that there was a fiduciary duty as a matter of law if it found that an agency relationship existed. As a matter of law, a principal is not a fiduciary of an agent. The principal is not "entrusted to act for the benefit of or in the interest of another." It is the principal who entrusts business to the agent to act for the principal's benefit. Any duties owed by a principal to an agent are not fiduciary. *Restatement (Third) of Agency,* § 1.01 comment e.

Judgment reversed in favor of CX.

Agency Concepts, Definitions, and Types

Agency law includes various concepts, definitions, and distinctions. These matters often determine the rights, duties, and liabilities of the principal, the agent, and third parties. In addition, they sometimes are important outside agency law. Because these basic topics are crucial in many different situations, we outline them together here.

Authority
Although agency law lets people multiply their dealings by employing agents, a principal is not always liable for his agent's acts. Normally, an agent can bind his principal on a contract or other matter only when the agent has **authority** to do so. Authority is an agent's ability to affect his principal's legal relations. It comes in two main forms: **actual authority** and **apparent authority.** Each is based on the principal's manifested consent that the agent may act for and bind the principal. For actual authority this consent must be communicated to the *agent,* while for apparent authority it must be communicated to the *third party.*

Actual authority comes in two forms: **express authority** and **implied authority.** *Express authority* is actual authority that the principal has manifested to the agent in very specific or detailed language. For example, a principal—a homeowner—may tell her agent—a tree removal expert—that the agent is authorized to "remove the diseased ash tree in my front yard."

Agency law also gives agents *implied authority* to bind their principals. An agent generally has implied authority to act in a way the agent reasonably believes the principal wants him to act. For example, the tree removal expert in the example above would have authority to choose a method for removing the tree, such as topping the tree first and removing it in sections or felling the tree with one cut. Relevant factors include the principal's express statements, the nature of the agency, the acts reasonably necessary to carry on the agency business, and the acts customarily done when conducting that business.

Sometimes an agent who lacks actual authority may still *appear* to have such authority, and third parties may reasonably rely on this appearance of authority. To protect third parties in such situations, agency law lets agents bind the principal on the basis of their apparent authority. *Apparent authority* arises when the *principal's* manifestations cause a third party to believe reasonably that the agent is authorized to act in a certain way.

Apparent authority depends on what the *principal* communicates to the third party—either directly or through the agent. A principal might clothe an agent with apparent authority by making direct statements to the third party, telling an agent to do so, or allowing an agent to behave in a way that creates an appearance of authority. The principal's communications to the agent are irrelevant unless they become known to the third party or affect the agent's behavior. Also, agents cannot give themselves apparent authority, and apparent authority does not exist where an agent creates an appearance of authority without the principal's consent. Finally, the third party must *reasonably* believe in the agent's authority. Trade customs and business practices can help courts determine whether such a belief is reasonable.

Authority is important in a number of agency contexts. Chapter 36 examines its most important agency application—determining a principal's liability on contracts made by his agent.

General and Special Agents Although it
may be falling out of favor with courts, the blurred distinction between general agents and special agents still has some importance. A **general agent** is continuously employed to conduct a series of transactions, while a **special agent** is employed to conduct a single transaction or a small, simple group of transactions. Thus, a continuously employed general manager of a McDonald's restaurant, a construction project supervisor for homebuilder Pulte, or a buyer of women's clothing for Macy's normally is a general agent. A person employed to buy or sell a few objects on a one-shot basis usually is a special agent. General agents often serve for longer periods, perform more acts, and deal with more parties than do special agents.

Gratuitous Agents An agent who receives no
compensation for his services is called a **gratuitous agent.** Gratuitous agents have the same power to bind their principals as do paid agents with the same authority. However, the fact that an agent is gratuitous sometimes lowers the duties principal and agent owe each other and also may increase the parties' ability to terminate the agency without incurring liability.

Subagents A **subagent** basically is an agent of an
agent. More precisely, a subagent is a person appointed by an agent to perform tasks that the agent has undertaken to perform for his principal. For example, if you retain accounting firm PricewaterhouseCoopers as your agent, the accountant actually handling your affairs is PWC's agent and your subagent. For a subagency to exist, an agent must have the authority to make the subagent *his agent* for conducting the principal's business. Sometimes, however, a party appointed by an agent is not a subagent because the appointing agent only had authority to appoint agents *for the principal.* For instance, sales agents appointed by a corporation's sales manager are agents of the corporation, not agents of the sales manager.

When an agent appoints a true subagent, the agent becomes a principal with respect to the subagent, his agent. Thus, the legal relations between agent and subagent closely parallel the legal relations between principal and agent. But a subagent is also the *original principal's* agent. Here, though, the normal rules governing principals and agents do not always apply. We occasionally refer to such situations in the pages ahead.

 LO2 Understand the distinction between employees and nonemployee agents.

Employees and Nonemployee Agents
Many legal questions depend on whether an agent or some other party who contracts with the principal is classed as an **employee** (or servant) or as a **nonemployee agent** (independent contractor). [The *Restatement (Third)* does not use the term *independent contractor*, because that term can designate either an agent or a nonagent, creating further ambiguity.] No sharp line separates employees from nonemployee agents; the *Eisenberg* case, which follows shortly, lists the factors considered in making such determinations. The most important of these factors is the principal's *right to control the manner and means* of the agent's performance or work. Employees typically are subject to such control. Nonemployee agents, on the other hand, generally

contract with the principal to produce a result, and determine for themselves how that result will be accomplished.

Although many employees perform physical labor or are paid on an hourly basis, corporate officers who do no physical work and receive salaries usually are employees as well. Professionals such as brokers, accountants, and attorneys often are nonemployee agents of their clients, although they are employees of the brokerage, accounting, or law firms that pay their salaries. Consider the difference between a corporation represented by an attorney engaged in her own practice (a nonemployee agent) and a corporation that maintains a staff of salaried in-house

counsel (employees). Finally, franchisees, like a KFC restaurant, usually are nonagents of their franchisors, like YUM! Brands.

As Chapter 36 makes clear, the employee–nonemployee agent distinction often is crucial in determining the principal's liability for an agent's torts. The distinction also helps define the coverage of some employment laws discussed in Chapter 51. Unemployment compensation, the Fair Labor Standards Act (the subject of *Eisenberg*), and workers' compensation are clear examples. Note that the *Eisenberg* case uses the historic term independent contractor to designate a nonemployee agent.

Eisenberg v. Advance Relocation & Storage, Inc.	237 F.3d 111 (2d. Cir. 2000)

In July 1998, Julianne Eisenberg discussed with Peter White and Mike Ewing working for Advance Relocation & Storage, Inc., a Danbury, Connecticut warehouse. White was involved in Advance's hiring process, and Ewing was the warehouse manager. The men discussed with Eisenberg the possibility of her working on a "permanent full-time" basis at Advance. They did not inquire into any special skills that Eisenberg may have had, and they did not ask about her prior work experiences. Instead, Eisenberg believed, the men were interested in her working at the warehouse because White knew that she was strong, having played football with her, and that she had been doing carpentry work for many years.

Eisenberg started work at Advance, where she and her co-workers were responsible for loading and unloading furniture from trucks at the warehouse and at residences. They were paid on an hourly basis, and were required to punch in and out. Eisenberg and her co-workers were occasionally sent home early if there was little to do, and they were sometimes asked to work on the weekend.

At the warehouse, Ewing gave Eisenberg orders, and if he was not going to be at the warehouse on a particular day, he told her on the prior day where to go and what to do. At job sites, an Advance representative told the crew what objects each crew member, including Eisenberg, was to move.

Eisenberg claimed that during much of the time that she worked at Advance, she was sexually harassed. She asserts that on September 16, 1998, she complained about this alleged sexual harassment to Joan Isaacson, the Advance office manager. Eisenberg also alleges that she told Isaacson that she had seen several Advance employees using cocaine in the warehouse.

The warehouse was closed by management the next day. Eisenberg then met again with Isaacson, at which point Isaacson allegedly told her that she would receive a job when the warehouse reopened and would be contacted and told when to return to work. However, Isaacson then told Eisenberg that she would not be called back to work at Advance if, based on her allegations of sexual harassment, she sought legal counsel or filed a complaint. Undeterred, Eisenberg hired an attorney and initiated an action against Advance on the grounds that she was sexually harassed in violation of the Civil Rights Act of 1964 (Title VII) and the New York Human Rights Law (NYHRL). After doing so, Eisenberg claimed that she was not called back to work at Advance by Issacson or anyone else. Eisenberg alleged that she was subjected to a hostile work environment at Advance, that her termination from the firm was discriminatory, and that Advance retaliated against her for complaining about the violation of her right to be free of sexual harassment—all in violation of Title VII and the NYHRL.

The district court granted Advance's motion for summary judgment on the grounds that Eisenberg was not an Advance employee, and thus could not invoke the protections of Title VII or the NYHRL. Eisenberg appealed to the Court of Appeals, arguing that she was an Advance employee.

Cabranes, Circuit Judge

Title VII and the NYHRL cover "employees," not independent contractors. For the purposes of these statutes, a decision on whether a worker is an "employee"—or whether he or she is

merely an independent contractor—requires the application of the common law of agency. In turn, whether a hired person is an employee under the common law of agency depends largely on the thirteen factors articulated by the Supreme Court in

Community for Creative Non-Violence v. Reid, 490 U.S. 730 (1989). These so-called "*Reid* factors," which are culled from the federal common law of agency, are as follows:

[1] the hiring party's right to control the manner and means by which the product is accomplished . . . ; [2] the skill required; [3] the source of the instrumentalities and tools; [4] the location of the work; [5] the duration of the relationship between the parties; [6] whether the hiring party has the right to assign additional projects to the hired party; [7] the extent of the hired party's discretion over when and how long to work; [8] the method of payment; [9] the hired party's role in hiring and paying assistants; [10] whether the work is part of the regular business of the hiring party; [11] whether the hiring party is in business; [12] the provision of employee benefits; and [13] the tax treatment of the hired party.

Though no single factor is dispositive, the "greatest emphasis" should be placed on the first factor—that is, on the extent to which the hiring party controls the "manner and means" by which the worker completes his or her assigned tasks. The first factor is entitled to this added weight because, under the common law of agency, an employer–employee relationship exists if the purported employer controls or has the right to control both the result to be accomplished and the "manner and means" by which the purported employee brings about that result.

Turning to the individual *Reid* factors, it is plain that the fifth, seventh, and ninth factors must be disregarded. As to the fifth factor, it is not disputed that Eisenberg worked at Advance for only 28–35 days. A relatively short tenure such as Eisenberg's ordinarily implies that a worker is an independent contractor. Here, however, the brevity of Eisenberg's stint at Advance does not suggest much of anything—her job lasted only 28–35 days because of the closing of the warehouse, not because of the nature of her work or her relationship to Advance. As to the seventh factor, the District Court found that Eisenberg had "some" control over her schedule, but not full control over it. Because this ambivalent finding does not seem to cut in any particular direction, we disregard it. Finally, the ninth factor is irrelevant to this case: Eisenberg hired no one to assist her with her work at Advance, and Advance hired no assistants for Eisenberg.

The remaining factors are the dispositive ones. As noted above, Eisenberg did not receive benefits such as medical insurance or vacation days, and Advance treated her as an independent contractor for tax purposes, giving her a "1099" tax form rather than a "W-2" form, and not deducting or withholding taxes from her wages. These factors favor characterizing Eisenberg as an independent contractor.

The remaining factors, however, suggest that Eisenberg was an Advance employee. As to the first factor, Advance exercised a great deal of control over the "manner and means" by which Eisenberg accomplished her assigned tasks. As we noted above,

at the warehouse White gave Eisenberg "orders" on a daily basis; if he was not going to be at the warehouse on a particular day, he told her on the prior day "where . . . to go and what . . . to do." Moreover, at job sites, an Advance representative—White, Ewing, or someone else—would direct the crew as to what objects each crew member, including Eisenberg was to move.

As to the second factor, Eisenberg's job at Advance—loading and unloading trucks—was not one that required relatively specialized skills. Other courts have held that the level of skill associated with being an architect, computer programmer, graphic artist, photographer, or treasurer suggests that workers who perform these jobs are independent contractors. In terms of the level of skill that it required, Eisenberg's moving work was not analogous to any of these jobs. Indeed, in this case White and Ewing all but offered Eisenberg a job without first asking her about moving-related work that she had done in the past, or about relevant skills that she might have developed over the years. That White seemed to view Eisenberg as qualified for the job solely on the basis of her football and carpentry abilities only emphasizes the point: While simple moving of the sort Eisenberg performed certainly requires skills—strength, for example, and agility—it does not demand *specialized* skills of the sort typically acquired through experience and/or education.

As to the third and fourth factors, the District Court found that "Advance supplied all of the [necessary] instrumentalities," including "trucks and other supplies," and that "the majority of plaintiff's work took place at Advance's warehouse or on Advance's trucks." Each of these findings suggests that Eisenberg was an Advance employee.

As to the sixth factor, the District Court found that Eisenberg "was not hired for a specific move or project." Instead, the District Court found that Eisenberg "was assigned to numerous moves or projects," and was required "to perform work on Advance's trucks and in its warehouse, on whatever moves or projects Advance undertook while she was there." This finding bolsters the conclusion that Eisenberg was an employee.

As to the eighth factor, the District Court found that Eisenberg was paid on an hourly basis. Compensation primarily or exclusively on the basis of time worked (rather than on the basis of projects completed) suggests that a worker is an employee. As to the ninth and tenth factors, the District Court found that Advance is "in the business of moving and storage" so that Eisenberg's work was "in the regular business of Advance," and that, "obviously, Advance is a business." Each of these findings favors characterizing Eisenberg as an employee.

Therefore, we conclude that Eisenberg was an "employee" within the meaning of Title VII and the NYHRL.

Judgment reversed in favor of Eisenberg.

L03 Recognize when an agent risks breaching a fiduciary duty.

Duties of Agent to Principal

An agent has a **fiduciary duty** to act loyally for the principal's benefit in all matters connected with the agency relationship. This duty supplements the duties created by an agency contract. A fiduciary duty exists because agency is a relationship of trust and confidence. The principal's many remedies for an agent's breach of her fiduciary duty include termination of the agency and recovery of damages from the agent.

A gratuitous agent usually has the same fiduciary duty as a paid agent, but need not perform as promised. She normally can terminate the agency without incurring liability. However, a gratuitous agent *is* liable for failing to perform as promised when her promise causes the principal to rely upon her to undertake certain acts, and the principal suffers losses because he refrained from performing those acts himself.

A subagent owes the agent (his principal) all the duties agents owe their principals. A subagent who knows of the original principal's existence also owes that principal all the duties agents owe their principals, except for duties arising solely from the original principal's contract with the agent. Finally, the agent who appointed the subagent generally is liable to the original principal when the principal is harmed by the subagent's conduct.

Agent's Duty of Loyalty

Because agency is a relationship of trust and confidence, an agent has a **duty of loyalty** to his principal. Thus, an agent must subordinate his personal concerns by (1) avoiding conflicts of interest with the principal, and (2) not disclosing confidential information received from the principal.

Conflicts of Interest An agent whose interests conflict with the principal's interests may be unable to represent his principal effectively. Therefore, an agent may not *acquire a material benefit* from a third party in connection with an agency transaction. When conducting the principal's business, an agent may **not deal with himself.** For example, an agent authorized to sell property cannot sell that property to himself. Many courts extend the rule to include transactions with the agent's relatives or business associates or with business organizations in which the agent has an interest. However, an agent may engage in self-dealing transactions if the principal consents. For this consent to be effective, the agent must disclose all

relevant facts to the principal before dealing with the principal on his own behalf.

Unless the principal agrees otherwise, an agent also may *not* **compete with the principal** regarding the agency business and not assist the principal's competitors, so long as he remains an agent. Thus, an agent employed to purchase specific property may not buy it himself if the principal desires it. Furthermore, an agent ordinarily may not solicit customers for a planned competing business while still employed by the principal.

Finally, an agent who is authorized to make a certain transaction may **not act on behalf of the other party** to the transaction unless the principal knowingly consents. Thus, one ordinarily may **not act as agent for both parties** to a transaction without first disclosing the double role to, and obtaining the consent of, both principals. Here, the agent must disclose to each principal all the factors reasonably affecting that principal's decision. Occasionally, though, an agent who acts merely as a middleman may serve both parties to a transaction without notifying either. For instance, an agent may simultaneously be employed as a "finder" by a firm seeking suitable businesses to acquire and a firm looking for prospective buyers, so long as neither principal expects the agent to advise it or negotiate for it.

An agent will not breach her duty of loyalty, however, if she acts in good faith, discloses to the principal all material facts regarding her conflict of interest, and deals fairly with the principal.

Confidentiality Unless otherwise agreed, an agent may not use or **communicate confidential information** of the principal for the agent's own purpose or that of a third party. Confidential information is the principal's information *entrusted* by the principal to the agent for purposes of the agent carrying out her duties. Confidential information includes facts that are valuable to the principal because they are not widely known or that would harm the principal's business if they became widely known. Examples include the principal's business plans, financial condition, contract bids, technological discoveries, manufacturing methods, customer files, and other trade secrets.

In the absence of an agreement to the contrary, after the agency ends almost all fiduciary duties terminate. For example, an agent may compete with her principal after termination of the agency. As the following *ABKCO* case illustrates, however, the duty not to use or disclose confidential information continues after the agency ends. The former agent may, however, utilize general knowledge and skills acquired during the agency.

ABKCO Music Inc. v. Harrisongs Music, Ltd.	722 F.2d 988 (2d Cir. 1983)

In 1963, a song called "He's So Fine" was a huge hit in the United States and Great Britain. In February 1971, Bright Tunes Music Corporation, the copyright holder of "He's So Fine," sued ex-Beatle George Harrison and Harrisongs, Music, Ltd. in federal district court. Bright Tunes claimed that the Harrison composition "My Sweet Lord" infringed its copyright to "He's So Fine." At this time, Harrison's business affairs were handled by ABKCO Music, Inc., and Allen B. Klein, its president. Shortly after the suit began, Klein unsuccessfully tried to settle it by having Harrison purchase Bright Tunes.

Shortly thereafter, Bright Tunes went into receivership, and it did not resume the suit until 1973. At this time, coincidentally, ABKCO's management contract with Harrison expired. In late 1975 and early 1976, however, Klein continued his efforts to have ABKCO purchase Bright Tunes. As part of these efforts, he gave Bright Tunes three schedules summarizing Harrison's royalty income from "My Sweet Lord," information he possessed because of his previous service to Harrison. Throughout the 1973–76 period, Harrison's attorneys had been trying to settle the copyright infringement suit with Bright Tunes. Because Klein's activities not only gave Bright Tunes information about the economic potential of its suit but also gave it an economic alternative to settling with Harrison, Klein may have impeded Harrison's efforts to settle.

When the copyright infringement suit finally came to trial in 1976, the court found that Harrison had infringed Bright Tunes' copyright. The issue of damages was scheduled for trial at a later date, and this trial was delayed for some time. In 1978, ABKCO purchased the "He's So Fine" copyright and all rights to the infringement suit from Bright Tunes. This made ABKCO the plaintiff in the 1979 trial for damages on the infringement suit. At trial, Harrison counterclaimed for damages resulting from Klein's and ABKCO's alleged breaches of the duty of loyalty. Finding a breach of duty, the district judge issued a complex order reducing ABKCO's recovery. ABKCO appealed.

Pierce, Circuit Judge

The relationship between Harrison and ABKCO prior to termination of the management agreement in 1973 was that of principal and agent. An agent has a duty not to use confidential knowledge acquired in his employment in competition with his principal. This duty exists as well after the employment as during its continuance. On the other hand, use of information based on general business knowledge is not covered by the rule, and the former agent is permitted to compete with his former principal in reliance on such publicly available information. The principal issue before us, then, is whether Klein (hence, ABKCO) improperly used confidential information, gained as Harrison's former agent, in negotiating for the purchase of Bright Tunes' stock in 1975–76.

One aspect of this inquiry concerns the nature of the schedules of "My Sweet Lord" earnings which Klein furnished to Bright Tunes in connection with the 1975–76 negotiations. It appears that at least some of [this] information was confidential.

The evidence is not at all convincing that the information was publicly available.

Another aspect of the breach of duty issue concerns the timing and nature of Klein's entry into the negotiation picture and the manner in which he became a plaintiff in this action. We find this case analogous to those where an employee, with the use of information acquired through his former employment, completes for his own benefit a transaction originally undertaken on the former employer's behalf. Klein had commenced a purchase transaction with Bright Tunes in 1971 on behalf of Harrison, which he pursued on his own account after termination of his fiduciary relationship with Harrison. Klein pursued the later discussions armed with the intimate knowledge not only of Harrison's business affairs, but also of the value of this lawsuit. Taking all of these circumstances together, we agree that Klein's conduct during the period 1975–78 did not meet the standard required of him as a former fiduciary.

Judgment in favor of Harrison affirmed.

Agent's Duty to Obey Instructions Because an agent acts under the principal's control and for the principal's benefit, she has a duty to **act within her actual authority** and to obey the principal's reasonable instructions for carrying out the agency business.

There are exceptions to the duty to obey instructions. A gratuitous agent need not obey his principal's order to continue to act as an agent. Also, agents generally have no duty to obey orders to behave illegally or unethically. Thus, a sales agent need not follow directions to misrepresent the quality of the principal's goods, and professionals such as attorneys and accountants are not obligated to obey directions that conflict with the ethical rules of their professions.

Usually a principal's instructions are clear and can be easily followed. Sometimes, however, the instructions are ambiguous. For example, an instruction may have terms

Ethics in Action

Corporations give special attention to rooting out conflicts of interests that result from kickbacks, bribes, and gifts to the corporations' employees. To ensure independence of auditors, auditing firms commonly have rules banning their audit staff from receiving anything of value from clients. In other contexts, most corporations permit their employees to receive items or services of nominal value only. Most firms have detailed rules, such as the following from Google's code of ethics:

Gifts, Entertainment, and Payments

Accepting gifts or entertainment from a Google customer, supplier, partner or competitor can easily create the appearance of a conflict of interest, especially if the value of the gift or entertainment is significant. As a result, Google policy prohibits Googlers accepting significant gifts, entertainment or any other business courtesy (including discounts or benefits that are not made available to all Googlers) from any of our customers, suppliers, partners or competitors. Acceptance of inexpensive "token" non-cash gifts, infrequent and moderate business meals and entertainment and infrequent invitations to local sporting events and celebratory meals can be appropriate aspects of many Google business relationships, provided that they aren't excessive and don't create the appearance of impropriety. However, tickets to something like the Olympics, Super Bowl, or World Cup, especially if travel and lodging are included, are a significant gift which, if accepted, could create at least the appearance of a conflict of interest. Don't accept significant gifts without getting the approval of your manager and Ethics & Compliance.

Gifts from customers, suppliers, partners, or competitors of cash or cash equivalents (e.g., gift certificates or prepaid gift cards) should never be accepted.

---

an agent does not understand. Or perhaps a cell phone conversation may be garbled due to poor signal strength. When a principal's instructions are unclear, the agent has a duty to communicate with the principal to clarify the instructions.

Agent's Duty to Act with Care and Skill

A paid agent must **act with the care, competence, and diligence** normally exercised by agents in similar circumstances. Paid agents who represent that they possess a higher than customary level of skill may be held to a correspondingly higher standard of performance. Similarly, an agent's duty may change if the principal and the agent agree that the agent must possess and exercise greater or lesser than customary care and skill.

Agent's Duty to Provide Information

An agent must use reasonable efforts to provide the principal with facts the agent knows or has reason to know, when the agent knows or should know the principal wants the facts or the facts are material to the agency. The basis for the duty to notify is the principal's interest in being informed of matters that are important to the agency business.

However, there is no duty to notify when the agent owes a superior duty to another person. For example, a consultant may acquire confidential information from a client and thus be obligated not to disclose it to a second client. If the consultant cannot properly represent the second client without revealing this information, he should refuse to represent that client.

Agent's Duties of Segregation, Record-Keeping, and Accounting

An agent's duties require that she not deal with the principal's property so that it appears to be the agent's, not mingle the principal's property with the agent's property or anyone else's, and keep accounts of the principal's money and other property. Agents must keep accurate records and accounts of all transactions and disclose these to the principal once the principal makes a reasonable demand for them. Also, an agent who obtains or holds property for the principal usually may not commingle that property with her own property. For example, an agent ordinarily cannot deposit the principal's funds in her own name or in her own bank account.

Duty Not to Receive a Material Benefit

Other than receiving the compensation the principal gives the agent for acting as her agent, an agent should not profit or receive any other benefit from acting on behalf of the principal. Improper material benefits include bribes, kickbacks, and gifts from parties with whom the agent deals on the principal's behalf. However, the principal and the agent may agree that the agent can retain certain benefits received during the agency. The Google code of ethics in the ethics box nearby is such an example. Courts may also imply such an agreement when it is customary for agents to retain tips or accept entertainment while doing the principal's business.

Duty of Good Conduct

The *Restatement (Third)* also includes a general duty that agents act reasonably and refrain from conduct that is likely to damage the principal's enterprise. While the scope of this general duty is not entirely clear, it encompasses, for example, an employee's duty not to damage the employer's computer system by exposing the system to harmful computer viruses while visiting unauthorized websites. It could also cover an agent who makes offensive statements to customers, resulting in the principal's loss of business.

Ordinarily, if a principal suffers no monetary damages from the agent's breach of duty, it is not entitled to any recovery from the agent, although termination of the agency may be justified. The following *Sanders* case shows how Madison Square Garden tried to circumvent the damage requirement by using the faithless servant doctrine.

Sanders v. Madison Square Garden L.P.
2007 U.S. Dist. LEXIS 48126 (S.D.N.Y. 2007)

Anuche Browne Sanders was vice president of marketing for the New York Knickerbockers, an NBA basketball team owned by Madison Square Garden (MSG). She was responsible for all aspects of the Knicks' marketing and media efforts, and she had access to confidential MSG financial and business proprietary material. When she was hired, Browne Sanders signed a copy of MSG's Confidentiality, Code of Business Conduct and Proprietary Property Agreement, which provided that during her employment, she may not engage in activities or have personal or financial interests that may impair, or appear to impair, her independence or judgment or otherwise conflict with her responsibilities to MSG. She also signed MSG's Employee Code of Conduct, which stated that "public trust and confidence are the greatest assets held by MSG."

In 2002, Browne Sanders was promoted to senior vice president, marketing and business operations, and her responsibilities expanded to include, among other things, oversight of the marketing and business operations budget. Browne Sanders remained in that position until she was fired in January 2006. Her total compensation for just over five years of employment with the Knicks exceeded $1,100,000. Shortly after being fired, Browne Sanders sued MSG and Knicks head coach and president, Isiah Thomas, among others, alleging that she was discriminated against on the basis of her sex and terminated in retaliation for her sexual harassment complaint against MSG and Thomas.

MSG obtained copies of Browne Sanders's federal, New York, and New Jersey tax returns for 2000–2005. The 2001–2004 returns included Schedule C deductions for the expenses of a "direct marketing" business, totaling approximately $73,000, seeming to indicate that she had conducted her own business on the side while working for the Knicks or that she had illegally deducted personal expenses as business expenses on her tax returns. Browne Sanders denied that she operated her own direct marketing business while working for the Knicks and claimed that the Schedule C deductions were due to accountant error and not a deliberate attempt to commit tax fraud. She filed amended tax returns for 2003 and 2004 that removed the Schedule C deductions. She did not amend the 2000 and 2001 tax returns on the advice of her current accountant, who informed her that there is a three-year statute of limitations for amending tax returns.

MSG counterclaimed against Browne Sanders for breach of fiduciary duty, claiming that she had breached her duty either by operating an outside business or by committing tax fraud while employed at MSG. MSG argued that under the faithless servant doctrine, it may recover all compensation paid to Browne Sanders while she was committing tax fraud or secretly operating an unauthorized direct marketing business while employed by MSG. MSG sought to amend its answer to Browne Sanders's complaint to include the faithless servant claim.

Lynch, District Judge

The faithless servant doctrine provides that an agent is obligated to be loyal to his employer and is prohibited from acting in any manner inconsistent with his agency or trust and is at all times bound to exercise the utmost good faith and loyalty in the performance of his duties. To show a violation of the faithless servant doctrine, an employer must show (1) that the employee's disloyal activity was related to the performance of his duties, and (2) that the disloyalty permeated the employee's service in its most material and substantial part.

Thus, the faithless servant doctrine, like the traditional fiduciary duty standard, is limited to matters relevant to affairs entrusted to the employee. However, unlike a traditional breach of fiduciary duty claim, which requires a showing of actual damages, to prove a violation of the faithless servant doctrine, an employer is not required to show that it suffered provable damage as a result of the breach of fidelity by the agent.

Here, MSG claims that Browne Sanders's tax returns show that she was either operating an outside business or that she committed tax fraud while employed at MSG. However, neither operating an outside business nor unethical conduct unrelated to employment violates the faithless servant doctrine unless such business or behavior adversely affects the employee's job performance. MSG neither claims nor has provided any evidence that Browne Sanders's alleged misconduct hurt her job performance.

Under MSG's interpretation of the faithless servant doctrine, an employee breaches her duty of loyalty any time she engages in conduct that is not condoned by her employer or that violates her employer's ethical standards, regardless of whether the employee's conduct was related to her job performance. However, the purpose of the doctrine is not to dissolve the well-established boundaries of an employee's fiduciary duty, but to provide a remedy for an employer if an employee breaches that duty and it is difficult to prove that harm resulted from the breach or the employee realizes no profit through the breach. *Restatement (Third) of Agency,* § 8.01 (2006). While employers may contractually obligate employees to act in an ethical manner, and condition continued employment on compliance with that requirement, an employee's alleged violation of that requirement does not result in a violation of the faithless servant doctrine unless the employee's unethical conduct materially and substantially infringed on her job performance. A faithless servant doctrine read as broadly as urged by MSG would allow an employer to sue an employee if the employee engaged in any conduct that fell short of the employer's ethical standards, no matter how disconnected to the employer's business the employee's misconduct might have been, simply because the employee's private misbehavior might reflect poorly on her employer.

MSG conspicuously fails to identify any way in which it suffered any such damage. As noted, it does not identify any way in which her alleged derelictions affected Browne Sanders's performance of her duties. Nevertheless, having accepted the fruits of Browne Sanders's labor for five years, MSG argues that it is entitled to obtain those fruits for free by forcing the forfeiture of all of Browne Sanders's pay for her entire period of employment. The remedies of the faithless servant doctrine are drastic, and appropriately so where the doctrine applies. An employee who works to undermine or covertly compete with her employer cannot be permitted to retain the benefits of an agency relationship she has betrayed. An employee who violates an incidental work rule, however, or who cheats the government out of taxes due, may have to respond in damages for breach of contract, but need not forfeit her entire salary.

MSG's motion to amend its answer denied.

Duties of Principal to Agent

If an agency is formed by a written contract, the contract normally states the duties the principal owes the agent. In addition, the law implies certain duties from the existence of an agency relationship, however formed. The most important of these duties are the principal's obligations to **compensate** the agent, to **reimburse** the agent for money spent in the principal's service, and to **indemnify** the agent for losses suffered in conducting the principal's business. These duties generally can be eliminated or modified by agreement between the parties.

Duty to Compensate Agent If the agency contract states the compensation the agent is to receive, it usually controls questions about the agent's pay. In other cases, the relationship of the parties and the surrounding circumstances determine whether and in what amount the agent is to be compensated. Where compensation is due but its amount is not expressly stated, the amount is the market price or the customary price for the agent's services or, if neither is available, their reasonable value.

Sometimes an agent's compensation depends on the accomplishment of a specific result. For instance, an investment banker may be retained on a contingent fee basis to find a buyer for its client's product line and be compensated with a percentage of the purchase price. In such cases, the agent is not entitled to compensation unless he achieves the result within the time stated or, if no time is stated, within a reasonable time. This is true no matter how much effort or money the agent expends. However, the principal must cooperate with the agent in achieving the result and must not do anything to frustrate the agent's efforts. Otherwise, the agent is entitled to compensation despite the failure to perform as specified.

A principal generally is not required to pay for undertakings that she did not request, services to which she did not consent, and tasks that typically are undertaken without pay. Also, a principal usually need not compensate an agent who has materially breached the agency contract or has committed a serious breach of a fiduciary duty, as the *Sanders* case on page 925 pointed out. Of course, there is no duty to compensate a gratuitous agent.

An agent's duties to a subagent are the same as a principal's duties to an agent. If there is no agreement to the contrary, however, the original principal has no contractual liability to a subagent. For example, such a principal normally is not obligated to compensate a subagent. But a

The Global Business Environment

While all modern nations regulate the relationship of agents and principals, associations of professional agents often reinforce or augment these legal duties with codes of ethics. For the real estate industry, you can find codes of ethics in 23 countries at the website of the International Consortium of Real Estate Associations, www.worldproperties.com.

Excerpts from the Code of Ethics of the Italian Federation of Real Estate Agents are below. Note how the listed rules relate to the agent's fiduciary duties we have studied.

- The Professional Real Estate Agent must know the real estate market and its development as well as the laws and regulations that govern his own activity.

- The Real Estate Agent must gather for any of his assignments all useful information in order to accomplish his task.
- The Real Estate Agent must not intermingle his own assets with the money received by a third party.
- The Real Estate Agent entrusted with the task of managing property must agree with the Client in advance on the amount of the compensation to be given to him and may not accept any amount of money from a third party at any time.
- The Real Estate Agent must examine the assignment entrusted to him and inform the Client of all the difficulties of the transaction.

---

principal must reimburse and indemnify subagents as he would agents.

Duties of Reimbursement and Indemnity

If an agent makes expressly or impliedly authorized expenditures while acting on the principal's behalf, the agent normally is entitled to **reimbursement** for those expenditures. Unless otherwise agreed, for example, an agent requested to make overnight trips as part of his agency duties can recover reasonable transportation and hotel expenses.

A principal's duty of reimbursement overlaps with her duty of **indemnity.** Agency law implies a promise by the principal to indemnify an agent for losses that should fairly be borne by the principal. These include authorized payments made on the principal's behalf and payments on contracts on which the agent was authorized to become liable. A principal may also have to indemnify an agent if the agent's authorized acts constitute a breach of contract or a tort for which the agent is required to pay damages to a third party.

So long as the principal did not benefit from such behavior, however, he is *not* required to indemnify an agent for losses resulting (1) from unauthorized acts, or (2) solely from the agent's negligence or other fault. Even where the principal directed the agent to commit a tortious act, moreover, there is no duty to indemnify if the agent knew the act was tortious. But the principal must indemnify the agent for tort damages resulting from authorized conduct that the agent did not believe was tortious. For example, if a principal directs his agent to repossess goods located on another's property and the agent, believing her acts legal, becomes liable for conversion or trespass, the

principal must indemnify the agent for the damages the agent pays.

LO4 Learn the way agency relationships are terminated.

Termination of an Agency

An agency can terminate in many ways that fall under two general headings: (1) termination by act of the parties, and (2) termination by operation of law.

Termination by Act of the Parties Termination by act of the principal and/or agent occurs:

1. *At a time or upon the happening of an event stated in the agreement.* If no such time or event is stated, the agency terminates after a reasonable time.

2. *When a specified result has been accomplished, if the agency was created to accomplish a specified result.* For example, if an agency's only objective is to sell certain property, the agency terminates when the property is sold.

3. *By mutual agreement of the principal and the agent,* at any time.

4. *At the option of either party.* This is called **revocation** when done by the principal and **renunciation** when done by the agent. Revocation or renunciation occurs when either party manifests to the other that he does not wish the agency to continue. This includes conduct inconsistent with the agency's continuance. For example, an agent may learn that his principal has hired another agent to perform the same job.

A party can revoke or renounce even if doing so violates the agency agreement. Although either party has the *power* to terminate in such cases, there is no *right* to do so. This means that where one party terminates in violation of the agreement, she need not perform any further, but she may be liable for damages to the other party. A gratuitous agency normally is terminable by either party without liability. Also, the terminating party is not liable when the revocation or renunciation is justified by the other party's serious breach of a fiduciary duty.

Termination by Operation of Law Termination by operation of law usually involves situations where it is reasonable to believe that the principal would not wish the agent to act further, or where accomplishment of the agency objectives has become impossible or illegal. The *Restatement (Third)* lists fewer specific instances that cause automatic termination than does the *Restatement (Second)*. Although courts may recognize exceptions in certain cases, an agency relationship usually is terminated by:

1. *The death of an individual principal.* Under the *Restatement (Third) of Agency,* this termination is effective only when the agent has notice of the principal's death.

2. *The death of an individual agent.*

3. *The principal's permanent loss of capacity.* This is a *permanent* loss of capacity occurring after creation of the agency—most often, due to the principal's insanity. The principal's permanent incapacity ends the agency even without notice to the agent.

4. The *cessation of existence or suspension of power* of an agent or principal that is not an individual, such as the dissolution of a corporation or partnership.

5. Upon the *occurrence of circumstances* from which the agent should reasonably conclude that the *principal no longer would want the agent to take action* for the principal. Changed circumstances include:

- *Changes in the value of the agency property or subject matter* (e.g., a significant decline in the value of land to be sold by an agent),
- *Changes in business conditions* (e.g., a much lower supply and a much increased price for goods to be purchased by an agent),
- *The loss or destruction of the agency property or subject matter or the termination of the principal's interest therein* (e.g., when a house to be sold by a real estate broker burns down or is taken by a mortgage holder to satisfy a debt owed by the principal).

There are other grounds for termination not listed in the *Restatement (Third):*

1. *The agent's loss of capacity to perform the agency business.* The scope of this basis for termination is unclear. As Chapter 36 states, an agent who becomes insane or otherwise incapacitated after the agency is formed still can bind his principal to contracts with third parties. Thus, it probably makes little sense to treat the agency as terminated in such cases. As a result, termination under this heading may be limited to such situations as the loss of a license needed to perform agency duties.

2. *Changes in the law that make the agency business illegal* (e.g., when drugs to be sold by an agent are banned by the government).

3. *The principal's bankruptcy*—as to transactions the agent should realize the principal no longer desires. For example, consider the likely effect of the principal's bankruptcy on an agency to purchase antiques for the principal's home versus its likely effect on an agency to purchase necessities of life for the principal.

4. *The agent's bankruptcy*—where the agent's financial condition affects his ability to serve the principal. This could occur when an agent is employed to purchase goods on his own credit for the principal.

5. *Impossibility of performance by the agent.* This covers various events, some of which fall within the categories just stated, for example, (*a*) destruction of the agency subject matter, (*b*) termination of the principal's interest in the agency subject matter (as, for example, by the principal's bankruptcy), and (*c*) changes in the law or in other circumstances that make it impossible for the agent to accomplish the agency's aims.

6. *A serious breach of the agent's duty of loyalty.*

7. *The outbreak of war*—when this leads the agent to the reasonable belief that his services are no longer desired. An example might be the outbreak of war between the principal's country and the agent's country.

Termination of Agency Powers Given as Security An agency power given as security for a duty owed by the principal, sometimes called an **agency coupled with an interest,** is an exception to some of the termination rules just discussed. Here, the agent has an interest in the subject matter of the agency that is distinct from the principal's interest and that is not exercised for the principal's benefit. This interest exists to benefit the agent or a third person by securing performance of an obligation owed by the principal. A common example is a **power of sale,** a secured loan agreement authorizing a lender (the agent) to sell property used as security if the borrower (the principal) defaults. For instance, suppose that Allen lends Peters $500,000 and Peters gives Allen a lien or security interest on Peters's land to secure the loan. The agreement might authorize Allen to act as Peters's "agent" to sell the land if Peters fails to repay the loan.

Because the power given the "agent" in such cases is not for the principal's benefit, it sometimes is said that an agency coupled with an interest is not truly an agency. In any event, courts distinguish it from genuine agency relations in which the agent is compensated from the profits or proceeds of property held for the principal's benefit. For example, if an agent is promised a commission for selling the principal's property, the relationship is not an agency coupled with an interest. Here, the power exercised by the agent (selling the principal's property) benefits the principal.

Why is the agency coupled with an interest important? The main reason is that it is not terminated by (1) the principal's revocation, (2) the principal's or the agent's loss of capacity, (3) the agent's death, and (4) the principal's death. However, unless an agency coupled with an interest is held for the benefit of a third party, the agent can voluntarily surrender it. Of course, an agency coupled with an interest terminates when the principal performs her obligation.

Effect of Termination on Agent's Authority

Sometimes former agents continue to act on their ex-principals' behalf even though the agency has ended. Once an agency terminates by any of the means just described, the agent's *actual authority* (expressed and implied) ends as well. Nonetheless, such "ex-agents" may retain *apparent authority* to bind their former principals.

Third parties who are unaware of the termination may reasonably believe that an ex-agent still has authority. To protect third parties who rely on such a reasonable appearance of authority, an agent's *apparent authority* often persists after termination. Thus, a former agent may be able to bind the principal under his apparent authority even though the agency has ended.

Notice to Third Parties Apparent authority ends only when the third party receives appropriate notice of the termination, that is, when it is no longer reasonable for a third party to believe that the agent has actual authority. Some bases for termination by operation of law (such as changed circumstances) may provide such notice.

Under the *Restatement (Third) of Agency*, an agent's apparent authority may continue even after the principal's death or loss of capacity. An agent may act with apparent authority following the principal's death or loss of capacity because the basis of apparent authority is a principal's manifestation to third parties, coupled with a third party's reasonable belief that the agent acts with actual authority. When third parties do not have notice that the principal has died or lost capacity, they may reasonably believe the agent to be authorized. The rule that the principal's death does not automatically terminate apparent authority is consistent with the interest of protecting third parties who act without knowledge of the principal's death or loss of capacity.

To protect themselves against unwanted liability, however, prudent principals will want to notify third parties themselves. The required type of notification varies with the third party in question.

1. *For third parties who have previously dealt with the agent or who have begun to deal with the agent,* **actual notification** is necessary. This can be accomplished by (1) a direct personal statement to the third party; or (2) a writing delivered to the third party personally, to his place of business, or to some other place reasonably believed to be appropriate.

2. *For all other parties,* **constructive notification** suffices. Usually, these other parties are aware of the agency but did no business with the agent. Constructive notification normally can be accomplished by advertising the agency's termination in a newspaper of general circulation in the place where the agency business regularly was carried on. If no suitable publication exists, notification by other means reasonably likely to inform third parties—for example, posting a notice in public places or at a website—may be enough.

In the next case, a summer camp counselor's actual authority terminated when the summer season ended. His apparent authority ceased when a camper learned that he had finished his stint at the camp. For that and other reasons, the camp that previously employed him was not liable for his assault of the camper.

LOG ON

Go to
www.wma.com
You can check out a career in the agency industry at the William Morris Agency website. WMA is the oldest and largest talent and literary agency in the world. Its business includes securing concert gigs for musicians and speaking engagements for authors. WMA clients include musician Lady Gaga, tennis player Serena Williams, late night host Conan O'Brien, and actor John Travolta.

Gniadek v. Camp Sunshine at Sebago Lake, Inc.
11 A.3d 308 (Me. Sup. Jud. Ct. 2011)

Camp Sunshine at Sebago Lake, Inc., is a nonprofit corporation providing a traditional summer camp experience in Maine for children with chronic or life-threatening illnesses. To attend a session, children must be accompanied by a parent or guardian who lodges with them. Katie Gniadek, who was 17 years old at the time, attended the camp with her mother, Kimberly Cooper-Morin. Gniadek had been attending Camp Sunshine annually for four years. During their week at the camp in 2005, Gniadek and Cooper-Morin met Michael Newton, a first-year volunteer counselor. Newton was 58 years old. On Gniadek's last day of camp, Newton gave her a card and gift and asked if they could stay in touch. Gniadek agreed, and Newton gave her his contact information. Gniadek, Cooper-Morin, and Newton also obtained copies of the contact lists for that week compiled by the camp, which recorded the name, address, and phone number of the counselors and parents in attendance. The camp had begun assembling these lists at the request of campers' families. Inclusion on the list was voluntary for parents. Cooper-Morin's contact information was on the parent-camper list.

After leaving Camp Sunshine on September 9, Gniadek had no contact with Newton until November 23, when he called to invite her to go with him to New York to visit a family who had attended camp. During their call, Gniadek learned that Newton had finished volunteering at Camp Sunshine for 2005. Gniadek obtained her mother's permission and agreed to go on the trip. Camp Sunshine had no knowledge of these plans. On November 25 around 6:00 p.m., Newton picked up Gniadek, and they left for New York. Gniadek and Cooper-Morin believed that there were two possible places where Gniadek and Newton would be staying that night, and both were the homes of former Camp Sunshine volunteers in New York. However, neither Gniadek nor Cooper-Morin had contacted these volunteers about this trip. Instead of staying with other volunteers, Gniadek and Newton stopped at a Connecticut motel. During the night, Newton assaulted Gniadek.

Newton was charged with assault and consented to a charge of assault in the third degree in the Connecticut Superior Court. He was sentenced to five years in jail.

Camp Sunshine was not operating or sponsoring any sessions in Maine on November 25 to 26, 2005, and at that point, Gniadek had not yet applied to attend Camp Sunshine in 2006. The camp had received Newton's 2006 volunteer application but had not acted on it. After learning about the sexual assault, the camp sent Newton a letter informing him that his volunteer services were no longer needed at Camp Sunshine. The letter also instructed him not to "solicit, recruit, speak on behalf of, or represent Camp Sunshine."

In 2008, Gniadek sued Camp Sunshine alleging, among other grounds, vicarious liability of Camp Sunshine for the acts of Newton. At the close of discovery, the trial court granted the camp's motion for summary judgment, finding that Newton was not Camp Sunshine's agent at the time of the sexual assault. Gniadek appealed to the Supreme Judicial Court of Connecticut.

Jabar, Judge

Gniadek contends that Newton committed his tort under the apparent authority of the Camp.

Apparent authority is authority which, though not actually granted, the principal knowingly permits the agent to exercise or which he holds him out as possessing. Apparent authority exists only when the conduct of the principal leads a third party to believe that a given party is its agent. Termination of actual authority will not alone end the apparent authority held by an agent. *Restatement (Third) of Agency* § 3.11(1) (2006). Instead, apparent authority ceases when it becomes unreasonable for the third party to believe that the agent continues to act with actual authority. Id. § 3.11(2)

The *Restatement (Third) of Agency* § 7.08 specifically addresses tortious liability for acts of agents cloaked with apparent authority. That section states:

A principal is subject to vicarious liability for a tort committed by an agent in dealing or communicating with a third party on or purportedly on behalf of the principal when actions taken by the agent with apparent authority constitute the tort or enable the agent to conceal its commission.

The commentary explains that section 7.08 applies to torts such as "fraudulent and negligent misrepresentation, defamation, tortious institution of legal proceedings, and conversion of property obtained by an agent purportedly at the principal's direction." § 7.08 comment a. In the commission of these torts, there must be a "close link between an agent's tortious conduct and the agent's apparent authority" in order for the principal to be liable. § 7.08 comment b. "Thus, a principal is not subject to liability when actions that an agent takes with apparent authority, although connected in some way to the agent's tortious conduct, do not themselves constitute the tort or enable the agent to mask its commission."

Our interpretation of a predecessor to section 7.08 recognized similar limitations. In *Mahar v. StoneWood Transport*, we interpreted the *Restatement (Second) of Agency* § 219(2)(d) (1958) as "limited in its application to cases within the apparent authority of the employee, or when the employee's conduct involves misrepresentation or deceit." 823 A.2d 540, 546 (Me. 2003). Although we had not "expressly adopted" that section, we nonetheless explained that it would not encompass assaultive and threatening conduct by an employee who did not purport to act on his employer's behalf.

Here, when Newton invited Gniadek to accompany him on a trip to New York, he told her that he had finished with Camp. By this statement, he conveyed that he was no longer acting with the actual authority of Camp Sunshine. Even assuming that after

learning this, it would still be reasonable for Gniadek to believe that Newton acted on behalf of Camp Sunshine, the assault was not committed with apparent authority. Newton's conduct does not fall within the scope of section 7.08.

Judgment for Camp Sunshine affirmed.

Problems and Problem Cases

1. When Del-Mar Development Corp. failed to pay real estate taxes on an office building it owned, the building was seized by tax authorities and sold to pay the taxes. The purchaser was Euclid Plaza Associates, LLC. The sale was not valid, however, until approved by a court. After the sale and before the court's approval of the sale, Del-Mar agreed to a three-year lease of the building with African American Law Firm LLC (AALF), which immediately began paying rent of $1,500 per month to Del-Mar. After the court approved the sale, Euclid claimed it was not bound by the lease made by Del-Mar with AALF. Euclid wanted to evict AALF unless it paid $2,033 in monthly rent. Was Del-Mar acting as Euclid's agent within Del-Mar's actual and apparent authority when Del-Mar leased the building to AALF?

2. Karsten was hired as a outside sales agent by Ling Company, a manufacturer of golf equipment and accessories. Karsten's duties required him to visit golf pro shops at golf courses and other golf equipment and accessory retailers. It was common for an outside sales agent in Karsten's position to have the power to make contracts to sell any item in his employer's line of products. However, Ling Company instructed Karsten that he could not contract to sell any Ling golf shoes without first getting permission from Ling's vice president of sales, Perez. Ling imposed this limit on Karsten's authority, because Ling was temporarily having problems getting shipments of golf shoes from its supplier in China. Neither Ling nor Karsten, however, had informed pro shops or retailers of the limitation on Karsten's authority. Nonetheless, Karsten, anxious to make a big sale, made a contract to sell 700 pairs of Ling golf shoes to Pro Golf Company. Was Ling bound to this contract with Pro Golf Company?

3. Circle C Investments operated two nightclubs featuring topless dancers. The secretary of labor sued

to compel Circle C to comply with the minimum-wage and maximum-hours provisions of the Fair Labor Standards Act, which applies only to employees, not independent contractors. Circle C required the dancers to comply with weekly work schedules, to charge at least $10 for table dances and $20 for couch dances, and to mingle with customers when not dancing. Circle C enforced the rules by fining infringing dancers. Dancers supplied their own costumes and padlocks for personal lockers. One dancer spent $600 per month on costumes, but another spent only $40 per month. A dancer's initiative, hustle, and costume contributed significantly to her tips. Circle C was responsible for advertising the club, choosing its location, and business hours, creating club aesthetics, and establishing a food and beverage menu, all of which attracted customers to the club. Dancers did not need long training or highly developed skills to dance at the club. Most dancers had a short-term relationship with Circle C. Were the dancers employees or independent contractors for purposes of the Fair Labor Standards Act?

4. Merrill Lynch, the investment firm, hired Elliot Jarvin as Director of Wealth Management Services. His duties included managing a team of 10 wealth managers who advised Merrill Lynch clients regarding their investment portfolios. When Jarvin joined Merrill Lynch, he brought with him 15 very wealthy clients to whom he provided investment services on behalf of Merrill Lynch. Unknown to Merrill Lynch, Jarvin had five additional clients, the five wealthiest of his clients. Jarvin continued to advise these clients on his own, retaining for himself all fees he charged for services provided to the five clients. In addition, to help him service the five personal clients, two members of his Merrill Lynch wealth management team frequently met with Jarvin's five personal clients to create investments plans for them. Has Jarvin breached a fiduciary duty owed to Merrill Lynch?

5. Catherine Creteau and her husband contracted with a travel agency, Liberty Travel, Inc., to arrange a trip to Jamaica. While staying in Jamaica in accommodations arranged by Liberty Travel, they were robbed at gunpoint. The Creteaus alleged that Liberty Travel either knew of safety issues with the accommodations or such information was available to Liberty Travel. What duty did the Creteaus allege their agent had breached?

6. When Perry Olsen died, his children placed his ranch in Vail, Colorado, for sale. Perry's children retained Vail Associates Real Estate, a real estate broker, to sell the land for them. Vail Associates introduced the children to Magnus Lindholm, who wanted to buy Perry's ranch along with adjacent land owned by Perry's children. The children eventually decided to sell only Perry's ranch and not the children's land. Their asking price for Perry's ranch was $400 per acre. Before committing to buying Perry's ranch (because he needed more land), Lindholm asked Vail Associates to introduce him to Del Rickstrew, whose land also abutted Perry's ranch. Rickstrew refused to negotiate the sale through a real estate agent, so Lindholm negotiated directly with Rickstrew. Vail Associates did, however, introduce Rickstrew to Lindholm and provide a model contract to Lindholm. A month later, Lindholm agreed to buy Rickstrew's land for $6,000 per acre, subject to his buying Perry's ranch also. Vail Associates was not aware that Lindholm and Rickstrew had a contract or that the price was $6,000 per acre. Two months later, with Vail Associates' assistance, the children sold Perry's ranch to Lindholm for $400 per acre. Vail Associates received a commission from the sale. When the children discovered later that Rickstrew received 15 times as much for his acreage as did they for Perry's ranch, they sued Vail Associates for failing to disclose material information, that is, that Lindholm was negotiating with Rickstrew. Did Vail Associates breach a fiduciary duty?

7. When Nitrogen Media was acquired by General Electric's NBC Universal unit, Nitrogen's Vice President of Finance, Babs Grogan, was terminated as a Nitrogen employee, but hired by NBCU as an outside consultant. The term of Grogan's contract was three months, and her engagement with NBCU required her to assess business opportunities presented to NBCU, such as the financial value of newly created television shows. Grogan represented to NBCU that she had an MBA degree in finance

and six years of experience in financial analysis. In fact, Grogan had falsified her academic record and possessed only an undergraduate degree in political science. In addition, she had no experience as a financial analyst, having delegated such work to coworkers for the past six years, although she took credit for their work. When NBCU asked Grogan to value the new TV show *Car Shop,* she delegated the task in part to a new MBA graduate, Roger Harvey, who was recently hired by NBCU and had virtually no on-the-job experience. As a result, Grogan and Harvey failed to perform a reasonable investigation into the facts regarding the TV show's value and to use appropriate valuations tools. Did Grogan and Harvey breach their fiduciary duty?

8. Lawrence is a clothing buyer for Federal Department Stores, a general merchandise retailer. Over the past five years, Lawrence has bought 75 percent of Federal's inventory of men's and women's denim pants from Worldwide Jeans Co. and 15 percent from Oskash Corp. Wanting to increase its sales of denim pants to Federal, Oskash contacts Lawrence and offers to sell 40,000 pairs of jeans to Federal for $320,000 and to make a contribution of $5,000 to the college education fund that Lawrence has established for his children. Should Lawrence accept this offer from Oskash?

9. Sheree Demming, a real estate investor, engaged Cheryl Underwood as a realtor to buy and sell properties on multiple occasions between July 2002 and April 2007. In 2002, Demming became particularly interested in purchasing two properties located on East Sixth Street in Bloomington, Indiana. The properties were owned by Marion and Frances Morris. The Morrises retained realtor Julie Costley to manage the properties, which were not listed for sale. Underwood first presented an offer to Costley on Demming's behalf in the fall of 2002. After the offer was declined, Underwood offered to contact Costley every few months to inquire about the properties' availability. Over the next few years, up until early 2007, Underwood contacted Costley on Demming's behalf regarding the properties every four of five months. Additionally, in May, August, and October 2006, Underwood contacted Costley to inquire into the availability of the properties after Demming specifically instructed her to do so. While Underwood was not compensated for these services, it was discussed and understood that Underwood would be paid a real estate commission, at closing,

in the customary amount of 7 percent of the sales price. However, unbeknownst to Demming, Underwood became interested in purchasing the properties for herself after she acquired a neighboring property in May 2006.

In February 2007, Demming again instructed Underwood to call Costley and inquire into the availability of the properties for purchase. Underwood responded, "Sheree, she's just not going to sell." Demming nevertheless insisted that Underwood contact Costley, and said that if Underwood refused, she would contact Costley herself. Underwood then agreed to call Costley, and when she did so, she asked Costley to contact Mrs. Morris, whose husband had recently passed away, to find out if she would be interested in selling. Costley responded that she would contact Mrs. Morris, but she expressed doubt as to whether Mrs. Morris would be willing to sell. The next day, Underwood told Demming that the properties were not for sale. Demming instructed Underwood to "stay on it" because she believed that Mrs. Morris would be willing to sell in the near future. A few days later, Costley contacted Mrs. Morris, who instructed Costley to request that anyone interested in purchasing the properties tender a written offer. When Costley informed Underwood that Mrs. Morris was willing to entertain an offer, Underwood did not relay this information to Demming. Instead, on March 9, 2007, Underwood and her partner Kinney tendered their own written offer to purchase the properties. A counteroffer was tendered and accepted, pursuant to which Underwood and Kinney agreed to purchase the properties for $650,000. Underwood and Kinney closed on the transaction on March 30, 2007. Does Demming have any recourse against Underwood?

10. On March 2, Bankers Life & Casualty Co. proposed in a letter addressed to Gaston Trepanier that he accept a lump-sum settlement of $20,000 in exchange for Bankers Life's release from a disability income policy that paid Trepanier a $400-a-month benefit as long as he lived. The letter stated that should

Mr. Trepanier decide "to accept our offer," he could "jot a note at the bottom of this letter and return it." Mrs. Trepanier discussed the idea with her husband, who decided to accept the offer and directed her to write a note on the bottom of the March letter as directed. She did so on April 6, and placed the letter in an envelope, intending to send it the following day. On April 7, Mr. Trepanier was hospitalized and the letter was not mailed. Mr. Trepanier fell into a coma on April 8. On April 12, Mrs. Trepanier tried to accept the offer by mailing the letter to Bankers Life. On April 14, Mr. Trepanier died. Bankers Life subsequently revoked its offer and issued a final disability payment. Was a contract formed when Mrs. Trepanier accepted the $20,000 offer on her husband's behalf?

Online Research

Investment Advisers' Fiduciary Duty

Conflicts of interest are a concern in the securities industry when securities brokers and investments advisers create investment plans and recommend securities purchases to their customers. Search the Internet for the website of the Investment Advisers Association. Under Investor Information, find IAA Standards of Practice. Click on IAA Standards of Practice. Scroll down and read the Fiduciary Duty section. Note how these duties reflect the fiduciary duties you studied in this chapter.

Consider completing the case "AGENCY: Duped by Duplication" from the You Be the Judge website element after you have read this chapter. Visit our website at www.mhhe.com/mallor15e for more information and activities regarding this case segment.

CHAPTER 36

THIRD-PARTY RELATIONS OF THE PRINCIPAL AND THE AGENT

You are vice president of acquisitions for a medium-sized consumer food products company, Bon Vivant Foods, Inc. The company's board of directors has given you authority to negotiate acquisitions of consumer food brands on behalf of Bon Vivant. The board has told you in written and oral instructions that you have the power to acquire any consumer products brand if the acquisition price is not greater than $30,000,000, which is the authority typically held by most vice presidents of acquisitions for businesses like yours. The board's written instructions also indicate, however, that you have no authority to purchase or negotiate the purchase of a cola drink brand. Others in your position in the consumer food industry typically have authority to purchase a cola drink brand for their companies. The board also tells you that the company wants to buy the Eddie's ice cream brand from its owner, Eddie Ghahraman, at a price not greater than $28,000,000. The board is fearful, however, that if Eddie knows the company wants to buy the Eddie's ice cream brand, he will demand a higher price. The board tells you, therefore, not to disclose to Eddie that you are buying for Bon Vivant, and instead to make it appear that you are buying for your own company. They suggest you make up a name for this fictitious company. You decide to use the name LHIW, Inc.

Assess the risks to you and Bon Vivant. Consider the following questions:

- If you make a contract in the name of Bon Vivant to buy a snack-cracker brand for $15,000,000, will Bon Vivant be bound on that contract?
- If you make a contract in the name of Bon Vivant to buy a cola brand for $13,500,000, will Bon Vivant be bound on that contract?
- If you make a contract in the name of Bon Vivant to buy an organic canned soup brand for $40,000,000, will Bon Vivant be bound on that contract? Will Bon Vivant be bound on that contract if you present the contract to the board, the board decides to accept the contract, and then the board later rejects the contract as too costly?
- Suppose you make a contract for Bon Vivant to purchase the Eddie's ice cream brand for $26,200,000. The contract is signed by Eddie. You sign LHIW's name and also your own name as agent for LHIW. Who is liable on that contract?

LO · LEARNING OBJECTIVES

After studying this chapter, you should be able to:

1. Know when an agent has authority to bind a principal to a contract.
2. Understand when an agent may be liable on contracts she makes for the principal.
3. Recognize when an agent is able to make a principal liable for torts committed by the agent.

BY LETTING PRINCIPALS CONTRACT through their agents and thereby multiply their dealings, agency law stimulates business activity. For this process to succeed, there must be rules for determining when the principal and the agent are liable on the agent's contracts. Principals need to predict and control their liability on agreements their agents make. Also, third parties need assurance that such agreements really bind the principal. Furthermore, both agents and third parties have an interest in knowing when an agent is bound on these contracts. The first half of this chapter discusses the principal's and the agent's contract liability.

While acting on the principal's behalf, agents sometimes harm third parties. Normally, this makes the agent liable to the injured party in tort. Sometimes, moreover, a principal is liable for his agent's torts. Because tort judgments can be expensive, the rules for determining the principal's and the agent's tort liability are of great concern to principals, their agents, and third parties. Thus, we examine these subjects in this chapter's second half.

The law in this chapter, as in Chapter 35, reflects the rules of the *Restatement (Third) of Agency*. The *Restatement (Third)* was adopted by the American Law Institute in 2006.

 L01 Know when an agent has authority to bind a principal to a contract.

Contract Liability of the Principal

A principal normally is liable on a contract made by his agent if the agent had **actual** or **apparent authority** to make the contract. Yet even when the agent lacks authority to contract, a principal may bind herself by later **ratifying** a contract made by an unauthorized agent.

Actual Authority An agent has **actual authority** to take an action designated or implied in the principal's **manifestations** *to the agent* and **acts necessary or incidental** to achieving the principal's objectives of the agency. The agent's reasonable understanding of the principal's manifestations and objectives determine the agent's actual authority. Actual authority, therefore, is the authority the principal wants the agent to possess. It is based on communications or manifestations from the principal to the agent.

Courts separate an agent's authority in two parts: express and implied. **Express authority** is actual authority that the principal has specified in very specific or detailed language. For example, suppose that Microsoft instructs its agent Gates to contract to sell a Windows XT software license for $400 or more. If Gates contracts to sell the software license to Dell for $425, Microsoft is liable to Dell on the basis of Gates's express authority. However, Gates would not have express authority to sell the software license for $375 or to sell a different software license.

An agent generally has **implied authority** to do whatever it is reasonable to assume that his principal wanted him to do, in light of the principal's manifestations to the agent and the principal's objectives of the agency. Relevant factors include the principal's express statements, the nature of the agency, the acts reasonably necessary to carry on the agency business, the acts customarily done when conducting that business, and the relations between principal and agent.

Implied authority usually derives from a grant of express authority by the principal. On occasion, however, implied authority may exist even though there is no relevant grant of express authority. Courts generally derive implied authority from the nature of the agency business, the relations between principal and agent, customs in the trade, and other facts and circumstances. There may be implied authority to make a certain contract if the agent has made similar past contracts with the principal's knowledge and without his objection or if the agent's position usually gives an agent the power to make a certain contract.

No matter what its source, an agent's implied authority cannot contradict the principal's express statements. Thus, there is no implied authority to contract when a principal has limited her agent's authority by express statement or clear implication and the contract would conflict with that limitation. But as we will see, apparent authority may still exist in such cases.

Examples of Implied Authority Courts have created general rules or presumptions for determining the implied authority of certain agents in certain situations. For example:

1. An agent hired to *manage a business* normally has implied authority to make contracts that are reasonably necessary for conducting the business or that are customary in the business. These include contracts for obtaining equipment and supplies, making repairs, employing employees, and selling goods or services. However, a manager ordinarily has no power to borrow money or issue negotiable instruments in the principal's name unless the principal is a banking or financial concern regularly performing such activities.

2. An agent given *full control over real property* has implied authority to contract for repairs and insurance and may rent the property if this is customary. But such an agent may not sell the property or allow any third-party liens or other interests to be taken on it.

3. Agents appointed to *sell the principal's goods* may have implied authority to make customary warranties on those goods. In states that still recognize the distinction, a general agent described in Chapter 35 is more likely to have such authority than a special agent.

Apparent Authority

Apparent authority arises when the principal's manifestations cause a third party to form a reasonable belief that the agent is authorized to act in a certain way. In other words, apparent authority is based on (1) *manifestations by the principal* to the third party (2) that cause the *third party* to *believe reasonably* that the agent has such authority. Background factors such as trade customs and established business practices often determine whether it is reasonable for the third party to believe that the agent has authority. In other words, apparent authority exists because it *appears* that the agent may act for the principal, based on what the principal has manifested to the third party.

Principals can give their agents apparent authority through the statements they make, or tell their agents to make, *to third parties* and through the actions they knowingly allow their agents to take *with third parties*. Thus, a principal might create apparent authority by telling a third party that the agent has certain authority or by directing the agent to do the same. A principal might also create apparent authority by appointing his agent to a position that customarily involves the authority to make certain contracts. For instance, if Exxon makes Alba its gasoline sales agent, and if that position customarily involves the power to sell gasoline, Alba would have apparent authority to sell gasoline. Here, Exxon's behavior in appointing Alba to the position of gasoline sales agent, as reasonably interpreted in light of business customs, gives Alba apparent authority. However, because agents cannot give themselves apparent authority, there would be no such authority if, without Exxon's knowledge or permission, Alba falsely told third parties that he was Exxon's gasoline sales agent.

Apparent authority protects third parties who reasonably rely on the principal's manifestations that the agent has authority. It assumes special importance in cases where the principal has told the agent not to make certain contracts that the agent ordinarily would have actual authority to make, but the third party knows nothing about this limitation and has no reason to know about it. Suppose that Prince employs Arthur as general sales agent for its tennis racquet manufacturing business. Certain warranties customarily accompany the racquets Prince sells, and agents like Arthur ordinarily are empowered to give these warranties. But Prince tells Arthur not to make any such warranties to buyers, thus cutting

---

The Global Business Environment

Electronic Agents

In the Internet Age, evolving business practices show an increasing use of software programs known as electronic agents in e-commerce transactions. A common definition of an electronic agent is a computer program or an electronic or other automated means used to initiate an action or to respond to electronic messages without review by an individual.

In the legal context, an electronic agent can be an automated means for making or performing contracts. In automated transactions, an individual does not deal with another individual, but one or both parties are represented by electronic agents. You have probably dealt with an electronic agent if you have ordered books, CDs, airline tickets, and other goods and services from an Internet site like Amazon.com.

The legal relationship between the principal and the automated agent is not fully equivalent to common law agency, but takes into account that the electronic agent is not a human actor. Nonetheless, parties who employ or deal with electronic agents are ordinarily bound by the results of their operations.

Most modern countries have laws that indicate when a person can be bound by the action of its electronic agent. In the United States, the Uniform Computer Information Transactions Act (2002) recognizes the ability of electronic agents to bind their principals, even if no individual is aware of or reviews the agent's operation or the results of the operation. Under the Philippines' Electronic Commerce Act, a contract may not be denied legal validity solely because it was created using an electronic agent, provided the electronic agent is under the control of or its actions attributable to the person sought to be bound. India's Electronic Commerce Act states that a contract may be formed between an individual and an electronic agent if the individual has reason to know she is dealing with an electronic agent. In Canada, the Uniform Electronic Commerce Act permits contracts to be formed by electronic agents, but if an individual deals with an electronic agent and makes an error, the individual will not be bound on the contract if the electronic agent provided no opportunity to correct the error and the individual immediately notifies the other party of the error.

off Arthur's express and implied authority. Despite Prince's orders, however, Arthur makes the usual warranties in a sale to Modell, who is familiar with customs in the trade. If Modell did not know about the limitation on Arthur's authority, Prince is bound by Arthur's warranties.

The following *Opp* case discusses whether an agent has express, implied, or apparent authority. Although decided under the *Restatement (Second) of Agency,* the case would have been resolved the same under the *Restatement (Third) of Agency.*

Opp v. Wheaton Van Lines, Inc.	231 F.3d 1060 (7th Cir. 2000)

Shelley Opp lived in California with her husband, Richard Opp, until they sought a divorce in August 1996. In June 1997, Ms. Opp contacted Soraghan Moving and Storage, an agent of Wheaton Van Lines, to move her personal property from California to Illinois. Ms. Opp told Soraghan she wanted to insure her property for its full value of $10,000. Soraghan faxed to Ms. Opp an "Estimate/Order for Service" form which stated that Ms. Opp intended to declare that the value of the goods shipped was $10,000. Ms. Opp signed the form. According to Soraghan, it explained to Ms. Opp that she or her representative must advise the mover at the time the shipment was picked up whether Ms. Opp would like full replacement coverage of $10,000. According to Ms. Opp, she was never informed that the person releasing her property in California would have to sign anything, declare any value for her property, or do anything other than give the movers access to her belongings. The estimate form also provided a location where Ms. Opp could designate someone as her "true and lawful representative," but she made no such designation.

On the day of the move, the movers in California called Ms. Opp in Illinois to tell her they would be late arriving at the California home due to a flat tire. Ms. Opp then phoned Mr. Opp at his office and asked him to go to the house, open the door, and let the movers in. Ms. Opp also told Soraghan that "someone" would be at the California home to give the movers access to her property. Mr. Opp met the movers at the house, and he signed the bill of lading on a line that indicated that he was Ms. Opp's authorized agent, and he allegedly agreed to limit the carriers' liability for her property at 60 cents per pound. Mr. Opp also signed an inventory of the property that indicated that he was its "owner or authorized agent."

On July 8, 1997, the truck carrying Ms. Opp's belongings was struck by a train, damaging most of her property. Ms. Opp inspected her damaged property and estimated its full replacement value to be over $10,000. Soraghan claimed that its liability was limited by the bill of lading to $2,625. Ms. Opp sued Sorghan and Wheaton to recover $10,000 for property damage. The carriers moved for summary judgment, which the district court granted, finding that Mr. Opp had the actual and apparent authority to sign the bill of lading as Ms. Opp's agent. Ms. Opp appealed.

Manion, Circuit Judge

An agent's authority may be either actual or apparent, and actual authority may be express or implied. Only the words or conduct of the alleged principal, not the alleged agent, establish the actual or apparent authority of an agent. We first note that Mr. Opp never received the express authority to represent Ms. Opp and to limit the carriers' liability. An agent has express authority when the principal explicitly grants the agent the authority to perform a particular act. There is no evidence that Ms. Opp explicitly granted authority to Mr. Opp to bind her to an agreement that limited the carriers' liability for her goods. Ms. Opp never requested or intended Mr. Opp to do anything other than to open the door and allow the movers to remove her property.

We next determine whether Mr. Opp had the implied authority to limit the carriers' liability. An agent has implied authority for the performance or transaction of anything reasonably necessary to effective execution of his express authority. *Restatement (Second) of Agency* § 35. Thus we must determine whether it was reasonably necessary for Mr. Opp to sign the bill of lading

in order to execute his express authority to open the door to give the movers access to Ms. Opp's property.

The carriers argue that because Ms. Opp allegedly knew that the bill of lading had to be signed when her property was picked up, but she arranged for Mr. Opp to be the only person present in California for the move, Ms. Opp's request for Mr. Opp to tender the goods to the movers also included the necessary authority for him to sign the bill of lading. But as noted above, Ms. Opp only told Mr. Opp to open the door. She made no request for him to sign anything, or to make any agreement as to the carriers' liability. Ms. Opp also testified that she was never informed that the person releasing her property in California would have to sign a bill of lading and declare a value for her property. Moreover, it is unclear whether Mr. Opp ever inferred from Ms. Opp's request that he was also authorized to limit the carriers' liability, or whether he merely thought that he was signing forms to confirm that Ms. Opp's goods were taken from the home. Thus we conclude that there is insufficient evidence to support a grant of summary judgment for the carriers on this issue.

We must then consider whether Mr. Opp had the apparent authority to sign the bill of lading and limit the carriers' liability. Under the doctrine of apparent authority, a principal will be bound not only by the authority that it actually gives to another, but also by the authority that it appears to give. Apparent authority arises when a principal creates, by its words or conduct, the reasonable impression in a third party that the agent has the authority to perform a certain act on its behalf. Thus we must determine whether the evidence demonstrates that Ms. Opp's words or conduct created a reasonable impression in the carriers that Mr. Opp had the authority to sign the bill of lading and limit their liability.

The carriers argue that they reasonably believed that Mr. Opp had the authority to sign the bill of lading because Ms. Opp allegedly knew that a bill of lading had to be signed when her goods were picked up, and she had also arranged for Mr. Opp to be the only person present at the California home to tender the goods. But material facts in the record also justify a reasonable inference that Mr. Opp did not have the apparent authority to limit the carriers' liability. It is undisputed that Ms. Opp told Soraghan that she wanted the full replacement value of $10,000 on her goods, which is reflected on the Estimate/Order for

Service form. Ms. Opp never designated a "lawful representative" on the space provided on the estimate form, and thus Soraghan's own form lacked any indication that Mr. Opp was her agent. And when the movers were delayed by a flat tire on their moving truck, they called to notify Ms. Opp in Illinois, not Mr. Opp in California. Additionally, Ms. Opp testified that the carriers never informed her that the person releasing her property in California would have to sign anything, declare any value for her property, or do anything other than to give the movers access to her belongings, which indicates that the carriers could not reasonably conclude that she knew that the bill of lading had to be signed in California, and that Mr. Opp had that authority. And there is no evidence in the record that the carriers had any knowledge that Ms. Opp ever discussed the valuation of her property with Mr. Opp. We conclude, therefore, that summary judgment is precluded because the record provides sufficient evidence to enable a reasonable jury to find that Mr. Opp lacked the apparent authority to limit the carriers' liability.

Judgment reversed in favor of Ms. Opp. Remanded to the district court.

Agent's Notification and Knowledge

Sometimes the general agency rules regarding *notification* and *knowledge* affect a principal's contract liability. If a third party gives proper notification to an agent with actual or apparent authority to receive it, the principal is bound as if the notification had been given directly to him. Similarly, notification to a third party by an agent with the necessary authority is considered notification by the principal.

In certain circumstances, an agent's knowledge of facts is *imputed* to the principal. This means that the principal's rights and liabilities are what they would have been if the principal had known what the agent knew. Generally, an agent's knowledge of facts or reason to know facts is imputed to a principal when it is material to the agent's duties to the principal. No imputation occurs, however, if the agent acts adversely to the principal with an intent to act solely for the agent's own purposes or those of another person. Suppose that Ames, acting on behalf of Sony, contracts with Target. Ames knows that Target is completely mistaken about a matter material to the contract to purchase TVs. Even though Sony knew nothing about Target's unilateral mistake, Target probably can avoid its contract with Sony.

Ratification

Ratification is a process whereby a principal binds himself to an unauthorized act done by an agent, or by a person purporting to act as an agent. Usually,

the act in question is a contract. Ratification relates back to the time when the contract was made. It binds the principal as if the agent had possessed authority at that time.

Conduct Amounting to Ratification   Ratification can be express or implied. An *express ratification* occurs when the principal manifests assent that his legal relations be affected, such as stating orally that he wishes to be bound by a contract that has already been made. *Implied ratification* arises when the principal's conduct justifies a reasonable assumption that he consents to the agent's act. Examples include the principal's part performance of a contract made by an agent, or the principal's acceptance of benefits under such a contract. Sometimes even a principal's silence, acquiescence, or failure to repudiate the transaction may constitute ratification. This can occur when the principal would be expected to object if he did not consent to the contract, the principal's silence leads the third party to believe that he does consent, and the principal is aware of all relevant facts.

Additional Requirements   Even if a principal's words or conduct indicate an intent to ratify, other requirements must be met before ratification occurs. These requirements have been variously stated; the following list is typical.

1. The act ratified must be one that was *valid* at the time it was performed. For example, an agent's illegal contract cannot be made binding by the principal's subsequent ratification. However, a contract that was voidable when made due to the principal's incapacity may be ratified by a principal who has later attained or regained capacity.

2. The principal must have been *in existence* at the time the agent acted. However, as discussed in Chapter 42, corporations may bind themselves to their promoters' *preincorporation* contracts by *adopting* such contracts.

3. When the contract or other act occurred, the agent must have indicated to the third party that she was acting for a principal and not for herself. The agent need not, however, have disclosed the principal's identity.

4. The principal must have *legal capacity* at the time of ratification. For instance, an insane principal cannot ratify.

5. As the following *Work Connection* case makes clear, the principal must have *knowledge of all material facts* regarding the prior act or contract at the time it is ratified. Here, an agent's knowledge is not imputed to the principal.

6. The principal must ratify the *entire* act or contract. He cannot ratify the beneficial parts of a contract and reject those that are detrimental.

7. In ratifying, the principal must use the *same formalities* required to give the agent authority to execute the transaction. As Chapter 35 stated, few formalities normally are needed to give an agent authority. But when the original agency contract requires a writing, ratification likewise must be written.

Note that a principal's ratification is binding even if not communicated to the third party. Also, once a principal has ratified a contract, the principal is estopped from denying its ratification if the other party has been induced to make a detrimental change in position.

Intervening Events Certain events occurring after an agent's contract but before the principal's ratification may cut off the principal's power to ratify. These include (1) the third party's *withdrawal* from the contract; (2) the third party's *death or loss of capacity;* (3) the principal's *failure to ratify within a reasonable time* (assuming that the principal's silence did not already work a ratification); and (4) where it would be *inequitable* to bind the third party.

The Work Connection, Inc. v. Universal Forest Products, Inc.
2002 Minn. App. LEXIS 659 (Minn. Ct. App. 2002)

The Work Connection, Inc. (Connection) is a temporary employment agency that provides workers to customers for a fee. In February 1995, Doyle Olson, a sales representative for Connection, contacted Universal Forest Products, Inc. (Universal). Olson spoke with Ken Von Bank, Universal's production manager who had direct supervisory authority over temporary workers. Universal hired some of Connection's employees, including Wayne DeLage, to construct fence panels at its Shakopee plant.

Olson gave to Universal work verification forms that were used as employee timecards. Universal filled out and signed the forms, which contained the worker's name, date, and hours worked. Submission of a completed, signed form was required for an employee to be paid, and Connection processed the forms through its payroll department. The work verification forms contained the following language:

CUSTOMER AGREES TO THE TERMS AND CONDITIONS SET FORTH ON THE REVERSE SIDE HEREOF AND CERTIFIES THAT THE LISTED EMPLOYEES HAVE SATISFACTORILY PERFORMED SERVICES FOR THE HOURS SHOWN ABOVE.

The back of the verification form stated the following:

CONDITIONS OF UNDERTAKING

* * * *

3. CUSTOMER agrees to indemnify, hold harmless and defend THE WORK CONNECTION against claims, damages, or penalties under the following circumstances:

* * * *

(b) From any claims for bodily injury (including death), or loss of, and loss of use of, or damage to, property arising out of the use of or operation of CUSTOMER'S owned, nonowned, or leased vehicles, machinery or equipment by

THE WORK CONNECTION employees.

The parties never discussed the language on the back of the work verification form. The parties' oral agreement did not include a term that required Universal to provide workers' compensation insurance for Connection's employees. Nonetheless, Von Bank signed the verification forms for Universal from March 1995 through July 1995, when the office manager, Yvonne Kohout, took over signing duties. At some point, Universal ran out of original work verification forms. Kohout simply photocopied the front side of the form and, thereafter, submitted forms that were blank on the back.

In August 1995, DeLage severed three of his fingers while operating a radial arm saw. DeLage received $75,000 in workers' compensation benefits from Connection. Connection then asked Universal to indemnify it pursuant to the language on the back of the verification form. Universal refused to pay, and Connection sued Universal for breach of contract. The trial court granted Universal's motion for a directed verdict. Connection appealed.

The Minnesota Court of Appeals held that Von Bank and Kohout had no actual or apparent authority to bind Universal to the indemnification clause. The court then considered whether Universal had ratified the indemnification clause by accepting the benefits of the employment contract for DeLage's labors.

Halbrooks, Judge

Connection contends that Universal agreed to be liable for workers' compensation costs based on a theory of ratification. Ratification occurs when a principal retains the benefits of an agent's unauthorized act. Once the principal has received the benefit, it is estopped from disclaiming liability based on the fact that the act was unauthorized. Connection contends that because Universal received the benefit of the temporary worker's labor, it also accepted the associated burden of the indemnification clause on the back of the verification form.

This argument is not viable. Ratification does not occur if the principal is ignorant of material facts surrounding the transaction.

Ratification by a party of another's unauthorized acts occurs where the party with full knowledge of all material facts confirms, approves, or sanctions the other's acts. Where a principal accepts and retains the benefits of an unauthorized act of an agent with full knowledge of all the facts he thereby ratifies the act.

Here Universal lacked knowledge of a material fact: that the original timecards that Kohout signed contained language committing Universal to indemnify Connection for a workers' compensation claim. Given that Universal lacked full information regarding Kohout's actions, it did not ratify her conduct.

Judgment for Universal affirmed.

Contracts Made by Subagents The rules governing a principal's liability for her agent's contracts generally apply to contracts made by her subagents. If an agent has authorized his subagent to make a certain contract and this authorization is within the authority granted the agent by his principal, the principal is bound to the subagent's contract.

Also, a subagent contracting within the authority conferred by her principal (the agent) binds the *agent* in an appropriate case. In addition, both the principal and the agent probably can ratify the contracts of subagents.

LOG ON

http://www.unidroit.org/english/
conventions/1983agency/1983agency-e.htm

http://frontpage.cbs.dk/law/commission_on_
european_contract_law

European Union Agency Law
Go to the first link, and you will find the "Unidroit Convention on Agency in the International Sale of Goods (1983)." The second link has the "Principles of European Contract Law in English." Article 3 covers agent's authority.

 L02 Understand when an agent may be liable on contracts she makes for the principal.

Contract Liability of the Agent

When are *agents* liable on contracts they make on their principals' behalf? For the most part, this question depends on a different set of variables than those determining the principal's liability. The most important of these variables is the *nature of the principal*. Thus, this section first examines the liability of agents who contract for several different kinds of principals. Then it discusses two ways that an agent can be bound after contracting for any type of principal.

The Nature of the Principal

Disclosed Principal A principal is **disclosed** if a third party knows or has reason to know (1) that the agent is acting for a principal, and (2) the principal's identity. Unless he agrees otherwise, an agent who represents a disclosed principal is *not liable* on authorized contracts made for such a principal. Suppose that Adkins, a sales agent for Google, calls on Toyota and presents a business card clearly identifying her as Google's agent. If Adkins contracts to sell Google's advertising space to Toyota with authority to do so, Adkins is not bound because Google is a disclosed principal. This rule usually is consistent with the third party's intention to contract only with the principal.

Unidentified Principal   A principal is **unidentified** if the third party (1) knows or has reason to know that the agent is acting for *a* principal, but (2) lacks knowledge or reason to know the principal's *identity*. This can occur when an agent simply neglects to disclose his principal's identity. Also, a principal may tell her agent to keep her identity secret to preserve her bargaining position, such as when a national retailer tries to buy land on which to build a large store.

Among the factors affecting anyone's decision to contract are the integrity, reliability, and creditworthiness of the other party to the contract. When the principal is unidentified, the third party ordinarily cannot judge these matters. As a result, he usually depends on the agent's reliability to some degree. For this reason, and to give the third party additional protection, an agent is liable on contracts made for an unidentified principal unless the agent and the third party agree otherwise.

Undisclosed Principal   A principal is **undisclosed** when the third party lacks knowledge or reason to know both the principal's existence *and* the principal's identity. This can occur when a principal judges that he will get a better deal if his existence and identity remain secret, or when the agent neglects to make adequate disclosure.

A third party who deals with an agent for an undisclosed principal obviously cannot assess the principal's reliability, integrity, and creditworthiness. Indeed, here the third party reasonably believes that the *agent* is the other party to the contract. Thus, the third party may hold an agent liable on contracts made for an undisclosed principal.

The undisclosed principal is also a party to the contract. The third party may not usually refuse to perform the contract merely because the principal was undisclosed, unless the contract excluded the possibility of an undisclosed principal.

Nonexistent Principal   Unless there is an agreement to the contrary, an agent who purports to act for a **legally nonexistent** principal, such as an unincorporated association, is personally liable when the agent knows or has reason to know the principal does not exist. Likewise, the agent is liable when she knows or has reason to know a principal has no capacity. This is true even when the third party knows that the principal is nonexistent or lacks capacity. See Chapter 42 for a more detailed discussion of the liability of those who transact on behalf of nonexistent corporations.

In the *Treadwell* case that follows, the court found that an agent acted for an unidentified principal when he disclosed he was transacting for a corporation, but gave the wrong corporate name to the third party with whom he transacted.

Treadwell v. J.D. Construction Co.   938 A.2d 794 (Me. Sup. Jud. Ct. 2007)

In the early 1990s, Jesse Derr created a corporation, JCDER, Inc., to operate his construction business. At some point, Derr began referring to the corporation as J.D. Construction Co., Inc., but no corporation by that name was ever created. JCDER, Inc., remained the official name for purposes of organization and filing with Maine's Secretary of State. Derr never filed with the Secretary of State a statement of intention to do business under the assumed name J.D. Construction Co., Inc.

In 2003, when Leah and William Treadwell decided to build a home, they were referred to Derr. The Treadwells brought their home plans to Derr's office to get a quote and left the plans with an employee, Jane Veinot. They did not meet with Derr, but received a quote from him in the mail. Soon after, the Treadwells signed a contract with J.D. Construction, with work to start in May 2003. Derr signed the contract, and his signature appeared on the contract as follows:

> J.D. Construction Co., Inc.
> By: Jesse Derr

The name JCDER, Inc., was nowhere in the contract, and the Treadwells were unaware of the existence of JCDER, Inc., when they signed the agreement. None of the documents the Treadwells received from J.D. Construction indicated that the company's real name was JCDER, Inc.

Mr. Treadwell testified that he spoke with Derr twice at the worksite, just as they were breaking ground. The Treadwells, who visited the site almost daily, never saw Derr again, even though they tried many times to contact him. They spoke to Veinot *often, but she would tell them that Derr was at another construction site. Derr had hired subcontractors to do the work on the Treadwells' property. Around Thanksgiving 2003, the Treadwells visited the site and found that Derr had abandoned the job with the house unfinished because the company was not making any money on the job. The Treadwells had paid Derr approximately $91,000 before construction halted.*

The Treadwells found many problems with the structure, including twisted studs and other lumber that had to be replaced. The Treadwells hired new contractors to fix and finish the project, for which they paid a significant sum.

To recover the additional costs, the Treadwells sued J.D. Construction Co., JCDER, Inc., and Derr for breach of contract and other grounds. The trial court awarded the Treadwells damages against J.D. Construction Co., Inc., and JCDER, Inc., but found that Derr was not personally liable for the damages. The Treadwells appealed to the Supreme Judicial Court of Maine, asking that Derr also be held liable.

Alexander, Judge

The Treadwells argue that the trial court should have awarded damages against Derr individually since he signed the contract for a non-existent corporation. In the alternative, they contend that the trial court should have pierced the corporate veil and held Derr responsible because he failed to disclose the existence of JCDER, Inc.

The question presented to us is whether, as a matter of law, an individual who signs a contract, purporting to act on behalf of a corporate entity that he knows does not exist, becomes personally liable for damages arising from failure to properly perform under that contract.

An agent who makes a contract for an undisclosed principal or a partially disclosed principal will be liable as a party to the contract. In order for an agent to avoid personal liability on a contract negotiated in his principal's behalf, he must disclose not only that he is an agent but also the identity of the principal. The term "partially disclosed" principal is synonymous with "unidentified" principal. *Restatement (Third) of Agency,* § 1.04 comment b (2006). "A principal is unidentified if, when an agent and a third party interact, the third party has notice that the agent is acting for a principal but does not have notice of the principal's identity." *Restatement (Third) of Agency,* § 1.04(2)(c) (2006). To avoid liability for the agent, the third party must have *actual* knowledge of the identity of the principal, and does not have a duty to investigate.

In *Maine Farmers Exch. v. McGillicuddy,* 697 A.2d 1266 (Me. 1996), the son of a potato seller signed a contract with a distributor for a certain grade potato. The father/seller furnished the potatoes, which turned out to be the wrong grade. In an action by the distributor against the father and son, the trial court found them to be jointly and severally liable. They appealed the finding of joint and several liability, arguing that the distributor should have been aware that the son was acting as an agent for his father. We affirmed that finding because the son did not disclose that he was an agent for his father, and the distributor believed he was buying potatoes from the son.

In the present case, Derr organized a corporation called JCDER, Inc., which he used to operate his construction business. Both Derr and JCDER, Inc., acted under the assumed name J.D. Construction Co., Inc., Derr signed the contract on behalf of J.D. Construction, hired the subcontractors, and was purported to be the contact-person for the project, although he was not available to the Treadwells. Derr's use of an assumed trade name was not sufficient to disclose his agency relationship with JCDER, Inc. JCDER, Inc., was therefore an unidentified or partially disclosed principal. As a matter of law, Derr is personally liable for performance of contracts entered into as agent for the non-existent J.D. Construction, Co., Inc., or the undisclosed principal JCDER, Inc.

Judgment reversed in favor of the Treadwells.

Liability of Agent by Agreement An agent may bind herself to contracts she makes for a principal by *expressly agreeing* to be liable. This is true regardless of the principal's nature. An agent may expressly bind herself by (1) making the contract in her own name rather than in the principal's name, (2) joining the principal as an obligor on the contract, or (3) acting as surety or guarantor for the principal.

Problems of contract interpretation can arise when it is claimed that an agent has expressly promised to be bound.

The two most important factors affecting the agent's liability are the wording of the contract and the way the agent has signed it. An agent who wishes to avoid liability should make no express promises in her own name and should try to ensure that the agreement obligates only the principal. In addition, the agent should use a signature form that clearly identifies the principal and indicates the agent's representative capacity—for example, "Parker, by Adkins," or "Adkins, for Parker." Simply adding the word "agent" when signing her name ("Adkins, Agent") or signing without any indication of her status ("Adkins") could subject the agent to liability. Sometimes, the body of the contract suggests one result and the signature form another. In such contexts, oral evidence or other extrinsic evidence of the parties' understanding may help resolve the uncertainty.

Implied Warranty of Authority
An agent also may be liable to a third party if he contracts for a legally existing and competent principal while lacking authority to do so. Here, the principal is not bound on the contract. Yet it is arguably unfair to leave the third party without any recovery. Thus, an agent normally is bound on the theory that he made an implied warranty of his authority to contract. This liability exists regardless of whether the agent is otherwise bound to the third party.

To illustrate, suppose that Allen is a salesman for Prine, a seller of furs. Allen has actual authority to receive offers for the sale of Prine's furs but not to make sale contracts, which must be approved by Prine himself. Prine has long followed this practice, and it is customary in the markets where his agents work. Representing himself as Prine's agent but saying nothing about his authority, Allen contracts to sell Prine's furs to Thatcher on Prine's behalf. Thatcher, who should have known better, honestly believes that Allen has authority to contract to sell Prine's furs. Prine is not liable on Allen's contract because Allen lacked actual or apparent authority to bind him. But Allen is liable to Thatcher for breaching his implied warranty of authority.

However, an agent is *not* liable for making an unauthorized contract if any of the following applies:

1. The third party *actually knows* that the agent lacks authority. Note from the previous example, however, that the agent still is liable where the third party merely had *reason to know* that authority was lacking.

2. The principal subsequently *ratifies* the contract. Here, the principal is bound, and there is no reason to bind the agent.

3. The agent adequately *notifies* the third party that he does not warrant his authority to contract.

In the following *Interbank Funding* case, the court found the president of a dissolved corporation liable for breaching the agent's implied warranty of authority.

In re Interbank Funding Corp. v. Chadmoore Wireless Group Inc.
2007 Bankr. LEXIS 3422 (Bank. Ct. S.D.N.Y. 2007)

Chadmoore Wireless Group was a Colorado corporation that sold substantially all of its assets to another company in early 2002. It was dissolved under Colorado law on February 23, 2002. Following Chadmoore's dissolution, there were only three remaining members on its board of directors. Robert Moore was president, CEO, and a director of the Chadmoore Board.

Purporting to act on behalf of Chadmoore, Moore signed the "Chadmoore Put," by which Chadmoore guaranteed the payment of the purchase price for the sale of US Mills, Inc., to Sunset Brands, Inc. The value of the Chadmoore Put was $2,500,000. One beneficiary of the Chadmoore Put was Fund LLC. The Chadmoore Put included a representation that Chadmoore had "full power, right and authority" to execute, deliver, and perform under the Chadmoore Put; that the execution, delivery, and performance by Chadmoore under the Chadmoore Put was "duly and validly authorized by all necessary actions on the part of Chadmoore" and would not conflict with Chadmoore's corporate formation documents or any applicable law; and that no further approvals, consents, or other actions by Chadmoore or any other person or entity were required. The Chadmoore Put included a representation that Moore was authorized to execute and deliver the Chadmoore Put, that Moore had obtained all required approvals, and that the Chadmoore Put was a binding obligation on Chadmoore.

Moore signed the Chadmoore Put on Chadmoore's behalf without approval of Chadmoore's board of directors. When Moore executed the Chadmoore Put, he inserted by hand the term "President" on the title line of the Chadmoore Put. Moore admits that he signed the Chadmoore Put intending that it would not be enforceable against Chadmoore. Moore concedes that he signed the Chadmoore Put to protect his friend, Todd Sanders, who allegedly led Moore to believe he would have serious financial difficulty and possibly be subject to physical harm if Moore did not sign the Chadmoore Put.

After the Chadmoore Put matured in November 2006, Fund LLC demanded that Chadmoore perform. Chadmoore refused to honor the Chadmoore Put and claimed that the two directors other than Moore had no prior knowledge of the Chadmoore Put. Fund LLC moved for summary judgment, asking the bankruptcy court to award it damages on the grounds that Moore breached an agent's implied warranty of authority.

Lifland, Judge

An action may lie in breach of implied warranty of authority when an agent executes an agreement purportedly on behalf of a principal; without authority from the principal; and damages result. The *Restatement of Agency* provides,

> A person who purports to make a contract, representation, or conveyance to or with a third party on behalf of another person, lacking power to bind that person, gives an implied warranty of authority to the third party and is subject to liability to the third party for damages for loss caused by breach of that warranty, including loss of the benefit expected from performance by the principal.

Restatement (Third) of Agency, § 6.10 (2006). New York courts recognize that a purported agent who signs a contract on behalf of his principal makes an implied warranty of authority to the other party to the contract.

Moore acknowledged that he signed the Chadmoore Put as President of Chadmoore and that he knew he did not have authority from the Board of Directors of Chadmoore at the time he executed the Chadmoore Put. In fact, Moore indicated that he signed the Chadmoore Put intending that it would never be enforceable. Yet he did sign the Chadmoore Put, and all of its accompanying representations and warranties.

Moore cites cases holding that an agent can only be held liable for contracts signed without authority to the extent the contract would have been enforceable against the principal but for the lack of authority of the agent. However, New York courts have specifically ruled that in the case of agents executing contracts on behalf of dissolved corporations, those agents are personally liable for the contracts. Fund LLC's motion for summary judgment on implied warranty of authority is granted. There are simply no facts asserted by Moore that would lead to a different result. Moore does not deny that he signed the Chadmoore Put as President of Chadmoore without actually having authority to do so. Moore does not deny that as a result of his signing the Chadmoore Put, Chadmoore defaulted on its obligation on the Chadmoore Put.

The damages resulting from Moore's breach of the implied warranty of authority include the third-party financial accommodations owed under the Chadmoore Put and all injury resulting from his want of power, including the costs of an unsuccessful action against the alleged principal.

Summary judgment granted in favor of Fund LLC.

Figure 1   *Liability of Principal and Agent: The Major Possibilities*

Principal	Agent's Authority		
	Actual	Apparent	None
Disclosed	P liable on the contract; A not liable on the contract unless agrees to be liable	P liable on the contract; A not liable on the contract unless agrees to be liable	P not liable on the contract; A usually liable for breach of the implied warranty of authority
Unidentified	P liable on the contract; A liable on the contract	P liable on the contract; A liable on the contract	P not liable on the contract; A liable on the contract or for breach of the implied warranty of authority
Undisclosed	P liable on the contract; A liable on the contract	Impossible	P not liable on the contract; A liable on the contract

---

 L03   Recognize when an agent is able to make a principal liable for torts committed by the agent.

Tort Liability of the Principal

Besides contracting on the principal's behalf, an agent may also commit torts while acting for the principal. A principal's liability for an agent's torts may be found on any one or more of four bases.

Respondeat Superior **Liability** Under the doctrine of ***respondeat superior*** (let the master answer), a principal who is an **employer** is liable for torts committed by agents (1) who are **employees** and (2) who commit the tort while acting within the **scope of their employment.** *Respondeat superior* makes the principal liable both for an employee's negligence and for her intentional torts. Chapter 35 outlined the main factors courts consider when determining whether an agent is an employee. The most important of these factors is a principal's right to control the manner and means of an agent's performance of work.

Respondeat superior is a rule of *imputed* or *vicarious* liability because it bases an employer's liability on her relationship with the employee rather than her own fault. This imputation of liability reflects the following beliefs: (1) that the economic burdens of employee torts can best be borne by employers; (2) that employers often can protect themselves against such burdens by self-insuring or purchasing insurance; and (3) that the resulting costs frequently can be passed on to consumers, thus "socializing" the economic risk posed by employee torts. *Respondeat superior* also motivates employers to ensure that their employees avoid tortious behavior. Because they typically control the physical details of the work, employers are fairly well positioned to do so.

Scope of Employment *Respondeat superior*'s scope-of-employment requirement has been stated in many ways and is notoriously ambiguous. Some courts considering this question asked whether the employee was on a "frolic" of his own, or merely made a "detour" from his assigned activity. According to the *Restatement*, an employee acts within the scope of employment when performing work assigned by the employer or when engaging in a course of conduct subject to the employer's control. An employee's act is not within the scope of employment when it occurs within an independent course of conduct not intended by the employee to serve any purpose of the employer. Most courts find that an employee's conduct is within the scope of his employment if it meets each of the following four tests:

1. It was of the *kind* that the employee was employed to perform. To meet this test, an employee's conduct need only be of the same general nature as work expressly authorized or be incidental to its performance.

2. It occurred substantially within the authorized *time* period. This is simply the employee's assigned time of work. Beyond this, there is an extra period of time during which the employment may continue. For instance, a security guard whose regular quitting time is 5:00 probably meets the time test if he unjustifiably injures an intruder at 5:15. Doing the same thing three hours later, however, would probably put the guard outside the scope of employment.

3. It occurred substantially within the *location* authorized by the employer. This includes locations not unreasonably distant from the authorized location. For example, a salesperson told to limit her activities to New York City probably would satisfy the location requirement while pursuing the employer's business in New Rochelle just north of the city limits but not while pursuing the same business in Philadelphia. Generally, the smaller the authorized area of activity, the smaller the departure from that area needed to put the employee outside the scope of employment. For example, consider the different physical distance limitations that should apply to a factory worker assigned to a single building and a traveling salesperson assigned to a five-state territory.

4. It was motivated *at least in part* by the *purpose* of serving the employer. This test is met when the employee's conduct was motivated *to any appreciable extent* by the desire to serve the employer. Thus, an employee's tort may be within the scope of employment even if the motives for committing it were partly personal. For example, suppose that a delivery employee is behind schedule and for that reason has an accident while speeding to make a delivery in his employer's truck. The employee would be within the scope of employment even if another reason for his speeding was to finish work quickly so he could watch his daughter's soccer game.

Ethics in Action

Principal's Liability for Agent's Torts

We have covered the reasons the law makes employers liable for the torts of employees under *respondeat superior*, including the ability of employers to bear the burden or to socialize the cost of paying for damages caused by an employee's tort.

- Do you think those are good reasons to make someone liable for the actions of another person? What kind of behavior is the rule of *respondeat superior* likely to foster? Does the rule encourage employers to train and supervise their employees better?

- Do you think *respondeat superior* makes employers liable for too many acts of their employees? Does the rule discourage some businesses from using employees? Does any discouragement affect both prospective employers and prospective employees?
- Do you think the law should make employers liable for all the torts of their employees?
- Do you think it is right for an employer to pay for all damages caused to others by the tort of an employee? When forming your answers, consider the ethical theories we covered in Chapter 4.

Direct Liability   A principal's **direct liability** for an agent's torts differs considerably from *respondeat superior* liability. Here, the principal himself is at fault, and there is no need to impute liability to him. Also, no scope-of-employment requirement exists in direct liability cases, and the agent need not be an employee. Of course, a principal might incur both direct liability and *respondeat superior* liability in cases where due to the principal's fault, an employee commits a tort within the scope of her employment.

A principal is directly liable for an agent's tortious conduct if the agent acts within her actual authority or the principal ratifies the agent's conduct. Usually this means the principal directs the agent's conduct and intends that it occur. In such cases, the *agent's* behavior might be intentional, reckless, or negligent. For instance if Lawn Mower Company directs its agent Agnew to sell defective lawn mowers to Landscape Company, Lawn Mower Company is directly liable to Landscape Company. Likewise, Procenture Consulting Company would be liable for harm to clients caused by its ordering its consulting employees to complete an engagement in an unreasonable, substandard manner.

www.toolkit.com
The CCH Business Owners Toolkit is a font of information on managing the liability of employers for the acts of employees. One article, "Negligent Hiring or Supervision," gives advice on how an employer may avoid vicarious and direct liability for the torts of employees.

The typical direct liability case, however, involves harm caused by the principal's negligence regarding the agent. Examples of direct liability for negligence include (1) giving the agent improper or unclear instructions; (2) failing to make and enforce appropriate regulations to govern the agent's conduct; (3) hiring an unsuitable agent; (4) failing to discharge an unsuitable agent; (5) furnishing an agent with improper tools, instruments, or materials; and (6) carelessly supervising an agent. Today, suits for negligent hiring are common.

The next case, *Millan*, covers both direct liability and *respondeat superior*.

Millan v. Dean Witter Reynolds, Inc.   90 S.W. 3d 760 (Tex. Ct. App 2002)

Maria Millan opened two brokerage accounts at Dean Witter Reynolds, Inc. One was for herself and the other for her as trustee for her son James. The broker for both accounts was her other son Miguel, an employee of Dean Witter. Over the course of the next three years, Miguel systematically looted his mother's account, ultimately stealing from her more than $287,000. He managed to do this by forging her signature on an account application form and opening an additional account in her name. This account had check-writing privileges and a credit card attached to it that Miguel used liberally. Dean Witter did not verify Millan's signature, as its policy required, when the bogus account was opened.

Miguel took his mother's periodic deposits, usually consisting of several thousand dollars, deposited these checks into this fictitious account, and wrote himself checks from the account, usually made out to "cash." Miguel covered his tracks by opening a post office box, filing a false change of address form on which he forged his mother's signature, and creating false account statements purporting to be from Dean Witter. In one instance, Miguel forged a check he stole from his mother's checkbook and made it payable to "cash" in the amount of $35,000. Disregarding Dean Witter written policy, a Dean Witter supervisor did not verify the check despite the high amount, the payment to "cash," and the concerns of a Dean Witter employee who first handled the check.

Millan sued her son and Dean Witter for unauthorized transactions, negligence, and gross negligence. The trial court directed a verdict for Dean Witter on the issues of vicarious liability. The jury was given the issue regarding Dean Witter's direct liability to Millan, and it found Dean Witter negligent and liable for 15 percent of her damages. Millan was found responsible for 85 percent of her damages on the grounds that she should have discovered the fraud earlier than she did. Millan appealed the trial court's decision to a Texas court of appeals. The court of appeals upheld the jury verdict that Dean Witter was only 15 percent responsible for Millan's damages under direct liability. The court then considered the vicarious liability issue using the doctrine of respondeat superior.

Angelini, Justice

Under the doctrine of *respondeat superior*, an employer is vicariously liable for the negligence of an agent or employee acting within the scope of his or her agency or employment. To determine whether an employee's acts are within the scope of his or her employment, we ask whether the employee's actions fall within the scope of the employee's general authority, are in furtherance of the employer's business, and are for the accomplishment of the object for which the employee was hired. In cases involving serious criminal activity, an employer is not liable for intentional and malicious acts that are unforeseeable considering the employee's duties. Our inquiry, therefore, must first focus on the scope of Miguel's general authority.

Miguel, in the course and scope of his employment for Dean Witter opened a brokerage account for his mother. It was within Miguel's general authority to open such accounts for clients, receive deposits to these accounts, and purchase and sell securities as directed by clients. Miguel's activities, however, went far beyond these general brokerage duties. Miguel greatly exceeded the scope of his authority when, through a litany of deceitful acts, he stole money from his mother. Those acts include stealing checks from his mother's bathroom drawer, writing checks on his mother's account, depositing his mother's checks into his own account, forging his mother's signature on numerous occasions, stealing statements from his mother's mailbox, creating and sending bogus statements to his mother, and opening a post office box so he could receive his mother's actual statements. These acts were not related to Miguel's duties and were not within his general scope of authority as a broker for Dean Witter.

We hold there was no evidence that Miguel acted within the scope of his authority as a broker at Dean Witter. Accordingly, there is no evidence to support the submission of the issue of Dean Witter's vicarious liability for fraud to the jury.

Judgment in favor of Dean Witter affirmed.

Liability for Torts of Nonemployee Agents

A principal ordinarily is *not* liable for torts committed by **nonemployee agents** (independent contractors). As compared with employees, nonemployee agents are more likely to have the size and resources to insure against tort liability and to pass on the resulting costs themselves. Sometimes, therefore, the risk still can be socialized if only the nonemployee agent is held responsible. Because the principal does not control the manner in which a nonemployee agent's work is performed, he has less ability to prevent the nonemployee agent's torts than an employer has to prevent an employee's torts. Thus, imposing liability on principals for the torts of nonemployee agents may do little to eliminate the nonemployee agent's torts. However, the rule that principals are not liable for torts committed by nonemployee agents has exceptions. For example:

1. A principal can be *directly* liable for tortious behavior connected with the retention of a nonemployee agent. One example is the hiring of a dangerously incompetent nonemployee agent.

2. A principal is liable for harm resulting from the nonemployee agent's failure to perform a *nondelegable duty*. A nondelegable duty is a duty whose proper performance is so important that a principal cannot avoid liability by contracting it away. Examples include a carrier's duty to transport its passengers safely, a municipality's duty to keep its streets in repair, a railroad's duty to maintain safe crossings, and a landlord's duties to make repairs and to use care in doing so. Thus, a landlord who retains a nonemployee agent to repair the stairs in an apartment building is liable for injuries caused by the agent's failure to repair the stairs properly.

3. A principal is liable for a nonemployee agent's negligent failure to take the special precautions needed to conduct certain *highly dangerous* or *inherently dangerous* activities. Examples of such activities include excavations in publicly traveled areas, the clearing of land by fire, the construction of a dam, and the demolition of a building. For example, a nonemployee agent engaged in demolishing a building presumably has duties to warn pedestrians and to keep them at a safe distance. If injury results from the nonemployee agent's failure to meet these duties, the principal is liable.

Liability for Agent's Misrepresentations

Special rules apply when a third party sues a principal for **misrepresentations** made by her agent. In most cases where the principal is liable under these rules, the third party can elect to recover in tort, or to rescind the transaction.

A principal is *directly* liable for misrepresentations made by her agent during authorized transactions if she *intended* that the agent make the misrepresentations. In some states, a principal also may be directly liable if she *negligently* allows the agent to make misrepresentations. Even where a principal is not directly at fault, she may be liable for an agent's misrepresentations if the agent had *actual or apparent authority to make true statements on the subject.* Suppose that an agent authorized to sell farmland falsely states that a stream on the land has never flooded the property when in fact it does so almost every year, and that this statement induces a third party to buy the land. The principal is directly liable if she intended that the agent make this false statement. Even if the principal is personally blameless, she is liable if the agent had actual or apparent authority to make true statements about the stream.

	CONCEPT REVIEW

An Outline of the Principal's Tort Liability

Respondeat Superior	1. Agent must be an employee, *and*
	2. Employee must act within scope of employment while committing the tort
Direct Liability	1. Principal intends and directs agent's intentional tort, recklessness, or negligence, or
	2. Principal is negligent regarding hiring or training of agent
Torts of Nonemployee Agents	1. Principal generally is *not* liable
	2. Exceptions exist for direct liability, highly dangerous activities, and nondelegable duties
Misrepresentation	1. Direct liability
	2. Vicarious liability when agent has authority to make true statements on the subject of the misrepresentation
	3. An exculpatory clause may eliminate the principal's tort liability, but the third party still can rescind the contract

After contemplating their potential liability under the rules just discussed, both honest and dishonest principals may try to escape liability for an agent's misrepresentations by including an **exculpatory clause** in contracts the agent makes with third parties. Such clauses typically state that the agent has authority only to make the representations contained in the contract and that only those representations bind the principal. Exculpatory clauses do not protect a principal who intends or expects that an agent will make false statements. Otherwise, though, they insulate the principal from *tort* liability if the agent misrepresents a material fact. But the third party still may rescind the transaction, because it would be unjust to let the principal benefit from the transaction while disclaiming responsibility for it.

Tort Liability of the Agent

Agents are usually liable for their own torts. Normally, they are not absolved from tort liability just because they acted at the principal's command. However, there are exceptions to this generalization.

1. An agent can escape liability if she is *exercising a privilege of the principal.* Suppose that Tingle grants Parkham a right-of-way to transport his farm products over a private road crossing Tingle's land. Parkham's agent Adams would not be liable in trespass for driving across Tingle's land to transport farm products if she did so at Parkham's command. However, an agent must not exceed the scope

of the privilege and must act for the purpose for which the privilege was given. Thus, Adams would not be protected if she took her Jeep on a midnight joyride across Tingle's land. Also, the privilege given the agent must be delegable in the first place. If Tingle had given the easement to Parkham exclusively, Adams would not be privileged to drive across Tingle's land.

2. A principal who is *privileged to take certain actions in defense of his person or property* may often authorize an agent to do the same. In such cases, the agent escapes liability if the principal could have done so. For example, a WalMart warehouse guard may use force to protect the property in WalMart's warehouse.

3. An agent who makes *misrepresentations* while conducting the principal's business is not liable in tort unless he either *knew or had reason to know* their falsity. Suppose Parker authorizes Arnold to sell his house, falsely telling Arnold that the house is fully insulated. Arnold does not know that the statement is false and could not discover its falsity through a reasonable inspection. If Arnold tells Thomas that the house is fully insulated and Thomas relies on this statement in purchasing the house, Parker is directly liable to Thomas, but Arnold is not liable.

4. An agent is not liable for injuries to third persons caused by *defective tools or instrumentalities* furnished by the principal unless the agent had actual knowledge or reason to know of the defect.

Tort Suits against Principal and Agent

Sometimes both principal and agent are liable for an agent's torts. Here, the parties are *jointly and severally* liable. This means that a third party may join the principal and the agent in one suit and get a judgment against each, or may sue either or both individually and get a judgment against either or both. However, once a third party actually collects in full from either the principal or the agent, no further recovery is possible.

In some cases, therefore, either the principal or the agent has to satisfy the judgment alone despite the other party's liability. Here, the other party sometimes is required to *indemnify* the party who has satisfied the judgment. As discussed in Chapter 35, for example, sometimes a principal is required to indemnify an agent for tort liability the agent incurs. On the other hand, some torts

committed by agents may involve a breach of duty to their principal, and the principal may be able to recover from an agent on this basis.

LOG ON

http://www.law.upenn.edu/bll/archives/ulc/uaaa/aaa1130.htm

Agents and College Athletes

The University of Pennsylvania law school maintains a website where you can read the Uniform Athlete Agent Act (2000), which is designed to regulate contacts between agents and college athletes and, thereby, to help college athletes maintain their eligibility to play college sports. Note that section 14 lists several prohibited actions, backed by section 15, which imposes criminal penalties on an agent who violates section 14.

Problems and Problem Cases

1. Jonas Bravario hires Suzanne Hermano, a securities broker, to manage his $700,000 portfolio of securities. When Bravario managed his own investments, his investment strategy was to own a large number of different companies, with no one company representing more than 5 percent of his total investments. Bravario also purchased all his investments for cash and did not borrow money to finance the purchase of any investment. Hermano is aware of Bravario's historical investment strategy, which Bravario informed Hermano that he wanted to continue in the future. Nonetheless, Hermano opts to purchase 1 million shares of Enron Corporation for $70,000. To finance the purchase, Hermano sells $40,000 of Bravario's current investments and borrows $30,000 from Wells Fargo Bank in the name of Bravario. The interest rate on the loan is 10 percent. When Bravario discovers the purchase and the loan, he attempts to repudiate both contracts. Is Bravario liable on the Enron purchase and loan contracts?

2. Kamitra Smith was a catering specialist for TLC Catering, a food service business. TLC's catering specialists were authorized to make catering contracts with customers and to serve food in compliance with those contacts. On behalf of TLC, Smith made a contract with Miller Clandon & Associates, a law firm, to cater a holiday party in Miller Clandon's

office. Smith signed a contract that was drafted by Miller Clandon. The contract provided that TLC would be liable for all damages suffered by Miller Clandon and its staff in connection with TLC's performance of the contract. Smith and three other TLC employees catered the Miller Clandon party for TLC. One of Miller Clandon's staff attorneys slipped on coffee spilled by a TLC employee during the catered party. The attorney sued TLC, arguing that TLC was bound by the contact signed by Smith. Did Smith have express, implied, or apparent authority to sign the contact that imposed liability on TLC?

3. Adventure Quest, Inc., a nonprofit school, was founded and operated by Peter Drutchal, its executive director and only full-time employee. From 1994 to 1996, Adventure Quest had liability coverage with Virginia Surety Company. The insurance policy included a "sexual abuse endorsement" that provided coverage for sexual abuse claims, but excluded from coverage any person or entity that personally participated in committing any sexual abuse. When Drutchal completed Adventure Quest's application for the insurance policy, he answered "no" in response to the question, "Have you ever had an incident which resulted in an allegation of sexual abuse?" In fact, Drutchal had previously sexually abused Adventure Quest's students, and additional abuse occurred during the coverage periods of the insurance policy. He kept the abuse secret from others until

2001. Drutchal's sexual abuse occurred in the course of school activities, while Drutchal was acting in his capacity as coach and chaperone. Drutchal's acts of sexual abuse were for his own purposes. The abuse was not done within the scope of his duties or authority as executive director and was not done in the best interests of Adventure Quest. Virginia Surety refused to pay for Adventure Quest's liability for Drutchal's abuse, arguing that Drutchal's knowledge of his own previous abuse was imputable to Adventure Quest, thereby excluding it from the policy's coverage. Was Virginia Surety right?

4. Richard Daynard, a Northeastern University law professor, contracted to provide tobacco litigation assistance to the Ness law firm in South Carolina. The Ness firm and the Scruggs law firm of Mississippi were plaintiffs' attorneys for tobacco litigation in Mississippi. Over a period of months, Daynard met in South Carolina and Boston, spoke over the phone, and communicated by fax with members of the Ness firm. He also communicated by phone and fax with members of the Scruggs firm. Based on their actions, Daynard believed that the Ness firm and Scruggs firm were agents of each other in directing the Mississippi tobacco litigation. In addition, both firms retained the benefits of his legal advice, which was provided in accordance with a contract he made with the Ness law firm and called for compensation equal to 5 percent of their legal fees. When the firms refused to pay Daynard, he sued in a federal district court in Massachusetts. The court had personal jurisdiction over the Ness firm, because of its contacts with Massachusetts, but the Scruggs firm asserted that it had no contacts with Massachusetts. May the contacts of the Ness firm be imputed to the Scruggs firm, giving the court jurisdiction over the Scruggs firm?

5. Sally Leiner was the sole shareholder, director, and president of Ecco Bella, Inc., a New Jersey corporation. On various occasions, African Bio-Botanica, Inc., sold Leiner and/or Ecco Bella merchandise. African gave little thought to the party with whom it was dealing. Initially, its records listed Sally Leiner as the customer; later, this was changed to Ecco Bella, but without any indication that Ecco Bella was a corporation. The checks with which Leiner paid for her orders and her firm's stationery bore the name Ecco Bella, but likewise did not indicate that the firm was a corporation.

Eventually, Leiner did not pay for a shipment from African, and African sued her personally for damages in a New Jersey trial court. Leiner's defense was that only the corporation, and not herself personally, was liable. Is Leiner correct?

6. Jerome Cohen was a youth counselor for Mellon Community Center (MCC). Needing paper supplies for a project he had planned for the youths he was counseling, Cohen went to a local Staples supplies store and selected $150 of paper goods. He paid for the goods with his personal credit card. He did not tell Staples that he was buying the paper goods for MCC. Cohen asked MCC to reimburse him for the cost of the paper goods, but it refused on the grounds that Cohen should have asked for permission in advance. Cohen then refused to pay the credit card bill for the paper purchase. He argued that since he bought the goods for MCC, only MCC was liable on the contract to buy the goods. Was Cohen right?

7. Mark Bradshaw, an agent for National Foundation Life Insurance Co. (NFLIC), tried to sell a health insurance policy to Bobby Reed. Bradshaw told Reed that his health insurance coverage would begin upon signing some forms and paying the first premium. On January 7, Reed signed but did not read the forms, which included language stating that Reed understood that Bradshaw could not change any NFLIC policy or make any policy effective, that the policy would not be effective until actually issued by NFLIC, and that it could take up to two weeks for Reed's application to be processed and the policy issued. NFLIC received Reed's application, including his payment for the first premium, on January 12. On January 19, NFLIC called Reed's home and was informed he had a heart attack on January 15. NFLIC declined to issue the policy to Reed. On what grounds did Reed sue Bradshaw? Was Reed's suit against Bradshaw successful?

8. Redford had been a backhoe operator for five years. Although he had worked for other sign companies, he had spent 90 percent of his time during the past three years working for Tube Art Display, Inc. Redford generally dug holes exactly as directed by the sign company employing him. He did, however, pay his own business taxes, and he did not participate in any of the fringe benefits available to Tube Art employees.

Tube Art obtained a permit to install a sign in the parking lot of a combination commercial and apartment building. Telling Redford how to proceed, Tube Art's service manager laid out the exact location of a 4 × 4 foot square on the asphalt surface with yellow paint and directed that the hole be 6 feet deep. After

Redford began the job, he negligently struck a small natural gas pipeline with the backhoe. He examined the pipe, and, finding no indication of a leak or break, concluded that the line was not in use and left the worksite. Later, an explosion and fire occurred in the building serviced by the line. As a result, a business owned by Massey was destroyed. Massey sued Tube Art for Redford's negligence under the doctrine of *respondeat superior*. Did Massey recover?

9. LaVar Johnson was a retail representative for the Wheaton Company, a processor of consumer packaged goods like cereals and canned goods. Johnson's job was to visit grocery stores in his territory to ensure that each store gave adequate shelf space to all Wheaton products sold by the store. Wheaton told Johnson that maintaining good relations with the general manager and assistant manager of each store was essential. It was important, Wheaton told him, to accommodate the managers to ensure that Wheaton got the shelf space it wanted in each store.

   While visiting a store in Springfield, Illinois, Johnson chatted for a few minutes with the manager, who got a phone call that his wife was in an auto accident while on her way to pick up the manager at the store. While the wife was not seriously injured, Johnson offered to take the manager to the scene of the accident, and the manager accepted. On the way to the accident scene, Johnson negligently ran a red light, resulting in his car being struck by another car. The grocery store manager received a broken leg, arm, and pelvis. Is Wheaton liable for the manager's injuries under the doctrine of *respondeat superior*?

10. Gary McCoy ordered a pizza from a Papa John's restaurant. The restaurant was owned by RWT, Inc., a franchisee of Papa John's International, Inc. RWT did business as Papa John's Pizza. Wendell Burke, an employee of RWT, Inc., delivered the pizza and obtained payment from McCoy at his place of business. Burke lingered for almost two hours after being paid, asking McCoy for a job and viewing a hunting videotape. When Burke returned to the Papa John's restaurant, to avoid criticism for being late he concocted the story that McCoy held him against his will. The police arrested McCoy for false imprisonment, which charges were eventually dropped. McCoy sued Burke, RWT, and Papa John's International for malicious prosecution based on Burke's false statements. Does the doctrine of *respondeat superior* impose liability on the franchisor, Papa John's International, in this case?

11. Tammy Bauer hires consulting firm Accent Pointe LLP to find a buyer for the formula and trade name of her pest repellent, NO BUGGZ. Bauer tells Accent Pointe to tell prospective buyers that NO BUGGZ is organic and has no health risks to humans. Bauer knows that NO BUGGZ has serious negative health effects on humans even when used as directed. Consequently, Accent Pointe tells Scotts Company that NO BUGGZ has no serious negative health risks to humans when used as directed. The written purchase contract that Scotts signs with Bauer does not represent that NO BUGGZ has no health risks to humans; the contract contains an exculpatory clause stating that Bauer is not bound by Accent Pointe's representations, unless they also appear in the written contract. Two years after Scotts buys NO BUGGZ, Scotts is subjected to consumer lawsuits claiming that NO BUGGZ is causing health problems for its users. Is Bauer liable to Scotts for misrepresentation?

12. Thule Drilling sued Jacob Schimberg based on business transactions between Thule and QGM Group, a corporation for which Schimberg was the CEO. Thule's contract with QGM required QGM to do repair and construction work on three of Thule's mobile drilling rigs. Thule agreed to loan QGM funds so that QGM's work on the rigs could be completed. Thule alleged that QGM breached the contracts with Thule and that Thule was entitled to take possession of the rigs. Thule also argued that Schimberg, as the corporate agent of QGM, was personally liable to Thule, because he directly denied Thule access to its rigs, committing the tort of conversion. Schimberg argued that he acted only at the behest of his QGM superiors and that he was never a party to any of the contracts between Thule and QGM. Are both QGM and Schimberg liable to Thule?

Online Research

Employer Liability for Workplace Violence

Search the Web to find the article by Steve Kaufer, "Corporate Liability: Sharing the Blame for Workplace Violence." Create a list of steps that an employer should take to protect its employees from violent fellow workers and thereby reduce the employer's risk of liability for the violent acts of employees.

Partnerships

Part Nine

Partnerships

CHAPTER 37

INTRODUCTION TO FORMS OF BUSINESS AND FORMATION OF PARTNERSHIPS

After working for a large company for 10 years, you decide to give expression to your entrepreneurial urges and start a business. Your business plan is to help small firms that are struggling with finding ways to make new information technologies affordable and effective for their business. You envision that your business will need a capital infusion of $500,000 for the first year, during which you project the business will have a net loss of $200,000, which reflects in part your salary of $80,000. Beginning with the second year, you believe that the business will generate enough cash flow to finance internally all its normal capital expenditures. You expect second-year losses to be $100,000. Beginning with the third year, the business will be profitable.

You have $120,000 of savings that you are willing to invest in the business. You hope to obtain the remaining $380,000 of initial capital from investors. While you are willing to give a portion of the equity of the business to the investors, you want to control the business, including day-to-day operations. It is especially important that the other investors not be able to expel you from the business or its management.

- What business forms are best for your business?
- How will you modify the default rules of some business forms to make those forms work best for you?

LEARNING OBJECTIVES

After studying this chapter, you should be able to:

1. Choose an appropriate form of business for a particular enterprise.
2. List the traits of each form of business.
3. Compare and contrast the various forms of business.
4. Apply the definition of partnership and avoid inadvertently being a partner of another person.
5. Appreciate the consequences of being a partner.
6. Understand the risks of being a purported partner and avoid being a purported partner.
7. Distinguish partner's property from partnership property.
8. List and compare the rights of a creditor having a charging order and the rights of a transferee of a partner's interest in a partnership.

IN THIS CHAPTER, YOU begin your study of business organizations. Early in this chapter, you will preview the basic characteristics of the most important forms of business and learn how to select an appropriate form of business and learn how to select an appropriate form for a business venture. Following that introduction, you will begin your in-depth study of partnerships, learning their characteristics and the formalities for their creation.

Choose an appropriate form of business for a particular enterprise.

Choosing a Form of Business

One of the most important decisions made by a person beginning a business is choosing a **form of business.** This decision is important because the business owner's liability and control of the business vary greatly among the many forms of business. In addition, some business forms offer significant tax advantages to their owners.

Although other forms of business exist, usually a person starting a business will wish to organize the business as a sole proprietorship, partnership, limited liability partnership, limited partnership, limited liability limited partnership, corporation, or limited liability company.

List the traits of each form of business.

Sole Proprietorship   A **sole proprietorship** has
only one owner. The sole proprietorship is merely an extension of its only owner, the **sole proprietor.**

As the only owner, the sole proprietor has the right to make all the management decisions of the business. In addition, all the profits of the business are his. A sole proprietor assumes great liability: He is personally liable for all the obligations of the business. All the debts of the business, including debts on contracts signed only in the name of the business, are his debts. If the assets of the business are insufficient to pay the claims of its creditors, the creditors may require the sole proprietor to pay the claims using his individual, nonbusiness assets such as money from his bank account and the proceeds from the sale of his house. A sole proprietor may lose everything if his business becomes insolvent. Hence, the sole proprietorship is a risky form of business for its owner.

Despite this risk, there are two reasons why a person may organize a business as a sole proprietorship. First, the sole proprietorship is formed very easily and inexpensively. No formalities are necessary. Second, few people consider the business form decision. They merely begin their businesses. Thus, by default, a person going into business by herself automatically creates a sole proprietorship when she fails to choose another business form. These two reasons explain why the sole proprietorship is the most common form of business in the United States.

Because the sole proprietorship is merely an extension of its owner, it has no life apart from its owner. Therefore,

while the business of a sole proprietorship may be freely sold to someone else, legally the sole proprietorship as a form of business cannot be transferred to another person. The buyer of the business must create his own form of business to continue the business.

A sole proprietorship is not a legal entity. It cannot sue or be sued. Instead, creditors must sue the owner. The sole proprietor—in his own name—must sue those who harm the business.

A sole proprietor may hire employees for the business, but they are employees of the sole proprietor. Under the law of agency, the sole proprietor is responsible for her employees' authorized contracts and for the torts they commit in the course of their employment. Also, a sole proprietorship is not a tax-paying entity for federal income tax purposes. All of the income of a sole proprietorship is income to its owner and must be reported on the sole proprietor's individual federal income tax return. Likewise, any business losses are deductible without limit on the sole proprietor's individual tax return. This loss-deduction advantage explains why some wealthier taxpayers use the sole proprietorship for selected business investments—when losses are expected in the early years of the business, yet the risk of liability is low. Such an investor may form a sole proprietorship and hire a professional manager to operate the business.

Many sole proprietorships have trade names. For example, Caryl Stanley may operate her bagel shop under the name Caryl's Bagel Shop. Caryl would be required to file the trade name under a state statute requiring the registration of fictitious business names. If she were sued by a creditor, the creditor would address his complaint to "Caryl Stanley, doing business as Caryl's Bagel Shop."

Partnership   A **partnership** has two or more owners,
called **partners.** The partners have the right to make all the management decisions for the business. In addition, all the profits of the business are shared equally by the partners.

The partners assume personal liability for all the obligations of the business. All the debts of the business are the debts of all the partners. Likewise, partners are liable for the torts committed in the course of business by their partners or by partnership employees. If the assets of the business are insufficient to pay the claims of its creditors, the creditors may require one or more of the partners to pay the claims using their individual, nonbusiness assets. Thus, a partner may have to pay more than his share of partnership liabilities.

Like the sole proprietorship, the partnership is not a tax-paying entity for federal income tax purposes. All of the income of the partnership is income to its partners and must be reported on the individual partners' federal income tax returns whether or not it is distributed to the partners. Likewise, any business losses are deductible without limit on the partner's individual tax return.

The partnership has a life apart from its owners. When a partner dies or otherwise leaves the business, the partnership usually continues. A partner's ownership interest in a partnership is not freely transferable: A purchaser of the partner's interest is not a partner of the partnership, unless the other partners agree to admit the purchaser as a partner.

Why would persons organize a business as a partnership? Formation of a partnership requires no formalities and may be formed by default. A partnership is created automatically when two or more persons own a business together without selecting another form. Also, each partner's right to manage the business and the deductibility of partnership losses on individual tax returns are attractive features.

Limited Liability Partnership A limited liability partnership is a partnership whose partners have elected limited liability status. Reacting to the large personal liability sometimes imposed on accountants and lawyers for the professional malpractice of their partners, Texas enacted in 1991 the first statute permitting the formation of **limited liability partnerships (LLPs).** An LLP is identical to a partnership except that an LLP partner has no liability for most LLP obligations; however, an LLP partner retains unlimited liability for his *own* wrongful acts, such as his malpractice liability to a client.

LLP partners may elect to have the LLP taxed like a partnership or a corporation. If an LLP is taxed like a corporation, it pays federal income tax on its income, but the partners pay federal income tax only on the compensation paid and the partnership profits distributed to the partners.

The formation of an LLP requires filing a form with the secretary of state; some states require LLPs to maintain adequate professional insurance or have a high net worth.

The LLP is an especially good form of business for professionals such as consultants and auditors, allowing them management flexibility while insulating them mostly from personal liability. The LLP is the preferred form of business for professionals.

Limited Partnership A **limited partnership** has one or more general partners and one or more limited partners. General partners have rights and liabilities similar to partners in a partnership. They manage the business of the limited partnership and have unlimited liability for the obligations of the limited partnership. Typically, however, the only general partner is a corporation, thereby protecting the human managers from unlimited liability.

Limited partners usually have no liability for the obligations of the limited partnership once they have paid their capital contributions to the limited partnership. Limited partners have no right to manage the business, but if they do manage, they nonetheless retain their limited liability.

Like an LLP, a limited partnership may elect to be taxed either as a partnership or as a corporation. If a limited partnership is taxed like a partnership, general partners report their shares of the limited partnership's income and losses on their individual federal income tax returns. For general partners, losses of the business are deductible without limit. A limited partner must pay federal income tax on his share of the profits of the business, but he may deduct his share of losses only to the extent of his investment in the business. As a passive investor, a limited partner may use the losses only to offset income from other passive investments.

If a limited partnership is taxed like a corporation, the limited partnership pays federal income tax on its net income. The partners pay federal income tax only on compensation paid and profits distributed to them.

A limited partnership may have a life apart from its owners. When a partner dies or otherwise leaves the business, the limited partnership is not dissolved, unless there is no remaining general partner or no remaining limited partner. A general or limited partner's rights may not be wholly transferred to another person unless the other partners agree to admit the new person as a partner.

Unlike a sole proprietorship or partnership—but like an LLP—a limited partnership may be created only by complying with a state statute permitting limited partnerships. Thus, no limited partnership may be created by default.

There are three main reasons why persons organize a business as a limited partnership. First, by using a corporate general partner, no human will have unlimited liability for the debts of the business. Second, if the limited partnership is taxed like a partnership, losses of the business are deductible on the owners' federal income tax returns. Third, investors may contribute capital to the business yet avoid unlimited liability and the obligation to manage the business. Thus, the limited partnership has the ability to attract large amounts of capital, much more than the sole proprietorship, which has only one owner, or the partnership, whose partners' fear of unlimited liability restricts the size of the business. Hence, for a business needing millions of dollars of capital, wanting only a few owners to manage the business, and expecting to lose money in its early years, the limited partnership is a particularly good form of business.

Limited Liability Limited Partnership A

limited liability limited partnership (LLLP) is a limited partnership whose partners have elected limited liability status for all the partners. An LLLP is created by making a filing with the secretary of state. The LLLP is designed to give the same limited liability advantages to general partners in a limited partnership as have been granted to partners who manage an LLP or a limited liability company (LLC). The LLC is explained shortly.

The LLLP is identical to a limited partnership in its management and the rights and duties of its partners. However, by electing LLLP status, both the limited partners and the general partners in a limited partnership will have no liability for most obligations of the LLLP. Nonetheless, a general partner will have unlimited liability for any torts he commits while acting for the LLLP.

Limited partnerships and LLLPs are covered in detail in Chapter 40.

Corporation A **corporation** is owned by shareholders who elect a board of directors to manage the business. The board of directors often selects officers to run the day-to-day affairs of the business. Consequently, ownership and management of a corporation may be completely separate: No shareholder has the right to manage, and no officer or director needs to be a shareholder.

Shareholders have limited liability for the obligations of the corporation, even if a shareholder is elected as a director or selected as an officer. Directors and officers have no liability for the contracts they or the corporation's employees sign only in the name of the corporation. While managers have liability for their own misconduct, they have no liability for corporate torts committed by other corporate managers or employees. Therefore, shareholders, officers, and directors have limited liability for the obligations of the business.

The usual corporation is a tax-paying entity for federal income tax purposes. The corporation pays taxes on its profits. Shareholders do not report their shares of corporation profits on their individual federal income tax returns. Instead, only when the corporation distributes its profits to the shareholders in the form of dividends or the shareholders sell their investments at a profit do the shareholders report income on their individual returns. This creates a double-tax possibility, as profits are taxed once at the corporation level and again at the shareholder level when dividends are paid.

Also, shareholders do not deduct corporate losses on their individual returns. They may, however, deduct their investment losses after they have sold their shares of the corporation.

There is one important exception to these corporate tax rules. The shareholders may elect to have the corporation and its shareholders taxed under Subchapter S of the Internal Revenue Code. By electing **S Corporation** status, the corporation and its shareholders are taxed nearly entirely like a partnership: Income and losses of the business are reported on the shareholders' individual federal income tax returns. A corporation electing S Corporation status may have no more than 100 shareholders, have only one class of shares, and be owned only by individuals and trusts.

A corporation has a life separate from its owners and its managers. When a shareholder or manager dies or otherwise leaves the business, the corporation is not dissolved. A shareholder may sell his shares of the corporation to other persons without limitation unless there is a contrary agreement. The purchaser becomes a shareholder with all the rights of the selling shareholder.

There are several reasons why persons organize a business as a corporation. First, no human has unlimited liability for the debts of the business. As a result, businesses in the riskiest industries—such as manufacturing—incorporate. Second, because investors may contribute capital to the business, avoid unlimited liability, escape the obligation to manage the business, and easily liquidate their investments by selling their shares, the corporation has the ability to attract large amounts of capital, even more than the limited partnership, or LLLP, whose partnership interests are not as freely transferable. Thus, the corporation has the capacity to raise the largest amount of capital.

The S Corporation has an additional advantage: Losses of the business are deductible on individual federal income tax returns. However, because the S Corporation is limited to 100 shareholders, its ability to raise capital is severely limited. Also, while legally permitted to sell their shares, S Corporation shareholders may be unable to find investors willing to buy their shares or may be restricted from selling their shares pursuant to an agreement between the shareholders.

Professional Corporation All states permit professionals such as accountants, physicians, and dentists to incorporate their professional practices. The **professional corporation** is identical to a business corporation in most respects. It is formed only by a filing with the secretary of state, and it is managed by a board of directors, unless a statute permits it to be managed like a partnership. The rigid management structure makes the professional corporation inappropriate for some smaller professional practices.

While professional shareholders have no personal liability for the obligations of the professional corporation, such as a building lease, they retain unlimited liability to their clients for their professional malpractice. A professional will have no personal liability, however, for the malpractice of a fellow shareholder or associate.

Typically, only professionals holding the same type of license to practice a profession may be shareholders of a professional corporation. For example, only physicians licensed to practice medicine may be shareholders of a professional corporation that practices medicine.

Professional corporation shareholders may elect for the corporation to be taxed like a corporation, or they may elect S Corporation tax treatment.

Fewer and fewer professionals incorporate each year. All of the liability and taxation advantages of the professional corporation have been assumed by the LLP. In addition, most professionals like the flexible management structure of the LLP better.

Limited Liability Company   A **limited liability company** (LLC) is a business form intended to combine the nontax advantages of corporations with the favorable tax treatment of partnerships. An LLC is owned by members, who may manage the LLC themselves or elect the manager or managers who will operate the business. Members have limited liability for the obligations of the LLC.

All states except California permit professionals to organize as LLCs. Professionals in a professional LLC have unlimited liability, however, for their own malpractice. Like an LLP or LLLP, members of an LLC may elect to have the LLC taxed like a partnership or a corporation.

There is limited free transferability of the LLC members' ownership interests. Transfer of a membership interest entitles the transferee to receive only the member's distributions from the LLC, unless all members or the LLC agreement permits the transferee to become a member. The death, retirement, or bankruptcy of any member usually does not dissolve or cause the liquidation of the LLC.

What are the advantages of the LLC? The LLC has the limited liability advantage and, if manager-managed, the management advantage of the corporation. The LLC and its members may elect to receive federal tax treatment similar to the S Corporation and its shareholders, yet the LLC has no limit on the number or type of owners, as does an S Corporation.

LLCs are covered in detail in Chapter 40.

 L03   Compare and contrast the various forms of business.

See Figure 1 for a summary of the general characteristics of business forms.

 LOG ON

http://www.sba.gov/category/navigation-structure/starting-managing-business

The Small Business Administration has valuable resources for anyone starting a business. Under "Starting a Business" you will find a link to "Establishing a Business." Click on the link "Incorporating and Registering Your Business." You will find sections describing some forms of business and listing some of the other steps to beginning a business. Go back to the menu under "Establishing a Business," click on "Taxes," and you will see some of the tax law requirements for new businesses.

The Global Business Environment

Globally, businesses have a wide choice of business forms, and many of them are forms shared by many countries. For example, the partnership is recognized not only in the United States but also in Australia, Canada, Cyprus, England, India, Israel, Russia, South Africa, Turkey, Zimbabwe, and many other nations. In the Chinese province of Hong Kong, the sole proprietorship, partnership, limited partnership, and company are the typical business forms. Limited liability partnerships and limited liability limited partnerships do not exist in Hong Kong as yet, or much of the world for that matter. Limited liability companies in Hong Kong are like American corporations.

German law recognizes the public stock corporation (*AG* or *Aktiengesellschaft*). Its shares are freely transferable like those of American corporations, so it may have an unlimited number of shareholders. More common is the limited liability company (*GmbH* or *Gesellschaft mit beschrankter Haftung*), first created in 1892. It permits the owners to restrict the transfer of its shares. The majority of German subsidiaries of foreign corporations are *GmbHs* rather than *AGs*. Owners of *AGs* and *GmbHs* have liability limited to their capital contributions. The German general commercial partnership (*OHG* or *offene Handelgesellschaft*) and the limited commercial partnership (*KG* or *Kommanditgesellschaft*) are essentially the same as the general and limited partnerships in the United States.

To find examples of forms of business in 60 countries, go to http://en.wikipedia.org/wiki/Types_of_business_entity.

Figure 1 *General Characteristics of Forms of Business*

	Sole Proprietorship	Partnership	Limited Liability Partnership	Limited Partnership	Limited Liability Limited Partnership	Corporation	S Corporation	Limited Liability Company
Formation	When one person owns a business without forming a corporation or LLC	By agreement of owners *or* by default when two or more owners conduct business together without creating another business form	By agreement of owners; must comply with limited liability partnership statute	By agreement of owners; must comply with limited partnership statute	By agreement of owners; must comply with limited liability limited partnership statute	By agreement of owners; must comply with corporation statute	By agreement of owners; must comply with corporation statute; must elect S Corporation status under Internal Revenue Code	By agreement of owners; must comply with limited liability company statute
Duration	Terminates on death or withdrawal of sole proprietor	Usually unaffected by death or withdrawal of partner	Usually unaffected by death or withdrawal of partner	Unaffected by death or withdrawal of partner	Unaffected by death or withdrawal of partner	Unaffected by death or withdrawal of shareholder	Unaffected by death or withdrawal of shareholder	Usually unaffected by death or withdrawal of member
Management	By sole proprietor	By partners	By partners	By general partners	By general partners	By board of directors	By board of directors	By members, unless choose to be manager-managed
Owner Liability	Unlimited	Unlimited	Limited to capital contribution, except for owner's individual torts	Unlimited for general partners; limited to capital contribution for limited partners	Limited to capital contribution, except for owner's individual torts	Limited to capital contribution, except for owner's individual torts	Limited to capital contribution, except for owner's individual torts	Limited to capital contribution, except for owner's individual torts
Transferability of Owners' Interest	None	Limited	Limited	Limited, unless agreed otherwise	Limited, unless agreed otherwise	Freely transferable, although shareholders may agree otherwise	Freely transferable, although shareholders usually agree otherwise	Limited, unless agreed otherwise
Federal Income Taxation	Only sole proprietor taxed	Only partners taxed	Usually only partners taxed; may elect to be taxed like a corporation	Usually only partners taxed; may elect to be taxed like a corporation	Usually only partners taxed; may elect to be taxed like a corporation	Corporation taxed; shareholders taxed on dividends (double tax)	Only shareholders taxed	Usually only members taxed; may elect to be taxed like a corporation

Ethics in Action

Two people who carefully consider which American business form to use for their business can achieve nearly any combination of attributes. For example, by choosing LLP status, they can limit their personal liability, totally control the business, and deduct business losses on their individual federal income tax returns. They can do the same with an LLC or S Corporation. They will have no liability for the contracts of the business, even though they make all business decisions and make all contracts for the business. When the business becomes profitable, they can elect to have the business form taxed like a corporation,

and if the corporate tax rate is lower than their individual tax rate, they will derive tax savings by retaining earnings in the business.

- Is it ethical for a business owner who controls the business to escape liability for the business's contracts and torts by hiding behind the veil of the business organization?
- Would you ever choose to use the partnership form when the LLP form is available?
- Is it ethical for a business owner to select a business form and elect a tax treatment that minimizes her tax liability?

Partnerships

The basic concept of partnership is as ancient as the history of collective human activity. Partnerships were known in ancient Babylonia, ancient Greece, and the Roman Empire. Hammurabi's Code of 2300 B.C. regulated partnerships. The definition of a partnership in the 6th-century Justinian Code of the Roman Empire does not differ materially from that in our laws today. The partnership was likewise known in Asian countries, including China. During the Middle Ages, much trade between nations was carried on by partnerships.

By the close of the 17th century, the partnership was recognized in the English common law. When the United States became an independent nation and adopted the English common law in 1776, the English law of partnerships became a part of American law. In the early part of the 19th century, the partnership became the most important form of association in the United States.

Today, the American common law of partnership has been largely replaced by statutory law. Every state has a statute on partnership law. The Revised Uniform Partnership Act (RUPA) of 1994, with the 1997 amendments, is a model partnership statute that is the product of the National Conference of Commissioners on Uniform State Laws, a group of practicing lawyers, judges, and law professors. The aims of the RUPA are to codify partnership law in one document, to make that law more nearly consistent with itself, and to attain uniformity throughout the country.

In recent years, the RUPA has supplanted the Uniform Partnership Act (UPA) of 1914 as the dominant source of partnership law in the United States. As of October 2011, 37 states plus the District of Columbia and the Virgin

Islands have adopted the RUPA. The RUPA is the framework of your study of partnerships and limited liability partnerships. (See Figure 2.)

Creation of Partnership

No formalities are necessary to create a partnership. Two or more persons may become partners in accordance with a written partnership agreement (articles of partnership), they may agree orally to be partners, or they may become partners merely by arranging their affairs as if they were partners. If partners conduct business under a trade name, they must file the name with the secretary of state in compliance with state statutes requiring the registration of fictitious business names.

When people decide to become partners, they should employ a lawyer to prepare a written partnership agreement. Although a partnership agreement is not required to form a partnership, it is highly desirable for the same reasons that written contracts are generally preferred. In addition, the statute of frauds requires a writing for a partnership having a term of a year or more.

More importantly, when partners do not define their relationship as partners, the default rules of the RUPA determine the rights of the partners vis-á-vis each other. While the RUPA rules are sensible and meet the needs of many partners, they may not meet the specific interests of other partners. Thus, having a written partnership agreement will allow the partners to define their rights and duties appropriately for them.

When there is no written partnership agreement, a dispute may arise over whether persons who are associated in some enterprise are partners. For example, someone may assert that she is a partner and, therefore, claim a share

Figure 2 *Principal Characteristics of Partnerships under the RUPA*

1. A partnership may be created with no formalities. Two or more people merely need to agree to own and conduct a business together in order to create a partnership.

2. Partners have unlimited liability for the obligations of the business.

3. Each partner, merely by being an owner of the business, has a right to manage the business of the partnership. He is an agent of the partnership and may make the partnership liable for contracts, torts, and crimes. Because partners are liable for all obligations of the partnership, in effect each partner is an agent of the other partners. Each partner may hire agents, and every partner is liable for the agents' authorized contracts and for torts that the agents commit in the course of their employments.

4. A partnership is not an employer of the partners, for most purposes. As a result, for example, a partner who leaves a partnership is not entitled to unemployment benefits.

5. Partners are fiduciaries of the partnership. They must act in the best interests of the partnership, not in their individual best interests.

6. The profits or losses of the business are shared by the partners, who report their shares of the profits or losses on their individual federal income tax returns, because the partnership does not pay federal income taxes. Nonetheless, a partnership does keep its own financial records and must file an information return with the Internal Revenue Service.*

7. A partnership may own property in its own name.

8. A partnership may sue or be sued in its own name. The partners may also be sued on a partnership obligation.

9. A partner may sue her partners during the operation of the partnership.

10. A partner's ownership interest in a partnership is not freely transferable. A purchaser of a partner's interest does not become a partner, but is entitled to receive only the partner's share of the partnership's profits.

11. Generally, a partnership has a life apart from its owners. If a partner dies, the partnership usually continues.

*The federal income tax return filed by a partnership, Schedule K-1, is merely an information return in which the partnership indicates its gross income and deductions and the names and addresses of its partners (IRC Sec. 6031). The information return allows the Internal Revenue Service to determine whether the partners accurately report partnership income on their individual returns.

of the value of a successful enterprise. More frequently, an unpaid creditor may seek to hold a person liable for a debt incurred by another person in the same enterprise. To determine whether there is a partnership in the absence of an express agreement, the courts use the definition of partnership in the RUPA.

 Apply the definition of partnership and avoid inadvertently being a partner of another person.

 Appreciate the consequences of being a partner.

RUPA Definition of Partnership The
RUPA defines a partnership as an "association of two or more persons to carry on as co-owners of a business for profit." If the definition is satisfied, then the courts will treat those involved as partners. A relationship may meet the RUPA definition of partnership even when a person does not believe he is a partner, and occasionally, even if the parties agree that they are not partners.

Association of Two or More Persons As an association, a partnership is a *voluntary and consensual relationship.* It cannot be imposed on a person; a person must agree expressly or impliedly to have a person associate with her. For example, a partner cannot force her partners to accept her daughter into the partnership.

No person can be a partner with herself—a partnership must have *at least two partners.* A person may be a partner with her spouse.

Nearly everyone or everything may be a partner. An individual, trust, partnership, limited partnership, corporation, or other association may be a partner.

Carrying On a Business Any trade, occupation, or profession may qualify as a business. Carrying on a business usually requires a series of transactions conducted over a period of time. For example, a group of farmers that buys supplies in quantity to get lower prices is not carrying on a business but only part of one. If the group buys harvesting equipment with which it intends to harvest crops for others for a fee for many years, it is carrying on a business.

Co-ownership Partners must *co-own the business* in which they associate. There is no requirement that the capital contributions or the assets of the business be co-owned.

Also, by itself, co-ownership of assets does not establish a partnership. For example, two persons who own a building as joint tenants are not necessarily partners. To be partners, they must co-own a business.

The two most important factors in establishing co-ownership of the business are the sharing of profits and the sharing of management of the business. The RUPA declares that a person's **sharing the profits** of a business is presumptive evidence that she is a partner in the business. This means that persons sharing profits are partners, unless other evidence exists to disprove they are partners. The rationale for this rule is that a person ordinarily would not be sharing the profits of a business unless she were a co-owner. This rule brings under partnership law many persons who fail to realize that they are partners. For example, two college students who purchase college basketball tickets, resell them, and split the profits are partners.

Sharing the gross revenues of a business does not create a presumption of partnership. The profits, not the gross receipts, must be shared. For example, a broker who receives a commission on a sale of land is not a partner of the seller of that land.

Although sharing profits usually is presumptive proof of a partnership, the RUPA provides that no presumption of partnership is made when a share of profits is received in payment

1. of a debt,
2. of wages to an employee or services to an independent contractor,
3. of rent,
4. of an annuity or other retirement or health benefit to a beneficiary or representative of a deceased partner,
5. interest on a loan, or
6. for the sale of the goodwill of a business or other property.

These exceptions reflect the normal expectations of the parties that no partnership exists in such situations.

Sharing management of a business is additional evidence tending to prove the existence of a partnership. However, by itself, participation in management is not conclusive proof of the existence of a partnership. For example, a creditor may be granted considerable control in a business, such as a veto power over partnership decisions and the right of consultation, without becoming a partner. Also, a sole proprietor may hire someone to manage his business, yet the manager will not be a partner of the sole proprietor.

However, when the parties claim that they share profits for one of the six reasons above, the sharing of management may overcome the presumption that they are not partners. When the parties arrange their affairs in a manner that otherwise establishes an objective intent to create a partnership, the courts find that a partnership exists. For example, when a nonmanagerial employee initially shares profits as a form of employment compensation, the employee is not a partner of his employer. But when the employer and employee modify their relationship by having the employee exercise the managerial control of a partner and fail to reaffirm that the manager is merely an employee, a partnership may exist.

Creditors occupy a special position. Many cases have permitted creditors to share profits and to exercise considerable control over a business without becoming partners. Creditor control is often justified on the grounds that it is merely reasonable protection for the creditor's risk.

For Profit The owners of an enterprise must *intend to make a profit* to create a partnership. If the enterprise suffers losses, yet the owners intend to make a profit, a partnership may result. When an endeavor is carried on by several people for charitable or other nonprofit objectives, it is not a partnership. For example, Alex and Geri operate a restaurant booth at a county fair each year to raise money for a Boy Scout troop. Their relationship is not a partnership but merely an association. (Nonetheless, like partners, they may be individually liable for the debts of the enterprise.)

Intent Frequently, courts say that there must be intent to form a partnership. This rule is more correctly stated as follows: *The parties must intend to create a relationship that the law recognizes as a partnership.* A partnership may exist even if the parties entered it inadvertently, without considering whether they had created a partnership. A written agreement to the effect that the parties do not intend to form a partnership is not conclusive if their actions provide evidence of their intent to form a relationship that meets the RUPA partnership test.

There are several important consequences of being a partner. See Figure 3 for a summary of the most important consequences.

The *Southex* case, which follows the next section, considers whether two businesses are partners.

Creation of Joint Ventures
Courts frequently distinguish **joint ventures** from partnerships. A joint venture may be found when a court is reluctant to

Figure 3   *Important Consequences of Being a Partner*

1. You share ownership of the business. For example, you want to bring an employee into your business, which is worth $250,000. If you and the employee conduct your affairs like partners, your employee will become your partner and own half of your business.
2. You share the profits of the business.
3. You share management of the business. Your partner must be allowed to participate in management decisions.
4. Your partner is an agent of the partnership. You are liable for your partner's torts and contracts made in the ordinary course of business.
5. You owe fiduciary duties to your partnership and your partner, such as the duties not to compete with the business, not to self-deal, and not to disclose confidential matters.
6. You have unlimited personal liability for all the obligations of the partnership.

call an arrangement a partnership because the purpose of the arrangement is not to establish an ongoing business involving many transactions; instead, it is limited to a single project. For example, an agreement to buy, develop, and resell for profit a particular piece of real estate is likely to be viewed as a joint venture rather than a partnership. In all other respects, joint ventures are created just as partnerships are created. The joint venturers may have a formal written agreement. In its absence, a court applies the RUPA definition of partnership—modified so as not to require the carrying on of a business—to determine whether a joint venture has been created.

The legal implications of the distinction between a partnership and a joint venture are not entirely clear. Generally, partnership law applies to joint ventures. For example, all of the participants in a joint venture are personally liable for its debts, and joint venturers owe each other the fiduciary duties imposed on partners. Joint ventures are treated as partnerships for federal income tax purposes. The most significant difference between joint venturers and partners is that joint venturers are usually held to have *less implied and apparent authority* to make contracts for the joint venture than partners, because of the limited scope of the enterprise.

Southex Exhibitions, Inc. v. Rhode Island Builders Association, Inc. **279 F. 3d 94 (1st Cir. 2002)**

The Rhode Island Builder's Association, Inc. (RIBA), is an association of home construction companies. In 1974, RIBA's executive director, Ross Dagata, made an agreement with Sherman Exposition Management, Inc. (SEM), a professional show owner and producer, regarding future productions of the RIBA home shows at the Providence Civic Center. The preamble in the 1974 Agreement announced that "RIBA wishes to participate in such shows as sponsors and partners." The term of the 1974 Agreement was five years, renewable by mutual agreement.

RIBA also agreed to sponsor and endorse only shows produced by SEM, to persuade RIBA members to exhibit at those shows, and to permit SEM to use RIBA's name for promotional purposes. In turn, SEM promised to obtain all necessary leases, licenses, permits, and insurance, to indemnify RIBA for show-related losses, to grant RIBA the right to accept or reject any exhibitor, to audit show income, and to advance all the capital required to finance the shows. Net show profits were to be shared: 55 percent to SEM; 45 percent to RIBA.

The 1974 Agreement provided that all show dates and admission prices, as well as the Rhode Island bank at which show-related business would be transacted, required agreement by both parties. If the Civic Center became unavailable for reasons beyond SEM's control, SEM was to be excused from its production duties, provided that SEM promoted no other home show in Rhode Island. RIBA retained the right to conduct a home show at another venue, after notice to SEM.

When the 1974 Agreement was being negotiated, SEM and RIBA had conversations relating to the meaning of the term "partners" in the agreement. Manual Sherman, SEM's president, informed RIBA's Ross Dagata that he "wanted no ownership of the show" because he was uncertain about the financial prospects for home shows in the Rhode Island market. Sherman advised Dagata: "After the first year, if I'm not happy, we can't produce the show properly or make any money, we'll give you back the show." Although SEM owned other home shows which it produced outside Rhode Island, Sherman consistently described himself simply as the "producer" of the RIBA shows.

In 1994, Southex Exhibitions, Inc., acquired SEM's interest under the 1974 Agreement. By 1998, Southex determined that in order to maintain its financial stake in the RIBA home shows, the 1974 Agreement either needed to be renegotiated or allowed to expire according to its terms in 1999. RIBA in turn expressed dissatisfaction with Southex's performance, and eventually entered into a management contract with another producer, Yoffee Exposition Services, Inc.

Southex sued RIBA to enjoin the RIBA 2000 home show on the grounds that the 1974 Agreement established a partnership between RIBA and Southex's predecessor, SEM. Southex argued that RIBA breached its fiduciary duties to Southex by its dissolution of their partnership and its subsequent appointment of another producer. The federal district court denied Southex's request for a preliminary injunction and found that the 1974 Agreement did not create a partnership. Southex appealed.

Cyr, Senior Circuit Judge

Under Rhode Island law, a partnership is an association of two or more persons to carry on as co-owners a business for profit. The receipt by a person of a share of the profits of a business is prima facie evidence that he or she is a partner in the business.

Southex insists that the 1974 Agreement contains ample indicia that a partnership was formed, including: (1) a 55–45 percent sharing of profits; (2) mutual control over designated business operations, such as show dates, admission prices, choice of exhibitors, and "partnership" bank accounts; and (3) the respective contributions of valuable property to the partnership by the partners. In our view, the evidence indicating a nonpartner relationship cannot be dismissed as insubstantial.

First, the 1974 Agreement is simply entitled "Agreement," rather than "Partnership Agreement." Second, rather than an agreement for an indefinite duration, it prescribed a fixed (albeit renewable) term. Third, rather than undertake to share operating costs with RIBA, SEM not only agreed to advance all monies required to produce the shows, but to indemnify RIBA for all show-related losses as well. State law normally presumes that partners share equally or at least proportionately in partnership losses. Although partners may agree to override such statutory "default" provisions, there is no evidence that SEM and RIBA meant to do so, notwithstanding an intent to form a partnership.

Similarly, although RIBA involved itself in some management decisions, SEM was responsible for the lion's share. Partners normally share equal rights in management. Furthermore, Southex not only entered into contracts but conducted business with third parties, in its own name, rather than in the name of the putative partnership. As a matter of fact, their mutual association was never given a name. It is noteworthy as well that Southex never filed either a federal or state partnership tax return.

Similarly, the evidence as to whether either SEM or RIBA contributed any corporate property with the intent that it become jointly-owned partnership property is highly speculative, particularly since their mutual endeavor simply involved a periodic event, i.e., an annual home show, which neither generated, nor necessitated, ownership interests in significant tangible properties, aside from cash receipts. Unlike tangible real and personal property, whose ownership is more readily established, the intangible intellectual property involved here, such as clientele lists, goodwill, and business expertise, did not so readily lend itself to evidentiary establishment. As a consequence, in the present circumstances the requisite mutual intent to convert intangible intellectual properties into partnership assets may well depend much more importantly upon a clear contractual expression of mutual intention to form a partnership.

Finally, even assuming that the 1974 Agreement, as a whole, is ambiguous, (i) Manual Sherman testified that he regarded SEM as simply the producer of the annual RIBA shows; and (ii) Dagata testified that SEM specifically disclaimed any ownership interest in the home shows in 1974.

Southex urges that the 1974 Agreement necessitated a finding of partnership formation, in that it unambiguously describes the contracting parties as "partners." The labels the parties assign to their intended legal relationship, while probative of partnership formation, are not necessarily dispositive as a matter of law, particularly in the presence of countervailing evidence—e.g., the provision in the 1974 Agreement indemnifying RIBA for all show-related losses—which would tend to refute the partnership characterization. Although the manner in which the parties themselves characterize the relationship is probative, the question ultimately is objective intent.

Although the courts should refrain from resorting to extrinsic evidence where a contract is utterly unambiguous, the lone reference to "partners" in the 1974 Agreement's prefatory clause is so inconclusive as to carry minimal interpretive weight, especially since it arguably conflicted with other contract provisions. Had the parties intended otherwise, it would seem entirely reasonable to expect the 1974 Agreement to have been entitled "Partnership Agreement," rather than simply "Agreement."

Judgment for RIBA affirmed.

Creation of Mining Partnerships Although similar to an ordinary partnership or a joint venture, a mining partnership is recognized as a distinct relationship in a number of states. Persons who cooperate in the working of either a mine or an oil or gas well are treated as mining partners if there is (1) joint ownership of a mineral interest, (2) joint operation of the property, and (3) sharing of profits and losses. Joint operation requires more than merely financing the development of a mineral interest, but it does not require active physical participation in operations; it may be proved by furnishing labor, supplies, services, or advice. The delegation of sole operating responsibility to one of the participants does not bar treatment as a mining partnership.

Creation of Limited Liability Partnerships Unlike an ordinary partnership, a limited liability partnership (LLP) may not be created merely by partners conducting a business together. The partners must expressly agree to create an LLP by complying with a limited liability partnership statute. The formation of an LLP requires filing a form with the secretary of state, paying an annual fee, and adding the words "Registered Limited Liability Partnership," "Limited Liability Partnership," or the acronym "RLLP" or "LLP" to the partnership's name. Some states also require an LLP to maintain a minimum level of professional liability insurance or net worth.

 LO6 Understand the risks of being a purported partner and avoid being a purported partner.

Purported Partners

Two persons may not be partners, yet in the eyes of a third person they may **appear** to be partners. If the third person deals with one of the apparent partners, he may be harmed and seek to recover damages from both of the apparent partners. The question, then, is whether the third person may collect damages from both of the apparent partners, even though they are not partners in fact.

For example, Thomas thinks that Wilson, a wealthy person, is a partner of Porter, a poor person. Thomas decides to do business with Porter on the grounds that if Porter does not perform as agreed, he can recover damages from Wilson. If Thomas is wrong and Wilson is not Porter's partner, Thomas ordinarily has no recourse against Wilson. RUPA Section 308(e) states that "persons who are not partners as to each other are not liable as partners to other persons." However, if Thomas can prove that Wilson misled him to believe that Wilson and Porter were partners, he may sue Wilson for damages suffered when

Porter failed to perform as agreed. This is an application of the doctrine of **purported partners.**

The liability of a purported partner is based on substantial, detrimental reliance on the appearance of partnership. A person will be a purported partner and have liability when the three elements of RUPA Section 308(a) are met:

1. A person purports to be or consents to being represented as a partner of another person or partnership.
2. A third party relies on the representation.
3. The third party transacts with the actual or purported partnership.

The third party may hold liable the persons who purported to be partners or consented to being represented as the partner of the actual or purported partnership.

Purporting to Be a Partner A person may purport to be a partner by referring to himself as another person's partner. Or he might appear frequently in the office of a purported partner and confer with him. Perhaps he and another person share office space, have one door to an office with both of their names on it, have one telephone number, and share a receptionist who answers the phone giving the names of both persons.

More difficult is determining when a person *consents* to being represented as another's partner. Mere knowledge that one is being held out as a partner is not consent. But a person's silence in response to a statement that the person is another's partner is consent.

For example, suppose Chavez tells Eaton that Gold is a partner in Birt's new restaurant. In fact, Gold is not Birt's partner. Later, Gold learns of the conversation between Chavez and Eaton. Gold does not have to seek out Chavez and Eaton to tell them that he is not Birt's partner in order to avoid being held liable as a partner for Birt's business debts. Had Chavez made the statement to Eaton in Gold's presence, however, Gold must deny the partnership relation or he will be held liable for Eaton's subsequent reliance on Gold's silence.

Note also that if a person makes a public representation that she is a partner of another, the purported partner is liable to any third person who relies on the representation, even if the purported partner is not aware of the reliance.

Reliance Resulting in a Transaction with the Partnership A purported partner is liable only to those persons who rely on the representation and enter into a transaction with the actual or purported partnership. This means that purported partnership is determined on a case-by-case basis. The third party must in fact rely on the appearance of partnership. For example, when Trump transacts with Doby based on Crabb's representation that Doby and Crabb are partners, Trump is able to hold both Doby and Crabb liable. If however, Trump had dealt with Doby believing Doby was in business by herself and later discovers that Crabb had purported to be Doby's partner, only Doby would be liable to Trump, because there was no reliance on Crabb's purporting to be Doby's partner when Trump transacted with Doby.

Effect of Purported Partnership

Once persons are proved to be purported partners, a person who purported to be the others' partner or who consented to being represented as the others' partner is liable as though he were a partner of those persons. He is liable on contracts entered into by third parties on their belief that he was a partner. He is liable for torts committed during the course of relationships entered by third parties who believed he was a partner. In addition, a partnership that represents that a person is a partner endows the purported partner with the apparent authority to make contracts for the partnership.

Although two persons are purported partners to a person who knows of the representation and who relies on it, the purported partners are not partners in fact and do not share the profits, management, or value of the business of the purported partnership. Purported partnership is merely a device to allow creditors to sue persons who mislead the creditors into believing that a partnership exists. It does not create an actual partnership.

In the following case, *McGregor v. Crumley,* the court found that a wife was not an actual or purported partner of her husband in his dairy business, despite her working in the business.

McGregor v. Crumley   775 N.W.2d 91 (S. Ct. S.D. 2009)

Clint and Paige Crumley lived on a dairy farm in Hand County, South Dakota. Clint managed the farm on a day-to-day basis, and Paige, a few hired hands, and Paige's mother and father also worked with the cattle. In August 2007, Clint purchased a herd of dairy cows from James McGregor. When McGregor delivered the dairy cows to Clint's dairy farm, Paige handed McGregor a check for payment. While at Clint's farm, McGregor observed Paige, her mother and father, and two farm hands working with the dairy cows on the farm.

In September 2007, McGregor and Clint had a series of telephone calls about the purchase of 25 dairy cows for Clint's milking operation. The calls were exclusively between McGregor and Clint. On September 13, 2007, McGregor and Clint entered into an oral contract for the purchase of dairy cows. McGregor's agent delivered 25 dairy cows to Clint's milking operation and assisted Clint in unloading the cattle. Paige was not present at the time of delivery. Nonetheless, the bill of lading prepared by McGregor's bookkeeper listed the purchasers as Clint and Paige Crumley. McGregor's agent gave the bill of lading to Clint.

A few days later, Clint returned to McGregor eight cows that were substandard. McGregor issued a second bill for the remaining 17 cows. The second bill listed both Clint and Paige as the purchasers. After the bill was not paid, McGregor sued both Clint and Paige. Eventually, Clint—via a letter from his attorney—offered to settle the suit filed by McGregor by returning the 17 cows. McGregor refused the offer.

At trial, Clint and Paige were represented by the same attorney. Paige was not present at the trial, did not testify, and was not called as a witness by either McGregor or Clint. McGregor testified at trial that he spoke with Clint several times concerning the outstanding bill. McGregor also testified that on one occasion he attempted to discuss the bill with Paige but was unable to get her to do so. McGregor testified that Clint became angry after finding out that McGregor had attempted to discuss the bill with Paige.

Clint testified at trial that he ran the dairy operation, and that he had gotten into the business on his own in early 2007. He further testified that Paige confronted him about the September 2007 purchase after McGregor tried to speak with her about the bill. Clint was not asked whether Paige was a partner in the operation with Clint. Clint also testified that, in the fall of 2007, he had signed over all the assets of the dairy farm—including the 17 cows purchased from McGregor—to his father-in-law to avoid losing the farm. He also testified that, after the transfer of the dairy operation's assets to his father-in-law, both he and Paige milked the dairy cows he had previously owned and were paid a bi-weekly salary of $1,000 by his father-in-law's limited liability company that assumed ownership of the operation.

McGregor did not ask questions concerning the business structure of Clint's dairy operation, or whether Paige was a partner in the business at the time of the cattle sale. Clint did not offer any evidence of the business structure of the operation. No financial statements, tax returns, or business formation documents were admitted at trial.

The trial court found that although the evidence was admittedly weak, McGregor thought he was doing business with Clint and Paige, Paige was a partner or purported partner in the dairy operation, and therefore, she was liable under the contract to buy the dairy cows. Paige appealed to the Supreme Court of South Dakota.

Gilbertson, Chief Justice

A partnership is formed when two or more persons carry on as co-owners a business for profit, whether or not the persons intend to form a partnership. SDCL 48-7A-202(a). SDCL 48-7A-202 provides in relevant part:

(c) In determining whether a partnership is formed, the following rules apply:

(1) Joint tenancy, tenancy in common, tenancy by the entireties, joint property, common property, or part ownership does not by itself establish a partnership, even if the co-owners share profits made by the use of the property.

(2) The sharing of gross returns does not by itself establish a partnership, even if the persons sharing them have a joint or common right or interest in property from which the returns are derived.

(3) A person who receives a share of the profits of a business is presumed to be a partner in the business, unless the profits were received in payment:

(ii) For services as an independent contractor or of wages or other compensation to an employee;

A purported partner may be found jointly and severally liable for certain transactions under SDCL 48-7A-308, which provides in relevant part:

(a) If a person, by words or conduct, purports to be a partner, or consents to being represented by another as a partner, in a partnership or with one or more persons not partners, the purported partner is liable to a person to whom the representation is made, if that person, relying on the representation, enters into a transaction with the actual or purported partnership. If the representation, either by the purported partner or by a person with the purported partner's consent, is made in a public manner, the purported partner is liable to a person who relies upon the purported partnership even if the purported partner is not aware of being held out as a partner to the claimant. If partnership liability results, the purported partner is liable with respect to that liability as if the purported partner were a partner.

No evidence was presented at trial to show that Paige shared in the title to the dairy farm. There was also no evidence presented that she shared in the gross returns generated by the dairy operation, or that she had a common right in the cattle. There was no evidence presented that Paige shared in the profits of the business, that there were any profits to share, or that she was compensated as an employee for her labor on the dairy farm.

Despite McGregor's contentions to the contrary, Clint made no admission at trial that Paige was a partner in the dairy operation. His testimony throughout the trial was that he had entered into the business on his own, that he was solely responsible for the debts incurred in the business, and that he made the decision to purchase the first herd from McGregor as well as the second herd over which the dispute occurred.

McGregor's argument that Clint and Paige admitted their partnership status in the letter of offer to McGregor and in their Answer and Counterclaim is also without merit. While both documents state that Clint and Paige operated the dairy farm at the time the contract was formed, neither document indicates Clint and Paige were partners, the dairy farm was operated as a partnership, Clint and Paige shared the profits, or Paige had property rights in the cattle. The fact that Clint and Paige ran the dairy farm does not address the type of business entity under which they operated. As Clint testified at trial, he and Paige managed the dairy farm after its assets were transferred to Paige's father's limited liability company. They did so as hired hands for which they were compensated at the bi-weekly rate of $1,000.

McGregor did not explore the type of business entity used by Clint at the time of the cattle sale during pre-trial discovery or at trial. McGregor assumed that because the husband and wife worked on the dairy farm together they were engaged in a partnership. However, the burden to show Clint and Paige were operating the dairy farm as a partnership was with McGregor.

McGregor's testimony and the billing statements issued by McGregor are likewise not conclusive evidence of the existence of a partnership between Clint and Paige. There was no testimony at trial to suggest that McGregor's decision to invoice Clint and Paige for the cattle was anything more than an assumption on his part that the couple operated the dairy farm as a partnership. There was no evidence Paige did or said anything to cause McGregor to place her name along with her husband's on the bill of lading for the August 2007 or the September 2007 cattle purchases.

McGregor also did not offer any testimony concerning anything Paige did or said to suggest to McGregor that a partnership existed. The only testimony he offered with regard to Paige's conduct was that she handed him a check for the first cattle order in August 2007, that she worked on the farm, and that she refused to discuss the bill for the second shipment of cattle. None of these actions suggest Paige held herself out to McGregor as a partner in the dairy operation, or constitute a direct admission by Paige of a partnership.

The trial court erred when it found the "admittedly weak" evidence was sufficient to establish the existence of a partnership between Clint and Paige given their status as husband and wife. There was insufficient evidence to establish that a partnership existed between Clint and Paige with regard to the operation of the dairy farm, or that Paige did anything to indicate to McGregor that she was a partner in the dairy farm.

Judgment reversed in favor of Paige Crumley.

Ethics in Action

Consider the ethical basis of the doctrine of purported partnership.

• Why does Kant's categorical imperative, which we studied in Chapter 4, suggest the rule of purported partnership is the right one?

• What steps will you take to avoid being a purported partner when you carry on business with an associate who is not your partner? Are those not only legal, but also ethical acts? Is there any distinction between law and ethics in this context?

Partnership Capital

When a partnership or limited liability partnership is formed, partners contribute cash or other property to the partnership. The partners' contribution is called **partnership capital.** To supplement beginning capital, other property may be contributed to the partnership as needed, such as by the partners permitting the partnership to retain some of its profits. Partnership capital is the equity of the business.

Loans made by partners to a partnership are not partnership capital but instead are liabilities of the business. Partners who make loans to a partnership are both owners and creditors.

 L07 Distinguish partner's property from partnership property.

Partnership Property

A partnership or limited liability partnership may own all or only a part of the property it uses. For example, it may own the business and perhaps a small amount of working capital in the form of cash or a checking account, yet own no other assets. All other tangible and intangible property used by the partnership may be individually or jointly owned by one or more of the partners or rented by the partnership from third parties. A determination of what is partnership property becomes essential when the partnership is dissolved and the assets are being distributed and when third persons claim that partnership property has been sold to them.

The RUPA provides that all property actually acquired by a partnership by transfer or otherwise is partnership property and, therefore, belongs to the partnership as an entity rather than to the partners. The RUPA has several rules that help determine when property is acquired by a partnership.

Property belongs to the partnership if the property is transferred (1) to the partnership in its name, (2) to any

partner acting as a partner by a transfer document that names the partnership, or (3) to any partner by a transfer document indicating the partner's status as a partner or that a partnership exists. In addition, property acquired with partnership funds is presumed to be partnership property.

The presumption is very strong that property purchased with partnership funds and used in the partnership belongs to the partnership. On the other hand, property used by the partnership is presumed to belong to an individual partner when the property is purchased by a partner with her own funds and in her own name with no indication in the transfer document of the partner's status as a partner or the existence of a partnership. However, in both situations, other factors such as an agreement among the partners may rebut the RUPA presumption of ownership.

The intent of the partners controls whether the partnership or an individual partner owns the property. It is best to have a written record of the partners' intent as to ownership of all property used by the partnership, such as a partnership agreement and partnership accounting records.

Examples A tax accountant discovers that a partnership is using a building to which a partner, Jacob Smith, holds title. The partnership pays rent monthly to Smith, but the partnership pays for all maintenance and repairs on the building. The accountant wants to know whether the partnership or Smith should be paying real property taxes on the building. Smith is the owner and should be paying taxes on it because his partners' intent to allow Smith to retain ownership is evidenced by the partnership's paying rent to Smith.

Changing the facts, suppose the partnership pays no rent to Smith, the partnership maintains and repairs the building, and the partnership pays real property taxes on the building, but the title is in Smith's name. Who owns the building? The property belongs to the partnership, because all the objective criteria of ownership point toward partnership ownership, especially the payment of taxes. Therefore, when the partnership is liquidated, the building will be sold along with other partnership assets, and the proceeds of its sale will be distributed to partnership creditors and to all of the partners.

Need for Partnership Agreement It would be best for the partnership agreement to remove all ambiguity regarding ownership of property used by a partnership. For example, if the partnership is using a partner's building and the partners want the owning partner to retain ownership, it would be best to have a lease agreement between themselves and the partner stating that the partner owns the building, the monthly rent, and who is responsible for property taxes, maintenance, and improvements to the building.

In the following case, *McCormick v. Brevig,* the court held that property listed on a partnership's tax returns was nonetheless property of a partner, not the partnership.

McCormick v. Brevig	96 P. 3d 697 (Mont. Sup. Ct. 2004)

Joan Brevig McCormick and Clark Brevig were sister and brother. Clark had been a partner with his father, Charles, until Charles's death in 1982. At that time, Joan became a partner with her brother in the Brevig Ranch, and eventually they were 50–50 partners.

Disagreements concerning management of the ranch caused Clark and Joan's relationship to deteriorate. By the early 1990s, cooperation between Clark and Joan had essentially ceased, and they began looking for ways to dissolve the partnership. In 1995, Joan brought suit against Clark and the partnership, alleging that Clark had converted partnership assets to his own personal use. The source of the dispute was cattle purchased by their mother, Helen.

In 1990, Helen Brevig purchased 10 head of Charolais cattle to live on the ranch. The following year, Helen transferred ownership of the cattle to Clark and his two sons. Thereafter, these cattle were listed and treated as partnership property for all tax purposes, and proceeds from the sale of the cattle's offspring were placed into a partnership account. At the time of Helen's lawsuit against Clark, all the Charolais cattle residing on the ranch were offspring of those cattle originally purchased by Helen in 1990.

At the district court trial, Clark argued that the Charolais cattle should be regarded as separate property due to the fact that his mother, who was not a partner, had given the cattle to Clark and his two sons, neither of whom were partners. The district court concluded, however, that since Clark had signed tax returns indicating that the cattle were partnership property, and had placed proceeds from the sale of calves into partnership accounts, the cattle should be treated as partnership assets.

Clark appealed, arguing that the mere inclusion of the cattle in the partnership tax returns is legally insufficient to transfer title of the cattle to the partnership.

Rice, Justice

Section 35–10–203, Montana Code, pertains to partnership property and provides as follows:

(1) Property transferred to or otherwise acquired by a partnership is property of the partnership and not of the partners individually.
(2) Property is partnership property if acquired in the name of:
    (a) the partnership; or
    (b) one or more partners with an indication in the instrument transferring title to the property of the person's capacity as a partner or of the existence of a partnership but without an indication of the name of the partnership.
(3) Property is acquired in the name of the partnership by a transfer to:
    (a) the partnership in its name; or
    (b) one or more partners in their capacity as partners in the partnership if the name of the partnership is indicated in the instrument transferring title to the property.

(4) Property is presumed to be partnership property if purchased with partnership assets even if not acquired in the name of the partnership or of one or more partners with an indication in the instrument transferring title to the property of the person's capacity as a partner or of the existence of a partnership.
(5) Property acquired in the name of one or more of the partners without an indication in the instrument transferring title to the property of the person's capacity as a partner or of the existence of a partnership and without use of partnership assets is presumed to be separate property even if used for partnership purposes.

(Emphasis added.) As reflected in the statute, property purchased with partnership assets, or transferred in the partnership's name, or to one or more of the partners in their capacity as partners of the partnership, is presumed to be partnership property. On the other hand, property acquired in the name of a partner without an indication that the property is being transferred to that person in his or her capacity as a partner of the partnership is presumed to be separate property, even if used for partnership purposes.

In the present case, the district court included the cattle as partnership assets in its accounting because they were listed on the partnership tax returns. However, nothing in the record suggests that the Charolais cattle were purchased with partnership assets or transferred to Clark and his two sons in their capacity as partners of the partnership. Nor has there been any assignment of the cattle to the partnership. Therefore, despite the fact that the cattle were included in the partnership tax returns, and proceeds from the sale of the cattle's offspring placed in partnership accounts, the cattle are to be presumed separate property.

As Joan correctly points out, this presumption is a rebuttable one. Nonetheless, Joan did not introduce any evidence to overcome the presumption but, rather, has relied upon the District Court's findings that money from the sale of calves had been

placed into partnership accounts, and that the cattle had been listed on partnership tax returns. However, we have previously considered and rejected arguments that a third party acquires an interest in cattle simply by feeding, watering, and pasturing them.

Here proceeds from the sale of calves had been deposited in partnership accounts and used for partnership purposes. Joan has not demonstrated any equitable interest in the cattle by virtue of the partnership's care and feeding of the cattle, nor has she provided any authority which would compel the conclusion that ownership of the cattle passed to the partnership. Because the presumption established by § 35–10–203(5), MCA, has not been overcome by evidence to the contrary, we conclude the District Court erred in categorizing the Charolais cattle as partnership assets, and reverse the court's determination in that regard.

Judgment reversed in favor of Clark Brevig.

Partner's Partnership Interest

As an owner of a partnership or LLP, a partner has an ownership interest in the partnership. A partner's ownership interest is called a **partnership interest,** which embodies all a partner's rights in a partnership:

1. The partner's transferable interest.
2. The partner's management and other rights.

The first right is discussed in this section. Partners' management and other rights are discussed in Chapter 38, Operation of Partnerships and Related Forms.

Note that a partner has no individual ownership rights in partnership property. The RUPA gives ownership of partnership property to the partnership only. Partners do, however, have the right to *use* partnership property for partnership purposes.

LO8   List and compare the rights of a creditor having a charging order and the rights of a transferee of a partner's interest in a partnership.

Partner's Transferable Interest Like a shareholder owning stock in a corporation, a partner owns his partnership interest. The only part of the partnership interest, however, that may be transferred to another person is the partner's **transferable interest:** the partner's share of profits and losses and his right to receive partnership distributions. The transferable interest may be

transferred or sold to any other person. It may also be used as collateral to secure a partner's debt.

Transfer The sale or transfer of a partner's transferable interest is a voluntary act of the partner. It entitles the buyer or transferee to receive the partner's distributions from the partnership, such as a share of profits. Although the transferee is the owner of the transferable interest, the transferee does not become a partner of the partnership. The transferee has no right to inspect the partnership's books and records or to manage the partnership. The transferee's only other right is to ask a court to dissolve and wind up the partnership, but only if the partnership is at will (i.e., has no term or objective). If the partnership dissolves and is wound up, the transferee will obtain the partner's claim against the partnership's assets.

By itself a partner's transfer of his transferable interest does not dissociate the partner from the partnership or effect a dissolution; the transferring partner remains a partner and may continue to manage the partnership.

The nontransferring partners may vote to expel the transferring partner from the partnership by their unanimous agreement (unless the partner merely granted a lien in the transferable interest to the partner's creditor), even if the term or objective of the partnership has not yet been met.

Charging Order A partner's personal creditor with a judgment against the partner may ask a court to issue a **charging order**—that is, an order charging all or part of the partner's transferable partnership interest with payment of the unsatisfied amount of the judgment. Unlike a transfer, a charging order is obtained without the partner's consent. As with a transfer, however, the partner remains a partner and may manage the partnership. The charging-order creditor is a lien creditor and is entitled to receive only the partner's share of the partnership distributions. If the distributions are insufficient to pay the debt, the creditor may ask the court to order foreclosure and to sell the partner's interest to satisfy the charging order.

Neither the issuance of a charging order nor the purchase of a transferable interest at a foreclosure sale dissociates the transferring partner from the partnership. But the purchaser of a transferable interest at the foreclosure sale becomes a transferee and therefore may ask a court to dissolve and wind up a partnership at will. The other partners may eliminate this potential threat to the continuation of the partnership by **redeeming the charging order.** To redeem a charging order, the other partners must pay the creditor the amount due on the judgment against the partner. If the other partners so choose, however, they may expel the partner suffering the charging order by their unanimous agreement, even if the term or objective of the partnership has not been met.

Effect of Partnership Agreement The

partners may believe that a partner's transferring her transferable partnership interest or suffering a charging order threatens the partnership. For example, they may believe that a partner may be less motivated to work for the partnership if the partner has transferred her partnership interest to a personal creditor, because she will not receive distributions from the partnership.

Consequently, the partners may restrict the transfer of a partner's transferable interest or impose negative consequences on a partner who transfers her transferable interest or suffers a charging order. For example, the partnership agreement may require a partner to offer to sell her partnership interest to the partnership prior to transferring it to any other person. Or the partnership agreement may effect a dissociation of any partner who suffers a charging order and fails to redeem the charging order within 30 days.

Note that any transfer restriction must not unreasonably limit the ability of a partner to transfer her property interest. For example, a transfer restriction that bans the transfer of a partner's interest would be unreasonable and therefore unenforceable against a partner. In addition, a transfer restriction will not be enforceable against a transferee who does not have notice of the restriction.

Joint Venturers and Mining Partners Transfers of interests in joint ventures are treated in the same way as transfers of partnership interests. However, a mining partner's interest is *freely transferable.* The transferee becomes a partner with all the rights of ownership and management, and the transferor loses all of his partnership rights. The other mining partners cannot object to the transfer, and their consent to a transfer is not required.

Problems and Problem Cases

1. One of your clients, a motion picture producer, has asked your firm to invest $2 million in her latest motion picture production, a movie based on the life of 1960s singing star Janis Joplin. In return for the contribution, your firm will receive a 10 percent interest in the limited partnership that will produce and own the movie. The movie is expected to be in preproduction for four years as rights to the subject matter, script, actors, and director are obtained. Production is expected to take three months, and postproduction editing and promotion will last another six months, after which the movie will be released into theaters domestically. Three months after its theater release, the movie will be released on pay-per-view and premium television channels like HBO. Six months after the theatrical release, the movie will be sold on DVD. As a consequence, the production company is not expected to make a profit for at least five years. Your client wants to form the production company as a limited partnership. Do you

believe that the limited partnership is the right business form? What business form may be better? How would you set up that business form to make sure your firm's interests are best protected?

2. You and nine of your wealthy friends decide to purchase a local minor league baseball team. The purchase price is $15 million, 60 percent of which you contribute to the business as capital. Your nine friends will contribute the remaining $6 million. All 10 of you agree that you will be the sole general manager of the business, making all business and baseball decisions, except as you delegate them to employees of the business, such as a team manager or vice president of baseball operations. Due to the way you will account for the purchase of the team and player salaries, you expect the business not to make a profit until year four. You expect that all 10 of you will remain owners of the business for at least 10 years, at which time you expect to sell the team at a profit. Which business form do you believe is best for this business?

3. Rick Yurko frequently purchased lottery tickets from Phyllis Huisel at the coffee shop she operated. In February 1990, Yurko bought 100 scratch-off lottery tickets, which revealed instant winners when a film covering was scratched off. Yurko asked Phyllis, Judy Fitchie, and Frances Vincent to help him scratch off the tickets. Yurko stated that if they helped him, they would be his partners and share in any winnings. Judy uncovered a ticket that gave its owner a chance to be on television and win $100,000. The owner had to complete a form on the back of the ticket and submit it for a drawing. Six tickets would be drawn for the TV appearance. Judy and Yurko urged Phyllis to fill out the ticket, but she did not want to appear on TV, so Yurko said he would. After a discussion, Frances, Judy, Phyllis, and Yurko agreed that Yurko would represent them on TV. Yurko then printed on the back of the ticket "F. J. P. Rick Yurko." F.J.P. stood for the first initials of Frances, Judy, and Phyllis. As Yurko completed the tickets, he told Phyllis that he was going to put all their initials and his name on the ticket and that they would be partners no matter what they might win.

   You can predict what happened next. The ticket was drawn for the TV show, and Yurko appeared on the show and won the $100,000 prize. He did not share the winnings with the three women. Were the three women able to share the winnings by proving they were partners with Yurko?

4. In August 2003, Tammy Duncan began working as a waitress at Bynum's Diner, which was owned by her mother, Hazel Bynum, and stepfather, Eddie Bynum. Tammy, Hazel, and Eddie signed an agreement stating the following:

   > As of September 6th, 2003, I, Eddie Bynum, lease Bynum's Diner to Hazel Bynum and Tammy Duncan for $800 a month. I am completely out of it for 6 months, at which time they (Hazel Bynum and Tammy) have the option of renewing this contract for another 6 months. They are responsible for all repairs, taxes, and expenses for Bynum's Diner.

   Tammy began doing paperwork and bookkeeping for the diner in addition to occasionally waiting tables and performing other duties. Tammy and Hazel's intention in their agreement was to make Tammy a co-manager and not a co-owner of the business. Tammy understood that she would take over her stepfather's duties as manager. She received wages for the performance of her duties. Although Tammy had no agreement to share in the

diner's profits, Hazel believed that she and Tammy were to split half of any profit. Hazel's intent, however, was not to transfer ownership of the business to Tammy until Hazel retired, whenever that might be. On October 30, 2003, Tammy was injured when she slipped off a ladder and fell onto both knees. The diner's insurer, Cypress Insurance Company, paid Tammy temporary total disability benefits beginning in November 2003. On April 2, 2004, however, Cypress notified Tammy that it would refuse to pay her disability claim on the grounds that she was not an employee of the diner, but a co-owner. Under the diner's insurance policy with Cypress, if Tammy were an owner of the diner, she would not have been entitled to workers' compensation benefits, because she did not notify Cypress that she elected to be included under the policy's coverage as a partner. Was Tammy a partner in the diner?

5. Don King and Scott Willson worked together on improving and selling an electronic payment system. To develop the system, they pooled their money and labor, with King providing financing and Willson contributing his time and expertise, amounting to about 2,000 hours of work over the period of a year. Willson was not paid by King for the work. Willson and King consulted with each other over pricing of equipment and services sold by the business. They made joint decisions to cut certain costs. Willson set up the invoice system used to bill customers. Willson made technical decisions on how best to assemble, repair, and maintain various aspects of the electronic payment system. King and Willson jointly addressed customer issues as they arose and jointly evaluated the systems' priorities as they went along. Willson and King also had an agreement to share profits. Are they partners?

6. John Williams was an assistant manager of a restaurant operated by Pizzaville, Inc. He was promoted to manager and later designated a managing partner with business cards describing him so. Williams's compensation was a salary of $270 per week plus 70 percent of the restaurant's gross sales less the cost of food purchases and employees' wages. Pizzaville fired Williams. Williams sued Pizzaville to receive a portion of the value of the restaurant business on the ground that he was a partner with Pizzaville. Was Williams a partner?

7. George Lawler and John Claydon were lawyers who maintained separate law practices in the same office space. They shared the expenses of that space,

but never shared clients, did not commingle their funds, and did not share profits or losses from their practices. A sign identified the office as "Claydon and Lawler," and the same joint listing of names appeared on stationery they both used and in their telephone listing. Claydon introduced Lawler to his clients as his partner. In phone conversations, Lawler identified himself as Claydon's partner. Is there a risk that Lawler will be liable on contracts and torts made by Claydon?

8. Karl Allen and Renee Galzo choose to be the sole owners and managers of a financial services business, Allen-Galzo & Associates LLP. Allen holds the copyright to investment analysis software that he developed three years ago. The LLP will use the software to service its clients. The software requires regular updating and improvement. What would you suggest the LLP agreement include regarding the software? Why?

9. Steve Holmes and his son Mike were partners in a construction business. Steve also owned a ranch, which he contributed to the partnership, even though Steve was still listed as the owner of record. Steve learned of a low-interest loan available for the purchase of property from a parent. Solely to obtain the benefits of the low-interest loan, Steve deeded the ranch to Mike. No money exchanged hands, however, and Mike never paid Steve or the partnership for the ranch. The transfer was not treated as a sale on Steve's or Mike's books, Mike did not claim ranch income as his own, and there were no changes in ranch operation. When Steve and Mike had disagreements, Steve asked a court to dissolve the partnership and to distribute its assets. Was the ranch an asset of the partnership or Mike?

10. Demas Yan and Dong Fu made an agreement to build condominiums on Yan's land in the Chinatown section of San Francisco. Their agreement provided that Yan would own 75 percent and Fu 25 percent of the property. Yan was responsible for the initial $300,000 construction cost, and Fu the remainder. They agreed to share the proceeds of the sale or rental of the condominiums according to the ownership percentage. Fu, however, had sole power to decide whether to sell or to rent the property. Afterward, Fu assigned his interest under the agreement to Wei Suen. Thereafter, the condominiums were sold for a combined price of $2.3 million. Was Suen entitled to a share of the condominium sale proceeds?

Online Research

The Revised Uniform Partnership Act and Your State

The National Conference of Commissioners on Uniform State Laws is the author of uniform state laws on forms of business.

- Find the website for the National Conference of Commissioners on Uniform State Laws.
- Find the link to the listing of the uniform state acts. This link will take you to the full text of the acts including the drafters' comments, which can help you understand why the acts were written as they are. Find the text of the Revised Uniform Partnership Act (1997) and its comments. Read section 202, which has the definition of partnership.
- Find the link to the "Legislative Fact Sheet" for the RUPA. Has your state adopted the RUPA?

CHAPTER 38

OPERATION OF PARTNERSHIPS AND RELATED FORMS

After many years working with a large consulting partnership, you and several of your business associates and friends decide to form your own consulting business as a limited liability partnership. You and five of your close friends have 20 to 25 years' experience in the consulting field. Each of you plans to contribute capital of $400,000 to the business. Each of you has a strong national reputation and expects to attract most of the firm's clients, at least in the first few years. You six partners will manage only a few of the firm's consulting engagements, but you six will bring to the firm clients generating $40,000,000 of annual revenue for the firm. Each of you also has experience managing consulting businesses, including expertise in personnel, financial, and marketing matters.

In addition, 15 other partners with 10 to 15 years' experience will join the new firm. Each of these 15 partners will contribute capital of $200,000. They are expected to bring few clients to the firm at this time, but they are expected to service the firm's clients and to bring in new clients as their reputations and skills expand and as the six older partners retire. Chiefly, these 15 partners will take charge of consulting engagements. They will directly supervise the firm's 50 associate consultants. The associate consultants will not be partners when the partnership is formed, but some expect to be offered partnership status within 5 to 10 years.

- What are the default rules regarding how the partnership will be managed?
- Why are those default rules inappropriate for this partnership?
- Write the management section of the partnership agreement. Accommodate the interests of all partners.
- What are the default rules regarding how the partners are compensated?
- Why are those default rules inappropriate for this partnership?
- Write the compensation section of the partnership agreement. Accommodate the interests of all partners.

LO LEARNING OBJECTIVES

After studying this chapter, you should be able to:

1. List and explain the duties partners owe to the partnership and each other.

2. Describe the default rules regarding partners' management and compensation rights.

3. Draft partnership agreements resolving management and compensation issues.

4. Explain the liability of partners for contracts and torts.

TWO RELATIONSHIPS ARE IMPORTANT during the operation of a partnership or limited liability partnership (LLP) business: (1) the relation of the partners to each other and the partnership; and (2) the relation of the partners to third parties who are affected by the business of the partnership. In the examination of the first relationship, partners owe duties to each other and the partnership and they share the management and profits of the partnership. As for the second relation, partners have the ability to make the partnership liable to third parties for contracts and torts.

 List and explain the duties partners owe to the partnership and each other.

Duties of Partners to the Partnership and Each Other

The relation between partners and the partnership is a fiduciary relation of the highest order. It is one of mutual trust, confidence, and honesty. Therefore, under the Revised Uniform Partnership Act (RUPA) partners owe to the partnership and each other the highest degree of *loyalty*. In addition, partners must act consistently with the obligation of *good faith and fair dealing*. The duties partners owe each other are the same in ordinary partnerships and in limited liability partnerships.

Having Interest Adverse to Partnership

Unless there is a contrary agreement, a partner's sole compensation from partnership affairs is a share of partnership profits. Therefore, a partner may not deal with the partnership when the partner has an interest adverse to the partnership or acts on behalf of another person with any adverse interest. For example, a partner may not profit personally by receiving an undisclosed kickback from a partnership supplier. In addition, a partner may not profit secretly when she makes a contract with her partnership, such as selling a building she owns to her partnership without disclosing her ownership and her profit to her partners.

When a partner receives a secret profit, she has a conflict of interests, and there is a risk that she may prefer her own interests over those of the partnership. Therefore, the law permits a partner to profit personally from partnership transactions only if she deals in good faith, makes a full disclosure of all material facts affecting the transaction, and obtains approval from her partners. The remedy for a breach of this duty not to make a secret profit is a return of the profit that she made in the transaction with the partnership.

Competing against the Partnership

A partner may not compete against his partnership unless he obtains consent from the other partners. For example, a partner of a retail clothing store may not open a clothing store nearby. However, he may open a grocery store and not breach his fiduciary duty. The partnership has the remedy of recovering the profits of the partner's competing venture.

Partnership agreements often define what conduct constitutes competing with the partnership. For example, a partnership agreement of a large auditing firm may state that no partner may provide auditing services except on behalf of the partnership. It may also state that a partner may provide other accounting services not offered by the partnership after disclosure to and approval by the partnership's managing partners.

Duty to Serve

The duty to serve requires a partner to undertake his share of responsibility for running the day-to-day operations of the partnership business. The basis of this duty is the expectation that all partners will work. Sometimes, this duty is termed the duty to devote full time to the partnership.

Partners may agree to relieve a partner of the duty to serve. So-called *silent partners* merely contribute capital to the partnership. Silent partners do not have the duty to serve, but they have the same liability for partnership debts as any other partner.

The remedies for breach of the duty to serve include assessing the partner for the cost of hiring a person to do his work and paying the other partners additional compensation.

Duty of Care

In transacting partnership business, each partner owes **a duty of care.** A partner is not liable to her partnership for losses resulting from honest errors in judgment, but a partner is liable for losses resulting from her gross negligence, reckless conduct, intentional misconduct, or knowing violation of the law. A partner also has an obligation of good faith and fair dealing when acting for the partnership. Collectively, these duties mean that a partner must make an **investigation** before making a decision so that she has an adequate basis for making the decision. The decision she makes must be one she has **grounds to believe is in the best interests of the partnership.**

In the partnership agreement, the partners may reduce or increase the duty of care owed to the partnership. They may not, however, eliminate the duty of care. It is common for partnership agreements to excuse partners from liability if they act in good faith and with the honest belief that their actions are in the best interests of the partnership. Such a provision is designed to encourage honest partners to take reasonable business risks without fearing liability.

Duty to Act within Actual Authority

A partner has the duty not to exceed the authority granted him by the partnership agreement or, if there is no agreement, the authority normally held by partners in his position. He is responsible to the partnership for losses resulting from unauthorized transactions negotiated in the name of the partnership. For example, suppose partners agree that no partner shall purchase supplies from Jasper Supply Company, which is unaware of the limitation on the partners' authority. When one partner purchases supplies from Jasper and the partnership suffers a loss because the supplies are of low quality, the wrongdoing partner must bear the loss caused by her breach of the partnership agreement.

Duty to Account

Partners have a duty to account for their use or disposal of partnership funds and partnership property, as well as their receipt of any property, benefit, or profit, without the consent of the other partners. Partnership property should be used for partnership purposes, not for a partner's personal use. In addition, a partner may not misappropriate a business opportunity in which the partnership had an interest or expectancy.

For example, when a partner of a firm that leases residential property to college students allows his daughter to live in a partnership-owned apartment, the partner must collect rent for the partnership from his daughter or risk breaching the duty to account.

Each partner owes a duty to keep a reasonable record of all business transacted by him for the partnership and to make such records available to the person keeping the partnership books. The books must be kept at the partnership's chief executive office. Every partner must at all times have access to them and may inspect and copy them.

Closely related to the duty to account is the right of a partner to be **indemnified** for payments made from personal funds and for personal liabilities incurred during the ordinary conduct of the business. For example, a partner uses her own truck to pick up some partnership supplies, which she pays for with her personal check. The partner is entitled to be reimbursed for the cost of the supplies and for her cost of picking up the supplies, including fuel.

Other Duties

A partner must maintain the **confidentiality** of partnership information such as a trade secret or a customer list. This means a partner should not disclose to third parties confidential information of the partnership unless disclosure benefits the partnership.

On the other hand, each partner owes a duty to disclose to the other partners all information that is material to the partnership business. She also owes a duty to inform the partners of notices she has received that affect the rights of the partnership. For example, Gordon Gekko, a partner of a stock brokerage firm, learns that National Motors Corporation is projecting a loss for the current year. The projection reduces the value of National stock, which the firm has been recommending that its customers buy. Gekko has a duty to disclose the projection to his partners to allow them to advise customers of the brokerage.

In *Spector v. Konover,* a case you'll read after the next section, the court found a managing partner liable for misusing partnership funds, self-dealing, and failing to disclose material information.

Joint Ventures and Mining Partnerships

The fiduciary duties of partners also exist in joint ventures and mining partnerships, although there are a few special rules regarding their enforcement. For example, a joint venturer may seek an accounting in a court to settle claims between the joint venturers, or he may sue his joint venturers to recover joint property or to be indemnified for expenditures that he has made on behalf of the joint venture. A mining partner's remedy against his partners is an accounting; however, a mining partner has a lien against his partners' shares in the mining partnership for his expenditures on behalf of the mining partnership. The lien can be enforced against purchasers of his partners' shares.

 Describe the default rules regarding partners' compensation rights.

Compensation of Partners

A partner's compensation for working for a partnership or limited liability partnership is a share of the profits of the business. The RUPA continues the UPA rule that a partner is not entitled to a salary or wages, even if he spends a disproportionate amount of time conducting the business of the partnership.

Profits and Losses

Unless there is an agreement to the contrary, partners share partnership profits equally, according to the number of partners, and not according to their capital contributions or the amount of time that each devotes to the partnership. For example, a partnership has two partners, Juarez, who contributes $85,000 of capital to the partnership and does 35 percent of the work, and Easton, who contributes $15,000 and does 65 percent of

The Global Business Environment

Partner's Relations and Fiduciary Duties

All modern societies share a common set of values that are reflected not only generally in their laws but also specifically in partnership law. Thus, there is substantial agreement from nation to nation in the duties partners owe each other under partnership law. In India and the United Kingdom, for example, partners' duties are nearly identical in name and substance to those in American law. Likewise in Canada, basic values of loyalty, good faith, honesty, and avoidance of conflicts of interest are fundamental to a partner's duties.

In other societies, there are mostly similarities but also a few differences. For example, among the Inuit and other aboriginal groups in Canada, the culture requires partners to "celebrate one another." In his book, *Hunters in the Barrens*: *The Naskapi on the Edge of the White Man's World,* Georg Henriken notes that in a joint venture, while the Naskapi partners watch one another, examine contracts and bank statements, and even sue one another, they should respect and recognize their respective contributions.

---

the work. If they have made no agreement how to share profits, when the partnership makes a $50,000 profit in the first year, each partner is credited with $25,000, half of the profits.

Although the default RUPA rule allocates profits equally to partners, the partners do not necessarily *receive* profits earned by the partnership or LLP. Profits are *allocated* to each partner's capital account as profits are recognized by the business. Profits are *distributed* to partners in an amount and at a time determined by a majority of the partners. Consequently, in a partnership or LLP that is taxed like a partnership for federal income tax purposes, a partner may have taxable income despite not receiving a distribution from the partnership.

Losses When the partnership agreement is silent on how to share losses, losses are shared in the same proportion that profits are shared. The basis of this rule is the presumption that partners want to share benefits and detriments in the same proportions. Nonetheless, the presumption does not work in reverse. If a partnership agreement specifies how losses are shared but does not specify how profits are shared, profits are shared equally by the partners, not as losses are shared.

Examples For example, when there is no agreement regarding how profits or losses are shared, profits are shared equally, and because losses are shared like profits, losses are shared equally as well. When two partners agree to share profits 70–30 and make no agreement on losses, both profits and losses are shared 70–30.

However, when two partners make no agreement how to share profits but agree to share losses 60–40, losses are shared in that proportion but profits are shared equally.

Partners may agree to split profits on one basis and losses on another basis for many reasons, including their

making different capital and personal service contributions or a partner's having higher outside income than the other partners, which better enables him to use a partnership loss as a tax deduction.

Effect of Agreement on Creditors' Rights Each partner has unlimited personal liability to partnership creditors. Loss-sharing agreements between partners do not bind partnership creditors unless the creditors agree to be bound. For example, two partners agree to share losses 60–40, the same proportion in which they contributed capital to the partnership. After the partnership assets have been distributed to the creditors, $50,000 is still owed to them. The creditors may collect the entire $50,000 from the partner who agreed to assume only 60 percent of the losses. That partner may, however, collect $20,000—40 percent of the amount—from the other partner.

 L03   Draft partnership agreements resolving management and compensation issues.

Compensation in Large Partnerships In a large accounting or other partnership that has thousands of partners, the partnership agreement often has a detailed section on the amount of partners' compensation and when it is paid. Usually, each partner is entitled to a monthly draw or salary. The amount of each partner's draw may be established yearly by the partnership's compensation committee or be determined by a rigid formula that takes into account a partner's capital contribution to the partnership, years of service as a partner, level of partner (such as managing partner, senior partner, or junior partner), area of practice (such as consulting, auditing, or tax), and other factors.

In addition, the compensation article will state how partners share profits and when profits are distributed to partners. While partners in a small partnership usually share profits according to each partner's capital contribution, in a large partnership the calculation may be very complex, including also the partner's area of practice, level of partner, and revenue received from a partner's clients. Usually, the profits are distributed four times a year, in January, April, June, and September, coinciding with the quarterly payment dates for estimated federal and state income taxes. In addition, the compensation

articles will provide for partners' expense accounts, vacations and leaves, and other fringe benefits, such as health insurance.

In the following case, involving all-too-common overreaching and misconduct in a partnership with active and passive partners, the court found that the managing partner was not entitled to receive special compensation for managing the business, absent agreement of the other partners. The court also found that the managing partner breached several fiduciary duties, including by refusing to distribute a higher amount of partnership profits.

| Spector v. Konover | 747 A.2d 39 (Conn. Ct. App. 2000) |

Martin Spector, Abner Rosenberg, Marvin Patron, and Simon Konover agreed to build a shopping plaza in Seymour, Connecticut. There was no written partnership agreement. The four orally formed Tri Town Realty Co., a partnership in which each partner received a 25 percent interest. Spector and Rosenberg contributed a land lease, while Patron and Konover were charged with building, operating, and managing the shopping plaza.

Konover and Patron initially managed the shopping plaza themselves, charging the partnership for any out-of-pocket expenses they incurred. Over time, as Konover and Patron amassed 20 to 30 shopping centers, they formed K and P Management Company. K and P Management hired managers and leasing agents to manage all of Konover and Patron's properties and charged management fees and leasing commissions to all of their properties, including Tri Town. Eventually, K and P Management was replaced by the Konover Management Corporation, which managed the Tri Town plaza for the last 10 years of the partnership.

Konover's duties in managing Tri Town included the preparation and distribution of monthly reports to each of the partners. In the early 1980s, Spector believed that Konover's reports did not adequately explain the finances of the partnership. Konover also determined the amount of money that was to be distributed to the partners as profit, and Spector felt that the amount being distributed was too low.

In June 1985, Spector requested an increase in the distributions. In September 1985, Konover increased the distributions from $500 per month to $1,200 per month. In February 1989, Spector again requested an increase in the distribution of profits and an explanation of various expenses appearing on the monthly report. Spector did not receive a response from Konover, and, in May 1989, Spector demanded that the partnership be terminated. Konover did not respond.

In April 1990, Konover stopped making profit distributions to Spector. In 1994, Spector hired a certified public accountant to review the financial records of the partnership. The accountant's review revealed that Konover did not maintain any account dedicated solely to the Tri Town partnership. Rather, the Tri Town partnership funds were commingled with funds from several other Konover entities, and all the funds were commingled in one account called the K and R Associates Trust Fund (K and R). The accountant further discovered that not only were the funds commingled in one account, but also the Tri Town funds were used by other properties owned by Konover. Even though Tri Town funds supposedly were kept in the K and R checking account, the balance of the entire K and R checking account actually was far less than the amount purported to be in the Tri Town partnership account. Additionally, interest earned on Tri Town funds was not credited to Tri Town's account.

Konover admitted to diverting funds between his various entities. He and several of his employees said that by sharing the funds in the K and R account, Konover could use one property's funds to cover expenses incurred by another property. For instance, if one property needed repairs but did not have enough cash to pay for the repairs, Konover would use cash from another property to pay for those repairs. It was, therefore, advantageous for him to commingle the funds of different Konover entities so that one property's funds could be used to cover an overdraft of another entity.

Spector sued Konover seeking damages stemming from Konover's alleged breaches of his fiduciary duties in managing the Tri Town partnership. The trial court found that Konover proved that he dealt with Spector fairly and breached no fiduciary duty. Spector appealed to the Appellate Court of Connecticut.

Foti, Judge

Konover's practice of diverting Tri Town funds to other entities and retaining interest earned on Tri Town partnership funds constitutes a breach of fiduciary duty. It is a thoroughly well-settled equitable rule that any one acting in a fiduciary relation shall not be permitted to make use of that relation to benefit his own personal interest. This rule is strict in its requirements and in its operation. It extends to all transactions where the individual's personal interests may be brought into conflict with his acts in the fiduciary capacity, and it works independently of the question whether there was fraud or whether there was good intention.

Konover's misuse of partnership property is a clear case of self-dealing and a violation of his fiduciary duty to Spector. As managing partner, Konover held a unique position of responsibility within the partnership. Spector trusted Konover to act in the best interest of the partnership. Instead, he used partnership funds to finance other entities owned by Konover and retained interest generated by Tri Town funds. This misuse of partnership funds for Konover's personal financial gain clearly constitutes a breach of fiduciary duty.

Spector also claims that Konover's commingling scheme affected his decisions regarding the disbursement of profits to the Tri Town partners. We agree with Spector and conclude that Konover's failure to make greater distributions of profits was a breach of his fiduciary duty. His proffered reason for withholding disbursements was that he wanted to create a large cash reserve to cover any expenses that might have arisen from the bankruptcy of one of Tri Town's largest tenants, Ames. According to the facts presented at trial, however, Konover did not actually maintain a reserve account dedicated to potential expenses related to Ames' bankruptcy. Rather, he continued the practice of diverting Tri Town funds to cover the expenses of other Konover properties. It is clear that his decision to withhold the disbursement of profits was, at least in part, motivated by his desire to use Tri Town funds to finance other Konover entities. This, too, was a breach of his fiduciary duty.

Spector also claims that Konover breached his fiduciary duty by billing the Tri Town partnership for management fees, leasing commissions, payroll maintenance fees, and undisclosed overhead charges included in Tri Town's insurance premiums. We agree. One of the factors to consider in determining whether a particular transaction is fair is whether the principal had competent and independent advice before completing that transaction. Implicit in this factor is the idea that the principal must consent to the transaction. With regard to the management fees and leasing commissions that Konover charged the partnership, the court found that there never were any meetings or partnership votes giving them the right to receive such compensation. In the absence of any agreement to the contrary, Konover and his management company were not entitled to any compensation, other than reimbursement for out-of-pocket expenses, for managing Tri Town. General Statutes § 34-335(c) provides that a partner is to be reimbursed for out-of-pocket partnership expenses. General Statutes § 34-335(h) provides in relevant part that "[a] partner is not entitled to remuneration for services performed for the partnership. . . ."

Even after Spector complained to Konover about the management fees, Konover began charging the partnership an additional "payroll maintenance fee." These new fees were clearly not authorized by Spector. Additionally, the insurance premiums charged to Tri Town included undisclosed overhead costs that were paid to another Konover entity. Thus, Konover did not make a free and frank disclosure of all the relevant information.

Konover, without the formal consent of his partners, compensated himself for managing Tri Town. He also added hidden charges to the insurance premiums charged to Tri Town. These acts of self-dealing were in breach of his fiduciary duty. Thus, we conclude that the trial court's finding that Konover proved fair dealing by clear and convincing evidence was clearly erroneous.

Judgment reversed in favor of Spector.

 L02 Describe the default rules regarding partners' management and compensation rights.

Management Powers of Partners

Individual Authority of Partners   In a partnership or limited liability partnership, every partner is a general manager of the business and may make contracts that bind the partnership. This power is expressed in the RUPA, which states that a partnership is bound by the act of every partner for apparently carrying on in the ordinary course the business of the partnership or business of the kind carried on by the partnership. Such authority to make contracts derives from the nature of the business. It permits a partner to bind the partnership and his partners for acts within the ordinary course of business. The scope of this **implied authority** is determined with reference to what is usual business for partnerships of the same general type.

Implied authority of a partner may not contradict a partner's **express authority,** which is created by agreement of the partners. An agreement among the partners can expand, restrict, or even completely eliminate the implied authority of a partner. For example, the partners in an online publishing business may agree that one partner shall have the authority to purchase a magazine business for the partnership and that another partner shall not have the authority to sell advertising space. The partners may agree also that all partners must consent to borrow money for the partnership. The partners' implied authority to be general managers is modified in accordance with these express agreements.

Express authority may be stated orally or in writing, or it may be obtained by acquiescence. Regardless of the method of agreement, all of the partners must agree to the modification of implied authority. Partners may give everyone notice of a partner's authority or limitation on a partner's authority by filing a **Statement of Partnership Authority** or **Statement of Denial** with the secretary of state or the real estate recording office. Together, a partner's express and implied authority constitute her **actual authority.**

Apparent Authority Apparent authority exists because it reasonably appears to a third party that a partner has authority to do an act. Often, the implied authority and apparent authority of a partner are coincident. However, when a partner's implied authority is restricted or eliminated, the partnership risks the possibility that **apparent authority** to do a denied act will remain. To prevent apparent authority from continuing when there is a limitation of a partner's actual authority, third persons with whom the partner deals must have knowledge of the limitation of his actual authority or have received notification of the limitation, such as receiving an e-mail or fax or otherwise having the limitation brought to their attention. Filing a Statement of Partnership Authority or Statement of Denial may help notify third parties of a partner's limited authority. Just as a principal must notify third persons of limitations of an agent's authority, so must a partnership notify its customers, suppliers, and others of express limitations of the actual authority of partners.

Suppose that Carroll, Melton, and Ramirez are partners and that they agree that Carroll will be the only purchasing agent for the partnership. This agreement must be communicated to third parties selling goods to the partnership, or Melton and Ramirez will have apparent authority to bind the partnership on purchase contracts. Melton and Ramirez do not have express authority to purchase goods, because they have agreed to such a restriction on their authority. They do not have implied authority to purchase, because implied authority may not contradict express authority.

Ratification A partnership may ratify the unauthorized acts of partners. Essentially, **ratification** occurs when the partners accept an act of a partner who had no actual or apparent authority to do the act when it was done.

For example, suppose Cabrillo and Boeglin are partners in an accounting firm. They agree that only Cabrillo has authority to make contracts to perform audits of clients, an agreement known by Mantron Company. Nonetheless, Boeglin and Mantron contract for the partnership to audit Mantron's financial statements. At this point, the partnership is not liable on the contract, because Boeglin has no express, implied, or apparent authority to make the contract. But suppose Boeglin takes the contract to Cabrillo, who reads it and says, "OK, we'll do this audit." Cabrillo, as the partner with express authority to make audit contracts, has ratified the contract and thereby bound the partnership to the contract.

Special Transactions The validity of some partner's actions is affected by special partnership rules that reflect a concern for protecting important property and the credit standing of partners. This concern is especially evident in the rules for conveying the partnership's real property and for borrowing money in the name of the partnership.

Power to Convey Partnership Real Property To bind the partnership, an individual partner's conveyance of a partnership's real property must be expressly, impliedly, or apparently authorized or be ratified by the partnership. For example, the partners may expressly agree that a partner may sell the partnership's real property.

The more difficult determination is whether a partner has *implied* and *apparent* authority to convey real property. A partner has implied and apparent authority to sell real property if a partnership sells real property in the usual course of the partnership business. Such would be the case with the partner of a real estate investment partnership that buys and sells land as its regular business. By contrast, a partner has no implied or apparent authority to sell the building in which the partnership's retail business is conducted. Here, unanimous agreement of the partners is required, since the sale of the building may affect the ability of the firm to continue. In addition, a partner has no implied or apparent authority to sell land held for investment not in the usual course of business. A sale of such land would be authorized only if the partners concurred.

When title to partnership real property is recorded in the name of the partners and not the partnership, those partners in whose name title is recorded have apparent authority to convey title to a bona fide purchaser unaware of the partnership's interest in the real property. However, purchasers are deemed to have knowledge of a limitation on a partner's authority to convey real property that is contained in a Statement of Partnership Authority or Statement of Denial that is filed in the real estate recording office.

Borrowing Money Partnership law restricts the ability of a partner to borrow money in the name of a partnership. Essentially, a partner must possess express, implied, or apparent authority to borrow. Express authority presents few problems. Finding implied and apparent authority to borrow is more difficult.

Although the RUPA does not explicitly recognize the distinction, a number of courts have distinguished between trading and nontrading partnerships for purposes of determining whether a partner has implied or apparent authority to borrow money on behalf of the partnership. A **trading partnership** has an inventory; that is, its regular business is buying and selling merchandise, such as retailing, wholesaling, importing, or exporting. For example, a toy store and a clothing store are trading partnerships. Since there is a time lag between the date they pay for their inventory and the date they sell inventory to their customers, these firms ordinarily need to borrow to avoid cash flow problems. Therefore, a partner of a trading partnership has implied and apparent authority to borrow money for the partnership.

A **nontrading partnership** has no substantial inventory and is usually engaged in providing services—for example, accounting services or real estate brokerage. Such partnerships have no normal borrowing needs. Therefore, a partner of a nontrading partnership has no implied or apparent authority to borrow money for the partnership.

The distinction between trading and nontrading partnerships is not always clear. Businesses such as general contracting, manufacturing, and dairy farming, although not exclusively devoted to buying and selling inventory, have been held to be trading partnerships. The rationale for their inclusion in this category is that borrowing is necessary in the ordinary course of business to augment their working capital.

This suggests why the distinction between trading partnerships and nontrading partnerships is useless or misleading. There is no necessary connection between borrowing money and buying and selling. The more important inquiry should be whether a partner's borrowing is in the ordinary course of business. When borrowing is in the ordinary course of business, a partner has implied and apparent authority to borrow money. If borrowing is not in the ordinary course of business, then no individual partner has implied or apparent authority to borrow money.

If a court finds that a partner has authority to borrow money, the partnership is liable for his borrowings on behalf of the partnership. There is a limit, however, to a partner's capacity to borrow. A partner may have authority to borrow, yet borrow beyond the ordinary needs of the business. A partnership will not be liable for any loan whose amount exceeds the ordinary needs of the business, unless otherwise agreed by the partners.

The power to borrow money on the firm's credit will ordinarily carry with it the power to grant the lender a lien or security interest in firm assets to secure the repayment of the borrowed money. Security interests are a normal part of business loan transactions.

Issuing Negotiable Instruments A partner who has the authority to borrow money also has authority to issue negotiable instruments such as promissory notes for that purpose. When a partnership has a checking account and a partner's name appears on the signature card filed with the bank, the partner has express authority to draw checks. A partner whose name is not on the signature card filed with the bank has apparent authority to issue checks, but only in respect to a third person who has no knowledge or notification of the limitation on the partner's authority.

Negotiating Instruments A partnership receives many negotiable instruments during the course of its business. For example, an accounting firm's clients often pay fees by check. Even though borrowing money and issuing negotiable instruments may be beyond a partner's implied and apparent authority, a partner usually has implied and apparent authority to transfer or negotiate instruments on behalf of the partnership.

For example, when a partnership has a bank account, a partner has implied and apparent authority to indorse and deposit in the account checks drawn payable to the partnership. As a general rule, a partner also has implied and apparent authority to indorse and cash checks drawn payable to the order of the partnership. Likewise, partners have implied authority to indorse drafts and notes payable to the order of the partnership and to sell them at a discount.

Admissions and Notice A partnership is bound by admissions or representations made by a partner concerning partnership affairs that are within her express, implied, or apparent authority. Likewise, notice to a partner is considered to be received by the partnership. Also, a partner's knowledge of material information relating to partnership affairs is **imputed** to the partnership. These rules reflect the reality that a partnership speaks, sees, and hears through its partners.

Disagreement among Partners: Ordinary Course of Business
Usually, partners will discuss management decisions among themselves before taking action, even when doing so is not required by a partnership agreement and even when a partner has the implied authority to take the action by herself. When partners discuss a prospective action, they will usually vote on what action to take. Under the default RUPA rules, each partner has one vote, regardless of the relative sizes of their partnership

interests or their shares of the profits. On matters in the ordinary course of business, the vote of a majority of the partners controls ordinary business decisions and, thereby, limits the actual authority of the partners. Nonetheless, the apparent authority of the partners to bind the partnership on contracts in the ordinary course of business is unaffected by the majority vote of partners, unless the limitation on the partners' actual authority is communicated to third parties.

When Unanimous Partners' Agreement Required

Some partnership actions are so important that one partner should not be able to do them by himself. To make clear that no single partner has implied or apparent authority to do certain acts, in the absence of a contrary agreement, the UPA requires unanimity for several actions. The RUPA, however, deletes such a list. Instead, the RUPA requires that any partnership act not in the ordinary course of business be approved by all partners, absent a contrary agreement of the partners.

For example, a decision to build a new executive office complex must be approved by all partners. Similarly, the decision of a small accounting partnership in Sacramento to open a second office in San Jose would require unanimity. When other actions, such as submitting a partnership claim to arbitration, are in the ordinary course of business, any partner has authority to do the actions.

Joint Ventures and Mining Partnerships

Most of the authority rules of partnerships apply to joint ventures and mining partnerships. These business organizations are in essence partnerships with limited purposes. Therefore, their members have less implied and apparent authority than do partners. Joint venturers have considerable apparent authority if third persons are unaware of the limited scope of the joint venture. A mining partner has no implied authority to borrow money or issue negotiable instruments. As with partners, joint venturers and mining partners may by agreement expand or restrict each other's agency powers.

 L03 Draft partnership agreements resolving management and compensation issues.

Effect of Partnership Agreement

The partners may modify the rules of management by their unanimous agreement. They may agree that a partner will relinquish his management right, thus removing the partner's express and implied authority to manage the partnership. They may grant sole authority to manage the business to one or more partners. Such removals or delegations of management powers will not, however, eliminate a partner's apparent authority to bind the partnership for his acts within the usual course of business unless a third party has knowledge or notification of the limitation.

A partnership agreement may create classes of partners, some of which will have the power to veto certain actions. Some classes of partners may be given greater voting rights. Unequal voting rights are often found in very large partnerships, such as an accounting firm with hundreds or thousands of partners.

For example, in a large accounting partnership, the partnership agreement will have a management section. This section usually begins with a restatement of the RUPA fiduciary duties that partners owe to the partnership, with exceptions or revisions, such as changes in the duty of care. The section also lists the duties of the partnership to the partners, such as the duty to indemnify.

Regarding the authority of partners, the management articles may give a managing partner or a managing partners' committee control over much of the firm's day-to-day management, such as the hiring, firing, and promotion of employees, investing the firm's excess cash, and drawing and indorsing partnership checks. The managing partners or a compensation committee may be given power to determine the partners' draws or salaries. Individual partners may have most of their management powers taken away but may be granted the power to hire a personal assistant or to make expenditures within limits from an expense account, such as buying a laptop computer. Other matters may require approval of all the partners (such as selling the partnership's real property and moving the partnership's place of business), a supermajority of partners (such as 75 percent approval to bind the partnership to a bank loan), a majority of partners (such as installing new carpeting), or the partners in a particular area of practice (such as requiring approval of a majority of consulting partners for a consulting engagement over $1,000,000).

In small partnerships of 10 or fewer partners, the partnership agreement often requires unanimous partners' agreement for many actions, such as hiring employees and making large contracts. In small partnerships, these and other actions have a greater impact on each partner. This impact is evident in the next case, *NBN Broadcasting,* in which a partnership agreement that was designed to prevent and resolve conflicts between the two partners eventually caused serious disagreements. The partners wanted to be equal essentially, but a deadlock provision allowed one partner to dominate, eventually causing a breakdown of the partners' relationship. It illustrates the necessity for careful drafting of partnership agreements, including anticipating that a part of the agreement may cause an undesired result.

> ## NBN Broadcasting, Inc. v. Sheridan Broadcasting Networks, Inc.
> ### 105 F.3d 72 (2d Cir. 1997)

NBN Broadcasting, Inc., and Sheridan Broadcasting Networks, Inc., operated competing radio networks. In 1991, NBN and Sheridan agreed to form American Urban Radio Network (AURN), a Pennsylvania partnership that combined NBN's and Sheridan's networks. Sheridan owned 51 percent of the partnership; NBN owned 49 percent. They agreed to maintain NBN's offices in New York and Sheridan's offices in Pittsburgh to allow direct oversight and input by AURN's cochairmen and co-CEOs, Sydney Small (chairman of NBN) and Ronald R. Davenport (chairman of Sheridan). NBN and Sheridan wanted equal rights in management of the partnership. The partners' equal right to manage AURN was modified by the partnership agreement in sections 5.2 and 5.3. Section 5.2 created a five-member Management Committee comprising two members selected by NBN and two by Sheridan; a seat on the Management Committee was to be vacant and would be filled only when the Management Committee was deadlocked. Section 5.2 also provided:

The Management Committee shall be responsible for the following functions of the partnership and contractual arrangements relating thereto:

(i)   Sales and marketing;
(ii) Promotions and public relations;
(iii) Affiliate relations and compensation;
(iv) Network programming;
(v)   Personnel administration; and
(vi) Budgeting, accounting, and finance.

Section 5.3 provides:

(a) In the event that three of the four members of the Management Committee are unable to reach agreement on any issue or issues relating to items (i) through (v) above and remain so unable for a period of thirty days, then Ronald R. Davenport, Chairman of Sheridan, shall have the right to fill the vacant seat on the Management Committee for the purpose of reaching an agreement, and only until an agreement is reached, on such issue or issues.

Section 5.3 did not authorize appointment of a fifth member of the Management Committee when there was a deadlock regarding budgeting, accounting, or finance or any matter other than those listed in Section 5.2(i) through (v). As to budgeting, accounting, and finance and matters not listed in Section 5.2(i) through (v), NBN and Sheridan were equal partners, and all decisions on such matters required their agreement.

At a Management Committee meeting on September 14, 1995, Davenport proposed that AURN open an expensive new office in Washington, D.C., hire Skip Finley as chief operating officer, and employ Richard Boland. When NBN's representatives opposed opening the new office and hiring Finley and Boland, Davenport scheduled a meeting solely to appoint a fifth member to break the deadlock. On September 15, NBN asked a Pennsylvania state trial court to grant a preliminary injunction and a permanent injunction against Sheridan's opening a new AURN office in Washington and hiring Finley and Boland, on the grounds that the proposals related to budgeting, accounting, and finance and were, therefore, not subject to the deadlock voting provision. On October 13, the state trial court denied NBN's motion for a preliminary injunction. The state trial court held that Sheridan had the right to invoke the deadlock provision to "make additions to personnel" by hiring Finley and Boland. The trial court did not rule on NBN's request for a permanent injunction.

At an October 16 Management Committee meeting, Davenport appointed a fifth member of the committee. By a 3–2 vote, the Management Committee voted to hire Finley and Boland, with NBN's representatives opposing. At that meeting, Davenport also proposed to relocate AURN's New York offices from NBN's office space in New York to other office space in the New York area; to transfer to Pittsburgh from New York AURN's traffic, billing, and collection functions; and to require Finley to make cuts in AURN's New York–based marketing and research personnel. NBN's representatives opposed the proposals, and Davenport scheduled a meeting on November 28 to break the deadlock.

Sensing that the Pennsylvania state trial court would dismiss its request for a permanent injunction and hoping to litigate the issues at a later time, NBN sought to withdraw its motion for a permanent injunction. On November 28, 1995, while the state trial court judge was considering NBN's request to withdraw its lawsuit, a meeting of AURN's Management Committee was held. Davenport again invoked the deadlock provision and appointed his son as fifth member of the Management Committee. By a 3–2 vote, the Management Committee agreed to relocate AURN's New York offices from NBN's office space, to transfer AURN functions to Pittsburgh from New York, and to authorize Finley to make cuts in AURN's New York–based marketing and research personnel. Davenport also proposed to promote Finley to chief executive officer and Boland to vice president of administration. NBN Chairman Small objected, and Davenport scheduled another meeting to break the deadlock.

On November 29 and 30, the state trial court, wanting to put "a final end to this unnecessary litigation," ordered the discontinuance of NBN's lawsuit with prejudice, meaning that NBN could appeal the ruling to an appellate court but would not be permitted to have another trial court litigate the same issues. NBN chose not to appeal the decision of the Pennsylvania state trial court.

After the November 28 meeting, Sheridan located new office space for AURN in New York and entered a new lease with a minimum annual liability of $900,000, yet Sheridan never revealed the location of the space to NBN or sought NBN approval of the relocation or new lease. On January 18, 1996, at the next Management Committee meeting, Davenport again appointed his son as the fifth member. By a 3–2 vote, with NBN's representatives opposing, the Management Committee appointed Finley as CEO and Boland as vice president of administration.

On January 31, 1996, NBN filed a federal lawsuit seeking an injunction against Sheridan's alleged violations of the equal management rights of the partners by hiring Finley and Boland, interfering with AURN's personnel and customer relations, and relocating AURN's New York offices. Sheridan asked the federal district court to dismiss the suit on the grounds of res judicata; that is, Sheridan argued that NBN was raising legal issues that the Pennsylvania state trial court had already considered or that NBN should have brought to the Pennsylvania trial court. Thus, Sheridan argued, because the Pennsylvania trial court had already dismissed NBN's request for an injunction with prejudice, the federal district court should not reconsider these issues. The federal district court agreed with Sheridan and dismissed NBN's lawsuit. NBN appealed to the federal court of appeal.

Pollack, Judge

A discontinuance with prejudice is deemed a final adjudication on the merits for res judicata purposes on the claims asserted or which could have been asserted in the suit. Any issue concerning the relocation of the New York Office could not have been raised in the State Court suit commenced on September 15, 1995, or until the voting deadlock thereon on November 28, 1995. The NBN claim on the relocation of the New York Office was a claim based on new conduct that could have only arisen long after the filing of NBN's State Court suit. Since a plaintiff has no obligation to expand its suit in order to add a claim that it could not have asserted at the time the suit was commenced, a later suit based on subsequent conduct is not barred by res judicata.

The res judicata effect is limited to those claims that had arisen at the time that NBN brought the State Court action. They did not include the relocation of the New York Office, which had not yet even been brought to an initial vote. There was no submission to the State Court of NBN's equal right to decide whether the New York Office should be moved from its existing location as part of NBN's premises.

The doctrine of res judicata embraces all claims of NBN, excluding those claims relating to the relocation of the New York Office, which were passed on by the Management Committee prior to the filing of NBN's State Court action; the claims asserted therein and the dismissal thereof on the grounds of res judicata is affirmed.

Judgment for Sheridan affirmed in part; judgment in part reversed in favor of NBN. Remanded to the district court.

LOG ON

Model Partnership Agreements
www.mhhe.com/mallor15e
    Go to your textbook's website above to find a model partnership agreement. Note that the agreement repeats the fiduciary duties we studied. A well-drafted partnership agreement will expand that section to make clear what each duty covers, such as stating what activities constitute competition with the partnership. In England and India, partnership agreements are called partnership deeds. See an example at **www.vakilno1.com/froms_html/partnership.html.**
There are several commercial websites that sell model partnership agreements. One is FindLegalForms.com. See a list of partnership agreements for sale at
www.findlegalforms.com/forms/partnership.

 LO4   Explain the liability of partners for contracts and torts.

Liability for Torts and Crimes

Torts   The standards and principles of agency law's *respondeat superior* are applied in determining the liability of the partnership and of the other partners for the torts of a partner and other partnership employees. See Chapter 36. In addition, the partnership and the other partners are liable jointly and severally for the torts of a partner committed within the ordinary course of partnership business or within the authority of that partner. Finally, when a partner commits a breach of trust, the partnership and all

Ethics in Action

You and your friends consider forming a consulting partnership. If you form the business as a partnership, each partner has personal liability for all the contacts and torts of the partnership. If you form the business as an LLP, in general you and the other partners have no liability for partnership obligations beyond the assets of the LLP, that is, beyond each partner's equity interest in the business.

• As your form of business, will you choose the partnership or LLP?

• Is it ethical to be an LLP partner and to have liability limited to your equity interest in the LLP? Would a profit maximizer find it ethical to form an LLP? Would a utilitarian or rights theorist find it ethical?

• Suppose that a bank knows the business is an LLP, lends money to the LLP, but does not obtain the LLP partners' individual promises to repay the loan. Is it ethical that the LLP partners are not liable to the bank on the loan if the LLP's assets are insufficient to repay the loan?

of the partners are liable. For example, all of the partners in a stock brokerage firm are liable for a partner's embezzlement of a customer's securities and funds.

Intentional Torts While a partnership and its partners are usually liable for a partner's negligence, they usually have no liability for a partner's intentional torts. The reason for this rule is that intentional torts are not usually within the ordinary scope of business or within the ordinary authority of a partner.

A few intentional torts impose liability on a partnership and its partners. For example, a partner who repossesses consumer goods from debtors of the partnership may trespass on consumer property or batter a consumer. Such activities have been held to be in the ordinary course of business. Also, a partner who authorizes a partner to commit an intentional tort is liable for such torts.

Partners' Remedies When a partnership and the other partners are held liable for a partner's tort, they may recover the amount of their vicarious liability from the wrongdoing partner, but only if the partner fails to comply with the fiduciary duty of care. For example, in the *Moren* case, which follows the next section, although a partner caused the harm for which the partnership was liable, she was not grossly negligent or reckless in causing the harm. Therefore, it was appropriate to deny the partnership a recovery against the partner and to require the partnership to assume ultimate liability to the victim.

Tort Liability and Limited Liability Partnerships

State legislatures created the limited liability partnership (LLP) as a means of reducing the personal liability of professional partners, such as accountants. Consequently, an innocent partner of an LLP has no liability for the professional malpractice of his partners. LLP statutes grant partners broad protection, eliminating an innocent

partner's liability for errors, omissions, negligence, incompetence, or malfeasance of his partners or employees.

Under the RUPA, the protection afforded LLP partners is even broader. LLP partners have no liability for other debts of the business, such as a supplier's bill, lease obligations, and bank loans.

That is the limit of protection, however. The LLP itself is liable for the tort of a wrongdoing partner or employee under the doctrine of *respondeat superior*. In addition, a wrongdoing partner is liable for his own malpractice or negligence. Also, the partner supervising the work of the wrongdoing partner may have unlimited liability for the wrongdoing partner's tort. Thus, the LLP's assets, the wrongdoing partner's personal assets, and the supervising partner's personal assets are at risk.

Crimes

When a partner commits a crime in the course and scope of transacting partnership business, rarely are his partners criminally liable. But when the partners have participated in the criminal act or authorized its commission, they are liable. They may also be liable when they know of a partner's criminal tendencies yet place him in a position in which he may commit a crime.

Until recent times, a partnership could not be held liable for a crime in most states because it was not viewed as a legal entity. However, modern criminal codes usually define a partnership as a "person" that may commit a crime when a partner, acting within the scope of his authority, engages in a criminal act.

Lawsuits by and against Partnerships and Partners

Under the RUPA, a partnership may sue in its own name. Since suing someone is usually an ordinary business decision, ordinarily any partner has authority to initiate a lawsuit.

The RUPA also permits a partnership to be sued in its own name. Partners may also be sued individually on partnership obligations. Partners are jointly and severally liable for partnership obligations, whether based in contract or tort. This means that in addition to suing the partnership, a creditor may sue all of the partners (jointly) or sue fewer than all the partners (severally). If a creditor sues the partnership and all of the partners, the judgment may be satisfied from the assets of the partnership and, if partnership assets are exhausted, from the assets of the partners. If the partnership and fewer than all the partners are sued severally, the judgment may be satisfied only from the assets of the partnership and the assets of the partners sued. Again, partners cannot be required to pay until partnership assets have been exhausted.

When fewer than all the partners are sued and made to pay a partnership obligation, the partners paying may seek **indemnification** and **contribution** from the other partners for their shares of the liability.

Limited Liability Partnerships

For LLP partners, only the LLP is liable on a contractual obligation, and only the LLP may be sued on such a claim. For tort obligations, the LLP is liable as well as the partner who committed the tort. LLP partners who had no role in the commission of the tort have no liability.

In the following case, *Ederer v. Gursky,* the court held that New York's LLP law, while mostly shielding LLP partners from liability to LLP creditors, did not shield LLP partners from liability to each other for breaches of contract or partner duties. While decided under New York law, the decision would be the same under the RUPA.

Ederer v. Gursky	881 N.E.2d 204 (N.Y. Ct. App. 2007)

Steven Gursky and Louis Ederer were law partners in a New York limited liability partnership, Gursky & Ederer LLP. In July 2003, Ederer withdrew from the LLP because he had a severe falling out with Gursky and the LLP was cash-strapped and unprofitable. In December 2003, Ederer sued Gursky alleging Gursky breached the LLP agreement by failing to pay Ederer his 30 percent share of the LLP's profits and other compensation that Ederer earned during the last months of the LLP. Gursky defended on several grounds, including that he, as a partner in an LLP, had no liability to Ederer because partnership law in New York shielded partners in an LLP from any personal liability. The New York trial court held that New York law placing limits on the personal liability of partners in an LLP applies to debts of the partnership or the partners to third parties and has nothing to do with a partner's duties to his partner. On appeal, the Appellate Division affirmed, and Gursky sought review by the New York Court of Appeals, the highest court in the State of New York.

Read, Judge

Partnership Law § 26, as originally enacted, and its prototype, section 15 of the UPA, have always been understood to mean what they plainly say: general partners are jointly and severally liable to nonpartner creditors for all wrongful acts and breaches of trust committed by their partners in carrying out the partnership's business, and jointly liable for all other debts to third parties. This proposition follows naturally from the very nature of a partnership, which is based on the law of principal and agent. Just as a principal is liable for the acts of its agents, each partner is personally responsible for the acts of other partners in the ordinary course of the partnership's business. In addition to this vicarious liability to nonpartner creditors, each partner concomitantly has an obligation to share or bear the losses of the partnership through contribution and indemnification in the context of an ongoing partnership.

The nationwide initiative to create a new business entity combining the flexibility of a partnership without the onus of this traditional vicarious liability originated with a law adopted in Texas in 1991, following the savings and loan crisis. At that time, a number of legal and accounting firms faced potentially ruinous judgments arising out of their professional services for banks and thrifts which thereafter failed. Because these professional firms were typically organized as general partnerships, this liability also threatened the personal assets of their constituent partners. The Texas LLP statute protected such partners from this unlimited personal exposure without requiring a reorganization of their business structure.

In New York, the Legislature enacted limited liability partnership legislation as a rider to the New York Limited Liability Company Law. This legislation eliminated the vicarious liability of a general partner in a registered limited liability partnership by amending section 26 of the Partnership Law .... providing that

"[e]xcept as provided by subdivisions (c) and (d) of this section, no partner of a partnership which is a registered limited liability partnership is liable or accountable, directly or indirectly (including by way of indemnification, contribution or otherwise), for any debts, obligations or liabilities of, or chargeable to, the registered limited liability partnership or each other, whether arising in tort, contract or otherwise, which are incurred, created or assumed by such partnership while such partnership is a registered limited liability partnership, solely by reason of being such a partner."

Section 26 (c) excludes from section 26 (b)'s liability shield "any negligent or wrongful act or misconduct committed by [a partner] or by any person under his or her direct supervision and control while rendering professional services on behalf of [the] registered limited liability partnership."

Gursky points out that section 26 (b) eliminates the liability of a partner in a limited liability partnership for "any debts" without distinguishing between debts owed to a third party or to the partnership or each other. As a result, he contends, the

Legislature did not "leave open to conjecture whether § 26 (b) was intended to cover debts which may be owed by the limited liability partnership (or one partner) to other partners." This argument ignores, however, that the phrase "any debts" is part of a provision (section 26) that has always governed only a partner's liability to third parties, and, in fact, is part of article 3 of the Partnership Law ("Relations of Partners to Persons Dealing with the Partnership"), not article 4 ("Relations of Partners to One Another"). The logical inference, therefore, is that "any debts" refers to any debts owed a third party, absent very clear legislative direction to the contrary.

Judgment for Ederer affirmed.

Problems and Problem Cases

1. Kyle Jauretz and Galina Marvano formed JM Solutions, a partnership that managed events for business clients. Jauretz had been an event manager for several years, and he insisted before the partnership was formed that Marvano agree that Jauretz could keep several clients to himself and not share the revenue or profits from those clients with Marvano. One such client was Bay Shores LLC, a golf community for which Jauretz had managed an annual golf tournament. When Jauretz was working for Bay Shores LLC, his personal client, he needed additional staff to manage the event. Jauretz directed two JM Solutions employees to work full-time on the Bay Shores event, which they did for three weeks. JM Solutions continued to pay the employees' wages while they worked on the Bay Shores event. Jauretz also used JM Solutions assets, including stakes and ropes, in the course of managing the Bay Shores event. He did not pay JM Solutions for the use of the stakes and ropes. Has Jauretz breached a fiduciary duty to JM Solutions?

2. Twelve accounting and financial services professionals opt to form a limited liability partnership. They have experience in the industry ranging from 15 to 35 years. Edie Fercano has the most professional and managerial experience and is bringing the most valuable clients to the business. She has one client that she has served for over 20 years. She is inclined to continue to serve that client by herself, not with the LLP's resources. What do you recommend Edie include in the partnership

agreement to avoid her having liability to the LLP? Why?

3. Dennis Ranzau and William Brosseau formed a partnership to purchase the Casa T, a house in Acapulco. Their intent was to use the Casa T as a vacation home for a few weeks each year, to lease it for the remainder of each year, and to share the rental income after expenses. Ranzau soon became concerned that Brosseau was not accounting for the expenses and income of the Casa T. Brosseau refused Ranzau's requests to provide receipts for expenses Brosseau claimed to have incurred on the house. Brosseau also let his friend have "total run of the house" over Ranzau's objection. On another occasion, Ranzau's wife and her friends were locked out of the house by an agent of Brosseau and had to make other accommodation arrangements. Has Brosseau breached his fiduciary duty to Ranzau?

4. Hal Carney and Trish Protura are two Web and software engineers seeking financial backing for further development of social networking technology they have created. Black Rock LLC is willing to commit $5 million to the venture, which will be formed as an LLP. The LLP is expected to generate no cash flow for the first 18 months and no profits for the first three years. The business will have minimal profits for years four and five. Starting in year six, its profits should exceed $1 million and grow steadily thereafter. Carney and Protura have no jobs, no income, and few assets beyond their investment and work for the LLP. Should they rely on the default rules of the RUPA to provide compensation to them for their work for the LLP?

5. Eric Wilmot and Renee Harmeau form WH & Associates Properties LLP, a limited liability partnership in Rochester, Minnesota, to purchase and manage commercial and residential real estate in the Rochester area. WH & Associates owns five residential apartment buildings, the largest of which has 32 units on two floors and has a value of $3 million. WH & Associates also owns seven strip shopping centers, of which the biggest has 12 stores and a value of $6 million. The total value of all the apartment buildings and shopping centers owned by WH & Associates is $31 million. Most of the residential buildings and shopping centers have been purchased partly with loans for which the properties are collateral.

   To escape the harsh Minnesota winters, Wilmot wants to move his home to Jacksonville, Florida. He also wants to move WH Associates' management office to Jacksonville. In addition, he has identified a mall in Jacksonville that he wants to buy for the LLP. The mall has 32 stores, and the asking price is $29 million. To purchase the mall, Wilmot wants to borrow $27 million. Does Wilmot have the authority to move WH Associates' office, to purchase the mall, and to borrow money to fund the purchase?

6. Jake Coombs, Yemi Ogarra, and Wade Stram formed a financial services consulting partnership. The partnership's ordinary business was to provide investment advice to businesses with assets between $500,000 and $40,000,000. The partnership operated from a small building that was owned by the partnership, even though title was held in the name of Yemi Ogarra, who had transferred the building to the partnership as her capital contribution. Because the partnership quickly became profitable, the partners chose to retain some of the earnings of the business and to invest it in commercial real estate in the community. Such investments, however, were not part of the partnership's regular business, which remained financial consulting. Title to investment property purchased by the partnership was held in the partnership's name. After a few years, the partners had a falling out. Ogarra wanted the partnership to move its offices to a bigger, more impressive building. She also believed that the commercial real estate market was in a bubble and that the partnership should sell some of its investment property. Without obtaining approval from her partners, Ogarra sold the building in which the partnership did its business to CFC Financial LLC. Because the building was titled only in Ogarra's name, CFC believed that she was the only person with an interest in the building. Ogarra also sold to CFC a commercial shopping mall that had been held by the partnership for investment. Title in the mall had been recorded in the partnership's name. Coombs and Stram sued to void the sales of the building and mall to CFC on the grounds that Ogarra had no authority to sell the properties. Were they right?

7. Roberto Frientas and Herman Graham formed an IT consulting business, which they organized as a limited liability partnership, Accent Pointe LLP. For the most part, each LLP client was assigned either to Frientas or Graham, but not both. On behalf of the LLP, Graham did an IT audit for Bemus, Inc., which required Graham to ensure that Bemus's IT controls complied with section 404 of the Sarbanes–Oxley Act. Graham failed to check whether the client had an off-site backup system for critical records like accounts receivable information, an omission that resulted in Bemus's failure to comply with section 404. As a result, when Bemus's system crashed internally, Bemus was unable to verify some of its receivables, resulting in a loss of $500,000. Bemus sued Graham, Accent Pointe LLP, and Frientas to recover its damages. Who is liable to Bemus?

8. Nicole Moren and her sister Amy Benedetti were partners in the JAX Restaurant in Foley, Minnesota. One afternoon, Nicole completed her day shift at JAX and left to pick up her two-year-old son, Remington, from day care. She returned to the restaurant with Remington after learning that Amy needed help. Nicole called her husband, Martin, who told her that he would pick Remington up in about 20 minutes. Because Nicole did not want Remington running around the restaurant, she brought him into the kitchen with her, set him on top of the counter, and began rolling out pizza dough using the dough-pressing machine. As she was making pizzas, Remington reached his hand into the dough press. His hand was crushed, and he sustained permanent injuries. On behalf of his son, Martin sued the partnership for damages, alleging that it negligently caused Remington's injuries. The partnership then brought a legal action against Nicole, claiming that if it was obligated to compensate Remington, the partnership was entitled to indemnity or contribution from Nicole for her negligence in allowing Remington to be on the counter where he could be injured by the pizza press. Was Nicole found liable to her partnership?

9. Upon his release from prison, Michael Clott, convicted of securities fraud and racketeering, retained a law firm partnership, Ross & Hardies, to provide Clott's company, Capital Financial Group, Inc., a legal framework to do financial, securities, and banking business in Maryland. Steven Kersner was the Ross & Hardies partner primarily assigned to Clott's account. Clott created the 7.5% Program, a mortgage program designed to provide lines of credit to minority homeowners. The 7.5% Program was a fraud by which Clott stole money that was borrowed by the homeowners participating in the program. Kersner helped perpetuate the fraud by assuring homeowners that the program was legitimate, aiding Clott in transferring borrowed funds to bank accounts, opening empty accounts in the name of homeowners to deceive them that lines of credit had been opened for them, preparing false statements to make it appear that the homeowners were no longer liable on the mortgages, telling lenders with questions to contact Kersner instead of homeowners, and forging and altering checks. Did Kersner's actions make his partnership liable to homeowners under the Racketeering Influenced Corrupt Organization Act?

10. Florence and Michael Acri were married and also partners in the Acri Café, which they jointly managed. For the first 15 years of their marriage, Michael had been in and out of sanitaria for the treatment of mental disorders. Although he had beaten Florence when they had marital problems, he had not attacked anyone else. Michael and Florence separated, and Michael assumed full control and management of the café. A few months after the Acris' separation, Stephen Vrabel and a friend went into the Acri Café. Without provocation, Michael shot and killed Vrabel's companion and seriously injured Vrabel while they were seated and drinking at the café's bar. Was Florence liable for Vrabel's injuries?

 Online Research

Complex Partnership Agreements

The NBN case on page 983 is an example of a complex partnership agreement that attempts to anticipate all future issues that partners may face. Often, but not always, these complex agreements are between two or more businesses. There are many other interesting examples you can find online at www.onecle.com. Under "Business Contracts from SEC Filings," find the link for "Partnership Agreement" and click on it. You will find partnership agreements involving Coca-Cola, Ticketmaster, and many others.

Examine these agreements. Note to whom management is entrusted and how management succession is planned. Determine the manner in which profits and other compensation are paid to the partners and the timing of payments. Note the statement of fiduciary duties.

Consider completing the case "PARTNERSHIP: You Sunk My Partnership" from the You Be the Judge website element after you have read this chapter. Visit our website at www.mhhe.com/mallor15e for more information and activities regarding this case segment.

CHAPTER 39

PARTNERS' DISSOCIATION AND PARTNERSHIPS' DISSOLUTION AND WINDING UP

You are planning the formation of a 50-partner venture capital limited liability partnership. Knowing the attributes, weaknesses, and faults of humans, you expect that some partners will die, become ill, and act irresponsibly during the term of the partnership. You know that some partners will want to leave the partnership for good reasons and some for bad reasons. You know that when a partner leaves the partnership, the leaving partner will want to be paid the value of her partnership interest. You also know it is human nature for partners to disagree about the value of a partnership interest. You are also concerned about how the partnership will fund its repurchase of the leaving partner's interest without causing severe liquidity problems for the firm. You know that some of the firm's clients have strong business and personal attachments to one or more firm partners; therefore, when those partners leave the partnership, the firm may lose the business of those partners' clients. Finally, you know that the firm will need to add new partners from time to time to ensure the firm's survival.

- What are the default rules that apply when partners leave and enter a partnership?
- Why may the default rules be unacceptable to you?
- Write the sections of your partnership agreement regarding partners' leaving and entering the partnership.

LO LEARNING OBJECTIVES

After studying this chapter, you should be able to:

1 Define dissociation and identify actions that cause wrongful and nonwrongful dissociations.

2 Understand the default consequences of dissociation.

3 Draft a partnership agreement that changes the rules applying when a partner dissociates.

4 Understand the causes of dissolution and the process of winding up.

5 Draft a partnership agreement that changes the rules applying when dissolution occurs.

6 Appreciate the default effects of continuing a partnership after dissolution.

7 Identify issues involved in adding new partners to existing partnerships.

THIS CHAPTER IS ABOUT the death of partnerships. Four terms are important in this connection: dissociation, dissolution, winding up, and termination. Dissociation of a partner is a change in the relation of the partners, as when a partner dies or retires from the firm. Dissolution of a partnership is the commencement of the winding up process. Winding up is the orderly liquidation of the partnership assets and the distribution of the proceeds to those having claims against the partnership. Termination, the end of the partnership's existence, automatically follows winding up. A partner in a limited liability partnership dissociates from the LLP and the LLP is dissolved, wound up, and terminated in the same manner as an ordinary partnership.

 LO1 Define dissociation and identify actions that cause wrongful and nonwrongful dissociations.

Dissociation

Dissociation is defined in the Revised Uniform Partnership Act (RUPA) as a change in the relation of the partners caused by any partner's ceasing to be associated in the carrying on of the business. A dissociation may be caused by a partner's retirement, death, expulsion, or bankruptcy filing, among other things. Whatever the cause of dissociation, however, it is characterized by a partner's **ceasing to take part in the carrying on of the partnership's business.**

Dissociation is the starting place for the dissolution, winding up (liquidation), and termination of a partnership. Although dissolution and winding up do not always follow dissociation, they often do. Winding up usually has a severe effect on a business: It usually ends the business, because the assets of the business are sold and the proceeds of the sale are distributed to creditors and partners.

A partner has the *power* to dissociate from the partnership *at any time,* such as by withdrawing from the partnership. A partner does not, however, always have the *right* to dissociate.

When a partner's dissociation does not violate the partnership agreement and otherwise is nonwrongful, the partner has the right to dissociate from the partnership: Such a dissociation is **nonwrongful.** When a partner's dissociation violates the partnership agreement or otherwise is wrongful, the partner has the power—but not the right—to dissociate from the partnership: Such a dissociation is **wrongful.** The consequences that follow a nonwrongful dissocation may differ from those that follow a wrongful dissociation.

Nonwrongful Dissociation

A dissociation is nonwrongful when the dissociation does not violate the partnership agreement and is not otherwise wrongful. The following events are nonwrongful dissociations:

1. Death of a partner.

2. Withdrawal of a partner at any time from a partnership at will. A partnership at will is a partnership whose partnership agreement does not specify any term or undertaking to be accomplished.

3. In a partnership for a term or completion of an undertaking, withdrawal of a partner within 90 days after another partner's death, adjudicated incapacity, appointment of a custodion over his property, or wrongful dissociation. This dissociation is deemed nonwrongful to protect a partner who may think her interests are impaired by the premature departure of an important partner.

4. Withdrawal of a partner in accordance with the partnership agreement. For example, a partnership agreement allows the partners to retire at age 55. A partner who retires at age 60 has dissociated from the partnership nonwrongfully.

5. Automatic dissociation by the occurrence of an event agreed to in the partnership agreement. For example, a partnership may require a partner to retire at age 70.

6. Expulsion of a partner in accordance with the partnership agreement. For example, the removal of a partner who has been convicted of a crime causes a dissociation from the partnership if the partnership agreement allows removal on such grounds.

7. Expulsion of a partner who has transferred his transferable partnership interest or suffered a charging order against his transferable interest. Under the RUPA, such an expulsion must be approved by all the other partners, absent a contrary partnership agreement.

8. Expulsion of a partner with whom it is unlawful for the partnership to carry on its business. Under the RUPA, this expulsion must be approved by all the other partners, absent a contrary agreement.

9. A partner's assigning his assets for the benefit of creditors or consenting to the appointment of a custodian over his assets.

10. Appointment of a guardian over a partner or a judicial determination that a partner is incapable of performing as a partner. For example, a court rules that a partner who has suffered a stroke and has permanent brain damage is unable to continue as a partner of a consulting partnership.

In addition, there are a few special rules for nonwrongful dissociations of nonhuman partners, such as corporations.

 LO2 Understand the default consequences of dissociation.

Consequences of Nonwrongful Dissociation A partner who nonwrongfully dissociates from the partnership is entitled to be paid the value of her partnership interest.

The partner or her representative has no power, however, to dissolve the partnership and to force winding up, unless it is a partnership at will, that is, a partnership with no term. If the partnership is not at will, the partnership will continue. If dissociation was caused by a partner's retirement in compliance with the partnership agreement, a partnership for a term may be dissolved only by all remaining partners agreeing to the dissolution. Dissociation caused by a partner's death, however, permits as few as 50 percent of the partners to dissolve a partnership for a term. See the Concept Review at the end of this chapter for a comprehensive summary of the consequences of dissociation due to death or retirement.

Wrongful Dissociation

A partner wrongfully dissociates from a partnership when she dissociates in violation of the partnership agreement or in any other wrongful way. The following are wrongful dissociations:

1. Withdrawal of a partner that breaches an express provision in the partnership agreement.

2. Withdrawal of a partner before the end of the partnership's term or completion of its undertaking, unless the partner withdraws within 90 days after another partner's death, adjudicated incapacity, appointment of a custodion over his property, or wrongful dissociation.

3. A partner's filing a bankruptcy petition or being a debtor in bankruptcy.

4. Expulsion of a partner by a court at the request of the partnership or another partner. The grounds for judicial dissolution are when

  a. A partner's wrongful conduct adversely and materially affects the partnership business,

  b. A partner willfully and persistently breaches the partnership agreement or her fiduciary duties, or

  c. A partner's conduct makes it not reasonably practicable to conduct partnership business with the partner.

For example, a partner may persistently and substantially use partnership property for his own benefit. Or three partners may refuse to allow two other partners to manage the partnership's business. The harmed partners may seek judicial dissolution. For the expelled, wrongdoing partners, the dissociation is wrongful.

In addition, there are a few wrongful dissociations that apply only to nonhuman partners, such as a corporation.

Consequences of Wrongful Dissociation A partner who wrongfully dissociates from a partnership has no right to demand that the partnership be dissolved and its business wound up. That means the remaining partners may continue the partnership and its business. If at least 50 percent of the remaining partners so choose, however, the partnership will be wound up.

Should the other partners choose to wind up the business, the wrongfully dissociated partner has no right to perform the winding up. Nonetheless, a wrongfully dissociated partner is entitled to his share of the value of his partnership interest, minus the damages he caused the partnership. Damages may include the cost of obtaining new financing and the harm to the partnership goodwill caused by the loss of a valuable partner. Moreover, the wrongfully dissociated partner is not entitled to receive the buyout price until the term of the partnership has expired.

Acts Not Causing Dissociation

Many events that you think may cause a dissociation in fact do not. For example, a partner's transfer of his transferable partnership interest, by itself, does not cause a dissociation from the partnership, and neither does a creditor's obtaining a charging order. Also, the addition of a partner to a partnership is not a dissociation, because no one ceases to be associated in the business.

Mere disagreements, even irreconcilable differences, between partners are expectable, and therefore by themselves are not grounds for dissociation. If the disagreements threaten the economic viability of the partnership, however, a court may order a dissolution, as will be discussed below.

 Draft a partnership agreement that changes the rules applying when a partner dissociates.

Effect of Partnership Agreement

The dissociations listed in the RUPA are merely default rules. The partners may limit or expand the definition of dissociation and those dissociations that are wrongful, and they may change the effects of nonwrongful and wrongful dissociations. For example, the partners may require dissociation if a partner transfers his transferable partnership interest, if a partner does not redeem a charging order within 15 days of the order, or if a partner fails to make a capital contribution required by the partnership agreement. The partnership agreement may also reduce the number of partners that must approve the expulsion of a partner, such as a two-thirds vote, and expand the grounds for expulsion. If one partner is very powerful, the partnership agreement might allow that partner to dissociate at any time without penalty.

LO4 Understand the causes of dissolution and the process of winding up.

Dissolution and Winding Up the Partnership Business

When a partner dissociates from a partnership, the next step may be dissolution and **winding up** of the partnership's business. This involves the orderly liquidation—or sale—of the assets of the business. Liquidation may be accomplished asset by asset; that is, each asset may be sold separately. It may also be accomplished by a sale of the business as a whole. Or it may be accomplished by a means somewhere between these two extremes.

Winding up does not always require the sale of the assets or the business. When a partnership has valuable assets, the partners may wish to receive the assets rather than the proceeds from their sale. Such *distributions-in-kind* are rarely permitted.

During winding up, the partners continue as fiduciaries to each other, especially in negotiating sales or making distributions of partnership assets to members of the partnership. Nonetheless, there is a termination of the fiduciary duties unrelated to winding up. For example, a partner who is not winding up the business may compete with his partnership during winding up.

Events Causing Dissolution and Winding Up
Recognizing that a partnership business is worth more as a going concern, the RUPA contemplates that the partnership business will usually continue after a partner's dissociation. Many dissociations, such as one caused by a partner's death or retirement, will *not* automatically result in the dissolution and winding up of a partnership.

Nonetheless, the RUPA provides that a partnership will be dissolved and wound up in the following situations:

1. When the partnership's term has expired.

2. When the partnership has completed the undertaking for which it was created.

3. When all the partners agree to wind up the business.

4. When an event occurs that the partnership agreement states will cause a winding up of the partnership.

5. For a partnership at will, when any partner expressly withdraws from the partnership, other than a partner who is deceased, was expelled, is a debtor in bankruptcy,

assigned his assets for the benefit of creditors, had a custodian appointed over his assets, or was automatically dissociated by the occurrence of an event agreed to in the partnership agreement.

6. For a partnership for a term or completion of an undertaking, when at least half the remaining partners vote to dissolve and wind up the partnership within 90 days after a partner dies, wrongfully dissociates, assigns his property for the benefit of his creditors, or consents to the appointment of a custodian over his property.

7. When the business of the partnership is unlawful.

8. Upon the request by a partner, when a court determines that the economic purpose of the partnership is likely to be unreasonably frustrated, a partner's conduct makes it not reasonably practicable to carry on the business with that partner, or it is not reasonably practicable to conform with the partnership agreement.

9. Upon the request of a transferee of a partner's transferable interest in a partnership at will or a partnership whose term or undertaking has been completed, when a court determines that it is equitable to wind up the partnership business.

 LO5 Draft a partnership agreement that changes the rules applying when dissolution occurs.

Effect of Partnership Agreement The above causes of winding up are the RUPA's default rules, which except for the last three may be changed by the partnership agreement. For example, the partnership agreement may provide that at any time two-thirds of the partners may cause a winding up or that upon the death or retirement of a partner no partner has the right to force a winding up. Partners will frequently want to limit the events that cause dissolution and winding up, because they believe the business will be worth more as a going concern than by being liquidated.

In addition, if dissolution has occurred, the partners may agree to avoid winding up and to continue the business. To avoid winding up after dissolution has occurred, under the RUPA all the partners who have not wrongfully dissociated must consent to continuing the business. That means that any partner who has not wrongfully dissociated may force winding up if dissolution has occurred. That RUPA rule gives great power to one partner who wants to wind up the business when all other partners want to continue the business. Many partnership agreements, therefore, prohibit a single partner from forcing not only dissolution but also winding up of the partnership's business.

In the following *Schwartz* case, we return to a recurrent theme: the importance of carefully drafting partnership agreements to make sure that the partners' intent is clearly expressed. In this case, the court interpreted the partnership agreement to allow two partners to expel a third partner from the partnership without cause.

Schwartz v. Family Dental Group, P.C.	943 A.2d 1122 (Conn. App. Ct. 2008)

In 1996, Steven Schwartz, Ken Epstein, and Peter Munk entered into a partnership agreement. All were dentists by profession. Under the partnership agreement, they formed Family Dental Group–Clinton Associates in Bridgeport, Connecticut. Their partnership agreement provided the following: The partnership was to continue until the year 2051, unless the partners agreed to an early dissolution. The partners wanted the partnership to survive their deaths. The partners were to devote full professional time and attention to the partnership during the first five years of its inception. The two practicing partners, Schwartz and Munk, were to receive 35 percent of their collections from patients. Additionally, any profit beyond expenses would be put into a profit pool of which the first 20 percent would be divided equally between all three partners and the remaining would be divided equally between Schwartz and Munk.

In 1997, Schwartz reduced his workload, decreasing his hours on Wednesdays and Thursdays, and eliminating Fridays. Munk, however, maintained a consistent, full-time work schedule. When Munk became aware of Schwartz's schedule change, he became upset and ceased communicating with Schwartz. Munk was dissatisfied with Schwartz's management style and the way he conducted his practice. Schwartz also refused to accept HMOs, take emergencies, and work on Saturdays. In addition, Munk was unhappy with Schwartz's appearance, the condition of his work space, and the amount of vacation time he took. He expressed his dissatisfaction to Epstein through letters he wrote to him over the course of several years; however, he did not approach Schwartz directly. Despite Munk's unhappiness, Schwartz was able to function normally in the office and interact appropriately with the remaining staff.

Munk was also dissatisfied with both his compensation and Schwartz's refusal to expand the partnership's dental facilities. Munk wanted to change the agreement to alter his compensation or alternatively terminate Schwartz as a partner. Schwartz did not accept either proposal and insisted that the parties submit to mediation pursuant to the agreement. The mediation resulted in an award of a management fee for Munk in the amount of two-thirds of 1 percent of the gross revenue.

In 2002, Epstein and Munk offered to buy out Schwartz's interest in the practice, or alternatively, to keep him as a partner while eliminating his management responsibilities and his share of the profits. Schwartz rejected the offer. On February 26, 2003, at a special meeting of the partners, Ken Epstein and Munk voted to terminate Schwartz from the practice "without cause" and provided him with 90 days notice pursuant to §12(a)(i) in the partnership agreement.

Section 12 of the partnership agreement is entitled "Other withdrawal from practice." Section 12(a)(i) states:

In the event that any Partner's association with the Partnership is terminated for any reason other than death or total disability, either party shall give the other not less than ninety (90) days written notice of such termination and the Partnership shall have the first option to retire the interest of the departing Partner by paying the departing Partner deferred compensation at the Formula Amount.

As a result of the termination, Schwartz sued Munk and Epstein seeking restoration of his partnership status. The trial court found that the partnership's termination date of December 31, 2051, implied that a reduction in workload was contemplated. The court rejected Munk and Epstein's argument that §12(a)(i) of the agreement provides for termination without cause, as long as a 90-day notice is provided. Instead, the court found the provision unenforceable on the ground that "no reasonable, educated person would sign an agreement whereby they could be stripped of their equitable interest in a business without a reasonable basis. Simply put, it is something a reasonably prudent person would not do." The trial court also found that §12(a)(i) of the agreement does not clearly state a majority of the partners can terminate another partner without any reasonable basis. The court concluded that Munk and Epstein did not provide a reasonable basis for Schwartz's termination. Munk and Epstein appealed to the Court of Appeals of Connecticut.

McLachlan, Judge

Munk and Epstein first claim that the court improperly concluded that §12(a)(i) of the parties' partnership agreement is unenforceable.

There is a strong public policy in Connecticut favoring freedom of contract. It is established well beyond the need for citation that parties are free to contract for whatever terms on which they may agree. This freedom includes the right to contract for the assumption of known or unknown hazards and risks that may arise as a consequence of the execution of the contract. Accordingly, in private disputes, a court must enforce the contract as drafted by the parties and may not relieve a contracting party from anticipated or actual difficulties undertaken pursuant to the contract, unless the contract is voidable on grounds such as mistake, fraud or unconscionability. If a contract violates public policy, this would be a ground not to enforce the contract. A contract, or in this instance, a partnership agreement, however, does not violate public policy just because the contract was made unwisely. Moreover, our Supreme Court has opined: "A provision of a partnership agreement does not violate public policy simply because it is susceptible of an application that is advantageous to one partner and disadvantageous to another." *Konover Development Corp. v. Zeller,* 228 Conn. 206, 231, 635 A.2d 798 (1994).

In the present case, it is clear that the provision in §12(a)(i) does not violate public policy and is enforceable. This provision was entered into by sophisticated and highly educated professionals.

Moreover, this provision, which Munk and Epstein argue is an involuntary termination clause, does not favor one partner over another because the majority of the parties voted to terminate Schwartz's association with the partnership. If the circumstances were different, Schwartz would have been able to rely on the same provision to terminate one of the other partners. Thus, this provision is not against public policy just because in the present case it was a disadvantage to Schwartz.

Munk and Epstein next claim that the court improperly concluded that §12(a)(i) of the parties' partnership agreement does not provide that a majority of the partners can terminate another partner without cause. Munk and Epstein maintain that, as the provision is written, the language refers to "termination resulting from any possible circumstance, excluding death or total disability, except as otherwise modified by another provision in the

agreement." In opposition, Schwartz argues that this provision is not a termination without cause provision; rather, it provides only the right of any partner to withdraw from the practice and voluntarily terminate his association in the event that a partner moved or relocated or for some other reason decided to terminate his association with the partnership. We disagree with Schwartz's assertion.

A contract must be construed to effectuate the intent of the parties, which is determined from the language used interpreted in the light of the situation of the parties and the circumstances connected with the transaction. The intent of the parties is to be ascertained by a fair and reasonable construction of the written words and the language used must be accorded its common, natural, and ordinary meaning and usage where it can be sensibly applied to the subject matter of the contract.

Munk and Epstein assert that the language in §12(a)(i) is clear and unambiguous and permits the partners to terminate another partner without cause. Under §12(a)(i), "[i]n the event that any Partner's association with the Partnership is terminated for any reason other than death or total disability, *either party shall give the other not less than ninety (90) days written notice....*" (Emphasis added.) Munk and Epstein argue that if the parties intended that §12(a)(i) would refer only to voluntary termination, they could have stated such intent. Munk and Epstein also refer to §9(a), which provides that "[a]ll decisions concerning the conduct of the Partnership business shall be made by a majority of the Partnership shares, except as otherwise expressly agreed to by the Partners."

The language of §12(a)(i), specifically, that *either party shall give the other* ninety days notice, clearly indicates that this provision does not simply apply to voluntary withdrawal. The term used in the provision, "either party," evidences the intent of the parties that this provision be a termination without cause provision. Furthermore, §12(a)(i) coupled with §9(a) permits the very action taken by Munk and Epstein: the majority of shares acting to terminate a partner without cause. Most significantly, Schwartz himself testified that §12(a)(i) permitted termination for reasons other than death, disability and termination for cause. Thus, we conclude that the provision is enforceable and that it permits the termination of Schwartz's association with the partnership in the manner taken by Munk and Epstein. Accordingly, we disagree with the conclusion of the trial court.

Judgment reversed in favor of Munk and Espstein.

Joint Ventures and Mining Partnerships

The partnership rules of dissociation and dissolution apply to joint ventures. Mining partnerships are difficult to dissolve, because of the free transferability of mining partnership

interests. The death of a mining partner does not effect a dissolution. In addition, a mining partner may sell his interest to another person and dissociate from the carrying on of the mining partnership business without causing a dissolution.

Understand the causes of dissolution and the process of winding up.

Performing Winding Up

For the well-planned partnership, the partnership agreement will indicate who may perform the process of winding up for the partnership, what is the power of the persons performing winding up, and what their compensation is for performing the service.

In the absence of a partnership agreement, the RUPA provides that any partner who has not wrongfully dissociated from the partnership may perform the winding up. A winding-up partner is entitled to reasonable compensation for her winding-up services, in addition to her usual share of profits.

Partner's Authority during Winding Up

Express and Implied Authority During winding up, a partner has the express authority to act as the partners have agreed. The implied authority of a winding up partner is the power to do those acts *appropriate for winding up* the partnership business. That is, he has the power to bind the partnership in any transaction necessary to the liquidation of the assets. He may collect money due, sue to enforce partnership rights, prepare assets for sale, sell partnership assets, pay partnership creditors, and do whatever else is appropriate to wind up the business. He may maintain and preserve assets or enhance them for sale, for example, by painting a building or by paying a debt to prevent foreclosure on partnership land. A winding-up partner may temporarily continue the business when the effect is to preserve the value of the partnership.

Performing Executory Contracts The implied authority of a winding up partner includes the power to perform executory contracts (made before dissolution but not yet performed). A partner may not enter into *new* contracts unless the contracts aid the liquidation of the partnership's assets. For example, a partner may fulfill a contract to deliver wind turbines if the contract was made before dissolution. She may not make a new contract to deliver wind turbines unless doing so disposes of wind turbines that the partnership owns or has contracted to purchase.

Borrowing Money Usually, the implied authority of a winding up partner includes no power to borrow money in the name of the partnership. Nonetheless, when a partner can preserve the assets of the partnership or enhance them for sale by borrowing money, he has implied authority to engage in new borrowing. For example, a partnership may have a valuable machine repossessed and sold far below its value at a foreclosure sale unless it can refinance a loan. A partner may borrow the money needed to refinance the loan, thereby preserving the asset. A partner may also borrow money to perform executory contracts.

Apparent Authority Winding-up partners have apparent authority to conduct business as they did before dissolution, when notice of dissolution is not given to those persons who knew of the partnership prior to its dissolution. For example, a construction partnership dissolves and begins winding up but does not notify anyone of its dissolution. After dissolution, a partner makes a contract with a customer to remodel the customer's building. The partner would have no implied authority to make the contract, because the contract is new business and does not help liquidate assets. Nonetheless, the contract may be within the partner's apparent authority, because to persons unaware of the dissolution, it appears that a partner may continue to make contracts that have been in the ordinary course of business.

To eliminate the apparent authority of a winding-up partner to conduct business in the ordinary way, the partnership must ensure that one of the following occurs:

1. A third party knows or has reason to know that the partnership has been dissolved.

2. A third party has received notification of the dissolution by delivery of a communication to the third party's place of business. For example, an e-mail message is sent to a creditor of the partnership.

3. The dissolution has come to the attention of the third party. For example, a partnership creditor was told of the dissolution by another creditor.

4. A partner has filed a Statement of Dissolution with the secretary of state, which limits the partners' authority during winding up. A third party is deemed to have notice of a limitation on a partner's authority 90 days after the filing of a Statement of Dissolution.

To be safe, a dissolved partnership should eliminate its partners' apparent authority to conduct business in the ordinary way by directly informing parties with whom it has previously conducted business, such as by e-mail, fax, or a phone call. The partnership should be able to identify such parties from its records. As for parties that may know about the partnership but with whom the partnership has not done business, the partnership should post notice of the dissolution at its place of business and in newspapers of general circulation in its area, increasing the chance that third parties will know of the dissolution. Also, the partnership should file a Statement of Dissolution: 90 days after its filing, no one should be able to rely on the apparent authority of a partner to conduct any business that is not appropriate to winding up. The partnership agreement of a well-planned partnership will require the partnership to take these steps when dissolution occurs.

Disputes among Winding-Up Partners When more than one partner has the right to wind up the partnership, the partners may disagree concerning which steps should be taken during winding up. For decisions in the ordinary course of winding up, the decision of a majority of the partners controls. When the decision is an extraordinary one, such as continuing the business for an extended period of time, unanimous partner approval is required.

In the following case, *Paciaroni v. Crane,* the court found that the business of the partnership to train and race a horse should continue during winding up. The drafters of the RUPA expressly noted that this case is a model for continuing a business during winding up.

Paciaroni v. Crane	408 A.2d 946 (Del. Ct. Ch. 1979)

Black Ace, a harness racehorse of exceptional speed, was the fourth best pacer in the United States in 1979. He was owned by a partnership: Richard Paciaroni owned 50 percent; James Cassidy, 25 percent; and James Crane, 25 percent. Crane, a professional trainer, was in charge of the daily supervision of Black Ace, including training. It was understood that all of the partners would be consulted on the races in which Black Ace would be entered, the selection of drivers, and other major decisions; however, the recommendations of Crane were always followed by the other partners because of his superior knowledge of harness racing.

In 1979, Black Ace won $96,969 through mid-August. Seven other races remained in 1979, including the prestigious Little Brown Jug and the Messenger at Roosevelt Raceway. The purse for these races was $600,000.

A disagreement among the partners arose when Black Ace developed a ringbone condition and Crane followed the advice of a veterinarian not selected by Paciaroni and Cassidy. The ringbone condition disappeared, but later Black Ace became uncontrollable by his driver, and in a subsequent race he fell and failed to finish the race. Soon thereafter, Paciaroni and Cassidy sent a telegram to Crane dissolving the partnership and directing him to deliver Black Ace to another trainer they had selected. Crane refused to relinquish control of Black Ace, so Paciaroni and Cassidy sued him in August 1979, asking the court to appoint a receiver who would race Black Ace in the remaining 1979 stakes races and then sell the horse. Crane objected to allowing anyone other than himself to enter the horse in races. Before the trial court issued the following decision, Black Ace had entered three additional races and won $40,000.

Brown, Vice Chancellor

It is generally accepted that once dissolution occurs, the partnership continues only to the extent necessary to close out affairs and complete transactions begun but not then finished. It is not generally contemplated that new business will be generated or that new contractual commitments will be made. This, in principle, would work against permitting Black Ace to participate in the remaining few races for which he is eligible.

However, in Delaware, there have been exceptions to this. Where, because of the nature of the partnership business, a better price upon final liquidation is likely to be obtained by the temporary continuation of the business, it is permissible, during the winding up process, to have the business continue to the degree necessary to preserve or enhance its value upon liquidation, provided that such continuation is done in good faith with the intent to bring affairs to a conclusion as soon as reasonably possible. And one way to accomplish this is through an application to the Court for a winding up, which carries with it the power of the Court to appoint a receiver for that purpose.

The business purpose of the partnership was to own and race Black Ace for profit. The horse was bred to race. He has the ability to be competitive with the top pacers in the country. He is currently "racing fit" according to the evidence. He has at best only seven more races to go over a period of the next six weeks, after which time there are established horse sales at which he can be disposed of to the highest bidder. The purse for these remaining stake races is substantial. The fact that he could possibly sustain a disabling injury during this six-week period appears to be no greater than it was when the season commenced. Admittedly, an injury could occur at any time. But this is a fact of racing life which all owners and trainers are forced to accept. And the remaining stake races are races in which all three partners originally intended that he would compete, if able.

Under these circumstances, I conclude that the winding up of the partnership affairs should include the right to race Black Ace in some or all of the remaining 1979 stakes races for which he is now eligible. The final question, then, is who shall be in charge of racing him.

On this point, I rule in favor of Paciaroni and Cassidy. They may, on behalf of the partnership, continue to race the horse through their new trainer, subject, however, to the conditions hereafter set forth. Crane does have a monetary interest in the partnership assets that must be protected if Paciaroni and Cassidy are to be permitted to test the whims of providence in the name of the partnership during the next six weeks. Accordingly, I make the following ruling:

1. Paciaroni and Cassidy shall first post security in the sum of $100,000 so as to secure to Crane his share of the value of Black Ace.

2. If Paciaroni and Cassidy are unable or unwilling to meet this condition, then they shall forgo the right to act as liquidating partners. In that event, each party, within seven days, shall submit to the Court the names of two persons who they believe to be qualified, and who they know to be willing, to act as receiver for the winding up of partnership affairs.

3. In the event that no suitable person can be found to act as receiver, or in the event that the Court should deem it unwise to appoint any person from the names so submitted, then the Court reserves the power to terminate any further racing by Black Ace and to require that he simply be maintained and cared for until such time as he can be sold as a part of the final liquidation of the partnership.

Judgment for Paciaroni and Cassidy.

Distribution of Dissolved Partnership's Assets

After the partnership's assets have been sold during winding up, the proceeds are distributed to those persons who have claims against the partnership. Not only creditors but also partners have claims against the proceeds. As you might expect, the claims of creditors must be satisfied first, yet a partner who is also a creditor of the partnership is entitled to the same priority as other creditors of the partnership. Thus a partner who has loaned money to the partnership is paid when other creditors of the partnership are paid.

After the claims of creditors have been paid, the remaining proceeds from the sale of partnership assets will be distributed to the partners according to the net amounts in their capital accounts. Over the life of a partnership, a partner's capital account is credited (increased) for any capital contributions the partner has made to the partnership plus the partner's share of partnership profits, including profits from the sale of partnership assets during winding up. The partner's capital account is charged (decreased) for the partner's share of partnership losses, including losses from the sale of partnership assets during winding up, and any distributions made to the partners, such as a distribution of profits or a return of capital. The net amount in the partner's account is distributed to the partner.

If the net amount in a partner's capital account is negative, the partner is obligated to contribute to the partnership an amount equal to the excess of charges over credits in the partner's account. Some partners may have a positive capital account balance and other partners may have a negative capital account balance. This means that during winding up, some partners may be required to contribute to enable the partnership to pay the claim of another partner.

In many partnerships that have been unprofitable, all the partners will have negative capital accounts. This means that the partnership assets have been exhausted and yet some of the partnership creditors have not been paid their claims. If partnership creditors cannot be paid from the partnership assets, the creditors may proceed against the partners, including a partner who may have already received a portion of partnership assets on account of her being a creditor also.

Since partners have liability for all the obligations of a partnership, if one partner fails to contribute the amount equal to her negative capital account balance, the other partners are obligated to contribute to the partnership in the proportions in which they share the losses of the partnership. The partner who fails to contribute as required is liable, however, to the partners who pay the defaulting partner's contribution.

The RUPA eliminates the old UPA's concept of marshaling of assets. While partnership creditors still have a priority over a partner's creditors with regard to partnership assets, partnership and partners' creditors share pro rata in the assets of individual partners.

Asset Distributions in a Limited Liability Partnership

The asset distribution rules are modified for a limited liability partnership, because in an LLP most partners have no liability for partnership obligations beyond the partnership's assets. If the LLP has been profitable, each partner will receive the net amount in her capital account. If creditors' claims exceed the LLP's assets, however, an LLP partner is not ordinarily required to contribute an amount equal to the negative balance in her account, and the creditors may not sue the partner to force the partner to pay the debt. This result is necessary to protect the limited liability of innocent partners who did not commit a wrong against the creditors.

If, however, a partner has committed malpractice or another wrong for which LLP statutes do not provide protection from liability, that wrongdoing partner must contribute to the LLP an amount equal to her share of the unpaid liability. Creditors may sue such a partner when the LLP fails to pay the liability. If more than one partner has liability, they must contribute to the LLP in proportion in which they share liability. If one is unable to pay, the other liable partners must contribute the shortfall. The partners who are not liable for the obligation cannot be forced to pay the debt.

Termination After the assets of a partnership have been distributed, **termination** of the partnership occurs automatically.

 Appreciate the default effects of continuing a partnership after dissociation.

When the Business Is Continued

Dissolution and winding up need not follow a partner's dissociation from a partnership. The partners may choose not to seek dissolution and winding up, or the partnership agreement may provide that the business may be continued by the remaining partners.

When there is no winding up and the business is continued, the claims of creditors against the partnership and the partners may be affected, because old partners are no longer with the business and new partners may enter the business.

Successor's Liability for Predecessor's Obligations

When the business of a partnership is continued after dissociation, creditors of the partnership are creditors of the person or partnership continuing the business. In addition, the original partners remain liable for obligations incurred prior to dissociation unless there is agreement with the creditors to the contrary. Thus, partners may not usually escape liability by forming a new partnership or a corporation to carry on the business of the partnership.

Dissociated Partner's Liability for Obligations Incurred While a Partner

Dissociated partners remain liable to partnership creditors for partnership liabilities incurred while they were partners; however, a dissociated partner's liability may be eliminated by the process of **novation.** Novation occurs when the following two conditions are met:

1. The continuing partners release a dissociated partner from liability on a partnership debt, and
2. A partnership creditor releases the dissociated partner from liability on the same obligation.

Continuing partners are required to indemnify dissociated partners from liability on partnership obligations. To complete the requirements for novation, a dissociated partner must also secure his release by the partnership's creditors. A creditor's agreement to release an outgoing partner from liability may be express, but usually it is implied. *Implied* novation may be proved by a creditor's knowledge of a partner's withdrawal and his continued extension of credit to the partnership. In addition, a *material modification* in the nature or time of payment of an obligation operates as a novation for an outgoing partner, when the creditor has knowledge of the partner's dissociation.

When former partners release a dissociated partner from liability but creditors do not, there is not a novation. As a result, creditors may enforce a partnership liability against a dissociated partner. However, the outgoing partner may recover from his former partners who have indemnified him from liability.

Dissociated Partner's Liability for Obligations Incurred after Leaving the Partnership

Ordinarily, a dissociated partner has no liability for partnership obligations incurred after he leaves the partnership. Nonetheless, a third party may believe that a dissociated partner is still a partner of the continuing partnership and transact with the partnership while holding that belief. In such a context, a dissociated partner could be liable to the third party even though the dissociated partner will not benefit from the transaction between the partnership and the third party.

The RUPA makes a dissociated partner liable as a partner to a party that entered into a transaction with the continuing partnership, unless:

1. The other party did not reasonably believe the dissociated partner was still a partner.
2. The other party knew or should have known or has received notification of the partner's dissociation.

3. The transaction was entered into more than 90 days after the filing of a Statement of Dissociation with the secretary of state, or

4. The transaction was entered into more than two years after the partner has dissociated.

Moreover, although a dissociated partner's right to manage the partnership has terminated upon his dissociation, unless one of the above can be proved the dissociated partner retains his apparent authority to bind the partnership on matters in the ordinary course of business.

This means that when dissociation occurs, a partnership should take steps similar to those it took to reduce the apparent authority of a winding-up partner: that is, the partnership should directly inform parties with whom it has previously conducted business, such as by e-mail, fax, or a phone call, that the partner has dissociated. It should also post notice of the dissociation at its place of business and in newspapers of general circulation in its area. Finally, the partnership should cause the filing of a Statement of Dissociation, limiting the authority of the dissociated partner and notifying the public that the partner is no longer a partner. Taking these steps will reduce the risk that the dissociated partner will be liable for future obligations of the partnership, and it will help eliminate the apparent authority of the dissociated partner to act on behalf of the partnership. The partnership agreement of a well-planned partnership will require that these steps be taken by the partnership immediately upon the dissociation of a partner.

Effect of LLP Status   In an LLP, a dissociated partner has less risk of continuing liability for contracts and torts occurring before or after the partner leaves the LLP, since the partner's liability is limited to the LLP's assets. However, a buyout payment made to a dissociated LLP partner may not impair the ability of the LLP to pay its creditors. If so, the dissociated partner will be required to return some or all of the buyout payment to creditors.

 L03   Draft a partnership agreement that changes the rules applying when a partner dissociates.

Buyout of Dissociated Partners   When the partnership is continued, the partnership is required to purchase the dissociated partner's partnership interest. In well-planned partnerships, the purchase price and timing of the buyout will be included in the partnership agreement. For example, the partnership agreement may require the payment of an amount equal to the current value of the partnership multiplied by the partner's proportionate share of profits or capital. The partnership agreement may specify how to value the partnership, such as average annual profits plus partners' salaries for the last three years multiplied by seven. Many professional partnerships, however, pay a dissociated partner only his capital contribution plus his share of undistributed profits. The agreement may also permit deductions against the value of the partnership interest if the dissociated partner acted wrongly.

The Global Business Environment

Dissolutions around the Globe

For most nations, partnership law on dissolutions is more like the old Uniform Partnership Act than the RUPA, which was drafted to create better default rules when partners leave a partnership. In countries other than the United States, dissolution is defined much like dissociation is defined under the RUPA, a change in the partners' relation. Unlike dissociation in the United States, dissolution in those countries (and in American states that still follow the UPA) often results in the end of the partnership and its business, absent a contrary agreement of the partners. Well-planned partnerships, however, have partnership agreements that in many situations provide for continuation of the partnership and its business by the remaining partners, despite dissolution.

In India, dissolution may be caused by a court, by agreement of the partners, automatically by operation of law, upon the happening of certain contingencies, and by notice.

An Indian court may dissolve a partnership due to a partner's insanity, permanent incapacity, conduct that prejudicially affects carrying on the business of the firm, willful or persistent breach of the partnership agreement, and transfer of his partnership interest, or if the partnership cannot be carried on except as a loss. Partners in an Indian partnership may dissolve the partnership by their unanimous agreement. An Indian partnership dissolves automatically if its term ends or undertaking is accomplished, if a partner dies or is insolvent, or if the partnership's business is illegal. Finally, a partnership at will in India may be dissolved by action of any partner.

In Austria, a partnership is dissolved by expiration of the period for which it was entered into, by resolution of the partners, by institution of bankruptcy proceedings against the partnership assets or the assets of a partner, by death of a partner, by notice of termination by a partner, and by judicial decision.

The agreement will state when the buyout is effected; for example, it may require the payment in a lump sum 30 days after dissociation, or it may allow the partnership to pay the amount in monthly installments over the course of three years.

In the absence of a partnership agreement, the RUPA spells outs the amount and timing of the buyout of the dissociated partner's interest. The buyout price is the greater of the amount that would have been in the dissociated partner's capital account had the partnership liquidated all its assets on the dissociation date *or* the amount in the capital account had it sold the entire business as a going concern on that date. If the partner has wrongfully dissociated from the partnership, the buyout price is reduced by any damages caused by the wrongfully dissociated partner, such as the reduction in the goodwill of the business caused by the loss of a valuable partner.

When the dissociated partner has not wrongfully dissociated and there is no partnership agreement on the issue, the RUPA requires the partnership to pay the dissociated partner in cash within 120 days after he has demanded payment in writing. The buyout amount must include interest from the date of dissociation. If the dissociated partner and the partnership cannot agree on the buyout price, the partnership must, within 120 days of the written demand for payment, pay in cash to the partner the partnership's estimate of the buyout price, plus interest. The partner may challenge the sufficiency of the buyout price tendered by the partnership by asking a court to determine the buyout price.

If a partner has wrongfully dissociated, the partnership may wait to buy out the partner until the end of the partnership's term, unless the partner shows that the partnership will suffer no undue hardship by paying earlier. The buyout price must include interest from the date of the dissociation.

In the following *Warnick* case between a son and his parents, we see again the risks of relying on the RUPA to resolve partnership issues. The case shows that the RUPA's less than unambiguous provision for valuing a partner's interest should be replaced in the partnership agreement by a concrete valuation method that covers every aspect of valuation the partners want to consider.

Warnick v. Warnick	133 P. 3d 997 (Wyo. S. Ct. 2006)

In 1978, Wilbur and Dee Warnick and their son Randall Warnick formed Warnick Ranches general partnership to operate a ranch in Sheridan County, Wyoming. The initial capital contributions of the partners totaled $60,000, paid 36 percent by Wilbur, 30 percent by Dee, and 34 percent by Randall. The partners over the years each contributed additional funds to the operation of the ranch and received cash distributions from the partnership. After 1983, Randall contributed very little new money. Almost all of the additional funds to pay off the mortgage on the ranch came from Wilbur and Dee Warnick. Wilbur also left in the partnership account two $12,000 cash distributions that were otherwise payable to him. The net cash contributions of the partners through 1999, considering the initial contributions, payments to or on behalf of the partnership, draws not taken, and distributions from the partnership were:

Wilbur $170,112.60 (51%)
Dee $138,834.63 (41%)
Randall $25,406.28 (8%)

After a dispute among the partners arose in 1999, Randall's lawyer sent a letter to Warnick Ranches stating:

I have been asked to contact you regarding [Randall's] desire either to sell his interest in the ranch to a third party or the partnership or to liquidate the partnership under Paragraph 12 of the partnership agreement. It would appear that it would be in the best interests of all to agree amicably to a selling price of his interest either to a third party or to the partnership as provided in the partnership agreement.

Warnick Ranches responded, treating the letter as Randall's intent to dissociate from the partnership. The partnership's response included an offer for Randall's interest, as provided under Wyo. Stat. Ann. § 17-21-701(e) and (g) [RUPA section 701(f) and (g)] in the case of a dissociating partner. Randall in turn exercised his right under § 17-21-701(j) [RUPA section 701(i)] to reject the offer and bring a lawsuit against the partnership to determine his interest in the partnership, including a buyout price if he was dissociated from the partnership.

A Wyoming district court found that dissociation of Randall as a partner was the appropriate remedy and awarded to Randall the amount of his cash contributions, plus 34 percent of the partnership assets' increase in value above all partners' cash *contributions. As a result of that calculation, $230,819, or 25.24 percent, of the undisputed value of the partnership was awarded to Randall, without provision of interest for any partner in the calculation.*

Warnick Ranch disputed the valuation and appealed to the Wyoming Supreme Court, which remanded the case to the district court, ordering it to take into account advances made by each partner to the partnership. Back in the district court again, Warnick Ranches asserted that for purposes of calculating the buyout price, the value of ranch assets should be less than the amount reflected in its appraisal. Specifically, it requested that the district court deduct $50,000 for real estate commissions and expenses of sale, including those associated with selling livestock and equipment. The district court rejected the deduction, ruling that possible costs associated with selling the assets of the partnership are too speculative.

The district court determined the amount to be paid to Randall by first valuing the partnership assets and deducting advances made to the partnership by each partner to arrive at a net value of the partnership of $133,901.68. Randall's percentage of ownership (34 percent) was then applied to the net value, to arrive at his proportionate share of the partnership of $45,526.57. Adding this amount to the amount of Randall's loan to the partnership, $70,256.56, the district court determined a buyout price of $115,783.13. Warnick Ranches appealed once more to the Wyoming Supreme Court.

Burke, Justice

The statute at issue is part of the Wyoming Revised Uniform Partnership Act (RUPA), Wyo. Stat. Ann. §§ 17-21-101 *et seq.* (2003). The district court was charged with calculating the amount owed to Randall Warnick pursuant to the applicable provisions of RUPA, Wyo. Stat. Ann. § 17-21-603(a) (2003) and Wyo. Stat. Ann. § 17-21-701. That amount, or the buyout price, is the amount that would have been paid to the dissociating partner following a settlement of partnership accounts upon the winding up of the partnership, if, on the date of dissociation, the assets of the partnership were sold at a price equal to the greater of the liquidation value or the value based on a sale of the business as a going concern without the dissociating partner. Wyo. Stat. Ann. § 17-21-701(b).

"[P]artnership assets must first be applied to discharge partnership liabilities to creditors, including partners who are creditors." Wyo. Stat. Ann. § 17-21-808(b) [RUPA section 807(a)]. The interplay between RUPA § 701(b) and § 808(b) requires that obligations to known creditors must be deducted before a partner distribution can be determined. Stated another way, in computing the buyout price, the amount the dissociating partner receives is reduced by his or her share of partnership liabilities.

Warnick Ranches claims that the district court erred in the first step of its calculation of the buyout price by overvaluing the ranch assets. The asserted error is the district court's failure to deduct estimated sales expenses of $50,000 from the value of the partnership assets. A common understanding of liquidation is the act or process of converting assets into cash. Warnick Ranches appears to assume that the liquidation value of the ranch is the amount of cash that would remain following a sale. This assumption is not supported by the pertinent statutory language and the circumstances of this case.

Critical to our determination in this case is the recognition that the assets of this partnership were not, in fact, liquidated. Instead, the record reflects that the assets were retained by Warnick Ranches. Randall Warnick's dissociation from the partnership

did not require the winding up of the partnership. The partnership's ranching operations had continued following Randall Warnick's departure. There was no evidence of any actual, intended, or pending sale before the district court at the time of dissociation, and, therefore, asset liquidation was only hypothetical. Accordingly, the deduction urged by Warnick Ranches is for *hypothetical* costs. Because of the hypothetical nature of the urged $50,000 deduction, we find that the district court's calculation was not erroneous.

If, in applying Wyo. Stat. Ann. § 17-21-701(b), we were to interpret the term "liquidation value" in isolation, we might envision an amount representing the net proceeds resulting from a distress sale. However, that interpretation is precluded by the language contained in the statute. The full text of Wyo. Stat. Ann. § 17-21-701(b) provides:

> The buyout price of a dissociated partner's interest is the amount that would have been distributable to the dissociating partner under W.S. 17-21-808(b) if, on the date of dissociation, the assets of the partnership were sold at a price equal to the greater of the liquidation value or the value based on a sale of the entire business as a going concern without the dissociated partner and the partnership were wound up as of that date. In either case, the sale price of the partnership assets shall be determined on the basis of the amount that would be paid by a willing buyer to a willing seller, neither being under any compulsion to buy or sell, and with knowledge of all relevant facts. Interest shall be paid from the date of dissociation to the date of payment.

Wyo. Stat. Ann. § 17-21-701(b) differs somewhat from the Uniform Laws version of the same provision, which does not include the second to last sentence. Revised Uniform Partnership Act § 701.

Liquidation value is one of two identified methods for valuing the partnership assets. Application of the two methods to the same partnership may yield two distinct values. The liquidation value looks to the value of the partnership's assets less its liabilities and determines each partner's appropriate share. When valuing a going concern, however, the market value of the partnership interest itself is what is at stake, rather than the percentage of net assets it represents.

Significantly, the buyout price under Wyo. Stat. Ann. § 17-21-701(b) involves use of the *greater* value resulting from the alternate valuation methods. Warnick Ranches' argument seems to assume that the district court's calculation incorporated the liquidation value of the partnership assets. We see room for disagreement based upon the record. The district court did not specify which valuation method was selected, and it was therefore possible that the value used in the buyout price calculation represented the going concern value of the ranch. Warnick Ranches makes no argument that costs of sale should also be deducted from the going concern value because, under its rationale, the $50,000 deduction is required only as part and parcel of liquidation value. Were we to conclude that the district court used a figure which represented the going concern value, our analysis could end here without further discussion of hypothetical costs of sale.

However, even if the district court valued the partnership assets using liquidation value, the deduction for costs associated with a hypothetical sale would not be warranted. Contrary to the interpretation asserted by Warnick Ranches, liquidation value is not the amount of the seller's residual cash following a sale. We find that the meaning of liquidation value in the statute is best understood by comparing it to the other method provided. When contrasted with "going concern value" it is clear that "liquidation value" simply means the sale of the separate assets rather than the value of the business as a whole.

Additionally, under either valuation method, Wyo. Stat. Ann. § 17-21-701(b) directs that the sale price be determined "on the basis of the amount that would be paid by a willing buyer to a willing seller, neither being under any compulsion to buy or sell, and with knowledge of all relevant facts." The legislature chose to supplement the Uniform Laws version of this provision by adding this sentence, lending added significance to this language. This "willing buyer" and "willing seller" language does not present a novel legal concept, as it sets forth precisely what has long been the legal definition or test of "fair market value." *Black's Law Dictionary* 1587 (8th ed. 2004). This language is similar to that found in commentary to RUPA, § 701(b).

Warnick Ranches does not provide any analysis concerning the fair market value language contained in Wyo. Stat. Ann. § 17-21-701(b) and does not explain how it can be reconciled with its urged meaning of liquidation value as involving a deduction for costs of sale. That reconciliation may be difficult. Simply stated, a deduction from fair market value yields an amount which is, by definition, less than fair market value.

Considering the language of RUPA § 701(b) as a whole, we conclude that "liquidation value" does not have the meaning that Warnick Ranches desires, i.e., the amount a seller would "net" upon liquidation. Rather, "liquidation value" represents the sale price of the assets based upon fair market value. Where it is contemplated that a business will continue, it is not appropriate to assume an immediate liquidation with its attendant transactional costs and taxes. We therefore hold that, under Wyo. Stat. Ann. § 17-21-701(b), purely hypothetical costs of sale are not a required deduction in valuing partnership assets. We find no error in the district court rejecting the $50,000 deduction urged by Warnick Ranches in calculating the buyout price.

Judgment for Randall Warnick affirmed.

 LO7 Identify issues involved in adding new partners to existing partnerships.

Partners Joining an Existing Partnership

Frequently, a partnership will admit new partners. For example, many of you hope to be admitted to a well-established consulting or accounting partnership after you graduate and have practiced for several years. The terms under which a new partner is admitted to a partnership are usually clearly stated in the partnership agreement and in the partner's admission agreement. The terms usually include the procedure for admission as well as the new partner's capital contribution, compensation including salary and share of profits, and power to manage the business. In the absence of a partnership agreement, the RUPA sets the rules for the partner's admission and rights and duties upon admission. For example, a new partner is admitted to a partnership only if all partners consent.

Liability of New Partners An important question is what level of liability a new partner should have for obligations of the new partnership. It makes sense for a new partner to be fully liable for all partnership obligations incurred *after* he becomes a partner, for he clearly benefits from the partnership during that time. This is the RUPA rule.

What should be his liability for partnership obligations incurred *before* he became a partner? The RUPA states that a new partner has no liability for partnership obligations incurred before he became a partner. However, many partnership agreements modify this rule by requiring a partner to assume liability for all the obligations of the business as a condition of being admitted to the partnership.

Effect of LLP Statutes If a new partner enters an LLP, however, the RUPA provides that the partner has no liability for the obligations of the LLP beyond his capital contribution, whether incurred before or after his admission, unless the new partner has committed malpractice or other wrong for which he is personally responsible. LLP partnership agreements should not change this rule.

LOG ON

www.nccusl.org

At the website for the National Conference of Commissioners on Uniform State Laws, you can find the complete text and comments of the RUPA. You can find the complex default rules regarding dissociation, dissolution, and buyouts of partners in Articles 6, 7, and 8. Pay particular attention to sections 601, 701, 801, and 802. Knowing the content of these sections will help you draft the partnership agreement dealing with a partner leaving the partnership.

Ethics in Action

The default rules of the RUPA provide that any partner who leaves the partnership is entitled to the value of her partnership interest. The default valuation method uses the greater of the partnership's liquidation or going concern value. If a partner wrongfully dissociates, however, damages are deducted from the partner's interest and the partner need not be paid until the partnership ends.

- Why would partners want a partnership agreement that sets out a different valuation method than the default rule?
- What risk is taken by relying on the default rule? Among other things, under the default rule a court will value a partnership interest when partners cannot agree on the valuation. Why would partners not want a court to valuate a partnership interest?
- Using profit maximization analysis, is it ethical to delay payment to a wrongfully dissociating partner for the value of her partnership interest until the partnership terminates? Does utilitarian analysis change your answer? What are the costs and benefits of delaying payment?
- When do you propose your partnership should pay a partner who dissociates due to death, disability, retirement at an expected age, and unexpected dissociations? What ethical arguments would you make to justify the rules you propose?

Consequences of Partner's Death or Retirement under the RUPA's Default Rules

Death of Partner

A. Is a nonwrongful dissociation

B. Does not by itself effect a dissolution

C. Rights of estate of deceased partner

    1. Receive the amount in the deceased partner's capital account at the time of death, valuing partnership or its assets at the greater of liquidation value or going concern value

    2. Payment must be made within 120 days after a written demand by the estate

D. Rights of other partners

    1. In a partnership at will, any other partner may dissociate at any time and effect a dissolution

    2. In a partnership for a term

        a. Any other partner may dissociate within 90 days of death

            1) Will not dissolve the partnership

            2) Dissociated partner must be paid amount in her capital account (valued as in C.1 above) within 120 days after a written demand

        b. By a vote of at least 50% of partners within 90 days of death, the partnership may be dissolved and its business wound up

Retirement (Withdrawal) of Partner

A. Is a dissociation

    1. Is a nonwrongful dissociation if the partnership is at will

    2. Is a wrongful dissociation, if the partnership is for a term and the term has not expired, unless the partnership agreement permits retirement before the end of the term

B. Effects a dissolution, only if a partnership at will

C. Rights of dissociated partner

    1. If nonwrongful dissociation, dissociated partner

        a. may wind up the business, if a partnership at will, or

        b. may receive the amount in the dissociated partner's capital account (valued same as for deceased partner) within 120 days after a written demand

    2. If wrongful dissociation, dissociated partner

        a. may not dissolve the partnership and

        b. may receive the amount in the dissociated partner's capital account, valuing partnership or its assets at the greater of liquidation value or going concern value, less damages, at the end of the partnership's term, unless no undue hardship to partnership to pay the partner earlier

D. Rights of other partners

    1. In a partnership at will, any other partner may dissociate at any time and effect a dissolution or dissociate and be paid the value in his capital account (valued same as for deceased partner) within 120 days

    2. In a partnership for a term when the partner has wrongly dissociated

        a. Any other partner may dissociate within 90 days of the retirement and be paid the amount in his capital account (valued same as for deceased partner)

        b. By a vote of at least 50% of partners within 90 days of the retirement, the partnership may be dissolved and its business wound up

    3. In a partnership for a term when the partner has not wrongfully dissociated, the remaining partners have no rights due to the dissociation

Problems and Problem Cases

1. Horizon/CMS Healthcare Corp., a large provider of both nursing home facilities and management for nursing homes, expanded into the Kissimmee, Florida, market by entering several 20-year partnerships with Southern Oaks Health Care, Inc. Within a few years, Horizon claimed that the partners had irreconcilable differences regarding how profits were to be determined and divided, resulting in the partners incapacity to operate in business together. Horizon asked a court to dissolve the partnership on these grounds. Did the court grant Horizon's request? Has Horizon wrongly dissociated by seeking judicial dissolution on these grounds?

2. Joe Costa and Nelson Borges orally agreed to associate together to purchase and develop a 15-acre parcel of real property located in Jerome County, Idaho. They intended to develop a subdivision with 41 residential lots and 3 commercial lots. Costa was to contribute his expertise in developing the real property, and Borges was to contribute his equipment to clear and level the land. They agreed to contribute equal capital and labor, with the exception that Borges could elect to contribute additional capital to hire someone to do his share of the labor. Within two years, their relationship broke down, and they stopped communicating with each other. Costa continued working on the development and hired his son to do some of the work. Borges did not perform any further labor at the site. Costa sued Borges claiming that Borges had breached the partnership agreement and that he should be expelled from the partnership. Was Costa's suit successful?

3. Brothers Don and Harley Shoemaker formed a partnership, D & H Real Estate. After 18 years, Harley withdrew from the partnership and asked for payment of the value of his partnership interest in accordance with the following provision in the partnership agreement:

    > In the event that the remaining partner(s) and the . . . retiring partner are unable to agree upon the value to be assigned to the partnership shares, all interested individuals shall select an appraiser and in the event they are not able to agree upon an appraiser, the remaining partner(s) and the . . . retiring partner shall be entitled to select an appraiser with the appraisers separately submitting their appraisals. If the appraisals are within ten percent of each other[,] the value shall be an average of the two appraisals. If the difference in the appraisals exceeds ten percent[,] the two appraisers shall together attempt to reach agreement on the value and if unable to do so shall obtain a third appraiser with the three appraisers together agreeing upon the value. The appraisers shall determine the value of the partnership as a going concern with all assets to be valued at their fair market value. . . . The value of the partner's interest as determined in the above section shall be paid without interest to the withdrawing or retiring partner . . . not later than 90 days after the effective date of the dissolution or termination.

    When Don failed to pay the appraisal amount within 90 days of Harley's withdrawal, Harley demanded that he receive not only the amount determined by the appraisal, but also a share of the profits earned by the partnership after his withdrawal, as well as interest on the late payment. Did the court agree with Harley?

4. Pietra Korda and Anna Kim were partners in an IT consulting business, K2 Solutions. They operated the business in a building owned by the partnership. The partnership purchased the building with the proceeds of a loan from Commerce Bank of Brunswick, which held a mortgage in the building. When Korda dissociated from the partnership, Kim paid Korda the value of her partnership interest, and Korda gave up all her claims against the partnership and its assets. Korda filed a Statement of Dissociation with the secretary of state, and she gave notice by a letter to Commerce Bank that she had left the partnership. Commerce Bank did not respond to the letter. Kim dissolved the partnership, filing a Statement of Dissolution, and continued the business under the name K-One Solutions LLC. For two years, Kim made monthly payments to Commerce Bank on the mortgage, paying with checks drawn on K-One Solutions' checking account at Commerce Bank. When Kim defaulted on the mortgage obligation, Commerce Bank sued K2 Solutions, Kim, and Korda. Was Korda liable on the mortgage obligation to Commerce Bank?

5. Labrum & Doak, LLP, was a law partnership that began in 1904 in Pennsylvania. John Seehousen, Jonathan Herbst, and James Hilly were partners of Labrum & Doak. They withdrew from the partnership in 1993, 1995, and 1997. They did not give creditors notice of their withdrawals from the LLP. In 1997, the LLP was dissolved. When the LLP's

assets were insufficient to pay creditors' claims, the LLP's creditors argued that Seehousen, Herbst, and Hilly were liable for the malpractice of the firm's partners, which malpractice occurred after the three former partners had left the partnership. Were they found liable?

6. Bertrand Barnes was one of three partners of NMB Associates, LLP, a limited liability partnership in the consulting and investment banking industries. When Barnes retired from the LLP, he sought to be released from liability on the $5,438,000 of outstanding bank loans the LLP had incurred during his tenure at NMB. Neither the partners nor the LLP nor the banks agreed to release Barnes from liability on the loans. What is the extent of Barnes's liability on the bank loans? Would his liability be different if NMB were a partnership and not an LLP?

7. Marc Senatre and Jacob Lewellen were partners in a business, Tavern Associates, which operated a bar in Des Moines, Iowa. The bar was located in a building that Tavern Associates leased from Graham Financial Corp. The term of the lease was five years. After two years, Senatre and Lewellen found a different building in a better location, and they moved the bar to the new location. They also reorganized the business as a limited liability company, named Tavern Associates II LLC. They transferred all the assets of Tavern Associates to Tavern Associates II. When Graham Financial sued Senatre, Lewellen, and Tavern Associates II for breaching the lease on the original building, Senatre and Lewellen argued that only Tavern Associates was liable on that lease. Were they right?

8. Joe Creel owned a NASCAR collectibles business named Joe's Racing Collectibles. In 1994, Creel brought Arnold Lilly and Roy Altizer into the business, which they reformed as a partnership named Joe's Racing. Creel contributed as capital to the partnership inventory and supplies of the old business, valued at $15,000. Lilly and Altizer each contributed $6,666 in cash to the partnership, and each paid $3,333 to Creel for his rights in the existing business. The partners agreed to share profits and losses with 52 percent going to Creel and 24 percent each to Lilly and Altizer. Less than a year later, Creel died and his wife sought to receive the value of his interest in the partnership. An accountant valued the

partnership at $44,589.44. The partnership's creditors were the accountant for $875, Mrs. Creel $495, Lilly $2,187, and Altizer $900. What was the value of the Creel's partnership interest?

9. Simon Weinberg and his brother were the only partners in Times Square Stationers LLP. The partners signed a 20-year lease with Tisch Leasing. After 12 years, Simon retired from the business and was replaced as a partner by his son, Seth. A year later, the business defaulted on its lease with Tisch Leasing. What is Seth's liability on the lease with Tisch? Would your answer change if the business were an ordinary partnership, not an LLP?

10. Herbert Lemon, Greg Clarkson, Adrienne Boysen, and five other marketing professionals decide to create a marketing consulting partnership. They expect the business will add partners from time to time, and they also know that it is likely one of the original partners will retire before the partnership is dissolved. They want to ensure that no partner entering the partnership is liable for obligations of the business that were incurred prior to the partner's entering the partnership. They also want to ensure that no partner leaving the partnership is liable for any obligation of the partnership that was incurred after she leaves. What should they do?

 Online Research

Complex Partnership Agreements Redux

This research task continues the task you started at the end of Chapter 38. Return to the website www.onecle.com. Find the link for "Partnership Agreement" and click on it. Also click on the link "All Partnership Agreements by Industry." As before, you will find many partnership agreements involving companies like Verizon Wireless, Trump Hotels, and stamps.com.

Examine these agreements. Note how they resolve the issues regarding partners leaving and entering a partnership. Compare the lists of grounds for dissociation and dissolution in the agreements with those in the RUPA. Note the dissociations that are wrongful. Read the provisions regarding the valuation of a partner's interest. Do you find that the partners' agreed upon valuations methods are less ambiguous than the RUPA's valuation method?

CHAPTER 40

LIMITED LIABILITY COMPANIES, LIMITED PARTNERSHIPS, AND LIMITED LIABILITY LIMITED PARTNERSHIPS

You are planning two business ventures. The first venture is a business that will own self-service businesses, such as laundromats, car washes, and warehouse storage. Due to start-up costs and accelerated write-offs of expenses and assets, you expect the business to generate losses in the first year or two, after which it should earn a yearly return on equity of over 20 percent. You prefer to own this business entirely yourself, yet you want to hire someone with experience in the business to do most of the day-to-day operations of the business. While you prefer that person not be an owner of the business, you may be willing to grant a small amount of ownership or a share of profits to her.

The other business venture will purchase and develop 320 acres of land on the outskirts of your city. You plan to construct several commercial buildings on the site and to lease the building space to several tenants. The venture will generate losses during the first four or five years of construction prior to full occupancy of the buildings. You want the business to be owned by members of your family. You want to be the only manager of the business; other family members will be passive owners only. You hope that this business will generate enough income to provide a moderate level of income to every member of your family in perpetuity.

- Why is the limited liability company an especially good business form for the first venture?
- Why should you choose the limited liability limited partnership for the family-owned commercial development?

LEARNING OBJECTIVES

After studying this chapter, you should be able to:

1 Explain the attributes of a limited liability company and the default rights and liabilities of a member in an LLC.

2 Draft an LLC operating agreement that changes the default rules regarding members' rights.

3 Explain the attributes of a limited partnership and limited liability limited partnership and the default rights and liabilities of partners in a limited partnership and LLLP.

4 Draft a limited partnership or LLLP agreement that changes the default rules regarding partners' rights.

STATE LEGISLATURES AND THE Internal Revenue Service have cooperated to permit the creation of three business forms that offer taxation advantages similar to the sole proprietorship and the partnership, yet have simple default rules that promote management of the business by fewer than all the owners and extend limited liability to some or all of the owners. These forms are the limited liability company (LLC), limited partnership, and limited liability limited partnership (LLLP).

> **LO1** Explain the attributes of a limited liability company and the default rights and liabilities of a member in an LLC.

Limited Liability Companies

The limited liability company (LLC) is the product of attempts by state legislators to create a new business organization that combines the nontax advantages of the corporation and the favorable tax status of the partnership. Wyoming, in 1977, passed the first LLC statute. Every state and the District of Columbia have adopted an LLC statute. The National Commissioners on Uniform State Laws has adopted the **Revised Uniform Limited Liability Company Act of 2006 (RULLCA).** The RULLCA provides default rules that govern an LLC in the absence of a contrary agreement of its owners. The RULLCA treats LLCs and their owners similarly to the way the Revised Uniform Partnership Act (RUPA) treats limited liability partnerships (LLPs) and their partners, with exceptions noted in this chapter. In general, the RULLCA has fewer rules than the RUPA, leaving more decisions to its members. As of October 2011, nine states and the District of Columbia have adopted or introduced the RULLCA.

> **LOG ON**
> **www.nccusl.org**
> You can find the Revised Uniform Limited Liability Company Act of 2006 at the website for the National Conference of Commissioners on Uniform State Laws.

The popularity of the LLC has grown dramatically since 2000. It is the preferred form for businesses with few owners, including high-profile sports firms such as Yankee Global Enterprises LLC. Many families use LLCs for estate planning purposes. Major corporations also form some of their subsidiaries as LLCs.

Tax Treatment of LLCs An LLC may elect to be taxed like a partnership or a corporation for federal income tax purposes. LLC members usually elect for the LLC to be recognized as a partnership for federal income tax purposes. As a result, the LLC pays no federal income tax. Instead, all income and losses of the LLC are reported by the LLC's owners on their individual income tax returns. Sometimes, the LLC is a tax shelter for wealthy investors, allowing such investors to reduce their taxable income by deducting LLC losses on their federal income tax returns to the extent they are *at risk,* that is, their capital contributions to the LLC. Moreover, passive investors in an LLC, like limited partners in a limited partnership, may use their shares of LLC losses to offset only income from other *passive* investments.

Formation of LLCs To create an LLC, one or more persons must file a **certificate of organization** with the secretary of state. The certificate must include the name of the LLC, and the name and address of its registered agent. The name of the LLC must include the words "limited liability company," "limited company," or an abbreviation such as "LLC" or "L.L.C.," indicating that the liability of its owners is limited.

The owners of an LLC are called **members.** An individual, partnership, corporation, and even another LLC may be a member of an LLC.

Although not required, an LLC will typically have an **operating agreement,** which is an agreement of the members. The operating agreement will usually state whether the LLC is member-managed or manager-managed. It also will cover how members share profits, manage the LLC, and withdraw from the LLC, among other things. Well-planned LLCs have detailed operating agreements that cover all aspects of the LLC's operation and members' relations, often restating much of what is contained in the RULLCA but with changes to suit the members' needs.

Once formed, an LLC may have perpetual existence and is an entity separate from its members. It may sue and be sued in its own name. It can buy, hold, and sell property. It can make contracts and incur liabilities. Figure 1 summarizes an LLC's characteristics.

>
> **LOG ON**
> **www.medlawplus.com/legalforms/instruct/ sample-llc.pdf**
> It is easy to find model and even actual LLC operating agreements on the Web. The link above is typical. You can find others by typing "LLC operating agreement" in a search engine. There are also websites that charge for downloads of LLC operating agreements. One such site is **www.uslegalforms.com.**

> ### Figure 1   *Principal Characteristics of LLCs under the RULLCA of 2006*
>
> 1. An LLC may be created only *in accordance with a statute.*
> 2. An LLC is owned by *members.* Members usually have *liability limited to their capital contributions* to the business.
> 3. LLC members *share equally in the profits* of the business, unless members agree otherwise.
> 4. An LLC may be *member-managed or manager-managed.* If it is member-managed, each member has an equal right to manage the business.
> 5. A member who manages the LLC owes *fiduciary duties* to the LLC and its members.
> 6. A member's ownership interest in an LLC is *not freely transferable.* A transferee of a member's distributional interest receives only the member's share of LLC distributions.
> 7. The death or other withdrawal of a member *does not usually dissolve an LLC.*
> 8. Members of an LLC may choose to have the LLC *taxed as a partnership or as a corporation.*

 L01   Explain the attributes of a limited liability company and the default rights and liabilities of a member in an LLC.

Members' Rights and Liabilities

Limited Liability   An LLC member has no individual liability on LLC contracts, unless she also signs LLC contracts in her personal capacity. Therefore, a member's liability is usually limited to her capital contributions to the LLC. She is, however, liable for torts she commits while acting for the LLC.

In addition, a member must make capital contributions to the LLC as she has agreed. This includes the initial capital she agreed to contribute and additional calls for capital that can be made on members according to the operating agreement.

Management Rights   Under the RULLCA, an LLC may choose to be member-managed or manager-managed. If it fails to make that choice in its operating agreement, the LCC is member-managed. Each member in a **member-managed LLC** shares equal rights in the management of the business merely by being a member of the LLC. Each member is an agent of the LLC with implied authority to carry on its ordinary business. If a member-managed LLC has limited the implied authority of one of its members, that member will retain apparent authority to transact for the LLC with a third party who did not know and had no notice that the member's authority was restricted.

 L02   Draft an LLC operating agreement that changes the default rules regarding members' rights.

The LLC operating agreement may modify the default rules of the RULLCA by granting more power to some

members, such as creating a class of members whose approval is required for certain contracts. The agreement could also provide that members share power in relation to their capital contributions.

Managers in a **manager-managed LLC** may be elected and removed *at any time* by a vote of a majority of LLC members. The powers of a manager to act for the LLC are similar to the power of members in a member-managed LLC. Each manager in a manager-managed LLC shares equal rights in the management of the business as an agent of the LLC with implied authority to carry on the LLC's ordinary business. If a manager-managed LLC has limited the implied authority of one of its managers, that manager retains apparent authority to transact for the LLC with a third party who did not know and had no notice that the manager's authority was restricted.

Under the RULLCA, most matters in an LLC may be conducted by individual managing members or managers, or by a vote of a majority of managing members or managers. This facilitates the conduct of ordinary business. Some matters, however, require the consent of all members, including amendment of the operating agreement, admission of new members, the redemption of a member's interest, and the sale of substantially all the LLC's assets.

In addition to being contractually liable for the acts of its members or managers acting within their express, implied, or apparent authority, the LLC is also liable for the torts and other wrongful acts of managing members and other managers acting within their authority. The LLC is not ordinarily liable for the wrongful acts of members not designated as managers in a manager-managed LLC.

Duties   Each member in a member-managed LLC and each manager in a manager-managed LLC is a fiduciary of the LLC and its members. The managing member or manager must account for LLC property and funds and not compete with the LLC. They owe a duty to act with the care that a person in a like position would reasonably exercise and with a reasonable belief that the act is in the best interest of the LLC. Managers must comply with the business judgment rule, a rule we cover in detail in our treatment of corporation law in Chapter 43. This duty of care can be increased or it can be decreased within limits set by the RULLCA.

Nonmanaging members of a manager-managed LLC owe no fiduciary duties to the LLC. Nonetheless, whether or not they are managers, all members owe a duty of good faith and fair dealing when exercising their rights as members. This means all members must act honestly and treat each other fairly.

In the following *Katris* case, the court held that while managers of an LLC owe fiduciary duties, a nonmanaging member of an LLC had no fiduciary duty, even when the LLC's manager delegated considerable power to him.

Katris v. Carroll	842 N.E. 2d 221 (Ill. Ct. App. 2005)

In the 1990s, Stephen Doherty wrote for Lester Szlendak a software program called Viper. On February 14, 1997, Doherty and Szlendak, along with Peter Katris and William Hamburg (both employees of Ernst & Company), formed Viper Execution Systems L.L.C. to exploit the software. Each member held a 25 percent interest in the LLC. Szlendak and Doherty assigned all their rights in Viper to the LLC. The operating agreement provided that the "business and affairs of the LLC shall be managed by its managers" and that the members agreed to elect Katris and Hamburg as the "sole managers" of the LLC. The operating agreement also listed the powers of the managers and the rights and obligations of the members. None of the rights and obligations of the members provided the members with any managerial authority. The operating agreement also stated it could "not be amended except by the affirmative vote of members holding a majority of the participating percentages."

Also on February 14, 1997, Katris and Hamburg, as managers of the LLC, adopted resolutions naming Hamburg as chief executive officer, Katris as chief financial officer, Szlendak as director of marketing, and Doherty as director of technical services. The written consent to the resolution contained signature lines for Hamburg and Katris, who were identified as "all of the managers" of the LLC.

Prior to and at the time of the LLC's formation, Doherty worked as an independent contractor for Hamburg and Patrick Carroll (also an Ernst employee). In late 1997, Ernst hired Doherty to work for Carroll. Working for Carroll and Ernst, Doherty helped to adapt a software program, Worldwide Options Web (WWOW).

By 2002, Katris came to believe that WWOW was functionally similar to Viper. He sued Doherty, Carroll, and Ernst arguing that Doherty usurped a corporate opportunity of the LLC by working in secret with Carroll to develop competing software for Ernst. He further contended that Carroll and Ernst colluded with Doherty in the breach of Doherty's fiduciary duties to the LLC. Doherty subsequently settled the case with Katris, leaving only Carroll and Ernst as defendants.

Carroll and Ernst filed a motion for summary judgment asserting that Katris's collusion claim failed because Doherty, as a nonmanaging member of the manager-managed LLC, did not owe Katris or the LLC a fiduciary duty under the Illinois Limited Liability Company Act; thus, Carroll and Ernst could not collude with Doherty to breach a fiduciary duty under that statute. Katris argued that the 1997 resolution of the managers amended the operating agreement to name Doherty as named Director of Technology and gave Doherty "sole management responsibility for developing, writing, revising and implementing the Viper software." Katris contended, therefore, that pursuant to the Illinois LLC Act, Doherty was subject to the standards of conduct imposed on managers by the act. The Illinois trial court disagreed with Katris, granting Carroll and Ernst's motion for summary judgment. Katris appealed to the Appellate Court of Illinois.

NcNulty, Justice

Summary judgment is appropriate where the pleadings, depositions, affidavits, admissions, and exhibits on file, when viewed in the light most favorable to the nonmoving party, show that there is no genuine issue as to any material fact and the moving party is entitled to judgment as a matter of law.

Katris' claim against Carroll and Ernst depended upon a finding that Doherty owed Katris and the LLC a fiduciary duty. We look to the applicable provisions of the Illinois Limited Liability Company Act in determining the fiduciary duties owed by the managers and members of the LLC. The parties here agree that section 15-3(g) of the Act (805 ILCS 180/15-3(g)) applies to determine Doherty's fiduciary duties.

Katris acknowledges that theirs was a manager-managed LLC and that, pursuant to the Act, a member of a manager-managed LLC "who is not also a manager owes no duties to the company or to the other members solely by reason of being a member." 805 ILCS 180/15-3(g)(1). Katris thus concedes that

Doherty did not owe any fiduciary duties solely by reason of being a member of the LLC.

Katris contends, however, that Doherty owed fiduciary duties to the LLC pursuant to section 15-3(g)(3) of the Act. Section 15-3(g)(3) provides:

> [A] member who pursuant to the operating agreement exercises some or all of the authority of a manager in the management and conduct of the company's business is held to the standards of conduct in subsections (b), (c), (d), and (e) of this Section to the extent that the member exercises the managerial authority vested in a manager by this Act[.]" 805 ILCS 180/15-3(g)(3).

Looking at the plain language of section 15-3(g)(3) of the Act, Doherty was subject to fiduciary duties if he exercised some or all of the authority of a manager pursuant to the LLC's operating agreement. 805 ILCS 180/15-3(g)(3). Looking to that operating agreement, it specifically provides that the business and affairs of the LLC "shall be managed by its managers," provides for the election of Katris and Hamburg as the "sole managers" of the LLC, and sets forth the powers of the managers of the LLC. Although the operating agreement also sets forth the rights and obligations of the members, these provisions do not provide for any managerial authority. Accordingly, Doherty did not exercise any managerial authority pursuant to the LLC's operating agreement.

Katris contends, however, that the managers amended the operating agreement by passing the February 14, 1997 written consent wherein they elected Doherty "Director of Technology." He contends that Doherty's designation as "Director of Technology" elevated him to a position beyond that of a mere member of the LLC and was sufficient to impart on him some managerial authority. This argument fails for two reasons.

First, Katris has provided no authority for his contention that the written consent constituted an amendment to the operating agreement. Pursuant to its own terms, an amendment to the operating agreement required the "affirmative vote of members holding a majority of the participating percentages." Katris and Hamburg were the sole participants to the February 14, 1997, written consent and held only a combined 50% interest in the LLC. They thus could not amend the operating agreement without an additional vote. Accordingly, the facts do not support Katris' contention that the written consent constituted an amendment to the operating agreement.

Second, even if the written consent were viewed as part of the operating agreement, it did not change and, indeed, it reaffirmed the terms of the operating agreement. Katris and Hamburg executed the written consent in their capacities as the managers of the LLC. In it, they specifically resolved to adopt the operating agreement the four members had executed that day as the operating agreement of the LLC. In the signature lines to the written consent, Katris and Hamburg designated themselves as "all of the managers" of the LLC. In light of these facts, something more than the managers' designation of Doherty as "Director of Technology" was required to change the terms of the operating agreement and grant Doherty managerial authority pursuant to it.

We find Katris' contentions inapposite under section 15-3(g)(3) of the Act. By its terms, that section applies where the nonmanager member exercises some or all of the authority of a manager *pursuant to the operating agreement*. To look beyond the operating agreement to Katris' affidavit would be to ignore the plain meaning of the statute and to render the express words used therein superfluous or meaningless. This we cannot do.

The undisputed facts of this case show that Doherty was a member of a manager-managed LLC and exercised no managerial authority pursuant to the LLC's operating agreement. Accordingly, the undisputed facts show that Doherty owed no fiduciary duties to Katris or the LLC pursuant to the Act. Katris's collusion claim against Carroll and Ernst fails as a matter of law.

Summary Judgment for Carroll and Ernst & Company affirmed.

 L02 Draft an LLC operating agreement that changes the default rules regarding members' rights.

Member's Distributions A member's most important right in an LLC is to receive distributions (usually profits) from the LLC. The RULLCA provides that members share profits and other distributions equally, regardless of differences in their capital contributions. No member, however, is entitled to a distribution of profits prior to the dissolution of the LLC, unless the LLC decides to make an interim distribution. The LLC members will usually state in the LLC operating agreement how and when profits are distributed. For example, the operating agreement may simply state that managing members are entitled to salaries and that all members share profits after salaries in proportion to their capital contributions to the LLC. At the other extreme, the LLC operating agreement may have complex rules determining how profits are allocated, including factors such as hours a member works for the LLC, the revenue from clients acquired for the LLC by a member, and a member's capital contribution.

Member's Ownership Interest An LLC member's ownership interest in an LLC is the personal property of the member. However, unlike a corporation in which a shareholder may freely transfer her shares and all her rights to another person, a member has limited ability to sell or transfer her rights in the LLC. Under the RULLCA, a member may transfer her **transferable interest** in the LLC to another person; however, the transferee is not a member of the LLC. (The member remains a member despite having transferred her transferable interest.) The transferee's most important right is to receive the transferring member's right to distributions from the partnership; that is, a share of profits and the value of the member's interest when the LLC is liquidated. A transferee has no right to manage the business and has only a limited right to information about the LLC's accounts.

The LLC operating agreement may provide that a transferee of a member's transferable interest becomes an LLC member. If so, the transferee has the rights, powers, and liabilities of the transferring member, which may include the right to manage the LLC, the right to access LLC records, and the duty to make additional capital contributions.

A personal creditor of a member may obtain from a court a charging order that charges the member's transferable interest with the payment of the debt owed to the creditor. The creditor with a charging order receives, therefore, the member's share of distributions for the life of the charging order. The creditor does not own the transferable interest, but instead only has a lien or security interest against it. To own the transferable interest and acquire all the rights of a transferee, the creditor must foreclose against the interest and purchase it at a foreclosure sale.

Members' Dissociations and LLC Dissolution

Under the RULLCA, members dissociate from an LLC in ways similar to those by which a partner dissociates from a partnership or LLP under the RUPA. Dissolution of an LLC is also similar to that of a partnership or LLP. Therefore, generally, when an LLC member dies or otherwise withdraws from the LLC, the LLC's business will continue, preserving its going concern value.

Member Dissociations A member's dissociation is a change in the relationship among the dissociated member, the LLC, and the other members caused by a member's ceasing to be associated in the carrying on of the business. Under the RULLCA, a partner has the power to dissociate by withdrawing from the LLC at any time.

Dissociations are also caused by a member's death, having a guardian appointed over her affairs, being adjudged legally incompetent by a court, being a debtor in bankruptcy, or being expelled by the other members. The other members may expel a member if it is unlawful to carry on business with her, she has suffered a charging order against her transferable interest, or she has transferred all her transferable interest in the LLC. At the request of the LLC or a member, a court may also expel a member because she has harmed the LLC's business, breached the LLC operating agreement, or engaged in conduct that makes it not practicable to carry on business with her. Judicial expulsion would be appropriate when a member persistently breaches the duty of good faith or competes against the LLC. There are also other causes of dissociation for nonhuman members.

A member's dissociation may be wrongful or nonwrongful. Wrongful dissociations breach the LLC operating agreement. Under the RULLCA, a member has wrongfully dissociated by withdrawing before an LLC's term expires, being a debtor in bankruptcy, or being expelled by a court. When dissolution is wrongful, the dissociating member is liable to the LLC for damages caused by the dissociation, such as the loss of business due to the member's withdrawal.

When a member dissociates, his right to manage the business terminates, as do his duties to the LLC, for the most part. He may, however, have apparent authority to transact for the LLC, unless notice of his dissociation is given to third parties. This apparent authority can be eliminated by giving personal notice to LLC creditors that a member has dissociated or by filing a Statement of Dissociation with the secretary of state.

Dissociation also terminates a member's status as a member. A dissociated member is treated as a transferee of a member's transferable interest.

Payment to a Dissociated Member Under the RULLCA, the dissociated member has no right after her dissociation to force the LLC to dissolve and to liquidate its assets. The RULLCA leaves such decisions to the operating agreement. In addition, a dissociated member is not entitled to receive the value of her LLC interest until the LLC dissolves, unless the members agree otherwise. The RULLCA expects members to resolve buyout issues in the operating agreement.

There is one exception. If the LLC is *at will* and is not dissolved, the LLC must purchase his interest at fair value within 120 days after the member's dissociation. If the LLC *has a term,* however, and is not dissolved, the LLC may continue its business and pay the dissociated member the value of his interest within 120 days after the end of the LLC's term.

LLC Dissolution When an LLC is dissolved, ordinarily it must be wound up. Since a business usually is worth more as a going concern, the RULLCA has few events that automatically cause dissolution of an LLC. For example, death and withdrawal of members do not by themselves cause dissolution of an LLC. Instead, the RULLCA mostly lets members decide the causes of dissolution.

The few grounds for dissolution in the RULLCA include an event making it unlawful for the LLC business to continue, judicial dissolution at the request of a member or transferee of a member's transferable interest, and administrative dissolution by the secretary of state. A member or dissociated member may ask for a judicial dissolution if, for example, the LLC cannot practicably carry on its business, the LLC is being managed illegally or oppressively, or the LLC failed to purchase a dissociated member's transferable interest on the date required. The RULLCA allows the members to state in the operating agreement the events that will dissolve the LLC. The operating agreement may also allow the members to dissolve the LLC by their vote, which may be any percentage of members that the members choose. In the absence of such a provision in the LLC agreement, all members must agree to dissolve an LLC.

When an LLC dissolves, any member who has not wrongly dissociated may wind up the business. Winding-up members should liquidate the assets, yet they may preserve the LLC's assets or business as a going concern for a reasonable time in order to optimize the proceeds from the liquidation.

The LLC is bound by the reasonable acts of its members during winding up, and may be liable for actions that continue the business and are inconsistent with winding up, unless the LLC gives third parties notice of dissolution. Notice can be given in a reasonable manner, such as by e-mail, letter, or phone call, and by filing a Notice of Dissociation with the secretary of state, which is effective against all parties 90 days after filing.

Distribution of Dissolved LLC's Assets After all the LLC assets have been sold, the proceeds will be distributed first to LLC creditors, including members who are creditors. If there are excess proceeds, members' contributions are returned next. Any remaining proceeds are distributed in proportion to how they share profits.

If the LLC's assets are insufficient to pay all creditors' claims, ordinarily creditors have no recourse, because the LLC's members have liability limited to the assets of the LLC. If an LLC member has not paid in all the capital she was required to pay, however, creditors may sue the member to force the member to contribute the additional capital.

 Draft an LLC operating agreement that changes the default rules regarding members' rights.

Effect of Operating Agreement The default dissociation and dissolution rules of the RULLCA may be unacceptable to members of an LLC. Therefore, a well-drafted operating agreement will cover this area completely, defining the grounds for dissociation, such as death, withdrawal, and disability of a member. The agreement should also state when a member may be expelled by the other members and a court. The RULLCA gives the members much flexibility to arrange their affairs the way they want.

The operating agreement may state the amount and timing of payments to a dissociated member for the value of her ownership interest. For example, the operating agreement may provide for a lump-sum payment within 90 days after a member dies, becomes disabled, or withdraws at age 55 or later. If a member withdraws before age 55, the agreement may provide for payment in quarterly installments over a five-year period.

The agreement may also state when dissolution and winding up occur. For example, the agreement may provide that no member has the power to seek dissolution at any time. Instead, the agreement may permit a vote of 75 percent of the members to commence winding up if any member dies or withdraws before the time permitted in the LLC operating agreement. It may require unanimous approval by the members in all other contexts. The agreement should also stipulate which members will have the right to participate in winding up.

The LLC operating agreement may also modify how proceeds are distributed to members during winding up after creditors are paid. For example, the agreement may state that all proceeds beyond creditors' claims are distributed equally to members, regardless of their capital contributions.

The following case considers both the effects of a member's dissociation and the management rights of a member in an LLC. It contains a good example of an LLC operating agreement that details the management powers of a managing member.

In re Garrison-Ashburn, LC	253 B.R. 700 (E. D. Va. 2000)

Cralle Comer and Stephen Chapman formed two manager-managed limited liability companies, Garrison-Ashburn, L. C. and Garrison-Woods, L. C. Comer and Chapman each owned a 50 percent membership interest in each LLC. While Chapman was the initial operating manager, Comer later replaced him as operating manager.

In 1999, Chapman filed a voluntary petition in bankruptcy under Chapter 11 of the United States Bankruptcy Code. In the course of the bankruptcy proceeding, Comer wished to sell a parcel of land owned by Garrison-Woods. Chapman argued that Garrison-Woods could not sell the land without his consent on the grounds that the LLC's operating agreement required all deeds and sales contracts be executed by both members. He refused to sign the contract of sale or the deed. Comer argued that as operating manager he was fully authorized to execute the contract. The bankruptcy court ruled in favor of Comer, and Chapman moved for the court to reconsider its judgment.

Mayer, Judge

The court is satisfied that Comer can bind Garrison-Woods and consummate the contract without Chapman's consent or participation.

The heart of Chapman's argument is Article IV, Section 6 of the Operating Agreement which addresses the powers of the Operating Manager. This section states in part:

> Operating Manager. The Operating Manager shall be the chief executive officer of the Company and shall have the general charge of the business and affairs of the Company, subject, however, to the right of the Members to confer specified powers on officers and subject generally to the direction of Members. . . . The Operating Manager shall also have the sole and complete control of the management and operation of the affairs and business of the Company. Without limiting the foregoing, the Operating Manager shall have full and complete authority in his sole and exclusive discretion to execute on behalf of the company, any listing agreement, contract or other paper.

Article IV, Section 11 of the Operating Agreement states in part:

> Signature Authority. Without limiting the foregoing, the signatures of both the Operating Manager and the Assistant Operating Manager shall be required for, and they shall have full and complete authority in their sole and exclusive discretion to:
>
> a. Execute on behalf of the Company, any bond or deed, execute or endorse promissory notes and renew the same from time to time;
>
> b. Draw upon any bank or banks or any corporations, associations, or individuals for any sum or sums of money that may be to the credit of the Company, or which the Company may be entitled to receive;
>
> c. Make all necessary deeds and conveyances thereof of Company real and/or personal property, wheresoever located, with all necessary covenants, warranties, and assurances, and to sign, seal, and acknowledge and deliver the same;

Chapman argues that pursuant to Article IV, Section 11, he along with Comer must also sign such a contract for it to be legally binding. This argument is contrary to the plain meaning of the Operating Agreement. The Operating Agreement plainly vests in the Operating Manager "the sole and complete control of the management and operation of the affairs and business of the Company" and the "full and complete authority . . . to execute on behalf of the Company" any contract. Operating Agreement, Article IV, Section 6. The Operating Manager controls the business affairs of the company pursuant to Section 6. This includes the ability to sell the principal property of the company thereby realizing the company's objective. Section 11 by its express terms does not limit this authority. Moreover, it does not require both members to execute a deed, as suggested in the Motion, but rather two officers, the Operating Manager and the Assistant Operating Manager. At best, if Chapman is the Assistant Operating Manager, Section 11 requires the deed that would be necessary to consummate the contract be signed by Comer as Operating Manager and Chapman as Assistant Operating Manager.

Chapman fails to consider the effect of the filing of his voluntary petition in bankruptcy on his rights in the limited liability company. The Code of Virginia provides that a member is "dissociated" from a limited liability company upon the occurrence of certain events, one of which is filing a petition in bankruptcy.

Dissociation of a member does not dissolve the company. The company continues in existence. The effect on a member of becoming dissociated from a limited liability company is to divest the member of all rights as a member to participate in the management or operation of the company. The only rights remaining are the dissociated member's economic rights, his membership interest. That is to say, the dissociated member is expelled from the company, but does not forfeit the value of his ownership interest.

The question presented by Chapman is whether Garrison-Woods can lawfully execute and consummate a contract for the sale of its real estate. Under present Virginia law, when Chapman filed his voluntary petition, he ceased to be a member and had no further voice or vote in the management of Garrison-Woods.

Comer, as the sole remaining member, has the unilateral power to remove Chapman as Assistant Operating Manager at any time and elect a new Assistant Operating Manager. The new Assistant Operating Manager need not be a member of the company. In any event, Comer could elect himself the new Assistant Operating Manager. Article IV, Section 1 of the Operating Agreement provides that any two or more offices may be held by the same person. The restriction Chapman raises in his motion to reconsider would not prevent Garrison-Woods from executing the sales contract for its parcel or from consummating the sale. The legal authority, and the intention, to execute the contract and consummate it are both present. The contract approved by the court can be fully consummated.

Chapman's motion to reconsider is denied. Judgment for Comer.

The Global Business Environment

The limited liability company is known in many countries throughout the world. However, LLCs formed under the laws of other nations are a bit different from American LLCs.

In Germany, which claims to be the first nation to permit them, in 1892, LLCs are known as *Gesellschaft mit beschrankter Haftung* (GmbH). Other countries soon followed Germany's lead, including Portugal (1917), Brazil (1919), Chile (1923), Turkey (1926), Uruguay (1933), Mexico (1934), and Belgium (1935). In France, the *societes de responsabilite limitee* is more popular than the more traditional stock corporation.

In these countries, LLC law confers limited liability on the members, requires use of the word *limited* in the entity's name, permits members to control admission of new members to the entity, and allows the entity to be dissolved by death of a member, unless otherwise expressly stated in the articles of association. Most countries provide for management of LLCs by one or more managing directors. Many countries also limit the number of members in an LLC, making the LLC an entity inappropriate for a publicly held company. Some experts refer to these LLCs as private limited companies, which more accurately describes what they are: corporations with a limited number of owners.

 L03 Explain the attributes of a limited partnership and limited liability limited partnership and the default rights and liabilities of partners in a limited partnership and LLLP.

Limited Partnerships and Limited Liability Limited Partnerships

The partnership form—with managerial control and unlimited liability for all partners—is not acceptable for all business arrangements. Often, business managers want an infusion of capital into a business yet are reluctant to surrender managerial control to those contributing capital. Investors wish to contribute capital to a business and share in its profits yet limit their liability to the amount of their investment and be relieved of the obligation to manage the business.

As you have already seen in this chapter and the other partnership chapters, an LLC may have an operating agreement and a limited liability partnership (LLP) may have a partnership agreement that accomplishes these objectives by limiting the management right to fewer than all of the LLC's members or LLP's partners. The **limited partnership,** however, has a basic, default structure that serves these needs. The limited partnership has two classes of owners: **general partners,** who contribute capital to the business, manage it, share in its profits, and possess unlimited liability for its obligations; and **limited partners,** who contribute capital and share profits, but possess no management powers and have liability limited to their investments in the business.

A variant of the limited partnership is the **limited liability limited partnership (LLLP).** An LLLP is a limited partnership that has elected limited liability status for all its partners, including general partners. Except for the liability of general partners, limited partnerships and LLLPs are identical. For that reason, every well-planned limited partnership should eliminate the unlimited liability of its human managers by having a corporate general partner or electing LLLP status, when available. Today, every state recognizes limited partnerships and many recognize LLLPs as well.

The Uniform Limited Partnership Acts

In 2001 the National Conference of Commissioners on Uniform State Laws drafted a new Uniform Limited

---

Figure 2   *Principal Characteristics of Limited Partnerships and LLLPs*

1. A limited partnership or LLLP may be *created only in accordance with a statute.*

2. A limited partnership or LLLP has two types of partners: *general partners* and *limited partners.* It must have one or more of each type.

3. All partners, limited and general, *share the profits* of the business *in relation to their capital contributions.*

4. Each limited partner has *liability limited to his capital contribution* to the business. Each general partner of a limited partnership has *unlimited liability* for the obligations of the business. A general partner in an LLLP, however, has *liability limited to his capital contribution.*

5. Each general partner has a *right to manage* the business, and she is an agent of the limited partnership or LLLP. A limited partner has *no right to manage* the business or to act as its agent, but he does have the right to vote on fundamental matters. A limited partner may manage the business, yet retain limited liability for partnership obligations.

6. General partners, as agents, are *fiduciaries* of the business. Limited partners are not fiduciaries.

7. A partner's rights in a limited partnership or LLLP *are not freely transferable.* A transferee of a general or limited partnership interest is not a partner, but is entitled only to the transferring partner's share of capital and profits, absent a contrary agreement.

8. The death or other withdrawal of a partner does not usually dissolve a limited partnership or LLLP, unless there is no surviving general partner.

9. Usually, a limited partnership or LLLP is taxed like a partnership. However, a limited partnership or LLLP may elect to be taxed like a corporation.

Partnership Act (ULPA) to replace the Revised Uniform Partnership Act of 1976 and its 1985 amendments. The ULPA of 2001 is the first comprehensive statement of American limited partnership law. As shown in Figure 2, many characteristics of a limited partnership under the ULPA are similar to those of a partnership or LLP under the Revised Uniform Partnership Act. While the ULPA copies much of the law of the RUPA, only the ULPA applies to limited partnerships.

Although most states at this time have enacted the RULPA, we will study the ULPA of 2001, which will soon be the dominant limited partnership law in the United States. As of October 2011, 18 states and the District of Columbia have adopted or introduced the ULPA. The ULPA governs both limited partnerships and LLLPs. Under the ULPA, limited partnerships and LLLPs are identical except for the liability of general partners. Therefore, when this chapter addresses limited partnership law (other than the rules regarding the liability of general partners), the law applies to LLLPs as well.

Use of Limited Partnerships and LLLPs

The limited partnership (or LLLP) form is used primarily in tax shelter ventures and activities such as real estate investment, oil and gas drilling, and professional sports. When the limited partnership elects to be taxed as a partnership, it operates as a tax shelter by allowing partners

to reduce their personal federal income tax liability by deducting limited partnership losses on their individual income tax returns. General partners, however, receive a greater tax shelter advantage than do limited partners. Losses of the business allocated to a general partner offset his income from any other sources. Losses of the business allocated to limited partners may be used to offset only income from other *passive* investments and only to the extent limited partners are *at risk,* that is, to the extent of their capital contributions to the limited partnership. If a limited partner has sold her limited partnership interest or the limited partnership has terminated, her loss offsets any income. Limited partnerships are also used by family businesses for estate planning purposes. The *Moser* case after the next section concerns a family limited partnership. Regardless of the use, the ULPA presumes that its partners want a highly centralized, strongly entrenched management (general partners) and passive investors with little control and little right to exit the limited partnership (limited partners).

LOG ON

www.nccusl.org
You can find the Uniform Limited Partnership Act of 2001 at the website for the National Conference of Commissioners on Uniform State Laws.

Creation of Limited Partnerships and LLLPs

A limited partnership (or LLLP) may be created only by complying with the applicable state statute. Yet the statutory requirements of the ULPA are minimal. A **certificate of limited partnership** must be executed and submitted to the secretary of state. The certificate must be signed by all general partners. A limited partnership begins its existence at the time the certificate is filed by the office of the secretary of state. The limited partnership may ask the secretary of state to issue a Certificate of Existence, which is conclusive proof the limited partnership exists.

The ULPA requires that the limited partnership certificate submitted by the limited partnership include its address, its registered agent for service of process, its general partners' names and addresses, and whether it is a limited partnership or an LLLP. The name of a limited partnership must include the words *limited partnership* or the letters *L.P.* or *LP*. The name of a limited liability limited partnership must contain the words *limited liability limited partnership* or the letters *L.L.L.P.* or *LLLP*. The name of a limited partnership or LLLP may include the name of any partner, general or limited.

It is expected that many limited partnerships (or LLLPs) will have unlimited duration. Therefore, the ULPA provides for the perpetual life of a limited partnership (or LLLP). The limited partnership certificate or limited partnership agreement, however, may place a limit on the limited partnership's duration.

The certificate is not required to address many other matters that are essential to the limited partnership, such as the limited partners' names, the partners' capital contributions, the partners' shares of profits and other distributions, or the acts that cause a dissolution of the limited partnership. A well-planned limited partnership will usually include those and other matters in the certificate or in a separate **limited partnership agreement.**

Any *person* may be a general or limited partner. Persons include a natural person, partnership, LLC, trust, estate, association, or corporation. Hence, as commonly occurs, a corporation may be the sole general partner of a limited partnership.

Creation of LLLPs

A well-planned limited partnership should shield all its partners from liability by electing LLLP status, when available. This election is simple, requiring no special filing. LLLP status is elected by making a statement in the limited partnership certificate submitted to the secretary of state that the business is an LLLP.

Defective Compliance with Limited Partnership Statute

The ULPA requires at least *substantial compliance* with the previously listed requirements to create a limited partnership. If the persons attempting to create a limited partnership do not substantially comply with the ULPA, a limited partnership does not exist; therefore, a limited partner may lose her limited liability and have unlimited liability for limited partnership obligations. A general partner in an LLLP will have unlimited liability if the LLLP was formed defectively.

A lack of substantial compliance might result from failing to file a certificate of limited partnership or from filing a defective certificate. A defective certificate might, for example, misstate the name of the limited partnership or erroneously identify the business form as a limited partnership when an LLLP was intended.

Limited Partners Infrequently, a person will believe that she is a limited partner but discover later that she has been designated a general partner or that the general partners have not filed a certificate of limited partnership. In such circumstances and others, she may be liable as a general partner unless she in good faith believes she is a limited partner and upon discovering she is not a limited partner she either:

1. Causes a proper certificate of limited partnership (or an amendment thereto) to be filed with the secretary of state, or

2. Withdraws from future equity participation in the firm by filing a certificate declaring such withdrawal with the secretary of state.

However, such a person remains liable as a general partner to third parties who previously believed in good faith that the person was a general partner.

General Partners The ULPA of 2001 has no provision protecting general partners who erroneously believe an LLLP has been formed. Consequently, a general partner in a limited partnership who believes wrongly that an LLLP has been created has unlimited liability for the obligations of the limited partnership.

In the following *Moser v. Moser* case, a husband and wife tried to use a family limited partnership to reduce taxes. Although they properly formed the limited partnership, they failed to comply with tax law and otherwise to keep the limited partnership's assets separate from themselves. Consequently, the court ruled that the husband and wife had not made a gift of the limited partnership's property to their children.

Moser v. Moser	2007 Ohio 4109 (Ohio Ct. App. 2007)

Terrance and Barbara Moser were married on October 11, 1980. Over the next 16 years, they had two children, Shannon and Joshua, and accumulated assets in excess of $2 million. On December 31, 1996, Terrance and Barbara signed a document creating the Moser Family Limited Partnership. A family limited partnership is an estate planning device designed to minimize tax liabilities. The Moser Family Limited Partnership was set up with Terrance, as trustee of a revocable trust holding his assets, as general partner; Barbara, as trustee of a revocable trust holding her assets, as a limited partner; Shannon and Joshua as limited partners, with Barbara as their custodian. Typically, a family partnership is funded with assets having a high potential for appreciation. Parents will then give to their children a certain number of units or a percentage interest in the limited partnership, without tax liability, taking advantage of the gift tax exclusion. At the time the Moser Family Limited Partnership was created, the annual gift tax exclusion was $10,000. In order to function properly as an estate planning device, the gifts of partnership interest to the children had to be completed, irrevocable gifts. In this way, wealth could be transferred to children during the parents' lifetime, thus avoiding estate taxes, while the parents would be able to maintain a certain amount of control of the wealth, by virtue of the general partner's control of the partnership. After its creation, the Moser Family Limited Partnership, in conjunction with Moser Construction and other business entities previously owned and operated by the Mosers, successfully oversaw several land development ventures.

Unfortunately, Terrance and Barbara had marital problems. On January 17, 2003, Barbara filed for divorce. In addition to naming Terrance as a defendant, she also named the Moser Family Limited Partnership as an additional defendant, arguing that its assets were part of the marital estate and that she should receive a portion of the limited partnership's assets. The trial court agreed with Barbara. The court determined the total value of the marital estate to be $3,778,764, of which $1,507,663 represented the net value of the Moser Family Limited Partnership. Terrance appealed the decision to an Ohio appellate court.

Grendell, Judge

Terrance raises two arguments. The first is that the trial court erred by invalidating the gifts of partnership interest to the Moser children. The second is that the trial court erred by treating partnership assets as marital property.

As any initial assets of the Partnership were marital, Terrance and Barbara were deemed to be equal partners, *i.e.*, fifty percent owners of the partnership shares. The trial court found that transfers of interest in the Moser Family Limited Partnership to the Moser children did not occur on December 31, 1996, and January 1, 1997, as purported in the federal gift tax returns. Leslie D. Smeach is a certified public accountant who did work for Terrrance. Smeach testified that the valuation of the partnership units allegedly given to the Moser children on December 31, 1996, and January 1, 1997, did not occur until April 1997. Prior to this valuation, it would have been impossible to determine the number of partnership units that could be given in accordance with the gift tax exclusion.

The trial court also found that Terrance operated the Moser Family Limited Partnership and its subsidiary companies as his own personal assets. The court noted the free transfer of funds between business entities that were part of, or associated with, the Moser Family Limited Partnership. For example, although the tax returns indicated the Moser Family Limited Partnership possessed a 50% interest in Rootstown Storage Partnership, Terrance continued to list Rootstown Storage as an asset on his personal financial statements. In April 2000, Terrance received a personal distribution of $55,000 from Rootstown Storage.

The trial court determined that Terrance and Barbara had not made valid, *inter vivos* gifts of their interests in the Moser Family Limited Partnership to the Moser children. In Barbara's case, the court relied upon her testimony that she did not intend to relinquish ownership interest in the Partnership until her death.

In Terrance's case, the court found the intent to make such a gift in the Memoranda of Gifts signed by Terrance on December 31, 1997. However, the court also found that there was no delivery of the Memorandum of Gift letters to the Moser children or to Barbara as their custodian. The court also concluded that Terrance had not relinquished control over his ownership interest in the Partnership in a manner consistent with the intent to make a gift.

There was considerable testimony from various witnesses at the hearings which likened Terrance's powers under the Moser Family Limited Partnership to those of "a benevolent dictator." There was also evidence at the hearings that Terrance exercised this power freely. When the marital residence was inadvertently transferred into the Partnership, Terrance transferred it out. Terrance used Partnership funds to meet the expenses of other businesses owned by him. As noted above, there was considerable "cash flow" between entities existing both within and without the Partnership.

Accordingly, the trial court had jurisdiction over the Moser Family Limited Partnership and its partners and could exercise that jurisdiction to order Terrance to assign specific partnership properties so as to effectuate a fair and equitable division of property.

Judgment for Barbara Moser affirmed.

Explain the attributes of a limited partnership and limited liability limited partnership and the default rights and liabilities of partners in a limited partnership and LLLP.

The ULPA makes it clear that limited partners have no inherent right to vote on any matter as a class. They may receive such a right only by agreement of the partners.

Draft a limited partnership or LLLP agreement that changes the default rules regarding partners' rights.

Rights and Liabilities of Partners in Limited Partnerships or LLLPs

The partners of a limited partnership (or LLLP) have many rights and liabilities. Some are common to both general and limited partners, while others are not shared.

Rights and Liabilities Shared by General and Limited Partners

Capital Contributions A partner may contribute any property or other benefit to the limited partnership. This includes cash, tangible or intangible property, services rendered, a promissory note, or a promise to contribute cash, property, or services. A partner is obligated to contribute as he promised. This obligation may be enforced by the limited partnership or by any of its creditors.

Share of Profits and Losses Under the ULPA, profits and losses are shared on the basis of the value of each partner's capital contribution unless there is a written agreement to the contrary. For example, if 2 general partners contribute $100,000 each and 20 limited partners contribute $2,000,000 each, and the profit is $2,010,000, each general partner's share of the profits is $5,000 and each limited partner's share is $100,000.

Because most limited partnerships are tax shelters, partnership agreements often provide for limited partners to take all the losses of the business, up to the limit of their capital contributions.

Voting Rights The ULPA of 2001 requires few actions to be approved by all the partners. Only amendment of the limited partnership agreement, amendment of the limited partnership certificate, and sale or other transfer of substantially all the limited partnership's assets outside the ordinary course of business require approval of all the partners. In a well-planned limited partnership, the limited partnership agreement may require that certain transactions be approved by general partners, by limited partners, or by all the partners. The agreement may give each general partner more votes than it grants limited partners, or vice versa.

Admission of New Partners Under the ULPA, the default rule is that no new partner may be admitted unless each partner has consented to the admission. The limited partnership agreement may provide for other admission procedures. For example, the general partners may be given the power to admit new limited partners without the consent of existing limited partners. Usually, this power is given to general partners to facilitate the ability of the limited partnership to raise capital, but the power should be restricted to prevent any significant dilution of the ownership interests of existing limited partners.

The limited partnership agreement may also provide for the election of new general partners, such as when a general partner dies or retires. Instead of requiring approval of all partners, the agreement may provide that a majority of the partners may elect a replacement general partner. Another option is to give to limited partners the power to replace a general partner. Another alternative is to grant such power to the partners owning a majority of the limited partnership, measured by their capital contributions.

In general, the ULPA does not grant partners much power to expel other partners from the partnership. When we discuss partners' dissociations later in the chapter, we will examine the few grounds for expulsion.

Partner's Transferable Interest Each partner in a limited partnership owns a transferable interest in the limited partnership. It is his personal property. He may sell or transfer it to others, such as his personal creditors. Or his personal creditor may obtain a charging order against it. Generally, a buyer or transferee—or a creditor with a charging order—is entitled to receive only the partner's share of distributions. The ULPA treats charging orders like ordinary partnership law does.

When the limited partnership agreement so provides or all the partners consent, a buyer or transferee of a partner's transferable interest may become a partner. The new partner then assumes all the rights and liabilities of a partner, except for liabilities unknown to her at the time she became a partner.

A partner's transfer of his transferable interest has no effect on his status as a partner, absent a contrary agreement. The partner has not dissociated, and the limited partnership has not dissolved merely as a result of the transfer. However, the limited partnership agreement may create consequences, such as expulsion of the transferring partner.

Power and Right to Withdraw Partners have the power to withdraw from the limited partnership at any time. The expectation, however, is that a limited partnership will have perpetual duration. Consequently, the ULPA gives the partners no right to withdraw, absent a contrary provision in the limited partnership agreement.

One result, therefore, under the ULPA, is that a withdrawing partner has no right to receive the value of her partnership interest. This means that a partner who withdraws from a limited partnership will not receive a return of her investment, unless the limited partnership agreement provides for a buyout of the withdrawing partner or the limited partnership dissolves and liquidates.

Other Rights of General Partners A general partner of a limited partnership or an LLLP has the same right to manage and the same agency powers as a partner in an ordinary partnership. He has the express authority to act as the partners have agreed he should and the implied authority to do what is in the ordinary course of business. In addition, he may have apparent authority to bind the partnership to contracts when his implied authority is limited yet no notice of the limitation has been given to third parties.

A general partner has no right to compensation beyond his share of the profits, absent an agreement to the contrary. Since most limited partnerships are tax shelters that are designed to lose money during their early years of operation, most limited partnership agreements provide for the payment of salaries to general partners.

Other Liabilities of General Partners

Liability A general partner in a limited partnership has unlimited liability to the creditors of the limited partnership. In an LLLP, however, a general partner's liability is limited to his capital contribution to the business.

Even so, in an LLLP a general partner may not escape liability for torts he commits in the course of the LLLP's business. Suppose a general partner drives a car on LLLP business and negligently injures a pedestrian. Not only may the LLLP be liable, but also the general partner will have personal liability to the pedestrian. Yet the LLLP form does protect the general partner from most torts of the business. For example, the general partner in an LLLP will not have personal liability for the torts of her fellow general partners or employees.

Fiduciary Duties Any general partner, whether in a limited partnership or an LLLP, is in a position of trust when she manages the business and therefore owes fiduciary duties to the limited partnership and the other partners. The general partner must account for limited partnership property, not compete against the partnership, and not self-deal with the partnership.

In addition, a general partner owes a duty of care when transacting for the partnership. The ULPA provides considerable protection for general partners under the duty of care, imposing liability to the limited partnership only if she engages in grossly negligent or reckless conduct, intentional misconduct, or knowing violations of the law. The limited partnership agreement may increase the general partners' duty of care, although that is not typical. The ULPA permits the partners to reduce the general partners' duty of care, if not unreasonable, but gives no clue to what is reasonable or unreasonable. The *Lach* case, which appears near the end of this chapter, found general partners breached their fiduciary duty by attempting to circumvent a limited partner's right to approve new general partners.

Other Rights of Limited Partners Limited partners have the right to be informed about partnership affairs. The ULPA obligates the general partners to provide financial information and tax returns to the limited partners on demand. In addition, a limited partner may inspect and copy a list of the partners, information concerning contributions by partners, the certificate of limited partnership, tax returns, and partnership agreements.

Other Liabilities of Limited Partners

Liability Once a limited partner has contributed all of his promised capital contribution, generally he has no further liability for partnership losses or obligations.

Under the RULPA of 1976, a limited partner who participates in the control of the business may be liable to creditors of the limited partnership. Under the RULPA, a limited partner who participates in control is liable only to those persons who transact with the limited partnership reasonably believing, based on the limited partner's conduct, that the limited partner is a general partner.

The ULPA of 2001 eliminates this liability risk. The ULPA extends to limited partners the same protection given to owners who manage LLCs and LLPs: liability limited to their capital contributions, regardless whether they manage the business.

Duties No limited partner owes fiduciary duties to the limited partnership or his partners solely by being a limited partner. That means, for example, a limited partner in an oil and gas limited partnership may also invest as a limited partner in other oil and gas limited partnerships. However, all limited partners owe a duty to act in good faith and to deal fairly with the limited partnership. For example, a limited partner who lends money to the partnership is expected to disclose his interest and to transact fairly with the limited partnership. In addition, a limited partner who is an agent of the limited partnership owes the fiduciary duties imposed by agency law. For example, a limited partner who is a leasing agent for a limited partnership that owns apartment buildings owes the duty to account for rental income and a duty of skill and care.

Partner Who Is Both a General Partner and a Limited Partner

Although unusual, a person may be both a general partner and a limited partner in a limited partnership or LLLP. A general partner may wish to be a limited partner to increase his share of limited partnership profits. A partner who is both a general and limited partner has the duties of a general partner when acting as a general partner and the duties of a limited partner when acting as a limited partner.

A general partner's liability in a limited partnership is not reduced merely because he is also a limited partner, but a limited partner who becomes a general partner would lose his limited liability. In an LLLP, liability is unaffected by whether a partner is both a general and limited partner, as the liability is the same for both types of partners in an LLLP.

Note, however, that ULPA section 102(11) indicates that the *only* limited partner and *only* general partner may *not* be the same person.

Explain the attributes of a limited partnership and limited liability limited partnership and the default rights and liabilities of partners in a limited partnership and LLLP.

Partners' Dissociations and Limited Partnership Dissolution

The ULPA of 2001 greatly changed the law regarding dissolutions of limited partnerships and LLLPs. The ULPA adopts much of the terminology and framework of partnership law in the RUPA. Reflecting the intent that limited partnerships and LLLPs are for long-term businesses, the ULPA makes it harder for a limited partnership to dissolve and provides few rights for partners who dissociate from the limited partnership before the partners expect.

Partners' Dissociations

Because the roles of limited partners and general partners are different in a limited partnership or LLLP, the ULPA's default rules for dissociations by a limited partner are in part different from the default rules for dissociations by a general partner.

Limited Partner Dissociations A limited partner will dissociate upon the limited partner's death, withdrawal, or expulsion from the partnership.

A limited partner may be expelled by the other partners or by a court. The other partners may expel a limited partner if she has transferred all of her transferable interest or suffered a charging order against her partnership interest. She can also be expelled if it is illegal to conduct business with the limited partner, such as a securities investment firm limited partner who has been convicted of securities fraud. The other partners' vote to expel must be unanimous.

At the request of the limited partnership, a court may also expel a limited partner if she has engaged in wrongful conduct that negatively affects the business or if she has willfully and persistently breached the partnership agreement or the limited partner's duty of good faith and fair dealing.

The ULPA also defines dissociations for nonhuman limited partners, such as corporations, LLCs, and trusts. For example, the other partners may expel an LLC that has been dissolved and is winding up its business.

A dissociated limited partner is not a limited partner, has no rights as a limited partner, and is treated as a mere transferee of the dissociated limited partner's transferable interest. That means the dissociated limited partner has no right to vote or exercise any other partners' powers, but does have the right to receive distributions (profits) from the limited partnership and has the right to receive the liquidation value of her transferable interest at the termination of the limited partnership.

General Partner Dissociations The ULPA treats general partners' dissociations the same as the RUPA treats partners' dissociations in a partnership. A general partner's death, withdrawal, or expulsion causes dissociation, just as with limited partners. In addition, a general partner dissociates if he becomes mentally or physically unable to care for himself (such as when a court appoints a guardian over his affairs) or he is unable to perform as a general partner (as determined by a court). A general partner also dissociates if he is a debtor in bankruptcy, assigns his assets for the benefit of creditors, or has a custodian appointed over his property. In addition, a general partner may be expelled by a vote of all the other partners or by a court for the same grounds that limited partners may be expelled. The ULPA also provides for dissociation of nonhuman general partners, such as the termination of a corporation that is a general partner.

Like a dissociated limited partner, a dissociated general partner is treated as a transferee of the dissociated general partner's transferable interest. He will receive the liquidation value of the partnership interest at the termination of the partnership.

While a general partner always has the power to dissociate, his dissociation may be wrongful. A general partner wrongfully dissociates by leaving the partnership before it terminates, violating the limited partnership agreement, being a debtor in bankruptcy, or being expelled by a court. A general partner who has wrongfully dissociated is liable to the limited partnership and other partners for damages caused by his dissociation.

Authority and Liability of Dissociated General Partners Dissociation ends a general partner's right to manage the limited partnership. The dissociated general partner is released from most of his fiduciary duties. For example, the duty not to compete would no longer apply, so the dissociated general partner could set up a competing business. The duty of confidentiality, however, exists after dissociation to protect the limited partnership's trade secrets and other proprietary information.

While a general partner's express and implied authority to act for the limited partnership terminates upon his dissociation, he may retain apparent authority to transact for the limited partnership. Moreover, his liability for partnership obligations does not terminate merely due to his dissociation. Therefore, the dissociated general partner and the limited partnership must take steps to notify creditors and other parties of the dissociation to protect the limited partnership and the dissociated general partner from liability.

The best way is for the limited partnership to give notice of the dissociation, such as by e-mail or phone calls. To give notice of a dissociation that is effective against everyone, the ULPA permits the filing of a Notice of Dissociation, which is effective 90 days after filing. In addition, two years after the dissociation, the apparent authority of a dissociated general partner automatically ends.

A dissociated general partner will remain liable on a limited partnership obligation incurred while he was a partner unless the creditor agrees to release him from liability. The dissociated general partner will not be liable for limited partnership obligations incurred after he dissociated, if notice has been given of his association or more than two years have passed since his dissociation.

In an LLLP, however, there is no need for the dissociated general partner to be released from liability by existing creditors or to give notice of the dissolution, because a general partner in an LLLP has liability limited to his contribution to the LLLP.

 LO4 Draft a limited partnership or LLLP agreement that changes the default rules regarding partners' rights.

Effect of Limited Partnership Agreement The partners may agree to modify the default dissociation rules in the ULPA. For example, the partners may agree that no limited partner may withdraw from the limited partnership. While such a provision will not prevent dissociation upon a limited partner's death, it would otherwise require a limited partner to remain with the limited partnership until its term ends. The partnership agreement may also state the events that cause dissociation, such as a general partner becoming a manager of a competing business. The partners may also provide grounds to expel a partner, such as when a partner fails to contribute additional capital as required by the partnership agreement. The agreement may also reduce the percentage of partners required to expel a partner, such as requiring only 80 percent approval or giving expulsion power to general partners.

While a limited partner's power to withdraw may be eliminated, the limited partnership agreement may not restrict a general partner's right to withdraw. The grounds for this distinction is that a general partner should be able to withdraw from his duties to manage the limited partnership, while the limited partner as a passive investor has no such need to be relieved of that burden.

It may be unacceptable to the partners in a limited partnership that the dissociated partners do not receive the value of their partnership interests until the partnership terminates. Therefore, the limited partnership agreement may provide for the buyout of a partner's interest. A well-written buyout agreement should state the events that trigger a buyout, the valuation method, and when and how the dissociated partner will be paid (for example, in a lump sum 120 days after dissociation or in quarterly installments for five years). To protect creditors, the ULPA prohibits any payment to a dissociated partner if the limited partnership is insolvent.

To protect the limited partnership's competitive position, the partners' agreement may also limit a dissociated general partner's ability to compete against the partnership.

For example, a noncompete agreement may prohibit a dissociated general partner from competing for five years in the geographic area served by the limited partnership.

Limited Partnership Dissolutions

Recognizing that a limited partnership is usually worth more as a going concern, the ULPA provides that a limited partnership (or LLLP) is not dissolved, its business is not wound up, and it does not terminate merely because a partner has dissociated from the limited partnership. The ULPA provides that a limited partnership is dissolved and its business wound up only if all general partners and limited partners owning a majority of the claims to limited partner distributions (such as profits) vote for dissolution, if a general partner dissociates and partners owning a majority of the claims to partners' distributions vote for dissolution, if the last general or limited partner dissociates and is not replaced within 90 days, or if a court dissolves the limited partnership because it is not reasonably practicable to carry on the business of the limited partnership. Administrative dissolution by the secretary of state is also possible if the limited partnership fails to pay fees and taxes due to the secretary of state or fails to deliver an annual report to the secretary.

When a limited partnership dissolves, winding up of its business follows automatically. The general partners have the power to wind up the business. Dissociated general partners have no right to wind up.

If there is no remaining general partner, the limited partners may appoint a general partner to conduct the winding up. The limited partnership is bound by the acts of a general partner that are appropriate to winding up, such as selling assets of the business and completing contracts. No new business should be conducted by the winding-up general partners.

After dissolution, a general partner has no express or implied authority to continue the business, except as necessary to liquidation. The general partners may have apparent authority to continue business in the usual way, however, and therefore bind the limited partnership. To avoid liability for the act of a general partner outside the scope of winding up, the limited partnership should give notice of its dissolution to all parties. One way to give notice is by filing a certificate of dissolution, which is effective against everyone after 90 days.

Distribution of Assets After the general partners have liquidated the assets of the limited partnership, the proceeds are distributed to those having claims against the limited partnership. First paid are creditors, which may include partners who, for example, have sold goods or made loans to the limited partnership.

If the proceeds from the sale of limited partnership assets exceed creditors' claims, the remainder is paid to the partners in the same proportions that they share distributions. This modifies the RULPA rule that repaid partners' capital contributions prior to distributing the remainder according to how partners share distributions. The ULPA rule may result in a wealth transfer from partners who have disproportionately larger contributions than their shares of distributions to partners who have disproportionately larger shares of distributions in relation to their capital contributions. If this is unacceptable, the partners may modify the ULPA rule in the limited partnership agreement, such as by requiring a return of capital contributions before distributing the remaining proceeds in the manner that partners share profits.

If a limited partnership's assets are insufficient to pay a creditor's claim, the persons who were general partners when the obligation was incurred must contribute cash to allow the limited partnership to pay the obligation. The general partners contribute in the same proportions that they shared distributions (considering only distributions to general partners) when the obligation was incurred.

In an LLLP, general partners are not required to contribute additional cash when the LLLP's assets are insufficient to pay creditors' claims, because the liability of general partners in an LLLP is limited to their capital contributions.

Mergers and Conversions

The ULPA and the RULLCA permit limited partnerships and LLCs to merge with other businesses, including other limited partnerships, LLCs, and corporations. All partners of a limited partnership and all members of an LLC must consent to the plan of **merger.**

In addition, those statutes also permit a limited partnership or an LLC to convert easily into another business form. For example, some limited partnerships will want to become LLCs in order to enjoy all the limited liability advantages of the LLC. By executing a plan of **conversion** to an LLC, the partners can change the form of business without the more expensive and time-consuming process of forming a new business to take over the old business and then dissolving the old one. All the owners need to do is adopt a plan of conversion to which all partners consent.

In the following *Lach* case, the court held that the general partners were not required to comply with the requirements for conversion, because a new LLC was formed and the limited partnership dissolved. However, the court found that the general partners breached their fiduciary duty by transferring the assets of the limited partnership to the LLC without the consent of a limited partner.

Lach v. Man O'War, LLC	256 S.W. 3d 563 (Ky. S. Ct. 2008)

In 1986, Shirley Lach and her then husband, Lynwood Wiseman, formed Man O'War Limited Partnership for the purpose of leasing real property and developing and operating shopping centers. Robert Miller became a general partner along with Wiseman. Lach was one of eight limited partners. The partners' ownership percentages were Miller, 1 percent, Wiseman, 32 percent, Lach, 27 percent, Jonathan Miller, 9 percent, Harry B. Miller, 12 percent, Harvey Morgan, 1 percent, Penny Miller, 3 percent, Jeffery Mullens, 1 percent, Jennifer Miller, 9 percent, and Sophie Wiseman, 5 percent. Wiseman, Lach, and Robert Miller also formed M.O.W. Place, Ltd., to lease a shopping center from the joint venture. In 1988, Wiseman and Lach were divorced, but continued in business together.

In the spring of 2002, Robert Miller became ill with cancer. With his approaching death, he met with Lach concerning the shopping center. Miller asked Lach to agree to naming Wiseman, Jeffery Mullens (brother-in-law of Robert Miller), and Jonathan Miller (son of Robert Miller), as the new general partners of the Partnership. Under the original Partnership agreement, new general partners could not be added without the consent of all the partners. Robert Miller also asked Lach to agree that when Wiseman died, the two remaining general partners will select a new general partner. Lach objected because it would allow the Miller family, which owned less than Lach's individual interest, to manage and control the shopping center. The Millers' would have two of the three general partners while Wiseman, who was then of advancing age, was alive. Upon his death, Jonathan Miller and Jeffery Mullens would then select the third general partner. Lach proposed substituting her daughter, Sherri McVay, an attorney, as a general partner in place of Jeffery Mullens. Her proposal was rejected.

Miller and Wiseman then sought to restructure the business form of the partnership to eliminate the need for Lach's consent to the proposed management change. They formed a new business entity, Man O'War Limited Liability Company. When operational, the LLC would be manager-managed and controlled only by a majority vote of the owners. The initial managers were to be Wiseman, Jonathan Miller, and Jeffery Mullens.

After forming the LLC, Robert Miller and Wiseman dissolved the Partnership, distributing its assets (the ownership of the LLC) to the partners in identical proportions to their previous ownership of the Partnership, that is—with one catch. Unless a partner signed the documents validating the restructuring, that partner would have no voting rights in the LLC. All the partners except Lach signed the agreement, leaving only Lach without any voting rights.

Lach then sued the LLC and Wiseman, among others. She asked the court to set aside the transfer of Partnership assets to the LLC on the grounds that the transfer and the Partnership's subsequent termination was a violation of KRS 362.490 and a breach by the general partners of their fiduciary duty to the Partnership and Lach. The trial court found for the LLC and Wiseman, granting them summary judgment. The Kentucky appellate court affirmed the trial court's decision. Lach appealed to the Supreme Court of Kentucky.

Scott, Justice

Lach argues that the restructuring of the Partnership business form was invalid without her consent for two reasons: (1) the restructuring was a conversion in violation of KRS 275.370, and (2) the restructuring made it impossible for the Partnership to carry on its business in violation of KRS 362.490.

KRS 275.370 provides, in pertinent part:

(1) A partnership or limited partnership may be converted to a limited liability company pursuant to this section.
(2) The terms and conditions of a conversion of a partnership or limited partnership to a limited liability company shall, in the case of a partnership, be approved by all the partners or by a number or percentage specified for conversion in the partnership agreement or, in the case of a limited partnership, by all the partners, notwithstanding any provision to the contrary in the limited partnership agreement.

While conceding that the statute, in this instance, requires the approval of all the limited partners before a limited partnership can be converted into a limited liability company, the LLC and Wiseman argue that the transformation constituted a "reorganization," not a "conversion" as envisioned under KRS 275.370(1). They illustrate their distinction of the word "conversion," by pointing out that the statute envisions a limited partnership *redesignating itself* as a limited liability company, whereas, in this instance, the limited liability company was created separately and existed concurrently with the Partnership (albeit without any assets). Thus, the fact that the LLC acquired all the assets of the Partnership and the Partnership then dissolved is simply immaterial.

KRS 275.375(1) acknowledges that "[a] partnership or limited partnership that has been converted pursuant to this chapter shall be for all purposes the same entity that existed before the conversion." KRS 275.375(2) recognizes that the property " *shall remain* vested in the converted [business entity] . . . [and] [a]ll obligations of the converting . . . limited partnership *shall continue* as obligations of the converted [business entity]." (Emphasis added.) All of which seem to confirm the LLC and Wiseman's argument that a "conversion" involves only one entity changing its legal form pursuant to statutory authorizations, rather than through interaction between *two* entities.

Looking at subsequent statutes for what light they cast on the question, we note that the Kentucky Legislature adopted the *new* Kentucky Uniform Limited Partnership Act in 2006. KRS 362.2-102, et. seq. This Act was adopted, with some changes, from the Uniform Limited Partnership Act (2001). The Act specifically provides "[i]n applying and construing this uniform act, consideration shall be given to the need to promote uniformity of the law with respect to its subject matter among states that enact it." KRS 362.2-1201.

When the need for uniformity is acknowledged, courts may consider the "Official Comments" to a Uniform Act, even where they have not been officially adopted. Looking at the Official Comments to §1102 of the Uniform Limited Partnership Act, which, with changes, corresponds to KRS 362.2-1102, the Comment acknowledges, "[i]n contrast to a merger, which involves at least two entities, a conversion involves only one. The converting and converted organizations are the same entity." Unif. Limited Partnership Act §1102–1105, GA U.L.A. 107 (2006).

Having thus considered the statutory scheme, its particular language, the subsequent statute and Official Comments, we answer the question that was presented to us—that the restructuring of the business form of the Partnership, to that of the LLC, in this instance, was not a conversion under, or subject to, KRS 275.370, for reasons that a conversion deals only with one entity. We have not been asked, nor have we considered, whether the restructuring of the Partnership into the LLC constituted a merger, pursuant to KRS 362.531.

Under Kentucky law, partners owe the utmost good faith to each and every other partner. The scope of the fiduciary duty has been variously defined as one requiring utter good faith or honesty, loyalty or obedience, as well as candor, due care, and fair dealing. Indeed, it has often been said, there is no relation of trust or confidence known to law that requires of the parties a higher degree of good faith than that of a partnership. Thus, the doing of an act proscribed by law is a breach of that duty.

KRS 362.490 provides, in pertinent part:

A general partner shall have all the rights and powers and be subject to all the restrictions and liabilities of a partner in a partnership without limited partners, except that without the written consent or ratification of the specific act by all the

limited partners, a general partner or all the general partners have no authority to

* * *

(2) do any act which would make it impossible to carry on the ordinary business of the partnership.

The LCC and Wiseman argue that Miller and Wiseman had the authority to perform all the acts constituting the restructuring without Lach's consent because they did not make it impossible to carry on the business of the partnership. They assert, *it was the only act which made it possible* to carry on the business of the partnership; suggesting that Lach would, by virtue of her right of rejection, have destroyed the partnership's business, something she hadn't done for the previous sixteen years. Moreover, the fact that a limited partner with significant ownership interests in a limited partnership would object to a transaction which would deprive her of her say in who might be able to successfully manage her business interest as a general partner, in return for a minority voting, or for that fact, a non-voting interest, in a limited liability company controlled by a majority vote, is not evidence that such limited partner has an interest in destroying the business, including the value of her interest therein.

They further argue that under the certificate of partnership and partnership agreement, the general partners had the absolute right to "(1) terminate the partnership, (2) execute documents agreements, contracts, leases, etc., on behalf of the partnership, and (3) to manage the partnership business in all aspects, which should include, but should not be limited to . . . take such other action, execute and deliver such other documents, and perform such other acts as the general partners may deem necessary, appropriate, or incidental to carrying out the business and affairs of the partnership." In this regard, they seek to distinguish *Mist Properties, Inc. v. Fitzsimmons Realty Co.,* 228 N.Y.S.2d 406 (Sup. Ct. 1962), in which the court approved the general partner's transfer of title to property owned by the limited partnership as against the claim of the receiver, because the limited partnership agreement allowed the general partners to do so.

Mist Properties, Inc., however, had a partnership agreement that gave the general partners the specific power to sell all of the partnership's property, subject to written approval of sixty-five percent of the limited partners. "There clearly appears to have been no violation of the statute since the conveyance was not without the written consent of the limited partners but was specifically contemplated and provided for by the agreement." *Id.* at 410. As the court recognized therein, the agreement the partners had made with themselves through their partnership agreement controlled. "There is no intervening public policy which prevents persons dealing at arm's length from entering into an agreement such as set forth above. It has been repeatedly held that where a limited partnership agreement has been entered into the partners cannot, *inter se,* set up that their rights are not governed thereby...." *Id.* at 410.

Simply put, we find that the general partners' rights under the partnership agreement to (1) terminate the partnership at any time upon agreement of the general partners, and (2) to act upon behalf of the Partnership in matters that are "necessary, appropriate, or incidental to carry out its business," can be not construed to allow them the power to transform the partnership into a limited liability company, in order to favor a majority of

the partners in their selection, or substitution, of the general partners/managers of the business, without the approval of all the limited partners.

We therefore conclude that the transfer of the partnership assets to the LLC was in violation of KRS 362.490 and thus a breach of the general partners' fiduciary duty to the non-consenting limited partner.

Judgment reversed in favor of Lach.

The Global Business Environment

Limited Partnerships in Other Countries

All modern commercial countries permit the creation of limited partnerships, but almost none allow the creation of LLLPs. England and its former colonies, including the United States, Canada, Singapore, and Australia, use the term *limited partnership.* In Italy, the limited partnership form is named *Societa in accomandita semplic*e (S.a.s.); in Latin American countries, the *Sociedad en comandita;* in Austria the *Kommanditgesellschaft* (Kg).

These business forms are mostly identical to American limited partnerships, having general partners who manage the business and possess unlimited liability and limited partners who may not manage and are granted limited liability. Most countries also permit the partners to restrict the transfer of a partner's interest and usually provide for the continuation of the business despite the death of a limited partner.

Ethics in Action

You now know the characteristics and default rules of LLCs, limited partnerships, and LLLPs. If you are a profit maximizer, which one of these forms would you find less desirable than the others? The answer is that the limited partnership is less desirable, because a limited partnership, LLLP, and LLC may have the same tax and management benefits, yet only the LLLP and LLC extend limited liability to all the owners. General partners in a limited partnership have unlimited liability for the limited partnership's obligations. Therefore, you reduce your risk and increase your return relative to risk by choosing the LLLP or LLC.

If you believe in utilitarianism, rights theory, or justice theory, does the distinction between limited partnerships and LLLPs and LLCs make sense to you? Why grant limited liability only to owners who know enough to create an LLLP or LLC? Is the business of an LLLP or LLC more important to society than the business of a limited partnership merely because the managers in a limited partnership have failed to acquire limited liability status? Is it fair for the law to protect someone better than others merely because she is more knowledgeable about the law?

Problems and Problem Cases

1. Racing Investment Fund 2000 LLC was created in August 2000 to purchase, train, and race thoroughbred horses. The LLC's operating agreement provided for 50 membership units to be sold for an initial capital contribution of $100,000 per unit and

allowed the LLC manager on an as-needed basis to call for additional capital from the members in order to pay operating, administrative, or other business expenses. Subsequently, the LLC failed to pay for insurance services provided by Clay Ward Agency, Inc. Clay Ward sued the LLC and its members and asked the court to require the LLC manager to make a call for additional capital in order to pay the debt to Clay Ward. Did the court order the call?

2. Bonnie Strickland and her husband Jake formed the Strickland Family Limited Liability Company as part of their estate plan. They transferred 83 percent of the equity shares of the LLC to their daughter Suzy Strickland Harbison. The Stricklands retained a 17 percent interest in the LLC and acted as comanagers of the LLC for the next two years. When Jake died, Bonnie became the only manager of the LLC. In 2002, Bonnie conveyed three parcels of real property belonging to the LLC to her son David Strickland. David was not a member of the LLC. Bonnie transferred the parcels of real property for an amount Suzy believed was less than fair market value. Suzy sued Bonnie, claiming that Strickland had breached her fiduciary duty to the LLC under the Alabama Limited Liability Company Act and that she had violated the terms of the operating agreement when she failed to make managerial decisions based on the best interests of the LLC and the equity owners. Bonnie defended by referring to the LLC's operating agreement, which clearly stated that the LLC was not formed for profit purposes:

> The managers do not, in any way guarantee a profit for the Equity Owners from the operations of the Company. Decisions with respect to the conduct, dissolution and winding up of the business of the company shall be made in the sole discretion of the Equity Owners and such other matters as the Managers consider relevant. There shall be no obligation on the part of the Managers to maximize financial gain or to make any or all of the Company Property productive.

Has Bonnie breached her fiduciary duty?

3. In 1999, Andreas Halvorsen, David Ott, and Brian Olson formed a hedge fund, Viking Global Investors LLC. The LLC's written agreement provided that the three founders would operate Viking, and divide all of its profits annually. If any one of them left Viking, he would receive only his capital account balance and earned compensation that had accrued and not been paid. In August 2005, the LLC management committee terminated Olson's membership in the LLC because the returns on his portfolio of investments were disappointing. The LLC bought out Olson by returning the amount in his capital account and paying his 2005 compensation, which amounted to over $100 million. Olson sued the LLC and the other members alleging that subsequent to executing the written agreement, they had agreed orally to pay the fair market value of a member's interest upon

his leaving the LLC. He also argued that Delaware's LLC statute required payment of fair value. Did the court agree with Olson?

4. Nabil Gamez was a member of Rock Angus LLC, a member-managed LLC that bred and sold beef cattle. Gamez was the most active of the member-managers, negotiating contracts with breeders, feed-lots, and banks on behalf of the LLC. One contract obligated Rock Angus LLC to purchase two Angus bulls for $624,000 from Shirlynne Farms, Inc. The contract was signed by Gamez as general manager acting on behalf of Rock Angus. Rock Angus defaulted on the contract with Shirlynne Farms, which sued Rock Angus LLC and Gamez. Was Gamez personally liable on the contract with Shirlynne Farms?

5. Tim Everest and Quinn Rider formed an LLC for the purpose of investing and managing commercial real estate properties. Everest drafted articles of organization for the LLC and gave the articles to Rider, who read them briefly. Rider told Everest "Everything looks OK to me," and signed the agreement. Everest submitted the LLC articles to the secretary of state, who filed the articles. After the LLC was formed, Everest operated the LLC as if he were the primary manager, excluding Rider from most of the day-to-day investment and management decisions of the LLC. When Rider protested, Everett showed him the LLC's articles of organization, which clearly stated that the LLC was manager-managed, with Everest listed as the sole manager. Rider argued that as a member of the LLC, he had the inherent right to manage the LLC. Was Rider correct?

6. Harlan Nesbitt was a member of Oak Creek Golf LLC, a limited liability company that owned and operated a golf course. Nesbitt wanted to dissociate from the LLC, but neither the LLC nor any other LLC member was willing to purchase his LLC interest. Nesbitt gave his LLC interest to his daughter, Eliza Portraro, and he notified the LLC that he was withdrawing from the LLC. Portraro sought to assert rights as a member of the LLC, including voting on matters submitted to LLC members, demanding a share of LLC profits, and inspecting the financial records of the LLC. The LLC operating agreement was silent on whether a transferee of a member's interest had those rights. Did Portraro have those rights?

7. Judith Carpenter was an experienced businesswoman and served on the board of directors of a bank. In 1984, Carpenter invested in Briargate Homes, a business that owned several condominiums. She believed

that Briargate was a limited partnership and that she was a limited partner. In fact, Briargate was a partnership and she was a general partner. No attempt had been made to comply with the North Carolina limited partnership statute. By 1987, Carpenter had possession of documents stating that Briargate was a partnership and she a partner. As an owner of condominiums, the partnership was liable to the condominium association for assessments for maintenance, repairs, and replacement of common areas in the complex. In 1988, the partnership failed to pay $85,000 in assessments. The partnership and its partners were sued by the condominium association. May Carpenter escape liability on the assessment because she thought she was a limited partner?

8. Virginia Partners, Ltd., a limited partnership organized in Florida, was in the business of drilling oil wells. When Virginia Partners injected acid into an oil well in Kentucky, a bystander, Robert Day, was injured by acid that sprayed on him from a ruptured hose. Virginia Partners had failed to register as a foreign limited partnership in Kentucky. Are the limited partners of Virginia Partners liable to Day for his injuries?

9. Brookside Realty, Ltd., was a limited partnership. In the limited partnership certificate filed with the secretary of state, four of its limited partners agreed to make capital contributions and be liable for future assessments in amounts ranging between $36,000 and $145,000. Brookside failed to pay for material Builders Steel sold to Brookside. Because the limited partners had not paid all the assessments required by the limited partnership certificate, Builders Steel claimed that it was entitled to require the limited partners to pay those assessments to the extent of the debt to Builders Steel. Did the court agree?

10. Blinder, Robinson & Co., as limited partner, and Combat Promotions, Inc., as general partner, created Combat Associates to promote an eight-round exhibition match between Muhammad Ali and Lyle Alzado, the pro football player. Combat Associates promised to pay Alzado $100,000 for his participation in the match.

Combat Promotions was owned entirely by Alzado, his accountant, and his professional agent. Alzado was

also vice president of Combat Promotions. Blinder, Robinson used its Denver office as a ticket outlet for the match, gave two parties to promote the match, and provided a meeting room for Combat Associates' meetings. Meyer Blinder, president of Blinder, Robinson, personally appeared on a TV talk show and gave TV interviews to promote the match.

Few tickets were sold, and the match was a financial debacle. Alzado received no payments for participating in the match. Alzado sued Blinder, Robinson claiming that since it acted like a general partner it had the liability of a general partner. The case was decided under the law of the RULPA. Was Blinder, Robinson liable to Alzado? Would Blinder, Robinson be liable to Alzado under the ULPA of 2001?

11. Virgina Mattson decides to form a limited partnership with herself as the sole general partner and with 10 friends and associates as the limited partners. She chooses the limited partnership form, because its default rules clearly grant sole management rights to her, the only general partner. Mattson is concerned, however, about having personal liability on contracts she signs on behalf of the limited partnership. What should she do to limit her personal liability for the obligations of the business to the amount of her capital contribution?

 Online Research

Your State and the RULLCA and the ULPA

Go to the website of the National Conference of Commissioners on Uniform State Laws.

- Check the legislative update to see whether your state has adopted the RULLCA and the ULPA.
- If your state has not adopted the RULLCA, find your state law for LLCs. Find the differences between the RULLCA and your state's LLC law.
- If your state has not adopted the ULPA, find the Revised Uniform Limited Partnership Act as amended in 1985. Note the differences between the RULPA and the ULPA of 2001, which are summarized in a table in the ULPA's Prefatory Note.

Corporations

Part Ten

Corporations

CHAPTER 41

HISTORY AND NATURE OF CORPORATIONS

You and three friends create an online retailer, which is incorporated in California under the name Gifts&Awards.com, Inc. The website will sell awards, clocks, desk sets, and other merchandise that businesses want as gifts for their clients and as promotional items for their employees. Physically, Gifts&Awards.com, Inc. will be located exclusively in San Jose, California. All its shareholders, employees, and assets will be in California. As an online retailer, however, Gifts&Awards.com's merchandise will be available to anyone anywhere in the world. Businesses worldwide will place orders through the website, which will be filled by the Gifts&Awards.com's staff. Gifts&Awards.com will ship about 20 percent of the merchandise ordered from a warehouse it leases in California. The other 80 percent will be shipped directly from the manufacturers or importers of the items. For that 80 percent, Gifts&Awards.com will take orders from customers and direct the orders to the appropriate manufacturers or importers, some of which will be in California but most of which will be dispersed throughout the United States.

You estimate that Gifts&Awards.com will have $4,000,000 in annual sales, $60,000 of which is to customers resident in Arizona. The goods will be delivered to customers by UPS, a third-party carrier whose fee will be added to the price of the goods. Some of the goods will be shipped from Gifts&Awards.com's warehouse in California, and some from manufacturers in other states, including Arizona. Consider the following questions regarding the State of Arizona's regulation of Gifts&Awards.com, Inc., a California corporation:

- May the State of Arizona require Gifts&Awards.com, Inc., to obtain a certificate of authority to do business in Arizona and collect a fee from Gifts&Awards.com for the privilege of doing business in the state?
- May the State of Arizona impose its state income tax on a portion of Gifts&Awards.com's worldwide income?
- May the State of Arizona require Gifts&Awards.com to collect the Arizona sales tax on sales to Arizona residents?
- If Gifts&Awards.com sells defective awards to a customer in Arizona, may the customer sue Gifts&Awards.com in an Arizona trial court? Will your answer affect Gifts&Awards.com policy on customers' returns and refunds?

LO LEARNING OBJECTIVES

After studying this chapter, you should be able to:

1 Discuss the history of the development of corporation law.

2 Recognize the types of corporations.

3 Understand the manner in which a state may regulate a foreign or alien corporation.

4 Prevent a court from piercing a corporation's veil.

THE MODERN CORPORATION HAS facilitated the rapid economic development of the last 200 years by permitting businesses to attain economies of scale. Businesses organized as corporations can attain such economies because they have a greater capacity to raise capital than do other business forms. This capital-raising advantage is ensured by corporation law, which allows persons to invest their money in a corporation and become owners without imposing unlimited liability or management responsibilities on themselves. Many people are willing to invest their savings in a large, risky business if they have limited liability and no management responsibilities. Far fewer are willing to invest in a partnership or other business form in which owners have unlimited liability and management duties.

 Discuss the history of the development of corporation law.

History of Corporations

Although modern corporation law emerged only in the last 200 years, ancestors of the modern corporation existed in the times of Hammurabi, ancient Greece, and the Roman Empire. As early as 1248 in France, privileges of incorporation were given to mercantile ventures to encourage investment for the benefit of society. In England, the corporate form was used extensively before the 16th century.

The famous British trading companies—such as the Massachusetts Bay Company—were the forerunners of the modern corporation. The British government gave these companies monopolies in trade and granted them powers to govern in the areas they colonized. They were permitted to operate as corporations because of the benefits they would confer on the British empire, such as the development of natural resources. Although these trading companies were among the few corporations of the time whose owners were granted limited liability, they sought corporate status primarily because the government granted them monopolies and governmental powers.

American Corporation Law Beginning in 1776, corporation law in the United States evolved independently of English corporation law. Early American corporations received **special charters** from state legislatures. These charters were granted one at a time by special action of the legislatures; few special charters were granted.

In the late 18th century, general incorporation statutes emerged in the United States. Initially, these statutes permitted incorporation only for limited purposes beneficial to the public, such as operating toll bridges and water systems. Incorporation was still viewed as a privilege, and many restrictions were placed on corporations: incorporation was permitted for only short periods of time; maximum limits on capitalization were low; ownership of real and personal property was often restricted.

During the last 150 years, such restrictive provisions have disappeared in most states. Today, modern incorporation statutes are mostly enabling, granting the persons who control a corporation great flexibility in establishing, financing, and operating it.

See Figure 1 for a summary of the characteristics of corporations.

 Recognize the types of corporations.

Classifications of Corporations

Corporations may be divided into three classes: (1) corporations **for profit,** (2) corporations **not for profit,** and (3) **government-owned** corporations. State and federal corporation statutes establish procedures for the incorporation of each of these classes and for their operation. In addition, a large body of common law applies to all corporations.

Most business corporations are **for-profit corporations.** For-profit corporations issue stock to their shareholders, who invest in the corporation with the expectation that they will earn a profit on their investment. That profit may take the form of dividends paid by the corporation or increased market value of their shares.

Nearly all for-profit corporations are incorporated under the **general incorporation law** of a state. All of the states require professionals who wish to incorporate, such as physicians, dentists, lawyers, and accountants, to incorporate under **professional corporation acts.** In addition, for-profit corporations that especially affect the public interest, such as banks, insurance companies, and savings and loan associations, are usually required to incorporate under special statutes.

For-profit corporations range from huge international organizations such as General Electric Company to small, one-owner businesses. GE is an example of a **publicly held corporation** because its shares are generally available to public investors. The publicly held corporation tends to be managed by professional managers who own small percentages of the corporation. Nearly all the shareholders of the typical publicly held corporation are merely investors who are not concerned in the management of the corporation.

Figure 1   *Principal Characteristics of Corporations*

1. *Creation.* A corporation may be created only by *permission of a government.*

2. *Legal status.* A corporation is a legal person and a legal entity independent of its owners (*shareholders*) and its managers (officers and the *board of directors*). Its life is unaffected by the retirement or death of its shareholders, officers, and directors. A corporation is a person under the Constitution of the United States.

3. *Powers.* A corporation may *acquire, hold, and convey property* in its own name. A corporation may *sue and be sued* in its own name. Harm to a corporation is not harm to the shareholders; therefore, with few exceptions, a shareholder may not sue to enforce a claim of the corporation.

4. *Management.* Shareholders elect a board of directors, which manages the corporation. The board of directors may delegate management duties to officers. A shareholder has *no right or duty to manage* the business of a corporation, unless he is elected to the board of directors or is appointed an officer. The directors and officers need not be shareholders.

5. *Owners' liability.* The shareholders have *limited liability.* With few exceptions, they are not liable for the debts of a corporation after they have paid their promised capital contributions to the corporation.

6. *Transferability of owner's interest.* Generally, the ownership interest in a corporation is *freely transferable.* A shareholder may sell her shares to whomever she wants whenever she wants. The purchaser becomes a shareholder with the same rights that the seller had.

7. *Taxation.* Usually, a corporation pays *federal income taxes* on its income. Shareholders have personal income from the corporation only when the corporation makes a distribution of its income to them. For example, a shareholder would have personal income from the corporation when the corporation pays him a dividend. This creates a *double-taxation* possibility: The corporation pays income tax on its profits, and when the corporation distributes the after-tax profits as dividends, the shareholders pay tax on the dividends.

Corporations with very few shareholders whose shares are not available to the general public are called **close corporations.** In the typical close corporation, the controlling shareholders are the only managers of the business.

Usually, close corporations and publicly held corporations are subject to the same rules under state corporation law. Many states, however, allow close corporations greater latitude in the operation of their internal affairs than is granted to public corporations. For example, the shareholders of a close corporation may be permitted to dispense with the board of directors and manage the close corporation as if it were a partnership.

A Subchapter S corporation, or **S corporation,** is a special type of close corporation. It is treated nearly like a partnership for federal income tax purposes. Its shareholders report the earnings or losses of the business on their individual federal income tax returns. This means that an S corporation's profits are taxed only once—at the shareholder level, eliminating the double-taxation penalty of incorporation. All shareholders must consent to an S corporation election. The Internal Revenue Code requires an S corporation to have only one class of shares and 100 or fewer shareholders. Shareholders may be only individuals or trusts.

Not-for-profit corporations do not issue stock and do not expect to make a profit. Instead, they provide services to their members under a plan that eliminates any profit motive. These corporations have **members** rather than shareholders, and none of the surplus revenue from their operations may be distributed to their members. Since they generally pay no income tax, nonprofit corporations can reinvest a larger share of their incomes in the business than can for-profit corporations. Examples of nonprofit corporations are charities, churches, fraternal organizations, community arts councils, cooperative grocery stores, and cooperative farmers' feed and supplies stores.

Some corporations are owned by governments and perform governmental and business functions. A municipality (city) is one type of **government-owned corporation.** Other types are created to furnish more specific services—for example, school corporations and water companies. Others—such as the Tennessee Valley Authority and the Federal Deposit Insurance Corporation—operate much like for-profit corporations except that at least some of their directors are appointed by governmental officials, and some or all of their financing frequently comes from government. The TVA and the FDIC are chartered by Congress, but government-owned corporations may also be authorized by states. Government-operated businesses seek corporate status to free themselves from governmental operating procedures, which are more cumbersome than business operating procedures.

Regulation of For-Profit Corporations

To become a corporation, a business must **incorporate** by complying with an incorporation statute. Incorporation is a fairly simple process usually requiring little more than paying a fee and filing a document with a designated government official—usually the secretary of state of the state of incorporation. Incorporation of for-profit businesses has been entrusted primarily to the governments of the 50 states.

State Incorporation Statutes State incorporation statutes set out the basic rules regarding the relationship between the corporation, its shareholders, and its managers. For example, an incorporation statute sets the requirements for a business to incorporate, the procedures for shareholders' election of directors, and the duties directors and officers owe to the corporation. Although a corporation may do business in several states, usually the relationship between the corporation, its shareholders, and its managers is regulated only by the state of incorporation.

The American Bar Association's Committee on Corporate Laws has prepared a *model* statute for adoption by state legislatures. The purpose of the model statute is to improve the rationality of corporation law. It is called the **Model Business Corporation Act (MBCA).** Its last major revision was in 2002.

The revised MBCA is the basis of corporation law in most states. Your study of statutory corporation law in this book concentrates on the revised MBCA. Delaware and several major commercial and industrial states such as New York and California do not follow the MBCA. Therefore, selected provisions of the Delaware and other acts will be addressed.

Several states have special provisions or statutes that are applicable only to close corporations. The ABA's Committee on Corporate Laws has adopted the *Statutory Close Corporation Supplement to the Model Business Corporation Act.* The Supplement is designed to provide a rational, statutory solution to the special problems facing close corporations.

LOG ON

Go to
http://delcode.delaware.gov/title8/c001/index.shtml
You can view the Delaware General Corporation Law at the State of Delaware website.

State Common Law of Corporations

Although nearly all of corporation law is statutory law, including the courts' interpretation of the statutes, there is a substantial body of common law of corporations (judge-made law). Most of this common law deals with creditor and shareholder rights. For example, the law of piercing the corporate veil, which you will study later in this chapter, is common law protecting creditors of corporations.

Regulation of Nonprofit Corporations

Nonprofit corporations are regulated primarily by the states. Nonprofit corporations may be created only by complying with a nonprofit incorporation statute. Incorporation under state law requires delivering articles of incorporation to the secretary of state. The existence of a nonprofit corporation begins when the secretary of state files the articles. Most states have statutes based on the revised **Model Nonprofit Corporation Act (MNCA).** Because of constitutional protection of freedom of religion, many states have special statutes regulating nonprofit religious organizations.

The law applied to nonprofit corporations is substantially similar to for-profit corporation law. At various points in the corporations chapters of this book, you will study the law of nonprofit corporations and examine how this form of business and its laws differ from the for-profit corporation and its laws. The Model Nonprofit Corporation Act will be the basis of your study of nonprofit corporation law.

The Global Business Environment

Corporations around the Globe

The corporate form of business is recognized throughout the world, and, regardless of the country, the form has essentially the same characteristics: limited liability for its owners, free transferability of shares, and separation of management from ownership. In Italy, the name is *Societa per azioni.*

In Zimbabwe and England, corporations are called limited companies. In Germany, the term is *Aktiengesellschaft* (AG). In Brazil, the name is *sociedade anonima.* You can learn a lot about Canadian corporations at www.ic.gc.ca/eic/site/cd-dgc.nsf/eng/home. This site has links to federal, provincial, and territorial websites that facilitate the incorporation process.

LO3 Understand the manner in which a state may regulate a foreign or alien corporation.

Regulation of Foreign and Alien Corporations

A corporation may be incorporated in one state yet do business in many other states in which it is not incorporated. The corporation's contacts with other persons in those states may permit the states to regulate the corporation's transactions with their citizens, to subject the corporation to suits in their courts, or to tax the corporation. The circumstances under which states may impose their laws on a business incorporated in another state is determined by the law of foreign corporations.

A corporation is a **domestic corporation** in the state that has granted its charter; it is a **foreign corporation** in all the other states in which it does business. For example, a corporation organized in Delaware and doing business in Florida is domestic in Delaware and foreign in Florida. Note that a corporation domiciled in one country is an **alien corporation** in other countries in which it does business. Many of the rules that apply to foreign corporations apply as well to alien corporations.

Generally, a state may impose its laws on a foreign corporation if such imposition does not violate the Constitution of the United States, notably the Due Process Clause of the Fourteenth Amendment and the Commerce Clause. The law discussed here also applies to foreign partnerships, LLPs, LLCs, limited partnerships, and LLLPs, forms of business discussed in Chapters 37–40.

Due Process Clause

The Due Process Clause requires that a foreign corporation have sufficient contacts with a state before a state may exercise jurisdiction over the corporation. The leading case in this area is the *International Shoe* case.[1] In that case, the Supreme Court ruled that a foreign corporation must have "certain minimum contacts" with the state such that asserting jurisdiction over the corporation does not offend "traditional notions of fair play and substantial justice." The Supreme Court justified its holding with a **benefit theory:** When a foreign corporation avails itself of the protection of a state's laws, it should suffer any reasonable burden that the state imposes as a consequence of such benefit. In other words, a foreign corporation should be required to pay for the benefits that it receives from the state.

---

[1] *International Shoe Co. v. State of Washington,* 326 U.S. 310 (1945).

Commerce Clause

Under the Commerce Clause, the power to regulate interstate commerce is given to the federal government. The states have no power to exclude or to discriminate against foreign corporations that are engaged solely in *interstate* commerce. Nevertheless, a state may require a foreign corporation doing interstate business in the state to comply with its laws if the application of these laws does not unduly burden interstate commerce. When a foreign corporation enters interstate commerce to do *intrastate* business in a state, the state may regulate the corporation's activities, provided again that the regulation does not unduly burden interstate commerce.

A state law regulating the activities of a foreign corporation does not unduly burden interstate commerce if (1) the law serves a legitimate state interest, (2) the state has chosen the least burdensome means of promoting that interest, and (3) that legitimate state interest outweighs the statute's burden on interstate commerce. Because conducting intrastate business increases a corporation's contact with a state, it is easier to prove that the state has a legitimate interest and that there is no undue burden on interstate commerce when the state regulates a corporation that is conducting intrastate business.

Doing Business   To aid their determination of whether a state may constitutionally impose its laws on a foreign corporation, courts have traditionally used the concept of **doing business.** Courts have generally held that a foreign corporation is subject to the laws of a state when it is doing business in the state. The activities that constitute doing business differ, however, depending on the purpose of the determination. There are four such purposes: (1) to determine whether a corporation is subject to a lawsuit in a state's courts, (2) to determine whether the corporation's activities are subject to taxation, (3) to determine whether the corporation must qualify to carry on its activities in the state, and (4) to determine whether the state may regulate the internal affairs of the corporation.

Subjecting Foreign Corporations to Suit

The Supreme Court of the United States has held that a foreign corporation may be brought into a state's court in connection with its activities within the state, provided that the state does not violate the corporation's due process rights under the Fourteenth Amendment of the Constitution and its rights under the Commerce Clause.

The *International Shoe* minimum contacts test must be met. Subjecting the corporation to suit cannot offend "traditional notions of fair play and substantial justice." A court must weigh the corporation's contacts within the state against the inconvenience to the corporation of requiring it to defend a suit within the state. The burden on the corporation must be reasonable in relation to the benefit that it receives from conducting activities in the state.

Under the minimum contacts test, even an isolated event may be sufficient to confer jurisdiction on a state's courts. For example, driving a truck from Arizona through New Mexico toward a final destination in Florida provides sufficient contacts with New Mexico to permit a suit in New Mexico's courts against the foreign corporation for its driver's negligently causing an accident within New Mexico.

Most of the states have passed **long-arm statutes** to permit their courts to exercise jurisdiction under the decision of the *International Shoe* case. These statutes frequently specify several kinds of corporate activities that make foreign corporations subject to suit within the state, such as the commission of a tort, the making of a contract, or the ownership of property. Most of the long-arm statutes grant jurisdiction over causes of action growing out of any transaction within the state. Later in this chapter, the court in *Ryan v. Cerullo* looks at Connecticut's long-arm statute.

In the following Global Business Environment box, the court considered whether the Turkish, French, and Luxembourgian subsidiaries of an American corporation may be sued in a North Carolina court. Note that the same law applies to both foreign and alien corporations.

The Global Business Environment

Goodyear Dunlop Tires Operations, S.A. v. Brown, 131 S. Ct. 2846 (2011)

On April 18, 2004, two 13-year-old soccer players from North Carolina, Julian Brown and Matthew Helms, were on a bus headed to Charles de Gaulle Airport in Paris, France, beginning their journey home from a soccer trip. When the bus overturned on a road outside Paris, the boys received fatal injuries. As administrators of the boys' estates, the boys' parents filed a suit for wrongful-death damages in a superior court in North Carolina. Attributing the accident to a tire that failed when its plies separated, the parents alleged negligence in the design, construction, testing, and inspection of the tire. The tire was manufactured at a Turkish plant owned by a Turkish subsidiary of The Goodyear Tire and Rubber Company (Goodyear USA). The parents sued Goodyear USA, an Ohio corporation, and three of its subsidiaries, organized and operating in Turkey, France, and Luxembourg. Goodyear USA, which had plants in North Carolina and regularly engaged in commercial activity there, did not contest the North Carolina court's jurisdiction over it. Goodyear USA's foreign subsidiaries, however, maintained that North Carolina lacked jurisdiction over them. The subsidiaries had no place of business, employees, or bank accounts in North Carolina. They did not design, manufacture, or advertise their products in North Carolina. They did not solicit business in North Carolina or sell or ship tires to North Carolina customers. A small percentage of the tires sold by the subsidiaries (tens of thousands out of tens of millions manufactured between 2004 and 2007) were distributed within North Carolina by other Goodyear USA affiliates. These tires were typically custom ordered to equip specialized vehicles such as cement mixers, waste haulers, and boat and horse trailers. The type of tire involved in the accident, a Goodyear Regional RHS tire manufactured by Goodyear Turkey, was never distributed in North Carolina.

The superior court found that North Carolina's court had jurisdiction over Goodyear USA's foreign subsidiaries, and the North Carolina Court of Appeals affirmed. After the North Carolina Supreme Court declined to review the case, the Supreme Court of the United States granted certiorari.

Ginsberg, Justice The Due Process Clause of the Fourteenth Amendment sets the outer boundaries of a state tribunal's authority to proceed against a defendant. The canonical opinion in this area remains *International Shoe Co. v. Washington*, 326 U.S. 310 (1945), in which we held that a State may authorize its courts to exercise personal jurisdiction over an out-of-state defendant if the defendant has "certain minimum contacts with [the State] such that the maintenance of the suit does not offend traditional notions of fair play and substantial justice." *Id.*, at 316.

Endeavoring to give specific content to the "fair play and substantial justice" concept, the Court in *International Shoe* classified cases involving out-of-state corporate defendants. First, as in *International Shoe* itself, jurisdiction unquestionably could be asserted where the corporation's in-state activity is "continuous and systematic" and that activity gave rise to the episode-in-suit. Further, the Court observed, the commission of certain "single or occasional acts" in a State may be sufficient to render a corporation answerable in that State with respect to those acts, though not with respect to matters unrelated to the forum connections. The heading courts today use to encompass these two *International Shoe* categories is "specific jurisdiction." Adjudicatory authority is "specific" when the suit arises out of or relates to the defendant's contacts with the forum.

International Shoe distinguished from cases that fit within the "specific jurisdiction" categories, instances in which the continuous corporate operations within a state are so substantial and of such a nature as to justify suit against it on causes of action arising from dealings entirely distinct from those activities. Adjudicatory authority so grounded is today called "general jurisdiction." For an individual, the paradigm forum for the exercise of general jurisdiction is the individual's domicile; for a corporation, it is an equivalent place, one in which the corporation is fairly regarded as at home.

Since *International Shoe*, this Court's decisions have elaborated primarily on circumstances that warrant the exercise of specific jurisdiction, particularly in cases involving "single or occasional acts" occurring or having their impact within the forum State. As a rule in these cases, this Court has inquired whether there was some act by which the defendant purposefully availed itself of the privilege of conducting activities within the forum State, thus invoking the benefits and protections of its laws. See, e.g., *World-Wide Volkswagen Corp. v. Woodson*, 444 U.S. 286 (1980) (Oklahoma court may not exercise personal jurisdiction "over a nonresident automobile retailer and its wholesale distributor in a products-liability action, when the defendants' only connection with Oklahoma is the fact that an automobile sold in New York to New York residents became involved in an accident in Oklahoma"); *Burger King Corp. v. Rudzewicz*, 471 U.S. 462 (1985) (franchisor headquartered in Florida may maintain breach-of-contract action in Florida against Michigan franchisees, where agreement contemplated on-going interactions between franchisees and franchisor's headquarters).

In only two decisions postdating *International Shoe* has this Court considered whether an out-of-state corporate defendant's in-state contacts were sufficiently "continuous and systematic" to justify the exercise of general jurisdiction over claims unrelated to those contacts: *Perkins v. Benguet Consol. Mining Co.*, 342 U.S. 437 (1952) (general jurisdiction appropriately exercised over Philippine corporation sued in Ohio, where the company's affairs were overseen during World War II); and *Helicopteros Nacionales de Colombia, S.A. v. Hall*, 466 U.S. 408 (1984) (helicopter owned by Colombian corporation crashed in Peru; survivors of U.S. citizens who died in the crash, the Court held, could not maintain wrongful-death actions against the Colombian corporation in Texas, for the corporation's helicopter purchases and purchase-linked activity in Texas were insufficient to subject it to Texas court's general jurisdiction).

To justify the exercise of general jurisdiction over petitioners, the North Carolina courts relied on the petitioners' placement of their tires in the "stream of commerce." The stream-of-commerce metaphor has been invoked frequently in lower court decisions permitting jurisdiction in products liability cases in which the product has traveled through an extensive chain of distribution before reaching the ultimate consumer. Typically, in such cases, a nonresident defendant, acting outside the forum, places in the stream of commerce a product that ultimately causes harm inside the forum.

The North Carolina court's stream-of-commerce analysis elided the essential difference between case-specific and all-purpose (general) jurisdiction. Flow of a manufacturer's products into the forum, we have explained, may bolster an affiliation germane to specific jurisdiction. See, e.g., *World-Wide Volkswagen*, 444 U.S. 286, at 297 (where "the sale of a product . . . is not simply an isolated occurrence, but arises from the efforts of the manufacturer or distributor to serve . . . the market for its product in [several] States, it is not unreasonable to subject it to suit in one of those States if its allegedly defective merchandise has there been the source of injury to its owner or to others"). But ties serving to bolster the exercise of specific jurisdiction do not warrant a determination that, based on those ties, the forum has general jurisdiction over a defendant.

A corporation's continuous activity of some sorts within a state, *International Shoe* instructed, is not enough to support the demand that the corporation be amenable to suits unrelated to

that activity. Our 1952 decision in *Perkins v. Benguet Consol. Mining Co.* remains the textbook case of general jurisdiction appropriately exercised over a foreign corporation that has not consented to suit in the forum.

Sued in Ohio, the defendant in *Perkins* was a Philippine mining corporation that had ceased activities in the Philippines during World War II. To the extent that the company was conducting any business during and immediately after the Japanese occupation of the Philippines, it was doing so in Ohio: the corporation's president maintained his office there, kept the company files in that office, and supervised from the Ohio office the necessarily limited wartime activities of the company. Although the claim-in-suit did not arise in Ohio, this Court ruled that it would not violate due process for Ohio to adjudicate the controversy.

We next addressed the exercise of general jurisdiction over an out-of-state corporation over three decades later, in *Helicopteros*. In that case, survivors of United States citizens who died in a helicopter crash in Peru instituted wrongful-death actions in a Texas state court against the owner and operator of the helicopter, a Colombian corporation. The Colombian corporation had no place of business in Texas and was not licensed to do business there. Basically, the company's contacts with Texas consisted of sending its chief executive officer to Houston for a contract-negotiation session; accepting into its New York bank account checks drawn on a Houston bank; purchasing helicopters, equipment, and training services from a Texas enterprise for substantial sums; and sending personnel to Texas for training. These links to Texas, we determined, did not constitute the kind of continuous and systematic general business contacts found to exist in *Perkins*, and were insufficient to support the exercise of jurisdiction over a claim that neither arose out of nor related to the defendant's activities in Texas.

Helicopteros concluded that mere purchases made in the forum State, even if occurring at regular intervals, are not enough to warrant a State's assertion of general jurisdiction over a nonresident corporation in a cause of action not related to those purchase transactions. We see no reason to differentiate from the ties to Texas held insufficient in *Helicopteros*, the sales of petitioners' tires sporadically made in North Carolina through intermediaries. Under the sprawling view of general jurisdiction urged by respondents and embraced by the North Carolina Court of Appeals, any substantial manufacturer or seller of goods would be amenable to suit, on any claim for relief, wherever its products are distributed.

Measured against *Helicopteros* and *Perkins*, North Carolina is not a forum in which it would be permissible to subject petitioners to general jurisdiction. Unlike the defendant in *Perkins*, whose sole wartime business activity was conducted in Ohio, petitioners are in no sense at home in North Carolina. Their attenuated connections to the State fall far short of the "the continuous and systematic general business contacts" necessary to empower North Carolina to entertain suit against them on claims unrelated to anything that connects them to the State.

Judgment reversed in favor of Goodyear USA's foreign subsidiaries.

Taxation A state may tax a foreign corporation if such taxation does not violate the Due Process Clause or the Commerce Clause. Generally, a state's imposition of a tax must serve a legitimate state interest and be reasonable in relation to a foreign corporation's contacts with the state. For example, a North Carolina corporation's property located in Pennsylvania is subject to property tax in Pennsylvania. The corporation enjoys Pennsylvania's protection of private property. It may be required to pay its share of the cost of such protection.

Greater contacts are needed to subject a corporation to state income and sales taxation in a state than are needed to subject it to property taxation. A state tax does not violate the commerce clause when the tax (1) is applied to an activity with a substantial connection with the taxing state, (2) is fairly apportioned, (3) does not discriminate against interstate commerce, and (4) is fairly related to the services provided by the state.[2]

For example, New Jersey has been permitted to tax a portion of the entire net income of a corporation for the privilege of doing business, employing or owning capital or property, or maintaining an office in New Jersey when the portion of entire net income taxed is determined by an average of three ratios: in-state property to total property, in-state to total receipts, and in-state to total wages, salaries, and other employee compensation.[3] However, Pennsylvania could not assess a flat tax on the operation of all trucks on Pennsylvania highways. The flat tax imposed a disproportionate burden on interstate trucks as compared with intrastate trucks because interstate trucks traveled fewer miles per year on Pennsylvania

---

[2]*Complete Auto Transit, Inc. v. Brady,* 430 U.S. 274 (1977).

[3]*Amerada Hess Corp. v. Director of Taxation,* 490 U.S. 66 (1989).

highways.[4] Nonetheless, the Supreme Court upheld a $100 fee levied by the state of Michigan on all trucks, whether or not owned by in-state or out-of-state companies, that made point-to-point hauls between Michigan cities, on the grounds that the fee taxed purely local activity and did not tax an interstate truck's entry into Michigan or transactions spanning multiple states.[5] Regarding sales and use taxes, the *Quill* case allows a state to tax an interstate sale by a foreign corporation to an in-state consumer if the seller has a physical presence in the state, such as a retail outlet.[6]

State taxation of interstate Internet transactions has become a potential source for state revenue. However, in 1998 the federal Congress placed a moratorium on new Internet access taxes. That moritorium has been extended to 2014. The states and Congress are currently debating whether states should be allowed to tax interstate Internet sales. Some states have been very aggressive in finding *Quill*-approved presences that allow them to tax Internet sales.

Qualifying to Do Business A state may require that foreign corporations **qualify** to conduct **intrastate** business in the state, that is, conducting business transaction *within* the state. The level of doing business that constitutes intrastate business for qualification purposes has been difficult to define. To help clarify the confusion in this area, the MBCA lists several activities that do *not* require qualification. For example, soliciting—by mail or through employees—orders that require acceptance outside the state is not doing intrastate business requiring qualification. That exception, for example, allows Amazon.com to

---

[4]*American Trucking Assns., Inc. v. Scheiner,* 483 U.S. 266 (1987).

[5]*American Trucking Assns., Inc. v. Mich. Pub. Serv. Comm.* 545 U.S. 429 (2005).

[6]*Quill Corp. v. North Dakota,* 504 U.S. 298 (1992).

Ethics in Action

Because consumers are tax sensitive, Internet sellers like amazon.com have tried to prevent the application of state sales taxes by avoiding the *Quill* court's physical presence requirement by having no facilities in most states. Nonetheless, as the business of an Internet company grows, it finds it must maintain physical presences such as warehouses and regional offices outside its state of incorporation, thereby subjecting to taxation sales between the Internet company and citizens within the state. Or does it?

Amazon.com has built three warehouses in the state of Indiana, yet amazon.com is not required to collect the 7 percent Indiana state sales tax on sales to Indiana residents. Why not?

In return for agreeing to build warehouses in Indiana, amazon .com obtained the state of Indiana's agreement that it would not require amazon.com to collect the Indiana sales tax.

Why would the state of Indiana make such a deal with amazon.com? Who, besides amazon.com and Indiana residents who buy from it, benefit from that deal? Is it fair that merchants who have had a physical presence in Indiana for decades, hired many employees, and sold large of amounts of useful goods—some of the very goods that amazon.com sells—do not receive the same exemption from collecting the Indiana sales tax? If you were amazon.com, what ethical argument would you make to justify amazon.com's exemption?

make Internet sales in many states outside its home state of Washington without needing to qualify in those states. In addition, selling through independent contractors or owning real or personal property does not require qualification.

Also classified as not doing business for qualification purposes is conducting an **isolated transaction** that is completed within 30 days and is not one in the course of repeated transactions of a like nature. This isolated transaction safe harbor allows a tree grower to bring Christmas trees into a state in order to sell them to one retailer. However, a Christmas tree retailer who comes into a state for 29 days before Christmas and sells to consumers from a street corner is required to qualify. Although both merchants have consummated their transactions within 30 days, the grower has engaged in only one transaction, but the retailer has engaged in a series of transactions.

Maintaining an office to conduct intrastate business, selling personal property not in interstate commerce, entering into contracts relating to local business or sales, or owning or using real estate for general corporate purposes does constitute doing intrastate business. Passive ownership of real estate for investment, however, is not doing intrastate business.

Maintaining a stock of goods within a state from which to fill orders, even if the orders are taken or accepted outside the state, is doing intrastate business requiring qualification. Performing service activities such as machinery repair and construction work may be doing intrastate business.

Qualification Requirements If required to qualify to do intrastate business in a state, a foreign corporation must apply for a **certificate of authority** from the secretary of state, pay an application fee, maintain a registered office and a registered agent in the state, file an annual report with the secretary of state, and pay an annual fee.

Doing intrastate business without qualifying usually subjects a foreign corporation to a fine, in some states as much as $10,000. The MBCA disables the corporation to use the state's courts to bring a lawsuit until it obtains a certificate of authority. The corporation may defend itself in the state's courts, however, even if it has no certificate of authority.

Go to
www.usregisteredagents.com
Several online businesses have been created to relieve corporations of the burden of qualifying to do business and maintaining a registered agent in each state in which it does business. US Registered Agents is one such business. Can you find the cost of hiring US Registered Agents to be a corporation's registered agent?

In the following case, *Ryan v. Cerullo,* the court found that a New York professional accounting corporation was not required to qualify to do business in Connecticut despite providing tax services to a Connecticut resident. Consequently, the New York corporation was not properly subject to a lawsuit in a Connecticut court.

Ryan v. Cerullo   918 A.2d 867 (Conn. S. Ct. 2007)

Thomas Ryan, a resident of Westport, Connecticut, was an investment banker in New York City. He also had an apartment in New York City. John Cerullo was a resident of New York. His accounting firm, Cerullo & Company, was a New York corporation with its principal office in Tarrytown, New York, and a satellite office in New York City.

Ryan retained Cerullo and his firm to prepare Ryan's 1998 and 1999 federal, Connecticut, and New York personal income tax returns. The New York tax returns Cerullo prepared for Ryan claimed that Ryan was a nonresident of New York. Because Ryan had an apartment in New York, the State of New York ruled that Ryan was not a nonresident and, therefore, assessed him an additional $149,654 in taxes, penalties, and interest.

To recover the penalties assessed by the New York tax department, Ryan sued Cerullo and his firm in a Connecticut court, alleging breach of contract and malpractice. Cerullo and his firm moved to dismiss Ryan's legal action, claiming that Connecticut lacked personal jurisdiction over them because they had insufficient contact with the State of Connecticut. Cerulo argued that all meetings between Ryan and Cerullo took place in New York, the tax services provided by Cerullo and his firm for Ryan included communications exclusively with New York tax department personnel, and the vast majority of the Cerullo's revenues were derived from persons residing or doing business in New York.

Ryan pointed out that Cerullo & Company had not obtained a certificate of authority to conduct intrastate business in Connecticut. Therefore, Ryan claimed that Connecticut's courts had jurisdiction over Cerullo & Company under Connecticut General Statutes § 33-929(e). General Statutes § 33-929(e) provides:

Every foreign corporation which transacts business in this state in violation of section 33-920 shall be subject to suit in this state upon any cause of action arising out of such business. . . .

General Statutes § 33-920 provides:

(a) A foreign corporation, other than an insurance, surety or indemnity company, may not transact business in this state until it obtains a certificate of authority from the Secretary of the State. . . .

(b) The following activities, among others, do not constitute transacting business within the meaning of subsection (a) of this section: (1) Maintaining, defending or settling any proceeding; (2) holding meetings of the board of directors or shareholders or carrying on other activities concerning internal corporate affairs; (3) maintaining bank accounts; (4) maintaining offices or agencies for the transfer, exchange and registration of the corporation's own securities or maintaining trustees or depositaries with respect to those securities; (5) selling through independent contractors; (6) soliciting or obtaining orders, whether by mail or through employees or agents or otherwise, if the orders require acceptance outside this state before they become contracts; (7) creating or acquiring indebtedness, mortgages and security interests in real or personal property; (8) securing or collecting debts or enforcing mortgages and security interests in property securing the debts; (9) owning, without more, real or personal property; (10) conducting an isolated transaction that is completed within thirty days and that is not one in the course of repeated transactions of a like nature; (11) transacting business in interstate commerce.

The trial court concluded that it lacked personal jurisdiction over Cerullo and Cerullo & Company under the applicable long-arm statutes on the grounds that the case involved preparation of New York state income tax returns by a New York firm for an individual who worked in New York. Ryan appealed to the Supreme Court of Connecticut. The Supreme Court first concluded that the trial court had no grounds for personal jurisdiction over Cerullo. The court then considered whether there were grounds for jurisdiction over Cerullo & Company.

Palmer, Judge

Cerullo and his firm derived only minimal income from Connecticut residents, did not solicit business in Connecticut and did not promote themselves as a national accounting firm. With respect to the professional accounting services that Ryan retained Cerullo and his firm to provide, they performed those services exclusively in New York, met with Ryan exclusively in New York, and corresponded exclusively with New York tax officials. Moreover, Ryan had retained them to prepare federal and state tax returns on income earned in New York. Although it is true, of course, that Ryan resides in Connecticut and that Cerullo prepared Ryan's Connecticut income tax returns, we agree with the trial court that those facts alone are insufficient to warrant a determination that the professional services rendered by Cerullo constituted the transacting of business in this state.

We next turn to Ryan's contention that the trial court incorrectly concluded that it lacks jurisdiction over Cerullo & Company under the corporate long-arm statute, namely, § 33-929(e), which vests our courts with jurisdiction over any foreign corporation that transacts business in this state without first having obtained a certificate of authority from the secretary of the state in accordance with § 33-920(a) when the cause of action arises out of such business. Our analysis under § 33-929(e) is twofold. We first must determine whether Cerullo & Company transacted business in this state without authorization to do so as required by § 33-920(a), and, if so, we then must determine whether Ryan's claim against Cerullo & Company arose out of such business.

We disagree with both prongs of Ryan's argument. With respect to his claim that Cerullo & Company transacted business in this state, this court previously has observed that the phrase "transacts any business" in General Statutes § 52-59b has a broader meaning than the phrases "transact business" or "transacts business" in the corporate long-arm statutes. In the absence of any claim or showing by Ryan that Cerullo & Company has a different, more substantial relationship to this state than Cerullo, and because we already have concluded that the trial court properly determined that it lacks personal jurisdiction over Cerullo under § 52-59b, it follows, a fortiori, that Cerullo & Company did not transact business in this state within the meaning of § 33-929(e).

Even if we assume, arguendo, that Cerullo & Company did transact business in this state within the meaning of § 33-929(e), Ryan cannot satisfy the second requirement of § 33-929(e), namely, that his claim against Cerullo arose out of that business. It is abundantly clear that Ryan's cause of action arises out of the allegedly negligent preparation of his New York income tax returns, not from the preparation of his Connecticut income tax returns. Indeed, Ryan's cause of action has no connection with or relationship to the preparation of his Connecticut income tax returns. Ryan, therefore, has failed to demonstrate that his claim arises out of any business that Cerullo & Company conducted in this state, as required by § 33-929(e).

Judgment affirmed for Cerullo & Company.

Regulation of a Corporation's Internal Affairs

Regulation of the internal affairs of a corporation—that is, the relation between the corporation and its directors, officers, and shareholders—is usually exercised only by the state of incorporation. Nonetheless, a foreign corporation may conduct most of its business in a state other than the one in which it is incorporated. Such a corporation is called a **pseudo-foreign corporation** in the state in which it conducts most of its business.

A few states subject pseudo-foreign corporations to extensive regulation of their internal affairs, regulation similar to that imposed on their domestic corporations. California's statute requires corporations that have more than 50 percent of their business and ownership in California to elect directors by cumulative voting, to hold annual directors' elections, and to comply with California's dividend payment restrictions. Foreign corporations raise many constitutional objections to the California statute, including violations of the Commerce Clause and the Due Process Clause.

Regulation of Foreign Nonprofit Corporations

The Model Nonprofit Corporation Act and other laws impose the same requirements and penalties on nonprofit corporations as are imposed on for-profit corporations. For example, the MNCA requires a foreign nonprofit corporation to qualify to do intrastate business in a state. The failure to qualify prevents the foreign nonprofit corporation from using the state's courts to bring lawsuits and subjects it to fines for each day it transacts intrastate business without a certificate of authority.

 Prevent a court from piercing a corporation's veil.

Piercing the Corporate Veil

A corporation is a legal entity separate from its shareholders. Corporation law erects an imaginary wall between a corporation and its shareholders that protects shareholders from liability for a corporation's actions. Once shareholders have made their promised capital contributions to the corporation, they have no further financial liability. This means that contracts of a corporation are not contracts of its shareholders, and debts of a corporation are not debts of its shareholders.

Nonetheless, in order *to promote justice and to prevent inequity,* courts will sometimes ignore the separateness of a corporation and its shareholders by **piercing the corporate veil.** The primary consequence of piercing the corporate veil is that a corporation's shareholders may lose their limited liability.

Two requirements must exist for a court to pierce the corporate veil: (1) **domination** of a corporation by its shareholders; and (2) use of that domination for an **improper purpose.**

As an entity separate from its shareholders, a corporation should act for itself, not for its shareholders. If a shareholder causes a corporation to act to the personal benefit of the shareholder, *domination*—the first requirement for piercing the corporate veil—is proved. For example, a majority shareholder's directing a corporation to pay the shareholder's personal expenses is domination. Domination is also proved if the controlling shareholders cause the corporation to fail to observe corporate formalities (such as failing to hold shareholder and director meetings or to maintain separate accounting records). Some courts say that shareholder domination makes the corporation the *alter ego* (other self) of the shareholders. Other courts say that domination makes the corporation an *instrumentality* of the shareholders.

To prove domination, it is not sufficient, or even necessary, to show that there is only one shareholder. Many one-shareholder corporations will never have their veils pierced. However, nearly all corporations whose veils are pierced are close corporations, since domination is more easily accomplished in a close corporation than in a publicly held one.

In addition to domination, there must be an *improper use* of the corporation. The improper use may be any of three types: defrauding creditors, circumventing a statute, or evading an existing obligation.

Defrauding Creditors Shareholders must organize a corporation with sufficient capital to meet the initial capital needs of the business. Inadequate capitalization, called **thin capitalization,** is proved when capitalization is very small in relation to the nature of the business of the corporation and the risks the business necessarily entails.

Thin capitalization defrauds creditors of a corporation. An example of thin capitalization is forming a business with a high debt-to-equity ratio, such as a $10 million–asset business with only $1,000 of equity capital, with the shareholders sometimes contributing the remainder of the needed capital as secured creditors. By doing so, the shareholders elevate a portion of their bankruptcy repayment priority to a level above that of general creditors, thereby reducing the shareholders' risk. The high debt-to-equity ratio harms nonshareholder-creditors by failing to provide an equity cushion sufficient to protect their claims. In such a situation, either the shareholders will be liable for the corporation's debts or the shareholders' loans to the corporation will be subordinated to the claims of other creditors. As a result, the nonshareholder-creditors are repaid all of their claims prior to the shareholder-creditors receiving payment from the corporation.

Transfers of corporate assets to shareholders for less than fair market value (called **looting**) also defraud creditors. For example, shareholder-managers loot a corporation by paying themselves excessively high salaries or by having the corporation pay their personal credit card bills. When such payments leave insufficient assets in the corporation to pay creditors' claims, a court will hold the shareholders liable to the creditors.

Frequently, the same shareholders may own two corporations that transact with each other. The shareholders may cause one corporation to loot the other. When such looting occurs between corporations of common ownership, courts pierce the veils of these corporations. This makes each corporation liable to the creditors of the other corporation. For example, a shareholder-manager operates two corporations from the same office. Corporation 1 transfers inventory to Corporation 2, but it receives less than fair market value for the inventory. Also, both corporations employ the same workers, but all of the wages are paid by Corporation 1. In such a situation, the veils of the corporations will be pierced, allowing the creditors of Corporation 1 to satisfy their claims against the assets of Corporation 2.

Looting may occur also when one corporation (called the **parent corporation**) owns at least a majority of the shares of another corporation (called the **subsidiary corporation**). Ordinarily, the parent is liable for its own obligations and the subsidiary is liable for its own obligations, but the parent is not liable for its subsidiary's debts and the subsidiary is not liable for the parent's debts. Nonetheless, because a parent corporation is able to elect the directors of its subsidiary and therefore can control the management of the subsidiary, the parent may cause its subsidiary to transact with the parent in a manner that benefits the parent but harms the subsidiary.

For example, a parent corporation may direct its subsidiary to sell its assets to the parent for less than fair value. Because the subsidiary has given more assets to the parent than it has received from the parent, creditors of the subsidiary have been defrauded. Consequently, a court will pierce the veil between the parent and its subsidiary and hold the parent liable to the creditors of the subsidiary.

To prevent the piercing of veils between them, affiliated corporations must not commingle their assets. Each corporation must have its own books of accounts. Transactions between affiliated corporations must be recorded on the books of both corporations, and such transactions must be executed at fair value.

Circumventing a Statute A corporation should not engage in a course of conduct that is prohibited by a statute. For example, a city ordinance may prohibit retail businesses from being open on consecutive Sundays. To avoid the statute, a retail corporation forms a subsidiary owned entirely by the retail corporation; on alternate weeks, it leases its building and inventory to the subsidiary. A court will pierce the veil because the purpose of creating the subsidiary corporation is to circumvent the statutory prohibition. Consequently, both the parent and the subsidiary will be liable for violating the statute.

Evading an Existing Obligation Sometimes, a corporation will attempt to escape liability on a contract by reincorporating or by forming a subsidiary corporation. The new corporation will claim that it is not bound by the contract, even though it is doing the same business as was done by the old corporation. In such a situation, courts pierce the corporate veil and hold the new corporation liable on the contract.

For example, to avoid an onerous labor union contract, a corporation creates a wholly owned subsidiary and sells its entire business to the subsidiary. The subsidiary will claim that it is not a party to the labor contract and may hire nonunion labor. A court will pierce the veil between the two corporations because the subsidiary was created only to avoid the union contract.

Nonprofit Corporations

Like a for-profit corporation, a nonprofit corporation is an entity separate and distinct from its members. A member is not personally liable for a nonprofit corporation's acts or liabilities merely by being a member. However, a court may pierce the veil of a nonprofit corporation if it is used to defraud creditors, circumvent a statute, or evade an existing obligation, the same grounds on which a for-profit corporation's veil may be pierced.

For a summary of the law of piercing the corporate veil, see Figure 2. Note that the law of veil piercing also applies to other business forms we studied in Chapters 37–40, including LLCs and LLPs.

In the next case, the Maryland Court of Appeals refused to pierce the corporate veil when the corporation was not used to defraud the creditor and the shareholder was not its alter ego. The court also held that the New Jersey corporation's failure to register to do business in Maryland did not impose personal liability on the foreign corporation's sole shareholder.

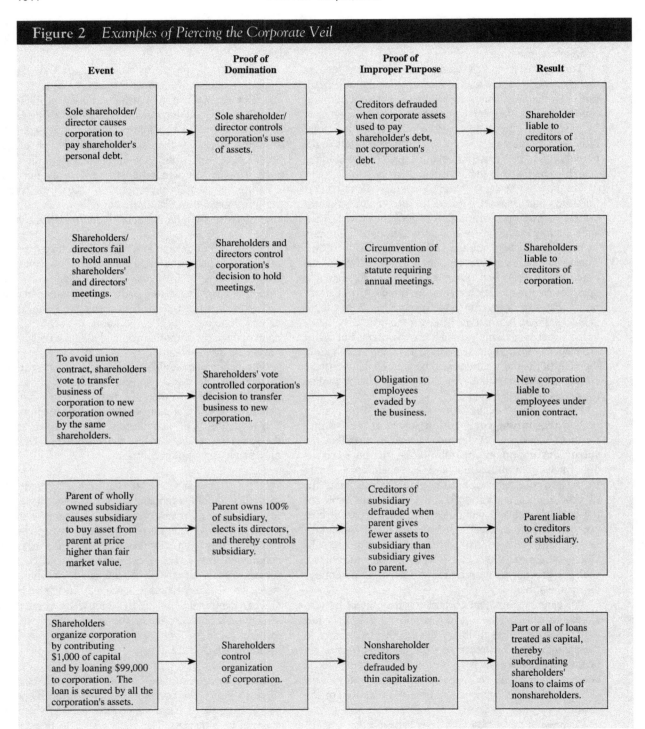

Figure 2   *Examples of Piercing the Corporate Veil*

Hildreth v. Tidewater Equipment Co.	**838 A.2d 1204 (Md. Ct. App. 2003)**

John Hildreth was the sole shareholder, director, and officer of a New Jersey corporation, HCE, Inc., also referred to as HCE-NJ. Engaged in the construction business, in late 1996 or early 1997, HCE-NJ began to do business in Maryland, opening an office in Columbia. However, Hildreth did not register HCE-NJ in Maryland, as required by Maryland Code, sections 7–202, 7–202.1, or 7–203 of the Corporations and Associations Article. Those sections require that foreign corporations register with the Maryland Department of Assessments and Taxation before doing any intrastate business in Maryland. Registration requires that the corporation have a resident agent in Maryland.

In February 1998, HCE-NJ rented a 20-ton capacity crane from Tidewater Equipment Company, Inc., for one or two days and paid the rental charge as agreed. In September 1998, HCE-NJ and Tidewater commenced negotiations for the long-term rental of a crane that HCE-NJ intended to use in connection with a construction project in Alexandria, Virginia.

Hildreth made clear he was acting for HCE, Inc., but neither said nor was asked where that company was incorporated. He informed Frank Kolbe, a Tidewater representative, that the company had an office in Columbia, Maryland. Kolbe visited both the Columbia office and a job site. He testified that the company "didn't appear to be a fly-by-night operation," but had "a nice office suite" and "numerous employees." The job site was also substantial, with "a huge warehouse," a rail siding, and "hundreds of metal building panels." Kolbe assumed that HCE-NJ was a Maryland corporation because it had an office in Columbia.

Tidewater and HCE-NJ signed a series of daily contracts. Hildreth did not sign the contracts, which were signed on behalf of HCE-NJ by some other employee. The charges for September, October, and November 1998, were paid in January and February 1999. When payments were not received thereafter, Tidewater repossessed the equipment. At the time, Tidewater was owed $47,246 for the months of December, January, February, and March, and for a few days in April.

Tidewater sued Hildreth on the grounds Hildreth was personally liable for the debts incurred by HCE-NJ. The court entered judgment against Hildreth for the entire corporate debt. Hildreth appealed to the Court of Special Appeals, arguing that officers and directors of a foreign corporation are not personally liable for corporate debts solely because the corporation fails to qualify to do business in Maryland and that Tidewater knew that it was dealing with a corporation.

On appeal, the intermediate appellate court pointed out that the only thing that was not disclosed to Tidewater was the fact that HCE-NJ was a foreign corporation that had not registered to do business in Maryland. Tidewater knew that it was dealing with a corporation engaged in the construction business; it knew the actual name of the corporation and that it had offices not just in Maryland but in New Jersey and New York as well.

The Court of Special Appeals also concluded that, as a general rule, officers and directors of a valid foreign corporation are not personally liable on corporate debts merely because the corporation fails to register to do business in the forum state, but held that the court could impose such liability "when justice requires." Although acknowledging that the traditional factors justifying veil piercing were not present, the court determined that the case presented a situation in which the corporate form must be disregarded to "enforce a paramount equity." After the court affirmed Hildreth's liability to Tidewater, Hildreth asked the Maryland Court of Appeals to review the decision.

Wilner, Judge

The only issue before us is whether there was a basis for piercing the corporate veil of HCE-NJ and imposing personal liability for the corporate obligation on Hildreth.

As the Court of Special Appeals recognized, there was no allegation here of fraud on the part of either Hildreth or HCE-NJ; nor was there any evidence or finding of fraud. Personal liability rested solely upon the notion of "paramount equity," which, in that court's view, arose from a combination of the following circumstances:

(1) Hildreth was the sole shareholder of HCE-NJ;
(2) Hildreth was "personally involved" in the business transaction with Tidewater, which the court viewed as "Hildreth's dirty hands";
(3) * * *

(4) Contracts made by unregistered foreign corporations, though valid, nonetheless constitute "illegal business transactions on the part of the unregistered foreign corporation, for which that corporation and its agents, officers, directors, and shareholders may be penalized," which the court characterized as "the public policy against illegal business transactions;"
(5) Maryland law precludes unregistered corporations doing business in Maryland from seeking relief in Maryland courts, which the court regarded as "the public policy against unregistered corporations using Maryland courts to protect their illegal business transactions."

Although we have not heretofore given any generic definition of "paramount equity" in this context, it is abundantly clear from our actual holdings in cases where attempts were made to pierce a corporate veil—to hold stockholders personally liable for corporate obligations—that those circumstances, individually or in combination, do not suffice.

In a number of cases, we made favorable reference to the synthesis supplied in the 1953 edition of Herbert Brune's work, *Maryland Corporation Law and Practice,* § 371, as to when a corporate entity will be disregarded:

> *First.* Where the corporation is used *as a mere shield for the perpetration of a fraud,* the courts will disregard the fiction of separate corporate entity.
>
> *Second.* The courts may consider a corporation as unencumbered by the fiction of corporate entity and deal with substance rather than form as though the corporation did not exist, *in order to prevent evasion of legal obligations.*
>
> *Third.* Where the stockholders themselves, or a parent corporation owning the stock of a subsidiary corporation, *fail to observe the corporate entity, operating the business or dealing with the corporation's property as if it were their own,* the courts will also disregard the corporate entity for the protection of third persons.
>
> (Emphasis added).

There is nothing in this record that could possibly justify the first of these circumstances. As already noted, there is no claim, no evidence, and no finding that Hildreth used HCE-NJ as "a mere shield for the perpetration of a fraud."

The third circumstance embodies what is sometimes called the "alter ego" doctrine. Fletcher observes that the "alter ego" doctrine has been applied "where the corporate entity has been used as a subterfuge and to observe it would work an injustice," the rationale being that "if the shareholders or the corporations themselves disregard the proper formalities of a corporation, then the law will do likewise as necessary to protect individual and corporate creditors." William Meade Fletcher, *1 Fletcher Cyclopedia of the Law of Private Corporations,* § 41.10 at 574–76 (1999 Rev. Vol.). Courts will apply the doctrine when the plaintiff shows (1) "complete domination, not only of the finances, but of policy and business practice in respect to the transaction so that the corporate entity as to this transaction had at the time no separate mind, will or existence of its own," (2) that "such control [was] used by the defendant to commit fraud or wrong, to perpetrate the violation of the statutory or other positive legal duty, or dishonest and unjust act in contravention of the plaintiff's legal rights," and (3) that such "control and breach of duty proximately caused the injury or unjust loss." *Id.* at 583–86. Because piercing the corporate veil is founded on equity, "where no fraud is shown, the plaintiff must show that an inequitable result, involving fundamental unfairness, will result from a failure to disregard the corporate form." *Id.* at 605.

Although there appears to be no universal rule as to the specific criteria that courts will consider in determining whether to apply the doctrine, Fletcher observes that some of the factors commonly considered, when dealing with a single corporation, are (1) whether the corporation is inadequately capitalized, fails to observe corporate formalities, fails to issue stock or pay dividends, or operates without a profit; (2) whether there is commingling of corporate and personal assets; (3) whether there are nonfunctioning officers or directors; (4) whether the corporation is insolvent at the time of the transaction; and (5) the absence of corporate records.

There is no support in this record for basing personal liability on the "alter ego" doctrine. There is no evidence that Hildreth exercised such complete domination over HCE-NJ to warrant a conclusion that the corporation had no separate mind, will, or existence of its own. There is no evidence that HCE-NJ was undercapitalized, that corporate formalities were not observed, that the corporation operated without a profit, that there were nonfunctioning officers or directors, that the company was insolvent when it entered into the arrangement with Tidewater, that there were no or inadequate corporate records.

What the record does show is that HCE-NJ was a valid, subsisting corporation which, until it suffered a reversal of fortunes, had substantial assets and business prospects. The relevant contracts, with the general contractor and with Tidewater, were in its name, and, indeed, the contracts with Tidewater were signed on its behalf not by Hildreth but by another employee. Although the conclusion is certainly warranted that Hildreth deliberately permitted HCE-NJ to operate in Maryland without benefit of registration, there is no evidence that that conduct in any way influenced Tidewater to enter into the contractual arrangement from which this debt arose. Tidewater knew that it was dealing with a corporation, and it had satisfied itself that the corporation had substantial contracts and assets, that it had two business locations in the state, that it had numerous employees, and that it was not a "one man show." Kolbe's assumption that HCE-NJ was a Maryland corporation did not come from anything Hildreth said. Indeed, much of the information apparently relied upon by Kolbe in agreeing to the contract came from another HCE-NJ employee, not Hildreth.

In sustaining liability on Hildreth's part, the Court of Special Appeals seemed to be applying the second in Brune's trilogy of circumstances, disregarding the corporate existence "in order to prevent the evasion of legal obligations." That, in turn, appears to rest on Hildreth's failure to register the corporation. Tidewater sees that set of circumstances as an independent basis for "paramount equity," urging that "paramount equity" need not rest solely on the "alter ego" doctrine.

Hildreth's conduct may have subjected him to a $1,000 fine pursuant to § 7–302(b) of the Corporations and Associations Article; it would have served as well to preclude the corporation from filing suit in Maryland, *see* § 7–301. Section 7–305 makes clear, however, that the failure of a foreign corporation to comply with the registration requirements "does not affect the validity of any contract to which the corporation is a party," and there is nothing in the registration statutes that permits a court to invade the corporate entity simply because of a failure to register.

We do not regard Brune's second proposition as a separate basis for piercing a corporate veil. It is, at best, subsumed, along with the "alter ego" doctrine, in the notion of paramount equity,

and has no application in this case. The record here reveals nothing more than the fact that a valid, subsisting corporation entered into a commercial contract and later became unable to satisfy its obligation under that contract. That is unfortunate, but it is not a basis for making someone else liable for the corporate debt.

Judgment reversed in favor of Hildreth.

Ethics in Action

Large multinational corporations and smaller closely held corporations use multiple corporations (and sometimes LLCs and limited partnerships) to manage their tax, contract, and tort liability. As we will learn in Chapter 42, American corporations set up subsidiaries in Delaware to take advantage of its low taxes. Also, if a corporation wants to engage in a risky new venture in a country with a volatile political climate, the corporation will almost always conduct the business in a wholly owned subsidiary.

Even in the absence of an abnormal risk, many corporations create a structure like the following, in which parts of the corporation's business, such as finance, sales, and manufacturing, are placed in separate corporations, each wholly owned by the parent corporation:

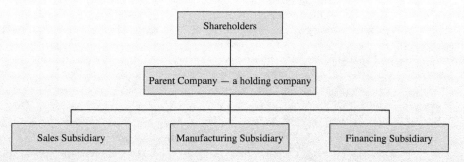

The parent company is a holding company that owns all the shares of the subsidiaries. Commonly, it also provides management services to the subsidiaries; in such cases, usually many employees working for the subsidiaries are actually employees of the parent, because the employees often work for more than one subsidiary. Employees are assigned by the parent holding company, which receives a management fee from the subsidiaries and allocates employees to the subsidiaries as needed. The holding company will also be the capital-raising arm of the business because its cost of capital is usually lower than the individual subsidiaries' costs of capital due to diversification of risk.

As far as corporation law is concerned, this parent–subsidiary structure allows the business to isolate liability. Thus, if one subsidiary is unable to pay its obligations and its assets lost, the assets of the other subsidiaries are preserved.

- Is it ethical for a business to set up such a parent–subsidiary structure? Would a profit maximizer be likely to set up such a structure?
- If a subsidiary becomes insolvent and is unable to pay its debts, would its creditors appreciate that neither the parent nor the other subsidiaries are liable to the creditors? Is it important that a creditor chose to do business with the subsidiary and could have examined its financial position before extending credit to the subsidiary?
- Would a tort victim who was injured by a product sold by the sales subsidiary appreciate that only its assets are available to pay his tort claim? Is it important that the victim is ignorant of corporation law and is not aware that the parent and subsidiaries are separate corporations? Does a tort victim have the same ability as a contract creditor to check out the corporate structure of the business before being injured by the product? Would a believer in justice theory see a difference between a contract creditor and a tort victim?

Problems and Problem Cases

1. You and four of your closest friends have decided to start a business that will purchase from banks and other financial institutions high-risk, subprime mortgage loans that are in default. You believe that you will be able to purchase the loans for no more than 40 percent of their face value. The plan is that the business will buy the loans by paying half the purchase amount in cash and the other half by issuing promissory notes due in six months to two years. You expect to turn a profit by restructuring the loans with the debtors, foreclosing against the real property securing the loans, or aggregating the loans and reselling them. You and your four friends are willing to invest $2 million each in the business. Needing an additional $10 million to start the venture, you and your four friends agree to allow 10 other investors to contribute equity of $1 million each to the business. Only you and the four friends will be the managers of the business. The five of you want to share equally all decisions regarding the acquisition, management, and sale of the loans. You want the other 10 investors to be passive investors only with no say in the management of the business. However, the 10 other investors, who are contributing half the equity of the business, are concerned about protecting their investments. You have proposed that the business be formed as a limited liability company (LLC), but some of your friends believe that the corporation or the limited partnership is a better form. One friend says that the advantages of the corporation make it a superior business form. List the usual advantages of the corporate form of business. Explain why some of the usual advantages of the corporation are not likely to be fully available in this context.

2. Hellyer Avenue Limited Partnership (HALP) was formed under California law for the purpose of developing, constructing, and managing a headquarters building in California for a communications company. The principal office and place of business of HALP also were in California. HALP's general partners were Mission West Properties, L.P. (MWLP), and Republic Properties Corporation. The three limited partners were Steven Grigg, David Peter, and Mentmore Partners LLC. Republic, Grigg, Peter, and Mentmore sued MWLP, the managing general partner of HALP, and Mission West Properties, Inc. (MWINC), the general partner of MWLP, for improperly diluting their interests in MWLP and failing to make owed distributions. The suit was brought in a Maryland state court. MWLP was formed as a limited partnership under Delaware law, but maintained its principal place of business in California. MWINC, the general partner of MWLP, was incorporated initially under the laws of California, but later was re-incorporated in 1999 under the laws of Maryland. As required under Maryland law, MWINC named a registered agent in Maryland as part of its re-incorporation under Maryland law. Were MWLP and MWINC correct in arguing that the Maryland court had no jurisdiction over them?

3. Dayton Furniture Fashions, Inc. (DFF), is incorporated in Ohio and operates three retail furniture stores in Dayton, Ohio. DFF advertises its stores on radio stations and in newspapers in Richmond, Indiana, a city near the Indiana border with Ohio. In response to DFF's advertisements, Greta Hammond, a resident of Richmond, drives to a DFF store in Dayton and purchases a sofa bed for $956. DFF agrees to deliver the sofa bed to Hammond's home in Richmond in three days. DFF's employees deliver the sofa bed to Hammond as promised, driving a delivery truck owned by DFF from its warehouse in Huber Heights, Ohio. A few days later, when Hammond attempts to use the sofa bed for the first time, she discovers the sofa bed is defective and is not usable. When DFF refuses to replace the sofa bed, Hammond sues DFF in an Indiana state court. Does the Indiana court have jurisdiction over DFF?

4. Barnesandnoble.com, LLC (BN Online), is an Internet retailer of books, movies, and music. The company accepts orders from customers across the country, including in St. Tammany Parish, Louisiana, and fills these orders through a national distribution system that has no physical presence in Louisiana, except for the use of third-party carriers like UPS and FedEx that deliver goods from out-of-state ordered online. The company did not maintain a mailing address or telephone number in Louisiana. It had no employees in Louisiana and owned no tangible property in Louisiana. From January 2001 through October 2003, Barnes & Noble, Inc., owned 40 percent of BN Online. Between October 2003 and May 2004, Barnes & Noble, Inc., owned 80 percent of BN Online through a wholly owned subsidiary. Between May 2004 and December 31, 2005, Barnes & Noble, Inc., owned 100 percent of BN Online through a wholly owned subsidiary, B&N Holding Corp. Barnes & Noble, Inc., also wholly owned Barnes &

Noble Booksellers, Inc. (BN Booksellers). BN Booksellers owned and operated retail stores throughout the country, including one in St. Tammany Parish, under the brand name "Barnes and Noble." The BN Booksellers retail outlet in St. Tammany Parish was located in the City of Mandeville. Although the two companies were both owned, in whole or in part, by the same parent corporation, BN Booksellers and BN Online did not share management, employees, offices, and other important elements of their businesses. In October 2005, the St. Tammany Parish Tax Collector sued BN Online in a Louisiana state court for sales taxes that BN online failed to collect on sales to Louisiana residents from 2001 to 2005. Did the court order BN Online or one of its owners to pay the sales tax?

5. Mead Corporation, an Ohio corporation in the business of producing and selling paper, packaging, and school and office supplies, also owned Lexis/Nexis, the electronic research service. Either as a separate subsidiary or as a division of Mead, Lexis was subject to Mead's oversight, but Mead did not manage its day-to-day affairs. Mead was headquartered in Ohio, while a separate management team ran Lexis out of its headquarters in Illinois. The two businesses maintained separate manufacturing, sales, and distribution facilities, as well as separate accounting, legal, human resources, credit and collections, purchasing, and marketing departments. Mead's involvement was generally limited to approving Lexis's annual business plan and any significant corporate transactions that Lexis wished to undertake. Mead managed Lexis's free cash, which was swept nightly from Lexis's bank accounts into an account maintained by Mead. The cash was reinvested in Lexis's business, but Mead decided how to invest it. Neither business was required to purchase goods or services from the other. Lexis, for example, was not required to purchase its paper supply from Mead and in fact purchased most of its paper from other suppliers. Neither received any discount on goods or services purchased from the other, and neither was a significant customer of the other.

In 1994, Mead sold Lexis for $1.5 billion, realizing a capital gain of over $1 billion. Mead did not report any of this gain as business income on its 1994 Illinois tax return, taking the position that it was non-business income and should be allocated entirely to Mead's domestic state, Ohio. Did the Supreme Court of the United States agree with Mead?

6. B & D Shrimp, Inc., a Delaware corporation, made a contract in Texas to sell a commercial shrimp boat to Donald Gosch and Jesse Bach. Gosch and Bach paid $5,000 down and received immediate possession of the boat in Texas, where they would shrimp in the coastal waters. The contract stated that Gosch and Bach would get title to the boat after transferring a cabin cruiser to Shrimp, Inc., and paying 15 percent of the cash proceeds from the boat's daily shrimp catches for the next calendar year. When Gosch and Bach defaulted on the contract, Shrimp, Inc., sued Gosch and won the case. Shrimp, Inc., however, had not obtained a certificate of authority to do business in Texas. Twenty days after the judgment was entered, Gosch contested the judgment on the grounds that Shrimp, Inc., by failing to qualify to do business, could not use Texas's courts to obtain a judgment against Gosch. Shrimp, Inc., decided at that time, therefore, to obtain a certificate of authority. Is the judgment for Shrimp, Inc., against Gosch valid?

7. The National Collegiate Athletic Association (NCAA) is a corporation organized in the State of Indiana. The NCAA conducts several championship events throughout the United States. The 2014 Men's Basketball Final Four will be held at Cowboys Stadium in Texas. The NCAA has contracted to lease Cowboys Stadium for two weeks up to and including the championship. The NCAA has also leased over 200 hotel rooms in Texas. To plan and conduct the championship event in Texas, over 20 NCAA employees will visit Texas over a two-year period, some of them spending over 75 days in Texas. Should the NCAA qualify to do business in Texas?

8. Lawrence Small formed Seatwo LLC to operate a Burger King restaurant in Wyoming. Seatwo was capitalized by $500 of contributions from its three members: Small, $500; his wife, $125; one of their children, $125. Gasstop Two LLC owned real property, which it leased to Seatwo beginning June 2000. The payments would total almost $1 million over the term of the lease. Seatwo also borrowed $350,000 to obtain furniture and equipment for the new Burger King operation and had a $15,000 line of credit. Unfortunately, Seatwo never turned a profit and ceased operations in October 2003 due to its poor location and lack of customers. Despite operating at a loss, Seatwo had made rental payments to Gasstop until it ceased business in 2003. Gasstop sued Small and his wife for the remaining $237,000 payments under

the lease, arguing that the veil should be pierced between the LLC and the Smalls. What grounds did Gasstop use to argue for piercing the veil? Did the court agree with Gasstop?

9. New York law required that every taxicab company carry $10,000 of accident liability insurance for each cab in its fleet. The purpose of the law was to ensure that passengers and pedestrians injured by cabs operated by these companies would be adequately compensated for their injuries. Carlton organized 10 corporations, each owning and operating two taxicabs in New York City. Each of these corporations carried $20,000 of liability insurance. Carlton was the principal shareholder of each corporation. The vehicles, the only freely transferable assets of these corporations, were collateral for claims of secured creditors. The 10 corporations were operated more or less as a unit with respect to supplies, repairs, and employees. Walkovszky was severely injured when he was run down by one of the taxicabs. He sued Carlton personally, alleging that the multiple corporate structure amounted to fraud upon those who might be injured by the taxicabs. Should the court pierce the corporate veil to reach Carlton individually?

10. REIS, Inc., owns, constructs, and manages 25 shopping malls throughout the United States and Canada. REIS is concerned that the failure of any one mall will be a substantial financial loss that will cause the entire business to fail. What parent-subsidiary structure do you recommend REIS, Inc., create to solve the liability risks of operating 25 malls? What roles will the parent corporation undertake after the subsidiary structure has been established? List the dos or don'ts that will help prevent a piercing of the veils between the subsidiaries and between the parent company and its subsidiaries.

11. Castleberry, Branscum, and Byboth each owned one-third of the shares of a furniture-moving business, Texan Transfer, Inc. Branscum formed Elite Moving Company, a business that competed with Texan Transfer. Castleberry objected and sued to claim part ownership of Elite Moving. Branscum threatened Castleberry that he would not receive any return on his investment in Texan Transfer unless he abandoned his claim of ownership of Elite Moving. Consequently, Castleberry sold his shares back to Texan Transfer for a $42,000 promissory note. Gradually, Elite Moving took over more and more of the business of Texan Transfer. Texan Transfer allowed Elite Moving to use its employees and trucks. Elite Moving advertised for business, while Texan Transfer did not. Elite Moving prospered, while Texan Transfer's business declined. As a result, Castleberry was paid only $1,000 of the $42,000 promissory note. Did Castleberry have any grounds to hold Branscum liable for the unpaid portion of the note?

12. Rachel Romano owns 90 percent of the stock of RRC, Inc. Romano is the president and CEO and the only voting member of the board of directors. Her husband and daughter each own 5 percent of the shares of RRC, and each is also an officer and non-voting director. When Romano receives payments from RRC's clients, she deposits the payments in her personal checking and savings accounts. She also pays all RRC's creditors with checks written on her personal account. She also pays all her personal expenses from the personal checking account into which she deposits RRC funds. For three years, Romano has not held a shareholders meeting or a meeting of the board of directors. Is Romano risking being held liable for the obligations of RRC?

Online Research

Your State's or Country's Corporation Law

Find a website that posts the corporation law of your state or country. All state governments have online access to their statutes, and a few countries do as well. When you find the statute, determine what a foreign or alien corporation must do in your state or country to qualify to do business.

CHAPTER 42

ORGANIZATION AND FINANCIAL STRUCTURE OF CORPORATIONS

A client has sought your assistance before incorporating a business that will buy and sell fine art. The client will enter the business with three other associates, all about 35 years old. They plan to own equal shares of the business and to manage it together. The business has not yet been incorporated.

- Your client and her associates identify five valuable paintings they want to purchase. To reduce their personal liability on the contracts to purchase the paintings, what do you recommend they do prior to signing the purchase contracts?
- Your client states that she wants to incorporate the business because a corporation's shares are freely transferable, making it easy for shareholders to liquidate their investments. You know better. Explain to your client why free transferability of the shares as a legal matter is a problem for her and her associates. Also explain to your client why free transferability of the shares as a practical matter does not exist. What should your client do to address the share transferability issues? Sketch the contents of a buy-sell agreement that addresses all the transferability issues.

LO   LEARNING OBJECTIVES

After studying this chapter, you should be able to:

1   Appreciate the risk of liability for corporate promoters.

2   Understand the process for incorporating a business.

3   Know the appropriate sources for financing a business.

4   Adopt appropriate share-transfer restrictions for a variety of contexts.

A PERSON DESIRING TO incorporate a business must comply with the applicable state or federal corporation law. Failing to comply can create various problems. For example, a person may make a contract on behalf of the corporation before it is incorporated. Is the corporation liable on this contract? Is the person who made the contract on behalf of the prospective corporation liable on the contract? Do the people who thought that they were shareholders of a corporation have limited liability, or do they have unlimited liability as partners of a partnership?

 L01 Appreciate the risk of liability for corporate promoters.

Promoters and Preincorporation Transactions

A **promoter** of a corporation incorporates a business, organizes its initial management, and raises its initial capital. Typically, a promoter creates or discovers a business or an idea to be developed, finds people who are willing to invest in the business, negotiates the contracts necessary for the initial operation of the proposed venture, incorporates the business, and helps management start the operation of the business. Consequently, a promoter may engage in many acts prior to the incorporation of the business. As a result, the promoter may have liability on the contracts he negotiates on behalf of the prospective corporation. In addition, the corporation may *not* be liable on the contracts the promoter makes on its behalf.

Corporation's Liability on Preincorporation Contracts

A nonexistent corporation has no liability on contracts made by a promoter prior to its incorporation. This is because the corporation does not exist.

Even when the corporation comes into existence, it does not automatically become liable on a preincorporation contract made by a promoter on its behalf. It cannot be held liable as a principal whose agent made the contracts because the promoter was not its agent and the corporation was not in existence when the contracts were made.

The only way a corporation may become bound on a promoter's preincorporation contracts is by the corporation's **adoption** of the promoter's contracts. Adoption is similar to the agency concept of ratification, which is covered in Chapter 36. For a corporation to adopt a promoter's contract, the corporation must accept the contract with knowledge of all its material facts.

Acceptance may be express or implied. The corporation's knowing receipt of the benefits of the contract is sufficient for acceptance. For example, a promoter makes a preincorporation contract with a genetic engineer, requiring the engineer to work for a prospective corporation for 10 years. After incorporation, the promoter presents the contract to the board of directors. Although the board takes no formal action to accept the contract, the board allows the engineer to work for the corporation for one year as the contract provides and pays him the salary required by the contract. The board's actions constitute an acceptance of the contract, binding the corporation to the contract for its 10-year term. The *SmithStearn* case is another example of a corporation adopting a preincorporation contract.

Promoter's Liability on Preincorporation Contracts

A promoter and her copromoters are jointly and severally liable on preincorporation contracts the promoter negotiates in the name of the nonexistent corporation. This liability exists even when the promoters' names do not appear on the contract. Promoters are also jointly and severally liable for torts committed by their copromoters prior to incorporation.

A promoter retains liability on a preincorporation contract until **novation** occurs. For novation to occur, the corporation and the third party must agree to release the promoter from liability and to substitute the corporation for the promoter as the party liable on the contract. Usually, novation will occur by express or implied agreement of all the parties.

If the corporation is not formed, a promoter remains liable on a preincorporation contract unless the third party releases the promoter from liability. In addition, the mere formation of the corporation does not release a promoter from liability. A promoter remains liable on a preincorporation contract even after the corporation's adoption of the contract, since adoption does not automatically release the promoter. The corporation cannot by itself relieve the promoter of liability to the third party; the third party must also agree, expressly or impliedly, to release the promoter from liability.

A few courts have held that a promoter is not liable on preincorporation contracts if the third party *knew of the nonexistence* of the corporation yet insisted that the promoter sign the contract on behalf of the nonexistent corporation. Other courts have found that the promoter is not liable if the third party clearly stated that he would *look only to the prospective corporation* for performance.

Recently, courts have held that the Model Business Corporation Act (MBCA) permits a promoter to escape liability for preincorporation contracts when the promoter has made some effort to incorporate the business and believes the corporation is in existence. The MBCA rule is discussed in the section titled Defective Attempts to Incorporate.

Obtaining a Binding Preincorporation Contract

While it may be desirable for the promoter to escape liability on a preincorporation contract, there is one disadvantage: Only when the promoter is liable on the preincorporation contract is the other party liable on the contract. This means that when the promoter is not liable on the contract, the other party to the contract may rescind the contract at any time prior to adoption by the corporation. Once the corporation has adopted the contract, the corporation and the third party are liable on it, and the contract cannot be rescinded without the consent of both parties.

To maintain the enforceability of a preincorporation contract prior to adoption, a promoter may want to be liable on a preincorporation contract at least until the corporation comes into existence and adopts the contract.

To limit his liability, however, the promoter may wish to have his liability cease automatically upon adoption. The promoter should ensure that the contract has an **automatic novation clause.** For example, a preincorporation contract may read that "the promoter's liability on this contract shall terminate upon the corporation's adoption of this contract."

Instead of using automatic novation clauses, today most well-advised promoters incorporate the business prior to making any contracts for the corporation. That is, the well-advised promoter makes *no* preincorporation contracts. Instead, she makes contracts only for existing corporations. As a result, only the corporation and the third party—and not the promoter—have liability on the contract.

SmithStearn Yachts, Inc. v. Gyrographic Communications, Inc.
2006 Conn. Super. LEXIS 1927 (Ct. Super. Ct. 2006)

SmithStearn Yachts, Inc., a Delaware corporation providing luxury yachting services in Connecticut, agreed to a contract with Gyrographic Communications, Inc., a California company, by which Gyrographic would provide advertising, marketing, and promotional services to SmithStearn. When SmithStearn sued Gyrographic for breaching the contract, Gyrographic countered that SmithStearn was not a party to the contact, because the contract was purportedly made with a limited liability corporation, SmithStearn Yachts, LLC, not the corporation that was suing Gyrographic.

Rodriguez, Judge

Leathern Stearn, the purported promoter and president of SmithStearn Yachts, Inc., executed the agreement with Gyrographic on behalf of SmithStearn, LLC, an entity that never came into existence. Rather, the plaintiff, SmithStearn Yachts, Inc. was formed. SmithStearn Yachts, Inc. contends that it has standing to bring this action because it assumed and ratified, both explicitly and implicitly, the agreement that was made on its behalf, prior to its formation.

Generally, a corporation is not bound by contracts entered into on its behalf prior to its existence. A corporation can, however, acquire rights and subject itself to duties with respect to preincorporation matters. A contract made in the name of an inchoate corporation can be enforced after the corporation is organized on the principle of ratification. Ratification is defined as the affirmance by a person of a prior act which did not bind him but which was done or professedly done on his account. Ratification requires acceptance of the results of the act with an intent to ratify, and with full knowledge of all the material circumstances.

A corporation may after its organization become liable on preliminary contracts made by its promoters by expressly adopting such contracts or by receiving the benefits from them. Although SmithStearn Yachts, Inc. was formed after the execution of the agreement, it received the benefit of the services pursuant to the agreement. Gyrographic worked toward developing letterheads, business cards, and other marketing material for SmithStearn Yachts, Inc. SmithStearn Yachts, Inc. made payments to Gyrographic, which SmithStearn Yachts, Inc. then recorded in its books. Thus, SmithStearn Yachts, Inc. received the benefits of the agreement and also fulfilled the obligations under it, thereby ratifying the agreement.

Furthermore, ratification, adoption, or acceptance of a preincorporation contract by a promoter need not be expressed, but may be implied from acts or acquiescence on the part of the corporation or its authorized agents. Thus, a corporation's act of suing on a preincorporation contract is in itself an adoption of the contract. SmithStearn Yachts, Inc. implicitly ratified the agreement when it brought this action. By suing under the agreement, SmithStearn Yachts, Inc. is also assuming the liabilities under it, thereby enforcing and adopting the agreement.

Judgment for SmithStearn Yachts, Inc.

Preincorporation Share Subscriptions

Promoters sometimes use **preincorporation share subscriptions** to ensure that the corporation will have adequate capital when it begins its business. Under the terms of a share subscription, a prospective shareholder offers to buy a specific number of the corporation's shares at a stated price.

Under the Model Business Corporation Act (MBCA), a prospective shareholder may not revoke a preincorporation subscription for a six-month period, in the absence of a contrary provision in the subscription. Generally, corporate acceptance of preincorporation subscriptions occurs by action of the board of directors after incorporation.

Promoters have no liability on preincorporation share subscriptions. They have a duty, however, to make a good faith effort to bring the corporation into existence. When a corporation fails to accept a preincorporation subscription or becomes insolvent, the promoter is not liable to the disappointed subscriber, in the absence of fraud or other wrongdoing by the promoter.

Today, most promoters incorporate the business and obtain promises to buy shares from prospective shareholders. These promises, which may take the form of postincorporation subscriptions, are discussed later in this chapter.

Relation of Promoter and Prospective Corporation

A promoter of a nonexistent corporation is not an agent of the prospective corporation. A promoter is not an agent of prospective investors in the business because they did not appoint him and they have no power to control him.

Although not an agent of the proposed corporation or its investors, a promoter owes a **fiduciary duty** to the corporation and to its prospective investors. A promoter owes such parties a duty of full disclosure and honesty. For example, a promoter breaches this duty when he diverts money received from prospective shareholders to pay his expenses, unless the shareholders agree to such payment. The fiduciary duty also prevents a promoter from diverting a business opportunity from the corporation and giving it to himself instead. In addition, the promoter may not purchase shares of the corporation at a price lower than that paid by the public shareholders.

A promoter may not profit personally by transacting secretly with the corporation in his personal capacity. The promoter's failure to disclose his interest in the transaction and the material facts permits the corporation to rescind the transaction or to recover the promoter's secret profit. On the other hand, the promoter's full disclosure of his interest and the material facts of the transaction to an independent board of directors that approves the transaction prevents the corporation from recovering the promoter's profit. Note, however, that when a promoter is a director, approval of the transaction by the board of directors may not be sufficient; the transaction may need to be intrinsically fair to the corporation.

Liability of Corporation to Promoter

Valuable as the services of a promoter may be to a prospective corporation and to society, a corporation is generally not required to compensate a promoter for her promotional services, or even her expenses, unless the corporation has agreed expressly to compensate the

promoter. The justification for this rule is that the promoter is self-appointed and acts for a corporation that is not in existence.

Nonetheless, a corporation may choose to reimburse the promoter for her reasonable expenses and to pay her the value of her services to the corporation. Corporations often compensate their promoters with shares. The MBCA permits the issuance of shares for a promoter's preincorporation services.

To ensure that she is compensated for her services, a promoter may tie herself to a person or property that the corporation needs to succeed. For example, a promoter may purchase the invention that the corporation was formed to exploit. Another way to ensure compensation is by the promoter's dominating the board of directors during the early months of its life. By doing so, the promoter may direct the corporation to compensate her, but only if the compensation is reasonable and, therefore, fair to the corporation.

 Understand the process for incorporating a business.

Incorporation

Anyone seeking to incorporate a business must decide where to do so. If the business of a proposed corporation is to be primarily *intrastate*, it is usually cheaper to incorporate in the state where the corporation's business is to be conducted. For the business that is primarily *interstate*, however, the business may benefit by incorporating in a state different from the state in which it has its principal place of business. Because few businesses qualify to incorporate under federal law, that option is rarely exercised.

Incorporation fees and taxes, annual fees, and other fees such as those on the transfer of shares or the dissolution of the corporation vary considerably from state to state. Delaware has been a popular state in which to incorporate because its fees and taxes tend to be low. It also has judges experienced in resolving corporate disputes.

Promoters frequently choose to incorporate in a state whose corporation statute and court decisions grant managers broad management discretion. For example, it is easier to pay a large dividend and to effect a merger in Delaware than in many other states.

Steps in Incorporation

There are only a few requirements for incorporation. It is a fairly simple process and can be accomplished inexpensively in most cases. The steps prescribed by the incorporation statutes of the different states vary, but they generally include the following, which appear in the MBCA:

1. Preparation of articles of incorporation.

2. Signing and authenticating the articles by one or more incorporators.

3. Filing the articles with the secretary of state, accompanied by the payment of specified fees.

4. Receipt of a copy of the articles of incorporation stamped "Filed" by the secretary of state, accompanied by a fee receipt. (Some states retain the old MBCA rule requiring receipt of a certificate of incorporation issued by the secretary of state.)

5. Holding an organization meeting for the purpose of adopting bylaws, electing officers, and transacting other business.

Articles of Incorporation The basic governing document of the corporation is the **articles of incorporation** (sometimes called the charter). The articles are similar to a constitution. They state many of the rights and responsibilities of the corporation, its management, and its shareholders. Figure 1 lists the contents of the articles.

The corporation must have a name that is distinguishable from the name of any other corporation incorporated or qualified to do business in the state. The name must include the word *corporation, incorporated, company,* or *limited,* or the abbreviation *corp., inc., co.,* or *ltd.*

The MBCA does not require the inclusion of a statement of purpose in the articles. When a purpose is stated, it is sufficient to state, alone or together with specific purposes, that the corporation may engage in "any lawful activity."

The MBCA permits a corporation to have perpetual existence. If desired, the articles of incorporation may provide for a shorter duration.

Most of the state corporation statutes require the articles to recite the initial capitalization of the business. Usually, the statutes require that there be a minimum amount of initial capital, such as $1,000. Since such a small amount of capital is rarely enough to protect creditors adequately, the MBCA dispenses with the need to recite a minimum amount of capital. Instead, the thin capitalization rule we studied in Chapter 41 protects creditors.

The articles may contain additional provisions not inconsistent with law for managing the corporation, regulating the internal affairs of the corporation, and establishing the powers of the corporation and its directors and shareholders. For example, these additional provisions may contain the procedures for electing directors, the quorum requirements for shareholders' and directors' meetings, and the dividend rights of shareholders.

The MBCA specifies that one or more persons, including corporations, partnerships, and unincorporated associations, may serve as the **incorporators.** Incorporators have no function beyond lending their names and signatures to the process of bringing the corporation into existence. No special liability attaches to a person merely because she serves as an incorporator.

Filing Articles of Incorporation The articles of incorporation must be delivered to the office of the secretary of state, and a filing fee must be paid. The office of the secretary of state reviews the articles of incorporation that are delivered to it. If the articles contain everything that is

Figure 1   *Contents of Articles of Incorporation (pursuant to MBCA)*

The following *must* be in the articles:

1. The name of the corporation.

2. The number of shares that the corporation has authority to issue.

3. The address of the initial registered office of the corporation and the name of its registered agent.

4. The name and address of each incorporator.

The following *may* be included in the articles:

1. The names and addresses of the individuals who are to serve as the initial directors.

2. The purpose of the corporation.

3. The duration of the corporation.

4. The par value of shares of the corporation.

5. Additional provisions not inconsistent with law for managing the corporation, regulating the internal affairs of the corporation, and establishing the powers of the corporation and its directors and shareholders.

Ethics in Action

Domestic Tax Havens

In the last 20 years, some American companies have reincorporated all or part of their businesses in states that offer favorable tax treatment. For example, Limited Brands Inc., the owner of the Limited, Bath & Body Works, and Victoria's Secret chains, has incorporated seven subsidiaries in Delaware. The primary function of the subsidiaries is to own the chains' trademarks. The subsidiaries charge the retail chains high fees to use the trademarks. This parent–subsidiary structure allows the business to transfer hundreds of millions of dollars each year from retail outlets in high-tax states like New York into Delaware subsidiaries that pay no state tax. Delaware is the most used domestic tax haven, but Nevada and Florida also provide favorable tax treatment for corporations.

- Is it ethical and socially responsible for an American corporation to incorporate its business wholly or in part in states that have low tax rates? Would a profit maximizer incorporate where tax rates are lowest? Would a believer in rights theory?
- If you were a state legislator in a state with high income taxes that is losing incorporations to Delaware, what legislation would you introduce? Would your answer depend on whether you were a utilitarian or a believer in justice theory?

required, the secretary of state stamps the articles "Filed" and returns a copy of the stamped articles to the corporation along with a receipt for payment of incorporation fees. Some states require a duplicate filing of the articles with an office—usually the county recorder's office—in the county in which the corporation has its principal place of business.

The existence of the corporation begins when the articles are filed by the secretary of state. Filing of the articles by the secretary of state is conclusive proof of the existence of the corporation.

Because the articles of incorporation embody the basic contract between a corporation and its shareholders, shareholders must approve most changes in the articles. For example, when the articles are amended to increase the number of authorized shares, shareholder approval is required.

The Organization Meeting After the articles of incorporation have been filed by the secretary of state, an organization meeting is held. Usually, it is the first formal meeting of the directors. Frequently, only bylaws are adopted and officers elected. The function of the bylaws is to supplement the articles of incorporation by defining more precisely the powers, rights, and responsibilities of the corporation, its managers, and its shareholders and by stating other rules under which the corporation and its activities will be governed. Its common contents are listed in Figure 2.

The MBCA gives the incorporators or the initial directors the power to adopt the initial bylaws. The board of directors holds the power to repeal and to amend the bylaws, unless the articles reserve this power to the shareholders. Under the MBCA, the shareholders, as the ultimate owners of the corporation, always retain the power to amend the bylaws, even if the directors also have such power. To be valid, bylaws must be consistent with the law and with the articles of incorporation.

Figure 2   *Contents of the Bylaws*

1. The authority of the officers and the directors, specifying what they may or may not do.
2. The time and place at which the annual shareholders' meetings will be held.
3. The procedure for calling special meetings of shareholders.
4. The procedures for shareholders' and directors' meetings, including whether more than a majority is required for approval of specified actions.
5. Provisions for special committees of the board, defining their membership and the scope of their activities.
6. The procedures for the maintenance of share records.
7. The machinery for the transfer of shares.
8. The procedures and standards for the declaration and payment of dividends.

If the organization meeting is the first meeting of the board of directors, the board may adopt a corporate seal for use on corporate documents, approve the form of share certificates, accept share subscriptions, authorize the issuance of shares, adopt preincorporation contracts, authorize reimbursement for promoters' expenses, and fix the salaries of officers.

Filing Annual Report To retain its status as a corporation in good standing, a corporation must file an annual report with the secretary of state of the state of incorporation and pay an annual franchise fee or tax. The amount of annual franchise tax varies greatly from state to state. While the annual report includes very little information and repeats information already filed in the articles of incorporation, failure to file an annual report or pay the annual fee or tax may result in a dissolution of the corporation and an imposition of monetary penalties.

Close Corporation Elections

Close corporations face problems that normally do not affect publicly held corporations. In recognition of these problems, 20 states and the District of Columbia have statutes that attend to the special needs of close corporations. For example, some corporation statutes allow a close corporation to be managed by its shareholders.

To take advantage of these close corporation statutes, most statutes require that a corporation make an *election* to be treated as a close corporation. The Statutory Close Corporation Supplement to the MBCA permits a corporation with *fewer than 50 shareholders* to elect to become a close corporation. The Close Corporation Supplement requires the articles of incorporation to state that the corporation is a statutory close corporation.

There is no penalty for a corporation's failure to make a close corporation election. The only consequence of a failure to meet the requirements is that the close corporation statutory provisions are inapplicable. Instead, statutory corporation law will treat the corporation as it treats any other general corporation.

Note, however, that even when a corporation fails to meet the statutory requirements for treatment as a close corporation, a court may decide to apply special *common law* rules applicable only to close corporations.

LOG ON

www.incorporate.com

The Company Corporation is one of many Internet businesses providing incorporation assistance to new businesses. While incorporation services do not facilitate the drafting of articles and bylaws meeting the special needs of a corporation and its shareholders, at least they reduce the cost and burden of incorporating.

Defective Attempts to Incorporate

When business managers attempt to incorporate a business, sometimes they fail to comply with all the conditions for incorporation. For example, the incorporators may not have filed articles of incorporation or the directors may not have held an organization meeting. These are examples of **defective attempts to incorporate.**

One possible consequence of defective incorporation is to make the managers and the purported shareholders *personally liable* for the obligations of the defectively formed corporation. For example, an employee of an insolvent corporation drives the corporation's truck over a pedestrian. If the pedestrian proves that the corporation was defectively formed, he may be able to recover damages for his injuries from the managers and the shareholders.

A second possible consequence of defective incorporation is that a party to a contract involving the purported corporation may claim nonexistence of the corporation in order to avoid a contract made in the name of the corporation. For example, a person makes an ill-advised contract with a corporation. If the person proves that the corporation was defectively formed, he may escape liability on the contract because he made a contract with a nonexistent person, the defectively formed corporation. As an alternative, the defectively formed corporation may escape liability on the contract on the grounds that its nonexistence makes it impossible for it to have liability.

The courts have tried to determine when these two consequences should arise by making a distinction between de jure corporations, de facto corporations, corporations by estoppel, and corporations so defectively formed that they are treated as being nonexistent.

De Jure Corporation

A de jure corporation is formed when the promoters substantially comply with each of the **mandatory conditions precedent** to the incorporation of the business. *Mandatory* provisions are distinguished from *directory* provisions by statutory language and the purpose of the provision. Mandatory provisions are those that the corporation statute states "shall" or "must" be done or those that are necessary to protect the public interest. Directory provisions are those that "may" be done and that are unnecessary to protect the public interest.

For example, statutes provide that the incorporators shall file the articles of incorporation with the secretary of state. This is a mandatory provision, not only because of the use of the word *shall* but also because of the importance of a filing to protect the public interest by informing the public that a business has shareholders with limited liability. Other mandatory provisions include conducting an organization meeting. Directory provisions include minor matters such as the inclusion of the incorporators' addresses in the articles of incorporation.

If a corporation has complied with each mandatory provision, it is a de jure corporation and is treated as a corporation for all purposes. The validity of a de jure corporation cannot be attacked, except in a few states in which the state, in a *quo warranto* proceeding, may attack the corporation for noncompliance with a condition subsequent to incorporation, such as a failure to file an annual report with the secretary of state.

De Facto Corporation

A de facto corporation exists when the incorporators fail in some material respect to comply with all of the mandatory provisions of the incorporation statute yet comply with most mandatory provisions. There are three requirements for a de facto corporation:

1. There is a valid statute under which the corporation could be organized.

2. The promoters or managers make an honest attempt to organize under the statute. This requires substantial compliance with the mandatory provisions taken as a whole.

3. The promoters or managers exercise corporate powers. That is, they act as if they were acting for a corporation.

Generally, failing to file the articles of incorporation with the secretary of state will prevent the creation of a de facto corporation. However, a de facto corporation will exist despite the lack of an organization meeting or the failure to make a duplicate filing of the articles with a county recorder.

A de facto corporation is treated as a corporation against either an attack by a third party or an attempt of the business itself to deny that it is a corporation. The state, however, may attack the claimed corporate status of the business in a *quo warranto* action.

Corporation by Estoppel

When people hold themselves out as representing a corporation or believe themselves to be dealing with a corporation, a court will estop those people from denying the existence of a corporation. This is called **corporation by estoppel.** For example, a manager states that a business has been incorporated and induces a third person to contract with the purported corporation. The manager will not be permitted to use a failure to incorporate as a defense to the contract because he has misled others to believe reasonably that a corporation exists.

Under the doctrine of estoppel, each contract must be considered individually to determine whether either party to the contract is estopped from denying the corporation's existence.

Liability for Defective Incorporation

If people attempt to organize a corporation but their efforts are so defective that not even a corporation by estoppel is found to exist, the courts have generally held such persons to be partners with unlimited liability for the contracts and torts of the business. However, most courts impose the unlimited *contractual* liability of a partner only on those who are *actively engaged in the management* of the business or who are responsible for the defects in its organization. *Tort* liability, however, is generally imposed on everyone—the managers and the purported shareholders of the defectively formed corporation.

Modern Approaches to the Defective Incorporation Problem

As you can see, the law of defective incorporation is confusing. It becomes even more confusing when you consider that many of the defective incorporation cases look like promoter liability cases, and vice versa. A court may have difficulty deciding whether to apply the law of promoter liability or the law of defective incorporation to preincorporation contracts. It is not surprising, therefore, that modern corporation statutes have attempted to eliminate this confusion by adopting simple rules for determining the existence of a corporation and the liability of its promoters, managers, and shareholders.

The MBCA states that incorporation occurs when the articles are filed by the secretary of state. The **filing** of the articles is **conclusive proof** of the existence of the corporation, except in a proceeding brought by the state. Consequently, the incorporators may omit even a mandatory provision, yet create a corporation, provided that the secretary of state has filed the articles of incorporation. Conversely, courts have held that a failure to obtain a filing of the articles is conclusive proof of the nonexistence of the corporation, on the grounds that the MBCA eliminates the concepts of de facto corporation and corporation by estoppel.

Liability for Defective Incorporation under the MBCA The MBCA imposes joint and several liability on those persons who purport to act on behalf of a corporation and know that there has been no incorporation. Thus, managers and shareholders who both (1) *participate* in the operational decisions of the business and (2) *know* that the corporation does not exist are liable for the purported corporation's contracts and torts.

The MBCA releases from liability shareholders and others who either (1) take no part in the management of the defectively formed corporation *or* (2) mistakenly believe that the corporation is in existence. Consequently, *passive* shareholders have no liability for the obligations of a defectively formed corporation even when they know that the corporation has not been formed. Likewise, managers of a defectively formed corporation have no liability when they believe that the corporation exists.

The following case found two owners of a business liable as partners when they failed to comply with Tennessee's corporation statute.

Christmas Lumber Co., Inc. v. Valiga	99 S.W.3d 585 (Tenn. Ct. App. 2002)

Robert Waddell decided to go into the home construction business. He entered into a contract with Robert Valiga on September 12, 1988. When he entered into the contract with Valiga, Waddell signed the contract on behalf of R. H. Waddell Construction, Inc. At the time the contract was entered into with Valiga, Waddell had no knowledge that the corporation's articles of incorporation had not been filed. Although Waddell had signed the articles of incorporation as the incorporator on August 19, 1988, the articles were not filed by the Secretary of State's office until December 9, 1988, and by the Registrar's Office in Knox County until January 12, 1989.

On September 12, 1988, the same day Waddell entered into the contract with Valiga, John Graves opened an account at Christmas Lumber Company in order to obtain building materials for the Valiga house. Graves opened the account in Waddell's name, and where the account information stated "type of customer," Graves marked "individual." Graves signed the document on behalf of Waddell.

In a letter from Valiga to Waddell dated November 9, 1988, Valiga made several requests about the construction of the house. In a letter dated the next day, Valiga terminated Waddell's services. Sensing potential litigation, Waddell and Graves on November 11, 1988, entered into a Joint Venture Agreement. The only parties to the Agreement were Waddell and Graves. R. H. Waddell Construction, Inc., was not a party to the agreement. Pursuant to the terms of the Agreement, Waddell and Graves divided funds received from Heritage Federal Credit Union for construction of the Valiga home.

After Waddell patched things up with Valiga, he returned to work on the project from November until February of the next year. On February 11, 1989, Waddell received a letter from Valiga expressing his shock regarding the cost of the construction job. Three days later, Waddell quit as Valiga's contractor.

On January 10, 1990, Christmas Lumber Company filed a lawsuit against Valiga, Waddell, and others seeking to enforce a materialmen's lien for building materials purchased by Waddell to be used on the house being built for Valiga. On December 2, 1992, Valiga filed a separate lawsuit against Waddell and Graves claiming there was no corporation chartered by the State of Tennessee named R. H. Waddell Construction, Inc., when the contract was entered into on September 12, 1988.

After the two lawsuits were consolidated, the trial court found that Waddell and Graves were liable as partners on the construction contract signed in the name of R. H. Waddell Construction, Inc., and awarded Valiga damages of $80,045.79. Waddell and Graves appealed to the Tennessee Court of Appeals. The court considered Waddell's argument that he did not know that the corporation was not formed at the time the construction contract was signed.

Swiney, Judge

Waddell relies on Tenn. Code Ann. § 48-12-104, which provides as follows:

48-12-104. Liability for preincorporation transactions.
All persons purporting to act as or on behalf of a corporation, knowing there was no incorporation under chapters 11–27 of this title, are jointly and severally liable for all liabilities created while so acting except for any liability to any person who knew or reasonably should have known that there was no incorporation.

Waddell argues he signed the necessary paperwork to have his business incorporated and was unaware of the delay in filing the charter with the Secretary of State's office. He claims, therefore, he did not "know" there was no incorporation.

Pursuant to Tenn. Code Ann. § 48-12-103, absent a delayed effective date, the "corporate existence begins when the charter is filed by the secretary of state."

Waddell apparently signed the charter on August 19, 1988. On September 12, 1988, the contract was signed between Valiga and R. H. Waddell Construction, Inc. Two months later, on November 11, 1988, Waddell and Graves entered into the Joint Venture Agreement. On December 9, 1988, the charter was filed with the Secretary of State's office. Waddell's claim he did not "know" the corporate charter had not been filed with the Secretary of State is belied by the fact he and Graves essentially memorialized their relationship in writing with the Joint Venture Agreement which was signed after Waddell claims he "thought" there was a corporation and before the corporation actually was formed. Waddell's assertion is made further suspect by his deposition testimony that he and Graves were "partners."

Based on the roles occupied by Waddell and Graves during the construction of Valiga's house, coupled with: (1) the terms of Joint Venture Agreement; (2) Waddell's deposition testimony he and Graves were "partners;" (3) Graves' testimony that he spent a significant amount of time at the work site; and (4) Waddell and Graves dividing the contractor's fee, we conclude the evidence does not preponderate against the Trial Court's findings leading to its conclusion that Waddell and Graves were partners.

Judgment for Valiga affirmed.

Incorporation of Nonprofit Corporations

Nonprofit corporations are incorporated in substantially the same manner as for-profit corporations. One or more persons serve as incorporators and deliver articles of incorporation to the secretary of state for filing. A nonprofit corporation's articles must include the name and address of the corporation and state its registered agent. Unlike a for-profit corporation, a nonprofit corporation must state that it is either a public benefit corporation, a mutual benefit corporation, or a religious corporation. A public benefit corporation is incorporated primarily for the benefit of the public—for example, a community arts council that promotes the arts. A mutual benefit corporation is designed to benefit its members—for example, a golf country club. An example of a religious corporation is a church.

A nonprofit corporation's articles must also state whether it will have members. While it is typical for nonprofit corporations to have members, the Model Nonprofit Corporation Act (MNCA) does not require a nonprofit corporation to have members. An example of a nonprofit corporation having no members is a public benefit corporation established to promote business development in a city, whose directors are appointed by the city's mayor.

A nonprofit corporation's articles may include the purpose of the corporation, its initial directors, and any matter regarding the rights and duties of the corporation and its directors and members. Each incorporator and director named in the articles must sign the articles.

A nonprofit corporation's existence begins when the secretary of state files the articles. After incorporation, the initial directors or incorporators hold an organization meeting to adopt bylaws and conduct other business.

Liability for Preincorporation Transactions

Nonprofit corporation status normally protects the members and managers from personal liability. However, when a nonprofit corporation is not formed or is defectively formed, promoters and others who transact for the nonexistent nonprofit corporation have the same liability as promoters and others who transact for a nonexistent for-profit corporation. The MNCA states the same rule as the MBCA: Persons who act on behalf of a corporation knowing there is no corporation are jointly and severally liable for all liabilities created while so acting.

Similarly, promoters have no authority to make contracts for a nonexistent nonprofit corporation. The corporation becomes liable on preincorporation contracts when its board of directors adopts the contracts.

 L03 Know the appropriate sources for financing a business.

Financing For-Profit Corporations

Any business needs money to operate and to grow. One advantage of incorporation is the large number of sources of funds that are available to businesses that incorporate. One such source is the sale of corporate **securities,** including shares, debentures, bonds, and long-term notes payable.

In addition to obtaining funds from the sale of securities, a corporation may be financed by other sources. A bank may lend money to the corporation in exchange for the corporation's short-term promissory notes, called commercial paper. Earnings provide a source of funds once the corporation is operating profitably. In addition, the corporation may use normal short-term financing, such as accounts receivable financing and inventory financing, that is, borrowing from banks or other financial institutions and using the corporation's receivables or inventory as collateral.

In this section, you will study only one source of corporate funds—a corporation's sale of securities. A corporate security may be either (1) a share in the corporation or (2) an obligation of the corporation. These two kinds of securities are called equity securities and debt securities.

Equity Securities

Every business corporation issues equity securities, which are commonly called stock or **shares.** The issuance of shares creates an ownership relationship: the holders of the shares—called stockholders or **shareholders**—are the owners of the corporation.

Modern statutes permit corporations to issue several classes of shares and to determine the rights of the various classes. Subject to minimum guarantees contained in the state business corporation law, the shareholders' rights are a matter of contract and appear in the articles of incorporation, in the bylaws, in a shareholder agreement, and on the share certificates.

Common Shares Common shares (or common stock) are a type of equity security. Ordinarily, the owners of common shares—called **common shareholders**—have the exclusive right to elect the directors, who manage the corporation.

The common shareholders often occupy a position inferior to that of other investors, notably creditors and preferred shareholders. The claims of common shareholders are subordinate to the claims of creditors and other classes of shareholders when liabilities and dividends are paid and when assets are distributed upon liquidation.

In return for this subordination, however, the common shareholders have an exclusive claim to the corporate earnings and assets that exceed the claims of creditors and other shareholders. Therefore, the common shareholders bear the major risks of the corporate venture, yet stand to profit the most if it is successful.

Preferred Shares   Shares that have preferences with regard to assets or dividends over other classes of shares are called preferred shares (or preferred stock). **Preferred shareholders** are customarily given liquidation and dividend preferences over common shareholders. A corporation may have several classes of preferred shares. In such a situation, one class of preferred shares may be given preferences over another class of preferred shares. Under the MBCA, the preferences of preferred shareholders must be set out in the articles of incorporation.

The **liquidation preference** of preferred shares is usually a stated dollar amount. During a liquidation, this amount must be paid to each preferred shareholder before any common shareholder or other shareholder subordinated to the preferred class may receive his share of the corporation's assets.

Dividend preferences may vary greatly. For example, the dividends may be cumulative or noncumulative. Dividends on **cumulative** preferred shares, if not paid in any year, accumulate until paid. The entire accumulation must be paid before any dividends may be paid to common shareholders. Dividends on **noncumulative** preferred shares do not accumulate if unpaid. For such shares, only the current year's dividends must be paid to preferred shareholders prior to the payment of dividends to common shareholders.

Participating preferred shares have priority up to a stated amount or percentage of the dividends to be paid by the corporation. Then, the preferred shareholders participate with the common shareholders in additional dividends paid.

Some close corporations attempt to create preferred shares with a **mandatory dividend** right. These mandatory dividend provisions have generally been held illegal as unduly restricting the powers of the board of directors. Today, a few courts and some special close corporation statutes permit mandatory dividends for shareholders of close corporations.

A **redemption** or **call** provision in the articles allows a corporation at its option to repurchase preferred shareholders' shares at a price stated in the articles, despite the shareholders' unwillingness to sell. Some statutes permit the articles to give the shareholders the right to force the corporation to redeem preferred shares.

Preferred shares may be **convertible** into another class of shares, usually common shares. A **conversion** right allows a preferred shareholder to exchange her preferred shares for another class of shares, usually common shares. The conversion rate or price is stated in the articles.

Preferred shares have **voting rights** unless the articles provide otherwise. Usually, most voting rights are taken from preferred shares, except for important matters such as voting for a merger or a change in preferred shareholders' dividend rights. Rarely are preferred shareholders given the right to vote for directors, except in the event of a corporation's default in the payment of dividends.

Authorized, Issued, and Outstanding Shares
Authorized shares are shares that a corporation is permitted to issue by its articles of incorporation. A corporation may not issue more shares than are authorized. **Issued shares** are shares that have been sold to shareholders. **Outstanding shares** are shares that are currently held by shareholders. The distinctions between these terms are important. For example, a corporation pays cash, property, and share dividends only on outstanding shares. Only outstanding shares may be voted at a shareholders' meeting.

Canceled Shares   Sometimes, a corporation will purchase its own shares. A corporation may cancel repurchased shares. Canceled shares do not exist: They are neither authorized, issued, nor outstanding. Since canceled shares do not exist, they cannot be reissued.

Shares Restored to Unissued Status   Repurchased shares may be restored to unissued status instead of being canceled. If this is done, the shares are merely authorized and they may be reissued at a later time.

Treasury Shares   If repurchased shares are neither canceled nor restored to unissued status, they are called **treasury shares.** Such shares are authorized and issued, but not outstanding. They may be sold by the corporation at a later time. The corporation may not vote them at shareholders' meetings, and it may not pay a cash or property dividend on them.

The MBCA abolishes the concept of treasury shares. It provides that repurchased shares are restored to unissued status and may be reissued, unless the articles of incorporation require cancellation.

Options, Warrants, and Rights

Equity securities include options to purchase common shares and preferred shares. The MBCA expressly permits the board of directors to issue **options** for the purchase of the corporation's shares. Options permit their holders to purchase a specific number of shares at a specified price during a specified time period, usually beginning months or years after the option is issued. Share options are often issued to top level managers as an incentive to increase the profitability of the corporation. An increase in profitability should increase the market value of the corporation's shares, resulting in increased compensation to the employees who own and exercise share options.

Warrants are options evidenced by certificates. They are sometimes part of a package of securities sold as a unit. For example, they may be sold along with notes, bonds, or even shares. Underwriters may receive warrants as part of their compensation for aiding a corporation in selling its shares to the public.

Rights are short-term certificated options that are usually transferable. Rights are used to give present security holders an option to subscribe to a proportional quantity of the same or a different security of the corporation. They are most often issued in connection with a **preemptive right** requirement, which obligates a corporation to offer each existing shareholder the opportunity to buy the corporation's newly issued shares in the same proportion as the shareholder's current ownership of the corporation's shares.

Debt Securities

Corporations have inherent power to borrow money necessary for their operations by issuing debt securities. Debt securities create a debtor–creditor relationship between the corporation and the security holder. With the typical debt security, the corporation is obligated to pay interest periodically and to pay the amount of the debt (the principal) on the maturity date. Debt securities include debentures, bonds, and promissory notes.

Debentures are long-term, unsecured debt securities. Typically, a debenture has a term of 10 to 30 years. Debentures usually have indentures. An **indenture** is a contract that states the rights of the debenture holders. For example, an indenture defines what acts constitute default by the corporation and what rights the debenture holders have upon default. It may place restrictions on the corporation's right to issue other debt securities.

Bonds are long-term, secured debt securities that usually have indentures. They are identical to debentures except that bonds are secured by collateral. The collateral for bonds may be real property such as a building, or personal property such as a commercial airplane. If the debt is not paid, the bondholders may force the sale of the collateral and take the proceeds of the sale.

Generally, **notes** have a shorter duration than debentures or bonds. They seldom have terms exceeding five years. Notes may be secured or unsecured.

It is not uncommon for notes or debentures to be **convertible** into other securities, usually preferred or common shares. The right to convert belongs to the holder of the convertible note or debenture. This conversion right permits an investor to receive interest as a debt holder and, after conversion, to share in the increased value of the corporation as a shareholder.

Consideration for Shares

The board of directors has the power to issue shares on behalf of the corporation. The board must decide at what *price* and for what *type of consideration* it will issue the shares. Corporation statutes restrict the discretion of the board in accepting specified kinds of consideration and in determining the value of the shares it issues.

Quality of Consideration for Shares

Not all kinds of consideration in contract law are acceptable as legal consideration for shares in corporation law. To protect creditors and other shareholders, the statutes require legal consideration to have *real value*. Modern statutes, however, place few limits on the type of consideration that may be received for shares. The MBCA permits shares to be issued in return for any tangible or intangible *property* or *benefit to the corporation,* including cash, promissory notes, services performed for the corporation, contracts for services *to be performed* for the corporation, and securities of the corporation or another corporation. The rationale for the MBCA rule is a recognition that future services and promises of future services have value that is as real as that of tangible property. Consequently, for example, a corporation may issue common shares to its president in exchange for the president's commitment to work for the corporation for three years or in exchange for bonds of the corporation or debentures issued by another corporation. In addition, the MBCA permits corporations to issue shares to their promoters in consideration for their promoters' preincorporation services. This rule acknowledges that a corporation benefits from a promoter's preincorporation services.

Several states' constitutions place stricter limits on permissible consideration for shares. They provide that shares may be issued only for money paid to the corporation, labor done for the corporation, or property actually received by the corporation. Such a rule prohibits a corporation from issuing its shares for a promise to pay money or a promise to provide services to the corporation in the future.

Quantity of Consideration for Shares

The board is required to issue shares for an adequate dollar amount of consideration. Whether shares have been issued for an adequate amount of consideration depends in part on the *par value* of the shares. The more important concern, however, is whether the shares have been issued for *fair value.*

Par Value Par value is an arbitrary dollar amount that may be assigned to the shares by the articles of incorporation. Par value does not reflect the fair market value of the shares, but par value is the minimum amount of consideration for which the shares may be issued.

Shares issued for less than par value are called **discount shares.** The board of directors is liable to the corporation for issuing shares for less than par value. A shareholder who purchases shares from the corporation for less than par value is liable to the corporation for the difference between the par value and the amount she paid.

Fair Value It is not always enough, however, for the board to issue shares for their par value. Many times, shares are worth more than their par value. In addition, many shares today do not have a par value. In fact, the MBCA purports to eliminate the concept of par value as it affects the issuance of shares. In all cases, the board must exercise care to ensure that the corporation receives the *fair value* of the shares it issues. If there are no par value problems, the board's judgment as to the amount of consideration

that is received for the shares is *conclusive* when the board acts in good faith, exercises the care of ordinarily prudent directors, and acts in the best interests of the corporation.

Disputes may arise concerning the value of property that the corporation receives for its shares. The board's valuation of the consideration is conclusive if it acts in good faith with the care of prudent directors and in a manner it reasonably believes to be in the best interests of the corporation. When the board impermissibly overvalues the consideration for shares, the shareholder receives **watered shares.** Both the board and the shareholder are liable to the corporation when there is a watered shares problem.

When a shareholder pays less than the amount of consideration determined by the board of directors, the corporation or its creditors may sue the shareholder to recover the deficit. When a shareholder has paid the proper amount of consideration, the shares are said to be *fully paid and nonassessable.*

Accounting for Consideration Received The consideration received by a corporation for its equity securities appears in the equity or capital accounts in the shareholders' equity section of the corporation's balance sheet. The **stated capital** account records the product of the number of shares outstanding multiplied by the par value of each share. When the shares are sold for more than par value, the excess or surplus consideration received by the corporation is **capital surplus.**

Under the MBCA, the terms *stated capital* and *capital surplus* have been eliminated. All consideration received for shares is lumped under one accounting entry for that class of shares, such as common equity.

The Global Business Environment

Corporation Law Worldwide: Proper Consideration for Shares

There is substantial similarity in corporation laws from country to country. Even in many countries where corporation law is different from American law, there are legislative attempts to modernize the law by making it more nearly consistent with U.S. law. One example is Israel, whose Knesset has adopted a corporation law in line with Western law, especially American law.

Examining the requirements to incorporate and the limits on consideration for shares, there are some differences globally, but generally not much more than one sees from state to state in the United States. For example, although the MBCA permits corporate shares to be issued for any benefit to the corporation, the laws of many countries retain the historic American rule

(which is still law in many states) that certain types of benefits are improper consideration. For example, the corporate law of the Dominion of Melchizedek (which comprises a slice of Antarctica and five Pacific islands) states that consideration for the issuance of shares shall consist of money or other property, tangible or intangible, or labor or services actually received by or performed for the corporation or for its benefit or in its formation or reorganization. Its law prohibits the issuance of shares for future payments or future services.

Chinese law is bit more restrictive, allowing shareholders to make their investments only in cash, in kind, in industrial property rights, in nonpatented technology, or land use rights. The Kingdom of Bhutan is more limiting, however, forbidding share issuances for consideration other than cash, unless shareholders approve.

Resales of Shares The par value of shares is important *only when the shares are issued* by the corporation. Since treasury shares are issued but not outstanding, the corporation does not issue treasury shares when it resells them. Therefore, the board may sell treasury shares for less than par, provided that it sells the shares for an amount equal to their fair value.

Because par value and fair value are designed to ensure only that the corporation receives adequate consideration for its shares, a shareholder may buy shares from another shareholder for less than par value or fair value and incur no liability. However, if the purchasing shareholder *knows* that the selling shareholder bought the shares from the corporation for less than par value, the purchasing shareholder is liable to the corporation for the difference between the par value and the amount paid by the selling shareholder.

Share Subscriptions

Under the terms of a **share subscription,** a prospective shareholder promises to buy a specific number of shares of a corporation at a stated price. If the subscription is accepted by the corporation and the subscriber has paid for the shares, the subscriber is a shareholder of the corporation, even if the shares have not been issued. Under the MBCA, subscriptions need not be in writing to be enforceable. Usually, however, subscriptions are written.

Promoters use written share subscriptions in the course of selling shares of a proposed corporation to ensure that equity capital will be provided once the corporation comes into existence. These are called **preincorporation subscriptions,** which were covered in this chapter's discussion of promoters. Preincorporation subscriptions are not contracts binding on the corporation and the shareholders until the corporation comes into existence and its board of directors accepts the share subscriptions.

Close corporations may use share subscriptions when they seek to sell additional shares after incorporation. These are examples of **postincorporation subscriptions,** subscription agreements made *after* incorporation. A postincorporation subscription is a contract between the corporation and the subscriber at the time the subscription agreement is made.

A subscription may provide for payment of the price of the shares on a specified day, in installments, or upon the demand of the board of directors. The board may not discriminate when it demands payment: It must demand payment from all the subscribers of a class of shares or from none of them.

A share certificate may not be issued to a share subscriber until the price of the shares has been fully paid. If the subscriber fails to pay as agreed, the corporation may sue the subscriber for the amount owed.

Issuance of Shares

Uniform Commercial Code (UCC) Article 8 regulates the issuance of securities. Under Article 8, a corporation has a duty to issue only the number of shares authorized by its articles. Overissued shares are void.

When a person is entitled to overissued shares, the corporation may not issue the shares. However, the person has two remedies. The corporation must obtain identical shares and deliver or register them to the person entitled to issuance or the corporation must reimburse the person for the value paid for the shares plus interest.

The directors may incur liability, including criminal liability, for an overissuance of shares. To prevent overissuance through error in the issuance or transfer of their shares, corporations often employ a bank or a trust company as a registrar.

A share certificate is evidence that a person has been issued shares, owns the shares, and is a shareholder. The certificate states the corporation's name, the shareholder's name, and the number and class of shares. A person can be a shareholder without receiving a share certificate, such as a holder of a share subscription.

Under the MBCA, a corporation is not required to issue share certificates. If a corporation does not issue share certificates, it must register the security in the name of its owner or his agent, usually a stockbroker. Today, most shareholders of public companies never receive certificates, especially those who have brokerage accounts at online brokers like E*TRADE.

Transfer of Shares

Because share certificates are evidence of the ownership of shares, their transfer is evidence of the transfer of the ownership of shares. The MBCA and UCC Article 8 cover the registration and transfer of shares, both certificated and uncertificated.

Shares are issued in *registered* form; that is, they are registered with the corporation in the name of a specific person. The indorsement of a share certificate on its back by its registered owner and the delivery of the certificate to another person transfers ownership of the shares to the other person. The transfer of a share certificate without naming a transferee creates a *street certificate.* The transfer of a street certificate may be made by delivery without indorsement. Any holder of a street certificate is presumed to be the owner of the shares it represents. Therefore, a transferee should ask the corporation to reregister the shares in his name.

Ownership of uncertificated securities is transferred by a corporation's registering the security in the new owner's name.

Under the UCC, a corporation owes a duty to register the transfer of any registered shares presented to it for registration, provided that the shares have been properly indorsed, or in the case of uncertificated shares, the corporation has received an **instruction** notifying it of the transfer of ownership. If the corporation refuses to make the transfer, it is liable to the transferee for either conversion or specific performance.

When an owner of shares claims that his registration or certificate has been lost, destroyed, or stolen, the corporation must register new shares to the owner if the corporation has not received notice that the shares have been acquired by a bona fide purchaser, the owner files with the corporation a sufficient indemnity bond, and the owner meets any other reasonable requirements of the corporation. A **bona fide purchaser** is a purchaser of the shares for value in good faith with no notice of any adverse claim against the shares.

If, after the issuance of the new certificated shares or registration of new uncertificated shares, a bona fide purchaser of the original shares presents them for registration, the corporation must register the transfer, unless overissuance would result. In addition, the corporation may recover the new certificated shares from the original owner or revoke the new registration.

 Adopt appropriate share-transfer restrictions for a variety contexts.

Restrictions on Transferability of Shares

Historically, a shareholder has been free to sell her shares to whomever she wants whenever she wants. Such free transferability is important to shareholders in a publicly held corporation. Because shares in a publicly held corporation are freely transferable, shareholders know that they can easily liquidate their investment by selling their shares, often on a stock exchange.

In close corporations, however, free transferability as a legal matter is a threat to the balance of power among shareholders. For example, if one of three shareholders owning a third of a corporation sells his shares to one of the other shareholders, the buying shareholder will own two-thirds of the corporation and may be able to dominate the third shareholder. In addition, as a practical matter, free transferability of close corporation shares is illusory, as few people other than existing shareholders are willing to purchase shares in a close corporation.

Consequently, many close corporations restrict the transfer of shares to ensure those in control of a corporation will continue in control. Share-transfer restrictions can also be used to guarantee a market for the shares when a shareholder dies or retires from the corporation.

The courts have been reluctant to allow restrictions on the free transferability of shares, even if the shareholder agreed to a restriction on the transfer of her shares. Gradually, the courts and the legislatures have recognized that there are good reasons to permit the use of some restrictions on the transfer of shares. Today, modern corporation statutes allow most transfer restrictions, especially for close corporations.

Types of Restrictions on Transfer There are four categories of transfer restrictions: (1) rights of first refusal and option agreements, (2) buy-and-sell agreements, (3) consent restraints, and (4) provisions disqualifying purchasers.

A **right of first refusal** grants to the corporation or the other shareholders the right to match the offer that a selling shareholder receives for her shares. An **option agreement** grants the corporation or the other shareholders an option to buy the selling shareholder's shares at a price determined by the agreement. An option agreement will usually state a formula used to calculate the price of the shares.

A **buy-and-sell agreement** compels a shareholder to sell his shares to the corporation or to the other shareholders at the price stated in the agreement. It also obligates the corporation or the other shareholders to buy the selling shareholder's shares at that price. The price of the shares is usually determined by a stated formula.

A **consent restraint** requires a selling shareholder to obtain the consent of the corporation or the other shareholders before she may sell her shares. A **provision disqualifying purchasers** may be used in rare situations to exclude unwanted persons from the corporation. For example, a transfer restriction may prohibit the shareholders from selling to a competitor of the business.

Uses of Transfer Restrictions A corporation and its shareholders may use transfer restrictions to maintain the balance of shareholder power in the corporation. For example, four persons may own 25 shares each in a corporation. No single person can control such a corporation.

If one of the four can buy 26 additional shares from the other shareholders, he will acquire control. The shareholders may therefore agree that each shareholder is entitled or required to buy an equal amount of any shares sold by any selling shareholder. The right of first refusal, option agreement, or buy-and-sell agreement may serve this purpose.

A buy-and-sell agreement is the preferred transfer restriction for nearly every context in well-planned close corporations, because certainty is obtained by both sides being obligated, one required to buy and the other to sell. For example, a buy-and-sell agreement may be used to guarantee a shareholder a market for his shares. In a close corporation, there may be no ready market for the shares of the corporation. To ensure that a shareholder can obtain the value of her investment when she leaves the corporation, the shareholders or the corporation may be required to buy a shareholder's shares upon the occurrence of a specific event, such as death, disability, or retirement.

A buy-and-sell agreement may also be used to determine who should be required to sell and who should be required to buy shares when there is a severe disagreement between shareholders that threatens the profitability of the corporation. It could also be worded to require majority shareholders to buy the shares of minority shareholders when a lucrative merger offer for the corporation is rejected by the majority but favored by the minority. The agreement could, but rarely does, set the buyout price as the price offered in the merger.

If minority shareholders are afraid of being frozen in a close corporation that will never go public and give shareholders a chance to sell their shares on the market and get a return on investment, a buy-and-sell agreement could require the corporation to repurchase the minority's shares if the corporation has not gone public after a specified number of years.

In a close corporation, the shareholders may want only themselves or other approved persons as shareholders. A buy-and-sell agreement or right of first refusal may be used to prevent unwanted persons from becoming shareholders.

A provision disqualifying purchasers may be used in limited situations only, such as when the purchaser is a competitor of the business or has a criminal background.

A consent restraint is used to preserve a close corporation or Subchapter S taxation election. Close corporation statutes and Subchapter S of the Internal Revenue Code limit the number of shareholders that a close corporation or S corporation may have. A transfer restriction may prohibit the shareholders from selling shares if, as a result of the sale, there would be too many shareholders to preserve a close corporation or S corporation election. A consent restraint is also used to preserve an exemption from registration of a securities offering. Under the Securities Act of 1933 and the state securities acts, an offering of securities is exempt from registration if the offering is to a limited number of qualified investors, usually 35 financially sophisticated investors. A transfer restriction may require a selling shareholder to obtain permission from the corporation's legal counsel, which permission will be granted upon proof that the shareholder's sale of the shares does not cause the corporation to lose its registration exemption.

Legality of Transfer Restrictions Corporation statutes permit the use of option agreements, rights of first refusal, and buy-and-sell agreements with virtually no restrictions. The MBCA authorizes transfer restrictions for any reasonable purpose. The reasonableness of a restraint is judged in light of the character and needs of the corporation.

Consent restraints and provisions disqualifying purchasers may be used if they are not *manifestly unreasonable*. The MBCA makes per se reasonable any consent restraint that maintains a corporation's status when that status is dependent on the number or identity of shareholders, as with close corporation or S corporation status. The MBCA also makes per se reasonable any restriction that preserves registration exemptions under the Securities Act of 1933 and state securities laws.

Enforceability To be enforceable against a shareholder, a transfer restriction must be contained in the articles of incorporation, the bylaws, an agreement among the shareholders, or an agreement between the corporation and the shareholders. In addition, the shareholder must either agree to the restriction or purchase the shares with notice of the restriction. Under the MBCA, a purchaser of the shares has notice of a restriction if it is noted conspicuously on the face or the back of a share certificate or a written statement provided to shareholders if no certificates were issued. A purchaser also has notice if he knows of the restriction when he buys the shares or otherwise has been notified.

In the next case, *Coyle v. Schwartz,* the court enforced a buy-sell agreement in which the shareholders were to agree from time to time on the price to be paid for the shares. It is a good example of a poorly drafted buy-sell agreement that failed to attain the objectives of all the shareholders.

Coyle v. Schwartz	2004 Ky. App. LEXIS 75 (Ky. Ct. App. 2004)

American Scale Corporation, a closely held Kentucky corporation with its principal place of business in Louisville, Kentucky, was incorporated in February 1985 to engage in the sale and repair of industrial and commercial scales. Daniel Coyle was president and Steven Schwartz was vice president. They were the sole shareholders. At the time of incorporation, Coyle and Schwartz each received 200 shares of stock in exchange for their capital contributions of $10,000.

In early March 1986 Schwartz had an automobile accident in which his passenger was seriously injured. Schwartz's passenger filed suit against American Scale, since it had provided insurance coverage on Schwartz's vehicle. Coyle became concerned that Schwartz's activities would expose American Scale to further liability. He was particularly displeased with Schwartz's actions in transporting an underage female, who was purportedly Schwartz's girlfriend, in a vehicle insured by American Scale.

As a result, Coyle informed Schwartz that he no longer desired to be in a 50–50 shareholder with him. Coyle told Schwartz that unless Schwartz agreed to transfer 1 percent of his shares to Coyle, thereby permitting Coyle to assume majority control of American Scale, Coyle would either seek dissolution of American Scale, or withdraw and begin operating a business in competition with American Scale. On March 21, 1986, Coyle and Schwartz executed a share-transfer agreement wherein Schwartz transferred 1 percent of his American Scale shares to Coyle. The agreement specifically stated that Coyle would thereafter own a 51 percent interest in American Scale, leaving Schwartz as owner of the remaining 49 percent of American Scale's shares.

About two years later, on August 25, 1988, Coyle and Schwartz made a buy-sell agreement that they titled, "Stockholders' Cross-Purchase Agreement." The agreement provided for the repurchase of a shareholder's stock in the event of death, disability, or voluntary withdrawal of that shareholder. Specifically, the agreement stated that if Coyle or Schwartz died, or otherwise attempted to dispose of his shares, the other shareholder would have the right to purchase those shares. In addition, the agreement gave the majority shareholder an option to purchase all of the minority shareholder's stock at any time upon a 60-day written notice.

The agreement provided a stock-valuation method for determining a per share price in the event either of the provisions was triggered:

> Unless altered as herein provided, for the purpose of determining the purchase price to be paid for the stock of a Stockholder, the fair market value of each share of stock shall be, as of August 25, 1988, $250.
>
> The Stockholders shall redetermine the value of the stock within 60 days following the end of each fiscal year. If the Stockholders fail to make the required annual redetermination of value for a particular year, the last previously recorded value shall control.

Over the course of the next 12 years, neither Coyle nor Schwartz attempted to revaluate the price of American Scale's shares as provided in the agreement. Hence, the initial buyout price of $250 per share was never changed.

In a letter dated November 20, 2000, Coyle informed Schwartz that he was exercising his option as majority shareholder to purchase Schwartz's stock for $250 per share. Schwartz refused to tender his shares to Coyle and filed suit against Coyle seeking to invalidate the buyout agreement. Schwartz argued that the shareholders had abandoned the agreement by not changing the buyout price for 12 years. Schwartz also argued that the buyout price was so low as to constitute a penalty. In response to Coyle's motion for summary judgment, the trial court ruled that the shareholders had not abandoned the agreement. However, the court agreed with Schwartz that forcing him to sell all of his stock at the price of $250 per share was a penalty and, therefore, unenforceable. The trial court ordered a current valuation of the stock be undertaken before Schwartz could be compelled to transfer his shares. Coyle appealed to the Kentucky Court of Appeals.

Johnson, Judge

In his appeal, Coyle argues that the trial court erred by finding that the stock-valuation provision was unenforceable as a penalty.

While Coyle and Schwartz never revaluated the stock, this fact alone does not render the provision unenforceable. Schwartz, as owner of 49% of American Scale's outstanding shares, had the right under the corporation's bylaws to call for a special meeting to revaluate the listed price of American Scale's shares. Schwartz has admitted in his deposition testimony that

he never made such a request. Hence, by sitting on his rights for over 12 years, Schwartz took the risk that Coyle would exercise the majority-purchase option at a time when the actual value of American Scale's shares was in excess of the $250 price originally listed in the stock-valuation provision. Schwartz is not entitled to have the courts rewrite the parties' agreement simply because he believes he is receiving the short end of the bargain. Accordingly, we reverse the trial court's finding that the stock-valuation provision listing a price of $250 per share was unenforceable.

The terms of the stock-valuation provision listed an original price of $250 per share. The provision further stated that the fair market value shall be $250 "unless altered as herein provided" via the "mutual agreement" revaluation method. Since the parties failed to revaluate the price of American Scale's shares, $250 is the "last recorded value" with respect to the price of the corporation's shares. Therefore, the majority-purchase option and the stock-valuation provision entitle Coyle to purchase all of Schwartz's stock at a price of $250 per share.

Finally, we address Schwartz's claim that the trial court erred by finding that Schwartz and Coyle did not abandon the stock-valuation provision of the cross-purchase agreement. Specifically, Schwartz argues that by completely ignoring the cross-purchase agreement's requirement that both shareholders "shall re-determine the value of the stock within 60 days following the end of each fiscal year" and record the same, as well as their intention to revalue their shares in American Scale, Schwartz and Coyle unequivocally acted in a manner inconsistent with the existence of the cross-purchase agreement.

We disagree and hold that the trial court did not err by finding that Coyle and Schwartz did not abandon their rights under the stock-valuation provision. A contract may be rescinded or discharged by acts or conduct of the parties inconsistent with the continued existence of the contract, and mutual assent to abandon a contract may be inferred from the attendant circumstances and conduct of the parties. While as a general rule a contract will be treated as abandoned or rescinded where the acts and conduct of one party inconsistent with its existence are acquiesced in by the other party, to be sufficient the acts and conduct must be positive and unequivocal.

In the instant case, while Coyle and Schwartz never revaluated American Scale's stock in the years following the execution of the cross-purchase agreement, this fact, standing alone, does not constitute "positive and unequivocal" acts which could lead to a finding of abandonment. The stock-valuation provision itself provided a default price for the stock in the event the parties failed to revaluate the shares. Therefore, Coyle and Schwartz contemplated that they might not always conduct a revaluation. Accordingly, the failure of Coyle and Schwartz to conduct an annual revaluation of American Scale's shares did not constitute an abandonment of the stock-valuation provision.

Judgment reversed in favor of Coyle.

Statutory Solution to Close Corporation Share-Transfer Problems Although transfer restrictions are important to close corporations, many close corporation shareholders fail to address the share transferability problem. Therefore, a few states provide statutory resolution of the close corporation transferability problem. In these states, statutes offer solutions to the transferability problem that are similar to the solutions that the shareholders would have provided had they thought about the problem. Not all transferability problems are settled by the Close Corporation Supplement, however. For example, there is no statutory buy-and-sell provision.

LOG ON

www.mhhe.com/mallor15e

Check out a model share transfer restriction at the website for this textbook. Note that the buy-sell agreement has four essential components: the events triggering a buyout, the persons obligated to buy and shareholders required to sell, the buyout price, and the timing of the payments to the selling shareholder.

Financing Nonprofit Corporations

Nonprofit corporations are financed differently from for-profit corporations. This is especially true of a public benefit corporation such as a public television station, which obtains annual financing from government sources, private foundations, members, and public contributors. A religious corporation such as a church receives weekly offerings from its congregation and may occasionally conduct capital drives to obtain additional funding from its members. A mutual benefit corporation, such as a fraternal or social organization like an Elks Club or golf country club, obtains initial funding from its original members to build facilities and assesses its members annually and monthly to pay operating expenses. In addition, nonprofit corporations have the power to obtain debt financing, such as borrowing from a bank or issuing notes and debentures.

A nonprofit corporation may admit members whether or not they pay consideration for their memberships. There is no statutory limit on the number of members a nonprofit corporation may admit, although the articles may place a limit on the number of members. Social clubs typically limit the number of members. Members must be admitted in compliance with procedures stated in the articles or the bylaws.

Generally, memberships in a nonpublic corporation are not freely transferable. No member of a public benefit corporation or religious corporation may transfer her membership or any rights she possesses as a member. A member of a mutual benefit corporation may transfer her membership and rights only if the articles or bylaws permit. When transfer rights are permitted, restrictions on transfer are valid only if approved by the members, including the affected member.

Problems and Problem Cases

1. You and three of your friends have entered negotiations with Toyota Motor Sales USA to acquire a Lexus automobile dealership. You plan to operate the dealership as a corporation, to be named Community Lexus, Inc. You and your three friends have not yet formed the corporation. You will be the president and CEO of the corporation. Among the many agreements that will be signed are a contract to purchase automobiles from Toyota, joint advertising agreements with Toyota, and loan contracts with Genesee National Bank. What should you do before you sign any of these contracts on behalf of Community Lexus, Inc.?

2. Roy Rose signed articles of incorporation for R&F Capital Corporation in December 1989, but Flaherty, who had been entrusted by Rose to create R&F, failed to file the articles until February 9, 1990. On January 12, 1990, purporting to act on behalf of R&F as its chairman, Rose signed a contract to lease a warehouse owned by Dennis Sivers. When R&F breached the lease, Sivers claimed that Rose was liable on the lease because he should have known on the basis of his vast experience as a businessman that R&F was not incorporated. Rose and another R&F director testified that they both believed R&F had been incorporated in December 1989, and Rose said he would not have invested in R&F or signed a document on its behalf if he had known that R&F was not incorporated. Was Rose found liable on the lease?

3. Hydro-Dynamics, Inc. (HDI), manufactured bed sheets, principally for waterbeds. HDI purchased cloth from Fieldcrest Cannon, Inc., on credit for several years. John Meyer was an officer and director of HDI from May 22, 1987, until HDI's dissolution on September 10, 1990. After HDI's dissolution, Meyer continued to act as if HDI was a corporation, and in the name of HDI, he continued for many months to make contracts and buy cloth on credit from Fieldcrest. Fieldcrest was not aware that HDI ceased to exist. Is Meyer personally liable on the contracts he made with Fieldcrest in the name of HDI after its dissolution?

4. George Richert agreed to retain Crye-Leike Realtors, Inc., as his sole and exclusive real estate agent to find a building for Richert's business. The agency contract was signed by Richert and by Colman Borosky for Crye-Leike. All parties understood that Richert would soon form a corporation that would be the actual party to lease the building found by Crye-Leike. A month later, Richert formed WDM, Inc. Richert was president and CEO. WDM never formally adopted the agency contract with Crye-Leike. However, Crye-Leike contacted various landlords for WDM, showed several properties to WDM, and prepared an offer to lease space on behalf of WDM. All these efforts were done with Richert's full knowledge. When WDM hired another real estate agent, Crye-Leike sued for breach of the exclusive agency contract. WDM claimed that it was not a party to the contract between Richert and Crye-Leike. Was WDM correct?

5. Two colleagues decide to incorporate their Internet social networking business. They want complete control of the business, yet they need additional capital to expand the business. The two colleagues enter negotiations with eight friends willing to provide capital to the corporation. The friends agree that they will not be allowed to elect directors, but they want to make sure that they will receive a return on their investments by receiving payments from the corporation quarterly or semiannually. What securities with what rights should the corporation create to achieve the objectives of the friends and colleagues? For each security you create, sketch the rights of the holders.

6. Pacific Coast Fisheries Corporation issued more than 5 percent of its public shares to Fujian Pelagic Fishery Group Company under the laws of the state of Washington. Fujian did not pay cash for the shares, instead issuing to Pacific Coast a promissory note committing it to pay in the future in the form of merchandise. Has Fujian paid a proper consideration for the shares?

7. Miranda Juarez is hired as the CEO of Spanata Corporation. Spanata's board of directors issues to Juarez 100,000 common shares of Spanata as part of her compensation package. Jaurez receives the shares in return for her giving a contractual promise to be Spanata's CEO for five years and her issuing to Spanata a promissory note in which Jaurez promises to pay $500,000 in five years. Has the board of directors issued the shares for a proper type of consideration?

8. Seven Springs Farm, Inc., is a Pennsylvanian corporation that owns and operates a 5,000-acre, year-round resort, with both skiing facilities and a conference center. The shareholders signed an agreement, providing that no stockholder "shall transfer, assign, sell, pledge, hypothecate, mortgage, alienate or in any other way encumber or dispose of all or any part of his stock in the Corporation . . . without first giving to all other Stockholders and the Corporation at least 30 days written notice . . . of his intention to make a disposition of his stock. . . . Within the 30 day period a special meeting of all of the Stockholders shall be called by the Corporation. . . . At such meeting all the stock of the Stockholders . . . shall be offered for sale and shall be subject to an option to purchase or to retire on the part of the Corporation, which option shall be exercised, if at all, at the time of such meeting. . . ." In 1998, two-thirds of the shareholders voted to merge the corporation with Booth Creek Ski Holding, Inc. Due to the merger, the existing shares of Seven Springs would be "converted" into the right to receive cash and certain deferred cash payments. The dissenting shareholder, Lynda Croker, sought to purchase the shares of the shareholders who approved the merger, arguing that the merger with Booth Creek invoked the shareholders' right of first refusal. Was Croker correct?

9. Stufft Farms, Inc., was a Montana corporation that owned and operated a family farm. The only shareholders were five family members. The bylaws included a share-transfer restriction stating that no shareholder had the right to sell her shares without first offering the shares to the corporation and shareholders at book value. Neil Johnson offered to purchase all of Stufft Farm's shares. His offer was contingent upon all of the shares being tendered to him. When four shareholders accepted Johnson's offer, the fifth shareholder, David Stufft, who did not accept the offer, argued that he had the right to buy the shares of the tendering four shareholders at book value. Was he correct?

10. Josh Thomas, Jack Wiley, and Will Regis are three close friends who have been offered the opportunity to invest $100,000 each and to become 10 percent shareholders each in a closely held corporation that will be controlled by their friends Leone and Teddy Battat, who will own the remaining the 70 percent of the shares. The business, to be named EZStreet.com, Inc., will be an online business networking site. Leone and Teddy's plan is to amass at least 500 million users worldwide, which they estimate will take five to seven years, after which they would like to take the company public or sell it to another company, like Google. Josh is a CPA with 10 years experience in business consulting and investment management. Jack is a software engineer who has designed more than 50 websites. Will has an MBA in consumer and business marketing with 12 years experience in public relations and ad sales. Sketch the terms of the agreement that Josh, Jack, and Will should ask of Leone and Teddy to ensure that they will obtain returns on their investments while they are shareholders before the company goes public or is sold to another company. In addition, what type of agreement should they have to make sure they can obtain capital appreciation of their shares when the corporation goes public or is sold to another company? Sketch the contents of that agreement. How do you suggest the agreement determine the value of the shares?

Online Research

Pricing Incorporation

Type "incorporate" in your Internet search engine and you will obtain a list of companies that assist persons who wish to incorporate a business. Most incorporation websites quote their fees for assisting incorporation and also fees assessed by the state of incorporation. Find which website offers the most services at the best price.

Note that some websites sell corporate kits. A corporate kit is a notebook with sample bylaws, organization meeting minutes, stock certificates, and a stock transfer ledger. Corporate kits usually include a corporate seal, which is used to emboss the corporation's name on official documents. Banks and other institutions may require that all documents signed by a corporation bear the corporate seal.

CHAPTER 43

MANAGEMENT OF CORPORATIONS

Clestra Corporation is a manufacturer of consumer products ranging from canned and packaged foods like spaghetti sauce and popcorn to over-the-counter health aids like toothpaste and mouthwash. Its annual worldwide revenues are just under $6 billion. Clestra brands are not among the top two in the industry in any of its product lines, each brand ranking from fourth to sixth in annual sales in countries in which it markets its products. Clestra's CEO has been discussing the company's future with its consultant, KRNP Consulting LLP. KRNP has suggested that Clestra consider acquiring Ballmax, Inc., a consumer products company with two billion dollars annual sales. Ballmax's brands are complementary to Clestra's brands, and while smaller than Clestra, Ballmax has a distribution system that will give Clestra access to markets in which Clestra is not currently a significant seller.

Clestra's CEO also wants to improve consumer recognition of the Clestra brand. She suggests that Clestra acquire naming rights to a stadium being built for a baseball team in northern Virginia, the Virginia Hatchets. The CEO thinks that Clestra has the inside track to acquire naming rights because the family of one of Clestra's board members owns the baseball team that will own and operate the stadium.

- What legal standard will determine whether Clestra's board of directors has acted properly when approving Clestra's acquisition of Ballmax, Inc.? What role may KRNP Consulting take in helping Clestra's board of directors meet its duties under that legal standard?
- What legal standard will judge whether Clestra's board of directors has acted properly when acquiring naming rights to the Virginia Hatchets' stadium? What role may KRNP Consulting take in helping Clestra's board of directors meet its duties under that legal standard?
- Suppose Clestra's CEO is concerned that Clestra may be a target for a takeover by one of the larger consumer goods companies. If Clestra wants to remain an independent company, what should Clestra's board of directors do now to increase the chances that it may fend off a hostile takeover? What legal standard will judge whether Clestra's board has acted properly in adopting defenses against a hostile takeover? What should Clestra's board do now to increase the likelihood that the board will comply with that legal standard when it opposes a hostile takeover?

LO LEARNING OBJECTIVES

After studying this chapter, you should be able to:

1 Understand the limits on the objectives and powers of corporations, especially the pressures corporate managers face in satisfying the interests of shareholders and other constituents.

2 Appreciate the roles of the board of directors and its various committees.

3 Describe recent developments in corporate governance.

4 Adapt the rules of corporate governance to the practical requirements of close corporations.

5 Know the legal standards that judge actions of officers and directors and apply the steps required to comply with each standard.

6 List and describe tactics a board of directors may adopt to defend against hostile takeovers.

7 Explain the legal limits of corporate liability for officers' and directors' actions.

ALTHOUGH SHAREHOLDERS OWN a corporation, they traditionally have possessed no right to manage the business of the corporation. Instead, shareholders elect individuals to a *board of directors,* to which management is entrusted. Often, the board delegates much of its management responsibilities to *officers.*

This chapter explains the legal aspects of the board's and officers' management of the corporation. Their management of the corporation must be consistent with the objectives and powers of the corporation, and they owe duties to the corporation to manage it prudently and in the best interests of the corporation and the shareholders as a whole.

 LO1 Understand the limits on the objectives and powers of corporations, especially the pressures corporate managers face in satisfying the interests of shareholders and other constituents.

Corporate Objectives

The traditional objective of the business corporation has been to *enhance corporate profits and shareholder gain.* According to this objective, the managers of a corporation must seek the accomplishment of the profit objective to the exclusion of all inconsistent goals. Interests other than profit maximization may be considered, provided that they do not hinder the ultimate profit objective.

Nonetheless, some courts have permitted corporations to take *socially responsible actions* that are *beyond the profit maximization requirement.* In addition, every state recognizes corporate powers that are not economically inspired. For example, corporations may make contributions to colleges, political campaigns, child abuse prevention centers, literary associations, and employee benefit plans, regardless of economic benefit to the corporations. Also, every state expressly recognizes the right of shareholders to choose freely the extent to which profit maximization captures all of their interests and all of their sense of responsibility.

Most states have enacted **corporate constituency statutes,** which broaden the legal objectives of corporations. Such statutes permit or require directors to take into account the interests of constituencies other than shareholders, including employees, suppliers, and customers. These statutes direct the board to act in the best interests of the corporation, not just the interests of the shareholders, and to maximize corporate profits *over the long term.* The new laws promote the view that a corporation is a collection of interests working together for the purpose of producing goods and services at a profit, and that the goal of corporate profit maximization over the long term is not necessarily the same as the goal of stock price maximization over the short term.

Ethics in Action

Corporate Constituency Statutes

About two-thirds of the states have enacted corporate constituency stakeholder laws that permit directors to weigh the interests of constituencies other than shareholders. Only Connecticut and Arizona require the consideration of other constituencies. The other states permit, but do not require, directors to consider interests other than those of shareholders.

- Would you recommend that board members consider the interests of stakeholders other than shareholders when making a corporate decision?
- Which ethical theories that we studied in Chapter 4 permit directors to consider the interests of constituencies other than shareholders?
- Under profit maximization, what is the significance of non-shareholders' interests? Can a corporation maximize its profits without considering the interests of persons other than shareholders?

Corporate Powers

The actions of management are limited not only by the objectives of business corporations but also by the *powers* granted to business corporations. Such limitations may appear in the state statute, the articles of incorporation, and the bylaws.

The primary source of a corporation's powers is the corporation statute of the state in which it is incorporated. Some state corporation statutes expressly specify the powers of corporations. These powers include making gifts for charitable and educational purposes, lending money to corporate officers and directors, and purchasing and disposing of the corporation's shares. Other state corporation statutes limit the powers of corporations, such as prohibiting the acquisition of agricultural land by corporations.

Modern statutes attempt to authorize corporations to engage in any activity. The Model Business Corporation Act (MBCA) states that a corporation has the power to do *anything that an individual may do.*

Purpose Clauses in Articles of Incorporation

Most corporations state their purposes in the articles of incorporation. The purpose is usually phrased in broad terms, even if the corporation has been formed with only one type of business in mind. Most corporations have purpose clauses stating that they may engage in any lawful business.

Under the MBCA, the inclusion of a purpose clause in the articles is optional. Any corporation incorporated under the MBCA has the purpose of engaging in any lawful business, unless the articles state a narrower purpose.

The Ultra Vires *Doctrine* Historically, an act of a corporation beyond its powers was a nullity, as it was *ultra vires,* which is Latin for "beyond the powers." Therefore, any act not permitted by the corporation statute or by the corporation's articles of incorporation was void due to lack of capacity.

This lack of capacity or power of the corporation was a defense to a contract assertable either by the corporation or by the other party that dealt with the corporation. Often, *ultra vires* was merely a convenient justification for reneging on an agreement that was no longer considered desirable. This misuse of the doctrine has led to its near abandonment.

Today, the *ultra vires* doctrine is of small importance for two reasons. First, nearly all corporations have broad purpose clauses, thereby preventing any *ultra vires* problem. Second, the MBCA and most other statutes do not permit a corporation or the other party to an agreement to avoid an obligation on the ground that the corporate action is *ultra vires.*

Under the MBCA, *ultra vires* may be asserted by only three types of persons: (1) by a shareholder seeking to enjoin a corporation from executing a proposed action that is *ultra vires;* (2) by the corporation suing its management for damages caused by exceeding the corporation's powers; and (3) by the state's attorney general, who may have the power to enjoin an *ultra vires* act or to dissolve a corporation that exceeds its powers.

Powers of Nonprofit Corporations

Nonprofit corporations, like for-profit corporations, have the power to transact business granted by the incorporation statute, the articles, and the bylaws. The Model Nonprofit Corporation Act (MNCA), like the MBCA, grants nonprofit corporations the power to engage in any lawful activity and to do anything an individual may do. Thus, a nonprofit corporation may sue and be sued, purchase, hold, and sell real property, lend and borrow money, and make charitable and other donations, among its many powers.

Commonly, a nonprofit corporation's articles will limit its powers pursuant to a purpose clause. For example, a nonprofit corporation established to operate a junior baseball league may limit its powers to that business and matters reasonably connected to it. When a nonprofit corporation limits its powers, a risk arises that the corporation may commit an *ultra vires* act. The MNCA adopts the same rules for *ultra vires* contracts as does the MBCA: Generally, neither the corporation nor the other party may use *ultra vires* as a defense to a contract.

 Appreciate the roles of the board of directors and its various committees.

The Board of Directors

Traditionally, the **board of directors** has had the authority and the duty to manage the corporation. Yet in a large publicly held corporation, it is impossible for the board to manage the corporation on a day-to-day basis, because many of the directors are high-level executives in other corporations and devote most of their time to their other business interests. Therefore, the MBCA permits a corporation to be managed *under the direction of* the board of directors. Consequently, the board of directors delegates major responsibility for management to committees of the board such as an executive committee, to individual board members such as the chairman of the board, and to the officers of the corporation, especially the chief executive officer (CEO). In theory, the board supervises the actions of its committees, the chairman, and the officers to ensure that the board's policies are being carried out and that the delegatees are managing the corporation prudently.

Board Authority under Corporation Statutes

A corporation's board of directors has the authority to do almost everything within the powers of the corporation. The board's authority includes not only the general power to manage or direct the corporation in the ordinary course of its business but also the power to issue shares of stock and to set the price of shares. Among its other powers, the board may repurchase shares, declare dividends, adopt and amend bylaws, elect and remove officers, and fill vacancies on the board.

Some corporate actions require *board initiative* and shareholder approval. That is, board approval is necessary to *propose such actions to the shareholders,* who then must approve the action. Board initiative is required for important changes in the corporation, such as amendment of the articles of incorporation, merger of the corporation, the sale of all or substantially all of the corporation's assets, and voluntary dissolution.

Committees of the Board

Most publicly held corporations have committees of the board of directors. These committees, which have fewer members than the board has, can more efficiently handle management decisions and exercise board powers than can a large board. Only directors may serve on board committees.

Although many board powers may be delegated to committees of the board, some decisions are so important that corporation statutes require their *approval by the board as a whole.* Under the MBCA, the powers that may not be delegated concern important corporate actions such as declaring dividends, filling vacancies on the board or its committees, adopting and amending bylaws, approving issuances of shares, and approving repurchases of the corporation's shares.

The most common board committee is the **executive committee.** It is usually given authority to act for the board on most matters when the board is not in session. Generally, it consists of the inside directors and perhaps one or two outside directors who can attend a meeting on short notice. An inside director is an officer of the corporation who devotes substantially full time to the corporation. Outside directors have no such affiliation with the corporation.

Audit committees are directly responsible for the appointment, compensation, and oversight of independent public accountants. They supervise the public accountants' audit of the corporate financial records. The Sarbanes–Oxley Act requires that all publicly held firms have audit committees comprising independent directors. That act was a response to allegations of unethical and criminal conduct by corporate CEOs and auditors at firms like Enron, WorldCom, and Arthur Andersen in the 1990s and early 2000s. Rules of the New York Stock Exchange (NYSE) and the National Association of Securities Dealers (NASD), which apply to firms listed on the NYSE or NASDAQ, require that independent directors approve audit committee nominations.

Nominating committees choose management's slate of directors that is to be submitted to shareholders at the annual election of directors. Nominating committees also often plan generally for management succession. Nominating committees wholly or largely comprise outside directors.

Compensation committees review and approve the salaries, bonuses, stock options, and other benefits of high-level corporate executives. Although compensation committees usually comprise directors who have no affiliation with the executives or directors whose compensation is being approved, compensation committees may also set the compensation of their members. Directors of a typical corporation receive annual compensation between $30,000 to $60,000.

The public and Congress have criticized board approvals of large compensation packages to CEOs and other top level officers, including stock options and bonus plans that sometimes allowed individual officers to earn more than $100 million in a single year. Hoping that board independence would rein in such compensation, the Securities and Exchange Commission (SEC) has adopted NYSE and NASD rules that require independent directors to approve executive compensation. The Dodd-Frank Wall Street Reform and Consumer Protection Act of 2010 also requires periodic shareholder approval of executive compensation.

A **shareholder litigation committee** is given the task of determining whether a corporation should sue someone who has allegedly harmed the corporation. Usually, this committee of disinterested directors is formed when a shareholder asks the board of directors to cause the corporation to sue some or all of the directors for mismanaging the corporation.

Powers, Rights, and Liabilities of Directors as Individuals

A director is not an agent of the corporation *merely* by being a director. The directors may manage the corporation only when they act as a board, unless the board of directors grants agency powers to the directors individually.

A director has the *right to inspect* corporate books and records that contain corporate information essential to the director's performance of her duties. The director's right of inspection is denied when the director has an interest adverse to the corporation, as in the case of a director who plans to sell a corporation's trade secrets to a competitor.

Normally, a director does not have any personal liability for the contracts and torts of the corporation.

Election of Directors

Generally, any individual may serve as a director of a corporation. A director need not even be a shareholder. Nonetheless, a corporation is permitted to specify qualifications for directors in the articles of incorporation.

A corporation must have the number of directors required by the state corporation law. The MBCA and several state corporation statutes require a minimum of one director, recognizing that in close corporations with a single shareholder-manager, additional board members are superfluous. Several statutes, including the California statute, require at least three directors, unless there are fewer than three shareholders, in which case the corporation may have no fewer directors than it has shareholders.

A corporation may have more than the minimum number of directors required by the corporation statute. The articles of incorporation or bylaws will state the number of directors of the corporation. Most large publicly held corporations have boards with 15 or more members.

Directors are elected by the shareholders at the annual shareholder meeting. Usually, each shareholder is permitted to vote for as many nominees as there are directors to be elected. The shareholder may cast as many votes for each nominee as he has shares. The top votegetters among the nominees are elected as directors. This voting process, called **straight voting,** permits a holder of more than 50 percent of the shares of a corporation to dominate the corporation by electing a board of directors that will manage the corporation as he wants it to be managed.

To avoid domination by a large shareholder, some corporations allow class voting or cumulative voting. **Class voting** may give certain classes of shareholders the right to elect a specified number of directors. **Cumulative voting** permits shareholders to multiply the number of their shares by the number of directors to be elected and to cast the resulting total of votes for one or more directors. As a result, cumulative voting may permit minority shareholders to obtain representation on the board of directors.

Directors usually hold office for only one year, but they may have longer terms. The MBCA permits **staggered terms** for directors. A corporation having a board of nine or more members may establish either two or three approximately equal classes of directors, with only one class of directors coming up for election at each annual shareholders' meeting. If there are two classes of directors, the directors serve two-year terms; if there are three classes, they serve three-year terms.

The original purpose of staggered terms was to permit continuity of management. Staggered terms also frustrate the ability of minority shareholders to use cumulative voting to elect their representatives to the board of directors.

The Proxy Solicitation Process Most individual investors purchase corporate shares in the public market to increase their wealth, not to elect or to influence the directors of corporations. Nearly all institutional investors—such as pension funds, mutual funds, and bank trust departments—have the same profit motive. Generally, they are passive investors with little interest in exercising their shareholder right to elect directors by attending shareholder meetings.

Once public ownership of the corporation's shares exceeds 50 percent, the corporation cannot conduct any business at its shareholder meetings unless some of the shares of these passive investors are voted. This is because the corporation will have a shareholder quorum requirement, which usually requires that 50 percent or more of the shares be voted for a shareholder vote to be valid. Since passive investors rarely attend shareholder meetings, the management of the corporation must solicit **proxies** if it wishes to have a valid shareholder vote. Shareholders who will not attend a shareholder meeting must be asked to appoint someone else to vote their shares for them. This is done by furnishing each such shareholder with a proxy form to sign. The proxy designates a person who may vote the shares for the shareholder.

Management Solicitation of Proxies To ensure its perpetuation in office and the approval of other matters submitted for a shareholder vote, the corporation's management solicits proxies from shareholders for directors' elections and other important matters on which shareholders vote, such as mergers. The management designates an officer, a director, or some other person to vote the proxies received. The person who is designated to vote for the shareholder is also called a proxy. Typically, the chief executive officer (CEO) of the corporation, the president, or the chairman of the board of directors names the person who serves as the proxy.

Usually, the proxies are merely signed and returned by the public shareholders, including the institutional shareholders. Passive investors follow the **Wall Street rule:** Either support management or sell the shares. As a result, management almost always receives enough votes from its proxy solicitation to ensure the reelection of directors and the approval of other matters submitted to the shareholders, even when other parties solicit proxies in opposition to management.

Management's solicitation of proxies may produce a result quite different from the theory of corporate management that directors serve as representatives of the shareholders. The CEO usually nominates directors of his choice, and they are almost always elected. The directors appoint officers chosen by the CEO. The CEO's nominees for director are not unduly critical of his programs or of his methods for carrying them out. This is particularly true if a large proportion of the directors are officers of the company and thus are more likely to be dominated by the CEO. In such situations, the board of directors may not function effectively as a representative of the shareholders in supervising and evaluating the CEO and the other officers of the corporation. The board members and the other officers are subordinates of the CEO, even though the CEO is not a major shareholder of the corporation.

L03 Describe recent developments in corporate governance.

Proposals for improving corporate governance in public-issue corporations seek to develop a board that is capable of functioning independently of the CEO by changing the composition or operation of the board of directors. Some corporate governance critics propose that a federal agency such as the SEC appoint one or more directors to serve as watchdogs of the public interest. Other critics would require that shareholders elect at least a majority of directors without prior ties to the corporation, thus excluding shareholders, suppliers, and customers from the board.

Other proposals recommend changing the method by which directors are nominated for election. One proposal would encourage shareholders to make nominations for directors. Supporters of this proposal argue that in addition to reducing the influence of the CEO, it would also broaden the range of backgrounds represented on the board. The SEC recommends that publicly held corporations establish a nominating committee composed of outside directors. Many publicly held corporations have nomination committees.

Due to pressure from the public and Congress after the corporate scandals of the 1990s and early 2000s, the SEC approved NYSE and NASD corporate governance rules that make corporate boards more nearly independent of the CEO in structure, if not in action. One rule requires boards to comprise mostly independent directors. Equally important, the independent directors must meet from time to time by themselves in executive session independent of the CEO. In addition, institutional investors—including mutual funds and hedge funds—are taking increasingly active roles in director elections.

For a complete treatment of the corporate social responsibility debate, including proposals to improve corporate governance, see Chapter 4.

LOG ON

http://blog.issgovernance.com/gov
Check out the Governance section of the Institutional Shareholder Services website to track current developments in corporate governance.

In the following case, *Grimes v. Donald,* the court considered whether a board of directors abdicated its duty to direct the corporation by delegating unlimited power to the CEO.

Grimes v. Donald   673 A.2d 1207 (Del. Sup. Ct. 1996)

James Donald was the chief executive officer of DSC Communications, a Delaware corporation headquartered in Plano, Texas. In 1990, DSC's board of directors entered an employment agreement with Donald that ran until his 75th birthday. The employment agreement provided that Donald "shall be responsible for the general management of the affairs of the company and report to the Board." Donald's employment could be terminated by death, disability, for cause, and without cause. The agreement provided, however, that Donald could declare a "Constructive Termination Without Cause" by DSC, if there was "unreasonable interference, in the good faith judgment of Donald, by the Board or a substantial stockholder of DSC, in Donald's carrying out of his duties and responsibilities." When there was termination without cause, the employment agreement provided that Donald was entitled to payment of his annual base salary ($650,000) for the remainder of the contract, his *annual incentive award ($300,000), and other benefits. The total amount of payments and benefits for the term of the contract was about $20,000,000.*

C. L. Grimes, a DSC shareholder, sued Donald on behalf of the corporation asking the court to invalidate the employment agreement between Donald and DSC on the grounds that the agreement illegally delegated the duties and responsibilities of DSC's board of directors to Donald. The Delaware Chancery Court dismissed the case, and Grimes appealed to the Supreme Court of Delaware.

Veasey, Chief Justice

Grimes claims that the potentially severe financial penalties which DSC would incur in the event that the Board attempts to interfere in Donald's management will inhibit and deter the Board from exercising its duties. We disagree.

Grimes has pleaded, at most, that Donald would be entitled to $20 million in the event of a Constructive Termination. In light of the financial size of DSC, this amount would not constitute a *de facto* abdication.

Directors may not delegate duties which lie at the heart of the management of the corporation. A court cannot give legal sanction to agreements which have the effect of removing from directors in a very substantial way their duty to use their own best judgment on management matters. The Donald agreement does not formally preclude the DSC board from exercising its statutory powers and fulfilling its fiduciary duty.

With certain exceptions, an informed decision to delegate a task is as much an exercise of business judgment as any other. Likewise, business decisions are not an abdication of directorial authority merely because they limit a board's freedom of future action. A board which has decided to manufacture bricks has less freedom to decide to make bottles. In a world of scarcity, a decision to do one thing will commit a board to a certain course of action and make it costly and difficult to change course and do

another. This is an inevitable fact of life and is not an abdication of directorial duty.

If the market for senior management, in the business judgment of the board, demands significant severance packages, boards will inevitably limit their future range of action by entering into employment agreements. Large severance payments will deter boards, to some extent, from dismissing senior officers. If an independent and informed board, acting in good faith, determines that the services of a particular individual warrant large amounts of money, whether in the form of current salary or severance provisions, the board has made a business judgment. That judgment normally will receive the protection of the business judgment rule unless the facts show that such amounts, compared with services to be received in exchange, constitute waste or could not otherwise be the product of a valid exercise of business judgment.

The Board of DSC retains the ultimate freedom to direct the strategy and affairs of DSC. If Donald disagrees with the Board, DSC may or may not be required to pay a substantial amount of money in order to pursue its chosen course of action. So far, we have only a rather unusual contract, but not a case of abdication.

Judgment for Donald affirmed.

The Global Business Environment

Corporate Governance in Germany

Corporate governance varies somewhat from country to country. In Germany, for example, the *Aktiengesellschaft* (AG) has a **management board** and a **supervisory board.** The AG's management board represents and manages the company. Its members are not directly answerable to shareholders, but are appointed by the AG's supervisory board. All members of the management board manage the company together. However, the articles may provide that the company may be represented by two members of the management board.

The members of the AG's supervisory board are like the outside directors of an American company. They are elected by the AG's shareholders and, if German co-determination rules apply,

by the employees. The supervisory board is charged with protecting the interests of the company, which may not coincide with those of the shareholders. To enable the supervisory board to carry out its oversight function, the management board is required to report regularly on the current status of the company's business and corporate planning. However, the supervisory board has no say in the day-to-day management of the company.

The Shop Constitution Act (*Betriebsverfassungsgesetz*) covers AGs with more than 500 employees. It provides that one-third of supervisory board members be employee representatives. Under the Co-determination Act (*Mitbestimmungsgesetz*), the supervisory boards of AGs with more than 2,000 employees must have equal numbers of shareholder and employee representatives.

Vacancies on the Board The MBCA permits the directors to fill vacancies on the board. A majority vote of the remaining directors is sufficient to select persons to serve out unexpired terms, even though the remaining directors are less than a quorum.

Removal of Directors Modern corporation statutes permit shareholders to remove directors *with or without cause.* The rationale for the modern rule is that the shareholders should have the power to judge the fitness of directors at any time.

However, most corporations have provisions in their articles authorizing the shareholders to remove directors *only for cause.* Cause for removal would include mismanagement or conflicts of interest. Before removal for cause, the director must be given notice and an opportunity for a hearing.

A director elected by a class of shareholders may be removed only by that class of shareholders, thereby protecting the voting rights of the class. A director elected by cumulative voting may not be removed if the votes cast against her removal would have been sufficient to elect her to the board, thereby protecting the voting rights of minority shareholders.

The MBCA also gives a court power to remove a director, upon petition of shareholders, when the court finds that the director engaged in fraudulent conduct with respect to the corporation or its shareholders, grossly abused the position of director, or intentionally inflicted harm on the corporation. The court must also find that removal of the director would be in the best interest of the corporation.

Directors' Meetings

For the directors to act, a *quorum* of the directors must be present. The quorum requirement ensures that the decision of the board will represent the views of a substantial portion of the directors. A quorum is usually a *majority* of the number of directors.

Each director has *one vote.* If a quorum is present, a vote of a majority of the directors present is an act of the board, unless the articles or the bylaws require the vote of a greater number of directors. Such *supermajority voting provisions* are common in close corporations but not in publicly held corporations. The use of supermajority voting provisions by close corporations is covered later in this chapter.

Directors are entitled to reasonable notice of all *special meetings,* but not of regularly scheduled meetings. The MBCA does not require the notice for a special meeting to state the purpose of the meeting. A director's attendance at a meeting waives any required notice, unless at the beginning of the meeting the director objects to the lack of notice.

Traditionally, directors could act only when they were properly convened as a board. They could not vote by proxy or informally, as by telephone. This rule was based on a belief in the value of consultation and collective judgment.

Today, the corporation laws of a majority of the states and the MBCA specifically permit action by the directors without a meeting if all of the directors consent in writing to the action taken. Such authorization is useful for dealing with routine matters or for formally approving an action based on an earlier policy decision made after full discussion.

The MBCA also permits a board to meet by telephone, television, or Internet hookup. This section permits a meeting of directors who may otherwise be unable to convene. The only requirement is that the directors be able to hear one another simultaneously.

Officers of the Corporation

The board of directors has the authority to appoint the officers of the corporation. Many corporation statutes provide that the officers of a corporation shall be the *president,* one or more *vice presidents,* a *secretary,* and a *treasurer.* Usually, any two or more offices may be held by the same person, except for the offices of president and secretary.

The MBCA requires only that there be an officer performing the duties normally granted to a corporate secretary. Under the MBCA, one person may hold several offices, including the offices of president and secretary.

The officers are agents of the corporation. As agents, officers have *express authority* conferred on them by the bylaws or the board of directors. In addition, officers have *implied authority* to do the things that are reasonably necessary to accomplish their express duties. Also, officers have *apparent authority* when the corporation leads third parties to believe reasonably that the officers have authority to act for the corporation. Like any principal, the corporation may *ratify* the unauthorized acts of its officers. This may be done expressly by a resolution of the board of directors or impliedly by the board's acceptance of the benefits of the officer's acts.

The most perplexing issue with regard to the authority of officers is whether an officer has *inherent authority* merely by virtue of the title of his office. Courts have held that certain official titles confer authority on officers, but such powers are much more restricted than you might expect.

Traditionally, a *president* possesses no power to bind the corporation by virtue of the office. Instead, she serves merely as the presiding officer at shareholder meetings and directors' meetings. A president with an additional title such as *general manager* or *chief executive officer* has broad implied authority to make contracts and to do other acts in the ordinary business of the corporation.

A *vice president* has no authority by virtue of that office. An executive who is vice president of a specified department, however, such as a vice president of marketing, will have the authority to transact the normal corporate business falling within the function of the department.

The *secretary* usually keeps the minutes of directors' and shareholder meetings, maintains other corporate records, retains custody of the corporate seal, and certifies corporate records as being authentic. Although the secretary has no authority to make contracts for the corporation by virtue of that office, the corporation is bound by documents certified by the secretary.

The *treasurer* has custody of the corporation's funds. He is the proper officer to receive payments to the corporation and to disburse corporate funds for authorized purposes. The treasurer binds the corporation by his receipts, checks, and indorsements, but he does not by virtue of that office alone have authority to borrow money, to issue negotiable instruments, or to make other contracts on behalf of the corporation.

Like any agent, a corporate officer ordinarily has *no liability on contracts* that he makes on behalf of his principal, the corporation, if he signs for the corporation and not in his personal capacity.

Officers serve the corporation at the pleasure of the board of directors, which may remove an officer at any time with or without cause. An officer who has been removed without cause has no recourse against the corporation, unless the removal violates an employment contract between the officer and the corporation.

 LO4 Adapt the rules of corporate governance to the practical requirements of close corporations.

Managing Close Corporations

Many of the management formalities that you have studied in this chapter are appropriate for publicly held corporations yet inappropriate for close corporations. For example, each close corporation shareholder may want to be *involved in management* of the corporation. If a close corporation shareholder is not involved in management, he may want to protect his interest by placing *restrictions on the managerial discretion* of those who do manage the corporation.

Modern close corporation statutes permit close corporations to dispense with most, if not all, management formalities. The Statutory Close Corporation Supplement to the MBCA permits a close corporation to *dispense with a board of directors* and to be *managed by the shareholders*. The California General Corporation Law permits the close corporation to be managed *as if it were a partnership*.

 **LOG ON**

www.sos.ca.gov/business/corp/pdf/articles/
corp_artsclose.pdf
This website for California's secretary of state will show you how to create a close corporation in California.

When a close corporation chooses to have a traditional board of directors, a minority shareholder may be dominated by the shareholders who control the board of directors. To protect minority shareholders, close corporations may impose **supermajority voting** requirements for board actions and **restrictions on the managerial discretion** of the board of directors.

Any corporation may require that board action be possible only with the approval of more than a majority of the directors, such as three-fourths or unanimous approval. A supermajority vote is often required to terminate the employment contract of an employee-shareholder, to reduce the level of dividends, and to change the corporation's line of business. Supermajority votes are rarely required for ordinary business matters, such as deciding with which suppliers the corporation should deal.

Traditionally, shareholders could not restrict the managerial discretion of directors. This rule recognized the traditional roles of the board as manager and of the shareholders as passive owners. Modern close corporation statutes permit shareholders to intrude into the sanctity of the boardroom. The Statutory Close Corporation Supplement grants the shareholders *unlimited* power to restrict the discretion of the board of directors. For example, the shareholders may agree that the directors may not terminate or reduce the salaries of employee-shareholders and must pay a mandatory dividend, if earned. And, as was stated above, close corporation statutes even permit the shareholders to dispense with a board of directors altogether and to manage the close corporation as if it were a partnership.

Of course, any article or bylaw protecting the rights of minority shareholders should not be changeable, unless the minority shareholders consent.

Managing Nonprofit Corporations

A nonprofit corporation is managed under the direction of a board of directors. The board of directors must have at least three directors. All corporate powers are exercised by or under the authority of the board of directors. Any person may serve as a director; however, the Model Nonprofit Corporation Act has an optional provision stating that no more than 49 percent of directors of a public service corporation may be financially interested in the business of the public service corporation. An interested person is, for example, the musical director of a city's symphony orchestra who receives a salary from the nonprofit corporation operating the orchestra.

If a nonprofit corporation has members, typically the members elect the directors. However, the articles may provide for the directors to be appointed or elected by other persons. Directors serve for one year, unless the articles or bylaws provide otherwise. Directors who are elected may not serve terms longer than five years, but appointed directors may serve longer terms.

Directors may be elected by straight or cumulative voting and by class voting. Members may elect directors in person or by proxy. Directors may be removed at any time with or without cause by the members or other persons who elected or appointed the directors. When a director engages in fraudulent or dishonest conduct or breaches a fiduciary duty, members holding at least 10 percent of the voting power may petition a court to remove the wrongdoing director. Generally, a vacancy may be filled by the members or the board of directors; however, if a removed director was elected by a class of members or appointed by another person, only the class or person electing or appointing the director may fill the vacancy.

The board is permitted to set directors' compensation. Typically, directors of public benefit corporations and religious corporations are volunteers and receive no compensation.

Directors of a nonprofit corporation usually act at a meeting at which all directors may simultaneously hear each other, such as a meeting in person or by telephone conference call. The board may also act without a meeting if all directors consent in writing to the action. The board has the power to do most actions that are within the powers of the corporation, although some actions, such as mergers and amendments of the articles, require member action also. Ordinarily, an individual director has no authority to transact for a nonprofit corporation.

The board of directors of a nonprofit corporation may delegate some of its authority to committees of the board and to officers. A nonprofit corporation is not required to have officers, except for an officer performing the duties of corporate secretary. If a corporation chooses to have more officers, one person may hold more than one office. The board may remove an officer at any time with or without cause.

Officers have the authority granted them by the bylaws or by board resolution. However, a nonprofit corporation is bound by a contract signed by both the presiding officer of the board and the president, when the other party had no knowledge that the signing officers had no authority. The corporation is also bound to a contract signed by either the presiding officer or the president which is also signed by either a vice president, the secretary, the treasurer, or the executive director.

Directors' and Officers' Duties to the Corporation

Directors and officers are in positions of trust; they are entrusted with property belonging to the corporation and with power to act for the corporation. Therefore, directors and officers owe **fiduciary duties** to the corporation. They are the duties to act within the authority of the position and within the objectives and powers of the corporation, to act with due care in conducting the affairs of the corporation, and to act with loyalty to the corporation.

Acting within Authority An officer or director has a duty to **act within the authority** conferred on her by the articles of incorporation, the bylaws, and the board of directors. The directors and officers must act within the scope of the powers of the corporation. An officer or a director may be liable to the corporation if it is damaged by an act exceeding that person's or the corporation's authority.

 Know the legal standards that judge actions of officers and directors and apply the steps required to comply with each standard.

Duty of Care Directors and officers are liable for losses to the corporation resulting from their lack of *care or diligence*. The MBCA expressly states the standard of care that must be exercised by directors and officers. MBCA section 8.30 states:

(a) Each member of the board of directors . . . shall act:
    (1) in good faith, and
    (2) in a manner the director reasonably believes to be in the best interests of the corporation.

(b) The members of the board of directors or a committee of the board, when becoming informed in connection with their decision-making function or devoting attention to their oversight function, shall discharge their duties with the care that a person in a like position would reasonably believe appropriate under similar circumstances.

The MBCA section 8.42 imposes almost the same duty on corporate officers:

(a) An officer . . . shall act:
(1) in good faith;
(2) with the care that a person in a like position would reasonably exercise under similar circumstances; and
(3) in a manner the officer reasonably believes to be in the best interests of the corporation.

Managers need merely meet the standard of the **ordinarily prudent person in the same circumstances,** a standard focusing on the basic manager attributes of common sense, practical wisdom, and informed judgment. The duty of care does not hold directors and officers to the standard of a prudent businessperson, a person of some undefined level of business skill. A director or officer's performance is evaluated at the time of the decision, thereby preventing the application of hindsight in judging her performance.

The MBCA duty of care test requires that a director or officer make a **reasonable investigation** and **honestly believe** that her decision is in the **best interests of the corporation.** For example, the board of directors decides to purchase an existing manufacturing business for $15 million without inquiring into the value of the business or examining its past financial performance. Although the directors may believe that they made a prudent decision, they have no reasonable basis for that belief. Therefore, if the plant is worth only $5 million, the directors will be liable to the corporation for its damages—$10 million—for breaching the duty of care.

The Business Judgment Rule The directors' and officers' duty of care is sometimes expressed as the **business judgment rule:** Absent bad faith, fraud, or breach of fiduciary duty, the judgment of the board of directors is conclusive. When directors and officers have complied with the business judgment rule, they are protected from liability to the corporation for their harmful decisions. The business judgment rule precludes the courts from substituting their business judgment for that of the corporation's managers. The business judgment rule recognizes that the directors and officers—not the shareholders and the courts—are best able to make business judgments and should not ordinarily be vulnerable to second-guessing. Shareholders and the courts are ill equipped to make better

business decisions than those made by the officers and directors of a corporation, who have more business experience and are more familiar with the needs, strengths, and limitations of the corporation.

Three requirements must be met for the business judgment rule to protect managers from liability:

1. The managers must make an **informed decision.** They must take the steps necessary to become informed about the relevant facts by making a **reasonable investigation** before making a decision.

2. The managers may have **no conflicts of interest.** The managers may not benefit personally—other than as shareholders—when they transact on behalf of the corporation.

3. The managers must have a **rational basis** for believing that the decision is in the **best interests of the corporation.** The rational basis element requires only that the managers' decision have a *logical connection to the facts* revealed by a reasonable investigation or that the decision *not be manifestly unreasonable.* Some courts have held that the managers' wrongdoing must amount to *gross negligence* for the directors to lose the protection of the business judgment rule.

If the business judgment rule does not apply because one or more of its elements are missing, a court may *substitute its judgment* for that of the managers.

Nonetheless, courts rarely refuse to apply the business judgment rule. As a result, the rule has been criticized frequently as providing too much protection for the managers of corporations. In one famous case, the court applied the business judgment rule to protect a 1965 decision made by the board of directors of the Chicago Cubs not to install lights and not to hold night baseball games at Wrigley Field.[1] Yet the business judgment rule is so flexible that it protected the decision of the Cubs' board of directors to install lights in 1988.

The *Trans Union* case[2] is one of the few cases that has held directors liable for failing to comply with the business judgment rule. The Supreme Court of Delaware found that the business judgment rule was not satisfied by the board's approval of an acquisition of the corporation for $55 per share. The board approved the acquisition after only two hours' consideration. The board received no documentation to support the adequacy of the $55 price. Instead, it relied entirely on a 20-minute *oral* report of the chairman of the board. No written summary of the acquisition was

[1]*Shlensky v. Wrigley,* 237 N.E.2d 776 (Ill. Ct. App. 1968).
[2]*Smith v. Van Gorkom,* 488 A.2d 858 (Del. Sup. Ct. 1985).

presented to the board. The directors failed to obtain an investment banker's report, prepared after careful consideration, that the acquisition price was fair.

In addition, the court held that the mere fact that the acquisition price exceeded the market price by $17 per share did not legitimize the board's decision. The board had frequently made statements prior to the acquisition that the market had undervalued the shares, yet the board took no steps to determine the intrinsic value of the shares. Consequently, the court found that at a minimum, the directors had been grossly negligent.

Complying with the Business Judgment Rule While the *Trans Union* case created some fear among directors that they could easily be held liable for making a decision that harms the corporation, nothing could be further from the truth. The *Trans Union* case and the business judgment rule provide a blueprint for how directors, with the assistance of investment bankers and other consultants, can avoid liability. First, to make an informed decision, the board must perform a reasonable investigation or reasonably rely on someone who has made a reasonable investigation, such as consultants, corporate officers, and employees. For example, few boards have the financial skills to value a product line that the corporation wants to sell, yet investment bankers are skilled at valuations. Therefore, a board will make an informed decision when an investment banker makes a reasonable investigation, informs the board of its finding in a written report delivered to the board several days prior to the board meeting, makes a presentation at the board meeting, and takes questions from the board, provided the

board makes its decision after giving sufficient time and care to its deliberation of the facts.

Second, the business judgment rule will not apply unless the board has no conflicts of interest. By compiling a list of questions and quizzing the board members, consultants can help the board determine whether any member has a financial or other improper interest in the matter before the board.

Third, for the board to have a rational basis to believe that the decision is in the best interests of the corporation, the decision must fit with the firm's corporate strategy and the facts revealed by a reasonable investigation. Investment bankers and consultants can help, first by defining the corporation's strategy and second by demonstrating the fit between the course of action, the facts, and the corporate strategy.

Changes in the Duty of Care Despite the low risk of liability, many state legislatures have changed the wording of the duty of care, typically imposing liability only for willful or wanton misconduct or for gross negligence. Some states allow corporations to reduce the duty of care in their articles of incorporation. For example, the MBCA allows corporations to reduce or eliminate directors' liability for monetary damages, unless a director has received an improper financial benefit or intended to violate the law or harm the corporation.

In the following case involving Disney's hiring and firing of Michael Ovitz, the Delaware court applied the business judgment rule. This case has a good explanation of the diligence directors should exercise in acquiring information before making a decision.

Brehm v. Eisner	906 A. 2d 27 (Del. S. Ct. 2006)

From the mid-1980s to the mid-1990s, The Walt Disney Company enjoyed remarkable success under the guidance of Chairman and CEO Michael Eisner and President and Chief Operating Officer Frank Wells. In 1994, Wells died in a helicopter crash, prematurely forcing the company to consider his replacement. Eisner promoted the candidacy of his long-time friend, Michael Ovitz. Ovitz was the head of Creative Artists Agency (CAA), which he and four others had founded in 1974. By 1995, CAA had grown to be the premier Hollywood talent agency. CAA had 550 employees and an impressive roster of about 1,400 of Hollywood's top actors, directors, writers, and musicians, clients that generated $150 million in annual revenues for CAA. Ovitz drew an annual income of $20 million from CAA. He was regarded as one of the most powerful figures in Hollywood.

To leave CAA and join Disney as its president, Ovitz insisted on an employment agreement that would provide him downside risk protection if he was terminated by Disney or if he was interfered with in his performance of his duties as president. After protracted negotiations, Ovitz accepted an employment package that would provide him $23.6 million per year for the first five years of the deal, plus bonuses and stock options. The agreement guaranteed that the stock options would appreciate at least $50 million in five years or Disney would make up the difference. The Ovitz employment agreement (OEA) also provided that if Disney fired Ovitz for any reason other than gross negligence or malfeasance, Ovitz would be entitled to a Non-Fault

Termination payment (NFT), which consisted of his remaining salary, $7.5 million a year for any unaccrued bonuses, the immediate vesting of some stock options, and a $10 million cash out payment for other stock options. While there was some opposition to the employment agreement among directors and upper management at Disney, Ovitz was hired in October 1995 largely due to Eisner's insistence.

At the end of 1995, Eisner's attitude with respect to Ovitz was positive. Eisner wrote, "1996 is going to be a great year—We are going to be a great team—We every day are working better together—Time will be on our side—We will be strong, smart, and unstoppable!!!" Eisner also wrote that Ovitz performed well during 1995, notwithstanding the difficulties Ovitz was experiencing assimilating to Disney's culture.

Unfortunately, such optimism did not last long. In January 1996, a corporate retreat was held at Walt Disney World in Orlando. At that retreat, Ovitz failed to integrate himself in the group of executives by declining to participate in group activities, insisting on a limousine when the other executives—including Eisner—were taking a bus, and making inappropriate demands of the park employees. In short, Ovitz was a little elitist for the egalitarian Disney and a poor fit with his fellow executives.

By the summer of 1996, Eisner had spoken with several directors about Ovitz's failure to adapt to the company's culture. In the fall of 1996, directors began discussing that the disconnect between Ovitz and Disney was likely irreparable, and that Ovitz would have to be terminated. In December 1996, Ovitz was officially terminated by action of Eisner alone. Eisner concluded that Ovitz was terminated without cause, requiring Disney to make the costly NFT payment.

Shareholders of Disney brought a derivative action on behalf of Disney against Eisner and other Disney directors. The shareholders alleged breaches of fiduciary duty in the hiring and firing of Ovitz. Eisner and the other directors defended on the grounds that they had complied with the business judgment rule. Because Disney was incorporated in Delaware, the case was brought in the Delaware Court of Chancery. The chancery court found that Eisner and the other directors had complied with the business judgment rule. The Disney shareholders appealed to the Delaware Supreme Court.

Jacobs, Justice

The shareholders' claims are subdivisible into two groups: (A) claims arising out of the approval of the OEA and of Ovitz's election as President; and (B) claims arising out of the NFT severance payment to Ovitz upon his termination.

A. Claims Arising from the Approval of the OEA and Ovitz's Election as President

The shareholders' core argument in the trial court was that the Disney directors' approval of the OEA and election of Ovitz as President were not entitled to business judgment rule protection, because those actions were either grossly negligent or not performed in good faith. The Court of Chancery rejected these arguments, and held that the shareholders had failed to prove that the Disney defendants had breached any fiduciary duty.

Our law presumes that in making a business decision the directors of a corporation acted on an informed basis, in good faith, and in the honest belief that the action taken was in the best interests of the company. Those presumptions can be rebutted if the shareholder shows that the directors breached their fiduciary duty of care or of loyalty or acted in bad faith. If that is shown, the burden then shifts to the director defendants to demonstrate that the challenged act or transaction was entirely fair to the corporation and its shareholders.

Because no duty of loyalty claim was asserted against the Disney defendants, the only way to rebut the business judgment rule presumptions would be to show that the Disney defendants had either breached their duty of care or had not acted in good faith. The Chancellor determined that the shareholders had failed to prove either. [The Delaware Supreme Court affirmed the Chancellor's finding.]

The shareholders next challenge the Court of Chancery's determination that the full Disney board was not required to consider and approve the OEA, because the Company's governing instruments allocated that decision to the compensation committee. This challenge also cannot survive scrutiny.

Under the Company's governing documents the board of directors was responsible for selecting the corporation's officers, but under the compensation committee charter, the committee was responsible for establishing and approving the salaries, together with benefits and stock options, of the Company's CEO and President. The compensation committee also had the charter-imposed duty to "approve employment contracts, or contracts at will" for "all corporate officers who are members of the Board of Directors regardless of salary." That is exactly what occurred here. The full board ultimately selected Ovitz as President, and the compensation committee considered and ultimately approved the OEA, which embodied the terms of Ovitz's employment, including his compensation.

The Delaware General Corporation Law (DGCL) expressly empowers a board of directors to appoint committees and to delegate to them a broad range of responsibilities, which may include setting executive compensation. Nothing in the DGCL mandates that the entire board must make those decisions. At Disney, the responsibility to consider and approve executive compensation was allocated to the compensation committee, as distinguished from the full board. The Chancellor's ruling—that executive compensation was to be fixed by the compensation committee—is legally correct.

In the Court of Chancery the shareholders argued that the board had failed to exercise due care, using a director-by-director, rather than a collective analysis. In this Court, however, the shareholders argue that the Chancellor erred in following that very approach. An about-face, the shareholders now claim that in determining whether the board breached its duty of care, the Chancellor was legally required to evaluate the actions of the old board collectively.

We reject this argument, without reaching its merits, for two separate reasons. To begin with, the argument is precluded by Rule 8 of this Court, which provides that arguments not fairly presented to the trial court will not be considered by this Court. The argument also fails because nowhere do shareholders identify how this supposed error caused them any prejudice. The Chancellor viewed the conduct of each director individually, and found that no director had breached his or her fiduciary duty of care (as members of the full board) in electing Ovitz as President or (as members of the compensation committee) in determining Ovitz's compensation. If, as shareholders now argue, a due care analysis of the board's conduct must be made collectively, it is incumbent upon them to show how such a collective analysis would yield a different result. The shareholders' failure to do that dooms their argument on this basis as well.

The shareholders next challenge the Chancellor's determination that although the compensation committee's decision-making process fell far short of corporate governance "best practices," the committee members breached no duty of care in considering and approving the NFT terms of the OEA. That conclusion is reversible error, the shareholders claim, because the record establishes that the compensation committee members did not properly inform themselves of the material facts and, hence, were grossly negligent in approving the NFT provisions of the OEA.

In our view, a helpful approach is to compare what actually happened here to what would have occurred had the committee followed a "best practices" (or "best case") scenario, from a process standpoint. In a "best case" scenario, all committee members would have received, before or at the committee's first meeting on September 26, 1995, a spreadsheet or similar document prepared by (or with the assistance of) a compensation expert (in this case, Graef Crystal). Making different, alternative assumptions, the spreadsheet would disclose the amounts that Ovitz could receive under the OEA in each circumstance that might foreseeably arise. One variable in that matrix of possibilities would be the cost to Disney of a non-fault termination for each of the five years of the initial term of the OEA. The contents

of the spreadsheet would be explained to the committee members, either by the expert who prepared it or by a fellow committee member similarly knowledgeable about the subject. That spreadsheet, which ultimately would become an exhibit to the minutes of the compensation committee meeting, would form the basis of the committee's deliberations and decision.

Regrettably, the committee's informational and decisionmaking process used here was not so tidy. That is one reason why the Chancellor found that although the committee's process did not fall below the level required for a proper exercise of due care, it did fall short of what best practices would have counseled.

The Disney compensation committee met twice: on September 26 and October 16, 1995. The minutes of the September 26 meeting reflect that the committee approved the terms of the OEA (at that time embodied in the form of a letter agreement), except for the option grants, which were not approved until October 16—after the Disney stock incentive plan had been amended to provide for those options. At the September 26 meeting, the compensation committee considered a "term sheet" which, in summarizing the material terms of the OEA, relevantly disclosed that in the event of a non-fault termination, Ovitz would receive: (i) the present value of his salary ($1 million per year) for the balance of the contract term, (ii) the present value of his annual bonus payments (computed at $7.5 million) for the balance of the contract term, (iii) a $10 million termination fee, and (iv) the acceleration of his options for 3 million shares, which would become immediately exercisable at market price.

Thus, the compensation committee knew that in the event of an NFT, Ovitz's severance payment alone could be in the range of $40 million cash, plus the value of the accelerated options. Because the actual payout to Ovitz was approximately $130 million, of which roughly $38.5 million was cash, the value of the options at the time of the NFT payout would have been about $91.5 million. Thus, the issue may be framed as whether the compensation committee members knew, at the time they approved the OEA, that the value of the option component of the severance package could reach the $92 million order of magnitude if they terminated Ovitz without cause after one year. The evidentiary record shows that the committee members were so informed.

On this question the documentation is far less than what best practices would have dictated. There is no exhibit to the minutes that discloses, in a single document, the estimated value of the accelerated options in the event of an NFT termination after one year. The information imparted to the committee members on that subject is, however, supported by other evidence, most notably the trial testimony of various witnesses about spreadsheets that were prepared for the compensation committee meetings.

The compensation committee members derived their information about the potential magnitude of an NFT payout from two sources. The first was the value of the "benchmark" options previously granted to Eisner and Wells and the valuations by Raymond Watson [a Disney director, member of Disney's compensation committee, and past Disney board chairman who had helped structure Wells's and Eisner's compensation packages] of the proposed Ovitz options. Ovitz's options were set at 75% of parity with the options previously granted to Eisner and to Frank Wells. Because the compensation committee had established those earlier benchmark option grants to Eisner and Wells and were aware of their value, a simple mathematical calculation would have informed them of the potential value range of Ovitz's options. Also, in August and September 1995, Watson and Irwin Russell [a Disney director and chairman of the compensation committee] met with Crystal to determine (among other things) the value of the potential Ovitz options, assuming different scenarios. Crystal valued the options under the Black-Scholes method, while Watson used a different valuation metric. Watson recorded his calculations and the resulting values on a set of spreadsheets that reflected what option profits Ovitz might receive, based upon a range of different assumptions about stock market price increases. Those spreadsheets were shared with, and explained to, the committee members at the September meeting.

The committee's second source of information was the amount of "downside protection" that Ovitz was demanding. Ovitz required financial protection from the risk of leaving a very lucrative and secure position at CAA, of which he was a controlling partner, to join a publicly held corporation to which Ovitz was a stranger, and that had a very different culture and an environment which prevented him from completely controlling his destiny. The committee members knew that by leaving CAA and coming to Disney, Ovitz would be sacrificing "booked" CAA commissions of $150 to $200 million—an amount that Ovitz demanded as protection against the risk that his employment relationship with Disney might not work out. Ovitz wanted at least $50 million of that compensation to take the form of an "up-front" signing bonus. Had the $50 million bonus been paid, the size of the option grant would have been lower. Because it was contrary to Disney policy, the compensation committee rejected the up-front signing bonus demand, and elected instead to compensate Ovitz at the "back end," by awarding him options that would be phased in over the five-year term of the OEA.

It is on this record that the Chancellor found that the compensation committee was informed of the material facts relating to an NFT payout. If measured in terms of the documentation that would have been generated if "best practices" had been followed, that record leaves much to be desired. The Chancellor acknowledged that, and so do we. But, the Chancellor also found that despite its imperfections, the evidentiary record was

sufficient to support the conclusion that the compensation committee had adequately informed itself of the potential magnitude of the entire severance package, including the options, that Ovitz would receive in the event of an early NFT.

The OEA was specifically structured to compensate Ovitz for walking away from $150 million to $200 million of anticipated commissions from CAA over the five-year OEA contract term. This meant that if Ovitz was terminated without cause, the earlier in the contract term the termination occurred the larger the severance amount would be to replace the lost commissions. Indeed, because Ovitz was terminated after only one year, the total amount of his severance payment (about $130 million) closely approximated the lower end of the range of Ovitz's forfeited commissions ($150 million), less the compensation Ovitz received during his first and only year as Disney's President. Accordingly, the Court of Chancery had a sufficient evidentiary basis in the record from which to find that, at the time they approved the OEA, the compensation committee members were adequately informed of the potential magnitude of an early NFT severance payout.

The shareholders' final claim in this category is that the Court of Chancery erroneously held that the remaining members of the old Disney board had not breached their duty of care in electing Ovitz as President of Disney. This claim lacks merit, because the arguments shareholders advance in this context relate to a different subject—the approval of the OEA, which was the responsibility delegated to the compensation committee, not the full board.

The Chancellor found and the record shows the following: well in advance of the September 26, 1995 board meeting the directors were fully aware that the Company needed—especially in light of Wells' death and Eisner's medical problems—to hire a "number two" executive and potential successor to Eisner. There had been many discussions about that need and about potential candidates who could fill that role even before Eisner decided to try to recruit Ovitz. Before the September 26 board meeting Eisner had individually discussed with each director the possibility of hiring Ovitz, and Ovitz's background and qualifications. The directors thus knew of Ovitz's skills, reputation and experience, all of which they believed would be highly valuable to the Company. The directors also knew that to accept a position at Disney, Ovitz would have to walk away from a very successful business—a reality that would lead a reasonable person to believe that Ovitz would likely succeed in similar pursuits elsewhere in the industry. The directors also knew of the public's highly positive reaction to the Ovitz announcement, and that Eisner and senior management had supported the Ovitz hiring. Indeed, Eisner, who had long desired to bring Ovitz within the Disney fold, consistently vouched for Ovitz's qualifications and told the directors that he could work well with Ovitz.

The board was also informed of the key terms of the OEA (including Ovitz's salary, bonus, and options). Russell reported this information to them at the September 26, 1995 executive session, which was attended by Eisner and all non-executive directors. Russell also reported on the compensation committee meeting that had immediately preceded the executive session. And, both Russell and Watson responded to questions from the board. Relying upon the compensation committee's approval of the OEA and the other information furnished to them, the Disney directors, after further deliberating, unanimously elected Ovitz as President.

Based upon this record, we uphold the Chancellor's conclusion that, when electing Ovitz to the Disney presidency the remaining Disney directors were fully informed of all material facts, and that the shareholders failed to establish any lack of due care on the directors' part.

B. Claims Arising from the Payment of the NFT Severance Payout to Ovitz

The shareholders contend that: (1) only the full Disney board with the concurrence of the compensation committee—but not Eisner alone—was authorized to terminate Ovitz; (2) because Ovitz could have been terminated for cause, Sanford Litvack [Disney's general counsel and member of the Disney board] and Eisner acted without due care and in bad faith in reaching the contrary conclusion; and (3) the business judgment rule presumptions did not protect the new Disney board's acquiescence in the NFT payout, because the new board was not entitled to rely upon Eisner's and Litvack's contrary advice.

The Chancellor determined that although the board as constituted upon Ovitz's termination (the "new board") had the authority to terminate Ovitz, neither that board nor the compensation committee was required to act, because Eisner also had, and properly exercised, that authority. The new board, the Chancellor found, was not required to terminate Ovitz under the company's internal documents. Without such a duty to act, the new board's failure to vote on the termination could not give rise to a breach of the duty of care or the duty to act in good faith.

Article Tenth of the Company's certificate of incorporation in effect at the termination plainly states that:

> The officers of the Corporation shall be chosen in such a manner, shall hold their offices for such terms and shall carry out such duties as are determined solely by the Board of Directors, subject to the right of the Board of Directors to remove any officer or officers at any time with or without cause.

Article IV of Disney's bylaws provided that the Board Chairman/CEO "shall, subject to the provisions of the Bylaws and the control of the Board of Directors, have general and active management, direction, and supervision over the business of the Corporation and over its officers. . . ."

Read together, the governing instruments do not yield a single, indisputably clear answer, and could reasonably be interpreted either way. For that reason, with respect to this specific issue, the governing instruments are ambiguous.

Here, the extrinsic evidence clearly supports the conclusion that the board and Eisner understood that Eisner, as Board Chairman/CEO had concurrent power with the board to terminate Ovitz as President. Because Eisner possessed, and exercised, the power to terminate Ovitz unilaterally, we find that the Chancellor correctly concluded that the new board was not required to act in connection with that termination, and, therefore, the board did not violate any fiduciary duty to act with due care or in good faith.

As the Chancellor correctly held, the same conclusion is equally applicable to the compensation committee. The only role delegated to the compensation committee was "to establish and approve compensation for Eisner, Ovitz and other applicable Company executives and high paid employees." The committee's September 26, 1995 approval of Ovitz's compensation arrangements "included approval for the termination provisions of the OEA, obviating any need to meet and approve the payment of the NFT upon Ovitz's termination."

Because neither the new board nor the compensation committee was required to take any action that was subject to fiduciary standards, that leaves only the actions of Eisner and Litvack for our consideration. The shareholders claim that in concluding that Ovitz could not be terminated "for cause," these defendants did not act with due care or in good faith. We next address that claim.

After considering the OEA and Ovitz's conduct, Litvack concluded, and advised Eisner, that Disney had no basis to terminate Ovitz for cause and that Disney should comply with its contractual obligations. Even though Litvack personally did not want to grant a NFT to Ovitz, he concluded that for Disney to assert falsely that there was cause would be both unethical and harmful to Disney's reputation. In conclusion, Litvack gave the proper advice and came to the proper conclusions when it was necessary. He was adequately informed in his decisions, and he acted in good faith for what he believed were the best interests of the Company.

With respect to Eisner, the Chancellor found that faced with a situation where he was unable to work well with Ovitz, who required close and constant supervision, Eisner had three options: (1) keep Ovitz as President and continue trying to make things work; (2) keep Ovitz at Disney, but in a role other than as President; or (3) terminate Ovitz. The first option was unacceptable, and the second would have entitled Ovitz to the NFT, or at the very least would have resulted in a costly lawsuit to determine whether Ovitz was so entitled. After an unsuccessful effort to "trade" Ovitz to Sony, that left only the third option, which was to terminate Ovitz and pay the NFT. The Chancellor found that in choosing this alternative, Eisner had breached no duty and had exercised his business judgment:

> . . . I conclude that Eisner's actions in connection with the termination are, for the most part, consistent with what is expected of a faithful fiduciary. Eisner unexpectedly found himself confronted with a situation that did not have an easy solution. He weighed the alternatives, received advice from counsel and then exercised his business judgment in the manner he thought best for the corporation. Eisner knew all the material information reasonably available when making the decision, he did not neglect an affirmative duty to act (or fail to cause the board to act) and he acted in what he believed were the best interests of the Company, taking into account the cost to the Company of the decision and the potential alternatives. Eisner was not personally interested in the transaction in any way that would make him incapable of exercising business judgment, and I conclude that the shareholders have not demonstrated by a preponderance of the evidence that Eisner breached his fiduciary duties or acted in bad faith in connection with Ovitz's termination and receipt of the NFT.

These determinations rest squarely on factual findings that, in turn, are based upon the Chancellor's assessment of the credibility of Eisner and other witnesses. Even though the Chancellor found much to criticize in Eisner's "imperial CEO" style of governance, nothing has been shown to overturn the factual basis for the Court's conclusion that, in the end, Eisner's conduct satisfied the standards required of him as a fiduciary.

The shareholders' third claim of error challenges the Chancellor's conclusion that the remaining new board members could rely upon Litvack's and Eisner's advice that Ovitz could be terminated only without cause. The short answer to that challenge is that, for the reasons previously discussed, the advice the remaining directors received and relied upon was accurate. Moreover, the directors' reliance on that advice was found to be in good faith. Although formal board action was not necessary, the remaining directors all supported the decision to terminate Ovitz based on the information given by Eisner and Litvack. The Chancellor found credible the directors' testimony that they believed that Disney would be better off without Ovitz, and the shareholders offer no basis to overturn that finding.

To summarize, the Court of Chancery correctly determined that the decisions of the Disney defendants to approve the OEA, to hire Ovitz as President, and then to terminate him on an NFT basis, were protected business judgments, made without any violations of fiduciary duty. Having so concluded, it is unnecessary for the Court to reach the shareholders' contention that the Disney defendants were required to prove that the payment of the NFT severance to Ovitz was entirely fair.

Judgment for Eisner and the other directors affirmed.

 LO6 List and describe tactics a board of directors may adopt to defend against hostile takeovers.

Board Opposition to Acquisition of Control of a Corporation
In the last 45 years, many outsiders have attempted to acquire control of publicly held corporations. Typically, these outsiders (called **raiders**) will make a **tender offer** for the shares of a corporation (called the **target**). A tender offer is an offer to the shareholders to buy their shares at a price above the current market price. The raider hopes to acquire a majority of the shares, which will give it control of the target corporation.

Most tender offers are opposed by the target corporation's management. The defenses to tender offers are many and varied, and they carry colorful names, such as the Pac-Man defense, the white knight, greenmail, the poison pill, and the lock-up option. See Figure 1 for definitions of these and other defenses.

When takeover defenses are successful, shareholders of the target may lose the opportunity to sell their shares at a price up to twice the market price of the shares prior to the announcement of the hostile bid. Frequently, the loss of this opportunity upsets shareholders, who then decide to sue the directors who have opposed the tender offer. Shareholders contend that the directors have opposed the tender offer only to preserve their corporate jobs. Shareholders also argue that the target corporation's interests would have been better served if the tender offer had succeeded.

Generally, courts have refused to find directors liable for opposing a tender offer because the business judgment rule applies to a board's decision to oppose a tender offer.

Nonetheless, the business judgment rule will not apply when the directors make a decision to oppose the tender offer before they have carefully studied it. In addition, if the directors' actions indicate that they opposed the tender offer in order to preserve their jobs, they will be liable to the corporation.

Figure 1   *Tender Offer Defenses*

Greenmail

The target's repurchase of its shares from the raider at a substantial profit to the raider, upon the condition that the raider sign a standstill agreement in which it promises not to buy additional shares of the target for a stated period of time.

White Knight

A friendly tender offeror whom management prefers over the original tender offeror — called a black knight. The white knight rescues the corporation from the black knight (the raider) by offering more money for the corporation's shares.

Pac-Man

The target corporation turns the tables on the tender offeror or raider (which is often another publicly held corporation) by making a tender offer for the raider's shares. As a result, two tender offerors are trying to buy each other's shares. This is similar to the Pac-Man video game, in which Pac-Man and his enemies chase each other.

Golden Parachutes

An incentive to attract top managers, a golden parachute requires a corporation to make a large severance payment to a top level executive such as the CEO when there is a change in control of the corporation. Payments to an individual executive may exceed $500 million. The severance agreement in *Grimes v. Donald* on page 1076 was a golden parachute.

Scorched Earth Tactics

Borrowed from a war tactic, scorched earth tactics attack the raider and its management directly and indiscriminately, like a tank with a flame thrower. These tactics include public relations campaigns in which the target points out the business, legal, and ethical failings of the raider and its management. The target typically warns its employees and communities that the raider will close the target's business in its current locations and move the jobs to another state or country. Finally, the target sues the raider alleging that the hostile takeover violates state corporation law, federal and state securities law, and antitrust law.

Long-Range Acquisition Strategy

A corporation should have a long-run strategy for expansion of its business, including by acquisition. That strategy may be to maintain a narrow business plan that allows the corporation and its management to focus on its core competencies. Or the strategy may be to seek new business opportunities that complement current business operations. An acquisition strategy allows the board of directors to oppose a hostile takeover that threatens the strategy, in accordance with the *Unocal* test. In the *Paramount* case on page 1089, Time, Inc., was better set to oppose Paramount's bid because Time's board had a long-range acquisition strategy requiring protection of the editorial integrity of Time's magazines.

Lock-Up Option

Used in conjunction with a white knight to ensure the success of the white knight's bid. The target and the white knight agree that the white knight will buy a highly valuable asset of the target at a very attractive price for the white knight (usually a below-market price) if the raider succeeds in taking over the target. For example, a movie company may agree to sell its film library to the white knight.

Friendly Shareholders

Establishing employee stock option plans (ESOPs), by which employees of the corporation purchase the corporation's shares, and selling the corporation's shares to other shareholders likely to be loyal to management, such as employee pension funds and people in the community in which the corporation conducts its business, may create a significant percentage of friendly shareholders that are not likely to tender their shares to a raider who may be perceived as hostile to the continuation of the corporation's business in the local community. Thus, building and maintaining a base of friendly shareholders make it easier to defeat a raider.

Poison Pill

Also called a shareholders' rights plan. There are many types, but the typical poison pill involves the target's issuance of a new class of preferred shares to its common share-holders. The preferred shares have rights (share options) attached to them. These rights allow the target's shareholders to purchase shares of the raider or shares of the target at less than fair market value. The poison pill deters hostile takeover attempts by threatening the raider and its shareholders with severe dilutions in the value of the shares they hold.

Stock Trading Surveillance Program

A target should watch the volume of trading in its stock, looking for unexplained spikes in volume that would indicate a future hostile bidder is acquiring a toe-hold in the target's stock prior to announcing a hostile takeover. By detecting abnormal trading in its stock, the target obtains advance knowledge of an impending hostile bid and will have additional time to implement its antitakeover strategy.

Control Share Law

A target company may incorporate in a state with a so-called Control Share Law. When a raider acquires 20 percent of the target's shares in a short period of time (say 90 days), the control share law renders the shares nonvoting, unless the target's board of directors opts out of the control share law or the target's shareholders vote to allow the raider to vote the shares. The effect is to diminish the ability of a raider to acquire voting control of the target without the consent of the target. Since most raiders are unwilling to risk that shareholders will deny them voting power, hostile takeovers of companies incorporated in control share law states are mostly deterred.

Court decisions have seemingly modified the business judgment rule as it is applied in the tender offer context. For example, in *Unocal Corp. v. Mesa Petroleum Co.,*[3] the Supreme Court of Delaware upheld the application of the business judgment rule to a board's decision to block a hostile tender offer by making a tender offer for its own shares that excluded the raider.[4] But in so ruling, the court held that the board may use only those defense tactics that are *reasonable* compared to the takeover threat. The board may consider a variety of concerns, including the inadequacy of the price offered, nature and timing of the offer, questions of illegality, the impact on constituencies other than shareholders (i.e., creditors, customers, employees, and perhaps even the community generally), the risk of nonconsummation, and the quality of securities being offered in the exchange.

In *Unocal,* the threat was a two-tier, highly coercive tender offer. In the typical two-tier offer, the raider first offers cash for a majority of the shares. After acquiring a majority of the shares, the offeror initiates the second tier, in which the remaining shareholders are forced to sell their shares for a package of securities less attractive than the first tier. Because shareholders fear that they will be forced to take the less attractive second-tier securities if they fail to tender during the first tier, shareholders—including those who oppose the offer—are coerced into tendering during the first tier. *Unocal* and later cases specifically authorize the use of defenses to defeat a coercive two-tier tender offer.

Since its decision in *Unocal,* the Supreme Court of Delaware has applied this modified business judgment rule to validate a poison pill tender offer defense tactic in *Moran v. Household Int'l, Inc.*[5] and *Versata Enterprises Inc.* v. *Selectica*[6] and to invalidate a lock-up option tender offer defense in the *Revlon*[7] case. These cases confirmed the *Unocal* holding that the board of directors must show that:

1. It had reasonable grounds to believe that a danger to corporate policy and effectiveness was posed by the takeover attempt.

2. It acted primarily to protect the corporation and its shareholders from that danger.

3. The defense tactic was reasonable in relation to the threat posed to the corporation.

Such a standard appeared to impose a higher standard on directors than the rational basis requirement of the business judgment rule, which historically has been interpreted to require only that a decision of a board not be manifestly unreasonable. In addition, the *Revlon* case required the board to establish an auction market for the company and to sell it to the highest bidder when the directors have abandoned the long-term business objectives of the company by embracing a bust-up of the company.

In the following *Paramount v. Time* case, the Supreme Court of Delaware expanded board discretion in fighting hostile takeovers, holding that a board may oppose a hostile takeover provided the board had a *preexisting, deliberately conceived corporate plan* justifying its opposition. The existence of such a plan enabled Time's board to meet the reasonable-tactic element of the *Unocal* test.

---

[3]493 A.2d 946 (Del. Sup. Ct. 1985).

[4]Discriminatory tender offers are now illegal pursuant to Securities Exchange Act Rule 13e-4.

[5]500 A.2d 346 (Del. Sup. Ct. 1985)

[6] 5 A.3d 586 (Del. Sup. Ct. 2010).

[7]*Revlon Inc. v. MacAndrews & Forbes Holdings, Inc.,* 506 A.2d 173 (Del. S. Ct. 1986).

Paramount Communications, Inc. v. Time, Inc.
571 A.2d 1140 (Del. Sup. Ct. 1989)

Since 1983, Time, Inc., had considered expanding its business beyond publishing magazines and books, owning Home Box Office and Cinemax, and operating television stations. In 1988, Time's board approved in principle a strategic plan for Time's acquisition of an entertainment company. The board gave management permission to negotiate a merger with Warner Communications, Inc. The board's consensus was that a merger of Time and Warner was feasible, but only if Time controlled the resulting corporation, preserving the editorial integrity of Time's magazines. The board concluded that Warner was the superior candidate because Warner could make movies and TV shows for HBO, Warner had an international distribution system, Warner was a giant in the music business, Time and Warner would control half of New York City's cable TV system, and the Time network could promote Warner's movies.

Negotiations with Warner broke down when Warner refused to agree to Time's dominating the combined companies. Time continued to seek expansion, but informal discussions with other companies terminated when it was suggested the other companies purchase Time or control the resulting board. In January 1989, Warner and Time resumed negotiations, and on March 4, 1989, they agreed to a combination by which Warner shareholders would own 62 percent of the resulting corporation, to be named Time-Warner. To retain the editorial integrity of Time, the merger agreement provided for a board committee dominated by Time representatives.

On June 7, 1989, Paramount Communications, Inc., announced a cash tender offer for all of Time's shares at $175 per share. (The day before, Time shares traded at $126 per share.) Time's financial advisers informed the outside directors that Time's auction value was materially higher than $175 per share. The board concluded that Paramount's $175 offer was inadequate. Also, the board viewed the Paramount offer as a threat to Time's control of its own destiny and retention of the Time editorial policy; the board found that a combination with Warner offered greater potential for Time.

In addition, concerned that shareholders would not comprehend the long-term benefits of the merger with Warner, on June 16, 1989, Time's board recast its acquisition with Warner into a two-tier acquisition, in which it would make a tender offer to buy 51 percent of Warner's shares for cash immediately and later buy the remaining 49 percent for cash and securities. The tender offer would eliminate the need for Time to obtain shareholder approval of the transaction.

On June 23, 1989, Paramount raised its offer to $200 per Time share. Three days later, Time's board rejected the offer as a threat to Time's survival and its editorial integrity; the board viewed the Warner acquisition as offering greater long-term value for the shareholders. Time shareholders and Paramount then sued Time and its board to enjoin Time's acquisition of Warner. The trial court held for Time. Paramount and other Time shareholders appealed to the Supreme Court of Delaware.

Horsey, Justice

Our decision does not require us to pass on the wisdom of the board's decision. That is not a court's task. Our task is simply to determine whether there is sufficient evidence to support the initial Time-Warner agreement as the product of a proper exercise of business judgment.

We have purposely detailed the evidence of the Time board's deliberative approach, beginning in 1983–84, to expand itself. Time's decision in 1988 to combine with Warner was made only after what could be fairly characterized as an exhaustive appraisal of Time's future as a corporation. Time's board was convinced that Warner would provide the best fit for Time to achieve its strategic objectives. The record attests to the zealousness of Time's executives, fully supported by their directors, in seeing to the preservation of Time's perceived editorial integrity in journalism. The Time board's decision to expand the business of the company through its March 4 merger with Warner was entitled to the protection of the business judgment rule.

The revised June 16 agreement was defense-motivated and designed to avoid the potentially disruptive effect that Paramount's offer would have had on consummation of the proposed merger were it put to a shareholder vote. Thus, we decline to apply the traditional business judgment rule to the revised transaction and instead analyze the Time board's June 16 decision under *Unocal*.

In *Unocal*, we held that before the business judgment rule is applied to a board's adoption of a defensive measure, the burden will lie with the board to prove (a) reasonable grounds for believing that a danger to corporate policy and effectiveness existed; and (b) that the defensive measure adopted was reasonable in relation to the threat posed.

Paramount argues a hostile tender offer can pose only two types of threats: the threat of coercion that results from a two-tier offer promising unequal treatment for nontendering shareholders; and the threat of inadequate value from an all-shares, all-cash offer at a price below what a target board in good faith deems to be the present value of its shares.

Paramount would have us hold that only if the value of Paramount's offer were determined to be clearly inferior to the value created by management's plan to merge with Warner could the offer be viewed—objectively—as a threat.

Paramount's position represents a fundamental misconception of our standard of review under *Unocal* principally because it would involve the court in substituting its judgment as to what is a "better" deal for that of a corporation's board of directors. The usefulness of *Unocal* as an analytical tool is precisely its flexibility in the face of a variety of fact scenarios. Thus, directors may consider, when evaluating the threat posed by a takeover bid, the inadequacy of the price offered, nature and timing of the offer, questions of illegality, the impact on constituencies other than shareholders, the risk of nonconsummation, and the quality of securities being offered in the exchange.

The Time board reasonably determined that inadequate value was not the only threat that Paramount's all-cash, all-shares offer could present. Time's board concluded that Paramount's offer posed other threats. One concern was that Time shareholders might elect to tender into Paramount's cash offer in ignorance or a mistaken belief of the strategic benefit which a business combination with Warner might produce.

Paramount also contends that Time's board had not duly investigated Paramount's offer. We find that Time explored the available entertainment companies, including Paramount, before determining that Warner provided the best strategic "fit." In addition, Time's board rejected Paramount's offer because Paramount did not serve Time's objectives or meet Time's needs.

Time's board was adequately informed of the potential benefits of a transaction with Paramount. Time's failure to negotiate cannot be fairly found to have been uninformed. The evidence supporting this finding is materially enhanced by the fact that 12 of Time's 16 board members were outside independent directors.

We turn to the second part of the *Unocal* analysis. The obvious requisite to determining the reasonableness of a defensive action is a clear identification of the nature of the threat. This requires an evaluation of the importance of the corporate objective threatened; alternative methods of protecting that objective; impacts of the defensive action; and other relevant factors.

The fiduciary duty to manage a corporate enterprise includes the selection of a time frame for achievement of corporate goals. Directors are not obliged to abandon a deliberately conceived corporate plan for a short-term shareholder profit unless there is clearly no basis to sustain the corporate strategy. Time's responsive action to Paramount's tender offer was not aimed at "cramming down" on its shareholders a management-sponsored alternative, but rather had as its goal the carrying forward of a preexisting transaction in an altered form. Thus, the response was reasonably related to the threat. The revised agreement did not preclude Paramount from making an offer for the combined Time-Warner company or from changing the conditions of its offer so as not to make the offer dependent upon the nullification of the Time-Warner agreement. Thus, the response was proportionate.

Judgment for Time affirmed

Complying with the Unocal *Test* To avoid liability when opposing a takeover of the corporation, the board of directors must act in a manner similar to which it complies with the business judgment rule. First, the board must make a reasonable investigation into the threats the takeover poses to the corporation's policies and effectiveness. Having a preexisting acquisition and expansion plan, as Time, Inc., had in the *Paramount* case, will provide a basis for determining whether there is an threat to the company's policies. An investment banker can help the company investigate the facts that reveal threats to the corporation and help define an acquisition strategy, if one does not currently exist.

Second, the board must be motivated primarily to protect the company from the raider's threat, not to save their positions as directors, including the compensation and power that go with the position of director. The *Unocal* test recognizes that directors may be conflicted by their interest in saving their jobs, yet it allows directors to oppose the takeover if they mostly are concerned about protecting the company from the takeover's threat to the company's policies, such as a preexisting acquisition or expansion strategy that would be frustrated by the takeover.

Third, the board may adopt only those takeover defenses that are reasonable in relation to the threat. While this requirement seems to limit board discretion, in practice once the board has identified a credible threat to the corporation's policies, the board may engage in nearly any legal maneuver to stop that threat. That is especially true if the threat is to a preexisting acquisition or expansion strategy, such as a long-existing corporate strategy to remain an independent company or to grow by purchasing smaller competitors.

Duties of Loyalty

Directors and officers owe a duty of **utmost loyalty and fidelity** to the corporation. Judge Benjamin Cardozo stated this duty of trust. He declared that a director:

> owes loyalty and allegiance to the corporation—a loyalty that is undivided and an allegiance that is influenced by no consideration other than the welfare of the corporation. Any adverse interest of a director will be subjected to a scrutiny rigid and uncompromising. He may not profit at the expense of his corporation and in conflict with its rights; he may not for personal gain divert unto himself the opportunities which in equity and fairness belong to his corporation.[8]

Directors and officers owe the corporation the same duties of loyalty that agents owe their principals, though many of these duties have special names in corporation law. The most important of these duties of loyalty are the duties not to *self-deal,* not to *usurp a corporate opportunity,* not to *oppress minority shareholders,* and not to *trade on inside information.*

Conflicting Interest Transactions

A director or officer has a conflicting interest when a director or officer deals with his corporation. The director or officer with a **conflict of interest** may prefer his own interests over those of the corporation. The director's or officer's interest may be *direct,* such as his interest in selling his land to the corporation, or it may be *indirect,* such as his interest in having another business of which

---

[8]*Meinhard v. Salmon,* 164 N.E.2d 545, 546 (N.Y. Ct. App. 1928).

he or his family is an owner, director, or officer supply goods to the corporation. When a director has a conflict of interest, the director's transaction with the corporation may be voided or rescinded.

Under the MBCA, a director's conflicting interest transaction will not be voided merely on the grounds of a director's conflict of interest when *any one* of the following is true:

1. The transaction has been approved by a majority of informed, disinterested directors,
2. The transaction has been approved by a majority of the shares held by informed, disinterested shareholders, or
3. The transaction is fair to the corporation.

Nonetheless, even when disinterested directors' or shareholders' approval has been obtained, courts will void a conflict-of-interest transaction that is unfair to the corporation. Therefore, every corporate transaction in which a director has a conflict of interest must be fair to the corporation. If the transaction is fair, the interested director is excused from liability to the corporation. A transaction is fair if reasonable persons in an *arm's-length bargain* would have bound the corporation to it. This standard is often called the **intrinsic fairness standard.**

The function of disinterested director or disinterested shareholder approval of a conflict-of-interest transaction is merely to shift the burden of proving unfairness. The burden of proving fairness lies initially on the interested director. The burden of proof shifts to the corporation that

is suing the interested officer or director if the transaction was approved by the board of directors or the shareholders. Nonetheless, when disinterested directors approve an interested person transaction, substantial deference is given to the decision in accordance with the business judgment rule, especially when the disinterested directors compose a majority of the board.

Generally, *unanimous* approval of an interested person transaction by informed shareholders *conclusively* releases an interested director or officer from liability even if the transaction is unfair to the corporation. The rationale for this rule is that fully informed shareholders should know what is best for themselves and their corporation.

Complying with the Intrinsic Fairness Standard
Complying with the intrinsic fairness standard is not much different than complying with the business judgment rule, despite the higher standard of conduct. The board must make a reasonable investigation to discover facts that will permit an informed decision. Almost always, the board will be aided in its investigation by officers and other employees of the corporation and by investment bankers, other consultants, and legal counsel. When relying on others' investigations, the board must receive written and oral reports in sufficient time to absorb the information, to ask questions of those who made the investigation, and to debate and to deliberate after receiving all relevant information.

Ethics in Action

Sarbanes–Oxley Act of 2002 Prohibits Loans to Management

Early corporation law prohibited loans by a corporation to its officers or directors, on the grounds that such loans may result in looting of corporate assets. Today, however, the MBCA and most other general corporation statutes allow loans to directors and officers, although they require either shareholder approval or compliance with conflicting interest transaction rules.

In 2002, Congress took steps to return to the past. After it was revealed that several executives of public companies were using their corporations as personal banks to fund extravagant lifestyles—some of which loans were never repaid and some of which corporations became bankrupt—Congress included in the Sarbanes–Oxley Act of 2002 a section generally prohibiting public companies from making loans to their directors

or executive officers. This includes the company's CEO and CFO, any vice president in charge of a principal business unit or function, and any other officer or other person who performs a policy-making function. If the corporation is not a public company or if the loan is made to a nonexecutive, the Sarbanes–Oxley Act does not prohibit the corporate loan.

- Do you think that Congress has gone too far in banning loans to directors and officers? What are the ethical justifications to ban loans? What would a rights theorist argue? What would a utilitarian argue? What would a profit maximizer argue?

- Do you think that the Sarbanes–Oxley Act should have banned all corporation loans to its employees? Would you prohibit a bank from making loans to its employees, officers, and directors?

Investment bankers, other consultants, and legal counsel are especially helpful in ascertaining and disclosing any director's conflict of interest. By compiling a list of questions and quizzing the board members, consultants can help the board determine the extent of a director's conflict and ensure that the conflict is fully disclosed to the board. They should also make sure that only board members who are independent of the conflicted directors approve the conflicting interest transaction.

Finally, the board must make a decision that is fair to the corporation. Investment bankers and other consultants can help with this determination by demonstrating the decision's close fit with the firm's corporate strategy and the facts revealed by a reasonable investigation. They must ensure the decision is one that a reasonable person would make acting at arm's length.

Parent–Subsidiary Transactions Self-dealing is a concern when a parent corporation *dominates* a subsidiary corporation. Often, the subsidiary's directors will be directors or officers of the parent also. When persons with dual directorships approve transactions between the parent and the subsidiary, the opportunity for *overreaching* arises. There may be *no arm's-length bargaining* between the two corporations. Hence, such transactions must meet the *intrinsic fairness* test.

Usurpation of a Corporate Opportunity

Directors and officers may steal not only assets of their corporations (such as computer hardware and software) but also *opportunities* that their corporations could have exploited. Both types of theft are equally wrongful. As fiduciaries, directors and officers are liable to their corporation for **usurping corporate opportunities.**

The opportunity must come to the director or officer *in her corporate capacity.* Clearly, opportunities received at the corporate offices are received by the manager in her corporate capacity. In addition, courts hold that CEOs and other high level officers are nearly always acting in their corporate capacities, even when they are away from their corporate offices.

The opportunity must have a *relation or connection* to an *existing or prospective* corporate activity. Some courts apply the *line of business test,* considering how closely related the opportunity is to the lines of business in which the corporation is engaged. Other courts use the *interest or expectancy test,* requiring the opportunity to relate to property in which the corporation has an existing interest or in which it has an expectancy growing out of an existing right.

The corporation must be *able financially* to take advantage of the opportunity. Managers are required to make a good faith effort to obtain external financing for the corporation, but they are not required to use their personal funds to enable the corporation to take advantage of the opportunity.

A director or officer is free to exploit an opportunity that has been rejected by the corporation.

In the following case, *Guth v. Loft,* the court found that an opportunity to become the manufacturer of Pepsi-Cola syrup was usurped by the president of a corporation that manufactured beverage syrups and operated soda fountains. Note that the court ordered the typical remedy for usurpation: the officers forfeiture to the corporation of all benefits the officer received.

Guth v. Loft, Inc.	**5 A. 2d 503 (Del. Sup. Ct. 1939)**

Loft, Inc., manufactured and sold candies, syrups, and beverages and operated 115 retail candy and soda fountain stores. Loft sold Coca-Cola at all of its stores, but it did not manufacture Coca-Cola syrup. Instead, it purchased its 30,000-gallon annual requirement of syrup and mixed it with carbonated water at its various soda fountains.

In May 1931, Charles Guth, the president and general manager of Loft, became dissatisfied with the price of Coca-Cola syrup and suggested to Loft's vice president that Loft buy Pepsi-Cola syrup from National Pepsi-Cola Company, the owner of the secret formula and trademark for Pepsi-Cola. The vice president said he was investigating the purchase of Pepsi syrup.

Before being employed by Loft, Guth had been asked by the controlling shareholder of National Pepsi, Megargel, to acquire the assets of National Pepsi. Guth refused at that time. However, a few months after Guth had suggested that Loft purchase Pepsi syrup, Megargel again contacted Guth about buying National Pepsi's secret formula and trademark for only $10,000. This time, Guth agreed to the purchase, and Guth and Megargel organized a new corporation, Pepsi-Cola Company, to acquire *the Pepsi-Cola secret formula and trademark from National Pepsi. Eventually, Guth and his family's corporation owned a majority of the shares of Pepsi-Cola Company.*

Very little of Megargel's or Guth's funds were used to develop the business of Pepsi-Cola. Instead, without the knowledge or consent of Loft's board of directors, Guth used Loft's working capital, credit, plant and equipment, and executives and employees to produce Pepsi-Cola syrup. In addition, Guth's domination of Loft's board of directors ensured that Loft would become Pepsi-Cola's chief customer.

By 1935, the value of Pepsi-Cola's business was several million dollars. Loft sued Guth, asking the court to order Guth to transfer to Loft his shares of Pepsi-Cola Company and to pay Loft the dividends he had received from Pepsi-Cola Company. The trial court found that Guth had usurped a corporate opportunity and ordered Guth to transfer the shares and to pay Loft the dividends. Guth appealed.

Layton, Chief Justice

Public policy demands of a corporate officer or director the most scrupulous observance of his duty to refrain from doing anything that would deprive the corporation of profit or advantage. The rule that requires an undivided and unselfish loyalty to the corporation demands that there shall be no conflict between duty and self-interest.

The real issue is whether the opportunity to secure a very substantial stock interest in a corporation to be formed for the purpose of exploiting a cola beverage on a wholesale scale was so closely associated with the existing business activities of Loft, and so essential thereto, as to bring the transaction within that class of cases where the acquisition of the property would throw the corporate officer purchasing it into competition with his company.

Guth suggests a doubt whether Loft would have been able to finance the project. The answer to this suggestion is twofold. Loft's net asset position was amply sufficient to finance the enterprise, and its plant, equipment, executives, personnel and facilities were adequate. The second answer is that Loft's resources were found to be sufficient, for Guth made use of no other resources to any important extent.

Guth asserts that Loft's primary business was the manufacturing and selling of candy in its own chain of retail stores, and that it never had the idea of turning a subsidiary product into a highly advertised, nationwide specialty. It is contended that the Pepsi-Cola opportunity was not in the line of Loft's activities, which essentially were of a retail nature.

Loft, however, had many wholesale activities. Its wholesale business in 1931 amounted to over $800,000. It was a large company by any standard, with assets exceeding $9 million, excluding goodwill. It had an enormous plant. It paid enormous rentals. Guth, himself, said that Loft's success depended upon the fullest utilization of its large plant facilities. Moreover, it was a manufacturer of syrups and, with the exception of cola syrup, it supplied its own extensive needs. Guth, president of Loft, was an able and experienced man in that field. Loft, then, through its own personnel, possessed the technical knowledge, the practical business experience, and the resources necessary for the development of the Pepsi-Cola enterprise. Conceding that the essential of an opportunity is reasonably within the scope of a corporation's activities, latitude should be allowed for development and expansion. To deny this would be to deny the history of industrial development.

We cannot agree that Loft had no concern or expectancy in the opportunity. Loft had a practical and essential concern with respect to some cola syrup with an established formula and trademark. A cola beverage has come to be a business necessity for soft drink establishments; and it was essential to the success of Loft to serve at its soda fountains an acceptable five-cent cola drink in order to attract into its stores the great multitude of people who have formed the habit of drinking cola beverages.

When Guth determined to discontinue the sale of Coca-Cola in the Loft stores, it became, by his own act, a matter of urgent necessity for Loft to acquire a constant supply of some satisfactory cola syrup, secure against probable attack, as a replacement; and when the Pepsi-Cola opportunity presented itself, Guth having already considered the availability of the syrup, it became impressed with a Loft interest and expectancy arising out of the circumstances and the urgent and practical need created by him as the directing head of Loft.

The fiduciary relation demands something more than the morals of the marketplace. Guth did not offer the Pepsi-Cola opportunity to Loft, but captured it for himself. He invested little or no money of his own in the venture, but commandeered for his own benefit and advantage the money, resources, and facilities of his corporation and the services of its officials. He thrust upon Loft the hazard, while he reaped the benefit. In such a manner he acquired for himself 91 percent of the capital stock of Pepsi-Cola, now worth many millions. A genius in his line he may be, but the law makes no distinction between the wrong doing genius and the one less endowed.

Judgment for Loft affirmed.

Oppression of Minority Shareholders

Directors and officers owe a duty to manage a corporation in the best interests of the corporation and the shareholders as a whole. When, however, a group of shareholders has been isolated for beneficial treatment to the detriment of another isolated group of shareholders, the disadvantaged group may complain of **oppression.**

For example, oppression may occur when directors of a close corporation who are also the majority shareholders pay themselves high salaries yet refuse to pay dividends or to hire minority shareholders as employees of the corporation. Since there is no market for the shares of a close corporation (apart from selling to the other shareholders), these oppressed minority shareholders have investments that provide them no return. They receive no dividends or salaries, and they can sell their shares only to the other shareholders, who are usually unwilling to pay the true value of the shares.

Generally, courts treat oppression of minority shareholders the same way courts treat director self-dealing: The transaction must be intrinsically fair to the corporation and the minority shareholders.

A special form of oppression is the **freeze-out.** A freeze-out is usually accomplished by merging a corporation with a newly formed corporation under terms by which the minority shareholders do not receive shares of the new corporation but instead receive only cash or other securities. The minority shareholders are thereby *frozen out as shareholders.*

Going private is a special term for a freeze-out of shareholders of *publicly owned corporations.* Some public corporations discover that the burdens of public ownership exceed the benefits of being public. For example, the SEC requires public companies to provide to shareholders annual reports that include audited financial statements. The Sarbanes–Oxley Act has increased the cost of being public by requiring, in section 404, that annual reports include an internal control report acknowledging management's responsibility to maintain "an adequate internal control structure and procedures for financial reports." For some firms, section 404 compliance consumes as much as 3 percent of profits. Today, therefore, some publicly owned companies choose to freeze out their minority shareholders to avoid such burdens.

Freeze-Out Methods The two easiest ways to freeze out minority shareholders are the freeze-out merger and the reverse share split. With the freeze-out merger, the majority shareholders form a new corporation owned only by the majority shareholders. Articles of merger are drafted that will merge the old corporation into the new

corporation. Under the merger terms, only shareholders of the new corporation will survive as shareholders of the surviving new corporation; the shareholders of the old corporation will receive cash only. Since the majority shareholders control both corporations, the articles of merger will be approved by the directors and shareholders of both corporations. The freeze-out merger was used in the *Coggins* case, which follows at the end of this section.

Using a reverse share split to freeze out the minority shareholders is simpler. Here the articles are amended to reduce the number of outstanding shares by a multiplier, say 1/50,000, that will result in the majority shareholders having whole shares but the minority shareholders having only fractional shares. The articles amendment will be approved by directors and shareholders since the majority shareholder controls the corporation. After the reverse share split, corporation law permits the corporation to repurchase any fractional shares, even if the shareholders don't consent. The corporation buys the minority shareholders' fractional shares for cash, leaving only the majority shareholder owning the corporation.

Legal Standard Often, going private transactions appear abusive because the corporation goes public at a high price and goes private at a much lower price. Some courts have adopted a fairness test and a business purpose test for freeze-outs. Most states apply the **total fairness test** to freeze-outs. In the freeze-out context, total fairness has two basic aspects: *fair dealing* and *fair price.* Fair dealing requires disclosing material information to directors and shareholders and providing an opportunity for negotiation. A determination of fair value requires the consideration of all the factors relevant to the value of the shares, except speculative projections.

Some states apply the **business purpose test** to freeze-outs. This test requires that the freeze-out accomplish some legitimate business purpose and not serve the special interests of the majority shareholders or the managers.

Other states place no restrictions on freeze-outs provided a shareholder has a **right of appraisal,** which permits a shareholder to require the corporation to purchase his shares at a fair price.

In addition, the SEC requires a *publicly held* company to make a statement on the fairness of its proposed going private transaction and to discuss in detail the material facts on which the statement is based.

In the *Coggins* case, the court required that a freeze-out of minority shareholders of the New England Patriots football team meet both the business purpose and intrinsic fairness tests. The court held that freezing out the minority

> ## Coggins v. New England Patriots Football Club, Inc.
> ### 492 N.E.2d 1112 (Mass. Sup. Jud. Ct. 1986)
>
> *In 1959, the New England Patriots Football Club, Inc. (Old Patriots), was formed with one class of voting shares and one class of nonvoting shares. Each of the original 10 voting shareholders, including William H. Sullivan, purchased 10,000 voting shares for $2.50 per share. The 120,000 nonvoting shares were sold for $5 per share to the general public in order to generate loyalty to the Patriots football team. In 1974, Sullivan was ousted as president of Old Patriots. In November 1975, Sullivan succeeded in regaining control of Old Patriots by purchasing all 100,000 voting shares for $102 per share. He again became a director and president of Old Patriots.*
>
> *To finance his purchase of the voting shares, Sullivan borrowed $5,350,000 from two banks. The banks insisted that Sullivan reorganize Old Patriots so that its income could be used to repay the loans made to Sullivan and its assets used to secure the loans. To make the use of Old Patriots' income and assets legal, it was necessary to freeze out the nonvoting shareholders. In November 1976, Sullivan organized a new corporation called the New Patriots Football Club, Inc. (New Patriots). Sullivan was the sole shareholder of New Patriots. In December 1976, the shareholders of Old Patriots approved a merger of Old Patriots and New Patriots. Under the terms of the merger, Old Patriots went out of business, New Patriots assumed the business of Old Patriots, Sullivan became the only owner of New Patriots, and the nonvoting shareholders of Old Patriots received $15 for each share they owned.*
>
> *David A. Coggins, a Patriots fan from the time of its formation and owner of 10 Old Patriots nonvoting shares, objected to the merger and refused to accept the $15 per share payment for his shares. Coggins sued Sullivan and Old Patriots to obtain rescission of the merger. The trial judge found the merger to be illegal and ordered the payment of damages to Coggins and all other Old Patriots shareholders who voted against the merger and had not accepted the $15 per share merger payment. Sullivan and Old Patriots appealed to the Massachusetts Supreme Judicial Court.*
>
> **Liacos, Justice**
>
> When the director's duty of loyalty to the corporation is in conflict with his self-interest, the court will vigorously scrutinize the situation. The dangers of self-dealing and abuse of fiduciary duty are greatest in freeze-out situations like the Patriots merger, when a controlling shareholder and corporate director chooses to eliminate public ownership. Because the danger of abuse of fiduciary duty is especially great in a freeze-out merger, the court must be satisfied that the freeze-out was for the advancement of a legitimate corporate purpose. If satisfied that elimination of public ownership is in furtherance of a business purpose, the court should then proceed to determine if the transaction was fair by examining the totality of the circumstances. Consequently, Sullivan
>
> and Old Patriots bear the burden of proving, first, that the merger was for a legitimate business purpose, and second, that, considering the totality of circumstances, it was fair to the minority.
>
> Sullivan and Old Patriots have failed to demonstrate that the merger served any valid corporate objective unrelated to the personal interests of Sullivan, the majority shareholder. The sole reason for the merger was to effectuate a restructuring of Old Patriots that would enable the repayment of the personal indebtedness incurred by Sullivan. Under the approach we set forth above, there is no need to consider further the elements of fairness of a transaction that is not related to a valid corporate purpose.
>
> ***Judgment for Coggins affirmed as modified.***

shareholders merely to allow the corporation to repay the majority shareholder's personal debts was not a proper business purpose.

Trading on Inside Information   Officers
and directors have *confidential access* to nonpublic information about the corporation. Sometimes, directors and officers purchase their corporation's securities with knowledge of confidential information. Often, disclosure of previously nonpublic, **inside information** affects the value of the corporation's securities. Therefore, directors and officers may make a profit when the prices of the securities increase after the inside information has been disclosed publicly. Shareholders of the corporation claim that they have been harmed by such activity, either because the directors and officers misused confidential information that should have been used only for corporate purposes or because the directors and officers had an unfair informational advantage over the shareholders.

In this century, there has been a judicial trend toward finding a duty of directors and officers to disclose information that they have received confidentially from the corporation before they buy or sell the corporation's securities. As will be discussed fully in Chapter 45, Securities

Regulation, the illegality of insider trading is already federal law under the Securities Exchange Act; however, it remains only a minority rule under state corporation law.

Director's Right to Dissent

A director who assents to an action of the board of directors may be held liable for the board's exceeding its authority or its failing to meet its duty of due care or loyalty. A director who attends a board meeting is deemed to have assented to any action taken at the meeting, unless he dissents.

Under the MBCA, to register his **dissent** to a board action, and thereby to protect himself from liability, the director must **not vote in favor** of the action and **must make his position clear** to the other board members. His position is made clear either by requesting that his dissent appear in the minutes or by giving written notice of his dissent to the chairman of the board at the meeting or to the secretary immediately after the meeting. These procedures ensure that the dissenting director will attempt to dissuade the board from approving an imprudent action.

Generally, directors are not liable for failing to attend meetings. However, a director is liable for *continually failing* to attend meetings, with the result that the director is unable to prevent the board from harming the corporation by its self-dealing.

Duties of Directors and Officers of Nonprofit Corporations

Directors and officers of nonprofit corporations owe fiduciary duties to their corporations that are similar to the duties owed by managers of for-profit corporations. Directors and officers owe a duty of care and duties of loyalty to the nonprofit corporation. They must act in good faith, with the care of an ordinarily prudent person, and with a reasonable belief that they are acting in the best interests of the corporation. In addition, a director should not have a conflict of interest in any transaction of the nonprofit corporation. As with for-profit corporations, conflict-of-interest transactions must meet the intrinsic fairness standard. Finally, a nonprofit corporation may not lend money to a director.

Liability concerns of directors of nonprofit corporations, especially public benefit corporations in which directors typically receive no compensation, have made it difficult for some nonprofit corporations to find and retain directors. Therefore, the Model Nonprofit Corporation Act permits nonprofit corporations to limit or eliminate the liability of directors for breach of the duty of care. The articles may not limit or eliminate a director's liability for failing to act in good faith, engaging in intentional misconduct, breaching the duty of loyalty, or having a conflict of interest.

 ## Ethics in Action

Sarbanes–Oxley Act Imposes Duties and Liabilities on Corporate Management

In the early 2000s, it was revealed that some high-level officers of public corporations reaped millions of dollars of bonuses and profits from their sale of their corporations' stock during periods in which the corporations' profits were fraudulently inflated. In the Sarbanes–Oxley Act, as amended by the Dodd-Frank Wall Street Reform and Consumer Protection Act in 2010, Congress has taken a two-barreled approach, increasing top management's responsibility for the accuracy of financial statements and eliminating management's ability to profit personally from misstated financial data.

First, the Sarbanes–Oxley Act requires the CEO and the CFO of public companies to certify that to their knowledge all financial information in annual and quarterly reports filed with the Securities and Exchange Commission fairly presents the financial condition of the company and does not include untrue or misleading material statements. The purpose of the certification requirement is to protect shareholders and investors who rely on corporate financial statements. If a CEO or

CFO certified materially false financial statements that she knew were false or misleading, she is subject to a fine of $5 million and 20 years' imprisonment. In addition, the officer could have civil liability to shareholders far exceeding the fine limitation.

Second, the act requires the executive officers of a public company to disgorge any bonus, incentive-based or equity-based compensation, and the profit from the sale of corporate securities received during the three-year period prior to which the corporation was required to restate a financial statement due to a wrongful material noncompliance with a financial reporting requirement. This reimbursement of the corporation applies to an executive officer even if the wrongdoing was by some other officer or employee and whether or not the executive officer had knowledge of the wrongdoing. In addition, the act expands the disgorgement remedy available against any wrongdoing officer who receives bonuses or stock profits during the period of time the stock price is inflated by false financial information. The act permits recovery of not only improper gains but also any other relief necessary to protect and to mitigate harm to investors.

The Global Business Environment

Directors' Duties around the Globe

The fiduciary duties that American directors owe to their corporations are echoed in corporate law throughout the world. In Brazil, for example, an officer must apply the same principles he would apply in his own business. A Brazilian director breaches the duty of loyalty if the director uses inside information for his own benefit or for that of third parties, acts negligently in the use or protection of the company's rights, or engages in a business opportunity to gain personal advantage. For public companies, Brazil adds a duty that does not exist under American corporation law: to supply information to the shareholders and the public. In the United States, this duty is generally imposed on the corporation, not the directors.

Under German law, the management board and supervisory board of an AG owe shareholders a duty of loyalty. Members of the management board have a statutory obligation of confidentiality, and each member of the management board must exercise the care of a diligent and prudent business executive.

L07   Explain the legal limits of corporate liability for officers' and directors' actions.

Corporate and Management Liability for Torts and Crimes

When directors, officers, and other employees of the corporation commit torts and crimes while conducting corporate affairs, the issue arises concerning who has liability. Should the individuals committing the torts and crimes be held liable, the corporation, or both?

Liability of the Corporation   For **torts,** the vicarious liability rule of *respondeat superior* applies to corporations. The only issue is whether an employee acted within the scope of her employment, which encompasses not only acts the employee is authorized to commit but may also include acts that the employee is expressly instructed to avoid. Generally, under the doctrine of *respondeat superior,* a corporation is liable for an employee's tort that is reasonably connected to the authorized conduct of the employee.

The traditional view was that a corporation could not be guilty of a **crime** because criminal guilt required intent. A corporation, not having a mind, could form no intent. Other courts held that a corporation was not a person for purposes of criminal liability.

Today, few courts have difficulty holding corporations liable for crimes. Modern criminal statutes either expressly provide that corporations may commit crimes or define the term *person* to include corporations. In addition, some criminal statutes designed to protect the public welfare do not require intent as an element of some crimes, thereby removing the grounds used by early courts to justify relieving corporations of criminal liability.

Courts are especially likely to impose criminal liability on a corporation when the criminal act is requested, authorized, or performed by:

1. The board of directors,

2. An officer,

3. Another person having responsibility for formulating company policy, or

4. A high level administrator having supervisory responsibility over the subject matter of the offense and acting within the scope of his employment.

In addition, courts hold a corporation liable for crimes of its agent or employee committed within the scope of his authority, even if a higher corporate official has no knowledge of the act and has not ratified it.

Directors' and Officers' Liability for Torts and Crimes   A person is always *liable for his own torts and crimes,* even when committed on behalf of his principal. Every person in our society is expected to exercise independent judgment and not merely to follow orders. Therefore, directors and officers are personally liable when they commit torts or crimes during the performance of their corporate duties.

A director or officer is usually not liable for the torts of employees of the corporation, since the corporation, not the director or the officer, is the principal. He will have **tort** liability, however, if he *authorizes* the tort or *participates* in its commission. A director or officer has **criminal** liability if she *requests, authorizes, conspires,* or *aids and abets* the commission of a crime by an employee.

The early 21st century has been a busy time for verdicts in criminal cases against CEOs accused of acceding to accounting irregularities or looting their companies in the late 1990s and early 2000s. Bernard Ebbers, former

CEO of WorldCom, was found guilty of helping to mastermind the $11 billion accounting fraud that saw the firm seek bankruptcy. Ebbers received a 25-year prison sentence. The jury rejected his defense that he knew nothing of the fraud that was orchestrated by WorldCom CFO Scott Sullivan. The jury believed that as CEO Ebbers must have known of the fraud and was motivated to prop up the price of WorldCom stock to increase the value of stock options he held. Sullivan, who pled guilty and testified against Ebbers, cooperated with the prosecution and received a five-year prison sentence, despite his central role in the fraud.

Also in 2005, Adelphia founder and former CEO John Rigas received a 15-year prison sentence and his son and former CFO Scott, 20 years, after being found guilty of looting Adelphia. According to prosecutors, the Rigases used Adelphia as their "private ATM" to provide $50 million in cash advances, buy $1.6 billion in securities, and repay $252 million in margin loans. Also, Tyco's former CEO Dennis Kozlowski received up to 25 years in prison for looting Tyco, including using company funds for his wife's $2 million birthday party. Kozlowski was also fined $70 million and ordered to repay $134 million to Tyco.

The following *Jensen* case involves one of the most highly publicized options backdating cases. The case is a primer on why corporations backdated options for their top executives and how courts determine an appropriate sentence, including imprisonment, for executives who willingly violate the law.

United States v. Jensen	537 F. Supp. 2d 1069 (N.D. Cal. 2008)

On March 18, 2006, The Wall Street Journal *published an article analyzing how some companies were granting stock options to their executives. According to the article, companies issued a suspiciously high number of options at times when the stock price hit a periodic low, followed by a sharp price increase. The odds of these well-timed grants occurring by chance alone were astronomical—less likely than winning the lottery. Eventually it was determined that such buy-low, sell-high returns simply could not be the product of chance. In testimony before Congress, Professor Erik Lie identified three potential strategies to account for these well-timed stock option grants. The first strategy included techniques called "spring-loading" and "bullet-dodging." The practice of "spring-loading" involved timing a stock option grant to precede an announcement of good news. The practice of "bullet-dodging" involved timing a stock option grant to follow an announcement of bad news. A second strategy included manipulating the flow of information—timing corporate announcements to match known future grant dates. A third strategy, backdating, involved cherry-picking past, and relatively low, stock prices to be the official grant date. Backdating occurs when the option's grant date is altered to an earlier date with a lower, more favorable price to the recipient.*

A company grants stock options to its officers, directors, and employees at a certain "exercise price," giving the recipient the right to buy shares of the stock at that price, once the option vests. If the stock price rises after the date of the grant, the options have value. If the stock price falls after the date of the grant, the options have no value. Options with an exercise price equal to the stock's market price are called "at-the-money" options. Options with an exercise price lower than the stock's market price are called "in-the-money" options. By granting in-the-money, backdated options, a company effectively grants an employee an instant opportunity for profit.

Granting backdated options has important accounting consequences for the issuing company. For financial reporting purposes, companies granting in-the-money options have to recognize compensation expenses equal to the difference between the market price and the exercise price. APB 25 is the accounting rule that governed stock-based compensation through June 2005; it required companies to recognize this compensation expense for backdated options. For options granted at-the-money, a company did not have to recognize any compensation expenses under APB 25.

Backdating stock options by itself is not illegal. Purposefully backdated options that are properly accounted for and disclosed are legal. On the other hand, the backdating of options that is not disclosed or does not result in the recognition of a compensation expense is fraud.

A motive for fraudulent backdating may be to avoid recognizing a compensation expense, or a hit to the earnings, while awarding in-the-money options. To accomplish the fraud, those responsible assign an earlier date to the stock options—a date where the stock price was attractively low—and pretend the option was awarded on that earlier date, rather than the real date. In other words, fraudulent backdating disguises in-the-money options (which require recognizing compensation expenses) as at-the-money options (which do not require recognizing compensation expenses). The paperwork and phony grant dates allow the company to avoid compensation expenses, while aware that the price on the true grant date is higher than the price on the phony grant date.

A company's failure to account properly for in-the-money options would inflate the bottom line such that the company's net income would be higher than it should have been from an accounting perspective. As a result, the company would report excessive earnings per share, one of the more important metrics that investors used to evaluate a company's performance.

After 2002, a company's ability to backdate fraudulently option grants became much more difficult. On August 29, 2002, Congress passed the Sarbanes–Oxley Act, which instituted new reporting requirements for stock option grants. Before Sarbanes–Oxley, an employee who received a stock option grant had to file financial forms with the SEC within 45 days after the company's fiscal year-end. After Sarbanes–Oxley, an employee must file financial forms with the SEC within two days of receiving the stock option grant. After Sarbanes–Oxley, a company fraudulently backdating stock options by a few weeks or months would not filed have the required SEC forms on time, raising red flags with the SEC.

There have been several highly publicized options backdating cases involving American corporations. One involved Brocade Communications issuing backdated options to its CEO Gregory Reyes. Not only were Brocade Communications and Reyes prosecuted for violating federal securities laws, but also Stephanie Jensen, a Brocade vice president and director of its human resources department. At their trial, Dr. John Garvey, an expert witness for the prosecution, provided testimony about the size of the compensation expenses that went unstated as a result of Brocade's options pricing practices. Dr. Garvey testified that Brocade failed to recognize more than $173 million of compensation expenses in 2001 and more than $161 million in 2002. He further testified that, if Brocade had properly accounted for the stock options it had backdated, then the company would have recorded a loss of $110 million in 2001, rather than the profit of $3 million it actually reported, and would have recorded a loss of $45 million in 2002, rather than the profit of nearly $60 million it actually reported.

In December 2007, a federal district court jury convicted Jensen of willingly and knowingly falsifying Brocade's records over a three-year period to conceal the actual date when stock options were granted to Reyes. The district court judge next considered whether a proper sentence for Jensen included imprisonment.

Breyer, Judge

The Securities Exchange Act's penalty provision, 15 U.S.C. § 78ff, precludes imprisonment "for the violation of any rule or regulation if [the defendant] proves that he had no knowledge of such rule or regulation." Concerned that a great mass of rules and regulations would be issued by the SEC in the wake of the Securities Act and Securities Exchange Act, Congress enacted the No Knowledge Clause, thereby rendering ludicrous a strict adherence to the fiction of presumed knowledge of the law.

The No Knowledge Clause is an affirmative defense to a sentence of imprisonment. As such, the defendant bears the burden of proving no knowledge by a preponderance of the evidence. To be more specific, Jensen bears the burden of proving that she did not know there was any applicable SEC rule prohibiting the falsification of books and records. It is not a defense for Jensen to argue that she did not know, for example, the precise number or common name of the rule, the book and page where it was to be found, or the date upon which it was promulgated.

Accordingly, the question becomes whether Jensen has satisfied her burden of proving by a preponderance that she was unaware of an SEC rule or regulation prohibiting the falsification of books and records. In the Court's opinion, she has not. Jensen argues that: (1) her background and experience are in

areas that have nothing to do with SEC rules and regulations; (2) her job responsibilities had nothing to do with SEC rules or regulations; (3) Jensen had nothing to do with the SEC reporting process; (4) none of the individuals who worked with Jensen drew any connection between their work on options grants and SEC regulations; and (5) none of the more than 50 deponents in the SEC action recall discussing anything connected to any SEC rule with Jensen.

There is no smoking gun conclusively demonstrating that Jensen was aware that falsification of books was outlawed by SEC regulation. However, the circumstantial evidence that Jensen offers up is insufficient to carry her burden in light of the evidence established at trial. There is substantial evidence that Jensen knew her conduct was wrongful, including the fact that Jensen attempted to minimize the obviousness of backdated options, concealed the way options were actually dated, and directed employees not to communicate about options over the phone or email. To be sure, Jensen can only be imprisoned if she knew her conduct was unlawful *and* knew that it was prohibited by SEC rule or regulation. But in light of the evidence demonstrating that Jensen knew her conduct affected Brocade finances, the Court is assured that Jensen also knew she was violating an SEC rule or regulation.

For example, Jensen received emails establishing that options had an effect on Brocade financials and audits. On January 28,

2002, Jensen received an email from Brocade comptroller Bob Bossi, asking for the stock grant list to support an upcoming quarter-end audit from Arthur Andersen. Similarly, Jensen received an email confirming that the stock options grant lists and compensation committee meetings would be used in Brocade's year-end audit. The only reasonable conclusion to draw is that Jensen knew that stock options, and how they were priced, affected the audited results of the company.

Moreover, there was evidence at trial that after Jensen shepherded options through the pricing process, the forms were then given to the finance department so that finance could ensure that the grants were accurate. It can be reasonably assumed that as director of human resources, Jensen understood the chain for processing option grants and that stock options went from human resources directly to finance. A reasonably intelligent corporate official would understand that if the options forms went directly to finance, that was so because the forms had an effect on Brocade's financials. Falsifying options grants would therefore impair the integrity of the company's financials, which a reasonable official would know is illegal under SEC rule and regulation.

In short, the Court does not believe that Jensen was so far removed from the financial side of the process that she would not know her conduct was prohibited by the SEC. Jensen clearly knew her conduct was unlawful and, the Court believes, knew that her conduct affected Brocade's finances and audits. Under the circumstances, Jensen has not persuasively established that she was unaware her conduct violated any SEC rule or regulation.

In determining the sentence of co-defendant Gregory Reyes, the Court concluded that it would be inappropriate to enhance the sentence for loss, number of victims, and sophisticated means. The Court reaches the same conclusion with respect to Jensen's sentence. As to other enhancements, the Court will impose a two-level abuse of trust enhancement and a two-level enhancement for obstruction of justice, but rejects the government's request for an aggravating role enhancement and a public officer enhancement.

In general, the government bears the burden of proving, by a preponderance of the evidence, the facts necessary to enhance a defendant's offense level under the Sentencing Guidelines. However, when a sentencing factor has an extremely disproportionate effect on the sentence relative to the offense of conviction, due process requires that the government prove the facts underlying the enhancement by clear and convincing evidence.

The government has *not* demonstrated—at least not by clear and convincing evidence—that Jensen was the kind of Vice President who owed a heightened fiduciary duty to shareholders. Brocade proxy statements, 10-Qs, and 10-Ks frequently listed corporate officers, including the Vice Presidents in charge of Engineering, Operations, and Sales—core decisional and

policy-making roles—but never Jensen. In addition, the government has identified no securities law that imposes heightened duties on executives in divisions such as human resources, as opposed to divisions more closely connected to the operational functions of the company.

To be sure, Jensen played an important *internal* role in the organization. Jensen was one of only nine executives who reported directly to Reyes, in contrast to sixteen Vice Presidents who did not. But the government has not pointed to persuasive evidence demonstrating that Jensen played the kind of role in relation to *shareholders* such that as head of Human Resources, she owed them a heightened fiduciary duty. Accordingly, the Court will not impose the four-level public officer enhancement.

Because the Court will not impose the public officer enhancement, it may consider whether to impose an enhancement for abuse of trust. To impose an enhancement for abuse of trust, the government must establish by clear and convincing evidence that: (1) Jensen occupied a position of trust; and (2) Jensen abused her position in a manner that significantly facilitated the commission or concealment of the offense.

Jensen used her managerial position to escort the backdated stock option grants through the necessary processes. It was Jensen who involved and oversaw employees in the human resources department tasked with the picking of lower dates, Jensen who ordered her employees to conceal the picking of past dates by not using email or phones, and Jensen who coordinated the signing of falsified dates by Reyes, providing the CEO with an array of earlier dates from which he could select. A lesser employee of the firm could not have accomplished these things which significantly facilitated the scheme's success and concealment.

Even if Jensen did not owe a heightened fiduciary duty to shareholders, she was entrusted with accurately maintaining books and records that affected the financials of the company. Thus, there can be no doubt that shareholders were obligated to trust that Jensen would properly maintain any books and records bearing on Brocade's assets. Because Jensen occupied a position of trust and abused that position to commit and conceal the falsification of books and records, a two-level enhancement is appropriate.

The Court will enhance Jensen's sentence by two levels because she impeded justice by proffering—through counsel—a false declaration in support of her motion to sever. Jensen's arguments that the declaration was truthful and that she should not be punished for the conduct of her attorney are unpersuasive.

In his declaration, Reyes declared, "I told Ms. Jensen that the option grant dates were the dates that I made the granting decisions. *Options were priced at the fair market value on the grant dates.*" (Emphasis added.) Jensen argues that no one obstructed justice because the declaration did not provide false information to the Court. According to Jensen, Reyes' declaration intended to convey that he *sometimes* priced grant dates on the same day he made granting decisions, but was not intended to deny that on other occasions, Reyes did backdate option grants with Jensen's help.

Even if Jensen is correct that, technically speaking, Reyes' statement was not per se false, the Court still finds that the declaration impeded justice because it was seriously misleading. Reyes' declaration, in combination with the statements of counsel, misled the Court into believing that Reyes' declaration related to *all* stock option grants. Whether or not Reyes and Jensen's counsel subjectively believed that the declaration only related to some grants, there was no way for the Court to discern that subtle distinction.

Jensen sat in court while her lawyer argued that Reyes' declaration provided "absolutely exculpatory" evidence that precluded the jury from convicting Jensen for backdating options. Jensen also sat idly by while her lawyer argued that there was no evidence Jensen actually knew that Reyes was backdating. But at the time, Jensen did know that Reyes had backdated, and therefore knew that Reyes' declaration was not "absolutely exculpatory."

Because Jensen has not carried her burden of proving that the No Knowledge Clause controls her sentence, the Court will impose a sentence with an eye towards—among other factors—the Sentencing Guidelines. With a base offense level of six, plus two-level enhancements for abuse of trust and obstruction of justice, the Guidelines recommend a sentence of 6–12 months. The minimum term may be satisfied by a sentence of imprisonment that includes a term of supervised release with a condition that substitutes community confinement or home detention, provided that at least one month is satisfied by imprisonment.

Order entered sentencing Jensen to imprisonment.

Note: Upon appeal in *U.S. v. Reyes*, 2009 U.S. Lexis 18426 (9th Cir. 2009), the court of appeals affirmed Jensen's conviction and sentence to imprisonment, but remanded the case for resentencing without enhancement for the obstruction of justice charge. The court held that it was inappropriate to enhance Jensen's sentence based on her silence in the face of her lawyer's argument when she did not help to bring about or cause Reye's declaration.

Insurance and Indemnification

The extensive potential liability of directors deters many persons from becoming directors. They fear that their liability for their actions as directors may far exceed their fees as directors. To encourage persons to become directors, corporations **indemnify** them for their outlays associated with defending lawsuits brought against them and paying judgments and settlement amounts. In addition, or as an alternative, corporations purchase **insurance** that will make such payments for the directors. Indemnification and insurance are provided for officers, also.

Mandatory Indemnification of Directors

Under the MBCA, a director is entitled to *mandatory indemnification* of her reasonable litigation expenses when she is sued and *wins completely* (is *wholly successful*). The greatest part of such expenses is attorney's fees. Because indemnification is mandatory in this context, when the corporation refuses to indemnify a director who has won completely, she may ask a court to order the corporation to indemnify her.

Ethics in Action

Expanding Indemnification

The MBCA permits a corporation to expand the grounds on which it may indemnify a director, within limits. For example, the corporation may provide for indemnification of a director's liability (including a judgment paid to the corporation) when the director acted carelessly and in bad faith, but did not intend to harm the corporation or its shareholders and did not receive an improper financial benefit.

- Do you think it is ethical for a corporation to indemnify a careless director for the amount for which she was liable to the corporation? Would a rights theorist support indemnification in that context? Would a utilitarian? Would a profit maximizer?
- Would you be a shareholder in a corporation that permits indemnification in the context above?
- Would you be a director in a corporation if it did not indemnify you in that context?

Permissible Indemnification of Directors

Under the MBCA, a director who loses a lawsuit *may* be indemnified by the corporation. This is called *permissible indemnification,* because the corporation is permitted to indemnify the director but is not required to do so.

The corporation must establish that the director acted in *good faith* and reasonably believed that she acted in the *best interests* of the corporation. When a director seeks indemnification for a *criminal* fine, the corporation must establish a third requirement—that the director had no reasonable cause to believe that her conduct was unlawful. Finally, any permissible indemnification must be approved by someone independent of the director receiving indemnification—a disinterested board of directors, disinterested shareholders, or independent legal counsel. Permissible indemnification may cover not only the director's reasonable expenses but also fines and damages that the director has been ordered to pay.

A corporation may not elect to indemnify a director who was found to have received a *financial benefit* to which he was not entitled. Such a rule tends to prevent indemnification of directors who acted from self-interest. If a director received no financial benefit but was held liable to his corporation or paid an amount to the corporation as part of a *settlement,* the director may be indemnified only for his reasonable expenses, not for the amount that he paid to the corporation. The purpose of these rules is to avoid the circularity of having the director pay damages to the corporation and then having the corporation indemnify the director for the same amount of money.

Advances A director may not be able to afford to make payments to her lawyer prior to the end of a lawsuit. More important, a lawyer may refuse to defend a director who cannot pay legal fees. Therefore, the MBCA permits a corporation to make advances to a director to allow the director to afford a lawyer, if the director affirms that she meets the requirements for permissible indemnification and she promises to repay the advances if she is found not entitled to indemnification.

Court-Ordered Indemnification A court may order a corporation to indemnify a director if it determines that the director meets the standard for *mandatory* indemnification or if the director is *fairly and reasonably* entitled to indemnification in view of all the relevant circumstances.

Indemnification of Nondirectors Under the MBCA, officers and employees who are not directors are entitled to the same mandatory indemnification rights as directors.

Insurance

The MBCA does not limit the ability of a corporation to purchase insurance on behalf of its directors, officers, and employees. Insurance companies, however, are unwilling to insure all risks. In addition, some risks are *legally uninsurable as against public policy.* Therefore, liability for misconduct such as self-dealing, usurpation, and securities fraud is uninsurable.

Nonprofit Corporations

A nonprofit corporation may obtain insurance and indemnify its officers and directors for liabilities incurred in the course of their performance of their official duties. The MNCA requires indemnification when the director or officer wins the lawsuit completely. A corporation is permitted to indemnify an officer or director who is found liable if he acted in good faith and reasonably believed he acted in the best interests of the corporation.

Problems and Problem Cases

1. Tri R Angus, Inc., a closely held corporation, was owned 80 percent by Jon and Frances Neiman, who were also directors of Tri R Angus. Troy Neiman and Carol Lewis owned 12 percent of Tri R Angus's shares. Troy and Carol asked a court to remove Jon and Frances as directors of the corporation on the grounds that they authorized Tri R Angus to distribute its assets in violation of state law, inappropriately mortgaged or sold corporate assets, misused corporate earnings, and wasted corporate assets. Jon and Frances denied the allegations. At trial, Troy and Carol entered as evidence pleadings from other actions against Jon and Frances and introduced no objective evidence of current conduct by Jon or Frances. What standard of misconduct did the court require Troy and Carol to prove in order to remove Jon and Frances? Did the court find they had proved their case?

2. Countrywide Financial Corporation created for its employees a pension plan that allowed employees to

select how their pension plan amounts are invested, including investing in the common stock of Country-wide. When the value of the common stock of Countrywide Financial Corporation declined from over $40 per share to $6 in a six-month period in 2007 and 2008 due to the collapse of the subprime lending market, Countrywide employees sued Countrywide and its directors for breaching a fiduciary duty to the employees by not exercising its discretion to suspend both offering Countrywide stock as a plan investment and matching employees' investment in Countrywide stock. Has the board of directors breached a fiduciary duty to the employees?

3. Lillian Pritchard was a director of Pritchard & Baird Corporation, a business founded by her husband. After the death of her husband, her sons took control of the corporation. For two years, they looted the assets of the corporation through theft and improper payments. The corporation's financial statements revealed the improper payments to the sons, but Mrs. Pritchard did not read the financial statements. She did not know what her sons were doing to the corporation or that what they were doing was unlawful. When Mrs. Pritchard was sued for failing to protect the assets of the corporation, she argued that she was a figurehead director, a simple housewife who served as a director as an accommodation to her husband and sons. Was Mrs. Pritchard held liable?

4. The Chicago National League Ball Club, Inc. (Chicago Cubs), operated Wrigley Field, the Cubs' home park. Through the 1965 baseball season, the Cubs were the only major league baseball team that played no home games at night because Wrigley Field had no lights for nighttime baseball. Philip K. Wrigley, director and president of the corporation, refused to install lights because of his personal opinion that baseball was a daytime sport and that installing lights and scheduling night baseball games would result in the deterioration of the surrounding neighborhood. The other directors assented to this policy. From 1961 to 1965, the Cubs suffered losses from their baseball operations. The Chicago White Sox, whose weekday games were generally played at night, drew many more fans than did the Cubs. A shareholder sued the board of directors to force them to install lights at Wrigley Field and to schedule night games. What did the court rule? Why?

5. James Gray was the president and managing officer of Peoples Bank and Trust Company. Frank Piecara was an old customer of the bank. Piecara was president of Mirage Construction, Inc. Gray directed Peoples Bank to make a $536,000 loan to a trust managed by Piecara, the loan proceeds to be used to provide working capital for Mirage. Gray obtained a security interest in Mirage's accounts receivable and contract rights for work Mirage was to perform for Rogers Construction. Gray did not perfect the security interest or notify Rogers that it should remit payments for Mirage's work directly to Peoples Bank. Piecara and Mirage defaulted on the loan to Peoples Bank. Gray was sued by his employer for breaching his fiduciary duty. Has Gray complied with the business judgment rule?

6. Selectica, Inc., a Delaware corporation, provides enterprise software solutions to business. It has never been profitable and has amassed net operating losses (NOLs) that it may use to offset future income for tax purposes. Trilogy, Inc., a Delaware corporation, also specializes in enterprise software solutions. Versata Enterprises, Inc., is a Delaware corporation and a subsidiary of Trilogy, providing technology-powered business services to clients. Versata and Trilogy owned 6.7 percent of Selectica's common stock. After they intentionally triggered Selectica's Shareholder Rights Plan through the purchase of additional shares, Versata's and Trilogy's joint beneficial ownership was diluted to approximately 3.3 percent. Selectica thereafter reduced the trigger of its poison pill to 4.99 percent of Selectica's outstanding shares and capped existing shareholders who held a 5 percent or more interest to a further increase of only 0.5 percent. Selectica's reason for taking such action was to protect the company's NOL carryforwards. When Trilogy, Inc., purchased shares above this cap, Selectica filed suit in the Delaware Court of Chancery, seeking a declaration that the poison pill was valid. Trilogy and its subsidiary Versata counterclaimed that the poison pill was unlawful on the grounds that, before acting, Selectica's board of directors failed to consider that its NOLs were unusable or that the poison pill was unnecessary given Selectica's unbroken history of losses and doubtful prospects of annual profits. Trilogy and Versata also asserted that the poison pill was impermissibly preclusive of a successful proxy contest for control of Selectica's board of directors,

particularly when combined with Selectica's staggered director terms. What rule did the court apply to judge the actions of Selectica's board of directors? Did the court conclude that the board complied with that rule?

7. Nook Pharmacies, Inc., is a small public company that operates 50 pharmacies in six states. Nook's board of directors is aware that CVS and Walgreens, the dominant companies in the pharmacy industry, are buying many of the remaining small pharmacy companies. Nook's directors prefer that Nook remain an independent company that will grow internally as it embraces new markets near its current pharmacies. The board wants to oppose any attempt by CVS or Walgreens to take over Nook. Nook's board has consulted you for advice on how to oppose a hostile takeover bid. In anticipation of a hostile bid, with what standard of conduct do you advise Nook's board to plan to comply? What do you advise Nook's board to do now to help Nook's board comply with that standard of conduct?

8. Lymon Properties Group, Inc., is a developer and operator of retail shopping malls. Lymon owns 75 percent of the shares of LDC, Inc., whose business is investing in undeveloped land. All of LDC's directors are appointed by Lymon. LDC owns 320 acres of land that Lymon wants to purchase for mall construction. LDC purchased the land two years ago for $6.4 million. Lymon has offered to purchase the land for $8.2 million. When approving the purchase, with what standard of conduct must Lymon's board comply? What should LDC's board of directors do before accepting the offer in order to reduce the likelihood that LDC's minority shareholders will be able to sue LDC's board successfully for selling the land for too low a price?

9. Gimble Hardt Corporation (GHC) is a manufacturer of aluminum wiring. Jason Gimble owns 82 percent of the 2 million outstanding shares of GHC. The remaining 360,000 shares are owned by 832 minority shareholders, none of whom owns more than 1,200 shares. Gimble wants to freeze out the minority shareholders using a reverse share split. Describe that procedure, including a statement of who must approve the transaction. What legal standard must the freeze-out transaction meet? Does it matter that Gimble wants to freeze out the minority shareholders so that GHC is no longer a public company that has to comply with the costly rules of the Sarbanes–Oxley Act?

10. Ian McCarthy was president and CEO of Beazer Homes USA, Inc., a publicly held home construction company that was required to restate its quarterly and annual financial statements due to a fraudulent earnings management scheme perpetrated by Beazer's CAO, Michael Rand, to satisfy analysts' quarterly and annual earnings expectations. Rand directed and supervised a reserve accounting scheme under which reserves for certain future homebuilding expenses were improperly established, inflated, or maintained, so that they could later be used in subsequent fiscal years, including 2006, to boost artificially income and earnings. In 2008, after uncovering the fraud, Beazer correctly restated its 2006 earnings. Even though McCarthy was not engaged in the fraud, the Securities and Exchange Commission demanded that McCarthy reimburse Beazer for cash bonuses, incentive and equity-based compensation, and profits from his sale of Beazer stock received during the 12-month period following the issuance of Beazer's quarterly and annual financial statements for its fiscal year 2006. Was the SEC's action successful?

11. In 1997, Peter Zaccagnino sold to investors historical bonds—issued by railroad and foreign governments—that he claimed were high-yield securities. In reality, the bonds had no value to anyone other than to collectors of historical documents. Peter obtained over $6.8 million from the sale of these bonds. During this time, his wife, Gigi, attended meetings where her husband represented to investors that the bonds could yield 7 to 30 percent of their valuation within a year. Zaccagnino sold the historical bonds through two corporate entities and deposited most of the sales proceeds into the corporations' accounts. One of those corporations was Wonder Glass Products, of which Gigi was the secretary, treasurer, and director. She received $5,200 a month from her employment with Wonder Glass. In March 1998, Gigi incorporated a business called Diamond in the Rough (DIR) in the British Virgin Islands, of which she was president, secretary, and director. Peter promoted DIR as a firm that placed client funds into high-yield offshore investment programs, promising investors substantial earnings. At one DIR meeting with prospective purchasers, Gigi sat at a table and made prospective investors promise that they would not record the meeting. Meanwhile, Peter told them that they could make huge

sums of money with the proposed investments and that he had been arranging similar investments successfully for so long that he was ready to retire. This foreign investment scheme earned Peter millions in addition to the money from the historical bond sales. When the federal government prosecuted Peter and Gigi for conspiracy and racketeering, Gigi claimed that she became aware of the criminal conduct only in December 1999, when she overheard her husband and one of his business partners laughing about the falsity of the statements they sent to investors. Did the court accept Gigi's argument or was she found to have willfully engaged in criminal conduct while acting for the corporations?

12. Shareholders of Barney Slaney, Inc., brought a derivative suit against the corporation's board of directors for failing to supervise adequately the corporation's loan officers, who made several high-risk loans to substandard borrowers. Almost 40 percent of the high-risk borrowers defaulted on the loans, resulting in a loss of $55 million to Barney Slaney. The directors asked the corporation to advance to them the cost of legal fees for defending themselves against the charges. Under what conditions may the corporation make advances of legal fees to the directors?

Online Research

The Credit Crisis and Directors' Fiduciary Duties

The credit crunch currently experienced in the United States and elsewhere was caused in part by decisions of banks like Countrywide Financial to make loans to borrowers who had insufficient income to repay the loans, as well as by investment banks like Bear Stearns which purchased many of those loans from banks in the secondary market. Check online to see how shareholders of banks and investment banks are faring in their lawsuits against the officers and directors who owed a fiduciary duty to make prudent decisions when issuing and purchasing loans.

Consider completing the case "LIABILITY: Office Party Blame Game" from the You Be the Judge website element after you have read this chapter. Visit our website at **www.mhhe.com/mallor15e** for more information and activities regarding this case segment.

CHAPTER 44

SHAREHOLDERS' RIGHTS AND LIABILITIES

Four business associates create a business that will develop and sell information technology software. The business will be incorporated. The four will provide 90 percent of the initial capital needs of the business, but none of them has the IT skills to develop marketable software. In addition, none of the four wants to be involved in the day-to-day management of the business. The four associates have found, however, an IT engineer to develop software and another person who is willing to manage the business. The engineer and the general manager each want a 5 percent equity interest in the corporation, which the four associates are willing to grant to them. Although the engineer and the GM would each like to elect a representative to the corporation's board of directors, the four associates want to control the business absolutely, with each associate owning an equal share of the corporation and sitting on the board.

- Using classes of shares, create an equity structure for the corporation that meets the wants of the four associates, the engineer, and the GM.
- In this context, why is using classes of shares preferable to using one class of shares with cumulative voting for directors?

LO   LEARNING OBJECTIVES

After studying this chapter, you should be able to:

1   Understand the rights and powers of shareholders and how shareholders exercise their powers.

2   Create classes of shares and delineate their rights to fit the needs of controlling and other shareholders.

3   Appreciate how shareholders may enforce corporate rights of actions, especially against corporate managers.

4   Explain the special liabilities of shareholders.

THE SHAREHOLDERS ARE THE owners of a corporation, but a shareholder has *no right to manage* the corporation. Instead, a corporation is managed by its board of directors and its officers for the benefit of its shareholders.

The shareholders' role in a corporation is limited to electing and removing directors, approving certain important matters, and ensuring that the actions of the corporation's managers are consistent with the applicable state corporation statute, the articles of incorporation, and the bylaws.

Shareholders also assume a few responsibilities. For example, all shareholders are required to pay the promised consideration for shares. Shareholders are liable for receiving dividends beyond the lawful amount. In addition, controlling shareholders may owe special duties to minority shareholders.

Close corporation shareholders enjoy rights and owe duties beyond the rights and duties of shareholders of publicly owned corporations. In addition, some courts have found close corporation shareholders to be fiduciaries of each other.

This chapter's study of the rights and responsibilities of shareholders begins with an examination of shareholders' meetings and voting rights.

Shareholders' Meetings

The general corporation statutes of most states and the Model Business Corporation Act (MBCA) provide that an annual meeting of shareholders shall be held. The purpose of an annual shareholders' meeting is to elect new directors and to conduct other necessary business. Often, the shareholders are asked to approve the corporation's independent auditors and to vote on shareholders' proposals.

Special meetings of shareholders may be held whenever a corporate matter arises that requires immediate shareholders' action, such as the approval of a merger that cannot wait until the next annual shareholders' meeting. Under the MBCA, a special shareholders' meeting may be called by the board of directors or by a person authorized to do so by the bylaws, usually the president or the chairman of the board. In addition, the holders of at least 10 percent of the shares entitled to vote at the meeting may call a special meeting.

Notice of Meetings To permit shareholders to arrange their schedules for attendance at shareholders' meetings, the MBCA requires the corporation to give shareholders notice of annual and special meetings of shareholders. Notice of a *special meeting* must list the purpose of the meeting. Under the MBCA, notice of an *annual meeting* need not include the purpose of the meeting unless shareholders will be asked to approve extraordinary corporate changes—for example, amendments to the articles of incorporation and mergers.

Notice need be given only to shareholders entitled to vote who are shareholders of record on a date fixed by the board of directors. Shareholders of record are those whose names appear on the share-transfer book of the corporation. Usually, only shareholders of record are entitled to vote at shareholders' meetings.

Conduct of Meetings To conduct business at a shareholders' meeting, a **quorum** of the outstanding shares must be represented at the meeting. If the approval of more than one class of shares is required, a quorum of each class of shares must be present. A quorum is a majority of shares outstanding, unless a greater percentage is established in

the articles. The president or the chairman of the board usually presides at shareholders' meetings. Minutes of shareholders' meetings are usually kept by the secretary.

A majority of the votes cast at the shareholders' meeting will decide issues that are put to a vote. If the approval of more than one class of shares is required, a majority of the votes cast by each class must favor the issue. The articles may require a greater than majority vote. Ordinarily, a shareholder is entitled to cast as many votes as he has shares.

Shareholders have a right of *full participation* in shareholders' meetings. This includes the right to offer resolutions, to speak for and against proposed resolutions, and to ask questions of the officers of the corporation.

Typical shareholder resolutions are aimed at protecting or enhancing the interests of minority shareholders and promoting current social issues. Proposals have included limiting corporate charitable contributions, restricting the production of nuclear power, banning the manufacture of weapons, and requiring the protection of the environment.

Shareholder Action without a Meeting
Generally, shareholders can act only at a properly called meeting. However, the MBCA permits shareholders to act without a meeting if *all of the shareholders entitled to vote consent in writing* to the action.

 Understand the rights and powers of shareholders and how shareholders exercise their powers.

Shareholders' Election of Directors

Straight Voting The most important shareholder voting right exercised at a shareholder meeting is the right to elect the directors. Normally, directors are elected by a single class of shareholders in **straight voting,** in which each share has one vote for each new director to be elected. With straight voting, a shareholder may vote for as many nominees as there are directors to be elected; a shareholder may cast for each such nominee as many votes as she has shares. For example, in a director election in which 15 people have been nominated for 5 director positions, a shareholder with 100 shares can vote for up to 5 nominees and can cast up to 100 votes for each of those 5 nominees.

Under straight voting, the nominees with the most votes are elected. Consequently, straight voting allows a majority shareholder to elect the entire board of directors. Thus, minority shareholders are unable to elect any representatives to the board without the cooperation of the majority shareholder.

Straight voting is also a problem in close corporations in which a few shareholders own equal numbers of shares. In such corporations, no shareholder individually controls the corporation, yet if the holders of a majority of the shares act together, those holders will elect all of the directors and control the corporation. Such control may be exercised to the detriment of the other shareholders.

Two alternatives to straight voting aid minority shareholders' attempts to gain representation on the board and prevent harmful coalitions in close corporations: cumulative voting and classes of shares.

Cumulative Voting

With cumulative voting, a corporation allows a shareholder to cumulate her votes by multiplying the number of directors to be elected by the shareholder's number of shares. A shareholder may then allocate her votes among the nominees as she chooses. She may vote for only as many nominees as there are directors to be elected, but she may vote for fewer nominees. For example, she may choose to cast all of her votes for only one nominee.

See Figure 1 for a further explanation of the mechanics of cumulative voting.

 LO2 Create classes of shares and delineate their rights to fit the needs of controlling and other shareholders.

Classes of Shares

A corporation may have several classes of shares. The two most common classes are *common shares* and *preferred shares,* but a corporation may have several classes of common shares and several classes of preferred shares. Many close corporations have two or more classes of common shares with different voting rights. Each class may be entitled to elect one or more directors, in order to balance power in a corporation.

For example, suppose a corporation has four directors and 100 shares held by four shareholders—each of whom owns 25 shares. With straight voting and no classes of shares, no shareholder owns enough shares to elect himself as a director, because 51 shares are necessary to elect a director. Suppose, however, that the corporation has four classes of shares, each with the right to elect one of the directors. Each class of shares is issued to only one

Figure 1   *Cumulative Voting Formula*

The formula for determining the minimum number of shares required to elect a desired number of directors under cumulative voting is:

$$X = \frac{S \times R}{D + 1} + 1$$

X = Number of shares needed to elect the desired number of directors

S = Total number of shares voting at the shareholders' meeting

R = Number of director representatives desired

D = Total number of directors to be elected at the meeting

Example: Sarah Smiles wants to elect two of the five directors of Oates Corporation. One thousand shares will be voted. In this case:

$S = 1,000$
$R = 2$
$D = 5$

Therefore:

$$X = 333.33$$

Fractions are ignored; thus, Sarah will need to hold at least 333 shares to be able to elect two directors.

shareholder. Now, as the sole owner of a class of shares entitling the class to elect one director, each shareholder can elect himself to the board.

Using classes of shares is the cleanest way to allocate among shareholders the power to elect directors, as well as allocate equity ownership of the corporation. To protect such allocations, however, the articles should require approval of every class of shares to change the rights of any class or to create a new class of shares.

Shareholder Control Devices

While cumulative voting and class voting are two useful methods by which shareholders can allocate or acquire voting control of a corporation, there are other devices that may also be used for these purposes: voting trusts; shareholder voting agreements; and proxies, especially irrevocable proxies.

Voting Trusts With a **voting trust,** shareholders transfer their shares to one or more voting trustees and receive voting trust certificates in exchange. The shareholders retain many of their rights, including the right to receive dividends, but the voting trustees vote for directors and other matters submitted to shareholders.

The purpose of a voting trust is to control the corporation through the concentration of shareholder voting power in the voting trustees, who often are participating shareholders. If several minority shareholders collectively own a majority of the shares of a corporation, they may create a voting trust and thereby control the corporation. You may ask why shareholders need a voting trust when they are in apparent agreement on how to vote their shares. The reason is that they may have disputes in the future that could prevent the shareholders from agreeing how to vote. The voting trust ensures that the shareholder group will control the corporation despite the emergence of differences.

The MBCA limits the duration of voting trusts to 10 years, though all or part of the participating shareholders may agree to extend the term for another 10 years. Also, a voting trust must be made public, with copies of the voting trust document available for inspection at the corporation's offices.

Shareholder Voting Agreements   As an alternative to a voting trust, shareholders may merely agree how they will vote their shares. For example, shareholders collectively owning a majority of the shares may agree to vote for each other as directors, resulting in each being elected to the board of directors.

A shareholder voting agreement must be written; only shareholders signing the agreement are bound by it. When a shareholder refuses to vote as agreed, courts specifically enforce the agreement.

Shareholder voting agreements have two advantages over voting trusts. First, their duration may be *perpetual.* Second, they may be kept secret from the other shareholders; they usually do not have to be filed in the corporation's offices.

Proxies   A shareholder may appoint a **proxy** to vote his shares. If several minority shareholders collectively own a majority of the shares of a corporation, they may appoint a proxy to vote their shares and thereby control the corporation. The ordinary proxy has only a limited duration—11 months under the MBCA—unless a longer term is specified. Also, the ordinary proxy is *revocable* at any time. As a result, there is no guarantee that control agreements accomplished through the use of revocable proxies will survive future shareholder disputes.

However, a proxy is *irrevocable* if it is coupled with an interest. A proxy is coupled with an interest when, among other things, the person holding the proxy is a party to a shareholder voting agreement or a buy-and-sell agreement. The principal use of irrevocable proxies is in conjunction with shareholder voting agreements.

In the *RHCS* case, the court found that the parties created only a revocable proxy when they wanted a long-term shareholder voting agreement. The case is a good example of the need for careful drafting of corporate documents.

Reynolds Health Care Services, Inc. v. HMNH, Inc.
217 S.W.3d 797 (Ark. Sup. Ct. 2005)

John Reynolds was the sole shareholder and manager of his family's longtime business, the Hillsboro Manor Nursing Home, Inc., in El Dorado, Arkansas. In 1993, Reynolds needed capital to expand the nursing home, so he approached Dr. James Sheppard, who contacted three additional investors: Sheppard's two brothers, Andrew and Courtney Sheppard, and his brother-in-law, Eugene Bilo. The Sheppards and Bilo formed a corporation called HMNH, Inc., to acquire 80 percent ownership of Hillsboro Manor. HMNH, Inc., made a contract with Reynolds Health Care Services, Inc. (RHCS), a corporation in which Reynolds was the sole shareholder. Under the contract, RHCS agreed to manage the nursing home in return for 6 percent of HMNH's gross revenues. HMNH agreed to provide adequate working capital and oversight on budgets, policies, and personnel. Of course, RHCS hired Reynolds as administrator of the facility.

To buy the nursing home, HMNH and Hillsboro Manor Nursing Home, Inc., entered into a stock purchase agreement by which HMNH purchased all of the stock of Hillsboro Manor Nursing Home, Inc., for $1,804,000. Hillsboro Manor Nursing Home, Inc., was merged into HMNH, Inc., with the three Sheppards, Bilo, and RHCS each receiving 20 shares of stock of the 100 outstanding shares of stock in HMNH. The Sheppards and Bilo also agreed to give RHCS the power to vote 7.5 of each of their shares on any matter submitted to shareholders in the next 20 years. The affect of the voting agreement was to give RHCS 50 percent voting control, which meant that Reynolds, who owned RHCS, could veto any matter submitted to HMNH's shareholders.

By 1999, HMNH had become concerned with the way Reynolds was running the nursing home. The shareholders held a meeting on September 14, 2000, at which the Sheppards and Bilo were present, but Reynolds was absent. The Sheppards voted their combined 60 shares to elect a new board of directors comprising the three Sheppards, Bilo, and Reynolds. At the directors' meeting, held immediately thereafter, all five men were elected as officers of HMNH, although Reynolds—while now present—abstained from the vote. Andrew Sheppard then made a motion that the board of directors authorize its attorney to institute a lawsuit in the name of HMNH against Reynolds and RHCS to recover damages caused by RHCS's breach of the management contract. The Sheppards and Bilo voted to adopt the resolution. On January 19, 2001, HMNH filed suit against RHCS and Reynolds, alleging that RHCS had breached the management contract. Reynolds and RHCS asked the trial court to dismiss the lawsuit on the grounds that HMNH's board had no authority to bring the lawsuit. Reynolds and RHCS argued that the directors were not properly elected, because the Sheppards voted all their shares to elect the new directors, a violation of the shareholder voting agreement that gave RHCS the power to vote 7.5 of each of their shares. The trial court disagreed, ruling that the voting agreement was merely a revocable proxy, which the Sheppards revoked at the September 2000 shareholder meeting, and therefore, the Sheppards could vote all of their shares. Reynolds and RHCS appealed to the Arkansas Supreme Court.

Glaze, Justice

RHCS argues that it entered into a voting agreement with the Sheppards and Bilo when they signed a document titled "Option to Purchase Stock." In particular, RHCS points to the following language in support of its contention that a voting agreement was created:

> [HMNH] shall grant to [RHCS] a proxy to vote one-half of the issued and outstanding shares of stock of HMNH, Inc. pending the term of this option to purchase stock, which proxy shall be reduced to twenty-five percent of the issued and outstanding shares of stock of the corporation for a period of twenty years from the effective date of the Agreement to Provide Management Services to a Health Care Facility executed the 8th day of January, 1993, as set forth in paragraph IV thereof, by and between Reynolds Health Care Services, Inc., and HMNH, Inc., upon the exercise of this option and transfer to [RHCS] of the shares of stock subject to this option.

A subsequent agreement among the shareholders, dated September 19, 1996, provided that the Sheppards and Bilo "shall execute a proxy to Reynolds Health Care Services, Inc., appointing Reynolds Health Care Services, Inc. as [their] proxy to vote 7.5 shares of each of the said shareholder's stock held in HMNH, Inc." Those proxies were executed by each of the Sheppards and Bilo on October 21, 1996; the proxy agreements provided as follows:

> I, the undersigned shareholder of HMNH, Inc., an Arkansas corporation, do hereby appoint Reynolds Health Care Services, Inc., an Arkansas corporation, my true and lawful attorney and agent, for me and in my name, place and stead to vote as my proxy 7.5 shares of stock held by me in HMNH, Inc. at any stockholders' meetings to be held between the date of this proxy and 20 years from the effective date of the Agreement to Provide Management Services to a Health Care Facility dated January 7, 1993, as set forth in Paragraph IV thereof, by and between

Reynolds Health Care Services, Inc., and HMNH, Inc., and I authorize Reynolds Health Care Services, Inc. to act for me and in my name and stead as fully as I could act if I were personally present, giving to Reynolds Health Care Services, Inc., attorney and agent, full power of substitution.

The trial court found that these agreements were not voting agreements, but rather were revocable proxies. Under Ark. Code Ann. §4-27-722 (Repl. 2001), proxies are revocable by a shareholder "unless the appointment form conspicuously states that it is irrevocable and the appointment is coupled with an interest." An appointment coupled with an interest includes the appointment of "a party to a voting agreement created under §4-27-731." None of the proxy agreements stated conspicuously on its face that it was irrevocable; indeed, in its reply brief, RHCS abandons its argument that the proxies were irrevocable. Nonetheless, RHCS maintains that the proxies "were merely the means of implementing the parties' foundational voting agreement," by which the Sheppards and Bilo gave RHCS the right to vote fifty percent of their shares in HMNH for twenty years.

However, we conclude that the document that RHCS calls a "voting agreement" is nothing more than a revocable appointment of proxy. The plain language of the agreement says nothing about how the stock is to be voted; it merely gives RHCS the right to vote a percentage of the stock. Because the agreement does not "provide for the manner in which" the shares are to be voted, it is not a voting agreement; it is a proxy.

Further, the proxies assigned to RHCS were revocable. Thus, the Sheppards and Bilo were acting within their rights as shareholders when they voted to revoke their proxies at the September 2000 shareholders' meeting. Accordingly, the trial court did not err when it concluded that the actions of the duly elected board of directors in voting to authorize the instant lawsuit were valid.

Judgment for HMNH affirmed.

Ethics in Action

By using classes of shares (or a perpetual shareholder voting agreement), shareholders that individually are minority shareholders but collectively control a majority of the corporation's shares may control the corporation absolutely. For example, suppose five shareholders create a corporation and decide at incorporation that it will have five classes of shares, one for each of the five shareholders. They decide that each of the five classes will elect its own director to the board of directors and that the consent of each class is required to amend the articles of incorporation, such as to increase the number of authorized shares of a class or to create a new class of shares. They also could agree that no shares may be issued without the consent of each class of shares. In the future, if they want to issue shares to employees of the corporation or public investors, by a vote of the five classes of shareholders they could create a class of shares that has a small (say, 20 percent) equity interest in the corporation,

either has no right to vote for directors or elects a nonvoting director, has a preferential right to dividends, and has no right to veto any action the five original classes of shares approve. The creation of the new share class would permit the five original shareholders to continue their control of the corporation while receiving an infusion of capital into the company.

- Do you think it is ethical for the five original shareholders to dominate the corporation in this way? If you were one of the five original shareholders, would you set up a different equity structure? Would you give more rights to the shareholders of the class with limited rights?
- Would you buy shares of the class that has limited rights? After you buy those shares, would it be ethical for you to argue for greater rights?
- Would your answers change if the corporation became a public company with over 2,000 shareholders?

Fundamental Corporate Changes

Other matters besides the election of directors require shareholder action, some because they make fundamental changes in the structure or business of the corporation.

Because the articles of incorporation embody the basic contract between a corporation and its shareholders, shareholders must approve most amendments of the articles of incorporation. For example, when the articles are amended to increase the number of authorized shares or reduce the dividend rights of preferred shareholders, shareholder approval is needed.

A **merger** is a transaction in which one corporation merges into a second corporation. Usually, the first corporation dissolves; the second corporation takes all the business and assets of both corporations and becomes liable for the debts of both corporations. Usually, the shareholders of the dissolved corporation become shareholders of the surviving corporation. Ordinarily, both corporations' shareholders must approve a merger.

Corporation law allows great flexibility in the terms of a merger. For example, a merger may freeze out minority shareholders by paying them cash only while allowing majority shareholders to remain as shareholders of the surviving corporation. Freeze-outs are covered in Chapter 43.

A consolidation is similar to a merger except that both old corporations go out of existence and a new corporation takes the business, assets, and liabilities of the old corporations. Both corporations' shareholders must approve

the consolidation. Modern corporate practice makes consolidations obsolete, since it is usually desirable to have one of the old corporations survive. The MBCA does not recognize consolidations. However, the effect of a consolidation can be achieved by creating a new corporation and merging the two old corporations into it.

A share exchange is a transaction by which one corporation becomes the owner of all of the outstanding shares of a second corporation through a *compulsory* exchange of shares: The shareholders of the second corporation are compelled to exchange their shares for shares of the first corporation. The second corporation remains in existence and becomes a wholly owned subsidiary of the first corporation. Only the selling shareholders must approve the share exchange.

A sale of all or substantially all of the assets of the business other than in the regular course of business must be approved by the shareholders of the selling corporation, since it drastically changes the shareholders' investment. Thus, a corporation's sale of all its real property and equipment is a sale of substantially all its assets, even though the corporation continues its business by leasing the assets back from the purchaser. However, a corporation that sells its building, but retains its machinery with the intent of continuing operations at another location, has not sold all or substantially all of its assets. Under the MBCA, a corporation that retains at least 25 percent of its business activity and either its income or revenue has not disposed of substantially all its assets.

A **dissolution** is the first step in the termination of the corporation's business. The typical dissolution requires

The Global Business Environment

In recent years, shareholder activism and discontent has been exported from the United States to affect corporations based in other nations. In some cases, American shareholders of non-American corporations have exercised their rights by attempting to oppose management through the ballot box or takeovers. In other cases, citizens of other nations have taken cues from their American cousins and attempted to assert their rights as shareholders.

For example, in late 2005, VNU NV, the Netherlands-based publishing and market research firm, faced pressure from a shareholder group that included Boston-based Fidelity Investments. The shareholder group, which held 40 percent of VNU's shares, opposed VNU's bid to acquire IMS Health, Inc., a Connecticut-based corporation. When shareholders first announced their opposition to the acquisition, VNU attempted to placate them by selling some assets, increasing a share buyback, and eventually replacing its CEO. Refusing to be appeased, the shareholders continued their opposition to VNU's acquisition of IMS Health.

Earlier in 2005, shareholders in Deutsche Borse AG, the German stock exchange company, prevented the company from completing an attempt to acquire London Stock Exchange PLC. The shareholders eventually forced the resignation of longtime CEO Werner Seifert. Despite Seifert's turning Deutsche Borse into the largest stock exchange during his 12-year tenure, his misjudgment of shareholder opposition to what he thought was the best strategy for the company ultimately led to his downfall.

Beginning in 2003 with HSBC's purchase of American subprime lender Household and escalating in 2007 and 2008 when HSBC suffered significant losses in the U.S. subprime loan market, U.S. activist investor Knight Vinke Asset Management engaged U.K.–based HSBC in a review of strategy. Knight Vinke called on HSBC's board to appoint independent financial advisers to review future subprime loan business, criticized its new executive compensation plan, and expressed concern about the independence of its board of directors. As a consequence of Knight Vinke's criticism that trying to be a world bank generated few cost savings, in 2011 HSBC refocused on trade and corporate banking and developed a new test for determining what businesses to acquire.

---

shareholder approval. Dissolution of corporations is covered more fully at the end of this chapter.

The articles of incorporation and the bylaws may require or permit other matters to be submitted for shareholder approval. For example, loans to officers, self-dealing transactions, and indemnifications of managers for litigation expenses may be approved by shareholders. Also, many of the states require shareholder approval of share option plans for high level executive officers, but the MBCA does not.

Procedures Required Similar procedures must be met to effect each of the above fundamental changes. The procedures include approval of the board of directors, notice to all of the shareholders whether or not they are entitled to vote, and majority approval of the votes held by shareholders entitled to vote under the statute, articles, or bylaws. Majority approval will be insufficient if a corporation has a supermajority shareholder voting requirement, such as one requiring two-thirds approval.

If there are two or more classes of shares, the articles may provide that matters voted on by shareholders must be approved by each class substantially affected by the proposed transaction. For example, a merger may have to be approved by a majority of the preferred shareholders and a majority of the common shareholders. As an alternative, the articles may require only the approval of the shareholders as a whole.

Under the MBCA, voting by classes is required for mergers, share exchanges, and amendments of the articles if these would substantially affect the rights of the classes. For example, the approval of preferred shareholders is required if a merger would change the dividend rights of preferred shareholders.

In many states, no approval of shareholders of the *surviving corporation* is required for a merger *if* the merger does not fundamentally alter the character of the business or substantially reduce the shareholders' voting or dividend rights.

Also, many statutes, including the MBCA, permit a merger between a parent corporation and its subsidiary without the approval of the shareholders of either corporation. Instead, the board of directors of the parent approves the merger and sends a copy of the merger plan to the subsidiary's shareholders. This simplified merger is called a short-form merger. It is available only if the parent owns a high percentage of the subsidiary's shares—90 percent under the MBCA and the Delaware statute.

Dissenters' Rights

Many times, shareholders approve a corporate action by less than a unanimous vote, indicating that some shareholders oppose the action. For the most part, the dissenting shareholders have little recourse. Their choice is to remain shareholders or to sell their shares. For close corporation shareholders, there is no choice—the dissenting close corporation shareholder has no ready market for her shares, so she will remain a shareholder.

Some corporate transactions, however, so materially change a shareholder's investment in the corporation or have such an adverse effect on the value of a shareholder's shares that it has been deemed unfair to require the dissenting shareholder either to remain a shareholder (because there is no fair market for the shares) or to suffer a loss in value when he sells his shares on a market that has been adversely affected by the news of the corporate action. Corporate law has therefore responded by creating **dissenters' rights** (right of appraisal) for shareholders who disagree with specified fundamental corporate transactions. Dissenters' rights require the corporation to pay dissenting shareholders the *fair value* of their shares.

Under the MBCA, the dissenters' rights cover mergers, short-form mergers, share exchanges, significant amendments of the articles of incorporation, and sales of all or substantially all the assets other than in the ordinary course of business. Some statutes cover consolidations also.

A dissenting shareholder seeking payment of the fair value of his shares must have the *right to vote* on the action to which he objects; however, a shareholder of a subsidiary in a short-form merger has dissenters' rights despite his lack of voting power. In addition, the shareholder must *not vote in favor* of the transaction. The shareholder may either vote against the action or abstain from voting.

The MBCA and 36 states' statutes exclude from dissenters' rights shares that can be sold in a liquid market such as the New York Stock Exchange. Instead, these statutes expect a shareholder to sell his shares on the stock exchange if he dissents to the corporate action. This *market-out exception* does not apply, however, if there is an "interested transaction." Delaware and 24 other states do not so limit the market-out exception.

Generally, a shareholder must notify the corporation of his intent to seek payment before the shareholders have voted on the action. Next, the corporation informs a dissenting shareholder how to demand payment. After the dissenting shareholder demands payment, the corporation and the shareholder negotiate a mutually acceptable price. If they cannot agree, a court will determine the fair value of the shares and order the corporation to pay that amount.

To determine fair value, most judges use the Delaware Block Method, a weighted average of several valuation techniques—such as market value, comparisons with other similar companies, net present value of future cash flows, and book value. Ironically, the Supreme Court of Delaware has abandoned the Delaware Block Method, recognizing the need for courts to value shares by methods generally considered acceptable to the financial community. The MBCA values shares using "customary and current valuation concepts and techniques generally employed for similar businesses."

The Delaware appraisal statute provides that a court:

> shall appraise the shares, determining their fair value exclusive of any element of value arising from the accomplishment or expectation of the merger or consolidation, together with a fair rate of interest, if any, to be paid upon the amount determined to be the fair value. In determining such fair value, the Court shall take into account all relevant factors. 8 Del. Code § 262(h).

In *Weinberger v. UOP*,[1] the Delaware Supreme Court reconciled the dual mandates of section 262(h), which direct a court to determine fair value based upon all relevant factors, yet exclude any element of value arising from the accomplishment or expectation of the merger. In making that reconciliation, the *Weinberger* court wrote:

> Only the speculative elements of value that may arise from the "accomplishment or expectation" of the merger are excluded. We take this to be a very narrow exception to the appraisal process, designed to eliminate use of *pro forma* data and projections of a speculative variety relating to the completion of a merger. But elements of future value, including the nature of the enterprise, which are known or susceptible of proof as of the date of the merger and not the product of speculation, may be considered. When the trial court deems it appropriate, fair value also includes any damages, resulting from the taking, which the stockholders sustain as a class. If that was not the case, then the obligation to consider "all relevant factors" in the valuation process would be eroded.[2]

In the following case, the court applied the *Weinberger* test when reviewing competing valuations of minority shares. The case is a model for sophisticated financial valuations in litigation.

---

[1]457 A.2d 701 (Del. S. Ct. 1983)
[2]457 A.2d at 713.

Montgomery Cellular Holding Co., Inc. v. Dobler
880 A.2d 206 (Del. S. Ct. 2005)

Price Communications Corporation (Price) owned all the shares of Price Communications Wireless (PCW). PCW owned all the shares of Palmer Wireless Holdings Inc. (Palmer). Palmer owned controlling interests in 16 cellular telephone systems in Georgia, Florida, and Alabama, including Montgomery Cellular Holding Company (MCHC). Palmer owned 94.6 percent of MCHC stock. MCHC was a holding company with no operating assets. MCHC's sole asset was 100 percent of the stock of

Montgomery Cellular Telephone Co. (Montgomery). Montgomery was a cellular telephone system located in the area around Montgomery, Alabama.

As a group, Palmer's holdings formed a valuable cluster of cellular systems in the southeastern United States. Price entered into discussions with various cellular telecommunications system operators about a possible sale of Palmer's cellular systems. Price hired the investment bank, Donaldson, Lufkin & Jenrette (DLJ), to solicit interest in acquiring Palmer. Verizon emerged as the potential acquirer.

In 2000, Price agreed to sell Palmer to Verizon for $2.06 billion. Because Palmer did not control 100 percent of the stock in MCHC and other subsidiaries, the agreement obligated Price to acquire those minority shareholder interests. If Palmer failed to acquire the minority interests, the agreement allowed Verizon to reduce the purchase price by an amount equal to the minority shareholders' pro rata share of fiscal year 2000 EBITDA multiplied by 13.5. To receive the full $2.06 billion purchase price, Price would have to freeze out all the minority shareholders of MCHC. As a result of the agreement, Price had a strong incentive to squeeze out all the minority shareholders at a price that was lower than Verizon's corresponding price reduction.

On June 30, 2001, Price caused Palmer to buy out MCHC's minority shareholders by a short-form merger under Delaware law. In determining the price to be paid to MCHC's minority shareholders, Price made no effort to obtain an independent valuation, which its CEO viewed as "very costly." Instead, Palmer relied on Price's settlement of an appraisal action with the dissenting minority shareholders of a different Palmer subsidiary, Cellular Dynamics (CD).

CD, like MCHC, was the operator of a cellular telephone company in the southeastern United States and, like MCHC, was majority-owned by Price. In 1999, Price bought out the minority shareholders of CD by a short-form merger. After a lengthy negotiation using POPs as the valuation tool, the minority shareholders agreed to a settlement based upon a value of CD derived by multiplying the estimated population by $470 per POP. POP is a shorthand reference to the census population of a specific geographic area. POPs are a common cellular industry metric for valuing cellular systems.

Despite overwhelming evidence that the CD settlement was negotiated using POPs and not EBITDA, Price claimed that it had valued CD's stock using an EBITDA multiplier of 10.05 to arrive at the $8,102.23 per share price that was offered to MCHC minority shareholders as fair value. In contrast, multiplying the $470 per POP metric by MCHC's POPs (323,675) would have yielded a value of $15,212.74 per share.

Although Price had bought out MCHC minority shareholders and was entitled to receive the full agreed merger price of $2.06 billion, the initial Verizon deal was not consummated. Later, Price and Verizon agreed to a reduced purchase price of $1.7 billion. That second transaction was consummated on August 15, 2002.

Gerhard Dobler and other minority MCHC shareholders challenged the buyout price of $8,102.23 per share, and they sued Price, Palmer, and MCHC in the Delaware Court of Chancery. At the trial, the minority shareholders' expert, Marc Sherman, previously a KPMG partner in charge of its corporate transactions practice, valued MCHC at $21,346 per share. MCHC's expert, Kenneth D. Gartrell, previously an Ernst & Young auditor, testified that the stand-alone value of MCHC was $7,840 per share.

Although both experts used similar methods to value MCHC, Sherman looked to third-party experts to create his forecasts, whereas Gartrell did not consult outside appraisers or other sources of relevant information. Moreover, only Sherman performed a comparable transaction analysis.

MCHC's expert, Gartrell, employed two valuation methodologies: a comparable company analysis and a discounted cash flow (DCF) analysis. The Court of Chancery found that Gartrell's valuation approach was legally and factually flawed, and must be disregarded in its entirety, for three reasons. First, Gartrell's overall theoretical framework was invalid as a matter of law, because Gartrell valued MCHC as if it were not a going concern that had contractual relationships with other cellular providers. Second, Gartrell's DCF analysis was flawed because he used a generic growth rate (the long-term growth rate of GNP) as his growth rate for MCHC without any valid, credible explanation and despite his having had access to industry-specific growth rates; Gartrell used a constant growth rate, which would yield the same value for MCHC regardless of the time frame; and Gartrell created the financial projections based entirely on his own judgment, without reference to other available sources of relevant information. Third, the Court of Chancery found that Gartrell's comparable company analysis was invalid because of his methodology and his data. Gartrell switched between the mean and the median at critical points. Had Gartrell used the mean numbers consistently throughout, the value of MCHC based on EBITDA would be over $163 million, which when added to the nonoperating assets, would be $183 million—a figure much closer to the value reached by the shareholders' expert.

The Court of Chancery accepted the shareholders' expert, Sherman's, valuation of MCHC with some modification, and it valued the minority shares at $19,621.74. MCHC asked the Delaware Supreme Court to review the chancery court's nearly full acceptance of Sherman's valuation. MCHC did not appeal the court's rejection of MCHC's expert's valuation.

Jacobs, Justice

The shareholders' expert, Marc Sherman, performed three different financial analyses of MCHC: a comparable transactions analysis, a DCF analysis, and a comparable company analysis. In his comparable transactions analysis, Sherman split the selected comparable transactions into three categories: similar sized transactions, the initial Verizon transaction, and the CD settlement. For the similar sized transactions category, Sherman considered five transactions that occurred between May 2000 and January 2001, each involving a cellular company with approximately the same number of POPs. The remaining two categories (the initial Verizon transaction and the CD settlement) involved single transactions that were included in the analysis because they were related to the sale of MCHC.

Sherman then analyzed each category using his four cellular system metrics (POPs, subscribers, EBITDA, and revenue). For each metric, Sherman computed a value of MCHC based on the category of comparable transactions, and then weighted these values to derive his final overall valuation. Sherman did that as follows: he first weighted the metrics based on their importance in valuing cellular companies. He then weighted the category of comparable transactions within each metric. The result of that process is shown *infra* on the table:

Category	Valuation	Metric Weighting	Category Weighting
POPs		45%	
Verizon Transaction	$199,278,316		20%
CD Settlement	$199,286,698		10%
Similar Sized Transactions	$136,352,297		15%
Subscribers		20%	
Verizon Transaction	$226,758,135		15%
CD Settlement	$225,865,136		5%
Operating Cash Flows		25%	
Verizon Transaction	$160,650,176		20%
CD Settlement	$226,738,142		5%
Revenue		10%	
Verizon Transaction	$236,517,971		7% (sic)
CD Settlement	$224,240,681		7% (sic)
Total		100%	100%

Multiplying the valuations by their respective weightings, Sherman computed a value of $192 million based on comparable transactions. To that figure he added the $20 million value of the non–operating assets to arrive at a comparable transactions value for MCHC of $212 million.

Sherman also performed a DCF analysis. Because of the lack of management projections, Sherman created forecasts of MCHC's cash flows based on predictions by others for the cellular industry and the economy. Sherman relied primarily on Paul Kagan, an outside industry expert. Sherman also looked to industry growth reports that showed an annual growth rate for the wireless industry of 16 percent.

The next step in Sherman's DCF analysis was to determine the discount rate using a weighted average cost of capital (WACC) approach. Applying that approach to the inputs he determined for each component of the WACC formula, Sherman arrived at a discount rate of 13.25 percent.

For his DCF projection period, Sherman used a ten-year period from June 1, 2001 to May 31, 2011. Before projecting the cash flows, however, Sherman first adjusted them by removing two "irregularities": (i) a nonrecurring $861,000 bad debt expense resulting from Montgomery having installed a new billing system, and (ii) the rent of $638,000 MCHC paid annually to Old North, a wholly owned subsidiary of Palmer. Lastly, using a capitalization rate of 9.25 percent and a growth rate of 4 percent, Sherman calculated a terminal value of $258 million.

From these inputs, Sherman arrived at a final enterprise (DCF) valuation of $150 million for Montgomery as a going concern, operating asset of MCHC. To that figure Sherman added the value of Montgomery's non–operating assets, which increased his valuation to $170 million. Finally, to that sum, Sherman applied a control premium of 31 percent, thereby increasing his DCF valuation to $216 million.

In his third (comparable company) analysis, Sherman found only two comparable companies, neither of which was similar in size to Montgomery. Sherman excluded companies that had international operations, multiple lines of business, or prepaid customers, as well as companies that used PCS technology. After selecting his comparable companies, Sherman applied the same metrics that he used in his comparable transactions analysis and gave them the same weight. That approach resulted in a valuation of $206 million. After adding in the value of the non–operating assets, Sherman's ultimate comparable company valuation of MCHC was $226 million.

Thus, Sherman's three analyses valued MCHC within a range of from $212 million to $226 million. Sherman derived his final fair value by combining the results of his three analyses into a weighted average, giving 80 percent weight to the comparable transactions value, 15 percent weight to the DCF value, and 5 percent weight to the comparable company value. Sherman's heavy weighting of the comparable transactions analysis reflected his judgment that the transaction data, particularly the initial Verizon transaction price, were the best indication of value for MCHC. In contrast, Sherman gave little weight to the DCF analysis because of his concerns about the reliability of MCHC's financial data and the lack of management projections. He gave even less weight to the comparable company valuation because of the scarcity of publicly traded companies to which MCHC could reliably be compared. Combining the results of the three analyses into a weighted average yielded a fair value for MCHC of $213,455,619, or $21,346 per share.

In making its independent determination of MCHC's fair value, the Court of Chancery adopted Sherman's overall valuation framework, and most of Sherman's inputs. The Court made adjustments to some of the inputs that it did not adopt. The result was to reduce Sherman's valuation of $213,455,619 ($21,346 per share) to a final valuation of MCHC of $196,217,373, or $19,621.74 per share.

First, with respect to the comparable transaction analysis, the Vice Chancellor determined that the Verizon transaction price and the CD settlement price were valid inputs. But, the Court adjusted Sherman's CD settlement price by eliminating what Sherman perceived (incorrectly, the Court determined) to be a minority discount. The Court then independently increased the CD settlement figure ($470 per POP) by 15 percent to eliminate a so-called "settlement haircut," to arrive at a value of $540.50 per POP.

Second, the Court adjusted Sherman's DCF valuation by eliminating the 31 percent control premium that Sherman had added to his DCF value. That adjustment reduced Sherman's DCF valuation of MCHC from $216 million to $170 million.

Third, and most significant, the Court adjusted the weights that Sherman had accorded to the values derived by his three valuation methods. Sherman had weighted the comparable transaction value at 80 percent of total fair value. Because the effect of that weighting was to give the Verizon transaction an overall weight of 50 percent—a weight the Court found to be "too significant"—the Vice Chancellor reduced the weight accorded to the comparable transactions valuation from 80 percent to 65 percent.

Finally, because Sherman had corrected the figures derived from MCHC's financial statements in a reasonable manner, and also had looked to third party authority for guidance on other

inputs, the Court determined that the 15 percent weight Sherman had accorded to the DCF valuation should be increased to 30 percent.

On appeal, MCHC does not challenge the Court of Chancery's adoption of Sherman's overall valuation framework. Instead, MCHC limits its attack to selected inputs to the valuation model that Sherman used.

Specifically, MCHC contends that the Court of Chancery erred in three different respects, namely by: (1) including in its comparable transactions analysis the price that Verizon Wireless initially agreed to pay to acquire Palmer; (2) adding a 15 percent premium to the price that the minority shareholders of CD, a separate Palmer subsidiary, had agreed to accept to settle their appraisal action; (3) subtracting the management fees that Palmer charged to MCHC, as reported in MCHC's financial statement.

We conclude that none of the challenged findings is clearly wrong, and indeed, all have firm support in the evidentiary record.

1. The Verizon Transaction

MCHC argues that the Court of Chancery erroneously included the Verizon transaction, because the transaction price contained synergistic elements of value whose inclusion is proscribed by 8 Del. C. § 262. That statute requires the Court of Chancery to appraise the subject shares by "determining their fair value exclusive of any element of value arising from the accomplishment or expectation of the merger or consolidation." In determining statutory "fair value," the Court must value the appraisal company as a "going concern." In performing its valuation, the Court of Chancery is free to consider the price actually derived from the sale of the company being valued, but only after the synergistic elements of value are excluded from that price.

The Court found Palmer offered *no business-related* combinatorial value to MCHC, and MCHC was probably the most valuable company in Palmer's cluster. Thus, the Vice Chancellor concluded, the only synergies included in the purchase price were dealmaking—not business-related—synergies.

That conclusion is supported by the evidence. The Verizon merger with Palmer did not add any synergistic business value to MCHC because Montgomery was a metropolitan statistical area (MSA), which is generally more valuable than a rural service area (RSA), and Montgomery had superior demographics relative to Palmer's other cellular holdings. Therefore, the only synergies required to be eliminated from the Verizon transaction price were the Palmer-related "deal-making" synergies. The question became how to determine the value of those synergies.

The Court of Chancery was unable precisely to quantify those "deal-making" synergies, because MCHC did not present any reliable evidence at trial of what those synergies were worth. Having received no helpful evidence from MCHC, the Court of Chancery had to—and did—account for the synergies in a different way, namely, by reducing the total weight accorded to the comparable transactions component of the overall valuation, from 80 percent to 65 percent. Although in a perfect world that may not have been the ideal solution, in this world it was the only one permitted by the record evidence, given MCHC's failure to obtain a pre–merger valuation and to present legally reliable expert valuation testimony during the trial.

MCHC next contends that including the Verizon transaction in its comparable transaction analysis led the Court of Chancery to commit reversible error by not valuing MCHC as a going concern. Delaware law requires that in an appraisal action, a corporation must be valued as a going concern based on the "operative reality" of the company as of the time of the merger. In determining a corporation's "operative reality," the use of "speculative" elements of future value arising from the expectation or accomplishment of a merger is proscribed, but elements of future value that are known or susceptible of proof as of the date of the merger may be considered. Any facts which were known or which could be ascertained as of the date of the merger and which throw any light on future prospects of the merged corporation are not only pertinent to an inquiry as to the value of the dissenting stockholder's interest, but must be considered by the agency fixing the value.

MCHC argues that the Verizon transaction was not part of MCHC's "operative reality." At the time of the MCHC–Palmer merger, the transaction was not expected to close. MCHC characterizes the Verizon transaction as a mere "option" whose exercise was entirely within Verizon's control and which neither Price nor Verizon realistically expected to close at the time the MCHC–Palmer merger occurred.

The Vice Chancellor rejected MCHC's argument that because the Verizon–Price agreement was conditional, it was impermissibly "speculative" and did not reflect MCHC's going concern value. The Court of Chancery found that the Verizon transaction was more than an offer. Rather, it was a validly executed enforceable transaction agreement which bound Verizon to the implied covenant of good faith and fair dealing that inheres in every contract.

2. Adjustment of the CD Settlement Price to Eliminate the Settlement Discount

MCHC's second claim of error is that the Court of Chancery improperly adjusted the "CD settlement" price to eliminate what the Court regarded as a "settlement haircut."

The CD settlement was a settlement of litigation that arose out of Price's elimination, in a short form merger, of the minority shareholders of Cellular Dynamics (CD), a cellular company located in the southeastern United States. The minority shareholders of CD sued, and after protracted negotiations the parties agreed to a settlement price of $470 per POP. For purposes of valuing MCHC, both parties agreed that the CD settlement was a comparable transaction. Accordingly, Sherman utilized the $470 per POP metric in performing his comparable transactions analysis.

The Vice Chancellor upheld Sherman's use of the CD settlement price, but adjusted that price to reflect what the Court described as a "settlement haircut"; that is, a discount that reflected factors unrelated to CD's fair value, such as the costs of litigation and the uncertainty of the appraisal action's outcome. To eliminate that settlement discount, the Court of Chancery increased the CD settlement price by 15 percent, thereby reaching a value of $540.50 per POP as more fairly reflective of the value of CD. The Court then included that upwardly–adjusted CD settlement value in the comparable transactions analysis.

There was ample evidence to support the Court of Chancery's finding that the CD settlement reflected a discount from CD's fair value. The record included an exchange of several letters between Price and CD during settlement negotiations. Those letters included an offer by CD, on December 19, 2000, to settle the litigation for $500 per POP. In that December 19 letter, the CD minority shareholders specifically stated that the $500 per POP offer was less than CD's fair value, but was being made in an effort to resolve the matter quickly. That letter evidences that CD's minority shareholders were willing to settle for an amount below fair value to avoid the costs and delays of litigation.

Although there was no evidence of the precise magnitude of the actual CD settlement discount, the Court of Chancery did not err by selecting 15 percent as a reasonable measure. That percentage was based on evidence that the CD minority shareholders had accepted a price lower than CD's fair value, as well as the Court of Chancery's extensive expertise in the appraisal of corporate enterprises—an expertise that this Court has recognized on several occasions. To reiterate, where, as here, one side of the litigation presents no competent evidence to aid the Court in discharging its duty to make an independent valuation, we will defer to the Vice Chancellor's valuation approach unless it is manifestly unreasonable, *i.e.*, on its face is outside a range of reasonable values.

3. Eliminating the Management Fees Paid by MCHC to Palmer as an Input to the DCF Valuation

MCHC's third claim of error challenges the Court of Chancery's adjustment of MCHC's financial statements to eliminate from the DCF valuation the management fees Palmer had charged MCHC. The Court found that those fees were essentially a pretext, unrelated to the actual furnishing of management services.

Because there were no management projections upon which Sherman could rely to project MCHC's future cash flows, Sherman had to create his own forecasts. To do that he relied upon various sources, including MCHC's financial statements. But Sherman did not accept MCHC's financial statements at face value. In his review of those statements, he identified several irregularities. The management fees that Palmer charged to MCHC represented one of those irregularities. The evidence established that since 1998, Palmer had charged MCHC more than $3 million in management fees, and that in the first five months of 2001 alone, those fees totaled $603,000. To determine MCHC's future cash flows more accurately, Sherman eliminated those fees.

None of Price's officers who testified were able to explain what management services Palmer had provided to MCHC, or how those management fees were calculated. Indeed, Price's CEO characterized the fees (under oath) as "accounting bullshit." The Court was also troubled by the fact that Palmer charged management fees only to its subsidiaries that had minority shareholders, but not to those subsidiaries that Palmer wholly owned. Tellingly, after Palmer eliminated MCHC's minority shareholders in the merger, Palmer stopped charging management fees to MCHC. That evidence strongly supports the elimination of the management fees as an expense.

Judgment for Dobler affirmed in part and reversed in part. Remanded to the Chancery Court.

 L01   Understand the rights and powers of shareholders and how shareholders exercise their powers.

Shareholders' Inspection and Information Rights

Inspecting a corporation's books and records is sometimes essential to the exercise of a shareholder's rights. For example, a shareholder may be able to decide how to vote in a director election only after examining corporate financial records that reveal whether the present directors are managing the corporation profitably. Also, a close corporation shareholder may need to look at the books to determine the value of his shares.

Many corporate managers are resistant to shareholders' inspecting the corporation's books and records, charging that shareholders are nuisances or that shareholders often have improper purposes for making such an inspection. Sometimes, management objects solely on the ground that it desires secrecy.

Most of the state corporation statutes specifically grant shareholders inspection rights. The purpose of these statutes is to facilitate the shareholder's inspection of the books and records of corporations whose managements resist or delay proper requests by shareholders. A shareholder's lawyer or accountant may assist the shareholder's exercise of his inspection rights.

The MBCA grants shareholders an absolute right of inspection of an alphabetical listing of the shareholders entitled to notice of a meeting, including the number of shares owned. Access to a shareholder list allows a shareholder to contact other shareholders about important matters such as shareholder proposals.

The MBCA also grants an absolute right of inspection of, among other things, the articles, bylaws, and minutes of shareholder meetings within the past three years.

Shareholders have a qualified right to inspect other records, however. To inspect accounting records, board and committee minutes, and shareholder minutes more than three years old, a shareholder must make the demand in *good faith* and have a *proper purpose*. Proper purposes include inspecting the books of account to determine the value of shares or the propriety of dividends. On the other hand, learning business secrets and aiding a competitor are clearly improper purposes.

Shareholders also have the right to receive from the corporation **information** that is important to their voting and investing decisions. The MBCA requires a corporation to furnish its shareholders *financial statements,* including a balance sheet, an income statement, and a statement of changes in shareholders' equity. The Securities Exchange Act of 1934 also requires publicly held companies to furnish such statements, as well as other information that is important to shareholders' voting and investing decisions. To protect shareholders of public companies, the Sarbanes–Oxley Act requires the CEO and the CFO of public companies to certify that to their knowledge all financial information filed with the Securities and Exchange Commission fairly presents the financial condition of the company and does not include untrue or misleading material statements.

In the following *Axcelis* case, the Delaware Supreme Court delineated some of the limits of the shareholder inspection right.

City of Westland Police & Fire Retirement System v. Axcelis Technologies, Inc.
1 A.3d 281 (Del. Sup. Ct. 2010)

Axcelis Technologies, Inc., is a Delaware corporation manufacturing ion implantation and semiconductor equipment. Westland Police & Fire Retirement System is a Michigan pension fund that owns Axcelis common stock on behalf of its beneficiaries, current and retired police and firemen. In early February 2008, Sumitomo Heavy Industries, Ltd. (SHI), a Japanese company, made an unsolicited bid to acquire Axcelis for $5.20 per share. That day, Axcelis shares closed on the NASDAQ at a price of $4.18 per share. Axcelis's board of directors rejected SHI's proposal on the grounds that the offered price was too low, in part because it did not assign any value for Axcelis's opportunity to take market share from its competitors or for the synergistic value of an Axcelis subsidiary.

A few weeks later, SHI made a second bid to acquire Axcelis, this time for $6 per share. That day, Axcelis shares closed at a price of $5.45 per share. On March 17, the Board rejected SHI's second proposal, stating that "the proposal undervalues Axcelis and is not in the best interests of Axcelis and its shareholders." Consequently, SHI was unsuccessful in its efforts to acquire Axcelis.

In December 2008, Westland sent a letter to Axcelis requesting seven categories of books and records of Axcelis and its subsidiaries. Westland's purpose for the demand was to investigate Axelis's board members' compliance with their fiduciary duty to Axcelis and its shareholders as related to SHI's acquisition proposals. Among the books and records requested by Westland were the following:

1. All minutes of agendas for meetings (including all draft minutes and agendas and exhibits to such minutes and agendas) of the Board at which the Board discussed, considered or was presented with information concerning SHI's acquisition proposals.
2. All documents reviewed, considered or produced by the Board in connection with SHI's acquisition proposals.
3. Any and all communications between and among Axcelis directors and/or officers and SHI directors and/or officers.
4. Any and all materials provided by SHI to the Board in connection with SHI's acquisition proposals.
5. Any and all valuation materials used to determine the Company's value in connection with SHI's acquisition proposal.

Axcelis rejected Westland's demand on the ground that it did not satisfy the standard under Delaware law. Westland filed an action in a Delaware Court of Chancery, asking the court to order Axcelis to grant Westland access to the books and records. The Vice Chancellor dismissed Westland's action, holding that Westland had failed to demonstrate a proper purpose for its demand for inspection Westland appealed to the Delaware Supreme Court.

Jacob, Justice

A stockholder seeking to inspect the books and records of a corporation must demonstrate a proper purpose for the inspection. A proper purpose is one that is reasonably related to such person's interest as a stockholder. 8 Del. C. § 220(b).

Our law recognizes investigating possible wrongdoing or mismanagement as a proper purpose. To obtain Section 220 relief based on that purpose, the plaintiff-stockholder must present some evidence to suggest a credible basis from which a court could infer possible mismanagement that would warrant further investigation. The "credible basis" standard strikes the appropriate balance between (on the one hand) affording shareholders access to corporate records that may provide some evidence of possible wrongdoing and (on the other) safeguarding the corporation's right to deny requests for inspection based solely upon suspicion or curiosity. Thus, a mere statement of a purpose to investigate possible general mismanagement, without more, will not entitle a shareholder to broad §220 inspection relief.

A plaintiff may establish a credible basis to infer wrongdoing through documents, logic, testimony or otherwise. Such evidence need not prove that wrongdoing, in fact, occurred. Because the "credible basis" standard sets the lowest possible burden of proof, any reduction of that burden would be tantamount to permitting inspection based on the plaintiff-stockholder's mere suspicion of wrongdoing.

Westland's evidence to support its purpose consisted of (1) the parties' Joint Stipulation of Uncontested Facts and exhibits thereto, and (2) Westland's "logical conclusions" from those facts and exhibits that the Axcelis Board had acted out of improper entrenchment motives. The Vice Chancellor, however, drew different "logical conclusions" from those same uncontested facts, and determined that there was "no support in the record of any entrenchment motive" other than Westland's "bare accusations" suggesting such a motive.

Westland claims that the Court of Chancery incorrectly applied the "credible basis" standard by requiring Westland to present "affirmative evidence" of wrongdoing. For support, Westland offers only its proposed interpretation of the uncontested facts, which (Westland asserts) create a "legitimate basis to believe" that the Board's decisions might have been the product of improper entrenchment motives. By way of example, Westland conclusorily asserts that "It cannot seriously be disputed . . . that SHI's acquisition proposals could have been deemed a 'threat' to the Axcelis Board's control over the Company," and that the Board's . . . denial of SHI's request for a "modest" extension, were made "in the face of this threat." Essentially, Westland disagrees with the Vice Chancellor's inferences from the undisputed facts. Westland's disagreement, without any further affirmative showing, is insufficient. The Vice Chancellor concluded that Axcelis' rejection of SHI's unsolicited acquisition proposals, without more, was not a "defensive action" under *Unocal Corp. v. Mesa Petroleum Co.*, 493 A.2d 946 (Del. S. Ct. 1985). That conclusion must stand, because the record provides no credible basis to infer that the Board's rejections of those proposals, and its refusal to extend the deadline for SHI to submit a revised acquisition bid, were other than good faith business decisions.

Judgment for Axcelis affirmed.

Preemptive Right

The market price of a shareholder's shares will be reduced if a corporation issues additional shares at a price less than the market price. In addition, a shareholder's proportionate voting, dividend, and liquidation rights may be adversely affected by the issuance of additional shares. For example, if a corporation's only four shareholders each own 100 shares worth $10 per share, then each shareholder has shares worth $1,000, a 25 percent interest in any dividends declared, 25 percent of the voting power, and a claim against 25 percent of the corporation's assets after creditors' claims have been satisfied. If the corporation subsequently issues 100 shares to another person for only $5 per share, the value of each shareholder's shares falls to $900 and his dividend, voting, and liquidation rights are reduced to 20 percent. In a worst-case scenario, the corporation issues 201 shares to one of the existing shareholders, giving that shareholder majority control of the corporation and reducing the other shareholders' interests to less than 17 percent each. As a result, the minority shareholders will be dominated by the majority shareholder and will receive a greatly reduced share of the corporation's dividends.

Such harmful effects of an issuance could have been prevented if the corporation had been required to offer each existing shareholder a percentage of the new shares equal to her current proportionate ownership. If, for example, in the situation described above, the corporation had offered 50 shares to each shareholder, each shareholder could have remained a 25 percent owner of the corporation: her interest in the corporation would not have been reduced, and her total wealth would not have been decreased.

Corporation law recognizes the importance of giving a shareholder the option of maintaining the value of his shares and retaining his proportionate interest in the corporation. This is the shareholder's **preemptive right,** an option to subscribe to a new issuance of shares in proportion to the shareholder's current interest in the corporation.

The MBCA adopts a comprehensive scheme for determining preemptive rights. It provides that the preemptive right does not exist except to the extent provided by the articles. The MBCA permits the corporation to state expressly when the preemptive right arises.

When the preemptive right exists, the corporation must notify a shareholder of her option to buy shares, the number of shares that she is entitled to buy, the price of the shares, and when the option must be exercised. Usually, the shareholder is issued a **right,** a written option that she may exercise herself or sell to a person who wishes to buy the shares.

Distributions to Shareholders

During the life of a corporation, shareholders may receive distributions of the corporation's assets. Most people are familiar with one type of distribution—dividends—but there are other important types of distributions to shareholders, including payments to shareholders upon the corporation's repurchase of its shares.

There is one crucial similarity among all the types of distributions to shareholders: Corporate assets are transferred to shareholders. Consequently, an asset transfer to shareholders may harm the corporation's creditors and others with claims against the corporation's assets. For example, a distribution of assets may impair a corporation's ability to pay its creditors. In addition, a distribution to one class of shareholders may harm another class of shareholders that has a liquidation priority over the class of shareholders receiving the distribution. The existence of these potential harms compels corporation law to restrict the ability of corporations to make distributions to shareholders.

Dividends One important objective of a business corporation is to make a profit. Shareholders invest in a corporation primarily to share in the expected profit either through appreciation of the value of their shares or through dividends. There are two types of dividends: *cash or property dividends* and *share dividends*. Only cash or property dividends are distributions of the corporation's assets. Share dividends are *not* distributions.

Cash or Property Dividends Dividends are usually paid in cash. However, other assets of the corporation—such as airline discount coupons or shares of another corporation—may also be distributed as dividends. Cash or property dividends are declared by the board of directors and paid by the corporation on the date stated by the directors. Once declared, dividends are *debts* of the corporation, and shareholders may sue to force payment of the dividends. The board's dividend declaration, including the amount of

dividend and whether to declare a dividend, is protected by the business judgment rule.

Preferred shares nearly always have a set dividend rate stated in the articles of incorporation. Even so, unless the preferred dividend is mandatory, the board has discretion to determine whether to pay a preferred dividend and what amount to pay. Most preferred shares are *cumulative preferred shares,* on which unpaid dividends cumulate. The entire accumulation must be paid before common shareholders may receive any dividend. Even when preferred shares are noncumulative, the current dividend must be paid to preferred shareholders before any dividend may be paid to common shareholders.

The following *Dodge v. Ford* case is one of the few cases in which a court ordered the payment of a dividend to common shareholders. The court found that Henry Ford had the wrong motives for causing Ford Motor Company to refuse to pay a dividend.

Dodge v. Ford Motor Co.   170 N.W. 668 (Mich. Sup. Ct. 1919)

In 1916, brothers John and Horace Dodge owned 10 percent of the common shares of the Ford Motor Company. Henry Ford owned 58 percent of the outstanding common shares and controlled the corporation and its board of directors. Starting in 1911, the corporation paid a regular annual dividend of $1.2 million, which was 60 percent of its capital stock of $2 million but only about 1 percent of its total equity of $114 million. In addition, from 1911 to 1915, the corporation paid special dividends totaling $41 million.

The policy of the corporation was to reduce the selling price of its cars each year. In June 1915, the board and officers agreed to increase production by constructing new plants for $10 million, acquiring land for $3 million, and erecting an $11 million smelter. To finance the planned expansion, the board decided not to reduce the selling price of cars beginning in August 1915 and to accumulate a large surplus.

A year later, the board reduced the selling price of cars by $80 per car. The corporation was able to produce 600,000 cars annually, all of which, and more, could have been sold for $440 instead of the new $360 price, a forgone revenue of $48 million. At the same time, the corporation announced a new dividend policy of paying no special dividend. Instead, it would reinvest all earnings except the regular dividend of $1.2 million.

Henry Ford announced his justification for the new dividend policy in a press release: "My ambition is to employ still more men, to spread the benefits of this industrial system to the greatest possible number, to help them build up their lives and their homes." The corporation had a $112 million surplus, expected profits of $60 million, total liabilities of $18 million, $52.5 million in cash on hand, and municipal bonds worth $1.3 million.

The Dodge brothers sued the corporation and the directors to force them to declare a special dividend. The trial court ordered the board to declare a dividend of $19.3 million. Ford Motor Company appealed.

Ostrander, Chief Justice

It is a well-recognized principle of law that the directors of a corporation, and they alone, have the power to declare a dividend of the earnings of the corporation, and to determine its amount. Courts will not interfere in the management of the directors unless it is clearly made to appear that they are guilty of fraud or misappropriation of the corporate funds, or they refuse to declare a dividend when the corporation has a surplus of net profits

which it can, without detriment to the business, divide among its stockholders, and when a refusal to do so would amount to such an abuse of discretion as would constitute a fraud, or breach of that good faith that they are bound to exercise towards the shareholders.

The testimony of Mr. Ford convinces this court that he has to some extent the attitude towards shareholders of one who has dispensed and distributed to them large gains and that they should be content to take what he chooses to give. His testimony creates the impression that he thinks the Ford Motor Company has made too much money, has had too large profits, and that, although large profits might be still earned, a sharing of them with the public, by reducing the price of the output of the company, ought to be undertaken. We have no doubt that certain sentiments, philanthropic and altruistic, creditable to Mr. Ford, had large influence in determining the policy to be pursued by the Ford Motor Company.

There should be no confusion of the duties that Mr. Ford conceives that he and the shareholders owe to the general public and the duties that in law he and his co-directors owe to protesting, minority shareholders. A business corporation is organized and carried on primarily for the profit of the shareholders. The powers of the directors are to be employed for that end.

We are not, however, persuaded that we should interfere with the proposed expansion of the Ford Motor Company. In view of the fact that the selling price of products may be increased at any time, the ultimate results of the larger business cannot be certainly estimated. The judges are not business experts. It is recognized that plans must often be made for a long future, for expected competition, for a continuing as well as an immediately profitable venture. We are not satisfied that the alleged motives of the directors, in so far as they are reflected in the conduct of the business, menace the interests of shareholders.

Assuming the general plan and policy of expansion were for the best ultimate interest of the company and therefore of its shareholders, what does it amount to in justification of a refusal to declare and pay a special dividend? The Ford Motor Company was able to estimate with nicety its income and profit. It could sell more cars than it could make. The profit upon each car depended upon the selling price. That being fixed, the yearly income and profit was determinable, and, within slight variations, was certain.

There was appropriated for the smelter $11 million. Assuming that the plans required an expenditure sooner or later of $10 million for duplication of the plant, and for land $3 million, the total is $24 million. The company was a cash business. If the total cost of proposed expenditures had been withdrawn in cash from the cash surplus on hand August 1, 1916, there would have remained $30 million.

The directors of Ford Motor Company say, and it is true, that a considerable cash balance must be at all times carried by such a concern. But there was a large daily, weekly, monthly receipt of cash. The output was practically continuous and was continuously, and within a few days, turned into cash. Moreover, the contemplated expenditures were not to be immediately made. The large sum appropriated for the smelter plant was payable over a considerable period of time. So that, without going further, it would appear that, accepting and approving the plan of the directors, it was their duty to distribute on and near the 1st of August 1916, a very large sum of money to stockholders.

Judgment for the Dodge brothers affirmed.

To protect the claims of the corporation's creditors, all of the corporation statutes limit the extent to which dividends may be paid. The MBCA imposes two limits: (1) the *solvency test* and (2) the *balance sheet test.*

Solvency Test A dividend may not make a corporation insolvent; that is, unable to pay its debts as they come due in the usual course of business. This means that a corporation may pay a dividend to the extent it has *excess solvency*—that is, liquidity that it does not need to pay its currently maturing obligations. This requirement protects creditors, who are concerned primarily with the corporation's ability to pay debts as they mature.

Balance Sheet Test After the dividend has been paid, the corporation's assets must be sufficient to cover its liabilities and the liquidation preference of shareholders having a priority in liquidation over the shareholders receiving the dividend. This means that a corporation may pay a dividend to the extent it has *excess assets*—that is, assets it does not need to cover its liabilities and the liquidation preferences of shareholders having a priority in liquidation over the shareholders receiving the dividends. This requirement protects not only creditors but also preferred shareholders. It prevents a corporation from paying to common shareholders a dividend that will impair the liquidation rights of preferred shareholders.

Example Batt Company has $27,000 in excess liquidity that it does not need to pay its currently maturing obligations. It has assets of $200,000 and liabilities of $160,000. It has one class of common shareholders. Its one class of preferred shareholders has a liquidation preference of $15,000. Examining these facts, we find that Batt's excess solvency is $27,000, but its excess assets are only $25,000 ($200,000 − 160,000 − 15,000). Therefore, Batt's shareholders may receive a maximum cash or property dividend of $25,000, which will eliminate all of Batt's excess assets and leave Batt with $2,000 of excess solvency.

Share Dividends and Share Splits Corporations sometimes distribute additional shares of the corporation to their shareholders. Often, this is done in order to give shareholders something instead of a cash dividend so that the cash can be retained and reinvested in the business. Such an action may be called either a *share dividend* or a *share split.*

A **share dividend** of a *specified percentage of outstanding shares* is declared by the board of directors. For example, the board may declare a 10 percent share dividend. As a result, each shareholder will receive 10 percent more shares than she currently owns. A share dividend is paid on outstanding shares only. Unlike a cash or property dividend, a share dividend may be revoked by the board after it has been declared.

A **share split** results in shareholders receiving a specified number of shares in exchange for each share that they currently own. For example, shares may be split two for one. Each shareholder will now have two shares for each share that he previously owned. A holder of 50 shares will now have 100 shares instead of 50.

The MBCA recognizes that a share split or a share dividend in the same class of shares does not affect the value of the corporation or the shareholders' wealth, because no assets have been transferred from the corporation to the shareholders. The effect is like that produced by taking a pie with four pieces and dividing each piece in half. Each person may receive twice as many pieces of the pie, but each piece is worth only half as much. The total amount received by each person is unchanged.

Therefore, the MBCA permits share splits and share dividends of the same class of shares to be made merely by action of the directors. The directors merely have the corporation issue to the shareholders the number of shares needed to effect the share dividend or split. The corporation must have a sufficient number of authorized, unissued shares to effect the share split or dividend; when it does not, its articles must be amended to create the required number of additional authorized shares.

Reverse Share Split A *reverse share split* is a decrease in the number of shares of a class such that, for example, two shares become one share. Most of the state corporation statutes require shareholder action to amend the articles to effect a reverse share split because the number of authorized shares is reduced. The purpose of a reverse share split is usually to increase the market price of the shares.

A reverse share split may also be used to freeze out minority shareholders. By the setting of a high reverse split ratio, a majority shareholder will be left with whole shares while minority shareholders will have only fractional shares. Corporation law allows a corporation to repurchase fractional shares without the consent of the fractional shareholders. Freeze-outs are discussed in Chapter 43.

Share Repurchases Declaring a cash or property dividend is only one of the ways in which a corporation may distribute its assets. A corporation may also distribute its assets by repurchasing its shares from its shareholders. Such a repurchase may be either a *redemption* or an *open-market repurchase.*

The right of **redemption** (or a call) is usually a right of the corporation to force an *involuntary* sale by a shareholder at a fixed price. The shareholder must sell the shares to the corporation at the corporation's request; in most states, the shareholder cannot force the corporation to redeem the shares.

Under the MBCA, the right of redemption must appear in the articles of incorporation. It is common for a corporation to issue preferred shares subject to redemption at the corporation's option. Usually, common shares are not redeemable.

In addition, a corporation may repurchase its shares on the open market. A corporation is empowered to purchase its shares from any shareholder who is willing to sell them. Such repurchases are usually *voluntary* on the shareholder's part, requiring the corporation to pay a current market price to entice the shareholder to sell. However, a corporation may force a shareholder with a fractional share to sell that fractional share back to the corporation.

A corporation's repurchase of its shares may harm creditors and other shareholders. The MBCA requires a corporation repurchasing shares to meet tests that are the same as its cash and property dividend rules, recognizing that financially a repurchase of shares is no different from a dividend or any other distribution of assets to shareholders.

Ensuring a Shareholder's Return on Investment

Obtaining a return on her investment in a corporation is important to every shareholder. In a publicly held corporation, a shareholder may receive a return in the form of dividends and more significantly an increase in the value of her shares, which she may sell in the public securities markets.

For a shareholder in a close corporation, obtaining a return on his investment is often a problem, especially for minority shareholders. The majority shareholders dominate the board of directors, who usually choose not to pay any dividend to shareholders. And since the close corporation has no publicly traded shares, minority shareholders have little if any ability to sell their shares. The majority shareholders in a close corporation don't suffer the same effect, because they are usually officers and employees of the corporation and receive a return on their investment in the form of salaries.

What can a minority shareholder do? Rarely will a court, as in *Dodge v. Ford,* require the payment of a dividend. The only way a minority shareholder can protect himself is to bargain well prior to becoming a shareholder. For example, a prospective minority shareholder may insist on a mandatory dividend, that he be employed by the corporation at a salary, or that the corporation or majority shareholders be required to repurchase his shares upon the occurrence of certain events, such as the failure of the corporation to go public after five years. There is a limit to what a minority shareholder may demand, however, for the majority shareholders may refuse to sell shares to a prospective shareholder who asks too much.

Shareholders' Lawsuits

Shareholders' Individual Lawsuits A shareholder has the right to sue in his own name to prevent or redress a breach of the shareholder's contract. For example, a shareholder may sue to recover dividends declared but not paid or dividends that should have been declared, to enjoin the corporation from committing an *ultra vires* act, to enforce the shareholder's right of inspection, and to enforce preemptive rights.

Shareholder Class Action Suits When several people have been injured similarly by the same persons in similar situations, one of the injured people may sue for the benefit of all the people injured. Likewise, if several shareholders have been similarly affected by a wrongful act of another, one of these shareholders may bring a **class action** on behalf of all the affected shareholders.

An appropriate class action under state corporation law would be an action seeking a dividend payment that has been brought by a preferred shareholder for all of the preferred shareholders. Any recovery is prorated to all members of the class.

A shareholder who successfully brings a class action is entitled to be reimbursed from the award amount for his *reasonable expenses,* including attorney's fees. If the class action suit is unsuccessful and has no reasonable foundation, the court may order the suing shareholder to pay the defendants' reasonable litigation expenses, including attorney's fees.

 Appreciate how shareholders may enforce corporate rights of actions, especially against corporate managers.

Shareholders' Derivative Actions When a corporation has been harmed by the actions of another person, the right to sue belongs to the corporation and any damages awarded by a court belong to the corporation. Hence, as a general rule, a shareholder has no right to sue in his own name when someone has harmed the corporation, and he may not recover for himself damages from that person. This is the rule even when the value of the shareholder's investment in the corporation has been impaired.

Nonetheless, one or more shareholders are permitted under certain circumstances to bring an action for the benefit of the corporation when the directors have failed to pursue a corporate cause of action. For example, if the corporation has a claim against its chief executive for wrongfully diverting corporate assets to her personal use, the corporation may not sue the chief executive because she controls the board of directors. Clearly, the CEO should not go unpunished. Consequently, corporation law authorizes a shareholder to bring a **derivative action** (or derivative suit) against the CEO on behalf of the corporation and for its benefit. Such a suit may also be used to bring a corporate claim against an outsider.

If the derivative action succeeds and damages are awarded, the damages ordinarily go to the corporate treasury for the benefit of the corporation. The suing shareholder is entitled only to reimbursement of his reasonable attorney's fees that he incurred in bringing the action.

Eligible Shareholders Although allowing shareholders to bring derivative suits creates a viable procedure for suing wrongdoing officers and directors, this procedure is also susceptible to abuse. **Strike suits** (lawsuits brought to gain out-of-court settlements for the complaining shareholders personally or to earn large attorney's fees, rather than to obtain a recovery for the corporation) have not been uncommon. To discourage strike suits, the person bringing the action must be a current shareholder who also held his shares at the time the alleged wrong occurred. In addition, the shareholder must fairly and adequately represent the interests of shareholders similarly situated in enforcing the right of the corporation.

One exception to these rules is the double derivative suit, a suit brought by a shareholder of a parent corporation on behalf of a subsidiary corporation owned by the parent. Courts regularly permit double derivative suits.

Demand on Directors Since a corporation's decision to sue someone is ordinarily made by its managers, a shareholder must first **demand** that the board of directors bring the suit. A demand informs the board that the corporation may have a right of action against a person that the board, in its business judgment, may decide to pursue. Therefore, if a demand is made and the board decides to bring the suit, the shareholder may not institute a derivative suit.

Ordinarily, a shareholder's failure to make a demand on the board prevents her from bringing a derivative suit. Nonetheless, the shareholder may initiate the suit if she proves that a demand on the board would have been useless or futile. Demand is futile, and therefore excused, if the board is unable to make a disinterested decision regarding whether to sue. Futility may be proved when all or a majority of the directors are interested in the challenged transaction, such as in a suit alleging that the directors issued shares to themselves at below-market prices.

If a shareholder makes a demand on the board and it refuses the shareholder's demand to bring a suit, ordinarily the shareholder is not permitted to continue the derivative action. The decision to bring a lawsuit is an ordinary business decision appropriate for a board of directors to make. The business judgment rule, therefore, is available to insulate from court review a board's decision not to bring a suit.

Of course, if a shareholder derivative suit accuses the board of harming the corporation, such as by misappropriating the corporation's assets, the board's refusal will not be protected by the business judgment rule because the board has a conflict of interest in its decision to sue. In such a situation, the shareholder may sue the directors despite the board's refusal.

Shareholder Litigation Committees In an attempt to ensure the application of the business judgment rule in demand refusal and demand futility situations, interested directors have tried to isolate themselves from the decision whether to sue by creating a special committee of the board, called a *shareholder* or *special litigation committee* (SLC) (or independent investigation committee) whose purpose is to decide whether to sue. The SLC should consist of directors who are not defendants in the derivative suit, who are not interested in the challenged action, are independent of the defendant directors, and, if possible, were not directors at the time the wrong occurred. Usually, the SLC has independent legal counsel that assists its determination whether to sue. Because the SLC is a committee of the board, its decision may be protected by the business judgment rule. Therefore, an SLC's decision not to sue may prevent a shareholder from suing.

Shareholders have challenged the application of the business judgment rule to an SLC's decision to dismiss a shareholder derivative suit against some of the directors. The suing shareholders argue that it is improper for an SLC to dismiss a shareholder derivative suit because there is a *structural bias*. That is, the SLC members are motivated by a desire to avoid hurting their fellow directors and adversely affecting future working relationships within the board.

When demand is not futile, most of the courts that have been faced with this question have upheld the decisions of special litigation committees that comply with the business judgment rule. The courts require that the SLC members be *independent* of the defendant directors, be *disinterested* with regard to the subject matter of the suit, make a *reasonable investigation* into whether to dismiss the suit, and act in *good faith*.

When demand is futile or excused, most courts faced with the decision of an SLC have applied the rule of the *Zapata* case, which follows.

The MBCA has adopted the *Zapata* rule in all contexts, whether or not an SLC is used. When a majority of directors are not independent, the corporation has the burden of proving that the *Zapata* test has been met: good faith and reasonable investigation by the directors making the decision to dismiss the action and a determination by those directors that the best interests of the corporation are served by dismissal. If, however, a majority of the directors are independent, the shareholders bringing the derivative action have the burden of proving that there was bad faith or no reasonable investigation or that bringing the action is in the best interest of the corporation.

Zapata Corp. v. Maldonado　　430 A.2d 779 (Del. Sup. Ct. 1981)

Zapata Corporation had a share option plan that permitted its executives to purchase Zapata shares at a below-market price. Most of the directors participated in the share option plan. In 1974, the directors voted to advance the share option exercise date in order to reduce the federal income tax liability of the executives who exercised the share options, including the directors. An additional effect, however, was to increase the corporation's federal tax liability.

*　William Maldonado, a Zapata shareholder, believed that the board action was a breach of a fiduciary duty and that it harmed the corporation. In 1975, he instituted a derivative suit in a Delaware court on behalf of Zapata against all of the directors. He failed to make a demand on the directors to sue themselves, alleging that this would be futile since they were all defendants.*

The derivative suit was still pending in 1979, when four of the defendants were no longer directors. The remaining directors then appointed two new outside directors to the board and created an Independent Investigation Committee consisting solely of the two new directors. The board authorized the committee to make a final and binding decision regarding whether the derivative suit should be brought on behalf of the corporation. Following a three-month investigation, the committee concluded that Maldonado's derivative suit should be dismissed as against Zapata's best interests.

Zapata asked the Delaware court to dismiss the derivative suit. The court refused, holding that Maldonado possessed an individual right to maintain the derivative action and that the business judgment rule did not apply. Zapata appealed to the Supreme Court of Delaware.

Quillen, Justice

We find that the trial court's determination that a shareholder, once demand is made and refused, possesses an independent, individual right to continue a derivative suit for breaches of fiduciary duty over objection by the corporation, as an absolute rule, is erroneous.

Derivative suits enforce corporate rights, and any recovery obtained goes to the corporation. We see no inherent reason why a derivative suit should automatically place in the hands of the litigating shareholder sole control of the corporate right throughout the litigation. Such an inflexible rule would recognize the interest of one person or group to the exclusion of all others within the corporate entity.

When, if at all, should an authorized board committee be permitted to cause litigation, properly initiated by a derivative stockholder in his own right, to be dismissed? The problem is relatively simple. If, on the one hand, corporations can consistently wrest bona fide derivative actions away from well-meaning derivative plaintiffs through the use of the committee mechanism, the derivative suit will lose much, if not all, of its effectiveness as an intracorporate means of policing boards of directors. If, on the other hand, corporations are unable to rid themselves of meritless or harmful litigation and strike suits, the derivative action, created to benefit the corporation, will produce the opposite, unintended result. It thus appears desirable to us to find a balancing point where bona fide shareholder power to bring corporate causes of action cannot be unfairly trampled on by the board of directors, but the corporation can rid itself of detrimental litigation.

We are not satisfied that acceptance of the business judgment rationale at this stage of derivative litigation is a proper balancing point. We must be mindful that directors are passing judgment on fellow directors in the same corporation and fellow directors, in this instance, who designated them to serve both as directors and committee members. The question naturally arises whether a "there but for the grace of God go I" empathy might not play a role. And the further question arises whether inquiry as to independence, good faith and reasonable investigation is sufficient safeguard against abuse, perhaps subconscious abuse.

We thus steer a middle course between those cases that yield to the independent business judgment of a board committee and this case as determined below, which would yield to unbridled shareholder control.

We recognize that the final substantive judgment whether a particular lawsuit should be maintained requires a balance of many factors—ethical, commercial, promotional, public relations, employee relations, fiscal, as well as legal. We recognize the danger of judicial overreaching but the alternatives seem to us to be outweighed by the fresh view of a judicial outsider.

After an objective and thorough investigation of a derivative suit, an independent committee may cause its corporation to file a motion to dismiss the derivative suit. The Court should apply a two-step test to the motion. First, the Court should inquire into the independence and good faith of the committee and the bases supporting its conclusions. The corporation should have the burden of proving independence, good faith, and reasonable investigation, rather than presuming independence, good faith, and reasonableness. If the Court determines either that the committee is not independent or has not shown reasonable bases for its conclusions, or if the Court is not satisfied for other reasons relating to the process, including but not limited to the good faith of the committee, the Court shall deny the corporation's motion to dismiss the derivative suit.

The second step provides the essential key in striking the balance between legitimate corporate claims as expressed in a derivative stockholder suit and a corporation's best interests as expressed by an independent investigating committee. The Court should determine, applying its own independent business judgment, whether the motion should be granted. The second step is intended to thwart instances where corporate actions meet the criteria of step one, but the result does not appear to satisfy its spirit, or where corporate actions would simply prematurely terminate a stockholder grievance deserving of further consideration in the corporation's interest. The Court of course must carefully consider and weigh how compelling the corporate interest in dismissal is when faced with a non-frivolous lawsuit. The Court should, when appropriate, give special consideration to matters of law and public policy in addition to the corporation's best interests.

The second step shares some of the same spirit and philosophy of the statement of the trial court: "Under our system of law, courts and not litigants should decide the merits of litigation."

Judgment reversed in favor of Zapata. Case remanded to the trial court.

Ethics in Action

After reading *Zapata Corp. v. Maldonado* and the MBCA rules for dismissal of shareholder derivative actions, you may predict that a court will almost always respect the recommendation of a special litigation committee, even when a former or existing board member is a defendant. That is not always the case because the corporation does not have a valid right of action against a director, but often because an SLC has adopted the right process (good faith and reasonable inquiry) and easily can justify that the expense of litigation and the distraction of current management outweigh the likely recovery to the corporation from the wrongdoing director.

• Do you think is it ethical for an SLC to recommend dismissal of an action against a director who has harmed the corporation? Is that sending the right message to other directors and officers? Are there other ways to discipline a

director or officer than by suing him? Are those alternatives sufficient deterrents or punishments?

• Do you think it would be justifiable for an SLC to recommend dismissal of an action against former officers who, like some top officers in Adelphia, Tyco, and Enron, either looted the corporation or caused it to overstate its earnings or understate its liabilities? Is it justifiable for a corporation not to sue directors and officers of corporations, like Apple Inc. and The Home Depot, Inc., who authorized or permitted the backdating of options given to the CEO and other officers, which nearly guaranteed that the officers would profit from the options? Is it clear that options backdating is unethical? Or is options backdating merely an alternative way of guaranteeing compensation to high quality officers? Would a utilitarian or profit maximizer be more likely to recommend dismissal than a rights theorist?

Litigation Expenses If a shareholder is successful in a derivative suit, she is entitled to a reimbursement of her reasonable litigation expenses out of the corporation's damage award. On the other hand, if the suit is unsuccessful and has been brought without reasonable cause, the shareholder must pay the defendants' expenses, including attorney's fees. The purpose of this rule is to deter strike suits by punishing shareholders who litigate in bad faith.

Defense of Corporation by Shareholder

Occasionally, the officers or managers will refuse to defend a suit brought against a corporation. If a shareholder shows that the corporation has a valid defense to the suit and that the refusal or failure of the directors to defend is a breach of their fiduciary duty to the corporation, the courts will permit the shareholder to defend for the benefit of the corporation, its shareholders, and its creditors.

 LO4 Explain the special liabilities of shareholders.

Shareholder Liability

Shareholders have many responsibilities and liabilities in addition to their many rights. In Chapters 41 and 42, we studied shareholder liability when a shareholder pays too little consideration for shares, when a corporation is defectively formed, and when a corporation's veil is pierced. In this section, four other grounds for shareholder liability are discussed.

Shareholder Liability for Illegal Distributions

Dividends and other distributions of a corporation's assets received by a shareholder with *knowledge of their illegality* may be recovered on behalf of the corporation. Under the MBCA, primary liability is placed on the directors who, failing to comply with the business judgment rule, authorized the unlawful distribution. However, the directors are entitled to contribution from shareholders who received an asset distribution knowing that it was illegally made. These liability rules enforce the limits on asset distributions that were discussed earlier in this chapter.

Shareholder Liability for Corporate Debts

One of the chief attributes of a shareholder is his *limited liability:* Ordinarily, he has no liability for corporate obligations beyond his capital contribution. Defective attempts to incorporate (in Chapter 42) and piercing the corporate veil (in Chapter 41) are grounds on which a shareholder may be held liable for corporate debts beyond his capital contribution. In addition, a few states impose personal liability on shareholders for *wages owed to corporate employees,* even if the shareholders have fully paid for their shares.

Sale of a Control Block of Shares

The per share value of the shares of a majority shareholder of a corporation is greater than the per share value of the shares of a minority shareholder. This difference in value is due to the majority shareholder's ability to control the corporation and to cause it to hire her as an employee at a high salary.

Therefore, a majority shareholder can sell her shares for a *premium* over the fair market value of minority shares.

Majority ownership is not always required for control of a corporation. In a close corporation it is required, but in a publicly held corporation with a widely dispersed, hard-to-mobilize shareholder group, minority ownership of from 5 to 30 percent may be enough to obtain control. Therefore, a holder of minority control in such a corporation will also be able to receive a premium.

Current corporation law imposes no liability on any shareholder, whether or not the shareholder is a controlling shareholder, *merely* because she is able to sell her shares for a premium. Nonetheless, if the premium is accompanied by wrongdoing, controlling shareholders have been held liable either for the amount of the premium or for the damages suffered by the corporation.

For example, a seller of control shares is liable for selling to a purchaser who harms the corporation if the seller had or should have had a *reasonable suspicion* that the purchaser would mismanage or loot the corporation. A seller may be placed on notice of a purchaser's bad motives by facts indicating the purchaser's history of *mismanagement and personal use of corporate assets,* by the purchaser's *lack of interest in the physical facilities* of the corporation, or the purchaser's great *interest in the liquid assets* of the corporation. These factors tend to indicate that the purchaser has a short-term interest in the corporation.

The mere payment of a premium is not enough to put the seller on notice. If the *premium is unduly high,* however, such as a $50 offer for shares traded for $10, a seller must doubt whether the purchaser will be able to recoup his investment without looting the corporation.

When a seller has, or should have, a reasonable suspicion that a purchaser will mismanage or loot the corporation, he must not sell to the purchaser unless a *reasonable investigation* shows there is no reasonable risk of wrongdoing.

A few courts find liability when a selling shareholder takes or sells a *corporate asset.* For example, if a purchaser wants to buy the corporation's assets and the controlling shareholder proposes that the purchaser buy her shares instead, the controlling shareholder is liable for usurping a corporate opportunity.

A more unusual situation existed in *Perlman v. Feldman.*[3] In that case, Newport Steel Corporation had excess demand for its steel production, due to the Korean War. Another corporation, in order to guarantee a steady supply of steel, bought at a premium a minority yet controlling block of shares of Newport from Feldman, its chairman and president. The court ruled that Feldman was required to share the premium with the other shareholders because he had sold a corporate asset—the ability to exploit an excess demand for steel. The court reasoned that Newport could have exploited that asset to its advantage.

Shareholders as Fiduciaries A few courts have recognized a fiduciary duty of controlling shareholders to use their ability to control the corporation in a fair, just, and equitable manner that benefits all of the shareholders proportionately. This is a duty to be impartial—that is, not to prefer themselves over the minority shareholders. For example, controlling shareholders have a fiduciary duty not to cause the corporation to repurchase their own shares or to pay themselves a dividend unless the same offer is made to the minority shareholder.

One of the most common examples of impartiality is the **freeze-out** or *squeeze-out* of minority shareholders, which is wrongful because of its **oppression** of minority shareholders. It occurs in close corporations when controlling shareholders pay themselves high salaries while not employing or paying dividends to noncontrolling shareholders. Since there is usually no liquid market for the shares of the noncontrolling shareholders, they have an investment that provides them no return, while the controlling shareholders reap large gains. Such actions by the majority are especially wrongful when the controlling shareholders follow with an offer to buy the minority's shares at an unreasonably low price.

Some courts have held that all close corporation shareholders—whether majority or minority owners—are fiduciaries of each other and the corporation, on the grounds that the close corporation is an incorporated partnership. Thus, like partners, the shareholders owe fiduciary duties to act in the best interests of the corporation and the shareholders as a whole.

Some statutes, such as the Statutory Close Corporation Supplement to the MBCA, permit close corporation shareholders to dispense with a board of directors or to arrange corporate affairs as if the corporation were a partnership. The effect of these statutes is to impose management responsibilities, including the fiduciary duties of directors, on the shareholders. In essence, the shareholders are partners and owe each other fiduciary duties similar to those owed between partners of a partnership.

The next case, *Brodie v. Jordan,* is a decision of the Supreme Judicial Court of Massachusetts, a leading court in fashioning rights for minority shareholders in close corporations. The court found that the majority shareholders who oppressed a minority shareholder by excluding her

[3]219 F.2d 173 (2d Cir. 1955).

from the business operations were required to permit the minority shareholder to enjoy the financial or other benefits from the business to the extent that her ownership interest justified. The court refused, however, to order the majority shareholders to repurchase the minority shareholder's shares.

| Brodie v. Jordan | 857 N.E.2d 1076 (Mass. Sup. Jud. Ct. 2006) |

Mary Brodie, Robert Jordan, and David Barbuto were the only shareholders of Malden Centerless Grinding Co., Inc., a Massachusetts corporation that operated a small machine shop. Mary's deceased husband, Walter Brodie, was one of the founding members of the company and served as its president from 1979 to 1992. Barbuto was a shareholder, director, and treasurer of the company since its formation. Jordan was an employee of the company since 1975 and a shareholder, director, and officer since 1984; he was in charge of the day-to-day operation of the business.

Beginning in 1984, Walter, Barbuto, and Jordan each held one-third of the shares of the corporation, and all three served as directors. By 1988, however, Walter was no longer involved in the company's day-to-day operation and only met with Barbuto and Jordan two to three times each year. After Walter disagreed with Barbuto and Jordan over management issues, Walter requested that the company purchase his shares, but those requests were rejected. Neither the articles of incorporation nor any corporate bylaw obligated Malden, Barbuto, or Jordan to purchase the stock of a shareholder.

The corporation had not paid any dividends to shareholders since 1989. As an employee, Jordan received a salary at a rate set by the board of directors (Barbuto and himself). Jordan participated in a profit-sharing plan made available by the corporation and had the use of a company vehicle. Barbuto received director's fees from the corporation until 1998. He owned the building that housed Malden's corporate offices and received rent from the corporation. Barbuto also owned a separate corporation, Barco Engineering, Inc., which was a customer of Malden and for which Malden regularly performed services. Walter received compensation from the company prior to 1992, when he was voted out as president and director of Malden. Walter was paid a consultant's fee in 1994 and 1995. He died in 1997, and Mary inherited his one-third interest in Malden. Neither Walter nor Mary received any compensation or other money from the corporation after 1995.

In July 1997, Mary attended a Malden shareholders' meeting, at which she nominated herself as a director; she was not elected as Barbuto and Jordan voted against her. At this same meeting, Mary asked Barbuto and Jordan to perform a valuation of the company so that she could value her shares, but a valuation was never performed.

In 1998, Mary sued Barbuto and Jordan claiming that they breached a fiduciary duty by freezing her out of the corporation. By the time the case came to trial, Barbuto and Jordan had failed to hold an annual shareholder's meeting for the previous five years, and Mary had not participated in any company decision making. The trial court found that Barbuto and Jordan had breached a fiduciary duty and oppressed Mary. The court ordered Barbuto and Jordan to purchase Mary's shares. After a court of appeals affirmed, Barbuto and Jordan appealed to the Massachusetts Supreme Judicial Court.

Cowin, Judge

The parties do not dispute that Malden is a close corporation, in that it has (1) a small number of stockholders; (2) no ready market for the corporate stock; and (3) substantial majority stockholder participation in the management, direction and operations of the corporation. "Stockholders in a close corporation owe one another substantially the same fiduciary duty in the operation of the enterprise that partners owe to one another" that is, a duty of "utmost good faith and loyalty." *Donahue v. Rodd Electrotype Co. of New England, Inc.,* 367 Mass. 578, 593, 328 N.E.2d 505 (1975).

Majority shareholders in a close corporation violate this duty when they act to "freeze out" the minority. We have defined freeze-outs by way of example: The squeezers (those who employ the freeze-out techniques) may refuse to declare dividends; they may drain off the corporation's earnings in the form of exorbitant salaries and bonuses to the majority shareholder-officers and perhaps to their relatives, or in the form of high rent by the corporation for property leased from majority shareholders; they may deprive minority shareholders of corporate offices and of employment by the company; they may cause the corporation to sell its assets at an inadequate price to the majority shareholders. What these examples have in common is that, in each, the majority frustrates the minority's reasonable expectations of benefit from their ownership of shares.

We have previously analyzed freeze-outs in terms of shareholders' "reasonable expectations" both explicitly and implicitly. See *Bodio v. Ellis,* 401 Mass. 1, 10, 513 N.E.2d 684 (1987) (thwarting minority shareholder's "rightful expectation" as to control of close corporation was breach of fiduciary duty); *Wilkes v. Springside Nursing Home, Inc.,* 370 Mass. 842, 850, 353 N.E.2d 657 (1976) (denying minority shareholders employment in corporation may "effectively frustrate their purposes in entering on the corporate venture").

In the present case, the Superior Court judge properly analyzed the defendants' liability in terms of the plaintiff's reasonable expectations of benefit. The judge found that the defendants had interfered with the plaintiffs reasonable expectations by excluding her from corporate decision-making, denying her access to company information, and hindering her ability to sell her shares in the open market. In addition, the judge's findings reflect a state of affairs in which the defendants were the only ones receiving any financial benefit from the corporation. The Appeals Court determined that the findings were warranted, and the defendants have not sought further appellate review with respect to liability. Thus, the only question before us is whether, on this record, the plaintiff was entitled to the remedy of a forced buyout of her shares by the majority. We conclude that she was not so entitled.

The proper remedy for a freeze-out is to restore the minority shareholder as nearly as possible to the position she would have been in had there been no wrongdoing. Because the wrongdoing in a freeze-out is the denial by the majority of the minority's reasonable expectations of benefit, it follows that the remedy should, to the extent possible, restore to the minority shareholder those benefits which she reasonably expected, but has not received because of the fiduciary breach.

If, for example, a minority shareholder had a reasonable expectation of employment by the corporation and was terminated wrongfully, the remedy may be reinstatement, back pay, or both. Similarly, if a minority shareholder has a reasonable expectation of sharing in company profits and has been denied this opportunity, she may be entitled to participate in the favorable results of operations to the extent that those results have been wrongly appropriated by the majority. The remedy should neither grant the minority a windfall nor excessively penalize the majority. Rather, it should attempt to reset the proper balance between the majority's conceded rights to what has been termed "selfish ownership" and the minority's reasonable expectations of benefit from its shares.

Courts have broad equitable powers to fashion remedies for breaches of fiduciary duty in a close corporation. Here, the Superior Court judge ordered the defendants to buy out the plaintiff at the price of an expert's estimate of her share of the corporation, a remedy that no Massachusetts appellate court has previously authorized. The problem with this remedy is that it placed the plaintiff in a significantly *better* position than she would have enjoyed absent the wrongdoing, and well exceeded her reasonable expectations of benefit from her shares.

The remedy in *Donahue v. Rodd Electrotype Co. of New England, Inc.*, 367 Mass. 578, 603, 328 N.E.2d 505 (1975), is readily distinguishable. There, the majority had caused the corporation to purchase majority shareholders' stock at a favorable price while denying minority shareholders the same opportunity. We held that, to comply with its fiduciary duties, the majority had to either rescind the sale of its own shares to the corporation or cause the corporation to purchase the minority's shares on the same terms. Here, there is no allegation that Malden purchased the defendants' shares without giving the plaintiff a similar opportunity.

One of the defining aspects of a close corporation is the absence of a ready market for corporate stock. It is well established that in the absence of an agreement among shareholders or between the corporation and the shareholder, or a provision in the corporation's articles of organization or by-laws, neither the corporation nor a majority of shareholders is under any obligation to purchase the shares of minority shareholders when minority shareholders wish to dispose of their interest in the corporation. In this case, it is undisputed that neither the articles of organization nor any corporate bylaw obligates Malden or the defendants to purchase the plaintiff's shares. Thus, there is nothing in the background law, the governing rules of this particular close corporation, or any other circumstance that could have given the plaintiff a reasonable expectation of having her shares bought out.

In ordering the defendants to purchase the plaintiffs stock at the price of her share of the company, the judge created an artificial market for the plaintiff's minority share of a close corporation—an asset that, by definition, has little or no market value. Thus, the remedy had the perverse effect of placing the plaintiff in a position superior to that which she would have enjoyed had there been no wrongdoing.

The remedy for the defendants' breach of fiduciary duty is one that protects the plaintiff's reasonable expectations of benefit from the corporation and that compensates her for their denial in the past. An evidentiary hearing is appropriate to determine her reasonable expectations of ownership; whether such expectations have been frustrated; and, if so, the means by which to vindicate the plaintiff's interests. For breaches visited upon the plaintiff resulting in deprivations that can be quantified, money damages will be the appropriate remedy. Prospective injunctive relief may be granted to ensure that the plaintiff is allowed to participate in company governance, and to enjoy financial or other benefits from the business, to the extent that her ownership interest justifies.

In devising a remedy that grants the plaintiff her reasonable expectations of benefit from stock ownership in Malden, the judge may consider the fact that the plaintiff has received no economic benefit from her shares. If the defendants have denied the plaintiff any return on her investment while draining off the corporation's earnings for themselves, the judge may consider, among other possibilities, the propriety of compelling the declaration of dividends.

Judgment for Mary Brodie affirmed in part and reversed in part. Remanded to the trial court.

LO1 Understand the rights and powers of shareholders and how shareholders exercise their powers.

Members' Rights and Duties in Nonprofit Corporations

In a for-profit corporation, the shareholders' rights to elect directors and to receive dividends are their most important rights. The shareholders' duty to contribute capital as promised is the most important responsibility. By contrast, in a nonprofit corporation, the members' rights and duties—especially in a mutual benefit corporation—are defined by the ability of the members to use the facilities of the corporation (as in a social club) or to consume its output (as in a cooperative grocery store) and by their obligations to support the enterprise periodically with their money (such as dues paid to a social club) or with their labor (such as the duty to work a specified number of hours in a cooperative grocery store).

Nonprofit corporation law grants a corporation and its members considerable flexibility in determining the rights and liabilities of its members. The Model Nonprofit Corporation Act (MNCA) provides that all members of a nonprofit corporation have equal rights and obligations with respect to voting, dissolution, redemption of membership, and transfer of membership, unless the articles or bylaws establish classes of membership with different rights and obligations. For other rights and obligations, the MNCA provides that all members have the same rights and obligations, unless the articles or bylaws provide otherwise.

For example, a mutual benefit corporation that operates a golf country club may have two classes of membership. A full membership may entitle a full member to use all the club's facilities (including the swimming pool and tennis courts), grant the full member two votes on all matters submitted to members, and require the full member to pay monthly dues of $500. A limited membership may give a limited member the right to play the golf course only, grant the limited member one vote on all matters submitted to members, and require the limited members to pay monthly dues of $300 per month.

While members are primarily concerned about their consumption rights and financial obligations—such as those addressed above—that are embodied in the articles and the bylaws, they have other rights and obligations as well, including voting, inspection, and information rights similar to those held by shareholders of for-profit corporations.

Members' Meeting and Voting Rights

A nonprofit corporation must hold an annual meeting of its members and may hold meetings at other times as well. Members holding at least 5 percent of the voting power may call for a special meeting of members at any time.

All members of record have one vote on all matters submitted to members, unless the articles or bylaws grant lesser or greater voting power. The articles or bylaws may provide for different classes of members. Members of one class may be given greater voting rights than the members of another class. The articles or bylaws may provide that a class has no voting power.

Members may not act at a meeting unless a quorum is present. Under the MNCA, a quorum is 10 percent of the votes entitled to be cast on a matter. However, unless at least one-third of the voting power is present at the meeting, the only matters that may be voted on are matters listed in the meeting notice sent to members. The articles or bylaws may require higher percentages.

Members may elect directors by straight or cumulative voting and by class voting. The articles or bylaws may also permit members to elect directors on the basis of chapter or other organizational unit, by region or other geographical unit, or by any other reasonable method. For example, a national humanitarian fraternity such as Lions Club may divide the United States into seven regions whose members are entitled to elect one director. Members also have the right to remove directors they have elected with or without cause.

In addition to the rights to elect and to remove directors, members have the right to vote on most amendments of the articles and bylaws, merger of the corporation with another corporation, sale of substantially all the corporation's assets, and dissolution of the corporation. Ordinarily, members must approve such matters by two thirds of the votes cast or a majority of the voting power, whichever is less. This requirement is more lenient than the rule applied to for-profit corporations. Combined with the 10 percent quorum requirement, members with less than 7 percent of the voting power may approve matters submitted to members.

However, the unfairness of such voting rules is offset by the MNCA's notice requirement. A members' meeting may not consider important matters such as mergers and articles amendments unless the corporation gave members fair and reasonable notice that such matters were to be submitted to the members for a vote.

In addition, the MNCA requires approval of each class of members whose rights are substantially affected by the matter. This requirement may increase the difficulty of obtaining member approval. For example, full members of a golf country club may not change the rights of limited members without the approval of the limited members. In addition, the articles or bylaws may require third-person approval as well. For example, a city industrial development board may not be permitted to amend its articles without the consent of the mayor.

Members may vote in person or by proxy. They may also have written voting agreements. However, member voting agreements may not have a term exceeding 10 years. Members may act without a meeting if the action is approved in writing by at least 80 percent of the voting power.

Member Inspection and Information Rights
A member may not be able to exercise his voting and other rights unless he is informed. Moreover, a member must be able to communicate with other members to be able to influence the way they vote on matters submitted to members. Consequently, the MNCA grants members inspection and information rights.

Members have an absolute right to inspect and copy the articles, bylaws, board resolutions, and minutes of members' meetings. Members have a qualified right to inspect and copy a list of the members. The member's demand to inspect the members' list must be in good faith and for a proper purpose—that is, a purpose related to the member's interest as a member. Improper purposes include selling the list or using the list to solicit money. Members also have a qualified right to inspect minutes of board meetings and records of actions taken by committees of the board.

A nonprofit corporation is required to maintain appropriate accounting records, and members have a qualified right to inspect them. Upon demand, the corporation must provide to a member its latest annual financial statements, including a balance sheet and statement of operations. However, the MNCA permits a religious corporation to abolish or limit the right of a member to inspect any corporate record.

Distributions of Assets
Because it is not intended to make a profit, a nonprofit corporation does not pay dividends to its members. In fact, a nonprofit corporation is generally prohibited from making any distribution of its assets to its members.

Nonetheless, a mutual benefit corporation may purchase a membership and thereby distribute its assets to the selling member, but only if the corporation is able to pay its currently maturing obligations and has assets at least equal to its liabilities. For example, when a farmer joins a farmers' purchasing cooperative, he purchases a membership interest having economic value—it entitles him to purchase supplies from the cooperative at a bargain price. The mutual benefit corporation may repurchase the farmer's membership when he retires from farming. Religious and public benefit corporations may not repurchase their memberships.

Resignation and Expulsion of Members
A member may resign at any time from a nonprofit corporation. When a member resigns, generally a member may not sell or transfer her membership to any other person. A member of a mutual benefit corporation may transfer her interest to a buyer if the articles or bylaws permit.

It is fairly easy for a nonprofit corporation to expel a member or terminate her membership. The corporation must follow procedures that are fair and reasonable and carried out in good faith. The MNCA does not require the corporation to have a proper purpose to expel or terminate a member but only to follow proper procedures. The MNCA places no limits on a religious corporation's expulsion of its members.

The MNCA does not require a nonprofit corporation to purchase the membership of an expelled member, and—as explained above—permits only a mutual benefit corporation to purchase a membership. Members of mutual benefit corporations who fear expulsion should provide for repurchase rights in the articles or bylaws.

Derivative Suits
Members of a nonprofit corporation have a limited right to bring derivative actions on behalf of the corporation. A derivative action may be brought by members having at least 5 percent of the voting power or by 50 members, whichever is less. Members must first demand that the directors bring the suit or establish that demand is futile. If the action is successful, a court may require the corporation to pay the suing members' reasonable expenses. When the action is unsuccessful and has been commenced frivolously or in bad faith, a court may require the suing members to pay the other party's expenses.

LOG ON

www.cipe.org
The Center for International Private Enterprise is a nonprofit affiliate of the U.S. Chamber of Commerce and one of the four core institutes of the National Endowment for Democracy. CIPE advocates for market-based democratic systems in foreign countries and has adopted Corporate Governance Initiatives in the Middle East and North Africa to help countries and territories like Bahrain, Yemen, and the Palestinian Territories advance their efforts to establish strong norms for corporate governance. Go to **www.cipe.org/regional/menacg/index.php**.

The Global Business Environment

Chapter 43 covered some of the corporate governance differences between the United States and other countries, specifically Germany, including the makeup of corporate boards. There are many similarities but also quite a few differences in the powers of shareholders, including matters that must be submitted for shareholder approval. In Germany, the management board must obtain the approval of the shareholders to create new shares of the corporation, to transfer major assets, and to liquidate the company. The differences include German law requiring shareholder approval to declare dividends, issue new shares, and waive shareholders' preemptive right. In addition, many matters that in the United States may be included by director action in the bylaws must be included in German articles of incorporation, which cannot be modified without shareholder approval.

Shareholders of German companies have limited power to force a corporate right of action against someone who has harmed the corporation. A German corporation must sue members of the management board if a shareholders' meeting decides or if shareholders holding at least 10 percent of the shares demand the action. Beyond that, German law rarely permits an *actio pro socio,* the equivalent of an American derivative action. Moreover, German corporation law does not provide for direct actions by shareholders against members of the management board for breach of duty, such as wrongfully providing false financial information to shareholders.

Dissolution and Termination of Corporations

The MBCA provides that a corporation doing business may be dissolved by action of its directors and shareholders. The directors must adopt a dissolution resolution, and a majority of the shares outstanding must be cast in favor of dissolution at a shareholders' meeting. For a voluntary dissolution to be effective, the corporation must submit articles of dissolution to the secretary of state. The dissolution is effective when the articles are filed by the secretary of state.

A corporation may also be dissolved without its consent by administrative action of the secretary of state or by judicial action of a court. The secretary of state may commence an administrative proceeding to dissolve a corporation that has not filed its annual report, paid its annual franchise tax, appointed or maintained a registered office or agent in the state, or whose period of duration has expired. Administrative dissolution requires that the secretary of state give written notice to the corporation of the grounds for dissolution. If, within 60 days, the corporation has not corrected the default or demonstrated that the default does not exist, the secretary dissolves the corporation by signing a certificate of dissolution.

The shareholders, secretary of state, or the creditors of a corporation may ask a court to order the involuntary dissolution of a corporation. Any **shareholder** may obtain judicial dissolution when there is a deadlock of the directors that is harmful to the corporation, when the shareholders are deadlocked and cannot elect directors for two years, or when the directors act illegally, oppressively, or fraudulently. The secretary of state may obtain judicial dissolution if it is proved that a corporation obtained its articles of incorporation by fraud or exceeded or abused its legal authority. **Creditors** may request dissolution if the corporation is insolvent.

Under the MBCA, a corporation that has not issued shares or commenced business may be dissolved by the vote of a majority of its incorporators or initial directors.

Many close corporations are nothing more than incorporated partnerships, in which all the shareholders are managers and friends or relatives. Corporation law reflects the special needs of those shareholders of close corporations who want to arrange their affairs to make the close corporation more like a partnership. The Close Corporation Supplement to the MBCA recognizes that a close corporation shareholder should have more dissolution power, like a partner had under the Uniform Partnership Act. This section, like similar provisions in many states, permits the articles of incorporation to empower any shareholder to dissolve the corporation at will or upon the occurrence of a specified event such as the death of a shareholder.

Winding Up and Termination A dissolved corporation continues its corporate existence but may not carry on any business except that appropriate to winding up its affairs. Therefore, winding up (liquidation) must follow dissolution. Winding up is the orderly collection and disposal of the corporation's assets and the distribution of the proceeds of the sale of assets. From these proceeds, the claims of creditors will be paid first. Next, the liquidation preferences of preferred shareholders will be paid. Then, common shareholders receive any proceeds that remain.

After winding up has been completed, the corporation's existence terminates. A person who purports to act on behalf of a terminated corporation has the liability of a person acting for a corporation prior to its incorporation. See Chapter 42. Some courts impose similar liability on a person

Roles of Shareholders and the Board of Directors

Corporate Action	Board's Role	Shareholders' Role
Day-to-Day Management	Selects officers; supervises management	Elect and remove directors
Issuance of Shares	Issues shares	Protected by preemptive right
Merger and Share Exchange	Adopts articles of merger or share exchange	Vote to approve merger or share exchange; protected by dissenters' rights
Amendment of Articles of Incorporation	Proposes amendment	Vote to approve amendment
Dissolution	Proposes dissolution	Vote to approve dissolution
Dividends	Declares dividends	Receive dividends
Board of Directors Harms Individual Shareholder Rights	Has harmed shareholders	Bring individual or class action against directors or the corporation
Directors Harm Corporation	Sues wrongdoing directors	Bring derivative action against wrongdoing directors

acting on behalf of a dissolved corporation, especially when dissolution is obtained by the secretary of state, such as for the failure to file an annual report or to pay annual taxes.

Dissolution of Nonprofit Corporations

A nonprofit corporation may be dissolved voluntarily, administratively, or judicially. Voluntary dissolution will usually require approval of both the directors and the members. However, a nonprofit corporation may include a provision in its articles requiring the approval of a third person also. For example, such a third person might be a state governor who appointed some of the directors to the board of a nonprofit corporation organized to encourage industrial development in the state. The dissolution is effective when the corporation delivers articles of dissolution to the secretary of state and the secretary of state files them. The dissolved corporation continues its existence, but only for the purpose of liquidating its assets and winding up its affairs.

The secretary of state may administratively dissolve a nonprofit corporation that fails to pay incorporation taxes or to deliver its annual report to the secretary of state, among other things. Minority members or directors may obtain judicial dissolution by a court if the directors are deadlocked, the directors in control are acting illegally or fraudulently, or the members are deadlocked and cannot elect directors for two successive elections, among other reasons.

Problems and Problem Cases

1. Wallace owned 50.25 percent of the shares of Capital Credit & Collection Service, Inc. (CCCS), with Jones and Gaarde each owning 24.8 percent. Those three shareholders also constituted the board of directors. At a directors' meeting, a majority of the directors, that is, Jones and Gaarde, removed Wallace as president and elected Jones president and Gaarde secretary of the corporation. The following month at a shareholders' meeting at which Gaarde was absent, Wallace voted his majority of the shares to remove Jones and Gaarde as directors of the corporation and to replace them with Roberts and Smith. Under the Oregon Business Corporation Act, a valid shareholders' meeting required a quorum of shares equal to a majority of the shares unless a different quorum is provided in the articles of incorporation. CCCS, however, in its corporate bylaws, had a requirement that a quorum for a shareholder meeting was equal to 100 percent of the shares. Wallace had agreed to the bylaw as a shareholder and director of CCCS. Was the shareholder meeting at which Wallace removed Jones and Gaarde invalid due to the lack of a quorum?

2. Kinetic Solutions, LLC, is an Internet software business with 15 members. Five members are the only managers of the business; the other 10 members are only investors. The five managing members want to sell part of the business to public investors. Before doing so, they opt to organize the business as a corporation. The five controlling shareholders want to be able to manage the corporation with little interference from other shareholders, and they want to continue to be compensated as managers of the business. The other 10 shareholders want some management control because of their sizable investments, especially if the business is not profitable. They are also concerned about being able to sell their shares at some point in the future. All 15 shareholders plan to raise an additional $50 million in capital by selling shares in the corporation to 1,000 wealthy public shareholders. The 15 original shareholders are unwilling to give the new investors any power to control the corporation or its management. The original shareholders expect that by having 1,000 new shareholders, a public market will be created in their shares. Sketch an ownership control structure (a structure that determines how shareholders own and control the corporation through their rights as shareholders) that serves the ownership control interests of the five controlling shareholders and the 10 other shareholders. What is the best way for the five controlling shareholders to receive returns on their investment in the corporation? What is the best way for the 10 other shareholders to receive returns on their investment in the corporation?

3. The Eliason family owned a majority (5,238) of the 9,990 shares of Brosius-Eliason Co., a building and materials company, with James Eliason (3,928 shares) and his sister Sarah Englehart (1,260) holding the controlling block. The Brosius family owned a total of 3,690 shares. Frank Hewlett owned the remaining 1,062 shares. On July 31, James Eliason executed a proxy giving his daughter, Louise Eliason, authority to vote his shares. Only in the notary public's acknowledgement verifying James's signature did the proxy state that it was irrevocable. The body of the proxy, the part signed by James, did not state it was irrevocable. Two weeks later, James and his sister Sarah made a voting agreement that ensured Eliason family control over the corporation by requiring their shares to be voted as provided in the agreement. The voting agreement was irrevocable, because it was coupled with an interest in each other's shares. Soon after, Sarah and Louise had a falling out when Louise tried to assert her family's

control of the company. Consequently, Sarah voted her shares with the Brosiuses and Hewlett in violation of the agreement with James. She argued that she was not bound by the voting agreement with James on the grounds that James could not make the agreement, because he had given Louise an irrevocable proxy two weeks earlier. Was Sarah right?

4. Myron Lasky was a shareholder in Kramett, Inc., a manufacturer of novelty candies. When Kramett's business declined, its board of directors chose to save the business by selling it to a larger candy company, Narron Confectioners, Inc. Narron's shares were trading on the market at $9.25 per share, while Kramett's shares traded at $0.50 per share. Kramett's and Narron's boards of directors approved a merger in which each Kramett shareholder would receive one share of Narron for each 20 shares of Kramett. Both the shareholders of Kramett and Narron approved the merger. What right should Lasky exercise if he objects to the merger terms? What must he do to exercise that right?

5. VeriFone Holdings, Inc., a Delaware corporation with its principal place of business in San Jose, California, designs, markets, and services electronic payment transaction systems. In 2006, VeriFone acquired Lipman Electronic Engineering Ltd. In 2007, VeriFone publicly announced that it would restate its reported earnings for the prior three fiscal quarters. Earnings had been materially overstated due to accounting and valuation errors made while Lipman's inventory systems were being integrated with VeriFone's. After that restatement announcement, VeriFone's stock price dropped over 45 percent. The next day, Charles King, a VeriFone shareholder filed a derivative action on behalf of VeriFone against certain of its officers and board of directors, asserting various federal securities fraud claims. A few months later, King demanded that VeriFone permit him to inspect the company's books and records, including VeriFone's Audit Committee Report, which contained the results of an internal investigation of VeriFone's accounting and financial controls conducted after the 2007 restatement announcement. VeriFone refused to grant to King access to the Audit Report on the grounds he lacked a proper purpose under Delaware law, because he had previously elected to bring a derivative action. Was VeriFone correct?

6. For 22 consecutive years, Marston Corporation, a steel producer, has paid a quarterly dividend to its common shareholders. The annual dividend amount

has ranged from 1 percent to 4 percent of the market price of Marston's common shares. Marston's board of directors decides not to declare a common dividend for the next three years. Its steel plants are over 40 years old, and several need to be updated or replaced. The board estimates the cost of updating or replacing its steel plants at $2.3 billion. Eliminating the common share dividend will result in Marston retaining an additional $634 million over a three-year period. Marston currently has retained earnings of $1.2 billion. Marston's minority shareholders sue Marton's to force the board of directors to declare the dividend. Will their action be successful?

7. Pomeroy Carnivals Co., Inc. (PCC), is a family-owned corporation that operates carnival rides at fairs and festivals. The founders of the business, Les and Clara Pomeroy, own 79 percent of the shares, and their three children own 21 percent. Les and Clara are the only members of the board of directors of PCC. Acting as directors of PCC, Les and Clara decide to sell 40 percent of its carnival rides and to reduce by 30 percent the number of fairs and festivals in which PCC will operate rides. The sale will result in a one-time cash infusion of $34,000,000, which Les and Clara plan to invest for PCC in commercial real estate. PCC's annual net income from carnivals will drop by $1,650,000, about 55 percent of current annual net income. The children want to sue PCC's board of directors to stop the sale of the carnival rides and the investment of the proceeds in real estate. What is the process by which the children will sue the directors? Can Les and Clara stop the suit?

8. Water Works, Inc., was a closely held corporation operating an automatic car wash in Wisconsin Rapids. Its 204 shares were issued to Duane and Sharon Jorgensen; their daughter, Doreen Barber, and her husband, James; and two family friends, Gary and Mary Tesch. Each received 34 shares, and each was a director. Duane was president; Sharon, Gary, and James were vice presidents; Mary was treasurer; and Doreen was secretary. The corporation's written business plan stated that Duane would be in charge of management and that the six shareholders would be permanent directors. An oral agreement of shareholders stated that Duane would oversee management as long as he lived. Each shareholder received weekly payments from the corporation, the amount of which was determined by the shareholders agreement. In 1995, Duane discovered that some of the officers and directors were engaged in illegal activity on property owned by the corporation and using the corporation's property for their own personal benefit. When Duane demanded the activities stop, the Barbers and Tesches removed the Jorgensens from the board of directors and stopped making payments to them. The Jorgensen's sued the Barbers and Tesches for breach of fiduciary duty. The Barbers and Tesches claimed they owed fiduciary duties only to the corporation and, therefore, the Jorgensens, as shareholders, could not sue in their own names. Were they right?

9. H. F. Ahmanson & Co. was the controlling shareholder of United Savings and Loan Association. There was very little trading in the Association's shares, however. To create a public market for their shares, Ahmanson and a few other shareholders of the Association incorporated United Financial Corporation and exchanged each of their Association shares for United shares. United then owned more than 85 percent of the shares of the Association. The minority shareholders of the Association were not given an opportunity to exchange their shares. United made two public offerings of its shares. As a result, trading in United shares was very active, while sales of Association shares decreased to half of the formerly low level, with United as virtually the only purchaser. United offered to purchase Association shares from the minority shareholders for $1,100 per share. Some of the minority shareholders accepted this offer. At that time, the shares held by the majority shareholders were worth $3,700. United also caused the Association to decrease its dividend payments. Has Ahmanson done anything wrong?

10. Cookietree, Inc., is a privately held Utah corporation that produces and retails baked goods. The company was formed in 1981, with Greg Schenck and his father, Boyd Schenck, among the original shareholders. From the beginning Greg was president of Cookietree, and after Boyd's death, Greg became majority shareholder. In 1992, Greg Schenck recruited Sam McLaughlin to work as the operations leader for Cookietree. McLaughlin's previous experience at Pillsbury and Quaker Oats made him a valuable employee, and he was quickly promoted to vice president of operations and then chief operating officer and vice president of operations. McLaughlin also invested his personal finances in the corporation by slowly purchasing increasing amounts of shares in the corporation. Nonetheless, McLaughlin's primary reason for joining Cookietree was employment. That employment allowed him to purchase stock in

Cookietree, but he was not required to do so. His ability to buy stock was offered to him as an incentive or reward for his work performance, but the purchase allowances were not tied to his employment; instead they were a separate investment in the company. McLaughlin was paid a competitive salary for his contributions to the company, and his investment in the company was separately rewarded through the payment of dividends. Unfortunately, the relationship between Greg and McLaughlin deteriorated, and eventually Greg terminated McLaughlin's employment. While McLaughlin no longer received a salary, he continued to receive dividends on his shares after his termination. McLaughlin sued Greg claiming that as a majority shareholder, Greg owed a fiduciary duty to McLaughlin, a minority shareholder, and that by terminating McLaughlin's employment, Greg had breached that duty. Did the court agree?

11. Sutter Ranch Corporation, an Oklahoma farming and ranching family corporation, had a provision in its articles of incorporation that provided the corporation could take action to dissolve only with the approval of 75 percent or more of the outstanding shares

of the corporation. After a dispute with his sisters, Owen Sutter, owner of 30 percent of the company, sought a judicial dissolution of the corporation on the grounds of shareholder dissension and oppression by his sisters, the majority shareholders. The sisters argued that Owen could not seek a judicial dissolution because his ownership of the corporation failed to meet the 75 percent minimum for dissolution by action of the shareholders. Did the court agree with the sisters?

Online Research

Corporate Governance Policies

The Council of Institutional Investors is an organization of large pension funds that addresses investment issues. As the representative of pension funds that are significant shareholders in public corporations, the council takes a strong stance in favor of shareholder rights. Log on to the CII's website, click on "Council Corporate Governance Policies" under "Council Policies" to find the CII's positions on shareholder voting rights, shareholder meeting rights, and board accountability to shareholders.

CHAPTER 45

SECURITIES REGULATION

You are the CEO of L'Malle LLC, a nonpublic company that builds and manages shopping malls. L'Malle plans to raise $4,400,000 for construction of L'Malle's newest shopping center complex, Grande L'Malle Geneva. In an effort to avoid the application of the Securities Act of 1933, L'Malle's CFO has proposed that L'Malle issue 22 Profit Participation Plans (PPPs) to two insurance companies, four mutual funds, and 16 individual investors. Under the PPPs, each owner will contribute $200,000 cash to finance the construction of Grande L'Malle Geneva (GLG) and receive 3 percent of the profits generated by GLG. L'Malle will be the exclusive manager of GLG, making all decisions regarding its construction and operation, for which L'Malle will receive a fee equal to 34 percent of GLG's profits.

- Are the PPPs securities under the Securities Act of 1933?
- If the PPPs are securities, may L'Malle sell them pursuant to a registration exemption from the Securities Act of 1933 under Regulation A, Rule 504, Rule 505, or 506?

L'Malle decides to sell the PPPs directly to investors by making a Regulation A offering. As CEO, you will accompany L'Malle's CFO and communications vice president when they visit prospective investors. During those visits, you and the other L'Malle's executives will present copies of the offering circular to prospective investors and make oral reports about the offering, GLG, and L'Malle's business and prospects. You will also answer the investors' questions about L'Malle and GLG.

- Should you be fearful about having liability to the investors under Section 12(a)(2) of the 1933 Act and Rule 10b–5 of the Securities Exchange Act of 1934?

L'Malle decides to make a public offering of its common shares by registering the offering under the Securities Act of 1933 and complying with the requirements of Section 5 of the 1933 Act. The shares will be sold by a firm commitment underwriting.

- Under what legal conditions may L'Malle release earnings reports and make other normal communications with its shareholders and other investors?
- After L'Malle has filed its 1933 Act registration statement with the Securities and Exchange Commission and before the SEC has declared the registration statement effective, under what legal conditions may you (the CEO) and L'Malle's CFO conduct a road show where you pitch the shares to mutual fund investment managers in several cities?
- During that waiting period, may L'Malle post its preliminary prospectus and have an FAQ page for prospective investors at the offering's website?
- After the SEC has declared the registration statement effective, under what legal conditions may L'Malle confirm the sale of shares to an investor?
- During that post-effective period, under what legal conditions may L'Malle direct prospective investors from the offering's website to L'Malle's corporate website, where investors may obtain additional information about L'Malle?

LEARNING OBJECTIVES

After studying this chapter, you should be able to:

1   Understand why and demonstrate how the law regulates issuances and issuers of securities.

2   Define a security and apply the definition to a variety of contracts.

3   Comply with the communication rules that apply to a public offering of securities.

4   List and apply the Securities Act's exemptions from registration.

5   Engage in behavior that avoids liability under the federal securities laws.

MODERN SECURITIES REGULATION AROSE from the rubble of the great stock market crash of October 1929. After the crash, Congress studied its causes and discovered several common problems in securities transactions, the most important ones being:

1. Investors lacked the necessary information to make intelligent decisions whether to buy, sell, or hold securities.

2. Disreputable sellers of securities made outlandish claims about the expected performance of securities and sold securities in nonexistent companies.

Faced with these perceived problems, Congress chose to require securities sellers to disclose the information that investors need to make intelligent investment decisions. Congress found that investors are able to make intelligent investment decisions if they are given sufficient information about the company whose securities they are to buy. This **disclosure scheme** assumes that investors need assistance from government in acquiring information but that they need no help in evaluating information.

L01   Understand why and demonstrate how the law regulates issuances and issuers of securities.

Purposes of Securities Regulation

To implement its disclosure scheme, in the early 1930s Congress passed two major statutes, which are the hub of federal securities regulation in the United States today. These two statutes, the **Securities Act of 1933** and the **Securities Exchange Act of 1934**, have three basic purposes:

1. To require the disclosure of meaningful information about a security and its issuer to allow investors to make intelligent investment decisions.

2. To impose liability on those persons who make inadequate and erroneous disclosures of information.

3. To regulate insiders, professional sellers of securities, securities exchanges, and other self-regulatory securities organizations.

The crux of the securities acts is to impose on issuers of securities, other sellers of securities, and selected buyers of securities the affirmative duty to disclose important information, even if they are not asked by investors to make the disclosures. By requiring disclosure, Congress hoped to restore investor confidence in the securities markets. Congress wanted to bolster investor confidence in the honesty of the stock market and thus encourage more investors to invest in securities. Building investor confidence would increase capital formation and, it was hoped, help the American economy emerge from the Great Depression of the 1930s.

Congress has reaffirmed the purposes of the securities law many times since the 1930s by passing laws that expand investor protections. Most recent are the enactments of the Sarbanes–Oxley Act of 2002 and the Dodd–Frank Wall Street Reform and Consumer Protection Act of 2010. The Sarbanes–Oxley Act was a response to widespread misstatements and omissions in corporate financial statements. Many public investors lost most of their life savings in the collapses of firms like Enron, while insiders profited. As we learned in Chapters 4 and 43 and will learn in this chapter and Chapter 46, the Sarbanes–Oxley Act imposes duties on corporations, their officers, and their auditors and provides for a Public Company Accounting Oversight Board to establish auditing standards.

The Dodd–Frank Act mostly regulates banks and consumer credit institutions, subject matter not within the scope of this chapter. Covered here and in Chapters 43 and 46 are the Dodd–Frank Act's provisions that impose new powers and responsibilities on the Securities and Exchange Commission, increase regulation of brokers and investment advisers, regulate asset-backed securities, require shareholder approval of executive compensation, and strengthen shareholder rights in director elections.

www.law.uc.edu/CCL/index.html
The Securities Lawyer's Deskbook is maintained by the Center for Corporate Law at the University of Cincinnati College of Law. You can find the text of all the federal securities statutes and SEC regulations.

Securities and Exchange Commission

The Securities and Exchange Commission (SEC) was created by the 1934 Act. Its responsibility is to administer the 1933 Act, 1934 Act, and other securities statutes. Like other federal administrative agencies, the SEC has legislative, executive, and judicial functions. Its legislative branch promulgates rules and regulations; its executive branch brings enforcement actions against alleged violators of the securities statutes and their rules and regulations; its judicial branch decides whether a person has violated the securities laws.

SEC Actions The SEC is empowered to investigate violations of the 1933 Act and 1934 Act and to hold hearings to determine whether the acts have been violated. Such hearings are held before an administrative law judge (ALJ), who is an employee of the SEC. The administrative law judge is a finder of both fact and law. Decisions of the ALJ are reviewed by the commissioners of the SEC. Decisions of the commissioners are appealed to the U.S. court of appeals. Most SEC actions are not litigated. Instead, the SEC issues consent orders, by which the defendant promises not to violate the securities laws in the future but does not admit to having violated them in the past.

The SEC has the power to impose civil penalties (fines) up to $500,000 and to issue **cease and desist orders.** A cease and desist order directs a defendant to stop violating the securities laws and to desist from future violations. Nonetheless, the SEC does not have the power to issue injunctions; only courts may issue injunctions. The 1933 Act and the 1934 Act empower the SEC only to ask federal district courts for injunctions against persons who have violated or are about to violate either act. The SEC may also ask the courts to grant ancillary relief, a remedy in addition to an injunction. Ancillary relief may include, for example, the disgorgement of profits that a defendant has made in a fraudulent sale or in an illegal insider trading transaction.

To reduce the risk that a securities issuer's or other person's behavior will violate the securities law and result in an SEC action, anyone may contact the SEC's staff in advance,

propose a transaction or course of action, and ask the SEC to issue a **no-action letter.** In the no-action letter, the SEC's staff states it will take no legal action against the issuer or other person if the issuer or other person acts as indicated in the no-action letter. Issuers often seek no-action letters before making exempted offerings of securities and excluding shareholder proposals from their proxy statements, issues we discuss later in the chapter. Since a no-action letter is issued by the SEC's staff and not the commissioners, it is not binding on the commissioners. Nonetheless, issuers that comply with no-action letters rarely face SEC action.

www.sec.gov
You can read more about the SEC at the SEC website.

 LO2 Define a security and apply the definition to a variety of contracts.

What Is a Security?

The first issue in securities regulation is the definition of a security. If a transaction involves no security, then the law of securities regulation does not apply. The 1933 Act defines the term **security** broadly:

> Unless the context otherwise requires the term "security" means any note, stock, treasury stock, security future, bond, debenture, evidence of indebtedness, certificate of interest or participation in any profit-sharing agreement, . . . preorganization certificate or subscription, . . . investment contract, voting trust certificate, . . . fractional undivided interest in oil, gas, or mineral rights, any put, call, straddle, option, or privilege on any security, . . . or, in general, any interest or instrument commonly known as a "security". . . .

The 1934 Act definition of security is similar, but excludes notes and drafts that mature not more than nine months from the date of issuance.

While typical securities like common shares, preferred shares, bonds, and debentures are defined as securities, the definition of a security also includes many contracts that the general public may believe are not securities. This is because the term **investment contract** is broadly defined by the courts. The Supreme Court's three-part test for an investment contract, called the *Howey* test, has been the guiding beacon in the area for more than 50 years.[1]

---

[1] *SEC v. W. J. Howey Co.*, 328 U.S. 293 (U.S. Sup. Ct. 1946).

The *Howey* test states that an investment contract is an **investment of money** in a **common enterprise** with an expectation of **profits solely from the efforts of others.**

In the *Howey* case, the sales of plots in an orange grove along with a management contract were held to be sales of securities. The purchasers had investment motives (they intended to make a profit from, not to consume, the oranges produced by the trees). There was a common enterprise, because the investors provided the capital to finance the orange grove business and shared in its earnings. The sellers, not the buyers, did all of the work needed to make the plots profitable.

In other cases, sales of limited partnership interests, Scotch whisky receipts, and restaurant franchises have been held to constitute investment contracts and, therefore, securities.

Courts define in two ways the common enterprise element of the *Howey* test. All courts permit horizontal commonality to satisfy the common enterprise requirement. Horizontal commonality requires that investors' funds be pooled and that profits of the enterprise be shared pro rata by investors. Some courts accept vertical commonality, in which the investors are similarly affected by the efforts of the person who is promoting the investment.

Courts have used the *Howey* test to hold that some contracts with typical security names are not securities. The courts point out that some of these contracts possess few of the typical characteristics of a security. For example, in *United Housing Foundation, Inc. v. Forman,*[2] the Supreme Court held that although tenants in a cooperative apartment building purchased contracts labeled as stock, the contracts were not securities. The "stock" possessed few of the typical characteristics of stock and the economic realities of the transaction bore few similarities to those of the typical stock sale: The stock gave tenants no dividend rights or voting rights in proportion to the number of shares owned, it was not negotiable, and it could not appreciate in value. More important, tenants bought the stock not for the purpose of investment but to acquire suitable living space.

However, when investors are misled to believe that the securities laws apply because a seller sold a contract bearing both the name of a typical security and significant characteristics of that security, the securities laws do apply to the sale of the security. The application of this doctrine led to the Supreme Court's rejection of the sale-of-business doctrine, which had held that the sale of 100 percent of the shares of a corporation to a single purchaser who would manage the corporation was not a security. The rationale for the sale-of-business doctrine was that the purchaser failed to meet element 3 of the *Howey* test because he expected to make a profit from his own efforts in managing the business. Today, when a business sale is effected by the sale of stock, the transaction is covered by the securities acts if the stock possesses the characteristics of stock.

In 1990, the Supreme Court further extended this rationale in *Reves v. Ernst & Young,*[3] adopting the **family resemblance test** to determine whether promissory notes were securities. The Supreme Court held that it is inappropriate to apply the *Howey* test to notes. Instead, applying the family resemblance test, the Court held that notes are presumed to be securities unless they bear a "strong family resemblance" to a type of note that is not a security.

The five characteristics of notes that are not securities are:

1. There is no recognized market for the notes.
2. The note is not part of a series of notes.
3. The buyer of the note does not need the protection of the securities laws.
4. The buyer of the note has no investment intent.
5. The buyer has no expectation that the securities laws apply to the sale of the note.

Types of notes that are not securities include consumer notes, mortgage notes, short-term notes secured by a lien on a small business, short-term notes secured by accounts receivable, and notes evidencing loans by commercial banks for current operations.

In the following case, the Supreme Court applied the *Howey* test.

---

[2]*United Housing Foundation Inc. v. Forman,* 421 U.S. 837 (U.S. Sup. Ct. 1975).

[3]494 U.S. 56 (U.S. Sup. Ct. 1990).

SEC v. Edwards   540 U.S. 389 (U.S. S. Ct. 2004)

Charles Edwards was the chairman, chief executive officer, and sole shareholder of ETS Payphones, Inc. ETS sold pay telephones to the public. The payphones were offered with a site lease, a five-year leaseback and management agreement, and a buyback agreement. All but a tiny fraction of purchasers chose this package, although other management options were offered. The purchase price for the payphone packages was approximately $7,000. Under the leaseback and management agreement, *purchasers were promised $82 per month, which was a 14 percent annual return on the purchase price. Purchasers were not involved in the day-to-day operation of the payphones they owned. ETS selected the site for the phone, installed the equipment, arranged for connection and long-distance service, collected coin revenues, and maintained and repaired the phone. Under the buyback agreement, ETS promised to refund the full purchase price of the package at the end of the lease or within 180 days of a purchaser's request.*

In its marketing materials and on its website, ETS trumpeted the "incomparable payphone" as "an exciting business opportunity," in which recent deregulation had "opened the door for profits for individual payphone owners and operators." According to ETS, "very few business opportunities can offer the potential for ongoing revenue generation that is available in today's pay telephone industry."

In reality, the payphones did not generate enough revenue for ETS to make the payments required by the leaseback agreements, so the company depended on funds from new investors to meet its obligations. In September 2000, ETS filed for bankruptcy protection. The SEC brought a civil enforcement action alleging that Edwards and ETS had violated the registration requirements of Section 5 of the Securities Act of 1933 and the antifraud provisions of the 1933 and 1934 securities acts. The district court concluded that the payphone sale-and-leaseback arrangement was an investment contract within the meaning of the federal securities laws. Edwards and ETS appealed to the court of appeals, which reversed the district court's decision. It held that ETS's scheme did not offer either capital appreciation or a participation in the earnings of the enterprise and that the purchasers' returns on their investments was not derived solely from the efforts of others because the purchasers had a contractual entitlement to the return. The SEC asked the Supreme Court of the United States to review the decision of the court of appeals.

O'Connor, Justice

"Opportunity doesn't always knock . . . sometimes it rings." And sometimes it hangs up. So it did for the 10,000 people who invested a total of $300 million in the payphone sale-and-leaseback arrangements touted by ETS under that slogan. In this case, we must decide whether a moneymaking scheme is excluded from the term "investment contract" simply because the scheme offered a contractual entitlement to a fixed, rather than a variable, return.

Congress' purpose in enacting the securities laws was to regulate *investments*, in whatever form they are made and by whatever name they are called. To that end, it enacted a broad definition of "security," sufficient to encompass virtually any instrument that might be sold as an investment. Section 2(a)(1) of the 1933 Act and § 3(a)(10) of the 1934 Act define "security" to include "any note, stock, treasury stock, security future, bond, debenture, . . . investment contract, . . . [or any] instrument commonly known as a 'security.'" "Investment contract" is not itself defined.

The test for whether a particular scheme is an investment contract was established in our decision in *SEC v. W. J. Howey Co.*, 328 U.S. 293 (1946). We look to whether the scheme involves an investment of money in a common enterprise with profits to come solely from the efforts of others.

When Congress included "investment contract" in the definition of security, it was using a term the meaning of which had been crystallized by the state courts' interpretation of their "blue sky" laws. The state courts had defined an investment contract as a contract or scheme for the placing of capital or laying out of money in a way intended to secure income or profit from its employment, and had uniformly applied that definition to a variety of situations where individuals were led to invest money in a

common enterprise with the expectation that they would earn a profit solely through the efforts of the promoter or a third party. Thus, when we held that "profits" must "come solely from the efforts of others," we were speaking of the profits that investors seek on their investment, not the profits of the scheme in which they invest. We used "profits" in the sense of income or return, to include, for example, dividends, other periodic payments, or the increased value of the investment.

There is no reason to distinguish between promises of fixed returns and promises of variable returns for purposes of the test, so understood. In both cases, the investing public is attracted by representations of investment income, as purchasers were in this case by ETS's invitation to watch the profits add up. Moreover, investments pitched as low-risk (such as those offering a "guaranteed" fixed return) are particularly attractive to individuals more vulnerable to investment fraud, including older and less sophisticated investors. Under the reading Edwards advances, unscrupulous marketers of investments could evade the securities laws by picking a rate of return to promise. We will not read into the securities laws a limitation not compelled by the language that would so undermine the laws' purposes.

Edwards protests that including investment schemes promising a fixed return among investment contracts conflicts with our precedent. We disagree. No distinction between fixed and variable returns was drawn in the blue sky law cases that the *Howey* Court used, in formulating the test. Indeed, two of those cases involved an investment contract in which a fixed return was promised. *People v. White*, 12 P.2d 1078 (Cal. 1932) (agreement between defendant and investors stated that investor would give defendant $5,000, and would receive $7,500 from defendant one year later); *Stevens v. Liberty Packing Corp.,* 161 A. 193 (N.J. 1932) ("ironclad contract" offered by defendant to investors entitled investors to $56 per year for 10 years on initial investment of $175, ostensibly in sale-and-leaseback of breeding rabbits).

None of our post-*Howey* decisions is to the contrary. In *United Housing Foundation, Inc. v. Forman,* 421 U.S. 837 (1975), we considered whether "shares" in a nonprofit housing cooperative were investment contracts under the securities laws. We identified the "touchstone" of an investment contract as "the presence of an investment in a common venture premised on a reasonable expectation of profits to be derived from the entrepreneurial or managerial efforts of others," and then laid out two examples of investor interests that we had previously found to be "profits." Those were "capital appreciation resulting from the development of the initial investment" and "participation in earnings resulting from the use of investors' funds." We contrasted those examples, in which "the investor is attracted solely by the prospects of a return on the investment," with housing cooperative shares, regarding which the purchaser "is motivated by a desire to use or consume the item purchased." Thus, *Forman* supports the commonsense understanding of "profits" in the *Howey* test as simply financial returns on investments.

The Eleventh Circuit's perfunctory alternative holding, that respondent's scheme falls outside the definition because purchasers had a contractual entitlement to a return, is incorrect and inconsistent with our precedent. We are considering investment *contracts.* The fact that investors have bargained for a return on their investment does not mean that the return is not also expected to come solely from the efforts of others. Any other conclusion would conflict with our holding that an investment contract was offered in *Howey* itself.

We hold that an investment scheme promising a fixed rate of return can be an "investment contract" and thus a "security" subject to the federal securities laws.

Judgment reversed in favor of the SEC; remanded to the Court of Appeals.

 LO1   Understand why and demonstrate how the law regulates issuances and issuers of securities.

Securities Act of 1933

The Securities Act of 1933 (1933 Act) is concerned primarily with public distributions of securities. That is, the 1933 Act regulates the sale of securities while they are passing from the hands of the issuer into the hands of public investors. An issuer selling securities publicly must make necessary disclosures at the time the issuer sells the securities to the public.

The 1933 Act has two principal regulatory components: (1) registration provisions and (2) liability provisions. The registration requirements of the 1933 Act are designed to give investors the information they need to make intelligent decisions whether to purchase securities when an issuer sells its securities to the public. The various liability provisions in the 1933 Act impose liability on sellers of securities for misstating or omitting facts of material significance to investors.

Registration of Securities under the 1933 Act

The Securities Act of 1933 is primarily concerned with protecting investors when securities are sold by an issuer to investors. That is, the 1933 Act regulates the process

during which issuers offer and sell their securities to investors, primarily public investors.

Therefore, the 1933 Act requires that *every* offering of securities be registered with the SEC prior to any offer or sale of the securities, unless the offering or the securities are exempt from registration. That is, an issuer and its underwriters may not offer or sell securities unless the securities are registered with the SEC or exempt from registration. Over the next few pages, we will cover the registration process. Then the exemptions from registration will be addressed.

 LO3   Comply with the communication rules that apply to a public offering of securities.

Mechanics of a Registered Offering

When an issuer makes a decision to raise money by a public offering of securities, the issuer needs to obtain the assistance of securities market professionals. The issuer will contact a managing underwriter, the primary person assisting the issuer in selling the securities. The managing underwriter will review the issuer's operations and financial statements and reach an agreement with the issuer regarding the type of securities to sell, the offering price, and the compensation to be paid to the underwriters. The issuer and the managing underwriter will determine what type of underwriting to use.

In a **standby underwriting,** the underwriters obtain subscriptions from prospective investors, but the issuer sells the securities only if there is sufficient investor interest in the securities. The underwriters receive warrants—options to purchase the issuer's securities at a bargain price—as compensation for their efforts. The standby underwriting is typically used only to sell common shares to existing shareholders pursuant to a preemptive rights offering.

With a **best efforts underwriting,** the underwriters are merely agents making their best efforts to sell the issuer's securities. The underwriters receive a commission for their selling efforts. The best efforts underwriting is used when an issuer is not well established and the underwriter is unwilling to risk being unable to sell the securities.

The classic underwriting arrangement is a **firm commitment underwriting.** Here the managing underwriter forms an underwriting group and a selling group. The underwriting group agrees to purchase the securities from the issuer at a discount from the public offering price—for example, 25 cents per share below the offering price. The selling group agrees to buy the securities from the underwriters also at a discount—for example, 12½ cents per share below the offering price. Consequently, the underwriters and selling group bear much of the risk with a firm commitment underwriting, but they also stand to make the most profit under such an arrangement.

Securities Offerings on the Internet Increasingly, issuers are using the Internet to make public securities offerings, especially initial public offerings (IPOs) of companies' securities. The Internet provides issuers and underwriters the advantage of making direct offerings to all investors simultaneously, that is, selling directly to investors without the need for a selling group. The first Internet securities offering that was approved by the SEC was a firm commitment underwriting. Internet offerings have increased dramatically since 1998. In the future, the Internet will become the dominant medium for marketing securities directly to investors.

Registration Statement and Prospectus

The 1933 Act requires the issuer of securities to register the securities with the SEC before the issuer or underwriters may offer or sell the securities. Registration requires filing a **registration statement** with the SEC. Historical and current data about the issuer, its business lines and the competition it faces, the material risks of the business, material litigation, its officers and directors experience and compensation, a description of the securities to be offered, the amount and price of the securities, the manner in which the securities will be sold, the underwriter's compensation for assisting in the sale of the

securities, and the issuer's use of the proceeds of the issuance, among other information, must be included in the registration statement prepared by the issuer of the securities with the assistance of the managing underwriter, securities lawyers, and independent accountants. Generally, the registration statement must include audited balance sheets as of the end of each of the two most recent fiscal years, in addition to audited income statements and audited statements of changes in financial position for each of the last three fiscal years.

The registration statement becomes effective after it has been reviewed by the SEC. The 1933 Act provides that the registration statement becomes effective automatically on the 20th day after its filing, unless the SEC delays or advances the effective date.

The **prospectus** is the basic selling document of an offering registered under the 1933 Act. Almost all of the information in the registration statement must be included in the prospectus. It must be furnished to every purchaser of the registered security prior to or concurrently with the sale of the security to the purchaser. The prospectus enables an investor to base his investment decision on all of the relevant data concerning the issuer, not merely on the favorable information that the issuer may be inclined to disclose voluntarily.

Although some prospectuses are delivered in person or by mail, the growth of the Internet as a communication tool has resulted in many issuers transmitting their prospectuses at their own or the SEC's website.

LOG ON

General Motors Preliminary Prospectus
   To see an example of a preliminary prospectus, log on the SEC's website and find the prospectus that General Motors Company filed when it again became a public company in 2010.
www.sec.gov/Archives/edgar/data/
1467858/000119312510192195/ds1.htm

Section 5: Timing, Manner, and Content of Offers and Sales

The 1933 Act restricts the issuer's and underwriter's ability to communicate with prospective purchasers of the securities. Section 5 of the 1933 Act states the basic rules regarding the timing, manner, and content of offers and sales. It creates three important periods of time in the life of a securities offering: (1) the pre-filing period, (2) the waiting period, and (3) the post-effective period.

The Pre-filing Period Prior to the filing of the registration statement (the pre-filing period), the issuer and any other person may **not offer or sell** the securities to be registered. The purpose of the pre-filing period is to prevent premature communications about an issuer and its securities, which may encourage an investor to make a decision to purchase the security before all the information she needs is available. The pre-filing period also marks the start of what is sometimes called the **quiet period,** which continues for the full duration of the securities offering. A prospective issuer, its directors and officers, and its underwriters must avoid publicity about the issuer and the prospective issuance of securities during the pre-filing period and the rest of the quiet period.

The SEC has created a few nonexclusive safe harbors that allow issuers about to make public offerings to continue to release information to the public yet not violate Section 5. Under Rule 168, public issuers are permitted to continue to release regularly released factual business and forward-looking information. The type of information, as well as the timing, manner, and form, must be similar to past releases by the public issuer. Under Rule 169, non-public issuers may release only factual business information of the type they have previously released. For both types of issuers, the information may not mention the offering or be a part of it.

In addition, Rule 163A now allows any issuer to communicate *any* information about itself more than 30 days prior to the filing of a registration statement, provided the issuer does not reference the upcoming securities offering.

During the 30 days prior to the filing date, however, Rule 163 allows only well-known, seasoned issuers to use a **free-writing prospectus.** Well-known seasoned issuers are public issuers with at least $700 million of public float, that is, the value of its common shares held by non-affiliates of the issuer, which excludes officers and directors. A free-writing prospectus is a written offer that may contain any information about the issuer or its securities that does not conflict with the registration statement. Unlike the preliminary prospectus, which must have all the information an investor needs to make an informed decision and may be hundreds of pages, the free-writing prospectus may be only a page or two or a short e-mail and have much less information, such as merely the issuer's financial results for the most recent quarter, a brief description of the securities, and reasons an investor should purchase the securities. It must include a legend that indicates an investor may obtain a prospectus at the SEC website. The free-writing prospectus must usually be filed with the SEC not later than the filing date of the registration statement.

SEC Rule 135 permits the issuer to publish a notice about a prospective offering during the pre-filing period. The notice may contain only the name of the issuer, the amount of the securities offered, and a basic description of the securities and the offering. It may not name the underwriters or state the price at which the securities will be offered.

The Waiting Period The waiting period is the time between the filing date and the effective date of the registration statement, when the issuer is waiting for the SEC to declare the registration statement effective. During the waiting period, Section 5 permits the securities to be **offered but not sold.** However, not all kinds of offers are permitted. Face-to-face oral offers (including personal phone calls) are allowed during the waiting period. However, written offers may be made only by a statutory prospectus, usually a **preliminary prospectus,** or a free-writing prospectus. During the waiting period, the preliminary prospectus omits the price of the securities and the underwriter's compensation. (A final prospectus will be available after the registration statement becomes effective. It will contain the price of the securities and the underwriter's compensation.) Other so-called free writings are not permitted during the waiting period.

The waiting period is part of the quiet period, but the issuer may continue to disclose regularly released factual business and forward looking information about itself.

In addition, one type of general advertisement, officially called Communications Not Deemed a Prospectus, but informally referred to as a **tombstone ad,** is permitted during the waiting period and thereafter. The tombstone ad, which appears in financial publications, is permitted by SEC Rule 134, which allows disclosure of the same information as is allowed by Rule 135 plus the general business of the issuer, the price of the securities, and the names of the underwriters who are helping the issuer to sell the securities. In addition, Rule 134 requires the tombstone ad to state where a hard copy of a prospectus may be obtained or downloaded from the Internet. See Figure 1.

Under Rules 433 and 164, well-known seasoned issuers may continue to use a free-writing prospectus with few limitations after the waiting period, including a legend that the investor may obtain a prospectus at the SEC website. Other issuers may use a free-writing prospectus only after the filing date and only after the investor receiving it has also received a prospectus or an e-mail with a hyperlink to the prospectus. Although the free-writing prospectus may include information not in the registration statement, it may not conflict with information in the registration statement or other documents filed with the SEC under the 1934 Act. All issuers must file the free-writing prospectus with SEC by the date of its first use.

Figure 1   Rule 134 Tombstone Ad

This announcement is neither an offer to sell nor solicitation of an offer to buy these securities. The offer is made only by the Prospectus. Copies of the Prospectus may be obtained in any State from only such of the underwriters as may lawfully offer these securities in compliance with the securities laws of such State.

September 14, 2005

$4,353,983,175

Google Inc.

14,759,265 Shares

Class A Common Stock

Price $295 Per Share

Morgan Stanley   Credit Suisse First Boston

Allen & Company LLC

Citigroup   JPMorgan
Lehman Brothers   UBS Investment Bank
Thomas Weisel Partners LLC   Blaylock & Company, Inc.

M.R. Beal & Company   William Blair & Company   CIBC World Markets

Capital Management Group Securities LLC   Deutsche Bank Securities

Lazard Capital Markets   Loop Capital Markets, LLC   Needham & Company, LLC

Piper Jaffray   Siebert Capital Markets   The Williams Capital Group, L.P.

CONCEPT REVIEW

Communications and Information That an Issuer or Underwriter May Provide to the Public or to Investors during a Registered Offering

Pre-filing Period		Waiting Period	Post-effective Period
More than 30 days prior to the filing date of the registration statement	Less than 30 days prior to the filing date of the registration statement	After the filing date of the registration statement and before the SEC has declared the registration statement effective	After the SEC has declared the registration statement effective
• Any information about the issuer, provided the information does not reference the prospective securities offering	• Negotiations between the issuer and underwriters who are in privity of contract with the issuer • Formation of the Selling Group, if every member of the Selling Group is also a retail division of a member of the Underwriting Group (that is, in privity of contract with the issuer) • Rule 135 Notice of a Prospective Offering • Regularly released factual business information about the issuer, provided it is released at the regular time and with regular emphasis and is not intended for investors or prospective investors • If the issuer is a public issuer, regularly released forward looking information about the issuer, provided it is released at the regular time and with regular emphasis and is not intended for investors or prospective investors • If the issuer is a well-known seasoned issuer, a free-writing prospectus that contains any information that does not conflict with the registration statement and contains a legend indicating that a prospectus will be available at the SEC website when the filing date arrives	• Formation of the Selling Group whether or not every member is also a member of the Underwriting Group (that is, in privity of contract with the issuer) • Rule 135 Notice of a Prospective Offering • Rule 134 Tombstone Ad • Oral offers (face-to-face either in person or on the phone) • Preliminary Prospectus • Regularly released factual business information about the issuer, provided it is released at the regular time and with regular emphasis and is not intended for investors or prospective investors • If the issuer is a public issuer, regularly released forward looking information about the issuer, provided it is released at the regular time and with regular emphasis and is not intended for investors or prospective investors • A free-writing prospectus that contains any information that does not conflict with the registration statement, if investors have a preliminary prospectus or an e-mail with a hyperlink to the preliminary prospectus • If the issuer is a well-known seasoned issuer, a free-writing prospectus that contains any information that does not conflict with the registration statement, if it contains a legend indicating that a prospectus is available at the SEC website • Road show, if it is provided live to a live audience, the attendees have a copy of the preliminary prospectus, or it meets the requirements of a free-writing prospectus	• Rule 135 Notice of a Prospective Offering • Rule 134 Tombstone Ad • Oral offers (face-to-face either in person or on the phone) • Final Prospectus • Sales of securities, if a final prospectus is delivered to the buyer prior to or simultaneous with the confirmation of sale • Any written offer, if the offeree has received a final prospectus • Regularly released factual business information about the issuer, provided it is released at the regular time and with regular emphasis and is not intended for investors or prospective investors • If the issuer is a public issuer, regularly released forward looking information about the issuer, provided it is released at the regular time and with regular emphasis and is not intended for investors or prospective investors • A free-writing prospectus that contains any information that does not conflict with the registration statement, if investors have a final prospectus or an e-mail with a hyperlink to the final prospectus • If the issuer is a well-known seasoned issuer, a free-writing prospectus that contains any information that does not conflict with the registration statement, if it contains a legend indicating that a prospectus is available at the SEC website • Road show, if it is provided live to a live audience, the attendees have a copy of a final prospectus, or it meets the requirements of a free-writing prospectus

Issuers making public offerings will typically send their CEOs and other top officers on the road to talk to securities analysts and institutional investors during the waiting period. These road shows are permissible, whether an investor attends in person or watches a webcast, provided it is a live, real-time road show to a live audience.

Road shows that are not viewed live in real-time by a live audience are considered written offers, but are permitted during the waiting period if they meet the requirements of free-writing prospectuses. That means that issuers other than well-known seasoned issuers must provide a prospectus to investors who view an electronic road show that is not live. Such issuers must also make a copy of the electronic road show available to any investor or file a copy of the electronic road show with the SEC.

The Internet is an exceptional medium to communicate with investors during the waiting period. Investors may easily view a tombstone ad, watch a road show, and download a prospectus from an offering web page.

The waiting period is an important part of the regulatory scheme of the 1933 Act. It provides an investor with adequate time (at least 20 days) to judge the wisdom of buying the security during a period when he cannot be pressured to buy it. Not even a contract to buy the security may be made during the waiting period.

The Post-effective Period After the effective date (the date on which the SEC declares the registration effective), Section 5 permits the security to be **offered and also to be sold,** provided that the buyer has received a **final prospectus** (a preliminary prospectus is not acceptable for this purpose). Road shows and free-writing prospectuses may continue to be used. Other written offers not previously allowed are permitted during the post-effective period, but only if the offeree has received a final prospectus.

The Internet can be used extensively during the post-effective period. From the issuer's web page, an investor may be required to download a final prospectus in order to obtain access to other written information about the issuer and the offering. Since the final prospectus download would be a delivery of the final prospectus to the investor, all communications thereafter would be legal even if they were written.

Liability for Violating Section 5 Section 12(a)(1) of the 1933 Act imposes liability on any person who violates the provisions of Section 5. Liability extends to any *purchaser* to whom an illegal offer or sale was made. The purchaser's remedy is *rescission* of the purchase or damages if the purchaser has already resold the securities.

 LO4 List and apply the Securities Act's exemptions from registration.

Exemptions from the Registration Requirements of the 1933 Act

Complying with the registration requirements of the 1933 Act, including the restrictions of Section 5, is a burdensome, time-consuming, and expensive process. Planning and executing an issuer's first public offering may consume six months and cost in excess of $1 million. Consequently, some issuers prefer to avoid registration when they sell securities. There are two types of exemptions from the registration requirements of the 1933 Act: securities exemptions and transaction exemptions.

Securities Exemptions Exempt securities never need to be registered, regardless who sells the securities, how they are sold, or to whom they are sold. The following are the most important securities exemptions.[4]

1. Securities issued or guaranteed by any government in the United States and its territories.

2. A note or draft that has a maturity date not more than nine months after its date of issuance.

3. A security issued by a nonprofit religious, charitable, educational, benevolent, or fraternal organization.

4. Securities issued by banks and by savings and loan associations.

5. An insurance policy or an annuity contract.

Although the types of securities listed above are exempt from the registration provisions of the 1933 Act, they are not exempt from the general antifraud provisions of the securities acts. For example, any fraud committed in the course of selling such securities can be attacked by the SEC and by the persons who were defrauded under

---

[4]Excluded from the list of securities exemptions are the intrastate offering and small offering exemptions. Although the 1933 Act denotes them (except for the section 4(6) exemption) as securities exemptions, they are in practice transaction exemptions. An exempt security is exempt from registration forever. But when securities originally sold pursuant to an intrastate or small offering exemption are resold at a later date, the subsequent sales may have to be registered. The exemption of the earlier offering does not exempt a future offering. The SEC treats these two exemptions as transaction exemptions. Consequently, this chapter also treats them as transaction exemptions.

Section 17(a) of the 1933 Act and Section 10(b) of the 1934 Act.

Transaction Exemptions
The most important 1933 Act registration exemptions are the transaction exemptions. If a security is sold pursuant to a transaction exemption, that sale is exempt from registration. Subsequent sales, however, are not automatically exempt. Future sales must be made pursuant to a registration or another exemption.

The transaction exemptions are exemptions from the registration provisions. The general antifraud provisions of the 1933 Act and the 1934 Act apply to exempted and nonexempted transactions.

The most important transaction exemptions are those available to issuers of securities. These exemptions are the intrastate offering exemption, the private offering exemption, and the small offering exemptions.

Intrastate Offering Exemption
Under Section 3(a)(11), an offering of securities solely to investors in one state by an issuer resident and doing business in that state is exempt from the 1933 Act's registration requirements. The reason for the exemption is that there is little federal government interest in an offering that occurs in only one state. Although the offering may be exempt from SEC regulation, state securities law may require a registration. The expectation is that state securities regulation will adequately protect investors.

The SEC has defined the intrastate offering exemption more precisely in Rule 147. An issuer must have at least 80 percent of its gross revenues and 80 percent of its assets in the state and use at least 80 percent of the proceeds of the offering in the state. Resale of the securities is limited to persons within the state for nine months.

Although Rule 147 is not an exclusive rule, the SEC scrutinizes closely an intrastate offering that does not comply with it.

Private Offering Exemption
Section 4(2) of the 1933 Act provides that the registration requirements of the 1933 Act "shall not apply to transactions by an issuer not involving any public offering." A private offering is an offering to a small number of purchasers who can protect themselves because they are wealthy or because they are sophisticated in investment matters and have access to the information that they need to make intelligent investment decisions.

To create greater certainty about what a private offering is, the SEC adopted Rule 506. Although an issuer may exempt a private offering under either the courts' interpretation of Section 4(2) or Rule 506, the SEC tends to treat Rule 506 as the exclusive way to obtain the exemption.

Rule 506 Under Rule 506, which is part of Securities Act Regulation D, investors must be qualified to purchase the securities. The issuer must reasonably believe that each purchaser is either (a) an accredited investor or (b) an unaccredited investor who "has such knowledge and experience in financial and business matters that he is capable of evaluating the merits and risks of the prospective investment." Accredited investors include institutional investors (such as banks and mutual funds), wealthy investors, and high-level insiders of the issuer (such as executive officers, directors, and partners). Issuers should have purchasers sign an **investment letter** or **suitability letter** verifying that they are qualified.

An issuer may sell to no more than 35 unaccredited purchasers who have sufficient investment knowledge and experience; it may sell to an unlimited number of accredited purchasers, regardless of their investment sophistication.

Each purchaser must be given or have access to the information she needs to make an informed investment decision. For a public company making a nonpublic offering under Rule 506 (such as General Motors sellings $5 billion of its notes to 25 mutual funds plus 5 other, unaccredited investors), purchasers must receive information in a form required by the 1934 Act, such as a 10-K or annual report. The issuer must provide the following audited financial statements: two years' balance sheets, three years' income statements, and three years' statements of changes in financial position.

For a nonpublic company making a nonpublic offering under Rule 506, the issuer must provide much of the same nonfinancial information required in a registered offering. A nonpublic company may, however, obtain some relief from the burden of providing audited financial statements to investors. When the amount of the issuance is $2 million or less, only one year's balance sheet need be audited. If the amount issued exceeds $2 million but not $7.5 million, only one year's balance sheet, one year's income statement, and one year's statement of changes in financial position need be audited. When the amount issued exceeds $7.5 million, the issuer must provide two years' balance sheets, three years' income statements, and three years' statements of changes in financial position. In any offering of any amount by a nonpublic issuer, when auditing would involve unreasonable effort or expense, only an audited balance sheet is needed. When a limited partnership issuer finds that auditing involves unreasonable effort or expense, the limited partnership may use financial statements prepared by an independent accountant in conformance with the requirements of federal tax law.

Rule 506 prohibits the issuer from making any general public selling effort. This prevents the issuer from using the radio, newspapers, and television. However, offers to an individual one-on-one are permitted.

In addition, the issuer must take reasonable steps to ensure that the purchasers do not resell the securities in a manner that makes the issuance a public distribution rather than a private one. Usually, the investor must hold the security for a minimum of six months.

In the *Mark* case, the issuer failed to prove it was entitled to a private offering exemption under Rule 506. The case features the improper use of an investment or suitability letter.

Mark v. FSC Securities Corp.   870 F.2d 331 (6th Cir. 1989)

FSC Securities Corp., a securities brokerage, sold limited partnership interests in the Malaga Arabian Limited Partnership to Mr. and Mrs. Mark. A total of 28 investors purchased limited partnership interests in Malaga. All investors were asked to execute subscription documents, including a suitability or investment letter in which the purchaser stated his income level, that he had an opportunity to obtain relevant information, and that he had sufficient knowledge and experience in business affairs to evaluate the risks of the investment.

When the value of the limited partnership interests fell, the Marks sued FSC to rescind their purchase on the grounds that FSC sold unregistered securities in violation of the Securities Act of 1933. The jury held that the offering was exempt as an offering not involving a public offering. The Marks appealed.

Simpson, Judge

Section 4(2) of the Securities Act exempts from registration with the SEC "transactions by an issuer not involving any public offering." There are no hard and fast rules for determining whether a securities offering is exempt from registration under the general language of Section 4(2).

However, the "safe harbor" provision of Regulation D, Rule 506, deems certain transactions to be not involving any public offering within the meaning of Section 4(2). FSC had to prove that certain objective tests were met. These conditions include the general conditions not in dispute here, and the following specific conditions:

(i) Limitation on number of purchasers. The issuer shall reasonably believe that there are no more than thirty-five purchasers of securities in any offering under this Section.

(ii) Nature of purchasers. The issuer shall reasonably believe immediately prior to making any sale that each purchaser who is not an accredited investor either alone or with his purchaser representative(s) has such knowledge and experience in financial and business matters that he is capable of evaluating the merits and risks of the prospective investment.

In this case, we take the issuer to be the general partners of Malaga. FSC is required to offer evidence of the issuer's reasonable belief as to the nature of each purchaser. The only testimony at trial competent to establish the issuer's belief as to the nature of the purchasers was that of Laurence Leafer, a general partner

in Malaga. By his own admission, he had no knowledge about any purchaser, much less any belief, reasonable or not, as to the purchasers' knowledge and experience in financial and business matters.

Q: What was done to determine if investors were, in fact, reasonably sophisticated?

A: Well, there were two things. Number one, we had investor suitability standards that had to be met. You had to have a certain income, be in a certain tax bracket, this kind of thing. Then in the subscription documents themselves, they, when they sign it, supposedly represented that they had received information necessary to make an informed investment decision, and that they were sophisticated. And if they were not, they relied on an offering representative who was.

Q: Did you review the subscription documents that came in for the Malaga offering?

A: No.

Q: So do you know whether all of the investors in the Malaga offering met the suitability and sophistication requirements?

A: I don't.

FSC also offered as evidence the Marks' executed subscription documents, as well as a set of documents in blank, to establish the procedure it followed in the Malaga sales offering. Although the Marks' executed documents may have been sufficient to establish the reasonableness of any belief the issuer may have had as to the Marks' particular qualifications, that does not satisfy Rule 506. The documents offered no evidence from which a jury could conclude the issuer reasonably believed each purchaser was suitable. Instead, all that was proved was the sale of 28 limited partnership interests, and the circumstances under which those sales were intended to have been made. The blank subscriptions documents simply do not amount to probative evidence, when it is the answers and information received from purchasers that determine whether the conditions of Rule 506 have been met.

Having concluded that the Malaga limited-partnership offering did not meet the registration exemption requirement of Rule 506 of Regulation D, we conclude that the Marks are entitled to the remedy of rescission.

Judgment reversed in favor of the Marks; remanded to the trial court.

Small Offering Exemptions

Small Offering Exemptions Sections 3(b) and 4(6) of the 1933 Act permit the SEC to exempt from registration any offering by an issuer not exceeding $5 million. Several SEC rules and regulations permit an issuer to sell small amounts of securities and avoid registration. The rationale for these exemptions is that the dollar amount of the securities offered or the number of purchasers is too small for the federal government to be concerned with registration. State securities law may require registration, however.

Rule 504 SEC Rule 504 of Regulation D allows a nonpublic issuer to sell up to $1 million of securities in a 12-month period and avoid registration. Rule 504 sets no limits on the number of offerees or purchasers. The purchasers need not be sophisticated in investment matters, and the issuer need disclose information only as required by state securities law. Rule 504 permits general selling efforts, and purchasers are free to resell the securities at any time but only if the issuer either registers the securities under state securities law or sells only to accredited investors pursuant to a state securities law exemption.

Rule 505 Rule 505 of Regulation D allows any issuer to sell up to $5 million of securities in a 12-month period and avoid registration. No general selling efforts are allowed, and purchasers may not resell the securities for at least six months or one year, depending on the type of issuer. Like Rule 506, the issuer may sell to no more than 35 unaccredited purchasers, and there is no limit on the number of accredited purchasers. The purchasers, however, need not be sophisticated in investment matters. Rule 505 has the same disclosure requirements as Rule 506.

Regulation A Regulation A permits a nonpublic issuer to sell up to $5 million of securities in a one-year period. There is no limit on the number of purchasers, no purchaser sophistication requirement, and no purchaser resale restriction.

The Regulation A disclosure document is the offering circular, which must be filed with the SEC. The offering circular is required to contain a balance sheet dated within 90 days before the filing date of the offering circular. It must also contain two years' income statements, cash flow statements, and statements of shareholder equity. Ordinarily, the financial statements need not be audited unless the issuer is otherwise required to have audited financial statements.

There is a 20-day waiting period after the filing of the offering circular, during which offers may be made. Oral offers are permitted, as are brief advertisements and written offers by an offering circular. Sales are permitted after the waiting period.

Regulation A also permits issuers to determine investors' interest in a planned offering prior to undertaking the expense of preparing an offering circular.

Securities Offerings on the Internet

Securities Offerings on the Internet With the emergence of the Internet as a significant communication tool, small issuers have sought to make offerings to investors over the Internet. Such offerings can easily run afoul of Rules 505 and 506 of Regulation D, which prohibit public solicitations of investors. Spring Street Brewing Company, the first issuer to offer securities via the Web in 1995, avoided registration by using the Regulation A exemption. Other issuers have used Rule 504, and some have made registered offerings exclusively over the Internet.

Transaction Exemptions for Nonissuers

Transaction Exemptions for Nonissuers Although it is true that the registration provisions apply primarily to issuers and those who help issuers sell their securities publicly, the 1933 Act states that every person who sells a security is potentially subject to Section 5's restrictions on the timing of offers and sales. You must learn the most important rule of the 1933 Act: **Every transaction in securities must be registered with the SEC or be exempt from registration.**

This rule applies to every person, including the small investor who, through the New York Stock Exchange, sells securities that may have been registered by the issuer 15 years earlier. The small investor must either have the issuer register her sale of securities or find an exemption from registration that applies to the situation. Fortunately, most small investors who resell securities will have an exemption from the registration requirements of the 1933 Act. The transaction ordinarily used by these resellers is Section 4(1) of the 1933 Act. It provides an exemption for "transactions by any person other than an issuer, underwriter, or dealer."

For example, if you buy GM common shares on the New York Stock Exchange, you may freely resell them without a registration. You are not an issuer (GM is). You are not a dealer (because you are not in the business of selling securities). And you are not an underwriter (because you are not helping GM distribute the shares to the public).

Application of this exemption when an investor sells shares that are already publicly traded is easy; however, it is more difficult to determine whether an investor can use this exemption when the investor sells **restricted securities.**

Sale of Restricted Securities Restricted securities are securities issued pursuant to Rules 505 and 506 and sometimes under Rule 504. Restricted securities are supposed to be held by a purchaser unaffiliated with the issuer for at least six months if the issuer is a public company and one year if the issuer is not public. If they are sold earlier, the investor may be deemed an underwriter who has assisted the issuer in selling the securities to the general public. Consequently, both the issuer and the investor may have violated Section 5 of the 1933 Act by selling nonexempted securities prior to a registration of the securities with the SEC. As a result, all investors who purchased securities from the issuer in the exempted offering may have the remedy of rescission under Section 12(a)(1), resulting in the issuer being required to return to investors all the proceeds of the issuance.

For example, an investor buys 10,000 common shares issued by Arcom Corporation pursuant to a Rule 506 private offering exemption. One month later, the investor sells the securities to 40 other investors. The original investor has acted as an underwriter because he has helped Arcom distribute the shares to the public. The original investor may not use the issuer's private offering exemption because it exempted only the issuer's sale to him. As a result, both the original investor and Arcom have violated Section 5. The 40 investors who purchased the securities from the original investor—and all other investors who purchased common shares from the issuer in the Rule 506 offering—may rescind their purchases under Section 12(a)(1) of the 1933 Act, receiving from their seller the return of their investment.

SEC Rule 144 allows purchasers of restricted securities to resell the securities and not be deemed underwriters. The resellers must hold the securities for at least six months if the securities issuer is a public company and for one year if the issuer is nonpublic, after which the investors may sell all or part of the restricted securities. After the passage of those time periods, investors not affiliated with the issuer may sell all or part of the restricted securities they hold. For investors affiliated with the issuers, such as an officer or director, the rules are more complex. In any three-month period, the affiliated reseller may sell only a limited number of securities—the greater of 1 percent of the outstanding securities or the average weekly volume of trading. The reseller must file a notice (Form 144) with the SEC.

Consequence of Obtaining a Securities or Transaction Exemption When an issuer has obtained an exemption from the registration provisions of the 1933 Act, the Section 5 limits on when and how offers and sales may be made do not apply. Consequently, Section 12(a)(1)'s remedy of rescission or damages is unavailable to an investor who has purchased securities in an exempt offering.

When an issuer has attempted to comply with a registration exemption and has failed to do so, any offer or sale of securities by the issuer may violate Section 5. Because the issuer has offered or sold nonexempted securities prior to filing a registration statement with the SEC, any purchaser may sue the issuer under Section 12(a)(1) of the 1933 Act.

Although the registration provisions of the 1933 Act do not apply to an exempt offering, the antifraud provisions of the 1933 Act and 1934 Act, which are discussed later, are applicable. For example, when an issuer gives false information to a purchaser in a Rule 504 offering, the issuer may have violated the antifraud provisions of the two acts. The purchaser may obtain damages from the issuer under the antifraud rules even though the transaction is exempt from registration.

Issuer's Exemptions from the Registration Requirements of the Securities Act of 1933

	Type of Issuer	Amount of Securities Sold	Number of Purchasers	Purchaser Qualifications
Rule 504	Nonpublic issuer	$1,000,000 in a 12-month period	No limit	None
Rule 505	Any issuer	$5,000,000 in a 12-month period	Same number of purchasers as Rule 506	None

Rule 506	Any issuer	Unlimited	• 35 unaccredited purchasers and
			• Unlimited accredited purchasers
			  • High-level insiders,
			  • Income > $200,000,
			  • NW (excluding primary residence) > $1,000,000, or
			  • Institutional investors
				Issuer must reasonably believe that each purchaser is either
				• accredited or
				• alone or with his purchaser representative has such knowledge and experience in financial and business matters to be capable of evaluating the merits and risks of the investment

Regulation A	Nonpublic issuer	$5,000,000 in a one-year period	No limit	None
Rule 147	• Issuer organized and doing business in the offerees' and purchasers' state • Issuer has 80% of its assets in the state • Issuer generates 80% of its gross revenues from the state • Issuer uses 80% of the offering's proceeds in the state	Unlimited	No limit	All offerees and purchasers must reside in the issuer's state

L05 Engage in behavior that avoids liability under the federal securities laws.

Liability Provisions of the 1933 Act

To deter fraud, deception, and manipulation and to provide remedies to the victims of such practices, Congress included a number of liability provisions in the Securities Act of 1933.

Liability for Defective Registration Statements Section 11 of the 1933 Act provides civil liabilities for damages when a 1933 Act registration statement on its effective date misstates or omits a material fact. A purchaser of securities issued pursuant to the defective registration statement may sue certain classes of persons that are listed in Section 11—the issuer, its chief executive officer, its chief accounting officer, its chief financial officer, the directors, other signers of the

Disclosure Requirements	General Solicitations	Resale Restrictions
None	Permitted, if the issuer registered the securities under state law or sold the securities only to accredited investors pursuant to a state securities exemption	No resale restrictions, if the issuer registered the securities under state law or sold the securities only to accredited investors pursuant to a state securities exemption
Same disclosure requirements as Rule 506	Not permitted	Same resale restrictions as Rule 506

If issuer sells only to accredited purchasers: the issuer must give the investors only the information requested by investors.
If issuer sells to any unaccredited purchasers, the issuer must give investors:
• the same nonfinancial information as required for a registered offering
• audited financial statements
  ◦ Public issuer: 2 balance sheets, 3 income statements, 3 statements of changes in financial position
  ◦ Nonpublic issuer: if amount of securities sold is
    ▪ ≤$2,000,000: 1 balance sheet
    ▪ >$2,000,000 but ≤$7,500,000: 1 balance sheet, 1 income statement, 1 statement of changes in financial position
    ▪ >$7,500,000: 2 balance sheets, 3 income statements, 3 statements of changes in financial position
  ◦ Nonpublic issuer, if auditing involves unreasonable effort or expense:
    ▪ 1 balance sheet
Any information given to one investor must be given to all investors.
	Not permitted	• Investors may not sell securities of a public issuer for at least six months
		• Investors may not sell securities of a nonpublic issuer for at least one year
		• After the passage of the time periods above, a nonaffiliated investor may sell the securities without volume restrictions
		• After the passage of the time periods above, an affiliated investor may sell in any three-month period the greater of
		  ◦ 1% of the issuer's outstanding shares or
		  ◦ the average weekly volume of the issuer's shares

The issuer must use an Offering Circular. Financial statements in the Offering Circular: • Need not be audited unless otherwise required • 1 balance sheet, 2 income statements, 2 cash flow statements, 2 statements of shareholder equity	Permitted	No resale restrictions
None	Permitted	Investors may not sell the securities outside the issuer's state for nine months

registration statement, the underwriter, and experts who contributed to the registration statement (such as auditors who issued opinions regarding the financial statements or lawyers who issued an opinion concerning the tax aspects of a limited partnership). The purchaser's remedy under Section 11 is for damages caused by the misstatement or omission. Damages are presumed to be equal to the difference between the purchase price of the securities less the price of the securities at the time of the lawsuit.

Section 11 is a radical liability section for three reasons. First, reliance is usually not required; that is, the purchaser need not show that she relied on the misstatement or omission in the registration statement. In fact, the purchaser need not have read the registration statement or have seen it. Second, privity is not required; that is, the purchaser need not prove that she purchased the securities from the defendant. All she has to prove is that the defendant is in one of the classes of persons liable under

Ethics in Action

Section 5 of the 1933 Act and many of the exemptions from registration put severe limits on an issuer's ability to inform prospective investors during a registered or exempted offering. For example, during the quiet period of a registered offering, the SEC takes a dim view of an issuer's attempt to publicize itself and its business. Rules 505 and 506 prohibit general solicitations.

- Are those limitations consistent with the principles of a country that has a market-based economy and elevates freedom of speech to a constitutional right? Would a rights theorist support American securities law? How about a profit maximizer?
- Might a believer in justice theory view be more likely to support American law regulating issuances of securities? Whom would a justice theorist want to see protected?
- Who is the typical securities purchaser? Is it not someone from the wealthier classes of citizens? Is securities regulation welfare for the wealthy?

Note that Section 5 of the 1933 Act does not require that investors receive a preliminary prospectus during the waiting period. In fact, an issuer can completely avoid giving investors a prospectus until a sale is confirmed during the post-effective period. That means an investor may not receive a prospectus until he has made his purchase decision. Moreover, many investors find the prospectus overwhelming to read, and if they do read it, it is often couched in legalese that is difficult to understand. Finally, the prospectus mostly comprises historical information. It is more correctly a "retrospectus," not a prospectus, and contains information that is already in the marketplace. Yet professionals like auditors and investment bankers make millions of dollars by being involved in the preparation of the prospectus, which is not received by investors at the right time, not read, not readable, and not relevant to investment decisions.

- Is it ethical for professionals to profit enormously from their role of putting together a prospectus that provides little real value to investors?

Section 11. Third, the purchaser need not prove that the defendant negligently or intentionally misstated or omitted a material fact. Instead, a defendant who otherwise would be liable under Section 11 may escape liability by proving that he exercised due diligence.

Section 11 Defenses A defendant can escape liability under Section 11 by proving that the purchaser knew of the misstatement or omission when she purchased the security. In addition, a defendant may raise the **due diligence defense.** It is the more important of the two defenses.

Any defendant except the issuer may escape liability under Section 11 by proving that he acted with due diligence in determining the accuracy of the registration statement. The due diligence defense basically requires the defendant to prove that he was not negligent. The exact defense varies, however, according to the class of defendant and the portion of the registration statement that is defective. Most defendants must prove that after a **reasonable investigation** they had **reasonable grounds to believe** and **did believe** that the registration statement was true and contained no omission of material fact.

Experts need to prove due diligence only in respect to the parts that they have contributed. For example, independent auditors must prove due diligence in ascertaining the accuracy of financial statements for which they issue opinions. Due diligence requires that an auditor at least comply with generally accepted auditing standards (GAAS). Experts are those who issue an opinion regarding information in the registration statement. For example, auditors of financial statements are experts under Section 11 because they issue opinions regarding the ability of the financial statements to present fairly the financial position of the companies they have audited. A geologist who issues an opinion regarding the amount of oil reserves held by an energy company is a Section 11 expert if her opinion is included in a registration statement filed by the limited partnership.

Nonexperts meet their due diligence defense for parts contributed by experts if they had no reason to believe and did not believe that the expertised parts misstated or omitted any material fact. This defense does not require the nonexpert to investigate the accuracy of expertised portions, unless something alerted the nonexpert to problems with the expertised portions.

The *BarChris* case is the most famous case construing the due diligence defense of Section 11.

Escott v. BarChris Construction Corp.   283 F.Supp. 643 (S.D.N.Y. 1968)

BarChris Construction Corporation was in the business of constructing bowling centers. With the introduction of automatic pinsetters in 1952, there was a rapid growth in the popularity of bowling, and BarChris's sales increased from $800,000 in 1956 to over $9 million in 1960. By 1960, it was building about 3 percent of the lanes constructed, while Brunswick Corporation and AMF were building 97 percent. BarChris contracted with its customers to construct and equip bowling alleys for them. Under the contracts, a customer was required to make a small down payment in cash. After the alleys were constructed, customers gave BarChris promissory notes for the balance of the purchase price. BarChris discounted the notes with a factor. The factor kept part of the face value of the notes as a reserve until the customer paid the notes. BarChris was obligated to repurchase the notes if the customer defaulted.

In 1960, BarChris offered its customers an alternative financing method in which BarChris sold the interior of a bowling alley to a factor, James Talcott, Inc. Talcott then leased the alley either to a BarChris customer (Type A financing) or to a BarChris subsidiary that then subleased to the customer (Type B financing). Under Type A financing, BarChris guaranteed 25 percent of the customer's obligation under the lease. With Type B financing, BarChris was liable for 100 percent of its subsidiaries' lease obligations. Under either financing method, BarChris made substantial expenditures before receiving payment from customers and, therefore, experienced a constant need of cash.

In early 1961, BarChris decided to issue debentures and to use part of the proceeds to help its cash position. In March 1961, BarChris filed with the SEC a registration statement covering the debentures. The registration statement became effective on May 16. The proceeds of the offering were received by BarChris on May 24, 1961. By that time, BarChris had difficulty collecting from some of its customers, and other customers were in arrears on their payments to the factors of the discounted notes. Due to overexpansion in the bowling alley industry, many BarChris customers failed. On October 29, 1962, BarChris filed a petition for bankruptcy. On November 1, it defaulted on the payment of interest on the debentures.

Escott and other purchasers of the debentures sued BarChris and its officers, directors, and auditors, among others, under Section 11 of the Securities Act of 1933. BarChris's registration statement contained material misstatements and omitted material facts. It overstated current assets by $609,689 (15.6 percent), sales by $653,900 (7.7 percent), and earnings per share by 10 cents (15.4 percent) in the 1960 balance sheet and income statement audited by Peat, Marwick, Mitchell & Co. The registration statement also understated BarChris's contingent liabilities by $618,853 (42.8 percent) as of April 30, 1961. It overstated gross profit for the first quarter of 1961 by $230,755 (92 percent) and sales for the first quarter of 1961 by $519,810 (32.1 percent). The March 31, 1961, backlog was overstated by $4,490,000 (186 percent). The 1961 figures were not audited by Peat, Marwick.

In addition, the registration statement reported that prior loans from officers had been repaid, but failed to disclose that officers had made new loans to BarChris totaling $386,615. BarChris had used $1,160,000 of the proceeds of the debentures to pay old debts, a use not disclosed in the registration statement. BarChris's potential liability of $1,350,000 to factors due to customer delinquencies on factored notes was not disclosed. The registration statement represented BarChris's contingent liability on Type B financings as 25 percent instead of 100 percent. It misrepresented the nature of BarChris's business by failing to disclose that BarChris was already engaged and was about to become more heavily engaged in the operation of bowling alleys, including one called Capitol Lanes, as a way of minimizing its losses from customer defaults.

Trilling, BarChris's controller, signed the registration statement. Auslander, a director, signed the registration statement. Peat, Marwick consented to being named as an expert in the registration statement. All three would be liable to Escott unless they could meet the due diligence defense of Section 11.

McLean, District Judge

The question is whether Trilling, Auslander, and Peat, Marwick have proved their due diligence defenses. The position of each defendant will be separately considered.

Trilling

Trilling was BarChris's controller. He signed the registration statement in that capacity. Trilling entered BarChris's employ in October 1960. He was Kircher's [BarChris's treasurer] subordinate. When Kircher asked him for information, he furnished it.

Trilling was not a member of the executive committee. He was a comparatively minor figure in BarChris. The description of BarChris's management in the prospectus does not mention him. He was not considered to be an executive officer.

Trilling may well have been unaware of several of the inaccuracies in the prospectus. But he must have known of some of them. As a financial officer, he was familiar with BarChris's finances and with its books of account. He knew that part of the cash on deposit on December 31, 1960, had been procured temporarily by Russo [BarChris's executive vice president] for window-dressing purposes. He knew that BarChris was operating Capitol Lanes in 1960. He should have known, although perhaps through carelessness he did not know at the time, that BarChris's contingent liability on Type B lease transactions was greater than the prospectus stated. In the light of these facts, I cannot find that Trilling believed the entire prospectus to be true.

But even if he did, he still did not establish his due diligence defenses. He did not prove that as to the parts of the prospectus expertised by Peat, Marwick he had no reasonable ground to believe that it was untrue. He also failed to prove, as to the parts of the prospectus not expertised by Peat, Marwick, that he made a reasonable investigation which afforded him a reasonable ground to believe that it was true. As far as appears, he made no investigation. He did what was asked of him and assumed that others would properly take care of supplying accurate data as to the other aspects of the company's business. This would have been well enough but for the fact that he signed the registration statement. As a signer, he could not avoid responsibility by leaving it up to others to make it accurate. Trilling did not sustain the burden of proving his due diligence defenses.

Auslander

Auslander was an outside director, i.e., one who was not an officer of BarChris. He was chairman of the board of Valley Stream National Bank in Valley Stream, Long Island. In February 1961, Vitolo [BarChris's president] asked him to become a director of BarChris. In February and early March 1961, before accepting Vitolo's invitation, Auslander made some investigation of BarChris. He obtained Dun & Bradstreet reports that contained sales and earnings figures for periods earlier than December 31, 1960. He caused inquiry to be made of certain of BarChris's banks and was advised that they regarded BarChris favorably. He was informed that inquiry of Talcott had also produced a favorable response.

On March 3, 1961, Auslander indicated his willingness to accept a place on the board. Shortly thereafter, on March 14, Kircher sent him a copy of BarChris's annual report for 1960. Auslander observed that BarChris's auditors were Peat, Marwick. They were also the auditors for the Valley Stream National Bank. He thought well of them.

Auslander was elected a director on April 17, 1961. The registration statement in its original form had already been filed, of course without his signature. On May 10, 1961, he signed a signature page for the first amendment to the registration statement which was filed on May 11, 1961. This was a separate sheet without any document attached. Auslander did not know that it

was a signature page for a registration statement. He vaguely understood that it was something "for the SEC."

At the May 15 directors' meeting, however, Auslander did realize that what he was signing was a signature sheet to a registration statement. This was the first time that he had appreciated the fact. A copy of the registration statement in its earlier form as amended on May 11, 1961, was passed around at the meeting. Auslander glanced at it briefly. He did not read it thoroughly. At the May 15 meeting, Russo and Vitolo stated that everything was in order and that the prospectus was correct. Auslander believed this statement.

In considering Auslander's due diligence defenses, a distinction must be drawn between the expertised and nonexpertised portions of the prospectus. As to the former, Auslander knew that Peat, Marwick had audited the 1960 figures. He believed them to be correct because he had confidence in Peat, Marwick. He had no reasonable ground to believe otherwise.

As to the nonexpertised portions, however, Auslander is in a different position. He seems to have been under the impression that Peat, Marwick was responsible for all the figures. This impression was not correct, as he would have realized if he had read the prospectus carefully. Auslander made no investigation of the accuracy of the prospectus. He relied on the assurance of Vitolo and Russo, and upon the information he had received in answer to his inquiries back in February and early March. These inquiries were general ones, in the nature of a credit check. The information which he received in answer to them was also general, without specific reference to the statements in the prospectus, which was not prepared until some time thereafter.

It is true that Auslander became a director on the eve of the financing. He had little opportunity to familiarize himself with the company's affairs. The question is whether, under such circumstances, Auslander did enough to establish his due diligence.

Section 11 imposes liability upon a director, no matter how new he is. He is presumed to know his responsibility when he becomes a director. He can escape liability only by using that reasonable care to investigate the facts that a prudent man would employ in the management of his own property. In my opinion, a prudent man would not act in an important matter without any knowledge of the relevant facts, in sole reliance upon general information which does not purport to cover the particular case. To say that such minimal conduct measures up to the statutory standard would, to all intents and purposes, absolve new directors from responsibility merely because they are new. This is not a sensible construction of Section 11, when one bears in mind its fundamental purpose of requiring full and truthful disclosure for the protection of investors.

Auslander has not established his due diligence defense with respect to the misstatements and omissions in those portions of the prospectus other than the audited 1960 figures.

Peat, Marwick

The part of the registration statement purporting to be made upon the authority of Peat, Marwick as an expert was the 1960 figures. But because the statute requires the court to determine Peat, Marwick's belief, and the grounds thereof, "at the time such part of the registration statement became effective," for the purposes of this affirmative defense, the matter must be viewed as of May 16, 1961, and the question is whether at that time Peat, Marwick, after reasonable investigation, had reasonable ground to believe and did believe that the 1960 figures were true and that no material fact had been omitted from the registration statement which should have been included in order to make the 1960 figures not misleading. In deciding this issue, the court must consider not only what Peat, Marwick did in its 1960 audit, but also what it did in its subsequent S–1 review. The proper scope of that review must also be determined.

The 1960 Audit

Peat, Marwick's work was in general charge of a member of the firm, Cummings, and more immediately in charge of Peat, Marwick's manager, Logan. Most of the actual work was performed by a senior accountant, Berardi, who had junior assistants, one of whom was Kennedy.

Berardi was then about 30 years old. He was not yet a CPA. He had had no previous experience with the bowling industry. This was his first job as a senior accountant. He could hardly have been given a more difficult assignment.

It is unnecessary to recount everything that Berardi did in the course of the audit. We are concerned only with the evidence relating to what Berardi did or did not do with respect to those items which I have found to have been incorrectly reported in the 1960 figures in the prospectus. More narrowly, we are directly concerned only with such of those items as I have found to be material.

First and foremost is Berardi's failure to discover that Capitol Lanes had not been sold. This error affected both the sales figure and the liability side of the balance sheet. Fundamentally, the error stemmed from the fact that Berardi never realized that Heavenly Lanes and Capitol were two different names for the same alley. Berardi assumed that Heavenly was to be treated like any other completed job.

Berardi read the minutes of the board of directors meeting of November 22, 1960, which recited that "the Chairman recommended that the Corporation operate Capitol Lanes." Berardi knew from various BarChris records that Capitol Lanes, Inc., was paying rentals to Talcott. Also, a Peat, Marwick work paper bearing Kennedy's initials recorded that Capitol Lanes, Inc., held certain insurance policies.

Berardi testified that he inquired of Russo about Capitol Lanes and that Russo told him that Capitol Lanes, Inc., was going to operate an alley someday but as yet it had no alley. Berardi testified that he understood that the alley had not been built and that he believed that the rental payments were on vacant land.

I am not satisfied with this testimony. If Berardi did hold this belief, he should not have held it. The entries as to insurance and as to "operation of alley" should have alerted him to the fact that an alley existed. He should have made further inquiry on the subject. It is apparent that Berardi did not understand this transaction.

He never identified this mysterious Capitol with the Heavenly Lanes which he had included in his sales and profit figures. The vital question is whether he failed to make a reasonable investigation which, if he had made it, would have revealed the truth.

Certain accounting records of BarChris, which Berardi testified he did not see, would have put him on inquiry. One was a job cost ledger card for job no. 6036, the job number which Berardi put on his own sheet for Heavenly Lanes. This card read "Capitol Theatre (Heavenly)." In addition, two accounts receivable cards each showed both names on the same card, Capitol and Heavenly. Berardi testified that he looked at the accounts receivable records but that he did not see these particular cards. He testified that he did not look on the job cost ledger cards because he took the costs from another record, the costs register.

The burden of proof on this issue is on Peat, Marwick. Although the question is a rather close one, I find that Peat, Marwick has not sustained that burden. Peat, Marwick has not proved that Berardi made a reasonable investigation as far as Capitol Lanes was concerned and that his ignorance of the true facts was justified.

I turn now to the errors in the current assets. As to cash, Berardi properly obtained a confirmation from the bank as to BarChris's cash balance on December 31, 1960. He did not know that part of this balance had been temporarily increased by the deposit of reserves returned by Talcott to BarChris conditionally for a limited time. I do not believe that Berardi reasonably should have known this. It would not be reasonable to require Berardi to examine all of BarChris's correspondence files [which contained correspondence indicating that BarChris was to return the cash to Talcott] when he had no reason to suspect any irregularity.

The S–1 Review

The purpose of reviewing events subsequent to the date of a certified balance sheet (referred to as an S–1 review when made with reference to a registration statement) is to ascertain whether any material change has occurred in the company's financial position which should be disclosed in order to prevent the balance sheet figures from being misleading. The scope of such a review, under generally accepted auditing standards, is limited. It does not amount to a complete audit.

Berardi made the S–1 review in May 1961. He devoted a little over two days to it, a total of 20½ hours. He did not discover any of the errors or omissions pertaining to the state of affairs in 1961, all of which were material. The question is whether, despite his failure to find out anything, his investigation was reasonable within the meaning of the statute.

What Berardi did was to look at a consolidating trial balance as of March 31, 1961, which had been prepared by BarChris, compare it with the audited December 31, 1960, figures, discuss with Trilling certain unfavorable developments which the comparison disclosed, and read certain minutes. He did not examine any important financial records other than the trial balance.

In substance, Berardi asked questions, he got answers which he considered satisfactory, and he did nothing to verify them. Since he never read the prospectus, he was not even aware that there had ever been any problem about loans from officers. He made no inquiry of factors about delinquent notes in his S–1 review. Since he knew nothing about Kircher's notes of the executive committee meetings, he did not learn that the delinquency situation had grown worse. He was content with Trilling's assurance that no liability theretofore contingent had become direct. Apparently the only BarChris officer with whom Berardi communicated was Trilling. He could not recall making any inquiries of Russo, Vitolo, or Pugliese [a BarChris vice president].

There had been a material change for the worse in BarChris's financial position. That change was sufficiently serious so that the failure to disclose it made the 1960 figures misleading. Berardi did not discover it. As far as results were concerned, his S–1 review was useless.

Accountants should not be held to a standard higher than that recognized in their profession. I do not do so here. Berardi's review did not come up to that standard. He did not take some of the steps which Peat, Marwick's written program prescribed. He did not spend an adequate amount of time on a task of this magnitude. Most important of all, he was too easily satisfied with glib answers to his inquiries.

This is not to say that he should have made a complete audit. But there were enough danger signals in the materials which he did examine to require some further investigation on his part. Generally accepted auditing standards require such further investigation under these circumstances. It is not always sufficient merely to ask questions.

Here again, the burden of proof is on Peat, Marwick. I find that burden has not been satisfied. I conclude that Peat, Marwick has not established its due diligence defense.

Judgment for Escott and the other purchasers.

Due Diligence Meeting Officers, directors, underwriters, accountants, and other experts attempt to reduce their Section 11 liability by holding a due diligence meeting at the end of the waiting period, just prior to the effective date of a registration statement. At the due diligence meeting, the participants obtain assurances and demand proof from each other that the registration statement contains no misstatements or omissions of material fact. If it appears from the meeting that there are inadequacies in the investigation of the information in the registration statement, the issuer will delay the effective date until an appropriate investigation is undertaken.

Statute of Limitations Under Section 11, a defendant has liability for only a limited period of time, pursuant to a statute of limitations. A purchaser must sue the defendant within one year after the misstatement or omission was or should have been discovered by the purchaser. In addition, the purchaser may sue the defendant not more than three years after the securities were offered to the public. Although the word "offered" is used in the statute, the three-year period does not usually begin until after the registered securities are first delivered to a purchaser. The Sarbanes–Oxley Act of 2002 arguably extends the statute of limitations to two years after discovery of facts constituting a violation of Section 11 and five years after the violation.

Other Liability Provisions Section 12(a)(2) of the 1933 Act prohibits misstatements or omissions of material fact in any written or oral communication in connection with the general distribution of any security by an issuer (except government-issued or government-guaranteed securities). Section 17(a) prohibits the use of any device or artifice to defraud, or the use of any untrue or misleading statement, in connection with the offer or sale of any security. Two of the subsections of Section 17(a) require that the defendant merely act negligently, while the third subsection requires proof of scienter. Scienter is the intent to deceive, manipulate, or defraud the purchaser. Some courts have held that scienter also includes recklessness.

Due Diligence Defenses under Section 11 of the 1933 Act

	For Expertised Portion of the Registration Statement	For Nonexpertised Portion of the Registration Statement
Expert Liable only for the expertised portion of the registration statement contributed by the expert. Examples: Auditor that issues an audit opinion regarding financial statements; Geologist that issues an opinion regarding mineral reserves; Lawyer that issues a tax opinion regarding the tax deductibility of losses	After a reasonable investigation, had reason to believe and did believe that there were no misstatements or omissions of material fact in the expertised portion of the registration statement contributed by the expert.	Not liable for this portion of the registration statement.
Nonexpert Liable for the entire registration statement. Examples: Directors of the issuer; CEO, CFO, and CAO of the issuer; Underwriters who assist in the sale of the securities and help prepare the registration statement	Had no reason to believe and did not believe that there were any misstatements or omissions of material fact in the expertised portions of the registration statement.	After a reasonable investigation, had reason to believe and did believe that there were no misstatements or omissions of material fact in the nonexpertised portion of the registration statement.

Since these liability sections are part of federal law, there must be some connection between the illegal activity and interstate commerce for liability to exist. Section 11 merely requires the filing of a registration statement with the SEC. Sections 12(a)(1), 12(a)(2), and 17(a) require the use of the mails or other instrumentality or means of interstate communication or transportation. Chapter 46 has more information on liability under Sections 11, 12(a)(2), and 17(a).

Criminal Liability Section 24 of the 1933 Act provides for criminal liability for any person who willfully violates the Act or its rules and regulations. The maximum penalty is a $10,000 fine and five years' imprisonment. Criminal actions under the 1933 Act are brought by the attorney general of the United States, not by the SEC.

 Understand why and demonstrate how the law regulates issuances and issuers of securities.

Securities Exchange Act of 1934

The Securities Exchange Act of 1934 is chiefly concerned with requiring the disclosure of material information to investors. Unlike the 1933 Act, which is primarily a one-time disclosure statute concerned with protecting investors when an issuer sells its shares to investors, the 1934 Act requires **periodic disclosure** by issuers with publicly held equity securities. That is, the 1934 Act is primarily concerned with protecting investors after the issuer becomes a public company. An issuer with publicly traded equity securities must report annually to its shareholders and submit annual and quarterly reports to the SEC. Also, any material information about the issuer must be disclosed as the issuer obtains it, unless the issuer has a valid business purpose for withholding disclosure.

In addition, the 1934 Act regulates insiders' transactions in securities, proxy solicitations, tender offers, brokers and dealers, and securities exchanges. The 1934 Act also has several sections prohibiting fraud and manipulation in securities transactions. The ultimate purpose of the 1934 Act is to keep investors fully informed to allow them to make intelligent investment decisions at any time.

Registration of Securities under the 1934 Act
Under the 1934 Act, issuers must **register classes of securities.** This is different from the 1933 Act, which requires issuers to register issuances of securities. Under the 1933 Act, securities are registered only for the term of an issuance. Under the 1934 Act, registered classes of securities remain registered until the issuer takes steps to deregister the securities. The chief consequence of having securities registered under the 1934 Act is that the issuer is required periodically to disclose information about itself to its owners and the SEC.

Registration Requirement Two types of issuers must register securities with the SEC under the 1934 Act.

1. An issuer whose total assets exceed $10 million must register a class of equity securities held by at least 500 holders if the securities are traded in interstate commerce.

2. An issuer must register any security traded on a national security exchange, such as common shares traded on the New York Stock Exchange or NASDAQ.

To register the securities, the issuer must file a 1934 Act **registration statement** with the SEC. The information required in the 1934 Act registration statement is similar to that required in the 1933 Act registration statement, except that offering information is omitted.

Termination of Registration An issuer may avoid the expense and burden of complying with the periodic disclosure and other requirements of the 1934 Act if the issuer terminates its registration. A 1934 Act registration of a class of securities may be terminated if the issuer has fewer than 300 shareholders of that class. In addition, a registration may be terminated if the issuer has fewer than 500 shareholders of the registered class of equity securities and assets of no more than $10 million for each of the last three years. However, an issuer with securities listed on a national securities exchange would not be able to terminate a registration of the listed securities.

Periodic Reporting Requirement To maintain a steady flow of material information to investors, the 1934 Act requires public issuers to file periodic reports with the SEC. Three types of issuers must file such reports:

1. An issuer whose total assets exceed $10 million and who has a class of equity securities held by at least 500 holders, if the securities are traded in interstate commerce.

The Global Business Environment

Securities Regulation of Global Issuers

All market-based economies have securities laws regulating the issuance and trading of securities. Even the Republic of China, which allows limited capitalism, has a comprehensive securities law, although not as extensive as United States law. All foreign laws regulate the issuance of securities, securities exchanges, and securities professionals.

Most countries' securities law applies equally to domestic and foreign issuers of securities. In the United States, for example, foreign issuers must register an issuance with the SEC in the same way a domestic company registers, under Regulation C.

Canadian securities law is similar to American law, although primarily enacted by the provinces and territories instead of the national government. Nonetheless, Canadian securities law is substantially similar throughout Canada. In general, domestic and foreign issuers must make securities offerings with a prospectus that has been filed with a securities commissioner. One exemption from registration is the private issuer exemption, which may be used by a nonpublic company with no more than 50 security holders. Another exemption is for offerings to a purchaser not exceeding C$150,000. While securities qualified by a prospectus may generally be freely traded in the secondary market, securities sold through an exemption must be held by the initial purchasers for 6 to 18 months, depending on the exemption.

For more information on international securities law, visit the website of the International Organization of Securities Commissions at www.iosco.org.

2. An issuer whose securities are traded on a national securities exchange.

3. An issuer who has made a registered offering of securities under the 1933 Act.

The first two types of issuers—which are issuers that must also register securities under the 1934 Act—must file several periodic reports, including an annual report (Form 10-K) and a quarterly report (Form 10-Q). They must file a current report (Form 8-K) when material events occur. Comparable reports must also be sent to their shareholders. The third type of issuer—an issuer who must disclose under the 1934 Act only because it has made a registered offering under the 1933 Act—must file the same reports as the other issuers, except that it need not provide an annual report to its shareholders. 1934 Act disclosure required of the third type of issuer is in addition to the disclosure required by the 1933 Act.

The 10-K annual report must include audited financial statements plus current information about the conduct of the business, its management, and the status of its securities. It includes management's description and analysis of the issuer's financial condition (the so-called MDA section) and the names of directors and executive officers, including their compensation (such as salary and stock options). The 10-K auditing requirements are the same as for a 1933 Act registration statement—two years' audited balance sheets, three years' audited income statements, and three years' audited statements of changes in financial position.

The quarterly report, the 10-Q, requires only a summarized, unaudited operating statement and unaudited figures on capitalization and shareholders' equity. The 8-K current report must be filed within four business days of the occurrence of the event, such as a change in the amount of securities, an acquisition or disposition of assets, a change in control of the company, a revaluation of assets, or "any materially important event."

The SEC permits issuers to file reports electronically, transmitting them by telephone or by sending computer tapes or disks to the SEC. These electronic filings are made with the SEC's Electronic Data Gathering, Analysis, and Retrieval system (EDGAR).

LOG ON

www.sec.gov/edgar.shtml
The SEC's Internet homepage gives anyone access to the EDGAR database.

Issuers have historically mailed to their shareholders written copies of their annual reports and other periodic disclosure statements. Today, issuers are able to transmit such reports over the Internet. The Internet increases investors' access to information and can reduce the issuer's costs as well.

Suspension of Duty to File Reports An issuer's duty to file periodic reports with regard to a class of securities is suspended if the issuer has fewer than 300 holders of that class. In addition, a suspension occurs if the issuer has fewer than 500 holders of that class of securities and assets of no more than $10 million. However, an issuer with securities traded on a national securities exchange would remain obligated to file periodic reports with respect to those securities.

Holdings and Trading by Insiders Section 16 of the 1934 Act is designed to promote investor confidence in the integrity of the securities markets by limiting the ability of insiders to profit from trading in the shares of their issuers. Section 16(a) requires statutory insiders to disclose their ownership of their company's securities within 10 days of becoming owners. In addition, statutory insiders must report any subsequent transaction in such securities within two business days after the trade.

A statutory insider is a person who falls into any of the following categories:

1. An officer of a corporation having equity securities registered under the 1934 Act.

2. A director of such a corporation.

3. An owner of more than 10 percent of a class of equity securities registered under the 1934 Act.

Section 16(b) prevents an insider from profiting from short-swing trading in his company's shares. Any profit made by a statutory insider is recoverable by the issuer if the profit resulted from the purchase and sale (or the sale and purchase) of any class of the issuer's equity securities within less than a six-month period. This provision was designed to stop speculative insider trading on the basis of information that "may have been obtained by such owner, director, or officer by reason of his relationship to the issuer." The application of the provision is without regard to intent to use or actual use of inside information. However, a few cases have held that sales made by a statutory insider without actual access to inside information do not violate Section 16(b).

Proxy Solicitation Regulation

In a public corporation, shareholders rarely attend and vote at shareholder meetings. Many shareholders are able to vote at shareholder meetings only by **proxy,** a document by which shareholders direct other persons to vote their shares. Just as investors need information to be able to make intelligent investment decisions, shareholders need information to make intelligent voting and proxy decisions.

The 1934 Act regulates the solicitation of proxies. Regulation 14A requires any person soliciting proxies from holders of securities registered under the 1934 Act to furnish each holder with a **proxy statement** containing voting information. Usually, the only party soliciting proxies is the corporation's management, which is seeking proxies from common shareholders to enable it to reelect itself to the board of directors.

If the management of the corporation does not solicit proxies, it must nevertheless inform the shareholders of material information affecting matters that are to be put to a vote of the shareholders. This **information statement,** which contains about the same information as a proxy statement, must be sent to all shareholders that are entitled to vote at the meeting.

The primary purpose of the SEC rules concerning information that must be included in the proxy or information statement is to permit shareholders to make informed decisions while voting for directors and considering any resolutions proposed by the management or shareholders. Information on each director nominee must include the candidate's principal occupation, his shareholdings in the corporation, his previous service as a director of the corporation, his material transactions with the corporation (such as goods or services provided), and his directorships in other corporations. The total remuneration of the five directors or officers who are highest paid, including bonuses, grants under stock option plans, fringe benefits, and other perquisites, must also be included in the proxy statement.

SEC rules regarding the content of proxies ensure that the shareholder understands how his proxy will be voted. The proxy form must indicate in boldface type on whose behalf it is being solicited—for example, the corporation's management. Generally, the proxy must permit the shareholder to vote for or against the proposal or to abstain from voting on any resolutions on the meeting's agenda. The proxy form may ask for discretionary voting authority if the proxy indicates in bold print how the shares will be voted. For directors' elections, the shareholders must be provided with a means for withholding approval for each nominee.

Modern technology has greatly increased the ease with which shareholders may participate in shareholder votes and meetings, as well as reducing the cost of counting shareholder votes. Shareholders can vote electronically by phone and on the Internet. Some companies broadcast their shareholder meetings by satellite, and others webcast their shareholder meetings.

SEC Rule 14a–9 prohibits misstatements or omissions of material fact in the course of a proxy solicitation. If a violation is proved, a court may enjoin the holding of the shareholders' meeting, void the proxies that were illegally obtained, or rescind the action taken at the shareholders' meeting.

Proxy Contests   A shareholder may decide to solicit proxies in competition with management. Such a competition is called a proxy contest, and a solicitation of this kind is also subject to SEC rules. To facilitate proxy contests, the SEC requires the corporation either to furnish a shareholder list to shareholders who desire to wage a proxy contest or to mail the competing proxy material for them. The Dodd–Frank Act goes one step further, authorizing the SEC to issue rules permitting a shareholder to use a corporation's proxy solicitation materials to nominate persons to stand for election to the board of directors.

Perhaps the most hotly contested proxy battle ever was fought in 2002 between the management of Hewlett-Packard, which wanted to merge with Compaq, and Walter Hewitt, the son of H-P's co-founder and leader of shareholders opposed to the merger. Both sides were well organized, and each deluged shareholders with proxy solicitation material. A mere 51 percent of H-P shareholders gave the merger a narrow victory. By contrast, about 90 percent of Compaq shareholders approved the merger.

Shareholder Proposals   In a large public corporation, it is very expensive for a shareholder to solicit proxies in support of a proposal for corporate action that she will offer at a shareholders' meeting. Therefore, she usually asks the management to include her proposal in its proxy statement. SEC Rule 14a–8 covers proposals by shareholders.

Under SEC Rule 14a–8, the corporation must include a shareholder's proposal in its proxy statement if, among other things, the shareholder owns at least 1 percent or $2,000 of the securities to be voted at the shareholders' meeting. A shareholder may submit only one proposal per meeting. The proposal and its supporting statement may not exceed 500 words.

Ethics in Action

Sarbanes–Oxley Act of 2002

In 2001 and 2002, the discovery of financial irregularities in financial statements of nearly two dozen companies—notably Enron, Global Crossing, and World-Com—led to the bankruptcy of some companies, cost investors billions of dollars, and contributed to the bear stock market of 2001 and 2002. While many ordinary investors lost a lifetime of savings, corporate insiders received and profited from lucrative stock options, bonuses, and favorable loans that were sometimes not repaid.

Consequently, Congress passed the Sarbanes–Oxley Act of 2002 (SOX), which was designed to restore integrity to corporate financial statements and revive investor confidence in the securities markets. The Sarbanes–Oxley Act attempts to accomplish these objectives by imposing a wide array of new responsibilities on public corporations and their executives and auditors. All the provisions result from the crisis of ethics, in which some corporate officers and auditors preferred their selfish interests over those of the corporation and its shareholders, creditors, and other stakeholders.

Because some public companies were manipulating their balance sheets by omitting liabilities of certain affiliate entities, SOX requires that 10-Ks and 10-Qs filed with the SEC disclose material off-balance sheet transactions. To increase the likelihood that auditors will not give in to corporate executives' pressure to account improperly for corporate transactions, SOX requires greater independence between the auditor and the corporation by prohibiting the audit firm from performing most types of consulting services for the corporation. Moreover, officers and directors are prohibited from coercing auditors into creating misleading financial statements. To ensure that auditors are serving the interests of shareholders and not those of corporate managers, SOX requires auditors to be hired and overseen by an audit committee whose members are independent of the CEO and other corporate executives.

In addition, the CEO and CFO of a public company must certify that the corporation's financial reports fairly present the company's operations and financial condition. To eliminate the CEO and CFO's incentive to manipulate earnings, the CEO and CFO must disgorge bonuses, other incentivebased compensation, and profits on stock sales that were received during the 12-month period before financial statements are restated due to material misstatements or omissions. Public corporations are also generally prohibited from making loans to officers and directors. To encourage the use of ethics codes, SOX requires public companies to disclose whether they have ethics codes for senior financial officers.

Finally, SOX gives the SEC several new powers, including the authority to freeze payments to officers and directors during any lawful investigation. The SEC may also bar "unfit" persons from serving as directors and officers of public companies. The previous standard was "substantial unfitness."

SOX Section 404

The most controversial part of the Sarbanes–Oxley Act has been Section 404, which requires that annual reports include an "internal control report" acknowledging management's responsibility to maintain "an adequate internal control structure and procedures for financial reports." The benefits of Section 404 are evident and substantial, yet the costs are as well. The benefits include more active participation by the board, audit committee, and management in internal controls; increased embedding of control concepts including a better understanding by operating personnel and management of their control responsibilities; improvements in the adequacy of audit trails; and a revival of basic controls such as segregation of duties and reconciliation of accounts that have been eroded as businesses downsized and consolidated.

The cost of initial compliance with Section 404 averaged about $3 million per company in 2004. That cost included an increase in employee hours, averaging about 26,000, when the SEC had estimated that only 383 staff hours would be required. In addition, companies paid higher fees to auditors, who have the additional Section 404 burden of attesting to the assessment made by management. At one extreme, General Electric estimated it spent $30 million to comply with Section 404. One study concluded that the total private cost of Section 404 compliance was $1.4 trillion. Another study found that only 14 percent of firms believed that the benefits of Section 404 exceeded the up-front costs of Section 404 compliance. By 2007, the cost of complying with Section 404 was an average of $1.7 million for companies with a market capitalization above $75 million. Nonetheless, Financial Executives International found that 69 percent of financial executives agreed that compliance with SOX Section 404 resulted in more investor confidence in their companies' financial reporting. Fifty percent agreed that financial reports were more accurate.

In 2010, a study by Protivity reported that executives found that the cost of complying with SOX had declined on average 50 percent from the first year of SOX compliance and that most executives found the benefits of SOX outweighed its costs. 23 percent of respondents reported cost reductions of at least 70 percent. sixty-three percent found their costs declined at least 30 percent, while only 7 percent experienced cost increases.

Nonetheless, a study by Dr. Ivy Zhang of the University of Minnesota raises concerns about SOX. Dr. Zhang concluded that SOX contributed significantly to wiping $1.4 trillion off the value of the stock market. Zhang says some indirect costs of SOX compliance were not included in budgets by managers. "While SOX likely imposed significant direct compliance costs on firms, the indirect costs could be even greater. Executives have complained that complying with the details of the rules diverts their attention from normal business practices. Also, as SOX increases the litigation risks for executives, managers are likely to behave more conservatively than shareholders would prefer. These changes could have long-lasting and far-reaching influence on business practices."

Under Rule 14a–8, a corporation's management may exclude many types of shareholder proposals from its proxy statement. For example, a proposal is excludable if:

1. The proposal deals with the ordinary business operations of the corporation. For example, Pacific Telesis Group was permitted on this ground to omit a proposal that the board consider adding an environmentalist director and designate a vice president for environmental matters for each subsidiary. However, TRW, Inc., was required to include in its proxy statement a proposal that it establish a shareholder advisory committee that would advise the board of directors on the interests of shareholders.

2. The proposal relates to operations that account for less than 5 percent of a corporation's total assets and is not otherwise significantly related to the company's business. For example, Harsco Corp. could not omit a proposal that it sell its 50 percent interest in a South African firm even though the investment was arguably economically insignificant—only 4.5 percent of net earnings—because the issues raised by the proposal were significantly related to Harsco's business.

3. The proposal requires the issuer to violate a state or federal law. For example, one shareholder asked North American Bank to put a lesbian on the board of directors. The proposal was excludable because it may have required the bank to violate antidiscrimination laws.

4. The proposal relates to a personal claim or grievance. A proposal that the corporation pay the shareholder $1 million for damages that she suffered from using one of the corporation's products would be excludable.

In addition, Rule 14a–8 prevents a shareholder from submitting a proposal similar to recent proposals that have been overwhelmingly rejected by shareholders in recent years.

 LO1 Engage in behavior that avoids liability under the federal securities laws.

Liability Provisions of the 1934 Act

To prevent fraud, deception, or manipulation in securities transactions and to provide remedies to the victims of such practices, Congress included provisions in the 1934 Act that impose liability on persons who engage in wrongful conduct.

Liability for False Statements in Filed Documents Section 18 is the 1934 Act counterpart to Section 11 of the 1933 Act. Section 18 imposes liability on any person responsible for a false or misleading statement of material fact in any document filed with the SEC under the 1934 Act. (Filed documents include the 10-K report, 8-K report, and proxy statements, but the 10-Q report is not considered filed for Section 18 purposes.) Any person who relies on a false or misleading statement in such a filed document may sue for damages. The purchaser need not prove that the defendant was at fault. Instead, the defendant has a defense that he acted in good faith and had no knowledge that the statement was false or misleading. This defense requires only that the defendant prove that he did not act with scienter.

Section 10(b) and Rule 10b–5 The most important liability section in the 1934 Act is Section 10(b), an extremely broad provision prohibiting the use of any manipulative or deceptive device in contravention of any rules that the SEC prescribes as "necessary or appropriate in the public interest or for the protection of investors." Rule 10b–5 was adopted by the SEC under Section 10(b). The rule states:

> It shall be unlawful for any person, directly or indirectly, by use of any means or instrumentality of interstate commerce or of the mails, or of any facility of any national securities exchange,
> (a) to employ any device, scheme, or artifice to defraud,
> (b) to make any untrue statement of a material fact or to omit to state a material fact necessary in order to make the statements made, in the light of the circumstances under which they were made, not misleading, or
> (c) to engage in any act, practice, or course of business which operates or would operate as a fraud or deceit upon any person, in connection with the purchase or sale of any security.

Rule 10b–5 applies to all transactions in all securities, whether or not registered under the 1933 Act or the 1934 Act.

Elements of a Rule 10b–5 Violation The most important elements of a Rule 10b–5 violation are a misstatement or omission of material fact and scienter. In addition, private persons suing under the rule must be purchasers or sellers of securities who relied on the misstatement or omission.

Misstatement or Omission of Material Fact Rule 10b–5 prohibits only *misstatements or omissions of material fact*. A person **misstates** material facts, for example, when a manager of an unprofitable business induces shareholders to sell their stock to him by stating that the business will fail, although he knows that the business has become potentially profitable.

Liability for an **omission of a material fact** arises when a person fails to disclose material facts when he has a duty to disclose. For example, a securities broker is liable to his customer for not disclosing that he owns the shares that he recommends to the customer. As an agent of the customer, he owes a fiduciary duty to his customer to disclose his conflict of interest. In addition, a person is liable for omitting to tell all of the material facts after he has chosen to disclose some of them. His incomplete disclosure creates the duty to disclose all of the material facts.

Materiality Under Rule 10b–5, the misstated or omitted fact must be **material.** In essence, material information is any information that is likely to have an impact on the price of a security in the market. A fact is material if there is a substantial likelihood that a reasonable investor would consider it important to his decision, that the fact would have assumed actual significance in the deliberations of the reasonable investor, and that the disclosure of the fact would have been viewed by the reasonable investor as having significantly altered the total mix of information made available.

When there is doubt whether an important event will occur, the *Texas Gulf Sulphur*[5] case holds that materiality of the doubtful event can be determined by "a balancing of both the indicated probability that the event will occur and the anticipated magnitude of the event in light of the totality of the company activity."

Scienter Under Rule 10b–5, the defendant is not liable unless he acted with **scienter.** Scienter is an intent to deceive, manipulate, or defraud. Scienter includes gross recklessness of the defendant in ascertaining the truth of his statements. Mere negligence is not scienter, but some courts hold that simple recklessness is sufficient proof of scienter.

Other Elements Rule 10b–5 requires that private plaintiffs seeking damages be **actual purchasers or sellers** of securities. Persons who were deterred from purchasing securities by fraudulent statements may not recover lost profits under Rule 10b–5.

Under Rule 10b–5, private plaintiffs alleging damages caused by misstatements by the defendant must prove that they **relied** on the misstatement of material fact. The SEC as plaintiff need not prove reliance. For private plaintiffs, reliance is not usually required in omission cases; the investor need merely prove that the omitted fact was material. In addition, the misstatement or omission must **cause the investor's loss.** The Supreme Court has held, however, that proof of loss causation is not required for certification of class action status.[6]

Several courts have held that an investor's reliance on the availability of the securities on the market satisfies the reliance requirement of Rule 10b–5 because the securities market is defrauded as to the value of the securities. This **fraud-on-the-market theory** is based on the hypothesis that, in an open and developed securities market, the price of a company's stock is determined by the available material information regarding the company and its business. With the presence of a market, the market is interposed between seller and buyer and, ideally, transmits information to the investor in the processed form of a market price. Thus, the market is performing a substantial part of the valuation process performed by the investor in a face-to-face transaction. The market is acting as the unpaid agent of the investor, informing him that given all the information available to it, the value of the stock is the same as the market price. Misleading statements will therefore defraud purchasers of stock even if the purchasers do not directly rely on the misstatements and even if the defendants never communicated with the plaintiffs.

In *Basic, Inc. v. Levinson,*[7] the Supreme Court held that the fraud-on-the-market theory permits a court to presume an investor's reliance merely from the public availability of material misrepresentations. That presumption, however, is rebuttable, such as by evidence that an investor knew the market price was incorrect.

For Rule 10b–5 to apply, the wrongful action must be accomplished *by the mails, with any means or instrumentality of interstate commerce,* or *on a national securities exchange.* This element satisfies the federal jurisdiction requirement. Use of the mails or a telephone within one state has been held to meet this element.

The scope of activities proscribed by Rule 10b–5 is not immediately obvious. While it is easy to understand that actual fraud and price manipulation are covered by the rule, two other areas are less easily mastered—the corporation's continuous disclosure obligation and insider trading.

---

[5]*SEC v. Texas Gulf Sulphur Co.,* 401 F.2d 833 (2d Cir.1968).

[6]*Erica P. John Fund, Inc. v. Halliburton Co.,* 131 S. Ct. 2179 (2011).
[7]*Basic, Inc. v. Levinson,* 485 U.S. 224 (1988).

A considerable amount of litigation under Rule 10b-5 has arisen in the wake of the recent credit crunch that began in 2007, including allegations that banks defrauded their shareholders and other investors who purchased their common shares and to whom they sold mortgage-backed securities. The following case involves Countrywide Financial Corporation, one of the companies hardest hit by the near financial collapse. The plaintiff, a hedge fund, was unsuccessful in its lawsuit against Countrywide, in part because of the hedge fund's investment sophistication.

SRM Global Fund L.P. v. Countrywide Financial Corp.
2010 U.S. Dist. LEXIS 60108 (S.D.N.Y. 2010)

Countrywide Financial Corporation billed itself an industry leader in originating and servicing subprime mortgages, that is, mortgage loans made to borrowers who did not qualify for the best market interest rates because of their poor credit histories. Countrywide offered pay-option adjustable rate mortgages, a type of ARM designed to give buyers flexibility in paying back their mortgage. The buyer could choose, in a given month, (1) to pay down the principal; (2) make an interest-only payment; or (3) make a minimum payment lower than the interest for the period. If a buyer chose option 3, the remaining interest was added to the loan principal.

SRM Global Fund Limited Partnership was a hedge fund, that is, a private investment company that invested in a variety of assets on behalf of its clients. Over time, SRM acquired 50 million shares of Countrywide common stock and other securities. In 2008, this investment lost nearly 90 percent of its value as Countrywide's financial condition deteriorated. SRM sued Countrywide and three of its officers under Securities Exchange Act Rule 10b-5. SRM alleged that the defendants knowingly misrepresented and omitted material facts.

SRM claimed that it relied on a variety of representations by Countrywide and its officers. In Countrywide's 2006 Form 10-K, filed on March 1, 2007, Countrywide represented that it had implemented a Liquidity Management Plan that would ensure Countrywide maintained adequate, appropriate, and cost-effective sources of liquidity under all market conditions. On May 23, 2007, Countrywide hosted a Fixed Income Investor Day meeting in New York City at which President and COO David Sambol represented that Countrywide's core fundamentals were strong. CFO Eric Sieracki's presentation at the Investor Day meeting touted Countrywide's strong asset liquidity and quality. On June 13, 2007, at Countrywide's annual shareholder meeting, Chairman and CEO Angelo Mozilo boasted of Countrywide's integration of strong capital and risk-management activities that kept the Company in excellent fiscal condition. Countrywide conducted a teleconference with SRM and others on July 24, 2007, concerning its earnings for the second quarter of 2007 during which Mozilo stated that "our Company is well-positioned to capitalize on opportunities during this transitional period in the mortgage business, which we believe will enhance the Company's long-term earnings growth prospects." During this teleconference, Sieracki stated that Countrywide had "adequate diversified and reliable sources of liquidity available."

Based upon these alleged misrepresentations, among others, SRM purchased 5.5 million shares of Countrywide common stock in the week following Countrywide's second quarter 2007 earnings call on July 24, 2007.

On August 2, 2007, Countrywide issued a press release entitled "Countrywide Comments on Its Strong Funding Liquidity and Financial Condition," stating that "our liquidity planning proved highly effective earlier during 2007 when market concerns first arose about subprime lending, and remains so today. Our mortgage company has significant short-term funding liquidity cushions. In fact, we have almost $50 billion of highly reliable short-term funding liquidity available as a cushion today." Countrywide's August 6, 2007, Form 8-K contained Countrywide's "Liquidity Source" schedule as of June 30, 2007, which reported that Countrywide's net available liquidity was $186.5 billion.

On August 13, 2007, Merrill Lynch issued an analyst report stating that Countrywide "has about $185 billion in available credit facilities, though the concern is that these facilities could be terminated or the terms changed meaningfully, thus impacting Countrywide's ability to operate normally. It is possible for Countrywide to go bankrupt." On August 23, 2007, Mozilo was interviewed on CNBC and during this interview he denounced the Merrill Lynch analysis of Countrywide as "baseless" and "irresponsible" and stated that "there is no more chance for bankruptcy today for Countrywide than there was six months ago, a year ago, two years ago. We are a very solid company."

SRM purchased more than 10.5 million shares of Countrywide common stock in the three weeks following Mozilo's CNBC interview.

On October 26, 2007, there was an unprecedented disruption in the capital markets and an abrupt loss in demand for loans and securities as well as increased credit costs related to continued deterioration in the housing market. On October 27, 2007,

Countrywide issued a press release and filed a Form 8-K announcing Countrywide's financial results for the third quarter of 2007, which included a quarterly loss of $1.25 billion, or $2.85 per share and a $1 billion write down of its loans and mortgage-backed securities. On February 29, 2008, Countrywide filed its Form 10-K for 2007 with the SEC, in which it disclosed that Countrywide held $28.42 billion of pay-option ARMs, and that the percentage of such loans which were at least 90 days past due had risen 800 percent from a year earlier, from 0.6 percent to 5.4 percent, and 71 percent of its pay-option adjustable rate mortgage borrowers were making only minimal payments that covered only part of the interest normally due, thus causing their loan principals to grow.

On December 28, 2007, SRM executives Ian Barclay, John Myers, and Jon Wood participated in a teleconference with Countrywide Investor Relations employee David Bigelow and Sieracki during which Bigelow and Sieracki confirmed Countrywide's public statements regarding Countrywide's financial condition, liquidity, and capital reserves and told SRM that Countrywide had sufficient liquidity to last for 12 months.

Based upon these misrepresentations, among others, SRM purchased over 8.4 million shares of Countrywide in a two-week period following SRM's December 28, 2007, teleconference with Bigelow and Sieracki.

On January 11, 2008, Bank of America announced an agreement to purchase Countrywide in an all-stock transaction worth approximately $4 billion, which represented less than 30 percent of Countrywide's most recently reported book value. In SRM's view, the agreed price was too low, given Countrywide's repeated reassurances in public statements and directly to SRM regarding Countrywide's financial condition. On January 14, 2008, BOA's CEO Kenneth Lewis spoke in support of the merger, telling the investing public on behalf of Bank of America that Countrywide's bankruptcy was just "a malicious rumor" and that, after having "conducted twice as much due diligence as Bank of America ordinarily might have," Bank of America concluded that "there is great long-term value embedded in Countrywide's business" and that Countrywide "had a very impressive liquidity plan and had its backup lines in place."

On June 3, 2008, Barclay, Myers, and Wood met with Mozilo, Sambol, and Sieracki. At that meeting, Mozilo told the SRM executives that Countrywide had gone from being a viable company to being not viable during one week nearly a year before, in July 2007. Sambol told SRM that liquidity disappeared in one day, on August 2, 2007.

Beginning June 24, 2008, SRM sold its Countrywide stock and thereby suffered substantial losses. On July 1, 2008, Bank of America completed its acquisition of Countrywide.

SRM sued Countrywide, Mozilo, Sambol, and Sieracki in a New York federal district court under Securities Exchange Act § 10(b) and Rule 10b-5, as well as the state common law of fraud. SRM's lawsuit focused on a September 26, 2006, e-mail that Mozilo sent to Sambol and Sieracki, which stated, "We have no way, with any reasonably certainty, to assess the real risk of holding pay-option ARM loans on our balance sheet. The bottom line is that we are flying blind on how these loans will perform in a stressed environment of higher unemployment, reduced values and slowing home sales." SRM alleged that the e-mail shows that Countrywide and its executives knew they were "flying blind" with respect to the value of Countrywide's substantial pay-option ARM portfolio and thus knew that Countrywide's true financial condition was precarious and had no reasonable basis for their assurances about Countrywide's financial condition.

Countrywide asked the district to dismiss the lawsuit on the ground it failed to state a claim on which relief may be granted.

Berman, Judge

To survive a motion to dismiss, a complaint must contain sufficient factual matter, accepted as true, to state a claim to relief that is plausible on its face. This standard is met when the plaintiff pleads factual content that allows the court to draw the reasonable inference that the defendant is liable for the misconduct alleged.

Section 10(b) and Rule 10b-5 Claims

To state a claim under §10(b) and the corresponding Rule 10b-5, a plaintiff must plead that the defendant, in connection with the purchase or sale of securities, made a materially false statement or omitted a material fact, with scienter, and that the plaintiff's reliance on the defendant's action caused injury to the plaintiff.

Securities fraud actions are subject to the heightened pleading requirements of the Private Securities Litigation Reform Act of 1995, as well as those of Federal Rule of Civil Procedure 9(b), which require that plaintiffs (1) specify the statements that the plaintiff contends were fraudulent, (2) identify the speaker, (3) state where and when the statements were made, and (4) explain why the statements were fraudulent.

Each of the misrepresentations alleged in SRM's Amended Complaint were made in financial disclosures, news articles, television programs, teleconferences, or press releases which (1) specify the statements that SRM contends were fraudulent, (2) identify the speaker and (3) state where and when the statements were made. SRM has satisfied the first three prongs of the Rule 9(b) requirements.

The "fourth prong" is critical to the analysis here. And, with respect to the fourth prong, the Court separately analyzes: (a) the flying blind email; (b) the June 3, 2008 meeting; (c) Mozilo's and Lewis's denials of rumors of bankruptcy.

Flying Blind Email

It is indisputable that there can be no omission where the allegedly omitted facts are disclosed. Countrywide warned investors in its 2006 Form 10-K, filed on March 1, 2007, i.e., approximately five months before SRM's first purchase of Countrywide securities, that "due to the lack of significant historical experience at Countrywide, the credit performance of pay-option ARM loans has not been established for the Company." SRM does not explain why or how this Form 10-K disclosure was deficient. While the term "flying blind" may more colorfully convey Countrywide's "lack of significant historical experience" with pay-option ARMs, Countrywide and its executives were under no duty to employ the characterization that SRM believes is more accurate.

Countrywide made additional disclosures regarding pay-option ARMs before and during the Relevant Period. For example, on July 26, 2005, Mozilo stated that although pay-option ARMs were Countrywide's "lowest delinquency product at the moment . . . you have to wait some time for loans to mature a year, two years, even three years to determine how they're going to perform." (Transcript of Second Quarter 2005 Earnings Call, dated July 26, 2005.) Similarly, on July 25, 2006, Mozilo warned that if "interest rates continue to rise significantly, then the resets and payments shocks will be substantial" on pay-option ARMs. He further explained that "we just need time to see how this is going to play out. . . . The test will be when the resets take place and I'm not certain exactly what's going to happen there." (Transcript of Second Quarter 2006 Earnings Call, dated July 25, 2006.) And, in Countrywide's 2007 Form 10-K, filed with the SEC on February 28, 2008, Countrywide disclosed that it "has a significant investment in pay-option loans. Pay-option loans represent 32 percent and 45 percent of the Company's investment in mortgage loans held for investment at December 31, 2007 and 2006, respectively." With respect to these loans, Countrywide also disclosed in its 2007 Form 10-K that "our borrowers' ability to defer portions of the interest accruing on their loans may expose us to increased credit risk. This is because when the required monthly payments for these loans eventually increase, borrowers may be less able to pay the increased amounts and may be more likely to default than a borrower with a loan whose initial payment provides for full amortization. Our exposure to this higher credit risk is increased by the amount of deferred interest that has been added to the principal balance."

The Court is aware that whether an allegedly omitted fact was available to the market often is a fact intensive inquiry that is rarely an appropriate basis for dismissing. However, "rarely appropriate" is not the same as "never appropriate." Here, Countrywide's lack of significant historical experience with pay-option

ARMs was clearly disclosed in a document filed with the SEC on March 1, 2007. (See 2006 Form 6-K, filed Mar. 1, 2007.) The facts here show that all the information SRM claims was concealed by Countrywide was publicly available and on these facts the law renders Countrywide's purported misstatements immaterial.

SRM's claim that certain statements made by the Countrywide defendants after Mozilo sent the flying blind email to Sambol and Sieracki were misleading is undermined also by the theory upon which it is based—namely, fraud-on-the-market theory—because the market price of a stock is presumed to reflect all publicly available information. Such publicly available information includes Countrywide's 2006 and 2007 Forms 10-K and statements made during a July 25, 2006 teleconference with Mozilo and analysts. Plaintiff acknowledges that the market for Countrywide securities efficiently digested current information regarding the company from all publicly available sources and reflected such information in the price of Countrywide's securities. Thus, SRM cannot use this presumption to argue that the market price reflected Countrywide's purported misstatements but not the true statements contained in its press releases and SEC filings.

June 3, 2008 Meeting

SRM's Amended Complaint does not contain any allegations of facts supporting SRM's contention that any defendant knew, prior to the June 3, 2008 meeting, that Countrywide had ceased to be a viable company in July 2007 and liquidity had disappeared on August 2, 2007. It is not sufficient for SRM to contend that Countrywide defendants must have had access to contrary facts. The compelling inference urged by SRM, i.e., that the Countrywide defendants could, nearly a year later, identify so precisely when Countrywide ceased to be viable and liquidity disappeared because they recognized those events at or about the time they happened, is unavailing because the mere disclosure of adverse information shortly after a positive statement does not support a finding that the prior statement was false at the time it was made. SRM must specifically identify the reports or statements containing this information that were allegedly available to defendants and which showed that Countrywide had ceased to be a viable company in July 2007 and liquidity had disappeared on August 2, 2007. SRM does not claim that either Mozilo or Sambol said at this meeting that they knew or believed, as of August 2007, that the company was no longer viable without liquidity. These were statements made in and as of June 2008, with the benefit of hindsight, after having lived through the mortgage and housing crisis for a year. The defendants, like so many other institutions floored by the housing market crisis, could not have been expected to anticipate the crisis with the accuracy SRM enjoys in hindsight.

Bankruptcy Rumors

SRM argues, among other things, that assurances that Countrywide's bankruptcy was "just a malicious rumor" omitted the material fact that Countrywide was not a viable company. SRM does not identify any document or statement made by any of the defendants which indicates that, during the Relevant Period, Countrywide was on the verge of or considering bankruptcy. Even assuming, arguendo, that SRM has sufficiently alleged (which it has not) that Countrywide had ceased to be a viable company in July 2007 and liquidity had disappeared on August 2, 2007, SRM fails to support its apparent assumption that bankruptcy was the only option for Countrywide as opposed, for example, to a merger (which, in fact, occurred), a sale of assets, a reduction in expenses or capital expenditures, a new business strategy, or an acquisition of additional credit lines.

Fraud

The elements of common law fraud are largely the same as those of a Rule 10b-5 claim. However, the two actions maintain meaningful distinctions. For example, common law fraud cases are to be distinguished from cases that involved a fraud-on-the-market theory or other theories in which reliance on a material omission is presumed to have existed. And, under New York law, the asserted reliance must be found to be justifiable under all the circumstances before a complaint can be found to state a cause of action in fraud. In evaluating whether a plaintiff has adequately alleged justifiable reliance, a court may consider, inter alia, the plaintiff's sophistication and expertise in finance, the existence of a fiduciary relationship, and whether the plaintiff initiated the transaction.

Countrywide's motion to dismiss is granted because SRM has failed to allege that the Countrywide defendants made a material misstatement or omission. But, even assuming, arguendo, that SRM had identified actionable misstatements or omissions, SRM has failed to state a claim for common law fraud because, as a very sophisticated investor, its reliance upon these alleged misstatements or omissions would not be considered justifiable. SRM is a multi-billion dollar hedge fund that takes a contrarian and long-term investment approach in companies or sections that have been through periods of stress and are out of favor with the market. Moreover, prior to SRM's first alleged purchase of Countrywide securities on July 24, 2007, Countrywide warned investors in its 2006 Form 10-K, filed on March 1, 2007, that "due to the lack of significant historical experience at Countrywide, the credit performance of pay-option ARM loans has not been established for the Company." As a sophisticated investor, SRM would be obligated to investigate information available to it with the care and prudence expected from people blessed with full access to information. Consequently, as a sophisticated institution contemplating the investment of tens of millions of dollars, it was unreasonable for SRM to rely upon the highly general statements alleged as misstatements in this case.

Motion to dismiss granted in favor of Countrywide, Mozilo, Sambol, and Sieracki.

Continuous Disclosure Obligation The purpose of the 1934 Act is to ensure that investors have the information they need in order to make intelligent investment decisions at all times. The periodic reporting requirements of the 1934 Act are especially designed to accomplish this result. If important developments arise between the disclosure dates of reports, however, investors will not have all of the information they need to make intelligent decisions unless the corporation discloses the material information immediately. Rule 10b–5 requires a corporation to disclose material information immediately, unless the corporation has a valid business purpose for withholding disclosure. When a corporation chooses to disclose information or to comment on information that it has no duty to disclose, it must do so accurately.

Until 1988, courts had disagreed on whether Rule 10b–5 requires disclosure of merger and other acquisition negotiations prior to an agreement in principle. In *Basic, Inc. v. Levinson,* the Supreme Court of the United States held that materiality of merger negotiations is to be determined on a case-by-case basis. The Court held that materiality depends on the probability that the transaction will be consummated

and on its significance to the issuer of the securities. In addition, the Court stated that a corporation that chooses to comment on acquisition negotiations must do so truthfully.

In response to the *Basic* decision, the SEC released guidelines to help public companies decide whether they must disclose merger negotiations. A company is not required to disclose merger negotiations if all three of the following requirements are met:

1. The company did not make any prior disclosures about the merger negotiations,

2. Disclosure is not compelled by other SEC rules.

3. Management determines that disclosure would jeopardize completion of the merger transaction.

Forward-Looking Statements Because the risk of liability has caused corporations to couch disclosures in sometimes obscure language and because companies were reluctant to provide highly valuable but difficult to justify predictions of the companies' future, Congress chose in the Private Securities Litigation Reform Act to provide a safe-harbor for forward-looking statements. When a private lawsuit is based on a misstatement or omission of a material fact, no liability shall exist with respect to any forward-looking statement identified as a forward-looking statement and accompanied by meaningful cautionary statements that state important factors that could cause actual results to differ materially from those in the forward-looking statement. A company will also not be liable if the forward-looking statement was not made by or with the approval of an executive officer of that entity or if that officer had no actual knowledge that the statement was false or misleading. Note that the safe harbor is written in the disjunctive; that is, a defendant is not liable if the forward-looking statement is **identified** *and* accompanied by **meaningful cautionary language** *or* is **immaterial** *or* it was made **without actual knowledge** that it was false or misleading.

Trading on Inside Information One of the greatest destroyers of public confidence in the integrity of the securities market is the belief that insiders can trade securities while possessing corporate information that is not available to the general public.

Rule 10b–5 prohibits insider trading on nonpublic corporate information. A person with nonpublic, confidential, inside information may not use that information when trading with a person who does not possess that information. He must either disclose the information before trading or refrain from trading. The difficult task in the insider trading area is determining when a person is subject to this **disclose-or-refrain** rule.

In *United States v. Chiarella,*[8] the Supreme Court laid down the test for determining an insider's liability for trading on nonpublic, corporate information:

---

[8]445 U.S. 222 (U.S. Sup. Ct. 1980).

The duty to disclose arises when one party has information that the other party is entitled to know because of a fiduciary or similar relation of trust and confidence between them. A relationship of trust and confidence exists between the shareholders of a corporation and those insiders who have obtained confidential information by reason of their position with that corporation. This relationship gives rise to a duty to disclose because of the necessity of preventing a corporate insider from taking unfair advantage of the uninformed stockholders.

Under this test, **insiders** include not only officers and directors of the corporation, but also anyone who is *entrusted with corporate information for a corporate purpose* and *the corporation has a proper purpose for keeping the information confidential.* Insiders include outside consultants, lawyers, independent auditors, engineers, investment bankers, public relations advisers, news reporters, and personnel of government agencies who are given confidential corporate information for a corporate purpose.

Tippees are recipients of inside information (tips) from insiders. Tippees of insiders—such as relatives and friends of insiders, stockbrokers, and security analysts—are forbidden to trade on inside information and are subject to recovery of their profits if they do.

In *Dirks v. SEC,* the Supreme Court stated the applicability of Rule 10b–5 to tippees. The Court held that a tippee has liability if (1) an insider has breached a fiduciary duty of trust and confidence to the shareholders by disclosing to the tippee and (2) the tippee knows or should know of the insider's breach. In addition, the Court held that an insider has not breached her fiduciary duty to the shareholders unless she has received a personal benefit by disclosing to the tippee. See the Concept Review after the *Dirks* case for a comprehensive explanation of insider and tippee liability.

Dirks v. SEC   463 U.S. 646 (U.S. Sup. Ct. 1983)

On March 6, 1973, Raymond Dirks, a security analyst in a New York brokerage firm, received nonpublic information from Ronald Secrist, a former officer of Equity Funding of America, a seller of life insurance and mutual funds. Secrist alleged that the assets of Equity Funding were vastly overstated as the result of fraudulent corporate practices. He also stated that the SEC and state insurance departments had failed to act on similar charges of fraud made by Equity Funding employees. Secrist urged Dirks to verify the fraud and to disclose it publicly.

Dirks visited Equity Funding's headquarters in Los Angeles and interviewed several officers and employees of the corporation. The senior management denied any wrongdoing, but certain employees corroborated the charges of fraud. Dirks openly discussed the information he had obtained with a number of his clients and investors. Some of these persons sold their holdings of Equity Funding securities.

Dirks urged a Wall Street Journal reporter to write a story on the fraud allegations. The reporter, fearing libel, declined to write the story.

During the two-week period in which Dirks investigated the fraud and spread the word of Secrist's charges, the price of Equity Funding stock fell from $26 per share to less than $15 per share. The New York Stock Exchange halted trading in Equity Funding stock on March 27. On that date, Dirks voluntarily presented his information on the fraud to the SEC. Only then did the

SEC bring an action for fraud against Equity Funding. Shortly thereafter, California insurance authorities impounded Equity Funding's records and uncovered evidence of the fraud. On April 2, The Wall Street Journal published a front-page story based largely on information assembled by Dirks. Equity Funding immediately went into receivership.

The SEC brought an administrative proceeding against Dirks for violating Rule 10b–5 by passing along confidential inside information to his clients. The SEC found that he had violated Rule 10b–5, but it merely censured him, since he had played an important role in bringing the fraud to light. Dirks appealed to the Court of Appeals, which affirmed the judgment. Dirks then appealed to the Supreme Court.

Powell, Justice

In *U.S. v. Chiarella* (1980), we accepted the two elements set out in *In Re Cady, Roberts,* 40 S.E.C. 907 (1961) for establishing a Rule 10b–5 violation: (i) the existence of a relationship affording access to inside information intended to be available only for a corporate purpose, and (ii) the unfairness of allowing a corporate insider to take advantage of that information by trading without disclosure. The Court found that a duty to disclose under Section 10(b) does not arise from the mere possession of nonpublic market information. Such a duty arises from the existence of a fiduciary relationship.

There can be no duty to disclose when the person who has traded on inside information was not the corporation's agent, was not a fiduciary, or was not a person in whom the sellers of the securities had placed their trust and confidence.

This requirement of a specific relationship between the shareholders and the individual trading on inside information has created analytical difficulties for the SEC and courts in policing tippees who trade on inside information. Unlike insiders who have independent fiduciary duties to both the corporation and its shareholders, the typical tippee has no such relationship. In view of this absence, it has been unclear how a tippee acquires the duty to refrain from trading on inside information.

Not only are insiders forbidden by their fiduciary relationship from personally using undisclosed corporate information to their advantage, but also they may not give such information to an outsider for the same improper purpose of exploiting the information for their personal gain. The transactions of those who knowingly participate with the fiduciary in such a breach are as forbidden as transactions on behalf of the trustee himself. Thus, the tippee's duty to disclose or abstain is derivative from that of the insider's duty. The tippee's obligation has been viewed as arising from his role as a participant after the fact in the insider's breach of a fiduciary duty.

A tippee assumes a fiduciary duty to the shareholders of a corporation not to trade on material nonpublic information only when the insider has breached his fiduciary duty to the shareholders by disclosing the information to the tippee and the tippee knows or should know that there has been a breach.

In determining whether a tippee is under an obligation to disclose or abstain, it thus is necessary to determine whether the insider's tip constituted a breach of the insider's fiduciary duty. Whether disclosure is a breach of duty therefore depends in large part on the purpose of the disclosure. Thus, the test is whether the insider personally will benefit, directly or indirectly, from his disclosure. Absent some personal gain, there has been no breach of duty to stockholders. And absent a breach by the insider, there is no derivative breach.

This requires courts to focus on objective criteria, i.e., whether the insider receives a direct or indirect personal benefit from the disclosure, such as a pecuniary gain or a reputational benefit that will translate into future earnings. For example, there may be a relationship between the insider and the recipient that suggests a *quid pro quo* from the latter, or an intention to benefit the particular recipient. The elements of fiduciary duty and exploitation of nonpublic information also exist when an insider makes a gift of confidential information to a relative or friend who trades. The tip and trade resemble trading by the insider himself followed by a gift of the profits to the recipient.

Under the inside-trading and tipping rules set forth above, we find that there was no violation by Dirks. Dirks was a stranger to Equity Funding, with no pre-existing fiduciary duty to its shareholders. He took no action, directly or indirectly, that induced the shareholders or officers of Equity Funding to repose trust or confidence in him. There was no expectation by Dirks's sources that he would keep their information in confidence. Nor did Dirks misappropriate or illegally obtain the information about Equity Funding. Unless the insiders breached their *Cady, Roberts* duty to shareholders in disclosing the nonpublic information to Dirks, he breached no duty when he passed it on to investors as well as to *The Wall Street Journal.*

It is clear that neither Secrist nor the other Equity Funding employees violated their *Cady, Roberts* duty to the corporation's shareholders by providing information to Dirks. Secrist intended to convey relevant information that management was unlawfully concealing, and he believed that persuading Dirks to investigate was the best way to disclose the fraud. The tippers received no monetary or personal benefit for revealing Equity Funding's secrets, nor was their purpose to make a gift of valuable information to Dirks. The tippers were motivated by a desire to expose the fraud. In the absence of a breach of duty to shareholders by the insiders, there was no derivative breach by Dirks. Dirks therefore could not have been a participant after the fact in an insider's breach of a fiduciary duty.

Judgment reversed in favor of Dirks.

CONCEPT REVIEW

Rule 10b–5 Liability for Trading on Inside Information

	For Trading by Insider	For Trading by Tippee
Insider-Tipper Liability	Liable if insider breached the fiduciary duty of confidentiality by receiving a personal benefit by using corporate information that was entrusted to insider solely for corporate purposes	Liable if insider breached the fiduciary duty of confidentiality (which breach requires that the tipper receive a personal benefit) by disclosing confidential corporate information to the tippee
Tippee Liability	Not liable	Liable if: 1. Insider-tipper breached the fiduciary duty of confidentiality by disclosing confidential corporate information to the tippee, and 2. The tippee knew or should have known of the insider-tipper's breach of the fiduciary duty of confidentiality

When is a person a corporate insider?
That is, when does a person owe a fiduciary duty of confidentiality to the corporation?
    1. The corporation **entrusts** corporate information to a person **for corporate purposes**, and
    2. The corporation has a **proper business purpose for keeping the information confidential**.

When does an insider breach the fiduciary duty of confidentiality?
    1. When the insider **uses** the entrusted corporate information **for his personal benefit**, or
    2. When the insider **discloses** the entrusted corporate information to someone **other than for corporate purposes** and the insider **receives a personal benefit**.

When does an insider **not** breach the fiduciary duty of confidentiality?
    1. When the insider discloses the entrusted corporate information to someone who needs the information **for corporate purposes**.
    2. When the **insider does not receive a personal benefit** by disclosing or using the entrusted corporate information.
    3. When the **corporation does not have a proper business purpose** for keeping the information confidential.

In June 1997, the Supreme Court held that Rule 10b–5 liability attaches to anyone who trades in securities for personal profit using confidential information misappropriated in a breach of fiduciary duty owed to the *source of the information*. Under the misappropriation theory, a person violates Rule 10b–5 not only when he steals confidential information from his company and trades in its shares, but also, for example, if he steals confidential information about his firm's intent to make a tender offer for another firm and buys securities of the second firm.

Extent of Liability for Insider Trading Section 20A of the 1934 Act allows persons who traded in the securities at about the same time as the insider or tippee to recover damages from the insider or tippee. Although there may be several persons trading at about the same time, the insider or tippee's total liability cannot exceed the profit she has made or the loss she has avoided by trading on inside information.

This limitation, which merely requires disgorgement of profits, has been assailed as not adequately deterring insider trading, because the defendant may realize an enormous profit if her trading is not discovered, but lose nothing beyond her profits if it is. In response to this issue of liability, Congress passed an amendment to the 1934 Act permitting the SEC to seek a civil penalty of three times the profit gained or the loss avoided by trading on inside information. This treble penalty is paid to the Treasury of the United States. The penalty applies only to SEC actions; it does not affect the amount of damages that may be recovered by private plaintiffs. The 1934 Act also grants the SEC power to award up to 10 percent of any triple-damage penalty as a bounty to informants who helped the SEC uncover insider trading.

Rewards to Whistleblowers The Dodd–Frank Act attempts to increase the likelihood that persons with knowledge of securities law violations will report them to the SEC. The act requires the SEC to pay a reward to individuals who provide original information resulting in SEC enforcement monetary sanctions exceeding $1 million. The award must range from 10 to 30 percent of the amount recouped.

Liability for Aiding and Abetting Persons who are not the primary actors that violate Rule 10b–5 but merely aid and abet another's violation of the rule nonetheless may be prosecuted by the SEC. To have aiding and abetting liability, there must be (1) a primary violation by another person, (2) the aider and abettor's knowing or reckless assistance of that violation, and (3) substantial assistance by the aider and abettor in the achievement of the primary violation. Although the SEC may prosecute aiders and abettors, investors harmed by a primary violation may recover their damages only from primary violators, not from aiders and abettors.

In the *Stoneridge* case, the Supreme Court considered whether actors who were aiders and abettors could be liable otherwise under Rule 10b–5.

Stoneridge Investment Partners, LLC v. Scientific-Atlanta, Inc.
552 U.S. 148 (U.S. Sup. Ct. 2008)

Stoneridge Investment Partners, LLC, was a shareholder in Charter Communications, Inc., a television cable service provider. Stoneridge sued Charter for engaging in a variety of fraudulent practices so that its quarterly reports would meet Wall Street expectations for cable subscriber growth and operating cash flow. The fraud included misclassification of its customer base, delayed reporting of terminated customers, improper capitalization of costs that should have been shown as expenses, and manipulation of the company's billing cutoff dates to inflate reported revenues.

Despite these efforts, in late 2000 Charter executives realized that the company would miss projected operating cash flow numbers by $15 to $20 million. To help meet the shortfall, Charter decided to alter its existing arrangements with Scientific-Atlanta and Motorola, which supplied Charter with the digital cable converter boxes that Charter furnished to its customers. Charter arranged to overpay Scientific-Atlanta and Motorola $20 for each set top box it purchased until the end of the year, with the understanding that Scientific-Atlanta and Motorola would return the overpayment by purchasing advertising from Charter. The transactions, it is alleged, had no economic substance, but because Charter would then record the advertising purchases as revenue and capitalize its purchase of the set top boxes, in violation of generally accepted accounting principles, the transactions would enable Charter to fool its auditor into approving a financial statement showing it met projected revenue and operating cash flow numbers. Scientific-Atlanta and Motorola agreed to the arrangement.

So that Charter's independent auditor, Arthur Andersen LLP, would not discover the link between Charter's increased payments for the boxes and the advertising purchases, the companies drafted documents to make it appear the transactions were unrelated and conducted in the ordinary course of business. Following a request from Charter, Scientific-Atlanta sent documents to Charter stating falsely that it had increased production costs. It raised the price for set top boxes for the rest of 2000 by $20 per box. As for Motorola, in a written contract Charter agreed to purchase from Motorola a specific number of set top boxes and pay liquidated damages of $20 for each unit it did not take. The contract was made with the expectation Charter would fail to purchase all the units and pay Motorola the liquidated damages.

To return the additional money from the set top box sales, Scientific-Atlanta and Motorola signed contracts with Charter to purchase advertising time for a price higher than fair value. The new set top box agreements were backdated to make it appear that they were negotiated a month before the advertising agreements. The backdating was important to convey the impression that the negotiations were unconnected, a point Arthur Andersen considered necessary for separate treatment of the transactions. Charter recorded the advertising payments to inflate revenue and operating cash flow by approximately $17 million. The inflated number was shown on financial statements filed with the Securities and Exchange Commission and reported to the public.

Scientific-Atlanta and Motorola had no role in preparing or disseminating Charter's financial statements. Their own financial statements booked the transactions as a wash, under generally accepted accounting principles.

Nonetheless, Stoneridge filed a securities fraud class action against Scientific-Atlanta and Motorola on behalf of purchasers of Charter stock. Stoneridge alleged that Scientific-Atlanta and Motorola, by entering wash transactions with Charter, violated § 10(b) of the Securities Exchange Act of 1934 and SEC Rule 10b–5, because they knew or were in reckless disregard of

Charter's intention to use the transactions to inflate its revenues and knew the resulting financial statements issued by Charter would be relied upon by research analysts and investors.

The district court granted Scientific-Atlanta and Motorola's motion to dismiss for failure to state a claim on which relief can be granted. The court of appeals affirmed on the grounds that the allegations did not show that Scientific-Atlanta and Motorola made misstatements relied upon by the public or that they violated a duty to disclose. At most, the court observed, Scientific-Atlanta and Motorola had aided and abetted Charter's misstatement of its financial results, but, it noted, there is no private right of action for aiding and abetting a § 10(b) violation. Stoneridge asked the United States Supreme Court to grant certiorari and review the decision.

Kennedy, Justice

Decisions of the Courts of Appeals are in conflict respecting when, if ever, an injured investor may rely upon §10(b) to recover from a party that neither makes a public misstatement nor violates a duty to disclose but does participate in a scheme to violate §10(b). Compare *Simpson v. AOL Time Warner Inc.*, 452 F.3d 1040 (9th Cir. 2006), with *Regents of Univ. of Cal. v. Credit Suisse First Boston (USA), Inc.*, 482 F.3d 372 (5th Cir. 2007). We granted certiorari.

Section 10(b) of the Securities Exchange Act makes it "unlawful for any person, directly or indirectly, by the use of any means or instrumentality of interstate commerce or of the mails, or of any facility of any national securities exchange . . . [t]o use or employ, in connection with the purchase or sale of any security . . . any manipulative or deceptive device or contrivance in contravention of such rules and regulations as the Commission may prescribe as necessary or appropriate in the public interest or for the protection of investors." 15 U.S.C. § 78j. The SEC, pursuant to this section, promulgated Rule 10b-5.

Rule 10b-5 encompasses only conduct already prohibited by §10(b). Though the text of the Securities Exchange Act does not provide for a private cause of action for §10(b) violations, the Court has found a right of action implied in the words of the statute and its implementing regulation. In a typical §10(b) private action a plaintiff must prove (1) a material misrepresentation or omission by the defendant; (2) scienter; (3) a connection between the misrepresentation or omission and the purchase or sale of a security; (4) reliance upon the misrepresentation or omission; (5) economic loss; and (6) loss causation.

In *Central Bank of Denver, N. A. v. First Interstate Bank of Denver, N. A.*, 511 U.S. 164 (1994), the Court determined that §10(b) liability did not extend to aiders and abettors. The Court found the scope of §10(b) to be delimited by the text, which makes no mention of aiding and abetting liability. The Court doubted the implied §10(b) action should extend to aiders and abettors when none of the express causes of action in the securities acts included that liability. It added the following: "Were we to allow the aiding and abetting action proposed in this case, the defendant could be liable without any showing that the plaintiff relied upon the aider and abettor's statements or actions. Allowing plaintiffs to circumvent the reliance requirement would

disregard the careful limits on 10b-5 recovery mandated by our earlier cases." *Central Bank,* at 180.

The decision in *Central Bank* led to calls for Congress to create an express cause of action for aiding and abetting within the Securities Exchange Act. Then-SEC Chairman Arthur Levitt, testifying before the Senate Securities Subcommittee, cited *Central Bank* and recommended that aiding and abetting liability in private claims be established. Congress did not follow this course. Instead, in §104 of the Private Securities Litigation Reform Act of 1995 (PSLRA), it directed prosecution of aiders and abettors by the SEC.

The §10(b) implied private right of action does not extend to aiders and abettors. The conduct of a secondary actor must satisfy each of the elements or preconditions for liability; and we consider whether the allegations here are sufficient to do so.

The Court of Appeals concluded Stoneridge had not alleged that Scientific-Atlanta and Motorola engaged in a deceptive act within the reach of the §10(b) private right of action, noting that only misstatements, omissions by one who has a duty to disclose, and manipulative trading practices are deceptive within the meaning of the rule. If this conclusion were read to suggest there must be a specific oral or written statement before there could be liability under §10(b) or Rule 10b-5, it would be erroneous. Conduct itself can be deceptive, as Scientific-Atlanta and Motorola concede. In this case, moreover, Scientific-Atlanta's and Motorola's course of conduct included both oral and written statements, such as the backdated contracts agreed to by Charter and Scientific-Atlanta and Motorola.

A different interpretation of the holding from the Court of Appeals opinion is that the court was stating only that any deceptive statement or act Scientific-Atlanta and Motorola made was not actionable because it did not have the requisite proximate relation to the investors' harm. That conclusion is consistent with our own determination that Scientific-Atlanta's and Motorola's acts or statements were not relied upon by the investors and that, as a result, liability cannot be imposed upon Scientific-Atlanta and Motorola.

Reliance by the plaintiff upon the defendant's deceptive acts is an essential element of the §10(b) private cause of action. It ensures that, for liability to arise, the requisite causal connection between a defendant's misrepresentation and a plaintiffs injury exists as a predicate for liability. We have found a rebuttable presumption of reliance in two different circumstances. First, if there is an omission of a material fact by one with a duty to disclose, the investor to whom the duty was owed need not provide specific proof of reliance. Second, under the fraud-on-the-market doctrine, reliance is presumed when the statements at issue become public. The public information is reflected in the market price of the security. Then it can be assumed that an investor who buys or sells stock at the market price relies upon the statement.

Neither presumption applies here. Scientific-Atlanta and Motorola had no duty to disclose; and their deceptive acts were not communicated to the public. No member of the investing public had knowledge, either actual or presumed, of Scientific-Atlanta's and Motorola's deceptive acts during the relevant times. Stoneridge, as a result, cannot show reliance upon any of Scientific-Atlanta's and Motorola's actions except in an indirect chain that we find too remote for liability.

Invoking what some courts call "scheme liability," Stoneridge nonetheless seeks to impose liability on Scientific-Atlanta and Motorola even absent a public statement. In our view this approach does not answer the objection that Stoneridge did not in fact rely upon Scientific-Atlanta's and Motorola's own deceptive conduct.

Liability is appropriate, Stoneridge contends, because Scientific-Atlanta and Motorola engaged in conduct with the purpose and effect of creating a false appearance of material fact to further a scheme to misrepresent Charter's revenue. The argument is that the financial statement Charter released to the public was a natural and expected consequence of Scientific-Atlanta's and Motorola's deceptive acts; had Scientific-Atlanta and Motorola not assisted Charter, Charter's auditor would not have been fooled, and the financial statement would have been a more accurate reflection of Charter's financial condition.

In effect Stoneridge contends that in an efficient market investors rely not only upon the public statements relating to a security but also upon the transactions those statements reflect. Were this concept of reliance to be adopted, the implied cause of action would reach the whole marketplace in which the issuing company does business; and there is no authority for this rule.

As stated above, reliance is tied to causation, leading to the inquiry whether Scientific-Atlanta's and Motorola's acts were immediate or remote to the injury. In considering Stoneridge's arguments, we note §10(b) provides that the deceptive act must be "in connection with the purchase or sale of any security." Though this phrase in part defines the statute's coverage rather than causation, the emphasis on a purchase or sale of securities does provide some insight into the deceptive acts that concerned the enacting Congress. In all events we conclude Scientific-Atlanta's and Motorola's deceptive acts, which were not disclosed to the investing public, are too remote to satisfy the requirement of

reliance. It was Charter, not Scientific-Atlanta and Motorola, that misled its auditor and filed fraudulent financial statements; nothing Scientific-Atlanta and Motorola did made it necessary or inevitable for Charter to record the transactions as it did.

Stoneridge's theory, moreover, would put an unsupportable interpretation on Congress' specific response to *Central Bank* in §104 of the PSLRA. Congress amended the securities laws to provide for limited coverage of aiders and abettors. Aiding and abetting liability is authorized in actions brought by the SEC but not by private parties. Stoneridge's view of primary liability makes any aider and abettor liable under §10(b) if he or she committed a deceptive act in the process of providing assistance. Were we to adopt this construction of §10(b), it would revive in substance the implied cause of action against all aiders and abettors except those who committed no deceptive act in the process of facilitating the fraud; and we would undermine Congress' determination that this class of defendants should be pursued by the SEC and not by private litigants.

The practical consequences of an expansion, which the Court has considered appropriate to examine in circumstances like these, see *Blue Chip Stamps v. Manor Drug Stores*, 421 U.S. 723, 737, n. 5 (1975), provide a further reason to reject Stoneridge's approach. In *Blue Chip*, the Court noted that extensive discovery and the potential for uncertainty and disruption in a lawsuit allow plaintiffs with weak claims to extort settlements from innocent companies. Adoption of Stoneridge's approach would expose a new class of defendants to these risks. As noted in *Central Bank*, contracting parties might find it necessary to protect against these threats, raising the costs of doing business. Overseas firms with no other exposure to our securities laws could be deterred from doing business here. This, in turn, may raise the cost of being a publicly traded company under our law and shift securities offerings away from domestic capital markets.

The history of the §10(b) private right and the careful approach the Court has taken before proceeding without congressional direction provide further reasons to find no liability here. The §10(b) private cause of action is a judicial construct that Congress did not enact in the text of the relevant statutes. It is settled that there is an implied cause of action only if the underlying statute can be interpreted to disclose the intent to create one. This is for good reason. In the absence of congressional intent the Judiciary's recognition of an implied private right of action necessarily extends its authority to embrace a dispute Congress has not assigned it to resolve. This runs contrary to the established principle that the jurisdiction of the federal courts is carefully guarded against expansion by judicial interpretation and conflicts with the authority of Congress under Art. III to set the limits of federal jurisdiction.

Concerns with the judicial creation of a private cause of action caution against its expansion. The decision to extend the cause of action is for Congress, not for us. Though it remains the law, the §10(b) private right should not be extended beyond its present boundaries.

Secondary actors are subject to criminal penalties and civil enforcement by the SEC. The enforcement power is not toothless. Since September 30, 2002, SEC enforcement actions have collected over $10 billion in disgorgement and penalties, much of it for distribution to injured investors. And in this case both parties agree that criminal penalties are a strong deterrent. In addition some state securities laws permit state authorities to seek fines and restitution from aiders and abettors. All secondary actors, furthermore, are not necessarily immune from private suit. The securities statutes provide an express private right of action against accountants and underwriters in certain circumstances and the implied right of action in §10(b) continues to cover secondary actors who commit primary violations. *Central Bank, supra,* at 191.

Here Scientific-Atlanta and Motorola were acting in concert with Charter in the ordinary course as suppliers and, as matters then evolved in the not so ordinary course, as customers. Unconventional as the arrangement was, it took place in the marketplace for goods and services, not in the investment sphere. Charter was free to do as it chose in preparing its books, conferring with its auditor, and preparing and then issuing its financial statements. In these circumstances the investors cannot be said to have relied upon any of Scientific-Atlanta's and Motorola's deceptive acts in the decision to purchase or sell securities; and as the requisite reliance cannot be shown, Scientific-Atlanta and Motorola have no liability to Stoneridge under the implied right of action. This conclusion is consistent with the narrow dimensions we must give to a right of action Congress did not authorize when it first enacted the statute and did not expand when it revisited the law.

Judgment for Scientific-Atlanta affirmed.

Securities Fraud and the Internet In recent years, the Internet has become a new source of securities fraud. In response, the SEC has included the investigation of Internet users in its antifraud arsenal. The SEC has announced that it will use search engines to conduct Internet searches of phrases such as "get high returns with low investment" to detect likely fraud. Some securities professionals have objected to the SEC tactics as an invasion of privacy.

Statute of Limitations A purchaser or seller bringing an action under Rule 10b–5 must file his suit in a timely fashion or else be precluded from litigating the issue. The Sarbanes–Oxley Act of 2002 extends the statute of limitation by requiring an action under Rule 10b–5 to be commenced within two years after discovery of the facts constituting a violation of Rule 10b–5 and within five years of the violation.

Regulation FD Regulation FD (Fair Disclosure) was passed by the SEC to allow general investors to have more nearly equal access to information that in the past was selectively disclosed to institutional investors and securities analysts. The regulation, which applies only to public companies, provides that when an issuer or person acting for the issuer discloses material nonpublic information to securities market professionals and holders of the issuer's securities, it must make public disclosure of that information. An *intentional* selective disclosure occurs when the discloser knows or is reckless in not knowing that the information is material and nonpublic. In such a situation,

the remedy is that the issuer must make public disclosure simultaneously, that is, at the same time it discloses the information selectively. When the disclosure of material nonpublic information is selective but *nonintentional,* the issuer must make the public disclosure promptly, that is, as soon as reasonably practical after a senior official learns of the disclosure and knows it is material and nonpublic. This must be no later than 24 hours after the selective disclosure or by the commencement of the next day's trading on the NYSE, whichever is later. The required public disclosure may be made by filing or furnishing a Form 8-K or by another method that is reasonably designed to effect broad, nonselective disclosure to the public.

The SEC has taken action against several firms under Regulation FD. Most make the same mistake: a material disclosure from corporate management to a select audience in private conversations or at an invitation-only meeting. In one case, the CEO said in a public conference call that the company had a negative business outlook. Three weeks later, at an invitation-only technology conference, he presented attendees with a positive view of the company's prospects, and the price of its stock immediately rose 20 percent. In fining the company $250,000, the SEC said the public did not have access to the technology conference and was unable to benefit from the information disclosed there. In another case, the SEC prosecuted one company for making material nonpublic disclosures to securities analysts following one of its investor conferences.

One other case shows the importance of taking quick action when an inadvertent selective disclosure is made. A company's CEO, working from his home, participated in a conference call with a portfolio manager and a salesperson from an investment advisory group. From her office, the company's director of investor relations also took part in the conversation. During the call, the director realized the CEO unwittingly disclosed nonpublic information, but she didn't interrupt him. As soon as the conference call ended, she tried to reach him by telephone but was able to leave him only a voice-mail message expressing her concern over his inadvertent selective disclosure. Not until an hour later did the CEO get her message. He then asked the other call participants to keep the information confidential, but took no further action. At the time the CEO learned of his disclosure error, he had 24 hours to publicly disseminate the material information. That much time was available because his selective release was unintentional. The next day, however, the CEO intentionally selectively disclosed the material information to analysts without issuing a press release. This intentionally selective disclosure invoked a different part of Regulation FD: it had to be accompanied by a simultaneous public announcement. The company did not meet this requirement, instead issuing a press release three hours later, thus violating the rule. By then its stock had risen nearly 15 percent since the CEO's first nonpublic disclosure.

How can companies comply with Regulations FD? They should

- Establish clear rules for the content of information that may be disclosed.
- Require previews of any material disclosure by a qualified team of executives, such as legal counsel and an investor relations officer.
- Use several mass communications outlets, including submissions to the SEC, press releases, and Internet-based sound and video presentations.
- Adopt procedures for appropriate corrective action as soon as possible after a selective disclosure occurs.

An issuer should adopt absolute rules that provide guidance to its CEO, CFO, and others who regularly communicate with securities analysts and institutional investors. Clear rules can help prevent errors in judgment that can lead to inadvertent violations during an unscripted conference call or presentation. For instance, a company may have a rule that after the CEO gives his outlook on the company earnings in a press release or conference call, the CEO does not update the earnings outlook unless the company finds that the earnings are so far off that another release is required.

As an example of a preview process, consider W. R. Grace & Co., which circulates draft press releases by e-mail to its financial, executive, and legal groups. For

Grace, the process consumes only a few hours typically and only a few days when the release is about a complex subject such as quarterly earnings.

Criminal Liability Like the 1933 Act, the 1934 Act provides for liability for criminal violations of the act. Section 32 provides that individuals may be fined up to $5 million and imprisoned up to 20 years for willful violations of the 1934 Act or the related SEC rules. Businesses may be fined up to $25 million.

Tender Offer Regulation

Historically, the predominant procedure by which one corporation acquired another was the merger, a transaction requiring the cooperation of the acquired corporation's management. Since the early 1960s, the **tender offer** has become an often used acquisition device. A tender offer is a public offer by a **bidder** to purchase a **subject company's** equity securities directly from its shareholders at a specified price for a fixed period of time. The offering price is usually well above the market price of the shares. Such offers are often made even though there is opposition from the subject company's management. Opposed offers are called hostile tender offers. The legality of efforts opposing a tender offer is covered in Chapter 43.

The Williams Act amendments to the 1934 Act require bidders and subject companies to provide a shareholder with information on which to base his decision whether to sell his shares to a bidder. The aim of the Williams Act is to protect investors and to give the bidder and the subject company equal opportunities to present their cases to the shareholder. The intent is to encourage an auction of the shares with the highest bidder purchasing the shares. The Williams Act applies only when the subject company's equity securities are registered under the 1934 Act.

The Williams Act does not define a tender offer, but the courts have compiled a list of factors to determine whether a person has made a tender offer. The greater the number of people solicited and the lower their investment sophistication, the more likely it is that the bidder will be held to have made a tender offer. Also, the shorter the offering period, the more rigid the price, and the greater the publicity concerning the offer, the more likely it is that the purchase efforts of the bidder will be treated as a tender offer. Given these factors, a person who offers to purchase shares directly from several shareholders at a set price for only a few days risks having a court treat the offer like a tender offer. The Williams Act does not regulate a tender offer unless the bidder intends to become a holder of at least 5 percent of the subject company's shares.

A bidder making a tender offer must file a tender offer statement (Schedule TO) with the SEC when the offer commences. The information in this schedule includes the terms of the offer (for example, the price), the background of the bidder, and the purpose of the tender offer (including whether the bidder intends to control the subject company).

The SEC requires the bidder to keep the tender offer open for at least 20 business days and prohibits any purchase of shares during that time. This rule gives shareholders adequate time to make informed decisions regarding whether to tender their shares. Tendering shareholders may withdraw their tendered shares during the entire term of the offer. This rule allows the highest bidder to buy the shares, as in an auction.

All tender offers, whether made by the issuer or by a third-party bidder, must be made to all holders of the targeted class of shares. When a bidder increases the offering price during the term of the tender offer, all of the shareholders must be paid the higher price even if they tendered their shares at a lower price. If more shares are tendered than the bidder offered to buy, the bidder must prorate its purchases among all of the shares tendered. This proration rule is designed to foster careful shareholder decisions about whether to sell shares. Shareholders might rush to tender their shares if the bidder could accept shares on a first-come, first-served basis.

After an initial offering period has expired, a bidder is permitted to include a "subsequent offering period" during which shareholders who tender will have no withdrawal rights. The SEC created the new offering period to allow shareholders a last opportunity to tender into an offer.

The management of the subject company is required to inform the shareholders of its position on the tender offer, with its reasons, within 10 days after the offer has been made. It must also provide the bidder with a list of the holders of the equity securities that the bidder seeks to acquire or mail the materials for the bidder.

SEC Rule 14e–3 prohibits persons who have knowledge of an impending tender offer from using such information prior to its public disclosure. The rule limits insider trading in the tender offer context.

Private Acquisitions of Shares

The Williams Act regulates private acquisitions of shares differently from tender offers. When the bidder privately seeks a controlling block of the subject company's shares on a stock exchange or in face-to-face negotiations with only a few shareholders, no advance notice to the SEC or disclosure to shareholders is required. However, a person making a private acquisition is required to file a Schedule 13D with the SEC and to send a copy to the subject company within 10 days after he becomes a holder of 5 percent of its shares. A Schedule 13G (which requires less disclosure than a 13D) must be filed when a 5 percent holder has purchased no more than 2 percent of the shares within the past 12 months.

State Regulation of Tender Offers

Statutes that apply to tender offers have been enacted by about two-thirds of the states. State statutes have become highly protective of subject companies. For example, the Indiana statute gives shareholders other than the bidder the right to determine whether the shares acquired by the bidder may be voted in directors' elections and other matters. The statute, which essentially gives a subject company the power to require shareholder approval of a hostile tender offer, has been copied by several states.

Other states, such as Delaware, have adopted business combination moratorium statutes. These statutes delay the effectuation of a merger of the corporation with a shareholder owning a large percentage of shares (such as 15 percent) unless the board of directors' approval is obtained. Because the typical large shareholder in a public company is a bidder who has made a tender offer, these state statutes primarily affect the ability of a bidder to effectuate a merger after a tender offer and, therefore, may have the effect of deterring hostile acquisitions.

 LO1 Understand why and demonstrate how the law regulates issuances and issuers of securities.

State Securities Law

State securities laws are frequently referred to as blue-sky laws, since the early state securities statutes were designed to protect investors from promoters and security salespersons who would "sell building lots in the blue sky." The first state to enact a securities law was Kansas, in 1911. All of the states now have such legislation.

The National Conference of Commissioners on Uniform State Laws has adopted the Uniform Securities Act of 1956. The act contains antifraud provisions, requires the registration of securities, and demands broker-dealer registration. About two-thirds of the states have adopted the act, but many states have made significant changes in it.

All of the state securities statutes provide penalties for fraudulent sales and permit the issuance of injunctions to protect investors from additional or anticipated fraudulent

The Global Business Environment

The Foreign Corrupt Practices Act

The Foreign Corrupt Practices Act (FCPA) was passed by Congress in 1977 as an amendment to the Securities Exchange Act of 1934. Its passage followed discoveries that more than 400 American corporations had given bribes or made other improper or questionable payments in connection with business abroad and within the United States. Many of these payments were bribes to high level officials of foreign governments for the purpose of obtaining contracts for the sale of goods or services. Officers of the companies that had made the payments argued that such payments were customary and necessary in business transactions in many countries. This argument was pressed forcefully with regard to facilitating payments. Such payments were said to be essential to get lower level government officials in a number of countries to perform their nondiscretionary or ministerial tasks, such as preparing or approving necessary import or export documents.

In a significant number of cases, bribes had been accounted for as commission payments, as normal transactions with foreign subsidiaries, or as payments for services rendered by professionals or other firms, or had in other ways been made to appear as normal business expenses. These bribes were then illegally deducted as normal business expenses in income tax returns filed with the Internal Revenue Service.

The Payments Prohibition

The FCPA makes it a crime for any American firm—whether or not it has securities registered under the 1934 Act—to offer, promise, or make payments or gifts of anything of value to foreign officials and certain others. Payments are prohibited if the person making the payment knows or should know that some or all of it will be used for the purpose of influencing a governmental decision, even if the offer is not accepted or the promise is not carried out. The FCPA prohibits offers or payments to foreign political parties and candidates for office as well as offers and payments to government officials. Payments of kickbacks to foreign businesses and their officers are not prohibited unless it is known or should be known that these payments will be passed on to government officials or other illegal recipients.

Facilitating or grease payments are not prohibited by the FCPA. For example, suppose a corporation applies for a radio license in Italy and makes a payment to the government official who issues the licenses. If the official grants licenses to every applicant and the payment merely speeds up the processing of the application, the FCPA is not violated.

Substantial penalties for violations may be imposed. A company may be fined up to $2 million. Directors, officers, employees, or agents participating in violations are liable for fines of up to $100,000 and prison terms of up to five years.

Record-Keeping and Internal Controls Requirements

The FCPA also establishes record-keeping and internal control requirements for firms subject to the periodic disclosure provisions of the Securities Exchange Act of 1934. The purpose of such controls is to prevent unauthorized payments and transactions and unauthorized access to company assets that may result in illegal payments.

The FCPA requires the making and keeping of records and accounts "which, in reasonable detail, accurately, and fairly reflect the transactions and dispositions of the assets of the issuer" of securities. It also requires the establishment and maintenance of a system of internal accounting controls that provides "reasonable assurances" that the firm's transactions are executed in accordance with management's authorization and that the firm's assets are used or disposed of only as authorized by management.

---

acts. Most of the statutes grant broad power to investigate fraud to some state official—usually the attorney general or his appointee as securities administrator. All of the statutes provide criminal penalties for selling fraudulent securities and conducting fraudulent transactions.

LOG ON

www.com.ohio.gov/secu
Many state securities commissioners maintain websites that warn investors of risky or fraudulent securities. Visit the Ohio Division of Securities website. Click on links under "Alerts" to see examples of investor warnings.

Comply with the communication rules that apply to a public offering of securities.

Registration of Securities

Most of the state securities statutes adopt the philosophy of the 1933 Act that informed investors can make intelligent investment decisions. The states with such statutes have a registration scheme much like the 1933 Act, with required disclosures for public offerings and exemptions from registration for small and private offerings. Other states reject the contention that investors with full information can make intelligent investment decisions. The securities statutes in these states have a **merit registration** requirement, giving a securities administrator power to deny registration on the merits of the security and its issuer. Only securities that are not unduly risky and promise an adequate return to investors may receive administrator approval.

All state statutes have a limited number of exemptions from registration. Most statutes have private offering exemptions that are similar to Securities Act Rule 506 of Regulation D. In addition, a person may avoid the registration requirements of state securities laws by not offering or selling securities.

Registration by Coordination The Uniform Securities Act permits an issuer to register its securities by coordination. Instead of filing a registration statement under the Securities Act of 1933 and a different one as required by state law, registration by coordination allows an issuer to file the 1933 Act registration statement with the state securities administrator. Registration by coordination decreases an issuer's expense of complying with state law when making an interstate offering of its securities.

Capital Markets Efficiency Act of 1996 Congress passed the Capital Markets Efficiency Act (CMEA) to facilitate offerings of securities by small investors. The CMEA preempts state registration of offers and sales of securities to "qualified purchasers," as defined by the SEC, as well as offerings exempt under Rule 506 of Regulation D. An issuance of securities listed on the New York Stock Exchange or NASDAQ is also exempted from state registration provisions. Nonetheless, states may apply their antifraud laws despite the preemption of their registration provisions.

Problems and Problem Cases

1. Marvie, Kim, Clarence, and Goldie Tschetter purchased units in Huron Kitchen LLC, a limited liability company, which would construct and own a Country Kitchen restaurant in South Dakota. As members of an LLC, they had management powers in proportion to their contributions of capital and could elect the managers of the LLC and set the managers' responsibilities. As LLC members, the Tschetters agreed to hire Country Hospitality Corporation to do much of the operation of the LLC. The LLC Operating Agreement required that the day-to-day decisions were made by two managers who were required to be members of the LLC, and selected by the other members. Members could authorize loans on behalf of the company by agreement. The members had the right to receive profits and distributions when warranted. The members could authorize incidental expenses within an aggregate of $12,500. The members were empowered to make any other routine actions incidental to the day-to-day activity of the LLC. The members were allowed to select officers for the LLC. Marvie, acting for all the Tschetters, exercised substantial control over the affairs of the LLC. Clarence and Goldie acquiesced in relying on Marvie and Kim for information and action. The minutes kept by the LLC showed that Tschetters were informed and active in the LCC. Unfortunately, the restaurant failed, and the Tschetters sued the person who sold them the interests in the LLC on the grounds that the LLC interests were securities, and therefore, the seller owed duties to them. Were the LLC interests securities?

2. Mickie Wenwoods, an outstanding collegiate golfer, graduates from college and decides to turn professional. To finance her effort to qualify for the LPGA Tour and to cover the cost of travel, housing, food, and a caddy, Wenwoods asks 20 of her family friends to contribute $10,000 each to her efforts. In return for their contributions, each friend will receive 1 percent of Wenwoods's revenues from her golfing efforts, including tournament prize money and endorsement fees from sponsors, less Wenwoods's expenses. Whether Wenwoods is able to generate revenue is dependent on how well she plays in golf tournaments and whether she is able to convince sponsors to sign her as an endorser. Wenwoods will also determine the amount of her expenses for travel, food, housing, and a caddy. Is Wenwoods selling a security when she asks for contributions from her friends?

3. AltaVerba, Inc., is a nonpublic company controlled by its majority shareholder, Robyn Streel. AltaVerba wants to make an initial public offering by selling 300 million Class B common shares in a firm commitment underwriting, with Goldman Sachs acting as the lead underwriter. AltaVerba is not a public company required to file periodic reports

with the SEC under the Securities Exchange Act of 1934. AltaVerba and Goldman are considering the communications they may have with existing and prospective investors and securities analysts before and during the registered offering and comply with Section 5 of the Securities Act of 1933. Seventy-two days before the 1933 Act registration statement will be filed with the SEC, AltaVerba wants to release historical information about its business and financial results. What are the restrictions on the release of such information at that time? Twenty-three days before the 1933 Act registration statement will be filed with the SEC, AltaVerba wants to release forward-looking information about its business and financial results. May AltaVerba do that? After the registration statement has been filed with the SEC, Streel and AltaVerba's vice president of finance want to speak on the phone about the issuance with an investment manager of Fidelity Magellan Fund. Is that communication legal at that time? At the same time, AltaVerba and Goldman want to conduct a road show in five cities. Selected very wealthy investors, securities analysts, and mutual fund managers will attend the road show in person. Under what conditions may AltaVerba and Goldman conduct a legal road show? After the registration statement has been declared effective by the SEC, AltaVerba wants to use a free-writing prospectus that includes historical and forward-looking information about AltaVerba. What conditions must the free-writing prospectus meet to be legal under Section 5?

4. EMG, Corp., a public corporation, decides to enter the Internet marketing business by creating a subsidiary corporation, GME, Inc., that will be 51 percent owned by EMG and 49 percent owned by other investors. The plan is that GME will not be not a public corporation required to file periodic reports with the Securities and Exchange Commission under the Securities Exchange Act of 1934. GME plans to sell 100 million shares for $20 each to EMG and to the following investors:

- An investor who has annual income of $4,080,000 and a net worth of $12,200,000.

- GME's chief operations officer, whose annual income is $175,000 and net worth is $350,000.

- A pension fund established for EMG's employees.

- 14 mutual funds, each of which has assets exceeding $20 billion.

GME wants to sell its common shares to the above investors in an exemption from the registration requirements of the Securities Act of 1933 under Rule 506. Is the $2 billion amount of the offering too large for Rule 506? Is the number of purchasers a problem under Rule 506? Are the listed investors qualified purchasers under Rule 506? Under Rule 506, for how long must GME restrict the purchasers' resales of the common shares? If GME is unsure whether the offering it proposes meets the requirements of Rule 506, what document should GME request from the staff of the SEC?

5. Real Options, Inc. (ROI), is a company not required to provide periodic reports to investors under the Securities Exchange Act of 1934. ROI wants to raise $700,000 by selling preferred shares to 150 investors, including its customers, suppliers, and employees. Is ROI eligible to make the offering under Rule 504 of the Securities Act of 1933? What must ROI do to comply with Rule 504?

6. Podcast Services Company is incorporated in Illinois. It has 200 employees that work in an office building leased by Podcast in Alton, Illinois. Most of Podcast's employees reside in Illinois, but a few reside in Missouri near St. Louis. All of Podcast's assets are in Illinois. It sells its services to clients in 20 states. About 35 percent of its business is conducted with clients in Missouri in the St. Louis area. Podcast wants to sell debentures to its employees, the proceeds of which will be used to purchase the building Podcast currently leases in Alton. May Podcast make the offering in compliance with Securities Act Rule 147? What must Podcast to do comply with Rule 147?

7. Commonwealth Edison Co. registered 3 million common shares with the SEC and sold the shares for about $28 per share. The price of the purchasers' stock dropped to $21 when the Atomic Safety and Licensing Board denied ComEd's application to license one of its reactors. It was the first and only time the Board had denied a license application. ComEd assumed that the license would be granted; therefore, its registration statement failed to disclose the pendency of the license application. Did ComEd violate Section 11 of the Securities Act?

8. Joseph Crotty was a vice president of United Artists Communications, Inc. (UA), a corporation with equity securities registered under the Securities Exchange Act of 1934. Crotty was the head film

buyer of UA's western division. He had virtually complete and autonomous control of film buying for the 351 UA theaters in the western United States, including negotiating and signing movie acquisition agreements, supervising movie distribution, and settling contracts after the movies had been shown. Crotty knew how many contracts were being negotiated at any one time and the price UA was paying for the rental of each movie. Crotty was required to consult with higher officers only if he wanted to exceed a certain limit on the amount of the cash advance paid to a distributor for a movie. This occurred no more than two or three times a year. The gross revenue from Crotty's division was about 35 percent of UA's gross revenue from movie exhibitions and around 17 percent of its total gross revenue. During a six-month period, Crotty purchased 7,500 shares of UA and sold 3,500 shares, realizing a large profit. Has Crotty violated Section 16(b) of the 1934 Act?

9. Shareholders of General Electric Company have asked the board of directors to include several shareholder proposals in its annual proxy statement. One proposal is that GE's articles of incorporation be amended to provide that shareholders will elect directors by cumulative voting of their shares. A second proposal asks that no GE director be permitted to serve on more than three corporate boards of directors, including GE's board. A third proposal asks GE to prepare a report outlining the vulnerability and substantial radiation risks of storage of irradiated fuel rods at all GE-designed nuclear reactor sites. May GE omit these shareholder proposals from its proxy statement under Rule 14a–8?

10. Michael Broudo and other investors purchased stock in Dura Pharmaceuticals, Inc., on the public securities market between April 15, 1997, and February 24, 1998. During this period, they allege that Dura or its officers made false statements concerning both Dura's drug profits and future Food and Drug Administration approval of a new asthmatic spray device. They also allege that Dura falsely claimed that it expected that its drug sales would prove profitable. Regarding the asthmatic spray device, they allege Dura falsely claimed that it expected the FDA would soon grant its approval. On February 24, 1998, Dura announced that its earnings would be lower than expected, principally due to slow drug sales. The next day Dura's shares lost almost half

their value falling from about $39 per share to about $21. Eight months later in November 1998, Dura announced that the FDA would not approve Dura's new asthmatic spray device. Soon after, Broudo and the other investors sued Dura and its officers under Rule 10b–5 of the Securities Exchange Act of 1934. In their complaint, they stated that in reliance on the integrity of the market, they paid artificially inflated prices for Dura securities and suffered damages. They did not specify or attempt to calculate the amount of damages caused by the alleged misstatements made by Dura. Dura defended on the grounds that Broudo and the other investors failed adequately to allege loss causation. Did the U.S. Supreme Court agree with Dura?

11. The managements of Combustion Engineering, Inc. (CEI), and Basic, Inc., entered negotiations regarding CEI's acquiring Basic. Despite the secrecy of the merger negotiations, there were repeated instances of abnormal trading in Basic's shares, with trading volume rising from 7,000 per day to 29,000. Basic issued a public statement that "the company knew no reason for the stock's activity and that no negotiations were under way with any company for a merger." Did Basic's statement violate Securities Exchange Act Rule 10b–5?

12. Plumbers & Steamfitters Local 773 Pension Fund sued Canadian Imperial Bank of Commerce and four of its officers on the grounds that they misled investors about CIBC's exposure to fixed-income securities backed by subprime residential mortgages. One example of a misstatement was in the 2006 Accountability Report, in which CIBC stated, "Although actual losses are not expected to be material, as of October 31, 2006, our maximum exposure to loss as a result of involvement with the CDOs [collateralized debt obligations] was approximately $729 million." Pension Fund alleges that this reference constituted false and misleading representations because CIBC's actual exposure to the U.S. real estate market was almost $12 billion. Pension Fund argued that CIBC and its officers were liable under Securities Exchange Act Rule 10b-5 because they failed to comply with generally accepted accounting principles in accounting for the CDO losses. Did the court agree?

13. In early May 2001, American Express Financial Advisors (AEFA) CEO James Cracchiolo received a fax from AEFA CFO Stuart Sedlacek advising

him that AEFA was facing additional losses on its high-yield debt investments beyond those already booked. American Express Company (AMEX) COO Kenneth Chenault was advised of the situation the next day. He was told that the deterioration of the high-yield debt portfolio was so bad that "even the investment-grade CDOs [collateralized debt obligations] held by American Express showed potential deterioration" because defaults on the underlying bonds had risen so sharply. Chenault asked, "What are we talking about here?" Cracchiolo replied, "We really don't know enough to even give you a range."

In the meantime, on May 15, 2001, AMEX filed its quarterly report (Form 10-Q) for the first quarter of 2001. In it, the Company reported the $182 million in first-quarter losses from AEFA's high-yield debt portfolio. The Company explained, "The high-yield losses reflect the continued deterioration of the high-yield portfolio and losses associated with selling certain bonds." Importantly, it added, "Total losses on these investments for the remainder of 2001 are expected to be substantially lower than in the first quarter."

In July 2001, however, AMEX recognized that losses from the debt portfolio would be $400 million. Investors who purchased AMEX stock between the 10-Q filing and the disclosure of the actual losses sued AMEX and certain officers under Securities Act Rule 10b-5 for making erroneous forward-looking statements. Were the investors successful?

14. In March 2004, Internet broadcasting pioneer and Dallas Mavericks owner Mark Cuban acquired 600,000 shares, a 6.3 percent stake, of Mamma.com. Later that spring, Mamma.com decided to sell more of its shares through a PIPE [private investment in public equity] offering. Shares issued in PIPE offerings are typically sold below the market price of the shares. Mamma.com's CEO called Cuban to invite him to participate. Before telling Cuban about the offering of shares, the CEO told Cuban he had confidential information for him, and Cuban agreed to keep whatever information the CEO shared confidential. The CEO then told Cuban about the PIPE offering. Cuban became very upset and said, among other things, that he did not like PIPEs because they dilute the existing shareholders. At the end of the call, Cuban told the CEO "Well, now I'm screwed. I can't sell." The CEO then sent Cuban a follow-up e-mail,

encouraging him to contact Mamma.com's investment banker handling the offering. Cuban called the banker and spoke for eight minutes. During that call, the banker supplied Cuban with additional confidential details about the PIPE. In response to Cuban's questions, the banker told him that the PIPE was being sold at a discount to the market price and that the offering included other incentives for the PIPE investors. With that information and one minute after speaking with the investment banker, Cuban called his broker and instructed him to sell his entire stake in Mamma.com. Cuban sold 10,000 shares during the evening of June 28, 2004, and the remainder during regular trading the next day. Did Cuban illegally trade on inside information under Rule 10b-5?

15. First City Financial Corp., a Canadian company controlled by the Belzberg family, was engaged in the business of investing in publicly held American corporations. Marc Belzberg identified Ashland Oil Company as a potential target, and on February 11, 1986, he secretly purchased 61,000 shares of Ashland stock for First City. By February 26, additional secret purchases of Ashland shares pushed First City's holdings to just over 4.9 percent of Ashland's stock. These last two purchases were effected for First City by Alan "Ace" Greenberg, the chief executive officer of Bear Stearns, a large Wall Street brokerage. On March 4, Belzberg called Greenberg and told him, "It wouldn't be a bad idea if you bought Ashland Oil here." Immediately after the phone call, Greenberg purchased 20,500 Ashland shares for about $44 per share. If purchased for First City, those shares would have increased First City's Ashland holdings above 5 percent. Greenberg believed he was buying the shares for First City under a put and call agreement, under which First City had the right to buy the shares from Bear Stearns and Bear Stearns had the right to require First City to buy the shares from it. Between March 4 and 14, Greenberg purchased an additional 330,700 shares. On March 17, First City and Bear Stearns signed a formal put and call agreement covering all the shares Greenberg purchased. On March 25, First City announced publicly for the first time that it intended to make a tender offer for all of Ashland's shares. First City filed a Schedule 13D on March 26. Has First City violated the Williams Act?

16. Amenity, Inc., was incorporated with 1 million authorized shares, which were issued to Capital

General Corporation (CGC) for $2,000. CGC distributed 90,000 of those shares to about 900 of its clients, business associates, and other contacts to create and maintain goodwill among its clients and contacts. CGC did not receive any monetary or other direct financial consideration from those receiving the stock. Amenity had no actual business function at this time, and its sole asset was the $2,000 CGC had paid for the 1 million shares. Through CGC's efforts, Amenity was acquired by another company, which paid CGC $25,000 for its efforts. The Utah Securities Division sought to suspend the public trading of Amenity stock on the grounds that when CGC distributed the shares it had sold them in violation of the Utah Securities Act. Was CGC's distribution a sale of securities?

Online Research

Internet Offerings of Securities

Using the term *Internet Securities Offerings*, you can find several websites and publications that explain how an issuer may make an Internet offering of securities without violating state or federal securities law. These resources can help you answer the following questions:

- Why will an Internet offering create problems if the issuer is trying to exempt the offering under Rules 505 or 506?
- Why are Rule 504 and Regulation A good exemptions for Internet offerings?
- What are the dos and don'ts for communications during an Internet registered offering?

CHAPTER 46

LEGAL AND PROFESSIONAL RESPONSIBILITIES OF AUDITORS, CONSULTANTS, AND SECURITIES PROFESSIONALS

Credit Deutsch First Chicago LLP (CDFC) is a financial consulting and investment banking firm. Angst & Yearn LLP (A&Y) is a public accounting firm. A client of both firms is Macrohard Corporation, a public issuer of securities required to file periodic reports with the Securities and Exchange Commission under the Securities Exchange Act of 1934. Because Macrohard has a short-term cash flow problem due to a downturn in the economy, CDFC advises Macrohard to issue 300 promissory notes, each with a face value of $10,000,000, interest of 4 percent, and a due date 11 months after issuance. CDFC recommends that the notes be sold to mutual funds, insurance companies, pension funds, and other institutional investors using the Rule 506 exemption from registration under the Securities Act of 1933.

The notes are offered in part by an offering circular, which includes financial statements audited by A&Y. A&Y's unqualified audit opinion is also included in the offering circular. A&Y receives a $6,500,000 fee for auditing Macrohard's financial statements and reviewing the financial statements for inclusion in the offering circular.

CDFC assists Macrohard with the offering of the notes by calling prospective investors on the phone, visiting investors in person, and sending e-mails to prospective investors urging them to buy the notes. In all three contacts, CDFC emphasizes that the notes carry an interest rate that is 3 percent higher than the 30-year Treasury bond rate and, therefore, offer an excellent return on investment. As compensation for its role in the notes offering, CDFC will receive 0.5 percent of the proceeds from the sale of the notes.

- What standard of care must CDFC meet when recommending that Marcrohard issue promissory notes as a solution to its liquidity problems?
- If one of CDFC's managing partners during the course of the offering negligently makes false statements about Macrohard's financial position to purchasers of the notes, does CDFC have potential liability to the purchasers under Section 12(a)(2) of the Securities Act of 1933? Especially consider whether CDFC is a proper type of defendant under that section.
- Is CDFC a proper type of defendant under Rule 10b–5 of the Securities Exchange Act of 1934 due to its communications with purchasers, if one of its partners negligently makes false statements?
- Should A&Y fear liability to the note purchasers under Section 12(a)(2) of the 1933 Act?
- If A&Y negligently audited Macrohard's financial statements and as a result the financial statements materially misstate Macrohard's financial position, does A&Y have potential liability to the purchasers under Rule 10b–5 of the 1934 Act? Especially consider whether A&Y is a proper type of defendant under that rule.

- Does CDFC have potential liability to any of the note purchasers under the state law of negligent misrepresentation in a state that has adopted the *Ultramares* test?
- If A&Y knows that the audited financial statements will be used in the offering circular to sell the notes, but it does not know to which institutional investors the notes will be sold, does A&Y have potential liability to any of the note purchasers under the state law of negligent misrepresentation in a state that adopted the *Ultramares* test? How about a state that has adopted the rule of the *Restatement (Second) of Torts*?

Suppose that instead of making a Rule 506 offering, Macrohard issues preferred stock in a public offering registered under the 1933 Act. CDFC is Macrohard's underwriter for the public offering, receiving a 25-cent spread for each share sold. The financial statements audited by A&Y and its audit opinion are included in the registration statement. Unknown to CDFC and A&Y, there are material misstatements of fact in the financial statements included in the registration statement, and there are also omissions of material facts in the portions of the registration statement that describe Macrohard's business and the material risks of investing in the preferred stock.

- Is CDFC a statutory defendant under Section 11 of the 1933 Act? For what portions of the registration statement is CDFC liable under Section 11? What is CDFC's due diligence defense for errors in the financial statements audited by A&Y? What is CDFC's due diligence defense for errors in the portions of the registration statement that describe Macrohard's business and material risks?
- Is A&Y a statutory defendant under Section 11 of the 1933 Act? For what portions of the registration statement is A&Y liable under Section 11? What is A&Y's due diligence defense?
- Compile a checklist that will help CDFC and A&Y meet their due diligence defenses under Section 11.

LO   LEARNING OBJECTIVES

After studying this chapter, you should be able to:

1   Appreciate the duties that accountants and securities professionals owe to their clients and third parties. and third parties under federal securities and other laws.

2   Engage in behavior that prevents you and your firm from having liability to clients

3   Take steps to protect a client's communications and the firm's working papers.

Each year, many accounting and finance students choose to become CPAs and seek jobs as auditors of public companies. Many students, however, opt for positions in consulting and other fields connected to the securities industry. Therefore, this chapter covers the legal responsibilities of not only accountants and auditors, but also consultants and securities professionals. The chapter's primary focus is on auditors of financial statements, tax accountants, consultants who provide management and financial advice to clients, investment

bankers, securities underwriters, securities analysts, and securities brokers.

This chapter will first cover the general standard of performance required of professionals. Next, we will study professionals' liability to their clients, especially under state law. The largest part of this chapter comprises liability to nonclient third parties. We will also examine criminal liability of professionals and end the chapter with coverage of the law protecting the integrity of communications between professionals and their clients.

LO1 Appreciate the duties that accountants and securities professionals owe to their clients and third parties.

General Standard of Performance

The general duty that auditors, consultants, and securities professionals owe to their clients and to other persons who are affected by their actions is to exercise the skill and care of the ordinarily prudent professional in the same circumstances. Hence, professionals must act carefully and diligently; they are *not* guarantors of the accuracy of their work or that the advice they give to clients will work out well. The professional's duty to exercise reasonable care is a subset of the negligence standard of tort law. Two elements compose the general duty of performance: skill and care.

A professional must have the **skill of the ordinarily prudent person in her profession.** This element focuses on education or knowledge, whether acquired formally at school or by self-instruction. For example, to audit financial records, an accountant must know generally accepted auditing standards (GAAS) and generally accepted accounting principles (GAAP). GAAS and GAAP are standards and principles embodied in the rules, releases, and pronouncements of the Securities and Exchange Commission, the American Institute of Certified Public Accountants (AICPA), the Financial Accounting Standards Board (FASB), the Public Company Accounting Oversight Board (PCAOB), and the International Accounting Standards Board (IASB). To assist a corporate client's development of an expansion strategy, a consultant must be knowledgeable of similar businesses and the opportunities for expansion. To assist a securities issuer making an initial public offering (IPO), an investment banker must know the mechanics of a public offering and the market for securities. In recommending stocks to an investor, a broker or investment adviser must know fundamental investment analysis and portfolio theory.

The care element requires a professional to act as carefully as the ordinarily prudent person in her profession. For example, in preparing a tax return, a tax accountant must discover the income exclusions, the deductions, and the tax credits that the reasonably careful accountant would find are available to the client. When recommending a corporate acquisition to a client, an investment banker must investigate the value of the acquired firm and check the acquired firm's fit with the business and strategy of the acquiring firm. A broker recommending a security to his customer must carefully investigate the security and its fit

with the customer's investment goals, securities portfolio, and financial status.

Courts and legislatures usually defer to the members of a profession in determining what the ordinarily prudent professional would do. Such deference recognizes the lawmakers' lack of understanding of the nuances of professional practice. However, a profession will not be permitted to establish a standard of conduct that is harmful to the interests of clients or other members of society.

 LO2 Engage in behavior that prevents you and your firm from having liability to clients and third parties under federal securities and other laws.

Professionals' Liability to Clients

Professionals are sometimes sued by their clients. For example, an accountant may wrongfully claim deductions on a client's tax return. When the IRS discovers the wrongful deduction, the individual will have to pay the extra tax, interest, and perhaps a penalty. The individual may sue his accountant to recover the amount of the penalty. For another example, consider a securities broker who churns the securities account of a 92-year-old investor by executing daily trades in risky Internet stocks. When the value of the investor's portfolio declines from $500,000 to near zero as high commissions and capital losses mount, the investor may sue the broker for making imprudent investment decisions and for churning the account merely to earn the commissions.

When clients sue professionals, there are three principal bases of liability: contract, tort, and trust.

Contractual Liability As a party to a contract with her client, a professional owes a duty to the client to perform as she has agreed to perform. This includes an implied duty to perform the contract as the ordinarily prudent person in the profession would perform it. If the professional fails to perform as agreed, ordinarily she is liable only for compensatory damages and those consequential damages that are contemplated by the client and the professional at the time the contract was made, such as the client's cost of hiring another consultant or auditor to complete the work. For example, an auditor agrees to provide audited financial statements for inclusion in a client's bank loan application. The loan will be used to expand the client's business. When the auditor fails to complete the audit on time, the auditor will not ordinarily be liable for the client's lost profits from the unexecuted

Ethics in Action

Public Company Accounting Oversight Board

One of the main features of the Sarbanes–Oxley Act (SOX) is the creation of an independent board that oversees the audits of public companies. Congress's perception was that auditing firms were not sufficiently independent of the public companies they audited due in part to the audit firms' receiving sizable nonaudit consulting fees from their audit clients. Thus, SOX created a Public Company Accounting Oversight Board (PCAOB). Public accounting firms that audit financial statements of public companies are required to register with PCAOB and submit to its rules. The board is charged with adopting rules establishing auditing, quality control, ethics, and independence standards. It has the power to regulate the nonaudit services that audit firms may perform for their clients. The PCAOB has the power to inspect periodically public accounting firms and to issue reports of the results of the reviews. The purpose of inspections is to assess the degree of compliance with the requirements of SOX, professional auditing standards, and the rules of the PCAOB and the SEC in the performance of audits and the issuance of audit reports of public companies. In addition, the PCAOB may investigate and discipline audit firms and their partners and employees.

The PCAOB is not a federal agency, but a nonprofit corporation with broad regulatory power like the National Association of Securities Dealers, a self-regulatory organization that regulates securities brokers and dealers. It has five members, only two of which may be CPAs. No board member may receive any share of profits or compensation from a public accounting firm.

• Do you think that the creation and work of the PCAOB results in greater independence of auditors of public companies?
• If auditing of financial statements is required primarily for the protection of public investors, should not all PCAOB members be taken from the investment community that uses audited financial statements?

The Global Business Environment

U.S. Moving to International Accounting Standards?

In 2008, the SEC announced that it would consider requiring American companies to comply with International Financial Reporting Standards (IFRS) adopted by the International Accounting Standards Board (IASB). The SEC proposal is designed to move the world to one set of accounting standards and, thereby, permit investors to compare more easily companies operating in differing parts of the world. The proposal, it is claimed, would also make it easier for companies to raise capital by allowing them to sell securities in securities markets anywhere in the world.

In 2011, the SEC withdrew its proposal and indicated it will not require American companies to comply with IFRS until 2015, at the earliest. It also withdrew permission for American firms to comply with IFRS voluntarily before 2015, although it has reserved the right to reconsider that decision.

• From time to time, the SEC has exercised its power to block an accounting standard issued by the FASB when it deems inappropriate the treatment required or permitted by the rule. Do you think the SEC will exercise the same power when it views as wrong an IASB standard?
• Under the Securities Exchange Act of 1934, the SEC has the power to set accounting standards for U.S. public companies. Do you think the SEC abdicated its responsibility by allowing the FASB today and the IASB in the future to set American accounting standards? Whom do you trust more to adopt reasonable accounting standards: the SEC, the FASB, or the IASB?

expansion, unless the auditor had agreed to be liable for such lost profits.

A professional is not liable for breach of contract if the client obstructs the performance of the contract. For example, an investment banker is not liable for failing to make a timely public offering of a client's securities if the client delays giving the investment banker the information it needs to complete the securities offering registration statement.

A professional may not delegate his duty to perform a contract without the consent of the client. Delegation is not permitted because the performance of a contract for profes-

sional services depends on the skill, training, and character of the professional. For example, PricewaterhouseCoopers, a public accounting firm, may not delegate to Ernst & Young, another public accounting firm, the contractual duty to audit the financial statements of Apple Inc., even though both firms are nearly equally skillful and careful.

Tort Liability Professionals' tort liability to their clients may be based on the common law concepts of negligence and fraud or on the violation of a statute, including the federal and state securities laws.

Negligence The essence of negligence is the failure of a professional to exercise the skill and care of the ordinarily prudent person in the profession. A professional is negligent when he breaches the duty to act skillfully and carefully and proximately causes damages to the client. For example, a corporate client may recover from an investment banker when the client overpays for an acquired firm due to the investment banker's careless valuation of the acquired firm.

Under the **suitability** and **know-your-customer rules** of the NASD and stock exchanges, a securities broker is required to know the financial circumstances and investment objectives of his client before recommending securities or executing securities transactions for the client. A broker who does not know his customer is negligent and may be liable for losses from securities transactions that are inappropriate for the client. A broker that warns a client of the risks and inappropriateness of an investment has met his duty and is not liable, for example, to a client that disregards the risk and authorizes trading in the risky investment. The suitability and know-your-customer rules may also justify a client's action on *contract* grounds when the customer signs an account agreement that requires a broker to handle the account in accordance with industry standards.

See *Millan v. Dean Witter Reynolds* on page 946 of Chapter 36 for a case in which a securities brokerage was held liable to its client for negligence and gross negligence.

Audit Duties Audit engagements are a unique area of professional liability. Sometimes, an accountant will audit a company, yet fail to uncover fraud, embezzlement, or other intentional wrongdoing by an employee of the company. Ordinarily, an accountant has no specific duty to uncover employee fraud or embezzlement. Nonetheless, an accountant must uncover employee fraud or embezzlement if an ordinarily prudent accountant would have discovered it. The accountant who fails to uncover such fraud or embezzlement is negligent and liable to his client. In addition, an accountant owes a duty to investigate suspicious circumstances that tend to indicate fraud, regardless of how he became aware of those circumstances. Also, an accountant has a duty to inform a proper party of his suspicions. It is *not enough* to inform or confront the person suspected of fraud.

When an accountant is hired to perform a fraud audit to investigate suspected fraud or embezzlement, she has a greater duty to investigate. She must be as skillful and careful as the ordinarily prudent auditor performing a fraud audit.

When an accountant negligently fails to discover embezzlement, generally he is liable to his client only for an amount equal to the embezzlement that occurred after he should have discovered the embezzlement. The accountant is usually not liable for any part of the embezzlement that occurred prior to the time he should have uncovered the embezzlement unless his tardy discovery prevented the client from recovering embezzled funds.

Contributory and Comparative Negligence of Client Courts are reluctant to permit a professional to escape liability to a client merely because the client was **contributorily negligent.** Since the accountant or consultant has skills superior to those of the client, courts generally allow clients to rely on an accountant's duty to discover employee fraud, a consultant's duty to make reasonable recommendations, and an underwriter's advice on what type of security to issue. The client is not required to exercise reasonable care to discover these things itself.

Nonetheless, some courts allow the defense of contributory negligence or the defense of **comparative negligence,** such as when clients negligently fail to follow a consultant's advice or when clients possess information that makes their reliance on an investment banker unwarranted.

In the following *Fehribach* case, the appeals court considered the scope of an auditor's duty when conducting an audit and the greater ability of the client to know its financial condition and, thereby, protect itself. Note also that the court, applying the *Ultramares* rule we will study later in this chapter, found that the bankruptcy trustee was a proper plaintiff only because he sued the auditor on behalf of the auditor's client.

Fehribach v. Ernst & Young LLP   493 F.3d 905 (7th Cir. 2007)

In October 1995, Ernst & Young LLP (E&Y) issued an audit report for fiscal year 1995 regarding its client, Taurus Foods, Inc., a small company engaged in the distribution of frozen meats and other foods. American Institute of Certified Public Accountants, Statement on Auditing Standards No. 59 (1988) requires an auditor report to indicate the auditor's substantial doubt about the audited company's ability to continue as a going concern for a reasonable period of time, not to exceed one year beyond the date of the financial statements being audited. E&Y's report on Taurus indicated that E&Y had "no substantial doubt" that Taurus would continue as a going concern until at least January 1996.

Several months after E&Y's audit report was received by Taurus, its chief lender, Bank One, became alarmed by the deterioration in Taurus's financial condition. The bank imposed restrictions on Taurus that increased the company's business troubles. To stave off disaster, Lisa Corry, the company's chief financial officer (and the daughter of one of Taurus's two owners), started defrauding Bank One by inflating the company's sales and accounts receivable in daily reports that Taurus was required to make to the bank. She was eventually caught, prosecuted, convicted, and sent to prison. Soon after, in 1998, Taurus entered in a bankruptcy proceeding.

Taurus's bankruptcy trustee, Gregory Fehribach, asked the district court to require E&Y to pay damages for failing to include a going concern qualification in its audit report for the 1995 fiscal year. The trustee argued that if E&Y had issued the qualification, the owners of Taurus—who were active owners who managed the company—would have realized that the company had no future and would immediately have liquidated, averting costs of some $3 million that the company incurred as a result of its continued operation under the restrictions imposed by Bank One. E&Y moved for summary judgment, which the district court granted. Taurus's bankruptcy trustee appealed to the Seventh Circuit Court of Appeals.

Posner, Circuit Judge

The trustee's damages claim is based on the theory of "deepening insolvency." This controversial theory allows damages sometimes to be awarded to a bankrupt corporation that by delaying liquidation ran up additional debts that it would not have incurred had the plug been pulled sooner. As originally formulated, the theory was premised on the notion that borrowing after a company becomes insolvent would "ineluctably" hurt the shareholders. That was a puzzling suggestion because by hypothesis a company harmed by *deepening* insolvency was insolvent before the borrowing spree, so what had the shareholders to lose? But a corporation can be insolvent in the sense of being unable to pay its bills as they come due, yet be worth more liquidated than the sum of its liabilities and so be worth something to the shareholders.

The theory could also be invoked in a case in which management in cahoots with an auditor or other outsider concealed the corporation's perilous state which if disclosed earlier would have enabled the corporation to survive in reorganized form. However, the theory makes no sense when invoked to create a substantive duty of prompt liquidation that would punish corporate management for trying in the exercise of its business judgment to stave off a declaration of bankruptcy, even if there were no indication of fraud, breach of fiduciary duty, or other conventional wrongdoing. Nor would it do to fix liability on a third party for lending or otherwise investing in a firm and as a result keeping it going, when management misused the opportunity created by that investment. Management could have instead used that opportunity to turn the company around and transform it into a profitable business. They did not, and therein lies the harm to the company.

The owners of Taurus lost their entire investment when the company became insolvent. They had nothing more to lose. The only possible losers from the prolongation of the corporation's miserable existence were the corporation's creditors. In a state that allows creditors (or shareholders) of the audited firm to sue the auditor for negligent misrepresentation, provided that the creditors' reliance on the auditor's report was foreseeable—or, in some states, was actually foreseen—Taurus's creditors could

sue E&Y directly. But Indiana adheres to a close approximation to *Ultramares Corp. v. Touche*, 255 N.Y. 170, 174 N.E. 441 (N.Y. 1931). And under the *Ultramares* doctrine, creditors in the position of Taurus's creditors, not having a contractual relation with the auditor, have no claim against it.

Taurus had the contractual relation, and thus could sue, though because it is in bankruptcy and has been liquidated the suit is really on behalf of the creditors; anything that reduces the liquidation value of the corporation hurts them. That doesn't make the suit an impermissible end run around Indiana's limitation of creditor (or shareholder) suits against auditors. Remember that under Indiana law E&Y has no duty of care to the creditors. But it does of course have such a duty to its client, Taurus, and that duty, on which this suit is founded, does not evaporate just because the client is bankrupt and any benefits from suing will accrue to its creditors.

The trustee's claim fails nevertheless, but fails on the facts, though not because Taurus survived for more than a year (in fact three years) after the audit period. A going-concern qualification is just a prediction; if it should have been included in the audit report and harm resulted as a foreseeable consequence of its omission, the auditor is liable to the firm audited for that harm. Such cases are rare because it is unusual for the audited firm to be able to make a plausible contention that it could not have been expected to recognize its financial peril on its own even though it supplied the financial information on which the audit was based. The purpose of an audit report is to make sure the audited company's financial statements—which are prepared by the company, not by the auditor—correspond to reality, lest they either have been doctored by a defalcating employee or innocently misrepresent the company's financial situation. The auditor is therefore required to state whether, in his opinion, the financial statements are presented in conformity with generally accepted accounting principles and to identify those circumstances in which such principles have not been consistently observed in the preparation of the financial statements of the current period in relation to those of the preceding period. There is no contention that E&Y failed to notice discrepancies

Business Law: The Ethical, Global, and E-Commerce Environment, 15th Edition

291

Chapter Forty-Six   **Legal and Professional Responsibilities of Auditors, Consultants, and Securities Professionals**   1193

between the statements and the company's actual financial situation. There were no discrepancies. And no information that the report contained or should have contained if the audit was carefully done indicated that Taurus couldn't limp through another year—the report revealed positive though slight net income in the most recent fiscal year and no obligations that would mature in the next year and by doing so might drive the firm under.

It is true that the report failed to warn Taurus of ominous trends in the frozen-meat distribution business. Intensified competition from national firms was causing Taurus to lose customers, thus depressing the firm's revenues; at the same time, the company's costs were rising because of higher workers' compensation premiums and other untoward developments. But predicting Taurus's future cash flow on any basis other than the financial statements for the audit year (which would for example reveal existing loan-repayment obligations) was not the function of the audit report. E&Y had not contracted to provide Taurus with management-consulting services. An auditor's duty is not to give business advice; it is merely to paint an accurate picture of the audited firm's financial condition, insofar as that condition is revealed by the company's books and inventory and other sources of an auditor's opinion.

But there is need to qualify what we have just said. The requirement that the auditor disclose in its report any substantial doubt it has that the firm will still be a going concern in a year expands the auditor's duty beyond that of verifying the accuracy of the company's financial statements. The accounting standards require the auditor to be on the lookout for certain conditions or events that, when considered in the aggregate, indicate there could be substantial doubt about the entity's ability to continue as a going concern for a reasonable period of time. The following are examples of such conditions and events:

Negative trends—for example, recurring operating losses, working capital deficiencies, negative cash flows from operating activities, adverse key financial ratios.

Other indications of possible financial difficulties—for example, default on loan or similar agreements, arrearages in dividends, denial of usual trade credit from suppliers, restructuring of debt, non-compliance with statutory capital requirements, need to seek new sources or methods of financing or to dispose of substantial assets.

Internal matters—for example, work stoppages or other labor difficulties, substantial dependence on the success of a particular project, uneconomic long-term commitments, need to significantly revise operations.

External matters that have occurred—for example, legal proceedings, legislation, or similar matters that might jeopardize an entity's ability to operate; loss of a key franchise, license, or patent; loss of a principal customer or supplier; uninsured or underinsured catastrophe such as a drought, earthquake, or flood.

American Institute of Certified Public Accountants, "The Auditor's Consideration of an Entity's Ability to Continue as a Going Concern," in *Codification of Statements on Accounting Standards*, § 341.06 (2007). It is the last bullet point, referring to "external matters," that stretches the auditor's duty—especially, so far as bears on this case, the reference to "loss of a principal customer or supplier." Elsewhere the standards emphasize that the auditor must have "an appropriate understanding of the entity *and its environment*" *Id.*, §§ 314.01-.02 (emphasis added).

Yet nowhere is the auditor required to *investigate* external matters as distinct from discovering them during the engagement. An accounting firm that conducts an annual audit of a multitude of unrelated firms in a multitude of different industries cannot be expected to be expert in the firms' business environments. Large accounting firms like E&Y do divide their practice into industry groups, and the accountants assigned to a particular group doubtless know a lot about the companies. But the auditor is not hired to assess the supply and demand conditions facing the audited firm. If the auditor is told by the firm or otherwise learns from the information that it collects in conducting the audit that the firm's near-term prospects are endangered by pending legislation, the loss of a customer, or other "conditions or events," then it must factor the information into its assessment of the firm's risk of going under within a year. But it is not expected to duplicate the expertise assumed to reside in the firms themselves and in management consultants specializing in the firm's industry. E&Y could not have been expected to know more about trends in the frozen-meat distribution business than Taurus, which had been in that business for more than 20 years.

Judgment for E&Y affirmed.

Fraud   A professional is liable to his client for fraud when he misstates or omits facts in communications with his client and acts with **scienter.** A person acts with scienter when he knows of the falsity of a statement or he recklessly disregards the truth. Thus, accountants are liable in fraud for their intentional or reckless disregard for accuracy in their work.

For example, an accountant chooses not to examine the current figures in a client's books of account, but relies on last year's figures because he is behind in his work for other clients. As a result, the accountant understates the client's income on an income statement that the client uses to apply for a loan. The client obtains a loan, but he has to pay a higher interest rate because his low stated income makes the loan a higher risk for the bank. Such misconduct by the accountant proves scienter and, therefore, amounts to fraud.

Scienter also includes recklessly ignoring facts, such as an auditor's finding obvious evidence of embezzlement yet failing to notify a client of the embezzlement. An investment banker defrauds its client when it withholds information concerning the value of the client's shares and causes the client to issue the shares for too little consideration, perhaps to an affiliate of the investment banker who, therefore, profits unreasonably. As you can see, fraud is extremely reprehensible conduct, and a defrauder deserves to be punished. Fraud actions are not designed to impose liability on honest professionals who sometimes make careless errors.

The chief advantage of establishing fraud is that the client may get a higher damage award than when the accountant is merely negligent. Usually, a client may receive only compensatory damages for a breach of contract or negligence. By proving fraud, a client may be awarded punitive damages as well.

Breach of Trust

A professional owes a duty of trust to his client. Information and assets that are entrusted to an accountant, broker, or investment banker, for example, may be used only to benefit the client. The duty of trust requires the professional to maintain the confidentiality of the client's information entrusted to the firm. Therefore, a professional may not disclose sensitive matters such as a client's income and wealth or use secret information about a client's new product to purchase the client's securities. In addition, for example, an accountant or securities broker may not use the assets of his client for his own benefit.

Securities Law

Federal and state securities law creates several rights of action for persons harmed in connection with the purchase or sale of securities. These rights of action are based in tort. Although some securities law sections permit clients to sue professionals, they are rarely used for that purpose. Usually, only third parties (nonclients) sue under the securities law. Therefore, the securities law sections that apply to professionals are discussed later in this chapter.

LOG ON

www.securitieslaw.com
The Securities Fraud & Investor Protection Resource Center provides information on the investor–broker relationship, including investors' rights of actions against brokers.

 LO2 Engage in behavior that prevents you and your firm from having liability to clients and third parties under federal securities and other laws.

Professionals' Liability to Third Persons: Common Law

Other persons besides a professional's clients may use her work product. Banks may use financial statements reviewed by a loan applicant's accountant in deciding whether to make a loan to the applicant. Investors may use financial statements audited by a company's auditors in deciding whether to buy or sell the company's securities. These documents prepared by an accountant may prove incorrect, resulting in damages to the nonclients who relied on them. For example, banks may lend money to a corporation only because an income statement prepared by an accountant overstated the corporation's income. When the corporation fails to repay the loan, the bank may sue the accountant to recover the damages it suffered.

Nonclient actions are rarer outside the accountant context because the work product of nonaccounting professionals is infrequently used by others in an expectable way. For example, consulting advice is almost never passed from a client to a third party. A securities broker's client rarely relays the broker's investment advice to a friend; when the friend attempts to sue the broker if the advice turns out to be bad, the friend usually is not able to recover damages from the broker.

However, investment bankers often prepare documents for their clients that are created expressly to sell securities to nonclients, that is, shareholders and other holders of the client's securities. Therefore, purchasers who buy the client's securities based on false statements in a document prepared for investors by an investment banker may sue the investment banker.

Nonclients may sue professionals for common law negligence, common law fraud, and violations of the securities laws. In this section, common law negligence and fraud are discussed.

Negligence and Negligent Misrepresentation

When a professional fails to perform as the ordinarily prudent professional would perform, she risks having liability for negligence. Many courts have restricted the ability of nonclients to sue a professional for damages proximately caused by the professional's negligent conduct. These courts limit nonclient suits on the grounds that nonclient users of a professional's work

Ethics in Action

The Sarbanes–Oxley Act: Auditor Independence Standards

When Congress studied the causes of financial statement irregularities in 2002, it became convinced that some auditors failed to challenge their clients' financial reporting practices for fear that the audit firms would lose lucrative consulting contracts with the clients. The belief was that firms undercharged for audit services to acquire valuable consulting clients. To ensure that audit firms are free from conflict-of-interest and lack of independence charges that can undermine the quality of their audits, the Sarbanes–Oxley Act (SOX) bans most types of services by audit firms for audit clients, including:

* Bookkeeping.
* Financial information system design.
* Appraisal or valuation services.
* Actuarial services.
* Internal audit outsourcing.

* Management or human resource services.
* Broker, dealer, investment banker, and investment adviser services.
* Legal and expert services related to the audit.
* Other services as determined by the Public Company Accounting Oversight Board.

The PCAOB also has power on a case-by-case basis to exempt services performed by an audit firm for an audit client. An audit firm may provide permissible nonaudit services for an audit client, such as tax services, only if the client's audit committee approves the services in advance.

In addition, SOX requires that the audit partner-in-charge be rotated every five years at a minimum. SOX also charges the General Accounting Office to study whether all public companies should be required to rotate audit firms on a regular basis. Finally, no audit firm may audit a public company that within the past year has hired an audit firm employee as a CEO, CFO, or CAO.

---

product have not contracted with the professional and, therefore, are not in **privity of contract** with her. Essentially, these courts hold that a professional owes no duty to nonclients to exercise ordinary skill and care.

This judicial stance conflicts with the usual principles of negligence law under which a negligent person is liable to all persons who are reasonably foreseeably damaged by his negligence. The rationale for the restrictive judicial stance was expressed in the *Ultramares* case,[1] a decision of the highest court in New York. In that case, Judge Benjamin Cardozo refused to hold an auditor liable to third parties for mere negligence. His rationale was stated as follows:

> If liability for negligence exists, a thoughtless slip or blunder, the failure to detect a theft or forgery beneath the cover of deceptive entries, may expose accountants to a liability in an indeterminate amount for an indeterminate time to an indeterminate class.

The *Ultramares* privity requirement protects an auditor or other professional who does not know the user or the extent of use of its work product and, therefore, is unable to assess the potential dollar amount of liability or the user's propensity to sue. *Ultramares* allows auditors and other professionals to manage the known risks of their work product being used by nonclients either by insuring

against the risk, increasing the client's engagement fee, or declining the engagement.

Ultramares dominated the thinking of judges for many years, and its impact is still felt today. However, many courts understand that many nonclients use and reasonably rely on the work product of professionals, especially accountants. To varying degrees, these courts have relaxed the privity requirement and expanded the class of persons who may sue an accountant or other professional for negligent conduct. Today, most courts adopt one of the following three tests to determine whether a nonclient may sue a professional for negligence.

Primary Benefit Test The *Ultramares* court adopted a primary benefit test for imposing liability for negligence. Under this test, a professional's duty of care extends only to those persons for whose primary benefit the professional audits or prepares financial reports and other documents. The professional must actually foresee the nonclient's use and prepare the document primarily for use by a specified nonclient. That is, the nonclient must be a **foreseen user** of the professional's work product. The professional must know four things: (1) the name of the person who will use her work product, (2) the particular purpose for which that person will use the work product, (3) the extent of the use, such as the dollar amount of the nonclient's transaction, and (4) the client has the primary intent that the user use the work product.

---

[1] *Ultramares Corp. v. Touche*, 174 N.E. 441 (N.Y.Ct.App. 1931).

Suppose an investment banker acts as a broker for a client issuing $100 million of securities to 10 mutual funds identified as prospective buyers. To assist the client's sale of the securities, the investment banker prepares an offering memorandum for the client, and the client tells the investment banker that the offering memo is being prepared for the benefit of the 10 mutual funds. If due to the investment banker's negligence the offering memorandum misstates material facts, and the client gives the offering memorandum to the previously identified mutual funds, the investment banker may have liability to the mutual funds that relied on the misstated facts.

Foreseen Users and Foreseen Class of Users Test By 1965, a draft of the *Restatement (Second) of Torts* proposed that the law of professional negligence expand the class of protected persons to **foreseen users** and **users within a foreseen class of users** of reports. Under this test, the professional must know the use and extent of use to be made of the work product. The protected persons are (1) those persons who a professional knows the client intends will use the work product and (2) those persons who use the work product in a way the professional knew the client intended the work product would be used.

For example, an accountant prepares an income statement that he knows his client will use to obtain a $50 million loan at Bank X. Any bank to which the client supplies the statement to obtain a similar loan, including Bank Y, may sue the accountant for damages caused by a negligently prepared income statement. Bank X is a foreseen user, and Bank Y is in a foreseen class of users. On the other hand, if an accountant prepares an income statement for a tax return and the client, without the accountant's knowledge, uses the income statement to apply for a loan from a bank, the bank is not among the protected class of persons—the accountant did not know that the tax return would be used for that purpose.

Also, if the accountant prepared the client's income statement for the purpose of aiding the client to obtain a $50 million loan, but instead the client obtained a $200 million loan, the accountant would not be liable to the nonclient bank: the accountant did not know the extent of the bank's use, that is, the dollar amount of risk to which she was exposed.

In the securities professional context, when an underwriter prepares an offering document for a client issuing a known amount of securities, the *Restatement* test extends an underwriter's liability for negligence to any purchaser of the securities whether known or not to the underwriter. This is because the underwriter knows the type of person who will use the offering document, that is, buyers of the securities, the use, and the extent of the use, that is, the dollar amount of securities to be bought.

Nonetheless, when the *Restatement* test is applied to securities brokers, liability rarely extends past the broker's client. A broker who gives investment advice to a client is rarely found liable to a nonclient who receives the advice secondhand on the grounds that investment advice is crafted specifically for the broker's client. That rationale is generally followed even in the context of a published investment newsletter, where usually only subscribers to the newsletter are permitted to sue the publisher of the newsletter.

Foreseeable Users Test A very few courts have applied traditional negligence causation principles to professional negligence. They have extended liability to **foreseeable users** of an accountant's audit and other reports who suffered damages that were proximately caused by the accountant's negligence. To be liable to a nonclient under this test, an accountant need merely be reasonably able to expect or foresee the nonclient's use of the accountant's work product. It is not necessary for the nonclient to prove that the accountant actually expected or foresaw the nonclient's use.

In the next case against accounting giant PricewaterhouseCoopers (PwC), the court reviewed the scope of *Ultramares* and other cases in the course of interpreting the Illinois statute defining those persons to whom a professional may be liable for negligent misrepresentation.

Tricontinental Industries, Ltd. v. PricewaterhouseCoopers, LLP
475 F.3d 824 (7th Cir. 2007)

Anicom, Inc., was a wire distribution company founded in the early 1990s. Its stock became publicly traded, and the company adopted a strategy to increase market share and to expand its operations. Between 1995 and 1997, Anicom acquired 12 companies. Each of these transactions involved some payment in the form of Anicom stock. During this time, PricewaterhouseCoopers, LLP, rendered accounting, audit, and various types of consulting services to Anicom.

In 1996, Anicom began engaging in improper accounting procedures to enable it to report that it had met sales and revenue goals. The procedures included the use of fictitious sales orders or prebills for goods that were not ordered. PwC became aware of these practices in July 1997 when it was asked to investigate Anicom's billing practices. After conducting its investigation, PwC reported to Donald C. Welchco, Anicom's vice president and CFO, that improper billing had occurred at Anicom branches and that, in the absence of controls, the practice might arise at other branches as well. No mention of these irregularities was made in PwC's audits of Anicom's 1998 and 1999 financial statements. Indeed, PwC issued opinions that Anicom's financial statements were accurate, complete, and conformed with GAAP and that its audits were performed according to GAAS.

In September 1998, Anicom made an Asset Purchase Agreement to acquire the wire and cable distribution assets of three companies: Texcan Cables Ltd. (known now as Tricontinental Distribution Ltd.), Texcan Cables, Inc., and Texcan Cables International, Inc. Anicom acquired those assets in exchange for cash and Anicom stock. After the transaction, Tricontinental Distribution and Texcan Cables, Inc., transferred their stock to Tricontinental Industries, Ltd.

On July 18, 2000, Anicom announced that it was investigating possible accounting irregularities that could result in revision of its 1998, 1999, and first quarter 2000 financial statements by as much as $35 million. Accordingly, Anicom announced that its 1998 and 1999 financial statements should no longer be relied upon. After conducting an internal investigation, Anicom further announced that, subject to audit, it believed that, for the period from the first quarter of 1998 to the first quarter of 2000, the company had overstated revenue by approximately $39.6 million. None of the company's announcements or disclosures ever stated that full-year 1997 revenue or net income had been materially misstated or that any of Anicom's prior financial results were inaccurate in any way. On January 5, 2001, Anicom filed for bankruptcy protection.

In July 2001, Tricontinental Industries filed an action against PwC for negligent misrepresentation. Tricontinental maintained that PwC knew that Tricontinental was relying on Anicom's audited financial statement for 1997 and, specifically, was relying on PwC's representation that the audit was performed in a manner consistent with GAAS and that Anicom's financial statements conformed with GAAP. These statements, Tricontinental alleged, were materially false, misleading, and without reasonable basis.

PwC moved to dismiss Tricontinental's complaint on the grounds that PwC owed no duty to Tricontinental, because the Illinois Public Accounting Act (IPAA) limited PwC's liability to persons who were either in privity of contract with PwC or for whose primary intent Anicom had secured PwC's services. The district court granted PwC's motion. Tricontinental appealed.

Ripple, Circuit Judge

In order to state a claim for negligent misrepresentation under Illinois law, a party must allege:

(1) a false statement of material fact; (2) carelessness or negligence in ascertaining the truth of the statement by the party making it; (3) an intention to induce the other party to act; (4) action by the other party in reliance on the truth of the statement; (5) damage to the other party resulting from such reliance; and (6) a duty on the party making the statement to communicate accurate information.

The Illinois courts have considered, on several occasions, the application of these requirements, specifically, the element of duty, as it applies to public accountants. The Illinois Appellate Court first spoke to this issue in *Brumley v. Touche, Ross & Co.*, 463 N.E.2d 195 (Ill. App. Ct. 1984) (*Brumley I*). In that case, the court reviewed the various approaches that courts around the country had adopted for accountant liability to third parties: (1) the standard set forth in *Ultramares Corp. v. Touche*, 174 N.E. 441 (N.Y. 1931), which held that public accountants could not be liable in negligence to third parties absent privity, (2) a reasonable

foreseeability standard; and (3) a more limited foreseeability rule that public accountants may be liable to plaintiffs, who are not exactly identifiable, but who belong to a limited class of persons whose reliance on the accountant's representations is specifically foreseen. The appellate court held that the plaintiff's complaint was insufficient to set forth a duty on the part of defendant to plaintiff because "the complaint did not allege Touche Ross knew of plaintiff or that the report was to be used by KPK to influence plaintiff's purchase decision nor does it allege that was *the primary purpose and intent* of the preparation of the report by Touche Ross for KPK." *Id.* (emphasis added).

In *Brumley v. Touche, Ross & Company*, 487 N.E.2d 641 (Ill. App. Ct. 1985) (*Brumley II*), the court revisited this standard. In *Brumley II*, the plaintiff had argued that the Supreme Court of Illinois had altered the standard for liability for attorneys, which necessitated a change by the appellate court with respect to accountant liability. The appellate court rejected this argument: it is apparent that to be sufficient plaintiff's complaint must allege facts showing that *the purpose and intent of the accountant-client relationship* was to benefit or influence the third-party plaintiff. 487 N.E.2d at 644–45 (emphasis added).

Shortly after *Brumley II,* the Illinois legislature enacted the Illinois Public Accounting Act, 225 ILCS 450/30.1, which provides:

> No person, partnership, corporation, or other entity licensed or authorized to practice under this Act . . . shall be liable to persons not in privity of contract with such person, partnership, corporation, or other entity for civil damages resulting from acts, omissions, decisions or other conduct in connection with professional services performed by such person, partnership, corporation, or other entity, except for:
>
> (1) such acts, omissions, decisions or conduct that constitute fraud or intentional misrepresentations, or
>
> (2) such other acts, omissions, decisions or conduct, if such person, partnership or corporation was aware that a primary intent of the client was for the professional services to benefit or influence the particular person bringing the action; provided, however, for the purposes of this subparagraph (2), if such person, partnership, corporation, or other entity (i) identifies in writing to the client those persons who are intended to rely on the services, and (ii) sends a copy of such writing or similar statement to those persons identified in the writing or statement, then such person, partnership, corporation, or other entity or any of its employees, partners, members, officers or shareholders may be held liable only to such persons intended to so rely, in addition to those persons in privity of contract with such person, partnership, corporation, or other entity.

Following IPAA's passage, there was some question regarding the effect of the IPAA on accountant liability. We are obliged, however, to follow the interpretation given the language by the state appellate court in *Chestnut Corp. v. Pestine, Brinati, Gamer, Ltd.,* 667 N.E.2d 543, 546-47 (Ill. App. Ct. 1996). The Illinois court took the view that the first clause of subparagraph (2) states the general rule of accountant liability as set out in *Brumley* while the second clause creates a legislative exception to the general rule. Continued the court:

> [T]o adopt the defendants' interpretation of the statute would require us to hold, as a matter of law, that accountants are never liable to third parties, absent fraud or intentional misrepresentation, unless they agree in writing to expose themselves to liability. The law in Illinois would have come full circle then and returned to the rationale of *Ultramares* in 1931. Absent a clear signal from the legislature or the supreme court that such a return is intended, we believe the observation of the trial court and the evolution of the law since *Ultramares* provides a useful background as one measures the statute's meaning.

Id. at 547.

Although the Supreme Court of Illinois has not spoken to the issue, Illinois Appellate Courts seem to agree that the IPAA embodies the rule applied to accountants in *Brumley II:* The plaintiff must show that a primary purpose and intent of the

accountant-client relationship was to benefit or influence the third-party plaintiff.

The primary intent rule, however, has proven to be somewhat difficult to define in practical terms. For instance, disputes have arisen regarding whether the "primary intent" of the client must be contemporaneous with the accountant's work product on which the third party relies. With respect to this issue, the Illinois Appellate Court has stated:

> In terms of timing, we do not read the statute to strictly require that an accountant be made aware of his client's intention to influence or benefit a third party only at the time the work product was created as defendant contends. The standard requires that a plaintiff prove that the primary purpose and intent of the client was to benefit or influence the third party. In *Brumley II,* we held that the plaintiff in that case met the standard because he alleged that the defendant knew of the plaintiff's reliance on the defendant's reports and that the defendant had subsequently verified its accuracy. We do not, however, read *Brumley II* as *per se requiring independent verification* in order to meet the standard in *Pelham. Other conduct* may be sufficient to satisfy *Pelham.*

Builders Bank v. Barry Finkel & Assocs., 790 N.E.2d 30, 37 (Ill. App. Ct. 2003) (emphasis added).

Further, although Illinois case law has established that "independent verification" is not a per se requirement, Illinois courts have not set forth in detail what "other conduct" may satisfy the "primary intent" standard. The cases, however, do establish that *some* affirmative action on behalf of the defendant-accountant is necessary. For instance, in *Builders Bank,* the record indicated that Finkel, the accountant, was told by Urkov, the company owner, that UMC was applying for a loan and requested that financial statements be furnished to UMC. The record further establishes that Finkel personally met with UMC on two occasions to discuss issues related to the loan. In at least one meeting, UMC was seeking an increase of $200,000 on a loan that had already been approved. In our view, it is reasonable to infer that Finkel played an active role in securing the loan or increasing the loan amount for UMC. From this evidence, a finder of fact could conclude, pursuant to the statute, that Finkel knew its work was being used to influence UMC at least at the time of the second meeting and that defendant, at minimum, presented its work as accurate. *Id.*

Similarly, in *Freeman, Freeman & Salzman, P.C. v. Lipper,* 812 N.E.2d 562 (Ill. App. Ct. 2004), the court held that the standard had been met by the allegation that the accountant to an investment fund had "issued clean audit opinions on each investment partner's capital accounts for those years"; had "addressed and sent its clean audit opinions to the partners who invested in those funds, including plaintiffs"; and had "prepared federal income tax Schedules K-1 for plaintiffs and the limited partners each year." *Id.* at 566–67. Furthermore, "each Schedule K-1 purported

Business Law: The Ethical, Global, and E-Commerce Environment, 15th Edition **297**

Chapter Forty-Six **Legal and Professional Responsibilities of Auditors, Consultants, and Securities Professionals** 1199

to reflect each partner's proportionate share of the partnership's net income for the year, as well as each partner's capital account balance at the beginning and end of each year." *Id.* at 567.

Finally, in *Chestnut Corp.*, the court held that the plaintiffs had stated a claim for negligent misrepresentation by alleging that the plaintiff's representatives had gone to the offices of the defendant-accountants to discuss their possible investment in the client company and to review its financial condition. In response to specific inquiries by the plaintiff's representatives, the defendants "stated that the audit was accurately performed according to generally accepted auditing standards." *Chestnut Corp.*, 667 N.E.2d at 545.

In sum, the duty owed by a professional accountant to non-client third-parties is the standard articulated in *Brumley II* and codified in the IPAA. The IPAA provides that an individual accountant, partnership or firm will be liable to a third party for negligence only "if such person, partnership or corporation was aware that a primary intent of the client was for the professional services to benefit or influence the particular person." This "primary intent" may be demonstrated by "independent verification" or by other affirmative actions taken by the accountant and directed to the third party.

With this standard in mind, we turn to the allegations set forth in the Amended Complaint to determine whether they state a claim for relief.

With respect to the negligent misrepresentation claim, Tricontinental alleged as follows:

163. Prior to the time that PwC conducted its 1997 audit, PwC had assisted Anicom in raising money for acquisitions and finding acquisition candidates. And, in 1997, PwC well knew that Anicom was seeking to complete additional acquisitions. PwC most certainly knew that acquisition candidates, such as Plaintiffs, would rely on the 1997 Form 10-K in making their decisions on whether to invest in Anicom's securities.

164. PwC knew prior to the closing of the Texcan transaction that Plaintiffs were negotiating to sell significant assets to Anicom in exchange in part for Anicom securities. PwC was on the circulation lists for drafts of the Asset Purchase Agreement and PwC conducted due diligence of Texcan for Anicom. PwC knew that Plaintiffs had received and were relying on Anicom's Form 10-K for 1997 and, in particular, PwC's unqualified audit report, and that Anicom intended

that Plaintiffs rely on the 10-K and PwC's audit report in assessing an investment in Anicom. Despite its awareness of these facts, and despite its knowledge from its own investigation and its involvement in the business of Anicom that Anicom was engaged in improper accounting practices and lacked adequate controls to prevent these irregular practices, PwC intentionally or recklessly failed to withdraw its audit opinion on the 1997 financial statements. Instead, PwC allowed Plaintiffs to rely on the false and misleading information contained in Anicom's Form 10-K for 1997.

As noted by the district court, these allegations do not demonstrate any "independent verification" provided by PwC to Tricontinental. However, such verification to the third party is not a per se requirement. "Other conduct" by PwC directed to Tricontinental also may satisfy the "primary intent" requirement of the IPAA. Tricontinental alleges that PwC knew of its reliance on the 1997 audit opinion, knew of the misrepresentation contained in the statement and "allowed plaintiffs to rely on the false and misleading information." However, Illinois cases, fairly read, make clear that the IPAA requires more. In order to state a claim under the IPAA, Tricontinental must allege that it was a primary purpose "of the accountant-client relationship . . . to benefit or influence" Tricontinental. None of the allegations contained in the above-recited paragraphs support such an inference. Indeed, the opposite appears to be the case. The actions taken by PwC—assisting Anicom in raising money for acquisitions, conducting due diligence "for Anicom," and being included on the circulation lists during the transaction—are examples of Anicom's use of PwC's services for its own benefit, not that of Tricontinental. Consequently, although we agree with Tricontinental that neither privity nor independent verification need be asserted or shown in order to state a claim, Tricontinental must set forth a short and plain statement of the claim showing that it is entitled to relief. Absent an allegation that fairly states that Anicom's primary intent in retaining and utilizing PwC's services and work product during the transaction was to influence Tricontinental, or absent factual allegations that support such an inference, Tricontinental has not stated a claim for negligent misrepresentation under Illinois law.

Judgment for PricewaterhouseCoopers affirmed.

Fraud Fraud is such reprehensible conduct that all courts have extended a professional's liability for fraud to all foreseeable users of his work product who suffered damages that were proximately caused by the fraud. Privity of contract, therefore, is not required when a person sues a professional for fraud, even in a state that has adopted the *Ultramares* test for negligence actions. To prove fraud, a nonclient must establish that a professional acted with scienter.

Some courts recognize a tort called constructive fraud that applies when a professional misstates a material fact. For a misstatement to amount to constructive fraud, the professional must have recklessly or grossly negligently failed to ascertain the truth of the statement. As with actual fraud, a professional's liability for constructive fraud extends to all persons who justifiably rely on the misstatement.

Common Law Bases of Liability of Professional to Nonclients for Use of Professional's Work Product

Privity Test Adopted by State	Basis of Liability	
	Negligence	Fraud
Primary Benefit Test (*Ultramares*)	Professional liable only to foreseen users for whose primary benefit the work product was provided (professional knew name of user, purpose of the user's use, extent of the use, and that the client has the primary intent that the user use the work product)	Professional liable to all persons whose damages were caused by their reliance on professional's fraud
Restatement (Second) of Torts **Test**	Professional liable to foreseen users and users in a foreseen class of users (professional knew at least the purpose and extent of the user's use)	
Foreseeable Users Test	Professional liable to all reasonably foreseeable users (professional can reasonably expect or foresee the purpose and extent of the user's use)	

L02 Engage in behavior that prevents you and your firm from having liability to clients and third parties under federal securities and other laws.

Professional's Liability to Third Parties: Securities Law

The slow reaction of the common law in creating a negligence remedy for third parties has led to an increased use of securities law by nonclients—that is, persons not in privity with a professional. Many liability sections in these statutes either eliminate the privity requirement or expansively define privity.

Securities Act of 1933 There are several liability sections under the Securities Act of 1933 (1933 Act). The most important liability section of the Securities Act of 1933 is Section 11, but Sections 12(a)(2) and 17(a) are also important, especially for securities professionals.

Section 11 Liability Section 11 imposes liability on underwriters and experts for misstatements or omissions of material fact in Securities Act registration statements. The 1933 Act registration statement must be filed with the Securities and Exchange Commission by an issuer making a public distribution of securities. The most common expert is an auditor who issues an opinion regarding financial statements. An underwriter, although knowledgeable, skillful, and experienced in securities offerings, is not an "expert" under Section 11.

An auditor or underwriter is liable to any purchaser of securities issued pursuant to a defective registration statement. The purchaser need not establish privity of contract with an underwriter or auditor. Because the underwriter is not an expert under Section 11, the underwriter is liable for errors in the *entire* registration statement. Since an auditor is an expert, the auditor is liable only for the part of the registration statement contributed by the auditor, that is, the auditor's opinion regarding the audited financial statements and those audited financial statements. Usually, the purchaser need not prove he relied on the misstated or omitted material fact; he need not even have read or seen the defective registration statement.

For example, an auditor issues an unqualified opinion regarding a client's income statement that overstates net income by 85 percent. The defective income statement is included in the client's registration statement pursuant to which the client sells its preferred shares. Without reading the registration statement or the income statement, a person buys from the client 1,000 preferred shares for $105 per share. After the correct income figure is released, the price of the shares drops to $25 per share. The auditor will most likely be liable to the purchaser for $80,000, unless the auditor proves the purchaser's damages were caused by other persons or factors.

Under Section 11, auditors and underwriters may escape liability by proving that they exercised due diligence. For auditors, who are experts, this **due diligence defense** requires that an auditor issuing an opinion regarding financial statements prove that she made a reasonable investigation and that she reasonably believed that there were no misstatements or omissions of material fact in the financial statements at the time the registration statement became effective. Because the effective date is often several months after an audit has been completed, an auditor must perform an additional review of the audited statements to ensure that the statements are accurate as of the effective date. In essence, due diligence means that an auditor was not negligent, which is usually proved by showing that she complied with GAAS and GAAP.

For underwriters, who are liable for the entire registration statement, the due diligence defense varies depending on the part of the registration statement. For parts of the registration statement contributed by experts (so-called expertised portions, such as an auditor's opinion and the financial statements covered by that opinion), underwriters are entitled to rely on the expert. Therefore, the underwriter's due diligence defense for errors in audited financial statements generally requires no independent investigation by the underwriter. The underwriter will have no liability for mistakes in an expertised portion if the underwriter had no reason to believe and did not believe that there were any misstatements or omissions of material fact in the audited financial statements. If, however, the underwriter has information leading her to believe that an audited financial statement misstates or omits material facts, she has a duty to investigate until she no longer has that belief and no longer has a reason to have that belief.

For errors in parts of the registration statement not contributed by experts (the nonexpertised portion), the underwriter's defense is that after a reasonable investigation, she had a reasonable belief that there were no misstatements or omissions of material fact in those parts. The nonexpertised portion constitutes the bulk of the registration statement and includes the description of the securities, the statement of the underwriter's compensation, the use of the proceeds of the securities issuance, the description of the issuer's business, the statement of the securities' material risks, and unaudited financial statements.

Standards for complying with the due diligence defense are explained more fully in *Escott v. BarChris Construction Corp.*, which appears in Chapter 45, Securities Regulation, at page 1157.

Section 12(a)(2) Section 12(a)(2) imposes liability on any person who misstates or omits a material fact in connection with an offer or sale of a security that is part of a general distribution of securities by an issuer. Privity of contract between the plaintiff and the defendant apparently is required, because Section 12(a)(2) states that the defendant is liable to the person *purchasing* the security *from him.*

Under Section 12(a)(2), a defendant must have direct contact with a buyer of a security to be liable. Merely performing professional services, such as auditing financial statements, is not enough for Section 12(a)(2) liability. A person must actively solicit the sale, motivated at least by a desire to serve his own financial interest. Such a financial interest is unlikely to be met by an auditor whose compensation is a fee unconnected to the proceeds of the securities sale. In addition, the *Central Bank* case[2] makes it fairly clear that auditors who merely *aid and abet* a client's Section 12(a)(2) violation will not have liability for damages under Section 12(a)(2).

Securities professionals have a greater risk of liability under Section 12(a)(2), because they frequently have direct contact with purchasers. Underwriters helping clients with public offerings sell securities or at least actively solicit sales by speaking with investors and writing the prospectus or other offering document. Since underwriters receive compensation for their services in the form of a commission or a spread (the difference between the amount underwriters pay the issuer and the price they sell at), they have the requisite financial stake in the sale. Securities brokers and dealers also are sellers or actively solicit securities sales and have a financial stake in the sale when they assist issuer distributions of securities and receive a commission or spread.

In the event that a person has sufficient contact with a purchaser to incur Section 12(a)(2) liability, the defendant may escape liability by proving that she did not know and could not reasonably have known of the untruth or omission; that is, she must prove that she was not negligent.

Section 17(a) Under Section 17(a), a purchaser of a security must prove his reliance on a misstatement or omission of material fact for which an accountant or securities professional is responsible. Under two of the subsections of Section 17(a), the investor need prove only negligence by the accountant, underwriter, broker,

---

[2]*Central Bank of Denver, N.A. v. First Interstate Bank of Denver, N.A.,* 511 U.S. 164 (1994).

or adviser. Under the third, the investor must prove the accountant or securities professional acted with scienter. Whether there is a private right of action for damages under Section 17(a) is unclear. The courts of appeals are in disagreement, and the Supreme Court has not ruled on the issue.

Securities Exchange Act of 1934

Two sections of the 1934 Act—Section 18 and Section 10(b)—especially affect the liability of professionals to nonclients.

Section 18 Section 18 of the 1934 Act imposes liability on persons who furnish misleading and false statements of material fact in any report or document filed with the Securities and Exchange Commission under the 1934 Act. Such reports or documents include the annual 10-K report—which includes auditors' opinions regarding financial statements—the 8-K current report, and proxy statements.

Under Section 18, a purchaser or seller of a security may sue an auditor if he relied on the defective statement in the filed document and it caused his damages. Usually, this means that a plaintiff must have *read and relied* on the defective statement in the filed document. The purchaser or seller may sue the auditor even if they are not in privity of contract.

An auditor may escape Section 18 liability by proving that she acted in *good faith* and had *no knowledge* that the information was misleading. That is, she must show that she acted *without scienter*. For this reason, as well as the difficulty of proving reliance, Section 18 liability for auditors is extremely rare.

Although securities professionals, such as brokers and dealers, may file reports under the 1934 Act, those documents are not the type normally used by investors making investment decisions. Section 18 liability is, therefore, not an issue for securities professionals.

Section 10(b) and Rule 10b–5 Securities Exchange Act Rule 10b–5, pursuant to Section 10(b), has been the basis for most of the recent suits investors have brought against auditors and securities professionals. Rule 10b–5 prohibits any person from making a misstatement or omission of material fact in connection with the purchase or sale of any security. Rule 10b–5 applies to misstatements or omissions in any communications with investors, including the use of audited financial statements resulting in a purchase or sale of a security. The wrongful act must have a connection with interstate commerce, the mails, or a national securities exchange.

A purchaser or seller of a security may sue an auditor, underwriter, or broker who has misstated or omitted a material fact. Privity is not required. The purchaser or seller must rely on the misstatement or omission. In omission cases, reliance may be inferred from materiality.

In addition, the defendant must act with scienter. In this context, scienter is an intent to deceive, manipulate, or defraud. For some courts, reckless misconduct is sufficient to prove scienter. Negligence, however, is not enough.

In the next case, the court found that the allegations against auditor Ernst & Young did not establish that E&Y had acted with scienter. The court gives several examples of what does and does not constitute scienter.

Ferris, Baker Watts, Inc. v. Ernst & Young, LLP
395 F.3d 851 (8th Cir. 2005)

MJK Clearing, Inc. (MJK), was a broker-dealer engaged in the risky business of securities borrowing. In securities borrowing, a party lent a security to MJK, which paid cash collateral slightly exceeding the value of the security. The cash collateral was "marked to market" so that if the market price of the security rose, MJK paid additional cash to the lender of the security. If the market price of the security fell, however, the lender owed MJK cash. In addition to borrowing securities, MJK was also a lender and therefore subject to the risk that it would be required to pay additional cash if the securities fell in value. MJK had lent securities to Ferris, Baker, Watts, Inc. (FBW), another broker-dealer, and received cash collateral.

By March 31, 2001, MJK had paid $ 160 million cash—representing nearly one-half of its accounts receivable and 21 percent of its total assets—to another broker-dealer, Native Nations Securities, Inc., in exchange for borrowed securities. These securities were mostly from three thinly traded issuers, including GenesisIntermedia, Inc. In 2001, the price of GenesisIntermedia fell, and Native Nations did not pay the cash collateral it owed MJK. As a result, MJK collapsed, and the Securities Investor Protection Corporation began the liquidation of MJK.

Consequently, FBW was unable to reclaim $20 million of cash collateral it had paid MJK. To recover its loss, FBW sued MJK's independent auditor, Ernst & Young, LLP. FBW argued that it dealt with MJK relying on E&Y's audit of MJK's financial statements, as of year-end March 31, 2001. FBW alleged that E&Y's audit violated Section 10(b) of the Securities Act of 1934 and SEC Rule 10b–5 by recklessly misrepresenting that its audit met generally accepted auditing standards and that MJK's financial statements were fairly presented in accordance with generally accepted accounting principles. The district court dismissed the action, holding that the complaint insufficiently alleged that E&Y had acted with scienter. FBW appealed.

Benton, Circuit Judge

Section 10(b) and Rule 10b–5 prohibit fraudulent conduct in the sale and purchase of securities. Claims require four elements: (1) misrepresentations or omissions of material fact or acts that operated as a fraud or deceit in violation of the rule; (2) causation, often analyzed in terms of materiality and reliance; (3) scienter on the part of the defendants; and (4) economic harm caused by the fraudulent activity occurring in connection with the purchase and sale of a security. Only scienter—the intent to deceive, manipulate, or defraud—is at issue here.

Mere negligence does not violate Rule 10b–5. Severe recklessness, however, may. Recklessness is limited to those highly unreasonable omissions or misrepresentations that involve not merely simple or even inexcusable negligence, but an extreme departure from the standards of ordinary care, and that present a danger of misleading buyers or sellers which is either known to the defendant or is so obvious that the defendant must have been aware of it. This level of recklessness requires that defendants make statements that they know, or have access to information suggesting, are materially inaccurate.

FBW argues it pleaded that E&Y knew of, or had access to, facts that permit a strong inference that its audit opinion was knowingly or recklessly false or misleading. It claims E&Y falsely stated that it conducted the audit in accordance with GAAS, when: (1) E&Y's review of internal control of MJK's securities-borrowing department—the largest and most rapidly growing part of the company—revealed a complete absence of internal control, imposing a duty of heightened scrutiny that E&Y ignored; (2) E&Y failed to investigate whether the $160 million receivable from Native Nations was impaired; and (3) E&Y failed to investigate any subsequent events after the audit (but before issuance of the audit opinion) as to the collectibility of MJK's account receivable from Native Nations, which investigation would have revealed defaults.

FBW further alleges that E&Y disregarded GAAP, which a reasonable accountant follows. Thus, FBW says, a strong inference of scienter arises that E&Y's audit opinion that MJK's financial statements conformed with GAAP was a knowing or reckless misstatement of fact. Specifically, FBW alleges that the financial statements do not disclose as required by GAAP: (1) the concentration of credit risk in the $160 million receivable from Native Nations; (2) the risk that the Native Nations receivable was impaired or uncollectible; and (3) the "going concern" risk from the Native Nations receivable.

Finally, FBW alleges that E&Y failed to disclose—as required by SEC Rule 17a–5—material inadequacies in MJK's internal controls known to E&Y, permitting a strong inference that the nondisclosure was knowing or reckless.

"Allegations of GAAP violations are insufficient, standing alone, to raise an inference of scienter. Only where these allegations are coupled with evidence of corresponding fraudulent intent might they be sufficient." *In re Navarre Corp. Sec. Litig.,* 299 F.3d 735, 745 (8th Cir. 2002). *See also Kushner v. Beverly Enters., Inc.,* 317 F.3d 820, 827, 831 (8th Cir. 2003) (affirming dismissal of complaint alleging failure to establish accounting reserves); *In re K-Tel Int'l, Inc. Sec. Litig.,* 300 F.3d 881, 894–95 (8th Cir. 2002) (affirming dismissal of complaint based on overstatement of assets and "sheer magnitude" of GAAP violations).

Assuming GAAP and GAAS violations occurred here, FBW's catch-all and blanket assertions that E&Y acted recklessly or knowingly are not evidence of corresponding fraudulent intent. This is not a case like Green Tree, where a defendant published statements knowing that crucial information in them was based on discredited assumptions. *Florida State Bd. of Admin, v. Green Tree Fin. Corp.,* 270 F.3d 645, 665 (8th Cir. 2001).

FBW asserts that the district court misreads *Kushner, K-Tel,* and *Navarre.* In fact, the lower court follows not only this court's cases, but also those from other Circuits. *See, e.g., Novak v. Kasaks,* 216 F.3d 300, 309 (2d Cir. 2000) (Allegations of GAAP violations or accounting irregularities, standing alone, are insufficient to state a securities fraud claim.); *Stevelman v. Alias Research Inc.,* 174 F.3d 79, 84 (2d Cir. 1999) (Allegations of a violation of GAAP provisions or SEC regulations, without corresponding fraudulent intent, are not sufficient to state a securities fraud claim.); *Fidel v. Farley,* 392 F.3d 220, 230 (6th Cir. 2004) (The failure to follow generally accepted accounting procedures does not in and of itself lead to an inference of scienter.); *DSAM Global Value Fund v. Altris Software, Inc.,* 288 F.3d 385, 387 (9th Cir. 2002) (affirming dismissal of allegations of a "seriously botched audit" and "a compelling case of negligence—perhaps even gross negligence"); *In re Software Toolworks Inc. Sec. Litig.,* 50 F.3d 615, 627–28 (9th Cir. 1994) (affirming summary judgment for auditor, stating that "mere publication of inaccurate accounting figures, or a failure to follow GAAP, without more, does not establish scienter").

FBW repeatedly asserts that E&Y's audit was so cursory and superficial as to amount to "no audit at all." *See Software Toolworks,* 50 F.3d at 628 (auditing that is "no audit at all" shows scienter). The facts alleged here show otherwise. FBW's complaint says that E&Y was fully aware of the risks associated with MJK's securities borrowing and lending operations, and had an audit plan that recognized the need for closer testing of securities borrowing. FBW states that E&Y did confirm the account receivable with Native Nations, noting its excess over the value of the collateral securities, and its concentration in three issuers. According to the complaint, E&Y did interview MJK's securities-borrowing department manager, who described the processes and procedures, and represented that he performed credit reviews "anywhere from monthly to annually by reviewing other Broker FOCUS reports." FBW

pleads that E&Y examined five files of MJK's (approximately) 60 customers for the presence of signed agreements and annual credit evaluations, inquired as to deficiencies in the files, and verified that securities-borrowing personnel prepared numerous reports, including daily "Balance Order Fail Reports." According to FBW, E&Y conducted tests of internal control activities, and identified reconciliations of balance-sheet cash accounts to bank accounts, and balance-sheet securities ledgers to securities accounts. E&Y concluded that internal controls were effective, and could be relied upon to reduce the substantive audit procedures (and increase reliance on management's representation that no subsequent events occurred after fieldwork, but before issue of the opinion). In sum, FBW alleges a poor audit, not the intent to deceive, manipulate, or defraud required for securities fraud.

Judgment for Ernst & Young affirmed.

Aiding and Abetting In 1994 in the *Central Bank* case discussed earlier, the Supreme Court of the United States held that those who merely aid and abet Rule 10b–5 violations have no liability for damages to those injured by the fraud. The court drew a distinction between those *primarily* responsible for the fraud—who retain Rule 10b–5 liability—and those *secondarily* responsible—who no longer have liability under Rule 10b–5. The distinction between primary and secondary responsibility is unclear. Issuing unqualified opinions regarding false financial statements is primary fault and would impose Rule 10b–5 liability on the auditor. However, an independent accountant's work in connection with false unaudited statements or other financial information released by a client may be only secondary and may not impose Rule 10b–5 liability on the accountant.

The Supreme Court affirmed and explained its *Central Bank* ruling in *Stoneridge Investment Partners.*[3] You can read that case in Chapter 45 on page 1175.

Although auditors are not liable to private litigants for merely secondary activities, Congress has made it clear that the SEC may prosecute accountants for aiding and abetting a client's violation of Rule 10b–5.

A person is subject to SEC sanctions for aiding and abetting under Rule 10b–5 if there is (1) a primary

violation by another person (such as a client fraudulently overstating its earnings), (2) the person's knowing or reckless assistance of the other person's primary violation, and (3) the person's substantial assistance in the achievement of the primary violation (such as an auditor's failure to disclose a client's fraud known to the auditor).

Securities professionals may be primarily responsible for misstatements or omissions of material facts in a variety of contexts, and therefore may have Rule 10b–5 liability to nonclients and clients. For example, an underwriter who drafts an offering memorandum for a client's Rule 506 securities offering is primarily responsible for that document, as well as oral statements the underwriter makes about the issuer and the securities to a prospective investor. Securities brokers may have Rule 10b–5 liability for churning their clients' accounts to generate high commissions for the broker. In addition, brokers may have liability under Rule 10b–5 for giving fraudulent advice to clients.

In 2011, however, the Supreme Court held in *Janus Capital Group, Inc. v. First Derivative Traders*[4] that an investment adviser was not liable for fraudulent statements in a prospectus of a mutual fund sponsored by the investment adviser, because the investment adviser was not the maker of those statements. The court came to this conclusion even though the mutual fund's officers were all

[3]*Stoneridge Investment Partners, LLC v. Scientific-Atlanta, Inc.,* 552 U.S. 148 (2008).

[4]131 S. Ct. 2296 (U.S. Sup. Ct. 2011)

employees of the adviser, and the adviser prepared and distributed the prospectus. The Supreme Court majority ruled that the adviser did not make the fraudulent statement, because the mutual fund was a legally separate entity from the adviser and had ultimate authority over the prospectus, including its content and whether and how to communicate it. In addition, the mutual fund, not the adviser, held the statutory duty to file the prospectus, and there was nothing on the face of the prospectus indicating that any statements therein came from the adviser rather than the mutual fund.

Extent of Liability The Private Securities Litigation Reform Act limits the liability of most auditors and securities professionals to the amount of an investor's loss for which the defendant is responsible. This means that a defendant has *proportionate liability* and need no longer fear being liable for investors' entire losses when a fraudulent client is unable to pay its share of the damages. The determination of the percentage of the loss for which a defendant is responsible is a question for the jury. Note, however, the Reform Act provides that when a person knowingly commits a violation of the securities laws, the defendant may be required to pay an investor's entire loss.

State Securities Law All states have securities
statutes with liability sections. Most of the states have a liability section similar to Section 12(a)(2) of the Securities Act.

Securities Analysts' Conflicts of Interest

For years, investors have known that stock recommendations and research reports by securities analysts in major investment banking firms are almost always overly optimistic. Few analysts have recommended that investors sell a stock. Almost all recommendations are strong buy, buy, accumulate, or hold, with a few sell recommendations sprinkled in. The reasons for such optimism vary from an unwillingness to say anything bad to a belief that a bull market will sustain rising securities prices. But the reason that caught the attention of securities regulators is that analysts may have a conflict of interest. The belief is that full-service investment firms that have securities research, brokerage, and investment banking departments discourage their securities analysts from giving poor recommendations for a public company's stock for fear that a poor recommendation will offend the company's management and cause the company to award valuable

investment banking business to a more cooperative investment firm. Some investment firms even threatened to lower public companies' stock recommendations unless the companies awarded investment banking business to the firms.

The Sarbanes–Oxley Act (SOX) directed the SEC to adopt or to direct the national securities exchanges and NASD to adopt rules to address research analysts' conflicts of interest. SOX requires the rules to accomplish the following:

- Restrict prepublication approval of analysts' research reports by investment banking or other nonresearch personnel in the firm.
- Limit supervision and evaluation of securities analysts' compensation to persons not in the investment banking side of the firm.
- Prohibit investment banking personnel from retaliating against a securities analyst because of a negative research report.
- Set time periods during which firms involved in an underwriting of public issuances may not publish research reports about the issuer and its securities.
- Place information partitions to separate research analysts from review, pressure, or oversight by those whose investment banking activities might bias their judgment.
- Require securities analysts to disclose in public appearances and research reports any conflict of interest, including whether the analyst owns the issuer's securities, whether compensation has been received by the firm or analyst, and whether the issuer is currently or has been a client of the firm in the last year.

The SEC has adopted Regulation AC (Analyst Certification). Although not designed to implement the requirements of SOX, Regulation AC requires an analyst's research report to include the analyst's certification that the views expressed in the report accurately reflect her personal views. Regulation AC also requires a securities analyst to certify whether or not any part of her compensation is related to her recommendation of a security or to her views contained in a company research report. The rule also restricts the relationship between research and investment banking departments of a securities firm, as well as their relationships with companies covered by a securities firm's research reports.

The SEC also has approved NYSE and NASD rules regarding analysts' conflicts of interest. The rules are substantially similar. They prohibit a securities firm from offering favorable research to a company in order to induce the company to use the securities firm's investment

CONCEPT REVIEW

Liability Sections of the 1933 Act and 1934 Act

	Wrongful Conduct	Covered Communications	Who May Sue? (Proper Plaintiff)	Must the Plaintiff Prove Reliance on the Wrongful Conduct?
Securities Act of 1933 Section 11	Misstatement or omission of material fact	1933 Act registration statement only	Any purchaser of securities issued pursuant to the registration statement	No
Securities Act of 1933 Section 12(a)(2)	Misstatement or omission of material fact	Any communication in connection with a general distribution of securities by an issuer (except government issued or guaranteed securities)	Any purchaser of the securities offered or sold	No
Securities Act of 1933 Section 17(a)	Misstatement or omission of material fact	Any communication in connection with any offer to sell or sale of any security	Any purchaser of the securities offered or sold	Yes
Securities Exchange Act of 1934 Section 10(b) and Rule 10b–5	Misstatement or omission of material fact	Any communication in connection with a purchase or sale of any security	Any purchaser or seller of the securities	Yes
Securities Exchange Act of 1934 Section 18	False or misleading statement of material fact	Any document filed with the SEC under the 1934 Act (includes the 1934 Act registration statement, 10-K, 8-K, and proxy statements)	Any purchaser or seller of a security whose price was affected by the statement	Yes

banking service. The rules increase analyst independence by prohibiting investment banking personnel from supervising analysts or approving research reports. Analyst compensation may not be tied to a specific investment banking services transaction. Also, an analyst is restricted in trading for his personal account in securities he recommends. The SEC release discussing and approving the NYSE and NASD rules may be viewed at www.sec.gov/rules/sro/34-48252.htm.

The NASD and the NYSE also passed rules on analysts' conflicts of interest prior to passage of SOX. The rules are substantially similar. They ban favorable research for pay, prohibit analyst compensation based on specific investment banking services, and limit the submission of a research report to an issuer prior to publication of the report.

Dodd–Frank Act and Broker-Dealers

In 2010, Congress passed the Dodd–Frank Wall Street Reform and Consumer Protection Act. The Dodd–Frank Act specifically authorizes the SEC to issue point-of-sale disclosure rules when investors purchase investment products or services, such as mutual fund and investment management services. These disclosures include costs, risks, and conflicts of interest. This authorization follows up the SEC's failure to implement proposed point-of-sale disclosure rules in 2004 and 2005. The SEC's proposed rules generated opposition because they were perceived as burdensome to broker-dealers. For example, they would have required oral

Business Law: The Ethical, Global, and E-Commerce Environment, 15th Edition   **305**

Chapter Forty-Six   **Legal and Professional Responsibilities of Auditors, Consultants, and Securities Professionals**   1207

Liability Sections of the 1933 Act and 1934 Act

Who May Be Sued? (Proper Defendant)	Must the Plaintiff and Defendant Be in Privity of Contract?	Defendant's Level of Fault	Who Has the Burden of Proving or Disproving Defendant's Level of Fault?
Issuer, underwriters, directors, signers (CEO, CFO, and CAO must sign), and experts who contribute to the registration statement (such as auditors of financial statements)	No	Negligence, except for the issuer. Issuer is liable without regard to fault.	Defendant, except issuer, may escape liability by proving due diligence. There are two defenses, but for most defendants for most parts of the registration statement, the defense is that he made a reasonable investigation and had reason to believe and did believe there were no misstatements or omissions of material fact.
Any person who sells a security or actively solicits a sale of a security	Yes (although met by a defendant who has a financial interest in a sale of securities)	Negligence	Defendant may escape liability by proving he did not know and could not reasonably have known of the misstatement or omission of material fact.
Any person responsible for the misstatement or omission	No	Negligence for some parts of Section 17(a); scienter for one part	Plaintiff must prove the defendant acted negligently or with scienter, depending on the subsection.
Any person primarily responsible for the misstatement or omission	No, but defendant must communicate with the plaintiff or know or should know plaintiff will receive the communication with the misstatement or omission	Scienter	Plaintiff must prove the defendant acted with scienter.
Any person who made or caused the statement to be made	No	Scienter	Defendant may escape liability by proving he acted in good faith with no knowledge that the statement was false or misleading.

disclosures for telephone transactions and could have allowed the customer to request disclosures specific to the amount of their investment. In determining the disclosure rules, the Act authorizes the SEC to do investor testing and rely on experts to study financial literacy among retail investors.

The Dodd–Frank Act also provides authority for the SEC to impose a fiduciary duty on broker-dealers and investment advisers in their dealings with their customer. Although the Act does not create such a duty immediately, the Act authorizes the SEC to establish such a standard and requires that the SEC study the standards of care that broker-dealers and investment

advisers apply to their customers and report the findings to Congress.

In addition, the Dodd–Frank Act adds new Section 9(a)(4) to the 1934 Act, making it unlawful for any broker, dealer, or other person selling or offering to sell or purchasing or offering to purchase any security (other than a government security), to make for the purpose of inducing the purchase or sale of such security any false or misleading misstatement of material fact, if the person knew or had reasonable ground to believe the statement was false or misleading. This new section tempers some of the effect of the *Janus* case, discussed on page 1204.

Ethics in Action

Securities and Investment Banking Firms Lose and Settle Conflict of Interest Cases

In the past few years, several securities firms and investment companies have settled or lost actions brought by investors, the SEC, the NASD, and other government and regulatory bodies in the face of allegations of conflicts of interest.

In 2003, securities firm and investment bank Goldman, Sachs & Co. agreed with the SEC, NASD, NYSE, and state regulators to pay $25 million in restitution and an additional $25 million in penalties, plus $50 million to provide the firm's clients with independent research and $10 million for investor education. The settlement stemmed from allegations that Goldman's research analysts were subject to inappropriate influence by Goldman's investment banking services. For example, Goldman required its analysts to prepare business plans that discussed the steps analysts planned to take to assist investment banking efforts. In preparing these business plans, analysts were required to answer such questions as "How much of your time will be devoted to IBD [investment banking division]?" and "How can you work more effectively with IBD to exploit the opportunities available to the firm?" In response to the question "What are the three most important goals for you in 2000?" one analyst replied, "1. Get more investment banking revenue. 2. Get more investment banking revenue. 3. Get more investment banking revenue."

A NASD arbitration panel ordered securities firm Merrill Lynch to pay $1 million to a Florida couple for failing to disclose that its analysts were recommending companies to Merrill Lynch customers that they privately disparaged. The analysts gave the companies positive recommendations in order for Merrill Lynch to obtain the companies' investment banking business.

Securities firm Morgan Stanley was charged by the NASD with improperly rewarding its brokers with tickets to concerts and sporting events in an attempt to boost sales of Morgan Stanley's mutual funds. Morgan Stanley agreed to pay a fine of $2 million.

In settlements with the SEC and state prosecutors, several mutual fund sellers, including Bank of America, FleetBoston Financial, and Putnam Investments agreed to pay hefty fines and make restitution to investors in light of allegations their employees engaged in "market timing" of the firms' mutual funds. Market timing involves frequent trading, usually in international funds, to exploit "stale" mutual fund prices that exist due to time zone differences. The practice allegedly hurts the returns of long-term shareholders of the mutual funds. Bank of America agreed to pay $250 million in restitution and $125 million in fines; FleetBoston, $70 million in restitution and $70 million in fines; Putnam, $10 million in restitution and $100 million in fines.

LO2   Engage in behavior that prevents you and your firm from having liability to clients and third parties under federal securities and other laws.

Limiting Professionals' Liability: Professional Corporations and Limited Liability Partnerships

Every state permits professionals to incorporate their business under a professional incorporation statute.

While there are significant taxation advantages to incorporation, the principal advantage of incorporation—*limited liability of the shareholders*—does not isolate professionals from liability for professional misconduct. For example, an accountant who injures his client by failing to act as the ordinarily prudent accountant would act has liability to his client, despite the incorporation of the accountant's business.

When two or more professionals conduct business as co-owners, however, the corporation—unlike the partnership—does offer them limited liability. While partners in a partnership are jointly and severally liable for each other's negligence, states permit incorporated professionals to escape liability for their associate's torts, unless the professional actually supervised the wrongdoing associate or participated in the tort.

Reacting to the large personal liability sometimes imposed on lawyers and accountants for the professional malpractice of their partners, Texas enacted in 1991 the first statute permitting the formation of limited liability partnerships (LLP). An LLP is similar to a partnership, except that a partner's liability for his partners' professional malpractice is limited to the partnership's assets, unless the partner supervised the work of the wrongdoing partner. A partner retains unlimited liability for his *own* malpractice and, in some states, for all *non*professional obligations of the partnership.

Nearly every state and the District of Columbia have passed LLP statutes. The LLP has become the preferred form of business for professionals who do not incorporate.

For more information on the limited liability partnership, see Chapters 37–39.

Qualified Opinions, Disclaimers of Opinion, Adverse Opinions, and Unaudited Statements

After performing an audit of financial statements, an independent auditor issues an opinion letter regarding the financial statements. The **opinion letter** expresses whether the audit has been performed in compliance with GAAS and whether, in the auditor's opinion, the financial statements fairly present the client's financial position and results of operations in conformity with GAAP. Usually, an auditor issues an unqualified *opinion*—that is, an opinion that there has been compliance with GAAS and GAAP. Sometimes, an auditor issues a qualified opinion, a disclaimer of opinion, or an adverse opinion. Up to this point, you have studied the liability of an auditor who has issued unqualified opinions yet has not complied with GAAS and GAAP.

What liability should be imposed on an auditor who discloses that he has not complied with GAAS and GAAP? An auditor is relieved of responsibility only to the extent that a qualification or disclaimer is specifically expressed in the opinion letter. Therefore, letters that purport to disclaim liability totally for false and misleading financial statements are too general to excuse an accountant from exercising ordinary skill and care.

For example, an auditor qualifies his opinion of the ability of financial statements to present the financial position of a company by indicating that there is uncertainty about how an antitrust suit against the company may be decided. He would not be held liable for damages resulting from an unfavorable verdict in the antitrust suit. He would remain liable, however, for failing to make an examination in compliance with GAAS that would have revealed other serious problems.

For another example, consider an auditor who, due to the limited scope of the audit, disclaims any opinion on the ability of the financial statements to present the financial position of the company. She would nonetheless be liable for the nondiscovery of problems that the limited audit should have revealed.

Likewise, an accountant who issued an adverse opinion that depreciation had not been calculated according to GAAP would not be liable for damages resulting from the wrongful accounting treatment of depreciation, but he would be liable for damages resulting from the wrongful treatment of receivables.

Merely preparing unaudited statements does not create a disclaimer as to their accuracy. The mere fact that the statements are unaudited only permits an accountant to exercise a lower level of inquiry. Even so, an accountant must act as the ordinarily prudent accountant would act under the same circumstances in preparing unaudited financial statements.

Criminal, Injunctive, and Administrative Proceedings

In addition to being held liable for damages to clients and third parties, a professional may be found criminally liable for his violations of securities, tax, and other laws. For criminal violations, he may be fined and imprisoned. His wrongful conduct may also result in the issuance of an injunction, which bars him from doing the same acts in the future. In addition, his wrongful conduct may be the subject of administrative proceedings by the Securities and Exchange Commission and state licensing boards. An administrative proceeding may result in the revocation of a professional's license to practice or the suspension from practice. Finally, disciplinary proceedings may be brought by professional societies and self-regulatory organizations such as the AICPA or NASD.

Criminal Liability under the Securities Laws
Both the Securities Act of 1933 and the Securities Exchange Act of 1934 have criminal provisions that can be applied to professionals. The 1933 Act imposes criminal liability for willful violations of any section of the 1933 Act, including Sections 11, 12(a)(2), and 17(a), or any 1933 Act rule or regulation. For example, willfully making an untrue statement or omitting any material fact in a 1933 Act registration statement imposes criminal liability on a person. The maximum penalty for a criminal violation of the 1933 Act is a $10,000 fine and five years' imprisonment.

The 1934 Act imposes criminal penalties for willful violations of any section of the 1934 Act, such as Sections 10(b) and 18, and any 1934 Act rule or regulation, such as Rule 10b–5. For example, willfully making false or misleading statements in reports that are required to be filed under the 1934 Act incurs criminal liability. Such filings include 10-Ks, 8-Ks, and proxy statements. An individual may be fined up to $5 million and imprisoned for up to 20 years for a criminal violation of the 1934 Act; however, an individual who proves that he had no knowledge of an SEC rule or regulation may not be imprisoned for violating that rule or regulation. A professional firm may be fined up to $25 million.

Most of the states have statutes imposing criminal penalties on professionals who willfully falsify financial statements or other reports in filings under the securities laws and who willfully violate the state securities laws or aid and abet criminal violations of these laws by others.

In *Natelli*, accountants permitting a client to book unbilled sales after the close of the fiscal period subjected the accountants to the criminal penalties of the 1934 Act.

United States v. Natelli	527 F.2d 311 (2d Cir. 1975)

Anthony Natelli was the partner in charge of the Washington, D.C., office of Peat, Marwick, Mitchell & Co., a large CPA firm. In August 1968, Peat, Marwick became the independent public auditor of National Student Marketing Corporation. Natelli was the engagement partner for the audit of Student Marketing. Joseph Scansaroli was Peat, Marwick's audit supervisor on that engagement.

Student Marketing provided its corporate clients with a wide range of marketing services to help them reach the lucrative youth market. In its financial statements for the nine months ended May 31, 1968, Student Marketing had counted as income the entire amount of oral customer commitments to pay fees in Student Marketing's "fixed-fee marketing programs," even though those fees had not yet been paid. They were to be paid for services that Student Marketing would provide over a period of several years. Standard accounting practice required that part of the unpaid fees be considered income in the present year but that part be deferred as income until the years when Student Marketing actually performed the services for which the fees were paid. Therefore, in making the year-end audit, Natelli concluded that he would use a percentage-of-completion approach on these commitments, taking as income in the present year only those fees that were to be paid for services in that year.

The customer fee commitments were oral only, making it difficult to verify whether they really existed. Natelli directed Scansaroli to try to verify the fee commitments by telephoning the customers but not by seeking written verification. However, Scansaroli never called Student's clients. Instead, Scansaroli accepted a schedule prepared by Student Marketing showing estimates of the percentage of completion of services for each corporate client and the amount of the fee commitment from each client. This resulted in an adjustment of $1.7 million for "unbilled accounts receivable." The adjustment turned a loss for the year into a profit twice that of the year before.

By May 1969, a total of $1 million of the customer fee commitments had been written off as uncollectible. The effect of the write-off was to reduce 1968 income by $209,750. However, Scansaroli, with Natelli's approval, offset this by reversing a deferred tax item of approximately the same amount.

Student Marketing issued a proxy statement in September 1969 in connection with a shareholders' meeting to consider merging six companies into Student Marketing. The proxy statement was filed with the Securities and Exchange Commission. It contained several financial statements, some of which had been audited by Peat, Marwick. Others had not been audited, but Peat, Marwick had aided in their preparation. In the proxy statement, a footnote to the financial statements failed to show that the write-off of customer fee commitments had affected Student Marketing's fiscal 1968 income.

The proxy statement required an unaudited statement of nine months' earnings through May 31, 1969. This statement was prepared by Student Marketing with Peat, Marwick's assistance. Student Marketing produced a $1.2 million commitment from the Pontiac Division of General Motors Corporation two months after the end of May, but it was dated April 28, 1969. At 3 AM on the day the proxy statement was to be printed, Natelli informed Randall, the chief executive officer and founder of Student Marketing, that this commitment could not be included because it was not a legally binding contract. Randall responded at once that he had "a commitment from Eastern Airlines" for a somewhat comparable amount attributable to the same period. Such a letter was produced at the printing plant a few hours later, and the Eastern commitment was substituted for the Pontiac sale in the proxy. Shortly thereafter, another Peat, Marwick accountant, Oberlander, discovered $177,547 in "bad" commitments from 1968. These were known to Scansaroli in May 1969 as being doubtful, but they had not been written off. Oberlander suggested to the company that these commitments plus others, for a total of $320,000, be written off, but Scansaroli, after consulting with Natelli, decided against the suggested write-off.

There was no disclosure in the proxy statement that Student Marketing had written off $1 million (20 percent) of its 1968 sales and over $2 million of the $3.3 million of unbilled sales booked in 1968 and 1969. A true disclosure would have shown that Student Marketing had made no profit for the first nine months of 1969.

Subsequently, it was revealed that many of Student Marketing's fee commitments were fictitious. The attorney general of the United States brought a criminal action against Natelli and Scansaroli for violating the Securities Exchange Act of 1934 by willfully and knowingly making false and misleading statements in a proxy statement. The district court jury convicted both Natelli and Scansaroli, and they appealed.

Business Law: The Ethical, Global, and E-Commerce Environment, 15th Edition   **309**

Chapter Forty-Six   **Legal and Professional Responsibilities of Auditors, Consultants, and Securities Professionals**   1211

Gurfein, Circuit Judge

The original action of Natelli in permitting the booking of un-billed sales after the close of the fiscal period in an amount sufficient to convert a loss into a profit was contrary to sound accounting practice. When the uncollectibility, and indeed, the nonexistence of these large receivables was established in 1969, the revelation stood to cause Natelli severe criticism and possible liability. He had a motive, therefore, intentionally to conceal the write-offs that had to be made.

Honesty should have impelled Natelli and Scansaroli to disclose in the footnote that annotated their own audited statement for fiscal 1968 that substantial write-offs had been taken, after year-end, to reflect a loss for the year. A simple desire to right the wrong that had been perpetrated on the stockholders and others by the false audited financial statement should have dictated that course.

The accountant owes a duty to the public not to assert a privilege of silence until the next audited annual statement comes around in due time. Since companies were being acquired by Student Marketing for its shares in this period, Natelli had to know that the 1968 audited statement was being used continuously.

Natelli contends that he had no duty to verify the Eastern commitment because the earnings statement within which it was included was unaudited. This raises the issue of the duty of the CPA in relation to an unaudited financial statement contained within a proxy statement where the figures are reviewed and to some extent supplied by the auditors. The auditors were associated with the statement and were required to object to anything they actually knew to be materially false. In the ordinary case involving an unaudited statement, the auditor would not be chargeable simply because he failed to discover the invalidity of booked accounts receivable, inasmuch as he had not undertaken an audit with verification. In this case, however, Natelli knew

the history of post-period bookings and the dismal consequences later discovered.

In terms of professional standards, the accountant may not shut his eyes in reckless disregard of his knowledge that highly suspicious figures, known to him to be suspicious, were being included in the unaudited earnings figures in the proxy statement with which he was associated.

There is some merit to Scansaroli's point that he was simply carrying out the judgments of his superior, Natelli. The defense of obedience to higher authority has always been troublesome. There is no sure yardstick to measure criminal responsibility except by measurement of the degree of awareness on the part of a defendant that he is participating in a criminal act, in the absence of physical coercion such as a soldier might face. Here the motivation to conceal undermines Scansaroli's argument that he was merely implementing Natelli's instructions, at least with respect to concealment of matters that were within his own ken. The jury could properly have found him guilty on the specification relating to the footnote.

With respect to the Eastern commitment, Scansaroli stands in a position different from that of Natelli. Natelli was his superior. He was the man to make the judgment whether or not to object to the last-minute inclusion of a new commitment in the nine-months statement. There is insufficient evidence that Scansaroli engaged in any conversations about the Eastern commitment or that he was a participant with Natelli in any check on its authenticity. Since in the hierarchy of the accounting firm it was not his responsibility to decide whether to book the Eastern contract, his mere adjustment of the figures to reflect it under orders was not a matter for his discretion.

Conviction of Natelli affirmed. Conviction of Scansaroli affirmed in part and reversed in part.

Other Criminal Law Violations

Tax Law Federal tax law imposes on professionals a wide range of penalties for a wide variety of wrongful conduct. At one end of the penalty spectrum is a $50 fine for an accountant's failing to furnish a client with a copy of his income tax return or failing to sign a client's return. At the other end is a fine of $250,000 for individuals and $500,000 for corporations and imprisonment of five years for tax fraud. In between is the penalty for promoting abusive tax shelters. The fine is $1,000, or 100 percent of the defendant's income from her participation in the tax shelter, whichever is lesser. In addition, all of the states impose criminal penalties for specified violations of their tax laws.

Mail Fraud Several other federal statutes also impose criminal liability on professionals. The most notable of these statutes is the general mail fraud statute, which prohibits the use of the mails to commit fraud. To be held liable, a professional must know or foresee that the mails will be used to transmit materials containing fraudulent statements provided by her.

In addition, the general false-statement-to-government-personnel statute prohibits fraudulent statements to government personnel. The false-statement-to-bank statute proscribes fraudulent statements on a loan application to a bank or other financial institution.

RICO The Racketeer Influenced and Corrupt Organizations Act (RICO) makes it a federal crime to engage in a pattern of racketeering activity. Although RICO was designed to attack the activities of organized crime enterprises, it applies to professionals who conduct or participate in the affairs of an enterprise in almost any pattern of business fraud. A pattern of fraud is proved by the commission of two predicate offenses within a 10-year period. Predicate offenses include securities law violations, mail fraud, and bribery. Individuals convicted of a RICO violation may be fined up to $250,000 and imprisoned up to 20 years.

A person who is injured in his business or property by reason of a professional's conduct or participation, directly or indirectly, in an enterprise's affairs through a pattern of racketeering activity may recover treble damages (three times his actual damages) from the professional. In *Reves v. Ernst & Young,*[5] the Supreme Court held that merely by auditing financial statements that substantially overvalued a client's assets, an accounting firm was not conducting or participating in the affairs of the client's business. The Court held that the accounting firm must participate in the "operation or management" of the enterprise itself to be liable under RICO.

Other Criminal Laws While there are many other criminal laws that may be violated by professionals, one final law bears mentioning: laws against the destruction of evidence that may be used against a professional in a criminal trial. All accounting and securities firms have rules regarding document retention and destruction. For the most part, retaining documents helps a firm prove that it has met its duty to its clients. Retained documents can establish that the firm acted in a reasonable manner when it conducted an audit or made an investment recommendation, for example.

On the other hand, documents may show that the professional or her client has acted inappropriately or even illegally. In general, professionals are not compelled to retain documents that prove their or a client's guilt, provided they do not destroy documents with the intent to obstruct a criminal prosecution. The *Andersen* case, which appears near the end of this chapter, held that Arthur Andersen LLP could not be found guilty when its employees shredded evidence regarding the Enron fraud, unless it was proved that Andersen intended to impede the prosecution of a particular criminal action at the time the shredding occurred.

Injunctions Administrative agencies such as the SEC and the Internal Revenue Service may bring injunctive actions against an auditor or securities professional in a federal district court. The purpose of such an injunction is to prevent a defendant from committing a future violation of the securities or tax laws.

After an injunction has been issued by a court, violating the injunction may result in serious sanctions. Not only may penalties be imposed for contempt, but also a criminal violation may also be more easily proven.

Administrative Proceedings The SEC has the authority to bring administrative proceedings against persons who violate the provisions of the federal securities acts. In recent years, the SEC has stepped up enforcement of SEC Rule of Practice 102(e). Rule 102(e) permits the SEC to bar temporarily or permanently from practicing before the SEC a professional who has demonstrated a lack of the qualifications required to practice before it, such as an accountant who has prepared financial statements not complying with GAAP. In the Sarbanes–Oxley Act, Congress amended the 1934 Act to include the language of Rule 102(e) almost word for word.

The SEC may discipline accountants who engage in a single instance of highly unreasonable conduct that leads to a violation of professional accounting standards. The SEC may also discipline an accountant who engages in repeated, unreasonable conduct that results in a violation of professional accounting standards. For example, an auditor's conduct in reviewing a client's financial statements is unreasonable when the auditor knew or should have known that heightened scrutiny is warranted yet failed to exercise the additional scrutiny while conducting an audit.

Rule 102(e) also permits the SEC to take action against a professional who has willfully violated or aided and abetted another's violation of the securities acts. An SEC administrative law judge hears the case and makes an initial determination. The SEC commissioners then issue a final order, which may be appealed to a federal court of appeals.

Rule 102(e) administrative proceedings can impose severe penalties on an accountant. By suspending an accountant from practicing before it, the SEC may take away a substantial part of an accountant's practice. Also, the SEC may impose civil penalties up to $500,000.

In addition, state licensing boards may suspend or revoke an accountant's license to practice if she engages in illegal or unethical conduct. If such action is taken, an accountant may lose her entire ability to practice accounting.

Securities Exchange Act Audit Requirements

The Private Securities Litigation Reform Act of 1995 imposes significant public duties on independent auditors that audit the financial statements of public companies. In part added to the Securities Exchange Act as Section 10A,

---

[5]507 U.S. 170 (1993).

the Reform Act requires auditors to take specific steps if they learn during the course of an audit that a client may have committed an illegal act (that is, a violation of any law, rule, or regulation). First, the auditor is required to determine whether an illegal act has in fact occurred. If the auditor determines that the client has committed an illegal act, the auditor must calculate the prospective impact on the client's financial statements, including fines, penalties, and liability costs such as damage awards to persons harmed by the client. As soon as practical, the auditor must inform the client's management and audit committee of the auditor's determination, unless the illegal act is clearly inconsequential.

If the client's management does not take appropriate remedial action with respect to an illegal act that has a material effect on the financial statements of the client—and if the failure to take remedial action is reasonably expected to result in the auditor's issuance of a nonstandard report or resignation from the audit engagement—the auditor must make a report to the client's board of directors. The board of directors has one business day to inform the SEC of the auditor's report; if the board does not submit a report to the SEC, the auditor has one additional business day to furnish a copy of its report to the SEC, whether or not the auditor also resigns from the audit engagement.

Section 10A imposes a significant whistle-blowing duty on independent auditors, consistent with the watchdog function that Congress and the courts have continually assigned to auditors. To encourage auditors to make such reports, Section 10A also provides that an auditor will have no liability to a private litigant for any statement in the auditor's reports given to management, the board of directors, or the SEC.

Section 10A is also the repository of many of the new securities provisions enacted under the Sarbanes–Oxley Act, including the list of services audit firms may not provide for audit clients, the audit partner rotation requirement, and the standards and duties of audit committees.

SOX Section 404

SOX Section 404   The most controversial part of the Sarbanes–Oxley Act has been Section 404, which requires public issuers to include in their annual reports an "internal control report" acknowledging management's responsibility to maintain "an adequate internal control structure and procedures for financial reports." The purpose of Section 404 is to improve the quality of accounting records and financial statements, which had eroded in the 1990s as management and audit committees lost control of internal accounting processes.

SOX Section 404 requires management's internal control report to include:

- A statement of management's responsibility for establishing and maintaining adequate internal control over financial reporting for the company;
- Management's assessment of the effectiveness of the company's internal control over financial reporting;
- A statement identifying the framework used by management to evaluate the effectiveness of the company's internal control over financial reporting; and
- A statement that the public accounting firm that audited the company's financial statements has issued an attestation report on management's assessment of the company's internal control over financial reporting.

Thus, SOX Section 404 requires not only that management maintain adequate internal controls, but also that auditors attest to management's assessment of internal controls. This requirement imposes new duties on auditors, yet at the same time provides new opportunities for providing services at a fee.

Auditors are experienced in performing attestation engagements on a broad variety of subjects. It was not surprising, therefore, that the rulemaking body charged with setting standards for Section 404, the Public Company Accounting Oversight Board, adopted the standard used in other contexts, SSAE No. 10, as the appropriate standard for Section 404 assessments. See Chapters 4 and 45 for additional materials on Section 404, including the benefits and costs of compliance.

LOG ON

http://www.aicpa.org/InterestAreas/
CenterForAuditQuality/Pages/CAQ.aspx
The AICPA and the Center for Audit Quality maintain the Sarbanes–Oxley Act Implementation Central. Here you will find a summary of the Sarbanes–Oxley Act and articles on how to comply with SOX.

  Take steps to protect a client's communications and the firm's working papers.

Ownership of Working Papers

The personal records that a client entrusts to a professional during an engagement, such as accounting records during an audit, remain the property of the client. A professional must return these records to his client. Nonetheless, material created by a professional, such as working papers produced by independent auditors, belong to the accountant, not the client.

Working papers are the records made during an audit. They include such items as work programs or plans for the audit, evidence of the testing of accounts, explanations of the handling of unusual matters, data reconciling the accountant's report with the client's records, and comments about the client's internal controls. The client has a right of access to the working papers. The accountant must obtain the client's permission before the working papers can be transferred to another accountant.

No doubt in reaction to the massive shredding of Enron-related documents by the Arthur Andersen audit firm, Congress included in the Sarbanes–Oxley Act a requirement that all audit or review working papers be retained for seven years. A knowing or willful violation of the document retention rule is subject to 10 years' imprisonment, and, if corruptly done, 20 years. The *Andersen* case follows the next section.

Professional–Client Privilege

The attorney–client privilege is well established as necessary to protect confidential communications between a lawyer and her client and to permit a lawyer to perform her professional duties for her client. The privilege protects communications between clients and their attorneys from the prying eyes of courts and government agencies. It also protects a lawyer's working papers from the discovery procedures available in a lawsuit.

Although other professionals owe a duty of confidentiality to their clients, in general communications between clients and nonlawyer professionals are not protected from judicial and administrative agency scrutiny when the professional's client is a party to legal or administrative action or the professional possesses evidence probative to an action. Thus, consultants, investment bankers, underwriters, brokers, and other securities professionals may be required to testify about client communications and produce documents concerning their clients, despite the objections of the client.

Accountants, however, enjoy a status somewhere between attorneys and other professionals. While the common law does not recognize an accountant–client privilege, a large number of states have granted such a privilege by statute. An accountant–client privilege of confidentiality protects communications between accountants and their clients as well as accountants' working papers. The provisions of the state statutes vary, but usually the privilege belongs to the client, and an accountant may not refuse to disclose the privileged material in a courtroom if the client consents to its disclosure.

Generally, the state-granted privileges are recognized in both state and federal courts deciding questions of state law. Nonetheless, federal courts do not recognize the privilege in matters involving federal questions, including antitrust, securities, and criminal matters.

In federal tax matters, for example, no privilege of confidentiality is recognized on the grounds that an accountant has a duty as a public watchdog to ensure that his client correctly reports his income tax liability. Consequently, an accountant can be required to bring his working papers into court and to testify as to matters involving the client's tax records and discussions with the client regarding tax matters. In addition, an accountant may be required by subpoena to make available his working papers involving a client who is being investigated by the IRS or who has been charged with tax irregularities. The same holds true for SEC investigations.

Although no accountant–client privilege exists in federal tax matters, an attorney–client privilege does exist. Moreover, the attorney–client privilege will protect communications between a client and a professional when the professional is assisting an attorney in rendering advice to the client.

As Enron Corporation's financial difficulties became public in 2001, Arthur Andersen LLP, Enron's auditor, instructed its employees to destroy Enron-related documents pursuant to its document retention policy, actions culminating in the following case. The Supreme Court mentions a concern regarding the professional–client privilege. The holding, however, focuses on when a professional can be found guilty for destroying working papers and other evidence.

Arthur Andersen LLP v. United States   544 U.S. 696 (U.S. S. Ct. 2005)

Enron Corporation, during the 1990s, switched its business from operation of natural gas pipelines to an energy conglomerate, a move that was accompanied by aggressive accounting practices and rapid growth. Arthur Andersen LLP audited Enron's publicly filed financial statements and provided internal audit and consulting services to it. Andersen's engagement team for Enron was headed by global managing partner David Duncan. Enron's financial performance began to suffer in 2000 and continued to worsen in 2001. On August 14, 2001, Jeffrey Skilling, Enron's CEO, unexpectedly resigned. Within days, Sherron

Watkins, a senior accountant at Enron, warned Kenneth Lay, Enron's newly reappointed CEO, that Enron could "implode in a wave of accounting scandals." She also informed Duncan and Michael Odom, an Andersen partner who supervised Duncan, of the problems.

A key accounting problem involved Enron's use of "Raptors," which were special-purpose entities used to engage in "off-balance-sheet" activities. Andersen's engagement team had allowed Enron to "aggregate" the Raptors for accounting purposes so that they reflected a positive return. This was a clear violation of generally accepted accounting principles.

On August 28, 2001, an article in The Wall Street Journal *suggested improprieties at Enron, and the SEC opened an informal investigation. By early September, Andersen had formed an Enron "crisis-response" team, which included Nancy Temple, an in-house lawyer. On October 8, Andersen retained outside counsel to represent it in any litigation that might arise from the Enron matter. The next day, Temple discussed Enron with other in-house lawyers. Her notes from that meeting reflect that "some SEC investigation" is "highly probable."*

On October 10, Odom spoke at a general training meeting attended by 89 employees, including 10 from the Enron engagement team. Odom urged everyone to comply with the firm's document retention policy. He added: "If it's destroyed in the course of normal policy and litigation is filed the next day, that's great. . . . We've followed our own policy, and whatever there was that might have been of interest to somebody is gone and irretrievable." On October 12, Temple entered the Enron matter into her computer, designating the "Type of Potential Claim" as "Professional Practice—Government/Regulatory Investigation." Temple also e-mailed Odom, suggesting that he "remind the engagement team of our documentation and retention policy."

Andersen's policy called for a single central engagement file, which "should contain only that information which is relevant to supporting our work." The policy stated that, "in cases of threatened litigation, . . . no related information will be destroyed." It also separately provided that, if Andersen is "advised of litigation or subpoenas regarding a particular engagement, the related information should not be destroyed." The policy statement set forth "notification" procedures for whenever "professional practice litigation against Andersen or any of its personnel has been commenced, has been threatened or is judged likely to occur, or when governmental or professional investigations that may involve Andersen or any of its personnel have been commenced or are judged likely."

On October 16, Enron announced its third quarter results, disclosing a $1.01 billion charge to earnings. The following day, the SEC notified Enron by letter that it had opened an investigation and requested certain information and documents. On October 19, Enron forwarded a copy of that letter to Andersen.

On the same day, Temple also sent an e-mail to a member of Andersen's internal team of accounting experts and attached a copy of the document retention policy. On October 20, the Enron crisis-response team held a conference call, during which Temple instructed everyone to "make sure to follow the [document] policy." On October 23, Enron CEO Lay declined to answer questions during a call with analysts because of "potential lawsuits, as well as the SEC inquiry." After the call, Duncan met with other Andersen partners on the Enron engagement team and told them that they should ensure team members were complying with the document retention policy. Another meeting for all team members followed, during which Duncan distributed the policy and told everyone to comply. These, and other smaller meetings, were followed by substantial destruction of paper and electronic documents.

On October 26, one of Andersen's senior partners circulated a New York Times *article discussing the SEC's response to Enron. His e-mail commented that "the problems are just beginning and we will be in the cross hairs. The marketplace is going to keep the pressure on this and is going to force the SEC to be tough." On October 30, the SEC opened a formal investigation and sent Enron a letter that requested accounting documents.*

Throughout this time period, Andersen continued to destroy documents, despite reservations by some of Andersen's managers. For example, on October 26, John Riley, another Andersen partner, saw Duncan shredding documents and told him "this wouldn't be the best time in the world for you guys to be shredding a bunch of stuff." On October 31, David Stulb, a forensics investigator for Andersen, met with Duncan. During the meeting, Duncan picked up a document with the words "smoking gun" written on it and began to destroy it, adding "we don't need this." Stulb cautioned Duncan on the need to maintain documents and later informed Temple that Duncan needed advice on the document retention policy.

On November 8, Enron announced that it would issue a comprehensive restatement of its earnings and assets. Also on November 8, the SEC served Enron and Andersen with subpoenas for records. On November 9, Duncan's secretary sent an e-mail that stated: "Per Dave—No more shredding. . . . We have been officially served for our documents." Enron filed for bankruptcy less than a month later. Duncan was fired and later pleaded guilty to witness tampering.

In March 2002, Andersen was indicted in the Southern District of Texas on one count of violating witness tampering provisions 18 U.S.C. §§1512(b)(2)(A) and (B). The indictment alleged that, between October 10 and November 9, 2001, Andersen knowingly, intentionally, and corruptly persuaded Andersen's employees, with intent to cause them to withhold documents from, and alter documents for use in, an official proceeding. The case went to a jury, which deadlocked after deliberating for seven days. The district court instructed the jury that it could find Andersen guilty if Andersen intended to "subvert, undermine, or impede" governmental factfinding by suggesting to its employees that they enforce the document retention policy. After three more days of deliberation, the jury returned a guilty verdict. Andersen appealed to the court of appeals, which affirmed the conviction. The court of appeals held that the jury instructions properly conveyed the meaning of "corruptly persuades" and "official proceeding" and that the jury need not find any consciousness of wrongdoing. The Supreme Court granted Andersen's request to review the decision.

Rehnquist, Chief Justice

Chapter 73 of Title 18 of the United States Code provides criminal sanctions for those who obstruct justice. Sections 1512(b)(2)(A) and (B), part of the witness tampering provisions, provide in relevant part:

> Whoever knowingly uses intimidation or physical force, threatens, or corruptly persuades another person, or attempts to do so, or engages in misleading conduct toward another person, with intent to . . . cause or induce any person to . . . withhold testimony, or withhold a record, document, or other object, from an official proceeding [or] alter, destroy, mutilate, or conceal an object with intent to impair the object's integrity or availability for use in an official proceeding . . . shall be fined under this title or imprisoned not more than ten years, or both.

In this case, our attention is focused on what it means to "knowingly . . . corruptly persuade" another person "with intent to . . . cause" that person to "withhold" documents from, or "alter" documents for use in, an "official proceeding."

We have traditionally exercised restraint in assessing the reach of a federal criminal statute, both out of deference to the prerogatives of Congress and out of concern that a fair warning should be given to the world in language that the common world will understand, of what the law intends to do if a certain line is passed.

Such restraint is particularly appropriate here, where the act underlying the conviction—"persuasion"—is by itself innocuous. Indeed, "persuading" a person "with intent to . . . cause" that person to "withhold" testimony or documents from a Government proceeding or Government official is not inherently malign. Consider, for instance, a mother who suggests to her son that he invoke his right against compelled self-incrimination or a wife who persuades her husband not to disclose marital confidences.

Nor is it necessarily corrupt for an attorney to "persuade" a client "with intent to . . . cause" that client to "withhold" documents from the Government. In *Upjohn Co. v. United States,* 449 U.S. 383 (1981), for example, we held that Upjohn was justified in withholding documents that were covered by the attorney–client privilege from the Internal Revenue Service. No one would suggest that an attorney who "persuaded" Upjohn to take

that step acted wrongfully, even though he surely intended that his client keep those documents out of the IRS' hands.

"Document retention policies," which are created in part to keep certain information from getting into the hands of others, including the Government, are common in business. It is, of course, not wrongful for a manager to instruct his employees to comply with a valid document retention policy under ordinary circumstances.

Acknowledging this point, the parties have largely focused their attention on the word "corruptly" as the key to what may or may not lawfully be done in the situation presented here. Section 1512(b) punishes not just "corruptly persuading" another, but "*knowingly* . . . corruptly persuading" another. The Government suggests that "knowingly" does not modify "corruptly persuades," but that is not how the statute most naturally reads. It provides the *mens rea*—"knowingly"—and then a list of acts—"uses intimidation or physical force, threatens, or corruptly persuades." The Government suggests that it is questionable whether Congress would employ such an inelegant formulation as "knowingly . . . corruptly persuades." Long experience has not taught us to share the Government's doubts on this score, and we must simply interpret the statute as written.

The parties have not pointed us to another interpretation of "knowingly . . . corruptly" to guide us here. In any event, the natural meaning of these terms provides a clear answer. "Knowledge" and "knowingly" are normally associated with awareness, understanding, or consciousness. "Corrupt" and "corruptly" are normally associated with wrongful, immoral, depraved, or evil. Joining these meanings together here makes sense both linguistically and in the statutory scheme. Only persons conscious of wrongdoing can be said to "knowingly . . . corruptly persuade." And limiting criminality to persuaders conscious of their wrongdoing sensibly allows §1512(b) to reach only those with the level of "culpability . . . we usually require in order to impose criminal liability."

The outer limits of this element need not be explored here because the jury instructions at issue simply failed to convey the requisite consciousness of wrongdoing. Indeed, it is striking how little culpability the instructions required. For example, the jury was told that, "even if Andersen honestly and sincerely believed

Business Law: The Ethical, Global, and E-Commerce Environment, 15th Edition **315**

Chapter Forty-Six **Legal and Professional Responsibilities of Auditors, Consultants, and Securities Professionals** 1217

that its conduct was lawful, you may find Andersen guilty." The instructions also diluted the meaning of "corruptly" so that it covered innocent conduct.

The District Court based its instruction on the definition of that term found in the Fifth Circuit Pattern Jury Instruction for §1503. This pattern instruction defined "corruptly" as "knowingly and dishonestly, with the specific intent to subvert or undermine the integrity" of a proceeding. The Government, however, insisted on excluding "dishonestly" and adding the term "impede" to the phrase "subvert or undermine." The District Court agreed over Andersen's objections, and the jury was told to convict if it found Andersen intended to "subvert, undermine, or impede" governmental factfinding by suggesting to its employees that they enforce the document retention policy.

These changes were significant. No longer was any type of "dishonesty" necessary to a finding of guilt, and it was enough for petitioner to have simply "impeded" the Government's factfinding ability. "Impede" has broader connotations than "subvert" or even "undermine," and many of these connotations do not incorporate any "corruptness" at all. The dictionary defines "impede" as "to interfere with or get in the way of the progress of" or "hold up" or "detract from." By definition, anyone who innocently persuades another to withhold information from the Government "gets in the way of the progress of" the Government.

The instructions also were infirm for another reason. They led the jury to believe that it did not have to find *any* nexus between the "persuasion" to destroy documents and any particular proceeding. In resisting any type of nexus element, the Government relies heavily on §1512(e)(1), which states that an official proceeding "need not be pending or about to be instituted at the time of the offense." It is, however, one thing to say that a proceeding "need not be pending or about to be instituted at the time of the offense," and quite another to say a proceeding need not even be foreseen. A "knowingly . . . corrupt persuader" cannot be someone who persuades others to shred documents under a document retention policy when he does not have in contemplation any particular official proceeding in which those documents might be material. If the defendant lacks knowledge that his actions are likely to affect the judicial proceeding, he lacks the requisite intent to obstruct.

For these reasons, the jury instructions here were flawed in important respects.

Judgment reversed in favor of Andersen.

Problems and Problem Cases

1. Lincoln Assurance Company engages audit firm Accent Pointe LLP to review its financial statements and internal controls. Accent Pointe examines Lincoln's expense ledger, which lists the creditors to whom Lincoln has made payments for supplies and services rendered to Lincoln, such as stationery, electricity, and phone. Accent Pointe makes no effort to verify that the payments were made to real creditors by randomly asking creditors to confirm that they had billed Lincoln and received payment. As a result, Accent Pointe fails to uncover an ongoing embezzlement by Lincoln's bookkeeper, who for the past six months has been writing checks to a fictitious creditor and then cashing the checks herself. The total amount of the checks is $155,000. When Lincoln uncovers the embezzlement scheme three months later, the bookkeeper has embezzled an additional $45,000. Is Accent Pointe liable to Lincoln for failing to uncover the embezzlement scheme?

2. Diversified Graphics, Ltd., hired Ernst & Whinney to assist it in obtaining a computer system to fit its data processing needs. DG had a long-standing relationship with E&W and developed great trust and reliance on E&W's services. Because DG lacked computer expertise, it decided to entrust E&W with the selection and implementation of an in-house computer data processing system. E&W promised to locate a "turnkey" system, which would be fully operational without the need for extensive employee training. Instead, DG received a system that was difficult to operate and failed to meet its needs. Is E&W liable to DG?

3. Al Rizek was a vice president of PaineWebber of Puerto Rico. One of his clients was Jorge Donato. Donato told Rizek that he was primarily interested in long-term bonds and the safety of his investment. In early 1993, Rizek recommended to Donato a strategy of short-term trading of zero-coupon bonds. Zero-coupon bonds are U.S. government instruments that accumulate interest until maturity, rather than paying interest periodically. The value of a zero-coupon bond is very sensitive to changes in interest rates. Rizek recommended that Donato purchase the bonds on margin, thus magnifying the potential gains and losses. Purchasing on margin meant that Donato had to make monthly margin interest payments to

PaineWebber; it also placed him at risk of being forced to sell at a loss to meet a margin call. During the 15-month period from January 1993 to March 1994, Donato's account had average monthly balances of $85,000. During this time, Rizek carried out $2 million in transactions on the account. Rizek's strategy led to losses of approximately $12,000. Rizek received about $15,000 in commissions. Donato sued Rizek and Paine Webber to recover the damages he suffered. Have Rizek and Paine Webber violated the common law of negligence or Securities Exchange Act Rule 10b-5?

4. Scioto Memorial Hospital Association, Inc., planned the construction of Richmond Place, a 170-unit retirement center in Lexington, Kentucky. Scioto hired Price Waterhouse to review the work of the architect, the financial underwriter, and the marketing consultant and to recommend whether Scioto should proceed with the Richmond Place investment. PW's engagement letter represented that PW would issue a preliminary feasibility study and review a detailed financial forecast of the project. Financial forecasts represent management's judgment of the most likely set of conditions and management's most likely course of action. Instead of reviewing a financial forecast for Richmond Place, PW reviewed only a financial projection compiled by the underwriter of the construction. As PW explained in its letter to Scioto, a projection "represents management's estimate of its possible, but not necessarily most probable, future course of action." PW's final report to Scioto assumed an occupancy rate of 98 percent. Unfortunately, construction of Richmond Place was slow and delayed by a fire. While Scioto used insurance proceeds to rebuild, sales of the units were slow, and a year after opening, only 15 residents occupied Richmond Place. Scioto sued PW for negligence and breach of contract. PW defended on the grounds that Scioto's delays in construction and its lack of business interruption insurance caused Scioto's damages. Was PW found liable to Scioto?

5. Piece Goods Shops Company, L.P., hired Price Waterhouse LLP to audit its 1992 financial statements. Piece Goods forwarded the audited 1992 financial statements to Marcus Brothers Textiles, Inc., which made several extensions of credit to Piece Goods up to April 1993 in reliance on the 1992 balance sheet. When Piece Goods filed for bankruptcy in April 1993, Piece Goods owed Marcus Brothers almost $300,000. Marcus Brothers sued PW for negligent misrepresentation under state law on the grounds PW negligently conducted the audit of the 1992 financial statements, which Marcus Brothers alleged contained several material misstatements. PW moved to dismiss the case on the grounds that PW did not know that Marcus Brothers would be using the financial statements to make credit extension to Piece Goods. Marcus Brothers produced evidence that PW had been Piece Goods's auditor since 1986. A PW internal memo stated that PW had historically reported on Piece Goods's financial statements and that its vendors were accustomed to receiving those financial statements. A PW audit partner signed a memo stating that some of PW's audit clients typically provided their audited financial statements to their trade creditors in reference to obtaining loans or extensions of credit. An audit manager who oversaw the audit of Piece Goods's 1992 financial statements testified that audited financial statements are used by management of the company and possibly outsiders and that such outsiders could include trade creditors such as Marcus Brothers. Piece Goods's bankruptcy filing revealed that 43 of its trade creditors had received the audited 1992 financial statements. Under the *Restatement (Second) of Torts,* is Marcus Brothers a proper plaintiff to whom PW owed a duty not to be negligent when conducting the audit?

6. Due to alleged overstatements of the value of loans held by First National Bank of Keystone (Keystone), the federal Office of the Comptroller of the Currency (OCC) began investigating Keystone. OCC required Keystone to retain an auditor to determine the appropriateness of Keystone's accounting treatments of its purchased loans and securitization of loans. Keystone hired Grant Thornton LLP to perform an audit of Keystone's financial statements. In April 1999, Grant Thornton issued an audit opinion to Keystone stating that its 1998 financial statements—which showed shareholder equity of $84 million—were fairly stated in accordance with GAAP. In fact, Keystone was insolvent. Grant Thornton's audit report stated that "This report is intended for the information and use of the Board of Directors and Management of The First National Bank of Keystone and its regulatory agencies and should not be used by third parties for any other purpose." Gary Ellis, a candidate to become Keystone's next president, reviewed in April 1999 the 1998 financial statements audited by Grant Thornton. At the time, Ellis was president of another bank and not an employee of Keystone.

He became a candidate for the Keystone presidency in late March 1999. Relying on the audit, Ellis decided to accept Keystone's offer to be its president at a base salary of $375,000. He also purchased $49,500 in Keystone stock. When Keystone failed, Ellis claimed he lost over $2 million in compensation he would have earned had he not taken the Keystone presidency, as well as losing the full amount of his investment in Keystone stock. He sued Grant Thornton for negligent misrepresentation. Under the *Restatement (Second) of Torts,* was Ellis a proper plaintiff to whom Grant Thornton owed a duty not to be negligent when conducting the audit?

7. AccentPoint LLP, an accounting firm, was hired by General Micron Company to audit its financial statements for inclusion in GMC's 1933 Act registration statement, pursuant to which GMC's common shares would be sold to investors. AccentPoint's sole compensation for performing the audit and issuing an opinion was a fee of $600,000. Due to AccentPoint's careless noncompliance with GAAS, the audited financial statements and AccentPoint's opinion contained material misstatements. AccentPoint, however, did not intentionally or recklessly mistate or omit any material fact. Does AccentPoint have potential liability to purchasers of the shares who bought GMC shares relying on AccentPoint's audit opinion under Section 12(a)(2) of the 1933 Act, Rule 10b–5 of the 1934 Act, and the common law of negligent misrepresentation? Does AccentPoint have potential liability to purchasers of the shares under Section 11 of the 1933 Act?

8. Kimon Daifotis was the lead portfolio manager of the YieldPlus Fund. In August 2007, when YieldPlus was suffering massive, unprecedented redemptions, Daifotis held two conference calls in which he allegedly falsely stated that "we've got very, very, very slight negative flows" and that "outflows have been minimal." Daifotis also allegedly made misrepresentations in YieldPlus's written materials in which he was directly quoted or in which statements were directly attributed to him, including a September 2005 brochure and a Spring 2006 brochure. When YieldPlus investors sued Daifotis for damages caused by the alleged misstatements, Daifotis argued that he had not "made" the statements and, therefore, could not be liable under Securities Exchange Act Rule 10b-5. Did the court agree?

9. Norman Cross was the independent auditor for Home-Stakes Production Company, a company that offered investors interests in oil and gas drilling programs. The programs offered investors both income and tax deductions. Cross issued unqualified opinions regarding Home-Stakes's financial statements. He prepared consolidated financial statements and start-up balance sheets for two programs. All these documents were included, with Cross's consent, in 1933 Act registration statements filed with the SEC and included in prospectuses and program books distributed to investors. When Home-Stakes collapsed after it was discovered that the oil and gas drilling programs were a classic Ponzi scheme (with investments from new investors providing the "profits" to old investors), purchasers of the programs sued Cross under Securities Exchange Act Section 10(b) and Rule 10b–5. Was Cross found liable, or was he only an aider and abettor to Home-Stakes's fraud with no Rule 10b–5 liability?

10. Floogle, Inc., a provider of a variety of Internet services, decides to make a public offering of its common shares. It retains investment bank Sturm & Drang Company to underwrite the offering and assist in the marketing of the common shares. Accounting firm Barnes Jonson LLP audits the financial statements that will be included in the 1933 Act registration statement that will be filed with the SEC. Floogle's income statement for the last fiscal year materially overstates Floogle's earnings, indicating that earnings were $1.25 per share when in reality earnings were only $0.03 per share. The earnings misstatement is known both to Sturm & Drang and Barnes Jonson. Nonetheless, when meeting with prospective investors, Sturm & Drang tells investors "last year's earnings were a robust $1.25 per share." Barnes Jonson also issues an opinion that Floogle's financial statements fairly present the financial position of Floogle. Investors purchase Floogle's common shares relying on Sturm & Drang's representation of Floogle's earnings and Barnes Jonson's audit opinion. When Floogle's real earnings are released three months later, the purchasers of Floogle's shares sue both Sturm & Drang and Barnes Jonson under Rule 10b–5 of the Securities Exchange Act of 1934. Both Strum & Drang and Barnes Jonson claim they are not liable under Rule 10b–5, because they merely aided and abetted Floogle's fraud. Are they correct?

11. Walter Piecyk, a broker and analyst with securities firm Fulcrum Global Partners, heard a rumor that Nokia Corp., the largest customer of RF Micro Devices Inc., was going to delay equipment orders from RF Micro.

After short-selling RF Micro stock, Piecyk spread the rumor, which was highly sensational. RF Micro's stock fell 5 percent that day. The next day, when RF Micro publicly denied the rumor (which was completely false), the stock fell another 8 percent, apparently because the market believed the rumor, not RF Micro. The market price continued to fall, as the rumor persisted, and Piecyk eventually covered his short sale, making a profit of about $8,000. RF Micro asked the NASD to take disciplinary action against Piecyk on the grounds that he had not adequately investigated whether there was a reasonable basis for the rumor. Did the NASD discipline Piecyk?

12. Accounting firm Procenture LLP was hired to audit fiscal year 2008 financial statements of Bard-Gramercy Corporation, a public company with assets of $7.3 billion and a market value of $2.7 billion. Procenture completed the audit, and its audit opinion was included in Bard-Gramercy's annual report filed with the SEC. Because of time constraints, Procenture did a cursory review of Bard-Gramercy's internal financial controls, essentially asking management and receiving oral confirmation that management was satisfied with Bard-Gramercy's processes for recording financial transactions. Although Procenture's audit opinion made no mention of Bard-Gramercy's internal controls, Procenture was confident based on its inquiries that Bard-Gramercy's internal controls were adequate. Did Procenture meet its duty under the Sarbanes–Oxley Act of 2002?

13. Ernst & Young, an accounting firm, was retained by Camelot Systems, Inc., to provide tax advice. Camelot also retained a law firm to provide tax and other legal advice. At all times, E&Y was working for and paid by Camelot. When the IRS investigated a merger transaction on which E&Y had worked for Camelot, it subpoenaed E&Y's records, including communications between E&Y and Camelot. Camelot sought to quash the subpoena on grounds that the communications between Camelot and E&Y were privileged and confidential. Did the court agree?

Online Research

Sarbanes–Oxley Act Section 404

The cost of initial compliance with SOX Section 404 has made it a lightning rod for criticism by companies, especially small issuers. Keep abreast of the current status of SOX Section 404, especially these issues:

- Has the cost of complying with SOX 404 fallen as management and auditors have become more experienced at performing assessments and attestations?
- Have the expected benefits of SOX 404 been realized?
- In light of the current credit crunch of, has Congress taken steps to lighten the burdens of SOX 404 or expand them?

Property, Estates and Bankruptcy

Part Five

Property

CHAPTER 23

PERSONAL PROPERTY AND BAILMENTS

Claudio is a skilled craftsman employed by the Goldcasters Jewelry to make handcrafted jewelry. Working after his normal working hours and using materials he paid for himself, Claudio crafts a fine ring by skillfully weaving together strands of gold wire. He presents the ring to his fiancé, Cheryl, as an engagement ring in anticipation of their forthcoming marriage. While visiting the restroom in a steak and ribs restaurant, Cheryl removes the ring so she can wash some barbecue sauce from her hands. In her haste to get back to her table, she leaves the ring on the washstand when she exits the restroom. Sandra, a part-time janitor for the restaurant, finds the ring and slips it into her purse. When Cheryl realizes she is missing the ring and returns to the restroom to look for it, neither the ring nor Sandra is still there. Later that evening Sandra sells the ring to her cousin, Gloria, who gives her $200 for it. Several days later, Cheryl breaks her engagement to Claudio, telling him that she no longer loves him. Claudio asks Cheryl to return the ring, indicating that he only intended for her to have it if their engagement led to marriage. This situation raises a number of questions concerning rights and interests in personal property that will be discussed in this chapter. They include:

- Between Claudio and Goldcasters, who was the owner of the ring at the time Claudio created it?
- Did Claudio make an effective gift of the ring to Cheryl? Or was it a conditional gift that he could revoke when Cheryl decided to call off the marriage?
- What was Sandra's responsibility when she found the ring? Between Sandra and the restaurant, who had the better right to the ring?
- Did Gloria become the owner of the ring when she paid the $200 to Sandra? Does Cheryl have the right to recover the ring from Gloria if she finds that Gloria has it?
- Was it ethical for Claudio to use this employer's tools and facilities for a personal project?

LO LEARNING OBJECTIVES

After studying this chapter, you should be able to:

1 Understand the concept of ownership of property as a bundle of rights that the law recognizes.

2 Differentiate personal property from real property.

3 List the primary ways to acquire ownership of personal property.

4 Explain how the rights of finders of abandoned, lost, and mislaid property differ.

5 List and discuss the elements that are necessary for making a valid gift of property.

6 List the three essential elements of a bailment.

7 List and compare the three different types of bailment.

8 Explain the basic duties of the bailee and the bailor of personal property.

9 Discuss the special rules applicable for bailments to common carriers and hotelkeepers.

10 Discuss the special rules applicable to bailments covered by negotiable documents of title, including warehouse receipts and bills of lading.

Understand the concept of ownership of property as a bundle of rights that the law recognizes.

Nature of Property

The concept of property is crucial to the organization of society. The essential nature of a particular society is often reflected in the way it views property, including the degree to which property ownership is concentrated in the state, the extent to which it permits individual ownership of property, and the rules that govern such ownership. History is replete with wars and revolutions that arose out of conflicting claims to, or views concerning, property. Significant documents in our Anglo-American legal tradition, such as the Magna Carta and the Constitution, deal explicitly with property rights.

The word **property** is used to refer to something that is capable of being owned. It is also used to refer to a right or interest that allows a person to exercise dominion over a thing that may be owned or possessed.

When we talk about property ownership, we are speaking of a *bundle of rights* that the law recognizes and enforces. For example, ownership of a building includes the exclusive right to use, enjoy, sell, mortgage, or rent the building. If someone else tries to use the property without the owner's consent, the owner may use the courts and legal procedures to eject that person. Ownership of a patent includes the rights to produce, use, and sell the patented item, and to license others to do those things.

In the United States, private ownership of property is protected by the Constitution, which provides that the government shall deprive no person of "life, liberty or property without due process of law." We recognize and encourage the rights of individuals to acquire, enjoy, and use property. These rights, however, are not unlimited. For example, a person cannot use property in an unreasonable manner that injures others. Also, the state has **police power** through which it can impose reasonable regulations on the use of property, tax it, and take it for public use by paying the owner compensation for it.

Property is divided into a number of categories based on its characteristics. The same piece of property may fall into more than one class. The following discussion explores the meaning of **personal property** and the numerous ways of classifying property.

Classifications of Property

Personal Property versus Real Property
Personal property is defined by process of exclusion. The term *personal property* is used in contrast to *real property*. Real property is the earth's crust and all things firmly attached to it.[1] For example, land, office buildings, and houses are considered to be real property. All other objects and rights that may be owned are personal property. Clothing, books, and stock in a corporation are examples of personal property.

Real property may be turned into personal property if it is detached from the earth. Personal property, if attached to the earth, becomes real property. For example, marble in the ground is real property. When the marble is quarried, it becomes personal property, but if it is used in constructing a building, it becomes real property again. Perennial vegetation that does not have to be seeded every year, such as trees, shrubs, and grass, is usually treated as part of the real property on which it is growing. When trees and shrubs are severed from the land, they become personal property. Crops that must be planted each year, such as corn, oats, and potatoes, are usually treated as personal property. However, if the real property on which they are growing is sold, the new owner of the real property also becomes the owner of the crops.

When personal property is attached to, or used in conjunction with, real property in such a way as to be treated as part of the real property, it is known as a **fixture.** The law concerning fixtures is discussed in the next chapter.

Tangible versus Intangible Personal Property
Personal property may be either tangible or intangible. Tangible property has a physical existence. Cars, animals, and computers are examples. Property that has no physical existence is called intangible property. For example, rights under a patent, copyright, or trademark would be intangible property.[2]

The distinction between tangible and intangible property is important primarily for tax and estate planning purposes. Generally, tangible property is subject to tax in the state in which it is located, whereas intangible property is usually taxable in the state where its owner lives.

Public and Private Property
Property is also classified as public or private, based on the ownership of the property. If the property is owned by the government or a governmental unit, it is public property. If it is owned

L02 Differentiate personal property from real property.

---
[1]The law of real property is treated in Chapter 24.
[2]These important types of intangible property are discussed in Chapter 8.

by an individual, a group of individuals, a corporation, or some other business organization, it is private property.

 L03 List the primary ways to acquire ownership of personal property.

Acquiring Ownership of Personal Property

Production or Purchase The most common ways of obtaining ownership of property are by producing it or purchasing it. A person owns the property that she makes unless the person has agreed to do the work for another party. In that case, the other party is the owner of the product of the work. For example, a person who creates a painting, knits a sweater, or develops a computer program is the owner unless she has been retained by someone to create the painting, knit the sweater, or develop the program. Another major way of acquiring property is by purchase. The law regarding the purchase of tangible personal property (that is, sale of goods) is discussed in Chapter 19.

The scenario set out at the start of this chapter posits that Claudio, a skilled craftsman employed by Goldcasters to make handcrafted jewelry, works after his normal working hours and uses materials he paid for himself to make a gold ring. Who should be considered to be the owner of the ring at the time Claudio created it, Claudio or Goldcasters? What are the critical factors that lead you to this conclusion?

Possession of Unowned Property In very early times, the most common way of obtaining ownership of personal property was simply by taking possession of unowned property. For example, the first person to take possession of a wild animal became its owner. Today, one may still acquire ownership of personal property by possessing it if the property is unowned. The two major examples of unowned property that may be acquired by possession are wild animals and abandoned property. Abandoned property will be discussed in the next section, which focuses on the rights of finders.

The first person to take possession of a wild animal normally becomes the owner.[3] To acquire ownership of a wild animal by taking possession, a person must obtain enough control over it to deprive it of its freedom. If a

person fatally wounds a wild animal, the person becomes the owner. Wild animals caught in a trap or fish caught in a net are usually considered to be the property of the person who set the trap or net. If a captured wild animal escapes and is caught by another person, that person generally becomes the owner. However, if that person knows that the animal is an escaped animal and that the prior owner is chasing it to recapture it, then he does not become the owner.

 L04 Explain how the rights of finders of abandoned, lost, and mislaid property differ.

Rights of Finders of Lost, Mislaid, and Abandoned Property The old saying "finders keepers, losers weepers" is not a reliable way of predicting the legal rights of those who find personal property that originally belonged—or still belongs—to another. The rights of the finder will be determined according to whether the property he finds is classified as abandoned, lost, or mislaid.

1. *Abandoned property.* Property is considered to be abandoned if the owner intentionally placed the property out of his possession with the intent to relinquish ownership of it. For example, Norris takes his TV set to the city dump and leaves it there. The finder who takes possession of abandoned property with intent to claim ownership becomes the owner of the property. This means he acquires better rights to the property than anyone else in the world, including the original owner. For example, if Fox finds the TV set, puts it in his car, and takes it home, Fox becomes the owner of the TV set.

2. *Lost property.* Property is considered to be lost when the owner did not intend to part with possession of the property. For example, if Barber's camera fell out of her handbag while she was walking down the street, it would be considered lost property. The person who finds lost property does not acquire ownership of it, but he acquires better rights to the lost property than anyone other than the true owner. For example, suppose Lawrence finds Barber's camera in the grass where it fell. Jones then steals the camera from Lawrence's bookbag. Under these facts, Barber is still the owner of the camera. She has the right to have it returned to her if she discovers where it is—or if Lawrence knows that it belongs to Barber. As the finder of lost property, however, Lawrence has a better right to the camera than anyone else except Barber. This means that

---

[3]As wildlife is increasingly protected by law, however, some wild animals cannot be owned because it is illegal to capture them (e.g., endangered species).

Lawrence has the right to require Jones to return it to him if he finds out that Jones has it.

If the finder does not know who the true owner is or cannot easily find out, the finder must still return the property when the real owner shows up and asks for the property. If the finder of lost property knows who the owner is and refuses to return it, the finder is guilty of **conversion** and must pay the owner the fair value of the property.[4] A finder who sells the property that he has found can pass to the purchaser only those rights that he has; he cannot pass any better title to the property than he himself has. Thus, the true owner could recover the property from the purchaser.

3. *Mislaid property.* Property is considered to be mislaid if the owner intentionally placed the property somewhere and accidentally left it there, not intending to relinquish ownership of the property. For example, Fields places her backpack on a coatrack at Campus Bookstore while shopping for textbooks. Forgetting the backpack, Fields leaves the store and goes home. The backpack would be considered mislaid rather than lost because Fields intentionally and voluntarily placed it on the coatrack. If property is classified as mislaid, the finder acquires no rights to the property. Rather, the person in possession of the real property on which the personal property was mislaid has the right to hold the property for the true owner and has better rights to the property than anyone other than the true owner.

For example, if Stevens found Fields's backpack in Campus Bookstore, Campus Bookstore would have the right to hold the mislaid property for Fields. Stevens would acquire neither possession nor ownership of the backpack.

The rationale for this rule is that it increases the chances that the property will be returned to its real owner. A person who knowingly placed the property somewhere but forgot to pick it up might well remember later where she left the property and return for it.

In the scenario set out at the start of this chapter, Cheryl visits the restroom in a steak and ribs restaurant in order to wash some barbecue sauce from her hands. She removes her engagement ring and places it on the washstand, but in her haste to get back to her table, she leaves the ring on the washstand when she exits the washroom. Sandra, a part-time janitor for the restaurant, finds the ring, slips it in her purse, and later sells the ring to her cousin, Gloria, for $200. When Cheryl returns to the restroom to look for the ring, neither the ring nor Sandra is still there.

At the time Sandra discovers the ring, should it be considered abandoned, lost, or mislaid property? What factors lead you to this conclusion? What should Sandra do with the ring at that point? Between Sandra and the owner of the restaurant, who has the best claim to the ring? Between the restaurant owner, Sandra, and Cheryl, who has the best claim to it? Why? If Cheryl discovers that Gloria has the ring, does she have the right to recover it from her? Why?

Some states have a statute that allows finders of property to clear their title to the property. The statutes,

---

[4]The tort of conversion is discussed in Chapter 6.

Rights of Finders of Personal Property

Character of Property	Description	Rights of Finder	Rights of Original Owner
Lost	Owner unintentionally parted with possession	Rights superior to everyone except the owner	Retains ownership; has the right to the return of the property
Mislaid	Owner intentionally put property in a place but unintentionally left it there	None; person in possession of real property on which mislaid property was found holds it for the owner, and has rights superior to everyone except owner	Retains ownership; has the right to the return of the property
Abandoned	Owner intentionally placed property out of his possession with intent to relinquish ownership of it	Finder who takes possession with intent to claim ownership acquires ownership of property	None

known as estray statutes, generally provide that the person must give public notice of the fact that the property has been found, perhaps by putting an ad in a local newspaper. All states have statutes of limitations that require the true owner of property to claim it or bring a legal action to recover possession of it within a certain number of years. A person who keeps possession of lost or unclaimed property for longer than that period of time will become its owner.

The *Corliss* case, which follows, discusses the relative rights of a person who finds property on land owned by someone else.

Corliss v. Wenner and Anderson	2001 Ida. App. LEXIS 79 (Ct. App. Idaho 2001)

In the fall of 1996, Jann Wenner hired Anderson Asphalt Paving to construct a driveway on his ranch. Larry Anderson, the owner of Anderson Asphalt Paving, and his employee, Gregory Corliss, were excavating soil for the driveway when they unearthed a glass jar containing paper-wrapped rolls of gold coins. Anderson and Corliss collected, cleaned, and inventoried the gold pieces dating from 1857 to 1914. The 96 coins weighed about four pounds. Initially, Anderson and Corliss agreed to split the coins among themselves, with Anderson retaining possession of all the coins. Subsequently, Anderson and Corliss argued over ownership of the coins, and Anderson fired Corliss. Anderson later gave possession of the coins to Wenner in exchange for indemnification on any claim Corliss might have against him regarding the coins.

Corliss sued Anderson and Wenner for possession of some or all of the coins. Corliss contended that the coins should be considered "treasure trove" and awarded to him pursuant to the "finders keepers" rule of treasure trove. Wenner, defending both himself and Anderson, contended that he had the better right to possession of the gold coins. The trial court held Idaho did not recognize "treasure trove" and that the coins, having been carefully concealed for safekeeping, fit within the legal classification of mislaid property, to which the right of possession goes to the landowner. Alternatively, the court ruled that the coins, like the topsoil being excavated, were a part of the property owned by Wenner and that Anderson and Corliss were merely Wenner's employees. Corliss appealed.

Schwartzman, Chief Judge

At common law all found property is generally categorized in one of five ways. Those categories are:

ABANDONED PROPERTY—that which the owner has discarded or voluntarily forsaken with the intention of terminating his ownership, but without vesting ownership in any other person.

LOST PROPERTY—that property which the owner has involuntarily and unintentionally parted with through neglect, carelessness, or inadvertence and does not know the whereabouts.

MISLAID PROPERTY—that which the owner has intentionally set down in a place where he can again resort to it, and then forgets where he put it.

TREASURE TROVE—a category exclusively for gold or silver in coin, plate, bullion, and sometimes its paper money equivalents, found concealed in the earth or in a house or other private place. Treasure trove carries with it the thought of antiquity, i.e., that the treasure has been concealed for so long as to indicate that the owner is probably dead or unknown.

EMBEDDED PROPERTY—that personal property which has become a part of the natural earth, such as pottery, the sunken wreck of a steamship, or a rotted-away sack of gold-bearing quartz rock buried or partially buried in the ground.

Under these doctrines, the finder of lost or abandoned property and treasure trove acquires a right to possess the property against the entire world but the rightful owner regardless of the place of finding. The finder of mislaid property is required to turn it over to the owner of the premises who has the duty to safeguard the property for the true owner. Possession of embedded property goes to owner of the land on which the property was found.

One of the major distinctions between these various categories is that only lost property necessarily involves an element of involuntariness. The four remaining categories involve voluntary and intentional acts by the true owner in placing the property where another eventually finds it. However, treasure trove, despite not being lost or abandoned property, is treated as such in that the right to possession is recognized to be in the finder rather than the premises owner.

On appeal, Corliss argues that the district court should have interpreted the undisputed facts and circumstances surrounding the placement of the coins in the ground to indicate that the gold coins were either lost, abandoned, or treasure trove. Wenner argues that the property was properly categorized as either embedded or mislaid property.

As with most accidentally discovered buried treasure, the history of the original ownership of the coins is shrouded in mystery and obscured by time. The coins had been wrapped in paper, like coins from a bank, and buried in a glass jar, apparently for safekeeping. Based on these circumstances, the district court determined that the coins were not abandoned because the condition in which the coins were found evidenced an intent to keep them safe, not an intent to voluntarily relinquish all possessory interest in them. The district court also implicitly rejected the notion that the coins were lost, noting that the coins were secreted with care in a specific place to protect them from the elements and from other people until such time as the original owner might return for them. There is no indication that the coins came to be buried through neglect, carelessness, or inadvertence. Accordingly, the district court properly concluded, as a matter of law, that the coins were neither lost nor abandoned.

The district court then determined that the modern trend favored characterizing the coins as property either embedded in the earth or mislaid—under which the right of possession goes to the landowner—rather than treasure trove—under which the right of possession goes to the finder. Although accepted by a number of states prior to 1950, the modern trend since then, as illustrated by decisions of the state and federal courts, is decidedly against recognizing the "finders keepers" rule of treasure trove.

We conclude that the rule of treasure trove is of dubious heritage and misunderstood application, inconsistent with our values and traditions. The danger of adopting the doctrine of treasure trove is laid out in *Morgan v. Wiser* (Tenn. 1985).

[We] find the rule with respect to treasure-trove to be out of harmony with modern notions of fair play. The common-law rule of treasure-trove invites trespassers to roam at large over the property of others with their metal detecting devices and to dig wherever such devices tell them property might be found. If the discovery happens to fit the definition of treasure-trove, the trespasser may claim it as his own. To paraphrase another court: The mind refuses consent to the proposition that one may go upon the lands of another and dig up and take away anything he discovers there which does not belong to the owner of the land.

The invitation to trespassers inherent in the rule with respect to treasure trove is repugnant to the common law rules dealing with trespassers in general. The common law made a trespass an actionable wrong without the necessity of showing any damage therefrom. Because a trespass often involved a breach of the peace and because the law was designed to keep the peace, the common law dealt severely with trespassers.

Recognizing the validity of the idea that the discouragement of trespassers contributes to the preservation of the peace in the community, we think this state should not follow the common law rule with respect to treasure trove. Rather, we adopt the rule suggested in the concurring opinion in *Schley v. Couch* . . . which we restate as follows:

Where property is found embedded in the soil under circumstances repelling the idea that it has been lost, the finder acquires no title thereto, for the presumption is that the possession of the article found is in the owner of the locus in quo.

Landownership includes control over crops on the land, buildings and appurtenances, soils, minerals buried under those soils. The average Idaho landowner would expect to have a possessory interest in any object uncovered on his or her property. And certainly the notion that a trespassing treasure hunter, or a hired handyman or employee, could or might have greater possessory rights than a landowner in objects uncovered on his or her property runs counter to the reasonable expectations of present-day landownership.

There is no reason for a special rule for gold and silver coins, bullion, or plate as opposed to other property. Insofar as personal property (money and the like) buried or secreted on privately owned realty is concerned, the distinctions between treasure trove, lost property, and mislaid property are anachronistic and of little value. The principal point of such distinctions is the intent of the true owner which, absent some written declaration indicating such, is obscured in the mists of time and subject to a great deal of speculation.

By holding that property classed as treasure trove (gold or silver coins, bullion, plate) in other jurisdictions is classed in Idaho as personal property embedded in the soil, subject to the same limitations as mislaid property, possession will be awarded to the owner of the soil as a matter of law. Thus, we craft a simple and reasonable solution to the problem, discourage trespass, and avoid the risk of speculating about the true owner's intent when attempting to infer such from the manner and circumstances in which an object is found. Additionally, the true owner, if any, will have the opportunity to recover the property.

We hold that the owner of the land has constructive possession of all personal property secreted in, on, or under his or her land. Accordingly, we adopt the district court's reasoning and conclusion melding the law of mislaid property with that of embedded property and conclude, as a matter of law, that the landowner is entitled to possession to the exclusion of all but the true owner, absence a contract between the landowner and finder.

Judgment for Wenner affirmed.

Legal Responsibilities of Finders

Some states go further and make it a criminal offense for a person who comes into control of property that he knows or learns has been lost or mislaid to appropriate the property to his own use without first taking reasonable measures to restore the property to the owner. For example under the Georgia Code, "A person commits the offense of theft of lost or mislaid property that he knows or learns to have been lost or mislaid property when he comes into control of property that he knows or learns to have been lost or mislaid and appropriates the property to his own use without first taking reasonable measures to restore the property to the owner" (O.C.G. A. section 16-8-6).

In a recent case[5] under that statute, an individual was convicted of the offense when she found a bank deposit bag containing checks, deposit slips, and over $500 in cash and subsequently attempted to cash one of the checks at a local check cashing business. The deposit bag had been misplaced while the victim was transporting it from her business located in a shopping mall to a car parked outside the mall. Some of the checks contained the victim's phone number and address, and the finder admitted that she never contacted the victim to restore the property to her.

Leasing   A lease of personal property is a transfer of the right to possess and use personal property belonging to another.[6] Although the rights of one who leases personal property (a lessee) do not constitute ownership of personal property, leasing is mentioned here because it is becoming an increasingly important way of acquiring the use of many kinds of personal property, from automobiles to farm equipment.

Articles 2 and 9 of the UCC may sometimes be applied to personal-property leases by analogy. However, rules contained in these articles are sometimes inadequate to resolve special problems presented by leasing. For this reason, a new article of the UCC dealing exclusively with leases of goods, Article 2A, was written in 1987. Forty-seven states and the District of Columbia have adopted Article 2A.

 L05 List and discuss the elements that are necessary for making a valid gift of property.

Gifts   Title to personal property may be obtained by **gift.** A gift is a voluntary transfer of property to the **donee** (the person who receives a gift), for which the **donor** (the person who gives the gift) gets no consideration in return. To have a valid gift, all three of the following elements are necessary:

1. The donor must *intend* to make a gift.

2. The donor must make *delivery* of the gift.

3. The donee must *accept* the gift.

The most critical requirement is delivery. The donor must actually give up possession and control of the property either to the donee or to a third person who is to hold it for the donee. Delivery is important because it makes clear to the donor that he is voluntarily giving up ownership without getting something in exchange. A promise to make a gift is usually not enforceable;[7] the person must actually part with the property. In some cases, the delivery may be symbolic or constructive. For example, handing over the key to a strongbox may be symbolic delivery of the property in the strongbox.

There are two kinds of gifts: gifts *inter vivos* and gifts *causa mortis.* A gift *inter vivos* is a gift between two living persons. For example, when Melissa's parents give her a car for her 21st birthday, that is a gift *inter vivos.* A gift *causa mortis* is a gift made in contemplation of death. For example, Uncle Earl, who is about to undergo a serious heart operation, gives his watch to his nephew, Bart, and says that he wants Bart to have it if he does not survive the operation.

A gift *causa mortis* is a conditional gift and is effective unless any of the following occurs:

1. The donor recovers from the peril or sickness under fear of which the gift was made, or

2. The donor revokes or withdraws the gift before he dies, or

3. The donee dies before the donor.

If one of these events takes place, ownership of the property goes back to the donor.

Conditional Gifts   Sometimes a gift is made on condition that the donee comply with certain restrictions or perform certain actions. A conditional gift is not a completed gift. It may be revoked by the donor before the donee complies with the conditions. Gifts in contemplation of marriage, such as engagement rings, are a primary example of a conditional gift. Such gifts are generally considered to have been made on an implied condition that marriage between the donor and donee will take place. The traditional rule applied in many states provides that if the donee breaks the engagement without legal justification or the engagement is broken by mutual consent, the donor will be able to recover the ring or other engagement gift. However, if the engagement is unjustifiably broken by the donor, the traditional rule generally bars the donor from recovering gifts made in contemplation of marriage. As illustrated by the *Lindh* case, which follows shortly, a growing number of courts have rejected the traditional approach and its focus on fault. Some states have enacted legislation prescribing the rules applicable to the return of engagement presents.

---

[5]*Shannon v. The State,* 574 S.E.2d 889 (Ct. App. Ga. 2002).
[6]A lease of personal property is a form of bailment, a "bailment for hire." Bailments are discussed later in this chapter.

---

[7]The idea is discussed in Chapter 12.

Ethics in Action

Finders Keepers: It May Be Legal, But Is It Ethical?

You're walking along the beach, and you find a toilet kit washed ashore. It contains some sodden cosmetics and a few dollars in change, but no identification. What should you do? The ordinarily ethical person probably tosses the potions and keeps the cash, persuaded by three arguments: Whatever drifts ashore falls under the heading of "finders, keepers," whatever has no identification is difficult to return, and whatever has trivial value would cost more to advertise for the proper owner than it's worth.

The next day on the same beach you find a dinghy with a small outboard motor attached, but no name or registration number. What should you do? While the finders-keepers and anonymity tests still hold, the triviality test does not: The dinghy clearly has significant value. The ordinarily ethical person probably, at the very least, contacts nearby harbormasters to see if anyone is missing a boat, leaving a phone number in case the owner calls.

The third day, astonishingly, you find 40 shipping containers that have washed off the deck of a vessel grounded on a sandbar in plain view a mile offshore. One contains a dozen brand-new BMW motorcycles, each worth more than $20,000. What should you do?

This third case is not hypothetical. The ship was the *Napoli,* a 62,000-ton cargo ship. On January 19, she encountered a terrific storm and was abandoned by her crew off the coast of Devon, England. As she was being towed to a nearby port, she began to list and was deliberately grounded. When the containers came loose, scores of people came from miles around, swarmed across Branscombe Beach under the eyes of helpless police, opened the containers, and made off with everything of value, including the motorcycles.

Why? They apparently saw this opportunity as somewhere between winning a lottery and finding money in a hollow tree. "It's great, isn't it?" one man told the *Guardian* newspaper, "a cross between a bomb site and a car boot [trunk] sale." Another said it was like finding "Aladdin's cave." In their view,

the stuff was there for the taking, and they were in the right place at the right time.

To call these people "looters" gives the wrong impression. These weren't professional second-story men, cat burglars, or back-alley thugs. By all accounts (and there were many in the news here last week), they were ordinary people. Two questions, then: Were their actions legal, and were they ethical?

What they did clearly fails the triviality test. As for anonymity, there's no doubt about the source of their loot, and no difficulty tracing its ownership. The finders-keepers test, however, is more complex. In fact, the police were legitimately flummoxed. English law allows salvagers to take whatever marine wreckage they find, as long as they fill out a form and take it to the Maritime and Coastguard Agency within 28 days. That entitles them to a reward if the property is claimed—and to legal ownership if, after a year, it is not. So the police felt they could do little more than hand out forms. By day's end, some of the items began showing up for sale on eBay, brazenly described as coming from the *Napoli,* suggesting that even the pretense of legality had been breached by some of these collectors.

What's being tested here, then, is not simply the law but the ethics underlying the law. Given the circumstances, would we expect a reasonably ethical person to remove objects clearly belonging to someone else, or would we want them to help restore lost property to its owners? Surely the latter. Cynics, of course, will yawp that if you don't take it, others will—a line of reasoning so thin that it also would permit you to slaughter your obnoxious neighbor if you thought others were also upset with him. Cynics also will argue that the shipper's insurance will recompense the owner for anything removed—an argument that, along with driving up insurance costs for everyone else, fails to account for one woman's loss of a collection of letters and pictures, personal and irreplaceable, that disappeared from Branscombe Beach as she was moving her home to South Africa.

So suppose we grant that, except for those who fenced their wares on eBay, the rest intended to behave legally by filing proper forms. Even so, does that make them ethical?

Source: Excerpted from the January 29, 2007, issue of *Ethics Newsline* (www.glopalethics.org/newsline/). A publication of the Institute for Global Ethics.

Lindh v. Surman   **742 A.2d 643 (Sup. Ct. Pa. 1999)**

In August 1993, Rodger Lindh (Rodger) proposed marriage to Janis Surman (Janis). Rodger presented her with a diamond engagement ring that he had purchased for $17,400. Janis accepted the marriage proposal and the ring. Two months later, Rodger broke the engagement and asked Janis to return the ring. She did so. Rodger and Janis later reconciled, with Rodger again proposing marriage and again presenting Janis with the engagement ring. Janis accepted the proposal and the ring. In March 1994, Rodger again broke the engagement and asked Janis to return the ring. This time, however, she refused. Rodger *sued her, seeking recovery of the ring or a judgment for its value. The trial court held in Rodger's favor and awarded him damages in the amount of the ring's value. When Janis appealed, the Pennsylvania Superior Court affirmed the award of damages and held that when an engagement is broken, the engagement ring must be returned even if the donor broke the engagement. Janis appealed to the Supreme Court of Pennsylvania.*

Newman, Justice

We are asked to decide whether a donee of an engagement ring must return the ring or its equivalent value when the donor breaks the engagement. We begin our analysis with the only principle on which the parties agree: that Pennsylvania law treats the giving of an engagement ring as a conditional gift. In *Pavlicic v. Vogtsberger* (Sup. Ct. Pa. 1957), the plaintiff supplied his ostensible fiancée with numerous gifts, including money for the purchase of engagement and wedding rings, with the understanding that they were given on the condition that she marry him. When the defendant left him for another man, the plaintiff sued her for recovery of these gifts. Justice Musmanno explained the conditional gift principle:

> A gift given by a man to a woman on condition that she embark on the sea of matrimony with him is no different from a gift based on the condition that the donee sail on any other sea. If, after receiving the provisional gift, the donee refuses to leave the harbor—if the anchor of contractual performance sticks in the sands of irresolution and procrastination—the gift must be restored to the donor.

The parties disagree, however, over whether fault [on the part of the donor] is relevant to determining return of the ring.

Janis contends that Pennsylvania law . . . has never recognized a right of recovery in a donor who severs the engagement. She maintains that if the condition of the gift is performance of the marriage ceremony, [a rule allowing a recovery of the ring] would reward a donor who prevents the occurrence of the condition, which the donee was ready, willing, and eagerly waiting to perform. Janis's argument that . . . the donor should not be allowed to recover the ring where the donor terminates the engagement has some basis in [decisions from Pennsylvania's lower courts and in treatises]. This Court, however, has not decided the question of whether the donor is entitled to return of the ring where the donor admittedly ended the engagement.

The issue we must resolve is whether we will follow the fault-based theory argued by Janis, or the no-fault rule advocated by Rodger. Under a fault-based analysis, return of the rings depends on an assessment of who broke the engagement, which necessarily entails a determination of why that person broke the engagement. A no-fault approach, however, involves no investigation into the motives or reasons for the cessation of the engagement and requires the return of the engagement ring simply upon the nonoccurrence of the marriage.

The rule concerning the return of a ring founded on fault principles has superficial appeal because, in the most outrageous instances of unfair behavior, it appeals to our sense of equity. Where one of the formerly engaged persons has truly "wronged" the other, justice appears to dictate that the wronged individual should be allowed to keep the ring or have it returned, depending on whether the wronged person was the donor . . . or the donee. However, the process of determining who is "wrong" and who is "right," when most modern relationships are complex circumstances, makes the fault-based approach less desirable. A thorough fault-based inquiry would not . . . end with the question of who terminated the engagement, but would also examine that person's reasons. In some instances the person who terminated the engagement may have been entirely justified in his or her actions. This kind of inquiry would invite the parties to stage the most bitter and unpleasant accusations against those whom they nearly made their spouse. A ring-return rule based on fault principles will inevitably invite acrimony and encourage parties to portray their ex-fiancées in the worst possible light. Furthermore, it is unlikely that trial courts would be presented with situations where fault was clear and easily ascertained.

The approach that has been described as the modern trend is to apply a no-fault rule to engagement ring cases. Courts that have applied this rule have borrowed from the policies of their respective legislatures that have moved away from the notion of fault in their divorce statutes. All fifty states have adopted some form of no-fault divorce. We agree with those jurisdictions that have looked toward the development of no-fault divorce law for a principle to decide engagement ring cases. In addition, the inherent weaknesses in any fault-based system lead us to adopt a no-fault approach to resolution of engagement ring disputes.

Decision of Superior Court in favor of Rodger Lindh affirmed.

Cappy, Justice, dissenting

The majority urges adoption of the no-fault rule to relieve trial courts from having the onerous task of sifting through the debris of the broken engagement in order to ascertain who is truly at fault. Are broken engagements truly more disturbing than cases where we ask judges and juries to discern possible abuses in nursing homes, day care centers, dependency proceedings involving abused children, and criminal cases involving horrific, irrational injuries to innocent victims? The subject matter our able trial courts address on a daily basis is certainly of equal sordidness as any fact pattern they may need to address in a simple case of who broke the engagement and why.

I can envision a scenario whereby the prospective bride and her family have expended thousands of dollars in preparation for the culminating event of matrimony and she is, through no fault of her own, left standing at the altar holding the caterer's bill. To add insult to injury, the majority would also strip her

of her engagement ring. Why the majority feels compelled to modernize this relatively simple and ancient legal concept is beyond the understanding of this poor man. As I see no valid reason to forego the [fault-based rule] for determining possession of the engagement ring under the simple concept of conditional gift law, I cannot endorse the modern trend advocated by the majority.

In the scenario set out at the beginning of this chapter, Claudio gave the ring to Cheryl as an engagement ring in anticipation of their forthcoming marriage. Later, Cheryl breaks off the engagement, telling Claudio that she no longer loves him. Claudio then asks Cheryl to return the ring to him.

What argument would Claudio make to support his claim that he has the legal right to have the ring returned to him? What argument might Cheryl make to support her contention that she should have the legal right to retain the ring? If Claudio and Cheryl lived in Pennsylvania, where the *Lindh v. Surman* case was decided, would Claudio be entitled to recover the ring from Cheryl? Why or why not? Would it make a difference if they lived in a state that used a fault-based approach concerning gifts given in anticipation of marriage?

Uniform Transfers to Minors Act

The Uniform Transfers to Minors Act, which has been adopted in one form or another in every state, provides a fairly simple and flexible method for making gifts and other transfers of property to minors.[8] As defined in this act, a minor is anyone under the age of 21. Under the act, an adult may transfer money, securities, real property, insurance policies, and other property. The specific ways of doing this vary according to the type of property transferred. In general, however, the transferor (the person who gives or otherwise transfers the property) delivers, pays, or assigns the property to, or registers the property with, a custodian who acts for the benefit of the minor "under the Uniform Transfers to Minors Act." The custodian is given fairly broad discretion to use the gift for the minor's benefit and may not use it for the custodian's personal benefit. The custodian may be the transferor himself, another adult, or a trust company, depending again on the type of property transferred. If the donor or other transferor fully complies with the Uniform Transfers to Minors Act, the transfer is considered to be irrevocable.

Will or Inheritance

Ownership of personal property may also be transferred upon the death of the former owner. The property may pass under the terms of a will if the will was validly executed. If there is no valid will, the property is transferred to the heirs of the owner according to state laws. Transfer of property at the death of the owner will be discussed in Chapter 26.

Confusion

Title to personal property may be obtained by **confusion**. Confusion is the intermixing of different owners' goods in such a way that they cannot later be separated. For example, suppose wheat belonging to several different people is mixed in a grain elevator. If the mixing was by agreement or if it resulted from an accident without negligence on anyone's part, each person owns his proportionate share of the entire quantity of wheat. However, a different result would be reached if the wheat was wrongfully or negligently mixed. Suppose a thief steals a truckload of Grade #1 wheat worth $8.50 a bushel from a farmer. The thief dumps the wheat into his storage bin, which contains a lower-grade wheat worth $4.50 a bushel, with the result that the mixture is worth only $4.50 a bushel. The farmer has first claim against the entire mixture to recover the value of the higher-grade wheat that was mixed with the lower-grade wheat. The thief, or any other person whose intentional or negligent act results in confusion of goods, must bear any loss caused by the confusion.

Accession

Ownership of personal property may also be acquired by **accession**. Accession means increasing the value of property by adding materials, labor, or both. As a general rule, the owner of the original property becomes the owner of the improvements. This is particularly likely to be true if the improvement was done with the permission of the owner. For example, Hudson takes his automobile to a shop that replaces the engine with a larger engine and puts in a new four-speed transmission. Hudson is still the owner of the automobile as well as the owner of the parts added by the auto shop.

---

[8]This statute was formerly called, and is still called in some states, the Uniform Gift to Minors Act.

Problems may arise if materials are added or work is performed on personal property without the consent of the owner. If property is stolen from one person and improved by the thief, the original owner can get it back and does not have to reimburse the thief for the work done or the materials used in improving it. For example, a thief steals Rourke's used car, puts a new engine in it, replaces the tires, and repairs the brakes. Rourke is entitled to get his car back from the thief and does not have to pay him for the engine, tires, and brakes.

The result is less easy to predict, however, if property is mistakenly improved in good faith by someone who believes that he owns the property. In such a case, a court must weigh the respective interests of two innocent parties: the original owner and the improver.

For example, Johnson, a stonecarver, finds a block of limestone by the side of the road. Assuming that it has been abandoned, he takes it home and carves it into a sculpture. In fact, the block was owned by Hayes. Having fallen off a flatbed truck during transportation, the block is merely lost property, which Hayes ordinarily could recover from the finder. In a case such as this, a court could decide the case in either of two ways. The first alternative would be to give the original owner (Hayes) ownership of the improved property, but to allow the person who has improved the property in good faith (Johnson) to recover the cost of the improvements. The second alternative would be to hold that the improver, Johnson, has acquired ownership of the sculpture, but that he is required to pay the original owner the value of the property as of the time he obtained it. The greater the extent to which the improvements have increased the value of the property, the more likely it is that the court will choose the second alternative and permit the improver to acquire ownership of the improved property.

 L06 List the three essential elements of a bailment.

Bailments

Nature of Bailments
A **bailment** is the delivery of personal property by its owner or someone holding the right to possess it (the **bailor**) to another person (the **bailee**) who accepts it and is under an express or implied agreement to return it to the bailor or to someone designated by the bailor. Only personal property can be the subject of bailments.

Although the legal terminology used to describe bailments might be unfamiliar to most people, everyone is familiar with transactions that constitute bailments. For example, Lincoln takes his car to a parking garage where

the attendant gives Lincoln a claim check and then drives the car down the ramp to park it. Charles borrows his neighbor's lawn mower to cut his grass. Tara, who lives next door to Kyle, agrees to take care of Kyle's cat while Kyle goes on a vacation. These are just a few of the everyday situations that involve bailments.

Elements of a Bailment
The essential elements of a bailment are:

1. The bailor owns personal property or holds the right to possess it.
2. The bailor delivers exclusive possession of and control over the personal property to the bailee.
3. The bailee knowingly accepts the personal property with the understanding that he owes a duty to return the property, or to dispose of it, as directed by the bailor.

Creation of a Bailment
A bailment is created by an express or implied contract. Whether the elements of a bailment have been fulfilled is determined by examining all the facts and circumstances of the particular situation. For example, a patron goes into a restaurant and hangs his hat and coat on an unattended rack. It is unlikely that this created a bailment, because the restaurant owner never assumed exclusive control over the hat and coat. However, if there is a checkroom and the hat and coat are checked with the attendant, a bailment will arise.

If a customer parks her car in a parking lot, keeps the keys, and may drive the car out herself whenever she wishes, a bailment has not been created. The courts treat this situation as a lease of space. Suppose, however, that she takes her car to a parking garage where an attendant, after giving her a claim check, parks the car. There is a bailment of the car because the parking garage has accepted delivery and possession of the car. However, a distinction is made between the car and packages locked in the trunk. If the parking garage was not aware of the packages, it probably would not be a bailee of them as it did not knowingly accept possession of them. The creation of a bailment is illustrated in the Concept Review box on page 623.

 L07 List and compare the three different types of bailment.

Types of Bailments
Bailments are commonly divided into three different categories:

1. Bailments for the sole benefit of the bailor.
2. Bailments for the sole benefit of the bailee.
3. Bailments for mutual benefit.

Chapter Twenty-Three **Personal Property and Bailments**   623

Creation of a Bailment

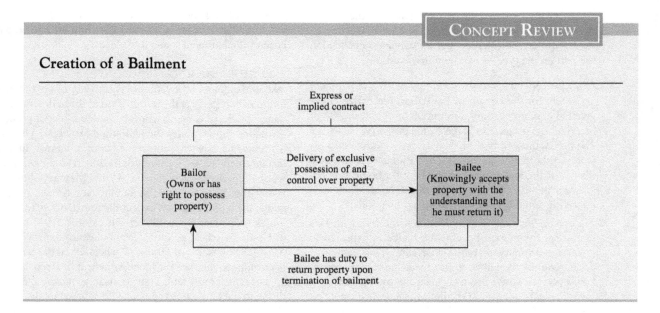

The type of bailment involved in a case can be important in determining the liability of the bailee for loss of or damage to the property. As will be discussed later, however, some courts no longer rely on these distinctions when they determine whether the bailee is liable.

Bailments for Benefit of Bailor A bailment for the sole benefit of the bailor is one in which the bailee renders some service but does not receive a benefit in return. For example, Brown allows his neighbor, Reston, to park her car in Brown's garage while she is on vacation. Brown does not ask for any compensation. Here, Reston, the bailor, has received a benefit from the bailee, Brown, but Brown has not received a benefit in return.

Bailments for Benefit of Bailee A bailment for the sole benefit of the bailee is one in which the owner of the goods allows someone else to use them free of charge. For example, Anderson lends a lawn mower to her neighbor, Moss, so he can cut his grass.

Bailments for Mutual Benefit If both the bailee and the bailor receive benefits from the bailment, it is a bailment for mutual benefit. For example, Sutton rents china for his daughter's wedding from E-Z Party Supplies for an agreed-on price. Sutton, the bailee, benefits by being able to use the china; E-Z benefits from his payment of the rental charge. On some occasions, the benefit to the bailee is less tangible. For example, a customer checks a coat at an attended coatroom at a restaurant. Even if no charge is made for the service, it

is likely to be treated as a bailment for mutual benefit because the restaurant is benefiting from the customer's patronage.

Special Bailments Certain professional bailees, such as innkeepers and common carriers, are treated somewhat differently by the law and are held to a higher level of responsibility than is the ordinary bailee. The rules applicable to common carriers and innkeepers are detailed later in this chapter.

 Explain the basic duties of the bailee and the bailor of personal property.

Duties of the Bailee The bailee has two basic duties:

1. To take care of the property that has been entrusted to her.

2. To return the property at the termination of the bailment.

The following discussion examines the scope of these duties.

Duty of Bailee to Take Care of Property
The bailee is responsible for taking steps to protect the property during the time she has possession of it. If the bailee does not exercise proper care and the property is lost or damaged, the bailee is liable for negligence. The bailee would then be required to reimburse the bailor for the amount of loss or damage. If the property is lost or

damaged without the fault or negligence of the bailee, however, the bailee is not liable to the bailor. The degree of care required of the bailee traditionally has depended in large part on the type of bailment involved.

1. *Bailment for the benefit of the bailor.* If the bailment is solely for the benefit of the bailor, the bailee is expected to exercise only a minimal, or slight, degree of care for the protection of the bailed property. He would be liable, then, only if he were grossly negligent in his care of the bailed property. The rationale for this rule is that if the bailee is doing the bailor a favor, it is not reasonable to expect him to be as careful as when he is deriving some benefit from keeping the goods.

2. *Bailment for mutual benefit.* When the bailment is a bailment for mutual benefit, the bailee is expected to exercise ordinary or reasonable care. This degree of care requires the bailee to use the same care a reasonable person would use to protect his own property in the relevant situation. If the bailee is a professional that holds itself out as a professional bailee, such as a warehouse, it must use the degree of care that would be used by a person in the same profession. This is likely to be more care than the ordinary person would use. In addition, a professional bailee usually has the obligation to explain any loss of or damage to property—that is, to show it was not negligent. If it cannot do so, it will be liable to the bailor.

3. *Bailment for the benefit of the bailee.* If the bailment is solely for the benefit of the bailee, the bailee is expected to exercise a high degree of care. For instance a person who lends a sailboat to a neighbor would probably expect the neighbor to be even more careful with the sailboat than the owner might be. In such a case, the bailee would be liable for damage to the property if his action reflected a relatively small degree of negligence.

A number of courts today view the type of bailment involved in a case as just one factor to be considered in determining whether the bailee should be liable for loss of or damage to bailed goods. The modern trend appears to be moving in the direction of imposing a duty of reasonable care on bailees, regardless of the type of bailment. This flexible standard of care permits courts to take into account a variety of factors such as the nature and value of the property, the provisions of the parties' agreement, the payment of consideration for the bailment, and the experience of the bailee. In addition, the bailee is required to use the property only as was agreed between the parties. For example, Jones borrows Morrow's lawn mower to mow his lawn. If Jones uses the mower to cut the weeds

on a trash-filled vacant lot and the mower is damaged, he would be liable because he was exceeding the agreed purpose of the bailment—to cut his lawn.

Bailee's Duty to Return the Property An essential element of a bailment is the duty of the bailee to return the property at the termination of the bailment. If the bailed property is taken from the bailee by legal process, the bailee should notify the bailor and must take whatever action is necessary to protect the bailor's interest. In most instances, the bailee must return the identical property that was bailed. A person who lends a 1999 Mercury Sable to a friend expects to have that particular car returned. In some cases, the bailor does not expect the return of the identical goods. For example, a farmer who stores 1,500 bushels of Grade #1 wheat at a local grain elevator expects to get back 1,500 bushels of Grade #1 wheat when the bailment is terminated, but not the identical wheat he deposited.

The bailee must return the goods in an undamaged condition to the bailor or to someone designated by the bailor. If the goods have been damaged, destroyed, or lost, there is a rebuttable presumption of negligence on the part of the bailee. To overcome the presumption, the bailee must come forward with evidence showing that he exercised the relevant level of care.

Bailee's Liability for Misdelivery The bailee is also liable to the bailor if he misdelivers the bailed property at the termination of the bailment. The property must be returned to the bailor or to someone specified by the bailor.

The bailee is in a dilemma if a third person, claiming to have rights superior to those of the bailor, demands possession of the bailed property. If the bailee refuses to deliver the bailed property to the third-party claimant and the claimant is entitled to possession, the bailee is liable to the claimant. If the bailee delivers the bailed property to the third-party claimant and the claimant is not entitled to possession, the bailee is liable to the bailor. The circumstances may be such that the conflicting claims of the bailor and the third-party claimant can be determined only by judicial decision. In some cases, the bailee may protect himself by bringing the third-party claimant into a lawsuit along with the bailor so that all the competing claims can be adjudicated by the court before the bailee releases the property. This remedy is not always available, however.

Limits on Liability Bailees may try to limit or relieve themselves of liability for the bailed property. Some examples include the storage receipts purporting to limit liability to a fixed amount such as $100, signs near checkrooms such as "Not responsible for loss of or damage to checked property," and disclaimers on claim checks such as "Goods left at owner's risk." The standards used to determine whether such limitations and disclaimers are enforceable are discussed in Chapter 15.

Any attempt by the bailee to be relieved of liability for intentional wrongful acts is against public policy and will not be enforced. A bailee's ability to be relieved of liability for negligence is also limited. Courts look to see whether the disclaimer or limitation of liability was communicated to the bailor at the time of the bailment. When the customer handed her coat to the checkroom attendant, did the attendant point out the "not responsible for loss or damage" sign? Did the parking lot attendant call the car owner's attention to the disclaimer on the back of the claim check?

If not, the court may hold that the disclaimer was not communicated to the bailor and did not become part of the bailment contract. Even if the bailor was aware of the disclaimer, it still may not be enforced on the ground that it is contrary to public policy.

If the disclaimer was offered on a take-it-or-leave-it basis and was not the subject of arm's-length bargaining,

it is less likely to be enforced than if it was negotiated and voluntarily agreed to by the parties. A bailee may be able to limit liability to a certain amount or to relieve himself of liability for certain perils. Ideally, the bailee will give the bailor a chance to declare a higher value and to pay an additional charge in order to be protected up to the declared value of the goods. Common carriers, such as railroads and trucking companies, often take this approach. Courts do not look with favor on efforts by a person to be relieved of liability for negligence. For this reason, terms limiting the liability of a bailee stand a better chance of being enforced than do terms completely relieving the bailee of liability.

An implied agreement as to the bailee's duties may arise from a prior course of dealing between the bailor and the bailee, or from the bailor's knowledge of the bailee's facilities or method of doing business. The bailee may, if he wishes, assume all risks incident to the bailment and contract to return the bailed property undamaged or to pay for any damage to or loss of the property.

In the case that follows, *Weissman v. City of New York*, the court concluded that an exculpatory clause was too vague to shield a bailor from liability for its negligence.

Weissman v. City of New York   860 N.Y.S.2d 393 (City of N.Y., Civil Court 2009)

In 2005, Ken Weissman rented storage space at the West 79th Street Boat Basin which is owned and operated by the City of New York Parks & Recreation Department. The written agreement contained an exculpatory clause which stated:

> I understand that the City of New York Parks & Recreation department will not be responsible for any damages incurred to my vessel while at the dinghy dock or while in the facility at the 79th Street Boat Basin, and that I store my vessel at my own risk.

The policy and practice at the facility was that users would store their vessels in an enclosed cage-like structure which had storage bins. Each user had a key to the storage area and had unrestricted access. Within the cage, users could further secure their vessels to the bin with their own devices such as chain and lock.

In 2007, Weissman had two brand new kayaks stolen from the caged area. The lock to the caged area was intact but his kayaks and locks were missing. Weissman reported this theft to the police, staff, and management. He indicated to the Boat Basin that he was no longer going to use the facility because of the theft. The manager of the facility spoke to him and urged him to continue to use the facility because they were changing their practice and policy by adding more security measures. Only West 79th Street Boat Basin employees would have keys to the caged storage area. Users no longer had unrestricted access and would have to get an employee to escort them, open the lock, and admit them to the storage area. Security cameras were going to be installed.

The Boat Basin posted a notice with the new changes, which said:

Attention Kayak Owners

Please see marina staff to gain access to kayak storage area. We have had a security issue and have temporarily changed the locks. We will be adding security cameras to the area shortly. We apologize for any inconvenience in the meantime.

Based on the assurances by the manager that the security would be better, Weissman purchased two used kayaks and again stored them in the caged area. He and the others no longer had keys to the area and had to be admitted and escorted by an employee to access the vessels in the storage area. On or about July 23, 2007, a week after the first two kayaks were stolen, one of Weissman's replacement kayaks, which cost $1,400, was missing from the storage area. He filed a notice of claim and then brought suit against the City of New York, seeking the value of the missing kayak and a refund of the unused portion of the storage fee.

Martion, Judge

The general rule is that a marina is not liable for negligence for loss of a vessel not due to the condition of the docking facility. The privilege of keeping a vessel in a marina without an agreement to keep daily or continuous guard over the vessel or without the marina taking over or assuming custody of the vessel does not constitute a bailment. This was initially the situation under the original arrangement between Weissman and the Boat Basin. Weissman had exclusive custody of his vessels and unrestricted access because he had a key to the storage area. He had the privilege of storing his kayaks there but Boat Basin was not an insurer.

However, the arrangement between the parties changed when Boat Basin took custody of the kayaks by retaining the key and controlling access to the kayaks, notifying users that this was the new temporary policy, promising better security, and urging Weissman to keep his kayaks there because of the new security measures. Under these facts, a bailment was established.

A bailment gives rise to the duty of exercising ordinary care in keeping and safeguarding property. In the instant case, Weissman has made out a prima facie case of breach of that duty by establishing that Boat Basin had exclusive possession of the kayak under lock and key and that the kayak is now missing. It then becomes the obligation of the Boat Basin to come forward with evidence to rebut the presumption of negligence. Here, Boat Basin did not come forward with any evidence and argues that it had no duty of care. However, when Boat Basin took exclusive possession of Weissman's kayak and urged him to continue using the facility because of its improved security, it created the duty of ordinary care in safeguarding the property.

Boat Basin argues that it cannot be held liable for negligence because of the exculpatory clause in the original 2005 contract, which Weissman concedes was subsequently renewed by his yearly payments. Although exculpatory clauses are enforceable, they are strictly construed against the party seeking exemption from liability. Unless the intention of the parties to insulate one of them from liability for its own negligence is expressed in unequivocal terms, the clause will not operate to have such an effect.

The exculpatory clause in this case is vague and does not suggest an intent to shield Boat Basin from its own negligence in carrying out its duty to care for Weissman's kayak. This makes perfect sense because the City did not initially have any duty to safeguard Weissman's vessel. There was no bailment. Weissman had the key to the storage cage and retained custody and control of his kayak. He stored the vessel at his own risk and the Boat Basin would not be responsible for any damages. This was the intent of the exculpatory clause.

However, the relationship changed when Boat Basin took it upon itself to secure and take control of Weissman's vessel. Boat Basin now had the only key and assured Weissman that his kayaks would be safer under Boat Basin's custody because of the heightened security. The initial contract could not have been meant to cover this new arrangement. The court holds that under the facts of this case, a bailment was created and Boat Basin was negligent by breaching its duty of care. The exculpatory clause in the original contract is too vague to shield Boat Basin from liability for its own negligence.

Judgment in favor of Weissman for $1,400, the value of the missing kayak.

Right to Compensation The express or implied contract creating the bailment controls whether the bailee has the right to receive compensation for keeping the property or must pay for having the right to use it. If the bailment is made as a favor, then the bailee is not entitled to compensation even though the bailment is for the bailor's sole benefit. If the bailment involves the rental of property, the bailee must pay the agreed rental rate. If the bailment is for the storage or repair of property, the bailee is entitled to the contract price for the storage or repair services. When no specific price was agreed on but compensation was contemplated by the parties, the bailee is entitled to the reasonable value of the services provided.

In many instances, the bailee will have a lien (a charge against property to secure the payment of a debt) on the bailed property for the reasonable value of the services. For example, Silver takes a chair to Ace Upholstery to

have it recovered. When the chair has been recovered, Ace has the right to keep it until the agreed price—or, if no price was set, the reasonable value of the work—is paid. This is an example of an **artisan's lien,** which is discussed in Chapter 29.

Bailor's Liability for Defects in the Bailed Property When personal property is rented or loaned, the bailor makes an implied warranty that the property has no hidden defects that make it unsafe for use. If the bailment is for the bailee's sole benefit, the bailor is liable for injuries that result from defects in the bailed property only if the bailor knew about the defects and did not tell the bailee. For example, Price lends his car, which he knows has bad brakes, to Sloan. If Price does not tell Sloan about the bad brakes and Sloan is injured in an accident because the brakes fail, Price is liable for Sloan's injuries.

If the bailment is a bailment for mutual benefit, the bailor has a greater obligation. The bailor must use reasonable care in inspecting the property and seeing that it is safe for the purpose for which it is intended. The bailor is liable for injuries suffered by the bailee because of defects that the bailor either knew about or should have discovered through reasonable inspection. For example, Acme Rent-All, which rents trailers, does not inspect the trailers after they are returned. A wheel has come loose on a trailer that Acme rents to Hirsch. If the wheel comes off while Hirsch is using the trailer and the goods Hirsch is carrying in it are damaged, Acme is liable to Hirsch.

In addition, product liability doctrines that apply a higher standard of legal responsibility have been applied to bailors who are commercial lessors of personal property.[9] Express or implied warranties of quality under either Article 2 or Article 2A of the UCC may apply. Liability under these warranties does not depend on whether the bailor knew about or should have discovered the defect. The only question is whether the property's condition complied with the warranty. Some courts have also imposed strict liability on the commercial lessor-bailor of defective, unreasonably dangerous goods that cause personal injury or property damage to the lessee-bailee. This liability is imposed regardless of whether the lessor was negligent.

 Discuss the special rules applicable for bailments to common carriers and hotelkeepers.

Special Bailments

Common Carriers

Bailees that are common carriers are held to a higher level of responsibility than are bailees that are private carriers. Common carriers are licensed by governmental agencies to carry the property of anyone who requests the service. Private contract carriers carry goods only for persons selected by the carrier.

Both common carriers and private contract carriers are bailees. However, the law makes the common carrier a near-absolute insurer of the goods it carries. The common carrier is responsible for virtually any loss of or damage to the entrusted goods, unless the common carrier shows that the loss or damage was caused by one of the following:

1. An act of God.
2. An act of a public enemy.
3. An act or order of the government.

4. An act of the person who shipped the goods.
5. The nature of the goods themselves.

Therefore, the common carrier is liable if goods entrusted to it are stolen by some unknown person, but not if the goods are destroyed when the warehouse is damaged by a hurricane.

If goods are damaged because the shipper improperly packaged or crated them, the carrier is not liable. Similarly, if perishable goods are not in suitable condition to be shipped and therefore deteriorate in the course of shipment, the carrier is not liable so long as it used reasonable care in handling them.

Common carriers are usually permitted to limit their liability to a stated value unless the bailor declares a higher value for the property and pays an additional fee.

Hotelkeepers

Hotelkeepers are engaged in the business of offering food and/or lodging to transient persons. They hold themselves out to serve the public and are obligated to do so. As is the common carrier, the hotelkeeper is held to a higher standard of care than that of the ordinary bailee. The hotelkeeper, however, is not a bailee in the strict sense of the word. The guest does not usually surrender the exclusive possession of his property to the hotelkeeper. Even so, the hotelkeeper is treated as the virtual insurer of the guest's property. The hotelkeeper is not liable for loss of or damage to property if she shows that it was caused by one of the following:

1. An act of God.
2. An act of a public enemy.
3. An act of a governmental authority.
4. The fault of a member of the guest's party.
5. The nature of the goods.

Most states have passed laws that limit the hotelkeeper's liability, however. Commonly, the law requires the hotel owner to post a notice advising guests that any valuables should be checked into the hotel vault. The hotelkeeper's liability is then limited, usually to a fixed amount, for valuables that are not so checked.

Safe-Deposit Boxes

If a person rents a safe-deposit box at a local bank and places property in the box, the box and the property are in the physical possession of the bank. However, it takes both the renter's key and the key held by the bank to open the box. In most cases, the bank does not know the nature, amount, or value of the goods in the box. Although a few courts have held that the rental of a safe-deposit box does not create a bailment,

---

[9]Product liability doctrines are discussed in Chapter 20.

Duties of Bailees and Bailors

Type of Bailment	Duties of Bailee	Duties of Bailor
Sole Benefit of Bailee	**1.** Must use great care; liable for even slight negligence. **2.** Must return goods to bailor or dispose of them at his direction. **3.** May have duty to compensate bailor.	**1.** Must notify the bailee of any known defects.
Mutual Benefit	**1.** Must use reasonable care; liable for ordinary negligence. **2.** Must return goods to bailor or dispose of them at his direction. **3.** May have duty to compensate bailor.	**1.** Must notify bailee of all known defects and any defects that could be discovered on reasonable inspection. **2.** Commercial lessors may be subject to warranties of quality and/or strict liability in tort. **3.** May have duty to compensate bailee.
Sole Benefit of Bailor	**1.** Must use at least slight care; liable for gross negligence. **2.** Must return goods to bailor or dispose of them at his direction.	**1.** Must notify bailee of all known defects and any hidden defects that are known or could be discovered on reasonable inspection. **2.** May have duty to compensate bailee.

most courts have concluded that the renter of the box is a bailor and the bank is a bailee. As such, the bank is not an insurer of the contents of the box. It is obligated, however, to use due care and to come forward and explain loss of or damage to the property entrusted to it.

Involuntary Bailments Suppose a person owns a cottage on a beach. After a violent storm, a sailboat washed up on his beach. As the finder of lost or misplaced property, he may be considered the involuntary bailee or constructive bailee of the sailboat. This relationship may arise when a person finds himself in possession of someone else's property without having agreed to accept possession.

The duties of the involuntary bailee are not well defined. The involuntary bailee does not have the right to destroy or use the property. If the true owner shows up, the property must be returned to him. Under some circumstances, the involuntary bailee may be under an obligation to assume control of the property or to take some minimal steps to ascertain the owner's identity, or both.

 LO10 Discuss the special rules applicable to bailments covered by negotiable documents of title, including warehouse receipts and bills of lading.

Documents of Title

Storing or shipping goods, giving a warehouse receipt or bill of lading representing the goods, and transferring such a receipt or bill of lading as representing the goods are practices of ancient origin. The warehouseman or the common carrier is a bailee of the goods who contracts to store or transport the goods and to deliver them to the owner or to act otherwise in accordance with the lawful directions of the owner. The warehouse receipt or the bill of lading may be either negotiable or nonnegotiable. To be negotiable, a warehouse receipt, bill of lading, or other document of title must provide that the goods are to be delivered to the bearer or to the order of a named person [7–104(1)]. The primary differences between the law of negotiable instruments and the law of negotiable documents of title are based on the differences between the obligation to pay money and the obligation to deliver specific goods.

Warehouse Receipts A warehouse receipt, to be valid, need not be in any particular form, but if it does not embody within its written or printed form each of the following, the warehouseman is liable for damages caused by the omission to a person injured as a result of it: (1) the location of the warehouse where the goods are stored; (2) the date of issue; (3) the consecutive number of the receipt; (4) whether the goods are to be delivered to the bearer or to the order of a named person; (5) the rate of storage and handling charges; (6) a description of the goods or of the packages containing them; (7) the signature of the warehouseman or his agent; (8) whether the warehouseman is the owner of the goods, solely, jointly, or in common with others; and (9) a statement of the amount of the advances made and of the liabilities incurred for which the warehouseman claims a lien or security interest. Other terms may be inserted [7–202].

A warehouseman is liable to a purchaser for value in good faith of a warehouse receipt for nonreceipt or misdescription of goods. The receipt may conspicuously qualify the description by a statement such as "contents, condition, and quantity unknown" [7–203].

Because a warehouseman is a bailee of the goods, he owes to the holder of the warehouse receipt the duties of a mutual benefit bailee and must exercise reasonable care [7–204]. The warehouseman may terminate the relation by notification where, for example, the goods are about to deteriorate or where they constitute a threat to other goods

The Global Business Environment

Liability of Carriers of Goods

When an American firm ships goods to a foreign buyer, the goods may be shipped by ground, air, or water carrier. The duties and extent of liability of these various carriers is largely determined by domestic statutes and international law.

Ground Carriers

American trucking and railroad companies are regulated by the Interstate Commerce Act. American carriers are liable for any loss or damage to the goods with few exceptions—for example, damage caused by acts of God and acts of the shipper (usually the seller of the goods), such as poorly packaging the goods. An American carrier may limit its liability by contract, provided it allows the shipper to obtain full liability by paying a higher shipping charge.

Most European trucking companies and railroads are covered by EU rules, which place liability on carriers for damages to goods they carry with few exceptions—for example, defective packaging by the shipper and circumstances beyond the carrier's control. EU rules also limit a carrier's liability unless the shipper agrees to pay for greater liability.

Air Carriers

The Warsaw Convention governs the liability of international air carriers. Most nations have ratified the Warsaw Convention in its original or amended form. Under the Convention, an air carrier is liable to the shipper for damages to goods with few exceptions, including that it was impossible for the carrier to prevent the loss or that the damage was caused by the negligence of the shipper. The Warsaw Convention limits a carrier's liability to a stated amount per pound, unless the shipper pays for greater liability.

Water Carriers

The Hague Rules govern the liability of international water carriers. The Hague Rules were amended in Vishy, Sweden,

in 1968. The United States codified the Hague Rules in the Carriage of Goods by Sea Act (COGSA), but has not ratified the Visby amendments, which do not substantially change the liability of international water carriers.

The Hague–Visby Rules and the COGSA impose on international water carriers the duties to (1) furnish a seaworthy ship and (2) stow the cargo carefully to prevent it from breaking loose during storms at sea. When these duties are met, a water carrier will not usually be liable for damages to cargo. Water carriers have no liability for damages caused by circumstances beyond their control—such as poor packaging, piracy, or acts of war. Under COGSA, liability is limited to $500 per package, unless the shipper agrees to pay a higher shipping fee. Under the Hague–Visby Rules, liability will be the value of the goods declared by the shipper. Sometimes a carrier will attempt to reduce or eliminate its liability in the shipping contract. However, COGSA does not permit a carrier to eliminate its liability for loss or damages to goods resulting from the carrier's negligence or other fault.

Under COGSA or the Hague–Visby Rules, the owner of cargo will be liable for damage his cargo does to other cargo. Also, under the ancient maritime doctrine of general average, when a carrier sacrifices an owner's cargo, such as throwing it overboard in order to save the ship and the other cargo, the other owners have liability to the owner whose cargo was sacrificed; liability is prorated to each owner according to the value of each owner's goods in relation to the value of the voyage (the value of the ship plus the value of the other owners' goods plus the carrier's total shipping fees).

The doctrine of general average is commonly expanded by the contract between the carrier and cargo owners in New Jason clauses. Typically, a New Jason clause provides that in *all* cases when goods are damaged and the carrier is not liable under COGSA, the goods owner is entitled to general average contributions from all other cargo owners. The doctrine of general average, bolstered by a New Jason clause, also requires cargo owners to pay for damages to the ship when not the result of the carrier's fault.

in the warehouse [7–206]. Unless the warehouse receipt provides otherwise, the warehouseman must keep separate the goods covered by each receipt; however, different lots of fungible goods such as grain may be mingled [7–207].

A warehouseman has a lien against the bailor on the goods covered by his receipt for his storage and other charges incurred in handling the goods [7–209]. The Code sets out a detailed procedure for enforcing this lien [7–210].

Bills of Lading

In many respects, the rights and liabilities of the parties to a negotiable bill of lading are the same as the rights and liabilities of the parties to a negotiable warehouse receipt. The contract of the issuer of a bill of lading is to transport goods, whereas the contract of the issuer of a warehouse receipt is to store goods. Like the issuer of a warehouse receipt, the issuer of a bill of lading is liable for nonreceipt or misdescription of the goods, but he may protect himself from liability where he does not know the contents of packages by marking the bill

of lading "contents or condition of packages unknown" or similar language. Such terms are ineffective when the goods are loaded by an issuer who is a common carrier unless the goods are concealed by packages [7–301].

Duty of Care

A carrier who issues a bill of lading, or a warehouse operator who issues a warehouse receipt, must exercise the same degree of care in relation to the goods as a reasonably careful person would exercise under similar circumstances. Liability for damages not caused by the negligence of the carrier may be imposed on him by a special law or rule of law. Under tariff rules, a common carrier may limit her liability to a shipper's declaration of value, provided that the rates are dependent on value [7–309].

In the case that follows, *Gyamfoah v. EG&G Dynatrend,* a warehouseman who was unable to return goods that had been entrusted to it for safekeeping or to account for their disappearance was held liable to the bailor for the value of the goods.

Gyamfoah v. EG&G Dynatrend (now EG&G Technical Services)
51 U.C.C. Rep. 2d 805 (E.D. Penn. 2003)

On May 7, 1999, Yaa Gyamfoah, a citizen of Ghana, arrived at JFK International Airport with two suitcases containing a number of watches she had purchased in Hong Kong. The suitcases were seized by U.S. Customs because it suspected the watches were counterfeit. Gyamfoah was given a receipt for 3,520 watches. The watches were transported to a warehouse operated by EG&G Dynatrend (EG&G), now known as EG&G Technical Services, under contract with the U.S. Department of Treasury to provide seized management services for all agencies of the department. The warehouse accepted and signed for the watches on June 2, 1999.

On October 13, U.S. Customs advised Gyamfoah's agent that the nonviolative (ones that were not counterfeit) portion of the seizure (2,940 watches) would be released upon payment of $1,470. On November 18, a Customs agent, observed by EG&G's warehouse supervisor, separated the watches into a group of 580 "violative" watches, which were placed in a carton, and 2,940 "nonviolative" watches, which were placed back in the suitcases. The carton and the suitcases were then returned to the custody of EG&G. When the Customs agent returned on November 24 to again, under the observation of the warehouse supervisor, examine the watches, there were only 1,002 watches in the carton and suitcases; some 2,518 were missing.

Gyamfoah subsequently brought suit against the United States and EG&G. The claim against the United States was dismissed, and the case went to trial on the claim against EG&G.

O'Neil, Jr., Judge

The duties of a warehouseman that existed under New Jersey common law have now been codified in *N.J.S.A. 12A: 7–101.* EG&G is a warehouseman under the definition in the statute: "a person engaged in the business of storing goods for hire." New Jersey requires that a warehouseman exercise reasonable care when storing bailed items. The statute imposes the following liability, in a provision adopted from the Uniform Commercial Code:

A warehouseman is liable for damages for loss of or injury to the goods caused by his failure to exercise such care in regard to them as a reasonably careful man would exercise under

like circumstances but unless otherwise agreed he is not liable for damages which could not have been avoided by the exercise of such care.

N.J.S.A. 12A: 7–204(1).

The warehouseman's statute has been interpreted to involve a burden-shifting scheme that reflects that common law of bailment. The bailor must present *a prima facie* case of conversion by proving (1) delivery of the bailed goods to the bailee; (2) demand for return of the bailed goods from the bailee; and (3) failure of the bailee to return the bailed goods. Once the bailee has proved these three points, the burden shifts to the bailee to show how the bailed goods were lost. If the bailee cannot prove how the bailed goods were lost it is liable under the New Jersey statute for conversion. Although the burden of proof regarding how the goods were lost shifts to the defendant, the burden of proving conversion rests at all times on the bailor as plaintiff.

The tort of conversion that can be proved under the statute is not necessarily an intentional tort. In this instance "[a] conversion can occur even when a bailee has not stolen the merchandise but has acted negligently in permitting the loss of the merchandise from its premises." In other words, if a bailor establishes that the bailed goods had disappeared while in the care of the bailee, there is a rebuttable presumption of conversion based either on the bailee's negligent conduct in permitting third parties to steal the goods, or by the negligent or intentional conduct of the bailee's employees or agents.

As established earlier, I find that Gyamfoah showed by a preponderance of the evidence that: (1) 3,520 watches were delivered to EG&G's warehouse; (2) when Gyamfoah's agent presented the papers entitling Gyamfoah to return of the watches 2,518 watches were missing; and (3) the U.S. Customs officers who manipulated the watches did not remove the missing watches.

Therefore, Gyamfoah has established delivery to EG&G and EG&G's failure to redeliver all of the items on Gyamfoah's demand. Under New Jersey law this creates a rebuttable presumption of conversion by EG&G.

EG&G produced evidence at trial of reasonable precautions against loss. Mr. Wenzcel testified that the watches were shrink-wrapped to a pallet and stored in a secured area on a high shelf that required a forklift to be reached. Paul Hehir, the EG&G district manager who oversaw operations in the New York district of the company, also testified about security. He testified that the area in which the watches were stored was armed and within a gated area that only EG&G employees could enter.

EG&G does not provide any evidence, however, regarding what happened to the missing watches. EG&G mentions the possibility that the missing watches were never delivered to the warehouse. This possibility is refuted, however, by evidence that U.S. Customs officers left the warehouse on November 18 thinking that there were 3,520 watches in storage. As I stated earlier, I find that Gyamfoah has proved by a preponderance of the evidence that there were 3,520 watches in the suitcases when the suitcases were delivered to EG&G's warehouse. There is no explanation for the disappearance of the watches other than EG&G's negligence. In fact, when asked "so it's fair to say that sitting here today, EG&G can offer no explanation of the loss of the majority of the contents of those two suitcases?" EG&G employee Mr. Herir testified "I cannot offer any explanation, no."

EG&G has not met its burden to rebut the presumption of negligence created by plaintiff's case. Gyamfoah has met her burden of proving by a preponderance of the evidence that EG&G is liable to her under New Jersey's law of bailment, as found in Section *7–204(1)* and the common law. EG&G is liable for the value of the lost watches.

Gyamfoah has proved by a preponderance of the evidence that EG&G is liable for the loss of 2,518 watches. For negligence, the measure of damages is the value of the lost goods.

The only evidence presented at trial regarding the value of the missing watches is a receipt from Andex Trading Limited. The receipt lists ten models of watches, the quantity bought by Gyamfoah, the unit price and the amount paid for the number of watches of each model bought. Because Gyamfoah has not shown which models the 2,518 missing watches were, I will calculate damages as if the least expensive 2,518 watches are missing.

The cost of the least expensive 2,518 watches is $3,781.30. That includes 300 watches at $0.90 each, 100 watches at $1.40 each, 350 watches at $1.55 each and 1,768 watches at $1.60 each.

Judgment in favor of Yaa Gyamfoah and against EG&G Dynatrend in the amount of $3,781.30.

Negotiation of Document of Title A negotiable document of title and a negotiable instrument are negotiated in substantially the same manner. If the document of title provides for the delivery of the goods to bearer, it may be negotiated by delivery. If it provides for delivery of the goods to the order of a named person, it must be endorsed by that person and delivered. If an order document of title is endorsed in blank, it may be negotiated by delivery unless it bears a special endorsement following the blank endorsement, in which event it must be endorsed by the special endorsee and delivered [7–501].

A person taking a negotiable document of title takes as a bona fide holder if she takes in good faith and in the regular course of business. The bona fide holder of a negotiable document of title has substantially the same advantages over a holder who is not a bona fide holder or over a holder of a nonnegotiable document of title as does a holder in due course of a negotiable instrument over a holder who is not a holder in due course or over a holder of a nonnegotiable instrument.

Rights Acquired by Negotiation A person who acquires a negotiable document of title by due negotiation acquires (1) title to the document, (2) title to the goods, (3) the right to the goods delivered to the bailee after the issuance of the document, and (4) the direct obligation of the issuer to hold or deliver the goods according to the terms of the document [7–502(1)].

Under the broad general principle that a person cannot transfer title to goods he does not own, a thief—or the owner of goods subject to a perfected security interest—cannot, by warehousing or shipping the goods on a negotiable document of title and then negotiating the document of title, transfer to the purchaser of the document of title a better title than he has [7–503].

Warranties of Transferor of Document of Title The transferor of a negotiable document of title warrants to his immediate transferee, in addition to any warranty of goods, only that the document is genuine, that he has no knowledge of any facts that would impair its validity or worth, and that his negotiation or transfer is rightful and fully effective with respect to the title to the document and the goods it represents [7–507].

Problems and Problem Cases

1. Bernice Paset, a customer of the Old Orchard Bank, found $6,325 in currency on the seat of a chair in an examination booth in the bank's safety-deposit vault. The chair was partially under a table. Paset notified officers of the bank and turned the money over to them. She was told by bank officials that the bank would try to locate the owner and that she could have the money if the owner was not located within one year. The bank wrote to everyone who had been in the safety-deposit vault either on the day of, or on the day preceding, the discovery. The bank's letter stated that some property had been found and invited the customers to describe any property they might have lost. No one reported the loss of any currency. The money remained unclaimed a year after it had been found. The bank refused to deliver the money to Paset, contending that it was mislaid, not lost, property and that it had a better right to it. Was the money mislaid property?

2. Alex Franks was staying at a Comfort Inn in Searcy, Arkansas, while working on a highway project. He checked into the hotel on Monday, September 10. Two days later, after he had checked out and returned to his room to retrieve some laundry, he discovered $14,200 in plain view in a drawer of the dresser in the room. It was wrapped tightly with masking tape, like a brick, with some of the money showing. Franks notified the hotel manager, who in turn notified the police. The police determined that there were two bundles of money separated by denominations and then bundled together. The bundle contained 46 one hundred dollar bills and 480 twenty dollar bills. The officer who took custody of the money testified that the money appeared to be intentionally and meticulously wrapped because all the bills faced in the same direction. Franks brought suit against the City

of Searcy claiming the money. The city joined the owners of the hotel as third-party defendants and then withdrew any claim on its part to the money. Should the court hold that the money is abandoned, lost, or mislaid? Between Franks and the owner of the hotel, who has the best right to it? Why?

3. Rick Kenyon purchased a painting by a noted Western artist, Bill Gollings, valued between $8,000 and $15,000 for $25 at a Salvation Army thrift store. Claude Abel filed suit against Kenyon seeking the return of the painting, which had belonged to his late aunt. Abel claimed that the Salvation Army mistakenly took the painting from his aunt's house when the box in which it was packed was mixed with items being donated to the thrift store. Abel's aunt, Billie Taylor, was a friend of the artist whose works were known for their accurate portrayal of the Old West. Sometime before his death in 1932, Gollings gave a painting to Taylor depicting a Native American on a white horse in the foreground with several other Native Americans on horses in the background traveling through a traditional Western prairie landscape. The painting remained in Taylor's possession at her home in Sheridan, Wyoming, until her death on August 31, 1999. After Taylor's death, Abel traveled from his home in Idaho to Sheridan for the funeral and to settle the estate. Abel was the sole heir of Taylor's estate, so he inherited all of her personal belongings, including the Gollings painting. Abel and his wife sorted through Taylor's belongings, selecting various items they would keep for themselves. Abel and his wife, with the help of a local moving company, packed those items into boxes marked for delivery to their home in Idaho. Items not being retained by Abel were either packed for donation to the Salvation Army or, if they had sufficient value, were taken by an antiques dealer for auction. The scene at the house was one of some confusion as Abel tried

to vacate the residence as quickly as possible while attempting to make sure all of the items went to their designated destinations. The painting was packed by Abel's wife in a box marked for delivery to Idaho. However, in the confusion and unbeknown to Abel, the box containing Gollings's painting was inadvertently picked up with the donated items by the Salvation Army. It was priced at $25 in its thrift store and sold to Kenyon. After returning to Idaho, Abel discovered that the box containing the painting was not among those delivered by the moving company. He also learned that the painting had gone to the Salvation Army and had been sold to Kenyon. When Kenyon refused to acknowledge he had the painting, Abel brought suit seeking its return. Kenyon claimed that he was a good faith purchaser of the painting that had been given to the Salvation Army. Was Abel entitled to have the painting returned to him on the grounds that not having made a gift of the painting, he was still the owner, and that its sale by the Salvation Army was a conversion of his property?

4. Jacqulyn Tubbs, who lived in Michigan, and Keith Church, who lived in England, began communicating over the internet in the fall of 1999. Soon they developed a long-distance relationship and in February of 2000 got engaged. At that time, Church gave Tubbs an engagement ring worth $7,274.42. In addition to the engagement ring, Church paid off Tubbs's credit cards and deposited $194,852.56 into Tubbs's bank account to purchase a home in Michigan. They were planning to get married in Las Vegas in July of 2000. In June, Tubbs discovered that Church was a bisexual cross-dresser. Tubbs was horrified at this discovery and e-mailed Church stating that their relationship was over. Tubbs consequently threw the ring into a river, and refused to return any of the property that Church had given her. In July Church died in England. Four years later Church's estate sued Tubbs in Michigan for the return of all the property, including the ring or its equivalent value. Tubbs argued that Church was responsible for the break up and was therefore precluded from recovering the ring and the gifts. Should the court order Tubbs to return the value of the engagement ring to Church's estate?

5. Faith Ballard's Corvette was substantially damaged in an accident and was being stored in her garage. Her son, Tyrone Ballard, told her that he would take the vehicle and have it restored. Instead he sold it to Lambert Auto Parts. Johnny Wetzel purchased the Corvette "hull" for $900 from Lambert, whose regular business is selling parts. Wetzel obtained a receipt documenting the purchase of the parts. He also checked the VIN numbers through the county clerk's office to make sure the parts were not stolen. Wetzel spent approximately $5,000 and 100 hours of labor restoring the vehicle. When completed, the restoration had a market value of $7,950. George Martin, an employee of Lambert, testified that he purchased only a "hull" of a car—rather than a whole vehicle—from Tyrone Ballard. Martin also testified that he usually received a title when he bought a "whole" vehicle but had not received one in this case where he had purchased only part of one. Under Tennessee law, a certificate of title is not required to pass ownership of a motor vehicle, but any owner dismantling a registered vehicle is to send the certificate of title back to the state. Faith Ballard brought suit against Wetzel to recover possession of the Corvette. Wetzel contended that he was a good faith purchaser for value and had become the owner of the restored auto hull by accession. Did Wetzel become the owner of the Corvette by accession?

6. On September 2, Deborah Jones signed a Storage Rental Agreement with Econo-Self Storage owned by Ernie Hanna. Jones needed to store her personal belongings and furniture because of the flooding of her apartment. The self-storage agreement was written as a lease and designated the parties as landlord and tenant. The warehouse space leased by Jones was 10 feet by 10 feet, on a monthly term of $45. The agreement provided in part: "All property kept, stored, or maintained within the premises by Tenant shall be at Tenant's sole risk."

On May 2, Jones learned that the lock to her storage unit had been cut and virtually all of her possessions were stolen. The circumstances of the theft were not known. The storage units, 180 in all, were protected by a 6-foot fence and a locked gate. The tenants placed their own locks on the units. No security dogs or watchmen were provided. Access could be made to the units between 6 A.M. and 9 P.M. daily. No inventory was made of the goods by the facility owner, and the goods were never placed in his hands and he did not know what was stored. Jones brought suit to recover damages for the loss of her property. Was Econo-Self Storage the bailee of Jones's goods?

7. Thompson discovered that the automatic transmission in his car was leaking even though it otherwise was operating properly. He took the car to Mr. Transmission, a transmission repair business, told the people

there he wanted the transmission seals replaced because the automatic transmission was leaking, signed a work order, and left the car with them expecting to pay their advertised fee of $69.95. When he returned to the shop several hours later, he found that the transmission, which did not have to be taken apart to replace the seals, had been removed from his car and was disassembled. An employee told him the fluid was burnt out and had metal particles in it. He also broke one of the transmission parts in Thompson's presence. Thompson was told that the transmission would have to be rebuilt or replaced and that installing a rebuilt transmission at a cost of $377 would be the quickest. In order to get his car back, Thompson had Mr. Transmission install a replacement rebuilt transmission and paid for it under protest as he had not authorized his transmission to be disassembled. The replaced transmission began to leak, and Thompson brought an action for unauthorized disassembly and destruction of his operating transmission resulting in his forced purchase of another transmission. He also sought punitive damages. Was Mr. Transmission liable to Thompson for the acts it took with respect to his transmission that had been entrusted to it?

8. On March 27, 2001, Felice Jasphy brought three fur coats to Illana Osinsky's establishment trading as Cedar Lane Furs in Teaneck, New Jersey, for storage and cleaning. The three coats included a ranch mink coat, a Shearling, and a blush mink. In addition to storage of the three coats, Jasphy also sought cleaning of the ranch mink. In 1997, the ranch mink had been appraised for $11,500; the Shearling for $3,500; and the blush mink for $3,995. Jasphy signed a written agreement, labeled "fur storage sales receipt," which included Jasphy's name and address, and the price of the storage and cleaning. On the back of the receipt, the following preprinted provision limiting Cedar Lane Furs' liability read:

> This receipt is a storage contract, articles listed are accepted for storage until December 31, of dated year, subject to the terms and conditions hereof, in accepting this receipt, the depositor agrees to be bound by all its terms and conditions and acknowledges that this receipt is the entire agreement with the furrier, which cannot be changed except by endorsement herein signed by the furrier. If no value is specified, or if no separate insurance covering the garment is declared at the time of issuance of this receipt, insurance in the amount of $1.00 will be placed on the garment.

Immediately above the location on the receipt for a customer's signature, the following was printed: "I understand and agree that Cedar Lane Furs' liability for loss or damage from any cause whatsoever, including their own negligence or that of employees and others, is limited to the declared valuation." Jasphy did not state the value of the coats or declare whether she had separate insurance coverage when the receipt was issued. There is no identifiable room provided on the receipt to specify such information. The limitation of the furrier's liability was not brought to Jasphy's attention, nor was she asked to furnish the value of her coats for storage. The following day, March 28, 2001, a fire swept through Cedar Lane Furs, causing Jasphy's furs to be completely destroyed. A hot iron, which Cedar Lane Furs' employees apparently forgot to unplug overnight, caused the fire. Jasphy subsequently learned that her furs had not been placed in the fur vault before the fire and were destroyed in the fire. Jasphy filed a claim form with Cedar Lane Furs' insurance company but never received any reimbursement. She then brought suit against Osinsky and Cedar Lane Furs. They contended that their liability was limited by the contract provision to $1 per garment. Should the court enforce the contractual provision limiting the furrier's liability to $1 per garment?

9. Marvin Gooden checked into a Day's Inn in Atlanta, paying in advance for two days' lodging. The next day he temporarily left his room. He left behind, in the room, a paper bag filled with approximately $9,000. Shortly after Gooden left, housekeeper Mary Carter entered his room to clean it. Carter found the bag of money. Because she saw no other personal effects, Carter assumed that Gooden had checked out. She therefore turned the bag of money over to her supervisor, Vivian Clark. Clark gave the bag to Dempsey Wilson, who was responsible for general supervision and maintenance of the grounds. During the three years he had worked for Day's Inn, Wilson had occasionally been given items of value to turn in at the hotel's office. In the past, he had always turned in the items. This time, however, he absconded with the bag of money. There was a safe on the Day's Inn premises. Day's Inn had posted, on the door of Gooden's room, a notice concerning the safe's availability for use by guests who had valuables with them. Gooden, who had never sought the use of the safe, brought a tort action against Day's Inn, Clark, and Carter in an effort to collect $9,000

in damages. Day's Inn argued that it was protected against liability by the following Georgia statute: "The innkeeper may provide a safe or other place of deposit for valuable articles and, by posting a notice thereof, may require the guests of the innkeeper to place such valuable articles therein or the innkeeper shall be relieved from responsibility for such articles." Gooden contended, however, that the statute could not insulate an innkeeper from liability when the loss of a guest's valuables is occasioned by the negligent (or other tortious) conduct of the innkeeper's employees. Should Gooden prevail against Day's Inn, Clark, and Carter?

10. Griswold and Bateman Warehouse Company stored 337 cases of Chivas Regal Scotch Whiskey for Joseph H. Reinfeld, Inc., in its bonded warehouse. The warehouse receipt issued to Reinfeld limited Griswold and Bateman's liability for negligence to 250 times the monthly storage rate, a total of $1,925. When Reinfeld sent its truck to pick up the whiskey, 40 cases were missing. Reinfeld then brought suit seeking the wholesale market value of the whiskey, $6,417.60. Reinfeld presented evidence of the delivery of the whiskey, the demand for its return, and the failure of Griswold and Bateman to return it. Reinfeld claimed that the burden was on Griswold and Bateman to explain the disappearance of the whiskey. Griswold and Bateman admitted that it had been negligent, but sought to limit its liability to $1,925: Is Griswold and Bateman's liability limited to $1,925?

Online Research

What Should You Do If You Find Valuable Property?

Use the Internet to determine whether your state has a law dealing with unclaimed or estray property. If you find a valuable item that appears to have been lost, what steps are you legally obligated to take in your state? What procedures does your state have for trying to locate the owner of such property?

Consider completing the case "PROPERTY: Subtracting the Addition" from the You Be the Judge website element after you have read this chapter. Visit our website at www.mhhe.com/mallor15e for more information and activities regarding this case segment.

CHAPTER 24

REAL PROPERTY

Joyce and John, a married couple with two young children, are in the process of buying a house. They made an offer on a single-family house in Greenwood, a new subdivision. The house has four bedrooms, one with custom-built bunk beds in it, four bathrooms, a swimming pool, and a large basement. There is a well-equipped kitchen and a large dining room with a vintage Tiffany lamp over the dining room table. The basement is perfect for Joyce, who plans to operate a small day care center in the house. Joyce and John notice that the next-door neighbors, the Fieldings, have been dumping their garden refuse in a ravine at the back of the property that they have offered to buy, but they assume that they will be able to stop that practice once they move in.

- Are the bunk beds and Tiffany lamp considered to be part of the real property that Joyce and John have offered to buy?
- If their offer is accepted, how will Joyce and John share ownership of the property? What form of ownership will they have?
- What are the steps involved in purchasing this property?
- What rights might others, such as the Fieldings, have in the property?
- What liability might John and Joyce have to others who are injured on their property?
- What controls does the legal system place on the use of property?
- Is it ethical for the Fieldings to dump their garden refuse on this property?

LO   LEARNING OBJECTIVES

After studying this chapter, you should be able to:

1. Define real property and explain what is included in the concept of real property.
2. Provide several examples of property that would be considered to be a fixture and explain the significance of classifying an item of property as a fixture.
3. Explain and distinguish among the various forms of ownership of real property.
4. Explain the legal effects of easements and restrictive covenants as well as the duties of property owners toward third persons.
5. Distinguish the various ways in which ownership of real property is transferred and how title to property can be assured.
6. Distinguish the different types of deeds, explain the purposes of recording deeds, and describe how state law determines priorities among those who claim competing rights in a parcel of real property.
7. Explain governmental powers to control and purchase private land and the constitutional limits on those powers.

LAND'S SPECIAL IMPORTANCE IN the law has long been recognized. In the agrarian society of previous eras, land served as the basic measure and source of wealth. In today's society, land functions not only as a source of food, clothing, and shelter but also as an instrument of commercial and industrial development. It is not surprising, then, that a complex body of law—the law of *real property*—exists regarding the ownership, acquisition, and use of land.

This chapter discusses the scope of real property and the various legal interests in it. In addition, the chapter examines the ways in which real property is transferred and the controls society places on an owner's use of real property.

 LO1 Define real property and explain what is included in the concept of real property.

Scope of Real Property

Real property includes not only land but also things firmly attached to or embedded in land. Buildings and other permanent structures thus are considered real property. The owner of a tract of real property also owns the air above it, the minerals below its surface, and any trees or other vegetation growing on the property.[1]

Unlike readily movable personal property, real property is immovable or attached to something immovable. Distinguishing between real and personal property is important because rules of law governing real property transactions such as sale, taxation, and inheritance are frequently different from those applied to personal property transactions.

Fixtures An item of personal property may, however, be attached to or used in conjunction with real property in such a way that it ceases being personal property and instead becomes part of the real property. This type of property is called a **fixture.**

Fixtures belong to the owner of the real property. One who provides or attaches fixtures to real property without a request to that effect from the owner of the real property is normally not entitled to compensation from the owner. A conveyance (transfer of ownership) of real property also transfers the fixtures associated with that property, even if the fixtures are not specifically mentioned.

People commonly install items of personal property on the real property they own or rent. Disputes may arise regarding rights to such property. Suppose that Jacobsen buys an elaborate ceiling fan and installs it in his home. When he sells the house to Orr, may Jacobsen remove

the ceiling fan, or is it part of the home Orr has bought? Suppose that Luther, a commercial tenant, installs showcases and tracklights in the store she leases from Nelson. May Luther remove the showcases and the lights when her lease expires, or do the items now belong to Nelson? If the parties' contracts are silent on these matters, courts will resolve the cases by applying the law of fixtures. As later discussion will reveal, Jacobsen probably cannot remove the ceiling fan because it is likely to be considered part of the real property purchased by Orr. Luther, on the other hand, may be entitled to remove the showcases and the lights under the special rules governing trade fixtures.

 LO2 Provide several examples of property that would be considered to be a fixture and explain the significance of classifying an item of property as a fixture.

Factors Indicating Whether an Item Is a Fixture There is no mechanical formula for determining whether an item has become a fixture. Courts tend to consider these factors:

1. *Attachment.* One factor helping to indicate whether an item is a fixture is the degree to which the item is attached or annexed to real property. If firmly attached to real property so that it cannot be removed without damaging the property, the item is likely to be considered a fixture. An item of personal property that may be removed with little or no injury to the property is less likely to be considered a fixture.

Actual physical attachment to real property is not necessary, however. A close physical connection between an item of personal property and certain real property may enable a court to conclude that the item is constructively annexed. For example, heavy machinery or remote control devices for automatic garage doors may be considered fixtures even though they are not physically attached to real property.

2. *Adaptation.* Another factor to be considered is adaptation—the degree to which the item's use is necessary or beneficial to the use of the real property. Adaptation is a particularly relevant factor when the item is not physically attached to the real property or is only slightly attached. When an item would be of little value except for use with certain real property, the item is likely to be considered a fixture even if it is unattached or could easily be removed. For example, keys and custom-sized window screens and storm windows have been held to be fixtures.

[1]Ownership of air above one's property is not an unlimited interest, however. Courts have held that the flight of aircraft above property does not violate the property owner's rights, so long as it does not unduly interfere with the owner's enjoyment of her land.

3. *Intent.* The third factor to be considered is the intent of the person who installed the item. Intent is judged not by what that person subjectively intended, but by what the circumstances indicate he intended. To a great extent, intent is indicated by the annexation and adaptation factors. An owner of real property who improves it by attaching items of personal property presumably intended those items to become part of the real estate. If the owner does not want an attached item to be considered a fixture,

he must specifically reserve the right to keep the item. For instance, if a seller of a house wants to keep an antique chandelier that has been installed in the house, she should either replace the chandelier before the house is shown to prospective purchasers or specify in the contract of sale that the chandelier will be excluded from the sale.

The following *Chevron* case illustrates the characteristics of a fixture.

Chevron U.S.A., Inc. v. Sheikhpour
2011 U.S. Dist. LEXIS 19566 (U.S. Dist. Ct. C.D. Cal. 2011)

In July 2007, Chevron sued to enforce a contract that it had made with Sheikhpour that entitled Chevron to buy and remodel Sheikhpour's Manhattan Beach gas station. The parties entered into a Settlement Agreement that required Sheikhpour to complete certain reconstruction obligations by October 31, 2009. When he failed to complete the reconstruction by the deadline, Chevron obtained an order enforcing the Settlement Agreement and ordering Sheikhpour to convey the station to Chevron. Chevron's efforts to possess the property were met with additional objections from Sheikhpour, however.

In December 2010, Sheikhpour requested continuing access to the property for fourteen days to remove his "personal property," including "equipment, supplies, materials, security fence, etc." The parties then executed a "Release and Indemnification Agreement," which authorized Sheikhpour to access the property during a two-week period for the sole purpose of removing his personal property. Several days after the agreement was formed, Sheikhpour informed Chevron that he intended to dig up and remove the fuel storage tanks. The tanks, which are valued at about $120,000, sit in a "tank pit area," and are covered with gravel.

Both parties filed motions with the court seeking an order resolving the question whether Sheikhpour was entitled to remove the fuel storage tanks.

Gutierrez, U.S. District Judge

The parties' Release and Indemnification Agreement, which authorized removal of Sheikhpour's "personal property," is the only viable source of Sheikhpour's putative right to remove the tanks. Thus, the inquiry before the Court is whether the tanks qualify as Sheikhpour's "personal property" within the meaning of the Agreement. Nothing in the express contractual language, the prior dealing between the parties, or the ordinary understanding of the term "personal property" gives rise to the conclusion that the parties understood "personal property" under the Agreement to include the underground fuel storage tanks in its definitional scope.

The Court's conclusion that the tanks do not constitute Sheikhpour's "personal property" is also consonant with California law regarding fixtures. In determining whether an item is a fixture, California courts consider three factors: (1) physical annexation; (2) adaptations to use with the property; and (3) intention to annex to realty. As to the first factor, California courts consider heavy machinery physically annexed to property even where the machinery is only attached by gravity. Thus, here, the first factor

is satisfied because the fuel tanks are heavy machinery that can be annexed to property, even if attached only by gravity. In fact, the tanks at issue here were not only annexed to the property by gravity due to their large size—they were actually buried under gravel.

Second, the Court concludes that the second factor, adaptation to use of the property, is satisfied. Here, the fuel tanks were specifically adapted to the use of the gas station because they were inserted into the ground and covered with gravel. The third element of intent, regarded as a crucial and overwhelming factor in the analysis, is likewise met. Given that the fuel storage tanks were highly necessary to the gas station and could serve almost no other use than gasoline storage, the Court finds it reasonable to infer that Defendant intended the tanks to become annexed to the property.

Therefore, as all three elements are satisfied, the Court concludes that the fuel tanks at issue are considered fixtures, not personal property, under California law.

Order in favor of Chevron.

Fixtures

Concept	A *fixture* is an item of personal property attached to or used in conjunction with real property in such a way that it is treated as being part of the real property.
Significance	A transfer of the real property will also convey the fixtures on that property.
Factors Considered in Determining Whether Property Is a Fixture	1. Attachment: Is the item physically attached or closely connected to the real property? 2. Adaptation: How necessary or beneficial is the item to the use of the real property? 3. Intent: Did the person who installed the item manifest intent for the property to become part of the real property?
Express Agreement	Express agreements clearly stating intent about whether property is a fixture are generally enforceable.
Trade Fixtures (Tenants' Fixtures)	Definition of *trade fixture:* personal property attached to leased real property by a tenant for the purpose of carrying on his trade or business. Trade fixtures can be removed and retained by the tenant at the termination of the lease except when any of the following applies: 1. Removal would cause substantial damage to the landlord's real property. 2. The tenant fails to remove the fixtures by the end of the lease (or within a reasonable time, if the lease is for an indefinite period of time). 3. An express agreement between the landlord and tenant provides otherwise.

Express Agreement If the parties to an express agreement have clearly stated their intent about whether a particular item is to be considered a fixture, a court will generally enforce that agreement. For example, the buyer and seller of a house might agree to permit the seller to remove a fence or shrubbery that would otherwise be considered a fixture.

Trade Fixtures An exception to the usual fixture rules is recognized when a tenant attaches personal property to leased premises for the purpose of carrying on her trade or business. Such fixtures, called **trade fixtures,** remain the tenant's personal property and may normally be removed at the termination of the lease. This trade fixtures exception encourages commerce and industry. It recognizes that the commercial tenant who affixed the item of personal property did not intend a permanent improvement of the leased premises.

The tenant's right to remove trade fixtures is subject to two limitations. First, the tenant cannot remove the fixtures if doing so would cause substantial damage to the landlord's realty. Second, the tenant must remove the fixtures by the end of the lease if the lease is for a definite period. If the lease is for an indefinite period, the tenant usually has a reasonable time after the expiration of the lease to

remove the fixtures. Trade fixtures not removed within the appropriate time become the landlord's property.

Leases may contain terms expressly addressing the parties' rights in any fixtures. A lease might give the tenant the right to attach items or make other improvements, and to remove them later. The reverse may also be true. The lease could state that any improvements made or fixtures attached will become the landlord's property at the termination of the lease. Courts generally enforce parties' agreements on fixture ownership.

Security Interests in Fixtures Special rules apply to personal property subject to a lien or security interest at the time it is attached to real property. Assume, for example, that a person buys a dishwasher on a time-payment plan from an appliance store and has it installed in his kitchen. To protect itself, the appliance store takes a security interest in the dishwasher and perfects that interest by filing a financing statement in the appropriate real estate records office within the period of time specified by the Uniform Commercial Code. The appliance store then is able to remove the dishwasher if the buyer defaults in his payments. The store could be liable, however, to third parties such as prior real estate mortgagees for any damage removal of the dishwasher caused to the real estate. The rules governing security interests in personal property that will become fixtures are explained more fully in Chapter 29.

LO3 Explain and distinguish among the various forms of ownership of real property.

Rights and Interests in Real Property

When we think of real property ownership, we normally envision one person owning all of the rights in a particular piece of land. Real property, however, involves a bundle of rights subject to ownership—sometimes by different people. This discussion examines the most common forms of present *possessory interests* (rights to exclusive possession of real property): *fee simple absolute* and *life estate*. It also explores the ways in which two or more persons may share ownership of a possessory interest. Finally, it discusses the interests and rights one may have in another person's real property, such as the right to use the property or restrict the way the owner uses it.

Estates in Land   The term **estate** is used to describe the nature of a person's ownership interest in real property. Estates in land are classified as either freehold estates or nonfreehold estates. Nonfreehold (or leasehold) estates are those held by persons who lease real property. They will be discussed in the next chapter, which deals with landlord–tenant law. Freehold estates are ownership interests of uncertain duration. The most common types of freehold estates are fee simple absolute and life estates.

Fee Simple Absolute   The **fee simple absolute** is what we normally think of as "full ownership" of land. One who owns real property in fee simple absolute has the right to possess and use the property for an unlimited period of time, subject only to governmental regulations or private restrictions. She also has the unconditional power to dispose of the property during her lifetime or upon her death. A person who owns land in fee simple absolute may grant many rights to others without giving up ownership. For example, she may grant a mortgage on the property to a party who has loaned her money, lease the property to a tenant, or grant rights such as those to be discussed later in this section.

Life Estate   The property interest known as a **life estate** gives a person the right to possess and use property for a time measured by his or another person's lifetime. For example, if Haney has a life estate (measured by his life) in a tract of land known as Greenacre, he has the right to use Greenacre for the remainder of his life. At Haney's death, the property will revert to the person who conveyed the estate to him or will pass to some other designated person. Although a life tenant has the right to use the property, he is obligated not to commit acts that would result in permanent injury to the property.

Co-ownership of Real Property   Co-ownership of real property exists when two or more persons share the same ownership interest in certain property. The co-owners do not have separate rights to any portion of the real property; each has a share in the whole property. Seven types of co-ownership are recognized in the United States.

Tenancy in Common   Persons who own property under a **tenancy in common** have undivided interests in the property and equal rights to possess it. When property is transferred to two or more persons without specification of their co-ownership form, it is presumed that they acquire the property as tenants in common. The respective ownership interests of tenants in common may be, but need not be, equal. One tenant, for example, could have a two-thirds ownership interest in the property, with the other tenant having a one-third interest.

Each tenant in common has the right to possess and use the property. Individual tenants, however, cannot exclude the other tenants in common from also possessing and using the property. If the property is rented or otherwise produces income, each tenant is entitled to share in the income in proportion to her ownership share. Similarly, each tenant must pay her proportionate share of property taxes and necessary repair costs. If a tenant in sole possession of the property receives no rents or profits from the property, she is not required to pay rent to her cotenant unless her possession is adverse to or inconsistent with her cotenant's property interests.

A tenant in common may dispose of his interest in the property during life and at death. Similarly, his interest is subject to his creditors' claims. When a tenant dies, his interest passes to his heirs or, if he has made a will, to the person or persons specified in the will. Suppose Peterson and Sievers own Blackacre as tenants in common. Sievers dies, having executed a valid will in which he leaves his Blackacre interest to Johanns. In this situation, Peterson and Johanns become tenants in common.

Tenants in common may sever the cotenancy by agreeing to divide the property or, if they are unable to agree, by petitioning a court for *partition*. The court will physically divide the property if that is feasible, so that each tenant receives her proportionate share. If physical division is not feasible, the court will order that the property be sold and that the proceeds be appropriately divided.

Joint Tenancy A **joint tenancy** is created when equal interests in real property are conveyed to two or more persons by means of a document clearly specifying that they are to own the property as joint tenants. The rights of use, possession, contribution, and partition are the same for a joint tenancy as for a tenancy in common. The joint tenancy's distinguishing feature is that it gives the owners the **right of survivorship,** which means that upon the death of a joint tenant, the deceased tenant's interest automatically passes to the surviving joint tenant(s). The right of survivorship makes it easy for a person to transfer property at death without the need for a will. For example, Devaney and Osborne purchase Redacre and take title as joint tenants. At Devaney's death, his Redacre interest will pass to Osborne even if Devaney did not have a will setting forth such an intent. Moreover, even if Devaney had a will that purported to leave his Redacre interest to someone other than Osborne, the will's Redacre provision would be ineffective.

When the document of conveyance contains ambiguous language, a court may be faced with determining whether persons acquired ownership of real property as joint tenants or, instead, as tenants in common.

A joint tenant may mortgage, sell, or give away her interest in the property during her lifetime. Her interest in the property is subject to her creditors' claims. When a joint tenant transfers her interest, the joint tenancy is severed and a tenancy in common is created as to the share affected by the transaction. When a joint tenant sells her interest to a third person, the purchaser becomes a tenant in common with the remaining joint tenant(s).

Tenancy by the Entirety Approximately half of the states permit married couples to own real property under a **tenancy by the entirety.** This tenancy is essentially a joint tenancy with the added requirement that the owners be married. As does the joint tenancy, the tenancy by the entirety features the right of survivorship. Neither spouse can transfer the property by will if the other is still living. Upon the death of the husband or wife, the property passes automatically to the surviving spouse.[2] You will see an application of this principle in the following *Tkachik* case, as well as an analysis of the surviving spouse's obligation to contribute to the expenses of property owned by the entireties.

---

[2]In states that do not recognize the tenancy by the entirety, married couples often own real property in joint tenancy, but they are not required to elect that co-ownership form.

Tkachik v. Mandeville	790 N.W.2d 260 (Sup. Ct. Mich. 2010)

Janet and Frank Mandeville were married in 1975 and remained so until Janet died in 2002, after a battle with breast cancer. The Mandevilles acquired two properties during their marriage, their home in Macomb County and a parcel of property in Ogamaw County. They owned both properties as tenants by the entirety. Accordingly, by the right of survivorship inherent in a tenancy by the entirety, both properties passed to Frank upon Janet's death, and he owns them in fee simple absolute.

In the last decade of their marriage Frank was often out of the country for extended periods. Specifically, he was absent for the 18 months preceding Janet's death. During this period, he did not try to call Janet or otherwise communicate with her, even though he knew she was seriously ill. He did not attend her funeral. In Frank's absence, Janet maintained the properties and was responsible for paying the taxes, insurance, and mortgage. She was cared for by her sister, Susan Tkachik.

In the months before she died, Janet executed a trust and will that stated the intent to disinherit her husband and leave everything to her mother. She also changed her retirement benefits so that they would not pass to Frank and she tried to defeat the right of survivorship in the real estate by transferring her interest in them by a quitclaim deed.

In November 2003, Tkachik filed suit on behalf of the estate to effectuate Janet's intent to disinherit Frank. She claimed the Mandevilles should be considered tenants in common with regard to their real property and Frank should not obtain full ownership of the properties. Tkachik later amended her petition to seek contribution from Frank for the expenses Janet incurred in maintaining the property before her death. The probate court denied this request and Tkachik appealed. The Michigan Court of Appeals affirmed, and Tkachik appealed to the Supreme Court of Michigan.

Markman, Justice

A tenancy by the entirety is a type of concurrent ownership in real property that is unique to married persons. A defining incident of this tenancy is that one tenant by the entirety has no interest separable from that of the other. Thus, when title to real estate is vested in a husband and wife by the entirety, separate [transfer] by one spouse only is barred. Furthermore, MCL 557.71 states, "a husband and wife shall be equally entitled to the rents, products, income, or profits, and to the control and management of real or personal property held by them as tenants by the entirety. In addition, both spouses have a right of survivorship, meaning that, in the event that one spouse dies, the remaining spouse automatically owns the entire property. Thus, entireties properties are not part of a decedent spouse's estate.

Contribution is an equitable remedy based on principles of natural justice. The general rule of contribution is that one who is compelled to bear more than his share of [a] common burden or obligation, upon which several persons are equally liable or which they are bound to discharge, is entitled to contribution against the others to obtain from their payment of their respective shares. This Court recognized the right of equitable contribution for tenants in common. Tkachik predicates her claim for contribution on a theory of unjust enrichment. Unjust enrichment is defined as the unjust retention of money or benefits which in justice and equity belong to another. No one is unjustly enriched unless the retention of the benefit would be unjust.

Frank argues, and the Court of Appeals agree[d], that he has not been unjustly enriched because he "has only received that which was given to him by operation of law, without any obligation." On the facts of this case, we conclude that equity, and the principles of natural justice embodied therein, call on Frank Mandeville to contribute his share of the property maintenance costs incurred by his wife, who bore these obligations alone in the 18 months before her death. In light of these facts, the conclusion that Frank received the properties "without any obligation" is an oversimplification that is at odds with the realities of this case. Significantly, this conclusion does not account for what *would* have happened to the properties had Janet not made mortgage, tax, and insurance payments. Simply put, but for Janet's payments, *there would be no property* to pass by operation of law.

What Tkachik is seeking as the personal representative of Janet's estate is contribution for the past monetary expenses that Janet incurred in maintaining the marital properties while Frank was willfully absent from Janet and the properties. Thus, the fact that the properties undisputedly passed to Frank automatically by operation of law does not defeat a finding that Frank was unjustly enriched or bar a claim for contribution. Permitting a contribution claim in these circumstances will not interfere with well-settled principles governing property held in a tenancy by the entirety and specifically will not affect the unencumbered right of survivorship. Janet and Frank Mandeville held their properties as tenants by the entirety; upon Janet's death, such properties passed to Frank solely and absolutely, at which point he owned them in fee simple absolute. The law of tenancy by the entirety, and specifically the right of survivorship, has already been given full effect in this case, a result that is unaltered when Frank is required to pay contribution to plaintiff for past monetary expenses. On these facts, we conclude that the firmly established doctrine of contribution can be appropriately applied between tenants by the entirety and, therefore, we will permit Tkachik's claim for contribution.

Reversed and remanded in favor of Tkachik.

A tenancy by the entirety cannot be severed by the act of only one of the parties. Neither spouse can transfer the property unless the other also signs the deed. Thus, a creditor of one tenant cannot claim an interest in that person's share of property held in tenancy by the entirety. Divorce, however, severs a tenancy by the entirety and transforms it into a tenancy in common. Figure 1 compares the features of tenancy in common, joint tenancy, and tenancy by the entirety.

Community Property A number of western and southern states recognize the community property system of co-ownership of property by married couples. This type of co-ownership assumes that marriage is a partnership in which each spouse contributes to the family's property base. Property acquired during the marriage through a spouse's industry or efforts is classified as *community* property. Each spouse has an equal interest in such property regardless of who produced or earned the property. Because each spouse has an equal share in community property, neither can convey community property without the other's joining in the transaction. Various community property states permit the parties to dispose of their interests in community property at death. The details of each state's community property system vary, depending on the specific provisions of that state's statutes.

Not all property owned by a married person is community property, however. Property a spouse owned before marriage or acquired during marriage by gift or

Figure 1 *Tenancy in Common, Joint Tenancy, and Tenancy by the Entirety*			
	Tenancy in Common	**Joint Tenancy**	**Tenancy by the Entirety**
Equal Possession and Use?	Yes	Yes	Yes
Share Income?	Yes	Yes	Presumably
Contribution Requirement?	Generally	Generally	Generally
Free Conveyance of Interest?	Yes; transferee becomes tenant in common	Yes, but joint tenancy is severed on conveyance and reverts to tenancy in common	Both must agree; divorce severs tenancy
Effect of Death?	Interest transferable at death by will or inheritance	Right of survivorship; surviving joint tenant takes decedent's share	Right of survivorship; surviving spouse takes decedent's share

inheritance is *separate* property. Neither spouse owns a legal interest in the other's separate property. Property exchanged for separate property also remains separately owned.

Tenancy in Partnership When a partnership takes title to property in the partnership's name, the co-ownership form is called **tenancy in partnership.** This form of co-ownership is discussed in Chapter 37.

Condominium Ownership Under condominium ownership, a purchaser takes title to her individual unit and becomes a tenant in common with other unit owners in shared facilities such as hallways, elevators, swimming pools, and parking areas. The condominium owner pays property taxes on her individual unit and makes a monthly payment for the maintenance of the common areas. She may generally mortgage or sell her unit without the other unit owners' approval. For federal income tax purposes, the condominium owner is treated as if she owned a single-family home, and is thus allowed to deduct her property taxes and mortgage interest expenses.

Cooperative Ownership In a cooperative, a building is owned by a corporation or group of persons. One who wants to buy an apartment in the building purchases stock in the corporation and holds his apartment under a long-term, renewable lease called a *proprietary lease.* Frequently, the cooperative owner must obtain the other owners' approval to sell or sublease his unit.

 LO4 Explain the legal effects of easements and restrictive covenants as well as the duties of property owners toward third persons.

Interests in Real Property Owned by Others

In various situations, a person may hold a legally protected interest in someone else's real property. Such interests, to be discussed below, are not possessory because they do not give their holder the right to complete dominion over the land. Rather, they give him the right to use another person's property or to limit the way in which the owner uses the property.

Easements An **easement** is the right to make certain uses of another person's property (*affirmative easement*) or the right to prevent another person from making certain uses of his own property (*negative easement*). The right to run a sewer line across someone else's property would be an affirmative easement. Suppose an easement prevents Rogers from erecting, on his land, a structure that would block his neighbor McFeely's solar collector. Such an easement would be negative in nature.

If an easement qualifies as an easement appurtenant, it will pass with the land. This means that if the owner of the land benefited by an easement appurtenant sells or otherwise conveys the property, the new owner also acquires the right contemplated by the easement. An easement appurtenant is primarily designed to benefit a certain tract of land, rather than merely giving an individual a personal right. For example, Agnew and Nixon are next-door neighbors. They share a common driveway that runs along the borderline of their respective properties. Each has an easement in the portion of the driveway that lies on the other's property. If Agnew sells his property to Ford, Ford also obtains the easement in the driveway portion on Nixon's land. Nixon, of course, still has an easement in the driveway portion on Ford's land.

Creation of Easements Easements may be acquired in the following ways:

1. *By grant.* When an owner of property expressly provides an easement to another while retaining ownership of the property, he is said to grant an easement. For example, Monroe may sell or give Madison, who owns adjoining property, the right to go across Monroe's land to reach an alley behind that land.

2. *By reservation.* When one transfers ownership of her land but retains the right to use it for some specified purpose, she is said to reserve an easement in the land. For example, Smythe sells land to Jones but reserves the mineral rights to the property as well as an easement to enter the land to remove the minerals.

3. *By prescription.* An easement by prescription is created when one person uses another's land openly, continuously, and in a manner adverse to the owner's rights for a period of time specified by state statute. The necessary period of time varies from state to state. In such a situation, the property owner presumably is on notice that someone else is acting as if she possesses rights to use the property. If the property owner does not take action during the statutory period to stop the other person from making use of his property, he may lose his right to stop that use. Suppose, for instance, that State X allows easements by prescription to be obtained through 15 years of prescriptive use. Tara, who lives in State X, uses the driveway of her next-door neighbor, Kyle. Tara does this openly, on a daily basis, and without Kyle's permission. If this use by Tara continues for the 15-year period established by statute and Kyle takes no action to stop Tara within that time span, Tara will obtain an easement by prescription. In that event, Tara will have the right to use the driveway not only while Kyle owns the property but also when Kyle sells the property to another party. Easements by prescription resemble *adverse possession,* a concept discussed later in this chapter.

4. *By implication.* Sometimes, easements are implied by the nature of the transaction rather than created by express agreement of the parties. Such easements, called easements by implication, take either of two forms: easements by prior use and easements by necessity.

An *easement by prior use* may be created when land is subdivided and a path, road, or other apparent and beneficial use exists as of the time that a portion of the land is conveyed to another person. In this situation, the new owner of the conveyed portion of the land has an easement to continue using the path, road, or other prior use running across the nonconveyed portion of the land. Assume, for example, that a private road runs through Greenacre from north to south, linking the house located on Greenacre's northern portion to the public highway that lies south of Greenacre. Douglas, the owner of Greenacre, sells the northern portion to Kimball. On these facts, Kimball has an easement by implication to continue using the private road even where it runs across the portion of Greenacre retained by Douglas. To prevent such an easement from arising, Douglas and Kimball would need to have specified in their contract of sale that the easement would not exist.

An *easement by necessity* is created when real property once held in common ownership is subdivided in such a fashion that the only reasonable way a new owner can gain access to her land is through passage over another's land that was once part of the same tract. Such an easement is based on the necessity of obtaining access to property. Assume, for instance, that Tinker, the owner of Blackacre, sells Blackacre's northern 25 acres to Evers and its southern 25 acres to Chance. In order to have any reasonable access to her property, Chance must use a public road that runs alongside and just beyond the northern border of the land now owned by Evers; Chance must then go across Evers's property to reach hers. On these facts, Chance is entitled to an easement by necessity to cross Evers's land in order to go to and from her property.

Easements and the Statute of Frauds As interests in land, easements are potentially within the coverage of the statute of frauds. To be enforceable, an express agreement granting or reserving an easement must be evidenced by a suitable writing signed by the party to be charged.[3] An express grant of an easement normally must be executed with the same formalities observed in executing the grant of a fee simple interest. However, easements not granted expressly (such as easements by prior use, necessity, or prescription) are enforceable despite the lack of a writing.

Profits A **profit** is a right to enter another person's land and remove some product or part of the land. Timber, gravel, minerals, and oil are among the products and parts frequently made the subject of profits. Generally governed by the same rules applicable to easements, profits are sometimes called *easements with a profit.*

---

[3]Chapter 16 discusses the statute of frauds and compliance with the writing requirement it imposes when it is applicable.

Licenses

A **license** is a temporary right to enter another's land for a specific purpose. Ordinarily, licenses are more informal than easements. Licenses may be created orally or in any other manner indicating the landowner's permission for the licensee to enter the property. Because licenses are considered to be personal rights, they are not true interests in land. The licensor normally may revoke a license at his will. Exceptions to this general rule of revocability arise when the license is coupled with an interest (such as the licensee's ownership of personal property located on the licensor's land) or when the licensee has paid money or provided something else of value either for the license or in reliance on its existence. For example, Branch pays Leif $900 for certain trees on Leif's land. Branch is to dig up the trees and haul them to her own property for transplanting. Branch has an irrevocable license to enter Leif's land to dig up and haul away the trees.

Restrictive Covenants

Within certain limitations, real estate owners may create enforceable agreements that restrict the use of real property. These private agreements are called **restrictive covenants.** For example, Grant owns two adjacent lots. She sells one to Lee subject to the parties' agreement that Lee will not operate any liquor-selling business on the property. This use restriction appears in the deed Grant furnishes Lee. As another illustration, a subdivision developer sells lots in the subdivision and places a provision in each lot's deed regarding the minimum size of house to be built on the property.

The validity and enforceability of such private restrictions on the use of real property depend on the purpose, nature, and scope of the restrictions. A restraint that violates a statute or other expression of public policy will not be enforced. For example, the federal Fair Housing Act (discussed later in this chapter) would make unlawful an attempt by a seller or lessor of residential property to refuse to sell or rent to certain persons because of an existing restrictive covenant that purports to disqualify those prospective buyers or renters on the basis of their race, color, religion, sex, handicap, familial status, or national origin.

Public policy generally favors the unlimited use and transfer of land. A restrictive covenant therefore is unenforceable if it effectively prevents the sale or transfer of the property. Similarly, ambiguous language in a restrictive covenant is construed in favor of the less restrictive interpretation. A restraint is enforceable, however, if it is clearly expressed and neither unduly restrictive of the use and transfer of the property nor otherwise violative of public policy. Restrictions usually held enforceable include those relating to minimum lot size, building design and size, and maintenance of an area as a residential community.

An important and frequently arising question is whether subsequent owners of property are bound by a restrictive covenant even though they were not parties to the original agreement that established the covenant. Under certain circumstances, restrictive covenants are said to "run with the land" and thus bind subsequent owners of the restricted property. For a covenant to run with the land, it must have been *binding* on the original parties to it, and those parties must have *intended that the covenant bind their successors.* The covenant must also *"touch and concern"* the restricted land. This means that the covenant must involve the use, value, or character of the land, rather than being merely a personal obligation of one of the original parties. The *Gardner* case, which follows, involves the analysis of whether a restrictive covenant runs with the land. In addition, a covenant will not bind a subsequent purchaser unless she had notice of the covenant's existence when she took her interest. This notice would commonly be provided by the recording of the deed (a subject discussed later in this chapter) or other document containing the covenant.

Restrictive covenants may be enforced by the parties to them, by persons meant to benefit from them, and—if the covenants run with the land—by successors of the original parties to them. If restrictive covenants amounting to a general building scheme are contained in a subdivision plat (recorded description of a subdivision), property owners in the subdivision may be able to enforce them against noncomplying property owners.

Gardner v. Jefferys	2005 Vt. LEXIS 86 (Vt. Sup. Ct. 2005)

In 1957, William Jefferys Jr. and his wife, Ena, the parents of William Jefferys III, purchased approximately 200 acres of farm land in Fayston, Vermont, known as the Strong Farm. Beginning in 1966, the elderly Jefferys began selling off parcels of the farm. In 1969, Sheldon and Carin Gardner purchased a 10-acre parcel of undeveloped land from the Jefferys. The deed contains a restrictive covenant providing that a specified part of the premises "shall forever be and remain open and free of all buildings and structures, except the right to construct on said open land a private swimming pool, and/or tennis court, and, the usual fences and structures appurtenant thereto and such other buildings and structures as meet the approval, in writing of the Grantors herein, their heirs and assigns." The provision further states that rights secured therein are "to be enjoyed by the Grantors, their heirs and assigns." In 1975, the Jefferys conveyed a five-acre parcel of land to Karin Souminen, who, in turn, sold the parcel to George and Janice Soules in 1987. The Soules built a house on the land and lived there. Their property is located above the Gardners' land. In 1979, the elderly Jefferys conveyed the remainder of their Fayston property to their son, William Jefferys III, and his wife, Susan.

In the late summer and early fall of 1999, the Gardners wrote to William and Susan Jefferys twice requesting approval to build a two-story structure within the area restricted by the covenant. The Jefferys gave the Soules a copy of the request. In June 2000, the Soules wrote the Gardners a letter stating that they were interested parties to the restrictive covenant. In September 2000, the Gardners filed a declaratory judgment action asking the court to determine the effect of the restrictive covenant in their deed. The Soules filed a counterclaim. In May 2001, the Gardners began building a shed in the restricted area. Shortly thereafter, the superior court granted the Soules' request for a preliminary injunction stopping the construction. In the fall of 2001, the Gardners began planting white pines in the restricted area directly in the Soules' view.

In July 2003, the superior court ruled that the benefit of the restrictive covenant ran with the land and was enforceable by both the Soules and the Jefferys, and that the Gardners had violated the covenant by beginning construction of the proposed shed and by planting trees in the restricted area. Accordingly, the court enjoined the continued existence of the shed and the trees. Further, the court prohibited the Gardners from allowing plants or crops in the restricted area to exceed six feet in height. The Gardners appealed.

Per Curiam

On appeal, Sheldon Gardner first contends that the restrictive covenant does not run with the land to the benefit of the Soules because the parties intended the covenant to bind only the grantors, their heirs and assigns, and neither the Soules nor the Jefferys are heirs or assigns of the grantors. We do not find this argument persuasive. Four requirements must be met for a restrictive covenant to "run with the land" so that successor property owners may enforce its burdens and benefits: (1) the covenant must be in writing; (2) the parties to the covenant must have intended that the covenant run with the land; (3) the covenant must "touch and concern" the land; and (4) privity of estate must exist between the parties.

Gardner argues only that the second requirement is not met in this case. Intent that a restrictive covenant is to run with the land may be either express or implied, and may be shown by extraneous circumstances. In some instances, a covenant is so intimately connected with the land as to require the conclusion that the necessary intention for the running of the benefit is present absent language clearly negating that intent. For example, we have held that a covenant prohibiting placing a particular type of structure on a property is such a restriction. Indeed, unless the terms of a restrictive covenant provide otherwise, when a property benefited by a restrictive covenant is divided into separately owned parcels, "each separately owned parcel is entitled to enforce [the] . . . covenant benefiting the property." *Restatement (Third) of the Law of Property* § 5.7(2) (2000).

Here, Gardner argues that the restrictive covenant in his deed does not run with the land because it expressly benefits only the grantors and their heirs and assigns, thereby implying an intent not to allow the covenant to be enforced by successors to the land who are not heirs or assigns. Gardner further states that neither the Soules' deed nor the Jefferys' deed includes an assignment from the elderly Jefferys, and that the Jefferys are not heirs because Ena Jefferys is still alive, and they did not obtain the land through inheritance. According to Gardner, they would never have purchased the property with the restrictive covenant if they thought that an indefinite number of successors could dictate how they used their property.

We conclude that the record in this case overwhelmingly demonstrates that the parties intended the restrictive covenant to run with the land. The testimony of several witnesses, including Ena Jefferys, unequivocally demonstrated that the covenant was intended to keep the restricted area, which had always been an open meadow, "forever" open and free of any obstructions that would diminish the view from the grantors' remaining lands located above the meadow. Moreover, the record, including evidence of negotiations surrounding the covenant and of the Gardners' subsequent conduct, demonstrates that the Gardners were aware of this intent. Notwithstanding Gardner's argument to the contrary, use of the term "assigns" rather than "successors" does not suggest that the parties intended to preclude subsequent owners of the dominant estate from enforcing the covenant. To the contrary, it is well settled that where a restrictive covenant contains words of succession, i.e., heirs and assigns, a presumption is created that the parties intended the restrictive covenant to run with the land.

Next, Gardner argues that the superior court erred by construing the restrictive covenant to prohibit him from planting trees in the restricted area, and that, by doing so, the court imposed a burden on his property greater than that imposed by the restrictive covenant. We disagree. We conclude that both the language of the covenant and evidence of the circumstances surrounding the making of the covenant support the court's determination. The word "open" refers to the land that had historically been maintained as an open field. The question, then, is what the parties meant by "open." The record demonstrates that most of the restricted area had been mowed or hayed for several decades or more when the restrictive covenant was signed. Ena Jefferys, one of the original grantors, testified that she always assumed that the phrase "open and free of all buildings and structures" meant that nothing would interfere with the view, which was "everything

up there" and the reason why people bought property there. Indeed, Gardner himself acknowledged that he bought his property, at least in part, for the view, and that the word "open" in the covenant did not necessarily refer to buildings and structures. In short, there was overwhelming evidence that the intent underlying the restrictive covenant at issue here was to maintain the restricted area as an open meadow, thereby allowing unobstructed views to the south for the benefit of adjoining neighbors.

Affirmed in favor of the Jefferys and Soules.

Termination of Restrictive Covenants Restrictive covenants may be terminated in a variety of ways, including voluntary relinquishment or *waiver*. They may also be terminated *by their own terms* (such as when the covenant specifies that it is to exist for a certain length of time) or *by dramatically changed circumstances*. If Oldcodger's property is subject, for instance, to a restrictive covenant allowing only residential use, the fact that all of the surrounding property has come to be used for industrial purposes may operate to terminate the covenant. When a restrictive covenant has been terminated or held invalid, the deed containing the restriction remains a valid instrument of transfer but is treated as if the restriction had been removed from the document.

  Distinguish the various ways in which ownership of real property is transferred and how title to property can be assured.

Acquisition of Real Property

Title to real property may be obtained in various ways, including purchase, gift, will or inheritance, tax sale, and adverse possession. Original title to land in the United States was acquired either from the federal government or from a country that held the land prior to its acquisition by the United States. The land in the 13 original colonies had been granted by the king of England either to the colonies or to certain individuals. The states ceded the land in the Northwest Territory to the federal government, which in turn issued grants or patents of land. Original ownership of much of the land in Florida and the Southwest came by grants from Spain's rulers.

Acquisition by Purchase Selling one's real property is a basic ownership right. Unreasonable restrictions on an owner's right to sell her property are considered

unenforceable because they violate public policy. Most owners of real property acquired title by purchasing the property. Each state sets the requirements for proper conveyances of real property located in that state. The various elements of selling and buying real property are discussed later in this chapter.

Acquisition by Gift Real property ownership may be acquired by gift. For a gift of real property to be valid, the donor must deliver a properly executed deed to the donee or to some third person who is to hold it for the donee. Neither the donee nor the third person needs to take actual possession of the property. Intent to make a gift is required. The gift's essential element is delivery of the deed. Suppose that Fields executes a deed to the family farm and leaves it in his safe-deposit box for delivery to his daughter (the intended donee) when he dies. The attempted gift will not be valid, because Fields did not deliver the gift during his lifetime.

Acquisition by Will or Inheritance The owner of real property generally has the right to dispose of the property by will. The requirements for a valid will are discussed in Chapter 26. If the owner of real property dies without a valid will, the property passes to his heirs as determined under the laws of the state in which the property is located.

Acquisition by Tax Sale If taxes assessed on real property are not paid when due, they become a *lien* on the property. This lien has priority over other claims to the land. If the taxes remain unpaid, the government may sell the land at a tax sale. Although the purchaser at the tax sale acquires title to the property, a number of states have statutes giving the original owner a limited time (such as a year) within which to buy the property from the tax sale purchaser for the price paid by the purchaser, plus interest.

Acquisition by Adverse Possession

Each state has a statute of limitations that gives an owner of land a specific number of years within which to bring suit to regain possession of her land from someone who is trespassing on it. This period varies from state to state, generally ranging from 5 to 20 years. If someone wrongfully possesses land and acts as if he were the owner, the actual owner must take steps to have the possessor ejected from the land. If the owner fails to do this within the statutory period, she loses her right to eject the possessor.

Assume, for example, that Titus owns a vacant lot next to Holdeman's house. Holdeman frequently uses the vacant lot for a variety of activities and appears to be the property's only user. In addition, Holdeman regularly mows and otherwise maintains the vacant lot. He has also placed a fence around it. By continuing such actions and thus staying in possession of Titus's property for the statutory period (and by meeting each other requirement about to be discussed), Holdeman may position himself to acquire title to the land by **adverse possession.**

To acquire title by adverse possession, one must possess land in a manner that puts the true owner on notice of the owner's cause of action against the possessor. The adverse possessor's acts of possession must be (1) *open,* (2) *actual,* (3) *continuous,* (4) *exclusive,* and (5) *hostile* (or adverse) *to the owner's rights.* The hostility element is not a matter of subjective intent. Rather, it means that the adverse possessor's acts of possession must be inconsistent with the owner's rights. If a person is in possession of another's property under a lease, as a cotenant, or with the permission of the owner, his possession is not hostile. In some states, the possessor of land must also pay the property taxes in order to gain title by adverse possession.

It is not necessary that the same person occupy the land for the statutory period. The periods of possession of several adverse possessors may be "tacked" together when calculating the period of possession if each possessor claimed rights from another possessor. The possession must, however, be continuous for the requisite time.

The following *Schlichting* case applies these criteria for adverse possession.

Schlichting v. Cotter | 2007 Conn. Super. LEXIS 461 (Conn. Super. Ct. 2007)

Angela Schlichting and her husband Walter acquired title to a piece of real estate in 1979. They had a cordial, neighborly relationship with their adjoining property owners, Fethon and Dorothy Nitsos. There had been no survey of the boundaries of the two properties, but it was believed that a certain section of the woods between the two houses contained the boundary line. The Schlichtings took care of an area that they believed was theirs. In 1993, Walter conveyed his interest in the Schlichtings' property to Angela. In 2005, the Nitsos conveyed their property to the Cotters. A dispute arose between Angela and the Cotters about whether Angela was encroaching on the Cotters property. The Cotters cut down trees, removed part of a stone wall, dug up the lawn, cut up the driveway, erected a fence, and otherwise disturbed part of the property that Angela claimed as hers. Angela applied for a temporary injunction against the Cotters.

Moraghan, Judge Trial Referee

Essentially, the elements of adverse possession are rather simple and uncomplicated. They are that the owners shall be ousted from possession and kept out uninterruptedly for a period of fifteen years under a claim of right by an open, visible and exclusive possession of the claimant without license or consent of the owner. At this point there seems to be little question that the "mutual agreement" non-memorialized and not marked with any type of surveying device was the product of a mutual mistake. In order to comprehend the concept of adverse possession, it might be appropriate to discuss and, to a degree, analyze the hostility of the taking.

Powell on Real Property, Sec. 91.05 et seq. In order to establish adverse possession, the possession must be openly hostile. Hostile possession can be understood as possession that is opposed and antagonistic to all other claims, and that

conveys the clear message that the possessor intends to possess the land as his or her own. . . . It is not necessary that the possessor intend to take away from the true owner something which he knows belongs to another, or even that he be indifferent as to the facts of the legal title. It is the intent to possess, and not the intent to take irrespective of his right, which governs.

The word "hostile," as employed in the law of adverse possession, is a term of art; it does not imply animosity, ill will or bad faith. Nor is the claimant required to make express declarations of adverse intent during the possessory period. "Hostile" use has been defined as use that is "inconsistent with the right of the owner, without permission asked or given, [to] use such as would entitle the owner to a cause of action against the intruder."

The modern position of American courts is that possession of land under the mistaken belief of legal ownership usually satisfies the hostility requirements, as long as the possessor does not hold in subordination to another and has no conscious doubt as to his or her rights. A large number of adverse possession disputes involve a mistaken belief on the part of a landowner as to the true boundary line between adjoining properties.

An occupation of land by a defendant as his own under an "owner" plaintiff's eye to what is supposed to be the dividing line between him and the "owner" plaintiff and which for many years the "owner" plaintiff permitted without any question challenging such action which flows from the mutual assent of the parties is strong presumptive evidence of the true place of the line. The very act itself has to be an assertion of his own title and thus equivalent to a denial of the title of all others and it does not matter that he was mistaken and if he had been better informed he would not have entered upon the land.

The testimony at trial and as set forth in the Nitsos' deposition clearly shows the Schlichtings continuously used the disputed area as their own from 1979 to March of 2006 in many ways in an open and visible fashion. Open and visible possession is a use calculated to let others know that the land is owned and occupied by the claimant. The use must be notorious and unconcealed so as to give the owner or any other claimant knowledge and the full opportunity to assert his rights, if any.

With respect to the open and visible ouster of the defendants there seems to be no evidence that contradicts Mrs. Nitsos concerning the action between 1979 and 2006. Suffice it to say that the fifteen-year limitation is satisfied. Use by the plaintiff in an open and visible possession consisted of spraying, pruning and removal of trees; planting and maintenance of pachysandra, German ferns, berry bushes, rhododendron; removal of poison ivy from the trees and the removal of sumac from the foliage in the area; utilization of gypsy moth traps and spraying; and the dumping, blowing and raking of leaves; the mowing and fertilizing and maintenance of the lawn area; the planting, cultivating and maintenance of the garden; and the paving, plowing, sealing and use of the driveway from 1979 to 2006 to the exclusion of others was open and notorious and put the Nitsos on notice that the property area was being occupied by the Schlichtings. Generally speaking, exclusive possession can and more often than not will be established by acts which at the time considering the state of the land comport with ownership, dominion and control such acts as would ordinarily be exercised by an owner in appropriating land to his own use to the exclusion of others.

Testimony unrefuted shows the Schlichtings maintained that they exclusively used up to the middle of the wooded area, and Mrs. Nitsos also testified that the Schlichtlings used that area exclusively as their own. There is a pond behind these two adjoining lots which was certainly attractive to children in terms of skating at least. The Nitsos would call the Schlichtings each time that one of their children or children's guests wanted to go skating. Permission was never denied but permission was always sought and granted. The reason for that was that the area behind the Nitsos' property tended to be swampy and muddy and the area behind the Schlichtings' property was more solid, less difficult to walk in and generally a cleaner path to the pond. The attitude of the abutting neighbor who enjoyed a friendly neighborly relationship with the Schlichtings lends strength to the recognition of the fact that they recognized the plaintiffs as the owners of the property.

The court finds by clear and convincing evidence that the plaintiff has proven her claim for adverse possession and is entitled to the property which she claims. The defendants are ordered to remove their fence, their piles of stone and to replace the ground cover and flowering bushes and shrubs and wall that they have destroyed within sixty (60) days of the date of this decision.

Judgment for Schlichtling.

Transfer by Sale

Steps in a Sale   The major steps normally involved in the sale of real property are:

1. Contracting with a real estate broker to locate a buyer.
2. Negotiating and signing a contract of sale.
3. Arranging for the financing of the purchase and satisfying other requirements, such as having a survey conducted or acquiring title insurance.
4. Closing the sale, which involves payment of the purchase price and transfer of the deed, as well as other matters.
5. Recording the deed.

LOG ON

For a variety of articles about practical aspects of buying, selling, or owning real estate, see Nolo.com Real Estate Law Center at **www.nolo.com/legal-encyclopedia/buying-house/**.

Contracting with a Real Estate Broker
Although engaging a real estate broker is not a legal requirement for the sale of real property, it is common for one who wishes to sell his property to "list" the property with a broker. A listing contract empowers the broker to act as the seller's agent in procuring a ready, willing, and able buyer and in managing details of the property

transfer. A number of states' statutes of frauds require listing contracts to be evidenced by a writing and signed by the party to be charged.

Real estate brokers are regulated by state and federal law. They owe *fiduciary duties* (duties of trust and confidence) to their clients. Chapter 35 contains additional information regarding the duties imposed on such agents.

Types of Listing Contracts Listing contracts specify such matters as the listing period's duration, the terms on which the seller will sell, and the amount and terms of the broker's commission. There are different types of listing contracts.

1. *Open listing.* Under an open listing contract, the broker receives a *nonexclusive* right to sell the property. This means that the seller and third parties (for example, other brokers) also are entitled to find a buyer for the property. The broker operating under an open listing is entitled to a commission only if he was the first to find a ready, willing, and able buyer.

2. *Exclusive agency listing.* Under an exclusive agency listing, the broker earns a commission if he *or any other agent* finds a ready, willing, and able buyer during the period of time specified in the contract. Thus, the broker operating under such a listing would have the right to a commission even if another broker actually procured the buyer. Under the exclusive agency listing, however, the seller has the right to sell the property himself without being obligated to pay the broker a commission.

3. *Exclusive right to sell.* An exclusive right to sell contract provides the broker the exclusive right to sell the property for a specified period of time and entitles her to a commission no matter who procured the buyer. Under this type of listing, a seller must pay the broker her commission even if it was the seller or some third party who found the buyer during the duration of the listing contract.

Contract of Sale The contract formation, performance, assignment, and remedies principles about which you read in earlier chapters apply to real estate sales contracts. Such contracts identify the parties and subject property, and set forth the purchase price, the type of deed the purchaser will receive, the items of personal property (if any) included in the sale, and other important aspects of the parties' transaction. Real estate sales contracts often make the closing of the sale contingent on the buyer's obtaining financing at a specified rate of interest, on the seller's procurement of a survey and title insurance, and

on the property's passing a termite inspection. Because they are within the statute of frauds, real estate sales contracts must be evidenced by a suitable writing signed by the party to be charged in order to be enforceable.

Financing the Purchase The various arrangements for financing the purchase of real property—such as mortgages, land contracts, and deeds of trust—are discussed in Chapter 28.

Fair Housing Act The Fair Housing Act, enacted by Congress in 1968 and substantially revised in 1988, is designed to prevent discrimination in the housing market. Its provisions apply to real estate brokers, sellers (other than those selling their own single-family dwellings without the use of a broker), lenders, lessors, and appraisers. Originally, the act prohibited discrimination on the basis of race, color, religion, sex, and national origin. The 1988 amendments added handicap and "familial status" to this list. The familial status category was intended to prevent discrimination in the housing market against pregnant women and families with children.[4] "Adult" or "senior citizen" communities restricting residents' age do not violate the Fair Housing Act even though they exclude families with children, so long as the housing meets the requirements of the act's "housing for older persons" exemption.[5]

The act prohibits discrimination on the above-listed bases in a wide range of matters relating to the sale or rental of housing. These matters include refusals to sell or rent, representations that housing is not available for sale or rental when in fact it is, and discriminatory actions regarding terms, conditions, or privileges of sale or rental or regarding the provision of services and facilities involved in sale or rental.[6] The act also prohibits discrimination in connection with brokerage services, appraisals, and financing of dwellings.

---

[4]"Familial status" is defined as an individual or individuals under the age of 18 who is/are domiciled with a parent, some other person who has custody over him/her/them, or the designee of the parent or custodial individual. The familial status classification also applies to one who is pregnant or in the process of attempting to secure custody of a child or children under the age of 18.

[5]The Fair Housing Act defines "housing for older persons" as housing provided under any state or federal program found by the Secretary of HUD to be specifically designed to assist elderly persons, housing intended for and solely occupied by persons 62 years old or older, or housing that meets the requirements of federal regulations and is intended for occupancy by at least one person 55 years old or older.

[6]Chapter 25 discusses the Fair Housing Act's application to rentals of residential property.

CYBERLAW IN ACTION

How does the Fair Housing Act apply to websites that permit users to post advertisements about the sale or rental of real estate? Advertisements about property for sale or lease that are posted by individuals sometimes make statements indicating a "preference, limitation, or discrimination, or an intention to make a preference, limitations, or discrimination, on the basis of race, color, national origin, sex, religion, and familial status" that could violate the Fair Housing Act if the statements were made offline. For example, in *Chicago Lawyers' Committee for Civil Rights under the Law, Inc. v. Craigslist, Inc.,* 519 F.3d 666 (7th Cir. 2008), the plaintiff alleged that Craigslist.com posted notices in violation of the Fair Housing Act such as "Apt. too small for families with small children," "NO MINORITIES," and "Christian single straight female needed." The content of advertisements on the website is created by Craigslist.com users, not by Craigslist, Inc. This is a legally significant point, because a federal statute, § 230 of the Communications Decency Act, states that "No provider or user of an interactive computer service shall be treated as the publisher or speaker of any information provided by another information content provider." This statute has been interpreted in many cases to immunize websites, ISPs, and other interactive computer services for liability for third-party content. In the *Craigslist* case, the Seventh Circuit held that under § 230 of the Communications Decency Act, Craigslist could not be treated as the publisher of information provided by others and, therefore, that § 230 shielded Craigslist from liability.

In *Fair Housing Council of San Fernando Valley v. Roommate .com, LLC,* 521 F.3d 1157 (9th Cir. 2008), however, the Ninth Circuit held that § 230 of the Communications Decency Act immunized Roommate for some but not all of its activities. Roommate.com operates a roommate-matching website. Prior to searching or posting listings, subscribers were required to disclose their sex, sexual orientation, and to indicate whether children would live with them. Subscribers also described their preferences in roommates with regard to the same three criteria and were encouraged to provide additional comments. Roommate.com would then compile information provided in the questionnaires into a profile for each user, which would be used to match subscribers with listings and which could be viewed by other subscribers. The plaintiffs alleged that these practices constituted Fair Housing Act violations. The Ninth Circuit emphasized that § 230 provides a shield for an interactive computer service for content created by third parties, but not for content developed by the interactive computer service itself. It characterized Roommate.com's creation and required use of the questionnaires as being "entirely its own" and the profiles created and displayed from the information provided in the questionnaire as information developed by Roommate. com. Since these practices involved content developed by Roommate.com and not a third party, they were not shielded from potential Fair Housing Act liability. However, § 230 did immunize Roommate.com from liability for discriminatory content authored by subscribers in the open-ended "additional comments" section of the questionnaire.

Prohibited discrimination on the basis of handicap includes refusals to permit a handicapped person to make (at his own expense) reasonable modifications to the property. It also includes refusals to make reasonable accommodations in property-related rules, policies, practices, or services when such modifications or accommodations are necessary to afford the handicapped person full enjoyment of the property. The act also outlaws the building of multifamily housing that is inaccessible to persons with handicaps.

A violation of the Fair Housing Act may result in a civil action brought by the government or the aggrieved individual. If the aggrieved individual sues and prevails, the court may issue injunctions, award actual and punitive damages, assess attorney's fees and costs, and grant other appropriate relief. Finally, the Fair Housing Act invalidates any state or municipal law requiring or permitting an action that would be a discriminatory housing practice under federal law.

 LO6 Distinguish the different types of deeds, explain the purposes of recording deeds, and describe how state law determines priorities among those who claim competing rights in a parcel or real property.

Deeds Each state's statutes set out the formalities necessary to accomplish a valid conveyance of land. As a general rule, a valid conveyance is brought about by the execution and delivery of a **deed,** a written instrument that transfers title from one person (the grantor) to another (the grantee). Three types of deeds are in general use in the United States: *quitclaim deeds, warranty deeds,* and *deeds of bargain and sale* (also called *grant deeds*). The precise rights contemplated by a deed depend on the type of deed the parties have used.

Quitclaim Deeds A **quitclaim deed** conveys whatever title the grantor has at the time he executes the deed. It does not, however, contain warranties of title. The grantor who executes a quitclaim deed does not claim to have good title—or any title, for that matter. The grantee has no action against the grantor under a quitclaim deed if the grantee does not acquire good title. Quitclaim deeds are frequently used to cure technical defects in the chain of title to property.

Warranty Deeds   A **warranty deed,** unlike a quitclaim deed, contains covenants of warranty. Besides conveying title to the property, the grantor who executes a warranty deed guarantees the title she has conveyed. There are two types of warranty deeds.

1. *General warranty deed.* Under a general warranty deed, the grantor warrants against (and agrees to defend against) all title defects and encumbrances (such as liens and easements), including those that arose before the grantor received her title.

2. *Special warranty deed.* Under a special warranty deed, the grantor warrants against (and agrees to defend against) title defects and encumbrances that arose after she acquired the property. If the property conveyed is subject to an encumbrance such as a mortgage, a long-term lease, or an easement, the grantor frequently provides a special warranty deed that contains a provision excepting those specific encumbrances from the warranty.

Deeds of Bargain and Sale   In a deed of bargain and sale (also known as a grant deed), the grantor makes no covenants. The grantor uses language such as "I grant" or "I bargain and sell" or "I convey" property. Such a deed does contain, however, the grantor's implicit representation that he owns the land and has not previously encumbered it or conveyed it to another party.

Form and Execution of Deed   Some states' statutes suggest a form for deeds. Although the requirements for execution of deeds are not uniform, they do follow a similar pattern. As a general rule, a deed states the *name of the grantee,* contains a *recitation of consideration and a description of the property conveyed,* and is *signed by the grantor.* Most states require that the deed be notarized (acknowledged by the grantor before a notary public or other authorized officer) in order to be eligible for recording in public records.

No technical words of conveyance are necessary for a valid deed. Any language is sufficient if it indicates with reasonable certainty the grantor's intent to transfer ownership of the property. The phrases "grant, bargain, and sell" and "convey and warrant" are commonly used.

Deeds contain recitations of consideration primarily for historical reasons. The consideration recited is not necessarily the purchase price of the property. Deeds often state that the consideration for the conveyance is "one dollar and other valuable consideration."

The property conveyed must be described in such a manner that it can be identified. This usually means that the legal description of the property must be used. Several methods of legal description are used in the United States. In urban areas, descriptions are usually by lot, block, and plat. In rural areas where the land has been surveyed by the government, property is usually described by reference to the government survey. It may also be described by a metes and bounds description that specifies the boundaries of the tract of land.

Recording Deeds   Delivery of a valid deed conveys title from a grantor to a grantee. Even so, the grantee should promptly record the deed in order to prevent his interest from being defeated by third parties who may claim interests in the property. The grantee must pay a fee to have the deed recorded, a process that involves depositing and indexing the deed in the files of a government office designated by state law. A recorded deed operates to provide the public at large with notice of the grantee's property interest.

Recording Statutes   Each state has a recording statute that establishes a system for the recording of all transactions affecting real property ownership. These statutes are not uniform in their provisions. In general, however, they provide for the recording of all deeds, mortgages, land contracts, and similar documents.

Types of Recording Statutes   State recording statutes also provide for priority among competing claimants to rights in real property, in case conflicting rights or interests in property should be deeded to (or otherwise claimed by) more than one person. (Obviously, a grantor has no right to issue two different grantees separate deeds to the same property, but if this should occur, recording statutes provide rules to decide which grantee has superior title.) These priority rules apply only to grantees who have given value for their deeds or other interest-creating documents (primarily purchasers and lenders), and not to donees. A given state's recording law will set up one of three basic types of priority systems: race statutes, notice statutes, and race-notice statutes. Figure 2 explains these priority systems. Although the examples used in Figure 2 deal with recorded and unrecorded deeds, recording statutes apply to other documents that create interests in real estate. Chapter 28 discusses the recording of mortgages, as well as the adverse security

Figure 2 *Three Basic Types of Priority Systems for Recording Deeds*	
Race Statutes	Under a race statute—so named because the person who wins the race to the courthouse wins the property ownership "competition"—the first grantee who records a deed to a tract of land has superior title. For example, if Grantor deeds Blackacre to Kerr on March 1 and to Templin on April 1, Templin will have superior title to Blackacre if she records her deed before Kerr's is recorded. Race statutes are relatively uncommon today.
Notice Statutes	Under a notice system of priority, a later grantee of property has superior title if he acquired his interest without notice of an earlier grantee's claim to the property under an unrecorded deed. For example, Grantor deeds Greenacre to Jonson on June 1, but Jonson does not record his deed. On July 1, Marlowe purchases Greenacre without knowledge of Jonson's competing claim. Grantor executes and delivers a deed to Marlowe. In this situation, Marlowe would have superior rights to Greenacre even if Jonson ultimately records his deed before Marlowe's is recorded.
Race-Notice Statutes	The race-notice priority system combines elements of the systems just discussed. Under race-notice statutes, the grantee having priority is the one who both *takes his interest without notice* of any prior unrecorded claim and *records first.* For example, Grantor deeds Redacre to Frazier on September 1. On October 1 (at which time Frazier has not yet recorded his deed), Grantor deeds Redacre to Gill, who is then unaware of any claim by Frazier to Redacre. If Gill records his deed before Frazier's is recorded, Gill has superior rights to Redacre.

interest–related consequences a mortgagee may experience if its mortgage goes unrecorded.

Methods of Assuring Title

In purchasing real property, the buyer is really acquiring the seller's ownership interests. Because the buyer does not want to pay a large sum of money for something that proves to be of little or no value, it is important for her to obtain assurance that the seller has good title to the property. This is commonly done in one of three ways:

1. *Title opinion.* In some states, it is customary to have an attorney examine an **abstract of title.** An abstract of title is a history of what the public records show regarding the passage of title to, and other interests in, a parcel of real property. It is not a guarantee of good title. After examining the abstract, the attorney renders an opinion about whether the grantor has marketable title, which is title free from defects or reasonable doubt about its validity. If the grantor's title is defective, the nature of the defects will be stated in the attorney's title opinion.

2. *Torrens system.* A method of title assurance available in a few states is the Torrens system of title registration. Under this system, one who owns land in fee simple obtains a certificate of title. When the property is sold, the grantor delivers a deed and a certificate of title to the grantee. All liens and encumbrances against the title are noted on the certificate, thus assuring the purchaser that the title is good except as to the liens and encumbrances

noted on the certificate. However, some claims or encumbrances, such as those arising from adverse possession, do not appear on the records and must be discovered through an inspection of the property. In some Torrens states, encumbrances such as tax liens, short-term leases, and highway rights are valid against the purchaser even though they do not appear on the certificate.

3. *Title insurance.* Purchasing a policy of title insurance provides the preferred and most common means of protecting title to real property. Title insurance obligates the insurer to reimburse the insured grantee for loss if the title proves to be defective. In addition, title insurance covers litigation costs if the insured grantee must go to court in a title dispute. Lenders commonly require that a separate policy of title insurance be obtained for the lender's protection. Title insurance may be obtained in combination with the other previously discussed methods of ensuring title.

Seller's Responsibilities regarding the Quality of Residential Property

Buyers of real estate normally consider it important that any structures on the property be in good condition. This factor becomes especially significant if the buyer intends to use the property for residential purposes. The rule of **caveat emptor** (let the buyer beware) traditionally applied to the sale of real property unless the seller committed misrepresentation or fraud or made express warranties about the property's condition. In addition, sellers had no duty to disclose hidden defects in the property. In recent years, however, the legal environment for sellers—especially real estate professionals such as developers and builder-vendors of residential property—has changed substantially. This section examines two important sources of liability for sellers of real property.

Implied Warranty of Habitability

Historically, sellers of residential property were not regarded as making any **implied warranty** that the property was habitable or suitable for the buyer's use. The law's attitude toward the buyer–seller relationship in residential property sales began to shift, however, as product liability law underwent rapid change in the late 1960s. Courts began to see that the same policies favoring the creation of implied warranties in the sale of goods applied with equal force to the sale of residential real estate.[7] Both goods and housing are frequently mass-produced. The disparity of knowledge and bargaining power often existing between a buyer of goods and a professional seller is also likely to exist between a buyer of a house and a builder-vendor (one who builds and sells houses). Moreover, many defects in houses are not readily discoverable during a buyer's inspection. This creates the possibility of serious loss, because the purchase of a home is often the largest single investment a person ever makes.

For these reasons, courts in most states now hold that builders, builder-vendors, and developers make an implied warranty of habitability when they build or sell real property for residential purposes. An ordinary owner who sells her house—in other words, a seller who was neither the builder nor the developer of the residential property—does not make an implied warranty of habitability.

The implied warranty of habitability amounts to a guarantee that the house is free of latent (hidden) defects that would render it unsafe or unsuitable for human habitation. A breach of this warranty subjects the defendant to liability for damages, measured by either the cost of repairs or the loss in value of the house.[8]

A related issue that has led to considerable litigation is whether the implied warranty of habitability extends to subsequent purchasers of the house. For example, PDQ Development Co. builds a house and sells it to Johnson, who later sells the house to McClure. May McClure successfully sue PDQ for breach of warranty if a serious

defect renders the house uninhabitable? Although some courts have rejected implied warranty actions brought by subsequent purchasers, many courts today hold that an implied warranty made by a builder-vendor or developer would extend to a subsequent purchaser.

May the implied warranty of habitability be *disclaimed* or *limited* in the contract of sale? It appears at least possible to disclaim or limit the warranty through a contract provision, subject to limitations imposed by the unconscionability doctrine, public policy concerns, and contract interpretation principles.[9] Courts construe attempted disclaimers very strictly against the builder-vendor or developer, and often reject disclaimers that are not specific regarding rights supposedly waived by the purchaser.

Duty to Disclose Hidden Defects

Traditional contract law provided that a seller had no duty to disclose to the buyer defects in the property being sold, even if the seller knew about the defects and the buyer could not reasonably find out about them on his own. The seller's failure to volunteer information, therefore, could not constitute misrepresentation or fraud. This traditional rule of nondisclosure was another expression of the prevailing *caveat emptor* notion. Although the nondisclosure rule was subject to certain exceptions,[10] the exceptions seldom applied. Thus, there was no duty to disclose in most sales of real property.

Today, courts in many jurisdictions have substantially eroded the traditional nondisclosure rule and have placed a duty on the seller to disclose any known defect that materially affects the property's value and is not reasonably observable by the buyer. The seller's failure to disclose such defects effectively amounts to an assertion that the defects do not exist—an assertion on which a judicial finding of misrepresentation or fraud may be based.[11]

Other Property Condition–Related Obligations of Real Property Owners and Possessors

In recent years, the law has increasingly required real property owners and possessors to take steps to further the safety of persons on the property and to make the property

---

[7]See Chapter 20 for a discussion of the development of similar doctrines in the law of product liability.

[8]Measures of damages are discussed in Chapter 18.

[9]The unconscionability doctrine and public policy concerns are discussed in Chapter 15. Chapter 16 addresses contract interpretation.

[10]These exceptions are discussed in Chapter 13.

[11]Misrepresentation and fraud are discussed in Chapter 13.

more accessible to disabled individuals. This section discusses two legal developments along these lines: the trend toward expansion of *premises liability* and the inclusion of property-related provisions in the *Americans with Disabilities Act*.

Expansion of Premises Liability

Premises liability is the name sometimes used for negligence cases in which property owners or possessors (such as business operators leasing commercial real estate) are held liable to persons injured while on the property. As explained in Chapter 7, property owners and possessors face liability when their *failures to exercise reasonable care* to keep their property reasonably safe result in injuries to persons lawfully on the property.[12] The traditional premises liability case was one in which a property owner's or possessor's negligence led to the existence of a potentially hazardous condition on the property (e.g., a dangerously slick floor or similar physical condition at a business premises), and a person justifiably on the premises (e.g., a business customer) sustained personal injury upon encountering that unexpected condition (e.g., by slipping and falling).

Security Precautions against Foreseeable Criminal Acts Recent years have witnessed a judicial inclination to expand premises liability to cover other situations in addition to the traditional scenario. A key component of this expansion has been many courts' willingness to reconsider the once-customary holding that a property owner or possessor had no legal obligation to implement security measures to protect persons on the property from the wrongful acts of third parties lacking any connection with the owner or possessor. Today, courts frequently hold that a property owner's or possessor's duty to exercise reasonable care includes the obligation to take *reasonable security precautions* designed to protect persons lawfully on the premises from *foreseeable* wrongful (including criminal) acts by third parties.

This expansion has caused hotel, apartment building, and convenience store owners and operators to be among the defendants held liable—sometimes in very large damage amounts—to guests, tenants, and customers on whom third-party attackers inflicted severe physical injuries. In such cases, the property owners' or possessors' negligent

failures to take security precautions restricting such wrongdoers' access to the premises served as at least a *substantial factor* leading to the plaintiffs' injuries.[13] The security lapses amounting to a lack of reasonable care in a particular case may have been, for instance, failures to install deadbolt locks, provide adequate locking devices on sliding glass doors, maintain sufficient lighting, or employ security guards.

Determining Foreseeability The security precautions component of the reasonable care duty is triggered only when criminal activity on the premises is foreseeable. It therefore becomes important to determine whether the foreseeability standard has been met. In making this determination, courts look at such factors as whether previous crimes had occurred on or near the subject property (and if so, the nature and frequency of those crimes), whether the property owner or possessor knew or should have known of those prior occurrences, and whether the property was located in a high-crime area. The fact-specific nature of the foreseeability and reasonable care determinations makes the outcome of a given premises liability case difficult to predict in advance. Nevertheless, there is no doubt that the current premises liability climate gives property owners and possessors more reason than ever before to be concerned about security measures.

Americans with Disabilities Act

In 1990, Congress enacted the broad-ranging Americans with Disabilities Act (ADA). This statute was designed to eliminate long-standing patterns of discrimination against disabled persons in matters such as employment, access to public services, and access to business establishments and similar facilities open to the public. The ADA's Title III focuses on places of *public accommodation*.[14] It imposes on certain property owners and possessors the obligation to take reasonable steps to make their property accessible to disabled persons (individuals with a physical or mental impairment that substantially limits one or more major life activities).

Places of Public Accommodation Title III of the ADA classifies numerous businesses and nonbusiness enterprises as places of **public accommodation.** These include hotels, restaurants, bars, theaters, concert halls,

---

[12]Chapter 7 explains the law's traditional view that real property owners and possessors owe persons who come on the property certain duties that vary depending on those persons' invitee, licensee, or trespasser status. It also discusses courts' increasing tendency to merge the traditional invitee and licensee classifications and to hold that property owners and possessors owe invitees and licensees the duty to exercise reasonable care to keep the premises reasonably safe.

[13]See Chapter 7's discussion of the *causation* element of a negligence claim.

[14]42 U.S.C. §§ 12181–12189. These sections examine only Title III of the ADA. Chapter 51 discusses the employment-related provisions set forth elsewhere in the statute.

auditoriums, stadiums, shopping centers, stores at which goods are sold or rented, service-oriented businesses (running the gamut from gas stations to law firm offices), museums, parks, schools, social services establishments (day care centers, senior citizen centers, homeless shelters, and the like), places of recreation, and various other enterprises, facilities, and establishments. Private clubs and religious organizations, however, are not treated as places of public accommodation for purposes of the statute.

Modifications of Property Under the ADA, the owner or operator of a place of public accommodation cannot exclude disabled persons from the premises or otherwise discriminate against them in terms of their ability to enjoy the public accommodation. Avoiding such exclusion or other discrimination may require alteration of the business or nonbusiness enterprise's practices, policies, and procedures. Moreover, using language contemplating the possible need for physical modifications of property serving as a place of public accommodation, the ADA includes within prohibited discrimination the property owner's or possessor's "failure to take such steps as may be necessary to ensure that no individual with a disability is excluded" or otherwise discriminated against in terms of access to what nondisabled persons are provided. The failure to take these steps does not violate the ADA, however, if the property owner or possessor demonstrates that implementing such steps would "fundamentally alter the nature" of the enterprise or would "result in an undue burden."

Prohibited discrimination may also include the "failure to remove architectural barriers and communication barriers that are structural in nature," if removal is "readily achievable." When the removal of such a barrier is not readily achievable, the property owner or possessor nonetheless engages in prohibited discrimination if he, she, or it does not adopt "alternative methods" to ensure access to the premises and what it has to offer (assuming that the alternative methods are themselves readily achievable). The ADA defines *readily achievable* as "easily accomplishable and able to be carried out without much difficulty or expense." The determination of whether an action is readily achievable involves consideration of factors such as the action's nature and cost, the nature of the enterprise conducted on the property, the financial resources of the affected property owner or possessor, and the effect the action would have on expenses and resources of the property owner or possessor.

New Construction Newly constructed buildings on property used as a place of public accommodation must contain physical features making the buildings *readily* *accessible* to disabled persons. The same is true of additions built on to previous structures. The ADA is supplemented by federal regulations setting forth property accessibility guidelines designed to lend substance and specificity to the broad legal standards stated in the statute. In addition, the federal government has issued technical assistance manuals and materials in an effort to educate public accommodation owners and operators regarding their obligations under the ADA.

Remedies A person subjected to disability-based discrimination in any of the respects discussed above may bring a civil suit for injunctive relief. An injunction issued by a court must include "an order to alter facilities" to make the facilities "readily accessible to and usable by individuals with disabilities to the extent required" by the ADA. The court has discretion to award attorney's fees to the prevailing party. The U.S. Attorney General also has the legal authority to institute a civil action alleging a violation of Title III of the ADA. In such a case, the court may choose to grant injunctive and other appropriate equitable relief, award compensatory damages to aggrieved persons (when the Attorney General so requests), and assess civil penalties (up to $50,000 for a first violation and up to $100,000 for any subsequent violation) "to vindicate the public interest." When determining the amount of any such penalty, the court is to give consideration to any good faith effort by the property owner or possessor to comply with the law. The court must also consider whether the owner or possessor could reasonably have anticipated the need to accommodate disabled persons.

 LO7 Explain governmental powers to control and purchase private land and the constitutional limits on those powers.

Land Use Control

Although a real property owner generally has the right to use his property as he desires, society has placed certain limitations on this right. This section examines the property use limitations imposed by nuisance law and by zoning and subdivision ordinances. It also discusses the ultimate land use restriction—the eminent domain power—which enables the government to deprive property owners of their land.

Nuisance Law One's enjoyment of her land depends to a great extent on the uses her neighbors make of their land. When the uses of neighboring landowners conflict, the aggrieved party sometimes institutes litigation to resolve the conflict. A property use that unreasonably interferes with another person's ability to use or enjoy her own property may lead to an action for **nuisance** against the landowner or possessor engaging in the objectionable use.

The term *nuisance* has no set definition. It is often regarded, however, as encompassing any property-related use or activity that unreasonably interferes with the rights of others. Property uses potentially constituting nuisances include uses that are inappropriate to the neighborhood (such as using a vacant lot in a residential neighborhood as a garbage dump), bothersome to neighbors (such as keeping a pack of barking dogs in one's backyard), dangerous to others (such as storing large quantities of gasoline in 50-gallon drums in one's garage), or of questionable morality (such as operating a house of prostitution). To amount to a nuisance, a use need not be illegal. The fact that relevant zoning laws allow a given use does not mean that the use cannot be a nuisance. The use's having been in existence before complaining neighbors acquired their property does not mean that the use cannot be a nuisance, though it does lessen the likelihood that the use would be held a nuisance.

The test for determining the presence or absence of a nuisance is necessarily flexible and highly dependent on the individual case's facts. Courts balance a number of factors, such as the social importance of the parties' respective uses, the extent and duration of harm experienced by the aggrieved party, and the feasibility of abating (stopping) the nuisance.

Nuisances may be private or public. To bring a *private nuisance* action, the plaintiff must be a landowner or occupier whose enjoyment of her own land is substantially lessened by the alleged nuisance. The remedies for private nuisance include damages and injunctive relief designed to stop the offending use. A *public nuisance* occurs when a nuisance harms members of the public, who need not be injured in their use of property. For example, if a power plant creates noise and emissions posing a health hazard to pedestrians and workers in nearby buildings, a public nuisance may exist even though the nature of the harm has nothing to do with any loss of enjoyment of property. Public nuisances involve a broader class of affected parties than do private nuisances. The action to abate a public nuisance must usually be brought by the government. Remedies generally include injunctive relief and civil penalties that resemble fines. On occasion, constitutional issues may arise in public nuisance cases brought by the government. Private parties may sue for abatement of a public nuisance or for damages caused by one only when they suffered unique harm different from that experienced by the general public.

Eminent Domain The Fifth Amendment to the Constitution provides that private property shall not be taken for public use without "just compensation." Implicit in this provision is the principle that the government has the power to take property for public use if it pays "just compensation" to the owner of the property. This power, called the power of **eminent domain,** makes it possible for the government to acquire private property for highways, water control projects, municipal and civic centers, public housing, urban renewal, and other public uses. Governmental units may delegate their eminent domain power to private corporations such as railroads and utility companies.

Although the eminent domain power is a useful tool of efficient government, there are problems inherent in its use. Determining when the power can be properly exercised presents an initial problem. When the governmental unit itself uses the property taken, as would be the case with property acquired for construction of a municipal building or a public highway, the exercise of the power is proper. The use of eminent domain is controversial, however, when the government acquires the property and transfers it to a private developer.[15] In the *Kelo* case, which follows shortly, the U.S. Supreme Court grappled with this issue.

Determining *just compensation* in a given case poses a second and frequently encountered eminent domain problem. The property owner is entitled to receive the "fair market value" of his property. Critics assert, however, that this measure of compensation falls short of adequately compensating the owner for her loss, because *fair market value* does not cover such matters as the lost goodwill of a business or one's emotional attachment to his home.

A third problem sometimes encountered is determining when there has been a "taking" that triggers the government's just compensation obligation. The answer is easy when the government institutes a formal legal action to exercise the eminent domain power (often called an action to *condemn* property). In some instances, however, the government causes or permits a serious physical invasion of a landowner's property without having instituted formal condemnation proceedings. For example, the government's dam-building project results in persistent flooding of a private party's land. Courts have recognized the right of property owners in such cases to institute litigation seeking compensation from the governmental unit whose actions effectively amounted to a physical taking of their land. In these so-called inverse condemnation cases, the property owner sends the message that "you have taken my land; now pay for it."

---

[15]This issue is discussed further in Chapter 3, as are other issues relating to eminent domain.

Kelo v. City of New London	125 S. Ct. 2655 (U.S. Sup. Ct. 2005)

The city of New London, Connecticut, had experienced decades of economic decline. In 1990, a state agency designated the city a "distressed municipality." In 1996, the federal government closed a U.S. naval facility in the Fort Trumbull area of the city that had employed over 1,500 people. In 1998, the city's unemployment rate was nearly double that of the rest of the state and its population of just under 24,000 residents was at its lowest since 1920. These conditions prompted state and local officials to target New London, and particularly its Fort Trumbull area, for economic revitalization.

To this end, New London Development Corporation (NLDC), a private nonprofit entity established some years earlier to assist the city in planning economic development, was reactivated. In January 1998, the state authorized a $5.35 million bond issue to support the NLDC's planning activities. In February, the pharmaceutical company Pfizer Inc. announced that it would build a $300 million research facility on a site immediately adjacent to Fort Trumbull; local planners hoped that Pfizer would draw new business to the area, thereby serving as a catalyst to the area's rejuvenation. In May, the city council authorized the NLDC to formally submit its plans to the relevant state agencies for review. Upon obtaining state-level approval, the NLDC finalized an integrated development plan focused on 90 acres of the Fort Trumbull area, which comprises approximately 115 privately owned properties, as well as the 32 acres of land formerly occupied by the naval facility.

The development plan called for the creation of restaurants, shops, marinas for both recreational and commercial uses, a pedestrian "riverwalk," 80 new residences, a new U.S. Coast Guard Museum, research and development office space, and parking. The NLDC intended the development plan to capitalize on the arrival of the Pfizer facility and the new commerce it was expected to attract. In addition to creating jobs, generating tax revenue, and helping to build momentum for the revitalization of downtown New London, the plan was also designed to make the city more attractive and to create leisure and recreational opportunities on the waterfront and in the park. The city council approved the plan in January 2000, and designated the NLDC as its development agent in charge of implementation. The city council also authorized the NLDC to purchase property or to acquire property by exercising eminent domain in the city's name.

The NLDC successfully negotiated the purchase of most of the real estate in the 90-acre area, but its negotiations with nine property owners, including the petitioners Susette Kelo, Wilhelmina Dery, and Charles Dery, failed. As a result, in November 2000, the NLDC initiated condemnation proceedings. Kelo had lived in the Fort Trumbull area since 1997. She had made extensive improvements to her house, which she prizes for its water view. Wilhelmina Dery was born in her Fort Trumbull house in 1918 and had lived there her entire life. Her husband, Charles, had lived in the house since they married some 60 years ago. In all, the nine petitioners own 15 properties in Fort Trumbull. There is no allegation that any of these properties is blighted or otherwise in poor condition; rather, they were condemned only because they happen to be located in the development area.

In December 2000, the petitioners brought this action claiming, among other things, that the taking of their properties would violate the "public use" restriction in the Fifth Amendment. The trial court granted a permanent restraining order prohibiting the taking of properties in one area of Fort Trumbull, but denied the order for properties in another area. Both sides appealed to the Supreme Court of Connecticut. That court held that all of the city's proposed takings were valid. The petitioners then appealed to the U.S. Supreme Court.

Stevens, Justice

Two polar propositions are perfectly clear. On the one hand, it has long been accepted that the sovereign may not take the property of *A* for the sole purpose of transferring it to another private party *B*, even though *A* is paid just compensation. On the other hand, it is equally clear that a State may transfer property from one private party to another if future "use by the public" is the purpose of the taking; the condemnation of land for a railroad with common-carrier duties is a familiar example. Neither of these propositions, however, determines the disposition of this case.

As for the first proposition, the City would no doubt be forbidden from taking petitioners' land for the purpose of conferring a private benefit on a particular private party. Nor would

the City be allowed to take property under the mere pretext of a public purpose, when its actual purpose was to bestow a private benefit. The takings before us, however, would be executed pursuant to a carefully considered development plan. The trial judge and all the members of the Supreme Court of Connecticut agreed that there was no evidence of an illegitimate purpose in this case. On the other hand, this is not a case in which the City is planning to open the condemned land—at least not in its entirety—to use by the general public. Nor will the private lessees of the land in any sense be required to operate like common carriers, making their services available to all comers. But although such a projected use would be sufficient to satisfy the public use requirement, this Court long ago rejected any literal requirement that condemned property be put into use for the general public. Indeed, while many state courts in the mid-19th century endorsed "use by the public" as the proper definition of public use, that narrow view steadily eroded over time. Not only was the "use by the public" test difficult to administer (e.g., what proportion of the public need have access to the property? at what price?), but it proved to be impractical given the diverse and always evolving needs of society. Accordingly, when this Court began applying the Fifth Amendment to the States at the close of the 19th century, it embraced the broader and more natural interpretation of public use as "public purpose." The disposition of this case therefore turns on the question whether the City's development plan serves a "public purpose."

Without exception, our cases have defined that concept broadly, reflecting our long-standing policy of deference to legislative judgments in this field. Viewed as a whole, our jurisprudence has recognized that the needs of society have varied between different parts of the Nation, just as they have evolved over time in response to changed circumstances. For more than a century, our public use jurisprudence has wisely eschewed rigid formulas and intrusive scrutiny in favor of affording legislatures broad latitude in determining what public needs justify the use of the takings power.

Those who govern the City were not confronted with the need to remove blight in the Fort Trumbull area, but their determination that the area was sufficiently distressed to justify a program of economic rejuvenation is entitled to our deference. The City has carefully formulated an economic development plan that it believes will provide appreciable benefits to the community, including—but by no means limited to—new jobs and increased tax revenue. As with other exercises in urban planning and development, the City is endeavoring to coordinate a variety of commercial, residential, and recreational uses of land, with the hope that they will form a whole greater than the sum of its parts. To effectuate this plan, the City has invoked a state statute that specifically authorizes the use of eminent domain to promote economic development. Given the comprehensive character of the plan, the thorough deliberation that preceded its adoption, and the limited scope of our review, it is appropriate for us to resolve the challenges of the individual owners, not on a piecemeal basis, but rather in light of the entire plan. Because that plan unquestionably serves a public purpose, the takings challenged here satisfy the public use requirement of the Fifth Amendment.

To avoid this result, petitioners urge us to adopt a new bright-line rule that economic development does not qualify as a public use. Putting aside the unpersuasive suggestion that the City's plan will provide only purely economic benefits, neither precedent nor logic supports petitioners' proposal. Promoting economic development is a traditional and long-accepted function of government. There is, moreover, no principled way of distinguishing economic development from the other public purposes that we have recognized. In our cases upholding takings that facilitated agriculture and mining, for example, we emphasized the importance of those industries to the welfare of the States in question. It would be incongruous to hold that the City's interest in the economic benefits to be derived from the development of the Fort Trumbull area has less of a public character than any of those other interests. Clearly, there is no basis for exempting economic development from our traditionally broad understanding of public purpose.

Petitioners contend that using eminent domain for economic development impermissibly blurs the boundary between public and private takings. Again, our cases foreclose this objection. Quite simply, the government's pursuit of a public purpose will often benefit individual private parties. It is further argued that without a bright-line rule nothing would stop a city from transferring citizen *A*'s property to citizen *B* for the sole reason that citizen *B* will put the property to a more productive use and thus pay more taxes. Such a one-to-one transfer of property, executed outside the confines of an integrated development plan, is not presented in this case. While such an unusual exercise of government power would certainly raise a suspicion that a private purpose was afoot, the hypothetical cases posited by petitioners can be confronted if and when they arise. They do not warrant the crafting of an artificial restriction on the concept of public use.

Alternatively, petitioners maintain that for takings of this kind we should require a "reasonable certainty" that the expected public benefits will actually accrue. Such a rule, however, would represent an even greater departure from our precedent. The disadvantages of a heightened form of review are especially pronounced in this type of case. Orderly implementation of a comprehensive redevelopment plan obviously requires that the legal rights of all interested parties be established before new construction can be commenced. A constitutional rule that required postponement of the judicial approval of every condemnation until the likelihood of success of the plan had been assured would unquestionably impose a significant impediment to the successful consummation of many such plans.

Just as we decline to second-guess the City's considered judgments about the efficacy of its development plan, we also decline to second-guess the City's determinations as to what lands it needs to acquire in order to effectuate the project. In affirming the City's authority to take petitioners' properties, we do not minimize the hardship that condemnations may entail, notwithstanding the payment of just compensation. We emphasize that nothing in our opinion precludes any State from placing further restrictions on its exercise of the takings power. Indeed, many States already impose "public use" requirements that are stricter than the federal baseline. Some of these requirements have been established as a matter of state constitutional law, while others are expressed in state eminent domain statutes that carefully limit the grounds upon which takings may be exercised. As the submissions of the parties make clear, the necessity and wisdom of using eminent domain to promote economic development are certainly matters of legitimate public debate. This

Court's authority, however, extends only to determining whether the City's proposed condemnations are for a "public use" within the meaning of the Fifth Amendment to the Federal Constitution.

Affirmed in favor of the City.

Zoning and Subdivision Laws

State legislatures commonly delegate to cities and other political subdivisions the power to impose reasonable regulations designed to promote the public health, safety, and welfare (often called the *police power*). Zoning ordinances, which regulate real property use, stem from the exercise of the police power. Normally, zoning ordinances divide a city or town into various districts and specify or limit the uses to which property in those districts may be put. They also contain requirements and restrictions regarding improvements built on the land.

Zoning ordinances frequently contain direct restrictions on land use, such as by limiting property use in a given area to single-family or high-density residential uses, or to commercial, light industry, or heavy industry uses. Other sorts of use-related provisions commonly found in zoning ordinances include restrictions on building height, limitations on the portion of a lot that can be covered by a building, and specifications of the distance buildings must be from lot lines (usually called *setback* requirements). Zoning ordinances also commonly restrict property use by establishing population density limitations. Such restrictions specify the maximum number of persons who can be housed on property in a given area and dictate the amount of living space that must be provided for each person occupying residential property. In addition, zoning ordinances often establish restrictions designed to maintain or create a certain aesthetic character in the community. Examples of this type of restriction include specifications of buildings' architectural style, limitations on billboard and sign use, and designations of special zones for historic buildings.

Many local governments also have ordinances dealing with proposed subdivisions. These ordinances often require the subdivision developer to meet certain requirements regarding lot size, street and sidewalk layout, and sanitary facilities. They also require that the city or town approve the proposed development. Such ordinances are designed to further general community interests and to protect prospective buyers of property in the subdivision by ensuring that the developer meets minimum standards of suitability.

Nonconforming Uses A zoning ordinance has *prospective* effect. This means that the uses and buildings already

existing when the ordinance is passed (nonconforming uses) are permitted to continue. The ordinance may provide, however, for the gradual phasing out of nonconforming uses and buildings that do not fit the general zoning plan.

Relief from Zoning Ordinances A property owner who wishes to use his property in a manner prohibited by a zoning ordinance has more than one potential avenue of relief from the ordinance. He may, for instance, seek to have the ordinance amended—in other words, attempt to get the law changed—on the ground that the proposed amendment is consistent with the essence of the overall zoning plan.

A different approach would be to seek permission from the city or political subdivision to deviate from the zoning law. This permission is called a variance. A person seeking a variance usually claims that the ordinance works an undue hardship on her by denying her the opportunity to make reasonable use of her land. Examples of typical variance requests include a property owner's seeking permission to make a commercial use of her property even though it is located in an area zoned for residential purposes, or permission to deviate from normal setback or building size requirements.

Attempts to obtain variances and zoning ordinance amendments frequently clash with the interests of other owners of property in the same area—owners who have a vested interest in maintaining the status quo. As a result, variance and amendment requests often produce heated battles before local zoning authorities.

Challenges to the Validity of the Zoning Ordinance A disgruntled property owner might also attack the zoning ordinance's validity on constitutional grounds. Litigation challenging zoning ordinances has become frequent in recent years, as cities and towns have used their zoning power to achieve social control. For example, assume that a city creates special zoning requirements for adult bookstores or other uses considered moral threats to the community. Such uses of the zoning power have been challenged as unconstitutional restrictions on freedom of speech. In *City of Renton v. Playtime Theatres, Inc.,* however, the Supreme Court upheld a zoning ordinance

Ethics in Action

The Jesus Center rented a two-story building in the City of Farmington Hills in a district zoned for single-family dwellings as well as churches and "other facilities normally incidental thereto." In its leased property, the church held services, Bible study, and prayer meetings as well as providing for collection and distribution of food, clothing, and other essentials for needy people. In 1991, The Jesus Center began to operate a homeless shelter.

After being notified that zoning approval was needed for this use of the property, The Jesus Center sought such approval, but it was denied on the ground that the provision of shelter services was not a permissible accessible use. What are the major ethical considerations suggested by such uses of zoning ordinances and restrictive covenants? What are the major ethical considerations suggested by attempts to place homeless shelters in primarily single-family residential locations?

that prohibited the operation of adult bookstores within 1,000 feet of specified uses such as residential areas and schools. The Court established that the First Amendment rights of operators of adult businesses would not be violated by such an ordinance so long as the city provided them a "reasonable opportunity to open and operate" their businesses within the city.

Other litigation has stemmed from ordinances by which municipalities have attempted to "zone out" residential facilities such as group homes for developmentally disabled adults. In a leading case, the Supreme Court held that the Constitution's Equal Protection Clause was violated by a zoning ordinance that required a special use permit for such a group home.[16] The Fair Housing Act, which forbids discrimination on the basis of disability and familial status, has also been used as a basis for challenging decisions that zone out group homes. Such a challenge has a chance of success when the plaintiff demonstrates that the zoning board's actions were a mere pretext for discrimination.[17] Certain applications of zoning ordinances that establish single-family residential areas may also raise Fair Housing Act–based claims of disability discrimination.

Many cities and towns have attempted to restrict single-family residential zones to living units of traditional families related by blood or marriage. In enacting ordinances along those lines, municipalities have sought to prevent the presence of groups of unrelated students, commune members, or religious cult adherents by specifically defining the term *family* in a way that excludes these groups. In *Belle Terre v. Boraas*,[18] the Supreme Court upheld such an ordinance as applied to a group of unrelated students.

The Court later held, however, that an ordinance defining *family* so as to prohibit a grandmother from living with her grandsons was an unconstitutional intrusion on personal freedom regarding family life.[19] Restrictive definitions of *family* have been held unconstitutional under state constitutions in some cases but narrowly construed by courts in other cases.

Land Use Regulation and Taking

Another type of litigation seen with increasing frequency in recent years centers around zoning laws and other land use regulations that make the use of property less profitable.[20] Affected property owners have challenged the application of such regulations as unconstitutional takings of property without just compensation, even though these cases do not involve the actual physical invasions present in the inverse condemnation cases discussed earlier in this chapter.

States normally have broad discretion to use their police power for the public benefit, even when that means interfering to some extent with an owner's right to develop her property as she desires. Some regulations, however, may interfere with an owner's use of his property to such an extent that they constitute a taking.

For instance, in *Nollan v. California Coastal Commission*,[21] the owners of a beach-front lot (the Nollans) wished to tear down a small house on the lot and replace that structure with a larger house. The California Coastal Commission conditioned the grant of the necessary coastal development permit on the Nollans' agreeing to allow the public an easement across their property. This easement would have allowed the public to reach certain nearby public beaches more easily. The Nollans challenged the validity of the Coastal Commission's action.

[16]*City of Cleburne v. Cleburne Living Centers*, 473 U.S. 432 (U.S. Sup. Ct. 1985).

[17]See, for example, *Baxter v. City of Nashville*, 720 F. Supp. 720 (S.D. Ill. 1989), which involves a challenge by a hospice for AIDS patients to a city's denial of a special use permit.

[18]416 U.S. 1 (U.S. Sup. Ct. 1974).

[19]*Moore v. City of East Cleveland*, 431 U.S. 494 (U.S. Sup. Ct. 1977).

[20]This issue is also discussed in Chapter 3.

[21]483 U.S. 825 (U.S. Sup. Ct. 1987).

Ultimately, the Supreme Court concluded that the Coastal Commission's placing the easement condition on the issuance of the permit amounted to an impermissible regulatory taking of the Nollans' property. In reaching this conclusion, the Court held that the state could not avoid paying compensation to the Nollans by choosing to do by way of the regulatory route what it would have had to pay for if it had followed the formal eminent domain route.

Regulations Denying Economically Beneficial Uses
What about a land use regulation that allows the property owner no *economically beneficial use* of his property? *Lucas v. South Carolina Coastal Commission*[22] was brought by a property owner, Lucas, who had paid nearly $1 million for two residential beach-front lots before South Carolina enacted a coastal protection statute. This statute's effect was to bar Lucas from building any permanent habitable structures on the lots. The trial court held that the statute rendered Lucas's property "valueless" and that an unconstitutional taking had occurred, but the South Carolina Supreme Court reversed. The U.S. Supreme Court, however, held that when a land use regulation denies "all economically beneficial use" of property, there normally has been a taking for which just compensation must be paid. The exception to this rule, according to the Court, would be when the economically productive use being prohibited by the land use regulation was already disallowed by nuisance law or other comparable property law principles. The Court therefore reversed and remanded the case for determination of whether there had been a taking under the rule crafted by the Court, or instead an instance in which the "nuisance" exception applied. On remand, the South Carolina Supreme Court concluded that a taking

calling for compensation had occurred (and, necessarily, that the nuisance exception did not apply to Lucas's intended residential use).[23]

The mere fact that a land use regulation deprives the owner of the *highest and most profitable use* of his property does not mean, however, that there has been a taking. If the regulation still allows a use that is economically beneficial in a meaningful sense—even though not the most profitable use—the *Lucas* analysis would seem to indicate that an unconstitutional taking probably did not occur. At the same time, *Lucas* offered hints that less-than-total takings (in terms of restrictions on economically beneficial uses) may sometimes trigger a right of compensation on the landowner's part. Thus, it appears that even as to land use regulations that restrict some but not all economically beneficial uses, property owners are likely to continue arguing (as they have in recent years) that the regulations go "too far" and amount to a taking.

There is no set formula for determining whether a regulation has gone too far. Courts look at the relevant facts and circumstances and weigh a variety of factors, such as the economic impact of the regulation, the degree to which the regulation interferes with the property owner's reasonable expectations, and the character of the government's invasion. The weighing of these factors occurs against the backdrop of a general presumption that state and local governments should have reasonably broad discretion to develop land use restrictions pursuant to the police power. As a result, the outcome of a case in which *regulatory taking* allegations are made is less certain than when a *physical taking* (a physical invasion of the sort addressed in the earlier discussion of inverse condemnation cases) appears to have occurred.

---

[22]505 U.S. 1003 (U.S. Sup. Ct. 1992).

[23]424 S.E. 2d 484 (S.C. Sup. Ct. 1992).

Problems and Problem Cases

1. Custer owns about 97 acres of land in Bedford County, where he operates a nursery business. In March 2001, he bought a used greenhouse for $1,500, disassembled it, transported it by flatbed truck to his property, and stored it there until 2004, when he reassembled it. The greenhouse is an arch-shaped structure that is 30 feet wide by 96 feet long and approximately 12 feet high. The greenhouse is constructed by 24 vertical pipes on each side that are inserted two feet into the ground and connected at the top to arch-shaped pipes. Plastic covering is attached to the arching pipes and serves as a covering for the structure. According to Custer,

he never intended this greenhouse to be permanent, but rather to serve as a "starter" greenhouse to be replaced in the future by a more permanent structure. He planned to take it apart and sell it or take it with him if he ever decided to quit the nursery business. Because of the addition of the greenhouse to Custer's property, the local Board of Assessment increased the assessed value of the buildings on the property for the 2004 tax year from $11,124 to $19,978, an increase of $8,854. Custer appealed this, contending that the greenhouse should not be assessed because it was not real estate. Is he correct?

2. In 1982, Green's grandmother, Billie Harrild, offered Green a piece of the family's land. Green selected a

parcel of land on a bluff, across a creek from her grand-parents' house. The alleged gift was not recorded, and Green's grandparents and cousin remained the owners of record. However, according to Green's testimony, in the 10 years following her entry onto the property, all three "absolutely" recognized the land as hers. Neighbors testified that Billie consistently referred to the land as Green's property. Between 1982 and 1992, Green gradually built a house and cultivated grounds on the bluff. She worked on the property over the summers, and worked as a nurse and glassmaker in California for the rest of the year. In 1982, she planned the site of her house and cleared trees on the lot. In the summers of 1983 and 1984, she lived in a camper on the property, cleared more trees and stumps, and over-saw hand excavation for the foundation of the house. In the following summers, she gradually expanded the cultivated section of the property, planting lilac bushes and fruit trees and installing a coop for chick-ens and turkeys. She and a neighbor worked on build-ing the house itself, and beginning in 1987, Green lived in the nearly complete house during the sum-mers. In 1986, Green worked in Fairbanks the whole year and visited the property by snow machine during the winter. In 1989 she lived on the property for eight or nine months. Green left trees standing on much of the property, but cleared undergrowth and planted native plants over an area of several acres. She also cut trees from a wide area on the southern hillside in order to clear the view from the cabin. She posted "No Trespassing" signs and built benches in some areas away from the house. She put up a chain across the road entering the property, but did not fence the entire area. In 1990, the house was considerably damaged by vandalism, and Green repaired the damage when she returned to Alaska in the spring. Green arranged with her grandparents that, for the remainder of their lives, they could extract and sell small quantities of rock from the property, but she strongly opposed use of such equipment on the property. Sometime between 1988 and 1991, the Harrilds signed a contract with an extraction company, Earthmovers, allowing them to excavate rock from the family property, including the bluff. Earthmovers excavated a trench on the bluff on a day when Green was not at home. When Green re-turned and found the workers and equipment on the property, however, she told them that they were not allowed to excavate there. Green granted the workers permission to finish the task at hand, insisted that they arrange to repair a telephone line that they had dam-aged, and ordered them to leave the property. In 1988,

Vezey became interested in properties in this area. Vezey approached the Harrilds about purchasing their land. In 1994, while Vezey was still in negotiations with the Harrilds, Green called him, and, according to Green, she told Vezey that the land belonged to her. In the winter of 1994–1995, Vezey purchased property that included the bluff area claimed by Green. Green brought suit, asserting that she owned the bluff area property. Will she win?

3. Aidinoff purchased land in 1979. It is adjacent to Sterling City Road but can only be reached by cross-ing land formerly owned by Rand. Other routes of ac-cess are impossible because of wetlands and a brook. A gravel driveway crosses the Rand land to Aidinoff's land. The person from whom Aidinoff purchased her land used the driveway for access to her land, and Aidinoff used the driveway from 1979 until 2003. She drove vehicles, walked, and brought animals across the driveway. She also used the power coming in over util-ity lines serving the property. After Aidinoff had begun using the driveway, she and Rand had had a conversa-tion about the driveway, and Rand had told her that he owned it and he had no problem with her using it but it was not "an open way for everybody to go through." In 2003, Rand sold his property to the Lathrops. After buying the property, the Lathrops blocked the drive-way and prevented Aidinoff from using it to access her property. Aidinoff claimed that she had the right to use the driveway because she had acquired an easement by prescription and an easement by necessity. Did she?

4. A declaration of restrictive covenants for the Mains Farm subdivision was recorded in 1962. Worthington purchased a residential lot in Mains Farm in 1987. A house already existed on the property. Before the pur-chase, Worthington obtained and read a copy of the restrictive covenants, which stated in part that all lots in Mains Farms "shall be designated as 'Residence Lots' and shall be used for single-family residential purposes only." Worthington later began occupying the residence along with four adults who paid her for 24-hour protective supervision and care. These four adults, who were not related to Worthington, were unable to do their own housekeeping, prepare their own meals, or attend to their personal hygiene. In pro-viding this supervision and care on a for-profit basis, Worthington complied with the licensing and inspec-tion requirements established by state law, but she ob-tained the permit by stating that only her family would be living with her. The Mains Farm Homeowners As-sociation, which consisted of owners of property in

the subdivision, filed suit against Worthington, asserting that her use of her property violated the restrictive covenant. Will the association prevail?

5. In 1968, JEP bought a fully functioning theater in the Lake of the Ozarks. The building was designed and constructed as a live theater. It contained a raked concrete floor, 1,000 seats bolted to the floor, stage and backstage areas, a concession stand, and a ticket booth. In 1970, the building was converted to a movie theater. On April 1, 1973, JEP agreed to a 20-year lease with Jablonow-Komm Theatres. Shortly thereafter, and with the approval of JEP, Jablonow removed the old wooden seats and installed 733 fabric-covered plastic theater seats. Jablonow then transferred its interest in the lease and property to RKO Mid-America Theatres, Inc. In May 1982, JEP and RKO amended the 1973 lease, giving RKO the right to remodel the theater so that it had two screens instead of one for an increase in monthly rent. Two years later, RKO transferred its interest in the lease and property to Commonwealth Theatres of Missouri. As part of this transfer, RKO gave Commonwealth a "Bill of Sale and Assignment" that purported to transfer to Commonwealth 654 theater seats, "free and clear of all liens, encumbrances, claims, clouds, charges, equities, or imperfections of any kind or nature. . . ." In May 1985, Commonwealth transferred its interest in the lease and property to Wehrenberg. In April 1993, after the lease had expired and without JEP's approval, Wehrenberg uprooted the theater seats from the floor, breaking sections of concrete and leaving behind only the inclined floor, pocked with 2,600 holes. Were these seats fixtures?

6. In May 1994, the Hubers rented a house to Lois Olbekson, who was the daughter of their friends, Loren and Alice May Olbekson. Lois hoped to be able to purchase the house from the Hubers one day. The primary source of heat for the rental house was a wood furnace located in the basement. Lois was not happy with the wood furnace. In the fall of 1995, she persuaded her parents to buy an oil furnace to replace the wood furnace in the rental house. During the process of installing the new oil furnace, the old wood furnace was removed from the rental house at the Olbeksons' direction and hauled to the landfill. Installation of the oil furnace required wiring in a thermostat and drilling a hole in the wall to accommodate the fuel line from the outside oil tank, and the Olbeksons had to widen an existing doorway into the basement in order to accommodate the new oil furnace. The Olbeksons paid $2,525 to have the new oil furnace installed. The Hubers acquiesced in the installation of the new furnace, but would not have done so if they had believed that they would be required to purchase it. During the time that Lois lived in the Hubers' rental house, the Hubers spent approximately $28,000 remodeling it, yet collected only $175 per month in rent. Lois admitted that before the remodeling was complete, the reasonable rental value of the house was probably $250 per month. In order to placate her husband about the rent, Emelia prepared an agreement that purported to tie the low rent to compensation for the cost of the furnace. The agreement, which Emelia and Lois signed, stated as follows:

> During October 1995, a fuel furnace for $2,525.00 was installed at 317 W. Lincoln and paid for by Loren and Alice May Olbekson. To compensate for the expense of this heating device, rent on this residence will remain at $175.00 per month thru the duration of Nov. 1st, 1995 thru Dec. 31st 1997.

Lois continued to rent the house until September 2000. Even though the written agreement provided that Lois would enjoy reduced rent only until December 31, 1997, the Hubers did not raise the rent at any time prior to the termination of the tenancy. At the end of Lois's tenancy, the Olbeksons removed the outside oil tank. Do they have the right to remove the oil furnace as well?

7. The Buzby Landfill was operated from 1966 to 1978. Although it was not licensed to receive liquid industrial or chemical wastes, large amounts of hazardous materials and chemicals were dumped there. Toxic wastes began to escape from the landfill because it had no liner or cap. Tests performed by a state environmental protection agency revealed ground water contamination caused by hazardous waste seepage from the landfill. The federal Environmental Protection Agency investigated the situation and recommended that the Buzby Landfill site be considered for cleanup under the federal Superfund law, but the cleanup did not take place. During the 1980s, Canetic Corp. and Canuso Management Corp. developed a housing subdivision near the closed Buzby Landfill. Some of the homes in the subdivision were within half a mile of the old landfill. Some of the homeowners filed a class action lawsuit alleging that Canetic and Canuso had substantial information about the dangers of placing a subdivision near the landfill, but they had not disclosed to buyers the fact that the subdivision was located near a hazardous waste dump. The defendants claimed that they did not have the duty to disclose conditions that happened on someone else's property. Will the defendants win?

8. Voyeur Dorm operates an Internet-based website that provides a 24-hour-a-day Internet transmission portraying the lives of the residents of 2312 West Farwell Drive, Tampa, Florida. Throughout its existence, Voyeur Dorm has employed 25 to 30 different women, most of whom entered into a contract that specifies, among other things, that they are "employees," on a "stage and filming location," with "no reasonable expectation of privacy," for "entertainment purposes." Subscribers to voyeurdorm.com pay a subscription fee of $34.95 a month to watch the women employed at the premises and pay an added fee of $16.00 per month to "chat" with the women. At a zoning hearing, Voyeur Dorm's counsel conceded that five women live in the house, that there are cameras in the corners of all the rooms of the house, that for a fee a person can join a membership to a website wherein a member can view the women 24 hours a day, seven days a week, that a member, at times, can see someone disrobed, that the women receive free room and board, and that the women are paid as part of a business enterprise. From August 1998 to June 2000, Voyeur Dorm generated subscriptions and sales totaling $3,166,551.35.

Section 27–523 of Tampa's City Code defines adult entertainment establishments as:

> any premises . . . on which is offered to members of the public or any person, for a consideration, entertainment featuring or in any way including specified sexual activities . . . or entertainment featuring the displaying or depicting of specified anatomical areas . . .; "entertainment" as used in this definition shall include, but not be limited to, books, magazines, films, newspapers, photographs, paintings, drawings, sketches or other publications or graphic media, filmed or live plays, dances or other performances either by single individuals or groups, distinguished by their display or depiction of specified anatomical areas or specified sexual activities.

The City of Tampa argues that Voyeur Dorm is an adult use business pursuant to the express and unambiguous language of section 27–523 and, as such, cannot operate in a residential neighborhood. Is the city correct?

9. In 2003, Hall acquired a sculpture by Anselm Kiefer, a German artist, and placed it on the lawn of his property fronting Harbor Road in the Southport Historic District, which is one of three historic districts in Fairfield, Connecticut. The sculpture is approximately 80 feet long and weighs more than six tons. It was placed on a specially prepared trench filled with more than 21 tons of gravel and stone. The Fairfield Historic District Commission regulates the use of historic property under a Connecticut statute that states, "No building or structure shall be erected or altered within an historic district until after an application for a certificate of appropriateness as to exterior architectural features has been submitted to the historic district commission and approved by said commission." Hall initially filed an application for a "certificate of appropriateness" with the Commission, but withdrew it before the Commission acted on it and went ahead and installed the sculpture. The Commission filed an action against Hall, seeking to force Hall to remove the sculpture or file an application for a certification of appropriateness within 30 days. Hall claims that the sculpture is not a "structure" because it is not affixed to the land by direct physical attachment nor embedded in the ground, and therefore, the Commission has no jurisdiction over the placement of the sculpture. Is the sculpture likely to be considered a "structure?"

10. Michael and Nora Hoth married, divorced, remarried, divorced again, then cohabited from 1998 to 2008 without further remarriage. In 2006, Michael bought a house and five acres with his own money. Without discussion with Nora, Michael put both of their names on the deed "in case something happened" to him. Thereafter, Nora, Michael, and Michael's mother lived on the property. Michael paid the real estate taxes and other bills. Nora and Michael ended their relationship in 2008. Nora moved out and sued to partition the property, claiming half ownership. The evidence indicated that Michael put Nora's name on the deed to give her the property only when and if she survived him, so that his mother and children would be provided for. Was Nora an owner of the property?

Online Research

Researching Real Property on the Web

1. Using your favorite search engine, locate a website that lists real estate for sale. Find a property listing on one of these sites. Using the concepts discussed in this chapter, identify the property features on the listing that would be considered fixtures.

2. Find an example online of each of the following kinds of deeds: quitclaim deed, general warranty deed, and special warranty deed.

CHAPTER 26

ESTATES AND TRUSTS

George, an elderly widower, has no children of his own but enjoys a very close relationship with his two stepdaughters, his late wife's children by her first marriage. George's only living blood relative is his brother, from whom he has been estranged for many years. George has a substantial amount of property—his home, two cars, stocks and bonds, rental property, bank accounts, and a valuable collection of baseball cards. Though retired, George is an active volunteer for, and supporter of, several community charities and organizations. Presently, George does not have a will, but he is considering writing one.

- What will happen to George's property upon his death if he does not have a will at that time?
- What are the requirements for executing a valid will?
- What can cause a will to be invalid?
- After George's death, how would his estate be probated?
- If George decided to create a trust to benefit his stepdaughters, what is required to create a trust, and what are the legal duties of a trustee? What are the *ethical* duties of a trustee?

LO   LEARNING OBJECTIVES

After studying this chapter, you should be able to:

1 List and explain the requirements for a valid will.

2 Explain how wills can be changed and revoked.

3 Identify and explain the legal tools ("advance directives") available for planning for possible future disability.

4 Explain and provide examples of how property is disposed of when a person dies without leaving a will.

5 Identify the steps in the process of administering an estate, and explain the responsibilities of the personal representative for the estate.

6 Explain the concept of trust, identify various types of trusts, and explain the powers and responsibilities of a trustee.

7 List the requirements for the formation of a trust, and describe how trusts can be revoked or modified.

ONE OF THE BASIC features of the ownership of property is the right to dispose of the property during life and at death. You have already learned about the ways in which property is transferred during the owner's life. The owner's death is another major event for the transfer of property. Most people want to be able to choose who will get their property when they die. There are a variety of ways in which a person may control the ultimate disposition of his property. He may take title to the property in a form of joint ownership that gives his co-owner a right of survivorship. He may create a trust and transfer property to it to be used for the benefit of a spouse, child, elderly parent, or other beneficiary. He may execute a will in which he directs that his real and personal property be distributed to persons named in the will. If, however, a person makes no provision for the disposition of his property at his death, his property will be distributed to his heirs as defined by state law. This chapter focuses on the transfer of property at death and on the use of trusts for the transfer and management of property, both during life and at death.

The Law of Estates and Trusts

Each state has its own statutes and common law regulating the distribution of property upon death. Legal requirements and procedures may vary from state to state, but many general principles can be stated. The Uniform Probate Code (UPC) is a comprehensive, uniform law that has been enacted in 16 states. It is intended to update and unify state law concerning the disposition and administration of property at death. Several relevant UPC provisions will be discussed in this chapter.

Estate Planning A person's **estate** is all of the property owned by that person. Estate planning is the popular name for the complicated process of planning for the transfer of a person's estate in later life and at death. Estate planning also concerns planning for the possibility of prolonged illness or disability. An attorney who is creating an estate plan will take an inventory of the client's assets, learn the client's objectives, and draft the instruments necessary to carry out the plan. This plan is normally guided by the desire to reduce the amount of tax liability and to provide for the orderly disposition of the estate.

Wills

Right of Disposition by Will The right to control the disposition of property at death has not always existed. In the English feudal system, the king owned all land. The lords and knights had only the right to use land for their lifetime. A landholder's rights in land terminated upon his death, and no rights descended to his heirs. In 1215, the king granted the nobility the right to pass their interest in the land they held to their heirs. Later, that right was extended to all property owners. In the United States, each state has enacted statutes that establish the requirements for a valid will, including the formalities that must be met to pass property by will.

LO1 List and explain the requirements for a valid will.

Nature of a Will A **will** is a document executed with specific legal formalities by a **testator** (person making a will) that contains his instructions about the way his property will be disposed of at his death. A will can dispose only of property belonging to the testator at the time of his death. Furthermore, wills do not control property that goes to others through other planning devices (such as life insurance policies) or by operation of law (such as by right of survivorship). For example, property held in joint tenancy or tenancy by the entirety is not controlled by a will, because the property passes automatically to the surviving cotenant by right of survivorship. In addition, life insurance proceeds are controlled by the insured's designation of beneficiaries, not by any provision of a will. (Because joint tenancy and life insurance are ways of directing the disposition of property, they are sometimes referred to as "will substitutes.")

LOG ON

For discussion of why it is important to have a will, see Peter Weaver, *10 Good Reasons Why You Should Have a Will*, **http://www.thirdage.com/estate-planning/ 10-good-reasons-why-you-should-have-a-will** and Rebecca Berlin, *Wills: Why You Need One*, **www.alllaw.com/articles/ wills_and_trusts/article2.asp**.

Common Will Terminology Some legal terms commonly used in wills include the following:

1. *Bequest.* A **bequest** (also called **legacy**) is a gift of personal property or money. For example, a will might provide for a bequest of a family heirloom to the testator's daughter. Since a will can direct only property that is owned by the testator at the time of his death, a specific bequest of property that the testator has disposed of before his death is ineffective. This is called **ademption**. For example, Samuel's will states that Warren is to receive Samuel's collection of antique guns. If the guns are destroyed before Warren's death, however, the bequest is ineffective because of ademption.

2. *Devise.* A **devise** is a gift of real property. For example, the testator might devise his family farm to his grandson.

3. *Residuary.* The **residuary** is the balance of the estate that is left after specific devises and bequests are made by the will. After providing for the disposition of specific personal and real property, a testator might provide that the residuary of his estate is to go to his spouse or be divided among his descendants.

4. *Issue.* A person's **issue** are his lineal descendants (children, grandchildren, great-grandchildren, and so forth). This category of persons includes adopted children.

5. *Per capita.* This term and the next one, *per stirpes,* are used to describe the way in which a group of persons are to share a gift. **Per capita** means that each of that group of persons will share equally. For example, Grandfather dies, leaving a will that provides that the residuary of his estate is to go to his issue or descendants *per capita.* Grandfather had two children, Mary and Bill. Mary has two children, John and James. Bill has one child, Margaret. Mary and Bill die before Grandfather (in legal terms, *predecease* him), but all three of Grandfather's grandchildren are living at the time of his death. In this case, John, James, and Margaret would each take one-third of the residuary of Grandfather's estate.

6. *Per stirpes.* When a gift is given to the testator's issue or descendants **per stirpes** (also called by right of representation), each surviving descendant divides the share that his or her parent would have taken if the parent had survived. In the preceding example, if Grandfather's will had stated that the residuary of his estate was to go to his issue or descendants *per stirpes,* Margaret would take one-half and John and James would take one-quarter each (that is, they would divide the share that would have gone to their mother).

Testamentary Capacity

The capacity to make a valid will is called testamentary capacity. To have testamentary capacity, a person must be *of sound mind* and *of legal age,* which is 18 in most states. A person does not have to be in perfect mental health to have testamentary capacity. Because people often delay executing wills until they are weak and in ill health, the standard for mental capacity to make a will is fairly low. To be of "sound mind," a person need only be sufficiently rational to be capable of understanding the nature and character of his property, of realizing that he is making a will, and of knowing the persons who would normally be the beneficiaries of his affection. A person could move in and out of periods of lucidity and still have testamentary capacity if he executed his will during a lucid period.

Lack of testamentary capacity is a common ground upon which wills are challenged by persons who were excluded from a will. *Fraud* and *undue influence* are also common grounds for challenging the validity of a will.[1]

Execution of a Will

Unless a will is executed with the formalities required by state law, it is *void.* The courts are strict in interpreting statutes concerning the execution of wills. If a will is declared void, the property of the deceased person will be distributed according to the provisions of state laws that will be discussed later.

The formalities required for a valid will differ from state to state. For that reason, an individual should consult the laws of his state before making a will. If he should move to another state after having executed a will, he should consult a lawyer in his new state to determine whether a new will needs to be executed. All states require that a will be *in writing.* State law also requires that a formal will be *witnessed,* generally by two or three *disinterested* witnesses (persons who do not stand to inherit any property under the will), and that it be *signed* by the testator or by someone else at the testator's direction. Most states also require that the testator *publish* the will—that is, declare or indicate at the time of signing that the instrument is his will. Another formality required by most states is that the testator sign the will in the presence and the sight of the witnesses and that the witnesses sign in the presence and the sight of each other. As a general rule, an attestation clause, which states the formalities that have been followed in the execution of the will, is written following the testator's signature. These detailed formalities are designed to prevent fraud. Section 2–502 of the UPC requires that a will must be in writing, signed by the testator (or in the testator's name by some other individual in the testator's conscious presence and by the testator's direction), and signed by at least two individuals, each of whom signed within a reasonable time after he witnessed either the signing of the will or the testator's acknowledgment of that signature or will. Also, under the UPC, any individual who is generally competent to be a witness may witness a will, and the fact that the witness is an interested party does not invalidate the will [2–505]. When a testator has made a technical error in executing a will, however, the UPC permits the document to be treated as if it had been executed properly if it can be proven by clear and convincing evidence that the testator intended the document to constitute his will [2–503]. The following *Zimmerman* case provides an example of how courts deal with technical problems in a will.

In some situations, a lawyer might arrange to have the execution of a will *videotaped* to provide evidence relating to the testator's capacity and the use of proper formalities. (Note that the will is executed in the normal way; the videotape merely records the execution of the will.) Some state probate codes specifically provide that videotapes of the executions of wills are admissible into evidence.

---

[1]Fraud and undue influence are discussed in detail in Chapter 13.

Zimmerman v. Allen	250 P.3d 558 (Ariz. Ct. App. 2011)

Gloria Waterloo belonged to a congregation of which Jack Zimmerman is the Senior Rabbi. In April 2008, Zimmerman and his wife, Sandie, visited Waterloo in a hospice facility. Because handwriting was difficult for Waterloo, she dictated to Sandie a document that stated:

To Whom It Concerns: April 11, 08

My name is Gloria Anne Waterloo. I live at [address]. The reason for this letter is so that my wishes are carried out by Jack Howard Zimmerman Also known as Rabbi Jack. He lives at [address].

1. I want Him Jack Zimmerman to have full guardianship of My Health Decisions along with Myself.
2. Also as far as my finances, and realestate transaction I want Jack Zimmerman to have full guardianship along with Myself.
3. Properties are in CCA As of 2003, I have properties in many countries in CCA.
4. After I am deceased Jack has full instructions frome me. Attached is a list of final instructions I want to leave Jack Howard Zimmerman A sum of $3,000,000 or more Three Million dollars, or More. He has full & final guardianship of my finances & realestate properties.
5. As far as a Memorial Service I want Rabbi Jack to organize All of it. I am to be buried next to my husband Dale Bec Waterloo at Sunny Slope Memorial in Sunny Slope, Phoenix.

In the presence of the Zimmermans, Waterloo reviewed the one-page document, initialed each of the five numbered paragraphs, and dated and signed the document at the bottom. Notwithstanding the document's reference to an "attached list of final instructions," Waterloo dictated no such list and no such list ever was attached to the instrument. About an hour after Waterloo dictated the document, another couple from the congregation arrived to visit her. One of them read the document aloud to Waterloo and confirmed with her that it represented her wishes.

Waterloo died less than a month later. After first petitioning for a declaration that Waterloo died intestate, Zimmerman petitioned the court to probate the document as a will.

Waterloo's heirs then moved for partial summary judgment, arguing that the document could not be admitted to probate because it was incomplete. They contended that because it referenced a "list of final instructions" that did not exist, the document failed as a will because it did not represent Waterloo's full testamentary intent. The court granted the heirs' motion, ruling it could not ascertain Waterloo's "complete intent . . . without knowing what was to be contained in the list of instructions." Zimmerman appealed.

Johnsen, Judge

A will is a "legal declaration of one's intentions, which he wills to be performed after death. It is not necessary that the testator use the word 'will' in his last testament. No particular words need be used, it being sufficient if it appears that the maker intended to dispose of his property after his death. . . . A letter written and signed by the author may serve as his last will where it contains testamentary language indicating that it was so intended." *In re: Miller's Estate* (Ariz. 1939).

To be treated as a will, an instrument that satisfies the requirement of testamentary intent must be properly executed. A non-holographic will must be signed by the testator or in the testator's name by some other individual in the testator's conscious presence and by the testator's direction, and must be signed by two witnesses. An instrument that demonstrates testamentary intent and complies with the statutory execution requisites should be admitted to probate as a will even though all of its terms are not capable of being enforced. The only issue in a will contest is whether the will is valid.

There is no question that Waterloo signed the document at issue (she even initialed each of the five numbered paragraphs that make up the substance of the document). As for the statutory witness

requirement, Waterloo's heirs did not cross-appeal from the superior court's decision accepting the affidavits of the Zimmermans and the other couple for that purpose. Thus, the only issue before the court in the contested will proceeding was whether the letter Waterloo dictated contained her testamentary intent.

The heirs correctly do not dispute that the document Waterloo dictated contains testamentary language indicating it was intended to constitute a will. Waterloo gave burial instructions in the letter and made provisions for what was to happen "[a]fter I am deceased." The use of certain formal phrases and the care that Waterloo took to initial the sections of substance and to sign and date the instrument also demonstrate testamentary intent. The superior court, however, refused to admit the will to probate based on its conclusion that the absence of the "list of final instructions" referenced in Waterloo's letter made it impossible to determine her "complete intent." On appeal, the heirs argue that we should affirm because the absence of the "list of final instructions" means that, as a matter of law, Waterloo lacked testamentary intent when she signed the letter.

In considering this argument, we are mindful that, as a general matter, an instrument will be admitted to probate even if it is vague or incomplete in some respects, as long as "there is a single portion of the instrument which is certain in its character." *In Re: Harris' Estate* (Ariz. 1931). Therefore, if some of an instrument's testamentary terms are clear, a court may not decline to admit the will to probate simply because other terms are indefinite.

Although this rule normally will doom the argument that an instrument that demonstrates testamentary intent is too ambiguous to admit to probate, we understand the heirs to argue not that the instrument is fatally ambiguous but that the omission of the "list of final instructions" necessarily means that Waterloo lacked testamentary intent when she created the letter. For the reasons set forth below, however, we conclude that the absence of the list does not disprove the presumption we are required to apply in favor of testacy.

Significantly, Waterloo executed the instrument knowing that she had not created the list. Waterloo placed the date and her signature at the bottom of the single page that contained what she had dictated. From that we conclude she was satisfied with what she had dictated and that she believed that the instrument she executed adequately expressed her testamentary intent even though it lacked the "list" that she apparently had once intended to create.

The heirs argue, however, that public policy requires us to affirm the order denying probate. They argue that a contrary ruling would encourage the filing of partial wills for probate, with petitioners submitting "only pages of a will that are advantageous to them, while withholding pages that are not in their favor." But the heirs do not allege any fraud on Zimmerman's part, and the situation the heirs posit is not present here, when the evidence is undisputed that the "missing" document never existed.

Zimmerman asks that beyond ordering that the letter be admitted to probate, we construe the instrument to contain a bequest to him of "$3,000,000 or more." The heirs argue that, at most, the letter is a direction that Zimmerman be appointed "guardian" of Waterloo's estate. We decline both sides' suggestions to construe the will and instead remand the matter to the superior court to conduct all further proceedings that may be required to determine the meaning of the instrument's various terms.

Vacated and remanded with instructions to admit Waterloo's will to probate.

Incorporation by Reference In some situations, a testator might want his will to refer to and incorporate an existing writing. For example, the testator may have created a list of specific gifts of personal property that he wants to incorporate in the will. A writing such as this is called an extrinsic document—that is, a writing apart from the will. In most states, the contents of extrinsic documents can be essentially incorporated into the will when the circumstances satisfy rules that have been designed to ensure that the document is genuine and that it was intended by the testator to be incorporated in the will. This is called incorporation by reference. For an extrinsic document to be incorporated by reference, it must have been *in existence at the time the will was executed.* In addition, the writing and the will must refer to each other so that the extrinsic document can be identified and so that it is clear that the testator intended the extrinsic document to be incorporated in the will. Under the UPC, incorporation by reference is allowed when the extrinsic document was in existence when the will was executed, the language of the will manifests the intent to incorporate the writing, and the will describes the writing sufficiently to identify it [2–510].

Informal Wills Some states recognize certain types of wills that are not executed with these formalities. These are:

1. *Nuncupative wills.* A nuncupative will is an oral will. Such wills are recognized as valid in some states, but only under limited circumstances and to a limited extent. In a number of states, for example, nuncupative wills are valid only when made by soldiers in military service and sailors at sea, and even then they will be effective only to dispose of personal property that was in the actual possession of the person at the time the oral will was made. Other states place low dollar limits on the amount of property that can be passed by a nuncupative will.

2. *Holographic wills.* **Holographic wills** are wills that are written and signed in the testator's handwriting. The fact that holographic wills are not properly witnessed makes them suspect. They are recognized in about half of the states and by section 2–502(b) of the UPC, even though they are not executed with the formalities usually required of valid wills. For a holographic will to be valid in the states that recognize them, it must evidence testamentary intent and must actually be *handwritten* by the testator. A typed holographic will would be invalid. Some states require that the holographic will be *entirely* handwritten—although the UPC requires only that the signature and material portions of the will be handwritten by the testator [2–502(b)]—and some also require that the will be dated.

Joint and Mutual Wills In some circumstances, two or more people—a married couple, for example—decide together on a plan for the disposition of their property at death. To carry out this plan, they may execute a joint will (a single instrument that constitutes the will of both or all of the testators and is executed by both or all) or they may execute mutual wills (joint or separate, individual wills that reflect the common plan of distribution).

Underlying a joint or mutual will is an agreement on a common plan. This common plan often includes an express or implied contract (a contract to make a will or not to revoke the will). One issue that sometimes arises is whether a testator who has made a joint or mutual will can later change his will. Whether joint and mutual wills are revocable depends on the language of the will, on state law, and on the timing of the revocation. For example, a testator who made a joint will with his spouse may be able to revoke his will during the life of his spouse, because the spouse still has a chance to change her own will, but he may be unable to revoke or change the will after the death of his spouse. The UPC provides that the mere fact that a joint or mutual will has been executed does *not* create the presumption of a contract not to revoke the will or wills [2–514].

Construction of Wills
Even in carefully drafted wills, questions sometimes arise as to the meaning or legal effect of a term or provision. Disputes about the meaning of the will are even more likely to occur in wills drafted by the testator himself, such as holographic wills. To interpret a will, a court will examine the entire instrument in an attempt to determine the testator's intent.

Limitations on Disposition by Will
A person who takes property by will takes it subject to all outstanding claims against the property. For example, if real property is subject to a mortgage or other lien, the beneficiary who takes the property gets it subject to the mortgage or lien. In addition, the rights of the testator's creditors are superior to the rights of beneficiaries under his will. Thus, if the testator was insolvent (his debts exceeded his assets), persons named as beneficiaries do not receive any property by virtue of the will.

Under the laws of most states, the surviving spouse of the testator has statutory rights in property owned solely by the testator that cannot be defeated by a contrary will provision. This means that a husband cannot effectively disinherit his wife, and vice versa. Even if the will provides for the surviving spouse, he or she can elect to take his or her elective share of the decedent's estate that would be provided by state law rather than the amount specified in the will. In some states, personal property, such as furniture, passes automatically to the surviving spouse.

At common law, a widow had the right to a life estate in one-third of the lands owned by her husband during their marriage. This was known as a widow's **dower right.** A similar right for a widower was known as **curtesy.** A number of states have changed the right by statute to give a surviving spouse a one-half to one-third interest in fee simple in the real and personal property owned by the deceased spouse at the time of his or her death. (Naturally, a testator can leave his spouse more than this if he desires.) Under UPC 2–201, the surviving spouse's elective share varies depending on the length of the surviving spouse's marriage to the testator—the elective share increases with the length of marriage.

As a general rule, a surviving spouse is given the right to use the family home for a stated period as well as a portion of the deceased spouse's estate. In community property states, each spouse has a one-half interest in community property that cannot be defeated by a contrary will provision. (Note that the surviving spouse will obtain *full* ownership of any property owned by the testator and the surviving spouse as joint tenants or tenants by the entirety.)

Ethics in Action

Dr. Coggins died in 1963. In his last will, Dr. Coggins gave the residue of his estate to the Mercantile–Safe Deposit & Trust Company, to be held by it as trustee under the will. The trust provided for monthly payments to four income beneficiaries until the death of the last of them. The last of these annuitants was Dr. Coggins's widow, who died in 1998. A provision of the will stated that, upon the death of the survivor of the four annuitants, the trust would terminate and the assets and all unpaid income shall be paid over "free of trust unto the Keswick Home, formerly Home for Incurables of Baltimore City, with the request that said Home use the estate and property thus passing to it for the acquisition or construction of a new building to provide additional housing accommodations to be known as the 'Coggins Building,' to house white patients who need physical rehabilitation. If not acceptable to the Keswick Home, then this bequest shall go to the University of Maryland Hospital to be used for physical rehabilitation." What are the major ethical considerations involved in determining whether this will provision should be enforced?

Children of the testator who were born or adopted after the will was executed are called **pretermitted** children. There is a presumption that the testator intended to provide for such a child, unless there is evidence to the contrary. State law gives pretermitted children the right to a share of the testator's estate. For example, under section 2–302 of the Uniform Probate Code, a pretermitted child has the right to receive the share he would have received under the state intestacy statute unless it appears that the omission of this child was intentional, the testator gave substantially all of his estate to the child's other parent, or the testator provided for the child outside of the will.

 L02 Explain how wills can be changed and revoked.

Revocation of Wills One important feature of a will is that it is *revocable* until the moment of the testator's death. For this reason, a will confers *no present interest* in the testator's property. A person is free to revoke a prior will and, if she wishes, to make a new will. Wills can be revoked in a variety of ways. Physical destruction and mutilation done with intent to revoke a will constitute revocation, as do other acts such as crossing out the will or creating a writing that expressly cancels the will.

In addition, a will is revoked if the testator later executes a valid will that expressly revokes the earlier will. A later will that does not *expressly* revoke an earlier will operates to revoke only those portions of the earlier will that are inconsistent with the later will. Under the UPC, a later will that does not expressly revoke a prior will operates to revoke it by inconsistency if the testator intended the subsequent will to *replace* rather than *supplement* the prior will [2–507(b)]. Furthermore, the UPC presumes that the testator intended the subsequent will to replace rather than supplement the prior will if the subsequent one makes a complete disposition of her estate, but it presumes that the testator intended merely to supplement and not replace the prior will if the subsequent will disposes of only part of her estate [2–507(c), 2–507(d)]. In some states, a will is presumed to have been revoked if it cannot be located after the testator's death, although this presumption can be rebutted with contrary evidence.

Wills can also be revoked by operation of law without any act on the part of the testator signifying revocation. State statutes provide that certain changes in relationships operate as revocations of a will. In some states, marriage will operate to revoke a will that was made when the testator was single. Similarly, a divorce may revoke provisions in a will made during marriage that leave property to the divorced spouse. Under the laws of some states, the birth of a child after the execution of a will may operate as a partial revocation of the will.

Codicils A **codicil** is an amendment of a will. If a person wants to change a provision of a will without making an entirely new will, she may amend the will by executing a codicil. One may *not* amend a will by merely striking out objectionable provisions and inserting new provisions. The same formalities are required for the creation of a valid codicil as for the creation of a valid will.

 L03 Identify and explain the legal tools ("advance directives") available for planning for possible future disability.

Advance Directives: Planning for Disability

Advances in medical technology now permit a person to be kept alive by artificial means, even in many cases in which there is no hope of the person being able to function without life support. Many people are opposed to their lives being prolonged with no chance of recovery. In response to these concerns, almost all states have enacted statutes permitting individuals to state their choices about the medical procedures that should be administered or withheld if they should become incapacitated in the future and cannot recover. Collectively, these devices are called **advance directives.** An advance directive is a written document (such as a living will or durable power of attorney) that directs others how future health care decisions should be made in the event that the individual becomes incapacitated.

Living Wills **Living wills** are documents in which a person states in advance his intention to forgo or obtain certain life-prolonging medical procedures. Almost all states have enacted statutes recognizing living wills. These statutes also establish the elements and formalities required to create a valid living will and describe the legal effect of living wills. Currently, the law concerning living wills is primarily a matter of state law and differs from state to state. Living wills are typically included with a

Figure 1 *Living Will*

LIVING WILL DECLARATION*

Declaration made this _____ day of _____ (month, year). I, _____, being at least eighteen (18) years of age and of sound mind, willfully and voluntarily make known my desires that my dying shall not be artificially prolonged under the circumstances set forth below, and I declare:

If at any time my attending physician certifies in writing that: (1) I have an incurable injury, disease, or illness; (2) my death will occur within a short time; and (3) the use of life prolonging procedures would serve only to artificially prolong the dying process, I direct that such procedures be withheld or withdrawn, and that I be permitted to die naturally with only the performance or provision of any medical procedure or medication necessary to provide me with comfort care or to alleviate pain, and, if I have so indicated below, the provision of artificially supplied nutrition and hydration. (Indicate your choice by initialing or making your mark before signing this declaration):

___I wish to receive artificially supplied nutrition and hydration, even if the effort to sustain life is futile or excessively burdensome to me.

___I do not wish to receive artificially supplied nutrition and hydration, if the effort to sustain life is futile or excessively burdensome to me.

___I intentionally make no decision concerning artificially supplied nutrition and hydration, leaving the decision to my health care representative appointed under IC 16–36–1–7 or my attorney in fact with health care powers under IC 30–5–5.

In the absence of my ability to give directions regarding the use of life prolonging procedures, it is my intention that this declaration be honored by my family and physician as the final expression of my legal right to refuse medical or surgical treatment and accept the consequences of the refusal.

I understand the full import of this declaration.

Signed: _____

City, County, and State of Residence

The declarant has been personally known to me, and I believe (him/her) to be of sound mind. I did not sign the declarant's signature above for or at the direction of the declarant. I am not a parent, spouse, or child of the declarant. I am not entitled to any part of the declarant's estate or directly financially responsible for the declarant's medical care. I am competent and at least eighteen (18) years of age.

Witness _____ Date _____

Witness _____ Date _____

*From Ind. Code § 16–36 4–10 (1999).

patient's medical records. Many states require physicians and other health care providers to follow the provisions of a valid living will. Because living wills are created by statute, it is important that all terms and conditions of one's state statute be followed. Figure 1 shows an example of a living will form.

Durable Power of Attorney Another technique of planning for the eventuality that one may be unable to make decisions for oneself is to execute a document that gives another person the legal authority to act on one's behalf in the case of mental or physical incapacity. This document is called a **durable power of attorney.**

A *power of attorney* is an express statement in which one person (the **principal**) gives another person (the **attorney in fact**) the authority to do an act or series of acts on his behalf. For example, Andrews enters into a contract to sell his house to Willis, but he must be out of state on the date of the real estate closing. He gives Paulsen a power of attorney to attend the closing and execute the deed on his behalf. Ordinary powers of attorney terminate upon the principal's incapacity. By contrast, the *durable power of attorney* is not affected if the principal becomes incompetent.

A durable power of attorney permits a person to give someone else extremely broad powers to make decisions and enter transactions such as those involving real and personal property, bank accounts, and health care, and to specify that those powers will not terminate upon incapacity. The durable power of attorney is an extremely important planning device. For example, a durable power of attorney executed by an elderly parent to an adult child at a time in which the parent is competent would permit the child to take care of matters such as investments, property, bank accounts, and hospital admission. Without the durable power of attorney, the child would be forced to apply to a court for a guardianship, which is a more expensive and often less efficient manner in which to handle personal and business affairs.

Durable Power of Attorney for Health Care

The majority of states have enacted statutes specifically providing for **durable powers of attorney for health care** (sometimes called **health care representatives**). This is a type of durable power of attorney in which the principal specifically gives the attorney in fact the authority to make certain health care decisions for him if the principal should become incompetent. Depending on state law and the instructions given by the principal to the attorney in fact, this could include decisions such as consenting or withholding consent to surgery, admitting the principal to a nursing home, and possibly withdrawing or prolonging life support. Note that the durable power of attorney becomes relevant only in the event that the principal becomes incompetent. So long as the principal is competent, he retains the ability to make his own health care decisions. This power of attorney is also revocable at the will of the principal. The precise requirements for creation of the durable power of attorney differ from state to state, but all states require a written and signed document executed with specified formalities, such as witnessing by disinterested witnesses.

Federal Law and Advance Directives

A federal statute, The Patient Self-Determination Act,[2] requires health care providers to take active steps to educate people about the opportunity to make advance decisions about medical care and the prolonging of life and to record the choices that they make. This statute, which became effective in 1991, requires health care providers such as hospitals, nursing homes, hospices, and home health agencies, to provide written information to adults receiving medical care about their rights concerning the ability to accept or refuse medical or surgical treatment, the health care provider's policies concerning those rights, and their right to formulate advance directives. The act also requires

the provider to document in the patient's medical record whether the patient has executed an advance directive, and it forbids discrimination against the patient based on the individual's choice regarding an advance directive. In addition, the provider is required to ensure compliance with the requirements of state law concerning advance directives and to educate its staff and the community on issues concerning advance directives.

 Explain and provide examples of how property is disposed of when a person dies without leaving a will.

Intestacy

If a person dies without making a will, or if he makes a will that is declared invalid, he is said to have died **intestate.** When that occurs, his property will be distributed to the persons designated as the intestate's heirs under the appropriate state's intestacy or intestate succession statute. The intestate's real property will be distributed according to the intestacy statute of the state in which the property is located. His personal property will be distributed according to the intestacy statute of the state in which he was **domiciled** at the time of his death. A domicile is a person's permanent home. A person can have only one domicile at a time. Determinations of a person's domicile turn on facts that tend to show that person's intent to make a specific state his permanent home.

Characteristics of Intestacy Statutes

The provisions of intestacy statutes are not uniform. Their purpose, however, is to distribute property in a way that reflects the *presumed intent* of the deceased—that is, to distribute it to the persons most closely related to him. In general, such statutes first provide for the distribution of most or all of a person's estate to his surviving spouse, children, or grandchildren. If no such survivors exist, the statutes typically provide for the distribution of the estate to parents, siblings, or nieces and nephews. If no relatives at this level are living, the property may be distributed to surviving grandparents, uncles, aunts, or cousins. Generally, persons with the same degree of relationship to the deceased person take equal shares. If the deceased had no surviving relatives, the property **escheats** (goes) to the state.

Figure 2 shows an example of a distribution scheme under an intestacy statute.

In the following *Estate of McDaniel v. McDaniel* case, you will see a court's determination of who should inherit from a person who died intestate.

___
[2]42 U.S.C. section 1395cc (1990).

Figure 2 *Example of a Distribution Scheme under an Intestacy Statute*

Person Dying Intestate Is Survived By	Result
1. Spouse* and child or issue of a deceased child	Spouse ½, Child ½
2. Spouse and parent(s) but no issue	Spouse ¾, Parent ¼
3. Spouse but no parent or issue	All of the estate to spouse
4. Issue but no spouse	Estate is divided among issue
5. Parent(s), brothers, sisters, and/or issue of deceased brothers and sisters but no spouse or issue	Estate is divided among parent(s), brothers, sisters, and issue of deceased brothers and sisters
6. Issue of brothers and sisters but no spouse, issue, parents, brothers and sisters	Estate is divided among issue of deceased brothers, and sisters
7. Grandparents, but no spouse, issue, parents, brothers, sisters, or issue of deceased brothers and sisters	All of the estate goes to grandparents
8. None of the above	Estate goes to the state

*Note, however, second and subsequent spouses who had no children by the decedent may be assigned a smaller share.

Estate of McDaniel v. McDaniel	73 Cal. Rptr. 3d 907 (Cal. Ct. App. 2008)

Troy and Marie McDaniel were married in August 2003. Their marriage was troubled, and Marie filed a petition for dissolution of the marriage in October 2004. Troy filed his response to the petition in April 2005. In May 2005, Marie and Troy each executed an "Interspousal Transfer Grant Deed," in which they released their interest in the other party's property. They also waived their right to appeal. On July 25, 2005, the court entered a stipulated judgment dissolving the marriage and ordering that the marital partnership be terminated and the parties be restored to the status of single persons effective October 29, 2005.

Nevertheless, Marie and Troy were apparently attempting to reconcile and end the dissolution proceedings before the marital partnership finally terminated on October 29, 2005. Both Marie and Troy attended counseling, and Marie attended Alcoholics Anonymous meetings with Troy. In April 2005, they each signed a private agreement providing that Marie would seek to vacate a restraining order against Troy, that they would attend counseling, that they would continue their marriage, and that they would keep their dissolution action open, "both knowing that we can cancel and dismiss anytime before the final date of termination." Troy and Marie also signed, but did not date or file, a request for dismissal of the dissolution action. According to Marie, they had intended to file the request after Troy attended a hearing on a criminal matter related to their marital differences on September 29.

Troy died in a motorcycle accident on September 23; however, and the request for dismissal of the dissolution action was never filed. Troy's mother, Marianne, filed a petition for entitlement of distribution of Troy's estate. Her petition alleged that Troy had died intestate, that he did not have and had not had any children, and that Marianne and Troy's father, Lyle, were entitled to have Troy's estate distributed equally between them. Marie opposed this position, arguing that, despite the dissolution proceeding, she was still Troy's wife at the time of his death and therefore entitled to inherit his estate.

The trial court held that Marie was not Troy's "surviving spouse" within the meaning of the Probate Code at the time of his death, and she was not entitled to inherit from his estate. The court granted Marianne's petition for distribution. Marie appealed.

Hull, Judge

Section 78, subdivision (d) provides that a "surviving spouse" for purposes of the Probate Code does not include "[a] person who was a party to a valid proceeding concluded by an order purporting to terminate all marital property rights." It is apparent that the parties divided their community property, confirmed their individual share of what was formerly community property as separate property, and waived spousal support, thus accounting for and terminating their marital property rights. It is equally apparent that, given the waiver of their right to appeal, the judgment dividing their marital property became final when entered by the court on July 25, 2005, and that the proceedings regarding their marital property were then concluded. Under the circumstances, we find that Marie was, by the time of Troy's death, "a party to a valid proceeding concluded by an order purporting to terminate all marital property rights" within the meaning of section 78, subdivision (d).

We find support for our holding in *Estate of Lahey*. In *Lahey*, Frances and Clarence Lahey were married in 1984 and they separated in March 1995. In April 1995 Frances petitioned for a legal separation alleging that there were no community debts or assets, waiving spousal support, and requesting that the court terminate any right of spousal support for Clarence. The court entered an order to that effect in July 1995. Clarence died intestate in December 1996 and Frances claimed one-half of his estate as the surviving spouse. While recognizing that a judgment of legal separation left the bonds of marriage intact, the Court of Appeal pointed out that a surviving spouse for purposes of intestate succession is different from a husband or wife of a decedent. The question before the *Lahey* court was whether the judgment of legal separation constituted an order purporting to terminate marital property rights within the meaning of section 78, subdivision (d). The court, noting that a judgment of legal separation is a final adjudication of the parties' property rights and is conclusive as to those rights, held that it did. There is no principled basis to reach a different result here.

Marie concedes that to the extent the judgment expressly divided marital property rights and recited the parties' agreement to waive spousal support, the judgment was final as to those matters at the time it was entered. But she attempts to avoid the effect of section 78, subdivision (d) by arguing that, although the July 25 judgment may have settled property rights, it did not settle inheritance rights. She enlists the support of a number of older cases—all of which were decided before the enactment of section 78, subdivision (d)—that construe the breadth of marital settlement agreements and decide whether those agreements were intended by the parties to determine inheritance rights. In this, Marie misses the mark. "Nothing in the language or meaning of [section 78, subdivision (d)] requires . . . an express termination of inheritance rights, for the obvious effect of the statute itself is to terminate the inheritance rights of such a spouse." *Lahey, supra.*

We agree with that reading of the statute. In whatever manner spousal inheritance rights might be determined under other circumstances, under the circumstances presented here, section 78, subdivision (d) determines such rights, denying them to a person in Marie's position because she is not deemed a surviving spouse within the meaning of the Probate Code and is therefore ineligible to inherit all or any of Troy's estate.

To the extent that Marie relies for relief on the provisions of Family Code section 2339, we must reject that argument also. That section provides that "no judgment of dissolution is final for the purpose of terminating the marriage relationship of the parties until six months have expired from the date of service of a copy of summons and petition or the date of appearance of the respondent, whichever occurs first." Both parties agree, and the judgment states, that Marie and Troy's marital status did not terminate, nor were they to be restored to the status of single persons until October 29, 2005. But Marie's reliance on Family Code section 2339 ignores the difference between her legal status as Troy's wife at the time of his death and her legal status as a "surviving spouse" at the time of his death. She was at that time legally his wife but she was not his surviving spouse.

Having been a party to a valid proceeding concluded by an order terminating all marital property rights, Marie was not Troy's surviving spouse at the time of his death and she could not share in his estate.

Affirmed in favor of Marianne.

Special Rules

Under intestacy statutes, a person must have a relationship to the deceased person through blood or marriage in order to inherit any part of his property. State law includes adopted children within the definition of "children," and treats adopted children in the same way as it treats biological children. Normally adopted children inherit from their adoptive families and not from their biological families, although some state's laws may allow them to inherit from both. Half brothers and half sisters are usually treated in the same way as brothers and sisters related by whole blood. An illegitimate child may inherit from his mother, but as a general rule, illegitimate children do not inherit from their fathers unless paternity has been either acknowledged or established in a legal proceeding.

A person must be alive at the time the decedent dies to claim a share of the decedent's estate. An exception may be made for pretermitted children or other descendants who are born *after* the decedent's death. If a person who is entitled to a share of the decedent's estate survives the decedent but dies before receiving his share, his share in the decedent's estate becomes part of his own estate.

Simultaneous Death

A statute known as the Uniform Simultaneous Death Act provides that where two persons who would inherit from each other (such as husband and wife) die under circumstances that make it difficult or impossible to determine who died first, each person's property is to be distributed as though he or she survived. This means, for example, that the husband's property will go to his relatives and the wife's property to her relatives.

Identify the steps in the process of administering an estate, and explain the responsibilities of the personal representative for the estate.

Administration of Estates

When a person dies, an orderly procedure is needed to collect his property, settle his debts, and distribute any remaining property to those who will inherit it under his will or by intestate succession. This process occurs under the supervision of a probate court and is known as the administration process or the probate process. Summary (simple) procedures are sometimes available when an estate is relatively small—for example, when it has assets of less than $7,500.

The Probate Estate
The probate process operates only on the decedent's property that is considered to be part of his probate estate. The probate estate is that property belonging to the decedent at the time of his death other than property held in joint ownership with right of survivorship, proceeds of insurance policies payable to a trust or a third party, property held in a revocable trust during the decedent's lifetime in which a third party is the beneficiary, or retirement benefits, such as pensions, payable to a third party. Assets that pass by operation of law and assets that are transferred by other devices such as trusts or life insurance policies do not pass through probate.

Note that the decedent's probate estate and his *taxable estate* for purposes of federal estate tax are two different concepts. The taxable estate includes all property owned or controlled by the decedent at the time of his death. For example, if a person purchased a $1 million life insurance policy made payable to his spouse or children, the policy would be included in his taxable estate, but not in his probate estate.

Determining the Existence of a Will
The first step in the probate process is to determine whether the deceased left a will. This may require a search of the deceased person's personal papers and safe-deposit box. If a will is found, it must be *proved* to be admitted to probate. This involves the testimony of the persons who witnessed the will, if they are still alive. If the witnesses are no longer alive, the signatures of the witnesses and the testator will have to be established in some other way. In many states and under UPC section 2–504, a will may be proved by an affidavit (declaration under oath) sworn to and signed by the testator and the witnesses at the time the

will was executed. This is called a self-proving affidavit. If a will is located and proved, it will be admitted to probate and govern many of the decisions that must be made in the administration of the estate.

Selecting a Personal Representative
Another early step in the administration of an estate is the selection of a personal representative to administer the estate. If the deceased left a will, it is likely that he designated his personal representative in the will. The personal representative under a will is also known as the **executor.** Almost anyone could serve as an executor. The testator may have chosen, for example, his spouse, a grown child, a close friend, an attorney, or the trust department of a bank.

If the decedent died intestate, or if the personal representative named in a will is unable to serve, the probate court will name a personal representative to administer the estate. In the case of an intestate estate, the personal representative is called an **administrator.** A preference is usually accorded to a surviving spouse, child, or other close relative. If no relative is available and qualified to serve, a creditor, bank, or other person may be appointed by the court.

Most states require that the personal representative *post a bond* in an amount in excess of the estimated value of the estate to ensure that her duties will be properly and faithfully performed. A person making a will often directs that his executor may serve without posting a bond, and this exemption may be accepted by the court.

Responsibilities of the Personal Representative
The personal representative has a number of important tasks in the administration of the estate. She must see that an inventory is taken of the estate's assets and that the assets are appraised. Notice must then be given to creditors or potential claimants against the estate so that they can file and prove their claims within a specified time, normally five months. As a general rule, the surviving spouse of the deceased person is entitled to be paid an allowance during the time the estate is being settled. This allowance has priority over other debts of the estate. The personal representative must see that any properly payable funeral or burial expenses are paid and that the creditors' claims are satisfied.

Both federal and state governments impose estate or inheritance taxes on estates of a certain size. The personal representative is responsible for filing estate tax returns. The federal tax is a tax on the deceased's estate, with provisions for deducting items such as debts, expenses of administration, and charitable gifts. In addition, an amount equal to the amount left to the surviving spouse may be deducted from the gross estate before the tax is computed. State inheritance taxes are imposed on the person who receives a gift or statutory share from an estate. It is common, however, for wills to provide that the estate will pay all taxes, including inheritance taxes, so that the beneficiaries will not have to do so. The personal representative must also make provisions for filing an income tax return and for paying any income tax due for the partial year prior to the decedent's death.

When the debts, expenses, and taxes have been taken care of, the remaining assets of the estate are distributed to the decedent's heirs (if there was no will) or to the beneficiaries of the decedent's will. Special rules apply when the estate is too small to satisfy all of the bequests made in a will or when some or all of the designated beneficiaries are no longer living.

When the personal representative has completed all of these duties, the probate court will close the estate and discharge the personal representative.

 Explain the concept of trust, identify various types of trusts, and explain the powers and responsibilities of a trustee.

Trusts

Nature of a Trust
A **trust** is a legal relationship in which a person who has legal title to property has the duty to hold it for the use or benefit of another person. The person benefited by a trust is considered to have equitable title to the property, because it is being maintained for his benefit. This means that he is the real owner even though the trustee has the legal title in his or her name. A trust can be created in a number of ways. An owner of property may *declare* that he is holding certain property in trust. For example, a mother might state that she is holding 100 shares of General Motors stock in trust for her daughter. A trust may also arise *by operation of law*. For example, when a lawyer representing a client injured in an automobile accident receives a settlement payment from an insurance company, the lawyer holds the settlement payment as trustee for the client. Most commonly, however, trusts are created through *express instruments* whereby an owner of property transfers title to the property to a trustee who is to hold, manage, and invest the property for the benefit of either the original owner or a third person. For example, Long transfers certain stock to First Trust Bank with instructions to pay the income to his daughter during her lifetime and to distribute the stock to her children after her death.

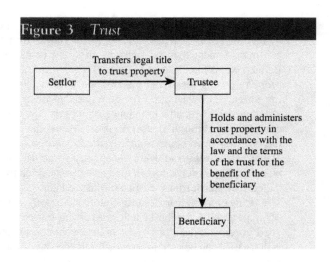

Figure 3   Trust

Settlor → Transfers legal title to trust property → Trustee

Trustee → Holds and administers trust property in accordance with the law and the terms of the trust for the benefit of the beneficiary → Beneficiary

Trust Terminology
A person who creates a trust is known as a **settlor** or trustor. The person who holds the property for the benefit of another person is called the **trustee.** The person for whose benefit the property is held in trust is the **beneficiary.** Figure 3 illustrates the relationship between these parties. A single person may occupy more than one of these positions; however, if there is only one beneficiary, he cannot be the sole trustee. The property held in trust is called the corpus or **res.** A distinction is made between the property in trust, which is the principal, and the income that is produced by the principal.

A trust that is established and effective during the settlor's lifetime is known as an **inter vivos** trust. A trust can also be established in a person's will. Such trusts take effect only at the death of the settlor. They are called testamentary trusts.

Why People Create Trusts
Bennett owns a portfolio of valuable stock. Her husband has predeceased her. She has two children and an elderly father for whom she would like to provide. Why might it be advantageous to Bennett to transfer the stock to a trust for the benefit of the members of her family?

First, there may be income tax or estate tax advantages in doing so, depending on the type of trust she establishes and the provisions of that trust. For example, she can establish an irrevocable trust for her children and remove the property transferred to her trust from her estate so that it is not taxable at her death. In addition, the trust property can be used for the benefit of others and may even pass to others after the settlor's death without the necessity of having a will. Many people prefer to pass their property by trust rather than by will because trusts afford more privacy:

unlike a probated will, they do not become an item of public record. Trusts also afford greater opportunity for post-gift management than do outright gifts and bequests. If Bennett wants her children to enjoy the income of the trust property during their young adulthood without distributing unfettered ownership of the property to them before she considers them able to manage it properly, she can accomplish this through a trust provision. A trust can prevent the property from being squandered or spent too quickly. Trusts can be set up so that a beneficiary's interest cannot be reached by his creditors in many situations. Such trusts, called spendthrift trusts, will be discussed later.

Placing property in trust can operate to increase the amount of property held for the beneficiaries if the trustee makes good investment decisions. Another important consideration is that a trust can be used to provide for the needs of disabled beneficiaries who are not capable of managing funds.

Creation of Express Trusts

There are five basic requirements for the creation of a valid express trust, although special and somewhat less restrictive rules govern the establishment of charitable trusts. The requirements for forming an express trust are:

1. *Capacity.* The settlor must have had the legal capacity to convey the property to the trust. This means that the settlor must have had the capacity needed to make a valid contract if the trust is an *inter vivos* trust or the capacity to make a will if the trust is a testamentary trust. For example, a trust would fail under this requirement if at the time the trust was created, the settlor had not attained the age required by state law for the creation of valid wills and contracts (age 18 in most states).

2. *Intent and formalities.* The settlor must *intend* to create a trust at the present time. To impose enforceable duties on the trustee, the settlor must meet certain formalities. Under the laws of most states, for example, the trustee must accept the trust by signing the trust instrument. In the case of a trust of land, the trust must be in writing so as to meet the statute of frauds. If the trust is a testamentary trust, it must satisfy the formal requirements for wills.

3. *Conveyance of specific property.* The settlor must convey *specific property* to the trust. The property conveyed must be property that the settlor has the *right to convey.*

4. *Proper purpose.* The trust must be created for a *proper purpose.* It cannot be created for a reason that is contrary to public policy, such as the commission of a crime.

5. *Identity of the beneficiaries.* The *beneficiaries* of the trust must be described clearly enough so that their identities can be ascertained. Sometimes, beneficiaries may be members of a specific class, such as "my children."

Charitable Trusts

A distinction is made between private trusts and trusts created for charitable purposes. In a private trust, property is devoted to the benefit of specific persons, whereas in a charitable trust, property is devoted to a charitable organization or to some other purposes beneficial to society. While some of the rules governing private and charitable trusts are the same, a number of these rules are different. For example, when a private trust is created, the beneficiary must be known at the time or ascertainable within a certain time (established by a legal rule known as the rule against perpetuities). However, a charitable trust is valid even though no definitely ascertainable beneficiary is named and even though it is to continue for an indefinite or unlimited period.

Doctrine of Cy Pres

A doctrine known as **cy pres** is applicable to charitable trusts when property is given in trust to be applied to a particular charitable purpose that becomes impossible, impracticable, or illegal to carry out. Under the doctrine of *cy pres,* the trust will not fail if the settlor indicated a general intention to devote the property to charitable purposes. If the settlor has not specifically provided for a substitute beneficiary, the court will direct the application of the property to some charitable purpose that falls within the settlor's general charitable intention.

In the following *Citizens National Bank* case, the court grapples with the issue of effectuating the donor's intent in a charitable trust.

Citizens National Bank of Paris v. Kids Hope United, Inc.
922 N.E.2d 1093 (Sup. Ct. Ill. 2009)

La Fern Blackman died in 1967. Her will provided that, after the death of her sister, Citizens National Bank of Paris would hold her farmland in trust and pay 75 percent of the income from the land to the Edgar County Children's Home (ECCH) and the other 25 percent to the trustees of the Embarrass Cemetery. The will further provided,

In the event either of the aforesaid organizations shall cease to exist, then said bank as trustee is to distribute said portion or portions of said net income to such charitable organization or organizations as it deems worthy of said money.

Blackman's sister, Etoile Davis, died in 1971. Her will directed the bank to hold her farmland in trust and give 75 percent of the net income to ECCH and the other 25 percent to the trustees of the Embarrass Cemetery. The will further provided,

In the event either of the aforesaid organizations shall cease to function in its present capacity, then the part of the trust fund which would have gone to this organization shall be divided equally between the FIRST METHODIST CHURCH OF PARIS MEMORIAL FOUNDATION, INC., THE EDGAR COUNTY CHAPTER OF THE AMERICAN CANCER SOCIETY, and THE EDGAR COUNTY HEART ASSOCIATION.

ECCH was incorporated in Illinois in 1803. Its charter stated that it was formed to "establish an institution for the education of dependent children of Edgar County, Illinois, and for the custody and maintenance of such children and to provide permanent homes for them in approved private families." In 1900, it erected a Children's Home facility on Eads Avenue to serve that purpose. In 1980, ECCH amended its articles of incorporation to allow it to become a residential placement resource for children throughout Illinois and to receive state funding. As a result of the amendment, ECCH's objective was to:

provide services to children and youth in the fields of health, welfare and education in the State of Illinois, including multi-treatment and educational programs for emotionally handicapped boys and girls of all races in residential treatment centers, day treatment services, counseling services to family, and such other related and auxiliary services as are necessary or desirable from time to time to accomplish these purposes; and to own or lease property, establish and maintain residential treatment centers, homes, schools and other facilities required.

In 2003, ECCH merged with the Hudelson Baptist Children's Home, and EECH dissolved as an entity and merged all its assets and programs into Hudelson. The Children's Home facility owned by ECCH also was transferred to Hudelson. In the merger agreement between ECCH and Hudelson, Hudelson "guaranteed that ECCH's mission of working with children in Edgar and the surrounding counties will be continued for as long as it is financially feasible to do so." In 2005, Hudelson changed its name to Kids Hope. The Children's Home that ECCH had built in 1900 closed and later was sold to a school district.

The bank, as trustee for the Blackman and Davis trusts, filed a petition in court stating that it believed that ECCH "had ceased to exist," and asked the court to determine whether this was true and, if so, to approve the distribution of 75 percent of the trust's net income to the alternate beneficiaries named in the Davis will. The bank and Kids Hope both filed motions for summary judgment. The trial court granted the bank's motion and found that ECCH had ceased to exist and directed the distribution of trust income to other beneficiaries. Kids Hope appealed, and the appellate court reversed. The bank appealed.

Freeman, Justice

In interpreting trusts, the goal is to determine the settlor's intent, which the court will effectuate if it is not contrary to law or public policy. Charitable gifts are viewed with peculiar favor by the courts, and every presumption consistent with the language contained in the instruments of gift will be employed in order to sustain them.

In the case at bar, it is true that ECCH ceased to exist as a separate corporate entity following its merger with Kids Hope. However, the important question here is not whether ECCH ceased to exist as a separate entity. Rather, in interpreting the restrictive condition to determine the testator's intent, the important question is whether the new corporation with which the original charitable organization merged was no longer suited to carry out the purposes of the bequest. If Kids Hope is not suited to carry out the purposes of Blackman's bequest, ECCH will have ceased to operate or exist within the meaning of Blackman's restrictive condition, and the gift to ECCH would lapse. If, however, Kids Hope *is* suited to carry out the purposes of the bequest, then in our view ECCH did not cease to operate or exist, as Blackman

meant those words, even if it did cease to exist as a separate corporate entity. We note that there is nothing in the language of Blackman's restrictive condition that would indicate that she meant "cease to operate or exist" to refer to ECCH's separate corporate existence.

In the 2003 merger agreement, Hudelson "guaranteed that ECCH's mission of working with children in Edgar and the surrounding counties will be continued for as long as it is financially feasible to do so." Moreover, part of the object for which ECCH was established was to "provide permanent homes for the dependent children of Edgar County in approved private families." According to the parties' agreed statement of facts, Kids Hope currently "has families in Edgar County who serve as approved foster homes." We agree with the appellate court that "the merger did not hinder Kids Hope's ability to carry out the purposes of the Blackman's original bequest." Kids Hope is suited to carry out these purposes, and ECCH did not cease to operate or exist as Blackman intended those words.

Affirmed in favor of Kids Hope.

Totten Trusts   A Totten trust is a deposit of money in a bank or other financial institution in the name of the depositor *as trustee* for a named beneficiary. For example, Bliss deposits money in First Bank in trust for his daughter, Bessie. The Totten trust creates a revocable living trust. At Bliss's death, if he has not revoked this trust, the money in the account will belong to Bessie.

Powers and Duties of the Trustee   In most express trusts, the settlor names a specific person to act as trustee. If the settlor does not name a trustee, the court will appoint one. Similarly, a court will replace a trustee who resigns, is incompetent, or refuses to act.

The trust codes of most states contain provisions giving trustees broad management powers over trust property. These provisions can be limited or expanded by express provisions in the trust instrument. The trustee must use a *reasonable degree of skill, judgment, and care* in the exercise of his duties unless he holds himself out as having a greater degree of skill, in which case he will be held to a higher standard. Section 7–302 of the UPC provides that the trustee is held to the standard of a prudent person dealing with the property of another, and if he has special skills or is named trustee based on a representation of special skills, he is required to use those special skills. He *may not commingle* the property he holds in trust with his own property or with that of another trust.

A trustee owes a *duty of loyalty* (fiduciary duty) to the beneficiaries. This means that he must administer the trust for the benefit of the beneficiaries and avoid any conflict between his personal interests and the interest of the trust. For example, a trustee cannot do business with a trust that he administers without express permission in the trust agreement. He must not prefer one beneficiary's interest to another's, and he must account to the beneficiaries for all transactions. Unless the trust agreement provides otherwise, the trustee must make the trust productive. He may not delegate the performance of discretionary duties (such as the duty to select investments) to another, but he may delegate the performance of ministerial duties (such as the preparation of statements of account).

A trust may give the trustee discretion as to the amount of principal or income paid to a beneficiary. In such a case, the beneficiary cannot require the trustee to exercise his discretion in the manner desired by the beneficiary.

Allocating between Principal and Income   One of the duties of the trustee is to distribute the principal and income of the trust in accordance with the terms of the trust instrument. Suppose Wheeler's will created a testamentary trust providing that his wife was to receive the income

from the trust for life, and at her death, the trust property was to be distributed to his children. During the duration of the trust, the trust earns profits, such as interest or rents, and has expenses, such as taxes or repairs. How should the trustee allocate these items as between Wheeler's surviving spouse, who is an income beneficiary, and his children, who are **remaindermen?**

The terms of the trust and state law bind the trustee in making this determination. As a general rule, ordinary profits received from the investment of trust property are allocated to income. For example, interest on trust property or rents earned from leasing real property held in trust would be allocated to income. Ordinary expenses such as insurance premiums, the cost of ordinary maintenance and repairs of trust property, and property taxes, would be chargeable to income. The principal of the trust includes the trust property itself and any extraordinary receipts, such as proceeds or gains derived from the sale of trust property. Extraordinary expenses—for example, the cost of long-term permanent improvements to real property or expenses relating to the sale of property—would ordinarily be charged against principal.

Liability of Trustee   A trustee who breaches any of the duties of a trustee or whose conduct falls below the standard of care applicable to trustees may incur personal liability. For example, if the trustee invests unwisely and imprudently, the trustee may be personally liable to reimburse the trust estate for the shortfall. The language of the trust affects the trustee's liability and the level of care owed by the trustee. A settlor might, for example, include language lowering the trustee's duty of care or relieving the trustee of some liability that he might otherwise incur.

The trustee can also have liability to third persons who are injured by the operation of the trust. Because a trust is not in itself a legal entity that can be sued, a third party who has a claim (such as a tort claim or a claim for breach of contract) must file his claim against the trustee of the trust. The trustee's actual personal liability to a third party depends on the language of the trust and of any contracts he might enter on behalf of the trust as well as the extent to which the injury complained of by the third party was a result of the personal fault or omission of the trustee.

Spendthrift Trusts   Generally, the beneficiary of a trust may voluntarily assign his rights to the principal or income of the trust to another person. In addition, any distributions to the beneficiary are subject to the claims of his creditors. Sometimes, however, trusts contain provisions known as spendthrift clauses, which restrict the voluntary or involuntary transfer of a beneficiary's interest.

Such clauses are generally enforced, and they preclude assignees or creditors from compelling a trustee to recognize their claims to the trust. The enforceability of such clauses is subject to four exceptions, however:

1. A person cannot put his own property beyond the claims of his own creditors. Thus, a spendthrift clause is not effective in a trust when the settlor makes himself a beneficiary.

2. Divorced spouses and minor children of the beneficiary can compel payment for alimony and child support.

3. Creditors of the beneficiary who have furnished necessaries can compel payment.

4. Once the trustee distributes property to a beneficiary, it can be subject to valid claims of others.

 List the requirements for the formation of a trust, and describe how trusts can be revoked or modified.

Termination and Modification of a Trust Normally, a settlor cannot revoke or modify a trust unless he reserves the power to do so at the time he establishes the trust. However, a trust may be modified or terminated with the consent of the settlor and all of the beneficiaries. When the settlor is dead or otherwise unable to consent, a trust can be modified or terminated by consent of all the persons with a beneficial interest, but only when this would not frustrate a material purpose of the trust. Because trusts are under the supervisory jurisdiction of a court, the court can permit a deviation from the terms of a trust when unanticipated changes in circumstances threaten accomplishment of the settlor's purpose.

Implied and Constructive Trusts Under exceptional circumstances in which the creation of a trust is necessary to effectuate a settlor's intent or avoid unjust enrichment, the law *implies* or imposes a trust even though no express trust exists or an express trust exists but has failed. One trust of this type is a resulting trust, which arises when there has been an incomplete disposition of trust property. For example, if Hess transferred property to Wickes as trustee to provide for the needs of Hess's grandfather and the grandfather died before the trust funds were exhausted, Wickes will be deemed to hold the property in a resulting trust for Hess or Hess's heirs. Similarly, if Hess had transferred the property to Wickes as trustee and the trust had failed because Hess did not meet one of the requirements of a valid trust, Wickes would not be permitted to keep the trust property as his own. A resulting trust would be implied.

A constructive trust is a trust created by operation of law to avoid fraud, injustice, or unjust enrichment. This type of trust imposes on the constructive trustee a duty to convey property he holds to another person on the ground that the constructive trustee would be unjustly enriched if he were allowed to retain it. For example, when a person procures the transfer of property by means of fraud or duress, he becomes a constructive trustee and is under an obligation to return the property to its original owner.

Problems and Problem Cases

1. John Irvine and Deana Dodge married in 1979. At the time of their marriage, Deana had a son from a previous marriage, Michael Dodge. During their marriage, John and Deana had no children together nor did they adopt any children. John did not adopt Dodge. In 1983, John and Deana executed wills. The lawyer who drafted the wills retained the wills in his file. When he retired, the law firm that took over his practice retained the files. Deana died in 2008 and John in 2009. At the time of John's death, she was survived by his stepson, Dodge, his brother, William, and his mother, Va Va. Under the laws of intestacy, Va Va stood to inherit all of John's property if John left no will. One week after John died, William—who believed his brother had died without at will—sought to be appointed personal representative of his brother's estate. Later, however, while going through John's belongings, William found a copy of John's will. He also obtained the original signed will from the law firm. The will purported to pass all of John's property to Dodge if Deana predeceased him. There was no indication that John had made another will or had destroyed the will or otherwise attempted to revoke it. Va Va filed an objection to the probate of John's will, challenging its validity. Will she win?

2. In 2003, Grubbs transferred his individual retirement account (IRA) to Raymond James and Associates, Inc., naming Nunnenman as the beneficiary to receive the residue in the event of his death. Grubbs was hospitalized in 2005. He summoned an attorney to the hospital, where he made and executed a last will and testament that did not mention the IRA account. The will left Grubbs' entire estate to his mother, Shervena, who was also named as executrix. Months after Grubbs' death,

Shervena stated that she found a handwritten note in Grubbs' Bible that stated:

> May 2005
>
> My Will
>
> I Donnie Grubbs want all of my estate All IRA and any SBC Telco and all other assets and worldly goods to go to my Mother Shervena Grubbs. Being of sound mind.
>
> Donnie Grubbs

In her capacity as executrix, Shervena filed an action for an injunction freezing the assets of the IRA account based on the handwritten note, which she claimed indicated the intent to make her the beneficiary of the account. Will she win?

3. Roy and Icie Johnson established two revocable *inter vivos* trusts in 1966. The trusts provided that upon Roy's and Icie's deaths, income from the trusts was to be paid in equal shares to their two sons, James and Robert, for life. Upon the death of the survivor of the sons, the trust was to be *"divided equally between all of my grandchildren, per stirpes."* James had two daughters, Barbara and Elizabeth. Robert had four children, David, Rosalyn, Catherine, and Elizabeth. James and Robert disclaimed their interest in the trust in 1979, and a dispute arose about how the trust should be distributed to the grandchildren. The trustee filed an action seeking instructions on how the trusts should be distributed. What should the court hold?

4. Elma Ward died in 2008. Frazier petitioned the court to probate a holographic will made by Ward. The document contains two typewritten sections, separated by one handwritten section. The document reads:

> [Typewritten section] October 14, 1987
>
> All of our worl[d]ly things, which we owne [sic] will not be sold, given away, borrowed or otherwise disposed of, until one year after either of our death. The one that is left can do what they think is best for them. This includes house, land, trucks, cars, boats, shop & all contents, and contents of the house.
>
> [A signature, purporting to be that of Elma Ward is located here]
>
> [Handwritten section] To whom it's [sic] concern[ed]:
>
> Everything we own will be sold at both our death[s]. Patricia B. Smith—leave to her $ 1,000 in cash. She has been a dear daughter to her stepdad and me. Jimmy Buchanan [$]200. Diane Buchanan Moorehead $200. The rest of the cash from the sale be divided between Sheila Willis, Teresa L. Ward Frazier, Robert E. Ward.

> [A notary seal, with the signature of Jimmy Wells, is located here. The date "2/2/99" is handwritten above Mr. Wells's signature, and the date "4/18/2001" is handwritten below Mr. Wells's signature.]
>
> [Typewritten section, identical to that above, is included a second time at this place in the document]
>
> [Following the typewritten section, the document contains the signature of Edward Ward and a second signature purported to be that of Elma K. Ward. A second notary seal follows these signatures, which seal is signed by Jimmy Wells with the handwritten dates of 2/12/99, and 4/18/2001.]

Two individuals familiar with Ward's handwriting provided affidavits that the signature on the alleged will was genuine. Ward's son objected to the probate of this document, arguing that it does not meet the statutory requirements for a will because his mother's signature was not directly below the handwritten portion of the will. Tennessee law provides that, "No witness to a holographic will is necessary, but the signature and all its material provisions must be in the handwriting of the testator and the testator's handwriting must be proved by two (2) witnesses." Was this a valid will?

5. Before 1985, Franklin Timmons and his wife, Kathryn, owned property that included a marina called the "Boatyard," where Timmons operated the family business. Timmons's primary income was derived from the Boatyard, and according to him, the business ran at a loss. In 1980, a court awarded a judgment against Timmons in a case involving the Boatyard. Timmons never paid the judgment. In 1985, with the judgment still outstanding and no improvement in their financial conditions, the Timmonses established a Joint Irrevocable Living Trust. They conveyed to the Trust the farm and the Boatyard, which comprised all the real property that they owned and the only significant assets that were capable of responding to a creditor judgment. Under the terms of the Trust, the Timmonses and their son, Jimmy, were named as trustees. The Trust instrument gave trustees discretion to invade the trust principal and to sell the land for their own benefit. Although his property was held by the Trust, Timmons never viewed the Trust as limiting his ability to use the land for himself or to rent it to others. Timmons believed that he could continue to live on the land, operate his business on it, and use the land as his own, as he had done in the past. In 1985, six months after the Trust was created, Kulp, Timmons's employee, was severely injured while working at the Boatyard. Timmons did not carry workers' compensation insurance, and he did not reimburse any of Kulp's medical

expenses. Kulp filed a petition for compensation due with the Industrial Accident Board (IAB), and the IAB ordered Timmons to post a $150,000 bond and to pay Kulp's medical expenses and other benefits. Timmons did not comply with the IAB order, and several years of litigation ensued. Timmons's son, Jimmy, died in October 1994, and Timmons's wife, Kathryn, died two years later. As a consequence, Timmons became the sole settlor, trustee, and lifetime beneficiary of the Trust. Kulp's IAB award still remained unpaid. In 1997, the Superior Court entered a money judgment in favor of Kulp, doubling the initial IAB award to $194,316.74 to compensate Kulp for the delay in payment. Kulp brought an action seeking a determination that the Trust was invalid and that its assets were subject to execution process. Less than one month after this action was filed, Timmons conveyed all his personal property to his daughter-in-law, Beverly, and his granddaughter, Brandi. Thereafter, Beverly and Brandi conveyed a life estate in the conveyed property to Timmons. Timmons argued that as a consequence of that conveyance, and the transfer of his (and his wife's) assets to the Trust in 1985, he has no assets from which to satisfy the judgment. Can Kulp reach the trust assets to collect his judgment?

6. Almost a century ago, Henry and Martha Kolb started a family-owned floral business in Storm Lake, Iowa. Both the business and the family grew into prominence. After their grandson, Robert, was tragically killed in a hunting accident, the Kolbs established an agreement with the City of Storm Lake to establish a flower garden in the memory of Robert. The agreement provided for the "establishment, installation and maintenance of a formal flower garden" at a specific location within the city park on the north shore of Storm Lake. The agreement made it clear that the garden was a gift to the city, and that the agreement was to "continue during the period of the trust as created in [Henry's] Will . . . providing for the continued maintenance of said formal flower garden." The trust was later supplemented for the addition of a water fountain in the garden. The Robert James Kolb Memorial Trust Fund was finally established in 1970. Henry and Martha established the trust by deeding a quarter section of farmland they owned to their sons "Robert H. Kolb and Norman J. Kolb, as Trustees for the use and benefit of the City of Storm Lake." The warranty deed stated in pertinent part:

It is the purpose of the grantors to hereby establish the Robert James Kolb Memorial Trust Fund out of the real

estate above described and the proceeds derived from the sale thereof and/or the income derived therefrom, or any investments created by said trust fund. . . .

The said trust fund shall be used in connection with improvements needed for the planting and upkeep of flower beds, such as annuals and perennials of all kinds, also flowering bulbs and rose bushes as may be put upon the tract of real estate hereinafter described.

In 1973, Henry and Martha deeded another quarter section of their farmland to their sons, Robert and Norman, as trustees, "for the use and benefit of the City of Storm Lake" to become a "part of the Robert James Kolb Memorial Trust Fund established by the grantors in the year 1970, in order that this trust and the previously established trust may be handled as a single trust." Neither warranty deed stated when the trust terminated. The trust operated without much trouble or question for over 30 years under the direction of Robert and Norman as trustees. The reports indicated the income produced from the farmland was more than enough to pay for the trust expenses. The trust disbursements mainly consisted of farm, garden, and fountain expenses, which often equaled $20,000–$30,000. On one occasion, however, the trustees used surplus trust funds to help the Storm Lake School District purchase additional school property. This transaction was memorialized in a 1980 agreement between Norman and the school district.

Henry died intestate in 1978 and Martha died a short time later. Despite their deaths, the garden and fountain survived for many years with the help of the city's maintenance and funds provided by the trust. It was a cherished location in Storm Lake, and often provided an ideal spot for weddings and celebrations. In 2003, however, the existence of the garden and fountain was placed in jeopardy. At this time the city was developing plans for an economic revitalization project called "Project Awaysis," funded with Vision Iowa grant money. The plans sought to turn the city's park on the north shore of Storm Lake and surrounding areas into a Midwest vacation destination. Among other things, the project was to provide a new public beach, a lighthouse, a family playground, a lodge, and an indoor/outdoor water park. Most importantly, the plans called for relocating the memorial gardens and fountain within the city's park. The project was viewed by its planners, and others, as a vital and necessary move for the city to grow and compete for jobs and residents in the future. Norman, as trustee of the Kolb trust, filed a petition for an injunction preventing the removal of the garden and fountain. The trial court ruled against Norman on the injunction and the city began the removal of the garden and fountain. After a later trial, however, the court found that the trust's purpose had been destroyed and that it therefore became a resulting trust to benefit the Kolbs' successors. Was this ruling correct?

7. John Henry Kirkpatrick was born Gion Rosetti to Joseph and Beatrice Rosetti in 1914. He had 10 siblings. On January 25, 1927, Edgar and Margaret Kirkpatrick adopted Gion and his brother, Leo. The Kirkpatricks changed Gion's name to John Henry Kirkpatrick and Leo's name to Edward Watson Kirkpatrick. The other nine birth siblings were either adopted away or remained with their birth parents. John Kirkpatrick was married briefly, divorced, and had no children. Edward Kirkpatrick married and, with his wife, raised a daughter, Karen Shippey. John and Edward Kirkpatrick's nine biological siblings produced eight children (the cousins). John Kirkpatrick died intestate on August 4, 2000, leaving a substantial estate consisting of stocks, bonds, real estate, and personal property. Shippey and Rick Rogers were appointed co-personal representatives of John Kirkpatrick's estate. Shippey and Rogers filed a document asking the court to determine the proper heirs for distribution of the estate. Shippey argued that she was John Kirkpatrick's sole heir because his adoption terminated the rights of any biological relative not adopted by his adoptive family. *Wyo. Stat. Ann.* §§ 2-4-101 and 2-4-107 establish the rules of intestate succession and, specifically, those that apply to persons in an adoptive family. The pertinent parts are:

> Except in cases above enumerated, the estate of any intestate shall descend and be distributed as follows:

> (ii) If there are no children, nor their descendents, then to his father, mother, brothers and sisters, and to the descendents of brothers and sisters who are dead, the descendents collectively taking the share which their parents would have taken if living, in equal parts[.]

> An adopted person is the child of an adopting parent *and of the natural parents for inheritance purposes only.*

> *An adopted person shall inherit from all other relatives of an adoptive parent as though he was the natural child of the adoptive parent and the relatives shall inherit from the adoptive person's estate as if they were his relatives*[.]

Will Karen prevail?

Online Research

Living Wills

Using your favorite search engine, find an example of a living will other than the form that appears in Figure 1 of this chapter.

CHAPTER 30

BANKRUPTCY

B ob and Sue Brown are a young couple with two small children. When they were students, they borrowed about $80,000 to finance their undergraduate educations, as well as an MBA for Bob and a teaching certificate for Sue. Within the past three years they stretched themselves further financially in the course of acquiring and furnishing their first home and starting their family. Recently, Bob was laid off from his job managing computer technology operations for a telecom company. Then, Sue was injured in an automobile accident and has been unable to continue substitute teaching. Bob's unemployment benefits are insufficient to provide for the ordinary family expenses, much less meet the heavy financial obligations the family has taken on. The bank has filed a notice of intent to foreclose the mortgage on their home, and other creditors have sent letters threatening to repossess their car and furnishings. A friend has suggested that Bob and Sue consult with an attorney who specializes in bankruptcy matters who may be able to get them some relief from their creditors and gain a new start financially.

This situation raises a number of questions that will be addressed in this chapter. They include:

- If the Browns file a petition in bankruptcy, what assets would they be able to retain as exempt from the claims of their creditors?
- Which of their debts could be discharged in a bankruptcy proceeding?
- What advantages and disadvantages would the Browns have if they filed under Chapter 7 (liquidation) as opposed to filing under Chapter 13 (consumer debt adjustment), which would require them to continue to make payments on their debts?

LO LEARNING OBJECTIVES

After studying this chapter, you should be able to:

1. Explain the purpose of the Bankruptcy Code.
2. List and describe the major types of bankruptcy proceedings.
3. Explain the procedure by which Chapter 7 (liquidation) proceedings are begun and the roles the court and the bankruptcy trustee play in managing the bankruptcy process.
4. Understand what assets are included in the bankruptcy estate and the nature of exemptions.
5. Understand when the trustee can avoid prior transactions made by the debtor to reclaim assets for the bankruptcy estate.

6. Distinguish among claims, allowable claims, secured claims, and priority claims of creditors.
7. Describe the process by which the property in a debtor's estate is distributed to creditors and the debtor is granted a discharge in bankruptcy.
8. List the kinds of debts that are not dischargeable.
9. Explain the purpose and basic procedure of Chapter 11 Reorganizations.
10. Explain the purpose and basic procedure of Chapter 13 Consumer Debt Adjustments.
11. Compare the major types of bankruptcy proceedings.

WHEN AN INDIVIDUAL, a partnership, or a corporation is unable to pay its debts to creditors, problems can arise. Some creditors may demand security for past debts or start court actions on their claims in an effort to protect themselves. Such actions may adversely affect other creditors by depriving them of their fair share of the debtor's assets. Also, quick depletion of the debtor's assets may effectively prevent the debtor who needs additional time to pay off his debts from having an opportunity to do so.

At the same time, creditors need to be protected against the actions a debtor in financial difficulty might be tempted to take to their detriment. For example, the debtor might run off with his remaining assets or might use them to pay certain favored creditors, leaving nothing for the other creditors. Finally, a means is needed by which a debtor can get a fresh start financially and not continue to be saddled with debts beyond his ability to pay. This chapter focuses on the body of law and procedure that has developed to deal with the competing interests when a debtor is unable to pay his debts in a timely manner.

 L01 Explain the purpose of the bankruptcy code.

The Bankruptcy Code

The Bankruptcy Code is a federal law that provides an organized procedure under the supervision of a federal court for dealing with insolvent debtors. Debtors are considered insolvent if they are unable or fail to pay their debts as they become due. The power of Congress to enact bankruptcy legislation is provided in the Constitution. Through the years, there have been many amendments to the Bankruptcy Code. Congress completely revised the code in 1978 and then passed significant amendments to it in 1984, 1986, and 1994. On April 20, 2005, President Bush signed the "Bankruptcy Abuse, Prevention and Consumer Protection Act of 2005," the most substantial revision of the bankruptcy law since the 1978 Bankruptcy Code was adopted. With a few exceptions, the revisions are effective for cases filed after October 17, 2005.

The Bankruptcy Code has several major purposes. One is to ensure that the debtor's property is fairly distributed to the creditors and that some creditors do not obtain unfair advantage over the others. At the same time, the code protects all of the creditors against actions by the debtor that would unreasonably diminish the debtor's assets to which they are entitled. The code also provides the honest

debtor with a measure of protection against the demands for payment by his creditors. Under some circumstances, the debtor is given additional time to pay the creditors, freeing him of those pressures creditors might otherwise exert. If the debtor makes a full and honest accounting of his assets and liabilities and deals fairly with his creditors, the debtor may have most—if not all—of the debts discharged so as to have a fresh start.

At one time, **bankruptcy** carried a strong stigma for the debtors who became involved in it. Today, this is less true. It is still desirable that a person conduct her financial affairs in a responsible manner. However, there is a greater understanding that such events as accidents, natural disasters, illness, divorce, and severe economic dislocations are often beyond the ability of individuals to control and may lead to financial difficulty and bankruptcy.

 L02 List and describe the major types of bankruptcy proceedings.

Bankruptcy Proceedings The Bankruptcy Code covers a number of bankruptcy proceedings. In this chapter, our focus will be on:

1. Straight bankruptcy (liquidations).
2. Reorganizations.
3. Family farms and commercial fishing operations.
4. Consumer debt adjustments.

The Bankruptcy Code also contains provisions regarding municipal bankruptcies, which are not covered in this chapter.

Liquidations A liquidation proceeding, traditionally called straight bankruptcy, is brought under Chapter 7 of the Bankruptcy Code. Individuals, as well as businesses, may file under Chapter 7. The debtor must disclose all of the property she owns and surrender this bankruptcy estate to the bankruptcy trustee. The trustee separates out certain property that the debtor is permitted to keep and then administers, liquidates, and distributes the remainder of the bankrupt debtor's estate. There is a mechanism for determining the relative rights of the creditors, for recovering any preferential payments made to creditors, and for disallowing any preferential liens obtained by creditors. If the bankrupt person has been honest in her business transactions and in the bankruptcy proceedings, she is usually given a **discharge** (relieved) of her debts.

Reorganizations Chapter 11 of the Bankruptcy Code provides a proceeding whereby a debtor can work out a plan to solve its financial problems under the supervision of a federal court. A reorganization plan is essentially a contract between a debtor and its creditors. The proceeding is intended for debtors, particularly businesses, whose financial problems may be solvable if they are given some time and guidance and if they are relieved of some pressure from creditors.

Family Farms Historically, farmers have been accorded special attention in the Bankruptcy Code. Chapter 12 of the Bankruptcy Code provides a special proceeding whereby a debtor involved in a family farming operation or a family-owned commercial fishing operation can develop a plan to work out his financial difficulties. Generally, the debtor remains in possession of the farm or fishing operations and continues to operate it while the plan is developed and implemented.

Consumer Debt Adjustments Under Chapter 13 of the Bankruptcy Code, individuals with regular incomes who are in financial difficulty can develop plans under court supervision to satisfy their creditors. Chapter 13 permits compositions (reductions) of debts and/or extensions of time to pay debts out of the debtor's future earnings.

The Bankruptcy Courts Bankruptcy cases and proceedings are filed in federal district courts. The district courts have the authority to refer the cases and proceedings to bankruptcy judges, who are considered to be units of the district court. If a dispute falls within what is known as a core proceeding, the bankruptcy judge can hear and determine the controversy. Core proceedings include a broad list of matters related to the administration of a bankruptcy estate. However, if a dispute is not a core proceeding but rather involves a state law claim, then the bankruptcy judge can only hear the case and prepare draft findings and conclusions for review by the district court judge.

Certain proceedings affecting interstate commerce have to be heard by the district court judge if any party requests that this be done. Moreover, even the district courts are precluded from deciding certain state law claims that could not normally be brought in federal court, even if those claims are related to the bankruptcy matter. Bankruptcy judges are appointed by the president for terms of 14 years.

LO3 Explain the procedure by which Chapter 7 (liquidation) proceedings are begun and the roles the court and the bankruptcy trustee play in managing the bankruptcy process.

Chapter 7: Liquidation Proceedings

Petitions All bankruptcy proceedings, including liquidation proceedings, are begun by the filing of a petition. The petition may be either a voluntary petition filed by the debtor or an involuntary petition filed by a creditor or creditors of the debtor. A voluntary petition in bankruptcy may be filed by an individual, a partnership, or a corporation. However, municipal, railroad, insurance, and banking corporations and savings or building and loan associations are not permitted to file for straight bankruptcy proceedings. A person filing a voluntary petition need not be insolvent—that is, her debts need not be greater than her assets. However, the person must be able to allege that she has debts. The primary purpose for filing a voluntary petition is to obtain a discharge from some or all of the debts.

The 2005 revisions establish a new "means test" for consumer debtors to be eligible for relief under Chapter 7. The purpose of the test is to ensure that individuals who will have income in the future that might be used to pay off at least a portion of their debts must pursue relief under Chapter 13 as opposed to pursuing relief and a discharge of liabilities through the liquidation provisions of Chapter 7. In general, debtors who earn more than the median income in their state and who can repay at least $7,025 of their debt over five years are required to use Chapter 13. This means test is discussed in detail later in this section under the subsection entitled "Substantial Abuse."

Involuntary Petitions An involuntary petition is a petition filed by creditors of a debtor. By filing it, they seek to have the debtor declared bankrupt and his assets distributed to the creditors. Involuntary petitions may be filed against many debtors. However, involuntary petitions in straight bankruptcy cannot be filed against (1) farmers; (2) ranchers; (3) nonprofit organizations; (4) municipal, railroad, insurance, and banking corporations; (5) credit unions; and (6) savings or building and loan associations.

If a debtor has 12 or more creditors, an involuntary petition to declare him bankrupt must be signed by at least 3 creditors. If there are fewer than 12 creditors, then an involuntary petition can be filed by a single creditor. The creditor or creditors must have valid claims against the debtor exceeding the value of any security they hold by $14,425 or more. To be forced into involuntary bankruptcy, the debtor must be generally not paying his debts as they become due—or have had a custodian for his property appointed within the previous 120 days.

If an involuntary petition is filed against a debtor engaged in business, the debtor may be permitted to continue to operate the business. However, the court may appoint an interim trustee if this is necessary to preserve the bankruptcy estate or to prevent loss of the estate. A creditor who suspects that a debtor may dismantle her business or dispose of its assets at less than fair value may apply to the court for protection.

Requirement for Credit Counseling and Debtor Education Under the 2005 revisions, individuals are ineligible for relief under any chapter of the Code unless within 180 days preceding their bankruptcy filing they received individual or group credit counseling from an approved nonprofit budget and credit counseling agency or obtain an exemption from the requirement. The required briefing, which may take place by telephone or on the Internet, must "outline" the opportunities for credit counseling and assist the debtor in performing a budget analysis. The debtor is required to file a certificate from the credit counseling agency that describes the services that were provided to the debtor and also to file any debt repayment plan developed by the agency. Because individuals who have not received the required briefing are not eligible for relief under the Bankruptcy Code, it is difficult for a creditor to force an individual debtor into bankruptcy by filing an involuntary petition against the debtor.

Attorney Certification The 2005 act increases the legal responsibilities for an attorney who signs a bankruptcy petition. The attorney's signature constitutes a certification that the attorney, after inquiry, has no knowledge that the information contained in the schedules filed by the debtor is incorrect. In addition, the attorney's signature on a petition, motion, or other written pleading constitutes a certification that the attorney, after inquiry, has determined that the pleading is well grounded in fact and is either warranted by existing law or is based on a good faith argument for extending existing law. In cases where the trustee files a motion to dismiss a case for substantial abuse, the court may order the debtor's attorney to reimburse the trustee for the reasonable costs, including attorney fees, for prosecuting the motion and may also order the attorney to pay a civil penalty to the trustee or the United States Trustee.

These provisions have raised concerns that bankruptcy practice will be less attractive to bankruptcy attorneys that handle a large volume of cases because the provisions will increase their costs and risks—and they operate on relatively thin margins.

Automatic Stay Provisions The filing of a bankruptcy petition operates as an **automatic stay,** holding in abeyance various forms of creditor action against a debtor or her property. These actions include (1) beginning or continuing judicial proceedings against the debtor; (2) actions to obtain possession of the debtor's property; (3) actions to create, perfect, or enforce a lien against the debtor's property; and (4) setoff of indebtedness owed to the debtor before commencement of the bankruptcy proceeding. A court may give a creditor relief from the stay if the creditor can show that the stay does not give her "adequate protection" and jeopardizes her interest in certain property. The relief to the creditor might take the form of periodic cash payments or the granting of a replacement lien or an additional lien on property.

Concerned that debtors were taking advantage of the automatic stay provisions to the substantial detriment of some creditors, such as creditors whose claims were secured by an interest in a single real estate asset, in 1994 Congress provided specific relief from the automatic stay for such creditors. Debtors must either file a plan of reorganization that has a reasonable chance of being confirmed within a reasonable time or must be making monthly payments to each such secured creditor that are in an amount equal to interest at a current fair market rate on the value of the creditor's interest in the real estate.

The automatic stay provisions are not applicable to actions to establish paternity, to establish or modify orders for domestic support obligations, for the collection of domestic support obligations from property that is not the property of the bankruptcy estate, or to withhold, suspend, or restrict a driver's license or professional, occupational, or recreational license.

In 2005, Congress added two additional exceptions from the automatic stay provisions for the benefit of landlords seeking to evict tenants. First, any eviction proceedings in which the landlord obtained a judgment of possession prior to the filing of the bankruptcy petition can be continued. Second, in cases where the landlord's claim for eviction is based on the use of illegal substances on the property or "endangerment" of the property, the eviction proceedings are exempt from the stay even if they are initiated after the bankruptcy proceeding was filed so long as the endangerment or illegal use occurred within 30 days before the filing. Debtors are able to keep the stay in effect by filing certifications that certain nonbankruptcy laws allow the lease to remain in effect and that they have cured any defaults within 30 days of the bankruptcy filing.

Order of Relief Once a bankruptcy petition has been filed, the first step is a court determination that relief should be ordered. If a voluntary petition is filed by the debtor, or if the debtor does not contest an involuntary petition, this step is automatic. If the debtor contests an involuntary petition, then a trial is held on the question of whether the court should order relief. The court orders relief only (1) if the debtor is generally not paying his debts as they become due, or (2) if within 120 days of the filing of the petition a custodian was appointed or took possession of the debtor's property. The court also appoints an interim trustee pending election of a trustee by the creditors.

Meeting of Creditors and Election of Trustee The bankrupt person is required to file a list of her assets, liabilities, and creditors and a statement of her financial affairs. The 2005 revisions impose a number of new production requirements on debtors. Now, individual debtors must file, along with their schedules of assets and liabilities:

- A certificate that they have received and/or have read the notice from the Clerk of the Bankruptcy Court that they must receive credit counseling to be eligible for relief under the Bankruptcy Code;
- Copies of all payment advices and other evidence of payments they have received from any employer within 60 days before the filing of the petition;
- A statement of the amount of monthly net income, itemized to show how the amount is calculated; and
- A statement showing any anticipated increase in income or expenditures over the 12-month period following the date of filing the petition.

Should an individual debtor in a voluntary Chapter 7 case or in a Chapter 13 case fail to file the required information within 45 days of the filing of the petition, the case is to be automatically dismissed. A court, upon finding that an extension is justified, can extend the time period to file for up to an additional 45 days.

Individual debtors also must provide copies of their most recent tax returns to the trustee and to creditors making a timely request; failure to do so can result in dismissal of the case. Debtors also must, at the request of the judge or a party in interest, file at the same time they file with the IRS copies of federal tax returns due while the bankruptcy case is pending and also file copies of tax returns (including any amended returns) for tax years that ended within the three years before the bankruptcy petition was filed.

Once the court receives the bankruptcy filing and the required schedules and certifications, the U.S. Trustee calls a meeting of the creditors. At the meeting, the U.S. Trustee is required to examine the debtor to make sure she is aware of (1) the potential consequences of seeking a discharge in bankruptcy, including the effects on credit history; (2) the debtor's ability to file a petition under other chapters (such as 11, 12, or 13) of the Bankruptcy Code; (3) the effect of receiving a discharge of debts; and (4) the effect of reaffirming a debt (discussed later in this chapter).

The creditors also elect a **trustee** who, if approved by the judge, takes over administration of the bankrupt's estate. The trustee represents the creditors in handling the estate. At the meeting, the creditors have a chance to ask the debtor questions about her assets, liabilities, and financial difficulties. These questions commonly focus on whether the debtor has concealed or improperly disposed of assets.

Duties of the Trustee The trustee takes possession of the debtor's property and has it appraised. The debtor must also turn over her records to the trustee. For a time, the trustee may operate the debtor's business. The trustee sets aside the items of property that a debtor is permitted to keep under state exemption statutes or federal law.

The 2005 act places restrictions on the authority of the trustee to sell personally identifiable information about individuals to persons who are not affiliated with the debtor. Congress was concerned about situations where individuals had provided information to persons and entities on the understanding and commitment that the information would remain in confidence with the recipient. These data files often are a valuable asset of a debtor involved in bankruptcy proceedings, but Congress concluded it was not reasonable to allow that information to be sold to a third party that was not in their contemplation when the individuals provided the information to the debtor under a promise of confidentiality.

The trustee examines the claims filed by various creditors and objects to those that are improper in any way. The trustee separates the unsecured property from the secured and otherwise exempt property. He also sells the bankrupt's nonexempt property as soon as possible, consistent with the best interest of the creditors.

The trustee is required to keep an accurate account of all the property and money he receives and to promptly deposit moneys into the estate's accounts. The trustee files a final report with the court, with notice to all creditors who then may file objections to the report.

Health Care Businesses The 2005 revisions reflect Congress's concern with what happens if a petition for bankruptcy is filed by a health care business and contain a number of provisions concerning that possibility.

First, the trustee is instructed to use his reasonable best efforts to transfer patients in a health care business that is in the process of being closed to an appropriate health care business in the vicinity of the one being closed that offers similar services and maintains a reasonable quality of care. Second, the actual, necessary costs of closing a health care business are considered administrative expenses entitled to priority. Third, the automatic stay provisions do not apply to actions by the Secretary of Health and Human Services to exclude the debtor from participating in Medicare and other federal health care programs. Finally, the act sets out requirements for the disposal of patient records where there are insufficient funds to continue to store them as required by law. The requirements include giving notice to the affected patients and specifying the manner of disposal for unclaimed records.

Liquidation of Financial Firms The Bankruptcy Code contains special provisions for the liquidation of stockbrokers, commodity brokers, and clearing banks that are designed to protect the interests of customers of the entities who have assets on deposit with the bankrupt debtor. These responsibilities are overseen by the trustee.

 Understand what assets are included in the bankruptcy estate and the nature of exemptions.

The Bankruptcy Estate
The commencement of a Chapter 7 bankruptcy case by the filing of a voluntary or involuntary petition creates a bankruptcy estate. The estate is composed of all of the debtor's legal and equitable interests in property, including certain community property. Certain property is exempted (see "Exemptions" section below). The estate also includes:

1. Profits, royalties, rents and revenue, along with the proceeds from the debtor's estate, received during the Chapter 7 proceeding.

2. Property received by the debtor in any of the following ways within 180 days of the filing of the Chapter 7 petition: (*a*) by bequest or inheritance; (*b*) as a settlement with a divorced spouse or as a result of a divorce decree; or (*c*) as proceeds of a life insurance policy.

3. Property recovered by the bankruptcy trustee because (*a*) creditor of the debtor received a voidable preferential transfer or (*b*) the debtor made a fraudulent transfer of her assets to another person. Preferential and fraudulent transfers are discussed later in this chapter.

Exemptions
Even in a liquidation proceeding, the bankrupt is generally not required to give up all of his property; he is permitted to **exempt** certain items of property. Under the Bankruptcy Code, the debtor may choose to keep certain items or property either exempted by state law, or exempt under federal law unless state law specifically forbids use of the federal exemptions. However, any such property concealed or fraudulently transferred by the debtor may not be retained.

The 2005 revisions specify that the state or local law governing the debtor's exemptions is the law of the place where the debtor was domiciled for 730 days before filing. If the debtor did not maintain a domicile in a single state for that period, then the law governing the exemptions is the law of the place of the debtor's domicile for the majority of the 180-day period preceding the filing of the petition that is between two and two and one-half years before the filing. For example, on January 1, 2007, Alex Smith was living in Florida. In March 2007 he moved to Georgia and in November 2007 he moved again and took up residence in Alabama. On July 1, 2009, Smith filed a petition in bankruptcy. Because Smith had not lived in Alabama for the 2 years (730 days) before he filed, he would not be able to claim the exemptions that Alabama provides. Rather, he would be entitled to claim the exemptions provided by Georgia where he lived for the majority of the 180 days between January 1, 2007 and July 1, 2007.

The debtor must elect to use *either* the set of exemptions provided by the state or the set provided by the federal bankruptcy law; she may not pick and choose between them. A husband and wife involved in bankruptcy proceedings must both elect either the federal or the state exemptions; where they cannot agree, the federal exemptions are deemed elected.

The **exemptions** permit the bankrupt person to retain a minimum amount of the assets considered necessary to life and to his ability to continue to earn a living. They are part of the fresh start philosophy that is one of the purposes of the Bankruptcy Code. The general effect of the federal exemptions is to make at least a minimum exemption available to debtors in all states. States that wish to be more generous to debtors can provide more liberal exemptions.

The specific items that are exempt under state statutes vary from state to state. Some states provide fairly liberal exemptions and are considered "debtors' havens." For example, in Florida none of the equity in the debtor's homestead can be used to pay off unsecured creditors, thus allowing even relatively well-off individuals to shield significant assets from creditors. Items that are commonly made exempt from sale to pay debts owed creditors include the family Bible; tools or books of the trade; life insurance policies; health aids, such as wheelchairs and hearing aids; personal and household goods; and jewelry, furniture, and motor vehicles worth up to a certain amount.

In the case that follows, *In re Rogers*, the court concluded that a debtor was entitled to claim a homestead exemption in property which she acquired more than 1,215 days before filing for bankruptcy, but which she began to use as her homestead within that period.

In re Rogers (Wallace v. Rogers)	**513 F.3d 212 (5th Cir. 2008)**

On January 17, 1994, Sarah Rogers inherited a 72.5-acre tract of real property in Forney, Texas. Rogers was single at the time she inherited the property from her mother. Subsequently, Rogers married George Rogers and they purchased a 5.1-acre property in Rockwall, Texas, and built a residence on it, which they claimed as their homestead.

In January 2004, Rogers separated from her husband, moved into a mobile home on the Forney property, and claimed it as her homestead. On April 6, Rogers and her husband divorced. Pursuant to the divorce decree, she gave up all right, title, and interest in the property in Rockwall, and no equity from that property was rolled into the property in Forney. The divorce decree awarded the Forney property to Rogers, reflecting the fact that it was her separate property, having inherited it from her mother before her marriage.

Prior to 2004, Rogers and her husband had borrowed money from Jack Wallace to embark on an ultimately unsuccessful business venture. Wallace sued to recover the unpaid balance on the loan and on April 19, 2004, he obtained a judgment against both Rogers and her then ex-husband for $316,180.95. On September 28, 2005, Rogers filed for relief under Chapter 7 of the Bankruptcy Code. She elected state law exemptions and claimed her homestead exemption on the Forney property in the amount of $359,000.

Wallace objected to the claimed homestead exemption, arguing that the Bankruptcy Code capped the exemption at the federal statutory amount of $125,000 because the debtor acquired her homestead interest in the Forney property within the 1,215-day period preceding the filing of her bankruptcy petition. Both the bankruptcy court and the district court held that Rogers was entitled to the homestead exemption, but gave different reasons for their holding. Wallace appealed the matter to the Fifth Circuit.

DeMoss, Circuit Judge

The bankruptcy estate is comprised of "all legal or equitable interests of the debtor in property as of the commencement of the case." Rogers elected to exempt the Forney property as her homestead under Texas state law. An exemption is an interest withdrawn from the estate (and hence from the creditors) for the benefit of the debtor.

Enacted as part of the Bankruptcy Abuse Prevention and Consumer Protection Act of 2005 (BAPCA), 11 U.S.C. section 522 (p) (1) limits the state law homestead exemption under certain circumstances. Section 522 (p) (1) prevents the debtor from exempting certain interests from the bankruptcy estate if they were acquired by the debtor during the statutory period and their aggregate value exceeds a certain dollar threshold. The statute reads, in pertinent part:

> As a result of electing . . . to exempt property under State or local law, a debtor may not exempt any amount of interest that was acquired by the debtor during the 1215-day period preceding the date of the filing of the petition that exceeds in the aggregate [$125,000][1] in value in real or personal property that the debtor or dependent of the debtor claims as a homestead.

---

[1] In 2007, the Judicial Conference of the United States adjusted the dollar amount from $125,000 to $136,875. At the time the bankruptcy petition was filed in this case, the relevant dollar amount was $125,000.

The statute further states that "any amount of such interest does not include any interest transferred from a debtor's previous principal residence (which was acquired prior to the beginning of such 1,215-day period) into the debtor's principal residence if the debtor's previous and current residences are located in the same state.

Based on the legislative history, the bankruptcy court concluded that the purpose of the statute was to close the "mansion loophole" and prevent debtors from moving to states with more generous homestead exemptions on the eve of bankruptcy in order to avail themselves of those exemptions. After observing that Rogers did not move to Texas in anticipation of bankruptcy and that her homestead designation of the Forney property was precipitated by divorce, the bankruptcy judge over-ruled Wallace's objection and held that Rogers may exempt the entirety of her homestead from the bankruptcy estate.

* * *

The legislative history indicates that Congress was concerned with the acquisition of vested economic interests in property during the statutory period.

On March 10, Senator Carper stated the following:

Today, under current law, a wealthy individual in a state such as Florida or Texas can go out, if they are a millionaire, and take those millions of dollars and invest the money in real estate, a huge house, and land in the State, file for bankruptcy, and basically protect all of their assets which they own because of a provision in Florida or Texas law.

With the legislation we have before us, someone has to figure out that 2-1/2 years ahead of time people are going to want to file for bankruptcy and be smart enough to put the money into a home, or an estate, or into a trust—not something you can do today—and file for bankruptcy tomorrow;

151 Cong. Rec. S2415-16 (daily ed. March 10, 2005).

Senator Carper's statement is also supported by language in the House Report which states that "the bill also restricts the so-called mansion loophole." Under current bankruptcy law, debtors living in certain states can shield from their creditors virtually all of the equity in their homes. In light of this, some debtors actually relocate to those states just to take advantage of their mansion loophole laws. In this case, it is undisputed that Rogers did not move to Texas to exploit the so-called mansion loophole.

According to Wallace, BAPCPA was intended to address fraudulent transfers in general, including conversions of nonexempt assets into exempt assets within the statutory period. We concur that Congress could have defined all the debtors exemptions to be whatever they would have been 1,215 days before the filing of the petition. Instead, Congress defined the cap more narrowly. We do not believe that Congress was concerned with the timing of the establishment of the homestead when it enacted section 522 (p) (1). The statutory text and legislative history indicate that the term "interest" refers to vested economic interests that were acquired by the debtor within the 1,215-day period preceding the filing of the petition. If Congress enacted into law something different from what it intended, then it should amend the statute to conform to its intent.

We hold that Rogers is entitled to her full homestead exemption.

Limits on State Homestead Exemptions Concerns that very generous homestead exemptions in a number of states were leading to abuses by debtors who transferred assets into large homes in those states and then filed for bankruptcy led Congress in 2005 to place some limits on state homestead exemptions. These limits include:

- The value of the debtor's homestead for purposes of a state homestead exemption is reduced to the extent that it reflects an increase in value on account of the disposition of nonexempt property by the debtor during the 10 years prior to the filing with the intent to hinder, delay, or defraud creditors.
- Any value in excess of $136,875—irrespective of the debtors intent—that is added to the value of a homestead during the 1,215 days (about 3 years, 4 months) preceding the bankruptcy filing may not be included in a state homestead exemption unless it was transferred from another homestead in the same state or the homestead is the principal residence of a family farmer.
- An absolute $136,875 homestead cap applies if either (*a*) the bankruptcy court determines that the debtor has been convicted of a felony demonstrating that the filing of the case was an abuse of the provisions of the Bankruptcy Code or (*b*) the debtor owes a debt arising from a violation of federal or state securities laws, fiduciary fraud, racketeering, or crimes or intentional torts that caused serious injury or death in the preceding five years. In certain cases, a discharge of a debtor under

Chapters 7, 11, or 13 may be delayed where the debtor is subject to a proceeding that might lead to a limitation of a homestead exemption.

Federal Exemptions Twelve categories of property are exempt under the federal exemptions, which the debtor may elect in lieu of the state exemptions. The federal exemptions include:

1. The debtor's interest (not to exceed $21,625 in value) in real or personal property that the debtor or a dependent of the debtor uses as a residence.
2. The debtor's interest (not to exceed $3,450 in value) in one motor vehicle.
3. The debtor's interest (not to exceed $550 in value for any particular item) up to a total of $11,525 in household furnishings, household goods, wearing apparel, appliances, books, animals, crops, or musical instruments that are held primarily for the personal, family, or household use of the debtor or a dependent of the debtor.
4. The debtor's aggregate interest (not to exceed $1,450 in value) in jewelry held primarily for the personal, family, or household use of the debtor or a dependent of the debtor.
5. $1,150 in value of any other property of the debtor's choosing, plus up to $10,825 of any unused homestead exemption.

6. The debtor's aggregate interest (not to exceed $2,175 in value) in any implements, professional books, or tools of the trade.

7. Life insurance contracts.

8. Interest up to $11,525 in specified kinds of dividends or interest in certain kinds of life insurance policies.

9. Professionally prescribed health aids.

10. Social Security, disability, alimony, and other benefits reasonably necessary for the support of the debtor or his dependents.

11. The debtor's right to receive certain insurance and liability payments.

12. Retirement funds that are in a fund or account that is exempt from taxation under the Internal Revenue Code. For certain individual retirement accounts, the aggregate amount exempted is limited to $1 million. Also protected are some contributions to certain education and college savings accounts made more than one year prior to bankruptcy.

The term **value** means "fair market value as of the date of the filing of the petition." In determining the debtor's interest in property, the amount of any liens against the property must be deducted.

Avoidance of Liens

The debtor is also permitted to **void** certain liens against exempt properties that impair her exemptions. Liens that can be voided on this basis are judicial liens or nonpossessionary, nonpurchase money security interests in (1) household furnishings, household goods, wearing apparel, appliances, books, animals, crops, musical instruments, or jewelry that are held primarily for the personal, family, or household use of the debtor or a dependent of the debtor; (2) implements, professional books, or tools of the trade of the debtor or a dependent of the debtor; and (3) professionally prescribed health aids for the debtor or a dependent of the debtor.

Under the 2005 revisions, the "household goods" as to which a nonpossessory, nonpurchase–money security interest can be avoided have been limited. The new definition limits electronic equipment to one radio, one television, one VCR, and one computer with related equipment. Specifically excluded are works of art other than those created by the debtor or family member, jewelry worth more than $600 (except wedding rings), and motor vehicles (including lawn tractors, motorized vehicles such as ORVs [off-road vehicles]), watercraft, and aircraft.

Redemptions

Debtors are also permitted to redeem exempt personal property from secured creditors by paying them the full value of the collateral at the time the property is redeemed. Then, the creditor is an unsecured creditor as to any remaining debt owed by the debtor. Under the 2005 revisions, the value of personal property securing a claim of an individual debtor in a Chapter 7 proceeding is based on the cost to the debtor of replacing the property—without deduction for costs of sale or marketing—and if the property was acquired for personal, family, or household purposes, the replacement cost will be the retail price for property of similar age and condition. The debtor is not permitted to retain collateral without redemption or reaffirmation of the debt (discussed later in this chapter) by just continuing to make the payments on the secured debt.

 Understand when the trustee can avoid prior transactions made by the debtor to reclaim assets for the bankruptcy estate.

Preferential Payments

A major purpose of the Bankruptcy Code is to ensure equal treatment for the creditors of an insolvent debtor. The code also seeks to prevent an insolvent debtor from distributing her assets to a few favored creditors to the detriment of the other creditors. Thus, the trustee has the right to recover for the benefit of the estate preferential payments above a certain threshold that are made by the bankrupt debtor in advance of the bankruptcy. In the case of an individual debtor whose debts are primarily consumer debts, the trustee is not entitled to avoid preferences unless the aggregate value of the property is $600 or more. In the case of a corporate debtor, a transfer by a debtor of less than $5,475 in the aggregate is not subject to avoidance. A preferential payment is a payment made by an insolvent debtor within 90 days before the filing of the bankruptcy petition that enables a creditor to obtain a greater percentage of a preexisting debt than other similar creditors of the debtor. It is irrelevant whether the creditor knew that the debtor was insolvent. A debtor is presumed to have been insolvent on and during the 90 days immediately preceding the filing of a petition.

For example, Fredericks has $1,000 in cash and no other assets. He owes $650 to his friend Roberts, $1,500 to a credit union, and $2,000 to a finance company. If Fredericks pays $650 to Roberts and then files for bankruptcy, he has made a preferential payment to Roberts. Roberts has had his debt paid in full, whereas only $350 is left to satisfy the $3,500 owed to the credit union and finance company. They stand to recover only 10 cents on each dollar that Fredericks owes them. The trustee has the right to get the $650 back from Roberts.

If the favored creditor is an insider—a relative of an individual debtor or an officer, director, or related party of a company—who had reasonable cause to believe the debtor was insolvent at the time the transfer was made, then a preferential payment made to that creditor up to one year prior to the filing of the petition can be recovered by the trustee.

The 1994 amendments to the Bankruptcy Code provided that the trustee may not recover as preferential payments any bona fide payments of debts to a spouse, former spouse, or child of the debtor for alimony, maintenance, or support pursuant to a separation agreement, divorce decree, or other court order.

Preferential Liens

Preferential liens are treated in a similar manner. A creditor might try to obtain an advantage over other creditors by obtaining a lien on the debtor's property to secure an existing debt. The creditor might seek to get the debtor's consent to a lien or to obtain a lien by legal process. Such liens are considered *preferential* and are invalid if they are obtained on property of an insolvent debtor within 90 days before the filing of a bankruptcy petition and if their purpose is to secure a preexisting debt. A preferential lien obtained by an insider up to one year prior to the filing of the bankruptcy petition can be avoided.

Transactions in the Ordinary Course of Business

The Bankruptcy Code provides several exceptions to the trustee's avoiding power that are designed to allow a debtor and his creditors to engage in ordinary business transactions. The exceptions include (1) transfers that are intended by the debtor and creditor to be a contemporaneous exchange for new value or (2) the creation of a security interest in new property where new value was given by the secured party to enable the debtor to obtain the property and where the new value was in fact used by the debtor to obtain the property and perfected within 20 days after the debtor took possession of the collateral.

For example, George Grocer is insolvent. He is permitted to purchase and pay cash for new inventory, such as produce or meat, without the payment being considered preferential. His assets have not been reduced. He has simply traded money for goods to be sold in his business. Similarly, he could buy a new display counter and give the seller a security interest in the counter until he

has paid for it. This would not be considered a preferential lien. The seller of the counter has not gained an unfair advantage over other creditors, and Grocer's assets have not been reduced by the transaction. The unfair advantage comes where an existing creditor tries to take a lien or obtain a payment of more than his share of the debtor's assets. Then, the creditor has obtained a preference over other creditors, which is what the trustee is allowed to avoid.

The Bankruptcy Code also provides an exception for transfers made in payment of a debt incurred in the ordinary course of the business or financial affairs of the debtor and the transferee (a) made in the ordinary course of business or (b) made according to ordinary business terms. Thus, for example, a consumer could pay her monthly utility bills in a timely fashion without the creditor/utility being vulnerable to having the transfer of funds avoided by a trustee. The purpose of this exception is to leave undisturbed normal financial relations, and it is consistent with the general policy of the preference section of the code to discourage *unusual action* by either a debtor or her creditors when the debtor is moving toward bankruptcy.

Exceptions to the trustee's avoidance power are also made for certain statutory liens, certain other perfected security interests, and cases filed by individual debtors whose debts are primarily consumer debts and the aggregate value of all property affected by the transfer is less than $600, and cases filed by a debtor where debts are not primarily consumer debts and the aggregate value of all property affected by the transfer is less than $5,000.

Fraudulent Transfers

If a debtor transfers property or incurs an obligation with *intent to hinder, delay, or defraud creditors,* the transfer is *voidable* by the trustee. Transfers of property for less than reasonable value are similarly voidable. Suppose Kasper is in financial difficulty. She "sells" her $15,000 car to her mother for $100 so that her creditors cannot claim it. Kasper did not receive fair consideration for this transfer. The transfer could be declared void by a trustee if it was made within two years before the filing of a bankruptcy petition against Kasper.

Some states provide longer periods of time; for example, New York allows trustees to avoid fraudulent transfers made in a six-year period before the bankruptcy filing.

Avoidance of Certain "Retention Bonuses" The 2005 revisions also explicitly authorize the trustee to avoid two types of transfers as fraudulent. First, he may avoid transfers to or for the benefit of an insider under an

Ethics in Action

Should the Homestead Exemption Be Limited?

As of June 2002, six states, including Florida and Texas, provide an unlimited household exemption that allows bankrupt debtors to shield unlimited amounts of equity in a residential estate. The unlimited exemption has come under increased scrutiny in recent years as a number of public figures as well as noted wrongdoers have taken advantage of the unlimited exemption to shield significant amounts of wealth from creditors. For example, a prominent actor who was declared bankrupt in 1996 was allowed to keep a $2.5 million estate located in Hobe Sound, Florida, and a corporate executive convicted of securities fraud kept his Tampa, Florida, mansion from the claims of his creditors in bankruptcy, including federal regulators seeking to collect civil fines. When the Enron and WorldCom corporate scandals broke in 2001 and 2002, the media called attention to a $15 million mansion under construction in Boca Raton, Florida, for the former CFO of WorldCom and to a $7 million penthouse owned by the former CEO of Enron as well as to the fact that the liberal exemption laws in Florida and Texas might be utilized by them to protect a significant amount of their wealth against claims from creditors and regulators.

As noted previously, in the 2005 act, Congress took some steps to limit the ability of debtors to shift assets into an expensive home in a state with an unlimited household exemption shortly before filing for bankruptcy and also to limit the

exemption for debtors convicted of violations of the federal securities laws. While the act was pending in the conference committee, a group of about 80 law professors who teach bankruptcy and commercial law wrote to the committee urging that it adopt a hard cap on the homestead exemption contained in the Senate version of the bill. They pointed out the fundamental unfairness created when residents of one state can protect in a supposedly "uniform" federal bankruptcy proceeding an asset worth millions while residents in other states face sharp limitations on what they can protect. As an example, they noted that a wealthy investor in Texas could keep an unencumbered home worth $10 million while a factory worker in Virginia puts at risk anything over $10,000 in equity.

The law professors described various ways that the formulation the conference committee had adopted could be gamed. They also asserted that the provisions to limit the homestead exemption for those who violate securities laws, who commit fraud while in a fiduciary capacity, or who commit certain felonies or intentional torts were too tightly drawn and would create a "playground of loopholes for wealthy individuals and clever lawyers." They noted, for example, that the provisions "would not cap the homestead exemption for someone who finds a dozen ways to bilk the elderly out of their money, someone who takes advantage of first-time home buyers, or someone who deceives people trying to set up college funds for their children."

Should Congress adopt a uniform cap on the homestead exemption?

---

employment contract and not in the ordinary course of business. Specifically addressed are "retention bonuses" which Congress believed had been abused in some recent high-profile corporate bankruptcies. Retention bonuses can be paid to insiders only where they are made in response to bona fide outside offers, the individual's services are essential to the survival of the business, and the amount of the bonus is not more than 10 times the mean of similar bonuses paid to nonmanagement employees during the year.

Avoidance of Transfers to Certain Asset Protection Trusts The second type of transfer that the trustee was explicitly suthorized to avoid as fraudulent is transfers to a self-settled trust made within 10 years of the filing by a debtor where the debtor is a beneficiary and the transfer was made with actual intent to hinder or delay. There is a particular focus on transfers made in anticipation of any money judgment, settlement, civil penalty, equitable

order, or criminal fine which the debtor believed would be incurred through any violation of federal or state securities laws or fraud, deceit or manipulation in a fiduciary capacity, or in connection with the purchase or sale of securities registered under the federal securities acts.

The provisions of law concerning fraudulent transfers are designed to prevent a debtor from concealing or disposing of his property in fraud of creditors. Such transfers may also subject the debtor to criminal penalties and prevent discharge of the debtor's unpaid liabilities.[1]

The case that follows, *In re Bernard Madoff Investment Securities LLC,* a Trustee, exercising powers under the Bankruptcy Code, sought to avoid monies paid out to certain investors pursuant to a Ponzi scheme as preferential and fraudulent transfers.

---

[1]Bulk sales of a debtor's materials, supplies, merchandise, or other inventory of the business in bulk and not in the ordinary course of business have the potential to defraud creditors.

In re Bernard Madoff Investment Securities LLC
445 B.R. 206 (U.S.B.C., S.D. N.Y. 2011)

For decades, Bernard L. Madoff operated a Ponzi scheme through his investment company, Bernard Madoff Investment Securities LLC (BLMIS). It was a fraud of unparalleled magnitude in which the only assets were other people's money or assets derived from such funds. During the course of the fraud, there were approximately 90,000 disbursements of fictitious profits to Madoff investors totaling $18.8 billion. Due to the longstanding nature of the Ponzi scheme, many of the customer accounts presented multiple generational investments, requiring the Trustee for the Liquidation of BLMIS, Irving Picard, to conduct a full forensic analysis of all of BLMIS's books and records dating back to at least the early 1980s. As of February 18, 2011, the Trustee had determined 16,267 claims under the Securities Investor Protection Act (SIPA), denied 2,740 claims (and 10,731 third-party claims), and allowed claims in the amount of $6,854,549.81.

As part of his effort to recoup monies that could be used to reimburse those who had been defrauded by Madoff, the Trustee brought suit against Stanley Chais, a sophisticated investment advisor who had been closely associated with Madoff since the 1970s, as well as against those who held accounts directed and controlled by Chais, including members of his family and related entitles. The Trustee sought to recover over $1 billion dollars as constituting preferential payments or fraudulent transfers under the Bankruptcy Code.

Prior to Madoff's arrest, Stanley Chais invested in BLMIS for over three decades through more than 60 entity or personal accounts. The Trustee alleged that from his investments with BLMIS, Chais withdrew hundreds of millions of dollars of other investors' money, funneling much of it to his children and their spouses, his grandchildren, and various entities he created for the benefit of his family. He served as the settlor and trustee for numerous trusts as well as the general partner and investment advisor to a number of companies.

As the general partner of Chais Funds, which invested heavily in BLMIS, Chais collected management fees equal to 25 percent of each of Chais Funds' entire net profit for every calendar year in which profits exceed 10 percent, which occurred every calendar year since at least 1996. The Trustee asserted that by virtue of his close and personal relationship with Madoff and expertise as an investment advisor, Stanley Chais knew or should have known that BLMIS was predicated on fraud.

The Trustee also asserted that the other defendants, whether independently or through Stanley Chais, knew or should have known that BLMIS was predicated on fraud and failed to exercise reasonable due diligence into BLMIS. In support of this allegation, the Trustee alleged the following indicia of irregularity and fraud: (1) that their accounts, directed and controlled by Stanley Chais, received fantastical rates of return from 1996 through 2007, including 125 instances of returns exceeding 50 percent, more than 35 instances of returns exceeding 100 percent, and one instance of returns exceeding 300 percent; (2) losses were manufactured after the dates when various transactions took place, including a purchase and sale of 125,000 shares of Micron Technology, Inc., for a loss of more than $1 million appearing for the first time 150 days after the purported purchase; (3) purported losses were generally remedied in subsequent periods with monumental rates of return that far outpaced the market, including a return in one defendant's account from negative 89 percent returns in 2003 to positive 165 percent returns the following year; (4) financial industry press reports questioned the legitimacy of BLMIS and Madoff and their ability to achieve promised returns, and many banks and advisors refused to deal with BLMIS and Madoff; (5) BLMIS lacked transparency to investors, regulars, and other outside parties by failing to provide customers with real-time online access to their accounts and excluding an independent custodian of securities; and (6) BLMIS, one of the world's largest hedge funds, was supposedly audited by Friehling & Horowitz, an accounting firm with only three employees, one of whom was semiretired, with offices in a strip mall.

Chais and a number of the family and related-party defendants filed a motion to dismiss the complaint filed by the Trustee for failure to state a claim on which relief can be granted. In considering such a motion, the court is required to accept all factual allegations in the complaint as true and draw all reasonable inferences in the plaintiff's [the Trustee's] favor.

Lifland, Bankruptcy Judge

The Trustee has sufficiently pled Count Three of the Complaint pursuant to sections 548(a)(1)(A), 550, and 551 of the [Bankruptcy] Code to avoid and recover fraudulent transfers.

Under the Code, "the trustee may avoid any transfer . . . of an interest of the debtor in property . . . made or incurred on or within 2 years before the date of the filing of the petition, if the debtor . . . made such transfer . . . with actual intent to hinder, delay, or defraud." To do this, the complaint must allege "(1) the property subject to the transfer, (2) the timing and, if applicable, frequency of the transfer and (3) the consideration paid with respect thereto." In contrast, fraudulent intent may be pled generally, and under the Code, the Trustee must show such intent on the part of the debtor-transferor.

Exhibit B to the Complaint specifically identifies the date, account number, transferor, transferee, method of transfer, and amount of each of the Transfers that the Trustee has thus far identified. In addition, the Trustee alleges that the Transfers represent redemptions of both principal and fictitious profits. The Six Year Transfers total $804 million, the Two Year Transfers total $377 million, and the Ninety Day Transfers total $46 million. Therefore, the Trustee's allegations sufficiently identify the specific Transfers sought to be avoided.

The Defendants do not dispute that the Trustee has sufficiently alleged the intent of the transferor, BLMIS, for purposes of section 548(a)(1)(A) of the Code. It is now well recognized that the existence of a Ponzi scheme establishes that transfers were made with the intent to hinder, delay, and defraud creditors.

The breadth and notoriety of the Madoff Ponzi scheme leave no basis for disputing the application of the Ponzi scheme presumption to the facts of this case, particularly in light of Madoff's criminal admission. Accordingly, BLMIS's fraudulent intent is established as a matter of law for purposes of the Trustee's Code-based actual fraudulent claims.

The trustee has sufficiently pled actual fraud under the Code, and the motion to dismiss is denied.

[At the same time, the Bankruptcy Judge ruled, among other things, that the Trustee had: (1) adequately alleged fraudulent intent on the part of the defendants; (2) sufficiently pled that transfers challenged as constructively fraudulent under the Code were not made in exchange for reasonably equivalent value.]

 Distinguish among claims, allowable claims, secured claims, and priority claims of creditors.

Claims If creditors wish to participate in the estate of a bankrupt debtor, they must file a proof of claim in the estate within a certain time, usually 90 days after the first meeting of creditors. Only unsecured creditors are required to file proofs of claims. However, a secured creditor whose secured claim exceeds the value of the collateral is an unsecured creditor to the extent of the deficiency. That creditor must file a proof of claim to support the recovery of the deficiency.

Allowable Claims The fact that a proof of claim is filed does not ensure that a creditor can participate in the distribution of the assets of the bankruptcy estate. The claim must also be allowed. If the trustee has a valid defense to the claim, he can use the defense to disallow or reduce it. For example, if the claim is based on goods sold to the debtor and the seller breached a warranty, the trustee can assert the breach as a defense. All of the defenses available to the bankrupt person are available to the trustee.

Under the 2005 revisions, the court is authorized to reduce claims based on unsecured consumer debt by 20 percent on motion by the debtor and a showing that the creditor refused to negotiate a reasonable alternative repayment schedule proposed on behalf of the debtor by an approved nonprofit budget and credit counseling agency. The offer had to have been made at least 60 days before filing of the petition and to have provided for the

payment of at least 60 percent of the debt over a period not to exceed the original period of the loan or a reasonable extension of the time.

Secured Claims The trustee must also determine whether a creditor has a lien or secured interest to secure an allowable claim. If the debtor's property is subject to a secured claim of a creditor, that creditor has first claim to it. The property is available to satisfy claims of other creditors only to the extent that its value exceeds the amount of the debt secured.

Priority Claims The Bankruptcy Code declares certain claims to have priority over other claims. The 10 classes of priority claims are:

1. Domestic support obligations of the debtor, including claims for debts to a spouse, former spouse, or child for alimony to, maintenance for, or support of such spouse or child in connection with a separation agreement, divorce decree, or other court order (but not if assigned to someone else other than a governmental unit). Expenses of a trustee in administering assets that might otherwise be used to pay the support obligations have priority before the support obligations themselves. And, support obligations owed directly to, or recoverable by, spouses and children have priority over support obligations that have been assigned to or are owed directly to a governmental unit.

2. Expenses and fees incurred in administering the bankruptcy estate.

3. Unsecured claims in involuntary cases that arise in the ordinary course of the debtor's business after the filing of the petition but before the appointment of a trustee or the order of relief.

4. Unsecured claims of up to $11,725 per individual (including vacation, severance, and sick pay) for employee's wages earned within 180 days before the petition was filed or the debtor's business ceased.

5. Contributions to employee benefit plans up to $11,725 per person (moreover, the claim for wages plus pension contribution is limited to $11,725 per person).

6. Unsecured claims up to $5,575 (*a*) for grain or the proceeds of grain against a debtor who owns or operates a grain storage facility or (*b*) by a U.S. fisherman against a debtor who operates a fish produce storage or processing facility and who has acquired fish or fish produce from the fisherman.

7. Claims of up to $2,600 each by individuals for deposits made in connection with the purchase, lease, or rental of property or the purchase of goods or services for personal use that were not delivered or provided.

8. Certain taxes owed to governmental units.

9. Allowed unsecured claims based on a commitment by the debtor to a federal depository institution regulatory agency (such as the FDIC).

10. Allowed claims for liability for death or personal injury resulting from operation of a motor vehicle where the operator was unlawfully intoxicated from alcohol, drugs, or other substances.

The 2005 act adds as a category of administrative expenses (see priority 2 above) "the value of any goods received by a debtor within 20 days before the petition date in which the goods have been sold to the debtor in the ordinary course of the debtor's business" The expectation is that a very significant percentage of claims arising from goods sold and received will qualify as administrative expenses. The 2005 revisions also extend the right of vendors to reclaim goods shipped before the petition. Any goods sold in the ordinary course of business and received by a debtor while insolvent may be reclaimed by the seller provided that the seller demands reclamation in writing not later than 45 days after the receipt of the goods or, if the debtor filed its petition during the 45 days, then not later than 20 days after the commencement of the bankruptcy case.

> **L07** Describe the process by which the property in a debtor's estate is distributed to creditors and the debtor is granted a discharge in bankruptcy.

Distribution of the Debtor's Estate The priority claims are paid *after* secured creditors realize on their collateral but *before* other unsecured creditors are paid. Payments are made to the 10 priority classes, in order, to the extent there are funds available. Each class must be paid in full before the next class is entitled to receive anything. To the extent there are insufficient funds to satisfy all the creditors within a class, each class member receives a pro rata share of his claim.

Unsecured creditors include (1) those creditors who had not taken any collateral to secure the debt owed to them; (2) secured creditors to the extent their debt was not satisfied by the collateral they held; and (3) priority claimholders to the extent their claims exceed the limits set for priority claims.

Unsecured creditors, to the extent any funds are available for them, share in proportion to their claims. Unsecured creditors frequently receive little or nothing on their claims. Secured claims, trustee's fees, and other priority claims often consume a large part of the bankruptcy estate.

Special rules are set out in the Bankruptcy Code for distribution of the property of a bankrupt stockbroker or commodities broker.

> **L08**   List the kinds of debts that are not dischargeable.

Discharge in Bankruptcy

Discharge A bankrupt person who has not been guilty of certain dishonest acts and has fulfilled his duties as a bankrupt is entitled to a discharge in bankruptcy. A discharge relieves the bankrupt person of further responsibility for dischargeable debts and gives him a fresh start. A corporation or a partnership is not eligible for a discharge in bankruptcy. A bankrupt person may file a written waiver of his right to a discharge. An individual may not be granted a discharge if she obtained one within the previous eight years.

Objections to Discharge After the bankrupt has paid all of the required fees, the court gives creditors and others a chance to file objections to the discharge of the bankrupt. Objections may be filed by the trustee, a creditor, or the U.S. attorney. If objections are filed, the court holds a hearing to listen to them. At the hearing, the court must determine whether the bankrupt person has committed any act that is a bar to discharge. If the

Distribution of Debtor's Estate (Chapter 7)

Secured creditors proceed directly against the collateral. If debt is fully satisfied, they have no further interest; if debt is only partially satisfied, they are treated as general creditors for the balance.

↓

Debtor's Estate Is Liquidated and Distributed

↓

Priority Creditors (10 classes)

1. Domestic support obligations of the debtor and expenses of administration of assets used to pay support obligations.
2. Costs and expenses of administration.
3. If involuntary proceeding, expenses incurred in the ordinary course of business after petition filed but before appointment of trustee.
4. Claims for wages, salaries, and commissions earned within 180 days of petition; limited to $11,725 per person.
5. Contributions to employee benefit plans arising out of services performed within 180 days of petition; limit of $11,725 (including claims for wages, salaries, and commissions) per person.
6. Unsecured claims (a) for grain or the proceeds of grain against a debtor who owns or operates a grain storage facility or (b) up to $5,775 by a United States fisherman against a debtor who operates a fish produce or processing facility and who has acquired fish or fish produce from the fisherman.
7. Claims of individuals, up to $2,600 per person, for deposits made on consumer goods or services that were not received.
8. Government claims for certain taxes.
9. Allowed unsecured claims based on a commitment by the debtor to a federal depository institution regulatory agency.
10. Allowed claims for liability for death or personal injury resulting from operation of a motor vehicle where the operator was intoxicated.

A. Distribution is made to 10 classes of priority claims in order.
B. Each class must be fully paid before next class receives anything.
C. If funds not sufficient to satisfy everyone in a class, then each member of the class receives same proportion of claim.

↓

General Creditors

1. General unsecured creditors.
2. Secured creditors for the portion of their debt that was not satisfied by collateral.
3. Priority creditors for amounts beyond priority limits.

If funds are not sufficient to satisfy all general creditors, then each receives the same proportion of their claims.

↓

Debtor

Debtor receives any remaining funds.

bankrupt has not committed such an act, the court grants the discharge. If the bankrupt has committed an act that is a bar to discharge, the discharge is denied. The discharge is also denied if the bankrupt fails to appear at the hearing on objections or if he refused earlier to submit to the questioning of the creditors.

Acts That Bar Discharge

Discharges in bankruptcy are intended for honest debtors. Therefore, the following acts bar a debtor from being discharged: (1) the unjustified falsifying, concealing, or destroying of records; (2) making false statements, presenting false claims, or withholding recorded information relating to the debtor's property or financial affairs; (3) transferring, removing, or concealing property in order to hinder, delay, or defraud creditors; (4) failing to account satisfactorily for any loss or deficiency of assets; and (5) failing to obey court orders or to answer questions approved by the court.

Nondischargeable Debts

Certain debts are not affected by the discharge of a bankrupt debtor. The Bankruptcy Code provides that a discharge in bankruptcy releases a debtor from all provable debts except for certain specified debts. These include, among others, debts that:

1. Are due as a tax or fine to the United States or any state or local unit of government.

2. Result from liabilities for obtaining money by false pretenses or false representations.

3. Were incurred by the debtor's purchase of more than $600 in luxury goods or services on credit from a single creditor within 90 days of filing a petition (presumed to be nondischargeable).

4. Are cash advances in excess of $875 obtained by use of a credit card or a revolving line of credit at a credit union and obtained within 70 days of filing a bankruptcy petition (presumed to be nondischargeable).

5. Were not scheduled in time for proof and allowance because the creditor holding the debt did not have notification of the proceeding even though the debtor was aware that he owed money to that creditor.

6. Were created by the debtor's larceny or embezzlement or by the debtor's fraud while acting in a fiduciary capacity.

7. Were for a domestic support obligation (unless excepting it from discharge would impose an undue hardship on the debtor's dependents).

8. Are due for willful or malicious injury to a person or his property.

9. Are educational loans.

10. Are judgments arising out of a debtor's operation of a motor vehicle while legally intoxicated.

11. Are debts incurred to pay a tax to the United States that would not be dischargeable.

12. Are property settlements arising from divorce or separation proceedings *other than* support provisions that are priority claims.

All of these nondischargeable debts are provable debts. The creditor who owns these claims can participate in the distribution of the bankrupt's estate. However, the creditor has an additional advantage: His right to recover the unpaid balance is not cut off by the bankrupt's discharge. All other provable debts are dischargeable; that is, the right to recover them is cut off by the bankrupt's discharge.

In the case that follows, *In re Gerhardt*, the court denied the request of a debtor that his student loans be discharged because their repayment would constitute an undue hardship to him.

In re Gerhardt   348 F.3d 89 (5th Cir. 2003)

Jonathon Gerhardt was a professional cellist who had obtained over $77,000 in government-insured student loans to finance his education at the University of Southern California, the Eastman School of Music, the University of Rochester, and the New England Conservatory of Music. He was 43 years old, healthy, and had no dependants. He subsequently defaulted on each loan owed to the United States government, having paid a total of only $755 on those loans. In 1999, Gerhardt filed for Chapter 7 bankruptcy and subsequently sought discharge of his student loans.

At the time he filed for bankruptcy, Gerhardt was earning $1,680.47 per month as the principal cellist for the Louisiana Philharmonic Orchestra (LPO), including a small amount of supplemental income earned as a cello teacher for Tulane University. His monthly expenses, which included a health club membership and Internet access, averaged $1,829.39. During the LPO off-season, Gerhardt collected unemployment.

The bankruptcy court discharged the student loans as causing undue hardship. On appeal, the district court reversed, holding that it would not be an undue hardship for Gerhardt to repay his loans. Gerhardt appealed that decision to the U.S. Circuit Court of Appeals.

Jones, Circuit Judge

This circuit has not explicitly articulated the appropriate test with which to evaluate the undue hardship determination. The Second Circuit in *Brunner v. New York State Higher Educational Service Corp.* (2nd Cir. 1987) crafted the most widely adopted test. To justify discharging the debtor's student loans, the *Brunner* test requires a three-part showing:

> (1) that the debtor cannot maintain, based on current income and expenses, a "minimal" standard of living for himself and his dependents if forced to repay the loans; (2) that additional circumstances exist indicating this state of affairs is likely to persist for a significant portion of the repayment period of the student loans; and (3) that the debtor has made good faith efforts to pay the loans.

Because the Second Circuit presented a workable approach to evaluating the "undue hardship" determination, this court expressly adopts the *Brunner* test for purposes of evaluating a section claims of "undue hardship".

Under the first prong of the *Brunner* test, the bankruptcy court determined that Gerhardt could not maintain a minimal standard of living if forced to repay his student loans. Evidence was produced at trial that Gerhardt earned $1,680.47 as the principal cellist for the Louisiana Philharmonic Orchestra (LPO), including a small amount of supplemental income earned as a cello teacher for Tulane University. His monthly expenses, which included a health club membership and Internet access, averaged $1,829.39. The bankruptcy court's factual findings are not clearly erroneous. Consequently, we agree with the bankruptcy court conclusion of law that flows from these factual findings. Given that Gerhardt's monthly expenses exceed his monthly income, he has no ability at the present time to maintain a minimal standard of living if forced to repay his loans.

The second prong of the *Brunner* test asks if "additional circumstances exist that this state of affairs is likely to persist for a significant period." "Additional circumstances" encompass "circumstances that impacted on the debtor's future earning potential but which were either not present when the debtor applied for the loans or have since been exacerbated." The second aspect of the test is meant to be a demanding requirement. Thus, proving that the debtor is currently in financial straights is not enough. Instead, the debtor must specifically prove "a total incapacity in the future to pay his debts for reasons not within his control."

Under the second prong of the test, the district court concluded that Gerhardt had not established persistent hardship entitling him to discharge his student loans. Gerhardt holds a masters degree in music from the New England Conservatory of Music. He is about 43 years old, healthy, well-educated, and has no dependants, yet has repaid only $755 of his over $77,000 debt. During the LPO's off-season, Gerhardt has collected unemployment, but he has somehow managed to attend the Colorado Music Festival. Although trial testimony tended to show that Gerhardt would likely not obtain a position at a higher-paying orchestra, he could obtain additional steady employment in a number of different arenas. For instance, he could attempt to teach full-time, obtain night-school teaching, or even work as a music store clerk. Thus, no reasons out of Gerhardt's control perpetuate his inability to repay his student loans.

In addition, nothing in the Bankruptcy Code suggests that a debtor may choose to work only in the field in which he was trained, obtain a low-paying job, and then claim that it would be an undue hardship to repay his student loans. Under the facts presented by Gerhardt, it is difficult to imagine a professional orchestra musician who would not qualify for an undue hardship discharge. Accordingly, Gerhardt has failed to demonstrate the type of exceptional circumstances that are necessary to meet his burden under the second prong of *Brunner*.

Judgment denying the discharge on the grounds of undue hardship affirmed.

Reaffirmation Agreements Sometimes, creditors put pressure on debtors to reaffirm, or to agree to pay, debts that have been discharged in bankruptcy. When the 1978 amendments to the Bankruptcy Code were under consideration, some individuals urged Congress to prohibit such agreements. They argued that reaffirmation agreements were inconsistent with the fresh start philosophy of the Bankruptcy Code. Congress did not agree to a total prohibition; instead, it set up a rather elaborate procedure for a creditor to go through to get a debt reaffirmed. Essentially, the agreement must be made *before* the discharge is granted and the debtor must receive certain specified disclosures at or before the time he signs the reaffirmation agreement. These disclosures include the "amount reaffirmed," the annual percentage rate of interest, the total of fees and costs accrued to date, that the agreement may be rescinded at any time prior to discharge or within 60 days after filing with the court, and a clear and conspicuous statement advising the debtor that the reaffirmation agreement is not required by the bankruptcy law or any other law.

The agreement must be filed with the court—and if the debtor is represented by an attorney, the agreement must be accompanied by a certification from the debtor's attorney that (1) it represents a voluntary agreement by the debtor, (2) that it does not impose an undue hardship on the debtor or any dependent of the debtor, and (3) the debtor was fully advised about the legal consequences of signing the agreement. Where the debtor is not represented by an attorney during the negotiation of the reaffirmation agreement, it is not effective unless approved by the court.

Until 60 days after a reaffirmation agreement is filed with the court, there is a presumption that the agreement will work an undue hardship on the debtor if the debtor's income less the monthly expenses as shown on the schedule she filed is less than the scheduled payments on the reaffirmed debt. The debtor has the opportunity to rebut the presumption, but where the debtor does not do so, the court may disapprove the reaffirmation agreement.

Dismissal for Substantial Abuse

In 1984, Congress, concerned that too many individuals with an ability to pay their debts over time pursuant to a Chapter 13 plan were filing petitions to obtain Chapter 7 discharges of liability, authorized the Bankruptcy Courts to dismiss cases that they determined were a substantial abuse of the bankruptcy process. The courts used this power to dismiss cases where it determined the debtor had acted in bad faith or had the present or future ability to pay a significant portion of her current debts. In the 2005 amendments Congress reduced the standard for dismissal from "substantial abuse" to just "abuse."

Means Testing In the 2005 act, Congress amended the Bankruptcy Code to provide for the dismissal of Chapter 7 cases—or with the debtor's consent their conversion to Chapter 13 cases—on a finding of abuse by an individual debtor with primarily consumer debts. The abuse can be established in two ways: (1) through an unrebutted finding of abuse based on a new "means test" that is included in the Code; or (2) on general grounds of abuse, including bad faith, determined under the totality of the circumstances.

The means test is designed to determine the debtor's ability to repay general unsecured claims. It has three elements: (1) a definition of "current monthly income"—which is the total income a debtor is presumed to have available; (2) a list of allowed deductions from the current monthly income for the purpose of supporting the debtor and his family and for repayment of higher priority debts; and (3) defined "trigger points" at which the income remaining after the allowed deductions would trigger the presumption of abuse. For example, if the debtor's current monthly income after the defined deductions is more than $166.66, the presumption of abuse arises irrespective of the amount of debt; and, if the debtor has at least $100 per month of current monthly income after the allowed deductions (which would amount to $6,000 over five years), then abuse is presumed if that income would be sufficient to pay at least 25 percent of the debtor's unsecured debts over 5 years. To rebut the presumption of abuse, the debtor must show "special circumstances" that would decrease the income or increase expected expenses so as to bring the debtor's income below the trigger points.

Debtors have to file a statement of their calculations under the means test as part of their schedule of current income and expenditures. If the presumption of abuse arises, then the court has to notify the creditors of this situation. While any party in interest generally has the right to bring a motion seeking dismissal of a Chapter 7 case for abuse, only the U.S. Trustee or bankruptcy administrator can bring the motion if the debtor's income is below the median income in the state. Moreover, the means test presumption is inapplicable to debtors whose income is below that state median and also to certain disabled veterans.

In the case that follows, *In re Siegenberg,* the court dismissed a Chapter 7 case on the grounds it was filed in bad faith.

| In re Siegenberg | **2007 LEXIS 2538 (U.S.B.C., C.D. Cal. 2007)** |

Commencing in 2000, when she was hired by Mariah Carey, a prominent entertainer, Nicole Siegenberg worked as a costumer in the entertainment business. Her duties were to buy clothes for and costume her employer. In 2004, she lost her job with Carey and began looking for other similar employment in the entertainment industry. In order to do that she had to build a portfolio which required purchases of clothing stock totaling $9,273 in 2004. Siegenberg's statement of financial affairs indicates that she earned $10,000 in 2004.

Since 2004, Siegenberg was employed only sporadically on temporary jobs such as television pilots. When employed, she earned about $2,000 per week. Unfortunately, since 2004 she was usually unemployed. Thus, in 2005 she earned $12,648, and in 2006 she earned $35,253.

Siegenberg lived with her parents in her parents' condominium in Pacific Palisades. During the 2004 to 2006 period she incurred debts to, among other things, assist her parents with a property they had bought as an investment to provide income when her father was unable to continue his job; to assist a boyfriend who was a realtor with expenses on properties he was seeking to market; travel with her boyfriend and her mother to South Africa to visit her sick grandmother; assist her mother with medical expenses; and provide living expenses for herself. Some of the expenses were reimbursed to her, while others were not.

Siegenberg filed a Chapter 7 bankruptcy on November 29, 2006. Siegenberg owed $82,597.12 in unsecured debt and $27,664 in secured debt on her car and her boyfriend's car (a 2001 BMW and a 1999 Cadillac Escalade, respectively). The United States Trustee (UST) filed a motion to dismiss Siegenberg's Chapter 7 petition as filed in bad faith and sought a one-year bar against refiling.

Donovan, U.S. Bankruptcy Judge

In considering whether a Chapter 7 case should be dismissed because granting relief would be an abuse of the provisions of Chapter 7, courts may consider (a) whether the debtor filed the petition in bad faith; or (b) whether the totality of the circumstances of the debtor's financial situation demonstrates abuse.

A. Dismissal for Bad Faith under 707(b)(3)(A)

Section 707(b)(3) was added to the Bankruptcy Code by the Bankruptcy Abuse Prevention and Consumer Protection Act of 2005 (BAPCPA). Since BAPCPA, the Ninth Circuit has not established a standard for determining a finding of "bad faith" in Chapter 7 cases under *§ 707(b)(3)(A)*. However, a few bankruptcy courts have addressed the issue. The court in *In re Mitchell,* a Chapter 7 case, used a nine-part test borrowing both from the Ninth Circuit's pre-BAPCPA "substantial abuse" test and from Chapter 11 and 13 bad faith cases. The court in *Mitchell* considered the following nine factors in determining whether "the debtor's intention in filing bankruptcy is inconsistent with the Chapter 7 goals of providing a 'fresh start' to debtors and maximizing return to creditors" and whether the case should thus be dismissed under *§ 707(b)(3)(A)*:

1. Whether the Chapter 7 debtor has a likelihood of sufficient future income to fund a Chapter 11, 12, or 13 plan which would pay a substantial portion of the unsecured claims;

2. Whether debtor's petition was filed as a consequence of illness, disability, unemployment, or other calamity;

3. Whether debtor obtained cash advances and consumer goods on credit exceeding his or her ability to repay;

4. Whether debtor's proposed family budget is excessive or extravagant;

5. Whether debtor's statement of income and expenses misrepresents debtor's financial condition;

6. Whether debtor made eve of bankruptcy purchases;

7. Whether debtor has a history of bankruptcy petition filings and dismissals;

8. Whether debtor has invoked the automatic stay for improper purposes, such as to delay or defeat state court litigation;

9. Whether egregious behavior is present.

1. Likelihood that the Chapter 7 debtor will have sufficient future income to fund a Chapter 11 or 13 plan. Siegenberg does not currently have income to fund a Chapter 11 or 13 plan. According to the pleadings, such future income is not foreseeable. This fact supports Siegenberg's position.

2. Consequence of illness, disability, unemployment or other calamity. Siegenberg claims, in part, that the bankruptcy petition was filed as a consequence of the disability of her father. His disability and surgery in April 2006 caused financial panic in her family, in response to which her parents bought a house in the hope of remodeling it and selling it quickly at a profit. Siegenberg contributed $35,000 to remodel that investment property under an agreement that promised her 50 percent of the profit. However, her parents sold the home at a loss and Siegenberg received no money in return for her investment.

Siegenberg did not experience an illness, disability, new unemployment, or other calamity. On the contrary, she provides evidence of only modest improvement in her employment status for the year 2006, not enough to match her greater expenditures. There was no change in her health status after 2004.

Further Siegenberg incurred thousands of dollars of new credit card debt on plane tickets, a car for her boyfriend, hotel stays, and other consumer items that are not convincingly attributable to any reasonably, potentially revenue-producing activities during May 2006, the month after her father's surgery and the month during which her parents purchased a house as an investment property, the alleged period of financial distress.

3. Obtaining cash advances and consumer goods on credit exceeding Siegenberg's ability to repay. Much of the argument between the two parties revolves around the question of consumer spending. The UST argues that Siegenberg purchased luxury consumer items on credit beyond her ability to repay at the expense of her creditors. Siegenberg urges in response that various expenditures were either for business purposes or were repaid.

Siegenberg asserts that she spent approximately $35,000 on her parent's residential investment; she repaid pre-bankruptcy almost two-thirds of the cost of the plane tickets to South Africa ($5,500); her parents wrote a check that she forwarded to her credit card company to repay $12,500 for the credit card charges for her mother's surgery; her expenditures on clothing were (a) a legitimate business expense and (b) some of the clothing was returned for credit; and she traveled to Mexico for the purpose of attaining a job.

On the other hand, Siegenberg provides no detail to explain $42,775 in cash advances she received on her credit card accounts between May 2005 and October 2006. She does not provide evidence of contractor payments she claims to have made that exceeded $19,607. She does not provide corroborating detailed evidence that during the period covered by the UST's motion she used the clothing she bought for demonstrable business purposes. Regarding her Mexican expenditures, it appears that she incurred credit card debt of more than $6,000 before July 2006, but only about $2,000 between July and October 2006, the period during which she claims she was interviewing for employment in Mexico. The pre-July Mexican expenditures appear to be for consumer items such as plane tickets, hotels, and restaurants for the personal pleasure of Siegenberg and her boyfriend, and Siegenberg offers no convincing evidence to persuade me otherwise.

Similarly, Siegenberg does not persuasively explain the reasonable business purpose of about $5,500 in car-related credit card debt creating expenditures (including $2,500 on her boyfriend's Cadillac down payment), as well as $2,129 on restaurants, and about $900 on hotels in Southern California, among other consumer items.

The sum of Siegenberg's justified business or personal expenditures, including contractor expenses, reimbursed tickets to South Africa, her mother's surgery, returned clothing, and spending to pursue employment in Mexico is about $59,000. On the other hand, the sum of her unexplained and unjustified cash advances, and other credit card debt for Mexican travel spending prior to her Mexican job interviews, on cars, Southern California hotels, and unexplained clothing expenditures is about $58,000. Further, if only the $19,607 in contractor charges are included in her explained expenditures, instead of her uncorroborated claim that she incurred $35,000 for such contractor charges, then her adequately explained expenditures are about $44,000 while her unexplained expenditures would appear to be about $73,000.

Whatever Siegenberg's business-oriented goals, her very substantial credit card charges for consumer goods and cash advances were incurred without any reasonable or foreseeable ability to repay them. I conclude, on balance, that such charges, under the circumstances, are evidence of Siegenberg's bad faith.

4. Excessive or extravagant proposed family budget. Siegenberg's budget appears to be excessive. In Schedules I and J, she claims average monthly income of $2,466.58 and average monthly expenditures of $5,368.60, including $1,824 to support her parents and $560.43 for car payments, as well as $652 in regular business operating expenses. In light of the thousands of dollars Siegenberg charged on her credit cards monthly during 2006, as well as minimal credit card payments she was required to make, the gap between her monthly income and budget appears excessive and is suggestive of a lack of good faith on her part.

5. Statement of income and expenses misrepresenting financial condition. The UST has not alleged any misrepresentation in Siegenberg's statement of financial condition.

6. Eve of bankruptcy purchases. Siegenberg claims that in fact she made an eve of bankruptcy payment rather than purchases, $12,500 toward her mother's surgery, militating in favor of a finding of good faith.

On the other hand, according to her Schedule F, Siegenberg opened at least three of her 11 credit cards in 2006, one in January and two in July. She owes $7,670 on the one opened in January, $10,925 on one opened in July, and $6,522 on the other opened in July. Thus, in under four months of use, Siegenberg became indebted for $17,447 on two cards that she opened within five months of filing. Also, she charged at least $6,759 in September and October 2006, within about two months of her bankruptcy petition. These are instances of eve of bankruptcy purchases that suggest a lack of good faith under the circumstances, regardless of alleged business purpose, given the wide gaps between her earnings and her new credit card debt.

7. Bankruptcy history. Siegenberg does not have a history of bankruptcy petition filing and dismissals.

8. Improper purpose for automatic stay: state litigation. There is no evidence that Siegenberg has invoked the automatic stay for an improper purpose, such as to defeat state court litigation.

9. Egregious behavior. Siegenberg argues that rather than exhibiting egregious behavior, the facts illustrate bad financial luck. She points to the fact that she has had a hard time finding a job in the entertainment industry, though she has spent a lot of money trying; her family's real estate investment flopped; and the interviews for a job selling Mexican time shares turned out to be a waste of time. In the end, she claims that despite her honest efforts to improve her income, she has been unlucky and, thus, is unable to pay off her debts.

Even assuming all of what Siegenberg says is true, those factors do not justify the spending detailed above. In light of her low rate of income over a three-year period preceding bankruptcy, her sizeable consumer-oriented expenditures and unexplained cash advance debt appear to be egregious under the circumstances, rather than legitimate startup business expenses.

Thus, analysis pursuant to five of nine *Mitchell* factors, factors 2, 3, 4, 6, and 9 supports a finding of a lack of good faith.

B. Dismissal under *707(b)(3)(B)*: Totality of the Circumstances

Additionally, dismissal would appear to be appropriate under § *707(b)(3)(B)*, considering the "totality of the circumstances" presented by the evidence. Bankruptcy courts that have addressed § *707(b)(3)* since the enactment of BAPCPA have found that the "totality of the circumstances" tests that were applicable under the former § *707(b)* remain applicable under BAPCPA. BAPCPA made changes, however, making it easier for the UST to prove a case for abuse because (a) there is no longer a presumption in favor of granting relief to a debtor, and (b) the standard for dismissal is reduced from "substantial abuse" to mere "abuse." The *In re Price* "totality of the circumstances" test includes the following six factors:

1. Whether there is a likelihood of future income to fund debtor's Chapter 11, 12, or 13 plan;

2. Whether the petition was filed as a consequence of illness, disability, unemployment, or other calamity;

3. Whether the schedules suggest debtor obtained cash advances and consumer goods without the ability to repay;

4. Whether debtor's proposed family budget is excessive or extravagant;

5. Whether debtor's papers misrepresent his or her financial condition; and

6. Whether debtor engaged in eve of bankruptcy purchases.

Here, *Price* factors 2, 3, 4, and 6 are unfavorable to Siegenberg, indicating a lack of good faith and supporting a conclusion of abuse under § *707(b)(3)(B)*.

1. Future income to fund a Chapter 11 or 13 plan. The UST has failed to establish that Siegenberg has a foreseeable likelihood of future income to fund a Chapter 11 or 13.

2. Consequence of illness, disability, unemployment, or calamity. This factor is unfavorable to Siegenberg because she does not present evidence that she herself experienced a grave illness, change in employment status, disability, or any other calamity that might explain the excess of her debt over her income.

3. Cash advances and consumer goods without ability to repay. As discussed above, Siegenberg incurred substantial credit card debt that might be considered business related or which may have been incurred in the attempt to improve her financial situation. However, a large portion of her credit card debt was incurred to acquire consumer goods and services and cash advances whose business purposes remain unexplained. Thus, on balance, this factor weighs against her.

4. Excessive or extravagant family budget. As discussed above, Siegenberg's monthly income is less than half of her monthly spending, which includes $560.43 on cars payments and $1,824 in support of her parents. Considering her high rate of debt accumulation, her budget is excessive and suggestive of a lack of good faith.

5. Misrepresentation of financial condition. The UST has not alleged any misrepresentation in Siegenberg's papers as to her financial condition.

6. Eve of bankruptcy purchases. As discussed above, Siegenberg opened two credit cards in July of 2006. During the four months in which those cards were in use she charged $17,447 on those two cards alone. Further, Siegenberg purchased at least $6,759 on various cards in September and October 2006. These facts are suggestive of a lack of good faith in her bankruptcy filing.

C. Dismissal with a One-Year Bar against Refiling

A bankruptcy court may, for cause, dismiss a bankruptcy case with a bar against later discharge of debt. A finding of bad faith based on egregious behavior can justify dismissal with prejudice. The bankruptcy court should consider the following factors when considering barring later discharge for bad faith:

1. Whether debtor misrepresented facts in her petition, unfairly manipulated the bankruptcy code, or otherwise filed in an inequitable manner;

2. Debtor's filing history;

3. Whether debtor only intended to defeat state court litigation;

4. Whether egregious behavior is present.

Here, while egregious behavior is present, the other three factors are not. There are no allegations of misrepresentation; Siegenberg has no bankruptcy history; and there has been no mention of state court litigation. Under the egregious circumstances outlined, it would appear to be appropriate to bar Siegenberg from refiling a bankruptcy petition for at least one year, as the UST has requested.

Conclusion

Siegenberg has used her credit cards in various efforts to extricate herself and her family from financial difficulties. She also used her credit cards for tens of thousands of dollars in personal expenditures, the purchase of consumer goods and services, and to obtain unexplained cash advances. The record contains significant evidence of these ostensibly excessive expenditures and contains only patchy, incomplete, and unconvincing evidence that most of these expenditures were made to further Siegenberg's business efforts. **I believe it is appropriate to grant the UST's motion to dismiss Siegenberg's Chapter 7 petition, and to impose a one-year bar on future bankruptcy filings by or against Siegenberg.**

L09 Explain the purpose and basic procedure of Chapter 11 Reorganizations.

Chapter 11: Reorganizations

Reorganization Proceeding Sometimes, creditors benefit more from the continuation of a bankrupt debtor's business than from the liquidation of the debtor's property. Chapter 11 of the Bankruptcy Code provides a proceeding whereby, under the supervision of the Bankruptcy Court, the debtor's financial affairs can be reorganized rather than liquidated. Chapter 11 proceedings are available to individuals and to virtually all business enterprises, including individual proprietorships, partnerships, and corporations (except banks, savings and loan associations, insurance companies, commodities brokers, and stockbrokers).

Chapter 11 cases for individuals look much like the Chapter 13 cases which are discussed later in this chapter but the amount of debt is usually much larger and it commonly is predominantly nonconsumer debt. The 2005 act created a special subclass of "small business debtors" debtors with less than $2 million in debts and provides special rules for them, including expedited decision making.

Petitions for reorganization proceedings can be filed voluntarily by the debtor or involuntarily by its creditors. Once a petition for a reorganization proceeding is filed and relief is ordered, the court usually appoints (1) a committee of creditors holding unsecured claims, and (2) a committee of equity security holders (shareholders). Normally, the debtor becomes the debtor in possession and the responsibility for running the debtor's business. It is also usually responsible for developing a plan for handling the various claims of creditors and the various interests of persons such as shareholders.

The reorganization plan is essentially a contract between a debtor and its creditors. This contract may involve recapitalizing a debtor corporation and/or giving creditors some equity, or shares, in the corporation in exchange for part or all of the debt owed to them. The plan must (1) divide the creditors into classes; (2) set forth how each creditor will be satisfied; (3) state which claims, or classes of claims, are impaired or adversely affected by the plan; and (4) provide the same treatment to each creditor in a particular class, unless the creditors in that class consent to different treatment.

For example, when Kmart's Chapter 11 reorganization plan was accepted by its creditors and approved by the bankruptcy court in 2003, the plan called for its banks who held secured claims to receive about 40 cents on each dollar they were owed and for the holders of unsecured claims to receive new stock valued at 14.4 percent of their claim.

The Bankruptcy Code provides for an initial 120-day period after the petition is filed during which only the debtor can file a reorganization plan, and a 180-day period within which only the debtor may solicit acceptances of the plan from creditors. The bankruptcy court, in its discretion, may extend these periods. The 2005 act limits the debtor's exclusive plan proposal period to 18 months and the exclusive solicitation period to 20 months. After the initial time periods pass, creditors are free to propose plans and seek acceptance of them by other creditors. In some cases, debtors develop what is known as a prepackaged plan whereby the debtor solicits acceptances of the plan prior to filing for bankruptcy. The 2005 act contains a number of provisions designed to facilitate the use of such plans.

A reorganization plan must be confirmed by the court before it becomes effective. Plans can be confirmed either through the voluntary agreement of creditors or alternatively through what is known as a cram down whereby the court forces dissenting creditors whose claims would be impaired by a proposed plan to accept the plan when the court can find that it is fair and equitable to the class of creditors whose claims are impaired. If the plan is confirmed, the debtor is responsible for carrying it out.

However, until a plan is confirmed, the bankruptcy court has no authority to distribute any portion of the bankruptcy assets to unsecured creditors.

Confirmation through Acceptance by Creditors A court must confirm a plan if the following requirements, among others, are met:

1. Each class of creditors or interests has either accepted the plan or such class is not impaired under the plan.

2. Each impaired class of claimants has either unanimously accepted the plan or will receive or retain under the plan property of a value not less than the holders of the claims would receive or retain if the debtor was liquidated under Chapter 7.

3. All secured creditors have either accepted the plan or their class of creditors is not impaired under the plan.

4. If any class of claims is impaired, then at least one class of impaired claims must have voted to accept the plan. A plan is deemed accepted by a class of creditors if more than one-half the number of creditors who vote

to accept the plan represent at least two-thirds of the dollar amount of allowed claims in the class.

5. The plan must be feasible. The court must be able to conclude that confirmation of the plan is not likely to be followed by the liquidation or the need for further financial reorganization of the debtor or any successor to the debtor unless the reorganization is proposed in the plan.

In addition, where the debtor is an individual, the amount of property to be distributed under the plan must not be less than the projected disposable income of the individual to be received during the period for which payments are to be made or five years, whichever is longer. Also, the debtor must have paid all domestic support obligations that became payable after the filing of the petition.

In the case below, *In re Made In Detroit,* the court was unable to conclude that a proposed plan was feasible and declined to confirm it.

Confirmation of a Plan by a Cram Down Where a class of creditors whose claims or interests are impaired does not accept the proposed plan, then the plan has not been accepted but the court may still confirm the plan under a "cram down" if it concludes that the plan is fair and equitable to the impaired class. A plan is considered to be fair and equitable to an impaired class of *secured creditors* if the reorganization plan (1) allows the class to retain its liens securing the claims (even where the property is transferred to a third person) and each holder of a claim in the class receives deferred cash payments totaling at least the allowed amount of claim, of value of at least the value of the holder's interest in the bankruptcy estate's interest in the property; *or* (2) provides for the sale of any property subject to liens securing such claims free and clear of such liens with the liens to attach to the proceeds of the sale; *or* (3) provides for the realization by the holders of the "indubitable equivalent" of such claims.

A plan is considered to be fair and equitable to *a class of impaired claimants with unsecured claims* if the plan (1) provides that each holder of a claim will receive or retain on account of the claim property of a value equal to the allowed amount of such claim *or* (2) the holder of any claim that is junior to the claims of such class will not receive or retain any property on account of the junior claim or interest.

A plan is considered to be fair and equitable to a *class of interests* (such as equity holders) if (1) the plan provides that each holder of an interest in the class receives or retains property of a value equal to the greatest of the amount of any fixed liquidation preference to which the holder is entitled, any fixed redemption price to which the holder is entitled, or the value of such interest; or (2) the holder of any interest that is junior to the interests of such class will not receive any property on account of such junior claim.

| In re Made in Detroit, Inc. | 299 B.R. 170 U.S.B.C. (E.D. Mich. 2003) |

In 1997, Made In Detroit, Inc., purchased approximately 410 acres of property for the purpose of development. The property is located on the Detroit River in Gibraltar and Trenton, Michigan, and is Made In Detroit's only significant asset. For the next five years, Made In Detroit attempted to develop the property. Due to problems obtaining permits, and because Made In Detroit was not generating income, it became delinquent to secured creditors. In 2002, the primary secured creditor, Standard Federal, commenced a foreclosure action against Made In Detroit. As a result, on October 23, 2002, Made In Detroit filed for bankruptcy protection under Chapter 11 of the Bankruptcy Code.

On July 15, 2003, Made In Detroit filed its Third Amended Combined Plan and Disclosure Statement (the "Debtor's Plan"). The Debtor's Plan provided that it would be funded with a $9 million loan from Kennedy Funding and that the Kennedy loan is contingent on certain conditions precedent, including the payment of a nonfundable $270,000 commitment fee and an appraisal of the property that indicated it would have a "quick sale" value of at least $15 million. The Kennedy commitment also provided a condition of its part; namely, that it intended to bring participants into the transaction and if it was unable to do so, it would only be obligated to refund the commitment fee less compensation for its time and expenses. The Debtor's Plan provided that once the $9 million loan was obtained, the secured creditors and administrative claimants would be paid in full, the unsecured creditors would receive an initial distribution of $750,000 (with the balance of the claims to be paid from the sale of lots), and equity shareholders would retain their interest.

The Official Committee of Unsecured Creditors (the "Committee") and the Wayne County Treasurer filed objections to confirmation of the Debtor's Plan. In addition, on July 9, 2003, the Committee filed its own plan of reorganization. The Committee's Plan provided that it would be financed by an "as is" immediate cash sale of the property to the Trust for Public Land for $4 million. Under the Plan, the Trust for Public Land would pay $4.8 million to the Debtor's Estate to settle all claims with *respect to the real property and would receive title to the property free of all liens, claims, and other encumbrances. Under the terms of the Committee's Plan, the secured creditors would be paid in full, the unsecured creditors would receive a pro rata payment (after payment of the administrative claims and higher classes of claims), and the equity shareholders would not receive any distribution nor would they retain any property interest.*

Made In Detroit objected to the Committees Plan, and the Bankruptcy Court held a hearing on confirmation of both the Debtor's and the Committee's Plans.

McIvor, Bankruptcy Judge

Debtor's Plan fails to meet the requirement that a plan must be feasible. Feasibility is a mandatory requirement for confirmation. Section 1129(a)(11) of the Bankruptcy Code provides that a plan can be confirmed only if "confirmation of the plan is not likely to be followed by the liquidation, or the need for further organization, of the debtor or any successor to the debtor under the plan, unless such liquidation or reorganization is proposed in the plan."

Section 1129(a)(11) prevents confirmation of visionary schemes which promise creditors more than the debtor can possibly attain after confirmation. A plan that is submitted on a conditional basis is not considered feasible, and thus confirmation of such a plan must be denied.

The plan does not need to guarantee success, but it must present reasonable assurance of success. To provide such reasonable assurance, a plan must provide a realistic and workable framework for reorganization. The plan cannot be based on "visionary promises"; it must be doable.

Sincerity, honesty and willingness are not sufficient to make the plan feasible, and neither are visionary promises. The test is whether the things which are to be done after confirmation can be done as a practical matter under the facts.

In re Hoffman (Bankr. D.N.D. 1985).

In *Hoffman*, the debtor's plan proposed to pay creditors within two years from the sale of real property. However, there was no potential purchaser and the plan did not set forth the terms of the proposed sale. The court found that the plan was not feasible because the proposed sale of the real estate was not "sufficiently concrete to assure either consummation within the two-years, or that even if sold within the two-year period the price obtained would be sufficient" to pay the secured creditor.

Similarly, in *In re Walker* (E.D. Va. 1994), the court also found a plan based on funding through a speculative sale of real estate was not feasible. There, the district court reversed the bankruptcy court's confirmation of a plan because the plan was not feasible. The plan proposed to pay creditors from the sale of two parcels of real estate. However, the plan did not provide any time frame within which the properties would be sold, did not set forth the terms of the proposed sale, and did not set forth a plan for the liquidation of other properties if the proceeds from the sale of the two identified properties was insufficient to pay

creditors. Based on these deficiencies, the court held that the proposed plan was not feasible.

Likewise, in *In re Thurmon* (Bankr. M.D. Fla. 1988), the court found that a plan conditioned on a sale of property which in turn was conditioned on financing was not feasible. In *Thurmon*, the plan proposed that funding would be obtained through a lease-purchase agreement. The lease-purchase agreement provided that a buyer would lease property from the debtor and would then purchase 147 acres from the debtor. The closing of the land sale was conditioned on the buyer's ability to obtain financing on favorable terms. The buyer had not yet applied for the financing but testified that he would do so within 30 days. The court found that the plan was not feasible because it was not reasonably likely that the money to fund the plan would come from the buyer.

While Debtor in this case is sincere, honest, and willing, the Debtor's Plan of Reorganization is not realistic, as it does not provide a reasonable assurance of success. The Plan is based on "wishful thinking" and "visionary promises." As a practical matter, the Debtor's Plan is not sufficiently concrete as to be feasible because it is contingent on exit financing from Kennedy and there is no reasonable assurance that the Kennedy loan will ever close or that the property will be appraised at a value high enough to provide a $9 million loan. Like in *Hoffman, Walker,* and *Thurmon,* it is not reasonably likely that Debtor's Plan will be funded. The conditions precedent to Kennedy's funding of the loan were not satisfied as of the date of the confirmation hearing. Further, the evidence did not show that the satisfaction of such conditions was reasonably likely in the foreseeable future.

The $270,000 loan commitment fee was never put into an escrow account or paid to Kennedy Funding. Even if Debtor had paid the commitment fee, there still were substantial obstacles to closing on the proposed Kennedy loan. First and foremost, in order for Kennedy to fund the required $9 million loan, it would need to value the property on an "as is" quick sale basis at $15 million. The evidence did not provide any reasonable assurance that the property would be valued at this amount; in fact, the evidence showed that the property, if sold "as is," was only worth approximately $4.2 million.

The best evidence of the value of the property, what a reasonable buyer would pay a reasonable seller for the property, is the Trust for Public Land's offer to purchase the property "as is" for

$4.8 million. Additional evidence that the "as is" value of the property is well below the $15 million value needed to obtain the Kennedy financing was provided by a current appraisal prepared by Integra Realty Resources.

The Integra appraisal report, dated on September 5, 2003, indicates that the "as is" market value of the property, if marketed from nine to twelve months, was $5,260,000. The report also stated the "disposition value" of the property, if only marketed for three to six months, was $4,210,000. The "as is" quick sale value as defined in the Kennedy commitment letter was based on a marketing period of "90 to 120 days," i.e., three to six months. Thus, for Kennedy to fund the $9 million loan proposed in Debtor's Plan, the "disposition value" of the property would have to be at least, $15 million. The appraiser who prepared the Integra report, Kenneth Blondell, testified at the confirmation hearing. Blondell is a certified MAI appraiser, and he was qualified as an expert. The Integra report and Blondell's testimony provided a credible expert opinion that the disposition value of the property is only $4.2 million.

In summary, the Debtor failed to show at confirmation that it had exit financing to fund its plan. The proposed financing had so many contingencies that Debtor's Plan was conditional at best. Thus, the Debtor's Plan is not feasible under 1129(a)(11), and the Court must deny confirmation of Debtor's Plan.

The Court denied confirmation of Debtor's Plan.

Use of Chapter 11 During the 1980s, attempts by a number of corporations to seek refuge in Chapter 11 as a means of escaping problems they were facing received considerable public attention. Some of the most visible cases involved efforts to obtain some protection against massive product liability claims and judgments for damages for breach of contract and to escape from collective bargaining agreements. Thus, for example, Johns-Manville Corporation filed under Chapter 11 because of the claims against it arising out of its production and sale of asbestos years earlier, while A. H. Robins Company was concerned about a surfeit of claims arising out of its sale of the Dalkon Shield, an intrauterine birth control device. And, in 1987, Texaco, Inc., faced with a $10.3 billion judgment in favor of Pennzoil in a breach of contract action, filed a petition for reorganizational relief under Chapter 11. Companies such as LTV and Allegheny Industries sought changes in retirement and pension plans, and other companies such as Eastern Airlines sought refuge in Chapter 11 while embroiled in labor disputes.

In the 1990s, a number of companies that were the subject of highly leveraged buyouts (LBOs) financed with so-called junk bonds, including a number of retailers, resorted to Chapter 11 to seek restructuring and relief from their creditors. Similarly, companies such as Pan Am and TWA that were hurt by economic slowdown and increase in fuel prices filed Chapter 11 petitions. In 2001, Enron and Kmart filed for reorganization under Chapter 11 as did WorldCom and USAirways in 2002.

In recent years, Chapter 11 has been the subject of significant criticism and calls for its revision. Critics point out that many of the Chapter 11 cases are permitted to drag on for years, thus depleting the assets of the debtor through payments to trustees and lawyers involved in administration and diminishing the assets available to creditors. For example, *The Wall Street Journal* noted in a July 11, 2003, article, "The Chapter 11 restructuring of Enron, whose controversial collapse became a symbol of corporate malfeasance, has dragged on for 19 months, generating more than 11,000 court filings and nearly $500 million in professional fees." This took the case to the point where the company was about to file its proposed reorganization plan and seek acceptance from creditors and approval by the bankruptcy court.

In the 2005 act, Congress responded to some of these concerns by establishing tighter time frames and placing some limits or restrictions on the availability of extensions of time. Examples include the limitations on the time period in which the debtor has the exclusive right to develop a reorganization plan and special rules forcing debtors to make decisions as to whether to assume or reject unexpired leases of nonresidential property such as space in shopping centers and office buildings.

Special Rules for Nonresidential Real Property Lessors Under the pre-2005 act, courts were allowed to grant, and often granted, repeated extensions of the 60-day period that debtors in Chapter 11 proceedings have to either assume or reject unexpired leases of nonresidential real property. Under the 2005 revisions, debtors must assume or reject unexpired leases of nonresidential real property by the earlier of 120 days from the date the petition is filed or the date a plan is confirmed. Failure to do so in a timely way results in the lease being deemed rejected. Courts are permitted to extend the time for an additional 90 days on a showing of good cause, but any further extensions can be granted only if the lessor consents in writing.

Ethics in Action

Using Bankruptcy to Manage Product Liability or to Change Labor Contracts

As noted above, in recent years a number of corporations have resorted to Chapter 11 to deal with their exposure to product liability claims or to seek changes in labor contracts. Is it ethical for a company like A. H. Robins Company that is faced with significant liability for birth-control devices it made and sold, or for a company like Johns-Manville that faces multimillion claims from individuals who were exposed to asbestos it made to seek the protection accorded by the bankruptcy laws? Similarly, is it ethical for a company that believes it is hampered by a labor contract under which it incurs higher costs than some of its competitors to try to use a Chapter 11 proceeding to get out of the labor contract?

These provisions help protect landlords who have leased property to individuals or entities that subsequently filed for bankruptcy protection. They require the bankrupt to decide relatively quickly whether they will go forward with the lease and fullfill their obligation or whether they will surrender the property to the landlord so he can secure a new paying tenant.

Collective Bargaining Agreements Collective bargaining contracts pose special problems. Prior to the 1984 amendments, there was concern that some companies would use Chapter 11 reorganizations as a vehicle to avoid executed collective bargaining agreements. The concern was heightened by the Supreme Court's 1984 decision in *NLRB v. Bildisco and Bildisco.* In that case, the Supreme Court held that a reorganizing debtor did not have to engage in collective bargaining before modifying or rejecting portions of a collective bargaining agreement and that such unilateral alterations by a debtor did not violate the National Labor Relations Act.

Congress then acted to try to prevent the misuse of bankruptcy proceedings for collective bargaining purposes. The act's 1984 amendments adopt a rigorous multistep process that must be complied with in determining whether a labor contract can be rejected or modified as part of a reorganization. Among other things that must be done before a debtor or trustee can seek to avoid a collective bargaining agreement are the submission of a proposal to the employees' representative that details the "necessary" modifications to the collective bargaining agreement and ensures that "all creditors, the debtor and all affected parties are fairly treated." Then, before the bankruptcy court can authorize a rejection of the original collective bargaining agreement, it must review the proposal and find that (1) the employees' representative refused to accept it without good cause, and (2) the balance of equities clearly favors the rejection of the original collective bargaining agreement.

Chapter 12: Family Farmers and Fishermen

Relief for Family Farmers and Fishermen Historically, farmers have been accorded special treatment in the Bankruptcy Code. In the 1978 act, as in earlier versions, small farmers were exempted from involuntary proceedings. Thus, a small farmer who filed a voluntary Chapter 11 or 13 petition could not have the proceeding converted into a Chapter 7 liquidation over his objection so long as he complied with the Code's requirements in a timely fashion. Additional protection was also accorded through the provision allowing states to opt out of the federal exemption scheme and to provide their own exemptions. A number of states used this flexibility to provide generous exemptions for farmers so they would be able to keep their tools and implements.

Despite these provisions, the serious stress on the agricultural sector in the mid-1980s led Congress in 1986 to further amend the Bankruptcy Code by adding a new Chapter 12 targeted to the financial problems of the family farm. During the 1970s and 1980s, farmland prices appreciated and many farmers borrowed heavily to expand their productive capacity, creating a large debt load in the agricultural sector. When land values subsequently dropped and excess production in the world kept farm product prices low, many farmers faced extreme financial difficulty. In the 2005 act, Chapter 12 proceedings were made available to family fishermen.

Chapter 12 is modeled after Chapter 13, which is discussed next. It is available only for family farmers and fishermen with regular income. To qualify, a farmer and spouse must have not less than 80 percent of their total noncontingent, liquidated debts arising out of their farming operations. The aggregate debt must be less than $3,792,650 and at least 50 percent of an individual's or couple's income during the year preceding the filing of the petition must have come from the farming operation and at least 80 percent of the assets must be related to the farming operation. A corporation or partnership can also qualify, provided that more than 50 percent of the stock or equity is held by one family or its relatives and they conduct the farming operation. Again, 80 percent of the debt must arise from the farming operation; the aggregate debt ceiling is $3,792,650.

In the case of a family fisherman, the debtor and spouse engaged in a commercial fishing operation are eligible for relief under Chapter 12 if their aggregate debts do not exceed $1,757,475 and not less than 80 percent of their aggregate noncontingent liquidated debts (excluding a debt for their principal residence) arise out of the commercial fishing operation. Again, a corporation or partnership can qualify so long as at least 50 percent is held by the family and relatives that conduct the fishing operation, its aggregate debts do not exceed $1,642,500, and at least 80 percent of the aggregate noncontingent liquidated debts arise out of a commercial fishing operation.

The debtor is usually permitted to remain in possession to operate the farm or fishing vessel. Although the debtor in possession has many of the rights of a Chapter 11 trustee,

a trustee is appointed under Chapter 12 and the debtor is subject to his supervision. The trustee is permitted to sell unnecessary assets, including farmland and farming or fishing equipment, without the consent of secured creditors and before a plan is approved. However, the secured creditor's interest attaches to the proceeds of the sale.

The debtor is required to file a plan within 90 days of the filing of the Chapter 12 petition—although the bankruptcy court has the discretion to extend the time. A hearing is held on the proposed plan, and it can be confirmed over the objection of creditors. The debtor may release to any secured party the collateral that secures the claim to obtain confirmation without the acceptance by that creditor.

Unsecured creditors are required to receive at least liquidation value under the Chapter 12 plan. If an unsecured creditor or the trustee objects to the plan, the court may still confirm the plan despite the objection so long as it calls for full payment of the unsecured creditor's claim or it provides that the debtor's disposable income for the duration of the plan is applied to making payments on it. A debtor who fulfills his plan, or is excused from full performance because of subsequent hardship, is entitled to a discharge.

The Global Business Environment

Transnational Insolvency Proceedings

As the volume of international trade and the number of multinational corporations have grown, there has been a concomitant increase in transnational insolvency cases. When a company engaged in international business transactions becomes insolvent, commonly some kind of insolvency proceeding will be initiated in each country where the company does business. Different laws and different national interests can produce a challenging—if not difficult—situation for creditors of the insolvent enterprise. Where and how should the creditor go about protecting its interests? Should it seek to have its claim allowed in any one—or more—of the various proceedings? What rights will it be accorded in those proceedings, particularly the foreign forums?

Historically, two different approaches have been used to deal with transnational insolvencies. The first uses the principle of "territoriality" where each country takes control of the enterprise's assets within that country and administers them according to the law of that country, giving little attention to what may be happening in other forums or to foreign interests. A second approach, often referred to as "universalism," seeks a cooperative or coordinated approach to transnational insolvency. This might be achieved through the identification of a single forum or proceeding where all assets of a company would be administered and all claims and interests addressed. Another variant

of this approach is to identify a primary proceeding that has the lead in conjunction with a number of coordinated ancillary proceedings in other countries.

In an effort to encourage cooperation among countries and to try to harmonize the competing and conflicting schemes, the United Nations Commission on International Trade Law has adopted a Model Law on Cross-Border Insolvency. On a regional level, the European Union has adopted a "Convention on Insolvency Proceedings" to coordinate and harmonize such proceedings in EU countries. And the American Law Institute has a Transnational Insolvency Project to develop principles of cooperation in transnational insolvency cases among the members (United States, Canada, and Mexico) of the North American Free Trade Agreement (NAFTA).

The 2005 Bankruptcy Act creates a new chapter of the Bankruptcy Code to deal with cross-border cases. The new sections incorporate the Model Code of Cross-Border Insolvency. The new chapter expands the scope of U.S. bankruptcy law and provides an explicit statutory mechanism for dealing with cross-border insolvency and for the U.S. courts, trustees, and debtors to cooperate with their foreign counterparts. It provides a framework for common cross-border situations such as providing access for foreign creditors to domestic cases and for the coordination of simultaneous domestic and foreign proceedings for the same debtor so that the relief afforded in different jurisdictions is consistent.

Explain the purpose and basic procedure of Chapter 13 Consumer Debt Adjustments.

Chapter 13: Consumer Debt Adjustments

Relief for Individuals Chapter 13 of the Bankruptcy Code, entitled Adjustments of Debts for Individuals, gives individuals who want to avoid the stigma of a Chapter 7 bankruptcy an opportunity to pay their debts in installments under the protection of a federal court. Under Chapter 13, the debtor has this opportunity free of such problems as garnishments and attachments of her property by creditors. Only individuals with regular incomes (including sole proprietors of businesses) who owe individually (or with their spouse) liquidated, unsecured debts of less than $360,475 and secured debts of less than $1,081,400 are eligible to file under Chapter 13.

Procedure Chapter 13 proceedings are initiated only by the voluntary petition of a debtor filed in the Bankruptcy Court. Creditors of the debtor may not file an involuntary petition for a Chapter 13 proceeding. Commonly, the debtor files at the same time a list of his creditors as well as a list of his assets, liabilities, and executory contracts. The court then appoints a trustee.

Following the filing of the petition, the trustee calls a meeting of creditors, at which time proofs of claims are received and allowed or disallowed. The debtor is examined, and she submits a plan of payment. If the court is satisfied that the plan is proposed in good faith, meets the legal requirements, and is in the interest of the creditors, the court approves the plan.

If the debtor's income is above the state median income for a family of the size of his family, then the plan must provide for payments over a period of five years unless all claims will be fully paid in a shorter period. In the case

of a debtor whose income is less than the median income of the applicable state, the plan may not provide for payments over a period that is longer than three years unless the court, for cause, approves a longer period, which is no case can be more than five years.

The plan must provide that all of the debtor's disposable income during the applicable commitment period will be applied to make payments to unsecured creditors under the plan. Unsecured creditors must receive at least what they would receive under Chapter 7. All priority claims must be paid in full.

No plan may be approved if the trustee or an unsecured creditor objects, unless the plan provides for the objecting creditor to be paid the present value of what he is owed or provides for the debtor to commit all of his projected disposable income for the applicable period to pay his creditors.

In the case below, *In re Burt,* the court agreed with an objection raised by a creditor to confirmation of a proposed Chapter 13 plan that would cram down the creditor's secured interest.

A Chapter 13 debtor must begin making the installment payments proposed in her plan within 30 days after the plan is filed. The interim payments must continue to be made until the plan is confirmed or denied. If the plan is denied, the money, less any administrative expenses, is returned to the debtor by the trustee. The interim payments give the trustee an opportunity to observe the debtor's performance and thus to be in a better position to make a recommendation about whether the plan should be approved.

Once approved, a plan may be subsequently modified on petition of a debtor or a creditor where there is a material change in the debtor's circumstances.

Suppose Curtis Brown has a monthly take-home pay of $1,000 and a few assets. He owes $1,500 to the credit union, borrowed for the purchase of furniture; he is supposed to repay the credit union $75 per month. He owes $1,800 to the finance company on the purchase of a used car; he is supposed to repay the company $90 a month. He has also run up charges of $1,200 on a MasterCard account, primarily

---

In re Burt   **378 B.R. 352 (U.S.B.C., D. Utah 2007)**

On December 31, 2005, Darin Burt purchased a 2006 Ford F-150, a pickup truck for his personal use, from LaPoint Automotive LLC. LaPoint financed the transaction through a Utah Simple Interest Retail Installment Contract. Under the contract, LaPoint retained a purchase money security interest (PMSI) in the truck. LaPoint later assigned its interest in the truck to Ford Motor Credit, which perfected its security interest by notation on the truck's title as required by the Utah Motor Vehicle Act.

The contract indicated that the cash price of the truck was $32,630 and the total amount financed was $45,628.14. The difference between the two amounts included charges of $2,425 for a service contract, $500 for gap insurance, $298 for document preparation fee, $1,149.46 for tax and license fees, and $11,021.68 to pay off the obligation owed on a trade-in vehicle (2004 Ford F-150). The negative equity rolled into the transaction, therefore, was the $11,021.68 payoff less the Burt's down payment *of $1,800 and the manufacturer's rebate of $3,000, yielding a net negative equity of $6,221. Because of the Burt's marginal credit, he was required to trade-in his 2004 Ford F-150 in order to qualify for financing on the new vehicle. The dealer would not have financed the purchase had Burt not agreed to all the terms of the contract, including the refinancing of negative equity.*

On July 13, 2007, Burt filed a petition under Chapter 13. On August 30, 2007, Ford Motor Credit filed a proof of secured claim for its security interest in the truck in the amount of $42,941.64. Burt filed his Chapter 13 plan on July 25, 2007, which proposed to bifurcate Ford Motor Credit's claim into a secured portion in the amount of $28,000 and an unsecured portion in the amount of the negative equity paid off by the financing transaction. Ford Motor Credit objected to confirmation of the debtor's plan, arguing that its entire claim qualified for treatment as a secured claim and could not be bifurcated.

Thurman, U.S. Bankruptcy Judge

In order to obtain confirmation of a Chapter 13 plan, the debtor must comply with provisions of *11 U.S.C. § 1325(a)*. Prior to the enactment of the Bankruptcy Abuse Prevention and Consumer Protection Act of 2005 (BAPCPA), *sections 506(a)(1)* and *1325(a)(5)(B)* allowed a Chapter 13 debtor to bifurcate an under-secured creditor's claim into secured and unsecured portions, with the result that a creditor's claim was allowed as secured only to the extent of the value of the collateral securing its debt. The portion of the creditor's claim allowed as secured would be paid in full with interest, whereas the unsecured portion of the claim would be paid pro-rata with all other general unsecured claims. This process of bifurcation is often referred to as "cram-down." BAPCPA, however, amended § *1325* to give special protection to creditors who finance automobile transactions that occur within 910 days prior to the debtors' filing for Chapter 13 relief.

Under BAPCPA, Congress added the "hanging paragraph" after § *1325(a)(9)*, which prevents the bifurcation of certain secured claims. It is commonly referred to as the "hanging paragraph" because it follows the numbered subsections of § *1325(a)* but has no numerical designation of its own. Specifically, the hanging paragraph states:

> For purposes of paragraph (5), section 506 shall not apply to a claim described in that paragraph if the creditor has a purchase money security interest securing the debt that is the subject of the claim, the debt was incurred within the 910-day [sic] preceding the date of the filing of the petition, and the collateral for that debt consists of a motor vehicle acquired for the personal use of the debtor, or if collateral for that debt consists of any other thing of value, if the debt was incurred during the 1-year period preceding that filing.

Thus, in order to avoid a cram-down, four conditions must be satisfied: (1) the creditor has a purchase money security interest (PMSI); (2) the debt was incurred within 910 days preceding the filing of the petition; (3) the collateral for the debt is a motor vehicle; and (4) the motor vehicle was acquired for the personal use of the debtor. If these requirements are satisfied, "then the creditor's claim is deemed fully secured" and cannot be bifurcated. The parties do not dispute that the collateral in this case

was a motor vehicle, purchased within 910 days of the debtor's petition, or that it was acquired for personal use. The only requirement that is in dispute is whether Ford Motor Credit's debt is secured by a purchase money security interest. To determine this issue, the Court must first decide whether the negative equity from the trade-in vehicle that was rolled into the financing for the Truck as well as the other costs associated with the purchase constitute a purchase money security interest as defined under Utah law.

In order to address the effect of the hanging paragraph, the Court must first determine the extent to which Ford Motor Credit's security interest is a purchase money security interest. The term "purchase money security interest," as used in the hanging paragraph, is not defined in the Bankruptcy Code. Therefore, courts uniformly refer to state law, and specifically to the state's version of the Uniform Commercial Code (UCC), to determine whether a creditor holds a purchase money security interest. The applicable statute in Utah is the *Utah Code Annotated § 9a-103(2)*, which provides that "[a] security interest in goods is a purchase-money security interest . . . to the extent that the goods are a purchase-money collateral with respect to that security interest. . . ." "Purchase-money collateral" is defined as "goods . . . that secures a purchase-money obligation incurred with respect to that collateral," and "purchase-money obligation" is defined as "an obligation of an obligor incurred as all or part of the *price of the collateral* or for *value given to enable* the debtor to acquire rights in or the use of the collateral if the value is in fact so used."

Whether a PMSI exists in this case, then, "turns on whether the negative equity on the debtor's trade-in vehicle constitutes 'part of the price of the collateral,' *i.e.* part of the price of the new vehicle, or whether it constitutes 'value given to enable the debtor to acquire rights in or the use of the collateral. . . .'" Although § *9a-103* does not define the terms "price" or "value given," Comment 3 to § *9a-103* states that "the 'price' of collateral or the 'value given to enable' includes obligations for expenses incurred in connection with acquiring rights in the collateral, sales, taxes, duties, finance charges, interest freight charges, costs of storage in transit, demurrage, administrative charges, expenses of collection and enforcement, attorney's fees, and other similar obligations."

The Court believes that this list is not exhaustive and the expenses identified in Comment 3 are merely examples or additional components of the "price of the collateral" or of "value given" by the debtor. Therefore, this Court cannot see how the refinancing of negative equity and the other transaction costs incurred in connection with the purchase of the debtor's new truck could not qualify as an "expense" within the meaning of Comment 3.

The debtor and the dealer in this case agreed that as part of the purchase of the truck and pursuant to the retail installment contract, the dealer would advance funds to payoff the lien on the debtor's trade-in vehicle and to cover tax, license and document preparation fees. Essentially, this was a package deal. Ford Motor Credit later stepped into the purchase-money lender shoes of the dealer. The Court concludes that the agreement and the dealings between the debtor and the dealer/creditor demonstrate that the costs of satisfying these outstanding obligations of the debtor were clearly incurred in connection with the purchase of the new vehicle.

Additionally, Comment 3 states that "[t]he concept of 'purchase money security interest' requires a close nexus between the acquisition of the collateral and the secured obligation." The Court finds that in the present case, there is a very close connection between the negative equity and the financing of the Debtor's new vehicle. As noted earlier, the financing transaction was a package deal where the negative equity in the trade-in was paid off by the dealer as part of its retail installment sale of the new vehicle and the related obligation was included in the Contract with the Debtor. All of the amounts financed in the contract, except the gap insurance and service contract, were directly connected to the Debtor's purchase of the new vehicle. In fact, the evidence before this Court shows that Ford Motor Credit would not have financed the total purchase price had the Debtor not agreed to all of the terms of the Contract including the negative equity and the add-on transaction costs. The Court, therefore, concludes that because of this close nexus between the negative equity and the financing of the Debtor's new vehicle, the entire transaction qualifies as a purchase money security interest.

Accordingly, Ford Motor Credit's entire claim including that portion of the claim attributable to the payoff of negative equity on the Debtor's trade-in vehicle and the other transaction costs, should be allowed as a fully secured claim that must be paid in full through the Debtor's Chapter 13 plan.

[Author's note—there is a significant split of authority concerning the issue in this case and other courts have reached a different conclusion, allowing the claim to be bifurcated. Sec, e.q., *In re Penrod*, 66 UCC Rep. 2d (U.S. Bank. App. Panel, 9th Cir. 2008) (negative equity not purchase money debt).]

for emergency repairs to his car; he must pay $60 per month to MasterCard. His rent is $350 per month, and food and other living expenses run him another $425 per month.

Curtis was laid off from his job for a month and fell behind on his payments to his creditors. He then filed a Chapter 13 petition. In his plan, he might, for example, offer to repay the credit union $50 a month, the finance company $60 a month, and Master-Card $40 a month—with the payments spread over three years rather than the shorter time for which they are currently scheduled.

Discharge As soon as practicable after the completion by the debtor of all payments under the plan, the court is required to grant the debtor a discharge of all debts provided for by the plan (or specifically disallowed) except:

- Debts covered by a waiver of discharge executed by the debtor and approved by the court;
- Debts that are for taxes required to be collected or paid and for which the debtor is liable;
- Certain debts that are not dischargeable under Chapter 7 such as those that result from liabilities for obtaining money by false pretenses or false representations (see page 804 for a more complete list);
- Debts for restitution or a criminal fine included in a sentence on the debtor's conviction of a crime; or
- For restitution or damages awarded in a civil action against the debtor as a result of willful or malicious injury by the debtor that caused personal injury to an individual or the death of an individual.

A debtor who is subject to a judicial or administrative order, or, by statute, to pay a domestic support obligation, must, in addition to making the payments pursuant to his plan, certify that all amounts under the order or statute have been paid up to the date of certification in order to be entitled to a discharge.

As is the situation under Chapter 7, the court is also prohibited from granting a discharge where there is reason to believe there is a pending proceeding in which the debtor may be found guilty of a violation of the federal securities laws or is liable for a debt based on the violation of those laws.

 Compare the major types of bankruptcy proceedings.

CONCEPT REVIEW

Comparison of Major Forms of Bankruptcy Proceedings

Purpose	Chapter 7 Liquidation	Chapter 11 Reorganization	Chapter 12 Adjustments of Debts	Chapter 13 Adjustments of Debts
Eligible Debtors	Individuals, and partnerships, and corporations *except* municipal corporations, railroads, insurance companies, banks, and savings and loan associations. Farmers and ranchers are eligible only if they petition voluntarily.	Generally, same as Chapter 7 except a railroad may be a debtor, and a stockbroker and commodity broker may not be a debtor under Chapter 11.	Family farmer with regular income, at least 50 percent of which comes from farming, and less than $3,792,650 in debts, at least 80 percent of which is farm related. Family fishermen with regular income whose aggregate debts do not exceed $1,757,475 and at least 80 percent of which arose out of the fishing operation.	Individual with regular income with liquidated unsecured debts less than $360,475 and secured debts of less than $1,081,400.
Initiation of Proceeding	Petition by debtor (voluntary). Petition by creditors (involuntary).	Petition by debtor (voluntary). Petition by creditors (involuntary).	Petition by debtor.	Petition by debtor.
Basic Procedure	1. Appointment of trustee. 2. Debtor retains exempt property. 3. Nonexempt property is sold and proceeds distributed based on priority of claims. 4. Dischargeable debts are terminated.	1. Appointment of committees of creditors and equity security holders. 2. Debtor submits reorganization plan. 3. If plan is approved and implemented, debts are discharged.	1. Trustee is appointed but debtor usually remains in possession. 2. Debtor submits a plan in which unsecured creditors must receive at least liquidation value. 3. If plan is approved and fulfilled, debtor is entitled to a discharge.	1. Trustee is appointed but debtor usually remains in possession. 2. Debtor submits a plan in which unsecured creditors must receive at least liquidation value. 3. If plan is approved and fulfilled, debts covered by plan are discharged.
Advantages	After liquidation and distribution of assets, most or all debts may be discharged and debtor gets a fresh start.	Debtor remains in business and debts are liquidated through implementation of approved reorganization plan.	Debtor generally remains in possession and has opportunity to work out of financial difficulty over period of time (usually three years) through implementation of approved plan.	Debtor has opportunity to work out of financial difficulty over period of time (usually three–five years) through implementation of approved plan.

Repeat Bankruptcies The 2005 act prohibits a court from granting a discharge of the debts provided for in the plan (or disallowed) if the debtor received a discharge in a case filed under Chapter 7, 11, or 12 of the Bankruptcy Code in the four-year period preceding the date of the order for relief under Chapter 13—or in a case filed under Chapter 13 during the two-year period preceding the date of the order of relief in the current case.

Advantages of Chapter 13 A debtor may choose to file under Chapter 13 to avoid the stigma of bankruptcy or to retain more of his property than is exempt from bankruptcy under state or federal law.

Nonexempt property would have to be surrendered to the trustee in a Chapter 7 liquidation proceeding. Chapter 13 can provide some financial discipline to a debtor as well as an opportunity to get his financial affairs back in good shape. It also gives him relief from the pressures of individual creditors so long as he makes the payments called for by the plan. The debtor's creditors may benefit by recovering a greater percentage of the debt owed to them than would be obtainable in straight bankruptcy.

Problems and Problem Cases

1. Gilbert and Kimberly Barnes filed a voluntary Chapter 7 petition in the U.S. Bankruptcy Court for the District of Maryland. Subsequently they moved to avoid a non–purchase money lien held by ITT Financial Services on their exempt "household goods." Among the goods that the Barneses were claiming as "household goods" were a videocassette recorder (VCR), a 12-gauge pump shotgun, a 20-gauge shotgun, a 30-06 rifle, and a 22 pistol. ITT contended that the VCR and the firearms were not household goods that they could exempt. Under Maryland law, household goods are items of personal property necessary for the day-to-day existence of people in the context of their homes. Should the court consider the VCR and firearms to be "household goods"?

2. In 2008 Virgil Hurd was kicked out of his home by his ex-wife. At that time he moved into his horse trailer (the "Trailer") to keep warm. The Trailer is twenty feet long and six feet wide. Virgil gets electricity for the Trailer from a socket and water from a barrel with a pump. He receives his mail at the land where the Trailer is parked. Since January of 2010, Virgil spends approximately 70 percent of his time at his girlfriend's house. In addition using the Trailer as a place to sleep, Virgil also uses it for transporting his horses and his girlfriend's horses. In April of 2010, he filed a voluntary petition for relief under Chapter 7 in the United States Bankruptcy Court for Western District of Missouri. In his schedule of exemptions, he listed the entire $3,000 value of the Trailer as exempt under a Missouri statute, which exempts any *mobile home* used as the principal residence that does not exceed $5,000 in value. The term mobile home in not defined in that statute. The Chapter 7 trustee objects to Virgil's claim of a Missouri exemption in a horse trailer used as his living quarters. The trustee contends that the Trailer was not Virgil's principal residence during the six- to twelve-month period before filing his bankruptcy petition, and that the Trailer does not qualify as a "mobile home" under the Missouri statute. Should the Trailer be exempt from the bankruptcy estate?

3. William Kranich, Jr., was the sole shareholder in the DuVal Finance Corporation (DFC). On November 10, Kranich filed a voluntary petition for relief under Chapter 7; on the following January 6, DFC also filed a voluntary petition under Chapter 7. Prior to the commencement of the Chapter 7 proceedings, Kranich conveyed his personal residence in Clearwater, Florida, to DFC. The transfer was wholly without consideration. Shortly thereafter, DFC transferred the property to William Kranich III and June Elizabeth Kranich, Kranich's son and daughter, as tenants in common. This transfer was also without consideration. The bankruptcy trustee brought suit to recover the property from the son and daughter on the grounds that the transfer was fraudulent. Could the trustee recover the property on the grounds that its transfer, without consideration, was fraudulent?

4. David Hott was a college graduate with a degree in business administration who was employed as an insurance agent. He and his wife graduated from college in 1996. At the time he graduated, Hott had outstanding student loans of $14,500 for which he was given a grace period before he had to repay them. Hott became unemployed. Bills began to accumulate, and a number of his outstanding bills were near the credit limits on his accounts. About that time, he received a promotional brochure by mail from Signal Consumer Discount Company, offering the opportunity to borrow several thousand dollars. The Hotts decided it appeared to be an attractive vehicle for them to use to consolidate their debts. Hott went to the Signal office and filled out a credit application. He did not list the student loan as a current debt. He later claimed that someone in the office told him he didn't have to list it if he owned an automobile, but there was significant doubt about the credibility of this claim. Had he listed it, he would not have met the debt-income ratio required by Signal, and it would not have made the loan. As it was, Signal agreed to make the loan on the condition Hott pay off a car debt in order to reduce his debt-income ratio and Hott agreed to do so. On March 30, 1997, Signal loaned the Hotts $3,458.01. On June 24, 1998, the Hotts filed for bankruptcy.

Signal objected to discharge of the balance remaining on its loan on the ground it had been obtained through the use of a materially false financial statement. Was discharge of the debt barred on the ground it had been obtained through the use of a materially false financial statement?

5. Brian Scholz was involved in an automobile collision with a person insured by The Travelers Insurance Company. At the time, Scholz was cited for, and pled no contest to, a criminal charge of driving under the influence of alcohol arising out of the accident. The Travelers paid its insured $4,303.68 and was subrogated to the rights of its insured against Scholz. Subsequently, The Travelers filed a civil action against Scholz to recover the amount it had paid, and a default judgment was entered against Scholz. Eleven months later, Scholz sought relief from the bankruptcy court by filing a voluntary petition under Chapter 7. One of the questions in the bankruptcy proceeding was whether the debt owing to The Travelers was nondischargeable. Is the debt dischargeable?

6. Bryant filed a Chapter 7 petition on January 7. On March 8, she filed an application to reaffirm an indebtedness owed to General Motors Acceptance Corporation (GMAC) on her Cadillac automobile. Bryant was not married, and she supported two teenage daughters. She was not currently employed, and she collected $771 a month in unemployment benefits and $150 a month in rental income from her mother. Her monthly house payments were $259. The present value of the Cadillac was $9,175; she owed $7,956.37 on it, and her monthly payments were $345.93. Bryant indicated that she wanted to keep the vehicle because it was reliable. GMAC admitted that Bryant had been, and continued to be, current in her payments. GMAC said that the car was in no danger of being repossessed but that, absent reaffirmation, it might decide to repossess it. Under the law at the time, permission of the court was required for a reaffirmation agreement. Should the court grant Bryant's petition to reaffirm her indebtedness to GMAC?

7. While attending college, Barbara Barrington obtained a student loan from the New York State Higher Education Services Corporation. Barrington had depressive illnesses all her life, as had previous generations in her family. Her grandmother was institutionalized, and her mother had been on medication for a long time. Barrington was discharged by Eastman Kodak Company because she could not face the problems and stress of her job. Since that time, she had stayed at home, slept a lot, and played with her dog. She made little or no effort to find other employment because of her depressed condition. She also filed for bankruptcy. In the bankruptcy proceeding, one of the questions was whether payment of her student loan would impose an undue hardship on Barrington, and thus whether the loan was dischargeable. Should the student loan be discharged?

8. Doug Boyce works as a claims adjuster for GEICO. He makes $57,000 a year as a base salary plus several thousand more as part of a discretionary annual profit sharing agreement. In 2008 he earned $67,961 from GEICO. GEICO also provides Boyce with a vehicle for his work and personal use. In 2007, Boyce took out a $16,000 loan from his 401(k) to purchase a house. He lives in the home and rents out some of the rooms for an additional rental income of approximately $5,800 a year. In October of 2007, Boyce finalized his divorce and assumed responsibility for $34,000 in student loans and $16,000 in credit card debt. By October of 2008 Boyce had added an additional $17,000 to his credit card debt. In March of 2008, Boyce purchased a Ford F350 with a $2,000 down payment and a monthly payment of $186. Boyce filed for bankruptcy protection under Chapter 7 on October 28, 2008. After filing for bankruptcy Boyce surrendered his Ford F350 and borrowed $14,750 from his 401(k) to purchase a Dodge Ram truck. He later sold the truck and purchased a Chevrolet truck and borrowed another $6,000 from his 401(k) to purchase a recreational camper. At the time of filing Boyce did not disclose the money he earned from the profit sharing agreement or his rental income and his reported monthly income was short by $109. In addition, Boyce did not include the $34,000 student loan debt on his schedules. The United States Trustee commenced a contested proceeding against Boyce seeking dismissal of the Chapter 7. Should the court dismiss Boyce's Chapter 7 bankruptcy filing or alternatively force him into Chapter 13?

9. The A. H. Robins Company is a publicly held company that filed a voluntary petition for relief under Chapter 11 of the Bankruptcy Code. Robins sought refuge in Chapter 11 because of a multitude of civil actions filed against it by women who alleged they were injured by use of the Dalkon Shield intrauterine device that it manufactured and sold as a birth control device. Approximately 325,000 notices of claim against Robins were received by the Bankruptcy Court.

Part Six   **Credit**

In 1985, the court appointed the Official Committee of Security Holders to represent the interest of Robins' public shareholders. In April 1987, Robins filed a proposed plan of reorganization but no action was taken on the proposed plan because of a merger proposal submitted by Rorer Group, Inc. Under this plan, Dalkon Shield claimants would be compensated out of a $1.75 billion fund, all other creditors would be paid in full, and the Robins stockholders would receive stock of the merged corporation. However, it being a time of other critical activity in the bankruptcy proceeding, no revised plan incorporating the merger proposal had been filed or approved.

Earlier, in August 1986, the court had appointed Ralph Mabey as an examiner to evaluate and suggest proposed elements of a plan of reorganization. On Mabey's suggestion, a proposed order was put before the district court supervising the proceeding that would require Robins to establish a $15 million emergency treatment fund "for the purpose of assisting in providing tubal reconstructive surgery or in-vitro fertilization to eligible Dalkon Shield claimants." The purpose of the emergency fund was to assist those claimants who asserted that they had become infertile as a consequence of their use of the product. A program was proposed for administering the fund and for making the medical decisions required.

On May 21, 1987, the district court ordered that the emergency treatment fund be created. This action was challenged by the committee representing the equity security holders. Was the court justified in ordering the distribution of some of the bankrupt's assets on an emergency basis before a reorganization plan was approved?

10. Winifred Doersam was the borrower on three student loans made to her by First Federal Savings and Loan and guaranteed by the state of Ohio Student Loan Commission (OSLC) totaling $10,000 to finance her graduate education at the University of Dayton. Doersam also signed as the cosigner for a $5,000 student loan for her daughter, also made by First Federal and guaranteed by OSLC. With the use of the loans, she was able to obtain a position as a systems analyst with NCR Corporation, which required her to obtain a master's degree in order to retain her position at an annual salary of $24,000. Approximately six weeks before her graduation, and before the first payment on her student loans was due, Doersam filed a petition and plan under Chapter 13. In her plan, she proposed to pay $375 a month to her unsecured creditors over a 36-month period. Doersam's total unsecured debt was $18,418, 81 percent of which was comprised of the outstanding student loans. Her schedules provided for payment of rent of $300 per month and food of $400 per month. Her listed dependents included her 23-year-old daughter and her 1-year-old granddaughter. At the time, her daughter was employed in the Ohio Work Program, a program designed to help welfare recipients, for which she was paid a small salary. The OLSC objected to the plan proposed by Doersam on the grounds that it was filed in bad faith. Should the bankruptcy court refuse to confirm the plan on the grounds it was not filed in good faith?

Online Research

Current Corporate Reorganizations

Use the Internet to locate articles from *The Wall Street Journal* and other financial publications concerning one of the recent major corporate bankruptcies and ascertain the following information concerning the bankruptcy case: (1) When was the bankruptcy petition filed? (2) Was the petition filed under Chapter 7 (liquidation) or under Chapter 11 (reorganization)? (3) Who were/are the major creditors or holders of claims against the bankrupt entity? (4) If the matter is in Chapter 11, has a reorganization plan been filed and what were/are its major elements? (5) Has the bankruptcy proceeding been completed? (6) If it has been completed, how did the major creditors appear to fare?

Business Ethics

CHAPTER 4

BUSINESS ETHICS, CORPORATE SOCIAL RESPONSIBILITY, CORPORATE GOVERNANCE, AND CRITICAL THINKING

You are a senior associate consultant at Accent Pointe Consulting LLP, a consulting firm. The engagement partner has asked you to prepare an engagement plan and budget. You make sure that your plan and budget are in line with your knowledge of what can and must be done to meet the client's needs. The proposed fee is $100,000. When you present the budget to the engagement partner, she goes ballistic. "What's this $100,000? This is Accent Pointe Consulting. This is the big time. What kind of consultant are you?"

"A good one," you reply. "I've created a reasonable plan, and for what we are doing for the client, that is a high-end fee."

The partner, however, does not buy your arguments. "You make this contract $200,000," she orders you, "and find a way in your engagement plan to back up that price."

- What action will you take?
- What process and guidelines will you use to determine what is the right thing to do in this context?
- If you decide that $100,000 is the correct contract price, how do you resist the partner's request to make you bill the client for $200,000?
- Will you take a different action if you know that a year from now the firm's partners will vote on whether you should be made a partner, and you believe the engagement partner's recommendation will be critical to your becoming a partner?
- Will you take a different action if you are the engagement partner and have been ordered to bill the client $200,000 by a managing partner? Note that as a partner, your share of firm profits is determined by the number of "units" you have, which is largely a function of the amount the firm bills clients for whom you are the engagement partner.
- What action will you take if you discover that the managing partner's request to bill more is a relatively isolated incident in a firm that generally bills clients accurately? You don't know the managing partner's motivation for asking you to overbill the client.
- What action will you take if you discover that the firm has a culture that encourages overbilling clients? The overbilling culture evolved within the last decade from a desire of managing partners to enjoy a financial status more nearly equal to the corporate executives of their clients, many of whom receive annual compensation in the millions of dollars.

Chapter Four   Business Ethics, Corporate Social Responsibility, Corporate Governance, and Critical Thinking   93

LO   LEARNING OBJECTIVES

After you have studied this chapter, you should be able to:

1   Appreciate the strengths and weaknesses of the various ethical theories.

2   Apply the Guidelines for Ethical Decision Making to business and personal decisions.

3   Recognize critical thinking errors in your own and others' arguments.

4   Utilize a process to make ethical decisions in the face of pressure from others.

5   Be an ethical leader.

Why Study Business Ethics?

Enron. WorldCom. Tyco. Adelphia. Global Crossing. ImClone. These business names from the front pages of the last decade conjure images of unethical and socially irresponsible behavior by business executives. The United States Congress, employees, investors, and other critics of the power held and abused by some corporations and their management have demanded that corporate wrongdoers be punished and that future wrongdoers be deterred. Consequently shareholders, creditors, and state and federal attorneys general have brought several civil and criminal actions against wrongdoing corporations and their executives. Congress has also got in on the action, passing the Sarbanes–Oxley Act, which increased penalties for corporate wrongdoers and established rules designed to deter and prevent future wrongdoing. The purpose of the statute is to encourage and enable corporate executives to be ethical and socially responsible.

But statutes and civil and criminal actions can go only so far in directing business managers down an ethical path. And while avoiding liability by complying with the law is one reason to be ethical and socially responsible, there are noble and economic reasons that encourage current and future business executives to study business ethics.

Although it is tempting to paint all businesses and all managers with the same brush that colors unethical and irresponsible corporations and executives, in reality corporate executives are little different from you, your friends, and your acquaintances. All of us from time to time fail to do the right thing, and we know that people have varying levels of commitment to acting ethically. The difference between most of us and corporate executives is that they are in positions of power that allow them to do greater damage to others when they act unethically or socially irresponsibly. They also act under the microscope of public scrutiny.

It is also tempting to say that current business managers are less ethical than managers historically. But as former Federal Reserve Chairman Alan Greenspan said, "It is not that humans have become any more greedy than in generations past. It is that the avenues to express greed have grown enormously."

This brings us to the first and most important reason why we need to study business ethics: to make better decisions for ourselves, the businesses we work for, and the society we live in. As you read this chapter, you will study not only the different theories that attempt to define ethical conduct, but more importantly you will learn to use a framework or strategy for making decisions. This framework will increase the likelihood you have considered all the facts affecting your decision. By learning a methodology for ethical decision making and studying common thinking errors, you will improve your ability to make ethical decisions.

Another reason we study ethics is to understand ourselves and others better. While studying the various ethical theories, you will see concepts that reflect your own thinking and the thinking of others. This chapter, by exploring ethical theories systematically and pointing out the strengths and weaknesses of each ethical theory, should help you understand better why you think the way you do and why others think the way they do. By studying ethical theories, learning a process for ethical decision making, and understanding common reasoning fallacies, you should also be better able to decide how you should think and whether you should be persuaded by the arguments of others. Along the way, by better understanding where others are coming from and avoiding fallacious reasoning, you should become a more persuasive speaker and writer.

There are also cynical reasons for executives to study business ethics. By learning how to act ethically and in fact doing so, businesses forestall public criticism, reduce lawsuits against them, prevent Congress from passing onerous legislation, and make higher profits. For many corporate actors, however, these are not reasons to act ethically, but instead the natural consequences of so acting.

While we are studying business ethics, we will also examine the role of the law in defining ethical conduct. Some argue that it is sufficient for corporations and executives to comply with the requirements of the law; commonly, critics of the corporation point out that since laws cannot and do not encompass all expressions of ethical behavior, compliance with the law is necessary but not sufficient to ensure ethical conduct. This introduces us to one of the major issues in the corporate social responsibility debate.

The Corporate Social Responsibility Debate

Although interest in business ethics education has increased greatly in the last few decades, that interest is only the latest stage in a long struggle to control corporate misbehavior. Ever since large corporations emerged in the late 19th century, such firms have been heroes to some and villains to others. Large corporations perform essential national and global economic functions, including raw material extraction, energy production, transportation, and communication, as well as providing consumer goods and entertainment to millions of people.

Critics, however, claim that corporations in their pursuit of profits ruin the environment, mistreat employees, sell shoddy and dangerous products, produce immoral television shows and motion pictures, and corrupt the political process. Critics claim that even when corporations provide vital and important services, business is not nearly as accountable to the public as are organs of government. For example, the public has little to say about the election of corporate directors or the appointment of corporate officers. This lack of accountability is aggravated by the large amount of power that big corporations wield in America and much of the rest of the world.

These criticisms and perceptions have led to calls for changes in how corporations and their executives make decisions. The main device for checking corporate misdeeds has been the law. The perceived need to check abuses of business power was a force behind the New Deal laws of the 1930s and extensive federal regulations enacted in the 1960s and 1970s. Some critics, however, believe that legal regulation, while an important element of any corporate control scheme, is insufficient by itself.

They argue that businesses should adhere to a standard of ethical or socially responsible behavior that is higher than the law.

One such standard is the stakeholder theory of corporate social responsibility. It holds that rather than merely striving to maximize profits for its shareholders, a corporation should balance the interests of shareholders against the interests of other corporate stakeholders, such as employees, suppliers, customers, and the community. To promote such behavior, some corporate critics have proposed changes that increase the influence of the various stakeholders in the internal governance of a corporation. We will study many of these proposals later in the chapter in the subsection on profit maximization. You will also learn later that an ethical decision-making process requires a business executive to anticipate the effects of a corporate decision on the various corporate stakeholders.

Despite concerns about abuses of power, big business has contributed greatly to the unprecedented abundance in America and elsewhere. Partly for this reason and partly because many businesses attempt to be ethical actors, critics have not totally dominated the debate about control of the modern corporation. Defenders of businesses argue that in a society founded on capitalism, profit maximization should be the main goal of businesses: the only ethical norms firms must follow are those embodied in the law or those impacting profits. In short, they argue that businesses that maximize profits within the limits of the law are acting ethically. Otherwise, the marketplace would discipline them for acting unethically by reducing their profits.

Former Fed Chairman Alan Greenspan wrote in 1963 that moral values are the power behind capitalism. He wrote, "Capitalism is based on self-interest and self-esteem; it holds integrity and trustworthiness as cardinal virtues and makes them pay off in the marketplace, thus demanding that men survive by means of virtue, not of vices." Note that companies that are successful decade after decade, like Procter & Gamble and Johnson & Johnson, adhere to society's core values.

We will cover other arguments supporting and criticizing profit maximization later in the chapter, where we will consider fully proposals to improve corporate governance and accountability. For now, however, having set the stage for the debate about business ethics and corporate social responsibility, we want to study the definitions of ethical behavior.

Ethics in Action

American physicist, mathematician, and futurist Freeman Dyson gave insight into why we humans may have difficulty determining which ethical viewpoint to embrace. His insights also help explain why different people have different ethical leanings.

The destiny of our species is shaped by the imperatives of survival on six distinct time scales. To survive means to compete successfully on all six time scales. But the unit of survival is different for each of the six time scales. On a time scale of years, the unit is the individual. On a time scale of decades, the unit is the family. On a time scale of centuries, the unit is the tribe or nation. On a time scale of millennia, the unit is the culture. On a time scale of tens of millennia, the unit is the species. On a time scale of eons, the unit is the whole web of life on our planet. That is why conflicting loyalties are deep in our nature. In order to survive, we need to be loyal to ourselves, to our families, to our tribes, to our culture, to our species, to our planet. If our psychological impulses are complicated, it is because they were shaped by complicated and conflicting demands.[1]

Dyson goes on to write, "Nature gave us greed, a robust desire to maximize our personal winnings. Without greed we would not have survived at the individual level." Yet he points out that Nature also gave us the connections and tools to survive at the family level (Dyson calls this tool love of family), the tribal level (love of friends), the cultural level (love of conversation), the species level (love of people in general), and the planetary level (love of nature).

If Dyson is correct, why are humans sometimes vastly different from each other in some of their ethical values? Why do some of us argue, for example, that universal health care is a right for each citizen, while others believe health care coverage should be an individual decision? The answer lies in the degree to which each of us embraces, innately or rationally, Dyson's six units of survival and the extent to which each of us possesses the connections and tools to survive on each of those levels.

---

[1]Freeman Dyson, *From Eros to Gaia*, (London: Penguin Books, 1993), pp. 341–42.

Ethical Theories

For centuries, religious and secular scholars have explored the meaning of human existence and attempted to define a "good life." In this section, we will define and examine some of the most important theories of ethical conduct.

L01   Appreciate the strengths and weaknesses of the various ethical theories.

As we cover these theories, much of what you read will be familiar to you. The names may be new, but almost certainly you have previously heard speeches and read writings of politicians, religious leaders, and commentators that incorporate the values in these theories. You will discover that your own thinking is consistent with one or more of the theories. You can also recognize the thinking of friends and antagonists in these theories.

None of these theories is necessarily invalid, and many people believe strongly in any one of them. Whether you believe your theory to be right and the others to be wrong, it is unlikely that others will accept what you see as the error of their ways and agree with all your values. Instead, it is important for you to recognize that people's ethical values can be as

diverse as human culture. Therefore, no amount of argumentation appealing to theories you accept is likely to influence someone who subscribes to a different ethical viewpoint.

This means that if you want to be understood by and to influence someone who has a different ethical underpinning than you do, you must first determine his ethical viewpoint and then speak in an ethical language that will be understood and accepted by him. Otherwise, you and your opponent are like the talking heads on nighttime cable TV news shows, whose debates often are reduced to shouting matches void of any attempt to understand the other side.

LOG ON

Go to
www.iep.utm.edu
    The Internet Encyclopedia of Philosophy gives you background on all the world's great philosophers from Abelard to Zizek. You can also study the development of philosophy from ancient times to the present. Many of the world's great philosophers addressed the question of ethical or moral conduct.

The four ethical theories we will study are rights theory, justice theory, utilitarianism, and profit maximization.

Some of these theories focus on results of our decisions or actions: do our decisions or actions produce the right results? Theories that focus on the consequences of a decision are teleological ethical theories. For example, a teleological theory may justify a manufacturing company laying off 5,000 employees, because the effect is to keep the price of manufactured goods low and to increase profits for the company's shareholders.

Other theories focus on the decision or action itself, irrespective of what results it produces. Theories that focus on decisions or actions alone are deontological ethical theories. For example, a deontological theory may find unacceptable that any competent employee loses his job, even if the layoff's effect is to reduce prices to consumers and increase profits.

First, we will cover rights theory, which is a deontological theory. Next will be justice theory, which has concepts common to rights theory, but a focus primarily on outcomes. Our study of ethical theories will conclude with two additional teleological theories, utilitarianism and profit maximization.

Rights Theory

Rights theory encompasses a variety of ethical philosophies holding that certain human rights are fundamental and must be respected by other humans. The focus is on each individual member of society and her rights. As an actor, each of us faces a moral compulsion not to harm the fundamental rights of others.

Kantianism Few rights theorists are strict deontologists, and one of the few is 18th-century philosopher Immanuel Kant. Kant viewed humans as moral actors that are free to make choices. He believed humans are able to judge the morality of any action by applying his famous categorical imperative. One formulation of the categorical imperative is, "Act only on that maxim whereby at the same time you can will that it shall become a universal law." This means that we judge an action by applying it universally.

Suppose you want to borrow money even though you know that you will never repay it. To justify this action using the categorical imperative, you state the following maxim or rule: "When I want money, I will borrow money and promise to repay it, even though I know I won't repay." According to Kant, you would not want this maxim to become a universal law, because no one would believe in promises to repay debts and you would not be able to borrow money when you want. Thus, your maxim or rule fails to satisfy the categorical imperative. You are compelled, therefore, not to promise falsely that you will repay a loan.

Kant had a second formulation of the categorical imperative: "Always act to treat humanity, whether in yourself or in others, as an end in itself, never merely as a means." That is, we may not use or manipulate others to achieve our own happiness. In Kant's eyes, if you falsely promise a lender to repay a loan, you are using that person because she would not agree to the loan if she knew all the facts.

Modern Rights Theories Strict deontological ethical theories like Kant's face an obvious problem: the duties are absolute. We can never lie and never kill, even though most of us find lying and killing acceptable in some contexts, such as in self-defense. Responding to these difficulties, some modern philosophers have proposed mixed deontological theories. There are many theories here, but one popular theory requires us to abide by a moral rule unless a more important rule conflicts with it. In other words, our moral compulsion is not to compromise a person's right unless a greater right takes priority over it.

For example, members of society have the right not to be lied to. Therefore, in most contexts you are morally compelled not to tell a falsehood. That is an important right, because it is critical to a society that we be able to rely on someone's word. If, however, you could save someone's life by telling a falsehood, such as telling a lie to a criminal about where a witness who will testify against him can be found, you probably will be required to save that person's life by lying about his whereabouts. In this context, the witness's right to live is a more important right than the criminal's right to hear the truth. In effect, one right "trumps" the other right.

What are these fundamental rights? How do we rank them in importance? Seventeenth-century philosopher John Locke argued for fundamental rights that we see embodied in the constitutions of modern democratic states: the protection of life, liberty, and property. Libertarians and others include the important rights of freedom of contract and freedom of expression. Modern liberals, like Bertolt Brecht, argued that all humans have basic rights to employment, food, housing, and education. Since the 1990s, the right to health care has become part of the liberal rights agenda.

Strengths of Rights Theory The major strength of rights theory is that it protects fundamental rights, unless some greater right takes precedence. This means that members of modern democratic societies have extensive liberties and rights that they need not fear will be taken away by their government or other members of society.

Criticisms of Rights Theory Most of the criticisms of rights theory deal with the near absolute yet relative value of the rights protected, making it difficult to articulate and administer a comprehensive rights theory. First, it is difficult to achieve agreement about which rights are protected. Rights fundamental to modern countries like the United States (such as many women's rights) are

The Global Business Environment

The Golden Rule in the World's Religions and Cultures

Immanuel Kant's categorical imperative, which is one formulation of rights theory, has its foundations in the Golden Rule. Note that the Golden Rule exists in all cultures and in all countries of the world. Here is a sampling.

BUDDHISM: Hurt not others in ways that you would find hurtful.

CHRISTIANITY: Do to others as you would have others do to you.

CONFUCIANISM: Do not to others what you would not like yourself.

GRECIAN: Do not that to a neighbor which you shall take ill from him.

HINDUISM: This is the sum of duty: do nothing to others which if done to you would cause you pain.

HUMANISM: Individual and social problems can only be resolved by means of human reason, intelligent effort, and critical thinking joined with compassion and a spirit of empathy for all living beings.

ISLAM: No one of you is a believer until he desires for his brother that which he desires for himself.

JAINISM: In happiness and suffering, in joy and grief, we should regard all creatures as we regard our own self.

JUDAISM: Whatever is hateful to you, do not to another.

NATIVE AMERICAN SPIRITUALITY: Respect for all life is the foundation.

PERSIAN: Do as you would be done by.

ROMAN: Treat your inferiors as you would be treated by your superiors.

SHINTOISM: The heart of the person before you is a mirror. See there your own form.

SIKHISM: As you deem yourself, so deem others.

TAOISM: Regard your neighbor's gain as your own gain, and your neighbor's loss as your own loss.

YORUBAN: One going to take a pointed stick to pinch a baby bird should first try it on himself to feel how it hurts.

ZOROASTRIANISM: That nature alone is good which refrains from doing to another whatsoever is not good for itself.

---

unknown or severely restricted in countries like Pakistan or Saudi Arabia. Even within one country, citizens disagree on the existence and ranking of rights. For example, some Americans argue that the right to health care is an important need that should be met by government or a person's employer. Other Americans believe funding universal health care would interfere with the libertarian right to limited government intervention in our lives.

In addition, rights theory does not concern itself with the costs or benefits of requiring respect for another's right. For example, rights theory probably justifies the protection of a neo-Nazi's right to spout hateful speech, even though the costs of such speech, including damage to relations between ethnic groups, may far outweigh any benefits the speaker, listeners, and society receives from the speech.

Moreover, rights theory promotes moral fanaticism and creates a sense of entitlement reducing innovation, entrepreneurship, and production. If, for example, I am entitled to a job, a place to live, food, and health care regardless of how hard I work, how motivated am I to work to earn those things?

Justice Theory In 1971, John Rawls published his book *A Theory of Justice,* the philosophical underpinning for the bureaucratic welfare state. Rawls reasoned

that it was right for governments to redistribute wealth in order to help the poor and disadvantaged. He argued for a just distribution of society's resources by which a society's benefits and burdens are allocated fairly among its members.

Rawls expressed this philosophy in his Greatest Equal Liberty Principle: each person has an equal right to basic rights and liberties. He qualified or limited this principle with the Difference Principle: social inequalities are acceptable only if they cannot be eliminated without making the worst-off class even worse off. The basic structure is perfectly just, he wrote, when the prospects of the least fortunate are as great as they can be.

Rawls's justice theory has application in the business context. Justice theory requires decision makers to be guided by fairness and impartiality. It holds that businesses should focus on outcomes: are people getting what they deserve? It would mean, for example, that a business deciding in which of two communities to build a new manufacturing plant should consider which community has the greater need for economic development.

Chief among Rawls's critics was his Harvard colleague Robert Nozick. Nozick argued that the rights of the individual are primary and that nothing more was justified than a minimal government that protected against violence and theft and ensured the enforcement of contracts. Nozick espoused a libertarian view that unequal distribution of wealth is moral if there is equal opportunity. Applied to the business context, Nozick's formulation of justice would permit a business to choose between two manufacturing plant sites after giving each community the opportunity to make its best bid for the plant. Instead of picking the community most in need, the business may pick the one offering the best deal.

Strengths of Justice Theory The strength of Rawls's justice theory lies in its basic premise, the protection of those who are least advantaged in society. Its motives are consistent with the religious and secular philosophies that urge humans to help those in need. Many religions and cultures hold basic to their faith the assistance of those who are less fortunate.

Criticisms of Justice Theory Rawls's justice theory shares some of the criticisms of rights theory. It treats equality as an absolute, without examining the costs of producing equality, including reduced incentives for innovation, entrepreneurship, and production. Moreover, any attempt to rearrange social benefits requires an accurate measurement of current wealth. For example, if a business is unable to measure accurately which employees are in greater need of benefits due to their wealth level, application of justice theory may make the business a Robin Hood in reverse: taking from the poor to give to the rich.

Utilitarianism
Utilitarianism requires a decision maker to maximize utility for society as a whole. Maximizing utility means achieving the highest level of satisfactions over dissatisfactions. This means that a person must consider the benefits and costs of her actions to everyone in society.

A utilitarian will act only if the benefits of the action to society outweigh the societal costs of the action. Note that the focus is on society as a whole. This means a decision maker may be required to do something that harms her if society as a whole is benefited by her action.

A teleological theory, utilitarianism judges our actions as good or bad depending on their consequences. This is sometimes expressed as "the ends justify the means."

Utilitarianism is most identified with 19th-century philosophers Jeremy Bentham and John Stuart Mill. Bentham argued that maximizing utility meant achieving the greatest overall balance of pleasure over pain. A critic of utilitarianism, Thomas Carlyle, called utilitarianism "pig philosophy," because it appeared to base the goal of ethics on the swinish pleasures of the multitude.

Mill thought Bentham's approach too narrow and broadened the definition of utility to include satisfactions such as health, knowledge, friendship, and aesthetic delights. Responding to Carlyle's criticisms, Mill also wrote that some satisfactions count more than others. For example, the pleasure of seeing wild animals free in the world may be a greater satisfaction morally than shooting them and seeing them stuffed in one's den.

How does utilitarianism work in practice? It requires that you consider not just the impact of decisions on yourself, your family, and your friends, but also the impact on everyone in society. Before deciding whether to ride a bicycle to school or work rather than to drive a car, a utilitarian would consider the wear and tear on her clothes, the time saved or lost by riding a bike, the displeasure of riding in bad weather, her improved physical condition, her feeling of satisfaction for not using fossil fuels, the cost of buying more food to fuel her body for the bike trips, the dangers of riding near automobile traffic, and a host of other factors that affect her satisfaction and dissatisfaction.

But her utilitarian analysis doesn't stop there. She has to consider her decision's effect on the rest of society. Will she interfere with automobile traffic flow and decrease the driving pleasure of automobile drivers? Will commuters be encouraged to ride as she does and benefit from doing so? Will her lower use of gasoline for her car reduce demand and consumption of fossil fuels, saving money for car drivers and reducing pollution? Will her and other bike riders' increased food consumption drive up food prices and make it less affordable for poor families? This only scratches the surface of her utilitarian analysis.

The process we used above, so-called act utilitarianism, judges each act separately, assessing a single act's benefits and costs to society's members. Obviously, a person cannot make an act utilitarian analysis for every decision. It would take too much time.

Utilitarianism recognizes that human limitation. Rule utilitarianism judges actions by a rule that over the long run maximizes benefits over costs. For example, you may find that taking a shower every morning before school or work maximizes society's satisfactions, as a rule. Most days, people around you will be benefited by not having to smell noisome odors, and your personal and professional prospects will improve by practicing good hygiene. Therefore, you are likely to be a rule utilitarian and shower each morning, even though some days you may not contact other people.

Many of the habits we have are the result of rule utilitarian analysis. Likewise, many business practices, such as a retailer's regular starting and closing times, also are based in rule utilitarianism.

Strengths of Utilitarianism   What are the strengths of utilitarianism as a guide for ethical conduct? It is easy to articulate the standard of conduct: you merely need to do what is best for society as a whole. It also coincides with values of most modern countries like the United States: it is capitalist in nature by focusing on total social satisfactions, benefits, welfare, and wealth, not on the allocations of pleasures and pains, satisfactions and dissatisfactions, and wealth.

Criticisms of Utilitarianism   Those strengths also expose some of the criticisms of utilitarianism as an ethical construct. It is difficult to measure one's own pleasures and pains and satisfactions and dissatisfactions, let alone those of all of society's members. In addition, those benefits and costs almost certainly are unequally distributed across society's members. It can foster a tyranny of the majority that may result in morally monstrous behavior, such as a decision by a 100,000-person community to use a lake as a dump for human waste because only one person otherwise uses or draws drinking water from the lake.

That example exhibits how utilitarianism differs from rights theory. While rights theory may protect a person's right to clean drinking water regardless of its cost, utilitarianism considers the benefits and costs of that right as only one factor in the total mix of society's benefits and costs. In some cases, the cost of interfering with someone's right may outweigh the benefits to society, resulting in the same decision that rights theory produces. But where rights theory is essentially a one-factor analysis, utilitarianism requires a consideration of that factor and a host of others as well.

A final criticism of utilitarianism is that it is not constrained by law. Certainly, the law is a factor in utilitarian analysis. Utilitarian analysis must consider, for example, the dissatisfactions fostered by not complying with the law and by creating an environment of lawlessness in a society. Yet the law is only one factor in utilitarian analysis. The pains caused by violating the law may be offset by benefits the violation produces. Most people, however, are rule utilitarian when it comes to law, deciding that obeying the law in the long run maximizes social utility.

Profit Maximization   Profit maximization as an ethical theory requires a decision maker to maximize a business's long-run profits within the limits of the law. It is based in the *laissez faire* theory of capitalism first expressed by Adam Smith in the 18th century and more recently promoted by economists such as Milton Friedman and Thomas Sowell. Laissez faire economists argue total social welfare is optimized if humans are permitted to work toward their own selfish goals. The role

of governments and law is solely to ensure the workings of a free market by not interfering with economic liberty, eliminating collusion among competitors, and promoting accurate information in the marketplace.

By focusing on results—maximizing total social welfare—profit maximization is a teleological ethical theory. It is closely related to utilitarianism, but it differs fundamentally in how ethical decisions are made. While utilitarianism maximizes social utility by focusing the actor on everyone's satisfactions and dissatisfactions, profit maximization optimizes total social utility by narrowing the actor's focus, requiring the decision maker to make a decision that merely maximizes profits for himself or his organization.

Strengths of Profit Maximization   How can we define ethical behavior as acting in one's selfish interest? As you probably already learned in a microeconomics course, this apparent contradiction is explained by the consequences of all of us being profit maximizers. By working in our own interests, we compete for society's scarce resources (iron ore, labor, and land, to name a few), which are allocated to those people and businesses that can use them most productively. By allocating society's resources to their most efficient uses, as determined by a free market, we maximize total social utility or benefits. Society as a whole is bettered if all of us compete freely for its resources by trying to increase our personal or business profits. If we fail to maximize profits, some of society's resources will be allocated to less productive uses that reduce society's total welfare.

In addition, profit maximization results in ethical conduct because it requires society's members to act within the constraints of the law. A profit maximizer, therefore, acts ethically by complying with society's mores as expressed in its laws.

Moreover, each decision maker and business is disciplined by the marketplace. Consequently, profit maximization analysis probably requires a decision maker to consider the rights protected by rights theory and justice theory. Ignoring important rights of employees, customers, suppliers, communities, and other stakeholders may negatively impact a corporation's profits. A business that engages in behavior that is judged unethical by consumers and other members of society is subject to boycotts, adverse publicity, demands for more restrictive laws, and other reactions that damage its image, decrease its revenue, and increase its costs.

Consider for example, the reduced sales of Martha Stewart branded goods at Kmart after Ms. Stewart was accused of trading ImClone stock while possessing inside information. Consider also the fewer number of college graduates willing to work for Waste Management, Inc., in the wake of adverse publicity and indictments against its executives for misstating its financial results. Note also the higher cost of capital for firms like Dell as investors bid down the stock price of companies accused of accounting irregularities and other wrongdoing.

All these reactions to perceived unethical conduct impact the business's profitability in the short and long run, motivating that business to make decisions that comply with ethical views that transcend legal requirements.

Criticisms of Profit Maximization The strengths of profit maximization as a model for ethical behavior also suggest criticisms and weaknesses of the theory. Striking at the heart of the theory is the criticism that corporate managers are subject to human failings that make it impossible for them to maximize corporate profits. The failure to discover and process all relevant information and varying levels of aversion to risk can result in one manager making a different decision than another manager. Group decision making in the business context introduces other dynamics that interfere with rational decision making. Social psychologists have found that groups often accept a higher level of risk than they would as individuals. There is also the tendency of a group to internalize the group's values and suppress critical thought.

Furthermore, even if profit maximization results in an efficient allocation of society's resources and maximization of total social welfare, it does not concern itself with how wealth is allocated within society. In America, more than 85 percent of all wealth is held by 20 percent of the population. To some people, that wealth disparity is unacceptable. To *laissez faire* economists, wealth disparity is a necessary component of a free market that rewards hard work, acquired skills, innovation, and risk taking. Yet critics of profit maximization respond that market imperfections and a person's position in life at birth interfere with his ability to compete.

Critics charge that the ability of laws and market forces to control corporate behavior is limited, because it requires lawmakers, consumers, employees, and other constituents to detect unethical corporate acts and take appropriate steps. Even if consumers notice irresponsible behavior and inform a corporation, a bureaucratic corporate structure may interfere with the information being received by the proper person inside the corporation. If instead consumers are silent and refuse to buy corporate products because of perceived unethical acts, corporate management may notice a decrease in sales, yet attribute it to something other than the corporation's unethical behavior.

Critics also argue that equating ethical behavior with legal compliance is a tautology in countries like the United States where businesses distort the lawmaking process by lobbying legislators and making political contributions. It cannot be ethical, they argue, for businesses to comply with laws reflecting the interests of businesses.

Profit maximization proponents respond that many laws restraining businesses are passed despite businesses lobbying against those laws. The Sarbanes–Oxley Act, which increases penalties for wrongdoing executives, requires CEOs to certify financial statements, and imposes internal governance rules on public companies, is such an example. So are laws restricting drug companies from selling a drug unless it is approved by the Food and Drug Administration and requiring environmental impact studies before a business may construct a new manufacturing plant. Moreover, businesses are nothing other than a collection of individual stakeholders, which includes employees, shareholders, and their communities. When they lobby, they lobby in the best interests of all these stakeholders.

Critics respond that ethics transcends law, requiring in some situations that businesses adhere to a higher standard than required by law. We understand this in our personal lives. For example, despite the absence of law dictating for the most part how we treat friends, we know that ethical behavior requires us to be loyal to friends and to spend time with them when they need our help. In the business context, a firm may be permitted to release employees for nearly any reason, except the few legally banned bases of discrimination (such as race, age, and gender), yet some critics will argue businesses should not terminate an employee for other reasons currently not banned by most laws (such as sexual orientation or appearance). Moreover, these critics further argue that businesses—due to their influential role in a modern society—should be leaders in setting a standard for ethical conduct.

Profit maximizers respond that such an ethical standard is difficult to define and hampers efficient decision making. Moreover, they argue that experience shows the law has been a particularly relevant definition of ethical conduct. Consider that all the recent corporate scandals would have been prevented had the executives merely complied with the law. For example, Enron executives illegally kept some liabilities off the firm's financial statements. Tyco and Adelphia executives illegally looted corporate assets. Had these executives simply complied with the law and maximized their firms' long-run profits, none of the recent ethical debacles would have occurred.

Critics of profit maximization respond that the recent corporate crises at companies like Enron and WorldCom prove that flaws in corporate governance encourage executives to act unethically. These examples, critics say, show that many executives do not maximize profits for their firms. Instead, they maximize their own profits at the expense of the firm and its shareholders. They claim that stock options and other incentives intended to align the interests of executives with those of shareholders promote decisions that raise short-term profits to the long-run detriment of the firms. They point out that many CEOs and other top executives negotiate compensation plans that do not require them to stay with the firm long term and which allow them to benefit enormously from short-term profits. Executive greed, encouraged by these perverse executive compensation plans, also encourage CEOs and other executives to violate the law.

Defenders of business, profit maximization, and capitalist economics point out that it is nearly impossible to stop someone who is bent on fraud. A dishonest executive will lie to shareholders, creditors, board members, and the public and also treat the law as optional. Yet enlightened proponents of the modern corporation accept that there are problems with corporate management culture that require changes. They know that an unconstrained CEO, ethically uneducated executives, perverse compensation incentives, and inadequate supervision of executives by the firm's CEOs, board of directors, and shareholders present golden opportunities to the unscrupulous person and make unwitting accomplices of the ignorant and the powerless.

Improving Corporate Governance and Corporate Social Responsibility Even if we cannot stop all fraudulent executives, we can modify the corporate governance model to educate, motivate, and supervise executives and thereby improve corporate social responsibility. Corporate critics have proposed a wide variety of cures, all of which have been implemented to some degree and with varying degrees of success.

Ethics Codes Many large corporations and several industries have adopted codes of ethics or codes of conduct to guide executives and other employees. The Sarbanes–Oxley Act requires a public company to disclose whether it has adopted a code of ethics for senior financial officers, and to disclose any change in the code or waiver of the code's application.

There are two popular views of such codes. One sees the codes as genuine efforts to foster ethical behavior within a firm or an industry. The other view regards them as thinly disguised attempts to make the firm function better, to mislead the public into believing the firm behaves ethically, to prevent the passage of legislation that would

impose stricter constraints on business, or to limit competition under the veil of ethical standards. Even where the first view is correct, ethical codes fail to address concretely all possible forms of corporate misbehavior. Instead, they often emphasize either the behavior required for the firm's effective internal function, such as not accepting gifts from customers, or the relations between competitors within a particular industry, such as prohibitions on some types of advertising.

Better corporate ethics codes make clear that the corporation expects employees not to violate the law in a mistaken belief that loyalty to the corporation or corporate profitability requires it. Such codes work best, however, when a corporation also gives its employees an outlet for dealing with a superior's request to do an unethical act. That outlet may be the corporate legal department or corporate ethics office. One example is Google's Code of Ethics, which appears on the next page.

Ethical Instruction Some corporations require their employees to enroll in classes that teach ethical decision making. The idea is that a manager trained in ethical conduct will recognize unethical actions before they are taken and deter herself and the corporation from the unethical acts.

While promising in theory, in practice many managers are resistant to ethical training that requires them to examine their principles. They are reluctant to set aside a set of long-held principles with which they are comfortable. Therefore, there are some doubts whether managers are receptive to ethical instruction. Even if the training is accepted, will managers retain the ethical lessons of their training and use it, or will time and other job-related pressures force a manager to think only of completing the job at hand?

Moreover, what ethical values should be taught? Is it enough to teach only one, a few, or all the theories of ethical conduct? Corporations mostly support profit maximization, because it maximizes shareholder value. But should a corporation also teach rights theory and expect its employees to follow it? Or should rights theory be treated as only a component of profit maximization?

Most major corporations today express their dedication to ethical decision making by having an ethics officer who is not only responsible for ethical instruction, but also in charge of ethical supervision. The ethics officer may attempt to instill ethical decision making as a component of daily corporate life by sensitizing employees to the perils of ignoring ethical issues. The ethics officer may also be a mentor or sounding board for all employees who face ethical issues.

Whether an ethics officer is effective, however, is determined by the level of commitment top executives make to ethical behavior and the position and power granted to

Ethics in Action

Google Code of Conduct

Internet giant Google Inc. is one of many international corporations to adopt an ethics code. Here are excerpts from Google's Code of Conduct. For the full code of behavior, go to http://investor.google.com/corporate/code-of-conduct.html.

Preface "Don't be evil." Googlers generally apply those words to how we serve our users. But "Don't be evil" is much more than that. Yes, it's about providing our users unbiased access to information, focusing on their needs and giving them the best products and services that we can. But it's also about doing the right thing more generally—following the law, acting honorably and treating each other with respect.

The Google Code of Conduct is one of the ways we put "Don't be evil" into practice. It's built around the recognition that everything we do in connection with our work at Google will be, and should be, measured against the highest possible standards of ethical business conduct. We set the bar that high for practical as well as aspirational reasons: Our commitment to the highest standards helps us hire great people, who then build great products, which in turn attract loyal users. Trust and mutual respect among employees and users are the foundation of our success, and they are something we need to earn every day.

So please do read the Code, and follow it, always bearing in mind that each of us has a personal responsibility to incorporate, and to encourage other Googlers to incorporate, the principles of the Code into our work.

I. Serve Our Users Our users value Google not only because we deliver great products and services, but because we hold ourselves to a higher standard in how we treat users and operate more generally. Keeping the following principles in mind will help us to maintain that high standard:

a. **Integrity** Our reputation as a company that our users can trust is our most valuable asset, and it is up to all of us to make sure that we continually earn that trust. All of our communications and other interactions with our users should increase their trust in us.

c. **Privacy and Freedom of Expression** Always remember that we are asking users to trust us with their personal information. Preserving that trust requires that each of us respect and protect the privacy of that information. Our security procedures strictly limit access to and use of users' personal information. Know your responsibilities under these procedures, and access data only as authorized by them, our Privacy Policy and applicable local data protection laws.

II. Respect Each Other We are committed to a supportive work environment, where employees have the opportunity to reach their fullest potential. Each Googler is expected to do his or her utmost to create a respectful workplace culture that is free of harassment, intimidation, bias and unlawful discrimination of any kind.

III. Avoid Conflicts of Interest In working at Google, we have an obligation to always do what's best for the company and our users. When you are in a situation where competing loyalties could cause you to pursue a personal benefit for you or your friends or family at the expense of Google or our users, you may be subject to a conflict of interest. All of us should avoid circumstances that present even the appearance of such a conflict.

When faced with a potential conflict of interest, ask yourself:

* Would this relationship or situation embarrass me or Google if it showed up on the front page of a newspaper or the top of a blog?
* Am I reluctant to disclose the relationship or situation to my manager, Legal or Ethics & Compliance?
* Could the potential relationship or situation create an incentive for me, or be perceived by others to create an incentive for me, to benefit myself, my friends or family or an associated business, at the expense of Google?

If the answer to any of these questions is 'yes,' the relationship or situation is likely to create a conflict of interest, and you should avoid it.

VI. Ensure Financial Integrity and Responsibility Financial integrity and fiscal responsibility are core aspects of corporate professionalism. This is more than accurate reporting of our financials, though that's certainly important. The money we spend on behalf of Google is not ours; it's the company's and, ultimately, our shareholders'. Each person at Google—not just those in Finance—has a role in making sure that money is appropriately spent, our financial records are complete and accurate and internal controls are honored.

VII. Obey the Law Google takes its responsibilities to comply with laws and regulations very seriously and each of us is expected to comply with applicable legal requirements and prohibitions. While it's impossible for anyone to know all aspects of every applicable law, you should understand the major laws and regulations that apply to your work. Take advantage of Legal and Ethics & Compliance to assist you here.

VIII. Conclusion Google aspires to be a different kind of company. It's impossible to spell out every possible ethical scenario we might face. Instead, we rely on one another's good judgment to uphold a high standard of integrity for ourselves and our company. We expect all Googlers to be guided by both the letter and the spirit of this Code. Sometimes, identifying the right thing to do isn't an easy call. If you aren't sure, don't be afraid to ask questions of your manager, Legal or Ethics & Compliance.

And remember . . . don't be evil, and if you see something that you think isn't right—speak up!

the ethics officer. For example, will top executives and the board of directors allow an ethics officer to nix an important deal on ethical grounds or will they replace the ethics officer with another executive whose ethical views permit the deal? Therefore, probably more important than an ethics officer is a CEO with the character to do the right thing.

Greater Shareholder Role in Corporations Since shareholders are the ultimate stakeholders in a corporation in a capitalist economy, some corporate critics argue that businesses should be more attuned to shareholders' ethical values and that shareholder control of the board of directors and executives should be increased. This decentralization of ethical decision making, the theory goes, should result in corporate decisions that better reflect shareholders' ethical values.

Yet this decentralization of power flies in the face of the rationale for the modern corporation, which in part is designed to centralize management in the board of directors and top officers and to free shareholders from the burden of managing their investments in the corporation. Significant efficiencies are lost if corporate executives are required to divine and apply shareholders' ethical values before making a decision.

In addition, divining the shareholders' ethical viewpoint may be difficult. While nearly all shareholders are mostly profit driven, a small minority of shareholders have other agendas, such as protecting the environment or workers' rights, regardless of the cost to the corporation. It is often not possible to please all shareholders.

Nonetheless, increasing shareholder democracy by enhancing the shareholders' role in the nomination and election of board members is essential to uniting the interests of shareholders and management. So is facilitating the ability of shareholders to bring proposals for ethical policy to a vote of shareholders. In the last several years, for public companies at least, the Securities and Exchange Commission has taken several steps to increase shareholder democracy. These steps, which are covered fully in Chapter 45, are having their intended effect. For example, shareholders of EMC Corporation approved a proposal recommending that the company's board comprise a majority of independent directors. Mentor Graphics Corporation shareholders voted in a resolution that any significant stock option plan be shareholder-approved. Moreover, the New York Stock Exchange and NASDAQ require companies listed on those exchanges to submit for shareholder approval certain actions, such as approval of stock option plans.

Consider All Stakeholders' Interests Utilitarianism analysis clearly requires an executive to consider a decision's impact on all stakeholders. How else can one determine all the benefits and costs of the decision? Likewise, modern rights theory also dictates considering all stakeholders' rights, including not compromising an important right unless trumped by another. Kant's categorical imperative also mandates a concern for others by requiring one to act as one would require others to act.

Critics of corporations and modern proponents of profit maximization argue that more responsible and ethical decisions are made when corporate managers consider the interests of all stakeholders, including not only shareholders, but also employees, customers, suppliers, the community, and others impacted by a decision. For profit maximizers, the wisdom of considering all stakeholders is apparent, because ignoring the interests of any stakeholder may negatively affect profits. For example, a decision may impact a firm's ability to attract high quality employees, antagonize consumers, alienate suppliers, and motivate the public to lobby lawmakers to pass laws that increase a firm's cost of doing business. This wisdom is reflected in the Guidelines for Ethical Decision Making, which you will learn in the next section.

Nonetheless, there are challenges when a corporate manager considers the interests of all stakeholders. Beyond the enormity of identifying all stakeholders, stakeholders' interests may conflict, requiring a compromise that harms some stakeholders and benefits others. In addition, the impact on each stakeholder group may be difficult to assess accurately.

For example, if a manager is considering whether to terminate the 500 least productive employees during an economic downturn, the manager will note that shareholders will benefit from lower labor costs and consumers may find lower prices for goods, but the manager also knows that the terminated employees, their families, and their communities will likely suffer from the loss of income. Yet if the employees terminated are near retirement and have sizable retirement savings or if the termination motivates employees to return to college and seek better jobs, the impact on them, their families, and their communities may be minimal or even positive. On the other hand, if the manager makes the decision to retain the employees, shareholder wealth may decrease and economic inefficiency may result, which harms all society.

Independent Boards of Directors In some of the instances in which corporate executives have acted unethically and violated the law, the board of directors was little more than a rubber stamp or a sounding board for the CEO and other top executives. The CEO handpicked a board that largely allowed the CEO to run the corporation with little board supervision.

CEO domination of the board is a reality in most large corporations, because the market for CEO talent has skewed the system in favor of CEOs. Few CEOs are willing to accept positions in which the board exercises real control. Often, therefore, a CEO determines which board members serve on the independent board nominating committee and selects who is nominated by the committee. Owing their positions to the CEO and earning handsome fees sometimes exceeding $100,000, many directors are indisposed to oppose the CEO's plans.

For more than four decades, corporate critics have demanded that corporate boards be made more nearly independent of the CEO. The corporate ethical crisis of recent years has increased those calls for independence. The New York Stock Exchange and NASDAQ require companies with securities listed on the exchanges to have a majority of directors independent of the company and top management. Their rules also require independent management compensation, board nomination, and audit committees. The Sarbanes–Oxley Act requires public companies to have board audit committees comprising only independent directors.

One criticism of director independence rules is the belief that no director can remain independent after joining the board, because every director receives compensation from the corporation. There is a concern that an independent director, whose compensation is high, will side with management to ensure his continuing nomination, election, and receipt of high fees.

More extreme proposals of corporate critics include recommendations that all corporate stakeholders, such as labor, government, environmentalists, and communities, have representation on the board or that special directors or committees be given responsibility over special areas, such as consumer protection and workers' rights. Other critics argue for contested elections for each board vacancy. Few corporations have adopted these recommendations.

While honestly motivated, these laws and recommendations often fail to produce greater corporate social responsibility because they ignore the main reason for management's domination of the board: the limited time, information, and resources that directors have. One solution is to give outside directors a full-time staff with power to acquire information within the corporation. This solution, while providing a check on management, also may produce inefficiency by creating another layer of management in the firm.

In addition, some of the recommendations complicate management by making the board less cohesive. Conflicts between stakeholder representatives or between inside and outside directors may be difficult to resolve. For example,
the board could be divided by disputes between shareholders who want more dividends, consumers who want lower prices, and employees who want higher wages.

Changing the Internal Management Structure Some corporate critics argue that the historic shift of corporate powers away from a public corporation's board and shareholders to its managers is irreversible. They recommend, therefore, that the best way to produce responsible corporate behavior is to change the corporation's management structure.

The main proponent of this view, Christopher Stone, recommended the creation of offices dedicated to areas such as environmental affairs and workers' rights, higher educational requirements for officers in positions like occupational safety, and procedures to ensure that important information inside and outside the corporation is directed to the proper person within the corporation. He also recommended that corporations study certain important issues and create reports of the study before making decisions.

These requirements aim to change the process by which corporations make decisions. The objective is to improve decision making by raising the competency of decision makers, increasing the amount of relevant information they hold, and enhancing the methodology by which decisions are made.

More information held by more competent managers using better tools should produce better decisions. Two of the later sections in this chapter in part reflect these recommendations. The Guidelines for Ethical Decision Making require a decision maker to study a decision carefully before making a decision. This includes acquiring all relevant facts, assessing a decision's impact on each stakeholder, and considering the ethics of one's decision from each ethical perspective. In addition, the Critical Thinking section below will help you understand when fallacious thinking interferes with a manager's ability to make good decisions.

Eliminating Perverse Incentives and Supervising Management Even if a corporation modifies its internal management structure by improving the decision-making process, there are no guarantees more responsible decisions will result. To the extent unethical corporate behavior results from faulty perception and inadequate facts, a better decision-making process helps. But if a decision maker is motivated solely to increase short-term profits, irresponsible decisions may follow. When one examines closely recent corporate debacles three things are clear: the corporate wrongdoers acted in their selfish interests; the corporate reward system encouraged them to act selfishly, illegally, and unethically; the wrongdoers acted without effective supervision. These facts suggest other changes that should be made in the internal management structure.

During the high flying stock market of the 1990s, stock options were the compensation package preferred by high level corporate executives. Shareholders and boards of directors were more than willing to accommodate them. On one level, stock options seem to align the interests of executives with those of the corporation and its shareholders. Issued at an exercise price usually far below the current market price of the stock, stock options have no value until the corporation's stock price exceeds the exercise price of the stock options. Thus, executives are motivated to increase the corporation's profits, which should result in an increase in the stock's market price. In the 1990s stock market, in which some stock prices were doubling yearly, the exercise price of executives' stock options was quickly dwarfed by the market price. Executives exercised the stock options, buying and then selling stock, and in the process generating profits for a single executive in the tens and hundreds of millions of dollars. Shareholders also benefited from the dramatic increase in the value of their stock.

So what is the problem with stock options? As executives accepted more of their compensation in the form of stock options and became addicted to the lifestyle financed by them, some executives felt pressure to keep profits soaring to ever higher levels. In companies like Enron and WorldCom, which had flawed business models and suspect accounting practices, some executives were encouraged to create business deals that had little if any economic justification and could be accounted for in ways that kept profits growing. In what were essentially pyramid schemes, once the faulty economics of the deals were understood by prospective partners, no new deals were possible and the schemes crashed like houses of cards. But until the schemes were discovered, many executives, including some who were part of the fraudulent schemes, pocketed tens and hundreds of millions of dollars in stock option profits.

The Sarbanes–Oxley Act, as amended by the Dodd-Frank Wall Street Reform and Consumer Protection Act of 2010, requires executive officers to disgorge any bonus and incentive-based or equity-based compensation received during the three-year period prior to which the corporation was required to restate its financial statements.

It is easy to see how fraudulent actions subvert the objective of stock options to motivate executives to act in the best interests of shareholders. Adolph Berle, however, has argued for more than 50 years that stock options are flawed compensation devices that allow executives to profit when stock market prices rise in general, even when executives have no positive effect on profitability. He proposed that the best way to compensate executives is to allow them to trade on inside information they possess about a corporation's prospects, information they possess because they helped produce those prospects. His proposal, however, is not likely ever to be legal compensation because insider trading creates the appearance that the securities markets are rigged.

Even with incentives in place to encourage executives to inflate profits artificially, it is unlikely that the recent fraudulent schemes at Enron, WorldCom, and other companies would have occurred had there been better scrutiny of upper management and its actions by the CEO and the board of directors. At Enron, executives were given great freedom to create partnerships that allowed Enron to keep liabilities off the balance sheet yet generate income that arguably could be recognized in the current period. It is not surprising that this freedom from scrutiny when combined with financial incentives to create the partnerships resulted in executives creating partnerships that had little economic value to Enron.

Better supervision of management is mostly the responsibility of the CEO, but the board of directors bears this duty also. We addressed earlier proposals to create boards of directors that are more nearly independent of the CEO and, therefore, better able to supervise the CEO and other top managers. Primarily, however, better supervision is a matter of attitude, or a willingness to devote time and effort to discover the actions of those under your charge and to challenge them to justify their actions. It is not unlike the responsibility a parent owes to a teenage child to scrutinize her actions and her friends to make sure that she is acting consistent with the values of the family. So too, boards must make the effort to scrutinize their CEOs and hire CEOs who are able and willing to scrutinize the work of the managers below them.

Yet directors must also be educated and experienced. Poor supervision of management has also been shown to be partly due to some directors' ignorance of business disciplines like finance and accounting. Unless board members are able to understand accounting numbers and other information that suggests management wrongdoing, board scrutiny of management is a process with no substance.

The Law The law has been a main means of controlling corporate misdeeds. Lawmakers usually assume that corporations and executives are rational actors that can be deterred from unethical and socially irresponsible behavior by the threats law presents. Those threats are fines and civil damages, such as those imposed and increased by the Sarbanes–Oxley Act. For deterrence to work, however, corporate decision makers must know when the law's penalties will be imposed, fear those penalties, and act rationally to avoid them.

To some extent, the law's ability to control executive misbehavior is limited. As we discussed earlier in this chapter, corporate lobbying may result in laws reflecting the views of corporations, not society as a whole. Some corporate executives may not know the law exists. Others may view the penalties merely as a cost of doing business. Some may think the risk of detection is so low that the corporation can avoid detection. Other executives believe they are above the law, that it does not apply to them out of arrogance or a belief that they know better than lawmakers. Some rationalize their violation of the law on the grounds that "everybody does it."

Nonetheless, for all its flaws, the law is an important means by which society controls business misconduct. Of all the devices for corporate control we have considered, only market forces and the law impose direct penalties for corporate misbehavior. Although legal rules have no special claim to moral correctness, at least they are knowable. Laws also are the result of an open political process in which competing arguments are made and evaluated. This cannot be said about the intuitions of a corporate ethics officer, edicts from public interest groups, or the theories of economists or philosophers, except to the extent they are reflected in law. Moreover, in mature political systems like the United States, respect for and adherence to law is a well-entrenched value.

Where markets fail to promote socially responsible conduct, the law can do the job. For example, the antitrust laws discussed in Chapter 49, while still controversial, have eliminated the worst anticompetitive business practices. The federal securities laws examined in Chapters 45 and 46 arguably restored investor confidence in the securities markets after the stock market crash of 1929. Although environmentalists often demand more regulation, the environmental laws treated in Chapter 52 have improved the quality of water and reduced our exposure to toxic substances. Employment regulations discussed in Chapter 51—especially those banning employment discrimination—have forced significant changes in the American workplace. Thus, the law has an accomplished record as a corporate control device.

Indeed, sometimes the law does the job too well, often imposing a maze of regulations that deter socially valuable profit seeking without producing comparable benefits. Former Fed chairman Greenspan once wrote,

"Government regulation is not an alternative means of protecting the consumer. It does not build quality into goods, or accuracy into information. Its sole 'contribution' is to substitute force and fear for incentive as the 'protector' of the consumer."

The hope was that the Sarbanes–Oxley Act would restore investor confidence in audited financial statements and corporate governance. A 2007 survey by Financial Executives International found that 69 percent of financial executives agreed that compliance with SOX section 404 resulted in more investor confidence in their companies' financial reports. Fifty percent agreed that financial reports were more accurate. Those results came despite the high cost of complying with the Act: an average of $1.7 million for 168 companies with market capitalization above $75 million.

Guidelines for Ethical Decision Making

Now that you understand the basics of ethical theories and the issues in the corporate governance debate, how do you use this information to make decisions for your business that are ethical and socially responsible? That is, what process will ensure that you have considered all the ethical ramifications and arrived at a decision that is good for your business, good for your community, good for society as a whole, and good for you.

 LO2   Apply the Guidelines for Ethical Decision Making to business and personal decisions.

Figure 1 lists nine factors in the Guidelines for Ethical Decision Making. Let's consider each Guideline and explain how each helps you make better decisions.

What Facts Impact My Decision?   This is such an obvious component of any good decision that it hardly seems necessary to mention. Yet it is common that people make only a feeble attempt to acquire *all* the facts necessary to a good decision.

Many people enter a decision-making process biased in favor of a particular option. As a result, they look only for facts that support that option. You have seen this done many times by your friends and opponents, and since you are an honest person, you have seen yourself do this as well from time to time. In addition, demands on our time, fatigue, laziness, ignorance of where to look for facts, and aversion to inconvenience someone who has information

Figure 1 *Guidelines for Ethical Decision Making*
1. What **FACTS** impact my decision?
2. What are the **ALTERNATIVES?**
3. Who are the **STAKEHOLDERS?**
4. How do the alternatives impact **SOCIETY AS A WHOLE?**
5. How do the alternatives impact **MY BUSINESS FIRM?**
6. How do the alternatives impact **ME, THE DECISION MAKER?**
7. What are the **ETHICS** of each alternative?
8. What are the **PRACTICAL CONSTRAINTS** of each alternative?
9. What **COURSE OF ACTION** should be taken and how do we **IMPLEMENT** it?

contribute to a reluctance or inability to dig deep for relevant facts.

Since good decisions cannot be made in a partial vacuum of information, it is important to recognize when you need to acquire more facts. That is primarily the function of your other classes, which may teach you how to make stock market investment decisions, how to audit a company's financial records, and how to do marketing research.

For our purposes, let's consider this example. Suppose we work for a television manufacturing company that has a factory in Sacramento, California. Our company has placed you in charge of investigating the firm's decision whether to move the factory to Juarez, Mexico. What facts are needed to make this decision, and where do you find those facts?

Among the facts you need are: What are the firm's labor costs in Sacramento and what will those costs be in Juarez? How much will labor costs increase in subsequent years? What is the likelihood of good labor relations in each location? What is and will be the productivity level of employees in each city? What are and will be the transportation costs of moving the firm's inventory to market? What impact will the move have on employees, their families, the communities, the schools, and other stakeholders in each community? Will Sacramento employees find other jobs in Sacramento or elsewhere? How much will we have to pay in severance pay?

How will our customers and suppliers be impacted by our decision? If we move to Juarez, will our customers boycott our products even if our televisions are better and cheaper than before? If we move, will our suppliers' costs increase or decrease? How will our profitability be affected? How will shareholders view the decision? Who are our shareholders? Do we have a lot of Mexican shareholders, or do Americans dominate our shareholder list? What tax concessions and other benefits will the

City of Sacramento give our firm if we promise to stay in Sacramento? What will Ciudad Juarez and the government of Mexico give us if we move to Juarez? How will our decision impact U.S.–Mexican economic and political relations?

This looks like a lot of facts, but we have only scratched the surface. You can probably come up with another 100 facts that should be researched. To give you another example of how thorough managers must be to make prudent decisions, consider that the organizers for the 2000 Summer Olympics in Sydney, Australia, created 800 different terrorist scenarios before developing an antiterrorism plan.

You can see that to some extent we are discussing other factors in the Guidelines as we garner facts. The factors do overlap to some degree. Note also that some of the facts you want to find are not facts at all, but estimates, such as cost and sales projections. We'll discuss in the Eighth Guideline the practical problems with the facts we find.

What Are the Alternatives? A decision maker must be thorough in listing the alternative courses of actions. For many of us, the temptation is to conclude that there are only two options: to do something or not to do something. Let's take our decision whether to move our factory to Juarez, Mexico. You might think that the only choices are to stay in Sacramento or to move to Juarez. Yet there are several combinations that fall in between those extremes.

For example, we could consider maintaining the factory in Sacramento temporarily, opening a smaller factory in Juarez, and gradually moving production to Mexico as employees in Sacramento retire. Another alternative is to offer jobs in the Juarez factory to all Sacramento employees who want to move. If per-unit labor costs in Sacramento are our concern, we could ask employees in

Sacramento to accept lower wages and fringe benefits or to increase their productivity.

There are many other alternatives that you can imagine. It is important to consider all reasonable alternatives. If you do not, you increase the risk that the best course of action was not chosen only because it was not considered.

Who Are the Stakeholders?

In modern societies, where diversity is valued as an independent virtue, considering the impacts of your decision on the full range of society's stakeholders has taken on great significance in prudent and ethical decision making. While a public corporation with thousands of shareholders obviously owes a duty to its shareholders to maximize shareholder wealth, corporate managers must also consider the interests of other important stakeholders, including employees, suppliers, customers, and the communities in which they live. Stakeholders also include society as a whole, which can be defined as narrowly as your country or more expansively as an economic union of countries, such as the European Union of 27 countries, or even the world as a whole.

Not to be omitted from stakeholders is you, the decision maker who is also impacted by your decisions for your firm. The legitimacy of considering your own selfish interests will be considered fully in the Sixth Guideline.

Listing all the stakeholders is not a goal by itself, but helps the decision maker apply more completely other factors in the Ethical Guidelines. Knowing whom your decision affects will help you find the facts you need. It also helps you evaluate the alternatives using the next three Guidelines: how the alternatives we have proposed impact society as whole, your firm, and the decision maker.

How Do the Alternatives Impact Society as a Whole?

We covered some aspects of this Guideline above when we made an effort to discover all the facts that impact our decision. We can do a better job discovering the facts if we try to determine how our decision impacts society as a whole.

For example, if the alternative we evaluate is keeping the factory in Sacramento after getting property tax and road building concessions from the City of Sacramento, how is society as a whole impacted? What effect will tax concessions have on the quality of Sacramento schools (most schools are funded with property taxes)? Will lower taxes cause the Sacramento infrastructure (roads and governmental services) to decline to the detriment of the ordinary citizen? Will the economic benefits to workers in Sacramento offset the harm to the economy and workers in Juarez?

Will our firm's receiving preferential concessions from the Sacramento government undermine the ordinary citizen's faith in our political and economic institutions? Will we contribute to the feelings of some citizens that government grants privileges only to the powerful? Will our staying in Sacramento foster further economic growth in Sacramento? Will staying in Sacramento allow our suppliers to stay in business and continue to hire employees who will buy goods from groceries and malls in Sacramento?

What impact will our decision have on efforts to create a global economy in which labor and goods can freely travel between countries? Will our decision increase international tension between the United States and Mexico?

Note that the impact of our decision on society as a whole fits neatly with one of the ethical theories we discussed earlier: utilitarianism. Yet profit maximization, rights theory, and justice theory also require a consideration of societal impacts.

How Do the Alternatives Impact My Firm?

The most obvious impact any alternative has on your firm is its effect on the firm's bottom line: what are the firm's profits. Yet that answer requires explaining, because what you really want to know is what smaller things leading to profitability are impacted by an alternative.

For example, if our decision is to keep the factory in Sacramento open temporarily and gradually move the plant to Juarez as retirements occur, what will happen to employee moral and productivity in Sacramento? Will our suppliers in Sacramento abandon us to serve more permanent clients instead? Will consumers in Sacramento and the rest of California boycott our televisions? Will they be able to convince other American laborers to boycott our TVs? Will a boycott generate adverse publicity and media coverage that will damage our brand name? Will investors view our firm as a riskier business, raising our cost of capital?

Again, you can see some redundancy here as we work through the guidelines, but that redundancy is all right, for it ensures that we are examining all factors important to our decision.

How Do the Alternatives Impact Me, the Decision Maker?

At first look, considering how a decision you make for your firm impacts *you* hardly seems to be a component of ethical and responsible decision making. The term "selfish" probably comes to mind.

Many of the corporate ethical debacles of the last few years comprised unethical and imprudent decisions that probably were motivated by the decision makers' selfish interests. Mortgage brokers' desires to earn large fees encouraged them to falsify borrowers' financial status and to make imprudent loans to high-risk clients. Several of Enron's off-balance-sheet partnerships, while apparently helping Enron's financial position, lined the pockets of conflicted Enron executives holding stock options and receiving management fees from the partnerships.

Despite these examples, merely because a decision benefits you, the decision maker, does not always mean it is imprudent or unethical. Even decisions by some Enron executives in the late 1990s, while motivated in part by the desire to increase the value of the executives' stock options, could have been prudent and ethical if the off-balance-sheet partnerships had real economic value to Enron (as they did when Enron first created off-balance-sheet partnerships in the 1980s) and accounting for them complied with the law.

At least two reasons explain why you can and should consider your own interest yet act ethically for your firm. First, as the decision maker, you are impacted by the decision. Whether deservedly or not, the decision maker is often credited or blamed for the success or failure of the course of action chosen. You may also be a stakeholder in other ways. For example, if you are an executive in the factory in Sacramento, you and your family may be required to move to Juarez (or El Paso, Texas, which borders Juarez) if the factory relocates. It is valid to consider a decision's impact on you and your family, although it should not be given undue weight.

A second, and more important, reason to consider your own interest is that your decision may be better for your firm and other stakeholders if you also consider your selfish interest. For example, suppose when you were charged to lead the inquiry into the firm's decision whether to move to Juarez, it was made clear that the CEO preferred to close the Sacramento factory and move operations to Juarez.

Suppose also that you would be required to move to Juarez. Your spouse has a well-paying job in Sacramento, and your teenage children are in a good school system and have very supportive friends. You have a strong relationship with your parents and siblings, who also live within 50 miles of your family in Sacramento. You believe that you and your family could find new friends and good schools in El Paso or Juarez, and the move would enhance your position in the firm and increase your chances of a promotion. Nonetheless, overall you and your spouse have determined that staying in the Sacramento area is best for your family. So you are considering quitting your job with the firm and finding another job in the Sacramento area rather than make an attempt to oppose the CEO's preference.

If you quit your job, even in protest, you will have no role in the decision and your resignation will likely have no impact on the firm's Sacramento–Juarez decision. Had you stayed with the firm, you could have led a diligent inquiry into all the facts that may have concluded that the prudent and ethical decision for the firm was to stay in Sacramento. Without your input and guidance, the firm may make a less prudent and ethical decision.

You can think of other examples where acting selfishly also results in better decisions. Suppose a top-level accounting executive, to whom you are directly responsible, has violated accounting standards and the law by pressuring the firm's auditors to book as income in the current year a contract that will not be performed for two years. You could quit your job and blow the whistle, but you may be viewed as a disgruntled employee and your story given no credibility. You could confront the executive, but you may lose your job or at least jeopardize your chances for a promotion while tipping off the executive, who will cover her tracks. As an alternative, the more effective solution may be to consider how you can keep your job and prospects for promotion while achieving your objective to blow the whistle on the executive. One alternative may be to go through appropriate channels in the firm, such as discussing the matter with the firm's audit committee or legal counsel.

Finding a way to keep your job will allow you to make an ethical decision that benefits your firm, whereas your quitting may leave the decision to someone else who would not act as prudently. The bottom line is this: while sometimes ethical conduct requires acting unselfishly, in other contexts consideration of your self-interest is not only consistent with ethical conduct, but also necessary to produce a moral result.

What Are the Ethics of Each Alternative?

Because our goal is to make a decision that is not only prudent for the firm but also ethical, we must consider the ethics of each alternative, not from one but a variety of ethical viewpoints. Our stakeholders' values comprise many ethical theories; ignoring any one theory will likely cause an incomplete consideration of the issues and may result in unforeseen consequences.

What Would a Utilitarian Do? A utilitarian would choose the alternative that promises the highest net welfare to society as a whole. If we define our society as the United States, moving to Juarez may nonetheless produce the highest net benefit, because the benefits to American citizens from a lower cost of televisions and to American shareholders from higher profits may more than offset the harm to our employees and other citizens of Sacramento. Another benefit of the move may be the reduced cost of the American government dealing with illegal immigration as Mexican workers decide to work at our plant in Juarez. Another cost may be the increased labor cost for a Texas business that would have hired Mexican workers had we not hired them.

If we define society as all countries in the North American Free Trade Agreement (NAFTA was signed by the United States, Mexico, and Canada), the benefit to workers in Juarez may completely offset the harm to workers in Sacramento. For example, the benefit to Juarez workers may be greater than the harm to Sacramento employees if many Juarez employees would otherwise be underemployed and Sacramento employees can find other work or are protected by a severance package or retirement plan.

As we discussed above in the discussion of ethical theories, finding and weighing all the benefits and costs of an alternative are difficult tasks. Even if we reject this theory as the final determinant, it is a good exercise for ensuring that we maximize the number of facts we consider when making a decision.

What Would a Profit Maximizer Do? A profit maximizer will choose the alternative that produces the most long-run profits for the company, within the limits of the law. This may mean, for example, that the firm should keep the factory in Sacramento if that will produce the most profits for the next 10 to 15 years.

This does not mean that the firm may ignore the impact of the decision on Juarez's community and workers. It may be that moving to Juarez will create a more affluent population in Juarez and consequently increase the firm's television sales in Juarez. But that impact is judged not by whether society as a whole is bettered (as with utilitarian analysis) or whether Juarez workers are more deserving of jobs (as with justice theory analysis), but is solely judged by how it impacts the firm's bottom line.

Nonetheless, profit maximization compels a decision maker to consider stakeholders other than the corporation and its shareholders. A decision to move to Juarez may mobilize American consumers to boycott our TVs, for example, or cause a public relations backlash if our Juarez employees receive wages far below our Sacramento workers. These and other impacts on corporate stakeholders may negatively impact the firm's profits.

Although projecting profits is not a precise science, tools you learned in finance classes should enhance your ability to select an alternative that maximizes your firm's profits within the limits of the law.

What Would a Rights Theorist Do? A follower of modern rights theory will determine whether anyone's rights are negatively affected by an alternative. If several rights are affected, the rights theorist will determine which right is more important or trumps the other rights, and choose the alternative that respects the most important right.

For example, if the alternative is to move to Juarez, the Sacramento employees, among others, are negatively affected. Yet if we do not move, potential employees in Juarez are harmed. Are these equal rights, a mere wash, or is it more important to retain a job one already has than to be deprived of a job one has never had?

Are other rights at work here, and how are they ranked? Is it more important to maintain manufacturing production in the firm's home country for national security and trade balance reasons than to provide cheaper televisions for the firm's customers? Does the right of all citizens to live in a global economy that spreads wealth worldwide and promotes international harmony trump all other rights?

While apparently difficult to identify and rank valid rights, this theory has value even to a utilitarian and a profit maximizer. By examining rights that are espoused by various stakeholders, we are more likely to consider all the costs and benefits of our decision and know which rights can adversely affect the firm's profitability if we fail to take them into account.

What Would a Justice Theorist Do? A justice theorist would choose the alternative that allocates society's benefits and burden most fairly. This requires the decision maker to consider whether everyone is getting what he deserves. If we follow the preaching of John Rawls, the firm should move to Juarez if the workers there are less advantaged than those in Sacramento, who may be protected by savings, severance packages, and retirement plans.

If we follow Nozick's libertarian approach, it is sufficient that the firm gives Sacramento workers an opportunity to compete for the plant by matching the offer the firm has received from Juarez workers. Under this analysis, if Sacramento workers fail to match the Juarez workers' offer of lower wages, for example, it would be fair to move the factory to Juarez, even if Sacramento workers are denied their right to jobs.

Even if the firm has difficulty determining who most deserves jobs with our firm, justice theory, like rights theory, helps the firm identify constituents who suffer from our decision and who can create problems impacting the firm's profitability if the firm ignores their claims.

What Are the Practical Constraints of Each Alternative?

As we evaluate alternatives, it is important to consider each alternative's practical problems before we implement it. For example, is it feasible for us to implement an alternative? Do we have the necessary money, labor, and other resources?

Suppose one alternative is to maintain our manufacturing plant in Sacramento as we open a new plant in Juarez, gradually shutting down the Sacramento plant as employees retire and quit. That alternative sounds like an ethical way to protect the jobs of all existing and prospective employees, but what are the costs of having two plants? Will the expense make that alternative infeasible? Will the additional expense make it difficult for the firm to compete with other TV manufacturers? Is it practicable to have a plant in Sacramento operating with only five employees who are 40 years old and will not retire for 15 years?

It is also necessary to consider potential problems with the facts that have led us to each alternative. Did we find all the facts relevant to our decision? How certain are we of some facts? For example, are we confident about our projections of labor and transportation costs if we move to Juarez? Are we sure that sales of our products will drop insubstantially due to consumer boycotts?

What Course of Action Should Be Taken and How Do We Implement It?

Ultimately, we have to stop our analysis and make a decision by choosing one alternative. Yet even then our planning is not over.

We must determine how to put the alternative into action. How do we implement it? Who announces the decision? Who is told of the decision and when? Do some people, like our employee's labor union, receive advance notice of our plans and have an opportunity to negotiate a better deal for our Sacramento employees? When do we tell shareholders, government officials, lenders, suppliers, investments analysts, and the media and in what order? Do we antagonize a friend or an enemy and risk killing a deal if we inform someone too soon or too late?

Finally, we have to prepare for the worst-case scenario. What do we do if, despite careful investigation, analysis, and planning, our course of action fails? Do we have backup plans? Have we anticipated all the possible ways our plan may fail and readied responses to those failures?

In 1985, the Coca-Cola Company decided to change the flavor of Coke in response to Coke's shrinking share of the cola market. Despite careful market research, Coca-Cola failed to anticipate Coke drinkers' negative response to the new Coke formula and was caught without a response to the outcry. Within three months, Coca-Cola realized it had to revive the old Coke formula under the brand name Coca-Cola Classic. In the meantime, Coke lost significant market share to rival Pepsi. Today, one would expect Coke executives introducing a reformulated drink to predict more consumers' reactions to the drink and to prepare a response to each reaction.

Knowing When to Use the Guidelines

You can probably see that following these factors will result in better decisions in a variety of contexts, including some that appear to have no ethical concerns. For example, in the next few years, most of you will consider what major course of study to select at college or what job to take with which firm in which industry. This framework can help you make a better analysis that should result in a better decision.

The Guidelines can be used also to decide mundane matters in your personal life, such as whether to eat a high-fat hamburger or a healthful salad for lunch, whether to spend the next hour exercising at the gym or visiting a friend in the hospital, and whether or not to brush your teeth every day after lunch. But for most of us, using the Guidelines every day for every decision would occupy so much of our time that little could be accomplished, what is sometimes called "paralysis by analysis."

Practicality, therefore, requires us to use the Guidelines only for important decisions and those that create a potential for ethical problems. We can identify decisions requiring application of the Guidelines if we carefully reflect from time to time about what we have done and are doing. This requires us to examine our past, current, and future actions.

It may not surprise you how seldom people, including business executives, carefully preview and review their actions. The pressures and pace of daily living give us little time to examine our lives critically. Most people are reluctant to look at themselves in the mirror and ask themselves whether they are doing the right thing for themselves, their families, their businesses, and their communities. Few know or follow the words of Socrates, "The unexamined life is not worth living."

Ask yourself whether you believe that mortgage brokers used anything like the Guidelines for Ethical Decision Making before signing low-income borrowers to loans exceeding $500,000. Did executives at bankrupt energy trader Enron consider any ethical issues before creating off-balance-sheet partnerships with no economic value to Enron? Do you think the employees at accounting firm Arthur Andersen carefully examined their decision to accept Enron's accounting for off-balance-sheet partnerships?

Merely by examining our past and prospective actions, we can better know when to apply the Guidelines. In the next to last section of this chapter, Resisting Requests to Act Unethically, you will learn additional tools to help you identify when to apply the Guidelines.

LOG ON

Go to
www.scu.edu/ethics
This website maintained by the Markkula Center for Applied Ethics at the University of Santa Clara has links to business ethics resources and guides for ethical/moral decision making.

Thinking Critically

Part of ethical decision making is being able to think critically, that is, to evaluate arguments logically, honestly, and without bias in favor of your own arguments and against those of others.

 L03 Recognize critical thinking errors in your own and others' arguments.

Even if someone uses the Guidelines for Ethical Decision Making, there is a risk that they have been misapplied if a person makes errors of logic or uses fallacious arguments. In this section, we want to help you identify when your arguments and thinking may be flawed and how to correct them. Equally important, we want to help you identify flaws in others' thinking. The purpose is to help you think critically and not to accept at face value everything you read or hear and to be careful before you commit your arguments to paper or voice them.

This chapter's short coverage of critical thinking covers only a few of the errors of logic and argument that are covered in a college course or book devoted to the subject. Here are 15 common fallacies.

Non Sequiturs

A *non sequitur* is a conclusion that does not follow from the facts or premises one sets out. The speaker is missing the point or coming to an irrelevant conclusion. For example, suppose a consumer uses a corporation's product and becomes ill. The consumer argues that because the corporation has lots of money, the corporation should pay for his medical expenses. Clearly, the consumer is missing the point. The issue is whether the corporation's product *caused* his injuries, not whether money should be transferred from a wealthy corporation to a poor consumer.

You see this also used when employees attempt to justify stealing pens, staplers, and paper from their employers. The typical *non sequitur* goes like this: "I don't get paid enough, so I'll take a few supplies. My employer won't even miss them."

Business executives fall prey to this fallacy also. Our firm may consider which employees to let go during a downturn. Company policy may call for retaining the best employees in each department, yet instead we release those employees making the highest salary in each position in order to save more money. Our decision does not match the standards the company set for downsizing decisions and is a *non sequitur,* unless we admit that we have changed company policy.

Appeals to Pity

A common fallacy seen in the American press is the appeal to pity or compassion. This argument generates support for a proposition by focusing on a victim's predicament. It usually is also a *non sequitur.* Examples are news stories about elderly, retired people who find it hard to afford expensive, life-prolonging drugs. None of these stories point out that many of these people squandered their incomes when working rather than saving for retirement.

Appeals to pity are effective because humans are compassionate. We have to be careful, however, not to be distracted from the real issues at hand. For example, in the trial against accused 9/11 co-conspirator Zacarias Moussaoui, federal prosecutors wanted to introduce testimony by the families of the victims. While what the families of 9/11 suffered is terrible, the victims' families hold no evidence of Moussaoui's role in 9/11. Instead, their testimonies are appeals to pity likely to distract the jury from its main task of determining whether Moussaoui was a part of the 9/11 conspiracy.

You see many appeals to pity used against corporations. Here is a typical argument: a corporation has a chemical plant near a neighborhood; children are getting sick and dying in the neighborhood; someone should pay for this suffering; the corporation should pay. You can also see that this reasoning is a *non sequitur.* Better reasoning requires one to determine not whether two events are coincidental or correlated, but whether one (the chemical plant) caused the other (the children's illnesses).

False Analogies

An analogy essentially argues that since something is like something else in one or more ways, it is also like it in another respect. Arguers often use analogies to make a point vividly, and therefore analogies have strong appeal. Nonetheless, while some analogies are apt, we should make sure that the two situations are sufficiently similar to make the analogy valid.

Suppose an executive argues that our bank should not make loans to lower-income borrowers because the bank will suffer huge losses like Countrywide Financial. This analogy may be invalid because we may do a better job verifying a borrower's income and ability to repay a loan than did Countrywide.

Analogies can also be used to generate support for a proposal, such as arguing that since Six Sigma worked for General Electric, it will work for our firm also. It is probable that factors other than Six Sigma contributed to GE's success, factors our firm may or may not share with GE.

Nonetheless, analogies can identify potential opportunities, which we should evaluate prudently to determine whether the analogy is valid. Analogies can also suggest potential problems that require us to examine a decision more carefully before committing to it.

Begging the Question

An arguer begs the question when she takes for granted or assumes the thing that she is setting out to prove. For example, you might say that we should tell the truth because lying is wrong. That is circular reasoning and makes no sense, because telling the truth and not lying are the same things. Another example is arguing that democracy is the best form of government because the majority is always right.

Examples of begging the question are difficult to identify sometimes because they are hidden in the language of the speaker. It is best identified by looking for arguments that merely restate what the speaker or questioner has already stated, but in different words. For an example in the business context, consider this interchange between you and someone working under you.

You: Can I trust these numbers you gave to me?

Co-worker: Yes, you can trust them.

You: Why can I trust them?

Co-worker: Because I'm an honest person.

The co-worker used circular reasoning, since whether the numbers can be trusted is determined by whether he is honest, yet he provided no proof of his honesty, such as his numbers being backed by facts.

Argumentum ad Populum

Argumentum ad populum means argument to the people. It is an emotional appeal to popular beliefs, values, or wants. The fallacy is that merely because many or all people believe something does not mean it is true. It is common for newspapers to poll its readers about current issues, such as support for a presidential decision. For example, a newspaper poll may show that 60 percent of Americans support the president. The people may be right, but it is also possible that the president's supporters are wrong: they may be uninformed or base their support of the president on invalid reasoning.

Arguments to the people are commonly used by corporations in advertisements, such as beer company ads showing friends having a good time while drinking beer. The point of such ads is that if you want to have a good time with friends, you should drink beer. While some beer drinkers do have fun with friends, you probably can also point to other people who drink beer alone.

Bandwagon Fallacy

The bandwagon fallacy is similar to *argumentum ad populum*. A bandwagon argument states that we should or should not do something merely because one or more other people or firms do or do not do it. *Sports Illustrated* quoted basketball player Diana Taurasi's objection to being arrested for driving drunk: "Why me? Everyone drives drunk!" Some people justify cheating on their taxes for the same reason.

This reasoning can be fallacious because probably not everyone is doing it, and even if many or all people do something, it is not necessarily right. For example, while some baseball players do use steroids, there are serious negative side effects including impotency and acute psychosis, which make its use risky. Cheating on taxes may be common, but it is still illegal and can result in the cheater's imprisonment.

Bandwagon thinking played a large part in the current credit crunch as many loan buyers like Bear Stearns bought high-risk loans only because their competitors were buying the loans, thereby encouraging lenders to continue to make high-risk loans.

Argumentum ad Baculum

Argumentum ad baculum means argument to club. The arguer uses threats or fear to bolster his position. This is a common argument in business and family settings. For example, when a parent asks a child to take out the garbage, the child may ask, "Why?" Some parents respond, "Because if you don't, you'll spend the rest of the afternoon in your room." Such an argument is a *non sequitur* as well.

In the business context, bosses explicitly and implicitly use the club, often generating support for their ideas from subordinates who fear they will not be promoted unless they support the boss's plans. An executive who values input from subordinates will ensure that they do not perceive that the executive is wielding a club over them.

Enron's CFO Andrew Fastow used this argument against investment firm Goldman Sachs when it balked at lending money to Enron. He told Goldman that he would not do anything with a presentation Goldman had prepared unless it made the loan.

By threatening to boycott a company's products, consumers and other interest groups use this argument against corporations perceived to act unethically. It is one reason that profit maximization requires decision makers to consider a decision's impact on all stakeholders.

Argumentum ad Hominem

Argumentum ad hominem means "argument against the man." This tactic attacks the speaker, not his reasoning. For example, a Republican senator criticizes a Democratic senator who supports the withdrawal of American troops from a war zone by saying, "You can't trust him. He never served in the armed forces." Such an argument attacks the Democratic senator's character, not the validity of his reasons for withdrawing troops.

When a CEO proposes a new compensation plan for corporate executives, an opponent may argue, "Of course he wants the new plan. He'll make a lot of money from it." Again, this argument doesn't address whether the plan is a good one or not; it only attacks the CEO's motives. While the obvious conflict of interest the CEO has may cause us to doubt the sincerity of the reasons he presents for the plan (such as to attract and retain better management talent), merely pointing out this conflict does not rebut his reasons.

One form of *ad hominem* argument is attacking a speaker's consistency, such as, "Last year you argued for something different." Another common form is appealing to personal circumstances. One woman may say to another, "As a woman, how can you be against corporate policies that set aside executive positions for women?" By personalizing the argument, the speaker is trying to distract the listener from the real issue. A proper response to the personal attack may be, "As a women and a human, I believe in equal opportunity for all people. I see no need for any woman or myself to have special privileges to compete with men. I can compete on my own. By having quotas, the corporation cheapens my accomplishments by suggesting that I need the quota. Why do you, as a woman, think you need a quota?"

Guilt by association is the last *ad hominem* argument we will consider. This argument attacks the speaker by linking her to someone unpopular. For example, if you make the libertarian argument that government should not restrict or tax the consumption of marijuana, someone may attack you by saying, "Mass murderer Charles Manson also believed that." Your attacker suggests that by believing as you do, you are as evil as Charles Manson. Some corporate critics use guilt by association to paint all executives as unethical people motivated to cheat their corporations. For example, if a CEO asks for stock options as part of her compensation package, someone may say, "Enron's executives wanted stock options also." The implication is that the CEO should not be trusted because some Enron executives who were corrupt also wanted stock options.

No *ad hominem* argument is necessarily fallacious, because a person's character, motives, consistency, personal characteristics, and associations may suggest further scrutiny of a speaker's arguments is necessary. However, merely attacking the speaker does not expose flaws in her arguments.

Argument from Authority

Arguments from authority rely on the quality of an expert or person in a position of authority, not the quality of the expert's or authority's argument. For example, if someone says, "The president says we need to stop drug trafficking in the United States, and that is good enough for me," he has argued from authority. He and the president may have good reasons to stop drug trafficking, but we cannot know that from his statement.

Another example is "Studies show that humans need to drink 10 glasses of water a day." What studies? What were their methodologies? Did the sample sizes permit valid conclusions? A form of argument to authority is argument to reverence or respect, such as "Who are you to disagree with the CEO's decision to terminate 5,000 employees?" The arguer is trying to get you to abandon your arguments, not because they are invalid, but because they conflict with the views of an authority. Your response to this question should not attack the CEO (to call the CEO an idiot would be *ad hominem* and also damage your prospects in the firm), but state the reasons you believe the company would be better off not terminating 5,000 employees.

It is natural to rely on authorities who have expertise in the area on which they speak. But should we give credibility to authorities speaking on matters outside the scope of their competency? For example, does the fact that Julia Roberts is an Academy Award–winning actress have any relevance when she is testifying before Congress about Rett Syndrome, a neurological disorder that leaves infants unable to communicate and control body functions? Is she any more credible as a Rett Syndrome authority because she narrated a film on the Discovery Health Channel about children afflicted with the disease?

This chapter includes several examples of arguments from authority when we cite Kant, Bentham, and others who have formulated ethical theories. What makes their theories valid, however, is not whether they are recognized as experts, but whether their reasoning is sound.

False Cause This fallacy results from observing two events and concluding that there is a causal link between them when there is no such link. Often we commit this fallacy because we do not attempt to find all the evidence proving or disproving the causal connection. For example, if as a store manager you change the opening hour for your store to 6 AM from 8 AM, records for the first month of operation under the new hours may show an increase in revenue. While you may be tempted to infer that the revenue increase is due to the earlier opening hour, you should not make that conclusion until at the very least you examine store receipts showing the amount of revenue generated between 6 AM and 8 AM. The increase in revenue could have resulted from improved general economic conditions unconnected to the new hours: people just had more money to spend.

The fallacy of false cause is important to businesses, which need to make valid connections between events in order to judge the effectiveness of decisions. Whether, for example, new products and an improved customer relations program increase revenues and profits should be subjected to rigorous testing, not some superficial causal analysis. Measurement tools you learn in other business classes help you eliminate false causes.

The Gambler's Fallacy This fallacy results from the mistaken belief that independent prior outcomes affect future outcomes. Consider this example. Suppose you flip a coin five times and each time it comes up heads. What is the probability that the next coin flip will be heads? If you did not answer 50 percent, you committed the gambler's fallacy. Each coin flip is an independent event, so no number of consecutive flips producing heads will reduce the likelihood that the next flip will also be heads. That individual probability is true even though the probability of flipping six consecutive heads is 0.5 to the sixth power, or only 1.5625 percent.

What is the relevance of the gambler's fallacy to business? We believe and are taught that business managers and professionals with higher skills and better decision-making methods are more likely to be successful than those with lesser skills and worse methods. Yet we have not discussed the importance of luck or circumstance to success. When a corporation has five years of profits rising by 30 percent, is it due to good management or

because of expanding consumer demand or any number of other reasons? If a mutual fund has seven years of annual returns of at least 15 percent, is the fund's manager an investment genius or is she lucky? If it is just luck, one should not expect the luck to continue. The point is that you should not be seduced by a firm's, manager's, or even your own string of successes and immediately jump to the conclusion that the successes were the result of managerial excellence. Instead, you should use measurement tools taught in your finance, marketing, and other courses to determine the real reasons for success.

Reductio ad Absurdum *Reductio ad absurdum* carries an argument to its logical end, without considering whether it is an inevitable or probable result. This is often called the slippery slope fallacy.

For example, if I want to convince someone not to eat fast food, I might argue, "Eating fast food will cause you to put on weight. Putting on weight will make you overweight. Soon you will weigh 400 pounds and die of heart disease. Therefore, eating fast food leads to death. Don't eat fast food." In other words, if you started eating fast food, you are on a slippery slope and will not be able to stop until you die. Although you can see that this argument makes some sense, it is absurd for most people who eat fast food.

Scientist Carl Sagan noted that the slippery slope argument is used by both sides of the abortion debate. One side says, "If we allow abortion in the first weeks of pregnancy, it will be impossible to prevent the killing of a full-term infant." The other replies, "If the state prohibits abortion even in the ninth month, it will soon be telling us what to do with our bodies around the time of conception."

Business executives face this argument frequently. Human resource managers use it to justify not making exceptions to rules, such as saying, "If we allow you time off to go to your aunt's funeral, we have to let anyone off anytime they want." Well, no, that was not what you were asking for. Executives who reason this way often are looking for administratively simple rules that do not require them to make distinctions. That is, they do not want to think hard or critically.

Pushing an argument to its limits is a useful exercise in critical thinking, often helping us to discover whether a claim has validity. The fallacy is carrying the argument to its extreme without recognizing and admitting that there are many steps along the way that are more likely consequences.

Appeals to Tradition Appeals to tradition infer that because something has been done a certain way in the past, it should be done the same way in the future. You probably have heard people say, "I don't know why we do it, but we've always done it that way, and it's always worked, so we'll continue to do it that way." Although there is some validity to continuing to do what has stood the test of time, the reasons a business strategy has succeeded in the past may be independent of the strategy itself. The gambler's fallacy would suggest that perhaps we have just been lucky in the past. Also, changed circumstances may justify departing from previous ways of doing business.

The Lure of the New

The opposite of appeals to tradition is the lure of the new, the idea that we should do or buy something merely because it is "just released" or "improved." You see this common theme in advertising that promotes "new and improved" Tide or Windows 7. Experience tells us that sometimes new products are better. But we can also recount examples of new car models with defects and new software with bugs that were fixed in a later version.

The lure of the new is also a common theme in management theories, as some managers have raced to embrace one new craze after another, depending on which is the hottest fad, be it Strategic Planning, Total Quality Management, Reengineering the Corporation, or Customer Relationship Management. The point here is the same. Avoid being dazzled by claims of newness. Evaluations of ideas should be based on substance.

Sunk Cost Fallacy

The sunk cost fallacy is an attempt to recover invested time, money, and other resources, by spending still more time, money, or other resources. It is sometimes expressed as "throwing good money after bad." Stock market investors do this often. They invest $30,000 in the latest tech stock. When the investment declines to $2,000, rather than evaluate whether it is better to withdraw that $2,000 and invest it elsewhere, an investor who falls for the sunk cost fallacy might say, "I can't stop investing now, otherwise what I've invested so far will be lost." While the latter part of the statement is true, the fallacy is in the first part. Of the money already invested, $28,000 is lost whether or not the investor continues to invest. If the tech stock is not a good investment *at this time,* the rational decision is to withdraw the remaining $2,000 and not invest more money.

There are other statements that indicate business executives may fall victim to the sunk cost fallacy: "It's too late for us to change plans now." Or "If we could go back to square one, then we could make a different decision." The best way to spend the firm's remaining labor and money may be to continue a project. But that decision should be unaffected by a consideration of the labor and money already expended. The proper question is this: What project will give the firm the best return on its investment of money and other resources *from this point forward.* To continue to invest in a hopeless project is irrational, and may be a pathetic attempt to delay having to face the consequences of a poor decision.

A decision maker acts irrationally when he attempts to save face by throwing good money after bad. If you want a real-world example of ego falling prey to the sunk cost fallacy, consider that President Lyndon Johnson committed American soldiers to the Vietnam Conflict after he had determined that America and South Vietnam could never defeat the Viet Cong. By falling for the sunk cost fallacy, the United States lost billions of dollars and tens of thousands of soldiers in the pursuit of a hopeless cause.

LOG ON

Go to
www.fallacyfiles.org
Maintained by Gary Curtis, *The Fallacy Files* cover more than 150 fallacies with links to explanations and valuable resources.
Go to
www.austhink.org/critical
Tim van Gelder's *Critical Thinking on the Web* lists some of the best websites with information about reasoning and critical thinking.

Common Characteristics of Poor Decision Making

Most business managers during the course of their formal education in school or informal education on the job have learned most of the techniques we have discussed in this chapter for making ethical and well-reasoned decisions. Yet business managers continue to make unethical and poor decisions, most often in disregard of the very principles that they otherwise view as essential to good decision making. Each of us can also point to examples when we have failed to analyze a situation properly before making a decision, even though at the time we possessed the ability to make better decisions.

Why do we and other well-intentioned people make bad decisions? What is it that interferes with our ability to use all the decision-making tools at our disposal, resulting sometimes in unethical and even catastrophic decisions? What causes a basically honest accountant to agree to cook the books for his corporation? What causes a drug company to continue to market a drug when internal tests and user experience show a high incidence of harmful side effects? What causes a corporation to continue to operate a chemical plant when its safety systems have been shut down? While business scholars and other writers have suggested several attributes that commonly interfere with good decision making, we believe they can be distilled into three essential traits that are useful to you, a decision maker who has already learned the Guidelines for Ethical Decision Making and the most common critical thinking errors.

Failing to Remember Goals Friedrich
Nietzsche wrote, "Man's most enduring stupidity is forgetting what he is trying to do." If, for example, our company's goal as a retailer is to garner a 30 percent market share in the retail market in five years, you may think that would translate into being dominant in each segment of our business, from housewares to video games. But should our retailer strive to dominate a market segment that is declining, such as portable cassette players, when the consumer market has clearly moved to iPods and other similar digital recorders? If we focus on the wrong goal—dominating the cassette player market, which may not exist in five years—we have failed to remember our goal of acquiring a 30 percent overall market share.

In another example, suppose we are a luxury homebuilder with two goals that go hand-in-hand: producing high quality housing and maintaining an annual 15 percent return on equity. The first goal supports the second goal: by having a reputation for producing high quality housing, we can charge more for our houses. Suppose, however, one of our project managers is under pressure to bring her development in line with cost projections. She decides, therefore, to use lower quality, lower cost materials. The consequence is we meet our profit target in the short run, but in the long run when the shoddy materials are detected and our reputation is sullied, both of our goals of building high quality housing and achieving a 15 percent return on equity will be compromised. Again, we have failed to remember the most important goal, maintaining high quality, which allowed us to achieve our ROE goal.

Overconfidence While confidence is a personal
trait essential to success, overconfidence or overoptimism is one of the most common reasons for bad decisions. We all have heard ourselves and others say, "Don't worry. Everything will work out OK." That statement is likely a consequence of overconfidence, not careful analysis that is necessary to make sure everything will work out as we hope.

There are several corollaries or other ways to express this overoptimism. Sometimes businesses executives will do something that they know to be wrong with the belief that it is only a small or temporary wrong that will be fixed next year. They may rationalize that no one will notice the wrongdoing and that only big companies and big executives get caught, not small companies and little managers like them.

Many of the accounting scandals of the last ten years started small, rationalized as temporary attempts to cook the books that would be corrected in the following years when business turned around. As we now know, finance managers and accountants who thought things would turn around were being overconfident about the economy and their companies.

Another aspect of overconfidence is confirmation bias; that is, we must be doing things the right way because all has gone well in the past. Or at least we have not been caught doing something wrong in the past, so we will not be caught in the future. In part this reveals a thinking error we have studied, appeal to tradition. In the homebuilder example above, the project manager's cutting quality in years past may not have been detected by homeowners who knew nothing about construction quality. And none of the project manager's workers may have told top management about the project manager's actions. That past, however, does not guarantee the future. New homeowners may be more knowledgeable, and future workers may inform management of the project manager's quality-cutting actions.

Another consequence of overoptimism is believing that complex problems have simple solutions. That leads to the next common trait of bad decision making.

Complexity of the Issues Closely aligned to
and aggravated by overconfidence is the failure of decision makers to understand the complexity of an issue. A manager may perceive that the facts are simpler than reality and, therefore, not see that there is little margin for error. Consequently, the executive has not considered the full range of possible solutions and has failed to find the one solution that best matches the facts.

Restated, the decision maker has not done all the investigation and thinking required by the Guidelines for Ethical Decision Making and, therefore, has not discovered all the facts and considered all the reasonable courses of action necessary to making a prudent decision.

The impediments to knowing all the facts, understanding the complexity of a problem, and doing the hard work to create and evaluate all possible solutions to a problem are known to all of us. Fatigue, laziness, overconfidence, and forgetting goals play roles in promoting ignorance of critical facts. We may also want to be team players, by following the lead of a colleague or the order of a boss. These human tendencies deter us from making the effort to find the facts and to consider all options.

Resisting Requests to Act Unethically

Even if we follow the Guidelines for Ethical Decision Making and avoid the pitfalls of fallacious reasoning, not everyone is a CEO or his own boss and able to make decisions that everyone else follows. Sure, if you control a firm, you will do the right thing. But the reality is that for most people in the business world, other people make many decisions that you are asked to carry out. What do you do when asked to do something unethical? How can you resist a boss's request to act unethically? What could employees at WorldCom have done when its CFO instructed them to falsify the firm's books, or mortgage brokers when their bosses asked them to falsify borrowers' incomes?

 LO4 Utilize a process to make ethical decisions in the face of pressure from others.

Recognizing Unethical Requests and Bosses A person must recognize whether he has been asked to do something unethical. While this sounds simple considering we have spent most of this chapter helping you make just that kind of decision, there are structural problems that interfere with your ability to perform an ethical analysis when a boss or colleague asks you to do something. Many of us are inclined to be team players and "do as we are told" by a superior. Therefore, it is important to recognize any tendency to accept appeals to authority and to resist the temptation to follow orders blindly. We do not want to be like the Enron accounting employee who returned to his alma mater and was asked by a student, "What do you do at Enron?" When considering that question, a question he never posed to himself, he realized that his only job was to remove liabilities from Enron's balance sheet.

For most bosses' orders, such an analysis will be unnecessary. Most of the time, a boss is herself ethical and will not ask us to do something wrong. But there are exceptions that require us to be on the lookout. Moreover, some bosses have questionable integrity, and they are more likely to give us unethical orders. Therefore, it will be helpful if we can identify bosses who have shaky ethics, for whom we should put up our ethical antennae when they come to us with a task.

Business ethicists have attempted to identify executives with questionable integrity by their actions. Ethical bosses have the ability to "tell it like it is" while those with less integrity say one thing and do another. Ethical bosses have the ability to acknowledge that they have failed, whereas those with low integrity often insist on being right all the time. Ethical bosses try to build a consensus before making an important decision; unethical bosses may generate support for their decisions with intimidation through anger and threats. Ethical bosses can think about the needs of others beside themselves. Bosses with low integrity who misuse their workers by asking them to act unethically often mistreat other people also, like secretaries and waiters.

If we pay attention to these details, we will be better able to consider the "source" when we are asked to do something by a boss and, therefore, more sensitive to the need to scrutinize the ethics of a boss's request.

Buying Time If we think a requested action is or might be unethical, what is done next? How can we refuse to do something a boss has ordered us to do? One key is to buy some time before you have to execute the boss's order. Buying time allows you to find more facts, to understand an act's impact on the firm's stakeholders, and to evaluate the ethics of the action. It also lets you find other alternatives that achieve the boss's objectives without compromising your values. Delay also gives you time to speak with the firm's ethics officer and other confidants.

How do you buy time? If the request is in an e-mail, you might delay responding to it. Or you could answer that you have received the e-mail and will give your attention to it when you finish with the task you are working on. Similar tactics can be used with phone calls and other direct orders. Even a few hours can help your decision. Depending on the order and your ability to stack delay on top of delay, you may be able to give yourself days or weeks to find a solution to your dilemma.

The most important reason for buying time is it allows you to seek advice and assistance from other people, especially those in the firm. That brings us to the next tactic for dealing with unethical requests.

Find a Mentor and a Peer Support Group Having a support system is one of the most important keys to survival in any organization, and it is

Resisting Requests to Do Unethical Acts

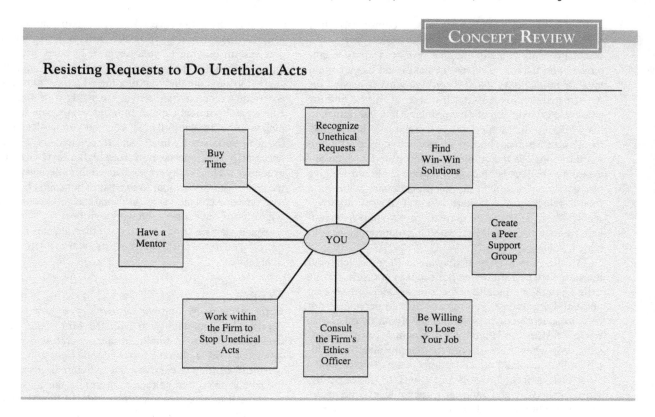

best to put a system in place when you start working at the firm. Your support system can improve and help defend your decisions. It can also give you access to executives who hold the power to overrule your boss. Your support system should include a mentor and a network of other employees with circumstances similar to your own.

A mentor who is well established, well respected, and highly placed in the firm will help you negotiate the pitfalls that destroy employees who are ignorant of a firm's culture. A mentor can be a sounding board for your decisions; he can provide information on those who can be expected to help you and those who could hurt you; he can advise you of the procedures you should follow to avoid antagonizing potential allies. A mentor can also defend you and provide protection when you oppose a boss's decision. Many firms have a mentorship program, but if not or if your assigned mentor is deficient, you should find an appropriate mentor soon after you join the firm. Be sure to keep him updated regularly on what you are doing. By letting a mentor know that you care to keep him informed, he becomes invested in you and your career.

You should also build a community of your peers by creating a network of other workers who share your values and interests. You may want to find others who joined the firm at about the same time you did, who are about the same age, who share your passion for the firm's products and services, and who have strong ethical values. To cement the relationship, your peer support group should meet regularly, such as twice a week at work during 15-minute coffee breaks. This group can give you advice, help with difficult decisions, and unite to back up your ethical decisions.

Find Win-Win Solutions

As we learned from the Guidelines for Ethical Decision Making, many times there are more than the two options of doing and not doing something. There are a number of choices in between those extremes, and the best solution may be one unconnected to them. For example, suppose your boss has ordered you to fire someone who works under you. The worker's productivity may be lagging, and perhaps he has made a few costly mistakes. Yet you think it would be wrong to fire the worker at this time. What do you do?

Find a win-win solution, that is, a compromise that works for you and your boss. First, discover your boss's wants. Probably you will find that your boss wants an employee who makes no or few mistakes and has a certain level of productivity. Next determine what is needed for the affected employee to reach that level. If you find the employee is having emotional problems that interfere with his work, are they temporary or can we help him handle them? Can we make him more productive by giving him more training? Is the employee unmotivated or is he unaware that he lags behind other workers? Should we give him a warning and place him on probationary status for a month, releasing him if there is no satisfactory improvement? These alternatives may address your boss's concerns about the employee without compromising your ethical values.

In other contexts, you may need to approach your boss directly and show that her order is not right for the firm. Using the Guidelines for Ethical Decision Making and valid arguments, you may be able to persuade your boss to accept your perspective and avoid an otherwise unethical decision. Finding a win-win solution is possible only when there is room for compromise. The Ethical Guidelines and logical arguments are effective when your boss respects reason and wants to act ethically. However, when you face an intractable executive demanding you do something illegal, a different response is needed.

Work within the Firm to Stop the Unethical Act

Suppose you receive an order from an executive you know or suspect to be corrupt. For example, a CFO is motivated to increase the price of the firm's stock in order to make her stock options more valuable. She orders you to book in the current year revenue that in fact will not be received for at least two years, if ever. Booking that revenue would be fraudulent, unethical, and illegal. You are convinced the CFO knows of the illegality and will find someone else to book the revenue if you refuse. You probably will lose your job if you do not cooperate. What do you do?

This is when your mentor, peer support group, and corporate ethics officer can help you. Your mentor may have access to the CEO or audit committee, who if honest, should back you and fire the CFO. Your peer support group might have similar access. The corporate ethics officer, especially if she is a lawyer in the firm's legal department, can also provide her backing and that of the legal department.

There is one large caveat, however. While the situation just described should and probably will result in your support system rallying to your support, in other situations that are ethically ambiguous, you, your mentor, and your support group may find that fighting a battle against a top corporate executive ineffectively expends your and your colleagues' political capital. In other words, you need to pick your battles carefully lest you and your colleagues at the firm be labeled whiners and troublemakers who unnecessarily seek intervention from higher level corporate executives. This is why we have listed this alternative near the end of our discussion. In most situations, it is better to rely on your colleagues as advisors and to execute win-win solutions in cooperation with your boss.

But if neither compromise nor other intrafirm tactics protect you from unethical requests, you are left with a final tactic.

Prepare to Lose Your Job

This is the last tactic, because by quitting or losing your job you are deprived of your ability to help the firm make ethical decisions. Only as an employee can you craft win-win solutions or work within the firm to do the right thing.

But if a firm's executives and its internal governance are so corrupted that neither compromise nor reason can steer the firm away from an unethical and illegal course, you must be willing to walk away from your job or be fired for standing up for your values. Do not want your job and the status it brings so much that you are willing to compromise more important values. It is tough losing a job when one has obligations to family, banks, and other creditors as well as aspirations for a better life. But if you prepare yourself financially from day one, putting away money for an ethical rainy day, you will protect more important values.

Leading Ethically

Some day, perhaps today, you will be in charge of other people in your business organization. You may be managing a four-person team, you may be a vice president of marketing in charge of a department, or you may eventually be a CEO directing an entire company. You give the people under your charge tasks to complete, supervise their work, help them complete the tasks, and provide motivation and feedback to ensure that the current job will be done well and that future work will be done better. So how do you also ensure that all those people under your charge act ethically? This is the daily challenge of ethical business leaders, who must not only act ethically themselves, but also promote ethical behavior of their workers.

 L05   Be an ethical leader.

Be Ethical No one can lead ethically who does not attempt and mostly succeed in behaving ethically in her business and personal life. Few underlings respect an unethical leader, and many will be tempted to rationalize their own unethical conduct when they see their leaders acting unethically. They fall prey to the bandwagon fallacy, arguing for example that since the CFO is doing something wrong, so may they. For the same reason, ethical behavior by good managers encourages ethical behavior by underlings, who often view their bosses as role models and guides for advancing in the corporation. If they see an ethical boss moving up in the business, they will believe that the system is fair and that they, too, by acting ethically, can advance at the firm.

Communicate the Firm's Core Ethical Values For CEOs, creating, communicating, and emphasizing the firm's core values are essential to creating an ethical environment that rubs off on all employees. For other managers, recommunicating and reemphasizing the firm's value are also important.

All public companies today have ethics codes, as do many smaller companies. Yet the CEO who leads ethically must continually emphasize in written messages and speeches the importance and necessity that everyone comply with the code. Other top level managers, such as the vice president of finance, should ensure that their staffs understand the ethics code's application to their corporate tasks and make ethical reviews part of the staffs' annual evaluations. A lower level manager who supervises a small staff for a single project should also do her part to encourage compliance with the ethics code by pointing out how the code relates to the project assignment and including ethics in the project team's progress reports.

Connect Ethical Behavior with the Firm's and Workers' Best Interests It is one thing to educate your staff about ethical behavior and another to obtain compliance. One good way to increase compliance with the firm's core ethical values is to convince the staff that their best interests—and the firm's—are met by acting ethically. Management should

help employees understand that the firm's profitability and the employee's advancement in the firm are optimized by each employee taking responsibility for acting ethically. Staff must understand that adverse publicity caused by unethical conduct harms a firm's ability to promote itself and its products and services. The ethical manager also clearly establishes ethical behavior as a prerequisite for salary increases and promotions, or at least that unethical behavior is a disqualifier.

Reinforce Ethical Behavior When a manager knows a staff member has acted ethically in a situation in which employees in less ethical firms would be tempted to act unethically, the manager should congratulate and find other ways to reinforce the staff member's behavior. For example, if a staff member reports that a supplier has attempted to bribe him in order to do business with the firm, the ethical manager will praise the staff member and may include a letter commending him in his employment file.

In addition, management should set up a mechanism for its employees to report instances of unethical behavior by the staff. While some employees will view whistle blowing as an act of disloyalty, management should recharacterize whistle blowing as necessary to the protection of the firm's decision-making processes and reputation. Undetected ethical decisions often lead to poor decisions and harm corporate profits. While management does not want witch hunts, good managers must garner evidence of alleged unethical behavior so they may investigate and stop conduct that is harmful to the firm.

A necessary corollary is not reinforcing unethical behavior, including behavior that may lead to an unethical act or foster an environment that appears tolerant of ethical missteps. As with childrearing, and so too with managing a staff, it is usually not acceptable to ignore bad behavior. The ethical leader must reprimand staff for unethical actions and must not tolerate statements that suggest the firm should engage in unethical conduct. For example, if during discussions about how to increase revenue for a product line, one staff member suggests obtaining competitors' agreements to fix prices, a manager running the meeting should make clear that the firm will not engage in that or any other conduct that is illegal. To let the price-fixing comment pass without comment may send the message that the manager and the firm condone illegal or unethical acts.

Collectively, these reinforcing mechanisms should create a culture in which ethical practices define the firm and its employees rather than being imposed on them.

Problems and Problem Cases

1. You are a middle manager with responsibility over a staff of 16 workers. One of your workers is six months pregnant. Over the last month, she has missed work an average of two days a week and seems to be frequently distracted at work. You are concerned about her welfare and about her work performance, but are unsure what to do. What do the Guidelines for Ethical Decision Making suggest you do first?

2. You are an outside director of Crowler Inc., a manufacturer of kitchen and bathroom fixtures such as faucets, shower heads, and shower doors. Crowler has 29,000 employees worldwide, including 18,000 manufacturing employees in the United States, Canada, and Mexico. Its headquarters is in Eden Prairie, Minnesota. The CEO has proposed that Crowler increase its manufacturing capacity by adding a large facility to manufacture kitchen faucets, thereby increasing manufacturing employment by 3,000 workers. The board of directors is considering whether Crowler should expand its manufacturing facility in Brownsville, Texas, open a new factory in Indonesia, or close the Brownsville facility and move its current operations and the new operations to Indonesia. Using the Guidelines for Ethical Decision Making, what do you want to know before you make a decision?

3. You are a debt collections officer for a credit card issuer, NationalOne Corporation. NationalOne generates 73 percent of its profits from credit card fees and interest charged to consumers with annual incomes between $15,000 and $125,000. NationalOne's business model is to charge its credit card customers a low initial interest rate of 10 percent and a nominal annual fee of $10. If a customer defaults on one payment, however, the interest rate jumps to 22 percent, and the annual fee to $100. In the course of collecting debts for NationalOne, you have noticed that once the typical customer defaults, she is able to pay about 50 percent of the original debt had the interest rate and annual fee not changed. NationalOne's policy is not to accept anything less than 100 percent of the amount of the debt until the debtor has been in default for at least two years, by which time you find the customers typically can pay only about 10 percent of the now much larger debt. Many customers threaten to file and do file for bankruptcy protection. Would a rights theorist suggest any changes in NationalOne's policies? Would a profit maximizer suggest changes?

4. You own a consulting firm with 32 employees and annual billings of $29,000,000. One of your clients, whom you bill an average of $1,200,000 annually, has asked you to hire her grandson. You know that the grandson has recently graduated from a top-20 business school. He is 31 years old, has a solid academic record, and possesses the personal and professional skills to be successful as a consultant. You also know, however, that he is a recovering cocaine addict, having struggled with the addiction for five years prior to his attending business school. Your firm has a strict no-drugs policy, which you usually interpret to exclude those who previously abused drugs. Using justice theory, justify a decision to exempt the grandson from your firm's no-drugs policy. Could you make the same decision as a profit maximizer?

5. Marigold Dairy Corporation sells milk products, including powdered milk formula for infants. Marigold hopes to increase sales of its powdered milk formula in Liberia and other African nations where mothers are often malnourished due to drought and civil war. Marigold's marketing department has created a marketing plan to convince mothers and expectant mothers not to breastfeed their babies and instead to use Marigold formula. Doctors generally favor breastfeeding as beneficial to mothers (it helps the uterus return to normal size), to babies (it is nutritious and strengthens the bonds between the infant and the mother), and to families (it is inexpensive). Marigold's marketing plan stresses the good nutrition of its formula and the convenience to parents of using it, including not having to breastfeed.

   You are the Senior Vice President of Marketing for Marigold. Do you approve this marketing plan? What would a rights theorist do? What would a utilitarian do? What would a profit maximizer do?

6. During World War II, the insecticide DDT was used successfully to halt a typhus epidemic spread by lice and to control mosquitoes and flies. After World War II, it was used extensively to control agricultural and household pests. Today, DDT may not be used legally in the United States and most other countries. Although DDT has a rather low immediate toxicity to humans and other vertebrates, it becomes concentrated in fatty tissues of the body. In addition, it degrades slowly, remaining toxic in the soil for years after its application. But there has never been any credible evidence that this residue has caused any harm. Even so, DDT has been blamed for the near extinction of bald eagles, whose population

has increased greatly since DDT was banned, although evidence tends to point to oil, lead, mercury, stress from noise, and other factors as the likely causes.

In 2010, over 980 people in the United States were infected by and 45 people killed after contracting West Nile virus, which is carried to humans by mosquitoes. CDC director Julie Gerberding called West Nile virus an "emerging, infectious disease epidemic" that could be spread all the way to the Pacific Coast by birds and mosquitoes. Pesticides such as malathion, resmethrin, and sumithrin can be effective in killing mosquitoes but are significantly limited because they do not stay in the environment after spraying. In Mozambique, indoor spraying of DDT has caused malaria rates to drop 88 percent among children.

As an executive for Eartho Chemical Company, you have been asked by Eartho's CEO to study whether Eartho should resume the manufacture of DDT. What would a utilitarian decide? What would a profit maximizer do?

7. You are assigned by your employer, Jay-Mart Corporation, an international discount retailer, to supervise the construction of ten new retail superstores in Shanghai, China. All construction is being done by a Chinese-owned contractor in compliance with Jay-Mart's construction standards. After an earthquake in China kills over 70,000 people, China's legislature passes a statute requiring new buildings to have a greater ability to withstand a large earthquake. The Chinese contractor has approached you and suggested that the new Chinese construction standards are unnecessarily high, that Jay-Mart's construction standards are sufficient to protect against any earthquake likely to occur, and that the cost of complying with the new Chinese construction standards will increase construction costs 20 percent.

What do you do if you believe that ethical behavior requires you to maximize Jay-Mart's profits?

8. You are the CFO of Ridgeway Bank, which makes loans to consumers and businesses totaling $870 million annually. Ridgeway Bank receives promissory notes from its borrowers, which notes the bank typically sells in bulk to investment banks, hedge funds, and other institutional investors within days after making the loans to its borrowers. By doing so, Ridgeway Bank is able to turn over its assets many times and optimize its profits. Finding buyers for the notes, however, can be challenging and depends in large part on the quality of the promissory notes, especially the collateral backing the notes and the borrowers' abilities to pay the notes. You are considering expanding Ridgeway's loan business by making loans to riskier borrowers. Before doing so, you want commitments from institutional investors that they will be willing to buy the risky notes. Because other banks made a large number of bad loans on which borrowers defaulted, Ridgeway has found it especially difficult to sell higher-risk notes, as institutional investors have greatly restricted their buying of risky notes. You know that if you can convince one institutional investor to purchase some of the risky notes, you can tell other institutional investors that they are missing an opportunity that one of their competitors is taking. Do you think it is ethical to use that tactic to convince institutional investors to buy the notes? What fallacy are you expecting the institutional investors to make when they agree to do what their competitors do?

9. In 2007, NFL Commissioner Roger Goodell determined that the New England Patriots and its head coach, Bill Belichick, had violated NFL rules by videotaping opposing teams' sideline signals during games. Goodell docked the Patriots a 2008 first-round draft pick, and he fined Belichick $500,000 and the team $250,000. In 2008, Goodell interviewed the Patriots' employee who had done the videotaping and concluded that the employee's information was consistent with the behavior for which the Patriots and Belichick had been disciplined in 2007. Therefore, Goodell termed the matter over and said it was not necessary to discipline further the Patriots or Belichick. Immediately thereafter, Arlen Specter, a U.S. senator from Pennsylvania, called the NFL investigation "neither objective nor adequate." Specter stated, "If the commissioner doesn't move for an independent investigation, . . . depending on the public reaction, I may ask the Senate Judiciary Committee to hold hearings on the NFL antitrust exemption." Specter further stated that Goodell has made "ridiculous" assertions that wouldn't fly "in kindergarten." The senator said Goodell was caught in an "apparent conflict of interest" because the NFL doesn't want the public to lose confidence in the league's integrity. Terming the videotaping of opposing teams' signals a form of cheating equivalent to steroid use, Specter called for an independent investigation similar to the 2007 Mitchell Report on performance enhancing drugs in baseball.

Can you identify the fallacies in Senator Specter's arguments?

10. You are hired as a corporate accountant for Ryco Industries, Inc., a public company with shares traded on the New York Stock Exchange. The company has enjoyed consistently higher earnings each quarter, meeting or exceeding the expectations of Wall Street analysts every quarter for the past seven years. Soon after being hired, you discover a "reserve" account in the accounting records. Your inquiry shows that the account is designed to accumulate earnings deficiencies or excesses, that is, to permit Ryco to adjust its earnings each quarter such that earnings not increase too little or too much. You bring your findings to the attention of Ryco's chief accounting officer, who tells you that the account merely allows Ryco to smooth or manage its earnings, something that Wall Street analysts want to see. If earnings fluctuated, she explains, analysts would make less optimistic estimates about the prospects of Ryco, and its stock price would take a hit. The CAO tells you, "Look, we're just doing this to avoid getting hammered in the stock market. Every company does this. And we're not making up earnings. When actual earnings are too high, we just withhold recognizing some of those earnings until we need them in the future. When actual earnings are too low, we know we'll have better quarters in the future from which we can borrow earnings now. It all evens out."

Can you identify the critical thinking errors and the characteristics of poor decision making that the CAO is exhibiting? Create a plan that will help you resist the CAO's request for you to continue to manage earnings as Ryco has done in the past.

11. You have been a director of sales at Privation Insurance Company for the last five years. Next week, you will be promoted to the position of Vice President of Sales, leading a staff of 35 sales professionals. Your immediate superior is the Senior Vice President of Marketing & Sales. What plan do you adopt for ethically leading your 35-person staff in your new position? List five things you'll do to lead you staff ethically.

Online Research

Josephson Institute Center for Business Ethics

Josephson Institute Center for Business Ethics is a leading source of materials for businesses and executives who want to act ethically.

- Locate the Josephson website.
- Find "The Seven-Step Path to Better Decisions" and the "Six Pillars of Character."
- List the "Obstacles to Ethical Decision Making: Rationalizations."

Glossary

abandonment To intentionally give up possession or claim to property with the intent of relinquishment of any ownership or claim.

abatement An action of stopping or removing.

ab initio From the beginning.

abstract of title A summary of the conveyances, transfers, and other facts relied on as evidence of title, together with all such facts appearing of record that may impair its validity.

abuse of process An intentional tort designed to protect against the initiation of legal proceedings for a primary purpose other than the one for which such proceedings were designed.

acceleration The shortening of the time for the performance of a contract or the payment of a note by the operation of some provision in the contract or note itself.

acceptance The actual or implied receipt and retention of that which is tendered or offered.

accession The acquisition of property by its incorporation or union with other property.

accommodation paper A negotiable instrument signed without consideration by a party as acceptor, drawer, or indorser for the purpose of enabling the payee to obtain credit.

accommodation party A person who signs a negotiable instrument for the purpose of adding his name and liability to another party to the instrument.

accord and satisfaction A legally binding agreement to settle a disputed claim for a definite amount.

account stated An account that has been rendered by one to another and which purports to state the true balance due and that balance is either expressly or impliedly admitted to be due by the debtor.

acquit To set free or judicially to discharge from an accusation; to release from a debt, duty, obligation, charge, or suspicion of guilt.

actionable Capable of being remedied by a legal action or claim.

act of God An occurrence resulting exclusively from natural forces that could not have been prevented or whose effect could not have been avoided by care or foresight.

act of state doctrine A doctrine of international law that no nation is permitted to judge the act of another nation committed within its own boundaries.

adjudge To give judgment; to decide.

adjudicate To adjudge; to settle by judicial decree.

ad litem During the pendency of the action or proceeding.

administrator The personal representative appointed by a probate court to settle the estate of a deceased person who died intestate (without leaving a valid will).

adoption In corporation law, a corporation's acceptance of a preincorporation contract by action of its board of directors, by which the corporation becomes liable on the contract.

advance directive A written document such as a living will or durable power of attorney that directs others how future health care decisions should be made in the event that the individual becomes incapacitated.

adverse possession Open and notorious possession of real property over a given length of time that denies ownership in any other claimant.

advised letter of credit The seller's bank acts as the seller's agent to collect against the letter of credit issued by the buyer's bank.

affidavit A signed writing containing statements of fact to whose accuracy the signing party has sworn. Used in a variety of judicial proceedings, including the motion for summary judgment.

affirm To confirm or uphold a former judgment or order of a court. Appellate courts, for instance, may affirm the decisions of lower courts.

after-acquired property Property of the debtor that is obtained after a security interest in the debtor's property has been created.

agency A legal relationship in which an agent acts under the direction of a principal for the principal's benefit. Also used to refer to government regulatory bodies of all kinds.

agent One who acts under the direction of a principal for the principal's benefit in a legal relationship known as agency. See *principal*.

aggregate theory In partnership law, the view that there is no distinction between a partnership and the partners who own it. See *entity theory*.

aggrieved One whose legal rights have been invaded by the act of another. Also, one whose pecuniary interest is directly affected by a judgment, or whose right of property may be divested by an action.

alienation The voluntary act or acts by which one person transfers his or her own property to another.

alien corporation A corporation incorporated in one country that is doing business in another country. See *foreign corporation*.

allegation A statement of a party to an action in a declaration or pleading of what the party intends to prove.

allege To assert a statement of fact.

alteration An addition or change in a document.

alter ego Other self. In corporation law, a doctrine that permits a court to pierce a corporation's veil and to hold a shareholder liable for the actions of a corporation dominated by the shareholder.

alternative dispute resolution (ADR) A general name applied to the many nonjudicial means of settling private disputes.

amortize   To provide for the payment of a debt by creating a sinking fund or paying in installments.

ancillary   Auxiliary to. An ancillary receiver is a receiver who has been appointed in aid of, and in subordination to, the primary receiver.

ancillary covenant not to compete   A promise that is ancillary to (part of) a valid contract whereby one party to a contract agrees not to compete with the other party for a specified time and within a specified location. Also called *noncompetition clause.*

answer   The pleading of a defendant in which he or she may deny any or all the facts set out in the plaintiff's declaration or complaint.

anticipatory breach   A contracting party's indication before the time for performance that he cannot or will not perform the contract.

appearance   The first act of the defendant in court.

appellant   The party making an appeal.

appellate jurisdiction   Jurisdiction to revise or correct the work of a subordinate court.

appellee   A party against whom a favorable court decision is appealed. May be called the *respondent* in some jurisdictions.

applicant   A petitioner; one who files a petition or application.

appurtenance   An accessory; something that belongs to another thing.

arbitrate   To submit some disputed matter to selected persons and to accept their decision or award as a substitute for the decision of a judicial tribunal.

argument   The discussion by counsel for the respective parties of their contentions on the law and the facts of the case being tried in order to aid the jury in arriving at a correct and just conclusion.

articles of incorporation   A document that must be filed with a secretary of state to create a corporation. Usually, it includes the basic rights and responsibilities of the corporation and the shareholders.

artisan's lien   A common law possessory security interest arising out of the improvement of property by one skilled in some mechanical art or craft; the lien entitles the improver of the property to retain possession in order to secure the agreed-on price or the value of the work performed.

assault   An intentional tort that prohibits any attempt or offer to cause harmful or offensive contact with another if it results in a well-grounded apprehension of imminent battery in the mind of the threatened person.

assent   To give or express one's concurrence or approval of something done.

assignable   Capable of being lawfully assigned or transferred; transferable; negotiable. Also, capable of being specified or pointed out as an assignable error.

assignee   A person to whom an assignment is made.

assignment   A transfer of property or some right or interest.

assignor   The maker of an assignment.

assumption of risk   A traditional defense to negligence liability based on the argument that the plaintiff voluntarily exposed himself to a known danger created by the defendant's negligence.

assurance   To provide confidence or to inform positively.

attachment   In general, the process of taking a person's property under an appropriate judicial order by an appropriate officer of the court. Used for a variety of purposes, including the acquisition of jurisdiction over the property seized and the securing of property that may be used to satisfy a debt.

attest   To bear witness to; to affirm; to be true or genuine.

attorney-in-fact   An agent who is given express, written authorization by his principal to do a particular act or series of acts on behalf of the principal.

at will   See *employment at will* or *partnership at will.*

audit committee   In corporation law, a committee of the board that recommends and supervises the public accountant who audits the corporation's financial records.

authentication   Such official attestation of a written instrument as will render it legally admissible in evidence.

authority   In agency law, an agent's ability to affect his principal's legal relations with third parties. Also used to refer to an actor's legal power or ability to do something. In addition, sometimes used to refer to a statute, case, or other legal source that justifies a particular result.

authorized shares   Shares that a corporation is empowered to issue by its articles of incorporation.

automatic stay   Under the Bankruptcy Act, the suspension of all litigation against the debtor and his property, which is triggered by the filing of a bankruptcy petition.

averment   A statement of fact made in a pleading.

avoid   To nullify a contractual obligation.

bad faith   A person's actual intent to mislead or deceive another; an intent to take an unfair and unethical advantage of another.

bailee   The person to whom a bailment is made.

bailment   The transfer of personal property by its owner to another person with the understanding that the property will be returned to the owner in the future.

bailor   The owner of bailed property; the one who delivers personal property to another to be held in bailment.

bankruptcy   The state of a person who is unable to pay his or her debts without respect to time; one whose liabilities exceed his or her assets.

bar   As a collective noun, those persons who are admitted to practice law, members of the bar. The court itself. A plea or defense asserted by a defendant that is sufficient to destroy a plaintiff's action.

battery   An intentional tort that prohibits the harmful or offensive touching of another without his consent.

bearer A person in possession of a negotiable instrument that is payable to him, his order, or to whoever is in possession of the instrument.

bench Generally used as a synonym for the term *court* or the judges of a court.

beneficiary The person for whose benefit an insurance policy, trust, will, or contract is established. In the case of a contract, the beneficiary is called a *third-party beneficiary.*

bequest In a will, a gift of personal property or money. Also called a *legacy.*

bid To make an offer at an auction or at a judicial sale. As a noun, an offer.

bilateral contract A contract in which the promise of one of the parties forms the consideration for the promise of the other.

bill of exchange An unconditional order in writing by one person to another, signed by the person giving it, requiring the person to whom it is addressed to pay on demand or at a fixed or determinable future time a sum certain in money to order or to bearer.

bill of lading A written acknowledgment of the receipt of goods to be transported to a designated place and delivery to a named person or to his or her order.

bill of sale A written agreement by which one person assigns or transfers interests or rights in personal property to another.

binder Also called a *binding slip.* A brief memorandum or agreement issued by an insurer as a temporary policy for the convenience of all the parties, constituting a present insurance in the amount specified, to continue in force until the execution of a formal policy.

blue sky laws The popular name for state statutes that regulate securities transactions.

bona fide Made honestly and in good faith; genuine.

bona fide purchaser An innocent buyer for valuable consideration who purchases goods without notice of any defects in the title of the goods acquired.

bond A long-term debt security that is secured by collateral.

bonus shares Also called *bonus stock.* Shares issued for no lawful consideration. See *discount shares* and *watered shares.*

breaking bulk The division or separation of the contents of a package or container.

brief A statement of a party's case or legal arguments, usually prepared by an attorney. Often used to support some of the motions described in Chapter 2, and also used to make legal arguments before appellate courts. Also, an abridgement of a reported case.

broker An agent who bargains or carries on negotiations in behalf of the principal as an intermediary between the latter and third persons in transacting business relative to the acquisition of contractual rights, or to the sale or purchase of property the custody of which is not entrusted to him or her for the purpose of discharging the agency.

bulk transfer The sale or transfer of a major part of the stock of goods of a merchant at one time and not in the ordinary course of business.

burden of proof Used to refer both to the necessity or obligation of proving the facts needed to support a party's claim, and the persuasiveness of the evidence used to do so. Regarding the second sense of the term, the usual burden of proof in a civil case is a preponderance of the evidence; in a criminal case, it is proof beyond a reasonable doubt.

business judgment rule A rule protecting business managers from liability for making bad decisions when they have acted prudently and in good faith.

buy-and-sell agreement A share transfer restriction compelling a shareholder to sell his shares to the other shareholders or the corporation and obligating the other shareholders or the corporation to buy the shareholder's shares.

buyer in ordinary course of business A person who, in good faith and without knowledge that the sale to him is in violation of a third party's ownership rights or security interest in the goods, buys in ordinary course from a person who is in the business of selling goods of that kind.

bylaws In corporation law, a document that supplements the articles of incorporation and contains less important rights, powers, and responsibilities of a corporation and its shareholders, officers, and directors.

call See *redemption.* Also, a type of option permitting a person to buy a fixed number of securities at a fixed price at a specified time. Compare *put.*

canceled shares Previously outstanding shares repurchased by a corporation and canceled by it; such shares no longer exist.

cancellation The act of crossing out a writing. The operation of destroying a written instrument.

C&F The price of the goods includes the cost of the goods plus the freight to the named destination.

capacity The ability to incur legal obligations and acquire legal rights.

capital Contributions of money and other property to a business made by the owners of the business.

capital stock See *stated capital.*

capital surplus Also called *additional paid in capital.* A balance sheet account; the portion of shareholders' contributions exceeding the par or stated value of shares.

case law The law extracted from decided cases.

cashier's check A draft (including a check) drawn by a bank on itself and accepted by the act of issuance.

causa mortis In contemplation of approaching death.

cause of action A legal rule giving the plaintiff the right to obtain some legal relief once certain factual elements are proven. Often used synonymously with the terms *claim* or *theory of recovery.*

caveat emptor "Let the buyer beware."

caveat venditor "Let the seller beware."

certificate of deposit An acknowledgment by a bank of the receipt of money with an engagement to pay it back.

certificate of limited partnership   A document that must be filed with a secretary of state to create a limited partnership.

certification   The return of a writ; a formal attestation of a matter of fact; the appropriate marking of a certified check.

certified check   A check that has been accepted by the drawee bank and has been so marked or certified that it indicates such acceptance.

chancellor   A judge of a court of chancery.

chancery   Equity or a court of equity.

charge   The legal instructions that a judge gives a jury before the jury begins its deliberations. In the prosecution of a crime, to formally accuse the offender or charge him with the crime.

charging order   A court's order granting rights in a partner's transferable interest to a personal creditor of the partner; a creditor with a charging order is entitled to the partner's share of partnership distributions.

charter   An instrument or authority from the sovereign power bestowing the right or power to do business under the corporate form of organization. Also, the organic law of a city or town, and representing a portion of the statute law of the state.

chattel   An article of tangible property other than land.

chattel mortgage   An instrument whereby the owner of chattels transfers the title to such property to another as security for the performance of an obligation subject to be defeated on the performance of the obligation. Under the UCC, called merely a *security interest.*

chattel paper   Written documents that evidence both an obligation to pay money and a security interest in particular goods.

check   A written order on a bank or banker payable on demand to the person named or his order or bearer and drawn by virtue of credits due the drawer from the bank created by money deposited with the bank.

chose in action   A personal right not reduced to possession but recoverable by a suit at law.

CIF   An abbreviation for cost, freight, and insurance, used in mercantile transactions, especially in import transactions.

citation of authorities   The reference to legal authorities such as reported cases or treatises to support propositions advanced.

civil action   An action brought to enforce a civil right; in contrast to a criminal action.

civil law   The body of law applicable to lawsuits involving two private parties.

class action   An action brought on behalf of the plaintiff and others similarly situated.

close corporation   A corporation with few shareholders generally having a close personal relationship to each other and participating in the management of the business.

COD   Cash on delivery. When goods are delivered to a carrier for a cash on delivery shipment, the carrier must not deliver without receiving payment of the amount due.

code   A system of law; a systematic and complete body of law.

codicil   Some addition to or qualification of one's last will and testament.

collateral   Property put up to secure the performance of a promise, so that if the promisor fails to perform as promised, the creditor may look to the property to make him whole.

collateral attack   An attempt to impeach a decree, a judgment, or other official act in a proceeding that has not been instituted for the express purpose of correcting or annulling or modifying the decree, judgment, or official act.

collateral contract   A contract in which one person agrees to pay the debt of another if the principal debtor fails to pay. See *guaranty.*

comaker   A person who with another or others signs a negotiable instrument on its face and thereby becomes primarily liable for its payment.

commercial impracticability   The standards used by the UCC, replacing the common law doctrine of impossibility, to define when a party is relieved of his or her contract obligations because of the occurrence of unforeseeable, external events beyond his or her control.

commercial law   The law that relates to the rights of property and persons engaged in trade or commerce.

commercial paper   Negotiable paper such as promissory notes, drafts, and checks that provides for the payment of money and can readily be transferred to other parties.

commercial unit   Under the UCC, any unit of goods that is treated by commercial usage as a single whole. It may, for example, be a single article or a set of articles such as a dozen, bale, gross, or carload.

common area   In landlord–tenant law, an area over which the landlord retains control but which is often used by or for the benefit of tenants. For example, hallways in an apartment building.

common carrier   One who undertakes, for hire or reward, to transport the goods of such of the public as choose to employ him.

common law   The law that is made and applied by judges.

common shareholders   Shareholders who claim the residual profits and assets of a corporation, and usually have the exclusive power and right to elect the directors of the corporation.

comparative fault   Often used synonymously with *comparative negligence.* But also sometimes used to refer to a defense that operates like comparative negligence but considers the plaintiff's and the defendant's overall fault rather than either's negligence alone.

comparative negligence   The contemporary replacement for the traditional doctrine of contributory negligence. The basic idea is that damages are apportioned between the parties to a negligence action in proportion to their relative fault. The details vary from state to state.

compensatory damages   Damages that will compensate a part for direct losses due to an injury suffered.

complaint   The pleading in a civil case in which the plaintiff states his claim and requests relief.

composition with creditors An agreement between creditors and their common debtor and between themselves whereby the creditors agree to accept the sum or security stipulated in full payment of their claims.

concealment In contract law, taking active steps to prevent another from learning the truth.

concurrent Running with; simultaneously with.

condemn To appropriate land for public use. To adjudge a person guilty; to pass sentence on a person convicted of a crime.

condition In contract law, a future, uncertain event that creates or extinguishes a duty of performance; a provision or clause in a contract that operates to suspend or rescind a party's duty to perform.

conditional acceptance An acceptance of a bill of exchange containing some qualification limiting or altering the acceptor's liability on the bill.

conditional gift A gift that does not become absolute or complete until the occurrence of some express or implied condition.

conditional sale The term is most frequently applied to a sale in which the seller reserves the title to the goods, although the possession is delivered to the buyer, until the purchase price is paid in full.

condition precedent A condition that operates to give rise to a contracting party's duty to perform.

condition subsequent A condition that operates to relieve or discharge one from his obligation under a contract.

confession of judgment An entry of judgment on the admission or confession of the debtor without the formality, time, or expense involved in an ordinary proceeding.

confirmed letter of credit The seller's bank agrees to assume liability on the letter of credit issued by the buyer's bank.

confusion The inseparable intermixture of property belonging to different owners.

consent decree or consent order Used to refer to the order courts or administrative agencies issue when approving the settlement of a lawsuit or administrative action against some party.

consent restraint A security transfer restriction requiring a shareholder to obtain the consent of the corporation or its shareholders prior to the shareholder's sale of her shares.

consequential damages Damages that do not flow directly and immediately from an act but rather flow from the results of the act; damages that are indirect consequences of a breach of contract or certain other legal wrongs. Examples include personal injury, damage to property, and lost profits.

conservator (of an incompetent person) A person appointed by a court to take care of and oversee the person and estate of an incompetent person.

consideration In contract law, a basic requirement for an enforceable agreement under traditional contract principles, defined in this text as legal value, bargained for and given in exchange for an act or promise. In corporation law, cash or property contributed to a corporation in exchange for shares, or a promise to contribute such cash or property.

consignee A person to whom goods are consigned, shipped, or otherwise transmitted, either for sale or for safekeeping.

consignment A bailment for sale. The consignee does not undertake the absolute obligation to sell or pay for the goods.

consignor One who sends goods to another on consignment. A shipper or transmitter of goods.

conspicuous Noticeable by a reasonable person, such as a term or clause in a contract that is in bold print, in capitals, or a contrasting color or type style.

constructive eviction In landlord–tenant law, a breach of duty by the landlord that makes the premises uninhabitable or otherwise deprives the tenant of the benefit of the lease and gives rise to the tenant's right to vacate the property and terminate the lease.

construe To read a statute or document for the purpose of ascertaining its meaning and effect, but in doing so the law must be regarded.

contempt Conduct in the presence of a legislative or judicial body tending to disturb its proceedings or impair the respect due to its authority, or a disobedience to the rules or orders of such a body, which interferes with the due administration of law.

continuation statement A document, usually a multicopy form, filed in a public office to indicate the continuing viability of a financing statement. See *financing statement.*

contra Otherwise; disagreeing with; contrary to.

contract A legally enforceable promise or set of promises.

contract of adhesion A contract in which a stronger party is able to dictate terms to a weaker party, leaving the weaker party no practical choice but to adhere to the terms. If the stronger party has exploited its bargaining power to achieve unfair terms, the contract is against public policy.

contribution In business organization law, the cash or property contributed to a business by its owners.

contributory negligence A traditional defense to negligence liability based on the plaintiff's failure to exercise reasonable care for his own safety.

conversion Any distinct act of dominion wrongfully exerted over another's personal property in denial of or inconsistent with his rights therein. That tort committed by a person who deals with chattels not belonging to him in a manner that is inconsistent with the ownership of the lawful owner.

convertible securities Securities giving their holders the power to exchange those securities for other securities without paying any additional consideration.

conveyance A written instrument transferring the title to land or some interest therein from one person to another.

copartnership A partnership.

copyright A set of exclusive rights, protected by federal law, pertaining to certain creative works such as books, musical compositions, computer programs, works of art, and so forth. The rights are (1) to reproduce the work in question, (2) to prepare derivative works based on it, (3) to sell or otherwise distribute it, and (4) to perform or display it publicly.

corporation A form of business organization that is owned by owners, called shareholders, who have no inherent right to manage the business, and is managed by a board of directors that is elected by the shareholders.

corporation by estoppel A doctrine that prevents persons from denying that a corporation exists when the persons hold themselves out as representing a corporation or believe themselves to be dealing with a corporation.

corporeal Possessing physical substance; tangible; perceptible to the senses.

counterclaim A legal claim made in response to the plaintiff's initial claim in a civil suit. Unlike a defense, the counterclaim is the defendant's affirmative attempt to obtain legal relief; in effect, it states a cause of action entitling the defendant to such relief. Often, the counterclaim must arise out of the occurrence that forms the basis for the plaintiff's claim.

counteroffer A cross-offer made by the offeree to the offeror.

countertrade A buyer's purchase of the seller's goods in exchange for the seller's agreement to purchase goods of the buyer or other person; usually required as a condition to selling goods to a foreign trade corporation.

course of dealing A sequence of previous conduct between the parties to a transaction that is fairly to be regarded as establishing a common basis for interpreting their contract.

covenant A contract; a promise.

cover To obtain substitute or equivalent goods.

credible As applied to a witness, competent.

creditor A person to whom a debt or legal obligation is owed, and who has the right to enforce payment of that debt or obligation.

crime An act prohibited by the state; a public wrong.

criminal law The body of law setting out public wrongs that the government attempts to correct by prosecuting wrongdoers.

culpable Blameworthy; denotes breach of legal duty but not necessarily criminal conduct.

cumulative voting A procedure for voting for a corporation's directors that permits a shareholder to multiply the number of shares she owns by the number of directors to be elected and to cast the resulting total of votes for one or more directors. See *straight voting*.

curtesy At common law, a husband's right in property owned by his wife during her life.

custody The bare control or care of a thing as distinguished from the possession of it.

cy pres As near as possible. In the law of trusts, a doctrine applied to prevent a charitable trust from failing when the application of trust property to the charitable beneficiary designated by the settlor becomes illegal or impossible to carry out; in such a case, cy pres allows the court to redirect the distribution of trust property for some purpose that is as near as possible to the settlor's general charitable intent.

damages The sum of money recoverable by a plaintiff who has received a judgment in a civil case.

date of issue As applied to notes, bonds, and so on of a series, the arbitrary date fixed as the beginning of the term for which they run, without reference to the precise time when convenience or the state of the market may permit their sale or delivery.

D/B/A Doing business as; indicates the use of a trade name.

deal To engage in transactions of any kind, to do business with.

debenture A long-term, unsecured debt security.

debtor A person who is under a legal obligation to pay a sum of money to another (the creditor).

decedent A person who has died.

deceit A tort involving intentional misrepresentation or cheating by means of some device.

decision The judgment of a court; the opinion merely represents the reasons for that judgment.

declaratory judgment One that expresses the opinion of a court on a question of law without ordering anything to be done.

decree An order or sentence of a court of equity determining some right or adjudicating some matter affecting the merits of the cause.

deed A writing, sealed and delivered by the parties; an instrument conveying real property.

deed of trust A three-party instrument used to create a security interest in real property in which the legal title to the real property is placed in one or more trustees to secure the repayment of a sum of money or the performance of other conditions.

de facto In fact; actual. Often used in contrast to *de jure* to refer to a real state of affairs.

de facto corporation A corporation that has complied substantially with the mandatory conditions precedent to incorporation, taken as a whole.

defalcation The word includes both embezzlement and misappropriation and is a broader term than either.

defamation An intentional tort that prohibits the publication of false and defamatory statements concerning another.

default Fault; neglect; omission; the failure of a party to an action to appear when properly served with process; the failure to perform a duty or obligation; the failure of a person to pay money when due or when lawfully demanded.

defeasible Regarding title to property, capable of being defeated. A title to property that is open to attack or that may be defeated by the performance of some act.

defend To oppose a claim or action; to plead in defense of an action; to contest an action suit or proceeding.

defendant The party who is sued in a civil case, or the party who is prosecuted in a criminal case.

defendant in error Any of the parties in whose favor a judgment was rendered that the losing party seeks to have reversed or modified by writ of error and whom he names as adverse parties.

defense A rule of law entitling the defendant to a judgment in his favor even if the plaintiff proves all elements of his claim or cause of action.

deficiency That part of a debt that a mortgage was made to secure, not realized by the liquidation of the mortgaged property. Something that is lacking.

defraud To deprive another of a right by deception or artifice.

de jure According to the law; legitimate; by legal right.

de jure corporation A corporation that has complied substantially with each of the mandatory conditions precedent to incorporation.

delegation In constitutional law and administrative law, a process whereby a legislature effectively hands over some of its legislative power to an administrative agency that it has created, thus giving the agency power to make law within the limits set by the legislature. In contract law, a transaction whereby a person who owes a legal duty to perform under a contract appoints someone else to carry out his performance.

deliver To surrender property to another person.

demand A claim; a legal obligation; a request to perform an alleged obligation; a written statement of a claim. In corporation law, a request that the board of directors sue a person who has harmed the corporation; a prerequisite to a shareholder derivative suit.

demurrer A civil motion that attacks the plaintiff's complaint by assuming the truth of the facts stated in the complaint for purposes of the motion, and by arguing that even if these facts are true, there is no rule of law entitling the plaintiff to recovery. Roughly similar to the motion to dismiss for failure to state a claim on which relief can be granted.

de novo Anew; over again; a second time. A trial de novo, for example, is a new trial in which the entire case is retried.

deposition A form of discovery consisting of the oral examination of a party or a party's witness by the other party's attorney.

deputy A person subordinate to a public officer whose business and object is to perform the duties of the principal.

derivative suit Also called *derivative action*. A suit to enforce a corporate right of action brought on behalf of a corporation by one or more of its shareholders.

descent Hereditary succession. It is the title whereby, upon the death of an ancestor, the heir acquires the ancestor's estate under state law.

detriment Any act or forbearance by a promisee. A loss or harm suffered in person or property.

devise In a will, a gift of real property.

dictum Language in a judicial opinion that is not necessary for the decision of the case and that, while perhaps persuasive, does not bind subsequent courts. Distinguished from *holding*.

directed verdict A verdict issued by a judge who has, in effect, taken the case away from the jury by directing a verdict for one party. Usually, the motion for a directed verdict is made at trial by one party after the other party has finished presenting his evidence.

disaffirm In contract law, a party's exercise of his power to avoid a contract entered before the party reached the age of majority; a minor's cancellation of his contract.

discharge Release from liability.

discharge in bankruptcy An order or decree rendered by a court in bankruptcy proceedings, the effect of which is to satisfy all debts provable against the estate of the bankrupt as of the time when the bankruptcy proceedings were initiated.

disclaimer A term in a contract whereby a party attempts to relieve itself of some potential liability associated with the contract. The most common example is the seller's attempt to disclaim liability for defects in goods that it sells.

discount A loan on an evidence of debt, where the compensation for the use of the money until the maturity of the debt is deducted from the principal and retained by the lender at the time of making the loan.

discount shares Also called *discount stock*. Shares issued for less than their par value or stated value. See *bonus shares* and *watered shares*.

discovery A process of information gathering that takes place before a civil trial. See *deposition* and *interrogatory*.

dishonor The failure to pay or accept a negotiable instrument that has been properly presented.

dismiss To order a cause, motion, or prosecution to be discontinued or quashed.

dissenter's rights A shareholder's right to receive the fair value of her shares from her corporation when she objects to a corporate transaction that significantly alters her rights in the corporation.

dissociation In partnership law, the change in the relation of the partners caused by any partner ceasing to be associated with the carrying on of the business.

dissolution In partnership law, the commencement of the winding up process.

distribution In business organization law, a business's gratuitous transfer of its assets to the owners of the business. Includes cash and property dividends and redemptions.

divided court A court is so described when there has been a division of opinion between its members on a matter that has been submitted to it for decision.

dividends, cash or property A corporation's distribution of a portion of its assets to its shareholders, usually corresponding to current or historical corporate profits; unlike a redemption, it is not accompanied by a repurchase of shares.

dividends, share Also called *stock dividends*. A corporation's pro rata issuance of shares to existing shareholders for no consideration.

documents of title A classification of personal property that includes bills of lading, warehouse receipts, dock warrants, and dock receipts.

domain The ownership of land; immediate or absolute ownership. The public lands of a state are frequently termed the *public domain*.

domicile A place where a person lives or has his home; in a strict legal sense, the place where he has his true, fixed, permanent home and principal establishment, and to which place he has, whenever he is absent, the intention of returning.

donee A person to whom a gift is made.

donor   A person who makes a gift.

double jeopardy clause   A constitutional provision designed to protect criminal defendants from multiple prosecutions for the same offense.

dower   The legal right or interest that a wife has in her husband's real estate by virtue of their marriage.

draft   A written order drawn on one person by another, requesting him to pay money to a designated third person.

drawee   A person on whom a draft is drawn by the drawer.

drawer   The maker of a draft.

due bill   An acknowledgment of a debt in writing, not made payable to order.

dummy   One posing or represented as acting for himself, but in reality acting for another. A tool or "straw man" for the real parties in interest.

dumping   The selling of goods by a seller in a foreign nation at unfairly low prices.

durable power of attorney   A power of attorney that is not affected by the principal's incapacity. See *power of attorney* and *attorney-in-fact.*

durable power of attorney for health care   A durable power of attorney in which the principal specifically gives the attorney-in-fact the authority to make health care decisions for her in the event that the principal should become incompetent. Also called *health care representative.*

duress   Overpowering of the will of a person by force or fear.

E

earned surplus   Also called *retained earnings.* A balance sheet account; a corporation's profits that have not been distributed to shareholders.

earnest money   Something given as part of the purchase price to bind the bargain.

easement   The right to make certain uses of another person's property or to prevent another person from making certain uses of his own property.

edict   A command or prohibition promulgated by a sovereign and having the effect of law.

e.g.   For example.

ejectment   By statute in some states, an action to recover the immediate possession of real property.

eleemosynary corporation   A corporation created for a charitable purpose or for charitable purposes.

emancipate   To release; to set free. In contract law, a parent's waiver of his rights to control and receive the services of his minor child.

embezzlement   A statutory offense consisting of the fraudulent conversion of another's personal property by one to whom it has been entrusted, with the intention of depriving the owner thereof, the gist of the offense being usually the violation of relations of a fiduciary character.

eminent domain   A governmental power whereby the government can take or condemn private property for a public purpose on the payment of just compensation.

employment at will   A rule stating that if an employment is not for a definite time period, either party may terminate the employment without liability at any time and for any reason that is not otherwise illegal.

enabling legislation   The statute by which a legislative body creates an administrative agency.

en banc (in banc)   By all the judges of a court, with all the judges of a court sitting.

encumbrance   A right in a third person that diminishes the value of the land but is consistent with the passing of ownership of the land by deed.

endorsement   See *indorsement.*

entity theory   In partnership law, the view that a partnership is a legal entity distinct from the partners who own it. See *aggregate theory.*

entry   Recordation; noting in a record; going on land; taking actual possession of land.

environmental impact statement   A document that the National Environmental Policy Act requires federal agencies to prepare in connection with any legislative proposals or proposed actions that will significantly affect the environment.

equity   A system of justice that developed in England separate from the common law courts. Few states in the United States still maintain separate equity courts, though most apply equity principles and procedures when remedies derived from the equity courts are sought. A broader meaning denotes fairness and justice. In business organization law, the capital contributions of owners plus profits that have not been distributed to the owners; stated capital plus capital surplus plus earned surplus.

equity of redemption   The right of a mortgagee to discharge the mortgage when due and to have title to the mortgaged property free and clear of the mortgage debt.

error   A mistake of law or fact; a mistake of the court in the trial of an action.

escheat   The reversion of land to the state in the event that a decedent dies leaving no heirs.

estate   An interest in land. Property owned by a decedent at the time of his death.

estop   To bar or stop.

estoppel   That state of affairs that arises when one is forbidden by law from alleging or denying a fact because of his previous action or inaction.

et al.   And another or and others. An abbreviation for the Latin *et alius,* meaning "and another"; also of *et alii,* meaning "and others."

eviction   Depriving the tenant of the possession of leased premises.

evidence   That which makes clear or ascertains the truth of the fact or point in issue either on the one side or the other; those rules of law whereby we determine what testimony is to be admitted and what rejected in each case and what is the weight to be given to the testimony admitted.

exception An objection; a reservation; a contradiction.

exclusionary rule The rule that bars the admissibility in criminal proceedings of evidence seized in violation of the Fourth Amendment's prohibition against unreasonable searches and seizures.

exculpatory clause A clause in a contract or trust instrument that excuses a party from some duty.

executed When applied to written instruments, synonymous with the word *signed;* more frequently, it means everything has been done to complete the transaction; that is, the instrument has been signed, sealed, and delivered. An executed contract is one in which the object of the contract is performed.

execution A process of enforcing a judgment, usually by having an appropriate officer seize property of the defendant and sell it at a judicial sale. The final consummation of a contract or other instrument, including completion of all the formalities needed to make it binding.

executive order A legal rule issued by a chief executive (e.g., the president or a state governor), usually pursuant to a delegation of power from the legislature.

executor The personal representative appointed to administer the estate of a person who died leaving a valid will.

executory Not yet executed; not yet fully performed, completed, fulfilled, or carried out; to be performed wholly or in part.

exemption A release from some burden, duty, or obligation; a grace; a favor; an immunity; taken out from under the general rule, not to be like others who are not exempt.

exhibit A copy of a written instrument on which a pleading is founded, annexed to the pleading and by reference made a part of it. Any paper or thing offered in evidence and marked for identification.

ex post facto After the fact. The U.S. Constitution prohibits ex post facto criminal laws, meaning those that criminalize behavior that was legal when committed.

express warranty A warranty made in words, either oral or written.

expropriation A government's taking of a business's assets, such as a manufacturing facility, usually without just compensation.

ex ship A shipping term that does not specify a particular ship for transportation of goods but does not place the expense and risk of transportation on the seller until the goods are unloaded from whatever ship is used.

F

face value The nominal or par value of an instrument as expressed on its face; in the case of a bond, this is the amount really due, including interest.

factor An agent who is employed to sell goods for a principal, usually in his own name, and who is given possession of the goods.

false imprisonment An intentional tort that prohibits the unlawful confinement of another for an appreciable time without his consent.

FAS An abbreviation for the expression free alongside ship.

federal supremacy The ability of federal laws to defeat inconsistent state laws in case they conflict.

fee simple absolute The highest form of land ownership, which gives the owner the right to possess and use the land for an unlimited period of time, subject only to governmental or private restrictions, and unconditional power to dispose of the property during his lifetime or upon his death.

felony As a general rule, all crimes punishable by death or by imprisonment in a state prison.

fiction An assumption made by the law that something is true that is or may be false.

fiduciary One who holds goods in trust for another or one who holds a position of trust and confidence.

field warehousing A method of protecting a security interest in the inventory of a debtor whereby the creditor or his agent retains the physical custody of the debtor's inventory, which is released to the debtor as he complies with the underlying security agreement.

financing statement A document, usually a multicopy form, filed in a public office serving as constructive notice to the world that a creditor claims a security interest in collateral that belongs to a certain named debtor.

firm offer Under the Uniform Commercial Code, a signed, written offer by a merchant containing assurances that it will be held open, and which is not revocable for the time stated in the offer, or for a reasonable time if no such time is stated.

fixture A thing that was originally personal property and that has been actually or constructively affixed to the soil itself or to some structure legally a part of the land.

FOB An abbreviation of free on board.

force majeure clause A contract provision, commonly encountered in international agreements for the sale of goods, that excuses nonperformance that results from conditions beyond the parties' control.

foreclosure To terminate the rights of the mortgagor/owner of property.

foreign corporation A corporation incorporated in one state doing business in another state. See *alien corporation.*

foreign trade corporation A corporation in a NME nation that is empowered by the government to conduct the whole business of exporting or importing a particular product.

forwarder A person who, having no interest in goods and no ownership or interest in the means of their carriage, undertakes, for hire, to forward them by a safe carrier to their destination.

franchise A special privilege conferred by government on individuals, and which does not belong to the citizens of a country generally, of common right. Also a contractual relationship establishing a means of marketing goods or services giving certain elements of control to the supplier (franchisor) in return for the right of the franchisee to use the supplier's tradename or trademark, usually in a specific marketing area.

fraud   Misrepresentation made with knowledge of its falsity and intent to deceive. See *misrepresentation*.

freeze-out   In corporation law, a type of oppression by which only minority shareholders are forced to sell their shares.

fungible goods   Goods, any unit of which is from its nature or by mercantile custom treated as the equivalent of any other unit.

future advances   Money or other value provided to a debtor by a creditor subsequent to the time a security interest in the debtor's collateral is taken by that creditor.

futures   Contracts for the sale and future delivery of stocks or commodities, wherein either party may waive delivery, and receive or pay, as the case may be, the difference in market price at the time set for delivery.

G

garnishee   Used as a noun, the third party who is subjected to the process of garnishment. Used as a verb, to institute garnishment proceedings; to cause a garnishment to be levied on the garnishee.

garnishment   A statutory proceeding whereby money, property, wages, or credits of the defendant that are in the hands of a third party are seized to satisfy a judgment or legally valid claim that the plaintiff has against the defendant.

general partnership   See *partnership*.

gift   A voluntary transfer of property for which the donor receives no consideration in return.

good faith   Honesty in fact; an honest intention to abstain from taking an unfair advantage of another.

goodwill   The value of a business due to expected continued public patronage of the business.

grantee   A person to whom a grant is made.

grantor   A person who makes a grant.

gravamen   The gist, essence, or central point of a legal claim or argument.

gray market goods   Goods lawfully bearing trademarks or using patented or copyrighted material, but imported into a foreign market without the authorization of the owner of the trademark, patent, or copyright.

guarantor   A person who promises to perform the same obligation as another person (called the *principal*), upon the principal's default.

guaranty   An undertaking by one person to be answerable for the payment of some debt, or the due performance of some contract or duty by another person, who remains liable to pay or perform the same.

guardian   A person (in some rare cases, a corporation) to whom the law has entrusted the custody and control of the person, or estate, or both, of an incompetent person.

H

habeas corpus   Any of several common law writs having as their object to bring a party before the court or judge. The only issue it presents is whether the prisoner is restrained of his liberty by due process.

hearing   The supporting of one's contentions by argument and, if need be, by proof.

hedging   A market transaction in which a party buys a certain quantity of a given commodity at the price current on the date of the purchase and sells an equal quantity of the same commodity for future delivery for the purpose of getting protection against loss due to fluctuation in the market.

heirs   Those persons appointed by law to succeed to the estate of a decedent who has died without leaving a valid will.

holder   A person in possession of a document of title or an instrument payable or indorsed to him, his order, or to bearer.

holder in due course   A person who is a holder of a negotiable instrument who took the instrument for value, in good faith, without notice that it is overdue or has been dishonored or that there is any uncured default with respect to payment of another instrument issued as part of the same series, without notice that the instrument contains an unauthorized signature or has been altered, without notice of any claim of a property or possessory interest in it, and without notice that any party has any defense against it or claim in recoupment to it.

holding   Language in a judicial opinion that is necessary for the decision the court reached and that is said to be binding on subsequent courts. Distinguished from *dictum*.

holding company   A corporation whose purpose or function is to own or otherwise hold the shares of other corporations either for investment or control.

holographic will   A will written in the handwriting of the testator.

homestead   In a legal sense, the real estate occupied as a home and also the right to have it exempt from levy and forced sale. It is the land, not exceeding a prescribed amount, upon which the owner and his family reside, including the house in which they reside as an indispensable part.

I

i.e.   That is.

illusory   Deceiving or intending to deceive, as by false appearances; fallacious. An illusory promise is a promise that appears to be binding but that in fact does not bind the promisor.

immunity   A personal favor granted by law, contrary to the general rule.

impanel   To place the names of the jurors on a panel; to make a list of the names of those persons who have been selected for jury duty; to go through the process of selecting a jury that is to try a cause.

implied warranty   A warranty created by operation of law.

implied warranty of habitability   Implied warranty arising in lease or sale of residential real estate that the property will be fit for human habitation.

impossibility   A doctrine under which a party to a contract is relieved of his or her duty to perform when that performance has become impossible because of the occurrence of an event unforeseen at the time of contracting.

inalienable Incapable of being alienated, transferred, or conveyed; nontransferable.

in camera In the judge's chambers; in private.

incapacity A legal disability, such as infancy or want of authority.

inception Initial stage. The word does not refer to a state of actual existence but to a condition of things or circumstances from which the thing may develop.

inchoate Imperfect; incipient; not completely formed.

incidental damages Collateral damages that result from a breach of contract, including all reasonable expenses that are incurred because of the breach; damages that compensate a person injured by a breach of contract for reasonable costs he incurs in an attempt to avoid further loss.

indenture A contract between a corporation and the holders of bonds or debentures issued by the corporation stating the rights of the holders and duties of the corporation.

independent contractor A person who contracts with a principal to perform some task according to his own methods, and who is not under the principal's control regarding the physical details of the work. Under the *Restatement (Second) of Agency,* an independent contractor may or may not be an agent.

indictment A finding by a grand jury that there is probable cause to believe an accused committed a crime.

indorsement Writing on the back of an instrument; the contract whereby the holder of an instrument (such as a draft, check, or note) or a document (such as a warehouse receipt or bill of lading) transfers to another person his right to such instrument and incurs the liabilities incident to the transfer.

infant See *minor.*

information A written accusation of crime brought by a public prosecuting officer to a court without the intervention of a grand jury.

injunction An equitable remedy whereby the defendant is ordered to perform certain acts or to desist from certain acts.

in pari delicto Equally at fault in tort or crime; in equal fault or guilt.

in personam Against a person. For example, in personam jurisdiction.

in re In the matter of.

in rem Against a thing and not against a person; concerning the condition or status of a thing; for example, in rem jurisdiction.

inside information Confidential information possessed by a person due to his relationship with a business.

insolvency In corporation law, the inability of a business to pay its currently maturing obligations.

instrument Formal or legal documents in writing, such as contracts, deeds, wills, bonds, leases, and mortgages.

insurable interest Any interest in property such that the owner would experience a benefit from the continued existence of the property or a loss from its destruction.

inter alia Among other things.

interlocutory Something not final but deciding only some subsidiary matter raised while a lawsuit is pending.

interpleader An equitable remedy applicable where one fears injury from conflicting claims. Where a person does not know which of two or more persons claiming certain property held by him has a right to it, filing a bill of interpleader forces the claimants to litigate the title between themselves.

interrogatory Written questions directed to a party, answered in writing, and signed under oath.

inter se Between or among themselves.

interstate Between or among two or more states.

intervening cause An intervening force that plays so substantial a role in causing a particular plaintiff's injury that it relieves a negligent defendant of any responsibility for that injury. Also called *superseding cause.*

intervention A proceeding by which one not originally made a party to an action or suit is permitted, on his own application, to appear therein and join one of the original parties in maintaining his cause of action or defense, or to assert some cause of action against some or all of the parties to the proceeding as originally instituted.

inter vivos A transaction between living persons.

intestate Having died without leaving a valid will.

in toto Wholly, completely.

intrastate Within a particular state.

investment contract In securities law, a type of security encompassing any contract by which an investor invests in a common enterprise with an expectation of profits solely from the efforts of persons other than the investor.

invitee A person who is on private premises for a purpose connected with the business interests of the possessor of those premises, or a member of the public who is lawfully on land open to the public.

ipso facto By the fact itself; by the very fact.

irrevocable letter of credit The issuing bank may not revoke the letter of credit issued by the buyer's bank.

issue Lineal descendants such as children and grandchildren. This category of persons includes adopted children.

issued shares A corporation's shares that a corporation has sold to its shareholders. Includes shares repurchased by the corporation and retained as treasury shares, but not shares canceled or returned to unissued status.

issuer In securities law, a person who issues or proposes to issue a security; the person whose obligation is represented by a security.

J

joint and several liability Liability of a group of persons in which the plaintiff may sue any member of the group individually and get a judgment against that person, or may sue all members of the group collectively.

joint bank account A bank account of two persons so fixed that they shall be joint owners thereof during their mutual lives, and the survivor shall take the whole on the death of other.

joint liability Liability of a group of persons in which, if one of these persons is sued, he can insist that the other liable parties be joined to the suit as codefendants, so that all must be sued collectively.

jointly Acting together or in concert or cooperating; holding in common or interdependently, not separately. Persons are jointly bound in a bond or note when both or all must be sued in one action for its enforcement, not either one at the election of the creditor.

joint tenancy An estate held by two or more jointly, with an equal right in all to share in the enjoyments of the land during their lives. An incident of joint tenancy is the right of survivorship.

joint venture A form of business organization identical to a partnership, except that it is engaged in a single project, not carrying on a business.

judgment A court's final resolution of a lawsuit or other proceeding submitted to it for decision.

judgment lien The statutory lien on the real property of a judgment debtor that is created by the judgment itself. At common law, a judgment imposes no lien on the real property of the judgment debtor, and to subject the property of the debtor to the judgment, it was necessary to take out a writ called an *elegit*.

judgment notwithstanding the verdict A judgment made by a judge contrary to a prior jury verdict whereby the judge effectively overrules the jury's verdict. Also called the *j.n.o.v.* or the *judgment non obstante veredicto*. Similar to the directed verdict, except that it occurs after the jury has issued its verdict.

judicial review The courts' power to declare the actions of the other branches of government unconstitutional.

jurisdiction The power of a court to hear and decide a case.

jurisprudence The philosophy of law. Also sometimes used to refer to the collected positive law of some jurisdiction.

jury A body of lay persons, selected by lot, or by some other fair and impartial means, to ascertain, under the guidance of the judge, the truth in questions of fact arising either in civil litigation or a criminal process.

kite To secure the temporary use of money by issuing or negotiating worthless paper and then redeeming such paper with the proceeds of similar paper. The word is also used as a noun, meaning the worthless paper thus employed.

laches The established doctrine of equity that, apart from any question of statutory limitation, its courts will discourage delay and sloth in the enforcement of rights. Equity demands conscience, good faith, and reasonable diligence.

land contract A conditional agreement for the sale and purchase of real estate in which the legal title to the property is retained by the seller until the purchaser has fulfilled the agreement, usually by completing the payment of the agreed-on purchase price.

larceny The unlawful taking and carrying away of personal property with the intent to deprive the owner of his property permanently.

last clear chance Under traditional tort principles, a doctrine that allowed a contributorily negligent plaintiff to recover despite his failure to exercise reasonable care for his own safety by arguing that the defendant had the superior opportunity (last clear chance) to avoid the harm.

law merchant The custom of merchants, or lex mercatorio, that grew out of the necessity and convenience of business, and that, although different from the general rules of the common law, was engrafted into it and became a part of it. It was founded on the custom and usage of merchants.

leading case The most significant and authoritative case regarded as having settled and determined a point of law. Often, the first case to have done so in a definitive and complete fashion.

leading questions Questions that suggest to the witness the answer desired or those that assume a fact to be proved that is not proved, or that, embodying a material fact, allow the witness to answer by a simple negative or affirmative.

lease A contract for the possession and use of land or other property, including goods, on one side, and a recompense of rent or other income on the other; a conveyance to a person for life, or years, or at will in consideration of a return of rent or other recompense.

legacy A bequest; a testamentary gift of personal property. Sometimes incorrectly applied to a testamentary gift of real property.

legal According to the principles of law; according to the method required by statute; by means of judicial proceedings; not equitable.

letter of credit An instrument containing a request (general or special) to pay to the bearer or person named money, or sell him or her some commodity on credit or give something of value and look to the drawer of the letter for recompense.

levy At common law, a levy on goods consisted of an officer's entering the premises where they were and either leaving an assistant in charge of them or removing them after taking an inventory. Today, courts differ as to what is a valid levy, but by the weight of authority there must be an actual or constructive seizure of the goods. In most states, a levy on land must be made by some unequivocal act of the officer indicating the intention of singling out certain real estate for the satisfaction of the debt.

libel The defamation action appropriate to printed or written defamations, or to those that have a physical form.

license A personal privilege to do some act or series of acts on the land of another, without possessing any ownership interest in the land. A permit or authorization to do something that, without a license, would be unlawful.

licensee A person lawfully on land in possession of another for purposes unconnected with the business interests of the possessor.

lien In its most extensive meaning, it is a charge on property for the payment or discharge of a debt or duty; a qualified right;

a proprietary interest that, in a given case, may be exercised over the property of another.

life estate   A property interest that gives a person the right to possess and use property for a time that is measured by his lifetime or that of another person.

limited liability limited partnership   A limited partnership that has elected to obtain limited liability status for all of its partners, including general partners, by filing with the secretary of state. Also called *LLLP*.

limited liability partnership   A partnership that has elected to obtain limited liability for its partners by filing with the secretary of state. Also called *LLP*.

limited partner   An owner of a limited partnership who has no right to manage the business but who possesses liability limited to his capital contribution to the business.

limited partnership   A form of business organization that has one or more general partners who manage the business and have unlimited liability for the obligations of the business and one or more limited partners who do not manage and have limited liability.

liquidated damages   The stipulation by the parties to a contract of the sum of money to be recovered by the aggrieved party in the event of a breach of the contract by the other party.

liquidated debt   A debt that is due and certain. That is, one that is not the subject of a bona fide dispute either as to its existence or the amount that is owed.

lis pendens   A pending suit. As applied to the doctrine of lis pendens, it is the jurisdiction, power, or control that courts acquire over property involved in a suit, pending the continuance of the action, and until its final judgment.

listing contract   A so-called contract whereby an owner of real property employs a broker to procure a purchaser without giving the broker an exclusive right to sell. Under such an agreement, it is generally held that the employment may be terminated by the owner at will, and that a sale of the property by the owner terminates the employment.

litigant   A party to a lawsuit.

living will   A document executed with specific legal formalities stating a person's preference that heroic life support measures should not be used if there is no hope of the person's recovery.

LLLP   See *limited liability limited partnership*.

LLP   See *limited liability partnership*.

long-arm statute   A state statute that grants to a state's courts broad authority to exercise jurisdiction over out-of-state persons who have contacts with the state.

looting   In corporation law, the transfer of a corporation's assets to its managers or controlling shareholders at less than fair value.

magistrate   A word commonly applied to the lower judicial officers such as justices of the peace, police judges, town recorders, and other local judicial functionaries. In a broader sense, a magistrate is a public civil officer invested with some part of the legislative, executive, or judicial power given by the Constitution. The president of the United States is the chief magistrate of the nation.

maker   A person who makes or executes an instrument. The signer of an instrument.

malfeasance   The doing of an act that a person ought not to do at all. It is to be distinguished from misfeasance—the improper doing of an act that a person might lawfully do.

malicious prosecution   An intentional tort designed to protect against the wrongful initiation of criminal proceedings.

mandamus   We command. It is a command issuing from a competent jurisdiction, in the name of the state or sovereign, directed to some inferior court, officer, corporation, or person, requiring the performance of a particular duty therein specified, which duty results from the official station of the party to whom it is directed, or from operation of law.

margin   A deposit by a buyer in stocks with a seller or a stockbroker, as security to cover fluctuations in the market in reference to stocks that the buyer has purchased but for which he has not paid. Commodities are also traded on margin.

marshals   Ministerial officers belonging to the executive department of the federal government, who with their deputies have the same powers of executing the laws of the United States in each state as the sheriffs and their deputies in such state may have in executing the laws of that state.

material   Important. In securities law, a fact is material if a reasonable person would consider it important in his decision to purchase shares or to vote shares.

materialman's lien   A claim created by law for the purpose of securing a priority of payment of the price or value of materials furnished in erecting or repairing a building or other structure.

mechanic's lien   A claim created by law for the purpose of securing a priority of payment of the price or value of work performed and materials furnished in erecting or repairing a building or other structure; as such, it attaches to the land as well as to the buildings erected therein.

memorandum   A writing.

mens rea   A guilty mind; criminal intent.

merchant   Under the Uniform Commercial Code, one who regularly deals in goods of the kind sold in the contract at issue, or holds himself out as having special knowledge or skill relevant to such goods, or who makes the sale through an agent who regularly deals in such goods or claims such knowledge or skill.

merchantable   Of good quality and salable, but not necessarily the best. As applied to articles sold, the word requires that the article shall be such as is usually sold in the market, of medium quality, and bringing the average price.

merger   In corporation law, traditionally, a transaction by which one corporation acquires another corporation, with the acquiring corporation being owned by the shareholders of both corporations and the acquired corporation going out of existence. Today, loosely applied to any negotiated acquisition of one corporation by another.

merger clause   A contract clause providing that the written contract is the complete expression of the parties' agreement. Also called *integration clause.*

mining partnership   A form of business organization used for mining and drilling mineral resources that is identical to a partnership, except that mining partnership interests are freely transferable.

minor   A person who has not reached the age at which the law recognizes a general contractual capacity (called *majority*), which is 18 in most states.

misdemeanor   Any crime that is punishable neither by death nor by imprisonment in a state prison.

misrepresentation   The assertion of a fact that is not in accord with the truth. A contract can be rescinded on the ground of misrepresentation when the assertion relates to a material fact or is made fraudulently and the other party actually and justifiably relies on the assertion.

mistrial   An invalid trial due to lack of jurisdiction, error in selection of jurors, or some other fundamental requirement.

mitigation of damages   A reduction in the amount of damages due to extenuating circumstances.

mortgage   A conveyance of property to secure the performance of some obligation, the conveyance to be void on the due performance thereof.

mortgagee   The creditor to whom property has been mortgaged to secure the performance of an obligation.

mortgagor   The owner of the property that has been mortgaged or pledged as security for a debt.

motion to dismiss   A motion made by the defendant in a civil case to defeat the plaintiff's case, usually after the complaint or all the pleadings have been completed. The most common form of motion to dismiss is the motion to dismiss for failure to state a claim on which relief can be granted, which attacks the legal sufficiency of the plaintiff's complaint. See *demurrer.*

motive   The cause or reason that induced a person to commit a crime.

mutuality   Reciprocal obligations of the parties required to make a contract binding on either party.

national ambient air quality standards   Federally established air pollution standards designed to protect the public health and welfare.

natural law   A body of allegedly existing ethical rules or principles that is morally superior to positive law and that prevails over positive law in case of a clash between it and the natural law. See *positive law.*

necessaries   That which is reasonably necessary for a minor's proper and suitable maintenance, in view of the income level and social position of the minor's family.

negligence   The omission to do something that a reasonable person, guided by those considerations that ordinarily regulate human affairs, would do, or doing something that a prudent and reasonable person would not do.

negligence per se   The doctrine that provides that a conclusive presumption of breach of duty arises when a defendant has violated a statute and thereby caused a harm the statute was designed to prevent to a person the statute was designed to protect.

negotiable   Capable of being transferred by indorsement or delivery so as to give the holder a right to sue in his or her own name and to avoid certain defenses against the payee.

negotiable instrument   An instrument that may be transferred or negotiated, so that the holder may maintain an action thereon in his own name.

negotiation   The transfer of an instrument in such form that the transferee becomes a holder.

NME   A nonmarket economy; a socialist economy in which a central government owns and controls all significant means of production, thereby setting prices and the levels of production.

nolo contendere   A no contest plea by the defendant in a criminal case that has much the same effect as a guilty plea but that cannot be used as an admission of guilt in other legal proceedings.

nominal damages   Damages that are recoverable when a legal right is to be vindicated against an invasion that has produced no actual present loss.

non compos mentis   Mentally incompetent.

nonfeasance   In the law of agency, the total omission or failure of an agent to enter on the performance of some distinct duty or undertaking that he or she has agreed with the principal to do.

non obstante veredicto   Notwithstanding the verdict. J.n.o.v. See *judgment notwithstanding the verdict.*

no-par value stock   Stock of a corporation having no face or par value.

novation   A mutual agreement, between all parties concerned, for the discharge of a valid existing obligation by the substitution of a new valid obligation on the part of the debtor or another, or a like agreement for the discharge of a debtor to his creditor by the substitution of a new creditor.

nudum pactum   A naked promise, a promise for which there is no consideration.

nuisance   That which endangers life or health, gives offense to the senses, violates the laws of decency, or obstructs the reasonable and comfortable use of property.

nuncupative will   An oral will. Such wills are valid in some states, but only under limited circumstances and to a limited extent.

oath   Any form of attestation by which a person signifies that he is bound in conscience to perform an act faithfully and truthfully.

obiter dictum   That which is said in passing; a rule of law set forth in a court's opinion but not necessary to decide the case. See *dictum.*

objection   In the trial of a case the formal remonstrance made by counsel to something that has been said or done, in order to obtain the court's ruling thereon.

obligee A person to whom another is bound by a promise or other obligation; a promisee.

obligor A person who is bound by a promise or other obligation; a promisor.

offer A proposal by one person to another that is intended to create legal relations on acceptance by the person to whom it is made.

offeree A person to whom an offer is made.

offeror A person who makes an offer.

opinion The opinion of the court represents merely the reasons for its judgment, while the decision of the court is the judgment itself.

oppression The officers, directors, or controlling shareholder's isolation of one group of shareholders for disadvantageous treatment to the benefit of another group of shareholders.

option A separate contract in which an offeror agrees not to revoke her offer for a stated period of time in exchange for some valuable consideration.

option agreement A share transfer restriction granting a corporation or its shareholders an option to buy a selling shareholder's shares at a price determined by the agreement.

ordinance A legislative enactment of a county or an incorporated city or town.

original jurisdiction The power to decide a case as a trial court.

outstanding shares A corporation's shares currently held by shareholders.

overdraft The withdrawal from a bank by a depositor of money in excess of the amount of money he or she has on deposit there.

overdue When an instrument is not paid when due or at maturity.

overplus That which remains; a balance left over.

owner's risk A term employed by common carriers in bills of lading and shipping receipts to signify that the carrier does not assume responsibility for the safety of the goods.

P

par Par means equal, and par value means a value equal to the face of a bond or a stock certificate.

parent corporation A corporation that owns a controlling interest of another corporation, called a *subsidiary corporation.*

parol Oral; verbal; by word of mouth.

parol evidence Where a written contract exists, evidence about promises or statements made prior to or during the execution of the writing that are not contained in the written contract.

parties All persons who are interested in the subject matter of an action and who have a right to make defense, control the proceedings, examine and cross-examine witnesses, and appeal from the judgment.

partition A proceeding the object of which is to enable those who own property as joint tenants or tenants in common to put

an end to the tenancy so as to vest in each a sole estate in specific property or an allotment of the lands and tenements. If a division of the estate is impracticable, the estate ought to be sold and the proceeds divided.

partners The owners of a partnership.

partnership A form of business organization; specifically, an association of two or more persons to carry on a business as co-owners for profit.

partnership agreement A formal written contract between the partners of a partnership that states the rights and the responsibilities of the partners.

partnership at will A partnership whose partnership agreement does not specify any term or undertaking to be accomplished.

partnership by estoppel See *purported partnership.*

partnership interest A partner's ownership interest in a partnership which embodies the partner's transferable interest and the partner's management and other rights.

partner's transferable interest In partnership law, a partner's share of the partnership's profits and losses and right to receive partnership distributions.

party to be charged The person against whom enforcement of a contract is sought; the person who is asserting the statute of frauds as a defense.

par value An arbitrary dollar amount assigned to shares by the articles of incorporation, representing the minimum amount of consideration for which the corporation may issue the shares and the portion of consideration that must be allocated to the stated capital amount.

patent A patent for land is a conveyance of title to government lands by the government; a patent of an invention is the right of monopoly secured by statute to those who invent or discover new and useful devices and processes.

patentee The holder of a patent.

pawn A pledge; a bailment of personal property as security for some debt or engagement, redeemable on certain terms, and with an implied power of sale on default.

payee A person to whom a payment is made or is made payable.

pecuniary Financial; pertaining or relating to money.

pendente lite During the litigation.

per capita A distribution of property in which each member of a group shares equally.

per curiam By the court as a whole, without an opinion signed by a particular judge.

peremptory challenge A challenge to a proposed juror that a defendant may make as an absolute right, and that cannot be questioned by either opposing counsel or the court.

perfection The process or method by which a secured party obtains a priority in certain collateral belonging to a debtor against creditors or claimants of a debtor; it usually entails giving notice of the security interest, such as by taking possession or filing a financial statement.

performance   The fulfillment of a contractual duty.

periodic tenancy   The tenancy that exists when the landlord and tenant agree that rent will be paid in regular successive intervals until notice to terminate is given but do not agree on a specific duration of the lease. A typical periodic tenancy is a tenancy from month to month.

perjury   The willful and corrupt false swearing or affirming, after an oath lawfully administered, in the course of a judicial or quasi-judicial proceeding, as to some matter material to the issue or point in question.

per se   In itself or as such.

personal property   All objects and rights, other than real property, that can be owned. See *real property*.

per stirpes   A distribution in which each surviving descendant divides the share that his or her parent would have taken if the parent had survived. Also called *by right of representation*.

petition   In equity pleading, a petition is in the nature of a pleading (at least when filed by a stranger to the suit) and forms a basis for independent action.

petition (bankruptcy)   The document filed with the appropriate federal court that initiates a bankruptcy proceeding. It may be either a voluntary petition (i.e., filed by the debtor) or an involuntary petition (i.e., filed by creditors).

piercing the corporate veil   Holding a shareholder responsible for acts of a corporation due to a shareholder's domination and improper use of the corporation.

plaintiff   The party who sues in a civil case.

plaintiff in error   The unsuccessful party to the action who prosecutes a writ of error in a higher court.

plea   A plea is an answer to a declaration or complaint or any material allegation of fact therein that, if untrue, would defeat the action. In criminal procedure, a plea is the matter that the accused, on his arraignment, alleges in answer to the charge against him.

pleadings   The documents the parties file with the court when they state their claims and counterarguments early in a civil case. Examples include the complaint and the answer.

pledge   A pawn; a bailment of personal property as security for some debt or engagement, redeemable on certain terms, and with an implied power of sale on default.

pledgee   A person to whom personal property is pledged by a pledgor.

pledgor   A person who makes a pledge of personal property to a pledgee.

police power   The states' power to regulate to promote the public health, safety, morals, and welfare.

positive law   Laws actually and specifically enacted or adopted by proper authority for the government of a jural society as distinguished from principles of morality or laws of honor.

possession   Respecting real property, exclusive dominion and control such as owners of like property usually exercise over it.

Manual control of personal property either as owner or as one having a qualified right in it.

postdated check   A check dated with a date later than its date of issue.

power of attorney   A written authorization by a principal to an agent to perform specified acts on behalf of the principal. See *attorney-in-fact*.

precedent   A past judicial decision relied on as authority in a present case.

preemptive right   A shareholder's option to purchase new issuances of shares in proportion to the shareholder's current ownership of the corporation.

preference   The act of a debtor in paying or securing one or more of his creditors in a manner more favorable to them than to other creditors or to the exclusion of such other creditors. In the absence of statute, a preference is perfectly good, but to be legal it must be bona fide, and not a mere subterfuge of the debtor to secure a future benefit to himself or to prevent the application of his property to his debts.

preferential   Having priority.

preferred shareholders   Shareholders who have dividend and liquidation preferences over other classes of shareholders, usually common shareholders.

prenuptial contract   A contract between prospective marriage partners respecting matters such as property ownership and division.

preponderance   Most; majority; more probable than not.

prerogative   A special power, privilege, or immunity, usually used in reference to an official or his office.

presentment   A demand for acceptance or payment of a negotiable instrument made on the maker, acceptor, drawee, or other payor by or on behalf of the holder.

presumption   A term used to signify that which may be assumed without proof, or taken for granted. It is asserted as a self-evident result of human reason and experience.

pretermitted   In the law of wills, an heir born after the execution of the testator's will.

prima facie   At first sight; a fact that is presumed to be true unless disproved by contrary evidence.

prima facie case   A case sufficiently strong that, unless rebutted by the defendant in some fashion, it entitles the plaintiff to recover against the defendant.

principal   In agency law, one under whose direction an agent acts and for whose benefit that agent acts.

priority   Having precedence or the better right.

privilege   Generally, a legal right to engage in conduct that would otherwise result in legal liability. Privileges are commonly classified as absolute (unqualified) or conditional (qualified). Occasionally, privilege is also used to denote a legal right to refrain from particular behavior (e.g., the constitutional privilege against self-incrimination).

privity of contract   The existence of a direct contractual relation between two parties.

probate A term used to include all matters of which probate courts have jurisdiction, which in many states are the estates of deceased persons and of persons under guardianship.

procedural law The body of law controlling public bodies such as courts, as they create and enforce rules of substantive law. See *substantive law.*

proceeds Whatever is received on the sale, exchange, collection, or other disposition of collateral.

process Generally, the summons or notice of beginning of suit.

proffer To offer for acceptance or to make a tender of.

profit An interest in land giving a person the right to enter land owned by another and remove natural resources (e.g., timber) from the land. Also called *profit à prendre.*

promisee The person to whom a promise is made.

promisor A person who makes a promise to another; a person who promises.

promissory estoppel An equitable doctrine that protects those who foreseeably and reasonably rely on the promises of others by enforcing such promises when enforcement is necessary to avoid injustice, even though one or more of the elements normally required for an enforceable agreement is absent.

promissory note Commercial paper or instrument in which the maker promises to pay a specific sum of money to another person, to his order, or to bearer.

promoter A person who incorporates a business, organizes its initial management, and raises its initial capital.

property Something that is capable of being owned. A right or interest associated with something that gives the owner the ability to exercise dominion over it.

pro rata Proportionate; in proportion.

prospectus In securities law, a document given to prospective purchasers of a security that contains information about an issuer of securities and the securities being issued.

pro tanto For so much; to such an extent.

proximate cause A legal limitation on a negligent wrongdoer's liability for the actual consequences of his actions. Such wrongdoers are said to be relieved of responsibility for consequences that are too remote or not the proximate result of their actions. Various tests for proximate cause are employed by the courts.

proxy A person who is authorized to vote the shares of another person. Also, the written authorization empowering a person to vote the shares of another person.

pseudoforeign corporation A corporation incorporated under the laws of a state but doing most of its business in one other state.

publicly held corporation A corporation owned by a large number of widely dispersed shareholders.

punitive damages Damages designed to punish flagrant wrongdoers and to deter them and others from engaging in similar conduct in the future.

purchase money security interest A security interest that is (1) taken or retained by the seller of collateral to secure all or part of its purchase price or (2) taken by a debtor to acquire rights in or the use of the collateral if the value is so used.

purported partnership The appearance of partnership when there is no partnership; it arises when a person misleads a second person into believing that the first person is a partner of a third person; a theory that allows the second person to recover from the first person all reasonable damages the second person has suffered due to his reliance on the appearance of partnership.

put A type of option permitting a person to sell a fixed number of securities at a fixed price at a specified time. Compare *call.*

Q

qualified acceptance A conditional or modified acceptance. In order to create a contract, an acceptance must accept the offer substantially as made; hence, a qualified acceptance is no acceptance at all, is treated by the courts as a rejection of the offer made, and is in effect an offer by the offeree, which the offeror may, if he chooses, accept and thus create a contract.

quantum meruit As much as is deserved. A part of a common law action in assumpsit for the value of services rendered.

quash To vacate or make void.

quasi-contract The doctrine by which courts imply, as a matter of law, a promise to pay the reasonable value of goods or services when the party receiving such goods or services has knowingly done so under circumstances that make it unfair to retain them without paying for them.

quasi-judicial Acts of public officers involving investigation of facts and drawing conclusions from them as a basis of official action.

quiet title, action to An action to establish a claimant's title in land by requiring adverse claimants to come into court to prove their claim or to be barred from asserting it later.

quitclaim deed A deed conveying only the right, title, and interest of the grantor in the property described, as distinguished from a deed conveying the property itself.

quorum That number of persons, shares represented, or officers who may lawfully transact the business of a meeting called for that purpose.

quo warranto By what authority. The name of a writ (and also of the whole pleading) by which the government commences an action to recover an office or franchise from the person or corporation in possession of it.

R

ratification The adoption or affirmance by a person of a prior act that did not bind him.

real property The earth's crust and all things firmly attached to it.

rebuttal Testimony addressed to evidence produced by the opposite party; rebutting evidence.

receiver One appointed by a court to take charge of a business or the property of another during litigation to preserve it and/or to dispose of it as directed by the court.

recklessness   Behavior that indicates a conscious disregard for a known high risk of probable harm to others.

recognizance   At common law, an obligation entered into before some court of record or magistrate duly authorized, with a condition to do some particular act, usually to appear and answer to a criminal accusation. Being taken in open court and entered on the order book, it was valid without the signature or seal of any of the obligors.

recorder   A public officer of a town or county charged with the duty of keeping the record books required by law to be kept in his or her office and of receiving and causing to be copied in such books such instruments as by law are entitled to be recorded.

redemption   The buying back of one's property after it has been sold. The right to redeem property sold under an order or decree of court is purely a privilege conferred by, and does not exist independently of, statute.

redemption right   Also called a call. In corporation law, the right of a corporation to repurchase shares held by existing shareholders.

redress   Remedy; indemnity; reparation.

reformation   An equitable remedy in which a court effectively rewrites the terms of a contract.

rejection   In contract law, an express or implied manifestation of an offeree's unwillingness to contract on the terms of an offer. In sales law, a buyer's refusal to accept goods because they are defective or nonconforming.

release   The giving up or abandoning of a claim or right to a person against whom the claim exists or the right is to be enforced or exercised. It is the discharge of a debt by the act of the party, in distinction from an extinguishment that is a discharge by operation of law.

remainderman   One who is entitled to the remainder of the estate after a particular estate carved out of it has expired.

remand   A process whereby an appellate court returns the case to a lower court (usually a trial court) for proceedings not inconsistent with the appellate court's decision.

remedy   The appropriate legal form of relief by which a remediable right may be enforced.

remittitur   The certificate of reversal issued by an appellate court upon reversing the order or judgment appealed from.

repatriation   An investor's removal to the investor's nation of profits from his investment in a foreign nation.

replevin   A common law action by which the owner recovers possession of his own goods.

repudiation   Indicating to another party to a contract that the party does not intend to perform his obligations.

res   The thing; the subject matter of a suit; the property involved in the litigation; a matter; property; the business; the affair; the transaction.

rescind   As the word is applied to contracts, to terminate the contract as to future transactions or to annul the contract from the beginning.

rescission   The rescinding or cancellation of a contract or transaction. In general, its effect is to restore the parties to their original precontractual position.

residue   Residuary; all that portion of the estate of a testator of which no effectual disposition has been made by his will otherwise than in the residuary clause.

res ipsa loquitur   Literally, the thing speaks for itself. A doctrine that, in some circumstances, gives rise to an inference that a defendant was negligent and that his negligence was the cause of the plaintiff's injury.

res judicata   A matter that has been adjudicated; that which is definitely settled by a judicial decision.

respondeat superior   A legal doctrine making an employer (or master) liable for the torts of an employee (servant) that are committed within the scope of the employee's employment.

respondent   A term often used to describe the party charged in an administrative proceeding. The party adverse to the appellant in a case appealed to a higher court. In this sense, often synonymous with *appellee.*

Restatement(s)   Collections of legal rules produced by the American Law Institute, covering certain subject matter areas. Although *Restatements* are often persuasive to courts, they are not legally binding unless adopted by the highest court of a particular state.

restitution   A remedy whereby one is able to obtain the return of that which he has given the other party, or an amount of money equivalent to that which he has given the other party.

restrictive covenant   An agreement restricting the use of real property.

reverse   To reject or overturn a judgment or order of a court. An appellate court, for example, may reverse the decision of a trial court. See *affirm.*

revocation   In general, the recalling or voiding of a prior action. In contract law, the withdrawal of an offer by the offeror prior to effective acceptance by the offeree.

right   An interest given and protected by law. In corporation law, an option to purchase shares given to existing shareholders, permitting them to buy quantities of newly issued securities in proportion to their current ownership.

right of appraisal   See *dissenter's rights.*

right of first refusal   In corporation law, a share transfer restriction granting a corporation or its shareholders an option to match the offer that a selling shareholder receives for her shares. See also *option agreement.*

right of survivorship   A feature of some types of co-ownership of property causing a co-owner's interest in property to be transferred on his death immediately and by operation of law to his surviving co-owner(s). See *tenancy by the entirety* and *joint tenancy.*

riparian   Pertaining to water rights or situated on the bank of a river.

S

sale of goods   The transfer of ownership to tangible personal property in exchange for money, other goods, or the performance of service.

sale on approval A conditional sale that is to become final only in case the buyer, after a trial, approves or is satisfied with the article sold.

sale or return A contract in which the seller delivers a quantity of goods to the buyer on the understanding that if the buyer desires to retain, use, or sell any portion of the goods, he will consider such part as having been sold to him, and that he will return the balance or hold it as bailee for the seller.

sanction The penalty that will be incurred by a wrongdoer for the violation of a law.

satisfaction A performance of the terms of an accord. If such terms require a payment of a sum of money, then satisfaction means that such payment has been made.

scienter In cases of fraud and deceit, the word means knowledge on the part of the person making the representations, at the time when they are made, that they are false. In an action for deceit, scienter must be proved.

S corporation Also called *subchapter S corporation*. A close corporation whose shareholders have elected to be taxed essentially like partners are taxed under federal income tax law.

seal At common law, a seal is an impression on wax or some other tenacious material, but in modern practice the letters *l.s.* (locus sigilli) or the word *seal* enclosed in a scroll, either written, or printed, and acknowledged in the body of the instrument to be a seal, are often used as substitutes.

security An instrument commonly dealt with in the securities markets or commonly recognized as a medium of investment and evidencing an obligation of an issuer or a share, participation, or other interest in an enterprise.

security agreement An agreement that creates or provides a security interest or lien on personal property. A term used in the UCC including a wide range of transactions in the nature of chattel mortgages, conditional sales, and so on.

security interest A lien given by a debtor to his creditor to secure payment or performance of a debt or obligation.

service As applied to a process of courts, the word ordinarily implies something in the nature of an act or proceeding adverse to the party served, or of a notice to him.

set off That right that exists between two parties, each of whom, under an independent contract, owes an ascertained amount to the other, to calculate their respective debts by way of mutual deduction, so that, in any action brought for the larger debt, the residue only, after such deduction, shall be recovered.

settlor A person who creates a trust. Also called *trustor*.

severable contract A contract that is not entire or indivisible. If the consideration is single, the contract is entire; but if it is expressly or by necessary implication apportioned, the contract is severable. The question is ordinarily determined by inquiring whether the contract embraces one or more subject matters, whether the obligation is due at the same time to the same person, and whether the consideration is entire or apportioned.

share An equity security, representing a shareholder's ownership of a corporation.

share dividend See *dividends, share.*

shareholder Also called *stockholder.* An owner of a corporation, who has no inherent right to manage the corporation but has liability limited to his capital contribution.

share split Also called *stock split.* Traditionally, a corporation's dividing existing shares into two or more shares, thereby increasing the number of authorized, issued, and outstanding shares and reducing their par value. In modern corporation law, treated like a share dividend.

sight A term signifying the date of the acceptance or that of protest for the nonacceptance of a bill of exchange; for example, 10 days after sight.

sinking fund A fund established by an issuer of securities to accumulate funds to repurchase the issuer's securities.

situs Location; local position; the place where a person or thing is, is his situs. Intangible property has no actual situs, but it may have a legal situs, and for the purpose of taxation, its legal situs is at the place where it is owned and not at the place where it is owed.

slander The defamation action appropriate to oral defamation.

sole proprietor The owner of a sole proprietorship.

sole proprietorship A form of business under which one person owns and controls the business.

sovereign immunity Generally, the idea that the sovereign (or state) may not be sued unless it consents to be sued. In antitrust law, the statutory immunity from antitrust liability for governmental actions that foreign governments enjoy under the Foreign Sovereign Immunities Act of 1976.

special damages Actual damages that would not necessarily but because of special circumstances do in fact flow from an injury.

specific performance A contract remedy whereby the defendant is ordered to perform according to the terms of his contract.

stale check A check more than six months past its date of issue.

standby letter of credit The seller's bank promises to pay the buyer if the seller defaults on his contract to deliver conforming goods.

standing The legal requirement that anyone seeking to challenge a particular action in court must demonstrate that such action substantially affects his legitimate interests before he will be entitled to bring suit.

stare decisis A doctrine whereby a court is said to be bound to follow past cases that are like the present case on the facts and on the legal issues it presents, and that are issued by an authoritative court.

stated capital Also called *capital stock.* A balance sheet account; shareholders' capital contributions representing the par value of par shares or stated value of no-par shares.

stated value An arbitrary dollar amount assigned to shares by the board of directors, representing the minimum amount of consideration for which the corporation may issue the shares and the portion of consideration that must be allocated to the stated capital account.

state implementation plan   A document prepared by states in which the emissions to the air from individual sources are limited legally so that the area will meet the national ambient air quality standards.

status quo   The existing state of things. In contract law, returning a party to status quo or status quo ante means putting him in the position he was in before entering the contract.

statute of frauds   A statute that provides that no lawsuit may be brought to enforce certain classes of contracts unless there is a written note or memorandum signed by the party against whom enforcement is sought or by his agent.

statute of limitations   A statute that requires that certain classes of lawsuits must be brought within defined limits of time after the right to begin them accrued or the right to bring the lawsuit is lost.

stipulation   An agreement between opposing counsel in a pending action, usually required to be made in open court and entered on the minutes of the court, or else to be in writing and filed in the action, ordinarily entered into for the purpose of avoiding delay, trouble, or expense in the conduct of the action.

stock   A business's inventory. Also, as used in corporation and securities law, see *share*.

stock dividend   See *dividends, share*.

stockholder   See *shareholder*.

stock split   See *share split*.

stoppage in transitu   A right that the vendor of goods on credit has to recall them, or retake them, on the discovery of the insolvency of the vendee. It continues so long as the carrier remains in the possession and control of the goods or until there has been an actual or constructive delivery to the vendee, or some third person has acquired a bona fide right in them.

stop-payment order   A request made by the drawer of a check to the drawee asking that the order to pay not be followed.

straight voting   A form of voting for directors that ordinarily permits a shareholder to cast a number of votes equal to the number of shares he owns for as many nominees as there are directors to be elected. See *cumulative voting*.

strict liability   Legal responsibility placed on an individual for the results of his actions irrespective of whether he was culpable or at fault.

strike suit   In corporation law, a derivative suit motivated primarily by an intent to gain an out-of-court settlement for the suing shareholder personally or to earn large attorney's fees for lawyers, rather than to obtain a recovery for the corporation.

subchapter S corporation   See *S corporation*.

sub judice   Before a court.

sublease   A transfer of some but not all of a tenant's remaining right to possess property under a lease.

sub nom   Under the name of.

subpoena   A process for compelling a witness to appear before a court and give testimony.

subrogation   The substitution of one person in the place of another with reference to a lawful claim or right, frequently referred to as the doctrine of substitution. It is a device adopted or invented by equity to compel the ultimate discharge of a debt or obligation by the person who in good conscience ought to pay it.

subscription   In corporation law, a promise by a person to purchase from a corporation a specified number of shares at a specified price.

subsidiary corporation   A corporation owned and controlled by another corporation, called a *parent corporation*.

substantive law   The body of law setting out rights and duties that affect how people behave in organized social life. See *procedural law*.

sui generis   Of its own kind, unique, peculiar to itself.

summary judgment   A method of reaching a judgment in a civil case before trial. The standard for granting a motion for summary judgment is that there be no significant issue of material fact and that the moving party be entitled to judgment as a matter of law.

summary proceedings   Proceedings, usually statutory, in the course of which many formalities are dispensed with. But such proceedings are not concluded without proper investigation of the facts, or without notice, or an opportunity to be heard by the person alleged to have committed the act, or whose property is sought to be affected.

summons   A writ or process issued and served on a defendant in a civil action for the purpose of securing his appearance in the action.

superseding cause   See *intervening cause*.

supra   Above; above mentioned; in addition to.

surety   A person who promises to perform the same obligation as another person (the principal) and who is jointly liable along with the principal for that obligation's performance. See *guarantor*.

T

T/A   Trading as, indicating the use of a trade name.

tacking   The adding together of successive periods of adverse possession of persons in privity with each other, in order to constitute one continuous adverse possession for the time required by the statute, to establish title.

takeover   A tender offer; also applied generally to any acquisition of one business by another business.

tangible   Having a physical existence; real; substantial; evident.

tariff   A tax or duty imposed on goods by a nation when the goods are imported into that nation.

tax haven   A nation that has no or minimal taxation of personal, business, and investment income.

tenancy   General term indicating a possessory interest in property. In landlord–tenant law, a property owner's conveyance to another person of the right to possess the property exclusively for a period of time.

tenancy at sufferance   The leasehold interest that occurs when a tenant remains in possession of property after the expiration of a lease.

tenancy at will   A leasehold interest that occurs when property is leased for an indefinite period of time and is terminable at the will of either landlord or tenant.

tenancy by the entirety   A form of co-ownership of property by a married couple that gives the owners a right of survivorship and cannot be severed during life by the act of only one of the parties.

tenancy for a term   A leasehold interest that results when the landlord and tenant agree on a specific duration for a lease and fix the date on which the tenancy will terminate.

tenancy in common   A form of co-ownership of property that is freely disposable both during life and at death, and in which the co-owners have undivided interests in the property and equal rights to possess the property.

tender   An unconditional offer of payment, consisting in the actual production in money or legal tender of a sum not less than the amount due.

tender offer   A public offer by a bidder to purchase a subject company's shares directly from its shareholders at a specified price for a fixed period of time.

testament   A will; the disposition of one's property to take effect after death.

testator   A deceased person who died leaving a will.

testimony   In some contexts, the word bears the same import as the word *evidence,* but in most connections it has a much narrower meaning. Testimony is the words heard from the witness in court, and evidence is what the jury considers it worth.

thin capitalization   In corporation law, a ground for piercing the corporate veil due to the shareholders' contributing too little capital to the corporation in relation to its needs.

third-party beneficiary   A person who is not a party to a contract but who has the right to enforce it because the parties to the contract made the contract with the intent to benefit him.

title   Legal ownership; also, a document evidencing legal rights to real or personal property.

tombstone advertisement   A brief newspaper advertisement alerting prospective shareholders that an issuer is offering to sell the securities described in the advertisement.

tort   A private (civil) wrong against a person or his property.

tortfeasor   A person who commits a tort; a wrongdoer.

tortious   Partaking of the nature of a tort; wrongful; injurious.

trade fixtures   Articles of personal property that have been annexed to real property leased by a tenant during the term of the lease and that are necessary to the carrying on of a trade.

trademark   A distinctive word, name, symbol, device, or combination thereof, which enables consumers to identify favored products or services and which may find protection under state or federal law.

trade secret   A secret formula, pattern, process, program, device, method, technique, or compilation of information that is used in its owner's business and affords that owner a competitive advantage. Trade secrets are protected by state law.

transcript   A copy of a writing.

transferee   A person to whom a transfer is made.

transfer of partner's transferable interest   A partner's voluntary transfer of her transferable interest to another person, such as the partner's creditor, giving the transferee the right to receive the partner's share of distributions from the partnership.

transferor   A person who makes a transfer.

treasury shares   Previously outstanding shares repurchased by a corporation that are not canceled or restored to unissued status.

treble damages   Three times provable damages, as may be granted to private parties bringing an action under the antitrust laws.

trespass   An unauthorized entry on another's property.

trial   An examination before a competent tribunal, according to the law of the land, of the facts or law put in issue in a cause, for the purpose of determining such issue. When the court hears and determines any issue of fact or law for the purpose of determining the rights of the parties, it may be considered a trial.

trust   A legal relationship in which a person who has legal title to property has the duty to hold it for the use or benefit of another person. The term is also used in a general sense to mean confidence reposed in one person by another.

trustee   A person in whom property is vested in trust for another.

trustee in bankruptcy   The federal bankruptcy act defines the term as an officer, and he is an officer of the courts in a certain restricted sense, but not in any such sense as a receiver. He takes the legal title to the property of the bankrupt and in respect to suits stands in the same general position as a trustee of an express trust or an executor. His duties are fixed by statute. He is to collect and reduce to money the property of the estate of the bankrupt.

ultra vires   Beyond the powers. In administrative law, it describes an act that is beyond the authority granted to an administrative agency by its enabling legislation. In corporation law, it describes a corporation's performing an act beyond the limits of its purposes as stated in its articles of incorporation.

unconscionable   In contract law, a contract that is grossly unfair or one-sided; one that "shocks the conscience of the court."

undisclosed principal   In agency law, a principal whom a third party lacks knowledge or the reason to know the principal's existence and identity.

unidentified principal   In agency law, a principal whom a third party knows or has reason to know exists but who lacks knowledge or reason to know the principal's identity.

unilateral contract   A contract formed by an offer or a promise on one side for an act to be done on the other, and a doing of the act by the other by way of acceptance of the offer or promise; that is, a contract wherein the only acceptance of the offer that is necessary is the performance of the act.

unliquidated   Undetermined in amount.

usage of trade   Customs and practices generally known by people in the business and usually assumed by parties to a contract for goods of that type.

usurpation   In corporation law, an officer, director, or shareholder's taking to himself a business opportunity that belongs to his corporation.

usury   The taking of more than the law allows on a loan or for forbearance of a debt. Illegal interest; interest in excess of the rate allowed by law.

valid   Effective; operative; not void; subsisting; sufficient in law.

value   Under the Code (except for negotiable instruments and bank collections), generally any consideration sufficient to support a simple contract.

vendee   A purchaser of property. The word is more commonly applied to a purchaser of real property, the word *buyer* being more commonly applied to the purchaser of personal property.

vendor   A person who sells property to a vendee. The words *vendor* and *vendee* are more commonly applied to the seller and purchaser of real estate, and the words *seller* and *buyer* are more commonly applied to the seller and purchaser of personal property.

venire   The name of a writ by which a jury is summoned.

venue   A requirement distinct from jurisdiction that the court be geographically situated so that it is the most appropriate and convenient court to try the case.

verdict   Usually, the decision made by a jury and reported to the judge on the matters or questions submitted to it at trial. In some situations, however, the judge may be the party issuing a verdict, as, for example, in the motion for a directed verdict. See *directed verdict.*

versus   Against.

vest   To give an immediate fixed right of present or future enjoyment.

vicarious liability   The imposition of liability on one party for the wrongs of another. Also called *imputed liability.* For example, the civil liability of a principal for the wrongs his agent commits when acting within the scope of his employment. See *respondeat superior.* Such liability is also occasionally encountered in the criminal context (e.g., the criminal liability that some regulatory statutes impose on managers for the actions of employees under their supervision).

void   That which is entirely null. A void act is one that is not binding on either party and that is not susceptible of ratification.

voidable   Capable of being made void; not utterly null, but annullable, and hence that may be either voided or confirmed. See *avoid.*

voidable title   A title that is capable of, or subject to, being judged invalid or void.

voting trust   A type of shareholder voting arrangement by which shareholders transfer their voting rights to a voting trustee.

waive   To throw away; to relinquish voluntarily, as a right that one may enforce, if he chooses.

waiver   The intentional relinquishment of a known right. It is a voluntary act and implies an election by the party to dispense with something of value, or to forgo some advantage that he or she might have demanded and insisted on.

warehouse receipt   A receipt issued by a person engaged in the business of storing goods for hire.

warrant   An order authorizing a payment of money by another person to a third person. Also, an option to purchase a security. As a verb, the word means to defend; to guarantee; to enter into an obligation of warranty.

warrant of arrest   A legal process issued by competent authority, usually directed to regular officers of the law, but occasionally issued to private persons named in it, directing the arrest of a person or persons on grounds stated therein.

warranty   An undertaking relating to characteristics of a thing being sold; a guaranty.

waste   The material alteration, abuse, or destructive use of property by one in rightful possession of it that results in injury to one having an underlying interest in it.

watered shares   Also called *watered stock.* Shares issued in exchange for property that has been overvalued. See *bonus shares* and *discount shares.*

will   A document executed with specific legal formalities that contains a person's instructions about the disposition of his property at his death.

winding up   In partnership and corporation law, the orderly liquidation of the business's assets.

writ   A commandment of a court given for the purpose of compelling certain action from the defendant, and usually executed by a sheriff or other judicial officer.

writ of certiorari   An order of a court to an inferior court to forward the record of a case for reexamination by the superior court.

wrongful use of civil proceedings   An intentional tort designed to protect against the wrongful initiation of civil proceedings.

Index

Page numbers with n indicate notes; A and B indicates appendices A and B respectively.

CONNECT
BUSINESS LAW

 STUDENTS...

Want to get **better grades**? *(Who doesn't?)*

Ready to do **online interactive assignments** that help you apply what you've learned? *(You need to know how to use this stuff in the real world...)*

Need **new ways** to **study** before the big test?
(A little peace of mind is a good thing...)

With McGraw-Hill's *Connect® Business Law*,

STUDENTS GET:

- **Interactive, engaging** content.
- **Interactive Applications** – chapter assignments that help you **APPLY** what you've learned in the course.
- **Immediate feedback** on how you're doing. (No more wishing you could call your instructor at 1 a.m.)
- **Quick access** to lectures, practice materials, eBook, and more. (All the material you need to be successful is right at your fingertips.)

 INSTRUCTORS...

Would you like your **students** to show up for class **more prepared**?
(Let's face it, class is much more fun if everyone is engaged and prepared...)

Want ready-made application-level **interactive assignments,** student p
reporting, and auto-assignment grading? *(Less time grading means more*

Want an **instant view of student or class performance** relative to le
objectives? *(No more wondering if students understand...)*

Need to **collect data and generate reports** required for administration
accreditation? *(Say goodbye to manually tracking student learning outcomes...)*

Want to **record and post your lectures** for students to view online?

 With McGraw-Hill's *Connect® Business Law*,

INSTRUCTORS GET:

- **Interactive Applications – book-specific interactive assignments** that require students to APPLY what they've learned.
- **Simple assignment management,** allowing you to spend more time teaching.
- **Auto-graded** assignments, quizzes, and tests.
- **Detailed Visual Reporting** where student and section results can be viewed and analyzed.
- Sophisticated **online testing** capability.
- A **filtering and reporting** function that allows you to easily assign and report on materials that are correlated to accreditation standards, learning outcomes, and Bloom's taxonomy.
- An easy-to-use **lecture capture** tool.

STUDENTS...

Want an online, **searchable version** of your textbook?

Wish your textbook could be **available online** while you're doing your assignments?

Connect® Plus Business Law eBook

If you choose to use *Connect® Plus Business Law*, you have an affordable and searchable online version of your book integrated with your other online tools.

Connect® Plus Business Law eBook offers features like:

- Topic search
- Direct links from assignments
- Adjustable text size
- Jump to page number
- Print by section

STUDENTS...

Want to get more **value** from your textbook purchase?

Think learning Business Law should be a bit more **interesting**?

Check out the STUDENT RESOURCES section under the *Connect®* Library tab.

Here you'll find a wealth of resources designed to help you achieve your goals in the course. You'll find things like **quizzes, PowerPoints, and Internet activities** to help you study. Every student has different needs, so explore the STUDENT RESOURCES to find the materials best suited to you.

Online Supplements

ConnectPlus Business Law Two-Semester Online Access for Business Law, 15th Edition

McGraw-Hill ConnectPlus® provides an online eBook and immediate feedback on online assignments, quizzes, and practice tests, providing a learning experience that is personalized for YOU. Study more efficiently and engage with your learning process – Connect with future success!

HOW TO REGISTER

Using a <u>Print Book</u>?
To register and activate your ConnectPlus account, simply follow these easy steps:
1. **Go to the ConnectPlus course web address provided by your instructor or visit the Connect link set up on your instructor's course within your campus learning management system.**
2. **Click on the link to register.**
3. **When prompted, enter the ConnectPlus code found on the inside back cover of your book and click Submit. Complete the brief registration form that follows to begin using Connect.**

Using an <u>eBook</u>?
To register and activate your ConnectPlus account, simply follow these easy steps:
1. **Upon purchase of your eBook, you will be granted automatic access to ConnectPlus.**
2. **Go to the ConnectPlus course web address provided by your instructor or visit the Connect link set up on your instructor's course within your campus learning management system.**
3. **Sign in using the same email address and password you used to register on the eBookstore. Complete your registration and begin using Connect.**

Note: Access Code is for one use only. If you did not purchase this book new, the access code included in this book is no longer valid.

Need help? Visit mhhe.com/support